INTERNATIONAL FINANCIAL MANAGEMENT

JEFF MADURA
Florida Atlantic University

ROLAND FOX
Salford University

CENGAGE
Learning®

Australia • Brazil • Japan • Korea • Mexico • Singapore • Spain • United Kingdom • United States

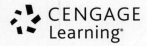

International Financial Management, 3rd Edition

Jeff Madura and Roland Fox

Publishing Director: Linden Harris

Publisher: Andrew Ashwin

Development Editor: Abigail Jones

Senior Production Editor: Alison Burt

Senior Manufacturing Buyer: Eyvett Davis

Marketing Manager: Amanda Cheung

Typesetter: Cenveo Publisher Services

Cover design: Adam Renvoize

For product information and technology assistance, contact **emea.info@cengage.com**

For permission to use material from this text or product, and for permission queries, email **emea.permissions@cengage.com**

British Library Cataloguing-in-Publication Data
A catalogue record for this book is available from the British Library.

ISBN: 978-1-4080-7981-2

Cengage Learning EMEA
Cheriton House, North Way, Andover, Hampshire, SP10 5BE, United Kingdom

Cengage Learning products are represented in Canada by Nelson Education Ltd.

For your lifelong learning solutions, visit **www.cengage.co.uk**

Purchase your next print book, e-book or e-chapter at **www.cengagebrain.com**

Printed in China by RR Donnelley
1 2 3 4 5 6 7 8 9 10 – 16 15 14

Jeff Madura:
To My Parents

Roland Fox:
To Marlene, Anna and Joe

Jeff Madura is presently the SunTrust Bank Professor of Finance at Florida Atlantic University. He has written several textbooks, including *Financial Markets and Institutions*. His research on international finance has been published in numerous journals, including *Journal of Financial and Quantitative Analysis, Journal of Money, Credit and Banking, Journal of Banking and Finance, Journal of International Money and Finance, Journal of Financial Research, Financial Review, Journal of Multinational Financial Management* and *Global Finance Journal*. He has received awards for excellence in teaching and research, and has served as a consultant for international banks, securities firms and other multinational corporations. He has served as a director for the Southern Finance Association and Eastern Finance Association, and also served as president of the Southern Finance Association.

Roland Fox graduated from Manchester University and joined PriceWaterhouseCoopers. He subsequently worked in insurance and for a multinational company, Invensys, before taking up a lecturing post. He is currently a senior lecturer in finance at Salford University. He has published a number of papers on management accounting, finance and education.

BRIEF CONTENTS

PART V SHORT-TERM ASSET AND LIABILITY MANAGEMENT

ONLINE ADDITIONAL READING

Go to our dedicated CourseMate platform for students.

CONTENTS

PART II: EXCHANGE RATE BEHAVIOUR   197

6 Exchange Rate History and the Role of Governments   198

PART 5: SHORT-TERM ASSET AND LIABILITY MANAGEMENT

17 Financing International Trade

18 Short-Term Financing

19 International Cash Management

20 Concluding Comments

ONLINE ADDITIONAL READING

1   Multinational Restructuring
2   Multinational Cost of Capital and Capital Structure
3   Multinational Capital Budgeting

Go to our dedicated CourseMate platform for students.

PREFACE

Multinational corporations (MNCs) continue to expand their operations globally. They must not only be properly managed to apply their comparative advantages in foreign countries, but must also manage their exposure to many forms and sources of risk. These firms' exposure is especially pronounced in developing countries where currency values and economies are volatile. As international conditions change, so do opportunities and risks. Those MNCs that are most capable of responding to changes in the international financial environment will be rewarded. The same can be said for today's students who become the MNC managers of the future.

LECTURER NOTES

Intended market and teaching strategy

This text presumes an understanding of basic corporate finance. It is suitable for both final year undergraduate and master's level courses in international financial management. The text is not directed at the wider business community but may nevertheless be of interest.

The text offers an intuitive and real world grasp of the concepts and issues in international finance. A wealth of examples are provided to enable the student to see the implications of the subject to business, mostly from an MNC perspective. This fuller explanation serves as a support for the lecturer who increasingly has to deliver to students from diverse backgrounds.

Links to the academic literature are provided by a selection of peer reviewed articles from academic journals with related questions provided at the end of each part of the book. These articles have been specially selected for their quality and accessibility to the typical final year and master's student. Giving academic articles a stronger pedagogic role in this way recognizes the now widely available e-journal access which allows such material to be an integral part of the learning programme.

The selection of academic articles is part of an extensive array of support material designed to ensure that the student is able to reflect on and evaluate issues and problems in the subject to a high academic level. Addressing the more technical aspects of the subject first, at the end of each chapter graded questions are provided. The last questions have been given the subtitle of 'Project Workshop'; they enable the student to apply ideas in the chapter directly to real world sources. These questions can be used as the basis of project work that can constitute part of the final assessment of the course. At master's level the workshop exercises may be used to form the element of research around which a dissertation can be written. A general framework for projects is provided in the 'Project Workshop Notes' section on the instructor online support resources. Spreadsheet and statistical packages combined with economic and exchange rate databases made available to your students by your institution can be used with good effect to support such work.

The more discursive aspects of the subject constitute a second route to achieving a high quality of academic study. The 'Critical Debate' topics at the end of each chapter give the student the opportunity to discuss contentious issues in the chapter. The continuing case study, also at the end of each chapter, may be used to help bring the subject within the students' grasp.

At the end of each of the five parts of the book there is an integrative problem that is mainly but not wholly technically based. As noted above, the more discursive elements are reviewed in a section titled 'Essays/Discussion and Articles' also at the end of each part. These articles, some 36 in total, can be read and understood without further support material by final year and master's level students. More particularly, they are not the listing of principal articles in the field which generally require specialist knowledge of a number of papers; such articles are widely quoted elsewhere. Most institutions have e-journal access and it will therefore be possible for all students in the class to have easy access to these papers. Essay questions, for the most part based exclusively on the article, follow many of the article references. Aligning student work directly with the sources in this way is an effective way of ensuring academic standards.

The difference between undergraduate level and master's is seen here as one of degree. Both levels require clear, extended explanations. However, final year undergraduate courses may omit some of the appendices and make occasional use of articles and workshop exercises and discussions; master's level courses can be expected to make greater use of the higher level material.

Appendix B titled 'Maths and Statistics Support' is a useful way of ensuring that all students have an adequate technical background for this subject.

Further support material for lecturers is available on the instructor online support resources. These include:

- Instructor's manual
- ExamView test generator and testbank
- PowerPoint lecture slides
- Multiple choice questions for students.

The instructor's manual contains chapter overviews and coverage of key chapter themes and topics to stimulate class discussion and answers to all the end-of-chapter questions.

The European edition

Existing users of the text may also be acquainted with the Madura US edition which this text replaces. Almost all of the changes are additions or alterations to the US text and hence this edition is slightly longer.

Examples have been changed to non-US contexts. In defence of the greater use of the pound rather than other currencies, all that can be said is that the text is in English and the second author is half French! A choice had to be made. Other changes add some topics of a slightly more advanced nature, generally for their real world relevance. Other sections have been rewritten mainly to give a rather more frank and at times sceptical approach that is more in line with the European tradition. Topics such as the euro and European financial integration and a history of exchange rates have been given fuller treatment for obvious reasons. Assessment material generally, and the academic paper programme in particular, has been added to develop the reflective and evaluative aspects of study as interpreted in academia on this side of the Atlantic.

A number of other changes have also been made. Diagrams are more self-contained. There have been some technical extensions. A fuller portfolio model is presented here simply so that students know how to handle more than two investments! Real exchange rates are given greater prominence; the role of the random walk in forecasting risk has been included; as has the calculation of optimal cross-currency hedges. Cylinder or range forward options have been added to the existing list. Volume effects in scenario analysis are worked out in greater detail. The international capital asset pricing model has been added. All of the content related developments have been taught to specialist and non-specialist students by the second author for many years. The project workshop exercises have been extended and reflect the second author's experience in supervising countless projects. The maths and statistics support section has been enlarged from the original, as has the project-based appendix (which can be found on CourseMate). And finally, the glossary has been extended particularly to include those statistical and technical terms that appear in articles and confuse the student. As most terms are defined throughout the text (highlighted in bold), the comprehensive glossary can be found on CourseMate.

The overall intention has been to preserve the clarity of the original text whilst offering a closer fit to the demands of Higher Education in Europe.

For the second edition of the adapted text, examples throughout the text have been updated in a more international context and the home currency is not always the British pound. The recent events of the global financial crisis have been covered, references to MNC practice brought up to date and more technical material has been added. The appendix to Chapter 3 now includes the formula for the variance of a portfolio of international risky foreign investments, which is oddly missing from most other texts. The appendix to Chapter 8 on exchange rate modelling goes even further into the mathematics of the analysis, explaining such issues as unit roots and half lives – terms that crop up increasingly in the literature. These additions provide extra optional material and offer greater support for lecturers who want to pursue a more technical explanation. The chapters on international restructuring and the multinational cost of capital have been placed on the accompanying CourseMate as it was felt that the international element was not sufficient to justify separate chapters. More generally, there is a greater awareness of the misbehaviour of markets that marks modern thinking.

For this third edition, the chapter on Multinational Capital Budgeting has been retired to the Internet site and the international element of that chapter has been integrated with the chapter on Foreign Direct Investment. This chapter has been extensively revised and extended to include host country-MNC relationships. The issues that are key elements of this relationship have strong financial implications and are essential to the broader picture that is international investment. Part of this broader perspective is a recognition that net present value is an incomplete model of project valuation. The value of post-investment decisions as represented by real options is recognized, as well as the importance of competitor reactions as addressed by game theory. Both developments are treated in non-mathematical form reflecting the current lack of a robust operational model.

The chapter on long-term financing has now been extended to medium- and long-term financing with particular reference to project finance. The definition of medium and long term is somewhat arbitrary especially given that outline plans of large companies rarely extend beyond 5 years.

There is now a new chapter on ethics. This departure gives overdue recognition of the many critiques of the financial market ethic of profit maximization. In this respect practice has been somewhat in advance of standard textbook treatment of financial management. MNCs are showing increasing sensitivity to the critique offered by alternative perspectives; this chapter recognizes the trend. We follow three major themes with strong financial implications. Firstly, the Green movement with its advocacy of renewable resources; secondly, Islamic finance affecting the very concept of a financial transaction; and finally, globalization and its discontents reflecting concerns that the existing management of international finance threatens self-destruction. Understanding and reacting to these alternative philosophies and viewpoints is essential in an international environment.

In addition, there have been a number of statistical updates and minor adjustments as well as further comments on current international financial affairs.

Taken together the changes to the third edition present a rather broader focus on financial management. Given that the international emphasis means that a much richer context is encountered, the broader focus seems appropriate.

Finally the style remains unchanged; I have attempted to explain issues in their basic elements before clothing them in the language of finance.

ACKNOWLEDGEMENTS

For the European edition I would like to thank the reviewers for their sterling work and the publishing team at Cengage Learning, in particular I would like to thank Annabel Ainscow and Abbie Jones for their supportive comments and efficiency. My colleagues at Salford University have also been very encouraging; my particular thanks go to Dr Neil Thompson and Dr Nazam Dzolkarnaini for comments on economic aspects and to Professor Rose Baker who checked over some of the more advanced statistics. I, of course, take responsibility for any inaccuracies.

Finally, I would like to thank my wife, Marlene, and two children, Anna and Joe, for their forbearance in what is a very time-consuming and absorbing process.

Roland Fox
Salford University

The publisher would like to thank the following reviewers for their comments in this and previous editions:

Dionysia Dionysiou, University of Stirling, UK

Daniel Makina, UNISA, South Africa

Carl-Gustaf Malmström, SBS Swiss Business School, Switzerland

Peter Morrison, University of Abertay Dundee, UK

Muhammad Azeem Qureshi, Oslo University College, Norway

Kami Rwegasira, Maastricht School of Management, The Netherlands

Kai-Hong Tee, University of Loughborough, UK

Konstantinos Tolikas, Cardiff University, UK

WALK-THROUGH TOUR

Part opening diagram A diagram at the beginning of each part illustrates how the key concepts relate to one another.

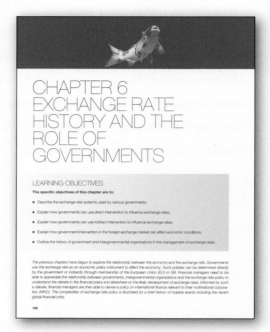

Objectives These define what you can expect to achieve as you read the chapter and what will be assessed by the exercises and other assessments as the chapter proceeds.

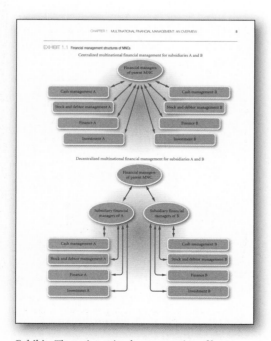

Exhibits These give a visual representation of key concepts or data.

Using the web Identifies websites that provide useful information related to key concepts.

Summary Found at the end of each chapter, the summary offers a useful method of reviewing knowledge for exams by reminding students of what they have learned so far.

Critical debate A controversial topic is introduced, two opposing views are provided and students must decide which view they support and why.

Self tests A self test at the end of each chapter challenges the students on the key concepts. The answers are provided in Appendix A.

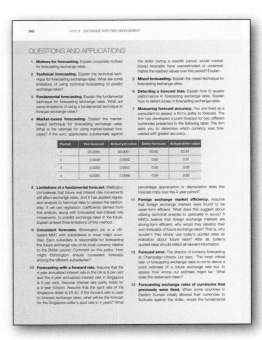

Questions and applications A variety of questions and other applications is designed to give students a thorough familiarity with the chapter material and to open up areas of further discovery.

BLADES PLC CASE STUDY

Consideration of foreign direct investment

For the last year, Blades plc has been exporting to Thailand in order to supplement its declining UK sales. Under the existing arrangement, Blades sells 180 000 pairs of roller blades annually to Entertainment Products, a Thai retailer, for a fixed price denominated in Thai baht. The agreement will last for another 2 years. Furthermore, to diversify internationally and to take advantage of an attractive offer by Jogs Inc., a US retailer, Blades has recently begun exporting to the USA. Under the resulting agreement, Jogs will purchase 200 000 pairs of 'Speedos', Blades' primary product, annually at a fixed price of $80 per pair.

Blades' suppliers of the needed components for its roller blade production are located primarily in the UK, where Blades incurs the majority of its cost of goods sold. Although prices for inputs needed to manufacture roller blades vary, recent costs have run approximately £70 per pair. Blades also imports components from Thailand because of the relatively low price of rubber and plastic components and because of their high quality. These imports are denominated in Thai baht, and the exact price (in baht) depends on prevailing market prices for these components in Thailand. Currently, inputs sufficient to manufacture a pair of roller blades cost approximately 3000 Thai baht per pair of roller blades.

Although Thailand had been among the world's fastest growing economies, recent events in Thailand have increased the level of economic uncertainty. Specifically, the Thai baht, which had been pegged to the dollar, is now a freely floating currency and has depreciated substantially in recent months. Furthermore, recent levels of inflation in Thailand have been very high. Hence, future economic conditions in Thailand are highly uncertain.

Ben Holt, Blades' financial director, is seriously considering FDI in Thailand. He believes that this is a perfect time to either establish a subsidiary or acquire an existing business in Thailand because the uncertain economic conditions and the depreciation of the baht have substantially lowered the initial costs required for FDI. Holt believes the growth potential in Asia will be extremely high once the Thai economy stabilizes.

Although Holt has also considered FDI in the USA, he would prefer that Blades invest in Thailand as opposed to the USA. Forecasts indicate that the demand for roller blades in the USA is similar to that in the UK, since Blades' UK sales have recently declined because of the high prices it charges. Holt expects that FDI in the USA will yield similar results. Furthermore, both domestic and foreign roller blade manufacturers are relatively well established in the USA, so the growth potential there is limited. Holt believes the Thai roller blade market offers more growth potential.

Blades can sell its products at a lower price but generate higher profit margins in Thailand than it can in the UK. This is because the Thai customer has committed itself to purchase a fixed number of Blades' products annually only if it can purchase Speedos at a substantial discount from the UK price. Nevertheless, since the cost of goods sold incurred in Thailand is substantially below that incurred in the USA, Blades has managed to generate higher profit margins from its Thai exports and imports than in the UK.

As a financial analyst for Blades plc you generally agree with Ben Holt's assessment of the situation. However, you are concerned that Thai consumers have not been affected yet by the unfavourable economic conditions. You believe that they may reduce their spending on leisure products within the next year. Therefore, you think it would be beneficial to wait until next year, when the unfavourable economic conditions in Thailand may subside, to make a decision regarding FDI in Thailand. However, if economic conditions in Thailand improve over the next year, FDI may become more expensive both because target firms will be more expensive and because the baht may appreciate. You are also aware that several of Blades' UK competitors are considering expanding into Thailand in the next year.

If Blades acquires an existing business in Thailand or establishes a subsidiary there by the end of next year, it would fulfil its agreement with Entertainment Products for the subsequent year. The Thai retailer has expressed an interest in renewing the contractual agreement with Blades at that time if Blades

Case studies Allow students to apply chapter concepts to a specific situation of an MNC.

SMALL BUSINESS DILEMMA

Developing a multinational sporting goods industry

In every chapter of this text, some of the key concepts are illustrated with an application to a small sporting goods firm that conducts international business. These 'Small Business Dilemma' features allow students to recognize the dilemmas and possible decisions that firms (such as this sporting goods firm) may face in a global environment. For this chapter, the application is on the development of the sporting goods firm that would conduct international business.

Last month, Jim Logan from Ireland completed his undergraduate degree in finance and decided to pursue his dream of managing his own sporting goods business. Jim had worked in a sporting goods shop while going to university in Ireland, and he had noticed that many customers wanted to purchase a low-priced basketball. However, the sporting goods store where he worked, like many others, sold only top-of-the-line basketballs. From his experience, Jim was aware that top-of-the-line basketballs had a high mark-up and that a low-cost basketball could possibly penetrate the UK market. He also knew how to produce cricket balls. His goal was to create a firm that would produce low-priced basketballs and sell them on a wholesale basis to various sporting goods stores in the UK. Unfortunately, many sporting goods stores began to sell low-priced basketballs just before Jim was about to start his business. The firm that began to produce the low-cost basketballs already provided many other products to sporting goods stores in the UK and therefore had already established a business relationship with these stores. Jim did not believe that he could compete with this firm in the UK market.

Rather than pursue a different business, Jim decided to implement his idea on a global basis. While basketball has not been a traditional sport in many countries, it has become more popular in some countries in recent years. Furthermore, the expansion of cable networks in many countries would allow for much more exposure to basketball games in those countries in the future. Jim asked many of his

friends from college days if they recalled seeing basketballs sold in their home countries. Most of them said they rarely noticed basketballs being sold in sporting goods stores but that they expected the demand for basketballs to increase in their home countries. Consequently, Jim decided to start a business of producing low-priced basketballs and exporting them to sporting goods distributors in foreign countries. Those distributors would then sell the basketballs at the retail level. Jim planned to expand his product line over time once he identified other sports products that he might sell to foreign sporting goods stores. He decided to call his business 'Sports Exports Company'. To avoid any rent and labour expenses, Jim planned to produce the basketballs in his garage and to perform the work himself. Thus, his main business expenses were the cost of the material used to produce basketballs and expenses associated with finding distributors in foreign countries who would attempt to sell the basketballs to sporting goods stores.

1 Is Sports Exports Company a MNC?

2 Why are the agency costs lower for Sports Exports Company than for most MNCs?

3 Does Sports Exports Company have any comparative advantage over potential competitors in foreign countries that could produce and sell basketballs there?

4 How would Jim Logan decide which foreign markets he would attempt to enter? Should he initially focus on one or many foreign markets?

5 The Sports Exports Company has no immediate plans to conduct direct foreign investment. However, it might consider other less costly methods of establishing its business in foreign markets. What methods might the Sports Exports Company use to increase its presence in foreign markets by working with one or more foreign companies?

Small business dilemma Students use the knowledge they have learned so far to make decisions about a small MNC.

Part 1 Integrative problem

THE INTERNATIONAL FINANCIAL ENVIRONMENT

Mesa Co. specializes in the production of small fancy picture frames, which are exported from the USA to the UK. Mesa invoices the exports in pounds and converts the pounds to dollars when they are received. The British pound for these frames is positively related to economic conditions in the UK. Assume that British inflation and interest rates are similar to the rates in the USA. Mesa believes that the US balance of trade deficit from trade between the USA and the UK will adjust to changing prices between the two countries, while capital flows will adjust to interest rate differentials. Mesa believes that the value of the pound is very sensitive to changing international capital flows and is moderately sensitive to changing international trade flows. Mesa is considering the following information:

- The UK inflation rate is expected to decline, while the US inflation rate is expected to rise.
- British interest rates are expected to decline, while US interest rates are expected to increase.

Questions

1 Explain how international trade flows should initially adjust in response to the changes in inflation (holding exchange rates constant). Explain how the international capital flows should adjust in response to the changes in interest rates (holding exchange rates constant).

2 Using the information provided, will Mesa expect the pound to appreciate or depreciate in the future? Explain.

3 Mesa believes international capital flows shift in response to changing interest rate differentials. Is there any reason why the changing interest rate differentials in this example will not necessarily cause international capital flows to change significantly? Explain.

4 Based on your answer to question 2, how would Mesa's cash flows be affected by the expected exchange rate movements? Explain.

5 Based on your answer to question 4, should Mesa consider hedging its exchange rate risk? If so, explain how it could hedge using forward contracts, futures contracts and currency options.

Integrative problem Found at the end of each part, this feature integrates the key concepts across chapters in that part.

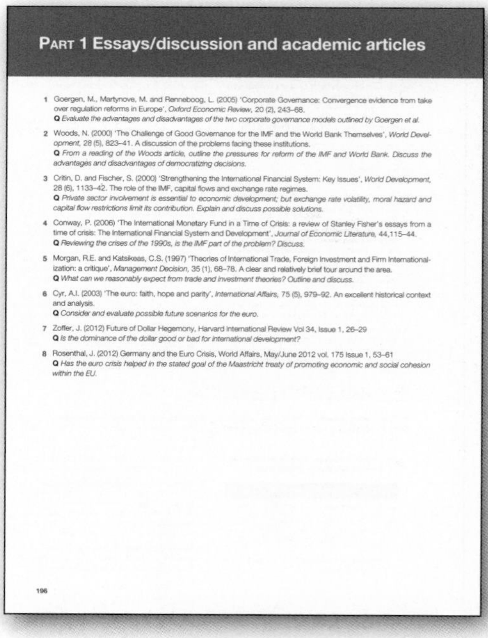

Part 1 Essays/discussion and academic articles

1 Goergen, M., Martynova, M. and Renneboog, L. (2005) 'Corporate Governance: Convergence evidence from take over regulation reforms in Europe', Oxford Economic Review, 20 (2), 243–68.
  Q Evaluate the advantages and disadvantages of the two corporate governance models outlined by Goergen et al.

2 Woods, N. (2000) 'The Challenge of Good Governance for the IMF and the World Bank Themselves', World Development, 28 (5), 823–41. A discussion of the problems facing these institutions.
  Q From a reading of the Woods article, outline the pressures for reform of the IMF and World Bank. Discuss the advantages and disadvantages of democratizing decisions.

3 Crittn, D. and Fischer, S. (2000) 'Strengthening the International Financial System: Key Issues', World Development, 28 (6), 1133–42. The role of the IMF, capital flows and exchange rate regimes.
  Q Private sector involvement is essential to economic development; but exchange rate volatility, moral hazard and capital flow restrictions limit its contribution. Explain and discuss possible solutions.

4 Conway, P. (2006) 'The International Monetary Fund in a Time of Crisis: a review of Stanley Fisher's essays from a time of crisis: The International Financial System and Development', Journal of Economic Literature, 44,115–44.
  Q Reviewing the crises of the 1990s, is the IMF part of the problem? Discuss.

5 Morgan, R.E. and Katsikeas, C.S. (1997) 'Theories of International Trade, Foreign Investment and Firm Internationalization: a critique', Management Decision, 35 (1), 68–78. A clear and relatively brief tour around the area.
  Q What can we reasonably expect from trade and investment theories? Outline and discuss.

6 Cyr, A.I. (2003) 'The euro: faith, hope and parity', International Affairs, 75 (5), 979–92. An excellent historical context and analysis.
  Q Consider and evaluate possible future scenarios for the euro.

7 Zoffer, J. (2012) Future of Dollar Hegemony, Harvard International Review Vol 34, Issue 1, 26–29
  Q Is the dominance of the dollar good or bad for international development?

8 Rosenthal, J. (2012) Germany and the Euro Crisis, World Affairs, May/June 2012 vol. 175 Issue 1, 53–61
  Q Has the euro crisis helped in the stated goal of the Maastricht treaty of promoting economic and social cohesion within the EU.

Essays/discussion and academic articles At the end of each Part, a list of articles allows students access to the literature and provides essay practice.

DIGITAL SUPPORT RESOURCES

Dedicated Instructor Resources

To discover the dedicated instructor online support resources accompanying this textbook, instructors should register here for access:

http://login.cengage.com

Resources include:

- Instructor's manual
- ExamView testbank
- PowerPoint slides.

Instructor access

Instructors can access CourseMate by registering at **http://login.cengage.com** or by speaking to their local Cengage Learning EMEA representative.

Instructor resources

Instructors can use the integrated Engagement Tracker in CourseMate to track students' preparation and engagement. The tracking tool can be used to monitor progress of the class as a whole, or for individual students.

Student access

Students can access CourseMate using the unique personal access card included in the front of the book.

Student resources

CourseMate offers a range of interactive learning tools tailored to the 3rd Edition of International Financial Management, including:

- Quizzes and self-test questions
- Interactive eBook
- Bonus chapters
- Glossary
- Flashcards
- Links to useful websites.

PART I
THE INTERNATIONAL FINANCIAL ENVIRONMENT

PART 1 (Chapters 1–5) provides an overview of the multinational corporation (MNC) and the environment in which it operates. Chapter 1 explains the goals of the MNC, along with the motives and risks of international business. Chapter 2 describes the international flow of funds between countries. Chapter 3 describes the international financial markets and how these markets facilitate ongoing operations. Chapter 4 explains how exchange rates are determined, while Chapter 5 provides a background on the currency futures and options markets. Managers of MNCs must understand the international environment described in these chapters in order to make proper decisions.

CHAPTER 1
MULTINATIONAL
FINANCIAL
MANAGEMENT:
AN OVERVIEW

LEARNING OBJECTIVES

The specific objectives of this chapter are to:

● Identify the main goal of the multinational corporation (MNC) and potential conflicts with that goal.

● Describe the key theories that seek to explain international business.

● Outline the common methods used to conduct international business.

The commonly stated goal of a firm is to maximize its value and thereby maximize shareholder wealth. This goal is applicable not only to firms that focus on domestic business, but also to firms that focus on international business. Developing business at an international level is an important means of enhancing value for many firms. Since foreign markets can be distinctly different from local markets, they create opportunities for improving the firm's cash flows. Many barriers to entry into foreign markets have been reduced or removed recently, thereby encouraging firms to pursue international business (producing and/or selling goods in foreign countries). Consequently, many firms have evolved into MNCs, which are defined as firms that engage in some form of international business. Their managers conduct international financial management, which involves international investing and financing decisions that are intended to enhance the value of the MNC.

Initially, firms may merely attempt to export products to a particular country or import supplies from a foreign manufacturer. Over time, however, many recognize additional foreign opportunities and eventually establish subsidiaries in foreign countries. Large European MNCs such as BP plc (UK), Renault (France), Koninklijke Philips Electronics NV *(the Netherlands) and many other firms have more than half of their assets in foreign (non-euro) countries. Businesses, such as Nokia (Finland), Diageo (UK), ThyssenKrupp Group (Germany), Alcatel (France), Tesco (UK) and Adidas (Germany), commonly generate more than a third of their sales outside Europe.*

An understanding of international financial management is crucial not only for the largest MNCs with numerous foreign subsidiaries but also for small and medium-sized enterprises (SMEs). They tend to penetrate specialty markets where they will not have to compete with large firms that could capitalize on economies of scale. While some SMEs have established subsidiaries, many of them penetrate foreign markets through exports. International financial management is important even to companies that have no international business because these companies must recognize how their foreign competitors will be affected by movements in exchange rates, foreign interest rates, labour costs and inflation. Such economic characteristics can affect the foreign competitors' costs of production and pricing policies.

Companies must also recognize how domestic competitors that obtain foreign supplies or foreign financing will be affected by economic conditions in foreign countries. If these domestic competitors are able to reduce their costs by capitalizing on opportunities in international markets, they may be able to reduce their prices without reducing their profit margins. This could allow them to increase market share at the expense of the purely domestic companies.

This chapter provides a background on the goals of an MNC and the potential risk and returns from engaging in international business.

GOAL OF THE MNC

The focus of this text is on MNCs that are quoted on the world's stock exchanges. They will almost always have numerous wholly owned foreign subsidiaries. The commonly accepted goal of such an MNC is to maximize shareholder wealth. Some MNCs are former state owned companies where governments remain an important shareholder (e.g. Renault and Petro China). Such companies seek stock market quotes to raise finance and therefore have to demonstrate by means of the annual accounts and report that they are maximizing shareholder wealth in the same way as a wholly private owned company. Such companies may benefit more from government support, but in all other respects there is little to suggest that they are in any way different from other MNCs.

Shareholder influence is another major difference between MNCs. Continental Europe has what has been termed the blockholder system: fewer, larger stakeholders in companies with corporate governance laws that seek to protect creditors and employees. The UK–US market-based approach has far more dispersed ownership and much greater emphasis on shareholders' rights. In the long run profit maximization is in the interests of all groups, but as ever it is the short term that provides key differences in areas such as employee rights and representation at Board level. In offering greater non-shareholder participation, the Continental system gives greater emphasis on long-term profitability, and this is borne out by the generally longer payback periods of Continental European companies compared to the UK.

Conflicts with the MNC goal

It has often been argued that managers of a firm may make decisions that conflict with the firm's goal to maximize shareholder wealth. For example, a decision to establish a subsidiary in one location versus another may be based on the location's appeal to a particular manager rather than on its potential benefits to shareholders. A decision to expand may be determined by a manager's desire to make the division grow in order to receive more responsibility and compensation. When a firm has only one owner who is also the sole manager, such a conflict of goals does not occur. However, when a corporation's shareholders differ from its managers, a conflict of goals can exist. This conflict is often referred to as the **agency problem**.

The costs of ensuring that managers maximize shareholder wealth (referred to as *agency costs*) are normally larger for MNCs than for purely domestic firms for several reasons. *First*, MNCs with subsidiaries scattered around the world may experience larger agency problems because monitoring managers of distant subsidiaries in foreign countries is more difficult. Financial managers of an MNC with several subsidiaries may be tempted to make decisions that maximize the values of their respective subsidiaries. This objective will not necessarily coincide with maximizing the value of the overall MNC. *Second*, foreign subsidiary managers raised in different cultures may treat the goals of its MNC in a different way from that intended by the senior management. *Third*, the sheer size of the larger MNCs can also create communication problems. The sales of the larger MNCs compare with the value of production of a small country. *Fourth*, the complexity of operations may result in decisions for foreign subsidiaries of the MNCs that are inconsistent with maximizing shareholder wealth.

EXAMPLE

A subsidiary manager obtained financing from the parent firm (headquarters) to develop and sell a new product. The manager estimated the costs and benefits of the project from the subsidiary's perspective and determined that the project was feasible. However, the manager neglected to realize that any earnings from this project remitted to the parent would be heavily taxed by the host government. The estimated after-tax benefits received by the parent were more than offset by the cost of financing the project. While the subsidiary's individual value was enhanced, the MNC's overall value was reduced.

If financial managers are to maximize the wealth of their MNC's shareholders, they must implement policies that maximize the value of the overall MNC rather than the value of their respective subsidiaries. Many MNCs require major decisions by subsidiary managers to be approved by the parent. However, it is difficult for the parent to monitor all decisions made by subsidiary managers.

At times it can appear that the headquarters of an MNC (the parent company) is pursuing other goals, for example, environmental concerns, funding community projects or maximizing market share or directors' bonuses. The counter argument is that these are really proxy or operational goals necessary for long-term profit maximization. The sheer size of MNCs makes what are small payments in relation to overall profits seem very large. Motives can always be questioned and there will always be the view that shareholders' interests could be more vigorously pursued. In some respects it is reassuring to note that the US company Enron's demise (the most recent major case of corporate misbehaviour where shareholders' wealth was being sacrificed for managerial rewards) involved misleading shareholders by false accounting and deception. If there had been a more honest disclosure of information, as is required, the abuses would most likely not have taken place. The same can be said of the Italian food giant Parmalat which collapsed in December 2003 with a 14.3 billion euro hole in its accounts. As with Enron the accounts had been materially misstated. The lesson to be learnt from such scandals is that relevant information must be disclosed to the market. Legislation (in the US, the Sarbanes–Oxley Act of 2002), an active financial press and improved accounting regulations help shareholders make informed decisions.

Impact of management control

The magnitude of agency costs can vary with the management style of the MNC. A centralized management style, as illustrated in the top section of Exhibit 1.1, can reduce agency costs because it allows managers of the parent direct control of foreign subsidiaries and therefore reduces the power of subsidiary managers. However, the parent's managers may make poor decisions for the subsidiary if they are not as informed as subsidiary managers about local financial conditions.

Alternatively, an MNC can use a decentralized management style, as illustrated in the bottom section of Exhibit 1.1. This style is more likely to result in higher agency costs because subsidiary managers may make decisions that do not focus on maximizing the value of the entire MNC. Yet, this style gives more control to those managers who are closer to the subsidiary's operations and environment.

EXHIBIT 1.1   Financial management structures of MNCs

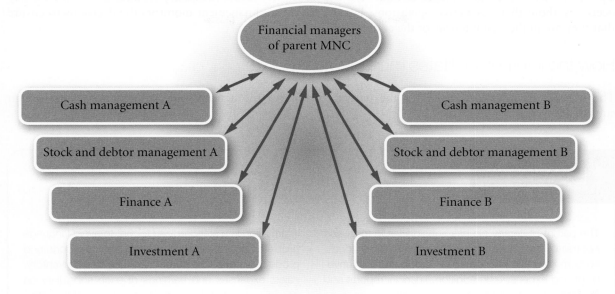

Centralized multinational financial management for subsidiaries A and B

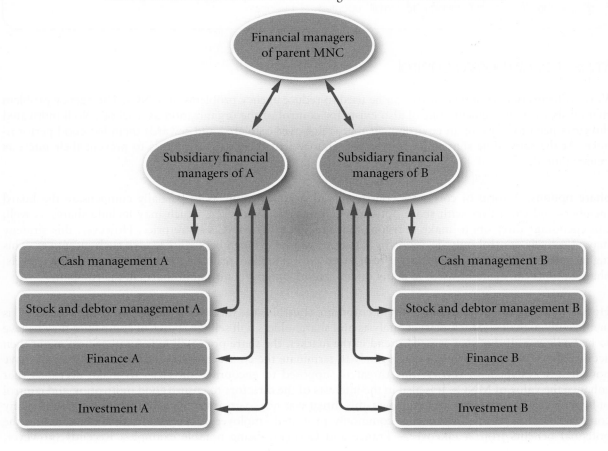

Decentralized multinational financial management for subsidiaries A and B

To the extent that subsidiary managers recognize the goal of maximizing the value of the overall MNC and are compensated in accordance with that goal, the decentralized management style can be more effective.

Given the obvious trade-off between centralized and decentralized management styles, some MNCs attempt to achieve the advantages of both styles. That is, they allow subsidiary managers to make the key decisions about their respective operations, but the parent's management monitors the decisions to ensure that they are in the best interests of the entire MNC.

How the Internet facilitates management control

The Internet is making it easier for the parent to monitor the actions and performance of its foreign subsidiaries.

EXAMPLE

The parent of Jersey plc has subsidiaries in India and Australia. The subsidiaries are in different time zones, so communicating frequently by telephone is inconvenient and expensive. In addition, financial reports and designs of new products or plant sites cannot be easily communicated over the telephone. The Internet allows the foreign subsidiaries to email updated information in a standardized format to avoid language problems and to send images of financial reports and product designs. The parent can easily track inventory, sales, expenses and earnings of each subsidiary on a weekly or monthly basis. Thus, the use of the Internet can reduce agency costs due to international business.

Impact of corporate control

Various forms of corporate control can be used to reduce agency problems in MNCs. The agency problem that exists for management control also exists for control of the organization as a whole. Well-motivated directors need to work in an environment that is not over-regulated and rewards them for good performance. At the same time shareholders need reassurance that there are safeguards to prevent their interests being ignored.

Share options. A form of corporate control, based on motivation, is to partially compensate the board members and executives with share options. Such incentive packages, which may include shares as well, can encourage directors to make decisions that maximize the MNC's share price. However, this strategy may effectively control only decisions by directors and board members who receive such incentives. This higher level of management is then in turn faced with a similar problem of motivating the lower levels. Share options can again be used. In many organizations employees also hold shares in the company.

Hostile takeover threat. A second form of corporate control is the threat of a hostile takeover if the MNC is inefficiently managed. Stock market analysts and shareholders will sell the shares of companies they believe to be badly run. If this view is widespread in the market, the share price will fall. Another firm might then acquire the MNC at a low price and is likely to terminate the contracts of the existing directors who have not already resigned. In theory, this threat is supposed to encourage directors to make decisions that enhance the value of MNCs. It is also in the interests of the directors to ensure good motivation and control of lower levels of management. In the past, this threat was not so great for managers of subsidiaries in many countries because their governments commonly protected employees, thereby effectively eliminating the potential benefits from a takeover – France and Germany being notable examples. Recently, however, governments have recognized that such protectionism may promote inefficiencies, and they are now more willing to accept takeovers and the subsequent layoffs that occur. In Europe there is currently much debate about the extent to which employee rights can be maintained in a world economy where production has to compete with goods made in countries with poor employee rights. **Hostile takeovers** are governed by the Thirteenth Directive of the European Union (EU). Generally it imposes more restrictions on both the raider and the target compared to the US legislation.

Investor monitoring. A third form of corporate control is monitoring by individuals, pressure groups and institutions, including investment trusts, pension funds and insurance companies, all of whom are major shareholders in the stock market. Their monitoring by means of the financial press, annual and interim reports and, rather more controversially, by investor briefings given by companies, tends to focus on broad issues such as: motivation packages; use of excess cash for repurchasing shares; investing in questionable projects; ethical behaviour; and attempts by MNCs to insulate themselves from the threat of a takeover (by implementing anti-takeover amendments, for example). An MNC whose decisions appear inconsistent with maximizing shareholder wealth will be subjected to shareholder activism as pension funds and other large institutional shareholders lobby for management changes and threaten votes of no confidence at the MNC's annual general meeting (AGM). MNCs that have been subjected to various forms of shareholder activism include Eastman Kodak, Adidas, Shell and IBM.

Non-US banks also maintain large share portfolios (unlike US commercial banks, which do not use deposited funds to purchase shares). Such banks are large and hold a sufficient proportion of shares of numerous firms (including some US-based MNCs) to have some influence on key corporate policies. In Germany, banks are often represented on the Supervisory Board of companies and will play a part in their management. The concern is that either as lender or as a member of the management, banks will have access to private or insider information. The relationship is uneasy in that stock markets around the world forbid the use of such information when taking investment decisions. If some investors used private information, other investors would be disadvantaged and may sell shares to the informed investor at a price that the informed investor knows for sure is undervalued. It would be like playing poker against someone who knew which cards were going to be dealt next. The banks are supposed to have 'Chinese walls' inside the organization so that insider information cannot be used to make investment decisions. Private information is not limited to banks. Rating agencies will be informed about important moves so that they can adjust their ratings immediately on announcement. Printing companies have the accounts prior to publication. Research findings may be shared with universities. The opportunity for leaks is extensive. Legal cases such as the conviction of Raj Rajaratnam (2009), have led to allegations against employees of many major companies. But without direct evidence that the investor knew that the information was as a result of a breach of trust, conviction is difficult.

Constraints interfering with the MNC's goal

When financial managers of MNCs attempt to maximize their firm's value, they are confronted with various constraints that can be classified as environmental, regulatory or ethical in nature.

Environmental constraints. Each country enforces its own environmental constraints. Building codes, disposal of production waste materials, and pollution controls are examples of restrictions that force subsidiaries to incur additional costs. The threat by MNCs to locate elsewhere in the face of overly harsh local environmental laws acts as a significant restraint to countries wishing to pursue a strong environmental policy. The failure of the USA and Australia to sign the Kyoto protocol on global warming further weakens the environmental movement.

Regulatory constraints. Each country also enforces its own regulatory constraints pertaining to taxes, currency convertibility, earnings remittance, employee rights and other policies that can affect cash flows of a subsidiary established there. Because these regulations can influence cash flows, financial managers must consider them when assessing policies. Also, any change in these regulations may require revision of existing financial policies, so financial managers should monitor the regulations for any potential changes over time.

To recognize the potential impact of regulations, consider the regulation of employee rights. Although it is understandable that every country attempts to ensure employee rights, countries are limited by the threat of multinationals investing elsewhere.

EXAMPLE

Bosch to quit South Wales with the loss of 900 jobs

About 900 jobs will be lost after the motor parts' maker Bosch announced the closure of its South Wales plant ... The firm says it has now decided to recommend closure to its board, transferring work to Hungary in 2011 ... Plant director Adam Willmott said the move was one of 'pure economics' after a feasibility study had concluded the switch to Hungary, where labour costs were 65 per cent of those at the plant in Wales, was necessary to gain the benefit of economies

of scale. He said: 'The decision today is one of pure economics and is really not a reflection at all on the workforce ... The problem is ... with the huge cost pressures that we are facing, we really have no other chance other than to bring the production together, consolidate it and really look for the economies of scale with the lower labour costs. The product we are producing is very much a commodity and it's a very, very tough market at the moment in the automotive industry.'

Source: © BBC News, http://news.bbc.co.uk/1/hi/wales/ 8458854.stm (15-01-10).

Ethical constraints. There is no consensus standard of business conduct that applies to all countries. A business practice that is perceived to be unethical in one country may be totally ethical in another. For example, MNCs are well aware that certain business practices that are accepted in some less developed countries would be illegal in their home country. Bribes to governments in order to receive special tax breaks or other favours are common in some countries. Dieter Frisch, a former director-general of development at the European Commission, estimates that on average at least 10–20 per cent of total government contract costs are bribes. The MNCs face a dilemma. If they do not participate in such practices, they may be at a competitive disadvantage. Yet, if they do participate, their reputations will suffer in countries that do not approve of such practices. One solution to this dilemma is to adopt a set of ethical conventions for all parties to adhere to, thus eliminating the competitive disadvantage and conforming to morally acceptable practice. The Equator principles, a voluntary set of relatively loosely defined commitments, represents one such initiative. But it remains voluntary and limited in scope to project finance. International organizations such as the UN and the International Monetary Fund (IMF) have as yet failed to develop a regulatory framework with a strong ethical foundation.

Managing within the constraints. Some MNCs have made the costly choice to refrain from business practices that are legal in certain foreign countries but not legal in their home country. Thus, they follow a worldwide code of ethics. This may enhance their worldwide credibility, which can increase global demand for their products. Recently, McKinsey & Co. found that investors assigned a higher value to firms that exhibit high corporate governance standards and are likely to obey ethical constraints. The premiums that investors would pay for these firms averaged 12 per cent in North America, 20 to 25 per cent in Asia and Latin America and more than 30 per cent in Europe.

THEORIES OF INTERNATIONAL BUSINESS

Theories in this area seek to explain the level and nature of international business. There are two broad categories, economic and business related theories. Economic theories address the problem at national level, looking at how countries can increase their overall level of wealth through international trade. In this respect the theories are normative, they examine the logic of international trade but do not necessarily explain actual trade levels. These theories are of particular importance in practice as a response to those who argue that international trade is creating poverty. Business theories are based on observation: they seek to find common patterns of development of international business and model these patterns into a coherent explanation. These theories are valuable in that they provide a compact explanation of observed practice.

Economic theories

Theory of absolute and comparative advantage. The theory of **absolute advantage** was first formally stated by Adam Smith and conforms to what most non-specialists would advance as an explanation and justification for international trade. Suppose that Country A is more efficient at producing food, and Country B is more efficient at producing machinery, in a two country world. The world production of food and machinery (the overall size of the 'cake') can be increased by specialization. Country A should produce more food than it needs at the expense of some machinery production; and country B should produce more machinery than it needs at the expense of some food production. Country A can then trade some of its surplus food for some of Country B's surplus machinery. The important point here is that through better use of resources by means of specialization, the world totals of food and machinery are now higher than before specialization. It is easy to show (see the example below) that from such trade, it is possible for both countries to increase their levels of consumption of food and machinery. This is termed a Pareto optimal solution; both parties are better off through specialization and international trade.

The economist David Ricardo extended this analysis to the law of **comparative advantage**. He asked the equivalent question to: 'what if A were less efficient at producing food as well as being less efficient at producing machinery?' He showed that if Country A produced more of the product at which it was comparatively *less inefficient*, it was still possible for world production levels of food and machinery to increase and both parties could still benefit through international trade. Suppose in this example that Country B developed its food production and became slightly more efficient than Country A and remained much more efficient at producing machinery. There would still be benefits to both parties if A specialized more in food and B more in machinery.

As well as productivity it may be the case that resources for production are more abundant in some countries than others. International trade allows use of resources that otherwise may have been unused. The Heckscher–Ohlin theorem translates these ideas of productivity and resource abundance to the price mechanism. Prices, unconstrained by tariffs and quotas, should guide the profit motive and result in specialization and international trade reflecting the comparative advantages of each country. Thus it is argued, in almost all cases countries can benefit through international trade providing that there is a free market and free price mechanism.

In practice, countries in the developed world have a technology advantage, while other countries, such as India and China, have an advantage in the cost of labour. Since these advantages cannot be easily transported, countries tend to use their advantages to specialize in the production of goods that can be produced with their relative advantages. This explains why Europe and the USA are large producers of aircraft, computer components and other highly technical equipment, while countries such as India and China are large producers of clothes, basic computers and other lower technology equipment. Many of the island economies (Martinique, the Seychelles and Virgin Islands), for example, specialize in tourism and rely completely on international trade for most products. Although these islands could produce some goods, it is more efficient for them to specialize in tourism. That is, the islands are better off using some revenues earned from tourism to import products rather than attempting to produce all the products that they need.

There are also more difficult to explain examples. Although there are exceptions with regard to individual products, on average, imports into the USA are more capital intensive than their exports. One would expect this of a developing country rather than the world's most developed country (this observation is known as the Leontief paradox). There are further developments to trade theory related to the pricing mechanism and availability of resources. The underlying rationale nevertheless remains the same. International trade increases world production and all can benefit through international trade. Thus trade theory provides a basic economic rationale and justification for multinational activity. Note that it does not say that all countries will necessarily benefit, only that countries *can* benefit. There is further support from history. Countries that have been excluded from international trade (e.g. North Korea, Libya, Cuba and arguably Eastern Europe) have all suffered from backward economies and there have been clear benefits when restrictions have been eased. Also, when there have been increased restrictions on international trade as in the 1930s, overall output and wealth have declined.

EXAMPLE

From the above discussion, suppose that Countries A and B produce all their own food and machinery, producing about as much food and as much machinery as each other – these equal size assumptions are to simplify calculations and are otherwise not important. Country A is more efficient at food production and Country B more efficient at machinery production. Then international trade is intro-

duced. Country A reduces its machinery production by 4 per cent to 96 per cent and with those resources increases its food production by 20 per cent to 120 per cent of before trade levels. Country B reduces its food production to 95 per cent and increases its machinery production to 114 per cent of before trade levels. They then trade as in the following diagram.

Gains from international trade	Country A		Country B	
	Machinery	Food	Machinery	Food
Before international trade, A and B self-sufficient producing about the same amounts of food and machinery as each other	100%	100%	100%	100%
Specialization due to international trade (A in food, B in machinery)	96%	120%	114%	95%
Exchange: B trades surplus machinery for A's surplus food	+7%	−10%	−7%	+10%
After international trade	103%	110%	107%	105%

Notes:

- Country A can reduce its production of machinery by 4 per cent and increase its production of food by 20 per cent because the resources released through reducing machinery production can be more productively used in producing food.
- Country B in similar fashion releases resources by reducing its food production by 5 per cent and uses those resources more productively to produce machinery.
- Country A exchanges 10 per cent of its food surplus in exchange for 7 per cent of B's machinery surplus. Both countries are now better off as they now have more food and machinery than before trade.
- Country A can be less productive than B at both machinery and food and there will still be gains from international trade, similarly B can be less productive than A. Alternatively, A may have more abundant food resources and B more abundant machinery resources.

Imperfect markets theory. Countries differ with respect to resources available for the production of goods. Yet, even with such differences, the volume of international business would be limited if all resources could be easily transferred among countries. If markets were perfect, factors of production (except land) would be mobile and freely transferable. The unrestricted mobility of factors would create equality in costs and returns and remove the comparative cost advantage. However, the real world suffers from **imperfect market** conditions where factors of production are somewhat immobile – people (labour) are not willing to move. There are also costs and restrictions related to the transfer of labour and other resources used for production. There may also be restrictions on transferring funds and other resources among countries. For example, tariffs and restrictions on imports that can only be overcome by producing in the relevant country. The EU is often cited as an example of such a restricted market. Because markets for the various resources used in production are 'imperfect', firms often capitalize on a foreign country's resources. Overall, wealth can be increased as imperfect markets provide an incentive for firms to seek out foreign opportunities and produce wealth that otherwise would not have been created.

Business theories

Product cycle theory. One of the more popular explanations as to why firms evolve into MNCs is the **product cycle theory**. According to this theory, firms first become established in the home market to meet local demand. A lack of information and a lack of resources creates a preference for single market development. Where the product is successful, the firm will experience foreign demand for its products from exporters, foreign companies or even via the Internet from foreign customers. As time passes, the firm may feel the only way to retain its advantage over competition in foreign countries is to produce the product in foreign markets, thereby reducing its transportation costs. The competition in the foreign markets may increase as other producers become more familiar with the firm's product. The firm may develop strategies to prolong the foreign demand for its product. A common approach is to attempt to differentiate the product so that other competitors cannot offer exactly the same product. These phases of the cycle are illustrated in Exhibit 1.2. Most of the established MNCs today have followed this route. Greater availability of finance, knowledge and better communications as well as the Internet suggests that in future more developments may start at an international level, but currently the product life cycle theory remains a good description.

Global strategies. International business is seen as a product of global strategies being pursued by MNCs. The large investments required for medical research can only be recouped by patenting and marketing the products worldwide. Similarly for the aircraft industry and big budget films. Prestigious brand names (France's Louis Vuitton, Ralph Lauren in the USA, Swiss Rolex watches) require a worldwide market as part of their attraction. Where there is already a strong international market, firms need to produce and sell internationally to protect their sales. For example, computer chip production and car production cannot be profitably viewed as single-country products unless catering for a niche market only.

INTERNATIONAL BUSINESS METHODS

Firms use several methods to conduct international business. The most common methods are:

- International trade
- Licensing
- Franchising

EXHIBIT 1.2   International product life cycle

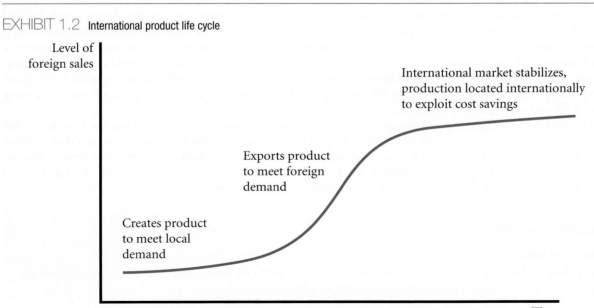

- Joint ventures
- Acquisitions of existing operations
- Establishing new foreign subsidiaries
- Special Purpose Vehicles.

Each method is discussed in turn, with emphasis on its risk and return characteristics.

International trade

Trading rather than investing abroad is a relatively conservative approach to international business that can be used by firms to penetrate markets (by exporting) or to obtain supplies at a low cost (by importing). The risk is minimal because the firm does not invest any of its capital abroad. If the firm experiences a decline in its exporting or importing, it can normally reduce or discontinue this part of its business at a low cost.

USING THE WEB

Trade conditions for industries

A comprehensive report on international trade conditions for industries in the USA is provided at www. trade.gov/mas/ian. Other countries tend to be less forthcoming in their reporting.

Many large MNCs, including Boeing (USA), BP (UK), DaimlerChrysler (Germany), France Telecom, Nestlé; (Switzerland), generate more than £3 billion in annual sales from exporting. Nonetheless, small businesses generally account for a significant proportion of exports (20 per cent in the USA).

How the Internet facilitates international trade. Many firms use their websites to list the products that they sell, along with the price for each product. This allows them to easily advertise their products to potential importers anywhere in the world without mailing brochures to various countries. In addition, a firm can add to its product line or change prices by simply revising its website. Thus, importers need only monitor an exporter's website periodically to keep abreast of its product information.

Firms can also use their websites to accept orders online. Some products such as software and music can be delivered directly to the importer over the Internet in the form of a file that lands in the importer's computer. Other products must be shipped, but the Internet makes it easier to track the shipping process. An importer can transmit its order for products via email to the exporter. The exporter's warehouse fills orders. When the warehouse ships the products, it can send an email message to the importer and to the exporter's headquarters. The warehouse may even use technology to monitor its inventory of products so that suppliers are automatically notified to send more supplies once the inventory is reduced to a specific level. If the exporter uses multiple warehouses, the Internet allows them to work as a network so that if one warehouse cannot fill an order, another warehouse will.

The Internet is particularly advantageous for small firms. Previously such firms would not have been able to consider international trade. As all access to websites is international, the Internet now means that all firms with a website are international. This has created 'mini–multinationals' small, often specialist firms, selling to an international market. As world markets are very much larger, small firms with a good idea can expand very quickly. Often such firms get bought out creating the phenomenon of 'Internet millionaires'.

USING THE WEB

Internet millionaires

For those who manage to exploit the new trading conditions the rewards are high. Anecdotes are provided at http://Internetmillionairesuccessstories.blogspot.co.uk/.

Licensing

Licensing involves selling copyrights, patents, trademarks, or trade names or legal rights in exchange for fees known as royalties. Thus a company is selling the right to produce their goods. For example, Pepsi-Cola licenses Heineken to make and sell Pepsi-Cola in the Netherlands. Oil companies need a licence from the host government to drill for oil. Eli Lilly & Co. (USA) has a licensing agreement to produce drugs for Hungary and other countries. Licensing allows firms to use their technology in foreign markets without a major investment in foreign countries and without the transportation costs that result from exporting. A major disadvantage of licensing is that it is difficult for the firm providing the technology to ensure quality control in the foreign production process.

How the Internet facilitates licensing. Some firms with an international reputation use their brand name to advertise products over the Internet. They may use manufacturers in foreign countries to produce some of their products subject to their specifications.

EXAMPLE

Springs SA (a fictitious French company) has set up a licensing agreement with a manufacturer in the Czech Republic. When Springs receives orders for its products from customers in Eastern Europe, it relies on this manufacturer to produce and deliver the products ordered. This expedites the delivery process and may even allow Springs to have the products manufactured at a lower cost than if it produced them itself. Springs has nevertheless to carefully monitor the quality of production in the Czech Republic.

Franchising

Under a **franchising** agreement the franchisor provides a specialized sales or service strategy, support assistance and possibly an initial investment in the franchise in exchange for periodic fees. For example, McDonald's, Pizza Hut, Subway sandwiches, Blockbuster video and Dairy Queen are franchisors who sell franchises that are owned and managed by local residents in many foreign countries. Like licensing, franchising allows firms to penetrate foreign markets without a major investment in foreign countries. The recent relaxation of barriers in foreign countries throughout Eastern Europe and South America has resulted in numerous franchising arrangements.

Joint ventures

A **joint venture** is a venture that is owned and operated by two or more firms. Many firms penetrate foreign markets by engaging in a joint venture with firms that reside in those markets. In China it is currently a requirement that one of the partners of a joint venture be a government owned company. Most joint ventures allow two firms to apply their respective comparative advantages in a given project. For example, General Mills, Inc. joined in a venture with Nestlé: SA, so that the cereals produced by General Mills could be sold through the overseas sales distribution network established by Nestlé. Xerox Corp. and Fuji Co. (of Japan) engaged in a joint venture that allowed Xerox Corp. to penetrate the Japanese market and allowed Fuji to enter the photocopying business. Joint ventures between automobile manufacturers are numerous, as each manufacturer can offer its technological advantages. General Motors has ongoing joint ventures with automobile manufacturers in several different countries, including Hungary and the former Soviet states.

Acquisitions of existing operations

Firms frequently acquire other firms in foreign countries as a means of penetrating foreign markets. Acquisitions allow firms to have full control over their foreign businesses and to quickly obtain a large portion of foreign market share.

EXAMPLE

Cadbury Schweppes has grown mainly through acquisitions in recent years including Wedel chocolate (Poland, 1999), Hollywood chewing gum (France, 2000), a buyout of minority shareholders of Cadbury India (2002), Dandy chewing gum from Denmark (2002) and the Adams chewing gum business ($4.2 billion, 2003). Clearly they were seeking synergies by being dominant in the chewing gum business. Then in early 2010 Cadbury Schweppes was taken over by Kraft Foods to create a 'global confectionary leader'.

An acquisition of an existing corporation is a quick way to grow. An MNC that grows in this way also partly protects itself from adverse actions from the host government of the acquired company. The MNC has control of a usually well-established firm with good connections to its government. The risk is that too much has been paid for the acquisition, also that there are unforeseen problems with the acquired company. It has to be remembered that the sellers of the company have a thorough knowledge of the business and the price at which they are selling is presumably higher than their estimate. The acquiring company is therefore to a certain extent outguessing the local owners – a risky proposition.

Some firms engage in partial international acquisitions in order to obtain a stake in foreign operations. This requires a smaller investment than full international acquisitions and therefore exposes the firm to less risk. On the other hand, the firm will not have complete control over foreign operations that are only partially acquired.

Establishing new foreign subsidiaries

Firms can also penetrate foreign markets by establishing new operations in foreign countries to produce and sell their products. Like a foreign acquisition, this method requires a large investment. Establishing new subsidiaries may be preferred to foreign acquisitions because the operations can be tailored exactly to the firm's needs. Development will be slower, however, in that the firm will not reap any rewards from the investment until the subsidiary is built and a customer base established.

Special Purpose Vehicles (SPV)

These are separate companies set up by the one or more sponsoring MNCs to exploit a particular project. This is part of what is termed project finance (see Chapter 15). The Special Purpose Vehicle (SPV) is legally and financially independent of the sponsors and other providers of capital. The success of the SPV depends on the project's ability to repay the contracted debt and reward the sponsors. Thus a SME can take on large projects. For larger companies the attraction is more in the way in which SPV isolates the MNC from downside risk (the risk of a loss). There is also the less virtuous motive of the activity being less visible ('off the balance sheet') as the SPV appears as an investment rather than the constituent assets and liabilities.

Summary of methods

The methods of increasing international business extend from the relatively simple approach of international trade to the more complex approach of acquiring foreign firms or establishing new subsidiaries. Any method of increasing international business that requires a direct investment in foreign operations normally is referred to as a **foreign direct investment (FDI)**. International trade and licensing usually are not considered to be FDI because they do not involve direct investment in foreign operations. Franchising and joint ventures tend to require some investment in foreign operations, but to a limited degree. Foreign acquisitions and the establishment of new foreign subsidiaries require substantial investment in foreign operations and represent the largest portion of FDI.

Many MNCs use a combination of methods to increase international business. Motorola and IBM, for example, have substantial **direct foreign investment (DFI)**, but also derive some of their foreign revenue from various licensing agreements, which require less FDI to generate revenue.

EXAMPLE

The evolution of Nike began in 1962, when Phil Knight, a business student at Stanford's business school, wrote a paper on how a US firm could use Japanese technology to break the German dominance of the athletic shoe industry in the USA. After graduation, Knight visited the Unitsuka Tiger shoe company in Japan. He made a licensing agreement with that company to produce a shoe that he sold in the USA under the name Blue Ribbon Sports (BRS). In 1972, Knight exported his shoes to Canada. In 1974, he expanded his operations into Australia. In 1977, the firm licensed factories in Asia to produce athletic shoes and then sold the shoes in Asian countries. In 1978, BRS became Nike, Inc., and began to export shoes to Europe and South America. As a result of its exporting and its direct foreign investment, Nike's international sales reached $1 billion by 1992 and were over $24 billion by 2012 – a 17.2 per cent annual growth rate.

INTERNATIONAL OPPORTUNITIES

Because of possible cost advantages from producing in foreign countries or possible revenue opportunities from demand by foreign markets, the growth potential becomes much greater for firms that consider international business.

Investment opportunities

Investment opportunities in real assets (i.e. factories, labour, machinery and offices) are greater for MNCs than for purely domestic companies in that MNCs supply world markets and take advantage of benefits on a worldwide basis. MNCs can take advantage of cheaper labour in one market and easily available natural resources in another. By supplying different markets, MNCs also benefit from greater diversification and hence lower risk. A decline in one market can be offset by an increase in demand in another market.

USING THE WEB

FDI analysis and trends can be obtained from the United Nations under the keywords 'UNCTAD World Investment report'. For a broader view see 'IMF World Economic Outlook' again by using the title as the keywords in a search engine.

Portfolio investment, that is investment in stocks and shares by banks and insurance companies, also offers better returns in the international markets. Investors can benefit from a booming economy in one part of the world and again spread their risk by investing in differing economies. But such profits come with greater risks: the world financial crisis that began in 2007 spread quickly due to international investments in new securities such as collateralized debt obligations. The risk of the American mortgage market that many such instruments were linked to was greatly underestimated. Yet the potential profits mean that to survive, investment companies must take an international perspective.

Financing opportunities

An MNC has greater access to funding than its smaller domestic counterpart. In particular the large foreign currency lending market in London (the Eurodollar market) is open to large companies only, at reduced interest rates. The security rating of large MNCs is also likely to be higher and therefore a lower risk premium is paid. A drawback is that individual international projects are riskier than their domestic equivalent. There are greater business risks in dealing with a less familiar market, greater financial risks when using a different currency and greater credit risk. As with investment, MNCs are more able to diversify exchange rate risk by borrowing in different currencies.

Opportunities in Europe

Over time, economic and political conditions can change, creating new opportunities in international business. Four events have had a major impact on opportunities in Europe: (1) the **Single European Act**, (2) the removal of the Berlin Wall, (3) the inception of the euro and (4) the expansion of the EU.

Single European Act. In the late 1980s, industrialized countries in Europe agreed to make regulations more uniform and to remove many taxes on goods traded between these countries. This agreement, supported by the Single European Act of 1987, was followed by a series of negotiations among the countries to achieve uniform policies by 1992. The act allows MNCs with subsidiaries in a given European country greater access to European markets than MNCs with no presence in Europe.

Many firms, including European subsidiaries of major MNCs, have capitalized on the agreement by streamlining their production within Europe and are now better able to achieve economies of scale.

Removal of the Berlin Wall. In 1989, another historic event occurred in Europe when the Berlin Wall separating East Germany from West Germany was torn down. This was symbolic of new relations between East Germany and West Germany and was followed by the reunification of the two countries. In addition, it encouraged free enterprise in all Eastern European countries and the privatization of businesses that were owned by the government. A key motive for pursuing opportunities in Eastern Europe was the lack of products available there. Coca-Cola Co., Reynolds Metals Co., General Motors and numerous other MNCs aggressively pursued expansion in Eastern Europe as a result of the momentum towards free enterprise.

While the Single European Act of 1987 and the move towards free enterprise in Eastern Europe offered new opportunities to MNCs, they also posed new risks. Firms doing business in Europe were subjected to more competition. As in other historical examples of deregulation, the more efficient firms have benefited at the expense of less efficient firms.

Inception of the euro. In 1999, the 11 EMU (European and Monetary Union) countries – the Netherlands, Germany, France, Austria, Luxembourg, Ireland, Portugal, Italy, Belgium, Finland and Spain – adopted the euro as their currency for business transactions between these countries (Greece joined later in 2001). The euro was phased in as a currency for other transactions during 2001 and completely replaced the currencies of the participating countries on 1 January 2002. Consequently, only the euro is used for transactions in these countries. MNCs now have reduced costs in having to deal with fewer currencies. There is also a benefit in not having to use the less stable currencies of smaller European countries. The single currency system in most of Europe should encourage more trade among European countries. In addition, the use of a single currency creates pressures for a single monetary policy across those countries (i.e. a single interest rate and increasing harmony in tax and financial regulations).

To understand this important point, take the UK as an example of a single currency area. Now suppose that the interest rate on deposits were higher for the Birmingham branch of a bank compared with the London branch. Obviously money would move to the Birmingham branch until that branch lowered its rate and/or London raised its rate. There would be similar forces for equalization if taxes and prices were different for people in Birmingham compared to London. However, these conclusions depend on the branches of the two banks having the same risk and the ability and willingness of people to move and trade, in our example, between Birmingham and London. The budget problems in Greece from 2010 illustrate that risk is not equal even with so-called safe investments such as government bonds (see Exhibit 1.3). Also, people are not willing to move without restriction within the EU and indeed regulations on labour mobility vary among the member countries. Therefore, in assessing the economic growth in Europe, MNCs must be aware that although there is greater unity among the countries of the Eurozone, differences remain and country risk analysis must still be carried out.

Expansion of the European Union. In the late 1990s, the European Union (EU) made plans to allow more countries to become members. In 2013, the Eurozone consisted of 17 member states of the EU: Austria, Belgium, Cyprus, Estonia, Finland, France, Germany, Greece, Ireland, Italy, Luxembourg, Malta, Netherlands, Portugal, Slovakia, Slovenia and Spain.

EU members who did *not* use the euro were: Bulgaria, Czech Republic, Denmark, Hungary, Latvia, Lithuania, Poland, Romania, Sweden and the UK. These countries continued to use their own currencies, but may be able to adopt the euro as their currency in the future if they meet specified guidelines regarding budget deficits and other financial conditions. Since wages in some of these countries are substantially lower than in Western European countries, many MNCs have established manufacturing plants there to

---

EXHIBIT 1.3 Interest rates on 10-year Government bonds as at November 2012

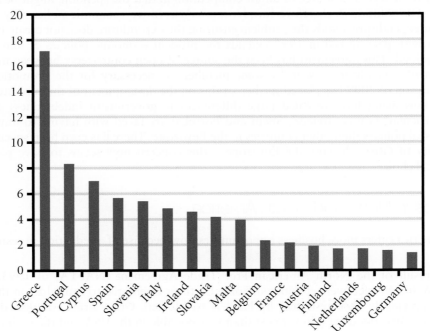

Source: European Central Bank.

produce products and export them to the rest of the EU (see the example of Bosch above). The governments in some of the new EU countries have also reduced corporate tax rates and offered other incentives to encourage MNCs to establish facilities there.

The conditions for joining the euro amount to a stable economy with relatively low levels of government intervention. The terms as set out in the 1992 Maastricht Treaty are as follows:

- Inflation no more than 1.5 per cent greater than the average of the three member countries with the lowest inflation rates.

- Long-term interest rates not in excess of 2 per cent above the average of the three member countries with the lowest inflation.

- Membership of the European mechanism of exchange rates for 2 years implying no change in the exchange rate with the euro by more than 15 per cent in 2 years.

- Net government spending (fiscal deficit) of no more than 3 per cent of GDP.

- A ratio of general government debt to GDP of no more than 60 per cent or approaching this value.

As national banks become an integral part of the European Central Bank, the process of integrating monetary policies is gradually taking shape. In June 2012 at the European Summit meeting, the EU decided to set up a Single Supervisory Mechanism as a major step towards a European banking union. Increasingly, the risk of investing in a MNC will be independent of its location; though as MNCs are located in their principal markets the risk is likely to be similar to country risk in many instances.

The UK, while not wanting to apply for euro membership, has nevertheless kept to within the spirit of the rules. The Bank of England's Monetary Policy Committee sets interest rates, a power previously held by the government. The Chancellor's 'Golden Rule' aimed at the start of the century to keep government spending on current as opposed to capital items at the same level as tax revenue over an economic cycle.

The central problem of economic integration between differing economies in the EU is that member countries are affected by each other's debt. A government that spends freely and borrows heavily damages confidence in the currency and increases interest rates for all member countries. High government expenditure is also likely to be seen as a source of unfair competition in that the spending might be indirectly subsidizing industry. The solution is therefore to advocate conservative economic policies by member states. Low government expenditure avoids the problem ensuring the expenditure does not create inequalities. The Stability and Growth pact agreed in 1997 extends the prudent economic policies of joining to members once they have joined. This agreement has been the source of open controversy between member states as greater government expenditure is seen by some members as necessary for the promotion of economic growth. The recession of 2009 has placed further strains on the development of the euro area as high levels of government borrowing have revealed large differences in government indebtedness among member countries. In particular, Greece, Ireland, Spain and Portugal are faced with having to implement harsher monetary and fiscal policies than other countries in the Eurozone. There has even been speculation concerning the possibility of Greece leaving the Eurozone – this concern now seems to have passed, though it remains a political choice.

Opportunities in North and South America

Like Europe, America offers more business opportunities now because of a reduction in restrictions.

NAFTA. As a result of the North American Free Trade Agreement (NAFTA) of 1993, trade barriers between the USA and Mexico were eliminated. Some US firms attempted to capitalize on this by exporting goods that had previously been restricted by barriers to Mexico. Other firms established subsidiaries in Mexico to produce their goods at a lower cost than was possible in the USA and then sell the goods in the USA. The removal of trade barriers essentially allowed US firms to penetrate product and labour markets that previously had not been accessible.

The removal of trade barriers between the USA and Mexico allows Mexican firms to export some products to the USA that were previously restricted. Thus, US firms that produce these goods are now subject to competition from Mexican exporters. Given the low cost of labour in Mexico, some US firms have lost some of their market share. The effects are most pronounced in the labour-intensive industries.

Within a month after the NAFTA accord, the momentum for free trade continued with a GATT (General Agreement on Tariffs and Trade) accord. This accord was the conclusion of trade negotiations from the so-called Uruguay Round that had begun 7 years earlier. It called for the reduction or elimination of trade restrictions on specified imported goods over a 10-year period across 117 countries. The accord has generated more international business for firms that had previously been unable to penetrate foreign markets because of trade restrictions.

Removal of investment restrictions. Many Latin American countries have made it easier for MNCs to engage in direct foreign investment thereby allowing MNCs more ownership rights if they acquire a local company. MNCs with technological advantages are now able to capitalize on their comparative advantages in Latin America with the possibility of creating lasting benefits.

Mercosur. This is in many respects the South American common market in emergent form. It is an alliance of Argentina, Brazil, Bolivia, Paraguay, Uruguay and Venezuela. Like the forerunner to the EU it has aims of reducing tariffs and other trade barriers between member states and moving towards common tariffs with non-member states. The free movement of capital and labour are also stated aims.

Opportunities in Asia

MNCs have commonly identified Asia as having tremendous business potential because of its large population base. Yet, MNCs had difficulty pursuing growth opportunities in Asia because of excessive restrictions on investment there. Some of the restrictions were explicit, while others were implicit (major bureaucratic delays).

Removal of investment restrictions. During the 1990s, many Asian countries reduced the restrictions imposed on investment by MNCs based in other countries. Consequently, MNCs can now acquire companies in Asia more easily or create licensing agreements with Asian companies without government interference.

Since the reduction in restrictions, MNCs have increased their international business in Asia. In 2012, 33 per cent of Adidas (Germany) footwear by volume was made in China, 31 per cent in Vietnam and 26 per cent in Indonesia, the remaining 10 per cent in other countries including Cambodia where production tripled in 2011. The fluidity of capital, in this case the ability to move factories and cite them anywhere in the world, is such that China's share of production has decreased from 49 per cent in 2007.

Investment in China. In 1992, China introduced a market based economy. Inward investment rose rapidly but then levelled off at the end of the 1990s. In response, China joined the World Trade Organisation in 2001 and has since seen a steady rise in inward investment. Both during the Asian crisis in 1997 and the current crisis, China has suffered less than other developing countries. The prospect of a growing economy has to a certain extent shielded it from world economic trends. Nevertheless the gradual opening up of the economy has lessened the isolation. In 2002 foreign investors were allowed into the Chinese stock market as Qualified Foreign Institutional Investors (QFIIs), the restrictions on their activities have gradually been lifted. Foreign banks now operate in China and are able to issue credit cards.

Investment in China was, in the 1990s, mainly greenfield as enterprises were state owned. The growing private sector has more recently encouraged increasing merger and acquisition activity motivated in part by the rapidly growing domestic market. The car market has, in particular, given rise to the establishment of factories by the major producers such as Daimler, Volkswagen, Hyundai and BMW. Investment is still controlled by the government which publishes lists of investment areas under categories of prohibited, restricted and encouraged. Foreign inward direct investment has always been below 20 per cent of overall direct investment, so it is significant but not dominant. Nevertheless, there are concerns that as local companies grow there might be increasing resistance to foreign investment given that the government is not ideologically committed to free trade.[1]

Data are difficult to estimate as much investment comes via Hong Kong and some via tax havens such as the British Virgin Islands and the Cayman Islands. Of the developing countries China has by far the greatest amount of inward investment but it is still far less than the USA or the Euro area. Shell (UK, the Netherlands) has a petrochemical complex in Nanhai, China. Heineken, Europe's largest brewer, has breweries in Shanghai and has acquired the major brewery in Guandong province. All major MNCs view China as the country with the most potential for growth and have invested billions of euros in projects.

There has also been a rise in Chinese multinationals with relatively unfamiliar names such as Haier, Lenovo, Huawei, TCL, UTStarcom, Galanz, Pearl River Piano, Chonghong, Ningbo Bird, Kelon, Baosteel, CNOOC and Sinopec. Case studies show that their behaviour and needs are similar to that of other multinationals. In particular they are constrained through competition to invest abroad and even in the USA, for example, fridges produced by Haier. Such developments create a motive for China to continue to participate in world trade.

Impact of the Asian crisis. In 1997, several Asian countries including Indonesia, Malaysia and Thailand experienced severe economic problems. Many local companies went bankrupt, and concerns about the countries caused financial outflows of funds. These outflows left limited funds to support the economy. Interest rates increased because of the outflow of funds; this placed even more strain on firms that needed to borrow money. This so-called Asian crisis lingered into 1998 and adversely affected numerous MNCs conducting business in South East Asia.

Yet, the crisis also created international business opportunities. The values of local firms were depressed, and Asian governments reduced restrictions on acquisitions, which allowed MNCs from Europe and the USA to pursue acquisitions in the Asian countries. Some MNCs were able to purchase local companies at a relatively low cost, improve the efficiency of the firms, and benefit from future economic growth. For example, during the Asian crisis in 1997–98, South Korea's large conglomerate firms (called *chaebols*) experienced financial problems and began to sell many of their business units to obtain cash.

USING THE WEB

Background material on the Asian crisis may be found from the PBS site at http://www.pbs.org/wgbh/pages/frontline/shows/crash/etc/cron.html

ASEAN. This is the Association of South East Asian States consisting of Brunei Darussalam, Cambodia, Indonesia, Lao PDR, Malaysia, Myanmar, Philippines, Singapore, Thailand and Vietnam. Founded in 1967 it pursues aims in political and cultural cooperation and economic integration. The ASEAN economic community (AEC) seeks regional integration with similar aspirations to the European Economic Community (the precursor to the EU) though without the common budgeting arrangements and tariff structures. The AEC emphasizes its openness to world trade and competitiveness.

EXPOSURE TO INTERNATIONAL RISK

Although international business can reduce an MNC's exposure to its home country's economic conditions, it usually increases an MNC's exposure to (1) exchange rate movements, (2) foreign economic conditions and (3) political risk. Each of these forms of exposure is briefly described here and is discussed in more detail in later sections of the text. MNCs that plan to pursue international business should consider these potential risks.

---

[1]For further details see Davies, K. (2009) *Inward FDI in China and its Policy Context*, Columbia FDI Profiles.

Exposure to exchange rate movements

Most international business results in the exchange of one currency for another to make the payment. Since exchange rates fluctuate on a daily basis, the cash outflows required to make payments change accordingly. Consequently, the number of units of a firm's home currency needed to purchase foreign supplies can change even if the suppliers have not adjusted their prices.

EXAMPLE

Burt plc, a UK importer, buys rice from the USA at $10 a sack. For each sack, Burt has to purchase $10 dollars with British pounds and then with the $10 buy the rice from the US company. The transaction is a double purchase, first the dollars then the rice. If the value of the dollar increases by 10 per cent, the effective cost of the sack of imported rice for Burt plc will also increase by 10 per cent. So both the cost of the foreign currency and the cost of the product are important to the overall cost of the rice for Burt.

Exporters selling goods in their own currency will be exposed to exchange rate fluctuations. A German company selling goods in euros to a British company, for example, will require the British company to purchase euros and then purchase the goods. In this case, if the value of the euro goes up (strengthens), the British company will have to pay more for the goods. The German exporter may well find that there is a decline in the order book as customers who do not use euros find the goods too expensive. To avoid the risk of currency changes for its customers, the German company may seek to invoice goods in the currency of its customers, in this case the British pound. In effect it would now be the German company that would bear the cost of exchange rate risk. If the value of the euro strengthens, the German company would now suffer in that the foreign currency would convert into fewer euros. In this case, the British pounds would convert into fewer euros. Either the exporter or the importer or the international financial markets must bear the exchange rate risk.

For MNCs with subsidiaries in foreign countries, exchange rate fluctuations affect the value of cash flows remitted by subsidiaries to the parent. When the parent's home currency goes up in value, the remitted foreign funds will convert to a smaller amount of the home currency.

EXAMPLE

The French subsidiary of Burt plc wishes to pay a dividend of 150 000 euros to Burt at an exchange rate of 1.5 euros for each British pound (£1) – a potential payment of £100 000 (being 150 000 euros / 1.5 = £100 000). If the value of the £ increases to 2 euros for each £1, the value of the payment will be only £75 000 (i.e. 150 000 euros / 2 = £75 000).

Exposure to foreign economies

When MNCs enter foreign markets to sell products, the demand for these products is dependent on the economic conditions in those markets. Thus, the cash flows of the MNC are subject to foreign economic conditions. For example, Michelin (France) the world's largest tyre manufacturer, experienced a 40 per cent drop in lorry tyre sales in South East Asia due to the Asian crisis in 1998 but in the USA that year their lorry tyre sales were up by 14 per cent.

Exposure to political risk

When MNCs establish subsidiaries in foreign countries, they become exposed to political risk, which arises because the host government or the public may take actions that affect the MNC's cash flows (political risk is often viewed as a subset of country risk, which is discussed in detail in a later chapter). For example, South Africa passed a law (the Medicines and Related Substances Control Amendment Act) in 1997 to allow generic substitutes (copies) of patented drugs to be used. The following year 41 pharmaceutical companies including large multinationals brought an action against the South African government. The law in South Africa had allowed their patented products to be copied legally – this is just one of the many forms of political risk. The US government sought to protect its pharmaceutical industry by putting the South African government on its special 'watch list' – but it was later removed. A compromise solution was eventually achieved. Generally, governments cannot act on the world stage in an unrestrained manner for fear of being isolated. Even where host governments have sought to nationalize subsidiaries of MNCs, compensation will be paid.

Terrorism and war. One form of an exposure to political risk is terrorism. A terrorist attack can affect a firm's operations or its employees. The September 11, 2001 terrorist attack on the World Trade Center reminded MNCs around the world of the exposure to terrorism. MNCs from more than 50 countries were directly affected because they occupied space in the World Trade Center. In addition, other MNCs were also affected because they engage in trade or have direct foreign investment in foreign countries that may also experience an increase in terrorism.

Wars can also adversely affect an MNC's cash flows. During the war in Iraq in 2003, anti-American protests against the war in countries in the Middle East and elsewhere forced some US-based MNCs to temporarily shut down their operations in some countries. In addition, the protests led to a decline in the demand for products produced by some US-based MNCs.

OVERVIEW OF AN MNC'S CASH FLOWS

Most MNCs have some local business similar to other purely domestic firms. Because of the MNCs' international operations, however, their cash flow streams differ from those of purely domestic firms. Exhibit 1.4 shows cash flow diagrams for three common profiles of MNCs. Profile A in this exhibit reflects an MNC whose only international business is international trade. Thus, its international cash flows result from either paying for imported supplies or receiving payment in exchange for products that it exports.

EXHIBIT 1.4   Cash flow diagrams for UK MNCs

Profile A: MNCs focused on international trade

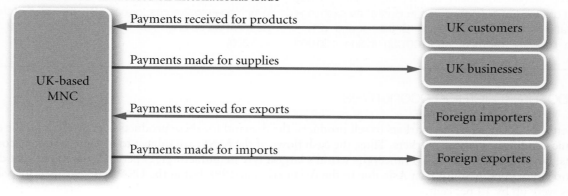

Profile B: MNCs focused on international trade and international arrangements

Profile C: MNCs focused on international trade international arrangements and direct foreign investment

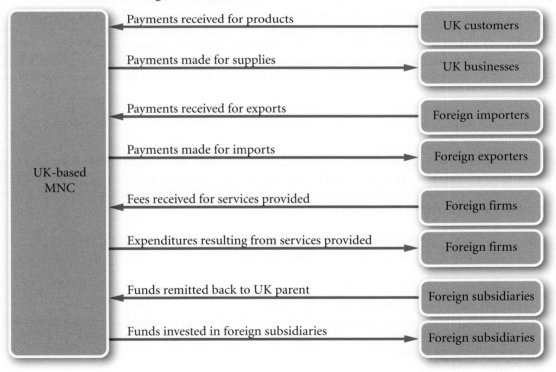

Profile B reflects an MNC that engages in both international trade and some international arrangements (which can include international licensing, franchising or joint ventures). Any of these international arrangements can require cash outflows by the MNC in foreign countries to comply with the arrangement, such as the expenses incurred from transferring technology or funding partial investment in a franchise or joint venture. These arrangements generate cash flows to the MNC in the form of fees for services (such as technology or support assistance) it provides.

Profile C reflects an MNC that engages in international trade, international arrangements and direct foreign investment. This type of MNC has one or more foreign subsidiaries. There can be cash outflows from the parent to its foreign subsidiaries in the form of invested funds to help finance the operations of the foreign subsidiaries. There are also cash flows from the foreign subsidiaries to the parent in the form of remitted earnings and fees for services provided by the parent, which can all be classified as remitted funds from the foreign subsidiaries. In general, the cash outflows associated with international business by the parent are to pay for imports, to comply with its international arrangements, or to support the creation or expansion of foreign subsidiaries. Conversely, it will receive cash flows in the form of payment for its exports, fees for the services it provides within its international arrangements, and remitted funds from the foreign subsidiaries.

Many MNCs initially conduct international business in the manner illustrated by Profile A. Some of these MNCs develop international arrangements and foreign subsidiaries over time; others are content to focus on exporting or importing as their only method of international business. Although the three profiles vary, they all show how international business generates cash flows.

VALUATION MODEL FOR AN MNC

The value of an MNC is relevant to its shareholders and debtholders. As shareholders are the owners of the company, when managers make decisions that maximize the value of the firm, they maximize shareholder wealth. Since international financial management should be conducted with the goal of increasing the value of the MNC, it is useful to review some basics of valuation. There are numerous methods of valuing an MNC, here we use the most widely accepted valuation model in finance. The model we generate here will be used throughout the text to relate various aspects of financial management to the overall goal of wealth maximization.

Domestic model

Before modelling an MNC's value, consider the valuation of a purely domestic firm that does not engage in any foreign transactions. The value of a purely domestic firm is commonly specified as the present value of its expected cash flows, where the discount rate used reflects the weighted average cost of capital and represents the required rate of return by investors:

$$V = \sum_{t=1}^{n} \left[\frac{E(CF_{\text{\pounds},t})}{(1+k)^t} \right]$$

where:
$V = $ MNC value
$E(CF_{\text{\pounds},t}) = $ expected home currency value of cash flows from all projects undertaken by the MNC received at the end of period t
$k = $ overall cost of capital
$n = $ distant time period.

In longer form: the value of a company (V) is the total (Σ) of the expected dividends for each period ($E(CF_{\text{\pounds},t})$), discounted by the cost of capital for that period $(1+k)^t$.

The required rate of return (k) in the denominator of the valuation equation represents the cost of capital to the firm and is essentially a weighted average of the cost of capital based on the risk of all the firm's projects. It can be calculated without reference to individual projects by calculating the cost of share capital and fixed interest debt and taking a weighted average based on their respective market values. Thus the overall cost of financing the projects can be worked out directly without reference to the cost of individual projects.

If the firm's credit rating is suddenly lowered because the market judges that its projects are now riskier, its cost of capital will increase as a result and so will the required rate of return for the now riskier projects. Holding other factors constant, an increase in the firm's required rate of return will reduce the value of the firm, because expected dividends must be discounted at a higher interest rate. Conversely, a decrease in the firm's required rate of return will increase the value of the firm because expected dividends are discounted at a lower required rate of return.

The two major factors in valuing an MNC are therefore returns as measured by the expected cash flows, and risk, as included in the discount rate. Expected cash flows are normally taken to be a matter of business estimation that is beyond the scope of finance and is therefore a given input into financial management. By far the greater emphasis in finance is on risk – the required discount rate.

MANAGING FOR VALUE

Yahoo!'s decision to expand internationally

Many MNCs have penetrated foreign markets in recent years. Like domestic projects, foreign projects involve an investment decision and a financing decision. The investment decision to engage in a foreign project results in revenue and expenses that are denominated in a foreign currency. The decision of how to finance a foreign project affects the MNC's cost of capital. Most foreign projects are assessed on the basis of their potential to attract new demand and therefore generate additional cash flows. Consider Yahoo! (US-based), which has expanded its portal services in numerous foreign countries. For example, it has established main pages in Canada, Latin America, Europe and Asia. It generates cash inflows from these foreign projects in the form of advertising fees paid by local merchants who purchase space on Yahoo!'s website. It incurs cash outflows from these foreign projects in the form of expenses incurred from providing information. It needs funding to finance these foreign projects and hopes that its cash flows will generate a return that exceeds the cost of financing.

Every foreign project considered by Yahoo! is subject to conditions specific to that country, resulting in a unique estimate of net cash flows. Every foreign project is also subject to a cost of financing that is specific to the country. Thus, Yahoo!'s decision regarding a possible project in Argentina may not necessarily be the same as its decision regarding a similar project in Australia.

Once an MNC such as Yahoo! has decided to pursue a foreign project, it must continually consider a set of multinational finance decisions, such as these:

● How to forecast exchange rates of the currencies it uses.

● How to assess its exposure to exchange rate movements.

● Whether and how to hedge its exposure to exchange rate movements.

● How to pursue additional foreign expansion.

● How to finance its foreign expansion.

● How to manage its international cash and liquidity.

These are the key multinational finance decisions that are made by Yahoo! and other MNCs, and they are therefore given much attention in this text. To the extent that Yahoo!'s managers can make multinational finance decisions that increase the overall present value of its future cash flows, they can maximize the firm's value.

Before financial managers of Yahoo! and other MNCs make these multinational finance decisions, they need to understand how international financial markets can facilitate their business and must recognize the forces that affect exchange rates. These macroeconomic concepts, which are discussed in the first two parts of the text, set the stage for understanding how the performance of any business is influenced by local country conditions. Then, in the last three parts of the text, multinational finance decisions are examined.

Valuing international cash flows

Unlike their domestic equivalents, MNCs engage in projects with a wider range of risk. Even where the product is relatively homogeneous, markets in different economies will differ more than in the same economy and, where relevant, the value of foreign currencies will affect revenues and costs. It is important therefore to distinguish between project discount rates and overall company discount rates: they will not be the same. Projects must be discounted using the risk premium relevant to that project and must not be discounted using the average rate or overall cost of capital irrespective of the project. Furthermore, the discount rate for a project is not affected by the financing of the project or the company – a point made by Modigliani and Miller. Fortunately these assertions make good common sense. A risky project does not become acceptable merely because it is being valued by a company that normally undertakes safe projects (i.e. has a low cost of capital). Nor is a safe project unacceptable because it is being considered by a company with a high cost of capital, i.e. that normally undertakes risky projects. Both such companies should discount the project at the same discount rate, which is derived from the risk of the project itself. The level of borrowing (gearing) of a company should not affect the acceptance or rejection of a project. As Modigliani and Miller[2] showed, shareholders can adjust their investments to effectively choose their own level of gearing, so it can hardly play a part in valuation. A minor exception to this picture are tax savings from borrowing, these affect the level of cash flows to shareholders and may make a moderate degree of borrowing more profitable for the MNC. The independence of shareholder risk preferences from the risk of the projects undertaken by the MNC is known as separation theorem. It means that directors do not have to ask the shareholders whether or not a project is too risky for them. They simply have to value each project according to its market risk and keep the stock market informed of any significant changes to the MNC's overall risk. This policy maximizes shareholder wealth whatever the risk preferences of the shareholders.

EXAMPLE

The Managing Director (MD) of Builders plc specializes in constructing apartments in the UK. The discount rate applied is normally the risk-free rate with a premium of 6 per cent. Recently, they have been approached with a project to build apartment blocks in a South American country. The MD applies the normal premium and finds the project very profitable. The Finance Director thinks that the project is far riskier and applies a 15 per cent premium. She calculates that the project has a negative value. The MD agrees that he should have applied a higher rate.

Part of the greater risk of foreign investment derives from variability in currency values. MNCs will be earning and paying amounts in various foreign currencies. The foreign currency cash flows will then be valued in the home currency. Thus, the expected home currency cash flows to be received at the end of period t are equal to the sum of the products of cash flows denominated in each currency j times the expected exchange rate at which currency j could be converted into pounds by the MNC at the end of period t.

$$E(CF_{£,t}) = \sum_{j=1}^{m} \left[E(CF_{j,t}) \times E(ER_{j,t}) \right]$$

Where:

$E(CF_{£,t})$ = expected value in home currency of the cash flows across all projects for period t

$\qquad CF_{j,t}$ = cash flow projects in currency j time t

$E(ER_{j,t})$ = expected exchange rate at time t for currency j in direct form, i.e. £s to a single foreign currency unit

[2]For example, see P. Vernimmen (2005) *Corporate Finance: Theory and Practice*, New York: Wiley, pp. 660 *et seq.*

To illustrate how the pound cash flows of an MNC can be measured, consider a UK firm that expects to earn £1 000 000 in the UK and 1 500 000 euros from the euro currency area. Assuming that a euro is worth 60 pence (£0.60), the expected cash flows are:

$$E(CF_{£,t}) = \sum_{j=1}^{m} \left[E(CF_{j,t}) \times E(ER_{j,t}) \right]$$
$$= [£1\,000\,000] + [1\,500\,000 \times 0.60]$$
$$= [£1\,000\,000] + [900\,000]$$
$$= £1\,900\,000$$

The earnings already in the home currency do not need to be converted.

The MNC's total pound and pound equivalent cash flows at the end of every period in the future can be estimated in the same manner. This example uses only two currencies, but if the MNC had transactions involving three or four currencies, the same process could be used. The expected pound cash flows for each of the currencies would be estimated separately for each future period. The expected pound cash flows for each of the currencies within each period could then be combined to derive the total pound cash flows per period. Finally, the cash flows in each period would be discounted to derive the present value of the expected cash flows.

The general formula for the cash flows received by an MNC in any particular period can be written as before:

$$E(CF_{£,t}) = \sum_{j=1}^{m} \left[E(CF_{j,t}) \times E(ER_{j,t}) \right]$$

The cash flows would then have to be discounted by a weighted average of the interest rates to be applied to each individual investment – the weighted average cost of capital (k) as shown here:

$$V = \sum_{t=1}^{} \frac{\sum_{j=1}^{n} \left[E(CF_{j,t}) \times E(ER_{j,t}) \right]}{(1 + k)^t}$$

where $CF_{j,t}$ represents the cash flow denominated in a particular currency (including pounds), and $ER_{j,t}$ represents the exchange rate at which the MNC can convert the foreign currency at the end of period t. Thus, the value of an MNC can be affected by a change in expectations about $CF_{j,t}$ or $ER_{j,t}$. Only those cash flows that are to be received by the MNC's parent in the period of concern should be counted. To avoid double-counting, cash flows of the MNC's subsidiaries are considered in the valuation model only when they reflect transactions with the parent company. Thus, any expected cash flows received by foreign subsidiaries should not be counted in the valuation equation until they are expected to be remitted to the parent.

In general, the valuation model shows that an MNC's value can be affected by forces that influence the amount of its cash flows in a particular currency (CF_j), the exchange rate at which that currency is converted into pounds (ER_j) or the MNC's weighted average cost of capital (k) which reflects the different risks of the international investments.

This view of projects as being wholly valued by cash flows is only part of the overall picture. The expected value of future cash flows discounted in this way allows for possible variation in the form of a normal distribution. However, some possible future cash flows are contingent on the outcome of the main project. If the project does well then the MNC might consider a further foreign investment. Such possibilities, contingent on outcomes, are known as **real options** – they are indeed options in the normal sense of the word. Valuing these possibilities is more complex as their probability depends on the outcome of the main project, their expected value changes with the outcome of the main project. Notwithstanding these problems such possibilities are sometimes referred to as the present value of growth opportunities or PVGO.

A further layer of complexity is added in that consideration so far has assumed that there is no specific reaction by competitors to the investment. In some cases this will be a reasonable assumption, any reaction being described by the normal distribution of possible outcomes. However, for large MNCs competing with each other across the world, competitive reaction seems a likely response. The added complexity is that now the competitors' cash flows need to be considered as well in order to understand their response.

There is no general model for valuing the possible effects of competition. In academic analysis, game theory addresses the competitive effects and offers a number of relevant concepts. In practice, competitive considerations are referred to as being part of an investment strategy. Formal valuation models do not exist for projects with significant strategic considerations; valuation is a matter of good business judgement. An approximate valuation model is therefore:

$$V_i = \sum_{t=1}^{n} \frac{E(CF_{£,t})}{(1+k)^t} + \text{PVGO} + \text{Strategic value}$$

Where:

V_i = value of project i

$E(CF_{£,i})$ = expected value in home currency of the cash flows converted in period t

PVGO = present value of growth opportunities.

Overall it is certainly important for the financial manager to map out the expected cash flows and their discounted value. Adding options is an important further consideration for which cash flows can be estimated but their value only approximated. Finally, competition may be decisive for which there is no formal model. Surveys of large MNCs suggest that managers are not paying as much attention to the valuation of cash flows in valuing investments as basic finance might advocate. The addition of PVGOs and competition offer convincing explanations. It may be that a company goes ahead with a project despite a negative net present value because the project offers growth opportunities conditional on the project outcome or that the project is part of a larger strategy. These matters are considered further in Chapter 13.

Impact of financial management and international conditions on value

MNCs recognize that they may increase their value by increasing their cash flows (return) or by reducing their cost of capital (risk). Hence, their challenge is to make decisions that will accomplish one or both of these objectives. An MNC's financial decisions include how much business to conduct in each country and how much financing to obtain in each currency. Its financial decisions determine its exposure to the international environment. If it conducts very little international business, its potential for enhancing its value is limited, but so is its vulnerability to changes in exchange rate movements or other international conditions. Conversely, if an MNC pursues substantial international business in markets where there are opportunities, it may be able to substantially increase its pound cash flows and therefore increase its value, but it will be highly exposed to exchange rate effects, economic conditions and political conditions in these markets. As in all finance, there is a trade off between risk and return. International investment entails higher risks; but higher returns. Effective international financial management minimizes the risk for the expected return net of interest charges.

The uncertainty surrounding an MNC's cash flows is influenced by the composition of its international business, as well as by the amount of that business. Exchange rates, economic conditions and political conditions are much more volatile in some countries than in others. Therefore, two MNCs of the same size and in the same industry may have the same volume of foreign business, but one of them might be less risky because it conducts business in more stable countries.

Though an MNC does not have control over a country's exchange rate, economic conditions or political conditions, it can control its degree of exposure to those conditions with its financial management. Two MNCs of the same size and in the same industry could have the exact same composition of international business, but one of them might be less risky because it makes financial decisions that reduce its exposure to exchange rates, economic conditions or political conditions.

ORGANIZATION OF THE TEXT

The organization of the chapters in this text is shown in Exhibit 1.5. Chapters 2 to 8 discuss international markets and conditions from a macroeconomic perspective, focusing on external forces that can affect the value of an MNC. Though financial managers may not have control over these forces, they do have some

EXHIBIT 1.5 Organization of chapters

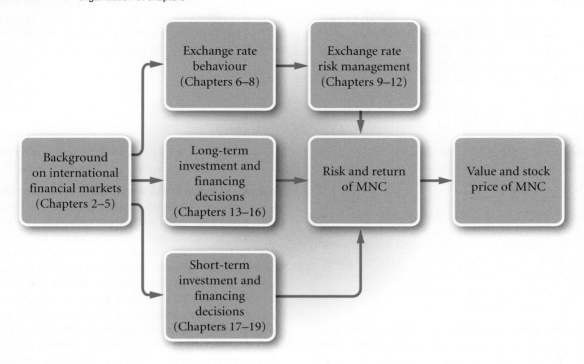

control over their degree of exposure to these forces. These macroeconomic chapters provide the background necessary to make financial decisions.

Chapters 9 to 20 take a microeconomic perspective and focus on how the financial management of an MNC can affect its value. Financial decisions by MNCs are commonly classified as either investing decisions or financing decisions. In general, investing decisions by an MNC tend to affect the numerator of the valuation model because such decisions affect expected cash flows. In addition, if investing decisions by the MNC's parent alter the firm's weighted average cost of capital, they may also affect the denominator of the valuation model. Long-term financing decisions by an MNC's parent tend to affect the denominator of the valuation model because they affect the MNC's cost of capital.

SUMMARY

- The main goal of an MNC is to maximize shareholder wealth. When managers are tempted to serve their own interests instead of those of shareholders, an agency problem exists. Managers also face environmental, regulatory and ethical constraints that can conflict with the goal of maximizing shareholder wealth.

- International business is justified by three key theories. The theory of comparative advantage suggests that each country should use its comparative advantage to specialize in its production and rely on other countries to meet other needs. The imperfect markets theory suggests that because of imperfect markets, factors of production are immobile, which encourages countries to specialize based on the resources they have. The product cycle theory suggests that after firms are established in their home countries, they commonly expand their product specialization in foreign countries.

The most common methods by which firms conduct international business are international trade, licensing, franchising, joint ventures, acquisitions of foreign firms and formation of foreign subsidiaries. Methods such as licensing and franchising involve little capital investment but distribute some of the profits to other parties. The acquisition of foreign firms and formation of foreign subsidiaries require substantial capital investments but offer the potential for large returns.

CRITICAL DEBATE

Proposition. When a European-based MNC competes in foreign countries it pays wages comparable with local rates and obeys environmental and other laws that can be less restrictive than in their home country. Bribes, in some countries regarded as a tradition, may also be paid to local government officials. In Europe, the picture is not so different: an MNC may contribute to local facilities and put pressure on local government not to oppose planning applications. MNCs do not exist to teach the world morality, they merely conform to local tradition – they have to do this in order to compete.

Opposing view. European-based MNCs should maintain a standard code of ethics that applies to any country, even if it is at a disadvantage in a foreign country that allows activities that might be viewed as unethical. In this way, the MNC establishes more credibility worldwide.

Critically evaluate these arguments. Which argument do you support? Offer your own opinion on this issue based on the information you have obtained.

To add content to your evaluation, review the annual reports of large European multinationals; where these are pdf files, conduct searches using the Acrobat 'binoculars' icon with the words 'responsibility' and 'environment' within the report. Some counter ideas may be gleaned from http://corporatewatch.com and from http://web.amnesty.org where you should search for 'UN Global Contract' as well as the previous keywords. All these sources are pursuing a particular goal and must be viewed critically.

SELF TEST

Answers are provided in Appendix A at the back of the text.

1 What are typical reasons why MNCs expand internationally?

2 Describe the changes in Europe that have created new opportunities for MNCs.

3 Identify the more obvious risks faced by MNCs that expand internationally.

QUESTIONS AND APPLICATIONS

1 **Agency problems of MNCs.**

   a Explain the agency problem of MNCs.
   b Why might agency costs be larger for an MNC than for a purely domestic firm?

2 **Comparative advantage.**

   a Explain how the theory of comparative advantage relates to the need for international business.
   b Explain how the product cycle theory relates to the growth of an MNC.

3 **Imperfect markets.**

   a Explain how the existence of imperfect markets has led to the establishment of subsidiaries in foreign markets.

   b If perfect markets existed, would wages, prices and interest rates among countries be more similar or less similar than under conditions of imperfect markets? Why?

4 **International opportunities.**

   a How does access to international opportunities affect the size of corporations?
   b Describe a scenario in which the size of a corporation is not affected by access to international opportunities.
   c Outline the opportunities available to MNCs.

5 International opportunities due to the Internet.

  a What factors cause some firms to become more internationalized than others?

  b Offer your opinion on why the Internet may result in more international business.

6 Impact of the euro. Explain how the adoption of the euro as the single currency by European countries could be beneficial to MNCs based in Europe and elsewhere.

7 Benefits and risks of international business. As an overall review of this chapter, identify possible reasons for growth in international business. Then, list the various disadvantages that may discourage international business.

8 Motives of an MNC. Describe constraints that interfere with an MNC's objective.

9 Centralization and agency costs. Would the agency problem be more pronounced for an MNC which has its parent company make most major decisions for its foreign subsidiaries, or for an MNC which uses a decentralized approach?

10 Global competition. Explain why more standardized product specifications across countries can increase global competition.

11 Impact of the euro on US subsidiaries. Drinkalot Ltd has a French subsidiary that produces wine and exports to various European countries. Explain how the subsidiary's business may have been affected since the conversion of many European currencies into a single European currency (the euro) in 1999.

12 Macro versus micro topics. Review the table of contents and indicate whether each of the chapters from Chapter 2 through Chapter 20 has a macro or micro perspective.

13 Methods used to conduct international business. Durve Ltd desires to penetrate a foreign market with either a licensing agreement with a foreign firm or by acquiring a foreign firm. Explain the differences in potential risk and return between a licensing agreement with a foreign firm and the acquisition of a foreign firm.

14 International business methods. Snyder GmbH a German firm that sells high-quality golf clubs in Europe, wants to expand further by selling the same golf clubs in Brazil.

  a Describe the trade-offs that are involved for each method (such as exporting, direct foreign investment, etc.) that Snyder could use to achieve its goal.

  b Which method would you recommend for this firm? Justify your recommendation.

15 Impact of political risk. Explain why political risk may discourage international business.

ADVANCED QUESTIONS

16 International joint venture. Scottish and Newcastle breweries (a real UK company) have joint ventures with United Breweries in India, Chongquin (the fifth largest brewer in China) and Baltic Beverages and Holdings in Eastern Europe.

  a Explain how the joint venture can enable Scottish and Newcastle breweries to achieve its objective of maximizing shareholder wealth.

  b Explain how the joint venture can limit the risk of the international business.

  c Many international joint ventures are intended to circumvent barriers (business and cultural) that normally prevent foreign competition. What barriers might Scottish and Newcastle breweries be circumventing as a result of the joint venture?

17 Impact of Eastern European growth. The managers of VGood Corp. (a US fictitious company) recently had a meeting to discuss new opportunities in Europe as a result of the recent integration among Eastern European countries. They decided not to penetrate new markets because of their present focus on expanding market share in the USA. VGood's financial managers have developed forecasts for earnings based on the 12 per cent market share (defined here as its percentage of total European sales) that VGood currently has in Eastern Europe. Is 12 per cent an appropriate estimate for next year's Eastern European market share? If not, does it likely overestimate or underestimate the actual Eastern European market share next year?

18 Valuation of an MNC. Turnip plc (a UK fictitious company), based in Birmingham, considers several international opportunities in Europe that could affect the value of its firm. The valuation of its firm is dependent on four factors: (1) expected cash flows in pounds, (2) expected cash flows in euros that are ultimately converted into pounds, (3) the rate at which it can convert euros to pounds and (4) Turnip's weighted average cost of capital. For each opportunity, identify the factors that would be affected.

a Turnip plans a licensing deal in which it will sell technology to a firm in Germany for £3 000 000; the payment is invoiced in pounds, and this project has the same risk level as its existing businesses.

b Turnip plans to acquire a large firm in Portugal that is riskier than its existing businesses.

c Turnip plans to discontinue its relationship with a US supplier so that it can import a small amount of supplies (denominated in euros) at a lower cost from a Belgian supplier.

d Turnip plans to export a small amount of materials to Ireland that are denominated in euros.

19 **Assessing motives for international business.** Pliny Inc. (a US fictitious company) specializes in manufacturing some basic parts for sports utility vehicles that are produced and sold in the USA. Its main advantage in the USA is that its production is efficient and less costly than that of some other unionized manufacturers. It has a substantial market share in the USA. Its manufacturing process is labour-intensive. It pays relatively low wages compared to US competitors, but has guaranteed the local workers that their job positions will not be eliminated for the next 30 years. It hired a consultant to determine whether it should set up a subsidiary in Mexico, where the parts would be produced. The consultant suggested that Pliny should expand for the following reasons. Offer your opinion on whether the consultant's reasons are logical.

a Theory of competitive advantage: There are not many SUVs sold in Mexico, so Pliny, Inc. would not have to face much competition there.

b Imperfect markets theory: Pliny cannot easily transfer workers to Mexico, but it can establish a subsidiary there in order to penetrate a new market.

c Product cycle theory: Pliny has been successful in the USA. It has limited growth opportunities because it already controls much of the US market for the parts it produces. Thus, the natural next step is to conduct the same business in a foreign country.

d Exchange rate risk: the exchange rate of the peso has weakened recently, so this would allow Pliny to build a plant at a very low cost (by exchanging dollars for the cheap pesos to build the plant).

e Political risk: the political conditions in Mexico have stabilized in the last few months, so Pliny should attempt to penetrate the Mexican market now.

20 **Valuation of Carrefour's international business.** In addition to all of its stores in France, Carrefour (a real French company) has 24 hypermarkets in Argentina, 85 in Brazil, 27 in Mexico, 41 in China, 27 in Korea, a total of 823 stores in 29 countries. Consider the value of Carrefour as being composed of two parts, a euro area part and a non-euro area part. Explain how to determine the present value (in euros) of the non-euro part assuming that you had access to all the details of Carrefour businesses outside the euro area.

21 **Impact of international business on cash flows and risk.** Slowman Travel Agency specializes in tours for American tourists. Until recently all of its business was in Switzerland. It has just established a subsidiary in Athens, Greece, which provides tour services in the Greek islands for American tourists. It rented a shop near the port of Athens. It also hired residents of Athens, who could speak English and provide tours of the Greek islands. The subsidiary's main costs are rent and salaries for its employees and the lease of a few large boats in Athens that it uses for tours. American tourists pay for the entire tour in dollars at Slowman's US office before they depart for Greece.

a Explain why Slowman may be able to effectively capitalize on international opportunities such as the Greek island tours.

b Slowman is privately owned by owners who reside in Switzerland and work in the main office. Explain possible agency problems associated with the creation of a subsidiary in Athens, Greece. How can Slowman attempt to reduce these agency costs?

c Greece's cost of labour and rent are relatively low. Explain why this information is relevant to Slowman's decision to establish a tour business in Greece.

d Explain how the cash flow situation of the Greek tour business exposes Slowman to exchange rate risk. Is Slowman favourably or unfavourably affected when the euro (Greece's currency) appreciates against the dollar? Explain.

e Slowman plans to finance its Greek tour business. Its subsidiary could obtain loans in euros from a bank in Greece to cover its rent, and its main office could pay off the loans over time. Alternatively, its main office could borrow dollars and would periodically convert dollars to euros to pay the expenses in Greece. Does either type of loan reduce the exposure of Slowman to exchange rate risk? Explain.

PROJECT WORKSHOP

22 **Assessing direct foreign investment trends.** The website address of the Bureau of Economic Analysis is http://www.bea.doc.gov.

For UK data see http://www.statistics.gov.uk/StatBase/Product.asp?vlnk=1140 or search for 'Pink Book' plus the year.

a   Use this website to assess recent trends in direct foreign investment (FDI) abroad by US or UK firms. Compare the FDI in the UK with the FDI in France. Offer a possible reason for the large difference.

b   Based on the recent trends in FDI, are UK-based MNCs pursuing opportunities in Asia? In Eastern Europe? In Latin America?

23 Select a firm from the top ten firms from a European country (exclude financial institutions, a list may be found at http://www.forbes.com/lists/ – choose the country option for selection). Go to the company website and download the most recent annual report. Before selecting the company, ensure that it is engaged in international business. From a reading of this document and with particular reference to this chapter:

f   Explain how the Greek island tour business could expose Slowman to country risk.

a   Review the Goals of the MNC. Is there a mission statement? Are there notes as to the company's policy towards the environment, its workforce etc.? Generally review statements of intent in the document.

b   How far do you think that the company development can be explained by theories of international business as outlined in this chapter?

c   What international business methods does this company principally employ? What do you think is the reason for their international business strategy (i.e. why do they not pursue other strategies)?

d   Outline the international opportunities and international risks faced by this company. Where these are not specifically stated, outline what you think are the likely opportunities and risks. In your view, how great are these international risks and international opportunities?

DISCUSSION IN THE BOARDROOM

This exercise can be found on our dedicated Course-Mate platform for students.

RUNNING YOUR OWN MNC

This exercise can be found on our dedicated Course-Mate platform for students.

Essays/discussion and articles can be found at the end of Part I.

BLADES PLC CASE STUDY

Decision to expand internationally

Blades plc is a UK-based company that has been incorporated in the UK for 3 years. Blades is a relatively small company, with total assets of only £15 million. The company produces a single type of product, roller blades. Due to the booming skateboard market in the UK at the time of the company's establishment, Blades has been quite successful. For example, in its first year of operation, it reported a net income of £3.5 million. Recently, however, the demand for Blades' 'Speedos', the company's primary product in the UK, has been slowly tapering off, and Blades has not been performing well. Last year, it reported a return on assets of only 7 per cent. In response to the company's annual report for its most recent year of operations, Blades' shareholders have been pressuring the company to improve its performance; its share price has fallen from a high of £20 per share 3 years ago to £12 last year. Blades produces high-quality skateboards and employs a unique production process, but the prices it charges are among the top 5 per cent in the industry.

In light of these circumstances, Ben Holt, the company's director of finance, is contemplating his alternatives for Blades' future. There are no other cost-cutting measures that Blades can implement in the UK without affecting the quality of its product. Also, production of alternative products would require major modifications to the existing plant setup. Furthermore, and because of these limitations, expansion within the UK at this time seems pointless.

Ben Holt is considering the following: if Blades cannot penetrate the UK market further or reduce costs here, why not import some parts from overseas and/or expand the company's sales to foreign countries? Similar strategies have proved successful for numerous companies that expanded into Asia in recent years to increase their profit margins. The Managing Director's initial focus is on Thailand. Thailand has recently experienced weak economic conditions, and Blades could purchase components there at a low cost. Ben Holt is aware that many of Blades' competitors have begun importing production components from Thailand.

Not only would Blades be able to reduce costs by importing rubber and/or plastic from Thailand due to the low costs of these inputs, but it might also be able to augment weak UK sales by exporting to Thailand, an economy still in its infancy and just beginning to appreciate leisure products such as roller blades. While several of Blades' competitors import components from Thailand, few are exporting to the country. Long-term decisions would also eventually have to be made; maybe Blades plc could establish a subsidiary in Thailand and gradually shift its focus away from the UK if its UK sales do not rebound. Establishing a subsidiary in Thailand would also make sense for Blades due to its superior production process. Ben Holt is reasonably sure that Thai firms could not duplicate the high-quality production process employed by Blades. Furthermore, if the company's initial approach of exporting works well, establishing a subsidiary in Thailand would preserve Blades' sales before Thai competitors are able to penetrate the Thai market.

As a financial analyst for Blades plc you are assigned to analyze international opportunities and risk resulting from international business. Your initial assessment should focus on the barriers and opportunities that international trade may offer. Ben Holt has never been involved in international business in any form and is unfamiliar with any constraints that may inhibit his plan to export to and import from a foreign country. Mr Holt has presented you with a list of initial questions you should answer.

1 What are the advantages Blades could gain from importing from and/or exporting to a foreign country such as Thailand?

2 What are some of the disadvantages Blades could face as a result of foreign trade in the short run? In the long run?

3 Which theories of international business described in this chapter apply to Blades plc in the short run? In the long run?

4 What long-range plans other than establishment of a subsidiary in Thailand are an option for Blades and may be more suitable for the company?

SMALL BUSINESS DILEMMA

Developing a multinational sporting goods industry

In every chapter of this text, some of the key concepts are illustrated with an application to a small sporting goods firm that conducts international business. These 'Small Business Dilemma' features allow students to recognize the dilemmas and possible decisions that firms (such as this sporting goods firm) may face in a global environment. For this chapter, the application is on the development of the sporting goods firm that would conduct international business.

Last month, Jim Logan from Ireland completed his undergraduate degree in finance and decided to pursue his dream of managing his own sporting goods business. Jim had worked in a sporting goods shop while going to university in Ireland, and he had noticed that many customers wanted to purchase a low-priced basketball. However, the sporting goods store where he worked, like many others, sold only top-of-the-line basketballs. From his experience, Jim was aware that top-of-the-line basketballs had a high mark-up and that a low-cost basketball could possibly penetrate the UK market. He also knew how to produce cricket balls. His goal was to create a firm that would produce low-priced basketballs and sell them on a wholesale basis to various sporting goods stores in the UK. Unfortunately, many sporting goods stores began to sell low-priced basketballs just before Jim was about to start his business. The firm that began to produce the low-cost basketballs already provided many other products to sporting goods stores in the UK and therefore had already established a business relationship with these stores. Jim did not believe that he could compete with this firm in the UK market.

Rather than pursue a different business, Jim decided to implement his idea on a global basis. While basketball has not been a traditional sport in many countries, it has become more popular in some countries in recent years. Furthermore, the expansion of cable networks in many countries would allow for much more exposure to basketball games in those countries in the future. Jim asked many of his foreign friends from college days if they recalled seeing basketballs sold in their home countries. Most of them said they rarely noticed basketballs being sold in sporting goods stores but that they expected the demand for basketballs to increase in their home countries. Consequently, Jim decided to start a business of producing low-priced basketballs and exporting them to sporting goods distributors in foreign countries. Those distributors would then sell the basketballs at the retail level. Jim planned to expand his product line over time once he identified other sports products that he might sell to foreign sporting goods stores. He decided to call his business 'Sports Exports Company'. To avoid any rent and labour expenses, Jim planned to produce the basketballs in his garage and to perform the work himself. Thus, his main business expenses were the cost of the material used to produce basketballs and expenses associated with finding distributors in foreign countries who would attempt to sell the basketballs to sporting goods stores.

1 Is Sports Exports Company a MNC?

2 Why are the agency costs lower for Sports Exports Company than for most MNCs?

3 Does Sports Exports Company have any comparative advantage over potential competitors in foreign countries that could produce and sell basketballs there?

4 How would Jim Logan decide which foreign markets he would attempt to enter? Should he initially focus on one or many foreign markets?

5 The Sports Exports Company has no immediate plans to conduct direct foreign investment. However, it might consider other less costly methods of establishing its business in foreign markets. What methods might the Sports Exports Company use to increase its presence in foreign markets by working with one or more foreign companies?

CHAPTER 2
INTERNATIONAL FLOW OF FUNDS

LEARNING OBJECTIVES

The specific objectives of this chapter are to:

● Explain the key components of the balance of payments.

● Explain how the international trade flows are influenced by economic and political factors.

● Explain how the international capital flows are influenced by country characteristics.

International business is facilitated by markets that allow for the flow of funds between countries. The principal international transactions are: borrowing from abroad, lending abroad, investing in foreign shares, setting up foreign subsidiaries, paying dividends to foreign parent companies, payments for imports and receipts for exports. The balance of payments is a record of these international money flows and is discussed in this chapter.

Financial managers of multinational corporations (MNCs) monitor the balance of payments so that they can determine the nature of international transactions for a particular country and how they are changing over time. The balance of payments is an indicator of the health of the economy and may even signal potential shifts in exchange rates.

BALANCE OF PAYMENTS

The **balance of payments** is a summary of transactions between domestic and foreign *residents* over a specified period of time. It represents an accounting of a country's international transactions for a period, usually a quarter or a year.

A resident is an individual or business or any organization operating in the particular country. For an organization, this will normally entail setting up a company in the country under the commercial company laws of that country. Individuals who earn their income and live in the country are residents though they might be foreign nationals. A business that is resident is registered in the country and is a legal, tax paying entity. Such businesses include all the national companies, so for the UK, British Petroleum plc, Tesco plc, Barclays Bank plc and so on are resident companies. Subsidiaries of foreign multinationals are also residents of the country like any other registered company in the country. For example, Matsushita Electric Industrial in Japan supplies consumer and business related electronics products in the UK. The operation is more than direct exporting from Japan, so they have set up Panasonic (UK) Ltd (a wholly owned subsidiary) to manage the operation. Panasonic (UK) Ltd is registered and located in the UK, pays taxes to the UK government on its profits and pays dividends to its parent company in Japan. Exports from Panasonic (UK) Ltd will count as UK exports in the balance of payments statement. In this way, multinationals play a full part in the economies in which they operate.

Data for the balance of payments are collected via questionnaires and returns to governments. Although it is described in terms of a double entry system, it is not the same as a set of accounts in this respect. The figures are therefore really estimates and there is a balancing account 'net errors and omissions'. In the UK 2011 accounts the net error was £11bn according to the International Monetary Fund (IMF). The figures will be adjusted over the years, so the figures for 2011 will be adjusted in subsequent publications.

A balance-of-payments statement can be broken down into various components. Those that receive the most attention are the current account and the financial account (sometimes referred to as the **capital account**). Taking the UK as an example, the **current account** represents mainly export and import payments for goods and services between the UK and the rest of the world. The **financial account** represents principally a summary of investments in stocks and shares between the UK and the rest of the world – investments into the UK and investments from the UK to the rest of the world. Balance of payments are normally prepared for individual countries, but may also be prepared for currency areas such as the euro, or for multinational entities such as the European Union (EU).

The transactions between home and foreign residents often involve different currencies, national residents offering their home currency in exchange for foreign currency and foreign residents offering their foreign currency for home currency. For countries trading in the euro area, many of the transactions will be in the same currency; but there is no fundamental difference to the recording process. The domestic or home currency side involved in the transaction (or more formally, currency held by the resident) is recorded twice in the balance of payments in a similar manner to **double entry book-keeping** (see Exhibit 2.1). It therefore does not matter how much or what currency is involved on the other side of the transaction, only what is happening to the currency held by residents is of interest.

Taking the British pound as the home currency, for an exchange of currencies to take place, foreign currency has to demand British pounds (say, €120 offered in exchange for £100 to buy British exports or invest in the UK) *and* there must be British pounds seeking foreign currency for the same amounts (so £100 seeking €120 to pay for imports or invest abroad). Only then will there be an exchange. Banks, travel agents and Bureaux de Change act as intermediaries in much the same way as a shop. They buy stocks of foreign currency and then sell it on at prices that attract domestic customers, but ultimately the transaction will be as outlined above. Examples of demand and supply are given in Exhibit 2.2.

Current account

Current accounts are described in various ways in differing balance of payments accounts. The distinguishing feature of current account transactions is that they are international payments for goods and services between nationals and non-nationals. The UK balance of payments reports a **balance of trade** (exports of

EXHIBIT 2.1 A foreign currency transaction

HOME CURRENCY
(currency held by residents
of home country)

TRANSACTION
(UK as the home currency)

FOREIGN CURRENCY
(currency held by residents
of foreign country)

Home currency offered mainly
to buy foreign goods or to
invest abroad (transactions
recorded as a "–" in the
balance of payments).

For every £1 supplied for
foreign currency (–£1)

Amount of foreign currency
depends on the exchange rate
– this changes on a daily basis

Home currency demanded by
non-residents to buy goods
from the home country or to
invest in the home country
(transactions recorded as a
"+") in the balance of
payments.

£1 must be demanded by
foreign currency (+£1)

Transactions should
balance and total £0

Notes:
- The Balance of Payments is a record of the demand and supply of currency held by home residents in transactions with non-residents.
- Particularly for EU countries, both the home currency and the foreign currency could be euros.

EXHIBIT 2.2 Examples of balance of payment transactions

International trade transaction with UK as the home country	Demand or supply of British pounds	Entry on UK balance of payments
UK importer purchases radios from Singapore	Supply of British pounds	Debit or –
Spanish importer pays UK company for goods supplied	Demand for British pounds	Credit or +
French company pays insurance premium to Lloyds insurance in London	Demand for British pounds	Credit or +
Foreign workers resident in the UK send money home	Supply of British pounds	Debit or –
French company buys shares on the London Stock Exchange	Demand for British pounds	Credit or +
UK company loans money to its American subsidiary	Supply of British pounds	Debit or –
Australian subsidiary pays dividends to its UK parent company	Demand for British pounds	Credit or +
Italian company lends money to its UK subsidiary	Demand for British pounds	Credit or +

goods less imports of goods); a balance of services (the export less import of insurance, banking, tourism and other services); a balance of income (the balance of dividend, interest payments and salary payments); and current transfers (sundry transactions including payments and receipts from the EU and charity payments). In total these balances add up to the overall current account balance.

> ## EXAMPLE
>
> Suppose, for the sake of clarity, that there are no financial intermediaries such as banks and therefore trading has to be direct. Wavy plc has to pay 150 euros for imports. It offers over the Internet £100 in exchange for 150 euros. That offer is accepted by Francophile SA of France who want £100 to pay for a British export. The supply of the £100 of UK currency by Wavy is recorded as a debit or negative in the imports account, and the demand for the £100 of UK currency by Francophile is recorded as an export – a plus or credit. Both transactions are at £100 – note that it does not matter as far as the balance is concerned how many euros were exchanged for the £100.

A deficit in the balance of trade means that the value of goods and services exported by the home country is less than the imports. On the financial markets there would have been a net supply of home currency seeking foreign currency to pay for the larger value of imported goods and services. A negative balance on the current account has to be met by a positive balance on the financial account. A positive balance on the financial account represents a net demand for the home currency to pay for investments into the home country. Taken together excess imports are being financed by borrowing from abroad (i.e. investments into the home country). The UK balance of payments (Exhibit 2.3) shows just such a picture.

Financial account

The key components of the financial account (sometimes called the capital account) are direct foreign investment, portfolio investment and other capital investment. Direct foreign investment represents the investment in fixed assets in foreign countries that can be used to conduct business operations. Examples of direct foreign investment include a firm's acquisition of part or all of a foreign company, the construction of a new manufacturing plant or the expansion of an existing plant in a foreign country. The investment will typically either be lending to an existing subsidiary or the acquisition of sufficient shares in a foreign company to be involved in the management (usually regarded as above 10 per cent) or setting up a new company and buying the shares and lending to that company to operate.

Portfolio investment represents transactions involving long-term financial assets (such as stocks and bonds) between countries. The key difference between portfolio investment and direct foreign investment is that with portfolio investment there is no participation in the management. The level of investment in any one company is therefore much lower than in the case of direct investment (below 10 per cent). Thus, a purchase of 1 per cent of Heineken (Netherlands) shares by a UK investor is classified as portfolio investment because it represents a purchase of foreign financial assets without changing control of the company. If a UK firm purchased all of Heineken's shares in an acquisition, this transaction would result in a transfer of control and therefore would be classified as direct foreign investment instead of portfolio investment.

A third component of the capital account consists of other capital investment, which represents transactions involving short-term financial assets (such as money market securities) between countries. These would include the net result of operations by governments in the market place in order to stabilize the value of the currency.

Overall balance of payments

The balance of payments account can be described in three broad categories:

● Current account in surplus, financial account in deficit.

● Current account in deficit, financial account in surplus.

● Current account and financial account in balance.

EXHIBIT 2.3 UK balance of payments 2011

	£ billion (thousand million)		
Goods: export	299		
Goods: import	−399		
Balance on goods		−100	A net importer of goods
Services export	184		
Services import	−114		
Balance on services		70	A net exporter of services
Investment income received	208		
Investment income paid	−207		
Balance on income		1	Dividends and interest received from abroad and received from abroad
A: CURRENT ACCOUNT		−29	
	Balanced by:		
Capital account: credit	6		
Capital account: debit	−3		
B: CAPITAL ACCOUNT		3	
Direct investment abroad	−50		
Direct investment inwards	17		
Balance on direct investments		−33	Net investment abroad for managerial purposes
Portfolio investment outward	−23		Outward investment
Portfolio investment inward	−26		A decline in inward investment
Balance on portfolio Investment		−49	
Other transactions		103	
C: FINANCIAL ACCOUNT		21	
NET TOTAL (B+C)		24	
D: CHANGE IN RESERVES OF FOREIGN CURRENCY		−7	An increase in reserves like exports
E: NET ERRORS AND OMISSIONS		12	Effectively a purchase of foreign currency
B+C+D+E = − A		29	

Notes:

- A negative figure represents an increase in the demand for foreign currency by British pounds. A positive figure is a demand for British pounds by foreign currency.
- To put these figures in perspective, gross domestic product (total value of output) was about £1 400 000m.

Source: IMF Balance of Payments, The Pink Book, ONS.

Current account in surplus, financial account in deficit (Type 1, Exhibit 2.4)

Ideally one would want to see these balances in a developed country. A mature economy should be able to generate surplus goods and surplus savings. A surplus on the current account would be expected from such a productive economy, more exports of high tech, high value added goods and imports of low tech goods and raw materials. The consequent deficit on the financial account means that there is a net demand for foreign currency. Such demand would be required if a developed country were to invest its surplus savings in a developing country.

However, an alternative less appealing scenario is of a developing country that has a surplus on the current account (a positive figure), driven by the need to earn foreign currency in order to repay loans on the financial account (equivalent to investment out, a balancing negative figure).

Current account in deficit, financial account in surplus (Type 2, Exhibit 2.4)

Reflecting the previous discussion, this result could be a good scenario for a developing nation. The current account deficit would ideally be due to imports of machinery. The finance for such imports would be through international borrowing resulting in a surplus on the financial account. A deficit on the current account can, however, all too easily be due to high interest payments on loans, or import of relatively unproductive goods.

Developed countries often over-consume resulting in excess imports leading to a current account deficit (a net supply of home currency for foreign currency on the current account). This deficit is financed by a demand by foreign currency for home currency to invest in deposit accounts, shares and bonds of the developed country – a capital account entry. Such investments are in a secure currency that may hold its value far better than the home currency of the MNC and be more useful to finance international trade. The developed country may even offer better interest rates to attract foreign deposits in order to finance the excess of imports.

The USA has for many years run a large currency account deficit, over 5 per cent of its gross national product. This net supply of US dollars for foreign currency is met by foreign investment in US Treasury bonds and other securities. Nearly 30 per cent of US Treasury bills are held by non-residents. There is also significant foreign investment in US real estate (ranches, shopping malls, etc.). The value of the US dollar is not affected; the supply of dollars for imports is met by a demand for dollars to invest in deposit accounts, bonds, etc. It may be argued that by running a deficit, the USA is providing a market for developing countries. Providing aid to developing countries can all too easily be siphoned off by corrupt officials or merely

EXHIBIT 2.4 **Types of balance of payments**

	Type 1	Type 2	Type 3
Defining characteristic:	**Positive current account balance, negative financial account balance**	**Negative current account balance, positive financial account balance**	**Both accounts more or less in balance**
Exports	+100	+65	+80
Imports	−60	−100	−78
Current account balance	**+40**	**−35**	**+2**
Investment in	+50	+80	−52
Investment out	−90	−45	+50
Financial account balance	**−40**	**+35**	**−2**

Note: The figures are illustrative only.

subsidize inefficiency. By contrast, a current account deficit provides demand, in effect payment that can only be met by investment, organization and production – a far more constructive form of aid. The resulting foreign holdings of dollar deposits also help international liquidity; effectively the dollar is acting as a world currency. In effect this gives the US great seigniorage, the gain from printing money or creating credit. The USA can buy foreign goods with the credit created by the money it prints and this credit is then invested back in the USA by foreign investors by buying US bonds thus saving in a stable well accepted currency. In this way the value of the dollar is maintained through a balance of supply and demand. But some may argue that there is a cost to the USA in that it could be seen as incurring foreign liabilities in the form of foreign deposits and investments to fund short-term purchases from abroad. Also, there is a concern that confidence in the value of the dollar may weaken if the deficit increase continues to grow.

Current account and financial account in balance (see Type 3, Exhibit 2.4)

The balance of payments must be seen within the context of the economy as a whole. Being in balance is not an especially desirable goal. Large deficits and surpluses may be quite small in the context of the economy as a whole. It is quite possible for a country to maintain a current account deficit in much the same way as a company can sustain an increasing overdraft as it grows in size.

INTERNATIONAL TRADE FLOWS

France, UK, Germany and other European countries rely more heavily on international trade than the USA. The trade volume of European countries is typically between 30 per cent and 40 per cent of their respective GDPs. The trade volume of the USA and Japan is typically between 10 per cent and 20 per cent of their respective GDPs. Nevertheless, for all countries, the volume of trade has grown over time (see Exhibits 2.5, 2.6 and 2.7).

Distribution of exports and imports for major countries

The themes to note from the bar charts (Exhibit 2.5) are:

1   The relatively low level of trade with Japan for the European countries.

2   The high levels of trade with Asia.

3   The relatively low involvement of France with the USA and Asia compared to Germany and the UK.

4   The generally low level of trade with Africa compared to other countries.

5   The much greater significance of the Pacific Rim (Japan and Asia) than Europe for the USA.

6   The persistence of traditional trading partners. The relatively high levels of French trade with Africa reflects its colonial ties with North Africa (Algeria) in particular. The UK's trade with Ireland and the US trade with Mexico are further examples.

Balance of trade trends

The themes on the balance of trade trends from Exhibit 2.6 are:

1   Germany has for many years operated with a surplus on the balance of payments account.

2   France's balance of payments has deteriorated in recent years.

3   The UK has operated for a number of years with a balance of payments deficit.

4   The USA runs an increasingly large balance of payments deficit.

Source: IMF Balance of Payments Yearbook.

EXHIBIT 2.5   Direction of trade statistics 2007

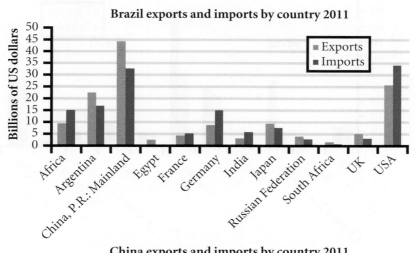

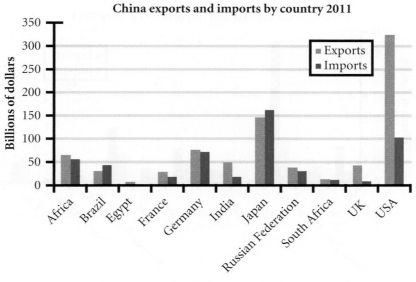

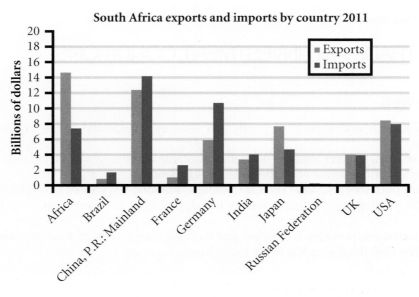

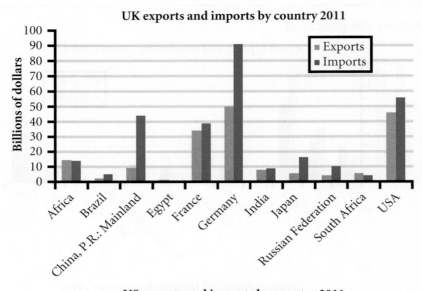

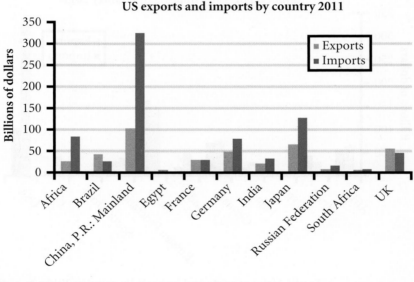

Source: IMF Direction of Trade Statistics.

UPDATED TRADE AND INVESTMENT CONDITIONS

USING THE WEB

An update of exports and imports of goods and services is provided at the WTO site at: http://www.wto.org.

An update of foreign direct investment (FDI) is available at: http://www.unctad.org/, the UNCTAD site (United Nations Conference on Trade and Development).

The IMF now publishes a survey 'The Co-Ordinated Portfolio Investment Survey' (CPIS) which lists by country the holdings of portfolio investments abroad, that is investments with no managerial involvement.

The UK government provides a detailed and well explained view of their investment and trade published as *The Pink Book* which is easily found from a browser.

EXHIBIT 2.6 Trends in trade

	Year	2005	2006	2007	2008	2009	2010	2011	% annual increase 2005 to 2011
USA	Exports	1288	1461	1656	1845	1582	1844	2105	9%
	Imports	1997	2214	2353	2544	1961	2339	2665	5%
UK	Exports	592	684	731	756	596	668	773	5%
	Imports	672	764	825	845	651	732	821	3%
Euro	Exports	2027	2309	2758	3082	2512	2789	3271	8%
	Imports	1920	2234	2624	3040	2404	2695	3165	9%
Germany	Exports	1108	1281	1533	1712	1368	1516	1761	8%
	Imports	962	1119	1299	1483	1205	1331	1578	9%
South Africa	Exports	68	78	90	99	79	100	118	10%
	Imports	69	84	98	108	81	100	120	10%
Egypt	Exports	31	37	44	55	45	49	47	7%
	Imports	34	41	54	67	54	60	61	10%
India	Exports	155 .	193	240	305	261	350	437	19%
	Imports	182	225	279	379	328	439	540	20%
China	Exports	770	973	1255	1494	1260	1648	1997	17%
	Imports	646	765	947	1145	1040	1425	1809	19%

Notes:
- Exports and imports of goods and services.
- Note that the increase in exports and imports exceeds the increase in GDP of each country. There is an increasing propensity for international trade.

Source: IMF Balance of Payments Yearbook.

Trade agreements

Many trade agreements have occurred over the years in an effort to reduce trade restrictions. Throughout the 1990s, trade restrictions between European countries were removed. One implicit trade barrier was the different regulations among countries. MNCs were unable to sell products across all European countries because each country required different specifications (related to the size or composition of the products). The standardization of product specifications throughout Europe during the 1990s removed a very large trade barrier. The adoption of the euro as a single currency in much of Europe also encouraged trade between European countries. It removed the transaction costs associated with the conversion of one currency to another. It also removed concerns about exchange rate risk for producers or customers based in Europe that were selling to other countries in Europe. The EU conducts a number of summits and meetings with countries and trading areas such as Latin America, Mercosur (Argentina, Brazil, Bolivia, Paraguay, Uruguay and Venezuela) designed to further trade relations by means of lowering tariffs (a tariff is a tax on imported goods), or in the case of a textile agreement with China in Shanghai, 10 June 2005, to limit the growth of textile imports from China until 2008.

EXHIBIT 2.7   Comparison of balance payments for selected countries 2011

	\$ billion (thousand million)							
	USA	UK	Euro area	Germany	South Africa	Egypt	India	China
Goods: export	1501	479	2469	1494	103	28	299	1812
Goods: import	−2236	−639	−2457	−1273	−100	−47	−416	−1570
Balance on goods	−735	−160	12	221	3	−19	−117	242
Services export	604	294	802	267	15	19	137	185
Services import	−429	−181	−708	−305	−20	−14	−125	−239
Balance on services	175	113	94	−38	−5	5	12	−54
Investment income received	849	333	866	304	7	16	74	200
Investment income paid	−755	−332	−956	−284	−18	−7	−30	−187
Balance on income	94	1	−90	20	−11	9	44	13
A: CURRENT ACCOUNT	−466	−46	16	203	−13	−5	−61	201
Balanced by:								
Capital account: credit		9	34	6	0	0	1	6
Capital account: debit	1	3	19	5	0	0	1	0
B: CAPITAL ACCOUNT	−1	6	15	1	0	0	0	6
Direct investment abroad	−443	−81	−564	−52	0	−1	−15	−101
Direct investment inwards	258	28	348	39	6	0	32	272
Balance on direct investments	−185	−53	−216	−13	6	−1	17	171
Portfolio investment outward	−83	−36	70	−35	−6	0	0	6
Portfolio investment inward	337	−42	316	90	7	−10	3	13
Balance on portfolio Investment	254	−78	386	55	1	−10	3	19
Other transactions	504	158	−281	−254	4	0	37	26
C: FINANCIAL ACCOUNT	572	33	−96	−211	11	−11	57	222
NET TOTAL (B+C)	571	39	−81	−210	11	−11	57	221
D: CHANGE IN RESERVES OF FOREIGN CURRENCY	−16	−11	35	−4	−5	19	5	−394
E: NET ERRORS AND OMISSIONS	−89	18	30	11	7	−3	−1	−35
B+C+D+E = −A	466	46	−16	−203	13	5	61	−201

Notes:
- Germany is a large part of the Euro area data.
- Sub totals are in bold; amounts in \$ billion.
- Increases in investment abroad are negative (a demand for foreign currency) and increases in inward investment are positive (a supply of foreign currency), opposite signs represent decreases.

  - The size of the Euro area.
  - The huge US balance of payments deficit.
  - The large portfolio inward investment into the USA.
  - The large portfolio inward investment into the Euro area other than Germany.
  - The huge increase in reserves of foreign exchange held by the Bank of China and invested abroad.

Source: IMF International Financial Statistics January 2012.

In 2003, the USA and Chile signed a free trade agreement to remove tariffs on more than 90 per cent of the products traded between the two countries. In June 2009 the EU concluded an interim Economic Partnership Agreement with Southern African Development Countries (SADC): Botswana, Lesotho, Namibia, Swaziland and Mozambique. It includes: no duties/quotas for SADC imports to the EU; no duties/quotas for 86 per cent of EU exports. South Africa signed a separate Trade Development and Co-operation Agreement with the EU in 2004.

General negotiations are now under the auspices of the World Trade Organization (WTO), which was set up after the Uruguay Round of trade talks (1986–94) held by the now disbanded **General Agreement on Tariffs and Trade (GATT)**. Currently the WTO is overseeing the Doha Development Agenda set up in November 2001 to focus in particular on the problems of developing nations.

USING THE WEB

For further information on trade agreements consult: the homepage of the World Trade Organization at http://www.wto.org/.

Trade disagreements

Countries seek to promote free trade so that their companies seeking to export goods are able to compete in foreign markets without discrimination. Economic theories (see above) also advocate free trade as the basis of greater wealth for all. For this reason countries are members of organizations such as the WTO and the Organization for Economic Cooperation and Development (OECD), which seek to encourage free trade for just these reasons. Yet countries also seek to restrict free trade in order to protect domestic industry from foreign competition and at the same time seek to promote exports and in doing so cause trade disagreements.

It is the specific task of the WTO to resolve multilateral trade disputes through an adjudication process. The main problems with this process are first, that it takes time, and second, the disputed unfair trade practice remains in place during the consultation procedure. The WTO itself gives as a case study of a dispute over discrimination against the import of Venezuelan petrol in January 1995 that took two and a half years to settle. Bringing cases may also be used as a way of justifying actions. The WTO allows a certain degree of retaliation including actions taken against dumping (selling at an unfairly low price), actions to counteract subsidies by foreign countries to promote their exports and emergency measures to limit imports in order to give temporary protection to domestic industries. Thus a kind of low level 'trade war' is permitted within the negotiating framework. It is important to remember that the WTO is a member driven organization, there are no powers of enforcement. All settlements are by agreement. Thus most countries, including the USA and EU, have at various times been accused of unfair trade practices. The job of the WTO is to prevent such actions escalating to the point where countries impose tariffs and quotas indiscriminately. The reason why countries do not want to be seen to be overtly in breach of WTO decisions is partly because of the risk of retaliation, but also history. The Smoot Hawley Act of 1930 raised tariffs to their highest level and provoked retaliation by other major industrialized countries, followed by a catastrophic collapse in world trade; thus in trying to protect against imports, the USA suffered a decline in exports as well and an overall adverse effect on economic activity. Real exports (after adjusting for general price changes) fell by over 30 per cent and GDP fell by over 25 per cent between 1930 and 1933, events that have always been seen as closely linked. This example above all others serves as a warning from history.

The argument about imports, however, remains. Foreign imports compete with local production causing unemployment, sometimes in areas of high unemployment. In theory, such workers should retrain for more productive employment and the unemployment should be temporary. The loss of salary should, therefore, only be short term and in the long run such workers should be better off. Unfortunately the theory does not specify the length of time for the short term. Governments are often in power only for the short term and have to address these problems. Thus the problem is finely balanced as countries try to argue that their exports should not be restricted but the exports of certain other countries (imports to them) should be restricted.

Consider the following situations that commonly occur:

1   The firms based in one country are not subject to environmental restrictions and, therefore, can produce at a lower cost than firms in other countries.

2   The firms based in one country are not subject to child labour laws and are able to produce products at a lower cost than firms in other countries by relying mostly on children to produce the products.

3   The firms based in one country are allowed by their government to offer bribes to large customers when pursuing business deals in a particular industry. They have a competitive advantage over firms in other countries that are not allowed to offer bribes.

4   The firms in one country receive subsidies from the government, as long as they export the products. The exporting of products that were produced with the help of government subsidies is commonly referred to as **dumping**. These firms may be able to sell their products at a lower price than any of their competitors in other countries.

5   The firms in one country receive tax breaks if they are in specific industries. This practice is not necessarily a subsidy, but it still is a form of government financial support.

In all of these situations, firms in one country may have an advantage over firms in other countries through lower social and environmental standards (e.g. 1 and 2), lower standards of governance (e.g. 3 and 4) and differences in regulatory regimes that have the effect of creating an advantage (e.g. 5). Every government uses strategies that may give its local firms an advantage in the fight for global market share. Thus, the playing field in the battle for global market share is probably not even across all countries. Yet, there is no formula that will ensure a fair battle for market share. Regardless of the progression of international trade treaties, governments will always be able to find strategies that can give their local firms an edge in exporting. Suppose, as an extreme example, that a new international treaty outlawed all of the strategies described above. One country's government could still try to give its local firms a trade advantage by attempting to maintain a relatively weak currency. This strategy can increase foreign demand for products produced locally because products denominated in a weak currency can be purchased at a low price.

Using the exchange rate as a policy. At any given point in time, a group of exporters may claim that they are being mistreated and lobby their government to adjust the currency so that their exports will not be so expensive for foreign purchasers. Note that when exports are purchased, the foreign purchaser has in effect to buy the currency and then with that currency buy the product or service. So a cheaper currency will be the same as lowering the price of the product. In 2004, European exporters claimed that they were at a disadvantage because the euro was too strong. Meanwhile, US exporters claimed that they could not compete with China because the Chinese currency (yuan) was maintained at an artificially weak level (8.277Yuan:$1). In July 2005 the Chinese yuan abandoned its peg to the dollar and has since revalued by over 20 per cent, potentially making Chinese exports more expensive and imports into China cheaper. Why should the Chinese government allow this to happen? As we have seen, competitive trading is sometimes seen as lowering standards but it also has a more virtuous side in that it requires cooperation between the buyer and seller. The USA as large 'customers' of Chinese exports and investments has considerable influence on Chinese policy. Broadly speaking it is in China's interests that the USA can still afford to buy Chinese goods.

Outsourcing. One of the most recent issues related to trade is outsourcing. Multinational companies relocate their production to countries such as Bulgaria, China, India, Vietnam to take advantage of lower labour costs. Even services can be outsourced, for example, telephone booking systems for airlines may be outsourced to India. This form of international trade allows MNCs to conduct operations at a lower cost. The consumer also benefits through lower prices. However, it shifts jobs to other countries and is criticized by the people who lose their jobs due to the outsourcing.

EXAMPLE

As a French citizen, Dominic says he is embarrassed by French firms that outsource their labour services to other countries as a means of increasing their value, because this practice eliminates jobs in France. Dominic is president of Atlantic Company and says the company will never outsource its services. Atlantic Company imports most of its materials from a foreign company. It also owns a factory in Morocco, and the clothing produced in Morocco is exported to France.

Dominic recognizes that outsourcing may replace jobs in France. Yet, he does not realize that importing materials or operating a factory in Morocco is outsourcing and may also have replaced jobs in France. If questioned about his use of foreign labour markets for materials or production, he would likely explain that the high manufacturing wages in France force him to rely on lower cost labour in foreign countries. Yet, the same argument could be used by other French firms that outsource services.

Dominic owns a Toyota, a Nokia cell phone, a Toshiba computer and Adidas clothing. He argues that these non-French products are better value for money than French products. Nicole, a friend of Dominic, suggests that his consumption choices are inconsistent with his 'create French jobs' philosophy. She explains that she only purchases French products. Yet she owns a Ford (produced in Morocco), a Motorola telephone (components produced in Asia), a Compaq computer (produced in China) and Nike clothing (produced in Indonesia)!

Trade policies and political issues. The actions of MNCs designed to maximize profits are seen by many as having strong political consequences for which governments and MNCs should be held to account. People expect imports to be restricted from countries that fail to enforce environmental laws or child labour laws or from countries whose governments commit large-scale abuse of human rights. Every international trade convention now attracts a large number of protesters, all of whom have their own agendas.

The problem for MNCs is whether they should follow relative or universal values. Should they respect or comply with the values and practices of the countries in which they operate, which may include low environmental standards, child labour and corrupt payments to government officials (relative values); or should they adopt universal values of good practice and behave in the same way wherever they operate? Relative values are in one sense non-political in that they respect the traditions and culture of the countries in which they operate. The counter argument is that MNCs become a strong moral force in these countries. Should a country wish to improve its environmental laws, for instance, there is the implied threat that a profit-making MNC will move to another location where the laws are more lax (an instance of the 'race to the bottom'). Thus countries feel pressured to maintain low standards. So it is argued that there is a political consequence even to relative values.

The other approach is to adopt universal values and standards, or at least minimum levels which MNCs apply wherever they operate. A small step was taken in this direction by the UN Sub-Commission on the Promotion and Protection of Human Rights, which in 2003 approved the UN Norms on the Responsibilities of Transnational Corporations and Other Business Enterprises with regard to human rights (search on the Internet for the paper's title). These appear to be no more than a set of aspirations, and as with much UN work, of uncertain practical implications. There would nevertheless be real difficulties if these values were to be actively enforced. Universal values are more obviously political and may be seen as interfering in the governance of countries. Also, the status of UN rules in a sense undermines that of governments in that many would argue that it is for governments to regulate MNCs, not the UN. Such initiatives are therefore likely to remain purely voluntary. In a similar vein the Equator Principles outline 'good behaviour' for international project finance initiatives.

Disagreements within the European Union. In 2004, ten countries from Eastern Europe joined the European Union (EU). Firms based in these newer participating countries in the EU are now subject to reduced trade barriers on EU-related trade. However, these countries are now also subject to the EU tariffs on products that enter the EU. For example, the EU places a 75 per cent tax (tariff) on bananas that are imported by all EU countries. Consequently, the retail price of bananas will likely increase, as the tax is passed on to the consumers. This type of tariff has caused some friction between EU countries that commonly import products and other EU countries.

The philosophy behind the EU trade agreements is that firms within the EU can compete on a level playing field with zero or standardized restrictions across countries. However, governments still claim that some countries have advantages over others. For example, the German government suggested that firms in Poland have an unfair advantage because the Polish government imposes a relatively lower corporate tax rate on its corporations than other EU countries.

FACTORS AFFECTING INTERNATIONAL TRADE FLOWS

Because international trade can significantly affect a country's economy, it is important to identify and monitor the important factors. The most influential factors are:

- Inflation
- National income
- Government restrictions
- Exchange rates.

Impact of inflation

If a country's inflation rate increases relative to the countries with which it trades, its current account will be expected to decrease, other things being equal. Consumers and corporations in that country will most likely purchase more goods overseas (due to high local inflation), while the country's exports to other countries will decline.

Impact of national income

If a country's income level (national income) increases by a higher percentage than those of other countries, its current account is expected to decrease, other things being equal. As the real income level (adjusted for inflation) rises, so does consumption of goods. A percentage of that increase in consumption (sometimes referred to as the marginal propensity to import) will most likely reflect an increased demand for foreign goods.

Impact of government restrictions

A country's government can prevent or discourage imports from other countries. By imposing such restrictions, the government disrupts trade flows. Among the most commonly used trade restrictions are tariffs and quotas.

Tariffs and quotas. If a country's government imposes a tax on imported goods (i.e. a **tariff**), the prices of foreign goods to consumers are effectively increased. Tariffs imposed by the US government are on average lower than those imposed by other governments. Some industries, however, are more highly protected by tariffs than others. American apparel products and farm products have historically received more protection against foreign competition through high tariffs on related imports.

In addition to tariffs, a government can reduce its country's imports by enforcing a **quota**, or a maximum limit that can be imported. Quotas have been commonly applied to a variety of goods imported by the USA and other countries.

Other types of restrictions. Some **trade sanctions** may be imposed on products for health and safety reasons.

In 2001, an outbreak of foot-and-mouth disease occurred in the UK and eventually spread to several other European countries. This disease can spread by direct or indirect contact with infected animals. The US government imposed trade restrictions on some products produced in the UK for health reasons. Consequently, UK exports to the USA declined abruptly. In 2004 the EU banned the import of tuna and swordfish products from countries that did not manage fish stocks in a sustainable manner.

These examples illustrate how uncontrollable factors besides inflation, national income, tariffs and quotas, and exchange rates can affect the balance of trade between two countries.

Impact of exchange rates

Each currency is valued in terms of other currencies through the use of exchange rates so that currencies can be exchanged to facilitate international transactions. The values of most currencies fluctuate over time because of market and government forces (as discussed in detail in Chapter 4). If a *currency*, for example Currency A as used by Country A, begins to rise in value against other currencies, goods exported in Currency A will become more expensive. As a consequence, the demand for such goods may well decrease and the value of exports for Country A will decline. But this is not certain, inflation in other countries may well mean that even after a revaluation, Country A's goods are still relatively cheaper compared to the equivalent domestic goods. On the import side, the higher value of currency A will mean that imports in foreign currency will cost less – the quantity of imports is likely to increase but whether the value of imports will increase or not depends on size of the volume increase. If, for example, imports are 10 per cent cheaper as a result of a revaluation and the quantity increases by only 6 per cent then there would be a reduction in the cost of imports. A revaluation changes the prices of imports and exports, if the quantity reactions to the change in price are sufficiently strong then a worsening of the balance of payments can be expected but such worsening is not inevitable.

EXAMPLE

A tennis racket that sells in the UK for £100 will require a payment of 110 euros by a French importer if the euro is valued at 1.1 euros = £1. If the British pound then becomes more expensive, costing say 1.2 euros, then the French importer will have to pay 120 euros to buy the tennis racket. The French importer may be willing to pay the extra 120 − 110 = 10 euros, in which case UK's exports will not be affected. But the cost of the racket for the French importer has increased by (120 − 110) / 110 = 0.09 or 9 per cent, so it seems likely that the French importer will look elsewhere and the UK will experience a fall in export quantities and value.

A devaluation or fall in the value of Currency A will make the currency cheaper and make imports denominated in foreign currency more expensive and exports less expensive. The hoped for improvement in the balance of payments is *not* inevitable. If a 10 per cent devaluation in Currency A results in only a

3 per cent reduction in imports then the import bill will have gone up; and if exports have only increased by 4 per cent in quantity then assuming that the current account was not in surplus, the balance of payments would worsen not improve (see Exhibit 2.8 for a summary).

The relationship between the balance of payments and currency devaluation crucially depends on the elasticity of demand for imports and exports. If demand is *very* price sensitive (highly elastic), then an increase in the value of Currency A will lead to export quantities falling dramatically and import quantities rising steeply; a devaluation will imply a steep rise in export quantities and a dramatic fall in imports. But if demand quantities did not change much as a result of the change in price (price inelasticity), a devaluation, for instance, could mean simply more expensive imports and no change in exports resulting in a worsening rather than an improvement in the balance of payments.

The elasticity argument is important because an increasing value of a currency (revaluation) does not always mean a worsening current account balance and a devaluation does not always improve the current account balance.

In the 1970s and 1980s the West German Deutschmark appreciated significantly in value on a number of occasions and yet the current account remained in surplus. So although a devaluing currency is normally associated with an improvement in the current account balance (and the opposite for an appreciation), the relationship is not automatic. A developing country exporting a basic commodity such as copper may experience an adverse rather than a positive effect from devaluation. Cheaper copper exports from a devaluation do not necessarily increase the demand as developed countries will not want to store up copper simply because it is cheap. On the other hand a devaluation will have made essential imports more expensive with little chance of switching supplies to home sources. So a devaluation could result in higher import costs and not much of an increase in exports, overall a fall in the current account balance. The elasticity of exports and imports must be such that when a currency devalues the favourable volume reactions, a decline in imports and a rise in exports, must be able to offset the increase in the cost of imports.

EXHIBIT 2.8 Current account balance for UK, effects of exchange rate revaluation and devaluation

Devaluation		Revaluation
Decrease in the value of the £ in relation to other currencies, e.g. 1.20 euros = £1	**Current spot rate, e.g. 1.40 euros = £1**	**Increase in the value of the £ in relation to other currencies, e.g. 1.60 euros = £1**
Imports are more expensive, demand falls and *probable* fall in total cost of imports		Imports are cheaper, demand increases and *probable* rise in total cost of imports
Exports cheaper for foreign buyers, demand increases and certain rise in £ value exports		Exports more expensive for foreign buyers, demand falls and certain fall in £ value exports
Probable current account improvement		**Probable current account worsening**

Notes:
- The total value of imports depends on the quantity reaction to changes in their price (elasticity) due to the change in the value of the pound.
- Although the increase and decrease in exports is certain, the size of the change is not certain.

EXAMPLE

During the 1997–98 Asian crisis, the exchange rates of Asian currencies declined substantially against the dollar, which caused the prices of Asian products to decline from the perspective of the USA and many other countries. Consequently, the demand for Asian products increased and sometimes replaced the demand for products of other countries. For example, the weakness of the Thai baht during this period caused an increase in the global demand for fish from Thailand and a decline in the demand for similar products from the USA (Seattle).

EXAMPLE

The President looked across the table at his Chief Economist and mused: 'So, if we devalue our currency from 1 lira to the US dollar to 1.15 liras to the dollar you are saying that all our exports will be cheaper to buy?' The Chief Economist looked pleased: 'Yes, holders of dollars will have to pay about 15 per cent less to buy a lira. Our tobacco, cars and clothing will all be much cheaper for them – we should be able to export more.' The President looked out of the window and eyed a passing plane: 'Imports are going to be more expensive – the dollar costs more, so fewer mobile phones and foreign cars.' 'Yes, if they want to buy a foreign car it is now going to cost them 15 per cent more.'

The President sensed that his Economist was simply trying to get him to agree: 'But what if they don't want to give up their phones and foreign cars, our import bill could go up.' The Chief Economist suddenly felt that the President was about to dismiss his advice: 'Sir, a cheaper currency should increase our exports, yet our existing levels of imports will be more expensive, but we confidently expect that the demand for imports on average will fall and that the increase in exports and fall in import quantities will offset the increase in import prices. Our balance of payments should improve.' The President noted the caution: 'Should, should . . . what are the other factors?'

Interaction of factors

Because the factors that affect the balance of trade interact, their simultaneous influence on the balance of trade is complex. For example, devaluing the home currency on its own will indeed make imports more expensive. But what if there is inflation in the home country? Imports may be more expensive; but home goods even more expensive.

CORRECTING A BALANCE OF TRADE DEFICIT

A balance of trade deficit is not necessarily a problem; it may be that a country's consumers benefit from imported products that are less expensive than locally produced products. However, the purchase of imported products implies less reliance on domestic production in favour of foreign production. Thus, it may be argued that a large balance of trade deficit causes a transfer of jobs to some foreign countries. Consequently, a country's government may attempt to correct a balance of trade deficit on the current account.

By reconsidering some of the factors that affect the balance of trade, it is possible to develop some common methods for correcting a deficit. Any policy that will increase foreign demand for the country's goods and services will improve its balance of trade position. Foreign demand may increase if export prices become more attractive. This can occur when the country's inflation is low or when its currency's value is reduced, thereby making the prices cheaper from a foreign perspective.

A floating exchange rate could possibly correct any international trade imbalances in the following way. A deficit in a country's balance of trade suggests that the country is spending more funds on foreign products than it is receiving from exports to foreign countries. Because it is selling its currency (to buy foreign goods) in greater volume than the foreign demand for its currency, the value of its currency should decrease. This decrease in value should encourage more foreign demand for its goods in the future. While this theory seems rational, it does not always work as just described. It is possible that, instead, a country's currency will remain stable or appreciate even when the country has a balance of trade deficit. The negative balance on the current account can be sustained by the positive balance on the financial account representing a net inflow of investment into the country.

The USA normally experiences a large balance of trade deficit, which should place downward pressure on the value of the dollar. Yet, in some years, there is substantial investment in dollar-denominated securities by foreign investors. This foreign demand for the dollar places upward pressure on its value, thereby offsetting the downward pressure caused by the trade imbalance. So, on the international exchanges the excess of dollars being offered for foreign currency to pay for imports is met by a demand by holders of foreign currency to buy dollars in order to buy bonds, shares and deposit accounts in the USA. The deficit on the current account due to the surplus imports is being met by a positive balance on the financial account due to surplus investment into the USA. Thus, a balance of trade deficit will not always be corrected by a currency adjustment.

This particular scenario is unique to the USA and possibly may be the case with the euro in the future. In effect, the US dollar is acting as a world currency. The USA can print dollars (expand its money supply), import goods with that money and the money is not exchanged but simply deposited back in the USA by a foreign institution and used for international trade. This relationship relies on the confidence of foreign investors in the dollar. If that confidence is lost, then the value of the dollar could fall rapidly as happened in the early 1970s. It is currently thought that these large imbalances may be a continuing feature of the world economy, especially as investment becomes increasingly international.

Why a weak home currency is not a perfect solution

Even if a country's home currency weakens, its balance of trade deficit will not necessarily be corrected for the following reasons.

Demand of imports and exports too inelastic. As discussed above, devaluing a currency does not necessarily mean that the increase in the quantity of exports and the reduction on the quantity of imports will offset the increase in the price of imports.

Counterpricing by competitors. When a country's currency weakens, its prices become more attractive to foreign customers, and many foreign companies lower their prices to remain competitive with the country's firms.

Impact of other weak currencies. The currency does not necessarily weaken against all currencies at the same time.

EXAMPLE

When the British pound weakens in Europe, the British pound's exchange rates with the currencies of Hong Kong, Singapore and South Korea may remain more stable. As some UK firms reduce their demand for supplies produced in European countries, they may increase their demand for goods produced in Asian countries. Consequently, the British pound's weakness in European countries causes a change in international trade behaviour but does not eliminate the UK trade deficit.

Prearranged international transactions. Many international trade transactions are prearranged and cannot be immediately adjusted. Thus, a weaker British pound may attract foreign purchasers who cannot immediately sever their relationships with suppliers from other countries. Over time, they may begin to take advantage of the weaker British pound by purchasing UK imports, if they believe that the weakness will continue. The lag time between the British pound's weakness and the foreign purchasers' increased demand for UK products could be as long as 18 months or even longer.

The UK balance of trade may actually deteriorate in the short run as a result of British pound depreciation. The price effects (increased cost of imports) are likely to occur more quickly than the more favourable quantity effects (reduction in quantity of imports and increase in the quantity of exports). This pattern is called the **J-curve effect**, and it is illustrated in Exhibit 2.9. The further decline in the trade balance before a reversal creates a trend that can look like the letter J.

Intercompany trade. A fifth reason why a weak currency will not always improve a country's balance of trade is that importers and exporters that are under the same ownership have unique relationships. Many firms purchase products that are produced by their subsidiaries in what is referred to as **intracompany trade** (intra means within and inter means between). This type of trade makes up a significant proportion of international trade, about a third of US exports are intra company transactions. This type of trade will normally continue regardless of exchange rate movements. Thus, the impact of exchange rate movements on intra-company trade patterns is limited.

INTERNATIONAL CAPITAL FLOWS

Capital flows on the balance of payments refers to investments abroad.

Direct foreign investment is typically the acquisition of shares with direct management interest (defined by the OECD as 10 per cent or more of the share ownership) and subsequent transactions with such entities. Such investments will typically then be classified as subsidiaries. From Exhibit 2.7 one can see the typical configuration that has prevailed in recent years. The US and the Euro area undertake large investments abroad as one would want from developed countries. Developing countries should show more investment in than out and that is again what is apparent from Exhibit 2.7.

Portfolio investments show a more marked difference between countries. Portfolio investments out are movements in mainly shares and bonds held abroad and investments in are changes in liabilities to foreign share and bond holders. A negative figure in investments out represents an increase in assets held abroad.

EXHIBIT 2.9 J-curve effect

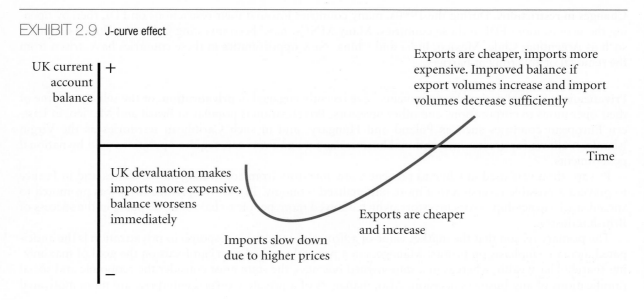

Exhibit 2.7 shows large purchases of shares and bonds in the US and the Euro area. The USA benefits from the safe haven argument whereas the Euro area has in recent years borrowed from abroad to finance government debt, but also some investments might well be seen as a safe investment as well.

There is also interaction between the balance of payments figures. The large net portfolio investment into the USA helps sustain the high net imports. Large new exporters to the USA such as China are saving a portion of their new wealth in the form of US bonds. The demand for dollars to buy the bonds in turn sustains the value of the dollar enabling further demand for Chinese exports. A fall in the value of the dollar would arguably do as much harm to China as to the USA.

In recent years average external assets and liabilities of major countries have tripled (these figures include direct investment). This increase has been accompanied by a decline in home bias of investments as the increase in overseas investments is much more than the increase in the total value of domestic investment markets. The cause of the increase has been largely due to the liberalization of capital markets in the 1980s and 1990s.

Finally, it is noticeable that capital flows are dominated by proximity and cultural ties hence the emergence of trading blocks such as the EU.

USING THE WEB

Information on FDI can be found in the UN Commission on Trade and Development (UNCTAD) World Investment Report, an annual report. The download is currently available at: http://www.unctad.org/; documents can be retrieved through using the local search engine.

Significant multinational investors abroad are: General Electric (US), Vodafone (UK), Ford Motor Co. (US), BP (UK), General Motors (USA), Royal Dutch/Shell Group (UK, Netherlands), Toyota (Japan), Total (France), France Telecom (France) and ExxonMobil (USA). The annual report of these companies and all major companies discloses the geographical location of foreign investments and reports on the investment policies of the company.

Factors affecting foreign direct investment

Capital flows resulting from FDI change whenever conditions in a country change the desire of firms to conduct business operations there. Some of the more common factors that could affect a country's appeal for FDI are identified here.

Changes in restrictions. During the 1990s, many countries lowered their restrictions on FDI, thereby opening the way to more FDI in those countries. Many MNCs, have been investing in less developed countries such as Argentina, Chile, Mexico, India and China. New opportunities in these countries have arisen from the removal of government barriers.

Privatization. Several national governments have recently engaged in privatization, or the selling of some of their operations to corporations and other investors. Privatization is popular in Brazil and Mexico, in Eastern European countries such as Poland and Hungary, and in such Caribbean territories as the Virgin Islands. It allows for greater international business as foreign firms can acquire operations sold by national governments.

Privatization was used in Chile to prevent a few investors from controlling all the shares and in France to prevent a possible reversion to a more nationalized economy. In the UK, privatization was promoted to spread stock ownership across investors, which allowed more people to have a direct stake in the success of British industry.

The primary reason that the market value of a firm may increase in response to privatization is the anticipated increase emphasis on profits. Managers in a privately owned firm can focus on the goal of maximizing shareholder wealth, whereas in a state-owned business, the state must consider the economic and social ramifications of any business decision. Also, managers of a privately owned enterprise are more motivated to ensure profitability because their careers and salaries are often closely linked to the profitability of the enterprise. For these reasons, privatized firms will search for local and global opportunities that could enhance their value. The trend towards privatization will undoubtedly create a more competitive global marketplace.

USING THE WEB

Foreign direct investment information

Further information on FDI can be obtained from the World Bank website at: www.worldbank.org. The 'Investment Policy Review' and 'The World Investment Directory' are useful further links from this page. The OECD offers a developed country viewpoint at http://www.oecd.org, choose the 'By Topic' option. Finally, the search engine at: http://www.corporatewatch.org offers a decidedly alternative (dissident) view of investment.

Potential economic growth. Countries that have greater potential for economic growth are more likely to attract FDI because firms recognize that they may be able to capitalize on that growth by establishing more business there.

Exchange rates. Firms typically prefer to direct FDI to countries where the local currency is expected to strengthen against their own. Under these conditions, they can invest funds to establish their operations in a country while that country's currency is relatively cheap (weak). Then, earnings from the new operations can periodically be converted back to the firm's currency at a more favourable exchange rate.

Tax rates. Countries that impose relatively low tax rates on corporate earnings are more likely to attract FDI. When assessing the feasibility of FDI, firms estimate the after-tax cash flows that they expect to earn.

Factors affecting international portfolio investment

The desire by individual or institutional investors to direct international portfolio investment to a specific country is influenced by the following factors.

Tax rates on interest or dividends. Investors normally prefer to invest in a country where the taxes on interest or dividend income from investments are relatively low. Investors assess their potential after-tax earnings from investments in foreign securities.

Interest rates. Portfolio investment can also be affected by interest rates. Money tends to flow to countries with high interest rates, as long as the local currencies are not expected to weaken.

USING THE WEB

Information on capital flows and international portfolio transactions is provided at: http://www.worldbank.org and at the website for the Bank for International Settlements http://www.bis.org/, follow the 'statistics' link.

Exchange rates. When investors invest in a security in a foreign country, their return is affected by: (1) the change in the value of the security and (2) the change in the value of the currency in which the security is denominated. If a country's home currency is expected to strengthen, foreign investors may be willing to invest in the country's securities to benefit from the currency movement. Conversely, if a country's home currency is expected to weaken, foreign investors may decide to purchase securities in other countries.

AGENCIES THAT FACILITATE INTERNATIONAL FLOWS

A variety of agencies have been established to facilitate international trade and financial transactions. These agencies often represent a group of nations. A description of some of the more important agencies follows.

International Monetary Fund

The United Nations Monetary and Financial Conference held in Bretton Woods, New Hampshire, in July 1944, was called to develop a structured international monetary system. As a result of this conference, the **International Monetary Fund (IMF)** was formed. The major objectives of the IMF, as set by its charter, are to: (1) promote co-operation among countries on international monetary issues, (2) promote stability in exchange rates, (3) provide temporary funds to member countries attempting to correct imbalances of international payments, (4) promote free mobility of capital funds across countries and (5) promote free trade. It is clear from these objectives that the IMF's goals encourage increased internationalization of business.

The IMF is overseen by a Board of Governors, composed of finance officers (such as the head of the central bank) from each of the 188 member countries. It also has an executive board composed of 24 executive directors representing the member countries. This board is based in Washington, DC, and meets at least three times a week to discuss ongoing issues.

One of the key duties of the IMF is its **compensatory financing facility (CFF)**, which attempts to reduce the impact of export instability on country economies. Although it is available to all IMF members, this facility is used mainly by developing countries. A country experiencing financial problems due to reduced export earnings must demonstrate that the reduction is temporary and beyond its control. In addition, it must be willing to work with the IMF in resolving the problem.

Each member country of the IMF is assigned a quota based on a variety of factors reflecting that country's economic size as an economy and involvement in international trade and investment. Members are required to pay this assigned quota. The amount of funds that each member can borrow from the IMF depends on its particular quota. Voting rights are also dependent on quotas.

The financing by the IMF is measured in **special drawing rights (SDRs)**. The SDR is an international reserve asset created by the IMF and allocated to member countries to supplement currency reserves. The SDR is not an issued currency but simply a unit of account, a weighted basket of currencies. It is like a currency for measuring only; to turn it into currency one has to convert it to an issued currency such as the euro at the calculated exchange rate. The SDR's value fluctuates in accordance with the value of the currencies in the basket.

The IMF played an active role in attempting to reduce the adverse effects of the Asian crisis. In 1997 and 1998, it provided funding to various Asian countries in exchange for promises from the respective governments to take specific actions intended to improve economic conditions. More recently in the world financial crisis its role has been more limited. The head of the IMF Madame Lagarde has called for better regulation, better supervision, better resolution of cross-border entities and better internal incentives in financial institutions. Actual action by the IMF has however been very limited.

Funding dilemma of the IMF. The IMF typically specifies economic reforms that a country must satisfy to receive IMF funding (the term 'conditionally' refers to IMF requests attached to lending). In this way, the IMF attempts to ensure that the country uses the funds responsibly. Although its lending powers have not kept pace with the growth of the international economy, the IMF retains great authority. Banks are generally unwilling to lend unless the IMF has agreed terms with the country.

During the Asian crisis, the IMF agreed to provide $43 billion to Indonesia. The negotiations were tense, as the IMF demanded that President Suharto break up some of the monopolies run by his friends and family members and close a number of weak banks. Citizens of Indonesia interpreted the bank closures as a banking crisis and began to withdraw their deposits from all banks. In January 1998, the IMF demanded many types of economic reform, and Suharto agreed to them. The reforms may have been overly ambitious, however, and Suharto failed to institute them. The IMF agreed to renegotiate the terms in March 1998 in a continuing effort to rescue Indonesia, but this effort signalled that a country did not have to meet the terms of its agreement to obtain funding. A new agreement was completed in April, and the IMF resumed its payments to support a bailout of Indonesia. In May 1998, Suharto abruptly discontinued subsidies for gasoline and food, which led to riots. Suharto blamed the riots on the IMF and on foreign investors who wanted to acquire assets in Indonesia at depressed prices.

The dilemma for the IMF is that its terms for lending (conditionality) have inevitable political consequences. Votes are proportional to SDR quotas, i.e. to the financial contribution of the country, it is therefore dominated by the richer countries. Developing countries feel aggrieved that a body with no democratic status should have a greater influence on their lives than the UN. The UN website has expressed the view that IMF and World Bank economic conditionality packages increase levels of poverty and inequality in developing countries.

World Bank

The **International Bank for Reconstruction and Development (IBRD)**, also referred to as the **World Bank**, was established in 1944. Its primary objective is to make loans to countries to enhance economic development. For example, the World Bank extended a loan to Mexico for about $4 billion over a 10-year period for environmental projects to facilitate industrial development near the US border. Its main source of funds is the sale of bonds and other debt instruments to private investors and governments. The World Bank has a profit-oriented philosophy. Therefore, its loans are not subsidized but are extended at market rates to governments (and their agencies) that are likely to repay them.

A key aspect of the World Bank's mission is the **Structural Adjustment Loan (SAL)**, established in 1980. A significant problem of international investment in developing countries is that foreign investment is in areas profitable to the developed world. Multinational companies cannot be expected to invest in schools, the judiciary or a proper social service and pension provision. The imbalance created by such commercial investment can lead to corruption, problems in contract enforcement, lawlessness and political unrest. The SALs are intended to counteract such tendencies. For example, a SAL to the Colombian government is described as having the particular aims of providing:

'New incentives for employers to create jobs for young, elderly, disabled and unemployed Colombians; Expansion of apprenticeship and training opportunities; More nutrition and child care assistance to poor families; Health insurance for more low-income workers.'

(World Bank website press release No:2003/82/LAC)

Given that the progress of developing countries has in many cases been very slow over the years, the effectiveness of such loans has been called into question.

Because the World Bank provides only a small portion of the financing needed by developing countries, it attempts to spread its funds by entering into **co-financing agreements**. Co-financing is performed in the following ways:

- *Official aid agencies.* Development agencies may join the World Bank in financing development projects in low-income countries.

- *Export credit agencies.* The World Bank co-finances some capital-intensive projects that are also financed through export credit agencies.

- *Commercial banks.* The World Bank has joined with commercial banks to provide financing for private-sector development. In recent years, more than 350 banks from all over the world have participated in co-financing.

The World Bank recently established the **Multilateral Investment Guarantee Agency (MIGA)**, which offers various forms of political risk insurance. This is an additional means (along with its SALs) by which the World Bank can encourage the development of international trade and investment.

World Trade Organization

The **World Trade Organization (WTO)** was created as a result of the Uruguay Round of trade negotiations that led to the GATT accord in 1993. This organization was established to provide a forum for multilateral trade negotiations and to settle trade disputes (see Trade disputes section above) related to the GATT accord. It began its operations in 1995 with 81 member countries, and now has 157. Member countries are given voting rights that are used to make judgements about trade disputes and other issues.

International Financial Corporation

In 1956 the **International Financial Corporation (IFC)** was established to promote private enterprise within countries. Composed of a number of member nations, the IFC works to promote economic development through the private rather than the government sector. It not only provides loans to corporations but also purchases stock, thereby becoming part owner in some cases rather than just a creditor. The IFC typically provides 10 to 15 per cent of the necessary funds in the private enterprise projects in which it invests, and the remainder of the project must be financed through other sources. Thus, the IFC acts as a catalyst, as opposed to a sole supporter, for private enterprise development projects. It traditionally has obtained financing from the World Bank but can borrow in the international financial markets.

International Development Association

The **International Development Association (IDA)** was created in 1960 with country development objectives somewhat similar to those of the World Bank. Its loan policy is more appropriate for less prosperous nations, however. The IDA extends loans at low interest rates to poor nations that cannot qualify for loans from the World Bank.

Bank for International Settlements

The **Bank for International Settlements (BIS)** attempts to facilitate co-operation among countries with regard to international transactions. It also provides assistance to countries experiencing a financial crisis. The BIS is sometimes referred to as the 'central banks' central bank' or the 'lender of last resort'. It played an important role in supporting some of the less developed countries during the international debt crisis in the early and mid-1980s. It commonly provides financing for central banks in Latin American and Eastern European countries.

An important role is to provide support for the Basel Committee on Banking Supervision (BCBS) which sets out regulations for international banking supervision. In particular, the BCBS recommends liquidity requirements for banks. Recently it has issued recommendations known as Basel III on banking supervision. The agreements are voluntary on the part of its members; but failure to comply would mean a loss of confidence in the particular bank that would have severe financial consequences.

Regional development agencies

Several other agencies have more regional (as opposed to global) objectives relating to economic development. These include, for example, the Inter-American Development Bank (focusing on the needs of Latin America), the Asian Development Bank (established to enhance social and economic development in Asia), and the African Development Bank (focusing on development in African countries).

In 1990, the European Bank for Reconstruction and Development was created to help the Eastern European countries adjust from communism to capitalism. It now helps to promote projects that lead towards open and democratic market economies, very much supporting the philosophy of free trade.

Western European countries taken together are the major shareholders with the USA as the biggest single country holding a 10 per cent interest. Japan, Italy, Germany and the UK are the next largest members with an 8.5 per cent subscription each.

BRICS

The recent BRICS alliance (Brazil, Russia, India, China and South Africa) is a representative group of the major (economically) developing nations. Whether this becomes a new voice in international finance has yet to be determined. The current world economic crisis is noticeably affecting developing countries less than developed countries. It may be that these economies develop a critical mass such that they are not reliant on the European and Western economies. BRICS could be a critical part of this development.

HOW INTERNATIONAL TRADE AFFECTS AN MNC'S VALUE

An MNC's value can be affected by international trade in several ways. The increased revenues from international trade are a clear source of increased value. International investments, exploiting resources and new investment opportunities should increase profits. The risk reduction effects of diversifying on the international stage serve to increase the value of the company by making its profits more stable.

SUMMARY

- The key components of the balance of payments are the current account and the financial account. The financial account is a broad measure of the country's international trade balance. The financial account is a measure of the country's long-term and short-term capital investments, including direct foreign investment and investment in securities (portfolio investment).

- A country's international trade flows are affected by inflation, national income, government restrictions and exchange rates. High inflation, a high national income, low or no restrictions on imports and a strong local currency tend to result in a strong demand for imports and a current account deficit.

- Although some countries attempt to correct current account deficits by reducing the value of their currencies, this strategy critically depends on import and export elasticities.

- A country's international capital flows are affected by any factors that influence direct foreign investment or portfolio investment. Direct foreign investment tends to occur in those countries that have no restrictions and much potential for economic growth. Portfolio investment tends to occur in those countries where taxes are not excessive, where interest rates are high, and where the local currencies are not expected to weaken.

CRITICAL DEBATE

Trade and human rights

Proposition. Some countries do not protect human rights in the same manner as European countries. At times, European countries should threaten to restrict EU imports from or investment to a particular country if it does not correct human rights violations. The EU should use its large international trade and investment as leverage to ensure that human rights violations do not occur. Other countries with a history of human rights violations are more likely to honour human rights if their economic conditions are threatened.

Opposing view. No. International trade and human rights are two separate issues. International trade should not be used as the weapon to enforce human rights. Firms engaged in international trade should not be penalized for the human rights violations of a government. If the EU imposes trade restrictions to enforce human rights, the country will retaliate. Thus, the EU firms that export to that foreign country will be adversely affected. By imposing trade sanctions, the EU is indirectly penalizing the MNCs that are attempting to conduct business in specific foreign countries. Trade sanctions cannot solve every difference in beliefs or morals between the more developed countries and the developing countries. By restricting trade, the EU will slow down the economic progress of developing countries.

Who has the better argument and why? Search the web under 'UN Norms on the Responsibilities of Transnational Corporations and Other Business Enterprises with regard to Human Rights' and 'UN Norms on the Responsibilities of Transnational Corporations problems'.

International finance and accountability

Proposition. The sheer size of the foreign currency markets make MNCs and their free market philosophy intimidating even for developed countries. Countries can in effect no longer regulate their financial institutions or their currencies. Only the IMF and the G8 have any influence and neither of those are democratic bodies. The UN has tried, but frankly, its charter for Transnational Corporations is not very strong. Although MNCs do not want to give the impression that they are above the law, it is difficult to see what law they are obeying.

Opposing view. Nonsense. Companies are registered in their home country and their subsidiaries are registered in their country of operation, they obey all the laws of those countries and more – the transgressions of MNCs, if you look on the Web, are remarkably few. MNCs in their Annual Reports demonstrate that not only do they comply with all local laws but also they have overriding concerns about the environment and working conditions. If countries wanted to stop trading in foreign assets, they could pass laws and ban the practice. But all countries know that MNCs are a source of wealth and prosperity and that their standards are higher than the local equivalent.

With whom do you agree? You may Google 'MNCs', 'accountability', '+OECD' and '+pdf' as one search and 'UN global Compact', 'OECD Guidelines for Multinational Enterprises' and finally 'FTSE4Good', but be aware that there is a bias towards the proposer's viewpoint.

SELF TEST

Answers are provided in Appendix A at the back of the text.

1 Briefly explain how changes in various economic factors affect the UK current account balance.

2 Explain why UK tariffs may change the composition of UK exports but will not necessarily reduce a UK balance of trade deficit.

3 Explain how a financial crisis can affect international trade.

QUESTIONS AND APPLICATIONS

1 **Balance of payments.**

  a What is the current account generally composed of?

  b What is the financial account generally composed of?

2 **Inflation effect on trade.**

  a How would a relatively high home inflation rate affect the home country's current account, other things being equal?

  b Is a negative current account harmful to a country? Discuss.

3 **Government restrictions.** How can government restrictions affect international payments among countries?

4 **IMF.**

  a What are some of the major objectives of the IMF?

  b How is the IMF involved in international trade?

5 **Exchange rate effect on trade balance.** Would the UK balance of trade deficit be larger or smaller if the pound depreciates against all currencies, versus

depreciating against some currencies but appreciating against others? Explain.

6 **Demand for exports.** A relatively small UK balance of trade deficit is commonly attributed to a strong demand for UK exports. What do you think is the underlying reason for the strong demand for UK exports?

7 **Demand for imports.** Explain why a devaluation may result in a higher total import value. Why do we expect it to be lower?

8 **Effects of the euro.** Explain how the euro may affect UK international trade.

ADVANCED QUESTIONS

11 **Free trade.** There has been considerable momentum to reduce or remove trade barriers in an effort to achieve 'free trade'. Yet, one disgruntled executive of an exporting firm stated, 'Free trade is not conceivable; we are always at the mercy of the exchange rate. Any country can use this mechanism to impose trade barriers.' What does this statement mean?

12 **International investments.** In recent years many UK-based MNCs have increased their investments in foreign securities, which are not as susceptible to the negative shocks of the UK market. Also, when MNCs believe that UK securities are overvalued, they can pursue non-UK securities that are driven by a different market. Moreover, in periods of low UK interest rates, UK corporations tend to seek investments in foreign securities. In general, the flow of funds into foreign countries tends to decline when UK investors anticipate a strong pound.

PROJECT WORKSHOP

14 **UK balance of trade.** Consult *The Pink Book* 2009 at: http://www.statistics.gov.uk/StatBase/Product. asp?vlnk=1140.

   a Use this website to assess recent trends in exporting and importing by UK firms. How has the balance of trade changed over the past 10 years?

   b Offer possible reasons for this change in the balance of trade.

9 **Currency effects.** When South Korea's export growth stalled, some South Korean firms suggested that South Korea's primary export problem was the weakness in the Japanese yen. How would you interpret this statement?

10 **Effects of tariffs.** Assume a simple world in which the UK exports soft drinks and beer to France and imports wine from France. If the UK imposes large tariffs on the French wine, explain the likely impact on the values of the UK beverage firms, UK wine producers, the French beverage firms and the French wine producers.

   a Explain how expectations of a strong pound can affect the tendency of UK investors to invest abroad.

   b Explain how low UK interest rates can affect the tendency of UK-based MNCs to invest abroad.

   c In general terms, what is the attraction of foreign investments to UK investors?

13 **Exchange rate effects on trade.**

   a Explain why a stronger dollar could enlarge the UK balance of trade deficit. Explain why a weaker dollar could affect the UK balance of trade deficit.

   b It is sometimes suggested that a floating exchange rate will adjust to reduce or eliminate any current account deficit. Explain why this adjustment would occur.

   c Why does the exchange rate not always adjust to a current account deficit?

15 Using the financial data packages at your institution or by consulting the *International Monetary Fund Balance of Payments Statistics Yearbook* and web references in the chapter, explore further the international trade and investment themes suggested in the notes to the bar charts.

16 Using the *UNCTAD World Investment Report 2009* or the Forbes lists at: http://www.forbes.com/lists/, consult the annual reports of ten large multinational

companies and examine their foreign investment policies. Forbes provides direct links, otherwise search using the companies' names and the word

'home page' then look for the download of the annual report.

DISCUSSION IN THE BOARDROOM

This exercise can be found on our dedicated Course-Mate platform for students.

RUNNING YOUR OWN MNC

This exercise can be found on our dedicated Course-Mate platform for students.

Essays/discussion and articles can be found at the end of Part I.

BLADES PLC CASE STUDY

Exposure to international flow of funds

Ben Holt, the finance director of Blades plc, has decided to counteract the decreasing demand for 'Speedos' roller blades by exporting this product to Thailand. Furthermore, due to the low cost of rubber and plastic in South-East Asia, Holt has decided to import some of the components needed to manufacture 'Speedos' from Thailand. Holt feels that importing rubber and plastic components from Thailand will provide Blades with a cost advantage (the components imported from Thailand are about 20 per cent cheaper than similar components in the UK). Currently, approximately $15 million, or 10 per cent, of Blades' sales are contributed by its sales in Thailand. Only about 4 per cent of Blades' cost of goods sold is attributable to rubber and plastic imported from Thailand.

Blades faces little competition in Thailand from other UK roller blades manufacturers. Those competitors that export roller blades to Thailand invoice their exports in British pounds. Currently, Blades follows a policy of invoicing in Thai baht (Thailand's currency). Ben Holt felt that this strategy would give Blades a competitive advantage, since Thai importers can plan more easily when they do not have to worry about paying differing amounts due to currency fluctuations. Furthermore, Blades' primary customer in Thailand (a retail store) has committed itself to purchasing a certain amount of 'Speedos' annually if Blades will invoice in baht for a period of 3 years. Blades' purchases of components from Thai exporters are currently invoiced in Thai baht.

Ben Holt is rather content with current arrangements and believes the lack of competitors in Thailand, the quality of Blades' products, and its approach to pricing will ensure Blades' position in the Thai roller blade market in the future. Holt also feels that Thai importers will prefer Blades over its competitors because Blades invoices in Thai baht.

As Blades' financial analyst, you have doubts as to Blades' 'guaranteed' future success. Although you believe Blades' strategy for its Thai sales and imports is sound, you are concerned about current expectations for the Thai economy. Current forecasts indicate a high level of anticipated inflation, a decreasing level of national income and a continued depreciation of the Thai baht. In your opinion, all of these future developments could affect Blades financially given the company's current arrangements with its suppliers and with the Thai importers. Both Thai consumers and firms might adjust their spending habits should certain developments occur.

In the past, you have had difficulty convincing Ben Holt that problems could arise in Thailand. Consequently, you have developed a list of questions for yourself, which you plan to present to the company's CFO after you have answered them. Your questions are listed here:

1 How could a higher level of inflation in Thailand affect Blades (assume UK inflation remains constant)?

2 How could competition from firms in Thailand and from UK and European firms conducting business in Thailand affect Blades?

3 How could a decreasing level of national income in Thailand affect Blades?

4 How could a continued depreciation of the Thai baht affect Blades? How would it affect Blades relative to UK exporters invoicing their roller blades in British pounds?

5 If Blades increases its business in Thailand and experiences serious financial problems, are there any international agencies that the company could approach for loans or other financial assistance?

SMALL BUSINESS DILEMMA

Developing a multinational sporting goods Industry

Recall from Chapter 1 that Jim Logan planned to pursue his dream of establishing his own business in Ireland (called the Sports Exports Company) of exporting basketballs to one or more foreign markets. Jim has decided to initially pursue the market in the UK because British citizens appear to have some interest in basketball as a possible hobby, and no other firm has capitalized on this idea in the UK. (The sporting goods shops in the UK do not sell basketballs but might be willing to sell them.) Jim has contacted one sporting goods distributor that has agreed to purchase basketballs on a monthly basis and distribute (sell) them to sporting goods stores throughout the UK. The distributor's demand for bas-

ketballs is ultimately influenced by the demand for basketballs by British citizens who shop in British sporting goods stores. The Sports Exports Company will receive British pounds when it sells the basketballs to the distributor and will then convert the pounds into euros. Jim recognizes that products (such as the basketballs his firm will produce) exported from Ireland to foreign countries can be affected by various factors.

Identify the factors that affect the current account balance between Ireland and the UK. Explain how each factor may possibly affect the British demand for the basketballs that are produced by the Sports Exports Company.

CHAPTER 3
INTERNATIONAL
FINANCIAL MARKETS

LEARNING OBJECTIVES

The specific objectives of this chapter are to describe the background and corporate use of the following international financial markets:

● Foreign exchange market

● International money market

● International credit market

● International bond market

● International stock markets.

Due to the growth in international business and investment over the past 30 years, there has been a large increase in the size and variety of international financial markets. The main functions of these markets are borrowing, lending and risk reduction. A complicating factor compared to their domestic equivalent is the exchange rate. Financial managers of MNCs need to understand these markets in order to operate effectively.

For technical support see Appendix B page 645.

MOTIVES FOR USING INTERNATIONAL FINANCIAL MARKETS

There are a number of barriers that prevent markets in different countries for real or financial assets from becoming completely integrated; these barriers include tax differentials, tariffs, quotas, labour immobility, cultural differences, financial reporting differences and significant costs of communicating information across countries. Nevertheless, the barriers can also create unique opportunities for specific geographic markets that will attract foreign creditors and investors. For example, barriers such as tariffs, quotas and labour immobility can cause a given country's economic conditions to be distinctly different from others. Investors and creditors may want to do business in that country to capitalize on favourable conditions unique to that country. At the same time these imperfections have also been a motive for developing larger international markets.

Motives for investing in foreign markets

Investors invest in foreign markets from one or more of the following motives:

- *Economic conditions.* Investors may expect firms in a particular foreign country to achieve a more favourable performance than those in the investor's home country. For example, the relaxing of restrictions in Eastern European countries created favourable economic conditions there. Such conditions attracted foreign investors and creditors.

- *Exchange rate expectations.* Some investors purchase financial securities denominated in a currency that is expected to appreciate against their own. The performance of such an investment is highly dependent on the currency movement over the investment horizon.

- *International diversification.* Investors may achieve benefits from internationally diversifying their asset portfolio. When an investor's entire portfolio does not depend solely on a single country's economy, cross-border differences in economic conditions can allow for risk-reduction benefits. A share portfolio representing firms across European countries is less risky than a share portfolio representing firms in any single European country. Furthermore, access to foreign markets allows investors to spread their funds across a more diverse group of industries than may be available domestically. This is especially true for investors residing in countries where firms are concentrated in a relatively small number of industries.

Motives for providing credit in foreign markets

Creditors (including individual investors who purchase debt securities) have one or more of the following motives for providing credit in foreign markets:

- *High foreign interest rates.* Some countries experience a shortage of loanable funds, which can cause market interest rates to be relatively high, even after considering default risk. Foreign creditors may attempt to capitalize on the higher rates, thereby providing capital to overseas markets. Often, however, relatively high interest rates are perceived to reflect relatively high inflationary expectations in that country. For example, in the year 2000, Turkey had an inflation rate of 55 per cent and an interest rate of 62 per cent. To the extent that inflation can cause depreciation of the local currency against others, high interest rates in the country may be somewhat offset by a weakening of the local currency, the Turkish lira devalued by 24 per cent in the year 2000 and 120 per cent the following year! The relation between a country's expected inflation and its local currency movements is not precise, however, several other factors can influence currency movements as well. Thus, some creditors may believe that the interest rate advantage in a particular country will not be offset by a local currency depreciation over the period of concern.

- *Exchange rate expectations.* Creditors may consider supplying capital to countries whose currencies are expected to appreciate against their own. Whether the form of the transaction is a bond or a loan, the creditor benefits when the currency of denomination appreciates against the creditor's home currency.

- *International diversification.* Creditors can benefit from international diversification, which may have the effect of reducing the probability of simultaneous bankruptcy across its borrowers. The effectiveness of such a strategy depends on the correlation between the economic conditions of countries. If the countries of concern tend to experience somewhat similar business cycles, diversification across countries will be less effective.

- *Crises.* Money may be invested in currencies that are expected to maintain their value in times of crises. This is the 'safe haven' argument; the dollar, the swiss franc and to a lesser extent the euro are seen by investors as currencies that are unlikely to suffer large devaluations.

Motives for borrowing in foreign markets

Borrowers may have one or more of the following motives for borrowing in foreign markets:

- *Exchange rate expectations.* When a company borrows from abroad, there are two 'costs' that must be taken into account. The first is the interest rate, as with any borrowing. The second is unique to international borrowing and is the effect of changes in the exchange rate. When money is borrowed in a foreign currency, it must be converted into the home currency to be usable. At the end of the borrowing period, the repayment must be in the foreign currency for the exact amount of the foreign currency loan. So the loan must be converted back into the foreign currency plus or minus amounts due to exchange rate changes. If the value of the foreign currency has, say, increased in the intervening period, the cost of borrowing will have effectively increased. If, for example, a UK company borrows from abroad and converts the loan into £100 000 at the start of the period, but at the end of the borrowing period it costs £120 000 to repay the amount lent in the foreign currency because the foreign currency has gone up in value, then the cost of borrowing from abroad is the £20 000 increase in repayment due to exchange rate movement, plus any interest payments made. On the other hand, if a foreign currency declines in value over the borrowing period, the cost of repayment could be less than the original converted cost of the loan. In the example above, if the foreign currency has fallen in value by say 5 per cent, then the cost of repayment will be £95 000 (i.e. $(1 - 0.05) \times 100\,000$), a saving of £100 000 − £95 000 = £5000. Such savings will reduce and even offset interest payments, making foreign borrowing potentially very cheap. So, because exchange rate movements can make borrowing cheaper or more expensive all that can be said overall is that it is more risky.

   When a foreign subsidiary of an MNC remits funds to its parent, the funds must be converted to the home currency and are subject to exchange rate risk. The MNC will be adversely affected if the foreign currency depreciates at that time. If the MNC expects that the foreign currency will depreciate against the dollar, it can reduce the exchange rate risk by having the subsidiary borrow funds locally to support its business. The subsidiary will remit fewer funds to the parent if it has to pay interest on local debt before remitting the funds. Thus, the amount of funds converted to home currency will be smaller, resulting in less exposure to exchange rate risk.

- *Low interest rates.* Some countries have a large supply of funds available to lend compared to the demand by borrowers for these funds. Interest rates, the price of borrowing, would in such circumstances, be low. Borrowers may attempt to borrow funds from creditors in these countries because the interest rate charged is lower. A country with relatively low interest rates is often expected to have a relatively low rate of inflation, which can place upward pressure on the foreign currency's value and offset any advantage of lower interest rates. The relation between expected inflation differentials and currency movements is not precise, however, so some borrowers will choose to borrow from a market where nominal interest rates (that is to say the interest rates in the newspapers) are low, since they do not expect an adverse currency movement to fully offset this advantage.

FOREIGN EXCHANGE MARKET

When MNCs or other participants invest or borrow in foreign markets, they commonly rely on the **foreign exchange market** to obtain the currencies that they need. By allowing currencies to be exchanged, the foreign exchange market facilitates international trade and financial transactions. MNCs rely on the foreign exchange market to exchange their home currency for a foreign currency that is needed to purchase imports or to use for direct foreign investment. Alternatively, they may need the foreign exchange market to convert foreign revenues to their home currency.

The difference between the market for foreign currency and any other market is that the price of currency has been subject to far more government intervention. The reason is simple. The price of a currency affects the price of all goods denominated in that currency. Thus if the value of the euro goes up in relation to the British pound, all goods in Europe will cost more for the British purchaser as the more expensive euro has to be purchased in order to purchase the goods. The pervasive effect of a change in the value of a currency naturally makes its price of great interest to a government.

Foreign exchange transactions

The foreign exchange market should not be thought of as a specific building or location where traders exchange currencies. Companies normally exchange one currency for another through a commercial bank over a telecommunications network.

Spot market. The most common type of foreign exchange transaction is for immediate exchange at the so-called **spot rate** (immediate is interpreted as being within 2 days). The market where these transactions occur is known as the **spot market**. The global foreign exchange market *daily* turnover in 2010 (the last survey by the Bank for International Settlements) was $4 trillion (million million) an increase of 20 per cent in 3 years. The daily turnover is larger than the annual gross domestic product of Germany, the fourth largest economy in the world. It is a hugely significant figure as it illustrates the powerlessness of governments to influence the market through intervention. The market has outgrown any single government.

Transactions are not just the spot trades but include forwards, futures, swaps and options. These are promises about future currency exchanges known as **derivatives** (see Chapter 5). The spot element made up 37 per cent of this market and had grown by 47 per cent over the 3 years from the previous survey. Some 85 per cent of transactions involve the dollar, 39 per cent the euro, 19 per cent the Japanese yen and 13 per cent the UK pound (the total is 200 per cent as there are two currencies to a transaction). Although there has been a very small decline in the use of the dollar, the currency remains by far the most influential in the world.

USING THE WEB

Historical exchange rates

Historical exchange rate movements are provided at: http://www.oanda.com. Data are available on a daily basis for most currencies.

Some commodities such as oil are traditionally traded in US dollars. The US dollar may also be an intermediary currency, for example British pounds could be converted to Malaysian ringgit by first converting to US dollars and then to Malaysian ringgit – simply because it is cheaper. Although banks in London, New York and Tokyo, the three largest foreign exchange trading centres, conduct much of the foreign exchange trading, many foreign exchange transactions occur outside these trading centres. Banks in virtually every major city facilitate foreign exchange transactions between MNCs. Trading also takes place outside the market, known as the over-the-counter (OTC) stock market. Here the trading takes place without a middle man, the process is also known as **disintermediation**. Buyers and sellers of currencies trade directly with each other, a process made much easier with the development of the Internet. The rate of growth in this market in the 2004–07 period was 83 per cent in notional amounts, whereas in the 2007–10 period it was more moderate at 9 per cent. The earlier growth included a ten-fold increase in credit derivatives, a market that subsequently failed in the global financial crisis. It is this kind of statistic that leads the IMF to call for better market monitoring and regulation. Any market growing at this rate will experience difficulties.

EXAMPLE

Max NV, a Dutch firm, purchases supplies priced at $100 000 from Amerigo, a US supplier, on the first day of every month. Max instructs its bank to transfer funds from its account to the supplier's account also on the first day of each month. It only has euros in its account, whereas Amerigo's invoices are in dollars. When payment was made 1 month ago, the dollar was worth 1.08 euros, so Max NV needed 108 000 euros to pay for the supplies ($100 000 × 1.08 = 108 000 euros). The bank reduced Max's account balance by 108 000 euros, which was exchanged at the bank for $100 000. The bank then sent the $100 000 electronically to Amerigo by increasing Amerigo's account balance by $100 000. Today, a new payment needs to be made. The dollar is currently valued at 1.12 euros, so the bank will reduce Max's account balance by 112 000 euros ($100 000 × 1.12 euros = 112 000 euros) and exchange it for $100 000, which will be sent electronically to Amerigo.

The bank not only executes the transactions but also serves as the foreign exchange dealer. Each month the bank receives euros from Max NVQ in exchange for the dollars it provides. In addition, the bank facilitates other transactions for MNCs in which it receives euros in exchange for dollars. The bank maintains a stock of euros, dollars and other currencies to facilitate these foreign exchange transactions. If the transactions cause it to buy as many euros as it sells to MNCs, its stock of euros will not change. If the bank sells more euros than it buys, however, its stock of euros will be reduced.

Other intermediaries also serve the foreign exchange market. Some other financial institutions such as securities firms can provide the same services described in the previous example. In addition, most major airports around the world have foreign exchange centres, where individuals can exchange currencies. In many cities, there are retail foreign exchange offices where tourists and other individuals can exchange currencies.

Use of the dollar in the spot market. Many foreign transactions do not require an exchange of currencies but will accept foreign currency. For example, the US dollar is commonly accepted as a medium of exchange by merchants in many countries, especially in countries such as Bolivia, Brazil, China, Cuba, Indonesia, Russia and Vietnam where the home currency is either weak or subject to foreign exchange restrictions. Many merchants accept US dollars because they are accepted internationally as direct payment and indeed in Ecuador, El Salvador, Liberia and Panama the dollar is the official currency.

Spot market structure. Hundreds of banks facilitate foreign exchange transactions, but the top 20 handle about 50 per cent of the transactions. Deutsche Bank (Germany), Citibank (a subsidiary of Citigroup, US) and JP Morgan Chase are the largest traders of foreign exchange. Some banks and other financial institutions have formed alliances (one example is FX Alliance LLC) to offer currency transactions over the Internet.

At any given point in time, the exchange rate between two currencies should be similar across the various banks that provide foreign exchange services. If there is a large discrepancy, customers or other banks will purchase large amounts of a currency from whatever bank quotes a relatively low price and immediately sell it to whatever bank quotes a relatively high price. Such actions cause adjustments in the exchange rate quotations that eliminate any discrepancy.

If a bank begins to experience a shortage in a particular foreign currency, it can purchase that currency from other banks. This trading between banks occurs in what is often referred to as the **interbank market**. Within this market, banks can obtain quotes, or they can contact brokers who sometimes act as intermediaries, matching one bank desiring to sell a given currency with another bank desiring to buy that currency. About ten foreign exchange brokerage firms handle much of the interbank transaction volume.

Although foreign exchange trading is conducted only during normal business hours in a given location, these hours vary among locations due to different time zones. Thus, at any given time on a weekday, somewhere around the world a bank is open and ready to accommodate foreign exchange requests.

When the foreign exchange market opens in the USA each morning, the opening exchange rate quotations are based on the prevailing rates quoted by banks in London and other locations where the foreign exchange markets have opened earlier. Suppose the quoted spot rate of the British pound was $1.80 at the previous close of the US foreign exchange market, but by the time the market opens the following day, the opening spot rate is $1.76. News occurring in the morning before the US market opened could have changed the supply and demand conditions for British pounds in the London foreign exchange market, reducing the quoted price for the pound.

With the newest electronic devices, foreign currency trades are negotiated on computer terminals, and a push of a button confirms the trade. Traders now use electronic trading boards that allow them to instantly register transactions and check their bank's positions in various currencies. Also, several US banks have established night trading desks. The largest banks initiated night trading to capitalize on foreign exchange movements at night and to accommodate corporate requests for currency trades. Even some medium-sized banks now offer night trading to accommodate corporate clients.

Spot market liquidity. The spot market for each currency can be described by its liquidity, which reflects the level of trading activity. The more willing buyers and sellers there are, the more liquid a market is. The spot markets for heavily traded currencies such as the euro, the British pound and the Japanese yen are very liquid. Conversely, the spot markets for currencies of less developed countries are less liquid. A currency's liquidity affects the ease with which an MNC can obtain or sell that currency. If a currency is illiquid, the number of willing buyers and sellers is limited, and an MNC may be unable to quickly purchase or sell that currency at a reasonable exchange rate.

Forward transactions. In addition to the spot market, a forward market for currencies enables an MNC to lock in the exchange rate (called a **forward rate**) at which it will buy or sell a currency. A **forward contract** specifies the amount of a particular currency that will be purchased or sold by the MNC at a specified future point in time and at a specified exchange rate. Commercial banks accommodate the MNCs that desire forward contracts. MNCs commonly use the forward market to hedge future payments that they expect to make or receive in a foreign currency. In this way, they do not have to worry about fluctuations in the spot rate until the time of their future payments. The liquidity of the forward market varies among currencies. The forward market for euros is very liquid because many MNCs take forward positions to hedge their future payments in euros. In contrast, the forward markets for Latin American and Eastern European currencies are less liquid because there is less international trade with those countries and therefore MNCs take fewer forward positions. For some currencies, there is no forward market.

Attributes of banks that provide foreign exchange. The following characteristics of banks are important to customers in need of foreign exchange:

1   *Competitiveness of quote.* For example, a saving of one pence per unit on an order of one million units of currency is worth £10 000.

2   *Special relationship with the bank.* The bank may offer cash management services or be willing to make a special effort to obtain even hard-to-find foreign currencies for the corporation.

3   *Speed of execution.* Banks may vary in the efficiency with which they handle an order. A corporation needing the currency will prefer a bank that conducts the transaction promptly and handles any paperwork properly.

4   *Advice about current market conditions.* Some banks may provide assessments of foreign economies and relevant activities in the international financial environment that relate to corporate customers.

5   *Forecasting advice.* Some banks may provide forecasts of the future state of foreign economies, the future value of exchange rates and the like.

This list suggests that a corporation needing a foreign currency should not automatically choose a bank that will sell that currency at the lowest price. Most corporations that often need foreign currencies develop a close relationship with at least one major bank in case they ever need favours from a bank.

Interpreting foreign exchange quotations

Exchange rate quotations for widely traded currencies are published in the *Financial Times* and in business sections of many newspapers on a daily basis. With some exceptions, most notably the EuroZone each country has its own currency.

A quote is written as so many units of one currency (the term or quote currency) for one unit of another (the base currency), so 60 pence or £0.60 to the dollar is written as £0.60:$1. To convert, say, $100 into British pounds at this rate is simply $100 × 0.60 = £60. To convert, say, £150 into dollars at this rate is £150 / 0.60 = $250. Note that conversion is achieved either by multiplying or dividing; it is important not to apply the wrong operation!

MANAGING FOR VALUE

Intel's currency trading

When Intel needs to exchange foreign currency, it no longer calls a bank to request an exchange of currencies. Instead, it logs on to an online currency trader that serves as an intermediary between Intel and member banks. One popular online currency trader is Currenex, which conducts more than $300 million in foreign exchange transactions per day. If Intel needs to purchase a foreign currency, it logs on and specifies its order. Currenex relays the order to various banks that are members of its system and are allowed to bid for the orders. When Currenex relays the order, member banks have 25 seconds to specify a quote online for the currency that the customer (Intel) desires. Then, Currenex displays the quotes on a screen, ranked from highest to lowest. Intel has 5 seconds to select one of the quotes provided, and the deal is completed. This process is much more transparent than traditional foreign exchange market transactions because Intel can review quotes of many competitors at one time.

Choosing the right operation, multiplying or dividing, always poses a small problem for most students. There are various ways of avoiding error, a simple mnemonic is offered here. If a currency conversion is seen as a source currency ('from') to a destination currency ('to'), then in the exchange rate quote, if the source currency is on the left (term) one divides; if the source currency is on the right (base) one multiplies. A number of examples are given in Exhibit 3.1.

EXHIBIT 3.1 Currency conversion

Conversion from (source)	To (*destination*)	Exchange rate	Operation	Converted value
£100	dollars	$1.85:£1	Multiply	£100 × 1.85 = $185
£60	euros	1.25 euro:£1	Multiply	£60 × 1.25 = 75 euros
250 euros	British pounds	1.25 euro:£1	Divide	250 euros /1.25 = £200
$1000	euros	$1.11:1 euro	Divide	$1000/1.11 = 901 euros

Direct and indirect quotations

- **Direct quote:** the number of units of home currency for one of the foreign currency.

- **Indirect quote:** the number of units of foreign currency for one unit of the home currency.

There is a reciprocal relationship between the two:

Indirect quotation = 1/Direct quotation

£ and euro indirect quotes			£ and euro direct quotes	
So	8 rand:£1	is the same as	£0.125:1 rand	as 1/8 = 0.125
	5 peso:£1	is the same as	£0.20:1 peso	as 1/5 = 0.20
	135 yen:1 euro	is the same as	0.0074 euro:1 yen	as 1/135 = 0.0074

A direct quote can be described as 'the value of foreign currency', and an indirect quote can be described as 'how much home currency will buy abroad'. The indirect quote tends to be used in the UK and parts of the former British Empire. It is a relic of the days when the British pound was non-decimal and it was easier to apply fractions to decimal currency than the then complex UK currency. Elsewhere it is normal to find the direct quote being used.

Much analysis in international finance seeks to explain the value of foreign currency and account for the variation in its value. The direct quote is the natural rate to use. If the value of foreign currency goes up, the direct rate goes up. So, taking the British pound as the home currency and an exchange rate of £0.56:$1, if the value of the dollar increases by 10 per cent then the new rate will be £0.56 × (1 + 0.10) = £0.616, that is £0.616:$1. Similarly, if the value of the dollar falls, the direct rate will fall. If the rates used were indirect, the relationship would be the opposite, an increase in the rate would mean a fall in the value of foreign currency – not surprisingly this is very confusing and should be avoided. In equations therefore, the more straightforward direct rate is used.

As a consequence of the direct and indirect methods of quoting, to write 'the exchange rate increased' is meaningless as it depends on the method of quoting. Far better to write: 'the *value* of the currency increased (or decreased)' this is clear.

EXAMPLE

Mr Y a Finance Director has been given the following rates from his bank: 4 zloty:1 euro; £0.68:1 euro and 6 zloty:£1. He wonders if he changed £1000 into Polish zloty, converted his Polish zloty into euros and then converted the euros back into British pounds, would he have the £1000 he started with? He works out that £1000 would buy him 6000 zloty, then 6000 zloty would buy 1500 euros (i.e. 6000 zloty / 4 = 1500) and finally 1500 euros would buy £1020 (i.e. 1500 euros × 0.68) a profit of £20 or 2 per cent ([1020 − 1000] / 1000). 'Great' he thinks, I can earn certain money just by picking up the telephone. When he tells the Bank Manager, she laughs: 'You've forgotten the transaction costs, we would charge nearly 2 per cent for those transactions and then your zloty euro rate is for converting euros into zloty not zloty into euros. All told, you would make a loss. Don't worry we would not allow you to make a profit for nothing – you've got to take a risk to do that.'

Quotations of spot and forward rates. The spot rate normally means delivery within 2 days and are quoted for all the major currencies in the financial press. Some quotations of exchange rates include forward rates for the most widely traded currencies. Other forward rates are not quoted in business newspapers but are quoted by the banks that offer forward contracts in various currencies. Quoted rates are normally for 1 month, 3 months and 1 year, but may be tailored by a bank to a MNC's individual needs. The extract opposite is the online quote given by the *Financial Times* at: http://news.ft.com/markets/spotpound.

The 'per cent PA' column is the calculation of the premium or **discount** in the rate compared to the spot expressed as an annual percentage rate. So for the Czech koruna, the 1 month rate is 28.3417 and the spot is 28.3290. If you invest £1 now in koruna you will receive 28.3290 koruna now and when you convert back 1 month later, you will receive 28.3290 / 28.3417 = £00.999551897. The annual interest rate equivalent is £0.999551897^{12} − 1 = −0.0053600536 or −0.5 per cent. Note that from the perspective of the pound, these are indirect quotes. The reason why the return is negative is because interest rates will be slightly higher in the Czech Republic, covered interest rate arbitrage (see later) will ensure that there can be no profit from using the forward rate.

Bid/ask spread of banks. Commercial banks charge fees for conducting foreign exchange transactions. At any given point in time, a bank's <u>bid</u> (<u>b</u>uy) direct quote for a foreign currency will be less than its a<u>s</u>k (<u>s</u>ell) direct quote. As with the retail of any other product the retailer (bank) will buy the product (currency) at the lower price and sell at the higher price. The service offered by the bank is availability, convenience and a competitive price. The bid/ask spread represents the differential between the bid and ask quotes, and is intended to cover the costs involved in accommodating requests to exchange currencies. The bid/ask spread is normally expressed as a percentage of the ask quote.

POUND SPOT FORWARD AGAINST THE POUND

Mar 3		Closing mid-point	Change on day	Bid/offer spread	Day's mid High	Day's mid Low	One month Rate	One month %PA	Three month Rate	Three month %PA	One year Rate	One year %PA	Bank of Eng. Index
Europe													
Czech Rep.	(Koruna)	28.3290	-0.0572	031 - 549	28.4960	28.2060	28.3417	-0.5	28.3609	-0.5	28.4552	-0.4	-
Denmark	(Danish Krone)	8.1898	-0.0025	871 - 925	8.2222	8.1758	8.1913	-0.2	8.1944	-0.2	8.2064	-0.2	-
Hungary	(Forint)	292.589	-0.5915	327 - 851	294.600	292.240	293.918	-5.4	296.040	-4.7	305.179	-4.1	-
Norway	(Nor. Krone)	8.8712	-0.0115	662 - 761	8.9326	8.8613	8.8822	-1.5	8.9058	-1.6	9.0174	-1.6	105.1
Poland	(Zloty)	4.2875	-0.0212	847 - 902	4.3372	4.2841	4.2979	-2.9	4.3165	-2.7	4.3986	-2.5	-
Russia	(Rouble)	44.8833	0.2740	706 - 960	44.9941	44.6212	45.0251	-3.8	45.3054	-3.7	46.8854	-4.3	-
Sweden	(Krona)	10.7719	0.0242	669 - 769	10.8390	10.7279	10.7688	0.3	10.7631	0.3	10.7572	0.1	78.7
Switzerland	(Fr)	1.6100	-0.0012	092 - 107	1.6165	1.6074	1.6092	0.5	1.6079	0.5	1.6002	0.6	122.1
Turkey	(New Lira)	2.3105	0.0173	096 - 113	2.3199	2.2983	2.3226	-6.3	2.3463	-6.1	2.4722	-6.5	-
UK	(£)	1.0000			-	-	-		-		-		76.9
Euro	(Euro)	1.1005	-0.0003	001 - 008	1.1049	1.0986	1.1002	0.2	1.0999	0.2	1.0990	0.1	100.3
SDR	-	0.9801	0.0041		-		-		-		-		-
Americas													
Argentina	(Peso)	5.8085	0.0523	068 - 102	5.8234	5.7633	5.8320	-4.8	5.9278	-8.0	6.6391	-12.5	-
Brazil	(Real)	2.6794	0.0195	782 - 806	2.7011	2.6784	2.6939	-6.5	2.7276	-7.1	2.9008	-7.6	-
Canada	(Canadian $)	1.5500	0.0086	494 - 506	1.5597	1.5485	1.5497	0.2	1.5492	0.2	1.5511	-0.1	110.1
Mexico	(Mexican Peso)	19.1212	0.1414	162 - 261	19.1775	19.0398	19.1783	-3.6	19.3073	-3.9	19.9763	-4.3	-
Peru	(New Sol)	4.2839	0.0402	824 - 853	-	-	4.2846	-0.2	4.2852	-0.1	4.2832	0.0	-
USA	(US $)	1.5066	0.0139	063 - 068	1.5107	1.4960	1.5062	0.3	1.5056	0.3	1.5026	0.3	83.1
Pacific/Middle East/Africa													
Australia	(A$)	1.6632	0.0106	624 - 639	1.6687	1.6556	1.6683	-3.7	1.6791	-3.8	1.7314	-3.9	98.6
Hong Kong	(HK $)	11.6944	0.1062	921 - 967	11.7265	11.6136	11.6891	0.5	11.6795	0.5	11.6360	0.5	-
India	(Indian Rupee)	69.0377	0.3534	187 - 566	69.2200	68.4880	69.1887	-2.6	69.5266	-2.8	70.7102	-2.4	-
Indonesia	(Rupiah)	13978.5	111.806	641 - 064	14004.2	13905.3	14052.8	-6.3	14210.2	-6.5	15008.3	-6.9	-
Iran	(Rial)	14907.3	137.541	546 - 600	14960.0	14855.3	-		-		-		-
Israel	(Shekel)	5.6752	0.0218	730 - 773	5.6949	5.6534	5.6773	-0.4	5.6813	-0.4	5.6969	-0.4	-
Japan	(Yen)	133.375	0.4843	323 - 427	133.900	132.780	133.327	0.4	133.230	0.4	132.506	0.7	159.8
Kuwait	(Kuwaiti Dinar)	0.4341	0.0014	338 - 343	0.4364	0.4318	0.4342	-0.5	0.4343	-0.2	0.4349	-0.2	-
Malaysia	(Ringgit)	5.0809	0.0268	762 - 855	5.0870	5.0506	5.0876	-1.6	5.1017	-1.6	5.1538	-1.4	-
New Zealand	(NZ $)	2.1751	0.0292	739 - 762	2.1835	2.1503	2.1792	-2.3	2.1876	-2.3	2.2347	-2.7	98.6
Philippines	(Peso)	69.3239	0.5277	898 - 580	69.4579	68.9437	69.5257	-3.5	69.9181	-3.4	71.3939	-2.9	-
Saudi Arabic	(Riyal)	5.6498	0.0522	486 - 510	5.6650	5.6104	5.6474	0.5	5.6432	0.5	5.6213	0.5	-
Singapore	($)	2.1091	0.0136	082 - 100	2.1141	2.0993	2.1090	0.1	2.1088	0.1	2.1061	0.1	-
South Africa	(Rand)	11.2973	-0.0376	878 - 067	11.4277	11.2777	11.3637	-7.0	11.4917	-6.8	12.0597	-6.3	-
Korea South	(Won)	1727.11	6.8670	652 - 770	1728.23	1718.46	1728.28	-0.8	1730.26	-0.7	1740.12	-0.7	-
Taiwan	($)	48.1810	0.3692	670 - 950	48.3041	47.9309	48.0565	3.1	47.7428	3.7	46.6033	3.4	-
Thailand	(Baht)	49.3019	0.4549	409 - 628	49.3550	48.9580	49.3176	-0.4	49.3315	-0.2	49.4266	-0.3	-
U A E	(Dirham)	5.5333	0.0507	322 - 343	5.5483	5.4956	5.5330	0.1	5.5334	0.0	5.5309	0.0	-

Euro Locking Rates: Austrian Schilling 13.7603, Belgium/Luxembourg Franc 40.3399, Cyprus 0.585274, Finnish Markka 5.94572, French Franc 6.55957, German Mark 1.95583, Greek Drachma 340.75, Irish Punt 0.787564, Italian Lira 1936.27, Malta 0.4293, Netherlands Guilder 2.20371, Portuguese Escudo 200.482, Slovakian Koruna 30.1260, Slovenia Tolar 239.64, Spanish Peseta 166.386. Bid/offer spreads in the Pound Spot table show only the last three decimal places Bid, offer, Mid spot rates and forward rates are derived from the WM/REUTERS CLOSING SPOT and FORWARD RATE services. Some values are rounded by the F.T.

EXAMPLE

To understand how a bid/ask spread could affect you, assume you live in France and have 1000 euros and plan to travel from France to the USA. Assume further that the bank's bid (buy) rate for the US dollar is 1.28 euros:$1 and its ask (sell) rate is 1.31 euros:$1. Before leaving on your trip, you go to this bank to exchange euros for dollars. Your 1000 euros will be converted to $763.36 as follows:

euros → US dollars: 1000 euros /1.31 euros: $1
= $763.36

The bank's ask rate is relevant here because that is the rate at which it is selling dollars. Note that the conversion is rounded to the smallest unit of currency $0.01 or 1 cent. Now suppose that because of an emergency you cannot take the trip, and you reconvert the $763.36 back to euros, just after purchasing the US dollars. If the exchange rate has not changed, you will be quoted the bank's bid rate for buying dollars and receive:

US dollars → euros: $763.36 × 1.28 euros: $1
= 977.10 euros

Due to the bid/ask spread, you have 22.90 euros less (1000 euros − 977.10 euros = 22.90 euros) or 2.29 per cent less. Obviously, the euro amount of the loss would be larger if you originally converted more than 1000 euros into dollars. The loss can be worked out directly as a percentage by measuring the percentage difference between the two rates thus:

(1.31 − 1.28) / 1.31 = 2.29%

Comparison of bid/ask spread among currencies. The differential between a bid quote and an ask quote will look much smaller for currencies that have a smaller value. As stated above, this differential can be standardized by measuring it as a percentage difference between the two rates divided by the ask rate (the first part of the transaction).

EXAMPLE

Somerset Bank quotes a bid price for yen of £0.005 and an ask price of £0.0052. In this case, the nominal bid/ask spread is £0.005 − £0.0052, or just two-hundredths of a penny. Yet, the bid/ask spread in percentage terms is actually slightly higher for the yen in this example than for the dollar in the previous example. To prove this, consider a traveller who sells £1000 for yen at the bank's ask price of £0.0052. The traveller receives about ¥192 308 (computed as £1000/ £0.0052). If the traveller cancels the trip and converts the yen back to pounds, then, assuming no changes in the bid/ask quotations, the bank will buy these yen back at the bank's bid price of £0.005 for a total of about £961.54 (computed by ¥192 308 × £0.005), this is £38.46 (or 3.846 per cent) less than what the traveller started with – measured directly as (0.0052 − 0.005) / 0.0052 = 0.03846 or 3.846 per cent. This spread exceeds that of the British pound (2.29 per cent in the previous example) although the figures are much smaller. The size of a currency unit is no more significant than whether your height is measured in metres or millimetres, it is the percentage movement in a currency that matters.

Both the previous examples calculated the bid/ask spread as a percentage. The following is the general formula for calculating the spread:

$$\text{Bid/Ask spread} = \frac{\text{Ask rate} - \text{Bid rate}}{\text{Ask rate}}$$

Using this formula, the bid/ask spreads are computed in Exhibit 3.2 for a selection of currency quotes.

EXHIBIT 3.2   Computation of the bid/ask spread

Currency	Bid rate	Ask rate	$\dfrac{\text{Ask rate} - \text{Bid rate}}{\text{Ask rate}} = \text{Spread}$
Dollar	£0.54:$1	£0.56:$1	$\dfrac{0.56 - 0.54}{0.56} = 0.03571 \text{ or } 3.571\%$
Nigerian naira	£0.004:1 naira	£0.0042:1 naira	$\dfrac{0.0042 - 0.004}{0.0042} = 0.04762 \text{ or } 4.762\%$
British pound	1.46 euro:£1	1.48:£1	$\dfrac{1.48 - 1.46}{1.48} = 0.01351 \text{ or } 1.351\%$

Notice that the spread represents the bank's profit margin. Sometimes travel firms who similarly buy and sell currencies will also add a commission or ostentatiously advertise zero commission. In all cases, however, money is made through buying more cheaply than selling. For larger so-called wholesale transactions between banks or for large corporations, the spread will be much smaller. The bid/ask spread for small retail transactions is commonly in the range of 3 per cent to 7 per cent; for wholesale transactions requested by MNCs, the spread is between 0.01 and 0.03 per cent. The spread is normally larger for illiquid currencies that are less frequently traded. Commercial banks are normally exposed to more exchange rate risk when maintaining these currencies.

In the following discussion and in examples throughout much of the text, the bid/ask spread will be ignored. That is, only one price will be shown for a given currency to allow you to concentrate on understanding other relevant concepts. These examples depart slightly from reality because the bid and ask prices are, in a sense, assumed to be equal. Although the ask price will always exceed the bid price by a small amount in reality, the implications from examples should nevertheless hold, even though the bid/ask spreads are not accounted for. In particular examples where the bid/ask spread can contribute significantly to the concept, it will be accounted for.

Various websites, including bloomberg.com, provide bid/ask quotations. To conserve space, some quotations show the entire bid price followed by a slash and then only the last two or three digits of the ask price (known as the 'pips').

EXAMPLE

Assume that the prevailing quote for wholesale transactions by a commercial bank for the euro is $1.0876/78. This means that a US commercial bank is willing to buy euros for $1.0876 per euro. Alternatively, it is willing to sell euros for $1.0878. The bid/ask spread in this example is:

$$\text{Bid/Ask spread} = \frac{\$1.0878 - \$1.0876}{\$1.0878}$$
$$= 0.00018386 \text{ or } 0.0184\%$$
$$\text{to 4 decimal places}$$

Factors that affect the spread. The spread on currency quotations is influenced by the following factors:

$$\text{Spread} = f(\text{Order costs}, \text{Inventory costs}, \text{Competition}, \text{Volume}, \text{Currency risk})$$
$$+ \qquad\qquad + \qquad\qquad - \qquad\qquad - \qquad\qquad +$$

● *Order costs.* Order costs are the costs of processing orders, including clearing costs and the costs of recording transactions.

● *Inventory costs.* Inventory costs are the costs of maintaining an inventory of a particular currency. Holding an inventory involves an opportunity cost because the funds could have been used for some other purpose. If interest rates are relatively high, the opportunity cost of holding an inventory should be relatively high. The higher the inventory costs, the larger the spread that will be established to cover these costs.

● *Competition.* The more intense the competition, the smaller the spread quoted by intermediaries. Competition is more intense for the more widely traded currencies because there is more business in those currencies.

● *Volume.* More liquid currencies are less likely to experience a sudden change in price. Currencies that have a large trading volume are more liquid because there are numerous buyers and sellers at any given time. This means that the market has sufficient depth that a few large transactions are unlikely to cause the currency's price to change abruptly.

● *Currency risk.* Some currencies exhibit more volatility than others because of economic or political conditions that cause the demand for and supply of the currency to change abruptly. For example, currencies in countries that have frequent political crises are subject to abrupt price movements. Intermediaries that are willing to buy or sell these currencies could incur large losses due to an abrupt change in the values of these currencies.

Cross exchange rates. Most tables of exchange rate quotations express currencies relative to the British pound, US dollar or euro or all three. But in some instances, a firm will want or be concerned about the exchange rate between two other currencies. For example, if a UK firm wants to convert earnings in Mexican pesos to Australian dollars (A$) to pay for imports from Australia, an estimate of the likely rate can be calculated as a **cross exchange rate**. The diagram in Exhibit 3.3 illustrates the relationship.

USING THE WEB

Cross exchange rates

Cross exchange rates for a range of currencies are provided at: http://www.bloomberg.com and OANDA.com.

EXHIBIT 3.3 Cross exchange rates

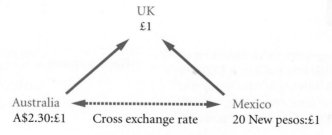

UK
£1

Australia ←----------------------------→ Mexico
A$2.30:£1   Cross exchange rate   20 New pesos:£1

A$2.30 = 20 New pesos (both worth £1)

(dividing both sides by 2.3)

$$A\$1 = \frac{20 \text{ New pesos:}£1}{A\$2.30:£1} = 8.70 \text{ New pesos:A\$1}$$

Note:
● For an implied or cross rate, the right-hand side of the quote (the base) must be the same currency for both rates and the denominator (lower half) of the ratio becomes the base of the new quote.

From Exhibit 3.3 if there are A$2.30:£1 and 20 New pesos:£1 then A$2.30 and 20 New pesos have the same value being both worth £1; so using the equation approach A$2.30 = 20 New pesos. To convert to an exchange rate with A$ as our base divide by 2.3 as in the example, or if New pesos is to be the base then divide both sides by 20. So to work out the cross exchange rate: 1) equate the currencies to one unit of a third currency; 2) use the equation approach to derive an exchange rate.

Currency futures and options markets

A **currency futures contract** specifies a standard volume of a particular currency to be exchanged on a specific **settlement date**. Some MNCs involved in international trade use the currency futures markets to hedge their positions.

Paris SA has ordered supplies from the USA that are denominated in dollars. It expects the dollar to increase in value over time and therefore desires to hedge its payables in dollars. Paris buys futures contracts on dollars to lock in the price that it will pay for dollars at a future point in time. Meanwhile, it will receive Mexican pesos in the future and wants to hedge these receivables. Paris sells futures contracts on pesos to lock in the euros that it will receive when it sells the pesos for euros at a specified point in the future.

Futures contracts are somewhat similar to forward contracts except that they are sold on an exchange whereas forward contracts are offered by commercial banks. Additional details on futures contracts, including other differences from forward contracts, are provided in Chapter 5.

Currency options contracts can be classified as calls or puts. A **currency call option** provides the right to buy a specific currency at a specific price (called the **strike price** or **exercise price**) within a specific period of time. It is used to hedge future payables. A **currency put option** provides the right to sell a specific currency at a specific price within a specific period of time. It is used to hedge future receivables.

Currency call and put options can be purchased on an exchange. They offer more flexibility than forward or futures contracts because they do not require any obligation. That is, the firm can elect not to exercise the option.

Currency options have become a popular means of hedging, particularly in the USA. The Coca-Cola Co. has replaced about 30 per cent to 40 per cent of its forward contracting with currency options. FMC, a US manufacturer of chemicals and machinery, now hedges its foreign sales with currency options instead of forward contracts. The annual reports of all the major companies now disclose their hedging policies. Additional details about currency options, including other differences from futures and forward contracts, are provided in Chapter 5.

INTERNATIONAL MONEY MARKET

Financial markets exist in every country to ensure that funds are transferred efficiently from surplus units (savers) to deficit units (borrowers). These markets are overseen by various regulators, the most immediate being the **clearing house**, that attempt to enhance the markets' creditworthiness (ensuring that purchasers are able to pay) and efficiency. The financial institutions that serve these financial markets exist primarily to provide information and expertise. The increase in international business has resulted in the development of an international money market. Financial institutions in this market serve MNCs by accepting deposits and offering loans in a variety of currencies. In general, the international money market is distinguished from domestic money markets by the types of transactions between the participating financial institutions and the MNCs. The financial transactions are in a wide variety of currencies, and large, often the equivalent of $1 million or more.

Market efficiency

One of the major concepts in finance is that of market efficiency. The term is not used to refer to the operational efficiency, though that is important. Rather, efficiency refers to how well information is used in the marketplace. The concepts apply to any market but are particularly relevant to the financial markets as the information relevant to valuing the asset (the information set) is very volatile and changes from hour to hour in some cases. By contrast, the information set for, say, cars is not volatile. The performance characteristics and product specification do not change greatly from day to day.

The currency market requires traders to look into the future, and using the information to hand, estimate the value of the currency. Information plays a key role in the valuation process. The value of a currency may fall if a current account deficit is larger than expected. The value may rise if there is an economic report that is better than expected. Or, the value may fall if a good economic forecast was not as good as expected. Thus, as information flows into the market on a daily basis, traders in the marketplace buy and sell currencies on the strength of that information and as a result, the price changes. Note that the definition of good and bad information is always in relation to expectations. In finance, information is not inherently good or bad. As noted above, a piece of good news may bring about a fall in the value of a currency if it is not as good as expected; bad news a rise in the value of the currency if it is not as bad as expected.

The role of the market is to ensure that information is available to all traders. In the market for shares this requirement implies strict rules on the disclosure of information to ensure that some traders do not have access to private company information and therefore have an unfair advantage. There is no real equivalent for currencies; private information of relevance to currencies is held by governments and major economic institutions. Governments are keen to avoid speculation in their currency and are therefore likely to ensure that private information is kept confidential until announced to the market as a whole. Major institutions would lose status if their reports were leaked to the market.

All information relevant to valuing a currency is about the future. It is tempting to think that a spot price only reflects current information and, say, a 1 month futures price will reflect future information. This would be wrong. All prices reflect the same information set. The only difference is that the information's effect on value will be discounted to the present for the spot price and will be discounted to the 1 month value for the 1 month futures price. Because these prices draw on the same information set, it is not unreasonable to suggest that a spot rate may be a good predictor of future rates. This and other consequences of market efficiency will be commented on in later chapters.

Tests for market efficiency have been developed in relation to the stock market, but here we apply the concepts to currencies. There are three types: weak form efficiency, semi strong form efficiency and strong form efficiency.

Weak form efficiency requires that currency prices move randomly, at least in the short term. It may seem strange that analysts would expect that such a sophisticated market should produce currency values that change randomly. Information, however, is by definition random because it is in relation to expectations. Tomorrow's information may be better than expected (implying a rise in currency value) or may be worse than expected (implying a fall in currency value), one cannot tell at the end of any particular trading day whether information will be better or worse than expected. If a rise or fall are equally likely at any point in time, one has a price that is moving randomly. Tests for randomness as such do not exist, one can only test for an absence of patterns (the opposite of randomness). In general, patterns are not found, so the market is weak form efficient.

The qualification made above was that this was at least in the short term. Indeed, until the 1990s, researchers could not distinguish exchange rate movements from a random information process as described. Nowadays, there is some belief that relative inflation rates offer some longer-term guidance as to the future exchange rate. The current debate is over the length of time of the adjustment process. Given that many studies indicate that half the adjustment would take 3 to 4 years, this is clearly a medium- to long-term process. Relevant research articles are given at the end of Part II.

The term weak sometimes causes confusion. Weak form efficiency is a necessary but not sufficient condition for market efficiency. Randomness does not of itself determine efficiency as it does not identify information itself, it only measures the 'footprint' of information.

The other two types of efficiency are called semi-strong efficiency and strong form efficiency. Both refer to the disclosure of information. Semi-strong efficiency requires that prices reflect all published information; strong form efficiency requires that prices reflect all published and private information. Markets desire semi strong form of efficiency, namely that the value of currencies reflect all known published information. If prices were influenced by private, unpublished information, market traders would feel that the market was unfair as they would lose profits to other traders who had such information. Such insider knowledge would lead to certain or near certain profits, an efficient market should *not* allow certain profits to be made when buying and selling an identical unchanged asset.

EXAMPLE

The trading department of Anybank plc is actively buying and selling Currency A. It expects good balance of payments figures to be announced tomorrow. The manager explains to a new recruit: 'Everyone expects that the figures will be good, we have already bought Currency A on this expectation. The point is, will it be better than the market expects or worse? I don't really know. The Prime Minister has been a bit pessimistic on the economy of late, maybe the results are very good and he is trying to lower our expectations so that the results are a nice surprise.' The recruit replies: 'Maybe the results aren't really that good and he is trying to avoid a big disappointment,' the manager responds: 'Mmm... who knows... OK, we haven't really got any fresh information on this currency, we will not make any further purchases or sales.'

Published information in the international arena is a matter for governments and international institutions. Generally, one can expect that the officials of both types of institutions will not trade on information before it is published.

Origins and development

The international money market includes large banks in countries around the world. Large financial institutions such as Deutsche Bank and JP Morgan Chase are major participants. Two other important elements of the international money market are the European money market and the Asian money market.

European money market. The origins of the European money market can be traced to the Eurocurrency market that developed during the 1960s and 1970s. As MNCs expanded their operations during that period, international financial intermediation emerged to accommodate their needs. Because the US dollar was widely used even between non US countries as a medium for international trade, there was a consistent need for dollars in Europe and elsewhere. Some foreign depositors in US banks were worried that their assets might be frozen for political reasons due to the Cold War. Other depositors were unhappy with the US government restrictions on banks. For example, when the USA limited foreign lending by US banks in 1968, foreign subsidiaries of US-based MNCs could obtain US dollars from banks in Europe via the Eurocurrency market. Similarly, when ceilings were placed on the interest rates paid on dollar deposits in the

USA, MNCs transferred their funds to European banks, which were not subject to the ceilings. A significant number of foreign depositors in US banks also transferred their dollar deposits to London. In effect they sold their accounts to a London bank who held the deposit in the US bank and in return gave the sellers an account in London denominated in US dollars. Soon, London banks were using their dollar deposits to lend to corporate customers based in Europe. These dollar deposits in banks in Europe (and on other continents as well) came to be known as **Eurodollars**, and the market for Eurodollars came to be known as the **Eurocurrency market**. ('Eurodollars' and 'Eurocurrency' should not be confused with the 'euro', which is the currency.)

The growing importance of the Organization of Petroleum Exporting Countries (OPEC) also contributed to the growth of the Eurocurrency market. Because OPEC generally requires payment for oil in dollars, the OPEC countries began to use the Eurocurrency market to deposit a portion of their oil reserves. These dollar-denominated deposits are sometimes known as **petrodollars**. Oil revenues deposited in banks have sometimes been lent to oil-importing countries that are short of cash. As these countries purchase more oil, funds are again transferred to the oil-exporting countries, which in turn create new deposits. This recycling process has been an important source of funds for some countries.

Today, the Eurocurrency market is not used as often as in the past because domestic markets are now more competitive. Governments are aware that they cannot restrict bank operations without distorting the market and disadvantaging their own banks. The European money market nevertheless remains an important part of the network of international money markets. Participation is limited to large MNCs and financial institutions who can benefit from rates that are better than elsewhere because the amounts traded are large and there is a very low risk of bankruptcy.

Asian money market. Like the European money market, the Asian money market originated as a market involving mostly dollar-denominated deposits. Hence, it was originally known as the **Asian dollar market**. The market emerged to accommodate the needs of businesses that were using the US dollar (and some other foreign currencies) as a medium of exchange for international trade. These businesses could not rely on banks in Europe because of the distance and different time zones. Today, the Asian money market, as it is now called, is centred in Hong Kong and Singapore, where large banks accept deposits and make loans in various foreign currencies.

Bitcoin Internet market. In 1998 a programmer working under the pseudonym Satoshi Nakamoto created the first truly Internet based currency. Like the Internet it has no central administration and is run by a network of computers acting as servers which is open to all to join (known as 'miners'). The currency is known as a bitcoin. Just as you have a username and password to access particular information on the Internet, so the purchaser by a similar process owns a bitcoin. A bitcoin is created by the miners. The process is deliberately made difficult by only allowing certain kinds of keys which are difficult to compute. As the miners computing power increases, so the keys become more demanding such that the rate of creation is more or less constantly decreasing until the total number reaches 21 million. This is designed to assure the market that there will be no overproduction. However, liquidity is ensured by allowing a bitcoin to be divided into units, the smallest being a Satoshi which is 100 millionth of a bitcoin!

The distinguishing feature of the bitcoin is that the market is the Internet and exchange is on a peer to peer basis with no necessary intermediary or identifiable record of the transaction – it cannot be identified with any particular user. This anonymity and freedom from government control initially made it attractive to illegal drug traders. More recently with disclosure of accounts in tax havens such as the British Virgin Islands and Switzerland it has been viewed as a potential store of wealth for money wishing to avoid scrutiny for whatever reason. In addition many legitimate businesses are beginning to accept bitcoins.

This market is still very small but it is interesting. In the 1960's the Eurodollar developed rapidly. Dollars accounts outside the control of the US authorities operated in London and initially were attractive to, amongst others, the Norodny Bank in Russia who feared that their accounts in New York would be frozen due to the cold war between the USA and Russia. The creation of the euro also saw the lessening of authority of, in this case, the participating governments. As part of this trend, the bitcoin market could further loosen government control of finance.

Functions of the international money market. Today, both the Asian money market and the European money market are key components of the international money market. The primary function of banks in this market is to channel funds from depositors to borrowers. For example, the major sources of deposits in the Asian money market are MNCs with excess cash and government agencies. Manufacturers are major borrowers in this market. Another function is interbank lending and borrowing. Banks that have more qualified loan applicants than they can accommodate use the interbank market to obtain additional funds. Banks in the Asian money market commonly borrow from or lend to banks in the European market.

Standardizing global bank regulations

The growing standardization of regulations around the world has contributed to the trend towards globalization in the banking industry. Four of the more significant regulatory events allowing for a more competitive global playing field are: the Single European Act, the Basel Accord, the Basel II Accord and the Basel III Accord.

Banks are central to international finance, exchanging currencies, speculating, investing internationally, trading in derivatives and so on. The balance sheet of banks is very unusual due to the nature of their trade. On the financing side, shareholder capital is relatively small compared to the very large current liabilities created by the deposit accounts. In effect the bank owes you the money you have deposited and that is much more than the shareholder value. On the assets side, most of the money is in lending to clients. In fact very little of the money deposited with banks is kept as cash. This is potentially a very risky position. If depositors all asked to withdraw their money (known as a run on the bank) the bank would not have the money. Also, if a few large clients went bankrupt, those loans would have to be written off against reserves, i.e. shareholder capital. Because shareholder capital is relatively small, it is possible that a bank could become bankrupt by having negative shareholder capital. This would occur if the amount of the write-off were larger than the shareholder value. Arguably, during the Third World Debt Crisis which began in 1982, many banks found that sovereign loans (loans to countries) of doubtful quality were greater in value than their shareholding. The share capital inadequacy of banks became apparent. Interest rates also became more volatile making it more possible that banks might be in a position of having to offer rates to customers that would threaten their profits. Off-balance sheet activities resulting in financial guarantees also increase the risk of banking.

Basel Accord. Before 1988, share capital standards imposed on banks varied across countries, which allowed some banks to have a comparative global advantage over others. As an example, suppose that banks in the USA were required to maintain more capital than foreign banks. Foreign banks would grow more easily, as they would need a relatively small amount of capital to support an increase in assets. Despite their low share capital, such banks were not necessarily perceived as too risky because the governments in those countries were likely to back banks that experienced financial problems. Therefore, some non-US banks had globally competitive advantages over US banks, without being subject to excessive risk. In December 1987, 12 major industrialized countries attempted to resolve the disparity by proposing uniform bank standards. In July 1988, in the Basel Accord, central bank governors of the 12 countries agreed on standardized guidelines. Under these guidelines, banks must maintain share capital equal (referred to as Tier 1 capital and subject to a detailed definition) to at least 8 per cent of their assets. For this purpose, banks' assets are weighted by risk — the higher the risk the higher the weighting. So, for example, government debt in the form of bonds (sovereign loans) that are rated AAA receive a zero weighting. Banks can invest in these bonds without needing to increase their reserves. If the bond is weighted BBB+ to BBB then the weight is 50 per cent under the Basel II standard approach. So if there is an 8 per cent requirement then if a bank invests £100 in such bonds then it must increase reserves by 50 per cent x 8 per cent = 4 per cent of the £100, i.e. £4 to provide against possible default. Thus there is a higher required capital ratio for riskier assets. Off-balance sheet items are also accounted for so that banks cannot circumvent capital requirements by focusing on services that are not explicitly shown as assets on a balance sheet.

Basel II Accord. Banking regulators that form the so-called Basel Committee have agreed a new accord (known as Basel II) to correct some inconsistencies that still existed. For example, banks in some countries have required better collateral (security) to back their loans — if the borrower from the bank cannot pay, the banks have a lien (ownership right) on the collateral and can sell the assets pledged to the bank in the event of non-payment.

The agreement, effective from December 2006, is based on three 'pillars':

- Minimum capital requirements. Share capital must be at least 8 per cent of a special valuation of lending. The formula for valuing lending is made up of credit risk (the risk that the borrower, e.g. a business, will not pay), market risk (exposure to uncertain market value of investments by the bank in shares, bonds, etc.) and operational risk (the risk from fraud and failing operational processes internal to the bank).

- Supervisory review. Banking supervisors have powers to ask a bank to increase its share capital requirements if there are found to be weaknesses in its capital assessment processes.

- Market discipline. Let investors decide on the risk of buying shares in the bank by requiring greater disclosure of their risk management policies in the annual report. Barclays Bank plc, for instance, prepares a Consolidated Basel 2 Pillar 3 Disclosure 2008 report of some 43 pages. For a non-bank operation the equivalent report would normally be about one to five pages. In its 2012 report it explains that it borrows in US dollars and euros to offset the effect of exchange rate movements in its investments in those currencies, thus minimizing the effect of currency movements on its regulatory capital ratios.

- Basel III Accord. This accord keeps the three pillars and makes further recommendations concerning their implementation. It introduces a minimum leverage ratio of 3 per cent defined as Tier 1 capital (mainly shares and retained earnings) divided by total assets. A bank is a much riskier operation than a commercial company!

Single European Act. One of the most significant events affecting international banking was the **Single European Act**, which was phased in by 1992 throughout the European Union (EU) countries. The following are some of the more relevant provisions of the Single European Act for the banking industry:

- Capital can flow freely throughout Europe.

- Banks can offer a wide variety of lending, leasing and securities activities in the EU.

- Regulations regarding competition, mergers and taxes are similar throughout the EU.

- A bank established in any one of the EU countries has the right to expand into any or all of the other EU countries.

As a result of this act, banks have expanded across European countries. Efficiency in the European banking markets has increased because banks can more easily cross countries without concern for country-specific regulations that prevailed in the past.

Another key provision of the act is that banks entering Europe receive the same banking powers as other banks there. Similar provisions apply to non-US banks that enter the USA.

INTERNATIONAL CREDIT MARKET

Multinational corporations (MNCs) and domestic firms sometimes obtain medium-term funds through loans from local financial institutions or through the issuance of notes (medium-term debt obligations) in their local markets. However, MNCs also have access to medium-term funds through banks located in foreign markets. Loans of 1 year or longer extended by banks to MNCs or government agencies in Europe are commonly called Eurocredits or **Eurocredit loans**. These loans are provided in the so-called **Eurocredit market**. The loans can be denominated in dollars or many other currencies and commonly have a maturity of 5 years.

Because banks accept short-term deposits and sometimes provide longer-term loans, their asset and liability maturities do not match. This can adversely affect a bank's performance during periods of rising interest rates, since the bank may have locked in a rate on its longer-term loans while the rate it pays on short-term deposits is rising over time. To avoid this risk, banks commonly use floating rate loans. The loan rate floats in accordance with the movement of some market interest rate, such as the

London Interbank Offer Rate (LIBOR), which is the rate commonly charged for loans between banks. For example, a Eurocredit loan may have a loan rate that adjusts every 6 months and is set at 'LIBOR plus 3 per cent'. The premium paid above LIBOR will depend on the credit risk of the borrower. The LIBOR varies among currencies because the market supply of and demand for funds vary among currencies.

The international credit market is well developed in Asia and is developing in South America. Periodically, some regions are affected by an economic crisis, which increases the credit risk. Financial institutions tend to reduce their participation in those markets when credit risk increases. Thus, even though funding is widely available in many markets, the funds tend to move towards the markets where economic conditions are strong and credit risk is tolerable.

Syndicated loans

Sometimes a single bank is unwilling or unable to lend the amount needed by a particular corporation or government agency. In this case, a **syndicate** of banks may be organized. Each bank within the syndicate participates in the lending. A lead bank is responsible for negotiating terms with the borrower. Then the lead bank organizes a group of banks to underwrite the loans. The syndicate of banks is usually formed in about 6 weeks, or less if the borrower is well known because the credit evaluation can then be conducted more quickly.

Borrowers that receive a syndicated loan incur various fees besides the interest on the loan. Front-end management fees are paid to cover the costs of organizing the syndicate and underwriting the loan. In addition, a commitment fee of about 0.25 per cent or 0.50 per cent is charged annually on the unused portion of the available credit extended by the syndicate.

Syndicated loans can be denominated in a variety of currencies. The interest rate depends on the currency denominating the loan, the maturity of the loan, and the creditworthiness of the borrower. Interest rates on syndicated loans are commonly adjustable according to movements in an interbank lending rate, and the adjustment may occur every 6 months or every year.

Syndicated loans not only reduce the default risk of a large loan to the degree of participation for each individual bank, but they can also add an extra incentive for the borrower to repay the loan. If a government defaults on a loan to a syndicate, word will quickly spread among banks, and the government will likely have difficulty obtaining future loans. Borrowers are therefore strongly encouraged to repay syndicated loans promptly. From the perspective of the banks, syndicated loans increase the probability of prompt repayment.

INTERNATIONAL BOND MARKET

Bonds or debentures or bills are issued by companies and governments. A bond typically offers a fixed interest payment for a number of years or term, combined with a repayment (redemption) of the nominal amount borrowed at the end of the term. They may be secured on the assets of the company in case of non-payment. Unlike shares, there is no ownership interest, and so no voting rights. Although MNCs, like domestic firms, can obtain long-term debt by issuing bonds in their local markets, MNCs can also access long-term funds in foreign markets. MNCs may choose to issue bonds in the international bond markets for three reasons. First, issuers recognize that they may be able to attract a stronger demand by issuing their bonds in a particular foreign country rather than in their home country. Some countries have a limited investor base, so MNCs in those countries seek financing elsewhere. Second, MNCs may prefer to finance a specific foreign project in a particular currency and therefore may attempt to obtain funds where that currency is widely used. Third, financing in a foreign currency with a lower interest rate may enable an MNC to reduce its cost of financing, although it may be exposed to exchange rate risk (as explained in later chapters). Some institutional investors prefer to invest in international bond markets rather than their respective local markets when they can earn a higher return on bonds denominated in foreign currencies.

International bonds are typically classified as either foreign bonds or Eurobonds. A **foreign bond** is issued by a borrower foreign to the country where the bond is placed. For example, a US corporation may issue a bond denominated in Japanese yen, which is sold to investors in Japan. In some cases, a firm may issue a variety of bonds in various countries. The currency denominating each type of bond is determined by the country where it is sold. These foreign bonds are sometimes specifically referred to as **parallel bonds**.

Eurobond market

Eurobonds are bonds that are sold in countries other than the country of the currency denominating the bonds. The emergence of the Eurobond market was partially the result of the **Interest Equalization Tax (IET)** imposed by the US government in 1963 to discourage US investors from investing in foreign securities. Thus, non-US borrowers that historically had sold foreign securities to US investors began to look elsewhere for funds. Further impetus to the market's growth came in 1984 when the US government abolished a withholding tax that it had formerly imposed on some non-US investors and allowed US corporations to issue bearer bonds directly to non-US investors.

Eurobonds have become very popular as a means of attracting funds, perhaps in part because they circumvent registration requirements. US-based MNCs such as McDonald's and Walt Disney commonly issue Eurobonds. Non-US firms such as Guinness, Nestlé and Volkswagen also use the Eurobond market as a source of funds.

In recent years, governments and corporations from emerging markets such as Croatia, Ukraine, Romania and Hungary have frequently utilized the Eurobond market. New corporations that have been established in emerging markets rely on the Eurobond market to finance their growth. They have to pay a risk premium of at least three percentage points annually above the US Treasury bond rate on dollar-denominated Eurobonds.

Features of eurobonds. Eurobonds have several distinctive features. They are usually issued in bearer form, and coupon payments are made yearly. Some Eurobonds carry a convertibility clause allowing them to be converted into a specified number of shares of common share. An advantage to the issuer is that Eurobonds typically have few, if any, protective covenants. Furthermore, even short-maturity Eurobonds include call provisions. Some Eurobonds, called **floating rate notes (FRNs)**, have a variable rate provision that adjusts the coupon rate over time according to prevailing market rates.

Denominations. Eurobonds are commonly denominated in a number of currencies. Although the US dollar is used most often, denominating 70 to 75 per cent of Eurobonds, the euro will likely also be used to a significant extent in the future. Recently, some firms have issued debt denominated in Japanese yen to take advantage of Japan's extremely low interest rates. Because interest rates for each currency and credit conditions change constantly, the popularity of particular currencies in the Eurobond market changes over time.

Underwriting process. Eurobonds are underwritten by a multinational syndicate of investment banks and simultaneously placed in many countries, providing a wide spectrum of fund sources to tap. The underwriting process takes place in a sequence of steps. The multinational managing syndicate sells the bonds to a large underwriting crew. In many cases, a special distribution to regional underwriters is allocated before the bonds finally reach the bond purchasers. One problem with the distribution method is that the second- and third-stage underwriters do not always follow up on their promise to sell the bonds. The managing syndicate is therefore forced to redistribute the unsold bonds or to sell them directly, which creates 'digestion' problems in the market and adds to the distribution cost. To avoid such problems, bonds are often distributed in higher volume to underwriters that have fulfilled their commitments in the past at the expense of those that have not. This has helped the Eurobond market maintain its desirability as a bond placement centre.

Secondary market. Eurobonds also have a secondary market. The market makers are in many cases the same underwriters who sell the primary issues. A technological advance called **Euro-clear** helps to inform all traders about outstanding issues for sale, thus allowing a more active secondary market. The intermediaries in the secondary market are based in ten different countries, with those in the UK dominating the action. They can act not only as brokers but also as dealers that hold inventories of Eurobonds. Many of these intermediaries, such as Bank of America International, Salomon Smith Barney and Citicorp International, are subsidiaries of US corporations.

Before the adoption of the euro in much of Europe, MNCs in European countries commonly preferred to issue bonds in their own local currency. The market for bonds in each currency was limited. Now, with the adoption of the euro, MNCs from many different countries can issue bonds denominated in euros, which allows for a much larger and more liquid market. MNCs have benefited because they can more easily obtain debt by issuing bonds, as investors know that there will be adequate liquidity in the secondary market.

Development of other bond markets

Bond markets have developed in Asia and South America. Government agencies and MNCs in these regions use international bond markets to issue bonds when they believe they can reduce their financing costs. Investors in some countries use international bond markets because they expect their local currency to weaken in the future and prefer to invest in bonds denominated in a strong foreign currency. The South American bond market has experienced limited growth because the interest rates in some countries there are usually high. MNCs and government agencies in those countries are unwilling to issue bonds when interest rates are so high, so they rely heavily on short-term financing.

COMPARING INTEREST RATES AMONG CURRENCIES

Interest rates vary between countries due to two factors: different inflation rates and different risk. Expectations related to inflation and risk drive changes in demand and supply.

The interest rates in debt markets, which are shown in Exhibit 3.4, are crucial because they affect the MNC's cost of financing. Since interest rates can vary substantially among currencies, the cost of local financing for foreign projects varies among countries. The interest rate on a debt instrument denominated in a specific currency is determined by the demand for funds denominated in that currency and the supply of funds available in that currency.

The supply and demand schedules for the British pound and for Mexico's currency (the peso) are compared for a given point in time in Exhibit 3.5. The demand schedule for loanable funds is downward sloping for any currency, which simply means that the quantity of funds demanded at any point in time is inversely related to the interest rate level. That is, the total amount of loanable funds demanded (borrowed) at a given point in time is higher if the cost of borrowing is lower.

The supply schedule for loanable funds denominated in a given currency is upward sloping, which means that the total amount of loanable funds supplied (such as savings by individuals) at a given point in time is positively related to the interest rate level. That is, the total amount of loanable funds supplied to the market is higher if the interest rate offered on savings accounts is higher.

Though the demand schedule for loanable funds should be downward sloping for every currency and the supply schedule of loanable funds should be upward sloping for every currency, the actual positions of these schedules vary among currencies. First, notice that the demand and supply curves are further to the right for the British pound than for the Mexican peso. The amount of British pound-denominated loanable funds supplied and demanded is much greater than the amount of peso-denominated loanable funds because the UK economy is much larger than Mexico's economy. Also notice that the positions of the demand and supply schedules for loanable funds are much higher for the Mexican peso than for the British pound. The supply schedule for loanable funds denominated in Mexican pesos shows that hardly any amount of savings would be supplied at low interest rate levels because the high inflation in Mexico encourages households to spend all of their disposable income before prices increase more. It discourages households from saving unless the interest rate is sufficiently high. In addition, the demand for loanable funds in pesos shows that borrowers are willing to borrow even at very high rates of interest because they would rather borrow funds to make purchases now before prices increase.

Because of the differences in the positions of the demand and supply schedules for the two currencies shown in Exhibit 3.5, the equilibrium interest rate for the Mexican peso is much higher than for the British pound.

EXHIBIT 3.4   Comparison of government market rates

Yield on 10–year bonds			
Country	Interest rate	Country	Interest rate
Greece	11.8	China	3.7
Nigeria	11.4	Latvia	3.3
Brazil	9.3	Bulgaria	3.3
India	7.9	Norway	2.2
Russia	6.4	Belgium	2.2
Romania	6.4	France	2.1
Portugal	6.3	UK	2.1
South Africa	6.3	Czech Republic	2.0
Hungary	6.2	Canada	1.9
Spain	5.0	USA	1.9
Croatia	4.9	Austria	1.9
Slovenia	4.8	Sweden	1.8
Ireland	4.4	Finland	1.8
Slovakia	4.3	Netherlands	1.7
Italy	4.2	Denmark	1.6
Lithuania	4.2	Germany	1.5
Israel	4.0	Japan	0.8
Poland	3.8	Switzerland	0.5

January 2012

EXHIBIT 3.5   Why UK interest rates differ from Mexican peso interest rates

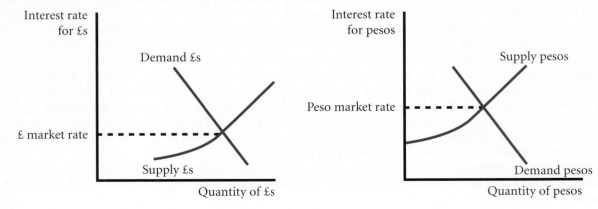

As the demand and supply schedules change over time for a specific currency, so will the equilibrium interest rate.

The fallacy of being attracted to higher interest rates. One might think that investors from other countries should invest in savings accounts in countries with higher interest rates. However, higher interest rates are given for a reason, and very often it is because of higher inflation. The currencies of these high-inflation countries usually weaken over time, which may more than offset the interest rate advantage as explained later in the text. Second, savings deposits in some of these countries are not insured, which presents another risk to foreign investors. Third, some emerging countries impose restrictions that discourage investors from investing funds there.

EXAMPLE

Suppose that Mexico's government is able to substantially reduce the local inflation. In that case, the supply schedule of loanable funds denominated in pesos would shift out (to the right). Conversely, the demand schedule of loanable funds denominated in pesos would shift in (to the left). The two shifts would result in a lower equilibrium interest rate.

Supply and demand conditions can explain the relative interest rate for any currency. Japan's very low interest rate is attributed to a large supply of savings by Japanese households relative to a weak demand for funds because of a weak economy (limited borrowing). The relatively high interest rate in Brazil is attributed both to high inflation, which encourages firms and consumers to borrow and make purchases before prices increase further, and to excessive borrowing by the government.

A change in one currency's interest rate can have an impact on another within the same day, week or month. The point is that the freedom to transfer funds across countries causes the demand and supply conditions for funds to be somewhat integrated, which can cause interest rate movements to be integrated. Interest rates in the European countries participating in the euro are similar because they are subject to the same money supply and demand conditions. For this reason as in Exhibit 3.4 above a EuroZone rate is quoted. The EuroZone however is a special case as it is made up of a number of distinct governments and economic areas. The fixed exchange rate ensures that banks will offer similar rates to investors across the EuroZone subject to regulations. However, government borrowing in the form of bonds does vary as there are perceived to be risks of leaving the EuroZone or default that are attached to individual governments. The Euro countries in Exhibit 3.4 illustrate the large differences in interest rates resulting from these uncertainties.

INTERNATIONAL STOCK MARKETS

MNCs and domestic firms commonly obtain long-term funding by issuing shares locally. Yet, MNCs can also attract funds from foreign investors by issuing shares in international markets. The shares offering may be more easily digested when it is issued in several markets. In addition, the issuance of shares in a foreign country can enhance the firm's image and name recognition there.

The conversion of many European countries to a single currency (the euro) has resulted in more share offerings in Europe by US- and European-based MNCs. In the past, an MNC needed a different currency in every country where it conducted business and therefore borrowed currencies from local banks in those countries. Now, it can use the euro to finance its operations across several European countries and may be able to obtain all the financing it needs with one share or bond offering denominated in euros. The MNCs can then use a portion of the revenue (in euros) to pay dividends to shareholders and interest to bondholders.

Issuance of foreign shares in the USA

Non-US corporations or governments that need large amounts of funds sometimes issue shares in the USA (these are called **Yankee stock offerings**, note that 'stock' is the US term for share in this context) due to the liquidity of the new-issues market there. In other words, a foreign corporation or government may be more likely to sell an entire issue of shares in the US market, whereas in other, smaller markets, the entire issue may not necessarily sell.

When a non-US firm issues shares in its own country, its shareholder base is quite limited, as a few large institutional investors may own most of the shares. By issuing shares in the USA, such a firm diversifies its shareholder base, which can reduce share price volatility caused when large investors sell shares.

The US investment banks commonly serve as underwriters of the shares targeted for the US market and receive underwriting fees representing about 7 per cent of the value of shares issued. Since many financial institutions in the USA purchase non-US shares as investments, non-US firms may be able to place an entire share offering within the USA.

Firms that issue shares in the USA typically are required to satisfy stringent disclosure rules on their financial condition. However, they are exempt from some of these rules when they qualify for a Securities and Exchange Commission guideline (called Rule 144a) through a direct placement of shares to institutional investors.

Many of the recent share offerings in the USA by non-US firms have resulted from privatization programmes in Latin America and Europe. Thus, businesses that were previously government owned are being sold to US shareholders. Given the large size of some of these businesses, the local stock markets are not large enough to digest the share offerings. Consequently, US investors are financing many privatized businesses based in foreign countries.

American depository receipts. Non-US firms also obtain equity financing by using **American depository receipts (ADRs)**, which are certificates representing bundles of shares. The use of ADRs circumvents some disclosure requirements imposed on share offerings in the USA, yet enables non-US firms to tap the US market for funds. The ADR market grew after businesses were privatized in the early 1990s, as some of these businesses issued ADRs to obtain financing.

Since ADR shares can be traded just like shares, the price of an ADR changes each day in response to demand and supply conditions. Over time, however, the value of an ADR should move in tandem with the value of the corresponding share that is listed on the foreign stock exchange, after adjusting for exchange rate effects. The formula for calculating the price of an ADR is:

$$P_{ADR} = Conv \times P_{fs} \times S$$

where:

P_{ADR} = the price of the ADR in dollars

$Conv$ = number of foreign shares that can be obtained for one ADR

P_{fs} = the price of the foreign shares measured in foreign currency

S = the spot rate of the foreign currency, i.e. foreign currency units:\$1

EXAMPLE

A share of the ADR of the French firm Pari represents one share of this firm that is traded on the French stock exchange. The share price of Pari was 20 euros when the French market closed. As the US stock market opens, the euro is worth \$1.05, so the ADR price should be:

$$\begin{aligned} P_{ADR} &= Conv \times P_{fs} \times S \\ &= 1 \times 20 \times \$1.05 \\ &= \$21 \end{aligned}$$

If there is a discrepancy between the ADR price and the price of the foreign share (after adjusting for the exchange rate), investors can use arbitrage to capitalize on the discrepancy between the prices of the two assets. The act of arbitrage should realign the prices.

EXAMPLE

Assume no transaction costs. If $P_{ADR} < (P_{fs} \times S)$, then ADR shares will flow back to France. They will be converted to shares of the French company and will be traded in the French market. Investors can engage in arbitrage by buying the ADR shares in the USA, converting them to shares of the French company, and then selling those shares on the French stock exchange where the share is listed.

The arbitrage will: (1) reduce the supply of ADRs traded in the US market, thereby putting upward pressure on the ADR price and (2) increase the supply of the French shares traded in the French market, thereby putting downward pressure on the share price in France. The arbitrage will continue until the discrepancy in prices disappears.

ADRs are a good example of the subtlety and international nature of financial markets. Their regulation has equally to be on an international scale to be effective.

Issuance of shares in foreign markets

The locations of an MNC's operations can influence the decision about where to place its shares, as the MNC may desire a country where it is likely to generate enough future cash flows to cover dividend payments. The shares of the largest MNCs are widely traded on numerous stock exchanges around the world. For example, Alcatel (France), Nokia (Finland), Coca-Cola Co., IBM and many other MNCs have their shares listed on several different stock exchanges. When an MNC's shares are listed on foreign stock exchanges, it can easily be traded by foreign investors who have access to those exchanges.

Impact of the euro. The adoption of the euro by many European countries has encouraged MNCs based in Europe to issue shares. Investors throughout Europe are more willing to invest in shares when they do not have to worry about exchange rate effects. For example, a German insurance company may be more willing to buy shares issued by a firm in Portugal now that the same currency is used in both countries. The secondary market for shares denominated in euros is more liquid as a result of the participation by investors from the countries that have adopted the euro.

Comparison of stock markets. Exhibit 3.6 provides a summary of the major stock markets by country. Stock markets vary considerably in relation to the size of the host economy. The relative size of the South African stock market reflects the perceived value of its mineral resources. Some stock markets are much smaller reflecting the greater reliance on debt financing than equity financing in the past. Recently, however, firms have been issuing shares more frequently, this has resulted in the growth of the smaller stock markets. The percentage of individual versus institutional ownership of shares varies across stock markets. Generally financial institutions and other firms own a much larger proportion of the shares than individuals. The concentration of ownership is lower on average in the USA and the UK compared with the rest of the world (see Chapter 16).

Large MNCs have begun to float new share issues simultaneously in various countries. Investment banks underwrite shares through one or more syndicates across countries. The global distribution of shares can reach a much larger market, so greater quantities of shares can be issued at a given price.

EXHIBIT 3.6   Stock market capitalization $billion (thousand million)

	Stock market	Gross domestic product
Brazil	1 230	2 396
China	3 697	8 227
France	1 823	2 609
Germany	1 486	3 401
India	1 263	1 825
Japan	3 681	5 964
Norway	253	501
South Africa	612	384
UK	3 019	2 441
USA	18 668	16 010

Source: various.

USING THE WEB

Stock market trading information

Information about the market capitalization, share trading volume and turnover for each stock market is provided at: www.worldbank.org by following the link for data.

In 2000, the Amsterdam, Brussels and Paris stock exchanges merged to create the Euronext market. Since then, the Lisbon stock exchange has joined as well. Most of the largest firms based in Continental Europe have listed their shares on the Euronext market. This market is likely to grow over time as other stock exchanges may join it. It is important to point out that stock exchanges are commercial not government enterprises. They can and are subject to takeovers. In 2004, for example, the Deutsche Borse (the German Stock Exchange based in Frankfurt) attempted a £1.35bn takeover of the London Stock Exchange that subsequently failed. As yet the attempt to develop a single European stock market has not happened and it is likely that there always will be, as in America, competing exchanges.

In recent years, many new stock markets have been developed. These so-called emerging markets enable foreign firms to raise large amounts of capital by issuing shares. These markets may enable MNCs doing business in emerging markets to raise funds by issuing shares there and listing their shares on the local stock exchanges. Market characteristics such as the amount of trading relative to market capitalization and the applicable tax rates can vary substantially among emerging markets.

INTERNATIONAL FINANCIAL MARKETS AND THE MNC

Exhibit 3.7 illustrates the foreign cash flow movements of a typical MNC. These cash flows can be classified into four corporate functions, all of which generally require use of the foreign exchange markets. The spot market, forward market, currency futures market and currency options market are all classified as foreign exchange markets.

EXHIBIT 3.7   Foreign cash flow chart of an MNC

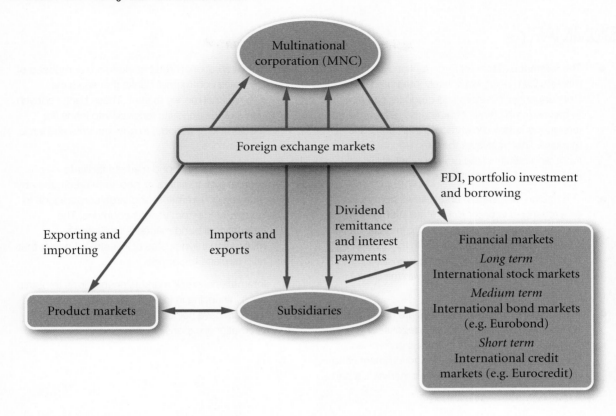

The first function is foreign trade with business clients. Exports generate foreign cash inflows, while imports require cash outflows. A second function is direct foreign investment, or the acquisition of foreign real assets. This function requires cash outflows but generates future inflows through remitted dividends back to the MNC parent or the sale of these foreign assets. A third function is short-term investment or financing in foreign securities. A fourth function is longer-term financing in the international bond or stock markets.

HOW FINANCIAL MARKERS AFFECT AN MNC'S VALUE

Since interest rates commonly vary among countries, an MNC's parent may use international money or bond markets to obtain funds at a lower cost than they can be obtained locally. By doing so, it reduces its cost of debt and therefore reduces its weighted average cost of capital, which results in a higher valuation. An MNC's parent may be able to achieve a lower weighted average cost of capital by issuing equity in some foreign markets rather than issuing equity in its local market. If the MNC achieves a lower cost of capital, it can achieve a higher valuation.

SUMMARY

- The existence of market imperfections prevents markets from being completely integrated. Consequently, investors and creditors can attempt to capitalize on unique characteristics that make foreign markets more attractive than domestic markets. This motivates the international flow of funds and results in the development of international financial markets.

- The foreign exchange market allows currencies to be exchanged in order to facilitate international trade or financial transactions. Commercial banks serve as financial intermediaries in this market. They stand ready to exchange currencies on the spot or at a future point in time with the use of forward contracts.

- The international money markets are composed of several large banks that accept deposits and provide short-term loans in various currencies. This market is used primarily by governments and large corporations. The European market is a part of the international money market.

- The international credit markets are composed of the same commercial banks that serve the international money market. These banks convert some of the deposits received into loans (for medium-term periods) to governments and large corporations.

- The international bond markets facilitate international transfers of long-term credit, thereby enabling governments and large corporations to borrow funds from various countries. The international bond market is facilitated by multinational syndicates of investment banks that help to place the bonds.

- International stock markets enable firms to obtain equity financing in foreign countries. Thus, these markets have helped MNCs finance their international expansion.

CRITICAL DEBATE

Should firms that go public engage in international offerings?

Proposition. Yes. When a firm issues shares to the public for the first time in an initial public offering (IPO), it is naturally concerned about whether it can place all of its shares at a reasonable price. It will be able to issue its shares at a higher price by attracting more investors. It will increase its demand by spreading the shares across countries. The higher the price at which it can issue shares, the lower is its cost of using equity capital. It can also establish a global name by spreading shares across countries.

Opposing view. No. If a firm spreads its shares across different countries at the time of the IPO, there will be less publicly traded shares in the home country. Thus, it will not have as much liquidity in the secondary market. Investors desire shares that they can easily sell in the secondary market, which means that they require that the shares have liquidity. To the extent that a firm reduces its liquidity in the home country by spreading its shares

across countries, it may not attract sufficient home demand for the shares. Thus, its efforts to create global name recognition may reduce its name recognition in the home country.

With whom do you agree? State your reasons. Use InfoTrac or some other search engine to learn more about this issue. Which argument do you support? Offer your own opinion on this issue.

Stock markets are inefficient

Proposition. I cannot believe that if the value of the euro in terms of, say, the British pound increases 3 days in a row, on the fourth day there is still a 50:50 chance that it will go up or down in value. I think that most investors will see a trend and will buy, therefore the price is more likely to go up. Also, if the forward market predicts a rise in value, on average, surely it is going to rise in value. In other words, currency prices are predictable. And finally, if it were so unpredictable and therefore unprofitable to the speculator, how is it that there is such a vast sum of money being traded every day for speculative purposes – there is no smoke without fire.

Opposing view. The simple answer is that if that is what you believe, buy currencies that have increased 3 days in a row and on average you should make a profit, buy currencies where the forward market shows an increase in value. The fact is that there are a lot of investors with just your sort of view. The market traders know all about such beliefs and will price the currency so that such easy profit (their loss) cannot be made. Look at past currency rates

for yourself, check all fourth day changes after 3 days of rises, any difference is going to be not enough to cover transaction costs or trading expenses and the slight inaccuracy in your figures which are likely to be closing day midpoint of the bid/ask spread. No, all currency movements are related to information and no one knows if tomorrow's news will be better or worse than expected.

With whom do you agree? Could there be undiscovered patterns? Could some movements not be related to information? Could some private news be leaking out?

SELF TEST

Answers are provided in Appendix A at the back of the text.

1 Sunny Bank quotes a bid rate of £0.58 for the US dollar and an ask rate of £0.60. What is the bid/ask percentage spread?

2 Cloudy Bank quotes an ask rate of £0.12 for the Peruvian currency (new sol) and a bid rate of £0.09.

Determine the bid/ask percentage spread. Briefly give reasons for the difference with Q1.

3 Briefly explain how MNCs can make use of each international financial market described in this chapter.

QUESTIONS AND APPLICATIONS

1 **Motives for investing in foreign money markets.** Explain why an MNC may invest funds in a financial market outside its own country.

2 **Motives for providing credit in foreign markets.** Explain why some financial institutions prefer to provide credit in financial markets outside their own country.

3 **Exchange rate effects on investing.** Explain how the appreciation of the Australian dollar against the euro would affect the return to a French firm that invested in an Australian money market security.

4 **Exchange rate effects on borrowing.** Explain how the appreciation of the Japanese yen against the UK pound would affect the return to a UK firm that borrowed Japanese yen and used the proceeds for a UK project.

5 **Bank services.** List some of the important characteristics of bank foreign exchange services that MNCs should consider.

6 **Bid/ask spread.** Delay Bank's bid price for US dollars is £0.53 and its ask price is £0.55. What is the bid/ask percentage spread?

7 **Bid/ask spread.** Compute the bid/ask percentage spread for Mexican pesos in which the ask rate is 20.6 new peso to the dollar and the bid rate is 21.5 new peso.

8 **Forward contract.** The Wolfpack Ltd is a UK exporter that invoices its exports to the USA in dollars. If it expects that the dollar will appreciate against the pound in the future, should it hedge its exports with a forward contract? Explain.

9 **Euro.** Explain the foreign exchange situation for countries that use the euro when they engage in international trade among themselves.

10 **Indirect exchange rate.** If the direct exchange rate of the euro is worth £0.685, what is the indirect rate of the euro? Note that the pound is the home currency.

11 **Cross exchange rate.** Assume Poland's currency (the zloty) is worth £0.17 and the Japanese yen is worth £0.005. What is the cross (implied) rate of the zloty with respect to the yen?

12 **Syndicated loans.** Explain how syndicated loans are used in international markets.

13 **Loan rates.** Explain the process used by banks in the Eurocredit market to determine the rate to charge on loans.

14 **International markets.** What is the function of the international money markets? Briefly describe the reasons for the development and growth of the European money market. Explain how the international money, credit and bond markets differ from one another.

15 **Evolution of floating rates.** Briefly describe the historical developments that led to floating exchange rates as of 1973.

16 **International diversification.** Explain how the Asian crisis would have affected the returns to a UK firm investing in the Asian stock markets as a means of international diversification. (See the Chapter Appendix.)

17 **Eurocredit loans.**

 a With regard to Eurocredit loans, who are the borrowers?

 b Why would a bank desire to participate in syndicated Eurocredit loans?

 c What is LIBOR, and how is it used in the Eurocredit market?

18 **Foreign exchange.** You just came back from Canada, where the Canadian dollar was worth £0.43. You still have C$200 from your trip and could exchange them for pounds at the airport, but the airport foreign exchange desk will only buy them for £0.40. Next week, you will be going to Mexico and will need pesos. The airport foreign exchange desk will sell you pesos for £0.055 per peso. You met a tourist at the airport who is from Mexico and is on his way to Canada. He is willing to buy your C$200 for 1500 new pesos. Should you accept the offer or cash the Canadian dollars in at the airport? Explain.

19 **Foreign stock markets.** Explain why firms may issue shares in foreign markets. Why might MNCs issue more shares in Europe since the conversion to a single currency in 1999?

20 **Stock market integration.** Bullet plc, a UK firm, is planning to issue new shares on the London Stock Exchange this month. The only decision still to be made is the specific day on which the shares will be issued. Why do you think Bullet monitors results of the Tokyo stock market every morning?

ADVANCED QUESTIONS

21 **Effects of September 11.** Why do you think the terrorist attack on the USA was expected to cause a decline in US interest rates? Given the expectations for a decline in US interest rates and share prices, how were capital flows between the USA and other countries likely to be affected?

22 **International financial markets.** Carrefour the French Supermarket chain has established retail outlets worldwide. These outlets are massive and contain products purchased locally as well as imports. As Carrefour generates earnings beyond what it needs abroad, it may remit those earnings back to France. Carrefour is likely to build additional outlets especially in China.

 a Explain how the Carrefour outlets in China would use the spot market in foreign exchange.

 b Explain how Carrefour might utilize the international money markets when it is establishing other Carrefour stores in Asia.

 c Explain how Carrefour could use the international bond market to finance the establishment of new outlets in foreign markets.

23 **Interest rates.** Why do interest rates vary among countries? Why are interest rates normally similar for those European countries that use the euro as their currency? Offer a reason why the government interest rate of one country could be slightly higher than that of the government interest rate of another country, even though the euro is the currency used in both countries.

PROJECT WORKSHOP

24 **Market information on the Internet.** Use your own institution's currency database or visit http://www.oanda.com/convert/fxhistory, to obtain exchange rate data covering at least 1 year, copy and paste the results into Excel and answer the following questions:

a Determine the cross exchange rate between the Japanese yen and the Australian dollar. Compare the cross exchange rate with the direct rate. Are there any differences? Evaluate the significance of your results.

b Select a pattern, for example 2 days of consecutive falls, then select and check the movements on the following day (the third day in this case). Are the following day movements unusual in any way? Evaluate the significance of your results.

It is helpful to use nested 'if' instructions in Excel. In this example 2 days of consecutive falls is the criteria for selecting the third day's price movement. An instruction placed in C4 and copied and pasted to C365 with exchange rates from B1 to B365 would be: =IF(B3>B2, IF(B2>B1, B4," ")," "), a run of 3 days would be:

=IF(B4>B3,IF(B3>B2,IF(B2>B1,B5," ")," ")," ")

note that " "; is simply a double inverted comma, Excel ignores gaps so " " will also work. Once applied, choose 'Data' and 'sort' from the toolbar to get rid of the blanks.

Note that the Excel formula can be varied so that for instance < may be used and other operands =, +, − and so on. Formulas may also be incorporated so that if only large movements were of interest one could write:

=IF(B4>B3*1.1,IF(B3>B2*1.1,IF(B2>B1*1.1, −B5," ")," ")," ")

Experiment with the formula to obtain the desired pattern.

25 From Appendix 3, imagine that you are a UK investor, construct an international portfolio of shares. Is the standard deviation of your international portfolio greater or less than an equivalent domestic portfolio? Evaluate the significance of your results.

You will need a database of a history of the share prices of large companies (Perfect Analysis and Datastream are examples). The history of exchange rates with the British pound for the currencies quoted, e.g. \$:£, euro:£, C\$:£ and so on.

The return on a share for a month will be (1 + R) × (1 + e) − see the appendix for more on the formula. You may then calculate the variance and covariance matrix of a portfolio of these returns month on month (the portfolio calculator may help).

26 From Appendix 3, compare the return and the risk of investing in the NYSE with investing in the London Stock Exchange for a UK investor. Evaluate the significance of your results.

You will need a FTSE stock exchange index, the Dow Jones index or NASDAQ index and the £:\$ exchange rate.

Analysis can be made using Excel. The process is to invest in the US index at the start of the period and convert back at the end of the period. Then work out the percentage change in the value. To 'buy the index' you can in effect treat the index as the dollar price of a share, so buy the currency, then buy the share at the beginning of the period, then at the end of the period reverse the process.

Alternatively, you can work out the percentage change in the index over the period and the percentage change in the value of the currency over the year, then use the formula as in the text:

$$R_£ = (1 + R)(1 + e)$$

Note that you can work out the risk in approximate fashion by working out the percentage changes in the value of the currency and index then applying the model for combining variances, as:

VAR(index) + Var(£:\$ rate) + 2 × SD(£:\$ rate) × SD(index) × Corr(£:\$ rate, index)

This is not exact but relies on the approximation that at low levels of change i.e. below 10 per cent:

$$(1 + R) × (1 + e) − 1 \text{ roughly equals } R + e$$

so the formula is the same as adding two investments as the returns are roughly additive.

27 From Appendix 3, calculate the percentage changes (returns on a period by period basis) between any two major currencies for a 10-year period on a rolling basis. You may choose the length of the return period. Thus, if your data is monthly, say, the last day of each month then your first return would be the

percentage change from 31 December to 31 January, the second return would be from the 31 January to 28 February and so on – there is a note on returns in Appendix B at the end of the book. Then calculate the variances and correlations between the returns.

a   Using graphs, examine the predictability of the standard deviation of each currency and the pre-

dictability of the correlation between the two currencies.

b   Examine a period where there has been a significant change in the value of the standard deviations and correlations. Look at the financial news about this time and see whether or not there is any suggestion in the press that might indicate a change in the behaviour of the currencies.

DISCUSSION IN THE BOARDROOM

This exercise can be found on our dedicated Course-Mate platform for students.

RUNNING YOUR OWN MNC

This exercise can be found on our dedicated Course-Mate platform for students.

Essays/discussion and articles can be found at the end of Part I.

BLADES PLC CASE STUDY

Decisions to use international financial markets

As a financial analyst for Blades plc you are reasonably satisfied with Blades' current setup of exporting 'Speedos' (roller blades) to Thailand. Due to the unique arrangement with Blades' primary customer in Thailand, forecasting the revenue to be generated there is a relatively easy task. Specifically, your customer has agreed to purchase 180 000 pairs of Speedos annually, for a period of 3 years, at a price of THB4594 (THB = Thai baht) per pair. The current direct quotation of the pound-baht exchange rate is £0.016.

The cost of goods sold incurred in Thailand (due to imports of the rubber and plastic components from Thailand) runs at approximately THB2871 per pair of Speedos, but Blades currently only imports materials sufficient to manufacture about 72 000 pairs of Speedos. Blades' primary reasons for using a Thai supplier are the high quality of the components and the low cost, which has been facilitated by a continuing depreciation of the Thai baht against the pound. If the pound cost of buying components becomes more expensive in Thailand than in the UK, Blades is contemplating providing its UK supplier with the additional business.

Your plan is quite simple; Blades is currently using its Thai-denominated revenues to cover the cost of goods sold incurred there. During the last year, excess revenue was converted to pounds at the prevailing exchange rate. Although your cost of goods sold is not fixed contractually as the Thai revenues are, you expect them to remain relatively constant in the near future. Consequently, the baht-denominated cash inflows are fairly predictable each year because the Thai customer has committed to the purchase of 180 000 pairs of Speedos at a fixed price. The excess pound revenue resulting from the conversion of baht is used either to support the UK production of Speedos if needed or to invest in the UK. Specifically, the revenues are used to cover the cost of goods sold in the UK manufacturing plant.

Ben Holt, Blades' finance director, notices that Thailand's interest rates are approximately 15 per cent (versus 8 per cent in the UK). You interpret the high interest rates in Thailand as an indication of the uncertainty resulting from Thailand's unstable economy. Holt asks you to assess the feasibility of investing Blades' excess funds from Thailand operations in Thailand at an interest rate of 15 per cent. After you express your opposition to his plan, Holt asks you to detail the reasons in a detailed report.

1 One point of concern for you is that there is a trade-off between the higher interest rates in Thailand and the delayed conversion of baht into pounds. Explain what this means.

2 If the net baht received from the Thailand operation are invested in Thailand, how will UK operations be affected? (Assume that Blades is currently paying 10 per cent on pounds borrowed and needs more financing for its firm.)

3 Construct a spreadsheet to compare the cash flows resulting from two plans. Under the first plan, net baht-denominated cash flows (received today) will be invested in Thailand at 15 per cent for a 1-year period, after which the baht will be converted to pounds. The expected spot rate for the baht in 1 year is about £0.0147 (Ben Holt's plan). Under the second plan, net baht-denominated cash flows are converted to pounds immediately and invested in the UK for 1 year at 8 per cent. For this question, assume that all baht-denominated cash flows are due today. Does Holt's plan seem superior in terms of pound cash flows available after 1 year? Compare the choice of investing the funds versus using the funds to provide needed financing to the firm.

SMALL BUSINESS DILEMMA

Developing a multinational sporting goods industry

Each month, the Sports Exports Company (an Irish firm) receives an order for basketballs from a British sporting goods distributor. The monthly payment for the basketballs is denominated in British pounds, as requested by the British distributor. Jim Logan, owner of the Sports Exports Company, must convert the pounds received into euros.

1 Explain how the Sports Exports Company could utilize the spot market to facilitate the exchange of currencies. Be specific.

2 Explain how the Sports Exports Company is exposed to exchange rate risk and how it could use the forward market to hedge this risk.

APPENDIX 3
INVESTING IN INTERNATIONAL FINANCIAL MARKETS

The trading of financial assets (such as shares or bonds) by investors in international financial markets has a major impact on MNCs. First, this type of trading can influence the level of interest rates in a specific country (and therefore the cost of debt to an MNC) because it affects the amount of funds available there. Second, it can affect the price of an MNC's shares (and therefore the cost of equity to an MNC) because it influences the demand for the MNC's shares. Third, it enables MNCs to sell securities in foreign markets. So, even though international investing in financial assets is not the most crucial activity of MNCs, international investing by individual and institutional investors can indirectly affect the actions and performance of an MNC. Consequently, an understanding of the motives and methods of international investing is necessary to anticipate how the international flow of funds may change in the future and how that change may affect MNCs.

BACKGROUND ON INTERNATIONAL STOCK EXCHANGES

The international trading of shares has grown over time but has been limited by three barriers: transaction costs, information costs and exchange rate risk. In recent years, however, these barriers have been reduced as explained here.

USING THE WEB

Stock exchange information

It is best to use a search engine to find the home page of the stock exchange. For example the London Stock Exchange can be found at: www.londonstockexchange.com, go to the bottom of the page and jump to statistics. Or choose the NYSE at: hwww.nyse.com. In both cases pdf or Excel files offer the best-quality data.

Reduction in transaction costs

Most countries tend to have their own stock exchanges, where the shares of local publicly held companies are traded. In recent years, exchanges have been consolidated within a country, which has increased efficiency and reduced transaction costs. Some European stock exchanges now have extensive cross-listings so that investors in a given European country can easily purchase shares of companies based in other European countries.

In particular, because of its efficiency, the stock exchange of Switzerland may serve as a model that will be applied to many other stock exchanges around the world. The Swiss stock exchange is now fully computerized, so a trading floor is not needed. Orders by investors to buy or sell flow to financial institutions that are certified members of the Swiss stock exchange. These institutions are not necessarily based in Switzerland. The details of the orders, such as the name of the shares, the number of shares to be bought or sold, and the price at which the investor is willing to buy or sell, are fed into a computer system. The system matches buyers and sellers and then sends information confirming the transaction to the financial institution, which informs the investor that the transaction is completed.

When there are many more buy orders than sell orders for a given share, the computer is unable to accommodate all orders. Some buyers will then increase the price they are willing to pay for the shares. Thus, the price adjusts in response to the demand (buy orders) for the shares and the supply (sell orders) of the shares for sale recorded by the computer system. Similar dynamics occur when a trading floor is used, but the computerized system has documented criteria by which it prioritizes the execution of orders; traders on a trading floor may execute some trades in ways that favour themselves at the expense of investors.

In recent years, electronic communications networks (ECNs) have been created in many countries to match orders between buyers and sellers. Like the Swiss stock exchange, ECNs do not have a visible trading floor: the trades are executed by a computer network. Examples of popular ECNs include Archipelago, Instinet, and Tradebook. With an ECN, investors can place orders on their computers that are then executed by the computer system and confirmed through the Internet to the investor. Thus, all parts of the trading process from the placement of the order to the confirmation that the transaction has been executed are conducted by computer. The ease with which such orders can occur, regardless of the locations of the investor and the stock exchange, is sure to increase the volume of international share transactions in the future.

Impact of alliances. Several stock exchanges have created international alliances with the stock exchanges of other countries, thereby enabling firms to more easily cross-list their shares among various stock markets. This gives investors easier and cheaper access to foreign shares. The alliances also allow greater integration between markets. At some point in the future, there may be one global stock market in which any shares of any country can be easily purchased or sold by investors around the world. A single global stock market would allow investors to easily purchase any shares, regardless of where the corporation is based or the currency in which the share is denominated. The international alliances are a first step toward a single global stock market. The costs of international share transactions have already been substantially reduced as a result of some of the alliances.

Reduction in information costs

The Internet provides investors with access to much information about foreign shares, enabling them to make more informed decisions without having to purchase information about these shares. Consequently, investors should be more comfortable assessing foreign shares. Although differences in accounting rules still limit the degree to which financial data about foreign companies can be interpreted or compared to data about firms in other countries, there is some momentum toward making accounting standards uniform across some countries.

Exchange rate risk

When investing in a foreign share that is denominated in a foreign currency, investors are subject to the possibility that the currency denominating the share may depreciate against the investor's currency over time.

The potential for a major decline in the share's value simply because of a large degree of depreciation is more likely for emerging markets, such as Indonesia or Russia, where the local currency can change by 10 per cent or more on a single day.

Measuring the impact of exchange rates The return to a UK investor from investing in a foreign share is influenced by the return on the share itself which includes the dividend, and the percentage change in the exchange rate, as shown here:

$$R_{t,UK} = (1 + R_t)(1 + e_t) - 1$$

where:

$R_{t,UK}$ = overall return to the UK investor over period t....

e_t = percentage change in the value of the foreign currency over period t

R_t = return on the foreign investment itself over period t measured as:

$$\frac{P_t - P_{t-1} + D_t}{P_t}$$

where:

P_t = price at the end of time t

p_{t-1} = price at the end of time $t - 1$

D_t = Dividend in time t.

EXAMPLE

A year ago, Rob Grady invested in the share of Vopka, a Russian company. Over the last year, the share increased in value by 35 per cent. Over this same period, however, the Russian rouble's value declined by 30 per cent. Rob sold the Vopka shares today. His return is:

$$R_{UK} = (1 + R)(1 + e) - 1$$
$$R_{UK} = (1 + 0.35)(1 - 0.30) - 1$$
$$= -0.055 \text{ or } -5.5\%$$

Even though the return on the share was more pronounced than the exchange rate movement, Rob lost money on his investment. The reason is that the exchange rate movement of −30 per cent wiped out not only 30 per cent of his initial investment but also 30 per cent of the share's return.

As the preceding example illustrates, investors should consider the potential influence of exchange rate movements on foreign shares before investing in those shares. Foreign investments are especially risky in developing countries, where exchange rates tend to be very volatile.

Reducing exchange rate risk of foreign shares. Although hedging the exchange rate risk of an international share portfolio can be effective, it has three limitations. First, the number of foreign currency units to be converted to the home currency at the end of the investment horizon is unknown as the exact price will not be known. Nevertheless, though the hedge may not be perfect for this reason, investors normally should be able to hedge most of their exchange rate risk.

A second limitation of hedging exchange rate risk is that the investors may decide to retain the foreign shares beyond the initially planned investment horizon. Of course, they can reverse (or close out) the existing position and create another forward sale for the extended period but this would be at a different rate.

A third limitation of hedging is that forward rates for currencies that are less widely traded may not exist or may exhibit a large discount. Here protection can be gained thorough cross hedging, that is hedging in a currency whose movements are correlated with the less widely traded currency (see Appendix 11A).

INTERNATIONAL SHARE DIVERSIFICATION

A substantial amount of research has demonstrated that investors in shares can benefit by diversifying internationally. The philosophy of diversification is very simple. An investor will normally invest in a portfolio, which is no more than saying that investment will be in the shares of more than one company. A well diversified portfolio will be made up of investments in shares whose performance is not well correlated. If the value of one share in the portfolio falls there will be other shares in the portfolio that will be increasing in value. Looking from the other point of view, there will be falls in the value of some shares in the portfolio which will limit the effect of rises. So a well diversified portfolio experiences lower overall falls in value but less steep rises in value than a poorly diversified portfolio. The general wisdom is that a portfolio should be well diversified to lessen the effect of individual problems of any one investment. Note that a well diversified portfolio may be risky if made up of volatile shares (i.e. prone to large gains or losses) or may be relatively safe depending on the nature of the shares in the portfolio. Diversification merely gets rid of individual share effects but keeps the common trait in the portfolio.

Investing in a portfolio is a choice between risk (as measured by expected **volatility** measures such as variance – see below) and return (as defined in the previous equation). Exhibit 3.8 outlines the choice for an investor. In an efficient market (where goods are priced according to all available information) the choice is between greater return and greater risk or lesser return but lesser risk. Portfolios C and E in Exhibit 3.8 are mispriced in relation to portfolio A – we will assume that A is correctly priced.

Portfolio E should be offering a higher return. As the future value is a given estimate, the only way to increase the return is to pay less for that future value – so portfolio E is overvalued with respect to A.

EXHIBIT 3.8   Risks return choice for an investor – a comparison of portfolios A, B, C, D and E

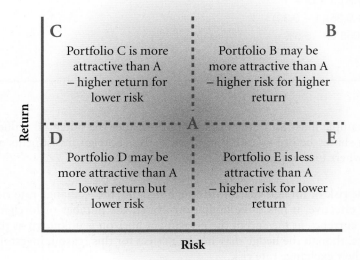

Lowering the amount paid for E and hence raising the return would move it into the B quadrant. By the same reasoning portfolio C is undervalued, more should be paid for the given expected value – the higher price of C would lower the return and move it down into the D quadrant. Portfolios B and D may or may not be attractive to the holder of portfolio A depending on the holder's level of risk aversion. A risk averse investor will prefer portfolio D to A and an investor wanting to take on more risk will prefer B to A. When selecting portfolios, choice and value depend on risk and return.

Measuring portfolio risk and return. As shown in the previous equation, the return on an individual share is measured by its movement in value plus any dividends all measured as a percentage return. Because the value of the currency may have changed, the return must be multiplied by currency movement. If the investment were in bonds, interest payments would replace dividends. Also, returns can be expressed in monetary terms as well.

EXAMPLE

Sunny investments plc, a UK company, has purchased 150 000 euros worth of shares in Sensible SA a French company when the exchange rate was 1.5 euros:£1. At the end of the year, Sunny receives 7000 euros from Sensible in dividend payments and sells its shares for 160 000 euros. Its returns are then converted at 1.4 euros:£1.

The returns calculated in monetary terms are:

Original investment 150 000 euros /1.5 = £100 000

Converted sale price of shares 160 000 euros / 1.4 = £114 285.71

Converted value of dividends 7000 euros / 1.4 = £5000

Monetary return = £114 285.71 + £5000 − £100 000 = £19 285.71 which is a return in percentage terms of £19 295.71 / £100 000 = 0.1928571 or 19.29%

Or

Percentage return on investment in Sensible: (160 000 euros − 150 000 euros + 7000 euros) / 150 000 euros = 11.3333%

Percentage movement in currency value: opening value of the euro 1 / 1.5 = £0.666666; closing value of the euro: 1 / 1.4 = £0.714285; percentage change in value of the euro: (£0.714285 − £0.666666) / £0.666666 = 0.071428571 or 7.14286%

Overall return is R_{UK}
$$= (1 + R)(1 + e) - 1$$
$$= (1 + 0.113333)(1 + 0.0714286) - 1$$
$$= 0.1928568 \text{ or } 19.29\%$$

Note that the difference between 0.1928571 and 0.1928568 of 0.0000003 is a rounding error!

The percentage approach as in the above example of Sunny investments plc will be used here.

The formula for the return on a portfolio is: the weighted average return on investments.

Weights are defined as the percentage original investment in a share. For international investments the return includes percentage changes in the value of the currency as outlined in the preceding example (Sunny Investments). The following example (Investor Morse) illustrates the calculation of the expected return on a portfolio.

EXAMPLE

If Investor Morse invests one-quarter of the initial sum in share A offering a 20 per cent return and three-quarters in share B offering a 10 per cent return, the

weights are 25 per cent and 75 per cent for shares A and B respectively and the overall return will be:

$0.25 \times 20\% + 0.75 \times 10\% = 12.5\%$ for the portfolio

The overall risk of a portfolio is, however, more problematic. Risk for an individual investment is normally thought of as an expected standard deviation – a measure of potential variability (sometimes termed volatility in the literature). For portfolios there is a need to combine the risk measure of differing investments to obtain the overall risk of the portfolio. If there were a perfect correlation between investments in a portfolio – see Appendix B for notes on correlation – the overall risk of a portfolio would be simply the weighted average of the expected standard deviations of the investments in the portfolio. However, in virtually all portfolios the returns on individual investments are not perfectly correlated. The more diversified the portfolio, the lower the overall variability of the portfolio. Diversification as well as standard deviation is therefore an important factor in taking into account the overall level of risk in a portfolio. It is not enough just to look at the individual variability of investments in a portfolio. Calculations must include correlation or covariability as a measure of diversification. Conceptually the formula is not difficult.

The formula for the overall standard deviation of a portfolio is: the square root of the weighted average of all possible variances and covariances in the portfolio.

A correlation is simply a covariance mapped onto a scale going from −1 to +1. A covariance can therefore be thought of as a correlation. Thus a high correlation or covariance exists between two shares A and B in a portfolio when the returns on share A are above its expected return, the return on share B is also almost always above its expected return; and similarly if share A is below its expected return, share B too will be below its expected return almost always. A low correlation would exist if share A were above its expected return, share B is only sometimes above its expected return. Thus correlation is the same idea as diversification, the advantage of a correlation or covariance is that it is a statistical measure. High correlation indicates low diversification, there is not much offsetting effect; low correlation indicates high diversification – when share A is performing badly share B may be performing well.

The calculation of the standard deviation of a portfolio of share A and share B can be written in the form of a matrix to ensure that all possible variances and covariances are included as shown in Exhibit 3.9.

Thus the standard deviation of a portfolio made up of two shares can also be written (with references to the matrix in Exhibit 3.9) as:

$$SD_P = \sqrt{\underbrace{w_A^2 \times Var(A)}_{\text{Top left}} + \underbrace{w_B^2 \times Var(B)}_{\text{Bottom right}} + \underbrace{2 \times w_A \times w_B SD_A \times SD_B \times Corr(A, B)}_{\text{Top right and bottom left}}}$$

This rather long formula is no more than the square root of the total of the cells in the matrix in Exhibit 3.9. The advantage of using a matrix is that it is easy now to see how to calculate the standard deviation of portfolios made up of three or more shares or, more generally, international investments.

An example of an extended matrix is shown in Exhibit 3.10. Note that this powerful formula, in many ways the basis of finance, applies to all types of investment: ADRs, Eurobonds, US treasury bonds, etc. Although the value of the cash flows in the foreign currency is almost certain for these particular instruments, the returns here are translated into the home currency of the investor and will therefore be subject to changes in the value of the foreign currency. The formula is extended later in this section to include uncertain foreign cash flows translated at variable exchange rates. Thus the formula applies to international investments in general.

The formula is the same as for domestic investment, the difference is that the sources of variability are increased as the returns are denominated in foreign currency and have to be translated.

Since stock markets partially reflect the current and/or forecasted state of their countries' economies, they do not move in tandem. Thus, the returns of shares in different markets are not expected to be highly correlated. In Exhibit 3.10 the off-diagonal values are therefore likely to be lower than for a purely domestic portfolio – the diversification effect larger.

Crucial to the measurement of risk is an understanding as to how to predict variances and covariances of shares. Also, as these investments are foreign, the variance and covariance of exchange rates as well as shares is important. Sophisticated techniques such as Generalized Autoregressive Conditional Heteroskedasticity (GARCH) can be employed to predict volatility (i.e. standard deviation). Predicting covariances or correlations, however, is currently on the frontier of statistical modelling.

EXHIBIT 3.9   Calculating the variance of a two share portfolio – the variance covariance matrix

	Share A	Share B
Share A	$w_A^2 \times Var(A)$	$w_A \times w_B \times Cov(A, B)$
Share B	$w_B \times w_A \times Cov(B, A)$	$w_B^2 \times Var(B)$

Notes:
- This is a variance (*Var*) and Covariance (*Cov*) matrix of returns, where returns are defined as:

   $R_{UK} = (1 + R)(1 + e) - 1$ (where R_{UK} are the translated foreign returns (*R*) affected by currency changes (*e*) – see above):
- w_A and w_B are weights, the percentage of original investment in share A and share B valued in the home currency
- The top right and bottom left values are the same i.e. $w_A \times w_B \times Cov(A, B) = w_B \times w_A \times Cov(B,A)$:
- Covariances can be written using more familiar terms:

$$Cov(A, B) = SD_A \times SD_B \times Corr(A, B)$$

Where:
   SD_A, SD_B = standard deviations of A and B
   $Corr(A, B)$ = correlation of *A* and *B*
- $SD(A)2 = Var(A)$
- The standard deviation of the portfolio is simply the square root of the total of all the values in the cells of the above matrix.

EXHIBIT 3.10   Calculating the variance of a portfolio of three or more international investments

	International investment A	International investment B	International investment C	International investment D	International investment E
International investment A	$w_A^2 \times Var(A)$	$w_A \times w_B \times Cov(A, B)$	$w_A \times w_C \times Cov(A, C)$	$w_A \times w_D \times Cov(A, D)$	$w_A \times w_E \times Cov(A, E)$
International investment B	$w_A \times w_B \times Cov(A, B)$	$W_B^2 \times Var(B)$	$w_B \times w_C \times Cov(B, C)$	$w_B \times w_D \times Cov(B, D)$	$w_B \times w_E \times Cov(B, E)$
International investment C	$w_A \times w_C \times Cov(A, C)$	$w_B \times w_C \times Cov(B, C)$	$W_C^2 \times Var(C)$	$w_C \times w_D \times Cov(C, D)$	$w_C \times w_D \times Cov(C, E)$
International investment D	$w_A \times w_D \times Cov(A, D)$	$w_B \times w_D \times Cov(B, D)$	$w_C \times w_D \times Cov(C, D)$	$W_D^2 \times Var(D)$	$w_D \times w_E \times Cov(D, E)$
International investment E	$w_A \times w_E \times Cov(A, E)$	$w_B \times w_E \times Cov(B, E)$	$w_C \times w_D \times Cov(C, E)$	$w_D \times w_E \times Cov(D, E)$	$W_E^2 \times Var(E)$

Notes:
- The overall variance is simply the total value of all the cells in the matrix, for an explanation of the symbols see previous exhibit. Note that this matrix simply extends the pattern of Exhibit 3.9.
- The pattern can be extended to any number of investments, the lead diagonal is top left to bottom right (in bold), the values above the lead diagonal are a mirror image (the same), as the values below the lead diagonal – hence the 2 in the equation above.
- Note that the lead diagonal represents individual risk of the investments and will become progressively less important compared to their joint risk as the portfolio grows – at present five cells compared to 20 covariance cells – hence the diversifying effect.
- The order of the investments in the covariance term is the same, but note that the operation is commutative i.e. Cov(A, B) = Cov(B, A) and so on.

As an alternative to statistical modelling, businesses have to resort to subjective judgements on the future value of these variables. Aids to such judgements can be gleaned from simply modelling volatilities and correlations over time in Excel. Even in these circumstances, the model is useful in that it provides the 'language' for estimating portfolio risk.

The concept of an efficient market says that prices move randomly in response to news that is by definition randomly better or worse than the expectations built into the current price; it may therefore seem that any prediction is not possible. However, the randomness refers to the direction of movement, variance is a non-directional statement and says nothing about whether the currency values will go up or down. So predicting variances and indeed covariances and the derived measures of correlations, standard deviations or volatilities does not mean that the markets are inefficient.

EXAMPLE

Guess Investments plc wants to invest £100 000 in a portfolio of two foreign shares. The following are estimates of their returns translated into British pounds:

Investment in: share X £60 000; share Y £40 000

Expected return: share X 15 per cent; share Y 45 per cent

Standard deviation: share X 10 per cent; share Y 50 per cent

Correlation share X with share Y: 0.25

The weights are: $w_X = 60 000 / 100 000 = 0.60$; $w_Y = 40 000 / 100 000 = 0.40$

The expected returns on the portfolio are: $0.60 \times 15\% + 0.40 \times 45\% = 27\%$

The standard deviation of the portfolio is:

$$\sqrt{\begin{array}{l} 0.60^2 \times 0.10^2 + 0.40^2 \times 0.50^2 + 2 \times 0.40 \\ \times 0.60 \times 0.10 \times 0.50 \times 0.25 \end{array}} = 0.22$$

or 22%

So, assuming that the returns are jointly normally distributed (that is when their returns are considered jointly the overall returns are normally distributed), the 95 per cent confidence interval (see Appendix B) for the expected portfolio returns is:

$$1.96 \times 0.22 = 43\%$$

$$-16\% \xleftarrow{-43\%} 27\% \xleftarrow{+43\%} 70\%$$

The Guess director observes: 'There isn't much of a diversification effect as the weighted average of the standard deviations (i.e. assuming perfect correlation and hence no diversification) is $0.6 \times 10\% + 0.4 \times 50\% = 26\%$ as opposed to the 22% above.' His bright young assistant replies: 'True, but two investments hardly make a portfolio. Now if you didn't invest in X as your "safe" share, but just looked for security in diversification and invested only in four shares similar to Y, in four different stock markets, with say a correlation of 0.1 between any two, your overall standard deviation would be about ... 0.285 or 28.5 per cent. An expected return of 45 per cent with a standard deviation of 28.5 per cent is not bad, certainly better than this expected return of 27 per cent for a standard deviation of 22 per cent.' (You may check this calculation on the Portfolio Calculator.) The Guess Director replies: 'And what if all the markets collapse together? It has happened.'

Limitations of international diversification

Correlations between share indexes in differing stock markets are a proxy measure for the kind of correlation of returns one can expect from investing in shares in the differing stock markets – the correlation is therefore important. In general, correlations between share indexes have been higher in recent years than they were several years ago. The general increase in correlations among stock market returns reduces the opportunity to lower risk through international diversification unless exchange rate movements offer further reductions in co-movement.

USING THE WEB

Stock market performance

Charts showing recent stock market performance for each market can be found at Yahoo! by following the finance link. The prevailing share index level is shown for each country, as well as the performance of each market during the previous day. For some markets, you can assess the performance over the last year by clicking on chart next to the country's name.

One reason for the increased correlations among stock market returns is increased integration of business between countries. Foreign portfolio investments since 1985 have increased globally as restrictions have been lifted as part of the liberalization of capital markets. Institutional investors are increasingly holding international portfolios. Increased integration also results in more inter-country trade flows. In particular, many European countries have become more integrated as regulations have been standardized throughout Europe to facilitate trade between countries. In addition, the adoption of the euro has removed exchange rate risk due to trade between participating countries.

The conversion to the euro also allows portfolio managers in European countries to invest in shares of other participating European countries without concern for exchange rate risk, because these shares are also denominated in euros. This facilitates a more regional approach for European investors, who are not restricted to shares within their respective countries.

Since some stock market correlations may become more pronounced during a crisis, international diversification will not necessarily be as effective during a downturn as it is during more favourable conditions. This is an important point. The statistics used to capture the idea of diversification (covariance and

EXHIBIT 3.11   Integration among foreign stock markets during the 1987 crash

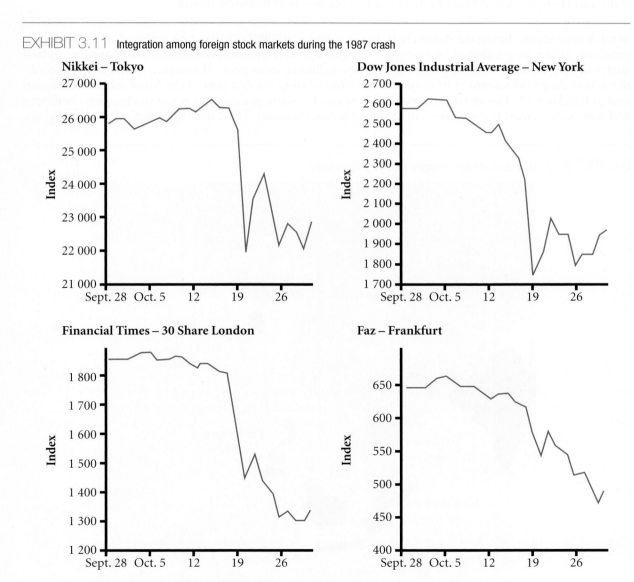

Source: Economic Trends Federal Reserve Bank of Cleveland (November 1987), p. 17.

correlation) are averages of co-movement. They assume that overall conditions are relatively constant and that the differing movements happen for temporary reasons. But clearly, if there is a major regime shift, as in a financial crisis, all markets are going to be affected and the kind of assumptions behind correlation measures may well not hold. Two such events that had just such an adverse effect on many markets, the 1987 crash and the Asian crisis, are discussed next.

Market movements during the 1987 crash. Further evidence on the relationships between stock markets is obtained by assessing market movements during the stock market crash in October 1987. Exhibit 3.11 shows the stock market movements for four major countries during the crash. While the magnitude of the decline was not exactly the same, all four markets were adversely affected. When institutional investors anticipated a general decline in shares, they sold some shares from all markets, instead of just their home market.

Many stock markets experienced larger declines in prices than US stock markets. For example, during the month of October 1987, the US market index declined by about 21 per cent, while the German market index declined by about 23 per cent and the UK index by 26 per cent. The stock market indexes of Australia and Hong Kong decreased by more than 50 per cent over this same month.

Market movements during the Asian crisis. In the summer of 1997, Thailand experienced severe economic problems, which were followed by economic downturns in several other Asian countries. Investors revalued shares downward because of weakened economic conditions, more political uncertainty and a lack of confidence that the problems would be resolved. The effects during the first year of the Asian crisis are summarized in Exhibit 3.12. This crisis demonstrated how quickly share prices could adjust to changing conditions and how adverse market conditions could spread across countries. Thus, diversification across Asia did not

EXHIBIT 3.12   How stock markets changed during the Asian crisis

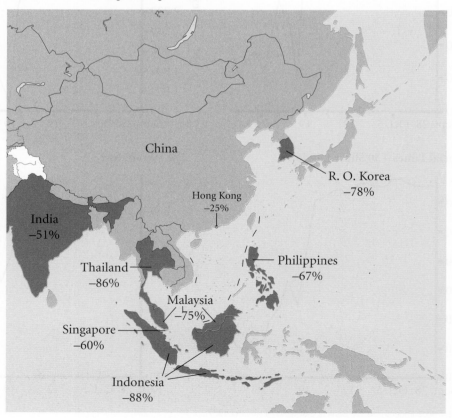

effectively insulate investors during the Asian crisis. Diversification across all continents would have been a more effective method of diversification during the crisis.

Although there has not been another world stock market crash since 1987, there have been several mini-crashes. For example, on 27 August 1998 (referred to as 'Bloody Thursday'), Russian shares and currency values declined abruptly in response to severe financial problems in Russia, and most stock markets around the world experienced losses on that day. US shares declined by more than 4 per cent on this day. The adverse effects extended beyond shares that would be directly affected by financial problems in Russia as paranoia caused investors to sell shares across all markets due to fears that all shares might be overvalued.

In response to the September 11, 2001, terrorist attacks on the USA, many stock markets experienced declines of more than 10 per cent over the following week. Diversification among markets was not very effective in reducing risk in this case. Note that the more recent world financial crisis of 2007 was not a stock market crisis as such.

VALUATION OF FOREIGN SHARES

When investors consider investing in foreign shares, they need methods for valuing those shares. The methods are no different from the valuation of domestic shares except that there are added complications from exchange rate movements.

Dividend discount model

One possibility is to use the dividend discount model with an adjustment to account for expected exchange rate movements. Foreign shares pay dividends in the currency in which they are denominated. Thus, the cash flow per period to European investors is the dividend (denominated in the foreign currency) converted to euros. Because of exchange rate uncertainty, the value of the foreign shares from a home investor's perspective is subject to exchange rate uncertainty as well as uncertainty over dividends.

Price-earnings method

An alternative method of valuing foreign shares is to apply price-earnings ratios. The expected earnings per share of the foreign firm are multiplied by the appropriate price-earnings ratio (based on the firm's risk and industry) to determine the appropriate price of the firm's shares. Although this method is easy to use, it is subject to some limitations when applied to valuing foreign shares. The price-earnings ratio for a given industry may change continuously in some foreign markets, especially when the industry is composed of just a few firms. Thus, it is difficult to determine the proper price-earnings ratio that should be applied to a specific foreign firm. In addition, the price-earnings ratio for any particular industry may need to be adjusted for the firm's country, since reported earnings can be influenced by the firm's accounting guidelines and tax laws. Furthermore, even if investors are comfortable with their estimate of the proper price-earnings ratio, the value derived by this method is denominated in the local foreign currency (since the estimated earnings are denominated in that currency). Therefore, investors would still need to consider exchange rate effects. Even if the share is undervalued in the foreign country, it may not necessarily generate a reasonable return for investors if the foreign currency depreciates against the home currency.

Other methods

Some investors adapt these methods when selecting foreign shares. For example, they may first assess the macroeconomic conditions of all countries to screen out those countries that are expected to experience poor conditions in the future. Then, they use other methods such as the dividend discount model or the price-earnings method to value specific firms within the countries that are appealing.

Why perceptions of share valuation differ among countries

A share that appears undervalued to investors in one country may seem overvalued to investors in another country. Some of the more common reasons why perceptions of a share's valuation may vary among investors in different countries are identified here.

Required rate of return. Some investors attempt to value a share according to the present value of the future cash flows that it will generate. The dividend discount model is one of many models that use this approach. The required rate of return that is used to discount the cash flows can vary substantially among countries. The rate is based on the prevailing risk-free interest rate available to investors, plus a risk premium.

Do countries apply the same risk premium to identical projects? Are some investment communities more risk averse than others? These are not settled questions. What can be said is that the more risky the project the lower the value of its share as a higher discount rate is applied. A foreign investor may think that the risk has been overpriced and that the share is a bargain and hence worth purchasing. Or the investor may see higher returns than are currently estimated for that share. Such judgements are the stuff of investment. For international investment it is this risk plus exchange rate risk.

The other element of the discount rate used to discount future dividends is the risk free rate. This interest rate is the newspaper rate quoted as the market rate between large banks. The rate includes an allowance for inflation and for the inconvenience of lending (sometimes called time preference). The rate is risk free in the sense that the investor is more or less guaranteed to receive the money as promised in the investment, as banks rarely go bankrupt. This rate differs between currencies (not countries). Thus, there is a single rate for the euro and a single rate for the British pound and one rate for the dollar, yen and so on. The rates differ, the 1-year rate for the euro LIBOR (London Interbank Offered Rate) is about 1.2 per cent, and is 1.29 per cent for the British pound and 0.85 per cent for the US dollar. Given that these are equilibrium rates in that they are determined by supply and demand in the marketplace, one might ask why everyone does not invest in the UK rather than in the euro, dollar and so on? From the point of view of the international investor on balance the higher rates are offset by concern that the value of the currency is less stable, and each interest rate requires the purchase of that particular currency.

One way of explaining the difference in the risk free rate is to look at differences in the constituent parts. Time preference probably does not vary between countries but inflation clearly does vary and may explain differences. But the fact that inflation may be higher in the UK is of little consequence to an investor who simply wants to buy shares, receive dividends and then convert the dividends to their home currency and then, at some later date, sell the shares and convert back. For the foreign investor the rationale for a difference lies in changes in the value of the currency between conversion dates – once again we return to the concept of exchange rate risk.

Exchange rate risk. Returns are determined by the rate earned in the local currency *and* any changes in the value of the currency between the investment date and the conversion back to the home currency date (see the Sunny Investments example above). The conversion process is termed exchange rate risk. The relationship between currency values, interest rates and inflation is explained further in the following chapter. But for the moment one can see that where a currency is suffering high inflation its value may well fall in relation to other currencies over time – as one unit of the currency buys less. A higher interest rate may well be needed to compensate for the expected loss in value of the currency. Hence interest rates between currencies may differ.

Taxes. The tax effects of dividends and capital gains also vary among countries. The lower a country's tax rates, the greater the proportion of the pre-tax cash flows received that the investor can retain. Other things being equal, investors based in low-tax countries should value shares higher. Differences in particular countries between the taxes levied on dividends and taxes on capital gains will create preferences within that country for shares that pay high dividends or shares that pay low dividends but have higher capital gains. A change in the tax laws of, say, the UK may make investments in that country more or less attractive to the UK.

METHODS USED TO INVEST INTERNATIONALLY

For investors attempting international share diversification, five common approaches are available:

- Direct purchases of foreign shares
- Investment in MNC shares
- American depository receipts (ADRs)
- Exchange-traded funds (ETFs)
- International mutual funds (IMFs).

Each approach is discussed in turn.

Direct purchases of foreign shares

Foreign shares can be purchased on foreign stock exchanges. This requires the services of brokerage firms that can contact floor brokers who work on the foreign stock exchange of concern. However, this approach is inefficient because of market imperfections such as insufficient information, transaction costs and tax differentials among countries.

An alternative method of investing directly in foreign shares is to purchase shares of foreign companies that are sold on the local stock exchange. In the USA, for example, Royal Dutch Shell (of the Netherlands), Sony (of Japan) and many other foreign shares are sold on US stock exchanges. Because the number of foreign shares listed on any local stock exchange is typically quite limited, this method by itself may not be adequate to achieve the full benefits of international diversification.

Investment in MNC shares

The operations of an MNC represent international diversification. Like an investor with a well-managed share portfolio, an MNC can reduce risk (variability in net cash flows) by diversifying sales not only among industries but also among countries. In this sense, the MNC as a single firm can achieve stability similar to that of an internationally diversified share portfolio. By investing in an MNC, the investor should gain from the diversification by having a share that behaves rather differently from local investments in non-MNCs. Perhaps surprisingly, the evidence is that MNC shares tend to behave in much the same way as less international shares on the same stock exchange and are not affected as might be expected by movements on other stock markets. This suggests that the diversification benefits from investing in an MNC are limited.

American depository receipts

Another approach is to purchase American depository receipts (ADRs), which are certificates representing ownership of foreign shares. More than 1000 ADRs are available in the USA, primarily traded on the OTC stock market. An investment in ADRs may be an adequate substitute for direct investment in foreign shares. Only a limited number of ADRs are available, however.

USING THE WEB

ADR performance

The performance of ADRs is provided at: http://www.adr.com. Click on Industry to review the share performance of ADRs within each industry. The website provides a table that shows information about the industry, including the number of ADRs in that industry, and the 6-month and 12-month returns. Click on any particular industry of interest to review the performance of individual ADRs in that industry.

Exchange-traded funds (ETFs)

Although investors have closely monitored international share indexes for years, they were typically unable to invest directly in these indexes. The index was simply a measure of performance for a set of shares but was not traded. Exchange-traded funds (ETFs) represent indexes that reflect composites of shares for particular countries; they were created to allow investors to invest directly in a share index representing any one of several countries. ETFs are sometimes referred to as world equity benchmark shares (WEBS) or as iShares.

International mutual funds

A final approach to consider is purchasing shares of **international mutual funds** (IMFs), which are portfolios of shares from various countries. Like domestic mutual funds, IMFs are popular due to: (1) the low minimum investment necessary to participate in the funds, (2) the presumed expertise of the portfolio managers and (3) the high degree of diversification achieved by the portfolios' inclusion of several shares. Many investors believe an IMF can better reduce risk than a purely domestic mutual fund because the IMF includes foreign securities. An IMF represents a pre-packaged portfolio, so investors who use it do not need to construct their own portfolios. Although some investors prefer to construct their own portfolios, the existence of numerous IMFs on the market today allows investors to select the one that most closely resembles the type of portfolio they would have constructed on their own. Moreover, some investors feel more comfortable with a professional manager managing the international portfolio.

Investment in risky foreign portfolios

For each investment in a portfolio of foreign shares there are *two* sources of risk, the exchange rate *and* the risk of the foreign investment itself. The following model addresses the problem of measuring the risk of a portfolio of assets where the price of the asset in the foreign currency and the price of the currency itself changes:

Consider an asset X_1 denominated in foreign currency, with exchange rate E_1 (in direct form). Let R_1 be the return on X_1 in its home country, so that $X_1 \rightarrow X_1(1 + R_1)$, and let R_{e1} be the return on the exchange rate, so that $E_1 \rightarrow E_1(1 + R_{e1})$. The X_1E_1 pounds invested becomes $X_1E_1(1 + R_1)(1 + R_{e1})$ pounds, or neglecting R_1Re_1 as being trivially small, it becomes $X_1E_1(1 + R_1 + Re_1)$ pounds.

Consider now an investment where a proportion w_1 of (home country currency) monies are invested in country 1, and w_2 in country 2, so that $w_1 + w_2 = 1$, and

$$w_1 = X_1E_1 / (X_1E_1 + X_2E_2)$$

Then the return is $R \approx w_1(R_1 + R_{e1}) + w_2(R_2 + R_{e2})$. Taking expectations, we get the same formula for expected return,

$$E(R) \approx w_1(E(R_1) + E(R_{e1})) + w_2(E(R_2) + E(R_{e2})):$$

Subtracting the expected return we get:

$$R - E(R) \approx w_1(R_1 - E(R_1) + R_{e1} - E(R_{e1})) + w_2(R_2 - E(R_2) + R_{e2} - E(R_{e2})).$$

Squaring this and taking the expectation across all possible returns, we obtain a formula for the variance σ^2 of the combined return. We write variances and covariances as e.g. σ_1^2, σ_{12}, and correlation as ρ so $\sigma_{12} = \sigma_1 \sigma_2 \rho_{12}$. With this notation, the overall risk (variance) of a portfolio of risky foreign investments can be given as:

$$\sigma^2 = w_1^2(\sigma_1^2 + \sigma_{e1}^2 + 2\sigma_{1e1}) + w_2^2(\sigma_2^2 + \sigma_{e2}^2 + 2\sigma_{2e2}) + 2w_1w_2(\sigma_{12} + \sigma_{1e2} + \sigma_{2e1} + \sigma_{e1e2}).$$

The matrix elements are therefore $w_1^2(\sigma_1^2 + \sigma_{e1}^2 + 2\sigma_{1e1})$ is the top left $w_2^2(\sigma_2^2 + \sigma_{e2}^2 + 2\sigma_{2e2})$, the bottom right and the remainder of the formula, the two off diagonal terms $2w_1w_2(\sigma_{12} + \sigma_{1e2} + \sigma_{2e1} + \sigma_{e1e2})$.

This extends to three countries using the matrix in Exhibit 3.10. Note that an inordinate number of correlations are required being 6 in the case of a two risky foreign asset portfolio (n = 2) and more generally $2n^2 - n$ so 15 correlations for three investments and so on.

The formula raises the empirical question as to how significant are the covariances, or can they be approximated as zero in some cases. Considering the case of a UK investor investing in French and US shares, the monthly correlation from February 1993 to December 2009 was 0.74 and the dollar and euro (or equivalent) movement in relation to the British pound was correlated at 0.29. There is clearly a rationale behind such co-movements: economic events can affect share values across countries and also across currencies. However, other correlations have no clear rationale, thus there is no reason why movements in the value of the dollar should be associated with movements in the value of the French Stock Exchange (0.12 correlation) or the euro with the US stock exchange (−0.07 correlation) and these might well be approximated to zero. Though one would expect that high nominal market returns to be associated with falls in the currency value, there clearly are other factors involved and over the period in question the correlations were −0.15 for the French Stock Market and the value of the euro and −0.07 for the US Stock Market and the value of the dollar. These are both very low and again might be approximated as zero. Added to this, of course, is the warning that calculating the overall variance of a portfolio (σ^2) does not fully describe actual variation. Extreme values in practice are more common than that predicted by the normal distribution (the so called 'fat tails' problem). In this particular example of investment in French and US shares there were 202 observations. Using the actual standard deviation over this period of 4.9 per cent with a mean return of 0.6 per cent one would expect to see 10 observations outside the 95 per cent confidence interval (5 per cent of the 202 observations); in fact there were 14 observations. Extreme variations are greater than predicted by the normal distribution. This is a consistent finding across all financial markets.

CHAPTER 4
EXCHANGE RATE DETERMINATION

LEARNING OBJECTIVES

The specific objectives of this chapter are to:

● Explain how exchange rate movements are measured.

● Explain how the equilibrium exchange rate is determined.

● Examine factors that affect the equilibrium exchange rate.

Financial managers of multinational corporations (MNCs) must continuously monitor exchange rates because their cash flows are highly dependent on changes in the rates. In a matter of days the value of a currency can fall by 5 per cent, 10 per cent or more. As a result, a potentially profitable contract or transaction can become unprofitable unless the risk has been managed in some way so that the effect is lessened without making the underlying business unprofitable. Financial managers therefore need to understand what factors influence exchange rates so that they can anticipate how exchange rates may change in response to specific conditions. This chapter provides a foundation for understanding how exchange rates are determined.

MEASURING EXCHANGE RATE MOVEMENTS

Exchange rate movements affect an MNC's value because they can affect the amount of cash inflows received from exporting or from a subsidiary, and the amount of cash outflows needed to pay for imports. An exchange rate measures the value of one currency in units of another currency. As economic conditions change, exchange rates can change substantially. A decline in a currency's value is often referred to as **depreciation** or **devaluation**. When the British pound depreciates against the US dollar, this means that the US dollar is strengthening relative to the pound. More pounds will be needed to buy a dollar. The increase in a currency value is often referred to as **appreciation**.

Unless stated otherwise, exchange rates will always be considered in direct form (see Chapter 3), that is so many units of home currency to one unit of foreign currency. Thus the exchange rate is a price of foreign currency and is in that way much like any other price. When a foreign currency's spot rates are compared at two specific points in time, the spot rate at the more recent date is denoted as S_t and the spot rate at the earlier date is denoted as S_{t-1}. The percentage change in the value of the foreign currency is computed as follows:

$$\text{Percentage change in a foreign currency value} = \frac{S_t - S_{t-1}}{S_{t-1}} \times 100$$

Using direct exchange rates, positive percentage change indicates that the foreign currency has appreciated, while a negative percentage change indicates that it has depreciated. As has been indicated, the values of currencies can vary greatly over a short time. For popular currencies there will be changes every day, indeed every hour on the foreign currency exchanges. Taking the euro as an example, on some days, most foreign currencies appreciate against the euro, although by different degrees. On other days, most currencies depreciate against the euro, but by different degrees. There are also days when some currencies appreciate while others depreciate against the euro; the media describe this scenario by stating that 'the euro was *mixed* in trading'.

Exhibit 4.1 shows how the euro changed against the South African rand on a quarterly basis from March 1993 to March 2010.

EXHIBIT 4.1   Quarterly changes in the value of the euro in terms of rand

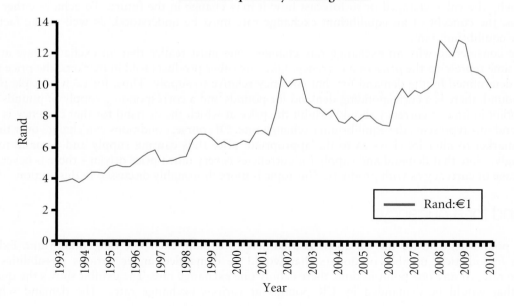

Rand: €1 quarterly exchange rates

EXAMPLE

Suppose a South African family goes skiing every year in France. If the bill in March of 2009 was €2000 the cost would have been 25 330 Rand (calculated as 12.6652R:€1 × €2000 – the approximate exchange rates are visible from the graph). However, the same holiday at the same price in euros the following March 2010 would have cost 19 760 Rand (calculated as 9.8801R:€1 × €2000). The holiday would have been 22 per cent cheaper (100 × (19 760 − 25 330) / 25 330) 1 year later solely due to the fall in value of the euro against the rand! By comparing March 2008 to March 2007 and assuming no change in the euro price, the holiday would have been 32 per cent more expensive – note the rise in value of the euro on the graph!

We are of course assuming that the price of the French holiday and the purchasing power of the rand are unchanged. Annual inflation in South Africa in March 2008 had been about 9½ per cent so in *relative* terms the cost of the holiday would have been only 22½ per cent (i.e. 32% − 9½%) more expensive (we assume that the family's salary kept pace with inflation). Also, the French hotel company (likely to be an MNC) might lower its euro price to take account of the appreciating euro (the euro had also appreciated 19 per cent against the dollar). The hotel may also advertise holidays priced in rands and increase the price by less than 32 per cent. More generally, a change in the exchange rate alters all prices between the two currencies. But the picture is not as simple as that, as the prices themselves which are both costs and revenues can alter due to inflation and competitive pricing.

It is important to understand the forces that can cause an exchange rate to change over time – the example illustrates some of the issues. MNCs that understand how currencies might be affected by existing forces can prepare for possible adverse effects on their expenses or revenue and may be able to reduce the impact on their profits.

EXCHANGE RATE EQUILIBRIUM

Although it is easy to measure the percentage change in the value of a currency, it is more difficult to explain why the value changed or to forecast how it may change in the future. To achieve either of these objectives, the concept of an **equilibrium exchange rate** must be understood, as well as the factors that affect the equilibrium rate.

Before considering why an exchange rate changes, one must realize that an exchange rate at a given point in time represents the *price* of a currency. Like any other products sold in markets, the price of a currency is determined by the demand for that currency relative to supply. Thus, for each possible price of a British pound, there is a corresponding demand for pounds and a corresponding supply of pounds for sale. At any point in time, a currency should exhibit the price at which the demand for that currency is equal to supply, and this represents the equilibrium exchange rate. Of course, conditions can change over time causing the market to alter its views as to the appropriate price thus causing supply and demand to change accordingly. Note that demand and supply for currencies is very much price driven – there is never a physical shortage of currency as with products. This topic is more thoroughly discussed in this section.

Demand for a currency

The UK pound demand for the US dollar is used here to explain exchange rate equilibrium. Exhibit 4.2 shows a hypothetical number of dollars that would be demanded under various possibilities for the exchange rate. At any one point in time, there is only one exchange rate. The exhibit shows the quantity of dollars that would be demanded by UK pounds at various exchange rates. The demand schedule is

EXHIBIT 4.2   UK demand schedule for US dollars

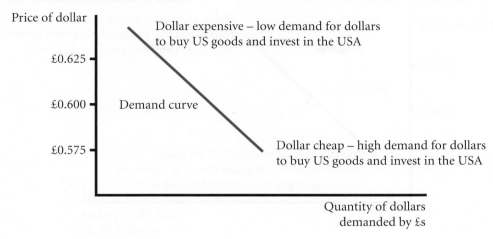

Note:
- Moving from an exchange rate of £0.625:$1 to £0.575:$1, US goods are (0.575 − 0.625)/0.625 = −0.08 or are 8 per cent cheaper.

downward sloping because UK corporations will be encouraged to purchase more US goods when the dollar is worth less, as it will take fewer British pounds to obtain the desired amount of dollars.

Supply of a currency for sale

Up to this point, only the UK demand for dollars has been considered, but the US demand for British pounds must also be considered. From the UK perspective, the US demand for the British pound results in a *supply of dollars for sale,* since dollars are supplied in the foreign exchange market in exchange for British pounds.

A supply schedule of dollars for sale in the foreign exchange market can be developed in a manner similar to the demand schedule for dollars. Exhibit 4.3 shows the quantity of dollars for sale (supplied to the foreign exchange market in exchange for pounds) corresponding to each possible exchange rate. Notice from the supply schedule in Exhibit 4.3 that there is a positive relationship between the value of the US dollar in British pounds and the quantity of US dollars for sale (supplied), which can be explained as follows. When the dollar is valued highly, US consumers and firms are more likely to purchase UK goods. Thus, they supply a greater number of dollars to the market, to be exchanged for pounds. Conversely, when the dollar is valued low, the supply of dollars for sale is smaller, reflecting less US desire to obtain the relatively more expensive UK goods.

Equilibrium

The demand and supply schedules for pounds by US dollars are combined in Exhibit 4.4. At an exchange rate of £0.575:$1, the quantity of dollars demanded would exceed the supply of dollars for sale. Consequently, banks providing foreign exchange services would experience a shortage of dollars at that exchange rate. At an exchange rate of £0.625:$1, the quantity of dollars demanded would be less than the supply of dollars for sale. Therefore, banks providing foreign exchange services would experience a surplus of dollars at that exchange rate. According to Exhibit 4.4, the equilibrium exchange rate is £0.600:$1 because this rate equates the quantity of dollars demanded with the supply of dollars for sale.

Impact of liquidity. For all currencies, the equilibrium exchange rate is reached through transactions in the foreign exchange market, but for some currencies, the adjustment process is more volatile than for others.

EXHIBIT 4.3 US supply schedule for British pounds

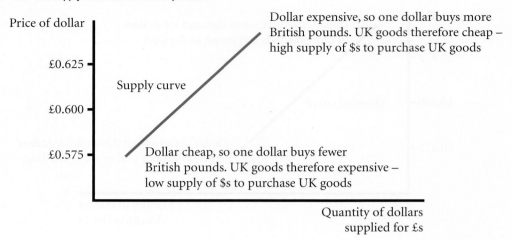

Price of dollar

Dollar expensive, so one dollar buys more
British pounds. UK goods therefore cheap –
high supply of $s to purchase UK goods

£0.625 —

Supply curve

£0.600 —

£0.575 —

Dollar cheap, so one dollar buys fewer
British pounds. UK goods therefore expensive –
low supply of $s to purchase UK goods

Quantity of dollars
supplied for £s

Notes:
- Adding some figures to the relationship, moving from an exchange rate of £0.625:$1 to £0.575:$1 means that for holders of US dollars the British pound will have increased in cost from $1.60:£1 to $1.74:£1 an increase of (1.74 – 1.60) / 1.60 ≈ 0.0875 or 8.75 per cent hence a low supply of dollars (note that these rates are the inverse of the $ rates, i.e. £0.625:$1 implies $1.60:£1 as 1/0.625 = 1.60 and 1/0.575 ≈ 1.74 see direct and indirect rates in the previous chapter).
- Compare these notes with the notes of Exhibit 4.2. For exactly the same change in exchange rates from £0.625:$1 to £0.575:$1, US goods have become 8 per cent cheaper for holders of British pounds; whereas UK goods have become 8.75 per cent more expensive for holders of US dollars. Surely the percentage changes should be the same! In fact they are not, the difference is known as Siegal's paradox and is currently thought to be of little consequence other than in explaining differences between calculations of the same events but viewed from differing home currencies.

EXHIBIT 4.4 Equilibrium exchange rate determination

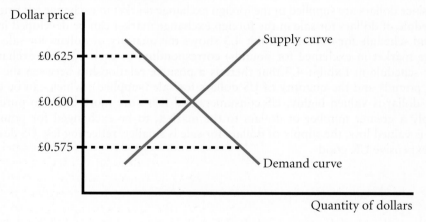

Dollar price

£0.625 ┄┄┄┄┄┄┄┄┄┄ Supply curve

£0.600 ┄ ┄ ┄ ┄ ┄ ┄

£0.575 ┄┄┄┄┄┄┄┄┄┄ Demand curve

Quantity of dollars

Note:
- The quantity of dollars now represents dollars demanded by British pounds and dollars offered or supplied for British pounds.

If the currency's spot market is liquid, its exchange rate will not be highly sensitive to a single large purchase or sale of the currency, such markets are termed 'deep'. Therefore, the change in the equilibrium exchange rate will be relatively small and the currency movement will not be volatile. With many willing buyers and sellers of the currency, transactions can be easily accommodated at the given rate. Conversely, if the currency's spot market is illiquid, its exchange rate may be highly sensitive to a single large purchase or sale transaction. There are not sufficient buyers or sellers to accommodate a large transaction, which means that the price of the currency must change to attract sufficient buyers and sellers to rebalance the supply and demand for the currency. Consequently, illiquid currencies tend to exhibit more volatile exchange rate movements, as the equilibrium prices of their currencies adjust to even minor changes in supply and demand conditions. Ideally, markets should be deep and broad. A deep market is liquid and can cope with large transactions. There is also the need for markets to be broad. A broad market has many different views as to the correct market price, and is not going to overreact to information. Therefore breadth is also important to stability.

FACTORS THAT INFLUENCE EXCHANGE RATES

The equilibrium exchange rate will change over time as supply and demand schedules change. The factors that cause currency supply and demand schedules to change are discussed here by relating each factor's influence to the demand and supply schedules graphically displayed in Exhibit 4.4. The following equation summarizes the factors that can influence a currency's spot rate:

$$e = f(\Delta INF, \Delta INT, \Delta INC, \Delta GC, \Delta EXP)$$

Where:

e = percentage change in the spot rate
Δ = Greek letter for delta where 'd' stands for difference or change
ΔINF = change in the differential between UK inflation and the foreign country's inflation
ΔINT = change in the differential between the UK interest rate and the foreign country's interest rate
ΔINC = change in the differential between the UK income level and the foreign country's income level
ΔGC = change in government controls
ΔEXP = change in expectations of future exchange rates

Relative inflation rates

Changes in relative inflation rates can affect international trade activity, which influences the demand for and supply of currencies and therefore influences exchange rates.

EXAMPLE

Consider how the demand and supply schedules displayed in Exhibit 4.4 would be affected if UK inflation suddenly increased substantially while US inflation remained the same. (Assume that both British and US firms sell goods that can serve as substitutes for each other.) The sudden jump in UK inflation should cause an increase in the UK demand for US goods, as they would be cheaper at the original exchange rate, leading to an increase in the UK demand for US dollars.

In addition, the jump in UK inflation should reduce the US desire for British goods and therefore reduce the supply of dollars wanting British pounds. These market reactions are illustrated in Exhibit 4.5. The increased UK demand for dollars and the reduced supply of dollars for

sale place upward pressure on the value of the dollar. According to Exhibit 4.5, the new equilibrium value is £0.610:$1.

If US inflation increased (rather than UK inflation), the opposite forces would occur. Assume there is a sudden and substantial increase in US inflation while UK inflation is low. Based on this information, answer the following questions: (1) How is the demand schedule for dollars affected? (2) How is the supply schedule of dollars for sale affected? (3) Will the new equilibrium value of the pound increase, decrease or remain unchanged? Based on the information given, the answers are (1) the demand schedule for dollars should shift inward, (2) the supply schedule of dollars

(Continued)

EXHIBIT 4.5   Impact of rising UK inflation on the equilibrium value of the US dollar

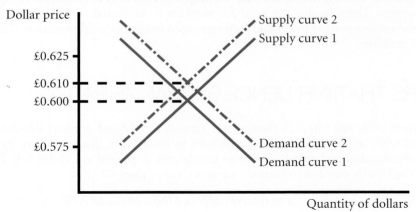

Note:
- The equilibrium rate changes from £0.600:$1 to £06610:$1.

for sale should shift outward and (3) the new equilibrium value of the dollar will decrease. Of course, the actual amount by which the dollar's value will decrease depends on the magnitude of the shifts. There is not enough information to determine their exact magnitude.

In reality, the actual demand and supply schedules, and therefore the true equilibrium exchange rate, will reflect several factors simultaneously. The point of the preceding example is to demonstrate how to logically work through the mechanics of the effect that higher inflation in a country can have on an exchange rate. Each factor is assessed one at a time to determine its separate influence on exchange rates, holding all other factors constant. Then, all factors can be tied together to fully explain why an exchange rate moves the way it does.

Relative interest rates

Changes in relative interest rates affect investment in foreign securities, which influences the demand for and supply of currencies and therefore influences exchange rates.

EXAMPLE

Assume that UK interest rates rise while US interest rates remain constant. In this case, UK investors are likely to reduce their demand for dollars, since UK rates are now more attractive relative to US rates, and there is therefore less desire for US bank deposits. Because UK rates will now look more attractive to US investors with excess cash, the supply of dollars for sale by US investors should increase as they establish more bank deposits in the UK. Due to an inward shift in the demand for dollars and an outward shift in the supply of dollars for sale, the equilibrium exchange rate or the value of the dollar should decrease. This is graphically represented in Exhibit 4.6. If UK interest rates decreased relative to US interest rates, the opposite shifts would be expected. This movement assumes that the expected change in the exchange rate would not wholly offset the higher interest rate. In effect the assumption is that the International Fisher Effect (Uncovered Interest Parity) does not hold. This form of trading is known as the carry trade.

EXHIBIT 4.6 Impact of rising UK interest rates on the equilibrium value of the US dollar in terms of British pounds

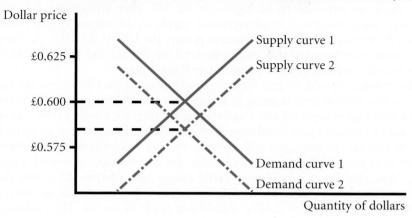

Notes:
- Demand and supply curves move from curve 1 to curve 2.
- Demand for dollars falls as home investments now seem relatively more attractive.
- Dollars supplied for British pounds increases in order to purchase UK securities offering the higher interest rate.

In some cases, an exchange rate between two countries' currencies can be affected by changes in a third country's interest rate, again assuming that the International Fisher Effect (Uncovered Interest Parity) does not hold.

EXAMPLE

When the euro interest rate increases, it can become more attractive to UK investors than the US rate. This encourages UK investors to purchase fewer dollar-denominated securities. Thus, the demand for dollars would be smaller than it would have been without the increase in euro interest rates for all given exchange rates, which places downward pressure on the value of the dollar in terms of the British pound.

It must be remembered that portfolio investment flows are very large in the international money markets, interest rates will therefore be an important part in determining the value of a currency.

Real interest rates. High interest rates on their own cannot be the only factor in determining the value of a currency, otherwise the currency offering the highest interest rate would attract all investment. So there must be factors that make a manager of a portfolio refrain from investing all funds in the currency offering the highest interest rate. That factor is a concern that although the interest rate is higher, there could well be an offsetting fall in the value of the currency with the higher interest rate. So if the UK is offering a LIBOR rate of 5 per cent and the USA is offering a rate of 3 per cent, a US portfolio manager who decides *not* to invest in the UK must be expecting the British pound to lose value against the dollar by at least 2 per cent (calculated as 5% − 3% = 2%), so that the net returns from investing in the UK would be the 5 per cent from the investment less at least the 2 per cent loss in the value of the British pound. The net return would therefore be no more than 5% − 2% = 3% the same as investing in the USA. So a higher interest rate would not attract all international investments as many investors would think that there is likely to be an even greater offsetting fall in the value of the currency.

Such reasoning leads to the question as to why the value of the British pound should be expected to fall if interest rates are higher? An American economist Irving Fisher suggested that interest rates were compensation for three elements: time, risk and inflation – the details are discussed in Chapter 7. For the LIBOR rates, time and risk elements of the interest rate (known as the **real interest rate**) should be the same between the USA and the UK; the only rationale for a difference is therefore inflation according to Fisher. If, for example, interest rates are expected to be higher in the UK after adjustment for inflation (i.e. higher expected real interest rates), there will be an increased supply of dollars for British pounds and a reduced demand for dollars by British pounds as investment prefers the UK to the USA. As shown in Exhibit 4.6 there would be a consequent leftward shift in the demand for dollars and rightward shift in the supply of dollars for British pounds resulting in a fall in the value of the dollar.

The US portfolio manager should, by this reasoning, only invest in the UK if he or she feels that the interest rate less inflation (or real interest rate) is going to be higher in the UK than in the USA. For the US portfolio manager, countries with higher expected real interest rates are offering a higher return after allowing for loss in currency value due to higher expected inflation. The currencies of such countries should be attractive and increase in value; though not all managers will agree, so the rise will be limited. But where a higher interest rate does not offset an expected fall in the currency value due to inflation, the overall return will be less than home investment. Note that Purchasing Power Parity theory (see Chapter 8) argues that exchange rates should exactly offset differences in inflation. The differences in inflations should in turn reflect differences in interest rates so *in theory* this form of trading should not result in profits. The evidence is, however, that exchange rate movements are poorly correlated with differences in interest and inflation rates. Exceptions to this finding are firstly in the long term, longer than the trading periods being considered here, and secondly, in extreme cases of hyper-inflation where economic instability becomes a dominating concern.

EXAMPLE

The investment manager at the UK company of BadGuess Investments plc is considering the interest rates offered in the USA (3.5 per cent), the UK (4 per cent), the euro (2 per cent) and Japan (0 per cent). She considers the inflation rates will be USA (2 per cent), the UK (3 per cent) the euro (0 per cent) and Japan (−1 per cent, deflation). She explains to her senior that: 'If I invest in the USA, inflation will be 1 per cent less than in the UK so the value of the dollar should rise by about 1 per cent against the British pound giving a return of 3.5% + 1% = 4.5%. The value of the euro should increase against the British pound by 3% − 0% = 3% a total return of 2% + 3% = 5% and for Japan the total return should be 4 per cent. So maybe we should be investing in the euro, it's offering 5 per cent as opposed to 4 per cent in the UK.' Her senior replies: 'Well OK, but your estimate is really a gamble that the value of the euro will rise against the British pound by 3 per cent, you say that this will happen because inflation is higher in the UK by 3 per cent, but there are many other factors that cause the value of currencies to change in relation to each other, such as the current problems of the constitution in the euro area.'

Such reasoning is flawed, although with a certain logic to it in that exchange rates *should* adjust to inflation and interest rate differences. In practice there is a large trade on the financial markets known as the carry trade whereby traders borrow in low interest countries and invest in higher interest countries. Borrowing in yen and investing in US dollars has been quite a frequent direction of trade. The trade is risky, however, in that the investment is converted back at the prevailing spot rate at the time and losses as well as profits can be made. But whenever governments attempt to manage interest rates or exchange they will indirectly fund the profits of financial institutions that identify the misalignment and engage in the carry trade.

Relative income levels

A third factor affecting exchange rates is relative income levels. Because income can affect the amount of imports demanded, it can affect exchange rates.

EXAMPLE

Assume that the UK income level rises substantially while the US income level remains unchanged. Consider the impact of this scenario on: (1) the demand schedule for dollars, (2) the supply schedule of dollars for sale and (3) the equilibrium exchange rate. First, the demand schedule for dollars will shift rightwards, reflecting the increase in UK income and therefore increased demand for US goods. Second, the supply schedule of dollars for sale is not expected to change as the US income level is constant. Therefore, the equilibrium exchange rate and value of the dollar are expected to rise, as shown in Exhibit 4.7.

EXHIBIT 4.7 **Impact of rising UK income levels relative to the USA on the equilibrium value of the US dollar**

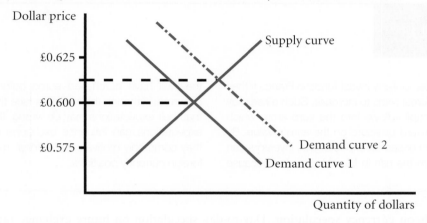

Note:
- Increase in UK income increases demand for goods generally including US imports, hence the higher demand for dollars.

Changing income levels can also affect exchange rates indirectly through effects on interest rates. When this effect is considered, the impact may differ from the theory presented here, as will be explained shortly.

Government controls

A fourth factor affecting exchange rates is government controls. The governments of foreign countries can influence the equilibrium exchange rate in many ways, including: (1) imposing foreign exchange barriers, (2) imposing foreign trade barriers, (3) intervening (buying and selling currencies) in the foreign exchange markets and (4) affecting macro variables such as inflation, interest rates and income levels. Chapter 6 covers these activities in detail.

EXAMPLE

Suppose the US real interest rates rose relative to British real interest rates. The expected reaction would an increase in the British supply of pounds for sale to obtain more US dollars (in order to capitalize on high US money market yields). Yet, if the British government placed a heavy tax on interest of income earned from foreign investments, this could discourage the exchange of pounds for dollars.

Expectations

A fifth factor affecting exchange rates is market expectations. Like other efficient financial markets, foreign exchange markets react immediately to any news that may have a future effect on demand and supply. By definition in finance, news is information that differs from expectations. This further complicates relationships in that an announcement of high inflation in the USA, if unexpected, may cause currency traders to sell dollars, anticipating a future decline in the dollar's value. But if the high inflation was less than expected then traders may buy dollars because the situation is better than at first thought. If in line with expectations, there may be no movement. So, an announcement of high inflation could have a positive, negative or no effect on the value of the dollar! The solution is that when analyzing the effect of factors on the value of a currency, the 'measure' should always be the difference between actual and expectations. Unfortunately expectations are hard to measure and for the most part academic models in using actual values implicitly assume that any actual change was unexpected. This is therefore a source of further inaccuracy in academic models as we do not really know whether or not an actual change in causal factors (interest or inflation rates) was expected.

EXAMPLE

Investors may temporarily invest funds in France if they expect euro interest rates to increase. Such a rise may cause further capital flows into the euro area, which could place upward pressure on the euro's value. By taking a position based on expectations, investors can fully benefit from the rise in the euro's value because they will have purchased euros before the change occurred. Although the investors face the obvious risk that their expectations may be wrong, the point is that expectations can influence exchange rates because they commonly motivate institutional investors to take foreign currency positions.

Impact of signals on currency speculation. Day-to-day speculation on future exchange rate movements is commonly driven by signals of future interest rate movements, but it can also be driven by other factors. Signals of the future economic conditions that affect exchange rates can change quickly, so the speculative positions in currencies may adjust quickly, causing unclear patterns in exchange rates. It is not unusual for the dollar to strengthen substantially on a given day, only to weaken substantially on the next day. This can occur when speculators overreact to news on one day (causing the dollar to be overvalued), which results in a correction on the next day. Overreactions occur because speculators are commonly taking positions based on signals of future actions (rather than the confirmation of actions), and these signals may be misleading.

When speculators speculate on currencies in emerging markets, they can have a substantial impact on exchange rates. Those markets have a smaller amount of foreign exchange trading for other purposes (such as international trade) and therefore are less liquid than the larger markets.

The abrupt decline in the Russian rouble on some days during 1998 was partially attributed to speculative trading (although the decline might have occurred anyway over time). The decline in the rouble created a lack of confidence in other emerging markets as well and caused speculators to sell off other emerging market currencies, such as those of Poland and Venezuela. The market for the rouble is not very active, so a sudden shift in positions by speculators can have a substantial impact. In June 2012 hedge funds were reported as taking out large short positions on the euro (borrowing in euros, selling them for, say, dollars, then repaying the euro loan at the expected lower euro rate). In fact the euro increased in value against the dollar over the next 6 months as much due to problems with the dollar.

Interaction of factors

Transactions within the foreign exchange markets facilitate either trade or financial flows. Trade-related foreign exchange transactions are generally less responsive to news. Financial flow transactions are very responsive to news, however, because decisions to hold securities denominated in a particular currency are often dependent on anticipated changes in currency values. Sometimes trade-related factors and financial factors interact and simultaneously affect exchange rate movements.

An increase in income levels sometimes causes expectations of higher interest rates. So, even though a higher income level can result in more imports, it may also indirectly attract more financial inflows (assuming interest rates increase). Because the favourable financial flows may overwhelm the unfavourable trade flows, an increase in income levels is frequently expected to strengthen the local currency.

Exhibit 4.8 separates payment flows between countries into trade-related and finance-related flows and summarizes the factors that affect these flows. Over a particular period, some factors may place upward pressure on the value of a foreign currency while other factors place downward pressure on the currency's value. The exact relationship between factors in practice is unclear allowing subjective processes such as market judgement to be significant in estimating future currency values.

The sensitivity of an exchange rate to these factors is dependent on the volume of international transactions between the two countries. If the two countries engage in a large volume of international trade but a very small

EXAMPLE

Assume the simultaneous existence of: (1) a sudden increase in UK inflation and (2) a sudden increase in UK interest rates. If the US economy is relatively unchanged, the increase in UK inflation will place upward pressure on the dollar's value while the increase in UK interest rates places downward pressure on the dollar's value.

EXHIBIT 4.8 Summary of factors affecting exchange rates

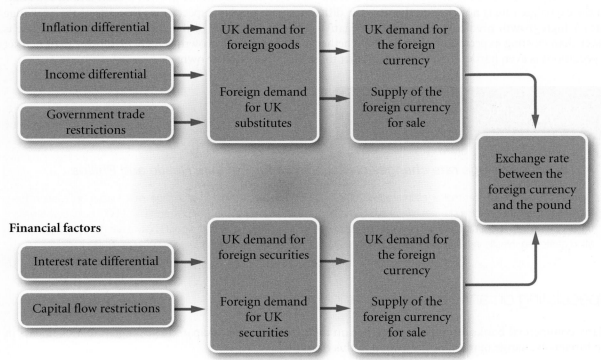

volume of international capital flows, the relative inflation rates will likely be more influential. If the two countries engage in a large volume of capital flows, however, interest rate fluctuations may be more influential.

EXAMPLE

Assume that Morgan AG, a German-based MNC, commonly purchases supplies from Venezuela and Bahrain and therefore desires to forecast the value of the Venezuelan bolivar and the Bahrain dinar in terms of euros.

Assume that Germany and Venezuela conduct a large volume of international trade but engage in minimal capital flow transactions. Venezuelan inflation is expected to be 5 per cent higher than in Germany.

Also, assume that Germany and Bahrain conduct very little international trade but frequently engage in capital flow transactions. Interest rates are expected to be 2 per cent higher in Germany than in Bahrain.

What should Morgan expect regarding the future value of the Venezuelan bolivar and the Bahrainian dinar?

The bolivar should be influenced most by trade-related factors because of Venezuela's assumed heavy trade with Germany. The expected inflationary changes should place downward pressure on the value of the bolivar. Interest rates are expected to have little direct impact on the bolivar because of the assumed infrequent capital flow.

The Bahrainian dinar should be most influenced by interest rates because of Bahrain's assumed heavy capital flow transactions with Germany. The expected interest rate changes should place upward pressure on the value of the euro in terms of the dinar. The inflationary changes are expected to have little direct impact on the dinar because of the assumed infrequent trade between the two countries.

Capital flows have become larger over time and can easily overwhelm trade flows. For this reason, the influence of factors such as inflation on interest rates has become increasingly important.

An understanding of exchange rate equilibrium does not guarantee accurate forecasts of future exchange rates because that will depend in part on how the factors that affect exchange rates will change in the future. Even if analysts fully realize how factors influence exchange rates, they may not be able to predict how those factors will change. Even if they can predict factors such as future economic growth and inflation, the effect on the exchange rate is not clear in that it is the difference with market expectations that affects the exchange rate. A high growth prediction may have a negative effect on the value of the currency if the growth rate is lower than existing expectations. Estimating whether or not economic growth is higher or lower than market expectations is even harder than trying to predict those variables on their own.

MANAGING FOR VALUE

Impact of exchange rate changes on cash flows for Renault, Nestlé and Philips

Renault SA the French car maker estimated in 2008 that there was a negative exchange-rate effect of €174 million on its operating margin, attributable mainly to the depreciation of sterling. Nestlé in 2009 made a 330 million Swiss franc provision for exchange rate losses. In relation to transactions the Philips group in 2009 held derivatives (see Chapter 5) that would show a net gain of €28m and in relation to loans the gain would be €302m.

Speculating on anticipated exchange rates

Many commercial banks attempt to capitalize on their forecasts of anticipated exchange rate movements in the foreign exchange market, as illustrated in this example.

- The European Bank expects the exchange rate of the New Zealand dollar (NZ$) to appreciate from its present level of 0.50 euros to 0.52 euros in 30 days. This is an increase in the value of the New Zealand dollar of 4 per cent (i.e. 0.52/0.5 − 1 = 0.04) over 30 days or an annualized increase of 60 per cent (i.e. using the exact method, $1.04^{360/30} - 1 = 0.601$, note that for large interest rates the simple method and exact method give widely differing rates). This is greatly in excess of the difference in interest rates, so the strategy is clear: buy into the New Zealand dollar and gain from the expected increase in value.

- The European Bank is able to borrow $20 million on a short-term basis from other banks.

- Present short-term interest rates (annualized) in the interbank market are as follows:

Currency	Lending rate	Borrowing
Euro	6.72%	7.20%
New Zealand dollar (NZ$)	6.48%	6.96%

Because brokers sometimes serve as intermediaries between banks, the lending rate differs from the borrowing rate. Given this information, the European Bank could:

1 Borrow 20 million euros.

2 Convert the 20 million euros to NZ$40 million (computed as 20 000 000 euros / 0.50).

3 Lend the New Zealand dollars at 6.48 per cent annualized, which represents a 0.54 per cent return over the 30-day period [computed as 6.48 per cent × (30/360)]. After 30 days, the bank will receive NZ$40 216 000 [computed as NZ$40 000 000 × (1 + 0.0054)].

4 Use the proceeds from the New Zealand dollar loan repayment (on day 30) to repay the euros borrowed. The annual interest on the euros borrowed is 7.2 per cent, or 0.6 per cent over the 30-day period [computed as 7.2 per cent × (30 / 360)]. The total NZ$ amount necessary to repay the loan is therefore NZ$38 692 308 [computed as 20 000 000 euros × (1 + 0.006)/0.52].

5 Given that the bank accumulated NZ$40 216 000 from its New Zealand dollar loan, it would earn a speculative profit of NZ$1 523 692 (being NZ$40 216 000 − NZ$38 692 308) or convert it to 792 320 euros (given a spot rate of 0.52 euros per New Zealand dollar on day 30 = 792 320 * 0.52). The bank would earn this speculative profit without using any funds from deposit accounts because the funds would have been borrowed through the interbank market.

A simple schema of the above events is shown below.

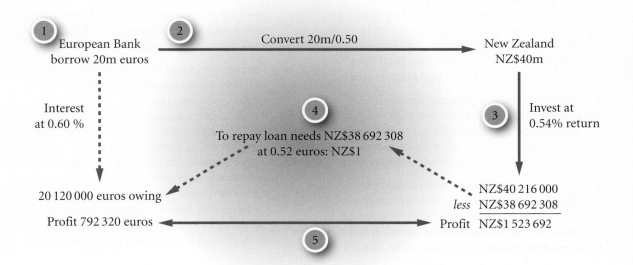

If instead the European Bank expects that the New Zealand dollar will depreciate, it can attempt to make a speculative profit by taking positions opposite to those just described. To illustrate, assume that the bank expects an exchange rate of 0.48 euros for the New Zealand dollar on day 30. It can borrow New Zealand dollars, convert them to euros, and lend the euros out. On day 30, it will close out these positions. Using the rates quoted in the previous example, and assuming the bank can borrow NZ$40 million, the bank takes the following steps:

1   Borrow NZ$40 million.

2   Convert the NZ$40 million to 20 million euros (computed as NZ$40 000 000 × 0.50 euro).

3   Lend the euros at 6.72 per cent, which represents a 0.56 per cent return over the 30-day period. After 30 days, the bank will receive 20 112 000 euros [computed as 20 000 000 euros × (1 + 0.0056)].

4   Use the proceeds of the euro loan repayment (on day 30) to repay the New Zealand dollars borrowed. The annual interest on the New Zealand dollars borrowed is 6.96 per cent, or 0.58 per cent over the 30-day period [computed as 6.96 × (30 / 360)]. The total New Zealand dollar amount necessary to repay the loan is therefore NZ$40 232 000 [computed as NZ$40 000 000 × (1 + 0.0058)].

5   Assuming that the exchange rate on day 30 is 0.48 euros per New Zealand dollar as anticipated, the number of euros necessary to repay the NZ$ loan is 19 311 360 euros (computed as NZ$40 232 000 × 0.48 euros per New Zealand dollar). Given that the bank accumulated 20 112 000 euros from its euro loan, it would earn a speculative profit of 800 640 euros without using any of its own money (computed as 20 112 000 euros −19 311 360 euros).

Most banks continue to take some speculative positions in foreign currencies. In fact, some banks' currency trading profits have exceeded $100 million per quarter lately.

The potential returns from foreign currency speculation are high for banks that have large borrowing capacity. Nevertheless, foreign exchange rates are very volatile and a poor forecast could result in a large loss. One of the best-known bank failures, Franklin National Bank in 1974, was primarily attributed to massive speculative losses from foreign currency positions.

SUMMARY

- Exchange rate movements are commonly measured by the percentage change in their values over a specified period, such as a month or a year. MNCs closely monitor exchange rate movements over the period in which they have cash flows denominated in the foreign currencies of concern.

- The equilibrium exchange rate between two currencies at any point in time is based on the demand and supply conditions. Changes in the demand for a currency or the supply of a currency for sale will affect the equilibrium exchange rate.

- The key economic factors that can influence exchange rate movements through their effects on demand and supply conditions are relative inflation rates, interest rates and income levels, as well as government controls. As these factors cause a change in international trade or financial flows, they affect the demand for a currency or the supply of currency for sale and therefore affect the equilibrium exchange rate.

- The two factors that are most closely monitored by foreign exchange market participants are relative inflation and interest rates.

    If a country experiences higher inflation than other countries, its exports should decrease (demand for its currency decreases), its imports should increase (supply of its currency increases), and there is downward pressure on its currency's equilibrium value.

    If a country experiences higher real interest rates (i.e. interest rate returns less expected loss in currency value due to inflation), the inflow of funds to purchase its securities should increase (demand for its currency increases), the outflow of its funds to purchase foreign securities should decrease (supply of its currency to be exchanged for foreign currency decreases), and there is upward pressure on its currency's equilibrium value.

- All relevant factors must be considered simultaneously to assess the likely movement in a currency's value.

CRITICAL DEBATE

The currencies of some Latin American countries depreciate against other currencies on a consistent basis. How can persistently weak currencies be stabilized?

Proposition. The governments of these countries need to increase the demand for their currency by attracting more capital flows. Raising interest rates will make their currencies more attractive to foreign investors. They also need to insure bank deposits so that foreign investors who invest in large bank deposits do not need to worry about default risk. In addition, they could impose capital restrictions on local investors to prevent capital outflows.

Opposing view. The governments of these countries print too much money because they make too many promises to the electorate that would otherwise have to be funded by higher taxes or borrowing at high interest rates. Printing money is the easy way out; but prices rise, exports decrease and imports increase. Thus, these countries could relieve the downward pressure on their local currencies by printing less money and thereby reducing the money supply and hence inflation. The outcome is likely to be a temporary reduction in economic growth and business failures. Higher interest rates would merely increase inflation.

Reply. Solutions that cause riots are not very clever.

With whom do you agree? Which argument do you support? Offer your own opinion on this issue.

SELF TEST

Answers are provided in Appendix A at the back of the text.

1 Briefly describe how various economic factors can affect the equilibrium exchange rate of the Japanese yen's value with respect to that of the pound.

2 A recent shift in the interest rate differential between the UK and Country A had a large effect on the value of Currency A. However, the same shift in the interest rate differential between the UK and Country B had no effect on the value of Currency B. Explain why the effects may vary.

3 Smart Banking plc can borrow £5 million at 6 per cent annualized. It can use the proceeds to invest in US dollars at 9 per cent per year over a 6-day period. The US dollar is worth £0.60 and is expected to be worth £0.59 in 6 days. Based on this information, should Smart Banking plc borrow pounds and invest in US dollars? What would be the gain or loss in pounds?

QUESTIONS AND APPLICATIONS

1 **Percentage depreciation.** Assume the spot rate of the US dollar is £0.54. The expected spot rate 1 year from now is assumed to be £0.51. What percentage depreciation does this reflect?

2 **Inflation effects on exchange rates.** Assume that the UK inflation rate becomes high relative to euro inflation. Other things being equal, how should this affect the: (a) UK demand for euros, (b) supply of euros for foreign currency and (c) equilibrium value of the euro?

3 **Interest rate effects on exchange rates.** Assume euro interest rates fall relative to British interest rates. Other things being equal, how should this affect the: (a) euro demand for British pounds, (b) supply of

pounds for sale and (c) equilibrium value of the pound?

4 **Income effects on exchange rates.** Assume that the income level in the euro area rises at a much higher rate than does the UK income level. Other things being equal, how should this affect the: (a) euro area demand for British pounds, (b) supply of British pounds for sale and (c) equilibrium value of the British pound in terms of the euro?

5 **Trade restriction effects on exchange rates.** Assume that the Japanese government relaxes its controls on imports by Japanese companies. Other things being equal, how should this affect the: (a) UK demand for Japanese yen, (b) supply of yen for sale and (c) equilibrium value of the yen?

6 **Effects of real interest rates.** What is the expected relationship between the relative real interest rates of two countries and the exchange rate of their currencies?

7 **Speculative effects on exchange rates.** Explain why a public forecast about the future value of the euro by a respected economist about future interest rates could affect the value of the euro today. Why do some forecasts by well-respected economists have no impact on today's value of the euro?

8 **Factors affecting exchange rates.** What factors affect the future movements in the value of the euro against the dollar?

9 **Interaction of exchange rates.** Assume that there are substantial capital flows between the UK, the USA and the euro area. If interest rates in the UK decline to a level below the US interest rate, and inflationary expectations remain unchanged, how could this affect the value of the euro against the US dollar? How might this decline in the UK's interest rate possibly affect the value of the British pound against the euro?

10 **Trade deficit effects on exchange rates.** Every month, the UK trade deficit figures are announced. Foreign exchange traders often react to this announcement and even attempt to forecast the figures before they are announced.

a Why do you think the trade deficit announcement sometimes has such an impact on foreign exchange trading?

b In some periods, foreign exchange traders do not respond to a trade deficit announcement, even when the announced deficit is very large. Offer an explanation for such a lack of response.

11 **Co-movements of exchange rates.** Explain why the value of the British pound against the dollar will not always move in tandem with the value of the euro against the dollar.

12 **Factors affecting exchange rates.** In the 1990s, Russia was attempting to import more goods but had little to offer other countries in terms of potential exports. In addition, Russia's inflation rate was high. Explain the type of pressure that these factors placed on the Russian currency.

13 **National income effects.** Analysts commonly attribute the appreciation of a currency to expectations that economic conditions will strengthen. Yet, this chapter suggests that when other factors are held constant, increased national income could increase imports and cause the local currency to weaken. In reality, other factors are not constant. What other factor is likely to be affected by increased economic growth and could place upward pressure on the value of the local currency?

14 **Factors affecting exchange rates.** If the Asian countries experience a decline in economic growth (and experience a decline in inflation and interest rates as a result), how will their currency values (relative to the British pound) be affected?

15 **Impact of crises.** Why do you think most crises in countries cause the local currency to weaken abruptly? Is it because of trade or capital flows?

16 How do you think the weaker economic conditions would affect trade flows in a **developing country**? How would weaker conditions affect the value of its currency (holding other factors constant)? How do you think interest rates would be?

ADVANCED QUESTIONS

17 **Measuring effects on exchange rates.** Tarheel Co. plans to determine how changes in UK and euro

real interest rates will affect the value of the British pound.

a Describe a regression model that could be used to achieve this purpose. Also explain the expected sign of the regression coefficient (see Appendix B).

b If Tarheel Co. thinks that the existence of a quota in particular historical periods may have affected exchange rates, how might this be accounted for in the regression model?

18 **Factors affecting exchange rates.** Mexico tends to have much higher inflation than the USA and also much higher interest rates than the USA. Inflation and interest rates are much more volatile in Mexico than in industrialized countries. The value of the Mexican peso is typically more volatile than the currencies of industrialized countries from a US perspective; it has typically depreciated from one year to the next, but the degree of depreciation has varied substantially. The bid/ask spread tends to be wider for the peso than for currencies of industrialized countries.

a Identify the most obvious economic reason for the persistent depreciation of the peso.

b High interest rates are commonly expected to strengthen a country's currency because they can encourage foreign investment in securities in that country, which results in the exchange of other currencies for that currency. Yet, the peso's value has declined against the dollar over most years even though Mexican interest rates are typically much higher than US interest rates. Thus, it appears that the high Mexican interest rates do not attract substantial US investment in Mexico's securities. Why do you think US investors do not try to capitalize on the high interest rates in Mexico?

c Why do you think the bid/ask spread is higher for pesos than for currencies of industrialized countries? How does this affect a US firm that does substantial business in Mexico?

19 **Aggregate effects on exchange rates.** Assume that the UK invests heavily in government and corporate securities of Country K. In addition, residents of Country K invest heavily in the UK. Approximately £10 billion worth of investment transactions occur between these two countries each year. The total value of trade transactions per year is about £8 million. This information is expected to also hold in the future.

Because your firm exports goods to Country K, your job as international cash manager requires you to forecast the value of Country K's currency (the 'krank') with respect to the dollar. Explain how each of the following conditions will affect the value of the krank, holding other things equal. Then, aggregate all of these impacts to develop an overall forecast of the krank's movement against the dollar.

a UK inflation has suddenly increased substantially, while Country K's inflation remains low.

b UK interest rates have increased substantially, while Country K's interest rates remain low. Investors of both countries are attracted to high interest rates.

c The UK income level increased substantially, while Country K's income level has remained unchanged.

d The UK is expected to impose a small tariff on goods imported from Country K.

e Combine all expected impacts to develop an overall forecast.

20 **Speculation.** Blue Demon Bank expects that the Mexican peso will depreciate against the dollar from its spot rate of $0.15 to $0.14 in *10 days*. The following *annual* interbank lending and borrowing rates exist:

Currency	Lending rate	Borrowing rate
US dollar	8%	8.3%
Mexican peso	8.5%	8.7%

Assume that Blue Demon Bank has a borrowing capacity of either $10 million or 70 million pesos in the interbank market, depending on which currency it wants to borrow.

a How could Blue Demon Bank attempt to capitalize on its expectations without using deposited funds? Estimate the profits that could be generated from this strategy.

b Assume all the preceding information with this exception: Blue Demon Bank expects the peso to appreciate from its present spot rate of $0.15 to $0.17 in 30 days. How could it attempt to capitalize on its expectations without using deposited funds? Estimate the profits that could be generated from this strategy.

21 **Speculation.** Diamond Bank expects that the Singapore dollar will depreciate against the euro from its spot rate of 0.48 euros to 0.45 euros in 60 days. The following interbank lending and borrowing rates exist:

Currency	Lending rate	Borrowing rate
Euro	7.0%	7.2%
Singapore dollar	22.0%	24.0%

Diamond Bank considers borrowing 10 million Singapore dollars in the interbank market and investing the funds in euros for 60 days. Estimate the profits (or losses) that could be earned from this strategy. Should Diamond Bank pursue this strategy?

PROJECT WORKSHOP

22 **Exchange rates online.** Download the exchange rate between any two major currencies on a daily basis for the last 5 years. You may download exchange rates either from your institution or from http://www.oanda.com. You will then need to load the figures into Excel.

a Select the days with the ten largest percentage changes in the exchange rate. Consult via online

newspapers (provided by your institution) the financial news related to the change in the exchange rate. Then examine and critically comment on the reasons for the change in the exchange rate as given in the financial press.

b How is the exercise in part (a) of this question related to the concept of market efficiency?

DISCUSSION IN THE BOARDROOM

This exercise can be found on our dedicated Course-Mate platform for students.

RUNNING YOUR OWN MNC

This exercise can be found on our dedicated Course-Mate platform for students.

Essays/discussion and articles can be found at the end of Part I.

BLADES PLC CASE STUDY

Assessment of future exchange rate movements

As the chief financial officer of Blades plc Ben Holt is pleased that his current system of exporting 'Speedos' to Thailand seems to be working well. Blades' primary customer in Thailand, a retailer called Entertainment Products, has committed itself to purchasing a fixed number of Speedos annually for the next 3 years at a fixed price denominated in baht, Thailand's currency. Furthermore, Blades is using a Thai supplier for some of the components needed to manufacture Speedos. Nevertheless, Holt is concerned about recent developments in Asia. Foreign investors from various countries had invested heavily in Thailand to take advantage of the high interest rates there. As a result of the weak economy in Thailand, however, many foreign investors have lost confidence in Thailand and have withdrawn their funds.

Ben Holt has two major concerns regarding these developments. First, he is wondering how these changes in Thailand's economy could affect the value of the Thai baht and, consequently, Blades. More specifically, he is wondering whether the effects on the Thai baht may affect Blades even though its primary Thai customer is committed to Blades over the next 3 years.

Second, Holt believes that Blades may be able to speculate on the anticipated movement of the baht, but he is uncertain about the procedure needed to accomplish this. To facilitate Holt's understanding of exchange rate speculation, he has asked you, Blades' financial analyst, to provide him with detailed illustrations of two scenarios. In the first, the baht would move from a current level of £0.0147 to £0.0133 within the next 30 days. Under the second scenario, the baht would move from its current level to £0.0167 within the next 30 days.

Based on Holt's needs, he has provided you with the following list of questions to be answered:

1 How are percentage changes in a currency's value measured? Illustrate your answer numeri-cally by assuming a change in the Thai baht's value from a value of £0.0147 to £0.0173.

2 What are the basic factors that determine the value of a currency? In equilibrium, what is the relationship between these factors?

3 How might the relatively high levels of inflation and interest rates in Thailand have affected the baht's value? (Assume a constant level of UK inflation and interest rates.)

4 How do you think the loss of confidence in the Thai baht, evidenced by the withdrawal of funds from Thailand, affected the baht's value? Would Blades be affected by the change in value, given the primary Thai customer's commitment?

5 Assume that Thailand's central bank wishes to prevent a withdrawal of funds from its country in order to prevent further changes in the currency's value. How could it accomplish this objective using interest rates?

6 Construct a spreadsheet illustrating the steps Blades' treasurer would need to follow in order to speculate on expected movements in the baht's value over the next 30 days. Also show the speculative profit (in pounds) resulting from each scenario. Use both of Ben Holt's examples to illustrate possible speculation. Assume that Blades can borrow either £7 million or the baht equivalent of this amount. Furthermore, assume that the following short-term interest rates (annualized) are available to Blades:

Currency	Lending rate	Borrowing rate
British pounds	8.10%	8.20%
Thai baht	14.80%	15.40%

SMALL BUSINESS DILEMMA

Assessment by the Sports Exports Company of factors that affect the British pound's value

Because the Sports Exports Company (an Irish firm) receives payments in British pounds every month and converts those pounds into euros, it needs to closely monitor the value of the British pound in the future. Jim Logan, owner of the Sports Exports Company, expects that inflation will rise substantially in the UK, while inflation in Ireland will remain low. He also expects that the interest rates in both countries will rise by about the same amount.

1 Given Jim's expectations, forecast whether the pound will appreciate or depreciate against the euro over time.

2 Given Jim's expectations, will the Sports Exports Company be favourably or unfavourably affected by the future changes in the value of the pound?

CHAPTER 5
CURRENCY
DERIVATIVES

LEARNING OBJECTIVES

The specific objectives of this chapter are to:

● Explain how forward contracts are used to hedge based on anticipated exchange rate movements.

● Describe how currency futures contracts are used to speculate or hedge based on anticipated exchange rate movements.

● Explain how currency options contracts are used to speculate or hedge based on anticipated exchange rate movements.

This chapter is devoted entirely to currency derivatives, often used by speculators interested in trading currencies simply to achieve profits but also used by firms to cover the risk of their foreign currency positions. A currency derivative is a contract whose price is derived from the value and price behaviour of the underlying currency that it represents. Multinational corporations (MNCs) commonly take positions in currency derivatives to reduce the risk of (or hedge) their exposure to exchange rate risk. Their managers must understand how these derivatives can be used to achieve corporate goals.

FORWARD MARKET

The forward market facilitates the trading of forward contracts on currencies. A forward contract is an agreement between a corporation and a commercial bank to exchange a specified amount of a currency at a specified exchange rate (called the forward rate) on a specified date in the future. When MNCs anticipate a future need for or future receipt of a foreign currency, they can set up forward contracts to lock in the rate at which they can purchase or sell a particular foreign currency. Virtually all large MNCs use forward contracts. Some MNCs have forward contracts of outstanding worth of more than £100 million to hedge various positions.

Because forward contracts accommodate large corporations, the forward transaction will often be valued for very large sums. Forward contracts normally are not used by consumers or small firms. In cases when a bank does not know a corporation well or fully trust it, the bank may request that the corporation make an initial deposit to assure that it will fulfil its obligation. Such a deposit is called a compensating balance and typically does not pay interest.

The most common forward contracts are for 30, 60, 90, 180 and 360 days, although other periods (including longer periods) are available. The forward rate of a given currency will typically vary with the length (number of days) of the forward period.

How MNCs use forward contracts

MNCs use forward contracts to hedge their imports. They can lock in the rate at which they obtain a currency needed to purchase imports.

EXAMPLE

Freeze plc is an MNC based in Birmingham that will need 1 000 000 Singapore dollars in 90 days to purchase Singapore imports. It can buy Singapore dollars for immediate delivery at the spot rate of £0.35 per Singapore dollar (S$). At this spot rate, the firm would need £350 000 (computed as S$1 000 000 × £0.35 per Singapore dollar). However, it does not have the funds right now to exchange for Singapore dollars. It could wait 90 days and then exchange pounds for Singapore dollars at the spot rate existing at that time. But Freeze does not know what the spot rate will be at that time. If the rate rises to £0.40 by then, Freeze will need £400 000 (computed as S$1 000 000 × £0.40 per Singapore dollar), an additional outlay of £50 000 due to the appreciation of the Singapore dollar.

To avoid exposure to exchange rate risk, Freeze can lock in the rate it will pay for Singapore dollars 90 days from now without having to exchange British pounds for Singapore dollars immediately. Specifically, Freeze can negotiate a forward contract with a bank to purchase S$1 000 000 at 90 days forward. Subsequent deals will have to be done at the new rate but by then Freeze will be able to adjust its selling prices to ensure a profit. The advantage of the forward rate is to seal the profit on existing deals.

The ability of a forward contract to lock in an exchange rate can create an opportunity cost in some cases.

EXAMPLE

Assume that in the previous example, Freeze negotiated a 90–day forward rate of £0.38 to purchase S$1 000 000. If the spot rate in 90 days is £0.37, Freeze will have paid £0.01 per unit or £10 000 (1 000 000 units × £0.01) more for the Singapore dollars as a result of taking out a forward contract. But this cost can also be seen as something of an insurance payment in that Freeze avoided the possibility of having to pay much more on the spot market.

Corporations also use the forward market to lock in the rate at which they can sell foreign currencies. This strategy is used to hedge against the possibility of those currencies depreciating over time.

EXAMPLE

Scanlon plc, based in the UK, exports products to a French firm and will receive payment of 400 000 euros in 4 months. It can lock in the value of the British pounds to be received from this transaction by selling euros forward. That is, Scanlon can negotiate a forward contract with a bank to sell the 400 000 euros for British pounds at a specified forward rate today. Assume the prevailing 4-month forward rate on euros is £0.60:1 euro. In 4 months, Scanlon will exchange its 400 000 euros for £240 000 (computed as 400 000 euros × £0.60 = £240 000).

Bid/Ask spread. Like spot rates, forward rates have a bid/ask spread. For example, a bank may set up a contract with one company agreeing to sell to the company Singapore dollars 90 days from now at £0.36 per Singapore dollar. This represents the ask rate. At the same time, the bank may agree to purchase (bid) Singapore dollars 90 days from now from some other company at £0.35 per Singapore dollar.

The spread between the bid and ask prices is wider for forward rates of currencies of developing countries, such as Chile, Mexico, South Korea and Thailand. Because these markets have relatively few orders for forward contracts, banks are less able to match up willing buyers and sellers. This lack of liquidity causes banks to widen the bid/ask spread when quoting forward contracts. The wider spread gives banks more profit to cope with the greater risk of having to buy the currency from another bank to complete the deal – an unprofitable course of action. The contracts in these countries are generally available only for short-term horizons.

Premium or discount on the forward rate. A forward rate for buying or selling currency is said to be at a premium or discount compared to the current spot rate.

Where the forward rate is at a premium, the foreign currency is more expensive than the current cost as given by the spot rate.

Where the forward rate is at a discount, the foreign currency is less expensive than the current cost as given by the spot rate.

The premium and discount are usually expressed as a percentage movement from the current spot price. Measuring the difference as a percentage helps in estimating the effect on proposed transactions. So if the US dollar is at a premium of 2 per cent in 60 days time against the euro, buying dollars in 60 days time will be 2 per cent more expensive than buying today.

More formally, the forward rate is equal to the spot rate multiplied by a premium or discount:

$$F_{t+1,\,t} = S_t(1+p)$$

Where:

$F_{t+1,\,t}$ = forward rate (in direct form, i.e. so many units of domestic currency for one unit of foreign currency) quoted at time t for exchange at time t+1

S_t = spot rate (in direct form, i.e. so many units of domestic currency for one unit of foreign currency) quoted at time t for exchange within 2 days

p = the forward premium (+) or discount (−) expressed as 0.05 for 5 per cent, etc.

For clarity, the subscripts will be omitted, thus the forward rate will be expressed as:

$$F = S(1+p)$$

EXAMPLE

If the euro's spot rate is £0.70, and its 1-year forward rate has a forward premium of 2 per cent, the 1-year forward rate is:

$$F = S(1 + p)$$
$$= 0.70(1 + 0.2)$$
$$= £0.714$$

Given quotations for the spot rate and the forward rate at a given point in time, the premium can be determined by rearranging the above equation:

$$F = S(1 + p)$$
$$F/S = 1 + p$$
$$F/S - 1 = p$$

EXAMPLE

If the euro's 1-year forward rate is quoted at £0.714 and the euro's spot rate is quoted at £0.70, the euro's forward premium is:

$$F/S - 1 = p$$
$$0.714/0.70 - 1 = 0.02 \text{ or } 2\%$$

When the forward rate is less than the prevailing spot rate, the **forward premium** is negative. Another term used for a negative premium is a discount.

EXAMPLE

If the euro's 1-year forward rate is quoted at £0.6596 and the euro's spot rate is quoted at £0.68, the euro's forward premium is:

Since p is negative, the forward rate contains a discount.

$$F/S - 1 = p$$
$$0.6596/0.68 - 1 = -0.03 \text{ or } -3\%$$

Assume the forward exchange rates of the British pound for various maturities as shown in the second column of Exhibit 5.1. Based on each forward exchange rate, the **forward discount** can be computed on an annualized basis, as shown in Exhibit 5.1.

In some situations, a firm may prefer to assess the premium or discount on an unannualized basis. In this case, it would not include the fraction that represents the number of periods per year in the formula. Note that the formula uses an approximate basis as often found in practice, the actuarial approach is also to be found (see Appendix B).

EXHIBIT 5.1 Computation of forward rate premiums or discounts

Type of exchange rate for the euro	Market quote: value of 1 euro	Maturity	Annualized premium (+) or discount (–)
Spot	£0.6813	now	0
30-day forward rate	£0.6829	30 days	$\frac{(0.6829 - 0.6813)}{0.6813} \times \frac{360}{30} = 2.8\%$
90-day forward rate	£0.6859	90 days	$\frac{(0.6859 - 0.6813)}{0.6813} \times \frac{360}{90} = 2.7\%$
180-day forward rate	£0.6977	180 days	$\frac{(0.6977 - 0.6813)}{0.677} \times \frac{360}{180} = 4.8\%$

Arbitrage. Forward rates typically differ from the spot rate for any given currency. The difference is dictated by arbitrage possibilities. It should *not* be possible to make a riskless profit through buying and selling currencies. In the case of forward rates, the arbitrageur could borrow in the country with the lower interest rate, invest in the country with the higher interest rate and arrange a conversion back into the original currency using the forward rate. So, borrow, convert to foreign currency, invest, then convert back at the forward rate. The 'round trip' would be without risk as interest rates and exchange rates would all be guaranteed at the outset. Although the arbitrageur would earn more interest than he or she is paying, that benefit would almost certainly be lost by the forward discount (or exchange rate loss) of the currency offering the higher interest rate. Transaction costs can also be significant in preventing profit possibilities. Consequently, the forward rate usually contains a premium (or discount) that reflects the difference between the home interest rate and the foreign interest rate.

Movements in the forward rate over time. Because of the arbitrage possibilities (above), the forward exchange rate between any two currencies will depend on the interest rates in those countries and the current spot rate. Any movement over time in the spot rate and the interest rates of the two countries will affect the forward rate. For example, if the spot rate of the euro (the value of the euro in terms of British pounds) increased by 4 per cent from a month ago, the forward rate would have also increased by 4 per cent providing that the difference between the interest rates remained the same. The effect of interest rates will be investigated further in Chapter 7. The forward rate is only a good predictor of the spot rate in so far as the difference in interest rates and the spot rate is a good predictor of the future spot rate. Arbitrage ties the forward rate to the spot and interest rates. As a result, although it sounds like a prediction, the forward rate is not an independent forecast.

USING THE WEB

Forward rates

Forward rates can be accessed on a day-by-day basis by following the market data tab on the *Financial Times* site at: http://www.ft.com/. The website shows the forward rate for 1 month, 3 months and 1 year for a range of currencies and interest rates for a wide range of countries.

Offsetting a forward contract. In some cases, an MNC may desire to offset a forward contract that it previously created. This is a common way in the financial markets of ending a contract. The simple idea is that if Company M owes 1 million Argentine pesos at some future point in time (t) as with a future contract to buy from Bank A (see Exhibit 5.2), the obligation can be effectively ended by taking out a future contract to sell 1 million pesos to, say, Bank B. Both contracts can be satisfied if Bank A sells to Bank B without any involvement of Company M. In the terminology, Company M's position will be 'closed out'. Importantly, if a bank negotiates a separate fee for ending a contract (and that may well be the case), that fee should be no more than the cost of closing out. Closing out is the underlying process that determines the cost. The following example

EXAMPLE

On 10 March, Green Bay plc hired a French construction company to expand its office and agreed to pay 200 000 euros for the work on 10 September. It negotiated a 6-month forward contract with Bank A to buy 200 000 euros at £0.70 per euro, which would be used to pay the French firm in 6 months. On 10 April, the French construction company informed Green Bay that it would not be able to perform the work as promised. Therefore, Green Bay offset its existing contract by negotiating a forward contract with Bank B to sell 200 000 euros for the date of 10 September. However, the spot rate of the euro had decreased over the last month, and the prevailing forward contract price for 10 September was £0.66. Green Bay now has a forward contract to sell 200 000 euros on 10 September, which offsets the other contract it has to buy 200 000 euros on 10 September. However, Green Bay is buying at £0.70 per euro and selling at £0.66 per euro, a loss of £0.04 per euro. The total loss on the contract would be £0.04 × 200 000 = 8000 euros. This loss would be paid by Green Bay to the holder of the first contract at £0.70 (Bank A) who would then be happy to sell to Bank B at the rate of the second contract of £0.66.

(Green Bay) illustrates that cost. Closing out is a general financial technique used in particular for futures contracts. Its use is not frequent for forward contracts but is most easily demonstrated using forwards.

If Green Bay in the preceding example negotiates the forward sale with the same bank where it negotiated the forward purchase, it may simply be able to request that its initial forward contract be offset. The bank will charge a fee of at least 8000 euros for this service, reflecting the underlying closing out process. Thus, the MNC cannot just ignore its obligation, but must pay a fee to offset its original obligation.

EXHIBIT 5.2 **Closing out**

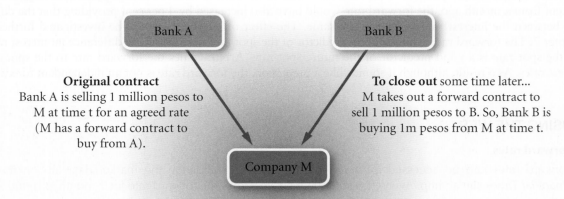

Original contract
Bank A is selling 1 million pesos to
M at time t for an agreed rate
(M has a forward contract to
buy from A).

To close out some time later...
M takes out a forward contract to
sell 1 million pesos to B. So, Bank B is
buying 1m pesos from M at time t.

Closed out position:
Bank A can sell 1 million pesos directly to Bank B at time t for the rate agreed between M and B.
M will have already settled with A any difference between the price with A and the price with B
(see Green Bay example).

Using forward contracts for swap transactions. A swap transaction involves a spot transaction along with a corresponding forward contract that will ultimately reverse the spot transaction. Many forward contracts are negotiated for this purpose.

EXAMPLE

Soho plc needs to invest 1 million Chilean pesos in its Chilean subsidiary for the production of additional products. It wants the subsidiary to repay the pesos in 1 year. Soho wants to lock in the rate at which the pesos can be converted back into British pounds in 1 year, and it uses a 1-year forward contract for this purpose. Soho contacts its bank and requests the following swap transaction:

1 *Today.* The bank should withdraw British pounds from Soho's UK account, convert the British pounds to pesos in the spot market, and transmit the pesos to the subsidiary's account.

2 *In 1 year.* The bank should withdraw 1 million pesos from the subsidiary's account, convert

them to British pounds at today's forward rate, and transmit them to Soho's UK account.

Soho plc is not exposed to exchange rate movements due to the transaction because it has locked in the rate at which the pesos will be converted back to British pounds. If the 1-year forward rate exhibits a discount, however, Soho will receive fewer British pounds in 1 year than it invested in the subsidiary today. It may still be willing to engage in the swap transaction under these circumstances in order to remove the possibility of receiving even fewer British pounds in 1-year's time.

Non-deliverable forward contracts

A new type of forward contract called a **non-deliverable forward contract (NDF)** is frequently used for currencies in emerging markets. Like a regular forward contract, an NDF represents an agreement regarding a position in a specified amount of a specified currency, a specified exchange rate, and a specified future settlement date. However, an NDF does not result in an actual exchange of the currencies at the future date. That is, there is no delivery. Instead, one party to the agreement makes a payment to the other party based on the exchange rate at the future date.

At first an NDF might sound rather odd as a contract, but it is really no more than a contract that is closed out at maturity date (see the Green Bay example above). The purpose of a forward contract is to protect against *changes* in the value of the currency. An NDF provides payment based on the change to the value of the currency, effectively locking in the purchaser (a multinational company) to a fixed rate. Thus if an MNC is buying a currency and takes out an NDF and the rate rises above the agreed future rate, the MNC will receive compensation for the difference. The cost of the currency less the compensation will be the same as purchasing at the agreed future rate. If there were a fall in the value of the currency, the MNC would have to pay the difference, again the total cost would be the equivalent of buying at the agreed future rate.

EXAMPLE

Jackson AG, a German company, determines as of 1 April that it will need 50 million Kenyan shillings to purchase coffee on 1 July. It can negotiate an NDF with a

local bank as follows. The NDF will specify the currency (Kenyan shilling), the settlement date (90 days from now), and a so-called reference rate, which

(Continued)

identifies the type of exchange rate that will be marked to market at the settlement. Specifically, the NDF will contain the following information:

- Buy 50 million Kenyan shilling.

- Settlement date: 1 July.

- Reference index: Kenyan shilling's closing exchange rate (in euros) quoted by Kenya's central bank in 90 days.

Assume that the Kenyan shilling (which is the reference index) is currently valued at 0.01 euros, so the euro amount of the position is 50 million × 0.01 = 500 000 euros at the time of the agreement. At the time of the settlement date (1 July), the value of the reference index is determined, and a payment is made between the two parties to settle the NDF. For example, if the shilling value increases to 0.012 euros by 1 July, the value of the position specified in the NDF will be 600 000 euros (0.012 euros × 50 million shillings). Since the cost of the 50 million shillings is 100 000 euros higher than when the agreement was created, Jackson will receive a payment of 100 000 euros from the bank.

Recall that Jackson needs 50 million shillings to buy imports. Since the shilling's spot rate rose from 1 April to 1 July, Jackson will need to pay 100 000 euros more for the imports than if it had paid for them on 1 April. At the same time, however, Jackson will have received a payment of 100 000 euros due to its NDF. Thus, the NDF hedged (offset) the exchange rate risk.

If the Kenyan shilling had depreciated to 0.009 euros instead of rising, Jackson's position in its NDF would have been valued at 450 000 euros (50 million shillings × 0.009 euros) at the settlement date, which is 50 000 euros less than the value when the agreement was created. Therefore, Jackson would have owed the bank 50 000 euros at that time to settle the NDF. However, the decline in the spot rate of the shilling means that Jackson would pay 50 000 euros less for the imports than if it had paid for them on 1 April. Thus, an offsetting effect would also occur in this example.

In both cases the net payment made by Jackson is 500 000 euros made up of purchasing the shilling at the market rate and then paying or receiving from the bank the difference between the market rate in euros and the NDF rate of 500 000 euros.

As these examples show, although an NDF does not involve delivery, it can effectively hedge future foreign currency payments that are anticipated by an MNC. The non-deliverable aspect of the contract may be attractive if the other party wants to be paid the equivalent value of their local currency in dollars, pounds or euros at the time of the transaction. There may therefore be no actual delivery of local currency in the underlying transaction.

CURRENCY FUTURES MARKET

Currency futures contracts are contracts specifying a standard volume of a particular currency to be exchanged on a specific settlement date. Thus, currency futures contracts are similar to forward contracts in terms of their obligation, but differ from forward contracts in the way they are traded. They are commonly used by MNCs to hedge their foreign currency positions. In addition, they are traded by speculators who hope to capitalize on their expectations of exchange rate movements. Unlike forward contracts, active trading determines the price of a futures contract. Trading is made possible because of the standard nature of the contracts.

The contracts are person to person, a buyer's gain is a seller's loss and vice versa. A buyer of a currency futures contract locks in the exchange rate to be paid for a foreign currency at a future point in time. Alternatively, a seller of a currency futures contract locks in the exchange rate at which a foreign currency can be sold for the home currency. In the UK, currency futures contracts are purchased to lock in the amount of British pounds needed to obtain a specified amount of a particular foreign currency; they are sold to lock in the amount of British pounds to be received from selling a specified amount of a particular foreign currency.

USING THE WEB

Futures trading with open outcry quotes can be found at the Chicago Mercantile Exchange site at: www.cme.com. The configuration of these sites changes frequently so some searching is required with the aid of the internal search engine. A more technical analysis can be found at: www.futuresmag.com with helpful notes.

Contract specifications

Currency futures contracts are available for several widely traded currencies at the Chicago Mercantile Exchange (CME – the original futures exchange and the market that serves as a model for all others); the contract for each currency specifies a standardized number of units (see Exhibit 5.3). The standard size of a contract enables traders to deal in contracts without having to ask for the size of the contract, this speeds up the trading process.

EXHIBIT 5.3   Currency futures contracts traded on the Chicago Mercantile Exchange

Currency	Units per contract
Australian dollar	100 000
Brazilian real	100 000
British pound	62 500
Canadian dollar	100 000
Euro	125 000
Japanese yen	12 500 000
Mexican peso	500 000
New Zealand dollar	100 000
Norwegian krone	2 000 000
Russian rouble	2 500 000
South African rand	500 000
Swedish krona	2 000 000
Swiss franc	125 000
Czech koruna	4 000 000
Polish zloty	500 000
Hungarian forint	30 000 000

Notes:
- The Czech Republic, Poland and Hungary joined the European Union in 2004 but have yet to announce a firm date for joining the euro.
- Underlying currencies are referred to as units, this practice avoids having to refer to too many currencies when specifying contracts.

Source: Chicago Mercantile Exchange.

On the Chicago Mercantile Exchange, the typical currency futures contract is based on a currency value in terms of US dollars. However, futures contracts are also available on some cross-rates, such as the exchange rate between the Australian dollar and the Canadian dollar. Thus, speculators who expect that the Australian dollar will move substantially against the Canadian dollar can take a futures position to capitalize on their expectations. In addition, Australian firms that have exposure in Canadian dollars or Canadian firms that have exposure in Australian dollars may use this type of futures contract to hedge their exposure.

Currency futures contracts typically specify the third Wednesday in March, June, September or December as the settlement date. There is also an over-the-counter currency futures market, where various financial intermediaries facilitate trading of currency futures contracts with specific settlement dates. As noted above, contracts have to be standardized to ensure that trading (nowadays carried out over computer screens) can be carried out quickly and efficiently.

Trading futures

When participants in the currency futures market take a position, they need to establish an initial margin (deposit an amount of money with the clearing house), which may represent as little as 10 per cent of the contract value. The margin required is in the form of cash for small investors or Treasury securities for institutional investors. In addition to the initial margin, participants are subject to a variation margin, which is intended to accumulate a sufficient amount of funds to back the futures position. Depositing such funds with the clearing house ensures that losses and gains are debited or credited to the customer account on the day they occur. This process is known as **marking to market** and **daily settlement**. The purpose of this process, common on most trading platforms, is to ensure that there are no bad debts. Full-service brokers typically charge a commission of about $50 for a round-trip trade in currency futures, while discount brokers charge a commission of about $20. Some Internet brokers also trade currency futures.

EXAMPLE

Assume that as of 10 February, a futures contract on $20 000 on the Euronext Liffe European market with a March settlement date is priced at 0.80 euros per dollar. Consider the positions of two different firms on the opposite sides of this contract. The buyer of this currency futures contract will receive $20 000 on the March settlement date and will pay 16 000 euros (computed as $20 000 × 0.80 euros per dollar). What will in fact happen is that the trade in March will take place at the spot rate and **daily settlement** (see later) will have ensured that the parties are paid or have paid up to date.

Comparison of currency futures and forward contracts

Currency futures contracts are similar to forward contracts in that they allow a customer to lock in the exchange rate at which a specific currency is purchased or sold for a specific date in the future. Nevertheless, there are some differences between currency futures contracts and forward contracts, which are summarized in Exhibit 5.4. Currency futures contracts are sold on an exchange, while each forward contract is negotiated between a firm and a commercial bank over a telecommunications network. Thus, forward contracts can be tailored to the needs of the firm, while currency futures contracts are standardized.

Corporations that have established relationships with large banks tend to use forward contracts rather than futures contracts because forward contracts are tailored to the precise amount of currency to be purchased or sold in the future and the precise forward date that they prefer. Conversely, small firms and individuals who do not have established relationships with large banks or prefer to trade in smaller amounts tend to use currency futures contracts.

EXHIBIT 5.4 Comparison of the forward and futures markets

	Forward	Futures
Size of contract	Tailored to individual needs.	Standardized.
Delivery date	Tailored to individual needs.	Standardized.
Participants	Banks, brokers and multinational companies. Public speculation not encouraged.	Banks, brokers and multinational companies. Qualified public speculation encouraged.
Security deposit	None as such, but compensating bank balances or lines of credit required.	Small security deposit required.
Clearing operation	Handling contingent on individual banks and brokers. No separate clearing house function.	Handled by exchange clearing house. Daily settlements to the market price.
Marketplace	Over the telephone worldwide.	Central exchange floor with worldwide communications.
Regulation	Self-regulating.	Commodity Futures Trading Commission; National Futures Association.
Liquidation	Most settled by actual delivery. Some by offset, at a cost.	Most by offset, very few by delivery.
Transaction costs	Set by 'spread' between bank's buy and sell prices.	Negotiated brokerage fees.

Pricing currency futures

The price of currency futures is determined by arbitrage (riskless trading) as with many prices in the financial markets. The alternative arbitrage process is very simple. In order to guarantee a future price for a currency (or any other type of underlying asset) simply buy the asset now and put it in 'storage'. For currencies, the storage cost (known as the **carry cost**) is the borrowing cost less interest earned through investment during the 'storage' period. The futures price should be identical as the end result is the same.

In the case of wanting the buy $150 dollars in, for example, 1-year's time with UK interest rates at 2 per cent, US interest at 1 per cent and the spot rate at $1.5:£1. The arbitrage process would need to:

1 Invest $148.51 (calculated as the present value of the $150: $150 / 1.01 = $148.51) which would cost £99 now (i.e. $148.51 / 1.5).

2 Borrow the £99 now at 2 per cent. So in 1-year's time the loan would be repaid costing £99 × 1.02 = £100.98.

3 In 1-year's time the dollar investment would mature at $150.

4 All cash flows would take place in 1-year's time being the repayment of the loan costing £100.98 and receiving the dollar investment of $150. In effect an exchange of £100.98 for $150 in 1-year's time, so a futures rate of $150 / £100.98 = $1.4854:£1.

This futures rate is enforced by the potential arbitrage activity that would occur if there were significant discrepancies, though transaction costs may account for small differences.

Credit risk of currency futures contracts

Each currency futures contract represents an agreement between a client and the exchange clearing house, even though the exchange has not taken a position (see Exhibit 5.5). To illustrate, assume you call a broker to request the purchase of a euro futures contract with a March settlement date. Meanwhile, another

EXHIBIT 5.5 Contractual positions for futures contract

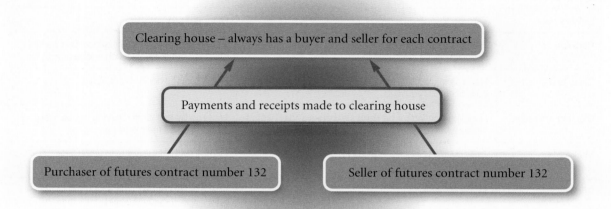

person unrelated to you calls a broker to request the sale of an identical futures contract. Neither party needs to worry about the credit risk of the counterparty. The exchange clearing house assures that you will receive whatever is owed to you as a result of your currency futures position.

To minimize its risk in such a guarantee, the CME imposes **margin requirements** to cover fluctuations in the value of a contract, meaning that the participants must make a deposit with their respective brokerage firms when they take a position. The initial margin requirement is typically between $1000 and $2000 per currency futures contract. There is a subsequent margin known as the **maintenance margin** which is usually slightly less. Charges and credits are made on a daily basis to the accounts of the buyer and seller depending on the movement of the value of the futures contract.

Thus if a US speculator purchases a futures contract on British pounds and the futures price of the pound goes up the following day by half a cent ($0.005), the purchaser has a potential gain as the contract enables him to buy British pounds for half a cent less than the market. The purchaser could 'close out' (see below) by taking out a futures contract to sell at the higher rate. As this is a zero sum game between the buyer and seller (one's loss is the other's gain) – the seller is selling at half a cent below the current futures price. So the seller (if nothing else happened) owes the purchaser half a cent per pound. The clearing house would charge the seller £62 500 × $0.005 = $312.5 and credit the amount to the purchaser *the next day*. The clearing house debits and credits each account in this way on a daily basis. This is a process used by most market trading organizations including those trading over the Internet (see Exhibit 5.6).

The obvious question is why settle on a daily basis? Why not wait to the end of the contract, after all the positions may reverse the following day and the payment be made in the other direction. The reason for daily settlement is to ensure the creditworthiness of both parties. If the seller's margin went below a safety level with the $312.5 payment and the seller refused to top up the account, the clearing house could terminate the contract and the purchaser buy a futures at the current price. Having already received the difference between the current price of the futures and the original purchase price from the daily settlement process, the purchaser will not lose out by having the contract at the higher price. In technical terms, the contract is effectively closed out on a daily basis. Exhibit 5.6 illustrates the daily closing out procedure.

Unlike futures contracts, margin requirements are not always required for forward contracts due to the more personal nature of the agreement; the bank knows the firm it is dealing with and may trust it to fulfil its obligation.

EXHIBIT 5.6   Currency futures contract on British pounds (£62 500), example of daily settlement on the Chicago Mercantile Exchange

Day	Price per £1 (or unit) of futures contract	Purchaser pays (–) or receives (1)	Seller pays (–) or receives (1)
0	$0.503		
1	$0.504	($0.504 – $0.503) × 62 500 = +$62.5 ⟵—— –$62.5	
2	$0.502	($0.502 – $0.504) × 62 500 =–$125 ——⟶ +$125	
3	$0.505	($0.505 – $0.502) × 62 500 = +$187.5 ⟵—— –$187.5	

Notes:
- Payments are based on price movements from the previous day (not from day 1), e.g. day 3 price movement is $0.505 – $0.502 = $0.003.
- Purchaser pays when prices fall, e.g. day 2 price falls from $0.504 to $0.502, amount calculated as movement × units i.e. ($0.502 – $0.504) × 62 500 = –$125. Purchaser receives when prices rise (days 1 and 3).
- Seller pays when prices rise (day 1 and day 3) and receives when prices fall (day 2).
- If, having paid on day 3, the seller became bankrupt, the purchaser could take out a new contract at $0.505 and continue unaffected.

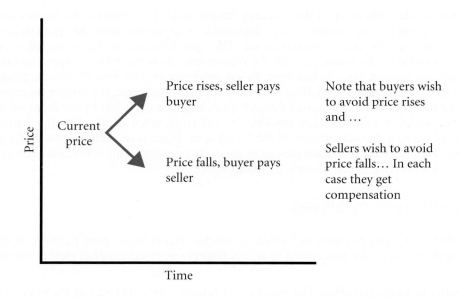

Speculation with currency futures

Currency futures contracts are often purchased by speculators who are simply attempting to capitalize on their expectation of a currency's future movement.

Assume that a UK speculator expects the US dollar to appreciate in the future. The speculator can purchase a futures contract that will lock in the price at which they buy dollars at a specified settlement date. On the settlement date, they can purchase their dollars at the rate specified by the futures contract and then sell these dollars at the spot rate. If the spot rate has appreciated by this time in accordance with their expectations, they will profit from the increase in value of the dollar. Alternatively, rather than actually dealing in the currencies, speculators can simply close out by selling an offsetting futures contract (similar to the offsetting forward contract, see below). Daily settlement will have ensured that they will have already received the gain.

Currency futures are often sold by speculators who expect that the spot rate of a currency will be less than the rate at which they would be obliged to sell it.

Assume that as of 4 April, a futures contract specifying 125 000 euros and a June settlement date is priced at £0.6813. On 4 April, speculators who expect the euro will decline sell futures contracts on euros. Assume that on 17 June (the settlement date), the spot rate of the euro is £0.6810. The gain on the futures position is £37.50, which represents the difference between the amount received (£85 162.5 = 125 000 × 0.6813) when selling the euros in accordance with the futures contract less the amount paid (£85 125 = 125 000 × 0.6810) to buy those euros in the spot market. In practice, the speculator will have received the £37.50 from daily settlement.

Of course, expectations are often incorrect. It is because of different expectations that some speculators decide to purchase futures contracts while other speculators decide to sell the same contracts at a given point in time.

Currency futures' market efficiency. If the currency futures market is efficient, the futures price for a currency at any given point in time should reflect all available information. Both the spot rate and the futures rate will be derived from the same information set. The only difference is that expected events of significance will be discounted to the future date for the futures and the present for the spot. An exception is the cost of time itself, the interest rate. As has been shown, arbitrage ensures that the futures price differs from the spot by the interest rate differential. If interest rates are higher in Brazil, the futures price will be at a discount so that the higher interest rate earned through investing in Brazil is lost by the discount on the futures price. Otherwise, riskless profits would be possible. By and large, when adjusted for this known difference, the futures should be an unbiased estimate of the future spot. But it is unlikely to be a better estimate than the present spot (i.e. the prediction of no change in the exchange rate). This is because there is nothing that the futures price 'knows' that is not 'known' by the spot rate.

How firms use currency futures

Corporations that have open positions in foreign currencies, that is to say have to make or receive foreign currency payments, can consider purchasing or selling futures con tracts to offset their positions.

Purchasing futures to hedge payables. The purchase of futures contracts locks in the price at which a firm can purchase a currency.

Tetoni SA (Italy) orders Canadian goods and upon delivery will need to send C$500 000 to the Canadian exporter. Thus, Tetoni purchases Canadian dollar futures contracts today, thereby locking in the price to be paid for Canadian dollars at a future settlement date. By holding futures contracts, Tetoni does not have to worry about changes in the spot rate of the Canadian dollar over time.

Selling futures to hedge receivables. The sale of futures contracts locks in the price at which a firm can sell a currency.

EXAMPLE

Karla Ltd sells futures contracts when it plans to receive a currency from exporting and wants to convert the currency back to its home currency of British pounds (it accepts a foreign currency when the importer prefers that type of payment). By selling a futures contract, Karla Ltd locks in the price at which it will be able to sell this currency as of the settlement date. Such an action can be appropriate if Karla expects the foreign currency to depreciate against Karla's home currency.

The use of futures contracts to cover, or **hedge**, a firm's currency positions is described more thoroughly in Chapter 11.

Closing out a futures position

If a firm holding a currency futures contract to purchase decides before the settlement date that it no longer wants to maintain its position, it can close out the position by selling an identical futures contract at a later date. The process is the same as the offsetting of forward contracts. With forward contracts closing out was unusual, with futures, closing out is normal. One reason is that a futures contract is much used for speculation where the interest is in the currency movements rather than actual buying or selling of the currency. A second reason, of interest to MNCs, is that a futures contract has fixed settlement dates (the third Wednesday of every quarter month). Companies will normally want protection to a different date; closing out enables a company to obtain protection up to a precise date and thereafter have no further obligations. Companies need to choose settlement dates beyond the date when a purchase or sale of currency is required. Closing out then enables protection to the precise date. The clearing house will offset the equal and opposite contracts and no further daily settlement receipts or payments will be made. The gain or loss to the firm will have been already paid or received from daily settlement before closing out.

The price of a futures contract changes over time in accordance with movements in the spot rate and interest rates and also with changing expectations about the spot rate and interest rates.

If the spot rate of a currency increases substantially over a 1-month period, the futures price is likely to increase by about the same amount. In this case, the purchase and subsequent sale of a futures contract would be profitable. Conversely, a decline in the spot rate over time will correspond with a decline in the currency futures price, meaning that the purchase and subsequent sale of a futures contract would result in a loss. While the purchasers of the futures contract could decide not to close out their position under such conditions, the losses from that position could increase over time.

EXAMPLE

On January 10, Tacoma Ltd anticipates that it will need Australian dollars (A$) in March when it orders supplies from an Australian supplier. Consequently, Tacoma purchases a futures contract specifying A$100 000 and a March settlement date (which is 19 March for this contract). On 10 January, the futures contract is priced at £0.41 per A$. On 15 February, Tacoma realizes that it will not need to order supplies because it has reduced its production levels. Therefore, it has no need for A$ in March. It sells a futures

(Continued)

contract on A$ with the March settlement date to offset the contract it purchased in January. At this time, the futures contract is priced at £0.39 per A$. On 19 March (the settlement date), Tacoma has off-setting positions in futures contracts. However, the price when the futures contract was purchased was higher than the price when an identical contract was sold, so Tacoma incurs a loss from its futures positions. Tacoma's transactions are summarized in Exhibit 5.7. Move from left to right along the time line to review the transactions. The example does not include margin requirements.

EXHIBIT 5.7   Closing out a futures contract

10 January	10 February	19 March
Futures contract price:		
£0.41	£0.39	£0.36
1. Takes out a contract to buy on 19 March A$100 000 at £0.41 per A$.	**2.** Will have paid out net £0.39 − £0.41 = − £0.02 × A$100 000 = £2000 in daily settlement charges. **3.** Takes out a contract to sell on 19 March on A$100 000 at £0.39 per A$. **4.** Contracts offset by clearing house, the holder will not have any further commitments.	**5.** The contracts are offset so no further payments are required. As a note, the contract to buy would have paid out a further (£0.36 − £0.39) × A$100 000 = £3000 but the contract to sell will have earned (£0.39 − £0.36) × A$100 000 = £3000. In fact, whatever the spot price on settlement, the contracts will have earned equal and opposite amounts. Closing out merely recognizes that the holder of equal and opposite contracts will not have to make further payments.

Sellers of futures contracts can close out their positions by purchasing currency futures contracts with similar settlement dates. Although most contracts are closed out before the settlement date, delivery is possible but the terms of delivery are usually not particularly attractive. The market prefers contracts to be closed out.

Transaction costs of currency futures

Brokers who fulfil orders to buy or sell futures contracts charge a transaction or brokerage fee in the form of a bid/ask spread. That is, they buy a futures contract for one price (their 'bid' price) and simultaneously sell the contract to someone else for a slightly higher price (their 'ask' price). The difference between a bid and an ask price on a futures contract may be as little as £5.00 in total. Yet, even this amount can be larger in percentage terms than the transaction fees for forward contracts.

CURRENCY OPTIONS MARKET

Currency options provide the right but not the obligation to purchase or sell currencies at specified prices. The main difference with futures and forward contracts is that, in the case of an option, a range of prices are offered and also the purchaser does not have to fulfil the contract, which can be allowed to lapse. For MNCs it can be used as a kind of insurance policy. When buying foreign currency an option contract can be used to ensure that the company will not have to pay more than a certain amount. When selling foreign currency, a minimum value can be established. Thus an MNC can limit its exposure to exchange rate fluctuations but not *eliminate* exposure as with a fully covered futures position. Where the market goes above or below the guaranteed price (known as the strike or exercise price) the options policy pays out the difference, as with any insurance policy where a claim is made. There are two types of options, an American option that allows the purchaser of the contract to buy or sell at any time before the settlement or exercise date, and a European option that allows purchase or sale of the currency only at the exercise date. Options are available for many currencies, including the US dollar, Australian dollar, British pound, Brazilian real, Canadian dollar, euro, Japanese yen, Mexican peso, New Zealand dollar, Russian rouble, South African rand and Swiss franc.

Option exchanges

In late 1982, exchanges in Amsterdam, Montreal and Philadelphia first allowed trading in standardized foreign currency options. Since that time, options have been offered on the Chicago Mercantile Exchange and the Chicago Board Options Exchange. Currency options are traded through the GLOBEX system at the Chicago Mercantile Exchange, even after the trading floor is closed. Thus, currency options are traded virtually around the clock.

The options exchanges in the USA are regulated by the Securities and Exchange Commission. Options can be purchased or sold through brokers for a commission. The commission per transaction is commonly $30 to $60 for a single currency option, but it can be much lower per contract when the transaction involves multiple contracts. Brokers require that a margin be maintained during the life of the contract and daily settlement is made as with futures contracts. The margin is increased for clients whose option positions have deteriorated. This protects against possible losses if the clients do not fulfil their obligations.

In September 2000 the exchanges of Amsterdam, Brussels and Paris merged to form Euronext NV, a Dutch holding company. In 2002 the LIFFE (London International Financial Futures and Options Exchange) was acquired. Subsequent years have seen the merger of clearing house services as well.

Over-the-counter market

In addition to the exchanges where currency options are available, there is an over-the-counter market where currency options are offered by commercial banks and brokerage firms. Unlike the currency options traded on an exchange, currency options are tailored to the specific needs of the firm. Since these options are not standardized, all the terms must be specified in the contracts. The number of units, desired strike price, and expiration date can be tailored to the specific needs of the client. When currency options are not standardized, there is less liquidity and a wider bid/ask spread.

The minimum size of currency options offered by financial institutions is normally more than £1 million. Since these transactions are conducted with a specific financial institution rather than an exchange, there are no credit guarantees. Thus, the agreement made is only as safe as the parties involved. For this reason, financial institutions may require some collateral from individuals or firms desiring to purchase or sell currency options.

Currency options are classified as either **calls** or **puts,** as discussed in the next section.

CURRENCY CALL OPTIONS

A currency call option grants the right to buy a specific currency at a designated price within a specific period of time if it is an American option or at a certain time if it is a European option. The price at which the owner is allowed to buy that currency is known as the exercise price or strike price, and there are monthly expiration dates for each option.

Call options are desirable when one wishes to lock in a maximum price to be paid for a currency in the future. If the spot rate of the currency rises above the strike price, owners of call options can 'exercise' their options by purchasing the currency at the strike price, which will be cheaper than the prevailing spot rate. This strategy is somewhat similar to that used by purchasers of futures contracts, except that:

- The futures contracts do not offer a range of prices; forward and futures only offer the expected price.

- Forward and future contracts require an obligation to buy or sell, while the currency option does not. The owner can choose to let the option expire on the expiration date without ever exercising it.

- Owners of expired call options will have lost the premium they initially paid, but that is the most they can lose. Losses are potentially unlimited for purchasers of futures contracts – though losses can be halted by closing out.

Although currency options typically expire near the middle of the specified month, some of them expire at the end of the specified month and are designated as EOM (end of month). Some options are listed as 'European style', which means that they can be exercised only upon expiration.

A currency call option is said to be *in the money* when the present exchange rate exceeds the strike price. The term 'in the money' is being used in the normal sense in that if the present exchange or spot rate exceeds the strike price, the holder of the call option is due to be paid the difference. In Exhibit 5.8 a quote on a range of call options on the dollar is given. Imagine that the situation is of a UK speculator wanting to buy dollars. Call options at strike prices of £0.60:$1 and £0.65:$1 are both in the money as the spot is £0.67:$1. At these lower strike prices, the holder is in effect able to buy dollars at below the spot or market price (note that the premium prevents an immediate profit being made). Options are *at the money* when the present exchange rate equals the strike price, and *out of the money* when the present exchange rate is less than the strike price (Exhibit 5.8 strike price of £0.70 is out of the money). For a given currency and expiration date, an in-the-money call option will require a higher premium than options that are at the money or out of the money. The premium will also be higher for longer expiration dates as evidenced in Exhibit 5.8.

Factors affecting currency call option premiums

The premium on a call option represents the cost of having the right to buy the underlying currency at a specified price. For MNCs that use currency call options to hedge, the premium reflects a cost of insurance or protection for MNCs.

The call option premium in general terms is influenced by the probability of a payout. Thus in Exhibit 5.8 the premium for the right to buy British pounds at £0.70:$1 is very small for December because it is very unlikely that the spot rate will increase by about four-and-a-half per cent from £0.67 to £0.70 in such a short space of time. Longer term options are more expensive because there is a greater probability of a payout, i.e. being in the money.

As with all insurance type contracts, the greater the likelihood of a payout, the higher the premium. Three factors influence the option premium (referred to as C):

$$C = f\,(S - X,\, T,\, \sigma,\, r_{f(H/F)})$$

EXHIBIT 5.8   Call option quote

Stock Exchange £/$ quote for call options for $50 000 – European style options		
Spot: £0.67:$1		
Current date: November		
Strike price value of $1 in pounds	**Premiums £s per $1**	
	December	**January**
£0.60	£0.076	£0.085
£0.65	£0.040	£0.052
£0.70	£0.017	£0.029

Notes:
- A January call option at a strike price of £0.65 would incur a cost £0.052 × 50 000 = £2600 known as the contract premium.
- The buyer of the January call option at a strike price of £0.65 will collect £0.01 × 50 000 = £500 for every penny (£0.01) the spot rate of the dollar is above £0.65 at the designated date in January. If the spot price remains £0.67:1$, the buyer will collect £1000 (£0.02*50 000).
- If the spot rate is below £0.65 in January, the option will not be exercised and will be allowed to lapse, the premium will have been forfeited by the purchaser of the call option.
- A European option can only be exercised at the exercise date – an American option any time up to the exercise date.

Where:

$S - X$ = the difference between the spot exchange rate (S) and the strike or exercise price (X)

T = the time to maturity

σ = the volatility of the currency, as measured by the standard deviation of the movements in the currency

$r_{f\,(H/F)}$ = the risk free rate in the home and foreign country.

The relationships between the call option premium and these factors are summarized next.

- *Level of existing spot price relative to strike price ($S - X$).* The higher the spot rate relative to the strike price, the more likely a payout. Where the spot is above the strike, the option contract is going to enable the holder to buy the currency at below the current price. The premium should at least cover this difference plus a small extra to cover for the possibility of being even deeper in the money (i.e. the payout being even higher).

- *Length of time before the expiration date (T, $r_{f,H/F}$).* It is generally expected that the spot rate has a greater chance of rising high above the strike price if it has a longer period of time to do so. The premiums for the January settlement dates are all higher than for the December dates. There is therefore a greater risk of a payout simply due to the passage of time. The risk free rate also prices the cost and reward of time itself including inflation. In currency option formulas the spot rate and the difference in home and foreign interest rates is often replaced by the forward rate which is a function of these variables.

- *Potential variability of currency.* The greater the variability of the changes in currency, the higher the probability that the spot rate will be above the strike price. Thus, more volatile currencies have higher call option prices. For example, changes in the euro Swiss franc exchange rate are more stable than most other currencies. If all other factors are similar, euro call options on Swiss francs should be less expensive than call options on other non-euro currencies.

The potential variability of returns or changes in the currency can also vary over time for a particular currency. For example, at the beginning of the Asian crisis in 1997, the Asian countries experienced financial problems, and their currency values were subject to much more uncertainty. Consequently, the premium on over-the-counter options of Asian currencies such as the Thai baht, Indonesian rupiah and Korean won increased. The higher premium was necessary to compensate those who were willing to sell options in these currencies, as the risk to sellers had increased because the currencies had become more volatile.

Note here that we are talking about volatility of the *changes* in the value of the currency, whether the daily *changes* in the value of the currency are high or low. This is closely linked to the standard deviation of the actual values of the currency, but there is an important difference. If there is a trend in the figures, the standard deviation of the actual values will be distorted upwards by out-of-date figures, whereas looking at just the movements will get rid of this distortion. The *changes* approach is sometimes referred to as detrended.

When the formula was first introduced by Fisher Black and Myron Scholes there was some surprise that there was no estimate of the future price. This is not true as one of the assumptions is that the price of the underlying asset follows a geometric Brownian motion in other words a **random walk**. This is the basis of an efficient market where the best estimate of the future price is the current spot.

How firms use currency call options

Corporations with open positions in foreign currencies can sometimes use currency call options to cover these positions.

Using call options to hedge payables. MNCs can purchase call options on a currency to hedge future payables.

EXAMPLE

When Pike Ltd (UK) orders Australian goods, it makes a payment in Australian dollars to the Australian exporter upon delivery. An Australian dollar call option locks in a maximum rate at which Pike can exchange British pounds for Australian dollars. The call option contract specifies the maximum price that Pike must pay to obtain these Australian dollars.

If the Australian dollar's value remains below the strike price, Pike can purchase Australian dollars at the prevailing spot rate when it needs to pay for its imports and simply let its call option expire.

If the Australian dollar's value is above the strike price then Pike can again purchase at the spot rate but this time Pike will exercise the option and claim the difference between the higher market price and the strike price.

Options may be more appropriate than futures or forward contracts for some situations. Adidas in their 2009 annual report state that they use options for about 25 per cent of their exposure for 12 to 24 months in the future to protect mainly against their significant dollar denominated purchases.

Using call options to hedge project bidding. MNCs bidding for foreign projects may purchase call options to lock in the cost of the potential expenses.

EXAMPLE

Kelly plc is an MNC based in Scotland that has bid on a project sponsored by the Canadian government. If the bid is accepted, Kelly will need approximately C$500 000 to purchase Canadian materials and services. However, Kelly will not know whether the bid is accepted until 3 months from now. Kelly expects the value of the Canadian dollar to fall; but it may rise. If it rises above a certain level the project will no longer be profitable. In this case, it can purchase call options with a 3-month expiration date at a strike price that will guarantee a minimum level of profit. Ten call option contracts will cover the entire amount of potential exposure. If the bid is accepted, Kelly can use the options to purchase the Canadian dollars needed if the value of the Canadian dollar has risen above the strike price. If the Canadian dollar has depreciated over time or has not risen above the strike price, Kelly will let the options expire.

Assume that the strike or exercise price on Canadian dollars is £0.43 and the call option premium is £0.005 per unit. Kelly will pay £250 per option (since there are 50 000 units per Canadian dollar option and 50 000 × 0.005 = £250), or £2500 for the ten option contracts. With options, the maximum amount necessary to purchase the C$500 000 is £215 000 (computed as £0.43 per Canadian dollar × C$500 000) plus the cost of the options £2500. So a *maximum* total of £217 500 would be needed. The cost of the options (£2500) would be less the higher the exercise price, simply because the protection would be less and therefore the probability of a payout less.

Even if Kelly's bid is rejected, it will exercise the currency call option if the Canadian dollar's spot rate exceeds the exercise price before the option expires and sell the Canadian dollars in the spot market. Any gain from exercising may partially or even fully offset the premium paid for the options. Alternatively, there is an active secondary market for options and they may simply be sold on that market.

The example of Kelly is quite common. When Air Products and Chemicals was hired to undertake some projects, it needed capital equipment from Germany. The purchase of equipment was contingent on whether the firm was hired for the projects. The company used options to hedge this possible future purchase.

Using call options to hedge target bidding. Firms can also use call options to hedge a possible acquisition.

EXAMPLE

Mumble plc is attempting to acquire a French firm and has submitted its bid in euros. Mumble has purchased call options on the euro because it will need euros to purchase the French company's stock. The call options hedge the UK firm against the potential appreciation of the euro by the time the acquisition occurs. Whether or not the acquisition goes ahead, if the euro remains below the strike price, Mumble can let the call options expire. If the euro exceeds the strike price at Speculating with currency call options maturity, Mumble can exercise the options and sell the euros in the spot market. Alternatively, Mumble can sell the call options it is holding. Either of these actions may offset part or all of the premium paid for the options. In these circumstances Mumble may also take out options on the price of the target company if they are traded or options on the Paris DAX index to provide partial protection against price rises in the shares of the target company.

Speculating with Currency Call Options

Because this text focuses on multinational financial management, the corporate use of currency options is more important than the speculative use. The use of options for hedging is discussed in detail in Chapter 11. Speculative trading is discussed here in order to provide a greater insight into the workings of the market. Speculators play an important role in setting prices and ensuring that the market is responsive to new information. Also, particularly with options, the dividing line between commercial and speculative use is somewhat blurred, only guaranteeing a price if it goes above a certain rate is to accept a degree of speculation on the future price.

Individuals may speculate in the currency options market based on their expectation of the future movements in a particular currency. Speculators who expect that a foreign currency will appreciate can purchase call options on that currency. Once the spot rate of that currency appreciates, the speculators can exercise their options by purchasing that currency at the strike price and then sell the currency at the prevailing spot rate. This assumes that the speculator holds an American option which can be exercised up to the expiration date. Holders of European options, which can only be exercised at the maturity date, can nevertheless sell their options on the secondary (second-hand) market before that date and achieve similar gains.

Just as with currency futures, for every buyer of a currency call option there must be a seller. A seller (called a **writer**) of a call option is obliged to sell a specified currency at a specified price (the strike price) up to a specified expiration date (in the case of an American option or at a specified date in the case of a European option) *if the option is exercised*. It is the buyer of the option who decides whether or not the option is exercised, not the writer. This is not a difficult decision, no more difficult than the decision to claim on a winning betting ticket or make an insurance claim.

Speculators may sometimes want to sell a currency call option on a currency that they expect will depreciate in the future. The only way a currency call option will be exercised is if the spot rate is higher than the strike price. Thus, a seller of a currency call option will receive the premium when the option is purchased and will profit by the entire amount if the option is not exercised.

A speculator may even profit from selling an option which is 'in the money', in other words, where there is a claim if the option were to mature immediately. The premium for such options will include the profit that can be made on the option now (assuming maturity now – the intrinsic element) plus an extra amount to pay for the risk of even higher profits being due at the actual maturity date (the time element).

The net profit to a speculator who purchases call options on a currency is based on a comparison of the selling price of the currency in the foreign exchange market versus the exercise price paid for the currency and the premium paid for the call option.

EXAMPLE

Jim is a speculator who buys a call option on euros with a strike price of £0.700 and a December settlement date. The current spot price as of that date is about £0.682. Jim pays a premium of £0.005 per unit (euro) for the call option. Assume there are no brokerage fees. At the expiration date, the spot rate of the euro reaches £0.724. *Where the spot rate is above the strike price, the call option will be exercised.* Jim exercises the call option and then immediately sells the pounds at the spot rate to a bank. To determine Jim's profit or loss, first compute his revenues from selling the currency. Then, subtract from this amount the purchase price of the euros when exercising the option, and also subtract the purchase price of the option (the premium). The computations follow. Assume one option contract specifies 150 000 units.

Position at settlement for Jim as PURCHASER per unit of a European call option on 150 000 euros	Per contract	Decision: EXERCISE OPTION 1
Selling price of euro (on the currency markets)	£0.724	£108 600 (£0.724 × 150 000 units)
− Purchase price of euro (by exercising the option)	−0.700	−£105 000 (£0.700 × 150 000 units)
− Premium paid for option	−0.005	−£750 (£0.005 × 150 000 units)
= Net profit	£0.019	£2850 (£0.019 × 150 000 units)

Assume that Linda was the seller of the call option purchased by Jim. Also assume that Linda would purchase euros only if and when the option was exercised, at which time she must provide the euros at the exercise price of £0.700. Using the information in this example, Linda's net loss from selling the call option is derived here:

Position at settlement for Linda as SELLER (or writer) of a European call option	Per unit	Per contract
Selling price of euro (as per option contract)	£0.700	£105 000 (£0.700 × 150 000 units)
− Purchase price of euro (on the currency markets)	−0.724	−£108 600 (£0.724 × 150 000 units)
+ Premium received for option	0.005	£750 (£0.005 × 150 000 units)
= Net profit (+) or loss (−)	−£0.019	−£2850 (£0.019 × 150 000 units)

As a second example, assume Jim tries his luck again:

- Call option premium on euros = £0.005 per unit.
- Strike price = $0.730.
- One option contract represents 150 000 euros.

In his previous contract Jim took out a strike price above the current spot and the value of the euro rose above the strike price and a profit was made. Here he is trying to do the same thing and hoping that the spot will rise above the level it was at the end of his

(Continued)

previous contract. Only this time, at the settlement date the spot rate is £0.720, well below the strike price. *Where the spot rate is below the strike price,* *the call option will not be exercised and allowed to lapse.* The net position to speculator Jim is computed as follows:

Position at settlement for Jim as PURCHASER of a European call option	Per unit	Per contract 1 decision: DO NOT EXERCISE OPTION
Selling price of euro (on the currency markets)	~~£0.720~~	Option allowed to lapse
− Purchase price of euro (by exercising the option)	~~£0.730~~	Option allowed to lapse
− Premium paid for option	−0.005	−£750 (£0.005 × 150 000 units)
= Net profit (+) or loss (−)	−£0.005	−£750 (£0.005 × 150 000 units)

For the seller or writer of the call option, Jim's losses are the writer's gains:

Position at settlement for Linda as SELLER or writer of a European call option	Per unit	Per contract
Selling price of euro (as per option contract)	~~£0.730~~	Option allowed to lapse by purchaser
Purchase price of euro (as per the markets)	~~£0.720~~	Option allowed to lapse by purchaser
+ Premium received for option	+0.005	£750 (£0.005 × 150 000 units)
= Net profit (+) or loss (−)	+£0.005	£750 (£0.005 × 150 000 units)

Further points

- When brokerage fees are ignored, the currency call purchaser's gain will be the seller's loss. The currency call purchaser's expenses represent the seller's revenues, and the purchaser's revenues represent the seller's expenses. Yet, because it is possible for purchasers and sellers of options to close out their positions, the relationship described here will not hold unless both parties begin and close out their positions at the same time.

  An owner of a currency option may simply sell the option to someone else before the expiration date rather than exercising it. The owner can still earn profits, since the option premium changes over time, reflecting the probability that the option can be exercised and the potential profit from exercising it.

- Where the spot rate is above the strike price, the call option will be exercised. Where the spot rate is below the strike price, the call option will not be exercised and allowed to lapse. This relationship holds even where there is an overall loss as exercising makes a contribution – the loss would be greater if the option were not exercised.

- The purchaser of the call option is the party that decides whether or not the option is to be exercised. The purchaser cannot lose more than his or her premium – it is a common error when making calculations of gains or losses to forget this point and forget that where an option is not exercised there will be no purchase or sale of currency.

Profit and break-even point from speculation. Regardless of the number of units in a contract, a purchaser of a call option will break even if the spot rate less the strike price equals the premium.

EXAMPLE

Based on the information in the previous example (a strike price of £0.73 and a premium of £0.005), the actions and profit or loss for the purchaser of a call option at varying strike prices including the break-even level would be as in the following table. Note that transaction costs have not been taken into account – the administration costs, brokerage fees, etc. Also, where the spot price equals the strike price, there is no benefit in exercising. As a check on the calculations, note that losses cannot exceed the premium.

Position at settlement for purchaser of a European call option for a range of potential selling prices	Per unit Do not exercise	Per unit Do not exercise	Per unit Do not exercise	Per unit Exercise	Per unit Exercise	Per unit Exercise
Selling price of euro (on the currency markets) if option exercised	£0.710	£0.720	£0.730	£0.732	£0.735	£0.740
− Purchase price of euro (by exercising the option)	£0.730	£0.730	£0.730	£0.730	£0.730	£0.730
− Premium paid for option	−0.005	−0.005	−0.005	−0.005	−0.005	−0.005
= Net profit (+) or loss (−) per unit	−£0.005	−£0.005	−£0.005	−£0.003	£0.000	+£0.005

Note that the purchaser of an option cannot lose more than the premium.

CURRENCY PUT OPTIONS

The purchaser of a currency put option receives the right to *sell* a currency at a specified price (the strike price) within a specified period of time for an American option or at the settlement date in the case of a European option. The reason for using the terms calls and puts should now be a little clearer. Options offer the right to buy and sell the right to buy, and buy and sell the right to sell! It is less confusing to say that options offer the right to buy and sell calls and puts. As with currency call options, the purchaser of a put option is not obliged to exercise the option. Therefore, the maximum potential loss to the owner of the put option is the price (or premium) paid for the option contract.

A currency put option is said to be *in the money* (i.e. profitable) when the present exchange rate is less than the strike price. Again the term 'in the money' simply refers to the fact that, at these prices, the purchaser of the option is due to be paid. This means that the purchaser of the put option has the right to sell at the strike price which is above the current market price. Where a put option is *at the money*, the present exchange rate equals the strike price, and *out of the money* when the present exchange rate exceeds the strike price. For a given currency and settlement or expiration date, an in-the-money put option will require a higher premium than options that are at the money or out of the money. The reason is simply that the probability of a payout is greater for an option that is already in-the-money.

Factors affecting currency put option premiums

The put option premium (referred to as P) is primarily influenced by three factors:

$$P = f(S - X, T, \sigma, r_{f\,(H/F)})$$

Where:

$S - X$ = the difference between the spot exchange rate (S) and the strike or exercise price (X)
T = the time to maturity
σ = the volatility of the currency changes, as measured by the standard deviation of the movements in the currency
$r_{f\,(H/F)}$ = the risk free rate in the home and foreign country.

The relationships between the put option premium and these factors, which also influence call option premiums as described earlier, are summarized next.

First, the spot rate of a currency relative to the strike price is important. The lower the spot rate relative to the strike price, the more valuable the put option will be, because there is a higher probability that the option will be exercised. Recall that just the opposite relationship held for call options. A second factor influencing put option premium is the length of time until the expiration date. As with currency call options, the longer the time to expiration, the greater the put option premium as a payout is more likely due to the greater uncertainty of prices over time. In other words we can be relatively sure that a spot rate that is, say, 5 per cent out of the money is not going to be in the money tomorrow. So if settlement were tomorrow the premium would be very small. But if settlement were to be a year hence, the possibility of being in the money is much greater. A longer period creates a higher probability that the currency will move into a range where it will be feasible to exercise the option (whether it is a put or a call). These relationships can be verified by assessing quotations of put option premiums for a specified currency (see Exhibit 5.9). A third factor that influences the put option premium is the variability of a currency. As with currency call options, the greater the variability, the greater the put option premium will be, again reflecting a higher probability that the option may be exercised. Finally the relative costs of time as measured by the risk free interest rates in the respective countries. As with call options sometimes the spot rate and the two risk free interest rates are expressed as the forward rate which is a function of these variables.

EXHIBIT 5.9 Put option quote

Stock Exchange £/$ quote for put options for $50 000 – European style options		
Spot: £0.67:$1		
Current date: November		
Strike price value of $1 in pounds	**Premium paid per $1**	
	December	**January**
£0.60	£0.003	£0.010
£0.65	£0.018	£0.027
£0.70	£0.044	£0.053

Notes:
- A January put option at a strike price of £0.65 would incur a cost £0.027 × 50 000 = £1350 known as the contract premium.
- The buyer of the January put option at a strike price of £0.65 will collect £0.01 × 50 000 = £500 for every penny (£0.01) the spot rate is below £0.65 at the designated date in January.
- If the spot rate is above £0.65 in January, the option will not be exercised and will be allowed to lapse, the premium will have been forfeited by the purchaser of the call option.
- A European option can only be exercised at the exercise date – an American option any time up to the exercise date.

Hedging with currency put options

Corporations with open positions in foreign currencies can use currency put options in some cases to cover these positions.

EXAMPLE

Assume that Hookway Ltd (UK) has exported products to Canada and invoiced the products in Canadian dollars (at the request of the Canadian importers). Hookway is concerned that the Canadian dollars it is receiving may depreciate to a level that would severely affect its profits. To insulate itself against possible depreciation, Hookway purchases Canadian dollar put options, which entitle it to sell Canadian dollars at a strike price that would avoid such losses. In essence, Hookway locks in the minimum rate at which it can exchange Canadian dollars for British pounds over a specified period of time. If the Canadian dollar appreciates over this time period, Hookway can let the put options expire and sell the Canadian dollars it receives at the prevailing spot rate.

Speculating with currency put options

Individuals may speculate with currency put options based on their expectations of the future movements in a particular currency. For example, speculators who expect that the British pound will depreciate can purchase British pound put options, which will entitle them to sell British pounds at a specified strike price. If the pound's spot rate depreciates as expected, the speculators can in theory purchase pounds at the spot rate and exercise their put options by selling these pounds at the strike price. In practice, the current market premium of the option they are holding will include this profit, so they could simply sell their put option.

Speculators can also attempt to profit from selling currency put options. The seller of such options is obliged to purchase the specified currency at the strike price from the owner who exercises the put option. Speculators who believe the currency will appreciate (or at least will not depreciate) may sell a currency put option. If the currency appreciates over the entire period, the option will not be exercised. This is an ideal situation for put option sellers, since they keep the premiums received when selling the options and bear no cost.

EXAMPLE

A put option contract on US dollars specifies the following information:

- Put option premium on the US dollar ($) = £0.02 per unit.
- Strike price = £0.60.
- One option contract represents $50 000.

A speculator who had purchased this put option decided to exercise the option at the expiration date, when the spot rate of the dollar was £0.55. The speculator purchased the pounds in the spot market at that time. Given this information, the net profit to the purchaser of the put option is calculated as follows:

Position at settlement for PURCHASER of a European put option	Per unit	Per contract
Selling price of $ from exercising the put option	£0.60	£30 000 (£0.60 × 50 000 units)
− Purchase price of $	−£0.55	−£27 500 (−£0.55 × 50 000 units)
− Premium paid	−£0.02	−£1 000 (−£0.02 × 50 000 units)
= Net profit	£0.03	£1 500 (£0.03 × 50 000 units)

(Continued)

Assuming that the seller of the put option sold the pounds received immediately after the option was exercised, the net loss to the seller of the put option is calculated as follows:

Selling price of $	£0.55	£27 500 (−£0.55 × 50 000 units)
− Purchase price of $ from the put option having been exercised	−£0.60	−£30 000 (£0.60 × 50 000 units)
+ Premium received	+£0.02	+£1 000 (−£0.02 × 50 000 units)
= Net profit	−£0.03	−£1 500 (£0.03 × 50 000 units)

The seller of the put options could simply refrain from selling the dollars (after being forced to buy them at £0.60 per dollar) until the spot rate of the dollar rises. However, there is no guarantee that the dollar will reverse its direction and begin to appreciate. The seller's net loss could potentially be greater if the dollar's spot rate continued to fall, unless the dollars were sold immediately.

MANAGING FOR VALUE

Cisco's dilemma when hedging with put options

When Cisco Systems' European subsidiaries remit funds to their US parent, Cisco may consider purchasing put options to lock in the rate at which the euros will convert to dollars. The put options also offer the flexibility of letting the options expire if the prevailing exchange rate of the euro is higher than the options' exercise price. Several put options are available to Cisco and other MNCs that wish to hedge their currency positions. At a given point in time, some put options are deep out of the money, meaning that the prevailing exchange rate is high above the exercise price. These options are cheaper (have a lower premium), as they are unlikely to be exercised because their exercise price is too low. At the same time, other put options have an exercise price that is currently above the prevailing exchange rate and are therefore more likely to be exercised. Consequently, these options are more expensive.

Cisco must weigh the tradeoff when using put options to hedge. It can create a hedge that is cheap, but the options can be exercised only if the currency's spot rate declines substantially. Alternatively, Cisco can create a hedge that can be exercised at a more favourable exchange rate, but it must pay a higher premium for the options. If Cisco's goal in using put options is simply to prevent a major loss if the currency weakens substantially, it may be willing to use an inexpensive put option (low exercise price, low premium). However, if its goal is to ensure that the currency can be exchanged at a more favourable exchange rate, Cisco will use a more expensive put option (high exercise price, high premium). By selecting currency options with an exercise price and premium that fits their objectives, Cisco and other MNCs can increase their value.

The net profit to a speculator from purchasing put options on a currency is based on a comparison of the exercise price at which the currency can be sold versus the purchase price of the currency and the premium paid for the put option.

With the simplifying assumptions of the previous example, whatever an owner of a put option gains, the seller loses and vice versa. This relationship would hold if brokerage costs did not exist and if the buyer and seller of options entered and closed their positions at the same time. Brokerage fees for currency options exist, however, and are very similar in magnitude to those of currency futures contracts.

Speculating with combined put and call options. For volatile currencies, one possible speculative strategy is to create a **straddle**, which uses both a put option and a call option at the same exercise price. This may seem unusual because owning a put option is appropriate for expectations that the currency will depreciate, while owning a call option is appropriate for expectations that the currency will appreciate. However, a company may simply wish to protect against volatility in the markets which of itself may affect profits. For example for a MNC producing in the USA, a sharply appreciating dollar will be good for the converted dollar revenues of a MNC, but may adversely affect its USA sales due to cheap imports into the USA. A depreciating dollar would be bad for converted dollar revenues but possibly good for sales if US imports decline. The overall effect of large changes may therefore be indeterminate and worthwhile hedging.

USING THE WEB

Options prices

Information on option quotes can be obtained on the website of Yahoo finance.

Alternatively, a speculator might anticipate that a currency will be substantially affected by current economic events yet be uncertain of the exact way it will be affected. By purchasing a put option and a call option, the speculator will gain if the currency moves substantially in either direction. Although two options are purchased and only one is exercised, the gains could more than offset the costs.

Currency options market efficiency. If the currency options market is efficient, the premiums on currency options properly reflect all available information. Under these conditions, it may be difficult for speculators to consistently generate abnormal profits when speculating in this market. Research has found that the currency options market is efficient after controlling for transaction costs. Although some trading strategies could have generated abnormal gains in specific periods, they would have generated large losses if implemented in other periods. It is difficult to know which strategy would generate abnormal profits in future periods.

CONTINGENCY GRAPHS FOR CURRENCY OPTIONS

A contingency graph for currency options illustrates the potential gain or loss for various exchange rate scenarios.

Contingency graph for a purchaser of a call option

A contingency graph for a purchaser of a call option compares the price paid for the call option to potential payoffs to be received for a range of future exchange rate rates.

Suppose a European style call option on dollars is available with a strike price of £0.65 and a call premium of £0.03. The speculator plans to exercise the option on the expiration date (if appropriate at that time) and then immediately sell the dollars received in the spot market. Under these conditions, a **contingency graph** can be created to measure the profit or loss per unit (see Exhibit 5.10A). Notice that if the future spot rate is £0.65 or less, the net loss per unit is £0.03 (ignoring brokerage fees). This represents the loss of the premium per unit paid for the option, as the option would not be exercised. At all rates above £0.65 per unit the option will be exercised. Between the future spot prices of £0.65 and £0.68 exercising the option reduces the losses and is therefore worthwhile. Note that it is a common mistake to think that because an overall loss per unit is being made the option should still not be exercised. The important point here is that the loss is reduced through exercising, i.e. it will be less than the premium of £0.03. Break-even is at £0.68. Here the gains from exercising the option are £0.68 – £0.65 = £0.03 and exactly match the premium paid. Break-even for a call option is therefore the strike price plus the premium.

Contingency graph for a seller of a call option

A contingency graph for the seller of a call option compares the premium received from selling a call option to the potential payoffs made to the buyer of the call option for various exchange rate scenarios. Remember that the seller or writer of an option hopes that the option will not be exercised and that the option will be out of the money for the purchaser.

EXAMPLE

Exhibit 5.10B provides a contingency graph for a speculator who sold the call option described in the previous example. It assumes that this seller, if the option were to be exercised, would purchase the pounds in the spot market at the exercise date (transaction costs have not been included). At future spot rates of less than £0.65, the net gain to the seller would be the premium of £0.03 per unit, as the option would not have been exercised. If the future spot rate is £0.67, the seller would gain £0.01 per unit on the option transaction paying £0.67 for the dollars in the spot market and selling dollars for £0.65 to fulfil the exercise request. This loss of £0.02 would be offset by the premium of £0.03 per unit received, resulting in a net gain of £0.01 per unit.

EXHIBIT 5.10A Contingency graph for the purchaser of the call option

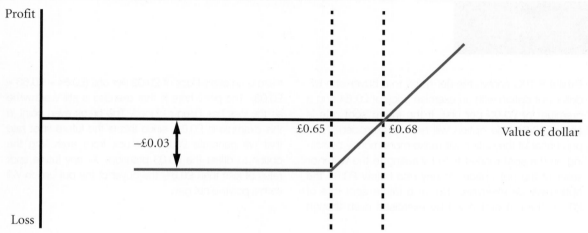

EXHIBIT 5.10B Contingency graph for the seller (or writer) of the call option

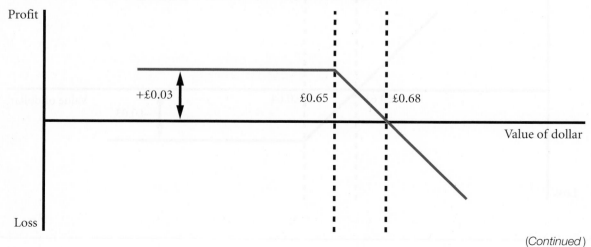

(Continued)

The break-even point is at £0.68 as outlined in the previous example, and the net gain to the seller of a call option becomes negative at all future spot rates higher than that point. Notice that the contingency graphs for the buyer and seller of call options are

The seller of the call option faces potentially unlimited losses. This exposure can be limited by buying a call option at a higher strike price (say, £0.72 for $1)

mirror images of one another. This reflects the fact that in this simplified scenario the seller's gain is the purchaser's loss and *vice versa* – this phenomenon is sometimes termed a zero sum game. The same applies to put options.

at rates above the higher strike price the losses from selling the call will be offset by the gains on the purchased call.

Contingency graph for a buyer of a put option

A contingency graph for a buyer of a put option compares the premium paid for the put option to potential payoffs received for a range of future exchange rates.

EXAMPLE

Exhibit 5.10C shows the net gains to a buyer of a US dollar put option with an exercise price of £0.64 and a premium of £0.03 per unit. If the future spot rate is above £0.64, the option will not be exercised – the purchaser of the option will make more money by selling on the spot market than by selling to the writer or seller of the put option. At any rate below £0.64 the option will be exercised. So, at a future spot rate of £0.63, the put option will be exercised even though

there is an overall loss of £0.02 per unit (£0.64 – £0.63 – £0.03). The point here is that exercise is still worthwhile as the loss has been reduced. The break-even point in this example is £0.61, since this is the future spot rate that will generate £0.03 per unit from exercising the option to offset the £0.03 premium. At any future spot rates of less than £0.61, the buyer of the put option will earn a positive net gain.

EXHIBIT 5.10C   Contingency graph for the purchaser of the put option

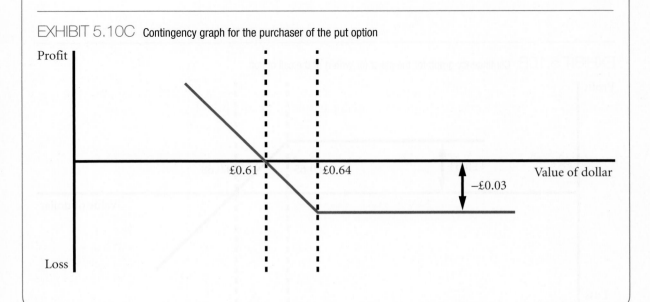

Contingency graph for a seller of a put option

A contingency graph for the seller of this put option (Exhibit 5.10D) compares the premium received from selling the option to the possible payoffs that the seller of the put option will have to make to the buyer of the put option for various exchange rate scenarios. As with call option writers, the hope is that the option will be out of the money and the seller will retain the premium.

Note that the graph for the seller of a put option is the mirror image of the contingency graph for the buyer of the same put option. Again as with call options, the seller's position is essentially speculative. Such speculation offers a service to MNCs who may be purchasing the option to protect against a loss of profits on international transactions.

EXHIBIT 5.10D Contingency graph for the seller (or writer) of the put option

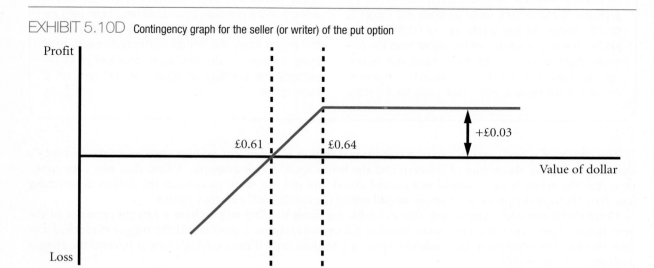

CONDITIONAL CURRENCY OPTIONS

A currency option can be structured with a conditional premium, meaning that the premium paid for the option is conditioned on the actual movement in the currency's value over the period of concern. This kind of option enables the instrument to compete more with futures where there is no premium (but remember that futures does not offer a range of strike prices nor the possibility of not exercising). The basic idea is to charge a higher premium than a traditional option when conditions are favourable and no premium when conditions are less favourable. It is rather like giving an option on an option!

EXAMPLE

Jensen Ltd, a UK-based MNC, needs to sell dollars that it will receive in 60 days. It can negotiate a traditional currency put option on dollars in which the exercise price is £0.60 and the premium is £0.03 per unit.

Alternatively, it can negotiate a conditional currency option with a commercial bank. The exercise price of £0.60 is supplemented by a so-called trigger of £0.62. If the dollar's value falls below the exercise price by the

(Continued)

expiration date, Jensen will exercise the option, thereby receiving £0.60 per dollar, and it will not have to pay a premium for the option. These will be unexpectedly bad circumstances for Jensen, so not paying the premium will be a welcome relief.

If the dollar's value is between the exercise price (£0.60) and the trigger (£0.62), the option will not be exercised, and Jensen will not need to pay a premium. For Jensen these will be circumstances that the company will judge to be very likely – so the judgement will be that the company will probably not have to pay the premium. If the dollar's value exceeds the trigger of £0.62, Jensen will pay a premium of £0.04 per unit. Notice that this premium will be higher than the premium that would be paid for a basic put option. Jensen may not mind this outcome, however, because it will be receiving a high price for the dollar

from converting its dollar receivables on the spot market.

Jensen must determine whether the potential advantage of the conditional option (avoiding the payment of a premium under some conditions) outweighs the potential disadvantage (paying a higher premium than the premium for a traditional put option on US dollars).

The potential advantages and disadvantages are illustrated in Exhibit 5.11. At exchange rates less than or equal to the trigger level (£0.62), the conditional option results in a larger payment to Jensen by the amount of the premium that would have been paid for the basic option. Conversely, at exchange rates above the trigger level, the conditional option results in a lower payment to Jensen, as its premium of £0.04 exceeds the premium of £0.03 per unit paid on a basic option.

The choice of a basic option versus a conditional option is dependent on expectations of the currency's exchange rate over the period of concern and the firm's level of risk aversion. A firm that was very confident that the pound's value would not exceed £0.64 and did not want to convert the dollars at anything less than £0.58 in the previous example would prefer the conditional currency option.

Conditional currency options are also available for firms needing to purchase a foreign currency in the near future. There are variations, some conditional options require a premium if the trigger is reached any time up until the expiration date; others require a premium only if the exchange rate is beyond the trigger as of the expiration date.

Another variation is a cylinder option (typically between a bank and an MNC) or zero cost option that guarantees an exchange rate between two agreed limits (see Appendix 5B for further details).

Taken together the zero cost option and the contingency option show that sophisticated insurance contracts can be built from using basic calls and puts. The term 'financial engineering' has been used to describe the complexity of such options.

EXHIBIT 5.11   Comparison of conditional and basic currency options

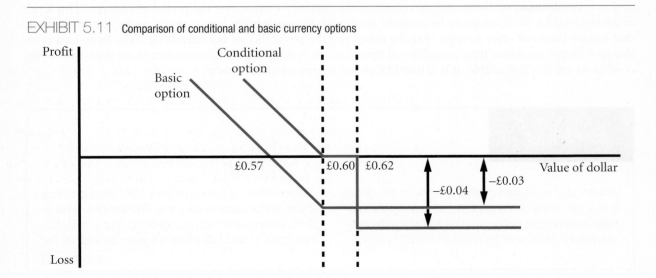

European and American currency options

The discussion of currency options has used a mixture of American and European style options. European style options can be exercised only at the settlement or expiration date, whereas American options can be exercised up to and including the settlement date. If a company wishes to terminate a European style option before the settlement date, the option can be sold in the secondary market. If the option is 'in the money' at the time of sale, the price of the option will take the 'in the money' position into account, so some but not all of the potential benefit will be recovered.

Asian options

Asian options offer the ability to take options out on assets that are not heavily traded. The problem here is that the price on maturity may be subject to considerable volatility due to a lower level of trading. The Asian option adjusts for this by taking an average price over a given period. The term Asian simply refers to the origin of the financial instrument and may be applied to any underlying asset. Because average prices are more stable the Asian option is cheaper than its European equivalent. In effect this option extends the market to a wider range of assets.

Options in Emerging Market Economies

One of the growth areas for derivative instruments has been in emerging market economies (EMEs)[1]. Trading is mainly over-the-counter (OTC) and now consists of some 12 per cent of total OTC derivative trading. About 80 per cent of this trade is in currencies being in the main currency swaps; there are several reasons for this phenomenon. Developing countries are more prone to suffering a balance of payments crisis and hence currency instability, secondly governments have tended to move away from fixed exchange rate regimes and thirdly pension funds in search of profits have been investing in developing countries and seek to limit their risk, fourthly foreign exchange markets are less open than the swap market and it is seen as a quick way of obtaining foreign currency. Credit default swaps are also seen as a particularly relevant form of protection for emerging economies. A credit default swap is a form of insurance contract against default. As with insurance, a regular premium is paid in return for a payout in the event of an 'accident' being in this case a default 'event' as defined in the contract. This is clearly of value when lending to developing economies, though the largest recent payout was on Greek debt.

SUMMARY

- A futures contract specifies a standard volume of a particular currency to be exchanged on a particular date. Such a contract can be purchased by a firm to hedge payables or sold by a firm to hedge receivables.

- A currency futures contract can be purchased by speculators who expect the currency to appreciate. Conversely, it can be sold by speculators who expect that currency to depreciate. If the currency depreciates, the value of

the futures contract declines, allowing those speculators to benefit when they close out their positions.

- Futures contracts on a particular currency can be purchased by corporations that have payables in that currency and wish to hedge against the possible appreciation of that currency. Conversely, these contracts can be sold by corporations that have receivables in that currency and wish to

---

[1]See Sweta Saxena, S. and Villar (2008) *Hedging Instruments in Emerging Market Economies*, BIS paper No. 44.

hedge against the possible depreciation of that currency.

- Currency options are classified as call options or put options. Call options allow the right to purchase a specified currency at a specified exchange rate by a specified expiration date. Put options allow the right to sell a specified currency at a specified exchange rate by a specified expiration date.

- Call options on a specific currency can be purchased by speculators who expect that

currency to appreciate. Put options on a specific currency can be purchased by speculators who expect that currency to depreciate.

- Currency call options are commonly purchased by corporations that have payables in a currency that is expected to appreciate. Currency put options are commonly purchased by corporations that have receivables in a currency that is expected to depreciate.

CRITICAL DEBATE

Hedging

Proposition. MNCs should not protect against currency changes. Investors take into account currency risks and the diversification benefits from investing in companies that conduct international business. But if these companies are going to protect themselves against one of the main sources of diversification, namely currency changes, they are in effect denying investors the opportunity to benefit from such diversification in order to protect their own positions as directors.

Opposing view. Companies specialize in certain activities that generally do not include currency speculation. Derivatives enable such companies to specialize in more clearly defined risks. The protection is in any case only

short term, no protection is being offered for long-term changes in the value of a currency. Derivatives simply avoid distortion to profits caused by unusual changes to currency values. Such currency shocks could lead to abnormal share price movements that might adversely affect individual shareholders who have to sell for personal reasons.

With whom do you agree? How should the investment community view business risk? Should shareholders be more aware of the currency risk policy of the company? Are directors protecting their own positions at the expense of the shareholder? Offer your own opinion on this issue.

SELF TEST

Answers are provided in Appendix A at the back of the text.

1 A call option on US dollars with a strike price of £0.60 is purchased by a speculator for a premium of £0.06 per unit. Assume there are 50 000 units in this option contract. If the US dollar's spot rate is £0.65 at the time the option is exercised, what is the net profit or loss per unit to the speculator if the option were to be exercised now? What is the net profit or loss for one contract? What would the spot rate need to be at the time the option is exercised for the speculator to break even? What is the net profit per unit to the seller of this option if exercised now?

2 A put option on Australian dollars with a strike price of £0.53 is purchased by a speculator for a premium of £0.02. If the Australian dollar's spot rate is £0.50 on the expiration date, should the speculator exercise the option on this date or let the option expire? What is the net profit or loss per unit to the speculator? What is the net profit or loss per unit to the seller of this put option?

3 Longer-term currency options are becoming more popular for hedging exchange rate risk. Why do you think some firms decide to hedge by using other techniques instead of purchasing long-term currency options?

QUESTIONS AND APPLICATIONS

1 **Forward versus futures contracts.** Compare and contrast forward and futures contracts.

2 **Using currency futures.**
   a How can currency futures be used by corporations?
   b How can currency futures be used by speculators?

3 **Currency options.** Differentiate between a currency call option and a currency put option.

4 **Forward premium.** Compute the forward discount or premium for the Mexican peso whose 90-day forward rate is £0.05 and spot rate is £0.051. State whether your answer is a discount or premium.

5 **Effects of a forward contract.** How can a forward contract backfire?

6 **Hedging with currency options.** When would a UK firm consider purchasing a call option on euros for hedging? When would a UK firm consider purchasing a put option on euros for hedging?

7 **Speculating with currency options.** When should a speculator purchase a call option on Australian dollars? When should a speculator purchase a put option on Australian dollars?

8 **Currency call option premiums.** List the factors that affect currency call option premiums and briefly explain the relationship that exists for each. Do you think an at-the-money call option in euros has a higher or lower premium than an at-the-money call option on dollars (assuming the expiration date and the total dollar value represented by each option are the same for both options)?

9 **Currency put option premiums.** List the factors that affect currency put options and briefly explain the relationship that exists for each.

10 **Speculating with currency call options.** Randy Rudecki purchased a call option on British pounds for 0.02 euros per unit. The strike price was 1.45 euros, and the spot rate at the time the option was exercised was 1.46 euros. Assume there are 31 250 units in a British pound option. What was Randy's net profit on this option?

11 **Speculating with currency put options.** Alice Duever purchased a put option on dollars for £0.04 per unit. The strike price was £0.55, and the spot rate at the time the dollar option was exercised was £0.63. Assume there are 50 000 units in a US dollar option. What was Alice's net profit on the option?

12 **Selling currency call options.** Mike Suerth sold a call option on Canadian dollars for £0.01 per unit. The strike price was £0.42, and the spot rate at the time the option was exercised was £0.46. Assume Mike did not obtain Canadian dollars until the option was exercised. Also assume that there are 50 000 units in a Canadian dollar option. What was Mike's net profit or loss on the call option?

13 **Selling currency put options.** Brian Tull sold a put option on Canadian dollars for £0.02 per unit. The strike price was £0.42, and the spot rate at the time the option was exercised was £0.40. Assume Brian immediately sold off the Canadian dollars received when the option was exercised. Also assume that there are 50 000 units in a Canadian dollar option. What was Brian's net profit on the put option?

14 **Forward versus currency option contracts.** What are the advantages and disadvantages to an MNC that uses currency options on dollars rather than a forward contract on dollars to hedge its exposure in dollars? Explain why an MNC may use forward contracts to hedge committed transactions and use currency options to hedge contracts that are anticipated but not committed. Why might forward contracts be advantageous for committed transactions, and currency options be advantageous for anticipated transactions?

15 **Speculating with currency futures.** Assume that the euro's spot rate has moved in cycles over time. How might you try to use futures contracts on euros to capitalize on this tendency? How could you determine whether such a strategy would have been profitable in previous periods?

16 **Hedging with currency derivatives.** Assume that the transactions listed in the first column of the following table are anticipated by UK firms that have no other foreign transactions. Place an 'X' in the table wherever you see possible ways to hedge each of the transactions.

17 **Price movements of currency futures.** Assume that on 1 November, the spot rate of the British pound was £0.63 and the price on a December futures contract was £0.64. Assume that the pound depreciated during November so that by 30 November it was worth £0.60.
   a What do you think happened to the futures price over the month of November? Why?
   b If you had known that this would occur, would you have purchased or sold a December futures contract in pounds on 1 November? Explain.

18 **Speculating with currency futures.** Assume that a March futures contract on Mexican pesos was available in January for $0.09 per unit. Also assume that forward contracts were available for the same settlement date at a price of $0.092 per peso. How could speculators capitalize on this situation, assuming zero transaction costs? How would such speculative activity affect the difference between the forward contract price and the futures price?

	Forward contract		Futures contract		Options contract	
	Forward purchase	Forward sale	Buy futures	Sell futures	Purchase call	Purchase put
a. George Ltd plans to purchase Japanese goods denominated in yen.						
b. Harvard Ltd will sell goods to Japan, denominated in yen.						
c. Yale plc has a subsidiary in Australia that will be remitting funds to the UK parent.						
d. Brown Ltd needs to pay off existing loans that are denominated in Canadian dollars.						
e. Princeton Ltd may purchase a company in Japan in the near future (but the deal may not go through).						

19 **Speculating with currency call options.** LSU Corp. purchased Canadian dollar call options for speculative purposes. If these options are exercised, LSU will immediately sell the Canadian dollars in the spot market. Each option was purchased for a premium of $0.03 per unit, with an exercise price of $0.80. LSU plans to wait until the expiration date before deciding whether to exercise the options. Of course, LSU will exercise the options at that time only if it is feasible to do so. In the following table, fill in the net profit (or loss) per unit to LSU Corp. based on the listed possible spot rates of the Canadian dollar on the expiration date.

Possible spot rate on Canadian dollar on expiration date	Net profit (loss) per unit to LSU Corporation
$0.76	
$0.78	
$0.80	
$0.82	
$0.85	
$0.87	

20 **Speculating with currency put options.** Auburn Ltd has purchased Canadian dollar put options for speculative purposes. Each option was purchased for a premium of £0.02 per unit, with an exercise price of £0.48 per unit. Auburn Ltd will purchase the Canadian dollars just before it exercises the options (if it is feasible to exercise the options). It plans to wait until the expiration date before deciding whether to exercise the options. In the following table, fill in the net profit (or loss) per unit to Auburn Ltd based on the listed possible spot rates of the Canadian dollar on the expiration date.

Possible spot rate on Canadian dollar on expiration date	Net profit (loss) per unit to Auburn Ltd
£0.42	
£0.44	
£0.46	
£0.48	
£0.50	
£0.52	

21 Speculating with currency call options. Bama plc has sold dollar call options for speculative purposes. The option premium was £0.04 per unit, and the exercise price was £0.54. Bama will purchase the dollars on the day the options are exercised (if the options are exercised) in order to fulfil its obligation. In the following table, fill in the net profit (or loss) to Bama plc if the listed spot rate exists at the time the purchaser of the call options considers exercising them.

Possible spot rate at the time the purchaser of the call option (American style) considers exercising them	Net profit (loss) per unit to Bama plc
£0.48	
£0.50	
£0.52	
£0.54	
£0.56	
£0.58	
£0.60	

22 Speculating with currency put options. Bulldog Ltd has sold Australian dollar put options at a premium of £0.01 per unit, and an exercise price of £0.42 per unit. It has forecasted the Australian dollar's lowest level over the period of concern as shown in the following table. Determine the net profit (or loss) per unit to Bulldog Ltd if each level occurs and the put options are exercised at that time.

Possible value of Australian dollar	Net profit (loss) per unit to Bulldog Ltd if value occurs
£0.38	
£0.39	
£0.40	
£0.41	
£0.42	

23 Hedging with currency derivatives. A US professional football team plans to play an exhibition game in the UK next year. Assume that all expenses will be paid by the British government, and that the team will receive a cheque for 1 million pounds. The team anticipates that the pound will depreciate substantially by the scheduled date of the game. In addition, the National Football League must approve the deal, and approval (or disapproval) will not occur for 3 months. How can the team hedge its position? What is there to lose by waiting 3 months to see if the exhibition game is approved before hedging?

ADVANCED QUESTIONS

24 Risk of currency futures. Currency futures markets are commonly used as a means of capitalizing on shifts in currency values, because the value of a futures contract tends to move in line with the change in the corresponding currency value. Recently, many currencies appreciated against the dollar. Most speculators anticipated that the dollar's value would continue to decline. However, the Fed intervened in the foreign exchange market by immediately buying dollars with foreign currency, causing an abrupt halt in the decline in the value of the dollar. Participants that had sold dollar futures contracts for a range of other currencies incurred large losses.

   a Explain why the central bank's intervention caused such panic among currency futures traders with sell positions.

   b Some traders with sell positions on dollars may have responded immediately to the central bank's intervention by buying futures contracts. Why would some speculators with buy positions leave their positions unchanged or even increase their positions by purchasing more futures contracts in response to the central bank's intervention?

25 Assume that on November 1 the spot rate of the British pound was $1.58 and the price on a December futures contract was $1.59. Assume that the pound depreciated over November, so that by November 30 it was worth $1.51

   a What do you think happened to the futures price over the month of November? Why?

   b If you would have known that this would occur, would you have purchased or sold a December futures contract in pounds on November 1? Explain.

26 Wrongdoer plc (a UK company) sells coffee in the UK and has signed a contract for the purchase of coffee from Brazil. As part of its financial risk management, the company takes out a Futures Contract at $106.00 per 60kg bag of coffee for 3 months for a quantity that represents its monthly purchase.

a Explain how this Futures Contract may contribute to the financial risk management of the company.

b Outline the payments and receipts that a financial manager would make if the price moved as follows on the days after the Futures Contract has been taken out:

	Day 1	Day 2	Day 3	Day 4
Price of 1 bag of coffee	$104	$102	$112	$95

c How might Wrongdoer manage the risk of a change in the price of coffee without resorting to the derivative markets?

27 **Currency straddles.** Reska Ltd has constructed a long euro straddle. A call option on euros with an exercise price of £0.61 has a premium of £0.015 per unit. A euro put option has a premium of £0.008 per unit. Some possible euro values at option expiration are shown in the following table (see Appendix 5B in this chapter).

a Complete the worksheet and determine the net profit per unit to Reska Ltd for each possible future spot rate.

Value of euro at option expiration				
	£0.50	£0.55	£0.60	£0.65
Call				
Put				
Net				

b Determine the break-even point(s) of the long straddle. What are the break-even points of a short straddle using these options?

28 **Currency straddles.** Refer to the previous question, but assume that the call and put option premiums are £0.01 per unit and £0.006 per unit, respectively (see Appendix 5B in this chapter).

a Construct a contingency graph for a long euro straddle (call options).

b Construct a contingency graph for a short euro straddle (put options).

29 **Currency option contingency graphs.** (See Appendix 5B in this chapter.) The current spot rate of the Singapore dollar (S$) is £0.34. The following option information is available:

● Call option premium on Singapore dollar (S$) = £0.015.

● Put option premium on Singapore dollar (S$) = £0.009.

● Call and put option strike price = £0.36.

● One option contract represents S$70 000.

Construct a contingency graph for a short straddle using these options.

30 **Speculating with currency straddles.** Maggie Hawthorne is a currency speculator. She has noticed that recently the dollar has depreciated substantially against the euro. The current exchange rate of the dollar is 0.78 euro. After reading a variety of articles on the subject, she believes that the dollar will continue to fluctuate substantially in the months to come. Although most forecasters believe that the dollar will depreciate against the euro in the near future, Maggie thinks that there is also a good possibility of further appreciation. Currently, a call option on dollars is available with an exercise price of 0.80 euro and a premium of 0.04 euro. A euro put option with an exercise price of 0.80 euro and a premium of 0.03 euro is also available (see Appendix 5B in this chapter).

a Describe how Maggie could use straddles to speculate on the dollar's value.

b At option expiration, the value of the dollar is 0.90 euro. What is Maggie's total profit or loss from a long straddle position?

c What is Maggie's total profit or loss from a long straddle position if the value of the dollar is 0.60 euro at option expiration?

d What is Maggie's total profit or loss from a long straddle position if the value of the dollar at option expiration is still 0.78 euro?

e Given your answers to the questions above, when is it advantageous for a speculator to engage in a long straddle? When is it advantageous to engage in a short straddle?

31 **Currency strangles.** (See Appendix 5B in this chapter.) Assume the following options are currently available for dollars:

- Call option premium on dollars = £0.04 per unit.
- Put option premium on dollars = £0.03 per unit.
- Call option strike price = £0.64.
- Put option strike price = £0.62.
- One option contract represents $50 000.

a Construct a diagram for a long strangle using these options.

b Determine the break-even point(s) for a strangle.

c If the spot price of the dollar at option expiration is £0.63, what is the total profit or loss to the strangle buyer?

d If the spot price of the dollar at option expiration is £0.51, what is the total profit or loss to the strangle writer?

32 Currency straddles. Refer to the previous question, but assume that the call and put option premiums are £0.035 per unit and £0.025 per unit, respectively (see Appendix 5B in this chapter).

a Construct a contingency graph for a long pound straddle.

b Construct a contingency graph for a short pound straddle.

33 Currency strangles. The following information is currently available for Canadian dollar (C$) options (see Appendix 5B in this chapter):

- Put option exercise price = £0.45.
- Put option premium = £0.014 per unit.
- Call option exercise price = £0.46.
- Call option premium = £0.01 per unit.
- One option contract represents C$50 000.

a What is the maximum possible loss the purchaser of a strangle can achieve using these options?

b What is the maximum possible gain the writer of a strangle can incur?

c Locate the break-even point(s) of the strangle.

   Currency strangles. For the following options available on Australian dollars (A$), construct a worksheet and contingency graph for a long strangle. Locate the break-even points for this strangle (see Appendix B in this chapter):

- Put option strike price = £0.42.
- Call option strike price = £0.40.
- Put option premium = £0.01 per unit.
- Call option premium = £0.02 per unit.

34 Speculating with currency options. Barry Egan is a currency speculator. Barry believes that the Japa-

nese yen will fluctuate widely against the euro in the coming month. Currently, 1-month call options on Japanese yen (¥) are available with a strike price of 0.0085 euro and a premium of 0.0007 euro per unit. One-month put options on Japanese yen are available with a strike price of 0.0084 euro and a premium of 0.0005 euro per unit. One option contract on Japanese yen contains ¥6.25 million (see Appendix 5B in this chapter).

a Describe how Barry Egan could utilize these options to speculate on the movement of the Japanese yen.

b Assume Barry decides to construct a long strangle in yen. What are the break-even points of this strangle?

c What is Barry's total profit or loss if the value of the yen in 1 month is 0.0070 euro?

d What is Barry's total profit or loss if the value of the yen in 1 month is $0.0090 euro?

35 Currency bull spreads and bear spreads. A call option on dollars exists with a strike price of £0.64 and a premium of £0.04 per unit. Another call option on dollars has a strike price of £0.66 and a premium of £0.03 per unit (see Appendix 5B in this chapter).

a Complete the worksheet for a bull spread below.

Value of US dollar at option expiration				
	£0.58	£0.64	£0.66	£0.72
Call@0.64				
Call@0.66				
Net				

b What is the breakeven point for this bull spread?

c What is the maximum profit of this bull spread? What is the maximum loss?

d If the dollar spot rate is £0.65 at option expiration, what is the total profit or loss for the bull spread?

e If the dollar spot rate is £0.63 at option expiration, what is the total profit or loss for a bear spread?

36 Bull spreads and bear spreads. Two dollar put options are available with exercise prices of £0.70 and £0.72. The premiums associated with these options are £0.02 and £0.03 per unit, respectively (see Appendix 5B in this chapter).

Value of US dollar at option expiration				
	£0.65	£0.70	£0.75	£0.80
Put@0.70				
Put@0.72				
Net				

a Describe how a bull spread can be constructed using these put options. What is the difference between using put options versus call options to construct a bull spread?

b Complete the worksheet.

c At option expiration, the spot rate of the pound is £0.70. What is the bull spreader's total gain or loss?

d At option expiration, the spot rate of the pound is £0.66. What is the bear spreader's total gain or loss?

37 Profits from using currency options and futures. On 2 July, the 2-month futures rate of the Argentine peso contained a 2 per cent discount (unannualized). There was a call option on pesos with an exercise price that was equal to the spot rate. There was also a put option on pesos with an exercise price equal to the spot rate. The premium on each of these options was 3 per cent of the spot rate at that time. On 2 September, the option expired. Go to http://www.oanda.com (or any website that has foreign exchange rate quotations) and determine the direct quote of the Argentine peso. You exercised the option on this date if it was feasible to do so.

a What was your net profit per unit if you had purchased the call option?

b What was your net profit per unit if you had purchased the put option?

c What was your net profit per unit if you had purchased a futures contract on 2 July that had a settlement date of 2 September?

d What was your net profit per unit if you sold a futures contract on 2 July that had a settlement date of 2 September?

38 A UK MNC takes out a cylinder option to buy dollars between the rates of £0.75 and £0.85 per US dollar (see Appendix 5B in this chapter).

a Describe the implied options in the contract.

b Explain potential payoffs from the options and their total effect on the MNC's cost of purchasing the dollar.

PROJECT WORKSHOP

39 Currency futures online. The website of the Chicago Mercantile Exchange provides information about currency futures and options. Its address is http://www.cme.com.

a Use this website to review the prevailing prices of currency futures contracts. Do today's futures prices (for contracts with the closest settlement date) generally reflect an increase or decrease from the day before? Is there any news today that might explain the change in the futures prices?

b Does it appear that futures prices among currencies (for the closest settlement date) are changing in the same direction? Explain.

c If you purchase a British pound futures contract with the closest settlement date, what is the futures price? Given that a contract is based on 62 500 pounds, what is the dollar amount you will need at the settlement date to fulfil the contract?

DISCUSSION IN THE BOARDROOM

This exercise can be found on our dedicated Course-Mate platform for students.

RUNNING YOUR OWN MNC

This exercise can be found on our dedicated Course-Mate platform for students.

Essays/discussion and articles can be found at the end of Part I.

BLADES PLC CASE STUDY

Use of currency derivative instruments

Blades plc needs to order supplies 2 months ahead of the delivery date. It is considering an order from a Japanese supplier that requires a payment of 12.5 million yen payable as of the delivery date. Blades has two choices:

- Purchase two call option contracts (since each option contract represents 6 250 000 yen).
- Purchase one futures contract (which represents 12.5 million yen).

The futures price on yen has historically exhibited a slight discount from the existing spot rate. However, the firm would like to use currency options to hedge payables in Japanese yen for transactions 2 months in advance. Blades would prefer hedging its yen payable position because it is uncomfortable leaving the position open given the historical volatility of the yen. Nevertheless, the firm would be willing to remain unhedged if the yen becomes more stable someday.

Ben Holt, Blades' finance director, prefers the flexibility that options offer over forward contracts or futures contracts because he can let the options expire if the yen depreciates. He would like to use an exercise price that is about 5 per cent above the existing spot rate to ensure that Blades will have to pay no more than 5 per cent above the existing spot rate for a transaction 2 months beyond its order date, as long as the option premium is no more than 1.6 per cent of the price it would have to pay per unit when exercising the option.

In general, options on the yen have required a premium of about 1.5 per cent of the total transaction amount that would be paid if the option is exercised. For example, recently the yen spot rate was £0.0048 and the firm purchased a call option with an exercise price of £0.00504, which is 5 per cent above the existing spot rate. The premium for this option was £0.000089, which is 1.5 per cent of the price to be paid per yen if the option is exercised.

A recent event caused more uncertainty about the yen's future value, although it did not affect the spot rate or the forward or futures rate of the yen. Specifically, the yen's spot rate was still £0.0048, but the option premium for a call option with an exercise price of $0.00504 was now £0.00010. An alternative call option is available with an expiration date of 2 months from now; it has a premium of £0.0000756 (which is the size of the premium that would have existed for the option desired before the event), but it is for a call option with an exercise price of £0.00528.

The table below summarizes the option and futures information available to Blades.

	Before event	After event	
Spot rate	£0.0048	£0.0048	£0.0048
Option information:			
Exercise price (£)	£0.00504	£0.00504	£0.00528
Exercise price (% above spot)	5%	5%	10%
Option premium per yen (£)	£0.000076	£0.00010	£0.0000756
Option premium (% of exercise price)	1.5%	2.0%	1.5%
Futures contract information:			
Futures price	£0.004608	£0.004608	

As an analyst for Blades, you have been asked to offer insight on how to hedge. Use a spreadsheet to support your analysis of questions 4 and 6.

1 If Blades uses call options to hedge its yen payables, should it use the call option with the exercise price of £0.00504 or the call option with the exercise price of £0.00528? Describe the trade-off.

2 Should Blades allow its yen position to be unhedged? Describe the trade-off.

3 Assume there are speculators who attempt to capitalize on their expectation of the yen's movement over the 2 months between the order and delivery dates by either buying or selling yen futures now and buying or selling yen at the future spot rate. Given this information, what is the *expectation* on the order date of the yen spot rate by the delivery date? (Your answer should consist of one number.)

4 Assume that the firm shares the market consensus of the future yen spot rate. Given this expectation and given that the firm makes a decision (i.e., option, futures contract, remain unhedged) purely on a cost basis, what would be its optimal choice?

5 Will the choice you made as to the optimal hedging strategy in question 4 definitely turn out to be the lowest-cost alternative in terms of actual costs incurred? Why or why not?

6 Now assume that you have determined that the historical standard deviation of the yen is about £0.0003. Based on your assessment, you believe it is highly unlikely that the future spot rate will be more than two standard deviations above the expected spot rate by the delivery date. Also assume that the futures price remains at its current level of £0.004608. Based on this expectation of the future spot rate, what is the optimal hedge for the firm?

SMALL BUSINESS DILEMMA

Use of currency futures and options by the Sports Exports Company

The Sports Exports Company receives pounds each month as payment for the footballs that it exports. It anticipates that the pound will depreciate over time against the dollar.

1 How can the Sports Exports Company use currency futures contracts to hedge against exchange rate risk? Are there any limitations of using currency futures contracts that would prevent the Sports Exports Company from locking in a specific exchange rate at which it can sell all the pounds it expects to receive in each of the upcoming months?

2 How can the Sports Exports Company use currency options to hedge against exchange rate risk? Are there any limitations of using currency options contracts that would prevent the Sports Exports Company from locking in a specific exchange rate at which it can sell all the pounds it expects to receive in each of the upcoming months?

3 Jim Logan, owner of the Sports Exports Company, is concerned that the pound may depreciate substantially over the next month, but he also believes that the pound could appreciate substantially if specific situations occur. Should Jim use currency futures or currency options to hedge the exchange rate risk? Is there any disadvantage of selecting this method for hedging?

APPENDIX 5A
CURRENCY OPTION PRICING

The premiums paid for currency options depend on various factors that must be monitored when anticipating future movements in currency option premiums. Since participants in the currency options market typically take positions based on their expectations as to how the premiums will change over time, they can benefit from understanding how options are priced.

BOUNDARY CONDITIONS

The first step in pricing currency options is to recognize boundary conditions that force the option premium to be within lower and upper bounds.

Lower bounds

The call option premium (C) has a lower bound of at least zero or the spread between the underlying spot exchange rate (S) and the exercise price (X), whichever is greater, as shown below:

$$C = MAX(0, S - X)$$

This floor is enforced by arbitrage restrictions. For example, assume that the premium on a British pound call option is $0.01, while the spot rate of the pound is $1.62 and the exercise price is $1.60. In this example, the spread (S – X) exceeds the call premium, which would allow for arbitrage. One could purchase the call option for $0.01 per unit, immediately exercise the option at $1.60 per pound, and then sell the pounds in the spot market for $1.62 per unit. This would generate an immediate profit of $0.01 per unit. Arbitrage would continue until the market forces realigned the spread (S – X) to be less than or equal to the call premium.

The put option premium (P) has a lower bound of zero or the spread between the exercise price (X) and the underlying spot exchange rate (S), whichever is greater, as shown below:

$$P = MAX(0, X - S)$$

This floor is also enforced by arbitrage restrictions. For example, assume that the premium on a British pound put option is $0.02, while the spot rate of the pound is $1.60 and the exercise price is $1.63. One could purchase the pound put option for $0.02 per unit, purchase pounds in the spot market at $1.60, and immediately exercise the option by selling the pounds at $1.63 per unit. This would generate an immediate profit of $0.01 per unit. Arbitrage would continue until the market forces realigned the spread $(X - S)$ to be less than or equal to the put premium.

Upper bounds

The upper bound for a call option premium is equal to the spot exchange rate (S):

$$C = S$$

If the call option premium ever exceeds the spot exchange rate, one could engage in arbitrage by selling call options for a higher price per unit than the cost of purchasing the underlying currency. Even if those call options are exercised, one could provide the currency that was purchased earlier (the call option was covered). The arbitrage profit in this example is the difference between the amount received when selling the premium and the cost of purchasing the currency in the spot market. Arbitrage would occur until the call option's premium was less than or equal to the spot rate.

The upper bound for a put option is equal to the option's exercise price (X):

$$P = X$$

If the put option premium ever exceeds the exercise price, one could engage in arbitrage by selling put options. Even if the put options are exercised, the proceeds received from selling the put options exceed the price paid (which is the exercise price) at the time of exercise.

Given these boundaries that are enforced by arbitrage, option premiums lie within these boundaries.

APPLICATION OF PRICING MODEL

Although boundary conditions can be used to determine the possible range for a currency option's premium, they do not precisely indicate the appropriate premium for the option. However, pricing models have been developed to price currency options. Based on information about an option (such as the exercise price and time to maturity) and about the currency (such as its spot rate, standard deviation and interest rate), pricing models can derive the premium on a currency option. The currency option pricing model of Biger and Hull[2] is shown below:

$$C = e^{-r^*T}S. \ N(d_1) - e^{-rT}X. \ N(d_1 - \sigma\sqrt{T})$$

Where:

$d_1 = \{[\ln(S / X) + (r (- r^* + (\sigma^2/2))\sqrt{T}] / \sigma\}$
C = price of the currency call option
S = underlying spot exchange rate
X = exercise price
r = home riskless rate of interest
r^* = foreign riskless rate of interest
σ = instantaneous standard deviation of the return on a holding of foreign currency
T = option's time maturity expressed as a fraction of a year
$N(\cdot)$ = standard normal cumulative distribution function.

---

[2]Nahum Biger and John Hull, 'The Valuation of Currency Options', *Financial Management* (Spring 1983), 24–8.

This equation is based on the stock option pricing model (OPM) when allowing for continuous dividends. Since the interest gained on holding a foreign security (r^*) is equivalent to a continuously paid dividend on a stock share, this version of the OPM holds completely. The key transformation in adapting the stock OPM to value currency options is the substitution of exchange rates for stock prices. Thus, the percentage change of exchange rates is assumed to follow a diffusion process with constant mean and variance.

Bodurtha and Courtadon[3] have tested the predictive ability of the currency option of the pricing model. They computed pricing errors from the model using 3326 call options. The model's average percentage pricing error for call options was −6.90 per cent, which is smaller than the corresponding error reported for the dividend-adjusted Black-Scholes stock OPM. Hence, the currency option pricing model has been more accurate than the counterpart stock OPM.

The model developed by Biger and Hull is sometimes referred to as the European model because it does not account for early exercise. European currency options do not allow for early exercise (before the expiration date), while American currency options do allow for early exercise. The extra flexibility of American currency options may justify a higher premium on American currency options than on European currency options with similar characteristics. However, there is not a closed-form model for pricing American currency options. Although various techniques are used to price American currency options, the European model is commonly applied to price American currency options because the European model can be just as accurate.

Bodurtha and Courtadon found that the application of an American currency options pricing model does not improve predictive accuracy. Their average percentage pricing error was −7.07 per cent for all sample call options when using the American model.

Given all other parameters, the currency option pricing model can be used to impute the standard deviation s. This implied parameter represents the option's market assessment of currency volatility over the life of the option.

Pricing currency put options according to put-call parity

Given the premium of a European call option (called C), the premium for a European put option (called P) on the same currency and same exercise price (X) can be derived from put-call parity, as shown below:

$$P = C + Xe^{-rT} - Se^{-r^*T}$$

Where:

r = home riskless rate of interest
r^* = foreign riskless rate of interest
T = option's time to maturity expressed as a fraction of the year

If the actual put option premium is less than what is suggested by the put-call parity equation above, arbitrage can be conducted. Specifically, one could: (1) buy the put option, (2) sell the call option and (3) buy the underlying currency. The purchases are financed with the proceeds from selling the call option and from borrowing at the rate r. Meanwhile, the foreign currency that was purchased can be deposited to earn the foreign rate r^*. Regardless of the scenario for the path of the currency's exchange rate movement over the life of the option, the arbitrage will result in a profit. First, if the exchange rate is equal to the exercise price such that each option expires worthless, the foreign currency can be converted in the spot market to dollars, and this amount will exceed the amount required to repay the loan. Second, if the foreign currency appreciates and therefore exceeds the exercise price, there will be a loss from the call option being exercised.

Although the put option will expire, the foreign currency will be converted in the spot market to dollars, and this amount will exceed the amount required to repay the loan and the amount of the loss on the call

---

[3]James Bodurtha and Georges Courtadon, 'Tests of an American Option Pricing Model on the Foreign Currency Options Market', *Journal of Financial Quantitative Analysis* (June 1987): 153–68.

option. Third, if the foreign currency depreciates and therefore is below the exercise price, the amount received from exercising the put option plus the amount received from converting the foreign currency to dollars will exceed the amount required to repay the loan. Since the arbitrage generates a profit under any exchange rate scenario, it will force an adjustment in the option premiums so that put-call parity is no longer violated.

If the actual put option premium is more than what is suggested by put-call parity, arbitrage would again be possible. The arbitrage strategy would be the reverse of that used when the actual put option premium was less than what is suggested by put-call parity (as just described). The arbitrage would force an adjustment in option premiums so that put-call parity is no longer violated. The arbitrage that can be applied when there is a violation of put-call parity on American currency options differs slightly from the arbitrage applicable to European currency options. Nevertheless, the concept still holds that the premium of a currency put option can be determined according to the premium of a call option on the same currency and the same exercise price.

APPENDIX 5B
CURRENCY OPTION COMBINATIONS

In addition to the basic call and put options just discussed, a variety of currency option combinations are available to the currency speculator and hedger. A currency option combination uses simultaneous call and put option positions to construct a unique position to suit the hedger's or speculator's needs. A currency option combination may include both long (buying) and short (selling) positions and will itself either cost money in the hope of earning revenue or earn revenue in the hope of not costing as much money, i.e. be either long or short. As a note, the term long can be equated with buying or owning assets and the term short with selling or incurring liabilities. Typically, a currency option combination will result in a unique contingency graph.

Currency option combinations can be used both to hedge cash inflows and outflows denominated in a foreign currency and to speculate on the future movement of a foreign currency. More specifically, both MNCs and individual speculators can construct a currency option combination to accommodate expectations of either appreciating or depreciating foreign currencies.

In this appendix, four of the most popular currency option combinations are discussed. These are straddles, strangles, spreads and zero premium options. For each of these combinations, the following topics will be discussed:

● The composition of combinations.

● The worksheet and contingency graph for long combinations.

● The worksheet and contingency graph for short combinations.

● Use of combinations to speculate on the movement of a foreign currency.

CURRENCY STRADDLES

Long currency straddle

A straddle is essentially a bet on the standard deviation or variability of a currency. To construct a long straddle in a foreign currency, an MNC or individual would buy (take a long position in) both a call option and a put option for that currency; the call and the put option have the same expiration date and strike price.

When constructing a long straddle, the buyer purchases both the right to buy the foreign currency and the right to sell the foreign currency at a given strike price. Since the call option will become profitable if the foreign currency appreciates, and the put option will become profitable if the foreign currency depreciates, a long straddle becomes profitable when the foreign currency *either* appreciates or depreciates. Obviously, this is a huge advantage for the individual or entity that constructs a long straddle, since it appears that it would benefit from the position as long as the foreign currency exchange rate does not remain constant. The disadvantage of a long straddle position is that it is expensive to construct, because it involves the purchase of two separate options, each of which requires payment of the option premium. Therefore, a long straddle becomes profitable only if the foreign currency appreciates or depreciates substantially. The holder of a straddle is therefore betting that the currency will become volatile.

Long currency straddle worksheet. To determine the profit or loss associated with a long straddle (or any combination), it is easiest to first construct a profit or loss worksheet for several possible currency values at option expiration. The worksheet can be set up to show each individual option position and the net position. The worksheet will also help in constructing a contingency graph for the combination.

Put and call options are available for dollars with the following information:

- Call option premium on dollar = £0.03 per unit.

- Put option premium on dollar = £0.02 per unit.

- Strike price = £0.60.

- One option contract represents $50 000.

To construct a long straddle, the buyer would purchase both a dollar call and a dollar put option, paying £0.03 + £0.02 = £0.05 per unit. If the value of the dollar at option expiration is above the strike price of £0.60, the call option is in the money, but the put option is out of the money. Conversely, if the value of the dollar at option expiration is below £0.60, the put option is in the money, but the call option is out of the money.

A possible worksheet for the long straddle that illustrates the profitability of the individual components is shown below:

Value of dollar at option expiration	£0.50	£0.55	£0.60	£0.65	£0.70
Profit (loss) from purchasing a call	−£0.03	−£0.03	−£0.03	+£0.02	+£0.07
Profit (loss) from purchasing a put	+£0.08	+£0.03	−£0.02	−£0.02	−£0.02
Net	+£0.05	£0.00	−£0.05	£0.00	+£0.05

Long currency straddle contingency graph. A contingency graph for the long currency straddle is shown in Exhibit 5B.1. This graph includes more extreme possible outcomes than are shown in the table. Either the call or put option on the foreign currency will be in the money at option expiration as long as the foreign currency value at option expiration differs from the strike price.

There are two overall break-even points for a long straddle position - one below the strike price and one above the strike price. The lower break-even point is equal to the strike price less both premiums; the higher break-even point is equal to the strike price plus both premiums. Thus, for the above example, the two break-even points are located at £0.55 = £0.60 − £0.05 and at £0.65 = £0.60 + £0.05 as for the long position.

The maximum loss for the long straddle in the example occurs at a dollar value at option expiration equal to the strike price, when both options are at the money. At that point, the straddle buyer would lose both option premiums. The maximum loss for the straddle buyer is thus equal to $0.05 = $0.03 + $0.02.

EXHIBIT 5B.1   Contingency graph for a long currency straddle (note that the break-even rates are for individual options, not the combined options)

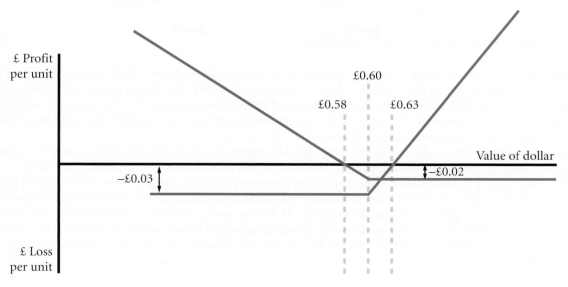

Short currency straddle

Constructing a short straddle in a foreign currency involves selling (taking a short position in) both a call option and a put option for that currency. As in a long straddle, the call and put options have the same expiration date and strike price.

The advantage of a short straddle is that it provides the option writer with income from two separate options. The disadvantage is the possibility of substantial losses if the underlying currency moves substantially away from the strike price.

Short currency straddle worksheet and contingency graph. A short straddle results in a worksheet and contingency graph that are exactly opposite to those of a long straddle.

Assuming the same information as in the previous example, a short straddle would involve writing both a call option on dollars and a put option on dollars. A possible worksheet for the resulting short straddle is shown below:

Value of dollar at option expiration	£0.50	£0.55	£0.60	£0.65	£0.70
Profit (loss) from selling a call	+£0.03	+£0.03	+£0.03	+£0.02	−£0.07
Profit (loss) from selling a put	−£0.08	−£0.03	+£0.02	+£0.02	+£0.02
Net	−£0.05	£0.00	+£0.05	£0.00	−£0.05

The worksheet also illustrates that there are two break-even points for a short straddle position – one below the strike price and one above the strike price. The lower break-even point is equal to the strike price less both premiums; the higher break-even point is equal to the strike price plus both premiums. Thus, the two break-even points are located at $1.00 = $1.05− $0.05 and at $1.10 = $1.05 + $0.05. This is the same relationship as for the long straddle position.

The maximum gain occurs at a dollar value at option expiration equal to the strike price of £0.60 and is equal to the sum of the two option premiums (£0.03 + £0.02 = £0.05).

The resulting contingency graph is shown in Exhibit 5B.2.

Speculating with currency straddles

Individuals can speculate using currency straddles based on their expectations of the future movement in a particular foreign currency. For example, speculators who expect that the British pound will appreciate or depreciate substantially can buy a straddle. If the pound appreciates substantially, the speculator will let the put option expire and exercise the call option. If the pound depreciates substantially, the speculator will let the call option expire and exercise the put option.

Speculators may also profit from short straddles. The writer of a short straddle believes that the value of the underlying currency will remain close to the exercise price until option expiration. If the value of the underlying currency is equal to the strike price at option expiration, the straddle writer would collect premiums from both options. However, this is a rather risky position; if the currency appreciates or depreciates substantially, the straddle writer will lose money. If the currency appreciates substantially, the straddle writer will have to sell the currency for the strike price, since the call option will be exercised. If the currency depreciates substantially, the straddle writer has to buy the currency for the strike price, since the put option will be exercised.

CURRENCY STRANGLES

Currency strangles are very similar to currency straddles, with one important difference: the call and put options of the underlying foreign currency have different exercise prices. Nevertheless, the underlying security and the expiration date for the call and put options are identical. They are in effect a cheap form of straddle offering lower payouts for a lower premium.

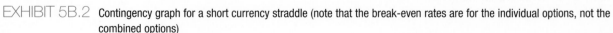

EXHIBIT 5B.2   Contingency graph for a short currency straddle (note that the break-even rates are for the individual options, not the combined options)

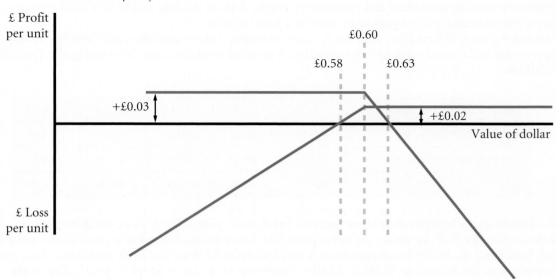

Long currency strangle

Since the call and put options used in a strangle can have different exercise prices, a long strangle can be constructed in a variety of ways. For example, a strangle could be constructed in which the call option has a higher exercise price than the put option and *vice versa*. The most common type of strangle, and the focus of this section, is a strangle that involves buying a put option with a lower strike price than the call option. To construct a long strangle in a foreign currency, an MNC or individual would thus take a long (buy) position in a call option and a long (buy) position in a put option for that currency. The call option has the higher exercise price.

An advantage of a long strangle relative to a comparable long straddle is that it is cheaper to construct. From previous sections, recall that there is an inverse relationship between the spot price of the currency relative to the strike price and the call option premium: the lower the spot price relative to the strike price, the lower the option premium will be. Therefore, if a long strangle involves purchasing a call option with a relatively high exercise price, it should be cheaper to construct than a comparable straddle, everything else being equal.

The disadvantage of a strangle relative to a straddle is that the underlying currency has to fluctuate for there to be a payout. As with a long straddle, the reason for constructing a long strangle is the expectation of a substantial currency fluctuation in either direction prior to the expiration date. However, since the two options involved in a strangle have different exercise prices, the underlying currency has to fluctuate to a larger extent before the strangle is in the money at future spot prices. The smaller likelihood of making a profit is matched by the lower cost of a strangle relative to the straddle.

Long currency strangle worksheet. The worksheet for a long currency strangle is similar to the worksheet for a long currency straddle, as the following example shows.

EXAMPLE

Put and call options are available for dollars with the following information:

- Call option premium on dollar = £0.015 per unit.
- Put option premium on dollar = £0.010 per unit.
- Call option strike price = £0.625.
- Put option strike price = £0.575.

Note that this example is almost identical to the earlier straddle example, except that the call option has a higher exercise price than the put option and the call option premium is slightly lower.

A possible worksheet for the long strangle is shown here:

Value of dollar at option expiration	£0.525	£0.575	£0.625	£0.675
Profit (loss) from buying a call	−£0.015	−£0.015	−£0.015	+£0.035
Profit (loss) from buying a put	+£0.040	−£0.010	−£0.010	−£0.010
Net	+£0.025	−£0.025	−£0.025	+£0.025

Long currency strangle contingency graph. Exhibit 5B.3 shows a contingency graph for the long currency strangle. Again, the graph includes more extreme values than are shown in the worksheet. The call option will be in the money when the foreign currency value is higher than its strike price at option expiration, and the put option will be in the money when the foreign currency value is below the put option strike price at option expiration. Thus, the long call position is in the money at dollar values above the £0.625 call option exercise price at option expiration. Conversely, the put option is in the money at dollar values below the put option exercise price of £0.575.

EXHIBIT 5B.3   Contingency graph for a long currency strangle (note that the break-even rates are for the individual options, not the combined options)

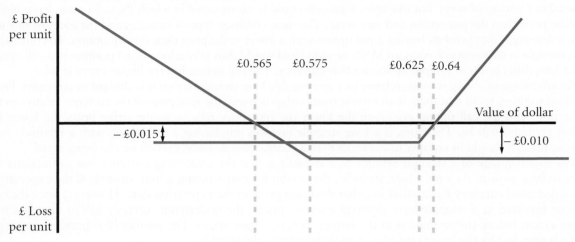

The two break-even points for a long strangle position are located below the put option premium and above the call option premium. The lower breakeven point for both the contracts together is equal to the put option strike price less both premiums (£0.55 = £0.575 − £0.025); the higher break-even point is equal to the call option strike price plus both premiums (£0.65 = £0.625 + £0.025).

The maximum loss for a long strangle occurs at dollar values at option expiration between the two strike prices. At any future spot price between the two exercise prices, the straddle buyer would lose both option premiums (−£0.025 = − (£0.010 + £0.015)).

The contingency graph for the long strangle illustrates that the dollar must fluctuate more widely than with a straddle before the position becomes profitable. However, the maximum loss is only £0.025 per unit, whereas it was £0.05 per unit for the long straddle.

Short currency strangle

Analogous to a short currency straddle, a short strangle involves taking a short position in both a call option and a put option for that currency. As with a short straddle, the call and put options have the same expiration date. However, the call option has the higher exercise price in a short strangle.

Relative to a short straddle, the disadvantage of a short strangle is that it provides less income, since the call option premium will be lower, everything else being equal. However, the advantage of a short strangle relative to a short straddle is that the underlying currency has to fluctuate more before the strangle writer is in danger of losing money.

Short currency strangle worksheet and contingency graph. The euro example is next used to show that the worksheet and contingency graph for the short strangle are exactly opposite to those of a long strangle.

Continuing with the information in the preceding example, a short strangle can be constructed by writing a call option on euros and a put option on euros. The resulting worksheet is shown below:

Value of euro at option expiration	£0.525	£0.575	£0.625	£0.675
Profit (loss) from writing a call	+£0.015	+£0.015	+£0.015	−£0.035
Profit (loss) from writing a put	−£0.040	+£0.010	+£0.010	+£0.010
Net	−£0.025	+£0.025	+£0.025	−£0.025

The table shows that there are two break-even points for the short strangle. The lower break-even point is equal to the put option strike price less both premiums; the higher break-even point is equal to the call option strike price plus both premiums. The two break-even points are thus identical to the break-even points for the long strangle position (see above).

The maximum gain for a short strangle (£0.025 = £0.015 + £0.010) occurs at a value of the euro at option expiration between the two exercise prices.

The short strangle contingency graph is shown in Exhibit 5B.4.

Speculating with currency strangles

As with straddles, individuals can speculate using currency strangles based on their expectations of the future movement in a particular foreign currency. For instance, speculators who expect the dollar to appreciate or depreciate substantially can construct a long strangle. Speculators can benefit from short strangles if the future spot price of the underlying currency is between the two exercise prices.

Compared to a straddle, the speculator who buys a strangle believes that the underlying currency will fluctuate even more widely prior to expiration. In return, the speculator pays less to construct the long strangle. A speculator who writes a strangle will receive both option premiums as long as the future spot price is between the two exercise prices. Compared to a straddle, the total amount received from writing the two options is less. However, the range of future spot prices between which no option is exercised is much wider for a short strangle. There is, therefore, a greater chance of gaining less. On the risk side the writer is exposed to potentially high losses and should buy deep out of the money call and deep out of the money put to protect against such losses.

CURRENCY SPREADS

A variety of currency spreads exist that can be used by both MNCs and individuals to hedge cash inflows or outflows or to profit from an anticipated movement in a foreign currency. This section covers two of the most popular types of spreads: bull spreads and bear spreads. Bull spreads are profitable when a foreign currency appreciates, whereas bear spreads are profitable when a foreign currency depreciates. The main advantage of a spread is that it is cheaper than an option but the potential gains are limited.

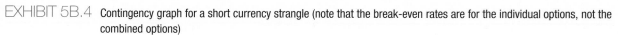

EXHIBIT 5B.4   Contingency graph for a short currency strangle (note that the break-even rates are for the individual options, not the combined options)

Currency bull spreads with call options

A currency bull spread is constructed by buying an at the money call option for a particular underlying currency and simultaneously writing an out of the money call option for the same currency with a higher exercise price (note that there is a net payment of premiums here, it is known as a debit spread). A bull spread can also be constructed using currency put options, as will be discussed shortly.

With a bull spread, the spreader believes that the underlying currency will appreciate modestly, but not substantially.

Assume two call options on Australian dollars (A$) are currently available. The first option has a strike price of £0.41 and a premium of £0.010. The second option has a strike price of £0.42 and a premium of £0.005. The bull spreader buys the £0.41 option and sells the £0.42 option (see Exhibit 5B.5).

Currency bull spread worksheet and contingency graph. For the Australian dollar example, a worksheet and contingency graph can be constructed. One possible worksheet is shown below:

Value of Australian dollar at option expiration	£0.40	£0.41	£0.415	£0.42	£0.43	£0.44
Profit (loss) from buying the call at £0.41 strike	−£0.010	−£0.010	−£0.005	£0.00	+£0.010	+£0.020
Profit (loss) from selling the call at £0.42 strike	+£0.005	+£0.005	+£0.005	+£0.005	−£0.005	−£0.015
Net	−£0.005	−£0.005	£0.000	+£0.005	+£0.005	+£0.005

The worksheet and contingency graph show that the maximum loss for the bull spreader is limited to the difference between the two option premiums of −£0.005 = −£0.010 + £0.005. This maximum loss occurs at future spot prices equal to the lower strike price or below.

Also note that for a bull spread the gain is limited to the difference between the strike prices less the difference in the option premiums and is equal to £0.005 = £0.42 − £0.41 − £0.005. This maximum gain occurs at future spot prices equal to the higher exercise price or above.

The break-even point for the bull spread is located at the lower exercise price plus the difference in the two option premiums and is equal to £0.415 = £0.41 + £0.005.

EXHIBIT 5B.5   Contingency graph for a currency bull spread

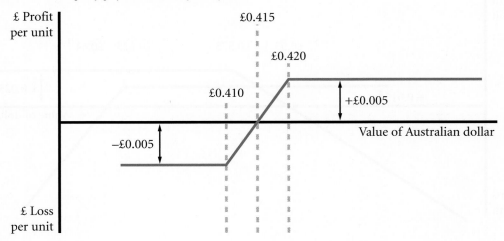

Currency bull spreads with put options

As mentioned previously, currency bull spreads can be constructed just as easily with put options as with call options. To construct a put bull spread, the spreader would buy an out of the money put option with a lower exercise price and write an in the money put option with a higher exercise price (note there is a net gain on the exercise prices here). The basic arithmetic involved in constructing a put bull spread is thus essentially the same as for a call bull spread, with one important difference, as discussed next.

Recall that there is a positive relationship between the level of the existing spot price relative to the strike price and the call option premium. Consequently, the option with the higher exercise price that is written in a call bull spread will have the lower option premium, everything else being equal. Thus, buying the call option with the lower exercise price and writing the call option with the higher exercise price involves a cash outflow for the bull spreader. For this reason, call bull spreads fall into a broader category of spreads called debit spreads. Also recall that the lower the spot rate relative to the strike price, the higher the put option premium will be. Consequently, the option with the higher strike price that is written in a put bull spread will have the higher option premium, everything else being equal. Thus, buying the put option with the lower exercise price and writing the put option with the higher exercise price in a put bull spread results in a cash inflow for the bull spreader. For this reason, put bull spreads fall into a broader category of spreads called credit spreads.

Speculating with currency bull spreads

The speculator who constructs a currency bull spread trades profit potential for a reduced cost of establishing the position. Ideally, the underlying currency will appreciate to the higher exercise price but not far above it. Although the speculator would still realize the maximum gain of the bull spread in this case, he or she would incur significant opportunity costs if the underlying currency appreciates much above the higher exercise price. Speculating with currency bull spreads is appropriate for currencies that are expected to appreciate slightly until the expiration date. Since the bull spread involves both buying and writing options for the underlying currency, bull spreads can be relatively cheap to construct and will not result in large losses if the currency depreciates.

Currency bear spreads

The easiest way to think about a currency bear spread is as a short bull spread. That is, a currency bear spread involves taking exactly the opposite positions involved in a bull spread. The bear spreader writes a call option for a particular underlying currency and simultaneously buys a call option for the same currency with a higher exercise price. Consequently, the bear spreader anticipates a modest depreciation in the foreign currency, but limits the losses should the currency move in the other direction.

Currency bear spread worksheet and contingency graph. For the Australian dollar example above, the bear spreader writes the £0.41 call option and buys the £0.42 option. A worksheet and contingency graph can be constructed (see Exhibit 5B.6). One possible worksheet is shown below:

Value of Australian dollar at option expiration	£0.40	£0.41	£0.415	£0.42	£0.43
Profit (loss) from selling a call at £0.41 premium £0.01	+£0.010	+£0.010	+£0.005	£0.00	−£0.010
Profit (loss) from buying a call at £0.42 premium £0.005	−£0.005	−£0.005	−£0.005	−£0.005	+£0.005
Net	+£0.005	+£0.005	£0.000	−£0.005	−£0.005

The corresponding contingency graph is shown in Exhibit 5B.6.

Notice that the worksheet and contingency graph for the bear spread are the mirror image of the worksheet and contingency graph for the bull spread. Consequently, the maximum gain for the bear spreader is

EXHIBIT 5B.6 Contingency graph for a currency bear spread

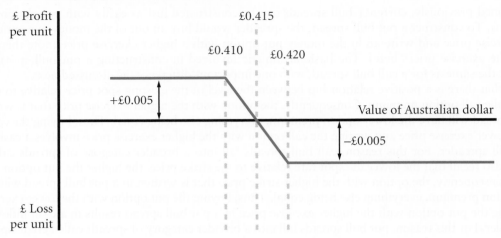

limited to the difference between the two exercise prices of £0.005 = £0.015 − £0.005, and the maximum loss for a bear spread (−£0.005 = £0.41 − £0.42 − £0.005) occurs when the Australian dollar's value is equal to or above the higher exercise price at option expiration.

Also, the break-even point is located at the lower exercise price plus the difference in the two option premiums and is equal to £0.415 = £0.41 + £0.05, which is the same break-even point as for the bull spread.

It is evident from the above illustration that the bear spreader hopes for a currency depreciation. An alternative way to profit from a depreciation would be to buy a put option for the currency. A bear spread, however, is typically cheaper to construct, since it involves buying one call option and writing another call option. The disadvantage of the bear spread compared to a long put position is that opportunity costs can be significant if the currency depreciates dramatically. Consequently, the bear spreader hopes for a modest currency depreciation.

USING THE WEB

Options prices

A wide variety of option combinations are explained at the Options guide at: http://www.theoptionsguide.com.

Cylinder or zero cost option

The Group claims hedge accounting in respect of certain forward foreign exchange contracts and options, or option strategies, which have zero net premium or a net premium paid, and where the critical terms of the bought and sold options within a collar or zero premium structure are the same and where the nominal amount of the sold option component is no greater than that of the bought option.

Nokia Annual Financial Report 2008, p. 16

This option is included because it is of interest to treasurers. If an MNC is purchasing goods, a useful form of protection would be if a bank guaranteed or compensated the MNC if the value of the currency went above a certain level. In effect a call option. The zero cost element (i.e. there is no charge for the options) exploits the fact that an MNC would probably not mind losing some of the benefits if a currency fell in value. If a treasurer of an MNC is purchasing, the concern is that the cost of the currency does not go above an upper limit. The MNC would be happy to see the rate fall, but if the currency fell below a lower limit the MNC would probably not be too worried if they did not benefit by the drop below the lower limit, so long as it is protected against rises above the upper limit. In effect the bank is saying: If the price of the currency goes above the upper limit, we will compensate you; but in return, if the price goes below the lower limit, you will have to buy at the lower limit price and we the bank will gain by the difference between the lower limit price at which we sell the currency to you and the even lower market price. Thus although the option itself does not cost money, the bank does stand to gain if the currency price moves in the case of buying currency to below the lower limit. A similar argument can be made out for revenues in foreign currency. Increases above the upper limit would be collected by the bank (the MNC writes a call to the bank); but if the value of the foreign currency fell below a lower limit, the bank would compensate the MNC for the difference (the MNC would hold a put funded by the bank). The limits are again set so that there is no net payment to be made.

EXAMPLE

Suppose a UK MNC is expecting to make a payment in dollars and takes out a cylinder option for zero cost against a bank with the purchase of a call option on dollars at a strike price of, say, £0.80 that could be financed by selling a put option on dollars at, say, £0.70. The upper limit is therefore £0.80, and the lower limit is £0.70 per dollar.

The arrangement would result in three possible scenarios: 1) the spot rate at settlement is above £0.80:$1 in which case the call option is exercised and the bank pays the MNC the difference between the spot and the strike of £0.80. The MNC is therefore guaranteed a maximum price of £0.80 to pay for a US dollar; 2) the spot price is at or between £0.80 and £0.70. Both contracts would be out of the money and

as the premiums offset, no payment would be required; 3) the spot rate is below £0.70 in which case the MNC honours the put option it sold to the bank and the bank sells the dollars to the MNC for £0.70. Thus possible payment by the MNC under (3) offsets possible payment to the MNC under (1). Put simply the treasurer of the MNC would be saying to the bank: 'You pay the difference in cost if the price of the dollar is above £0.80 and in return I will pay you the difference if the price falls below £0.70.' The value of expressing this arrangement in terms of options, is that the appropriate strike prices can be approximated reasonably well using the option pricing formula. The contingency position is shown in Exhibit 5B.7 and Exhibit 5B.8.

The guaranteed limits can also apply to MNCs intending to sell currency. Suppose a UK MNC wanted to sell dollars earned in the USA for British pounds and was offered an upper limit to the value of the dollars converted of £0.80, in return the bank would guarantee a lower limit to the value of the dollars of £0.70. The MNC would in effect purchase a put at the lower limit to benefit from falls below £0.70, and sell or write a call at the higher limit where the bank would now benefit by being able to buy dollars from the MNC at a top limited rate of £0.80 if the market rate is even higher. Between those limits the transaction would be at the market rate.

EXHIBIT 5B.7 **Using a cylinder option contract – a UK MNC seeking to buy dollars**

Column number	1	2	3	4	5
Value of US dollar at settlement to pay	−£0.65	−£0.70	−£0.75	−£0.80	−£0.85
MNC profit (loss) from purchasing a call on dollars	not exercised	not exercised	not exercised	not exercised	+£0.05
MNC profit (loss) from selling a put on dollars	−£0.05	not exercised	not exercised	not exercised	not exercised
Net rate for the US dollar for MNC	−£0.70	−£0.70	−£0.75	−£0.80	−£0.80

EXHIBIT 5B.8 Contingency graph for a cylinder option guaranteeing purchase cost of dollars of between £0.70 and £0.80

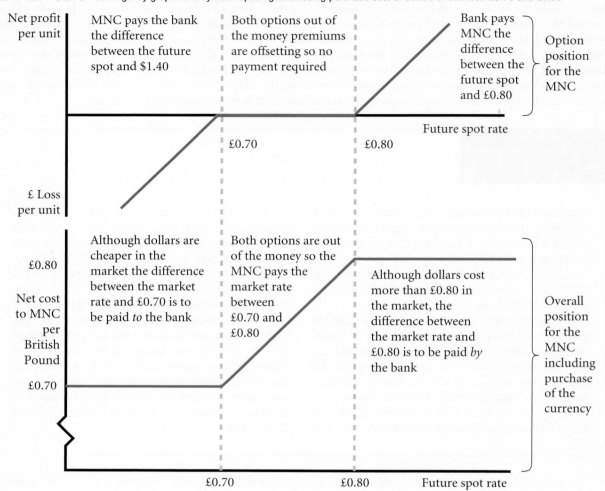

PART 1 Integrative problem

THE INTERNATIONAL FINANCIAL ENVIRONMENT

Mesa Co. specializes in the production of small fancy picture frames, which are exported from the USA to the UK. Mesa invoices the exports in pounds and converts the pounds to dollars when they are received. The British demand for these frames is positively related to economic conditions in the UK. Assume that British inflation and interest rates are similar to the rates in the USA. Mesa believes that the US balance of trade deficit from trade between the USA and the UK will adjust to changing prices between the two countries, while capital flows will adjust to interest rate differentials. Mesa believes that the value of the pound is very sensitive to changing international capital flows and is moderately sensitive to changing international trade flows. Mesa is considering the following information:

● The UK inflation rate is expected to decline, while the US inflation rate is expected to rise.

● British interest rates are expected to decline, while US interest rates are expected to increase.

Questions

1 Explain how the international trade flows should initially adjust in response to the changes in inflation (holding exchange rates constant). Explain how the international capital flows should adjust in response to the changes in interest rates (holding exchange rates constant).

2 Using the information provided, will Mesa expect the pound to appreciate or depreciate in the future? Explain.

3 Mesa believes international capital flows shift in response to changing interest rate differentials. Is there any reason why the changing interest rate differentials in this example will not necessarily cause international capital flows to change significantly? Explain.

4 Based on your answer to question 2, how would Mesa's cash flows be affected by the expected exchange rate movements? Explain.

5 Based on your answer to question 4, should Mesa consider hedging its exchange rate risk? If so, explain how it could hedge using forward contracts, futures contracts and currency options.

PART 1 Essays/discussion and academic articles

1 Goergen, M., Martynove, M. and Renneboog, L. (2005) 'Corporate Governance: Convergence evidence from take over regulation reforms in Europe', *Oxford Economic Review,* 20 (2), 243–68.
   Q *Evaluate the advantages and disadvantages of the two corporate governance models outlined by Goergen et al.*

2 Woods, N. (2000) 'The Challenge of Good Governance for the IMF and the World Bank Themselves', *World Development,* 28 (5), 823–41. A discussion of the problems facing these institutions.
   Q *From a reading of the Woods article, outline the pressures for reform of the IMF and World Bank. Discuss the advantages and disadvantages of democratizing decisions.*

3 Critin, D. and Fischer, S. (2000) 'Strengthening the International Financial System: Key Issues', *World Development,* 28 (6), 1133–42. The role of the IMF, capital flows and exchange rate regimes.
   Q *Private sector involvement is essential to economic development; but exchange rate volatility, moral hazard and capital flow restrictions limit its contribution. Explain and discuss possible solutions.*

4 Conway, P. (2006) 'The International Monetary Fund in a Time of Crisis: a review of Stanley Fisher's essays from a time of crisis: The International Financial System and Development', *Journal of Economic Literature,* 44,115–44.
   Q *Reviewing the crises of the 1990s, is the IMF part of the problem? Discuss.*

5 Morgan, R.E. and Katsikeas, C.S. (1997) 'Theories of International Trade, Foreign Investment and Firm Internationalization: a critique', *Management Decision,* 35 (1), 68–78. A clear and relatively brief tour around the area.
   Q *What can we reasonably expect from trade and investment theories? Outline and discuss.*

6 Cyr, A.I. (2003) 'The euro: faith, hope and parity', *International Affairs,* 75 (5), 979–92. An excellent historical context and analysis.
   Q *Consider and evaluate possible future scenarios for the euro.*

7 Zoffer, J. (2012) Future of Dollar Hegemony, Harvard International Review Vol 34, Issue 1, 26–29
   Q *Is the dominance of the dollar good or bad for international development?*

8 Rosenthal, J. (2012) Germany and the Euro Crisis, World Affairs, May/June 2012 vol. 175 Issue 1, 53–61
   Q *Has the euro crisis helped in the stated goal of the Maastricht treaty of promoting economic and social cohesion within the EU.*

PART II
EXCHANGE RATE BEHAVIOUR

PART 2 (Chapters 6–8) focuses on the critical factors that affect exchange rates. Chapter 6 explains how governments can influence exchange rate movements and how such movements can affect economic conditions. Chapter 7 explores further the relationship between currency value and interest rates. Chapter 8 discusses prominent theories about the links between inflation, exchange rates and interest rates.

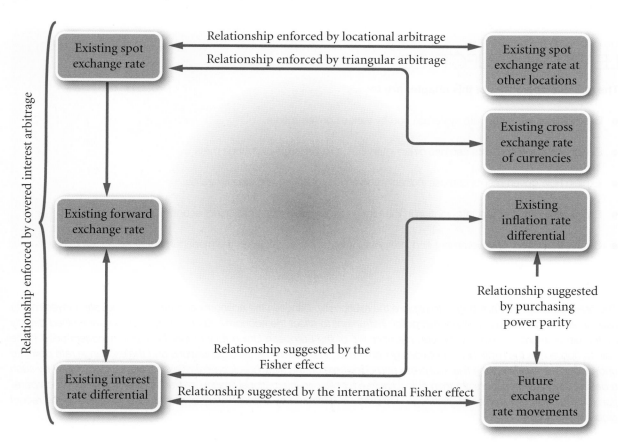

CHAPTER 6
EXCHANGE RATE HISTORY AND THE ROLE OF GOVERNMENTS

LEARNING OBJECTIVES

The specific objectives of this chapter are to:

- Describe the exchange rate systems used by various governments.

- Explain how governments can use *direct* intervention to influence exchange rates.

- Explain how governments can use *indirect* intervention to influence exchange rates.

- Explain how government intervention in the foreign exchange market can affect economic conditions.

- Outline the history of government and intergovernmental organizations in the management of exchange rates.

The previous chapters have begun to explore the relationship between the economy and the exchange rate. Governments use the exchange rate as an economic policy instrument to affect the economy. Such policies can be determined directly by the government or indirectly through membership of the European Union (EU) or G8. Financial managers need to be able to appreciate the relationship between governments, intergovernmental organizations and the exchange rate policy to understand the debate in the financial press and elsewhere on the likely development of exchange rates. Informed by such a debate, financial managers are then able to devise a policy on international finance relevant to their multinational corporation (MNC). The complexities of exchange rate policy is illustrated by a brief history of notable events including the recent global financial crisis.

EXCHANGE RATE SYSTEMS

Exchange rate systems can be classified according to the degree by which exchange rates are controlled by the government. Exchange rate systems normally fall into one of the following categories:

- Fixed
- Managed float
- Pegged
- Freely floating.

Each of these exchange rate systems is discussed in turn.

Fixed exchange rate system

In a **fixed exchange rate system**, exchange rates are either held constant or allowed to fluctuate only within very narrow boundaries. If an exchange rate begins to move too much, governments, via their central banks, intervene to maintain it within the boundaries. In some situations, a government will devalue or reduce the value of its currency against other currencies. In other situations, it will revalue or increase the value of its currency against other currencies. A central bank's actions to devalue a currency is referred to as devaluation. The term *depreciation* is also used, but in a different context. Devaluation refers to a downward adjustment of the exchange rate by the central bank. Depreciation refers to a change caused by exchange rate markets. Revaluation refers to an upward adjustment of the exchange rate by the central bank. An upward adjustment by the market is referred to as an *appreciation* in the value of the currency.

USING THE WEB

Visit the EU site at: http://europa.eu for access to the server of the EU's Parliament, Council, Commission, Court of Justice and other bodies. It includes basic information on all related political and economic issues.

Advantages of a fixed exchange rate system. In a fixed exchange rate environment, MNCs can engage in international trade without worrying about the future exchange rate. Consequently, the managerial duties of an MNC are less difficult.

EXAMPLE

When UK companies imported materials from abroad during the fixed exchange rate era after World War II (see history below), it could anticipate the amount of British pounds it would need to pay for the imports. When the British pound devalued in the late 1960s, however, UK companies needed more British pounds to purchase imports.

A second advantage is that where the currency of a small economy with high inflation fixes its exchange rate to a large currency with low inflation, the inflation in the small currency is restrained. Prices in the small currency are now in direct competition with imports that are not increasing in price because of the fixed exchange rate. As the economy is smaller, the possible extra demand for imports from the large economy will not affect the price of imports.

Disadvantages of a fixed exchange rate system. Although an MNC is not exposed to continual movements in an exchange rate, it does continuously face the possibility that the government will devalue or revalue its currency. In this respect the difference with a variable exchange rate system is not so great.

A second disadvantage is that from a macro viewpoint, a fixed exchange rate system may make each country more vulnerable to economic conditions in other countries.

EXAMPLE

Assume that there are only two countries in the world: the USA and the UK. Also assume a fixed exchange rate system, and that these two countries trade frequently with each other. If the USA experiences a much higher inflation rate than the UK, US consumers should buy more goods from the UK and British consumers should reduce their imports of US goods (due to the high US prices). This reaction would force US production down and unemployment up. It could also cause higher inflation in the UK due to the excessive demand for British goods relative to the supply of British goods produced. Thus, the high inflation in the USA could cause high inflation in the UK. In the mid- and late 1960s, the USA experienced relatively high inflation and was accused of 'exporting' that inflation to some European countries due to the fixed exchange rate.

Alternatively, a high unemployment rate in the USA will cause a reduction in US income and a decline in US purchases of British goods. Consequently, productivity in the UK may decrease and unemployment may rise. In this case, the USA may 'export' unemployment to the UK.

However if a fixed exchange rate is accompanied by appropriate policies, good rather than bad economic conditions may spread.

EXAMPLE

Rerun the previous example and assume that there is only the USA and the UK. The much higher inflation in the USA causes the demand for British pounds to rise and the exchange rate to move outside its set limits. Initially, the USA will use its reserves of British pounds to meet the demand in the marketplace; but reserves of British pounds are bound to run low. Subsequently, the USA raises interest rates to make the dollar more attractive. The higher interest rates reduces spending in the USA as consumers lower their credit card debt and companies borrow less and defer investment spending plans. Demand decreases in the USA, inflation slows down and as a result unemployment increases temporarily. Financial stability is restored, some may say at the expense of economic activity.

Where different countries share the same currency as in the EU it is very clearly the case that members are subject to the economic conditions in each other's countries. If a member government such as Italy decided to borrow excessively to promote its own economy, interest rates may well increase. As a common currency area can only support one interest rate for a given level of risk, it would mean that people in France could be paying more on their borrowing for credit cards and houses etc. due to the excessive borrowing in Italy. The solution in the EU is to harmonize economic policies. To this end, member states signed up to the Growth and Stability Pact in 1997. The main terms are that government budgets must balance in the medium term and that there are penalties for excessive annual borrowing (more than 3 per cent of GDP) and excessive total government debt (more than 60 per cent of GDP). Due to the recent economic downturn, even Germany has had to increase its borrowing to more than 3 per cent and the Eurozone as a whole has not met this condition since the third quarter of 2008.

Thus a fixed currency implies interdependency of the economic systems. It is possible for good economic conditions such as low inflation to spread, or bad conditions such as high inflation and unemployment to spread. The relative size of the countries, or rather, currency areas is an important factor as well as the economic policies of the countries concerned and the nature of the cooperation between the policies.

Managed float exchange rate system

The exchange rate system that exists today for the major currencies lies somewhere between fixed and freely floating. It resembles the freely floating system in that exchange rates are allowed to fluctuate on a daily basis and there are no official boundaries. It is similar to the fixed rate system in that governments can and sometimes do intervene to prevent their currencies from moving too far in a certain direction. This type of system is known as a **managed float** or 'dirty' float (as opposed to a 'clean' float where rates float freely without government intervention).

Criticism of a managed float system. The main problem of a managed float is whether or not it works. Interventions at the time of the Louvre Accord (1987) were not found to be statistically significant. Economic fundamentals, that is the view that the dollar economy was being undervalued, was probably more responsible for stabilizing the value of the dollar. At best it seems a very weak form of control of variable rate systems that achieves little. However, it is probably all that is available given that market volumes greatly exceed reserves of foreign exchange held by governments.

Pegged exchange rate system

Some countries use a **pegged exchange rate** arrangement, in which their home currency's value is pegged to a foreign currency or a basket of foreign currencies. While the home currency's value is fixed in terms of the foreign currency to which it is pegged, it moves in line with that currency against other currencies.

Some Asian countries such as Malaysia and Thailand had pegged their currency's value to the dollar. During the Asian crisis (1997), they were unable to maintain the peg and allowed their currencies to float against the dollar.

Currency boards

A **currency board** is a system for pegging the value of the local currency to some other specified currency. The board must maintain currency reserves of the specified currency for all the local currency that it has issued. In one sense it may appear that the currency value is safe in that the currency board can replace the currency it has issued with the foreign currency. Cash is, however, only a small part of the total 'money' or credit in an economy. Banks hold only about 10 per cent of deposits in the form of cash. The currency board could therefore only convert 10 per cent of bank balances into the chosen foreign currency.

EXAMPLE

Hong Kong has tied the value of its currency (the Hong Kong dollar) to the US dollar (HK$7.80 = $1.00) since 1983. Every Hong Kong dollar in circulation is backed by a US dollar in reserve.

A currency board can stabilize a currency's value. This is important because investors generally avoid investing in a country if they expect the local currency will weaken substantially. If a currency board is expected to remain in place for a long period, it may reduce fears that the local currency will weaken and thus may encourage investors to maintain their investments within the country. However, a currency board is worth considering only if the government can convince investors that the exchange rate will be maintained.

When Indonesia was experiencing financial problems during the 1997–98 Asian crisis, businesses and investors sold the local currency (rupiah) because of expectations that it would weaken further. Such actions perpetuated the weakness, as the exchange of rupiah for other currencies placed more downward pressure on the value of the rupiah. Indonesia considered implementing a currency board to stabilize its currency and discourage the flow of funds out of the country. Businesses and investors had no confidence in the Indonesian government's ability to maintain a fixed exchange rate and feared that economic pressures would ultimately lead to a decline in the rupiah's value. Therefore, Indonesia's government did not implement a currency board.

A currency board is effective only if investors believe that it will last. If investors expect that market forces will prevent a government from maintaining the local currency's exchange rate, they will attempt to move their funds to other countries where they expect the local currency to be stronger. When foreign investors withdraw their funds from a country and convert the funds into a different currency, they place downward pressure on the local currency's exchange rate. If the supply of the currency for sale continues to exceed the demand, the government will be forced to devalue its currency.

EXAMPLE

In 1991, Argentina established a currency board that pegged the Argentine peso to the dollar. In 2002, Argentina was suffering from major economic problems, and its government was unable to repay its debt. Foreign investors and local investors began to transfer their funds to other countries because they feared that their investments would earn poor returns. These actions required the exchange of pesos into other currencies such as the dollar and caused an excessive supply of pesos for sale in the foreign exchange market. The government could not maintain the exchange rate of 1 peso = 1 dollar, because the supply of pesos for sale exceeded the demand at that exchange rate. In March 2002, the government devalued the peso to 1 peso = $0.71 (1.4 pesos per dollar). Even at this new exchange rate, the supply of pesos for sale exceeded the demand, so the Argentine government decided to let the peso's value float in response to market conditions rather than set the peso's value.

The dominance of the markets over government management is evident. Where the market takes the view that the currency is overvalued, the volume of selling of that currency is such that governments are unable to resist the pressure for a devaluation.

Exposure of a pegged currency to interest rate movements. A country that uses a currency board does not have complete control over its local interest rates, because its rates must be aligned with the interest rates of the currency to which it is tied.

Recall that the Hong Kong dollar is pegged to the US dollar. If Hong Kong lowers its interest rates to stimulate its economy, its interest rate would then be lower than US interest rates. Investors based in Hong Kong would be enticed to exchange Hong Kong dollars for US dollars and invest in the USA where interest rates are higher. Since the Hong Kong dollar is tied to the US dollar, the investors could exchange the proceeds of their investment back to Hong Kong dollars at the end of the investment period without concern about exchange rate risk because the exchange rate is fixed.

If the USA raises its interest rates, Hong Kong would be forced to raise its interest rates (on securities with similar risk as those in the USA). Otherwise, investors in Hong Kong could invest their money in the USA and earn a higher rate.

Even though a country may not have control over its interest rate when it establishes a currency board, its interest rate may be more stable than if it did not have a currency board. Its interest rate will move in tandem with the interest rate of the currency to which it is tied. The interest rate may include a risk premium that could reflect either default risk or the risk that the currency board will be discontinued.

EXAMPLE

While the Hong Kong interest rate moves in tandem with the US interest rate, specific investment instruments may have a slightly higher interest rate in Hong Kong than in the USA. For example, a Treasury bill may offer a slightly higher rate in Hong Kong than in the USA. While this allows for possible arbitrage by US investors who wish to invest in Hong Kong, they will face two forms of risk.

First, some investors may believe that there is a slight risk that the Hong Kong government could default on its debt. Second, if there is sudden downward pressure on the Hong Kong dollar, the currency board could be discontinued. In this case, the Hong Kong dollar's value would be reduced, and US investors would earn a lower return than they could have earned in the USA.

Exposure of a pegged currency to exchange rate movements. A currency that is pegged to another currency cannot be pegged against all other currencies. If it is pegged to the US dollar, it is forced to move in tandem with the dollar against other currencies. Since a country cannot peg its currency to all currencies, it is exposed to movements of currencies against the currency to which it is pegged. In 2005 the Chinese announced that the yuan would no longer be pegged to the dollar but to a basket of currencies. As well as the dollar, the euro, the yen and the South Korean won, the basket includes the Australian, Canadian and Singapore dollars, the British pound, the Malaysian ringgit, the Russian rouble and the Thai baht. The weights in the basket have not been disclosed other than to say that the weights in general reflect the level of trade with those currencies. In effect, the yuan will only be presenting a soft target to the foreign exchange market. Traders will not know exactly what value the Bank of China seeks against any one currency. Such a strategy is designed to deter speculators in the manner of the soft targets in the Exchange Rate Mechanism (see below).

EXAMPLE

As mentioned earlier, from 1991 to 2002, the Argentine peso's value was set to equal 1 US dollar. Thus, if the dollar strengthened against the Brazilian real by 10 per cent in a particular month, the Argentine peso strengthened against the Brazilian real by the exact same amount. During the 1991–2002 period, the dollar commonly strengthened against the Brazilian real and some other currencies in South America;

therefore, the Argentine peso also strengthened against those currencies. Many exporting firms in Argentina were adversely affected by the strong Argentine peso because it made their products too expensive for importers. Now that Argentina's currency board has been eliminated, the Argentine peso is no longer forced to move in tandem with the dollar against other currencies.

Pressures can also exist for appreciation. The Chinese central bank revalued the yuan against the dollar (to which it was then pegged) in July 2005. The Chinese government faces speculative purchase of Chinese securities to profit from an expected further appreciation in the value of the yuan. Exporters will also find that their products cost more and must decide whether to compensate by lowering their prices or pass the higher cost on to the foreign importer.

Dollarization

Dollarization is the replacement of a foreign currency with US dollars. This process is a step beyond a currency board, because it forces the local currency to be replaced by the US dollar. Although dollarization and a currency board both attempt to peg the local currency's value, the currency board does not replace the local currency with dollars. The decision to use US dollars as the local currency cannot be easily reversed because the country no longer has a local currency.

From 1990 to 2000, Ecuador's currency (the sucre) depreciated by about 97 per cent against the dollar. The weakness of the currency caused unstable trade conditions, high inflation and volatile interest rates. In 2000, in an effort to stabilize trade and economic conditions, Ecuador replaced the sucre with the US dollar as its currency. By November 2000, inflation had declined and economic growth had increased. Thus, it appeared that dollarization had favourable effects.

Freely floating exchange rate system

In a **freely floating exchange rate system**, exchange rate values are determined by market forces without intervention by governments. Whereas a fixed exchange rate system allows no flexibility for exchange rate movements, a freely floating exchange rate system allows complete flexibility. A freely floating exchange rate adjusts on a continual basis in response to demand and supply conditions for that currency.

Advantages of a freely floating exchange rate system. One advantage of a freely floating exchange rate system is that a country is more insulated from the inflation of other countries.

EXAMPLE

Return to the previous example in which there are only two countries, but now assume a freely floating exchange rate system. If the USA experiences a high rate of inflation, the increased US demand for British goods will place upward pressure on the value of the British pound. As a second consequence of the high US inflation, the reduced British demand for US goods will result in a reduced supply of pounds for sale (exchanged for dollars), which will also place upward pressure on the British pound's value. The pound will appreciate due to these market forces (it was not allowed to appreciate under the fixed rate system).

This appreciation will make British goods more expensive for US consumers, even though British producers did not raise their prices. The higher prices will simply be due to the pound's appreciation; that is, a greater number of US dollars are required to buy the same number of pounds as before.

In the UK, the actual price of the goods as measured in British pounds may be unchanged. Even though US prices have increased, British consumers will continue to purchase US goods because they can exchange their pounds for more US dollars (due to the British pound's appreciation against the US dollar).

Another advantage of freely floating exchange rates is that a country is more insulated from unemployment problems in other countries.

EXAMPLE

Under a floating rate system, the decline in US purchases of British goods, caused by US unemployment, will reflect a reduced US demand for British pounds. Such a shift in demand can cause the pound to depreciate against the dollar (under the fixed rate system, the pound would not be allowed to depreciate). The depreciation of the pound will make British goods look cheap to US consumers, offsetting the possible reduction in demand for these goods resulting from a lower level of US income. As was true with inflation, a sudden change in unemployment will have less influence on a foreign country under a floating rate system than under a fixed rate system.

As these examples illustrate, in a freely floating exchange rate system, problems experienced in one country will not necessarily be contagious. The exchange rate adjustments serve as a form of protection against 'exporting' economic problems to other countries.

An additional advantage of a freely floating exchange rate system is that a central bank is not required to constantly maintain exchange rates within specified boundaries. It can therefore hold lower levels of foreign exchange that would be needed under a fixed rate regime to meet surplus demand for foreign currency at the fixed rate. It also need not adjust interest rates and the money supply just to control exchange rates. Furthermore, governments can implement policies without concern as to whether the policies will maintain the exchange rates within specified boundaries. Restrictions on investments can be reduced and markets as a result are free-er and more efficient.

Disadvantages of a freely floating exchange rate system. In the previous example, the UK was somewhat insulated from the problems experienced in the USA due to the freely floating exchange rate system. Although this is an advantage for the country that is protected (the UK), it can be a disadvantage for the country that initially experienced the economic problems.

EXAMPLE

If the UK experiences high inflation, the British pound may weaken. A weaker UK British pound causes import prices to be higher. This can increase the price of UK materials and supplies causing 'cost push' inflation. In addition, higher foreign prices (from the UK perspective) can force UK consumers to purchase domestic products. As UK producers recognize that foreign competition has been reduced due to the weak British pound, they can more easily raise the prices of their finished goods without losing their customers to foreign competition.

In a similar manner, a freely floating exchange rate system can adversely affect a country that has high unemployment.

EXAMPLE

If the UK unemployment rate is rising, UK demand for imports will decrease. As a result, the reduced supply of British pounds on the foreign exchange will place upward pressure on the value of the British pound. A

(Continued)

stronger British pound will then cause UK consumers to purchase foreign products rather than UK products because the foreign products can be purchased cheaply. Yet, such a reaction can actually be detrimental to the UK during periods of high unemployment.

As these examples illustrate, a country's economic problems can sometimes be compounded by freely floating exchange rates. Under such a system, MNCs will need to devote substantial resources to measuring and managing exposure to exchange rate fluctuations. Thus although cheaper for governments, variable rates are more expensive for industry.

Comparing fixed and floating rates in outline, governments want the certainty of fixed rates with the low cost and greater independence of variable rates. Managed floats offer the prospect of benefiting from both systems.

Classification of exchange rate arrangements

Exhibit 6.1 identifies the currencies and exchange rate arrangements used by various countries. Many countries allow the value of their currency to float against others but intervene periodically to influence its value. Several small countries peg their currencies to the US dollar.

The Mexican peso has a controlled exchange rate that applies to international trade and a floating market rate that applies to tourism. The floating market rate is influenced by central bank intervention. Chile intervenes to maintain its currency within 10 per cent of a specified exchange rate with respect to major currencies. Venezuela intervenes to limit exchange rate fluctuations within wide bands.

Some Eastern European countries that recently opened their markets have tied their currencies to a single widely traded currency. The arrangement was sometimes temporary, as these countries were searching for the proper exchange rate that would stabilize or enhance their economic conditions. For example, in 1998 when the currency account deficit of the Slovakian balance of payments exceeded 10 per cent of GDP, the government unpegged to a currency and allowed it to devalue in an attempt to reduce demand for foreign goods and increase foreign demand for its own goods.

Many governments attempt to impose exchange controls to prevent their exchange rates from fluctuating. When these governments remove the controls, however, the exchange rates abruptly adjust to a new market-determined level. For example, in October 1994, the Russian authorities allowed the Russian rouble to fluctuate, and the rouble depreciated by 27 per cent against the dollar on that day. In April 1996, Venezuela's government removed controls on the bolivar (its currency), and the bolivar depreciated by 42 per cent on that day.

After the 2001 war in Afghanistan, an exchange rate system was needed. In October 2002, a new currency, called the new afghani, was created to replace the old afghani. The old currency was exchanged for the new money at a ratio of 1000 to 1. Thus, 30 000 old afghanis were exchanged for 30 new afghanis. The new money was printed with watermarks to deter counterfeits.

At the end of the 2003 war in Iraq, an exchange rate system was also needed. At that time, three different currencies were being used in Iraq. The Swiss dinar (so called because it was designed in Switzerland) was created before the Gulf War, but had not been printed since then. It traded at about eight dinars per dollar and was used by the Kurds in northern Iraq. The Saddam dinar, which was used extensively before 2003, was printed in excess to finance Iraq's military budget and was easy to counterfeit. Its value relative to the dollar was very volatile over time. The US dollar was frequently used in the black market in Iraq even before the 2003 war. Just after the war, the dollar was used more frequently, as merchants were unwilling to accept Saddam dinars out of fear that their value was declining.

Although Iraq is not the best example, mention should be made of the possibility of multicurrency arrangements. In 1989 the UK government proposed a 'hard ecu', a European currency to be used as an alternative alongside the domestic currencies that made up the European Currency Unit (ECU). Indeed, in the UK and in most other countries there is nothing to stop MNCs and individuals settling their debts in any currency, providing both parties are agreed. A number of retail chains in the UK will accept euros as

EXHIBIT 6.1   Exchange rate arrangements

Floating rate system			
Country	**Currency**	**Country**	**Currency**
Afghanistan	new afghani	Norway	krone
Argentina	peso	Paraguay	guarani
Australia	dollar	Peru	new sol
Bolivia	boliviano	Poland	zloty
Brazil	real	Romania	leu
Canada	dollar	Russia	rouble
Chile	peso	Singapore	dollar
Euro participants (17 European countries)	euro	South Africa	rand
Hungary	forint	South Korea	won
India	rupee	Sweden	krona
Indonesia	rupiah	Switzerland	franc
Israel	new shekel	Thailand	baht
Jamaica	dollar	UK	pound
Japan	yen	Venezuela	bolivar
Mexico	peso		

Pegged rate system		
The following currencies are pegged to a currency or a composite of currencies.		
Country	**Currency**	**Currency is pegged to**
Bahamas	dollar	US dollar
Cameroon	Central African CFA Franc	Euro
China	yuan	Basket of currencies
Denmark	Danish krone	Euro with two-and-a-quarter per cent variation band
Hong Kong	dollar	US dollar
Saudi Arabia	riyal	US dollar

payment and it may be that the UK converts to the euro in this way. The process is known as dollarization even when it refers to the euro. The danger of such arrangements is that individuals become exposed to currency fluctuations in their own personal finances, for example, earning in one currency and borrowing in another. This was the case in the Argentinian crisis of 2001–02 where some 70 per cent of loans were denominated in dollars and earnings were in pesos.

GOVERNMENT INTERVENTION – THE PROCESS

Each country has a central bank that may intervene in the foreign exchange markets to control its currency's value. In the USA, for example, the central bank is made up of a network of major banks referred to as the Federal Reserve System (the Fed). In Europe the European Central Bank (ECB) is a separate bank situated in Frankfurt, Germany. The main decision-making body, the Governing Council, includes the governors of all the national central banks from the 12 euro area countries. Central banks have other duties besides intervening in the foreign exchange market. In particular, they control interest rates and attempt to control the growth of the money supply. The central bank is in charge of printing the money and controlling the amount of lending in the currency. The immediate objectives are to maintain stable prices, economic growth and low unemployment. The precise nature of government spending is, of course, the responsibility of governments. The Central Bank's role is to control the overall levels.

USING THE WEB

Central bank website links

The Bank for International Settlements website http://www.bis.org/cbanks.htm provides links to websites of central banks around the world.

Reasons for government intervention

The degree to which the home currency is controlled, or 'managed', varies among central banks. Central banks commonly manage exchange rates for three reasons:

- To smooth exchange rate movements.
- To establish implicit exchange rate boundaries.
- To respond to temporary disturbances.

Smooth exchange rate movements. If a central bank is concerned that its economy will be affected by abrupt movements in its home currency's value, it may attempt to smooth the currency movements over time. Its actions may keep business cycles less volatile. The central bank may also encourage international trade by reducing exchange rate uncertainty. Furthermore, smoothing currency movements may reduce fears in the financial markets and speculative activity that could cause a major decline in a currency's value.

Establish implicit exchange rate boundaries. Some central banks attempt to maintain their home currency rates within some unofficial, or implicit, boundaries. Analysts are commonly quoted as forecasting that a currency will not fall below or rise above a particular benchmark value because the central bank would intervene to attempt to prevent that. It should be remembered that the volumes of transactions on the international financial markets are very much greater than the reserves of the central banks. Any attempt by central banks to influence the value of its currency may well fail.

Respond to temporary disturbances. In some cases, a central bank may intervene to insulate a currency's value from a temporary disturbance. Because of the size of the international currency markets, central banks will often act in unison. The ECB may therefore use its reserves of euros to buy British pounds to support the value of the pound at the request of the Bank of England.

EXAMPLE

News that oil prices might rise could cause expectations of a future decline in the value of the Japanese yen because Japan exchanges yen for dollars to purchase oil from oil-exporting countries (oil was always paid for in dollars – this is still generally the case). Foreign exchange market speculators may exchange yen for dollars in anticipation of this decline. Central banks may therefore intervene to offset the immediate downward pressure on the yen caused by such market transactions.

Several studies have found that government intervention does not have a permanent impact on exchange rate movements. In many cases, intervention is overwhelmed by market forces. In the absence of intervention, however, currency movements would be even more volatile.

Direct intervention

To force the British pound to depreciate, the Bank of England can intervene directly by exchanging pounds that it holds as reserves for other foreign currencies in the foreign exchange market. By 'flooding the market with pounds' in this manner, the Bank of England puts downward pressure on the pound. If the Bank of England desires to strengthen the pound, it can use its reserves of foreign exchange to buy pounds in the foreign exchange market, thereby putting upward pressure on the pound.

The effects of direct intervention on the value of the British pound are illustrated in Exhibit 6.2. To strengthen the pound's value, the Bank of England draws on its reserves of foreign currency (an item in the balance of payments account) to buy British pounds. As a result, there is an outward shift in the demand for pounds in the foreign exchange market (as shown in the graph on the left). Conversely, to weaken the pound's value, the Bank of England sells pounds for foreign currency, which causes an outward shift in the supply of pounds for sale in the foreign exchange market (as shown in the graph on the right).

EXHIBIT 6.2   Effects of direct central bank intervention in the foreign exchange market

Bank of England exchanges reserves of foreign currency for £s thereby increasing the demand for £s by foreign currency

Bank of England exchanges £s for foreign currency thereby increasing the supply of £s for foreign currency

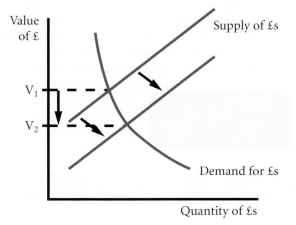

During early 2004, Japan's central bank, the Bank of Japan, intervened on several occasions to lower the value of the yen. In the first 2 months of 2004, the Bank of Japan sold yen in the foreign exchange market in exchange for $100 billion. Then, on 5 March, 2004, the Bank of Japan sold yen in the foreign exchange market in exchange for $20 billion, which put immediate downward pressure on the value of the yen.

Direct intervention is usually most effective when there is a co-ordinated effort among central banks. If all central banks simultaneously attempt to strengthen or weaken the currency in the manner just described, they can exert greater pressure on the currency's value.

Reliance on reserves. The effectiveness of a central bank's direct intervention depends on the amount of reserves it can use. If the central bank has a low level of reserves, it may not be able to exert much pressure on the currency's value. Market forces are likely to overwhelm its actions.

As foreign exchange activity has grown, central bank intervention has become less effective. The volume of foreign exchange transactions on a single day now exceeds the combined values of reserves at all central banks. Consequently, the number of direct interventions has declined. In 1989, for example, the Fed (the US central banking system) intervened on 97 different days. Since then, the Fed has not intervened on more than 20 days in any year.

Nonsterilized versus sterilized intervention. When central banks intervene in the foreign exchange market without adjusting for the change in the money supply, they are engaging in a **nonsterilized intervention**. For example, if the Bank of England sells pounds for foreign currencies in the foreign exchange markets in an attempt to weaken the pound, the pound money supply increases. Effectively, the Bank of England as the printer of the currency, has created the reserve of pounds to use on the exchange markets.

In a **sterilized intervention**, the central bank intervenes in the foreign exchange market and simultaneously engages in offsetting transactions in the treasury securities markets. As a result, the money supply is unchanged. When intervening in the foreign exchange market, the central bank can either buy its own currency with its reserves of foreign currency or sell its currency from the reserves that it creates by virtue of being the issuer of the currency.

If the central bank buys its own currency, it creates an artificial demand that will help to maintain its value. There will also be a reduction in the money supply as the central bank in effect 'buys back' its own currency. This effect can be negated by using the money it has bought back to purchase its own treasury securities from commercial banks. Redeeming treasury securities in this way increases the money supply in the economy as money is paid by the central bank to the commercial banks for the securities.

If the central bank, in simple terms, prints money and sells it for foreign currency, the effect is to increase the money supply. This effect can be negated by issuing treasury securities. Payment for securities by banks will reduce the money supply as banks pay the central bank for the securities. The central bank can then retire the payments it receives from circulation.

If the Bank of England desires to strengthen the British pound without affecting the pound money supply, it:

(1) buys pounds with foreign currency, thus maintaining the foreign currency demand for pounds and

(Continued)

hence the pound's value and (2), with the pounds it receives for foreign currency buy or redeem its own treasury bills (securities). Thus there will be no net change in the holding of pounds in the economy (see Exhibit 6.3, top right-hand section).

The balance of payments would show a reduction in the Bank of England's reserves of foreign currency. This would be noted with a plus sign indicating the resulting demand for pounds (similar to the effect of exports).

The difference between nonsterilized and sterilized intervention is illustrated in Exhibit 6.3. In the top half of the exhibit, the Bank of England attempts to strengthen the British pound, and in the bottom half, the Bank of England attempts to weaken or lower the value of the pound. For each scenario, the right-hand side shows a sterilized intervention involving an exchange of Treasury bills for British pounds that offsets the pound flows resulting from the exchange of currencies. Thus, the sterilized intervention achieves the same exchange of currencies in the foreign exchange market as the nonsterilized intervention, but it involves an additional transaction to prevent changes to the pound money supply.

EXHIBIT 6.3 Forms of central bank intervention in the foreign exchange market

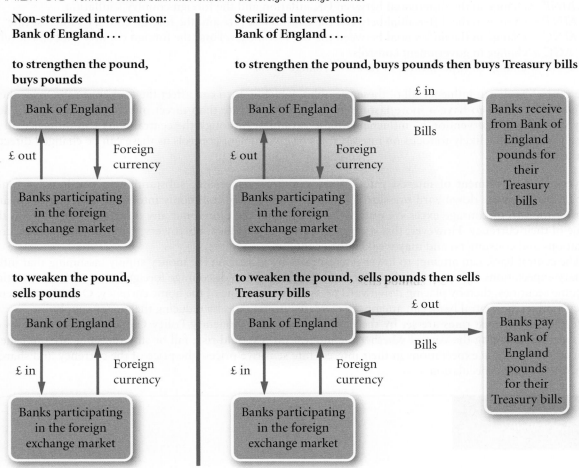

Notes:

£ out = £s taken out of circulation and held by the Bank of England.

£ in = £s put into circulation by the Bank of England.

Speculating on direct intervention. Some traders in the foreign exchange market attempt to determine when central bank intervention is occurring, and the extent of the intervention, in order to capitalize on the anticipated results of the intervention effort. Normally, the central banks attempt to intervene without being noticed. However, dealers at the major banks often pass the information to other market participants. Also, when central banks deal directly with the numerous commercial banks, markets are well aware that the central bank is intervening. To hide its strategy, a central bank may pretend to be interested in selling when it is actually buying or vice versa. It calls commercial banks and obtains both bid and ask quotes on currencies, so the banks will not know whether the central bank is considering purchases or sales of these currencies.

Intervention strategies vary among central banks. Some arrange for one large order when they intervene; others use several smaller orders equivalent to 5 million euros to 10 million euros. Even if traders determine the extent of central bank intervention, they still cannot know with certainty what impact it will have on exchange rates.

Indirect intervention

A central bank can also affect its currency's value indirectly by influencing the factors that determine it. Recall that the change in a currency's spot rate is influenced by the following factors in the case of the UK and the British pound:

ΔINF = change in the differential between UK inflation and the foreign country's inflation
ΔINT = change in the differential between the UK interest rate and the foreign country's interest rate
ΔINC = change in the differential between the UK income level and the foreign country's income level
ΔGC = change in government controls
ΔEXP = change in expectations of future exchange rates.

The central bank can influence all of these variables, which in turn can affect the exchange rate. Since these variables are likely to have a more lasting impact on a spot rate than direct intervention, a central bank may use indirect intervention by influencing these variables. Although the central bank can influence all of these variables, it is likely to focus on interest rates or government controls as these can be changed directly by the central bank.

Government adjustment of interest rates. When countries experience substantial net outflows of funds (which places severe downward pressure on their currency), they commonly intervene indirectly by raising interest rates to discourage excessive outflows of funds and therefore limit any downward pressure on the value of their currency. However, this strategy adversely affects local borrowers (government agencies, corporations and consumers) and may weaken the economy.

The central bank can attempt to lower interest rates by increasing the money supply (assuming that inflationary expectations are not affected). Lower interest rates tend to discourage foreign investors from investing in home securities, thereby placing downward pressure on the value of the home currency. Or, to boost a currency's value, the central bank can attempt to increase interest rates by reducing the money supply.

In the UK, interest rates are set by the Bank of England's Monetary Policy Committee. The minutes of the meeting including the vote of whether the interest rates should rise, fall or stay the same are published. Markets can include expectations in their interest rate sensitive prices (the price of the currency and shares) thus discouraging speculation.

EXAMPLE

In October 1997, there was concern that the Asian crisis might adversely affect Brazil and other Latin American countries. Speculators pulled funds out of Brazil and reinvested them in other countries, causing major capital

(Continued)

outflows and therefore placing extreme downward pressure on the Brazilian currency (the real). The central bank of Brazil responded at the end of October by doubling its interest rates from about 20 per cent to about 40 per cent. This action discouraged investors from pulling funds out of Brazil because they could now earn twice the interest from investing in some securities there. Although the bank's action was successful in defending the real, it reduced economic growth because the cost of borrowing funds was too high for many firms.

In another example, during the Asian crisis in 1997 and 1998, central banks of some Asian countries increased their interest rates to prevent their currencies from weakening. The higher interest rates were expected to make the local securities more attractive and therefore encourage investors to maintain their holdings of securities, which would reduce the exchange of the local currency for other currencies. This effort was not successful for most Asian countries, although it worked for China and Hong Kong.

As a third example, in May 1998, the Russian currency (the rouble) had consistently declined, and Russian stock prices had fallen by more than 50 per cent from their level 4 months earlier. Fearing that the lack of confidence in Russia's currency and stocks would cause massive outflows of funds, the Russian central bank attempted to prevent further outflows by tripling interest rates (from about 50 per cent to 150 per cent). The rouble was temporarily stabilized, but stock prices continued to decline because investors were concerned that the high interest rates would reduce economic growth.

Government use of foreign exchange controls. Some governments attempt to use foreign exchange controls (such as restrictions on the exchange of the currency) as a form of indirect intervention to maintain the exchange rate of their currency. A control exists where a resident has to obtain permission to buy foreign currency and where a foreign national needs permission to buy a currency. Exchange controls tend to affect the capital account rather than the current account. China, for example, allowed its currency to be bought and sold for current account transactions involving goods and services in 1996. But only in 2001 were Chinese residents allowed to purchase foreign exchange to pay for their own studies abroad. In 2002 the Qualified Foreign Investor Initiative was introduced in China to allow non-residents, under certain conditions, to invest in the Chinese Stock Market. Exchange rate controls require government permission to exchange the domestic currency for foreign currency. Sometimes the rates may differ depending on the purpose of the transaction. Under severe pressure, however, governments tend to let the currency float temporarily towards its market-determined level and set new bands around that level.

EXAMPLE

During the mid-1990s, Venezuela imposed foreign exchange controls on its currency (the bolivar). In April 1996, Venezuela removed its controls on foreign exchange, and the bolivar declined by 42 per cent the next day. This result suggests that the market-determined exchange rate of the bolivar was substantially lower than the exchange rate at which the government artificially set the bolivar.

EXCHANGE RATE TARGET ZONES

In recent years, many economists have criticized the present exchange rate system because of the wide swings in exchange rates of major currencies. Some have suggested that **target zones** be used for these currencies. An initial exchange rate would be established, with specific boundaries surrounding that rate. Such a target zone is similar to the bands used in a fixed exchange rate system, but would likely be wider. Proponents of the target zone system suggest that it would stabilize international trade patterns by reducing exchange rate volatility.

Implementing a target zone system could be complicated, however. First, what initial exchange rate should be established for each country? Second, how wide should the target zone be? The ideal target zone would allow exchange rates to adjust to economic factors without causing wide swings in international trade and arousing fear in financial markets.

If target zones were implemented, governments would be responsible for intervening to maintain their currencies within the zones. If the zones were sufficiently wide, government intervention would rarely be necessary; however, such wide zones would basically resemble the exchange rate system as it exists today. Governments tend to intervene when a currency's value moves outside some implicitly acceptable zone. Unless governments could maintain their currency's value within the target zone, this system could not ensure stability in international markets. A country experiencing a large balance of trade deficit might intentionally allow its currency to float below the lower boundary in order to stimulate foreign demand for its exports. Wide swings in international trade patterns could result. Furthermore, financial market prices would be more volatile because financial market participants would expect some currencies to move outside their zones. The result would be a system no different from what exists today.

In February 1987, representatives of the USA, Japan, West Germany, France, Canada, Italy and the UK (also known as the Group of Seven or G7 countries) signed the Louvre Accord to establish acceptable ranges (not disclosed to the public) for the dollar's value relative to other currencies. The Federal Reserve intervened heavily in the foreign exchange market for 2 years after the Louvre Accord, but it has generally intervened only in small doses in recent years.

INTERVENTION AS A POLICY TOOL

The government of any country can implement its own fiscal and monetary policies to control its economy. In addition, it may attempt to influence the value of its home currency in order to improve its economy, weakening its currency under some conditions and strengthening it under others. In essence, the exchange rate becomes a tool, like tax laws and the money supply, that the government can use to achieve its desired economic objectives.

Influence of a weak home currency on the economy

A weak home currency can stimulate foreign demand for products. A weak euro, for example, can substantially boost Eurozone exports and Eurozone jobs. In addition, it may also reduce imports.

Though a weak currency can reduce unemployment at home, it can lead to higher inflation. In the early 1990s, the US dollar was weak, causing US imports from foreign countries to be highly priced. This situation priced firms such as Bayer, Volkswagen and Volvo out of the US market. Under these conditions, US companies were able to raise their domestic prices because it was difficult for foreign producers to compete. In addition, US firms that are heavy exporters, such as Goodyear Tire & Rubber Co., Litton Industries, Merck and Maytag Corp., also benefit from a weaker dollar.

Influence of a strong home currency on the economy

A strong home currency can encourage consumers and corporations of that country to buy goods from other countries. This situation intensifies foreign competition and forces domestic producers to refrain from increasing prices. Therefore, the country's overall inflation rate should be lower if its currency is stronger, other things being equal.

Though a strong currency is a possible cure for high inflation, it may cause higher unemployment due to the attractive foreign prices that result from a strong home currency. The ideal value of the currency depends on the perspective of the country and the officials who must make these decisions. The strength or weakness of a currency is just one of many factors that influence a country's economic conditions.

By combining this discussion of how exchange rates affect inflation with the discussion in Chapter 4 of how inflation can affect exchange rates, a more complete picture of the dynamics of the exchange rate-inflation relationship can be achieved. A weak pound places upward pressure on UK inflation, which in turn places further downward pressure on the value of the pound. A strong pound places downward pressure on inflation and on UK economic growth. The interaction among exchange rates, government policies and economic factors is illustrated in Exhibit 6.4. As already mentioned, factors other than the home currency's strength affect unemployment and/or inflation. Likewise, factors other than unemployment and the inflation level influence a currency's strength. The cycles that have been described here will often be interrupted by these other factors and therefore will not continue indefinitely.

A BRIEF HISTORY OF EXCHANGE RATES

The history of exchange rates is mainly an account of the attempt by governments to manage exchange rates in increasingly free market economies. Exchange rates are primarily affected by economic developments. The exchange rate accompanies these developments, but on occasion can be the cause when there is a financial crisis. For financial managers knowledge of the history of exchange rates is important in that it shows in a way that theory does not, what can happen to exchange rates. Although transactions have become increasingly sophisticated over the years, the role of money in the economy has little changed. Solutions in the past are therefore still relevant today. Also, history suggests social and political dimensions to exchange rate behaviour that is not reflected in the primarily economic exchange rate models.

Perhaps the simplest question to ask is why there are so many changes to the exchange rate system? Why is there not one system that has slowly evolved over time? Part of the answer lies in James Tobin's suggestion of an impossibility theorem. He maintains that governments try to achieve a set of policies that are not

EXHIBIT 6.4 Impact of government actions on exchange rates

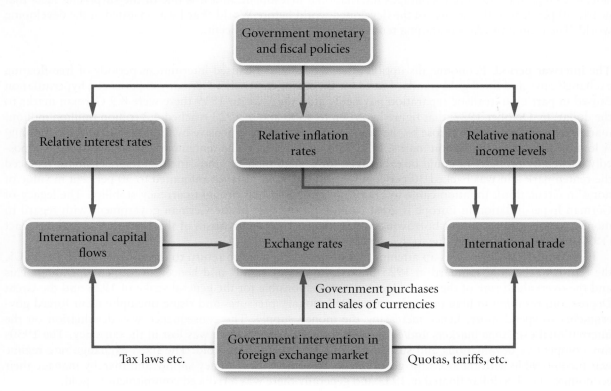

consistent, being: (1) a fixed exchange rate, (2) unregulated convertibility – the freedom to convert unrestricted amounts of home currency into any other currency and (3) an independent monetary policy, allowing control over interest rates, inflation rates and government spending. A fixed exchange rate is desirable to avoid the negative effects of devaluation and revaluation and to encourage trade and economic stability. There is also a political dimension, a variable rate means that the government is under the constant scrutiny of the exchange rate markets. If the markets are displeased with government policy, the value of the currency will fall on the foreign currency markets causing a loss of economic confidence. But the cost of maintaining a fixed exchange rate, as Tobin points out, is either to regulate the conversion of the currency, as in the post-World War II era (see below), or to lose sovereignty over economic policy – the experience of countries within the Eurozone (again discussed below). The following history is a brief outline of this dilemma.

Pre-World War I – the gold standard. The gold standard is the earliest fixed rate system of the developed world. Currencies under a full gold standard are convertible into a fixed weight of gold of a defined fineness (quality). Before World War I, the Bank of England sold gold at £3 17s 10½d (£3.89375) per ounce (28.35 grammes). Gold could serve as an alternative currency: if businesses feared that their paper money would buy less gold in future (a devaluation), they could always convert their money into gold now. The gold standard was an insurance against the temptation by central banks to print too much money – the main cause of a devaluation. As all currencies adopting the gold standard were convertible into an ounce of gold at a set price, the exchange rate between these currencies was also fixed. As stated in an earlier chapter, a currency unit that could buy twice as much gold as a unit of another currency had to be worth twice as much as the other currency unit.

The UK adopted the gold standard in 1816 and the USA and Europe converted in the 1870s. This was a period of great financial stability, although there were large fluctuations in economic activity trade cycles. As exchange rates were fixed and free trade was actively encouraged, an excess of imports could only be corrected by reducing the level of economic activity in order to reduce imports. This was achieved automatically in that excess imports meant money and gold flowing out of the economy to pay for the imports. The consequent reduction in the money supply led directly to a reduction in economic activity. On the plus side, exchange rate stability encourages international investment, and it is one of the surprising facts that nearly 50 per cent of the savings of the developed world before World War I was invested in the developing world. The ratio nowadays is about a tenth of that figure, i.e. 5 per cent.

The interwar period. Economic disruption after World War I caused intermittent periods of free floating exchange rates and fixed gold standard rates for the major currencies. Germany experienced hyperinflation caused in part by unrealistic reparation payments after the War. In 1919 there were 8.9 German marks to the dollar, by October 1922, that figure had risen to 4500 and in 1923 reached 4.2 trillion (million million) marks to the dollar! Inflation rose by the hour, a meal was more expensive by the end than at the beginning. A loaf of bread cost 200 billion marks. In 1923 a new currency, the rentenmark, was introduced, supposedly backed by property (it could be exchanged for a small piece of land). In 1924 the reichsmark replaced the rentenmark and was backed 30 per cent by gold (i.e. gold reserves amounted to 30 per cent in value of notes in circulation). Inflation came to an abrupt end, gold had brought currency stability. The legacy of German hyper-inflation in Europe is great caution on the part of the German government with regard to monetary policy (government borrowing and lending). The conservatism of the Growth and Stability pact (1997 – see below) is in part due to this experience.

In the mid-1920s there was an attempt by European countries to return to the gold standard. In the UK the return to the gold standard in 1925 limited the money supply and hence government spending. This and the overvalued rate of the pound were in part responsible for the general strike of 1926 and the Great Depression, resulting in high unemployment. Deflationary pressures and rising unemployment forced governments to spend more, hence increasing the money supply. The consequence was devaluation on the international exchange markets and/or shortage of gold as confidence was lost in the currency. The 1930s saw competitive devaluations and suspension of convertibility into gold. The fixed exchange rate regime was incompatible with the need for governments to control their money supply and thereby manage their economies. The US dollar floated in 1933 and generally there was a reduced commitment to gold.

Bretton Woods Agreement. Towards the end of World War II, there was a desire to establish a stable exchange rate system. In particular, countries wanted to avoid the financial chaos after World War I. The Bretton Woods Conference resulted in the setting up of the International Monetary Fund (IMF) and the International Bank for Reconstruction and Development (now the World Bank). The IMF was charged with overseeing a fixed exchange rate with the dollar. From 1944 to 1971, exchange rates were typically fixed to within 1 per cent of the dollar which alone was redeemable into gold at 35 dollars an ounce. Governments intervened in the foreign exchange markets to ensure that the exchange rates remained within the 1 per cent band. As with the gold standard, a fixed exchange rate with the dollar implies a fixed exchange rate with all other currencies in the system. In addition to the fixed exchange rate there were also restrictions on the amount of currency that could be used in international transactions. These restrictions on convertibility helped to support the currency in the marketplace. For example, until 1967 foreign investors in the UK were allowed to sell their stocks and shares to other foreign investors but not to UK residents. Such a sale would have created a demand for foreign currency to pay the foreign investors. There were also restrictions on investments abroad that were only lifted in 1979.

Smithsonian Agreement. The problem with the Bretton Woods Agreement was that all currencies except the dollar were pegged or fixed in a way that was tested by market trading each day. The dollar's peg was with gold, and that link was not tested as few in the immediate post-war era wanted to change dollars for the far less easily handled commodity, gold. The Fed or Federal Reserve Board in the USA, charged with managing monetary policy, was constrained by the need to ensure that there were sufficient gold reserves to meet any demands to convert dollars into gold. In 1958 their reserves of gold were more than the rest of the world's banks put together and were ample, though the reserves were not sufficient to change all dollars into gold. But as there were very few demands to convert dollars into gold, the Fed found that in practice the dollars could be issued without increasing the reserves of gold, and that the gold to dollar ratio could be allowed to fall. The resulting increase in the money supply was needed to finance large current account deficits and the Vietnam War.

In effect the USA was benefiting from international seigniorage. The dollar was becoming a world currency and the US was able to profit from issuing the currency. In very simple terms, the US could print dollars and spend the money and associated credit created on imports. For other currencies this would have resulted in an oversupply of domestic currency and devaluation. But the US position was different. Because international trade needed accounts denominated in a stable, acceptable currency, the dollars offered for imports were deposited back in the USA in the form of short-term deposits. The current account deficits therefore did not appear to lead to devaluation pressures. Increased supply was met by increased demand. The deficit on the current account was met by a surplus on the financial or capital account due to the demand for deposits in the USA. When the IMF was set up at Bretton Woods, a plan by the British economist J.M. Keynes wanted to create a world currency, the bancor. It was intended that the benefits from issuing the bancor would go to developing countries. In the event this plan was rejected and the numeraire currency of the SDR (Special Drawing Right) was created which did not have a separate seigniorage effect. It was the dollar that became the prime beneficiary of the increase in world trade.

Eventually the US current account deficits and evident over issuing of dollars led to a loss of confidence in its value and two European countries, Germany and France, began to prefer gold as a reserve to dollars. The resulting loss of confidence ending the long period of relative calm in exchange rates, came to an abrupt end on 14 March 1968 when President Johnson suspended the gold pool operation as it was known. $2.8 billion had been converted into gold in the previous 6 months. The price of gold was allowed to float freely, though central banks continued to trade gold at $35 an ounce.

Eventually, the USA on 15 August 1971, suspended convertibility into gold, imposed a 10 per cent surcharge on imports, and limited tax relief on imported machinery. Unfortunately these measures prompted restrictions on the international flow of investments, as investment institutions sought to move their funds out of dollars in anticipation of a devaluation of the dollar. A meeting was called of the ten largest economies at the Smithsonian Institute in Washington. As a result, the dollar was devalued against the yen by 17 per cent, the German mark by 14 per cent and the French franc and the UK pound by 8 per cent. The margin of variation around the dollar was increased to two-and-a-quarter per cent from 1 per cent. The official price of gold was raised to $38 an ounce. This move was of little significance as the market price was well above this rate – newly mined gold went on to the non-bank market, and banks were unwilling to use gold at this rate to settle accounts. Finally, in August 1971, with much depleted gold reserves, convertibility of the dollar into gold between Central Banks was suspended.

The fixed exchange rates between currencies continued in this now weakened form. However, there was still an excessive demand by dollar holders for foreign currency. As of February 1973, the dollar was again devalued. By March 1973, most governments of the major countries were no longer attempting to maintain their home currency values within the boundaries established by the Smithsonian Agreement. The world financial system had changed from a fixed rate regime to a freely floating exchange rate system between the major currencies.

The members of what is now termed the EU, at this point, set up a system of managing exchange rates between their currencies in what proved to be the start of the long road that led to the creation of the euro (see below). Their reasons were simply that a fixed exchange rate between members was seen as necessary for promoting free trade.

Creation of Europe's snake arrangement. In the late 1960s it became evident that the gold exchange standard was not going to last in its present form. The European Economic Community (EEC) (now the EU) commissioned the Werner report which came out in 1970. The report recommended a process of monetary union within Europe by means of a parity grid system. By narrowing the band of variation, a single currency was planned to be achieved by 1980 – some 19 years before the actual achievement of fixed rates on 1 January 1999. In the spirit of the Werner plan, and in response to the Smithsonian arrangements, the EEC set up what came to be known as the 'snake in the tunnel' or simply, the 'snake' system. Currencies, as under the Smithsonian Agreement, were allowed to vary two-and-a-quarter per cent either side of the dollar, allowing currencies to rise or fall a total of four-and-a-half per cent. If a currency moved from its ceiling to its floor while another currency went from the floor to the ceiling the total movement between the two currencies would be $2 \times 4\frac{1}{2}\% = 9$ per cent. Such potential variation was considered to be too much between members of the EEC. They therefore agreed in addition that they would maintain a two-and-a-quarter per cent (half the Smithsonian band) with each other. When one currency rose to the top of its band with the dollar, it would buy the weakest of the currencies. The snake came into operation in March 1972; the UK, Denmark and Ireland joined in May 1972. The UK left the following month when the £ was floated, Italy left in 1973 and France in 1976. When the European monetary system was established in 1979 (see below), members of the snake were Germany, Benelux, Denmark and Norway.

The failure to develop a stable system in the 1970s was in no small part due to the large increases in oil prices. In response to the Arab–Israeli war in October 1973 oil prices were increased by the Arab dominated Organization of Petroleum Exporting Countries (OPEC). Prices increased in real terms (after adjusting for inflation) by 126 per cent in 1974. Over the 1970s oil prices increased by 300 per cent again in real terms. Oil is paid for in dollars, therefore the devaluation of the dollar helped to offset the oil price changes. Being linked to the dollar, however, meant that the beneficial effect of dollar devaluation was less than if currencies floated freely against the dollar.

Creation of the European Monetary System (EMS). Despite the gradual disintegration of the snake, the UK president of the European Commission, Roy Jenkins, relaunched the monetary union project by initiating the European Monetary System in March 1979. This was a parity grid system that did not include the dollar. Thus each country faced a central rate, upper and lower rates with each other member of the system. Originally, the currencies were allowed to diverge by two-and-a-quarter per cent above and below the central rate and a wider band of 6 per cent for the Italian lira. The system became known as the Exchange Rate Mechanism or ERM. In addition a numeraire currency (a weighted basket of currencies) was created known as the ECU. The new currency, later to become the euro, was used in the parity system as a measure for determining intervention and also served to measure expenditure of the EEC.

A weighted basket of currencies can be thought of literally as a basket containing currencies. In this case there were 1.15 French francs, 109 Italian lira, 0.82 of a German mark and so on. The value of the ECU could be translated into any one currency simply by converting the currencies in the basket at the market exchange rates to the desired currency. The amount of each currency in the basket was determined by the level of trade undertaken by each country within the community. The lira had a low value, so 109 lira amounted to less than 10 per cent of the value of the ECU in 1979. The German mark had a high value and was about 33 per cent of the value of the ECU. The currency values in the basket were periodically readjusted. The Special Drawing Right (SDR) is also a numeraire currency and serves a similar purpose for the International Monetary Fund. The value of the ECU was originally set at 1SDR, and the value of the euro was set at the then value of an ECU in 1999.

Managed float. This system is usually dated from the Plaza Accord (September 1985) between the USA, France, Germany and the UK. The view was expressed at the meeting that the dollar was overvalued, but no specific targets or timetable was offered. By early 1987 the dollar had lost more than 40 per cent against its highs in 1985 with the German mark and the Japanese yen. In February 1987 there was another meeting in Paris (the Louvre Accord, this time including Canada) where it was jointly agreed that the value of the dollar should be stabilized, but gave no indication as to how this was to be achieved. The dollar continued to fall and only began to stabilize following a further meeting among the major nations that Christmas (the 'Telephone Accord'). Unlike previous attempts to influence the exchange rate, no specific targets were given to the market. The concept of soft targets was born. The advantage was that the very large funds on the foreign exchange markets had no targets against which to speculate. Intervention by the central banks initially tried to oppose market movements but later was refined to move rates in relatively quiet periods with market trends that they approved of rather than contest bouts of speculation. The technique was later adopted by the Exchange Rate Mechanism of the EU to good effect.

Demise of the European Monetary System. At first the system worked well. Between 1979 and 1983 there were 27 realignments averaging 5.3 per cent and between 1984 and 1987, 12 realignments averaging 3.8 per cent. The UK joined the ERM on 8 October 1990 after a period of high interest rates in order to maintain the value of the British pound. The consensus was that the British pound was overvalued in the parity grid. This was, in fact, a deliberate policy designed to keep inflation low. The reason was that by making the British pound relatively expensive, prices in the UK would have to compete with imports that were at an artificially low price. France had taken much the same action when it joined in 1979 and had successfully reduced its inflation. The stratagem was nevertheless vulnerable. Measures needed to protect the value of the British pound would now have to be that much stronger given that the starting point was already one of overvaluation. Needless to say, the market tested this vulnerability in 1992. A major difference between 1979 and 1992 was that the international financial markets were much larger and hence powerful, boosted in part by the relaxation of restrictions on portfolio investment. The breaking point came as a result of German unification following the fall of the Berlin Wall in 1989. East Germany was allowed to convert its currency to West German marks at a very favourable rate causing a 20 per cent jump in the money supply. Growth was insufficient to absorb this increase. Government borrowing in Germany was also higher to help finance the rebuilding of East Germany following years of neglect under communist rule. As a result, the German government increased its interest rates. In order to prevent the value of the British pound falling against the other currencies in the ERM, it was necessary to increase UK interest rates as well. The currencies in the ERM were having to pay higher interest rates for reasons that were purely concerned with the German economy.

The effect of an interest rate rise in the UK is very different from other members due to the tradition of borrowing to purchase houses in the UK. On the continent renting is the norm. Householders in the UK typically borrow up to 5 years' income to purchase their house on variable interest loans (mortgages). A 1 per cent increase in a 6 per cent 25 year loan of £100 000 to buy a house (i.e. a mortgage) is approximately £64 per month, a 2 per cent increase is £129 per month. An increase in interest rates directly affects householders far more in the UK than in the rest of Europe. Against this background, the market came to believe that UK politicians would prefer to devalue the British pound rather than raise interest rates. The trial of strength with the markets came on 16 September 1992 ('Black Wednesday'). Speculators, treasurers of MNCs, and investors all converted British pounds into foreign currency in the belief that the pound was about to devalue. At 2.15 pm interest rates were raised to 15 per cent from 10 per cent that morning. By 5.15 pm after using over £8 billion in the foreign currency reserves of the Bank of England and other

European central banks to support the value of the pound, it was suspended from the ERM and allowed to devalue. The British pound devalued by over 5 per cent in one day and by a further 5 per cent over the next month. The Italian lira suffered a similar fate (Italy had also followed the UK out of the snake system). An attempt was then made to speculate on a fall in the value of the French franc. The attempt failed, though at 30 January 1993 central bank interest rates were: France 10 per cent, Germany 8.25 per cent and the UK 6.0625 per cent. The fluctuation margins were increased to 15 per cent in August 1993 effectively ending the rigid form of the ERM. Italy later rejoined the ERM. However, for the British pound, Black Wednesday marked the end of formal participation in the European currency project - a position that is little changed today.

USING THE WEB

The website http://www.ecb.int/home/html/index.en.html provides information on the euro and monetary policy conducted by the ECB.

After 1992, greater variation of currencies in the looser form of the ERM did not ensue. A policy of soft exchange rate targets was pursued. Occasional variations were not contested by the central banks; when the market was quieter, intervention was made to encourage the markets to move in the approved direction.

The relative calm among European currencies after 1992 was in part due to the clear commitment to create a single European currency by the end of the decade. The Maastricht Treaty was signed in February 1992 and among other provisions 'Resolved to achieve the strengthening and the convergence of their economies and to establish an economic and monetary union including, in accordance with the provisions of this Treaty, a single and stable currency.' By stressing economic convergence, the lesson had been learnt that exchange rate policy had to reflect economic realities.

Unlike many previous exchange rate agreements, the ERM came to an orderly end with the creation of the euro in 1999.

European Monetary Union. The creation of the euro on 1 January 1999 meant the fixing of exchange rates of the then 11 participating nations: Austria, Belgium, Finland, France, Germany, Ireland, Italy, Luxembourg, the Netherlands, Portugal, Spain and later, Greece. Subsequently, in January and early February 2002 these nations withdrew their national currencies and issued a common currency.

Together, the participating countries in the euro comprise almost 20 per cent of the world's gross domestic product – a proportion similar to that of the USA. Three countries that were members of the EU in 1999 (the UK, Denmark and Sweden) decided not to adopt the euro at that time. The ten countries in Eastern Europe (including the Czech Republic and Hungary) that joined the EU in 2004 will be eligible to participate in the euro in the future if they meet specific economic goals. Countries that participate in the EU are supposed to abide by the Growth and Stability pact before they adopt the euro. This pact requires, as mentioned above, that the country's annual budget deficit be less than 3 per cent of its gross domestic product and government total borrowing be less than 60 per cent. These targets have, however, not generally been met since the 2008–09 recession.

To join the euro, a country must restrict the movements of the euro relative to its home currency within a range of plus or minus 15 per cent from an initially set exchange rate. This will allow it to convert to euros at a particular exchange rate with some assurance of stability. Assuming that the country also complies with other specified macroeconomic conditions, such as limiting inflation and its budget deficit, a member state will be allowed to join the euro. Currently the euro is the official currency in 17 of the member states of the EU being: Austria, Belgium, Cyprus, Estonia, Finland, France, Germany, Greece, Ireland, Italy, Luxembourg, Malta, the Netherlands, Portugal, Slovakia, Slovenia and Spain. States that are part of the EU but not part of the Eurozone include: Denmark, Sweden, the UK, Bulgaria, the Czech Republic, Estonia, Hungary, Latvia, Lithuania, Poland and Romania.

As an historical note suggesting that little is new in finance, a similar form of standardization was attempted in 1865 with the formation of the Latin Monetary Union. The principal members were France,

Belgium, Switzerland, Italy and Greece. Each member issued standard coins that were allowed to circulate freely throughout the Union. Later, other countries, in particular, Austria, Bulgaria, Romania, Spain and Venezuela issued coins of similar denomination and value without formally joining.

Greek crisis and beyond. This is the third of the major crises to affect the development of the euro, the previous two being the collapse of the snake in the 1970s and the effect of German unification in the early 1990s. In both the previous cases the euro project continued principally because the alternatives were worse. In the case of the Greek crisis there is the prospect of Greece leaving the euro because the Greek government is unable to repay loans made by, amongst others, banks in the Eurozone.

Such a scenario is problematic not only for Greece but also for those within the euro. If Greece left the euro and defaulted on its debts but eventually recovered (and there are similarities with the Argentinian crisis of 2002, see below), then Greece would be part of the EU in much the same way as the UK. However, any attempt to impose discipline within the euro would be undermined. If it did not recover then the whole notion of social cohesion in the Maastricht Treaty would be undermined, it would be little more than a club of developed nations. The alternative of staying in is the current option of both the EU and the majority of Greek people after two elections in 2012. The prospects are nevertheless very uncertain and it may be that in the future the Greek people decide to secede from the euro.

The problem that the EU and the IMF face is how much of the Greek debt should be rolled over and refinanced with further loans and how much should be written off. From the perspective of the IMF, in 2012 Greece was effectively in default. Fitch, a credit rating agency, reduced Greece to 'Restricted Default' status and the ISDA (International Swaps and Derivatives Association) declared Greek debt a 'credit event', triggering credit default payments. In the same year, in order to respond to Greek government requests for funding to repay its debts, a 'troika' was formed made up of the EU, the IMF and the ECB. This body has overseen the implementation of a number of conditionality packages (extensive economic reforms) in much the same way as the IMF on its own has demanded from other countries in default. It has been argued that Greece has been in receipt of preferred treatment compared to a developing country subject to IMF sponsored reforms. The effect of the reforms have, however, been devastating. Youth unemployment at over 50 per cent and general unemployment at 25 per cent, cuts in pensions and public sector salaries, the minimum wage and a 27 per cent increase in bankruptcies in 2012 is testimony to the severity of the reforms. Perhaps worst of all is that there is no prospect of a recovery, the cutbacks required to receive extra bailout monies reduce Greece's ability to grow its economy to repay its debts.

The problems experienced by Greece have also been experienced by most other developing countries to varying degrees as part of the 2007 world financial crisis (see below). Exhibit 6.4 shows the recent experience of other EU countries. Portugal and Ireland have also been in receipt of troika administered bailout packages and Spain and Italy have been on the verge of requesting EU and IMF support. In effect, where a country loses the confidence of the international financial markets, the governments concerned lose a substantial part of their sovereignty through loan renegotiation. As the table of interest rates shows in Exhibit 6.4A being in the Eurozone appears to offer little protection. This might be criticized as 'rule by the markets' an undemocratic process; others see this as an important counterbalance to profligate government spending and ill advised sovereign lending by banks, hedge funds and government institutions. This has happened before, the Third World Debt Crisis was another example of over-borrowing by governments and overestimating the creditworthiness of sovereign (country) lending.

The difference between the Greek position and that of a sovereign state is that Greece does not control its currency. Regaining control of the national currency is a mixed blessing as the experience of Argentina subsequent to its reinstatement of a freely floating peso in 2002. Previously the peso had been pegged to the dollar at a rate of 1 peso to the US dollar. The rate changed to nearly 4 pesos to the dollar when the peg was removed. The result was inflation.

Inflation in many countries serves as a cheap form of taxation. Instead of going through the long and expensive process of filling in tax returns then paying over to the government a percentage of income and profits, governments can fund themselves by simply creating credit. The tax system can then serve as a lesser form of raising taxes. From the individual's point of view the effect is similar. The value of one's income can be reduced either by paying taxes or through inflation. From the governments' perspective they can fund expensive electoral promises without the unpopular measure of raising taxes and without the

EXHIBIT 6.4A   Comparative European statistics

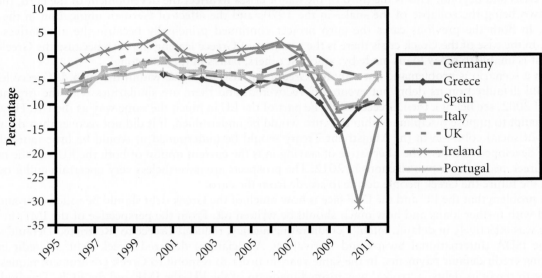

Government deficit (revenues less expenditure) as a percentage of GDP

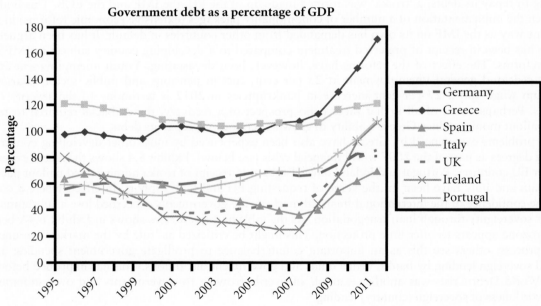

Government debt as a percentage of GDP

10-year government bonds in European countries Jan-2013					
Country	%	Currency	Country	%	Currency
Greece	10.72	euro	Latvia	3.34	lat
Iceland	6.64	krona	Bulgaria	2.97	lev
Russia	6.63	rouble	Norway	2.39	krone

10-year government bonds in European countries Jan-2013					
Country	%	Currency	Country	%	Currency
Turkey	6.57	lira	Belgium	2.3	euro
Hungary	6.36	forint	France	2.18	euro
Portugal	6.15	euro	UK	2.06	pound
Romania	5.9	new leu	Czech Republic	2.01	koruna
Spain	5.14	euro	Austria	1.92	euro
Slovenia	5	euro	Sweden	1.84	krona
Croatia	4.76	kuna	Finland	1.74	euro
Slovakia	4.31	euro	Netherlands	1.73	euro
Italy	4.22	euro	Denmark	1.68	euro
Ireland	4.2	euro	Germany	1.53	euro
Lithuania	4.05	litas	Switzerland	0.61	Swiss franc
Poland	3.92	zloty			

expense of a fully operational tax system. The disadvantage of the inflation approach is that it is a form of deception and inevitably gets out of control.

Returning to the example of Argentina, official inflation since 2004 has been around 10 per cent. However, currently that figure is being questioned by the IMF and most experts believe it is close to 25 per cent. So dissatisfied is the IMF with the reporting of inflation by the Argentinian government that the IMF is considering excluding the country from its membership. This would in effect exclude Argentina from international funding.

Unfortunately the Greek experience is similar. Like Argentina the Greek government has been accused of false information, in this case, hiding the levels of government borrowing. Defence spending at one time was omitted. A more subtle technique was cross currency swaps at artificial rates. As an example, suppose bank B borrows three-quarters-of-a-billion euros from country A and in return 'swaps' $1bn to A at what would be a wholly artificial exchange rate. If they swapped back at the end of the period, country A would have in effect received a loan of slightly less than one-quarter-of-a-billion euros without the transaction actually appearing as a loan. The bank would gain by the difference in interest payments on the loan amount. Poor regulation, in particular rules that are clear, are an invitation to such avoidance schemes in much the same way as taxation.

A second similarity is that like Argentina, the country has experienced high inflation. The tax system in Greece is poorly administered. Greeks were happy to admit on television that they did not pay their taxes. On the Greek island of Hydra tax inspectors had to be rescued by riot police following attempts to arrest a restaurant owner who failed to issue receipts, the basis for declaring income. This black economy in a developed country has little justification; but the general counter argument that is put forward is that tax is funding a corrupt or inefficient, wasteful government. Such a rationale is however achieving little more than fighting corruption with corruption. In Greece in 2011 the black (non-tax paying) economy was estimated to be about 25 per cent of GDP whereas in the UK it was about 10 per cent and Germany 13 per cent. Were Greece to leave the Eurozone, the prospect of high inflation and ironically negotiations with the IMF part of the 'troika' seem highly likely. As with the Argentinian experience, one might reflect that there are no financial solutions to problems that are in essence political and social.

USING THE WEB

One of the best sources of the events of the EU debt crisis is Wikipedia. Follow 'Greek government-debt crisis' and subsequent links.

The Greek crisis has stressed the need for economic integration in Europe that may or may not reshape the EU. In the debate about the euro that took place in the early 1990s there was concern about whether there should be economic integration followed by monetary integration or whether it should be the other way around. In the event, monetary integration first was preferred in part because it provided the clearer goal in the formation of a single currency. The vision was very radical. The term 'subsidiarity' was coined to refer to a Europe of the regions that would be directly governed by the EU and the eventual withering away of the state – a very ambitious concept. The formation of the euro was a fist step in that integration; it was supported by the Growth and Stability pact in 1997 which provided limitations on borrowing that were designed to further integrate monetary policies. The strategy again opted for clarity (as mentioned before, debt no more than 60 per cent of GDP and annual budget deficit to be no more than 3 per cent of GDP). In practice these rules were broken by all countries. The lack of economic integration in employment, pensions, tax and social policy meant that governments had to take responsibility and perform something of a balancing act between the EU and national demands. In the long period of growth from the formation of the euro to 2007 the differences seemed unimportant. But in the more stringent times brought on by the crisis they became significant. Cultural differences also became important. In the 1990s the Greek inflation rate was on average 8.5 per cent per year higher than France. In effect the Greek government financed itself in part by printing money. As explained in a section above, the tax payment regime was accordingly lax. Being a member of the euro took away the government's ability to finance itself through inflation but did nothing to change the over-reliance on the government leading to unrealistic demands, and also the attitude of the country towards the payment of taxes. To sustain both cultural traits the government borrowed. This now is being reversed partly by extreme cuts in the Greek government budget and partly by the ECB and the EU member countries adjusting the bailout packages to alleviate the worst effects of the cutbacks. The euro project continues with perhaps a greater understanding of the true implications of monetary and economic integration.

How Mexico's pegged system led to the Mexican peso crisis. In 1994, Mexico's central bank used a special pegged exchange rate system that linked the peso to the US dollar but allowed the peso's value to fluctuate against the dollar within a band. The Mexican central bank enforced the link through frequent intervention. In fact, it partially supported its intervention by issuing short-term debt securities denominated in dollars and using the dollars to purchase pesos in the foreign exchange market. Limiting the depreciation of the peso was intended to reduce inflationary pressure that can be caused by a very weak home currency. The argument is that a weak home currency leads to more expensive imports creating a cost push effect thereby increasing inflation. Keeping the price of imports down, however, led in part to a large balance of trade deficit in 1994. Because the peso was stronger than it should have been, Mexican firms and consumers were encouraged to buy an excessive amount of imports.

Many speculators based in Mexico recognized that the peso was being maintained at an artificially high level, and they speculated on its potential decline by investing their funds in the USA. They planned to sell their US investments if and when the peso's value weakened so that they could convert the dollars from their US investments into pesos at a favourable exchange rate. As with the speculation against the British pound on Black Wednesday, the selling of the peso for the dollar put even more downward pressure on the peso.

On 20 December 1994, Mexico's central bank devalued the peso by about 13 per cent. Mexico's stock prices plummeted, as many foreign investors sold their shares and withdrew their funds from Mexico in anticipation of further devaluations. On 22 December the central bank allowed the peso to float freely, and it declined by 15 per cent. This was the beginning of the so-called Mexican peso crisis. In an attempt to discourage foreign investors from withdrawing their investments in Mexico's debt securities, the central bank increased interest rates. However the higher rates increased the cost of borrowing for Mexican firms and consumers, thereby slowing economic growth.

As Mexico's short-term debt obligations denominated in dollars matured, the Mexican central bank used its weak pesos to obtain dollars and repay the debt. Since the peso had weakened, the effective cost of financing with dollars was very expensive for the central bank. Mexico's financial problems caused investors to lose confidence in peso-denominated securities, so they liquidated their peso-denominated securities and transferred their funds to other countries. These actions put additional downward pressure on the peso. In the 4 months after 20 December 1994, the value of the peso declined by more than 50 per cent. Over time, Mexico's economy improved, and the paranoia that had led to the withdrawal of funds by foreign investors subsided. The Mexican crisis might not have occurred if the peso had been allowed to float throughout 1994, because the peso would have gravitated towards its natural level. The crisis illustrates that central bank intervention will not necessarily be able to overwhelm market forces; thus, the crisis may serve as an argument for letting a currency float freely.

The end of Argentina's pegged system. In 1991 Argentina set up a currency board which linked the peso to the dollar on a one to one basis. The money supply was limited to purchasing dollars. Strong economic growth was checked in 1994 by the Mexican crisis and a decline in Argentina's GDP. Growth subsequently resumed but at the cost of increasing indebtedness. In 1998, Argentina was in recession made worse by the devaluation of the Brazilian real. About a third of Argentina's exports were to Brazil. In 2001 Argentina defaulted on its international loan repayments. As many loans were denominated in dollars and earnings were in pesos, loss of confidence in the peso led to a run on the banks. Withdrawals were limited to $1000 per month. In early 2002 the currency board was terminated and the peso was allowed to devalue; by March the peso had lost nearly 70 per cent of its value. The government implemented legislation on the conversion rate to be used in converting dollar debts to pesos. The burden of devaluation was mainly placed on the lender, especially for the smaller debts.

In many ways the Argentina crisis is an illustration of Tobin's proposition that a fixed exchange rate is incompatible with free convertibility *and* an independent money supply and hence borrowing policy. It also illustrates the risk involved of a supposedly riskless fixed exchange rate. As noted above, inflation has returned to Argentina and the country appears to be returning to the hyperinflation that the currency board was designed to cure. Pegging a currency to reduce inflation is, however, an attempt to treat the symptoms only, the cause undoubtedly lies in the social and political tensions within societies. Unfortunately mainstream economic modeling offers little by way of such analysis.

The Asian crisis. From 1990 to 1997, Asian countries achieved higher economic growth than any of the other countries. They were viewed as models for advances in technology and economic improvement. In the summer and fall of 1997, however, they experienced financial problems, leading to what is commonly referred to as the 'Asian crisis', and resulting in bailouts of several countries by the International Monetary Fund (IMF).

Much of the crisis is attributed to the substantial depreciation of Asian currencies, which caused severe financial problems for firms and governments throughout Asia, as well as some other regions. This crisis demonstrated how exchange rate movements can affect country conditions and therefore affect the firms that operate in those countries.

Crisis in Thailand. Until July 1997, Thailand was one of the world's fastest growing economies. In fact, Thailand grew faster than any other country over the 1985–94 period. Thai consumers spent freely, which resulted in lower savings compared to other South East Asian countries. The high level of spending and low level of saving put upward pressure on prices of real estate and products, and on the local interest rate. Normally, countries with high inflation tend to have weak currencies because of forces from purchasing power parity. Prior to July 1997, however, Thailand's currency was linked to the dollar, which made Thailand an attractive site for foreign investors; they could earn a high interest rate on invested funds while being protected (until the crisis) from a large depreciation in the baht.

Normally, countries desire a large inflow of funds because it can help support the country's growth. In Thailand's case, however, the inflow of funds provided Thai banks with more funds than the banks could use for making loans. Consequently, in an attempt to use all the funds, the banks made many very risky loans. Commercial developers borrowed heavily without having to prove that the expansion was feasible.

Lenders were willing to lend large sums of money based on the previous success of the developers. The loans may have seemed feasible based on the assumption that the economy would continue its high growth, but such high growth could not last forever. The corporate structure of Thailand also led to excessive lending. Many corporations are tied in with banks, such that some bank lending is not an 'arm's-length' business transaction, but a loan to a friend that needs funds.

In addition to the lending situation, the large inflow of funds made Thailand more susceptible to a massive outflow of funds if foreign investors ever lost confidence in the Thai economy. Given the large amount of risky loans and the potential for a massive outflow of funds, Thailand was sometimes described as a 'house of cards', waiting to collapse.

While the large inflow of funds put downward pressure on interest rates, the supply was offset by a strong demand for funds as developers and corporations sought to capitalize on the growth economy by expanding. Thailand's government was also borrowing heavily to improve the country's infrastructure. Thus, the massive borrowing was occurring at relatively high interest rates, making the debt expensive to the borrowers.

During the first half of 1997, the dollar strengthened against the Japanese yen and European currencies, which reduced the prices of Japanese and European imports. Although the dollar was linked to the baht over this period, Thailand's products were not priced as competitively to US importers.

Pressure on the Thai baht. The baht experienced downward pressure in July 1997 as some foreign investors recognized its potential weakness. The outflow of funds expedited the weakening of the baht, as foreign investors exchanged their baht for their home currencies. The baht's value relative to the dollar was pressured by the large sale of baht in exchange for dollars. On 2 July 1997, the baht was detached from the dollar. Thailand's central bank then attempted to maintain the baht's value by intervention. Specifically, it swapped its baht reserves for dollar reserves at other central banks and then used its dollar reserves to purchase the baht in the foreign exchange market (this swap agreement required Thailand to reverse this exchange by exchanging dollars for baht at a future date). The intervention was intended to offset the sales of baht by foreign investors in the foreign exchange market, but market forces overwhelmed the intervention efforts. As the supply of baht for sale exceeded the demand for baht in the foreign exchange market, the government eventually had to surrender in its effort to defend the baht's value. In July 1997, the value of the baht plummeted. Over a 5-week period, it declined by more than 20 per cent against the dollar.

Thailand's central bank used more than $20 billion to purchase baht in the foreign exchange market as part of its direct intervention efforts. Due to the decline in the value of the baht, Thailand needed more baht to be exchanged for the dollars to repay the other central banks.

Thailand's banks estimated the amount of their defaulted loans at over $30 billion. Meanwhile, some corporations in Thailand had borrowed funds in other currencies (including the dollar) because the interest rates in Thailand were relatively high. This strategy backfired because the weakening of the baht forced these corporations to exchange larger amounts of baht for the currencies needed to pay off the loans. Consequently, the corporations incurred a much higher effective financing rate (which accounts for the exchange rate effect to determine the true cost of borrowing) than they would have paid if they had borrowed funds locally in Thailand. The higher borrowing cost was an additional strain on the corporations.

On 5 August 1997, the IMF and several countries agreed to provide Thailand with a $16 billion rescue package. Japan provided $4 billion, while the IMF provided $4 billion. At the time, this was the second largest bailout plan ever put together for a single country (Mexico had received a $50 billion bailout in 1994). In return for this monetary support, Thailand agreed to reduce its budget deficit, prevent inflation from rising above 9 per cent, raise its value-added tax from 7 per cent to 10 per cent, and clean up the financial statements of the local banks, which had many undisclosed bad loans.

The rescue package took time to finalize because Thailand's government was unwilling to shut down all the banks that were experiencing financial problems as a result of their overly generous lending policies. Many critics have questioned the efficacy of the rescue package because some of the funding was misallocated due to corruption in Thailand.

Spread of the crisis throughout South East Asia. The crisis in Thailand was contagious to other countries in South East Asia. The South East Asian economies are somewhat integrated because of the trade between countries. The crisis was expected to weaken Thailand's economy, which would result in a reduction in the demand for products produced in the other countries of South East Asia. As the demand for those countries' products declined, so would their national income and their demand for products from other South East Asian countries. Thus, the effects could perpetuate. Like Thailand, the other South East Asian countries had very high growth in recent years, which had led to overly optimistic assessments of future economic conditions and thus to excessive loans being extended for projects that had a high risk of default.

These countries were also similar to Thailand in that they had relatively high interest rates, and their governments tended to stabilize their currencies. Consequently, these countries had attracted a large amount of foreign investment as well. Thailand's crisis made foreign investors realize that such a crisis could also hit the other countries in South East Asia. Consequently, they began to withdraw funds from these countries.

In July and August of 1997, the values of the Malaysian ringgit, Singapore dollar, Philippine peso, and Indonesian rupiah also declined. The Philippine peso was devalued in July. Malaysia initially attempted to maintain the ringgit's value within a narrow band but then surrendered and let the ringgit float to its market-determined level. In August 1997, Bank Indonesia (the central bank) used more than $500 million in direct intervention to purchase rupiah in the foreign exchange market in an attempt to boost the value of the rupiah. By mid-August, however, it gave up its effort to maintain the rupiah's value within a band and let the rupiah float to its natural level. This decision by Bank Indonesia to let the rupiah float may have been influenced by the failure of Thailand's costly efforts to maintain the baht. The market forces were too strong and could not be offset by direct intervention. On 30 October 1997, a rescue package for Indonesia was announced, but the IMF and Indonesia's government did not agree on the terms of the $43 billion package until the spring of 1998. One of the main points of contention was that President Suharto wanted to peg the rupiah's exchange rate, but the IMF believed that Bank Indonesia would not be able to maintain the rupiah's exchange rate at a fixed level and that it would come under renewed speculative attack.

As the South East Asian countries gave up their fight to maintain their currencies within bands, they imposed restrictions on their forward and futures markets to prevent excessive speculation. For example, Indonesia and Malaysia imposed a limit on the size of forward contracts created by banks for foreign residents. These actions limited the degree to which speculators could sell these currencies forward based on expectations that the currencies would weaken over time. In general, efforts to protect the currencies failed because investors and firms had no confidence that the fundamental factors causing weakness in the currencies were being corrected. Therefore, the flow of funds out of the Asian countries continued; this outflow led to even more sales of Asian currencies in exchange for other currencies, which put additional downward pressure on the values of the currencies.

As the values of the South East Asian currencies declined, speculators responded by withdrawing more of their funds from these countries, which led to further weakness in the currencies. As in Thailand, many corporations had borrowed in other countries (such as the USA) where interest rates were relatively low. The decline in the values of their local currencies caused the corporations' effective rate of financing to be excessive, which strained their cash flow situation.

Due to the integration of South East Asian economies, the excessive lending by the local banks across the countries, and the susceptibility of all these countries to massive fund outflows, the crisis was not really focused on one country. What was initially referred to as the Thailand crisis became the Asian crisis.

Impact of the Asian crisis on Hong Kong. On 23 October 1997, prices in the Hong Kong stock market declined by 10.2 per cent on average; considering the three trading days before that, the cumulative 4-day effect was a decline of 23.3 per cent. The decline was primarily attributed to speculation that Hong Kong's currency might be devalued and that Hong Kong could experience financial problems similar to the South East Asian countries. The fact that the market value of Hong Kong companies could decline by almost one-quarter over a 4-day period demonstrated the perceived exposure of Hong Kong to the crisis.

During this period, Hong Kong maintained its pegged exchange rate system with the Hong Kong dollar tied to the US dollar. However, it had to increase interest rates to discourage investors from transferring their funds out of the country.

Impact of the Asian crisis on Russia. The Asian crisis caused investors to reconsider other countries where similar effects might occur. In particular, they focused on Russia. As investors lost confidence in the Russian currency (the rouble), they began to transfer funds out of Russia. In response to the downward pressure this outflow of funds placed on the rouble, the central bank of Russia engaged in direct intervention by using dollars to purchase roubles in the foreign exchange market. It also used indirect intervention by raising interest rates to make Russia more attractive to investors, thereby discouraging additional outflows.

In July 1998, the IMF (with some help from Japan and the World Bank) organized a loan package worth $22.6 billion for Russia. The package required that Russia boost its tax revenue, reduce its budget deficit, and create a more capitalist environment for its businesses.

During August 1998, Russia's central bank commonly intervened to prevent the rouble from declining substantially. On 26 August, however, it gave up its fight to defend the rouble's value, and market forces caused the rouble to decline by more than 50 per cent against most currencies on that day. This led to fears of a new crisis, and the next day (called 'Bloody Thursday'), paranoia swept stock markets around the world. Some stock markets (including the US stock market) experienced declines of more than 4 per cent.

Impact of the Asian crisis on South Korea. By November 1997, seven of South Korea's conglomerates (called *chaebols*) had collapsed. The banks that financed the operations of the *chaebols* were stuck with the equivalent of $52 billion in bad debt as a result. Like banks in the South East Asian countries, South Korea's banks had been too willing to provide loans to corporations (especially the chaebols) without conducting a thorough credit analysis. The banks had apparently engaged in such risky lending because they assumed that economic growth would continue at a rapid pace and therefore exaggerated the future cash flows that borrowers would have available to pay off their loans. In addition, South Korean banks had traditionally extended loans to the conglomerates without assessing whether the loans could be repaid. In November, South Korea's currency (the won) declined substantially, and the central bank attempted to use its reserves to prevent a free fall in the won but with little success. Meanwhile, the credit ratings of several banks were downgraded because of their bad loans.

On 3 December 1997, the IMF agreed to enact a $55 billion dollar rescue package for South Korea. The World Bank and the Asian Development Bank joined with the IMF to provide a standby credit line of $35 billion. If that amount was not sufficient, other countries (including Japan and the USA) had agreed to provide a credit line of $20 billion. The total available credit (assuming it was all used) exceeded the credit provided in the Mexican bailout of 1994 and made this the largest bailout ever. In exchange for the funding, South Korea agreed to reduce its economic growth and to restrict the conglomerates from excessive borrowing. This restriction resulted in some bankruptcies and unemployment, as the banks could not automatically provide loans to all conglomerates needing funds unless the funding was economically justified.

Impact of the Asian crisis on China. Ironically, China did not experience the adverse economic effects of the Asian crisis because it had grown less rapidly than the South East Asian countries in the years prior to the crisis. The Chinese government had more control over economic conditions because it still owned most real estate and still controlled most of the banks that provided credit to support growth. Thus, there were fewer bankruptcies resulting from the crisis in China. In addition, China's government was able to maintain the value of the yuan against the dollar, which limited speculative flows of funds out of China. Though interest rates increased during the crisis, they remained relatively low. Consequently Chinese firms could obtain funding at a reasonable cost and could continue to meet their interest payments.

Nevertheless, concerns about China mounted because it relies heavily on exports to stimulate its economy; China was now at a competitive disadvantage relative to the South East Asian countries whose currencies had depreciated. Thus, importers from the USA and Europe shifted some of their purchases to those countries. In addition, the decline in the other Asian currencies against the Chinese yuan encouraged Chinese consumers to purchase imports instead of locally manufactured products.

Lessons about exchange rates and intervention from the Asian crisis. The Asian crisis demonstrated the degree to which currencies could depreciate in response to a lack of confidence by investors and firms in a central bank's ability to stabilize its local currency. If investors and firms had believed the central banks could prevent the free fall in currency values, they would not have transferred their funds to other countries, and South East Asian currency values would not have experienced such downward pressure.

Exhibit 6.5 shows how exchange rates of some Asian currencies changed against the US dollar during one year of the crisis (from June 1997 to June 1998). In particular, the currencies of Indonesia, Malaysia, South Korea and Thailand declined substantially.

The Asian crisis also demonstrated how interest rates could be affected by flows of funds out of countries. Exhibit 6.6 illustrates how interest rates changed from June 1997 (just before the crisis) to June 1998 for various Asian countries. The increase in interest rates can be attributed to the indirect interventions intended to prevent the local currencies from depreciating further, or to the massive outflows of funds, or to both of these conditions. In particular, interest rates of Indonesia, Malaysia and Thailand increased substantially from their pre-crisis levels. Those countries whose local currencies experienced more depreciation had higher upward adjustments. Since the substantial increase in interest rates (which tends to reduce economic growth) may have been caused by the outflow of funds, it may have been indirectly due to the lack of confidence by investors and firms in the ability of the Asian central banks to stabilize the local currencies.

The Asian crisis demonstrated how integrated country economies are, especially during a crisis. Just as the US and European economies can affect emerging markets, they are susceptible to conditions in emerging markets. Even if a central bank can withstand the pressure on its currency caused by conditions in other countries, it cannot necessarily insulate its economy from other countries that are experiencing financial problems.

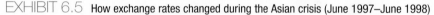

EXHIBIT 6.5 How exchange rates changed during the Asian crisis (June 1997–June 1998)

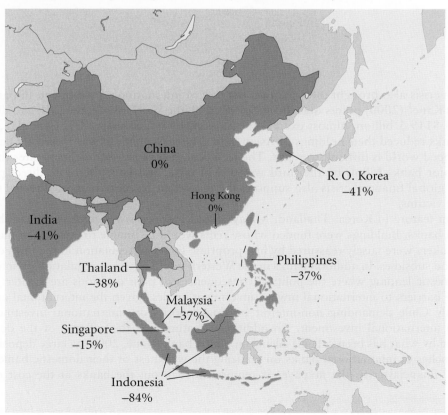

EXHIBIT 6.6   How interest rates changed during the Asian crisis (number before '/' represents annualized interest rate as of June 1997; number after the '/' represents annualized interest rate as of June 1998)

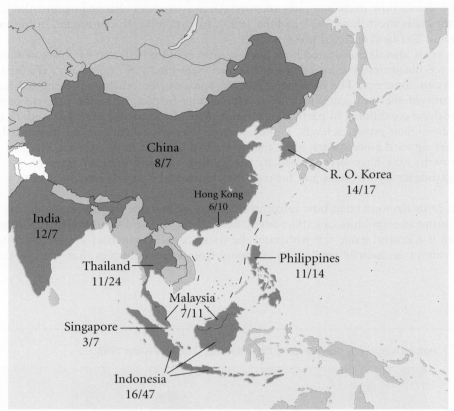

The Asian crisis also brought into question the role of international investment, in particular the role of banks. As Kane[1] (2000) points out, the aid pledged by the World Bank, the IMF and directly by countries totalled $119.5 billion, almost exactly the amount by which major US, Canadian, European and Japanese banks reduced their holdings of Asian debt. The view that aid was indirectly paid to the banks of the developed world is difficult to reject. The technical insolvency (bad debts greater than shareholder value) of major banks following the third world debt crisis and later the more direct problems of the banks in the global financial crisis also supports the thesis that rescues are more directed to the perpetrators than the victims.

A common feature in Korea, Thailand, Malaysia and Indonesia was massive private borrowing from international banks. Buildings were funded whose rents would be unable to cover even the interest on the loan. The bankers were falsely reassured by inappropriate financial regulation in the form of inappropriate guarantees and subsidies. In addition banks in the Western world have less regulation on international lending than domestic lending where the political consequences of poor decisions are greater. For developing countries the barriers to international inward investment are less given the international emphasis on free markets. Only Chile demanding non-interest bearing deposits on international investment offers some resistance to international investment. An additional feature was the collapse of the domestic banking system caused by what has been called a silent run on the bank (Kane, 2000) as large depositors transferred funds to branches of international banks on realizing the weakness of their domestic banks. Ultimately as in the global financial crisis the taxpayer is required to bail out the banks at the cost of an economic

---

[1]Kane, E. (2000) 'Capital Movements, Banking Insolvency and Silent Runs in the Asian Financial Crisis', *NBER Working Paper Series*, No. 7514.

recession. Poor bank regulation, inappropriate guarantees that make unprofitable investments seem profitable, rapidly attract foreign loans in the knowledge that governments will eventually have to pay for any significant bad outcomes. In a sense Black Wednesday in 1992 where the British government inappropriately guaranteed membership of the exchange rate mechanism (forerunner of the euro) resulting in huge payments on bets to the contrary was an instance in microcosm of the same phenomenon. The fluidity of international funds makes any profits whose risks are lowered by government guarantees the subject of huge speculation. The appearance of above-normal profits is usually a signal of economic need and in an efficient market should attract funds. But the Asian crisis demonstrated that it can also be a signal of inappropriate regulation. Distinguishing between the two is not always simple; are increases in land prices indicating a genuine shortage or favourable regulations for such investments, in many cases the cause may be regulations in apparently unrelated areas.

●   **The recent history of the dollar.** Between January 2001 and January 2005 the dollar had lost 30 per cent against the euro and over 22 per cent against the British pound. The US government, as part of its management strategy, chose not to attempt to reverse this change. One explanation for the fall was that the balance of payments in goods and services had risen from $363 billion (i.e. $363 000 000 000) to $618 billion in 2004. From the end of 2004 to 2012 the dollar has been stable against the euro and has appreciated by 15 per cent against the British pound. The 2011 balance of payments account recorded a deficit of $559 billion due mainly to a positive balance on the services account helping to offset the negative balance on the international trade in goods.

There are concerns that the persistent indebtedness of the USA to the rest of the world, caused by the positive balance on the financial account and deficit on the current account, will become unsustainable. As happened at the end of the 1960s, a loss of confidence could cause rapid selling of the dollar that could bring about a collapse in its value. However, a more optimistic scenario is that the USA could continue to provide a secure place for the world's surplus savings and although a beneficiary in terms of being able to create credit in this way (seigniorage) nevertheless the dollar could help growth in the world economy.

The problems created when a currency is both a reserve currency for other countries and also a national currency was first examined by Robert Triffin in the 1960s. He predicted that the international demand for a currency would weaken the balance of payments for that country in this case the USA (known as the Triffin dilemma). This is in effect what has happened since the 1970s. The dollar is seen as a safe currency for reserves and the US balance of payments has been poor certainly over the last 10 years.

The SDR was created as the end of the 1960s to supplement the shortfall in dollar and gold reserves when the USA was reluctant to allow the dollar to be used as a reserve currency. The currency is restricted to dealings between countries in the IMF. If a country is given a loan denominated in SDRs then it can convert it, but other countries have to accept it as payment for their reserves of dollar, yen, pounds or euros which in effect happens with their accounts with the IMF. Countries may also simply be allocated SDRs as happened in 2009 for a long list of more recent IMF members many of which were developing countries. In effect, this is an international increase in the money supply with the benefits of seigniorage being spread internationally rather than accruing mostly to the USA. In 2009 China raised questions about the role of the dollar suggesting that the SDR could play a greater role, in particular, that those holding dollar reserves could exchange their reserves for SDRs. This would have to have the agreement of the IMF and in effect the USA as it and its allies control the votes which are proportional to involvement in world trade. Only if the USA accepted the Triffin analysis and sought to improve the current account balance by retiring the dollar from its role as a reserve currency might such a suggestion be acceptable. Even then, it seems likely that other currencies such as the euro would seek to replace the dollar and compete with the SDR. The immediate rewards of being a world reserve currency are considerable as the reluctance of the USA to change the role of the dollar testifies.

In 2011 Standard and Poor downgraded the USA to AA+ from AAA giving it a lower rating than the UK, Germany and Australia. The markets however have not reacted greatly to the change. Ten-year government bond rates in 2013 were lower than that of the UK though only marginally so. Like many countries, the US government is facing debt problems termed in the case of the USA 'the fiscal cliff', this topic is addressed in the next section.

USING THE WEB

The Trading Economics website at: www.tradingeconomics.com is an easily accessible source of national statistics collected for the most part by the IMF.

The global financial crisis 2007 onwards

It is instructive to begin by briefly recalling two previous crises with features in common with the global financial crisis. The first concerned the convertibility of dollars into gold, suspended first in 1968, as noted previously, and then finally abandoned in 1971. In simple terms the USA was creating too much credit on the promise of being able to convert dollars into gold at a guaranteed rate ($35 an ounce). They did not have enough gold even to convert a small proportion of the dollars. The excess dollars had been building up throughout the 1960s and was used to finance large government expenditure such as the Vietnam war. There was also a large international demand for dollars to finance growing world trade. Central banks and MNCs kept dollar accounts and investments to finance their activities. The ratio of dollar credit to gold eventually became unrealistic (the conversion promise was no longer believable particularly when the French government decided to convert its dollar reserves into gold) and a period of freely floating exchange rates ensued. The market had become overconfident in the value of poorly backed dollar accounts.

The second instance was the Third World Debt Crisis that began in 1982 with Mexico being unable to repay government debt, in effect asking for an easier repayment schedule. Subsequently most of the developing world sought to reschedule its government (sovereign) debt. The root cause was the dramatic rise in oil prices in the 1970s which in turn led to huge deposits in Western banks from the oil producing Arab countries. This is turn was lent by Western banks as something of a new venture to developing countries in the belief that though risky, the investment was diversified across countries. It was believed at the time that the IMF could reduce its funding role and hand over the process to capitalist economies. The sudden collapse of sovereign debt took the markets by surprise. In particular Mexico, an oil producing country itself, was not seen as a high risk country. The fact that so many other countries quickly followed Mexico's example across the developing world is a good instance of the markets tendency to underestimate the correlation of different risks (the contagion effect) – particularly when there are large movements. Short term rewards also encourage the market not to consider these unlikely but dramatic changes. This was the first post 1945 instance of contagion on an international scale and served as an important warning for all future national crises.

The global financial crisis had elements of both previous crises. The actual reduction in risk through diversification in a new form of lending (collateralized debt obligations or CDOs) was greatly underestimated, and secondly, too much credit was being created by the dollar – a condition that persists.

The first phase of the crisis (June 2007 to mid-March 2008) was caused by a housing boom in the USA. Rising house prices and low interest rates enabled borrowers to borrow ever increasing amounts for a house purchase. A new form of lending, sub prime mortgage backed securities often in the form of bonds, enabled investors, typically foreign banks, to engage in lending to this market without a great knowledge of the actual loans. There are obvious comparisons with the Asian crisis also fuelled by foreign investment. Mortgages were pooled into bonds and then securitized in the form of CDOs. Although the mortgages were sub prime, meaning that the borrowers were a poor risk, by dividing the debt pool into tranches (slices), low risk paper (AAA credit rating) could be created. The top or senior tranche (AAA) would only have to start suffering bad debts if more than 24 per cent of loans went bad (in a typical arrangement). The bottom or equity tranche would take on all of the first 8 per cent of the bad loans and was held by the originating bank. Typically, this tranche would not receive a credit rating. A huge moral hazard problem was created in the sense that those offering the mortgages were not going to be responsible for the risk; it was sold on in the form of the CDOs. Compounding the problem was the fact that those taking on the risk assumed that the loans were being issued responsibly and underestimated the riskiness of the CDOs. Low interest rates at the time enabled estate agents and banks with breathtaking indifference to their 'customers' to sell houses to people who were highly unlikely to be able to repay the mortgage – this is an instance of what is termed predatory lending. An increase in interest rates and a surplus of houses led to a decline in house prices and difficulty in repaying the mortgages. The collateralized mortgage obligations were suddenly seen as being far more risky. Although the AAA tranche went up in risk relatively moderately, the rate of return on the lower tranches went up to rates that were difficult to estimate but were around 30 per cent. Of particular note was the prevention of withdrawals from funds managed by BNP Paribas in August 2007 as they warned of 'The complete evaporation of liquidity in certain market segments of the US securitization market has made it impossible to value certain assets fairly regardless of their quality or credit rating.' BNP was holding AAA paper and higher risks that they were unable to sell and hence unable to value. This was the start of concerns over bank liquidity, leading ultimately to the collapse of Lehman Brothers in September 2008. Only direct government intervention and guarantees of support prevented a complete collapse. The UK government became majority shareholders in Lloyds Bank, HBOS and RBS, appointing directors to the board. From October 2008 to March 2009 saw the second phase as the market adjusted to gloomy growth prospects.

The third phase from March 2009 to the present (January 2013) has seen some signs of recovery as countries report growth in output. But also there are concerns as to how countries are going to repay the government borrowing needed to rescue the banking system and more generally, borrowing undertaken in the early years of this century when it was assumed that repayment would be financed by economic growth. Riots in Greece in February 2010 (see above) at the prospect of cutting government services illustrate the dangers.

Generally government borrowing in the developed countries has increased in recent years (see Exhibit 6.7); the problem of the Greek deficit is not so different from the US fiscal cliff and the problem facing many developed countries. Governments are attempting to reduce the deficit by increasing taxes and reducing government spending; but in doing so they risk a continuation of slow economic growth that threatens to increase

EXHIBIT 6.7   Gross government debt as a percentage of GDP

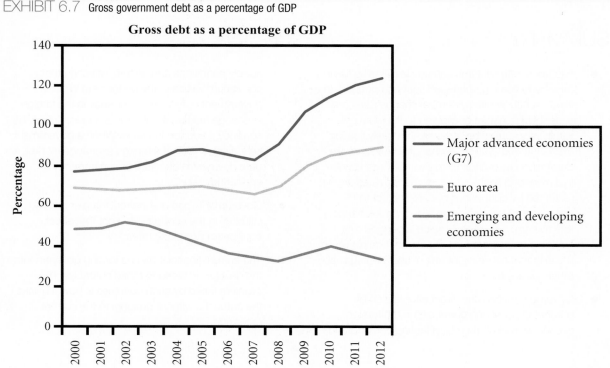

Source: IMF

government spending to meet social security commitments (unemployment pay, etc). In addition therefore, social security rights are being reduced, including pensions, pensionable age and welfare payouts in the developed world. To some this may appear to be part of the 'race to the bottom' ultimately one cannot compete with developing countries without having to adopt their lower standards of social care; to others it is a necessary rebalancing of government spending promises that were always unrealistic – the financial system is calling countries to account. Both views have considerable empirical support.

At the time of writing, with the exception of Greece, countries are still only beginning to face the measures needed to reduce government spending. The hope is that economic recovery will alleviate many of the proposed reforms. Recovery will increase the revenue from taxes and reduce government cutbacks. The worry is that the cutbacks in themselves will hamper recovery. Cutbacks therefore have to be sufficient to convince the markets that government spending is under control and that the deficit as a percentage of GDP will fall; but not so severe as to cause concerns that GDP itself will not recover. Taking the ratio 'government debt /GDP' reducing the numerator (government debt) may cause the denominator (GDP) to fall hence worsening the ratio. In 2012 the chief economist at the IMF warned the UK that their cutbacks were in danger of putting a recovery at risk, the concern with some other countries, notably the USA, is that they will not achieve cutbacks seen as necessary by the marketplace.

The global financial crisis has been a crisis of the developed world rather than the developing world. As with the Third World Debt Crisis, high risk innovative lending was thought to be low risk. The cause of the misestimating of the risk of these international investments is not clear. Poor market regulation, poor accounting practices and excessive employee bonuses for short term lending have all been cited. Whether trading practices will be reformed is a matter of current debate at international level. The Third World debt crisis gave rise to the Basel agreements on bank reserves designed to curb excessively risky portfolios. Basel III is a continuation of that process only this time informed by the global financial crisis. How does one rein back on a culture of innovation and risk taking without damaging the international financial system itself? How does one repay debt without damaging the economic 'engine' that will repay that debt? There is no clear answer to these questions.

SUMMARY

- Exchange rate systems can be classified as fixed rate, freely floating, managed float and pegged. In a fixed exchange rate system, exchange rates are either held constant or allowed to fluctuate only within very narrow boundaries. In a freely floating exchange rate system, exchange rate values are determined by market forces without intervention. In a managed float system, exchange rates are not restricted by boundaries but are subject to government intervention. In a pegged exchange rate system, a currency's value is pegged to a foreign currency or a unit of account and moves in line with that currency (or unit of account) against other currencies.

- Governments can use direct intervention by purchasing or selling currencies in the foreign exchange market, thereby affecting demand and supply conditions and, in turn, affecting the equilibrium values of the currencies. When a government purchases a currency in the foreign exchange market, it puts upward pressure on the currency's equilibrium value. When a government sells a currency in the foreign exchange market, it puts downward pressure on the currency's equilibrium value.

- Governments can use indirect intervention by influencing the economic factors that affect equilibrium exchange rates.

- The current financial crisis is forcing governments in the developed world to make cutbacks. The problem faced by such countries is how to make the cutbacks without prolonging the current recession.

CRITICAL DEBATE

To join or not to join …

Proposition. The position of the UK within the EU is untenable. Whereas the UK enjoys the economic trade and investment benefits of being in the EU, by having a separate currency, it reserves for itself the right to make all its goods cheaper than other countries within the EU by devaluing against the euro. Since 2001 it has been as high as 1.6 euros:£1 and as low as 1.4 euros:£1. Harmonizing taxation, trade and competition within the EU makes little sense when one of the players has this enormous advantage. Furthermore, the ability of the UK to lower its prices is slowly forcing the EU to adopt the 'Anglo-Saxon' model of the economy (low wages, little worker protection and wider gaps between rich and poor) in order to compete. The whole EU project is being undermined.

Opposing view. The status of the British pound does not confer benefits, rather it avoids injustice. UK residents borrow far more than in the EU, the euro interest rate policy could easily severely disadvantage the UK as was illustrated by 'Black Wednesday'. The UK also trades heavily with non-EU countries and is more exposed to world trade factors than other EU countries. Given that the UK is a net contributor to the EU and that it runs a trade deficit with the EU, the benefits seem rather limited.

With whom do you agree? (Remember to include Appendix 6 in your reading.)

1 Is a single currency necessary for further EU integration?

2 Does the UK economy necessarily need a separate currency?

3 Is a separate currency really the cause of the spread of the Anglo-Saxon model; what other factors underlie the Anglo-Saxon model?

The gold standard

Proposition. Developing countries should adopt the gold standard! History shows that a lack of confidence in the currencies of developing countries is the major cause of the financial crises. Under the gold standard currencies would be convertible into gold. Currency value would be more stable, countries would be less likely to borrow excessively. More investment would be attracted to developing countries as in the pre-World War I era.

Opposing view. Credit would be restricted to the reserves of gold and would arrest development. Alternatively, convertibility would be limited. The large level of imports needed for a developing country would lead to balance of payments difficulties which in turn would lead to a reduction in the money supply as sterilization would not be possible. The consequent deflation would be disastrous for a developing country.

SELF TEST

Answers are provided in Appendix A at the back of the text.

1 Explain why it would be difficult to maintain a fixed exchange rate between the euro and the dollar.

2 Assume the European Central Bank (ECB) believes that the dollar should be weakened against the euro. Explain how the ECB could use direct and indirect intervention to weaken the dollar's value with respect to the euro. Assume that future inflation in the EU is expected to be low, regardless of the ECB's actions.

3 Briefly explain why a central bank may wish to weaken the value of its currency.

QUESTIONS AND APPLICATIONS

1 **Exchange rate systems.** Compare and contrast the fixed, freely floating, and managed float exchange rate systems. What are some advantages and disadvantages of a freely floating exchange rate system versus a fixed exchange rate system?

2 **Intervention with euros.** Assume that Belgium, one of the European countries that uses the euro as its currency, would prefer that its currency depreciate against the dollar. Can it apply central bank intervention to achieve this objective? Explain.

3 **Direct intervention.** How can a central bank use direct intervention to change the value of a currency? Explain why a central bank may desire to smooth exchange rate movements of its currency.

4 **Indirect intervention.** How can a central bank use indirect intervention to change the value of a currency?

5 **Intervention effects.** Assume there is concern that the USA may experience a recession. How should the Federal Reserve influence the dollar to prevent a recession? How might US exporters react to this policy (favourably or unfavourably)? What about US importing firms?

6 **Currency effects on economy.** What is the impact of a weak home currency on the home economy, other things being equal? What is the impact of a strong home currency on the home economy, other things being equal?

7 **Feedback effects.** Explain the potential feedback effects of a currency's changing value on inflation.

8 **Indirect intervention.** Why would indirect intervention by a central bank have a stronger impact on some currencies than others? Why would a central bank's indirect intervention have a stronger impact than its direct intervention?

9 **Effects on currencies tied to the dollar.** The Hong Kong dollar's value is tied to the US dollar. Explain how the following trade patterns would be affected by the appreciation of the Japanese yen against the dollar:

   a Hong Kong exports to Japan.
   b Hong Kong exports to the USA.

10 **Intervention effects on Treasury bills (bonds).** UK Treasury bill prices are normally inversely related to UK Treasury bill. If the Bank of England planned to use intervention to weaken the British pound, how might bill prices be affected?

11 **Direct intervention in Europe.** If most countries in Europe experience a recession, how might the European Central Bank use direct intervention to stimulate economic growth?

12 **Sterilized intervention.** Explain the difference between sterilized and non-sterilized intervention.

13 **Effects of indirect intervention.** Suppose that the government of Chile reduces one of its key interest rates. The values of several other Latin American currencies are expected to change substantially against the Chilean peso in response to the news.

   a Explain why other Latin American currencies could be affected by a cut in Chile's interest rates.
   b How would the central banks of other Latin American countries likely adjust their interest rates? How would the currencies of these countries respond to the central bank interventions?
   c How would a US firm that exports products to Latin American countries be affected by the central bank interventions? (Assume the exports are denominated in the corresponding Latin American currency for each country.)

14 **Freely floating exchange rates.** Should the governments of Asian countries allow their currencies to float freely? What would be the advantages of letting their currencies float freely? What would be the disadvantages?

15 **Indirect intervention.** During the Asian crisis, some Asian central banks raised their interest rates to prevent their currencies from weakening. Yet, the currencies weakened anyway. Offer your opinion as to why the central banks' efforts at indirect intervention did not work.

ADVANCED QUESTIONS

16 **Monitoring of the central bank intervention.** Why do foreign market participants attempt to monitor the European Central Bank's (ECB's) direct intervention efforts? How does the ECB attempt to hide its intervention actions? The media frequently report that 'the euro's value strengthened ahead of moves by the ECB to . . .' Explain why the euro's value may change even before the ECB takes action (for example a change in interest rates).

17 **Effects of September 11.** Within a few days after the September 11, 2001 terrorist attack on the USA, the Federal Reserve reduced short-term interest rates to stimulate the US economy. How might this action have affected the foreign flow of funds into the USA and affected the value of the dollar? How could such an effect on the dollar have increased the probability that the US economy would strengthen?

18 **Intervention effects on corporate performance.** Assume you have a subsidiary in Australia. The subsidiary sells mobile homes to local consumers in Australia, who buy the homes using mostly borrowed funds from local banks. Your subsidiary purchases all of its materials from Hong Kong. The Hong Kong dollar is tied to the US dollar. Your subsidiary

borrowed funds from the US parent, and must pay the parent $100 000 in interest each month. Australia has just raised its interest rate in order to boost the value of its currency (Australian dollar, A$). The Australian dollar appreciates against the dollar as a result. Explain whether these actions would increase, reduce, or have no effect on:

a   The volume of your subsidiary's sales in Australia (measured in A$).

b   The cost to your subsidiary of purchasing materials (measured in A$).

c   The cost to your subsidiary of making the interest payments to the US parent (measured in A$).

Briefly explain each answer.

19 **Pegged currencies.** Why do you think a country suddenly decides to peg its currency to the dollar or some other currency? When a currency is unable to maintain the peg, what do you think are the typical forces that break the peg?

20 **Impact of intervention on currency option premiums.** Assume that the central bank of the country Zakow periodically intervenes in the foreign exchange market to prevent large upward or downward fluctuations in its currency (called the zak) against the US dollar. Today, the central bank announced that it will no longer intervene in the foreign exchange market. The spot rate of the zak against the dollar was not affected by this news. Will the news affect the premium on currency call options that are traded on the zak? Will the news affect the premium on currency put options that are traded on the zak? Explain.

PROJECT WORKSHOP

21 **Bank of Japan.** The website for Japan's central bank, the Bank of Japan, provides information about its mission and its policy actions. Its address is http://www.boj.or.jp/en/index.htm.

a   Use this website to summarize the mission of the Bank of Japan. How does this mission relate to intervening in the foreign exchange market?

b   Review the minutes of recent meetings by Bank of Japan officials. Summarize at least one recent meeting that was associated with possible or actual intervention to affect the yen's value.

c   Why might the foreign exchange intervention strategies of the Bank of Japan be relevant to the European governments and to European-based MNCs?

22 Use newspaper resources at your institution to summarize the arguments around one of the following groups of keywords:

a   'Polish plumber' and 'euro'. In particular, focus on the need for cohesion in Europe to support the euro.

b   'yuan' and 'revaluation' and 'trade restrictions'. In particular, focus on the issues surrounding a revaluation (increase in value) of the Chinese currency.

c   'imf' and 'conditionally' and 'Africa' and 'exchange rate'. In particular, focus on the problems of managing a weak currency.

One year, 2005, should be sufficient. You will need to choose the articles carefully. Avoid articles that are too detailed or not relevant. Try to sort out the main themes surrounding the issue. Include detailed references to source articles – it is a good idea to cut and paste all articles referred to into one Word file. Try to include at least one very recent article as evidence against plagiarism. Finally, you may vary the keywords to refine your theme; but do not spend hours looking for the elusive perfect article.

DISCUSSION IN THE BOARDROOM

This exercise can be found on our dedicated Course-Mate platform for students.

RUNNING YOUR OWN MNC

This exercise can be found on our dedicated Course-Mate platform for students.

Essays/discussion and articles can be found at the end of Part II.

BLADES PLC CASE STUDY

Assessment of government influence on exchange rates

Recall that Blades, the UK manufacturer of roller blades, generates most of its revenue and incurs most of its expenses in the UK. However, the company has recently begun exporting roller blades to Thailand. The company has an agreement with Entertainment Products, Inc., a Thai importer, for a 3-year period. According to the terms of the agreement, Entertainment Products will purchase 180 000 pairs of 'Speedos', Blades' primary product, annually at a fixed price of 4594 Thai baht per pair. Due to quality and cost considerations, Blades is also importing certain rubber and plastic components from a Thai exporter. The cost of these components is approximately 2871 Thai baht per pair of Speedos. No contractual agreement exists between Blades plc and the Thai exporter. Consequently, the cost of the rubber and plastic components imported from Thailand is subject not only to exchange rate considerations but to economic conditions (such as inflation) in Thailand as well.

Shortly after Blades began exporting to and importing from Thailand, Asia experienced weak economic conditions. Consequently, foreign investors in Thailand feared the baht's potential weakness and withdrew their investments, resulting in an excess supply of Thai baht for sale. Because of the resulting downward pressure on the baht's value, the Thai government attempted to stabilize the baht's exchange rate. To maintain the baht's value, the Thai government intervened in the foreign exchange market. Specifically, it swapped its baht reserves for dollar reserves at other central banks and then used its dollar reserves to purchase the baht in the foreign exchange market. However, this agreement required Thailand to reverse this transaction by exchanging dollars for baht at a future date. Unfortunately, the Thai government's intervention was unsuccessful, as it was overwhelmed by market forces. Consequently, the Thai government ceased its intervention efforts, and the value of the Thai baht declined substantially against the dollar over a 3-month period.

When the Thai government stopped intervening in the foreign exchange market, Ben Holt, Blades' finance director, was concerned that the value of the Thai baht would continue to decline indefinitely. Since Blades generates net inflow in Thai baht, this would seriously affect the company's profit margin. Furthermore, one of the reasons Blades had expanded into Thailand was to appease the company's shareholders. At last year's annual shareholder meeting, they had demanded that senior management take action to improve the firm's low profit margins. Expanding into Thailand had been Holt's suggestion, and he is now afraid that his career might be at stake. For these reasons, Holt feels that the Asian crisis and its impact on Blades demand his serious attention. One of the factors Holt thinks he should consider is the issue of government intervention and how it could affect Blades in particular. Specifically, he wonders whether the decision to enter into a fixed agreement with Entertainment Products was a good idea under the circumstances. Another issue is how the future completion of the swap agreement initiated by the Thai government will affect Blades. To address these issues and to gain a little more understanding of the process of government intervention, Holt has prepared the following list of questions for you, Blades' financial analyst, since he knows that you understand international financial management.

1 Did the intervention effort by the Thai government constitute direct or indirect intervention? Explain.

2 Did the intervention by the Thai government constitute sterilized or non-sterilized intervention? What is the difference between the two types of intervention? Which type do you think would be more effective in increasing the value of the baht? Why? (Hint: think about the effect of non-sterilized intervention on UK interest rates.)

3 If the Thai baht is virtually fixed with respect to the dollar, how could this affect UK levels of inflation? Do you think these effects on the UK economy will be more pronounced for companies such as Blades that operate under trade arrangements involving commitments or for firms that do not? How are companies such as Blades affected by a fixed exchange rate?

4 What are some of the potential disadvantages for Thai levels of inflation associated with the floating exchange rate system that is now used in Thailand? Do you think Blades contributes to these disadvantages to a great extent? How are companies such as Blades affected by a freely floating exchange rate?

5 What do you think will happen to the Thai baht's value when the swap arrangement is completed? How will this affect Blades?

SMALL BUSINESS DILEMMA

Assessment of central bank intervention by the Sports Exports Company

Jim Logan, owner of the Sports Exports Company, is concerned about the value of the British pound over time because his firm receives pounds as payment for basketballs exported to the UK. He recently read that the Bank of England (the central bank of the UK) is likely to intervene directly in the foreign exchange market by flooding the market with British pounds.

1 Forecast whether the British pound will weaken or strengthen based on the information provided.

2 How would the performance of the Sports Exports Company be affected by the Bank of England's policy of flooding the foreign exchange market with British pounds (assuming that it does not hedge its exchange rate risk)?

APPENDIX 6
ECONOMIC CONSIDERATIONS OF THE EURO

Optimum currency areas. In 1961 Robert Mundell advanced the notion of an optimal currency area. He argued that if either labour and machinery were mobile and/or prices were flexible, the cost of joining a monetary union would be very low. The benefits of a union are those of a fixed exchange rate regime, in particular, less uncertainty and more competition.

Labour mobility has been questioned during the referendums that led to the recent rejection of a new constitution for Europe. The possibility of labour mobility was expressed in the form of a 'Polish plumber' in the French referendum. The notion that the local plumber might come from Poland caught the public imagination and was seen by many in France as unacceptable. Price flexibility is another difficulty. The high cost of labour in France and Germany compared to Spain and East European countries is in part responsible for the increase in unemployment in those countries. A lower cost of employment along with the resultant lower protection of workers rights is seen by many countries as leading to US-style or 'Anglo-Saxon' economy.

The picture is not brighter with regard to capital mobility. One way to assess such mobility is to measure the correlation of savings with investment within a country. If it is high, then investment is self funded within a country and there is deemed to be low capital mobility. Studies in the 1990s suggest that countries within the then European Monetary System had a low correlation compared to European countries outside the system (Sarno and Taylor, 1998 and Bayoumi *et al.*, 1999). Such results suggest that capital moves relatively freely within the currency area and therefore would not be correlated with any one country's savings. The sharing out of capital within the EU is helped by regional development grants giving aid to poorer areas. This is a relatively static part of EU expenditure being between 32 per cent to 38 per cent of EU operating expenditure compared to agriculture which is between 55 per cent and 60 per cent. However, capital mobility is not beneficial for all. In 2009 Bosch announced that it was moving its starter motor production facility to Hungary with the loss of some 900 jobs. Reasons given were a downturn in demand but also labour costs in Hungary were about 65 per cent of those in the UK.

Reasons for joining a currency area in the case of the EU include wanting to create ever closer economic and social cohesion. Capital and labour mobility within a currency area has social as well as economic consequences that are entirely in line with the original aims of the EU as laid out in the Maastricht Treaty. There are also more immediate financial gains and some costs. On the plus side, there are the gains of having a fixed exchange rate with other countries in the exchange rate area – low price uncertainty and lower reserves of foreign exchange are needed. On the negative side is the centralization and potential loss of seigniorage (the profit from printing money). Regional grants from the EU offer limited recompense. Another benefit of being able to print money is that governments can fund operations. Where this is to excess, the result is inflation. But such inflation can be seen as a tax on the real value of savings. The decline in value of a balance of, say, 1000 units of local currency due to inflation is the cost or 'tax' that funds the excessive government money creation to fund projects. A higher inflation, lower direct tax country may have to alter its taxes to compensate the loss of the 'inflation tax' as it is sometimes called. More generally, the loss of seigniorage is part of the development of a single monetary policy which is a direct consequence of a currency area such as the EU.

Impact on European monetary policy

The euro allows for a single money supply throughout the Eurozone, rather than a separate money supply for each participating currency. This means that levels of government borrowing must be similar across participating countries. To this end the Growth and Stability pact was signed in 1997. The conditions of the pact, a balanced budget in the medium term and limited government borrowing to 3 per cent of GDP, are very restrictive and have presented difficulties especially to members of the Eurozone facing an economic slowdown. Even the UK in 2005 had to redefine the medium term in order to claim a balanced budget in the medium term under its parallel 'Golden Rule'. There is a certain irony in the fact that Germany, the country seen as sponsoring the pact, was in fact the country that in the early 1990s through monetary indiscipline during the unification of Germany was the cause of the break-up of the narrow form of the ERM and to a certain extent the cause of Black Wednesday as explained above.

European Central Bank. The **European Central Bank (ECB)** is based in Frankfurt and is responsible for setting monetary policy for all participating European countries. Its objective is to control inflation in the participating countries and to stabilize (within reasonable boundaries) the value of the euro with respect to other major currencies. Thus, the ECB's monetary goals of price stability and currency stability are similar to those of individual countries around the world, but differ in that they are focused on a group of countries instead of a single country.

Implications of a European monetary policy. Although a single European monetary policy may allow for more consistent economic conditions across countries, it prevents any individual European country from solving local economic problems with its own unique monetary policy. European governments may disagree on the ideal monetary policy to enhance their local economies, but they must agree on a single European monetary policy.

The degree to which countries can pursue different *economic* policies while maintaining a common currency and monetary policy is something of an unanswered question. Crucial to any government policy is the level of government spending. Given that the amount of borrowing is controlled by being in the euro, further spending has to be financed by taxation (fiscal policy). For high tax countries (often cited as the Scandinavian countries and more generally all EU countries apart from the UK) the concern is that as barriers come down, businesses and higher earners will opt for lower tax countries within the EU (such an economy is often referred to as the 'Anglo-Saxon model'). For governments wishing to increase spending to help a sluggish economy (France and Germany being examples in 2005), raising taxes is not a good policy as it takes money out of the economy that the government is trying to energize. Thus it is perhaps understandable that the Growth and Stability pact rules are being broken by a number of countries and also that the next step in integration that was represented by the European Constitution has met considerable resistance. The danger for the EU is that exchange rate policy (in this case the euro and the implied common monetary policy) and economic policy are beginning to diverge. At the heart of many a crisis is just such a divergence.

Impact on business within Europe

The euro enables residents of participating countries to engage in cross-border trade flows and capital flows throughout the Eurozone (participating countries) without converting to a different currency. The elimination of currency movements among European countries also encourages more long-term business arrangements between firms of different countries, as they no longer have to worry about adverse effects due to currency movements. Thus, firms in different European countries are increasingly engaging in all types of business arrangements including licensing, joint ventures and acquisitions.

Prices of products are now more comparable among European countries, as the exchange rate between the countries is fixed. Thus, buyers can more easily determine where they can obtain products at the lowest cost.

Trade flows between the participating European countries have increased because exporters and importers can conduct trade without concern about exchange rate movements. To the extent that there are more trade flows between these countries, economic conditions in each of these countries should have a larger impact on the other European countries, and economies of these countries may become more integrated. Yet, as noted above, the degree of integration and its speed are now in question.

Impact on the valuation of businesses in Europe

When non-EU firms consider acquiring targets in Europe, they can more easily compare the prices (market values) of targets among countries because their values are denominated in the same currency (the euro). In addition, the future currency movements of the target's currency against any non-European currency will be the same. Therefore, MNCs can more easily conduct valuations of firms across the participating European countries.

European firms face more pressure to perform well because they can be measured against all other firms in the same industry throughout the participating countries, not just within their own country. The influence of firms on individual governments is less in that specific help is likely to breach European competition rules. On the other hand the collective bargaining strength of the EU is much greater than the individual power of the constituent governments. As such, EU firms offer stronger competition in the international marketplace than prior to the introduction of the euro and can be expected to increase in value.

Impact on financial flows

A single European currency forces the risk free interest rate offered on government securities to be similar across the participating European countries. Any discrepancy in rates would encourage investors within these European countries to invest in the currency with the highest rate, which would realign the interest rates among these countries. Any small differences are most likely due to technical reasons such as slightly differing conditions on the bond. That at least was the conventional wisdom. In January 2010, however, when there were suspicions that the Greek government might be forced to withdraw from the Eurozone, differences opened up between the returns being demanded on Greek bonds compared to, say, German bonds. This gap reached 396 basis points or 3.96 per cent. This does not contradict the conventional view as investment in Greek bonds was seen by the market as riskier, an outcome not originally envisaged.

Stock prices are now more comparable among the European countries because they are denominated in the same currency. Investors in the participating European countries are now able to invest in stocks throughout these countries without concern about exchange rate risk. Thus, there is more cross-border investing than there was in the past.

Since stock market prices are influenced by expectations of economic conditions, the stock prices among the European countries may become more highly correlated if economies among these countries become more highly correlated. Investors from other countries who invest in European countries may not achieve as much diversification as in the past because of the integration and because the exchange rate effects will be the same for all markets whose stocks are denominated in euros. Stock markets in these European countries are also likely to consolidate over time now that they use the same currency. Bond investors based in these European countries can now invest in bonds issued by governments and corporations in these countries without concern about exchange rate risk, as long as the bonds are denominated in euros. Some European governments have already issued bonds that are redenominated in euros, because the secondary market for some bonds issued in Europe with other currency denominations is now less active. The bond yields in participating European countries are not necessarily similar even though they are now denominated in the same currency; the credit risk may still be higher for issuers in a particular country.

Impact on exchange rate risk

One major advantage of a single European currency is the complete elimination of exchange rate risk between the participating European countries, which could encourage more trade and capital flows across European borders. In addition, foreign exchange transaction costs associated with transactions between European countries have been eliminated. The single European currency is consistent with the goal of the Single European Act to remove trade barriers between European borders, since exchange rate risk is an implicit trade barrier.

The euro's value with respect to other currencies changes continuously. The euro's value is influenced by the trade flows and capital flows between the set of participating European countries and the other countries, since these flows affect supply and demand conditions. Its value with respect to the Japanese yen, for instance, is influenced by the trade flows and capital flows between the set of participating European countries and Japan.

Status report on the euro

The euro has experienced a volatile ride since it was introduced in 1999. Its value initially declined substantially against the British pound, the dollar, and many other currencies. In October 2001, for example, 33 months after it was introduced, its value was $0.88, or about 27 per cent less than its initial value. The weakness was partially attributed to capital outflows from Europe. By June 2004, however, the euro was valued at $1.22, or 42 per cent above its value in October 2001. The strength in the euro was partially due to the relatively high European interest rates compared to US interest rates in this period, which attracted capital inflows into Europe.

The main problem for the euro is the status of the Growth and Stability pact, in particular its borrowing restrictions. Germany, since 2005, has yet to comply with restrictions on government borrowing, and the same is true for France, a problem that will continue for the foreseeable future. There is now open criticism of the euro and its attendant borrowing restrictions, first voiced at ministerial level in Italy (Roberto Maroni, the Italian Welfare Minister in 2005). The governor of the Bank of France, Christian Noyer, has also in 2005 openly discussed the possibility of countries leaving the euro. The restrictions of the Growth and Stability pact, designed to maintain order between countries were set at a very conservative level – too conservative even for the German government. Many members of the Eurozone regard a measure of increased borrowing and government intervention as being needed to help sluggish economies. The European Commission in response has eased the restrictions of the Growth and Stability pact and some now regard it as effectively inoperative. At a time when a Eurozone macroeconomic policy needs to be negotiated to replace the pact, there is no effective forum and level of agreement among member states to decide on a policy. The issue is in some ways a playing out of the debate in the early 1990s at to whether there should be economic union (sometimes termed political union as the union is essentially about agreeing common economic policies – a political process) before monetary union or, as happened, monetary union before economic union. The European Constitution was designed to allow greater central decision-making powers that would have eased political and economic union. Its rejection, along with an easing of the Growth and Stability pact, now leaves a currency with an uncertain management structure made up of the ECB, the Commission and individual governments all having a significant independent influence. To be optimistic, the need for a co-ordinated fiscal policy (borrowing and taxation) is now self-evident and is being called for by academics and the IMF. A process of informal co-operation between central banks, the

ECB, the Commission and individual governments may well emerge to provide, de facto, the level of co-ordination not achieved by more formal agreement. In 2010 the Greek financial crisis was seen as a major cause of weakness in the value of the euro that could only be met by coordinated action.

The response to the Greek crisis has been for the IMF, ECB and the European Commission to form a coordinated group known as the 'Troika' to oversee what are in effect conditionality packages for IMF backed loans. This is proving to be highly unpopular as it is in effect reducing the government sector and creating short term unemployment. Leaving the EU has been one response but this would have little effect on the debt position, loans would still be required from the IMF and there is little difference between the approach of the Troika and the IMF.

REFERENCES

Sarno, L. and Taylor, M.P. (1998) 'Savings – Investment Correlations: Transitory versus Permanent', *Manchester Business School,* 66, 17–38.

Bayoumi, T.A., Sarno, L. and Taylor, M.P. (1999) 'Macro Economic Shocks, the ERM, and Tripolarity', *Review of Economics and Statistics*, 77, 321–31.

Mundell, R.A. (1961) 'A Theory of Optimal Currency Areas', *American Economic Review,* 51, 657–65.

CHAPTER 7
INTERNATIONAL ARBITRAGE AND INTEREST RATE PARITY

LEARNING OBJECTIVES

The specific objectives of this chapter are to:

- Explain the conditions that will result in various forms of international arbitrage, along with the realignments that will occur in response to various forms of international arbitrage.

- Explain the concept of interest rate parity and how it prevents arbitrage opportunities.

The foreign exchange market is one of the most sophisticated of all world markets. If inconsistencies occur within the foreign exchange market, rates will be realigned by market traders. The process is driven by international arbitrage which offers the highly attractive prospect of being able to make a profit without taking a risk. Financial managers of multinational corporations (MNCs) must understand how international arbitrage realigns exchange rates in order to begin to predict exchange rate behaviour. Arbitrage processes are therefore fundamental to assessing the foreign exchange risk faced by MNCs.

INTERNATIONAL ARBITRAGE

Arbitrage can be loosely defined as making a profit from a discrepancy in quoted prices. The strategy does not involve risk (or at least the risk is trivially small) and, in many cases, does not require an investment of funds to be tied up for any length of time.

EXAMPLE

Two coin shops buy and sell coins. If Shop A is willing to sell a particular coin for £120, while Shop B is willing to buy that same coin for £130, a person can execute arbitrage by purchasing the coin at Shop A for £120 and selling it to Shop B for £130. The profit is certain (£10 less any travel costs) and the risk trivial – the trader might be mugged going from one shop to the other! The prices at coin shops can nevertheless vary because demand conditions may vary among shop locations. But if two coin shops are not aware of each other's prices and are sufficiently close to each other, the opportunity for arbitrage may occur. The act of arbitrage will cause prices to realign. In our example, arbitrage would cause Shop A to raise its price (due to high demand for the coin). At the same time, Shop B would reduce its buying price after receiving a surplus of coins as arbitrage occurs. The beauty of the process is that Shop A and Shop B need not know even of each other's existence, they simply have to react to demand and supply.

Arbitrage is therefore a very simple mechanism for determining prices and price behaviour and is a fundamental process in many financial proofs. The reasoning is that if the price in shop A can be calculated, then by arbitrage processes, it should be possible to predict the price in Shop B. In finance, the two 'shops' may be two financial packages that offer the same benefits. Modigliani and Miller's[1] propositions use this argument, personal gearing acting as the 'Shop A' price to value shares in companies with leverage (borrowing), and the Black Scholes option pricing model where a leveraged portfolio (borrowing and investing) again acts as a 'Shop A' price to predict option prices in the binomial version.

The type of arbitrage discussed in this chapter is primarily international in scope; it is applied to foreign exchange and international money markets and takes three common forms:

- Locational arbitrage
- Triangular arbitrage
- Covered interest arbitrage.

Each form will be discussed in turn.

Locational arbitrage

Commercial banks providing foreign exchange services normally quote about the same rates as each other on currencies, so shopping around may not necessarily lead to a more favourable rate. If the demand and supply conditions for a particular currency vary among banks, the banks may price that currency at different rates, and market forces will force realignment. That is to say, traders will change the market conditions when exploiting the price differences, ultimately forcing the same price for the same 'product'.

When quoted exchange rates vary among locations, participants in the foreign exchange market can capitalize on the discrepancy. Specifically, they can use **locational arbitrage**, which is the process of buying a currency at the location where it is priced cheaply and immediately selling it at another location where the price is higher.

---

[1]For example see Vernimmen, P. (2005) *Corporate Finance: Theory and Practice*, New York: Wiley, pp. 660 *et seq.*

EXAMPLE

Akron Bank and Zyn Bank serve the foreign exchange market by buying and selling currencies. Assume that there is no bid/ask spread. The exchange rate quoted at Akron Bank is £0.62 for $1, while the exchange rate quoted at Zyn Bank is £0.63. You could conduct locational arbitrage by purchasing dollars at Akron Bank for £0.62 per dollar and then selling them to Zyn Bank for £0.63 per dollar. Under the condition that there is no bid/ask spread and there are no other costs to conducting this arbitrage strategy, your gain would be £0.01 per dollar. The gain is risk-free in that you knew when you purchased the dollars how much you could sell them for. Also, you did not have to tie your funds up for any length of time.

Locational arbitrage is normally conducted by banks or other foreign exchange dealers whose computers can continuously monitor the quotes provided by other banks. If other banks noticed a discrepancy between Akron Bank and Zyn Bank, they would quickly engage in locational arbitrage to earn an immediate risk-free profit. Since banks have a bid/ask spread on currencies, this next example accounts for the spread.

EXAMPLE

The information on British pounds at both banks is revised to include the bid/ask spread in Exhibit 7.1. Based on these quotes, you can no longer profit from locational arbitrage. If you buy pounds from Akron Bank at £0.62 (the bank's ask price) and then sell the pounds at Zyn Bank at its bid price of £0.62, you just break even. If you try it the other way around and buy from Zyn bank at £0.63 and sell to Akron bank at £0.61 you will make a loss. As this example demonstrates, even when the bid or ask prices of two banks are different, locational arbitrage will not always be possible. To achieve profits from locational arbitrage, the bid price of one bank must be higher than the ask price of another bank.

Gains from locational arbitrage. Gains from locational arbitrage are based on the amount of money used to capitalize on the exchange rate discrepancy, along with the size of the discrepancy.

EXAMPLE

Quotations for the New Zealand dollar (NZ$) at two banks are shown in Exhibit 7.2. You can obtain New Zealand dollars from North Bank at the ask price of £0.38 and then sell New Zealand dollars to South Bank at the bid price of £0.39. This represents one 'round-trip' transaction in locational arbitrage. If you start with £10 000 and conduct one round-trip transaction, how many British pounds will you end up with? The £10 000 is initially exchanged for NZ$26 316 (£10 000/£0.38 per New Zealand dollar) at North Bank. Then the NZ$26 316 are sold for £0.39 each, for a total of £10 263. Thus, your gain from locational arbitrage is £263.

A briefer calculation is to observe that for every £0.38 a profit of £0.39 − £0.38 = £0.01 is made. As a percentage, this profit is £0.01 / £0.38 = 2.63 per cent, which for £10 000 is £10 000 × 0.0263 = £263. As a note of caution, it is advisable to avoid short cuts unless very familiar with the calculation, the safer, longer route of calculating a 'round-trip' is preferable!

EXHIBIT 7.1   Currency quotes for locational arbitrage example

	Akron Bank			Zyn Bank	
	Bid (bank buys dollars)	Ask (bank sells dollars)		Bid (bank buys dollars)	Ask (bank sells dollars)
Dollar quote	£0.61	£0.62	Dollar quote	£0.62	£0.63

EXHIBIT 7.2   Locational arbitrage

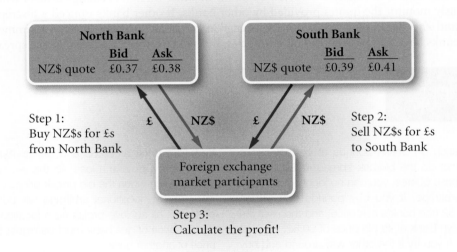

The gain of £263 in the example above may appear to be small relative to the investment of $10 000. However, consider that funds were not tied up for any length of time and that there was no risk. The round-trip transaction could take place over a telecommunications network within a matter of seconds for hundreds of times a day. Also, if a larger sum of money were used the gain would be larger each 'round-trip'. In financial terms, this transaction amounts to earning limitless amounts of money for no risk – the financial equivalent of a 'free lunch' and there are no 'free lunches' in finance! It is important to emphasize, therefore, that such a misalignment of prices is only likely to last for a very short period of time.

If you notice an apparent misalignment of prices in the financial press, the likely explanations are that:

1   The prices are not accurate (for example they may have been taken at different times of the day).

2   There are regulations and restrictions concerning the purchase and selling of the currencies that make the pro-posed round-trip impossible.

3   The difference does not cover transaction costs which include commissions.

4   You have not identified the element of risk.

Unfortunately, the press often uses the word 'arbitrage' for transactions that are risky and therefore give the impression that such profits are common. In any event do not attempt to pay for your education through part-time locational arbitrage!

Realignment due to locational arbitrage. Quoted prices will react to the locational arbitrage strategy used by foreign exchange market participants.

EXAMPLE

In the previous example, the high demand for New Zealand dollars at North Bank (resulting from arbitrage activity) will cause a shortage of New Zealand dollars there. As a result of this shortage, North Bank will raise its ask price for New Zealand dollars. The excess supply of New Zealand dollars at South Bank (resulting from sales of New Zealand dollars to South Bank in exchange for US dollars) will force South Bank to lower its bid price. As the currency prices are adjusted, gains from locational arbitrage will be reduced. Once the ask price of North Bank is not any lower than the bid price of South Bank, locational arbitrage will no longer occur. Prices may adjust in a matter of seconds or minutes from the time when locational arbitrage occurs.

The concept of locational arbitrage is relevant in that it explains why exchange rate quotations among banks at different locations normally will not differ by a significant amount. This applies not only to banks on the same street or within the same city but to all banks across the world. Technology allows banks to be electronically connected to foreign exchange quotations at any time. Thus, banks can ensure that their quotes are in line with those of other banks. They can also immediately detect any discrepancies among quotations as soon as they occur, and capitalize on those discrepancies. Thus, technology enables more consistent prices among banks and reduces the likelihood of significant discrepancies in foreign exchange quotations among locations.

Triangular arbitrage

Cross exchange rates represent the relationship between two currencies that are different from the chosen base currency. Taking the UK as the base currency, the term *cross exchange rate* refers to the implied exchange rate between two foreign currencies that exists when there are two quotes for foreign currencies in terms of British pounds. The calculation is illustrated by the following example.

EXAMPLE

If the US dollar is worth £0.50 and the euro is worth £0.80 there is an implied or cross exchange rate between the euro and the dollar. This is because the holder of euros wanting to convert to dollars could do so indirectly by converting into British pounds and then converting the pounds into dollars. This method uses the cross exchange rate, the implied rate. To calculate the rate we can use a simple equation approach.

The above exchange rates can be written as:

£0.50 = $1 or taking the inverse £1 = $2.00
(see Chapter 3)

£0.80 = 1 euro or taking the inverse £1 = 1.25 euro

Therefore $2.00 = 1.25 euro as they are both worth £1

(Continued)

Putting this exchange rate in more traditional form:

$2.00 = 1.25 euro → divide both sides by 1.25 →
    $1.60 equals 1 euro

or

$2.00 = 1.25 euro → divide both sides by 2.00 → $1
        equals 0.625 euro

Therefore, to calculate the cross exchange rate, find out the value of the currencies to one unit of the common currency. Then equate those values and convert the equation to traditional form.

If a quoted direct exchange rate differs from the appropriate cross exchange rate (as determined by the preceding formula), you can attempt to capitalize on the discrepancy. Specifically, you can use **triangular arbitrage**, in which currency transactions are conducted in the spot market to capitalize on a discrepancy in the cross exchange rate between two currencies.

EXAMPLE

Assume that a UK bank has quoted the US dollar at $1.60 to the British pound, the Malaysian ringgit (MYR) at 8.10MYR to the pound, and the third exchange rate at $0.20 for 1 Malaysian ringgit. If, as a UK businessman or businesswoman, you wanted to convert 100 000 ringgit to pounds, would it be preferable to convert at the direct rate of £1 = 8.10MYR or use the cross exchange rate by converting the ringgit into dollars and then the dollars into pounds (see Exhibit 7.3)?

Looking at the rates involved in the cross rate calculation, $0.20 = 1MYR and $1.60 = £1 or taking the inverses $1 = £0.625 and $1 = 5MYR the implied

EXHIBIT 7.3 Converting ringgit to pounds

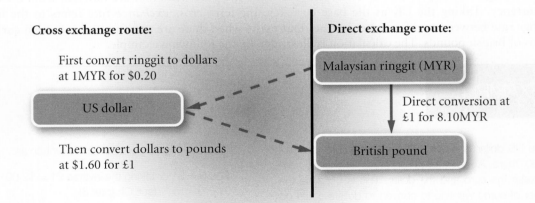

Cross exchange route:

First convert ringgit to dollars at 1MYR for $0.20

US dollar

Then convert dollars to pounds at $1.60 for £1

Direct exchange route:

Malaysian ringgit (MYR)

Direct conversion at £1 for 8.10MYR

British pound

(Continued)

pound to ringgit rate is £0.625 = 5MYR or (dividing both sides by 0.625) 8MYR = £1. So the pound is cheaper when the cross exchange route (8MYR) is taken compared to the direct route (8.10MYR). Taking the calculation step by step:

1 Convert ringgit to dollars: 100 000MYR × $0.20 = $20 000.

2 Convert the $20 000 to pounds: $20 000 / $1.60 = £12 500.

3 Compare with direct conversion: 100 000MYR / 8.10MYR = £12 346. So using the cross exchange rate is better by £12 500 − £12 346 = £154.

Speculators using the arbitrage process could borrow in pounds for a very short period. Convert to ringgit at the rate of 8.10MYR, convert the ringgit to dollars and then from dollars back into pounds (anticlockwise around the triangle). This is equivalent to converting into ringgit at 8.10MYR to the pound and converting back at 8MYR to the pound (the cross exchange rate calculated above). For every £100 converted in this way the gain would be £1.25 or 1.25 per cent of the initial investment. Assuming no transaction costs, the rates would eventually change so that there was no profit to be gained in this way.

Like locational arbitrage, triangular arbitrage does not tie up funds. Also, the strategy is risk-free, since there is no uncertainty about the prices at which you will buy and sell the currencies. As the market does not like profit to be earned for no risk, any gains are likely to be for a very short period of time.

Accounting for the bid/ask spread. As noted, the previous example was simplified in that it did not account for transaction costs. In reality, there is a bid and ask quote for each currency, which means that the arbitrageur incurs transaction costs that can reduce or even eliminate the gains from triangular arbitrage. The following example illustrates how bid and ask prices can affect arbitrage profits.

EXAMPLE

Using Exhibit 7.4, you can determine whether or not a fictitious amount (say £10 000) of British pounds and

triangular arbitrage is possible by starting with some estimating of the number of pounds you would

EXHIBIT 7.4   Currency quotes for a triangular arbitrage example

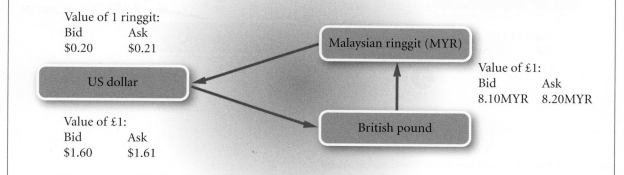

(Continued)

generate by going 'around the triangle' in Exhibit 7.4. Note that the task has changed from the previous example only in that the speculator is simply interested in the consistency of the exchange rates and can test the rates by converting pounds to ringgit, then ringgit to dollars and finally dollars to pounds. If the rates are not aligned, a profit or loss will be made. If there is a loss, then going the other way around the triangle will yield a profit.

The initial £10 000 will be converted into ringgit at the bid rate (bank buys) of 8.10MYR so 81 000MYR. Then convert the ringgit to dollars at the bid rate of $0.20 yielding 81 000MYR × $0.20 = $16 200. Finally, convert the $16 200 into pounds at the ask rate (bank sells) of $1.61, so $16 200 / 1.61 = £10 062.11, a profit of £62.11. This profit is less than the previous example due to the bid ask spread (which is a profit margin or transaction cost) charged by the banks.

Realignment due to triangular arbitrage. The realignment that results from the triangular arbitrage activity is summarized in Exhibit 7.5. The realignment is likely to occur quickly to prevent continued benefits from triangular arbitrage. The discrepancies assumed here are unlikely to occur within a single bank. More likely, triangular arbitrage would require three transactions at three separate banks.

The exchange rate between the three currencies is displayed in Exhibit 7.5. If any two of these three exchange rates are known, the exchange rate of the third pair can be determined. When the actual exchange rate differs from the implied cross exchange rate, the exchange rates of the currencies are not in equilibrium. Triangular arbitrage would force the exchange rates back into equilibrium.

Like locational arbitrage, triangular arbitrage is a strategy that few of us can ever take advantage of because the computer technology available to foreign exchange dealers can easily detect misalignments in cross exchange rates. It is because of triangular arbitrage that cross exchange rates are usually aligned correctly. If they are not, triangular arbitrage will take place until the rates are aligned correctly.

EXHIBIT 7.5   Currency quotes for a triangular arbitrage example

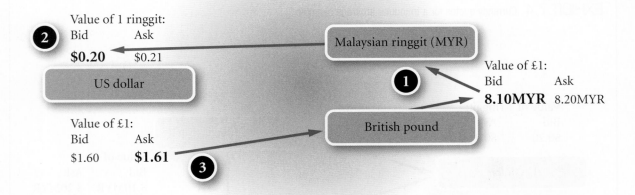

One or more of these should occur such that profits are no longer possible:
1   High demand for ringgit from pounds, results in pressure for a fall in ringgit offered to make it less attractive. Arbitrageur gets fewer ringgit.
2   High demand for dollars from ringgit, results in pressure for a fall in dollars offered to make it less attractive. Arbitrageur gets fewer dollars.
3   High demand for pounds at this rate, bank makes pound more expensive by raising the rate. Arbitrageur gets fewer pounds.

Covered interest arbitrage

Covered interest arbitrage is the process of capitalizing on interest rate differences between two countries while covering exchange rate risk. The logic of the term *covered interest arbitrage* becomes clear when it is broken into two parts: 'interest arbitrage' refers to the process of capitalizing on the difference between the interest rates of two countries; 'covered' refers to hedging your position against exchange rate risk by converting at today's quote for a forward exchange transaction rather than taking a risk and converting at whatever the spot rate is at the future point in time.

Covered interest arbitrage differs from conventional arbitrage in that investment and a period of time is required in the process. However, the profit is made at the moment of concluding the arbitrage package in much the same way as any other arbitrage operation. An arbitrageur can always sell the package and obtain the discounted value of the profit immediately as with other arbitrage arrangements. The following is an example of such an arbitrage operation:

EXAMPLE

As a UK currency trader, you desire to capitalize on relatively high rates of interest in the USA compared with the UK and have funds available for 90 days. The interest rate is certain; only the future exchange rate from dollars into pounds is uncertain. You can use a forward sale of dollars to guarantee the rate at which you can exchange dollars for pounds at a future point in time (see Exhibit 7.6). The strategy is as follows:

1 On day 1, convert your British pounds into dollars and set up a 90-day deposit account in a US bank. Work out the value of the account after 90 days.

2 On day 1, engage in a 90-day forward contract to sell the dollars accumulated in step 1 for pounds. The arbitrage deal is now complete and the profit guaranteed.

3 In 90 days, when the deposit matures, fulfil the 90-day forward contract and convert the dollars back into pounds at the agreed forward rate.

EXHIBIT 7.6 **Covered interest arbitrage**

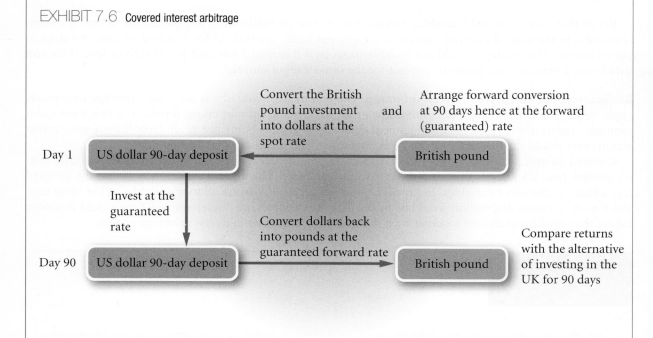

If the proceeds from engaging in covered interest arbitrage exceed the proceeds from investing in a domestic bank deposit, and assuming neither deposit is subject to default risk, covered interest arbitrage is feasible. The feasibility of covered interest arbitrage is based on the interest rate differential and the forward rate premium. To illustrate, consider the following numerical example.

EXAMPLE

Assume the following information:

- You have £800 000 to invest.
- The current spot rate of the dollar is £0.625.
- The 90-day forward rate of the pound is £0.625.
- The 90-day interest rate in the UK is 2 per cent.
- The 90-day interest rate in the USA is 4 per cent.

These interest rates are rather high and are for illustrative purposes only. 90 days is 90/360 or one-quarter of a year so the annual rate in the USA is approximately 16 per cent (i.e. 4 × 4 per cent)!

Based on this information, you should proceed as follows:

1   On day 1, convert the £800 000 to $1 280 000 and deposit the $1 280 000 in a US bank.

2   On day 1, sell $1 331 200 at the 90-days forward rate at the contract rate of £0.625 to the dollar.

Note that by the time the deposit matures, you will have $1 280 000 × 1.04 = $1 331 200 (including interest).

3   In 90 days when the deposit matures, you can fulfil your forward contract obligation by converting your $1 331 200 into £832 000 (based on the forward contract rate of £0.625 per dollar).

This reflects a 4 per cent return over the 3-month period (calculated as (£832 000 − £800 000) / £800 000 = 4 per cent), which is twice as much as the 2 per cent return on the UK investment over a similar period. The return on the foreign deposit is known on day 1, since you know when you make the deposit exactly how many dollars you will get back from your 90-day investment.

Recall that locational and triangular arbitrage do not tie up funds; thus, any profits are achieved instantaneously. In the case of covered interest arbitrage, the funds are tied up for a period of time (90 days in our example). This strategy would not be advantageous if it earned 2 per cent per annum or less, since you could earn 2 per cent on a domestic deposit for the same level of (no) risk.

Realignment due to covered interest arbitrage. The comments made about previous arbitrage operations apply here as well. The market does not allow profit to be made without taking a risk. So if this were a real example, one would only see the misalignment very briefly and probably not at all. Only if there were transaction costs would the forward rate not be in alignment with the interest rate differential.

Covered interest arbitrage affects four variables, taking the UK and USA they are: pound spot rate, British interest rate, US interest rate, and the pound forward rate. The normal assumption is that the forward rate adjusts to the other variables. In practice, future expectations drives all four variables at the same time and a more accurate description would be to say that the variables are co-determined. One would therefore expect the variables to change together such that there is a reduction in excess arbitrage profits.

EXAMPLE

Using the information from the previous example, Exhibit 7.7 summarizes the potential impact of covered interest arbitrage on exchange rates and interest rates and the forward rate. For the sake of explanation, the

(Continued)

EXHIBIT 7.7 Covered interest arbitrage market pressures from profitable arbitrage (in italics)

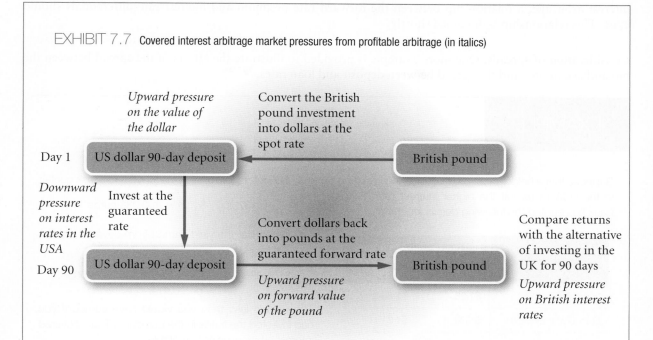

assumption is made here that all variables except the forward rate are fixed and that it is the forward rate alone that adjusts. But it should be remembered that in practice the process of adjustment is more complex.

In the previous example, if we assume no adjustment to interest rates, covered interest arbitrage will be feasible until the loss in value of the dollar on the forward exchange exactly offsets the gain in interest rates. Here we work out the forward rate that yields no profit. Given that the US interest rate is 2 per cent above the British rate, UK investors can benefit from covered interest arbitrage until the forward rate of the dollar is 2 per cent less in value than the spot rate.

The spot rate is £0.625 to the dollar. The offsetting 2 per cent fall in the value of the dollar on the forward market is calculated as follows:

£0.625 × (1.02/1.04) = £0.61298 to the dollar

(Note that the approximate approach is to say that the value of the dollar will be 2% − 4% = −2% or 2% less, so 98% of £0.625 is £0.6125. The exact relationship is to divide rather than subtract so 1.02 / 1.04 =

0.980769, so 98.0769% of £0.625 which is £0.61298. The very small rounding error of £1 is due to rounding to five decimal places! See the interest rate parity derivation below for a more formal derivation of this relationship.)

The arbitrage operation now appears as follows:

1 On day 1, convert the £800 000 to $1 280 000 and deposit the $1 280 000 in a US bank.

2 On day 1, arrange to sell in 90 days the amount deposited plus the interest that will be credited to the account, i.e. $1 331 200 (note that $1 280 000 × 1.04 = $1 331 200) at the new 90-day forward rate of £0.61298 to the dollar.

3 In 90 days when the deposit matures, you can fulfill your forward contract obligation by converting your $1 331 200 at the forward rate of £0.61298 into £816 000 (there is a £1.024 rounding error).

The £816 000 is a return of (£816 000 − £800 000) / £800 000 = 0.02 or 2 per cent the same return as investing in the UK. So there are now no gains through interest rate arbitrage.

As this example shows, those individuals who initially conduct covered interest arbitrage cause exchange rates and possibly interest rates to move in such a way that future attempts at covered interest arbitrage provide a return that is no better than what is possible domestically. Due to the market forces from covered interest arbitrage, a relationship between the forward rate premium and interest rate differentials should exist. This relationship is discussed shortly.

Consideration of spreads. One more example is provided to illustrate the effects of the spread between the bid and ask quotes and the spread between deposit and loan rates.

EXAMPLE

Suppose that a holder of euros is considering investing in the USA to exploit the higher interest rate. A US bank has quoted the following details for euros:

	Bid quote (bank buys euros)	Ask quote (bank sells euros)
Euro spot	$1.28	$1.30
Euro 1-year forward	$1.30	$1.31
	Deposit Rate	
Interest rate on dollars	7.5%	
Interest rate on euros	6.5%	

You have 100 000 euros to invest for 1 year. Would you benefit from engaging in covered interest arbitrage?

1 Convert 100 000 euros to dollars (**b**id quote – the US bank **b**uys euros for $1.28:1 euro):

$100 000$ euros $\times$ $1.28 = $128 000$

2 Calculate accumulated dollars over 1 year at 7.5%:

$128 000 \times 1.075 = $137 600$

3 Sell dollars for euros at the forward rate (ask quote):

$137 600 / $1.31 = 105 038$ euros

4 Determine the yield earned from covered interest arbitrage:

$($105 038 – $100 000) / $100 000 = 0.05038$, or 5.038%

The yield is less than you would have earned if you had invested the funds in the Eurozone. Thus, covered interest arbitrage is not profitable.

There are two sources of gain or loss in covered interest arbitrage, the first is the interest rate differential and the second is the gain or loss from currency conversion. The two can be separated in approximate terms:

Interest rate differential   7.5% – 6.5%   =   1% gain

from investing in the USA.

Currency conversion: the investment was multiplied by 1.28 and converted back by dividing by 1.31.

The net change is:

$1.28/1.31 - 1 = \underline{2.3\% \text{ loss}}$

Approximate net gain or loss   1.3% loss

The actual loss in the example above would have been $6.5\% - 5.038\% = 1.462\%$. The approximate analysis is useful in that it shows that the gain in interest rates is more than offset by the loss in value of the dollar on the forward market. At the start of the period the bank bought euros for $1.28 but at the end of the period it was selling them for $1.31. The euro was at a premium (higher value) in the forward market.

Could a profit have been made if someone with $100 000 invested for a year in euros? We can see that this also would not be possible. The spot ask rate of $1.30 is the same as the forward bid rate so there would be no gain to be had on the exchange rates. Interest rates are the only other source of gain. As the euro interest rates are lower than the dollar rates there would be no gain.

Finally, note that the arbitrage operation shows that there are powerful market forces to ensure that the forward rate does not allow a riskless profit to be made. Thus the spot rate, the forward rate and the interest rates are linked or co-determined to ensure that this does not happen. Interest rates are rather slow to move, being adjusted once a month in the UK by the Bank of England. Reasons for moving the rates will often have little to do directly with the future value of the currency. Therefore, any news about the future value of a currency that affects the forward rate will almost certainly affect the spot rate. They both look to the future value of the currency. Using the current spot rate to predict changes to the future spot rate (i.e. a prediction of no change in the rate) may therefore be a good predictor in practice and no worse than using the forward rate. The only exception would be where there is high inflation in one of the currencies. The forward rate alone would capture the devaluation (see Chapter 9).

COMPARISON OF ARBITRAGE EFFECTS

Exhibit 7.8 provides a comparison of the three types of arbitrage. The threat of locational arbitrage ensures that quoted exchange rates are similar across banks in different locations. The threat of triangular arbitrage ensures that exchanging money via another currency is in line with direct conversion. The threat of covered interest arbitrage ensures that forward exchange rates offset interest rate differentials.

INTEREST RATE PARITY (IRP)

Once market forces cause interest rates and exchange rates to adjust such that covered interest arbitrage is no longer feasible, there is an equilibrium state referred to as **interest rate parity (IRP)**. In equilibrium, the forward rate differs from the spot rate by a sufficient amount to offset the interest rate differential between two currencies. In the previous example, the European investor receives a higher interest rate from the investment in the USA, but there is an offsetting effect because the investor finds that the euro has increased in value against the dollar over the period (or equivalently, the dollar has fallen in value or devalued against the euro).

Derivation of interest rate parity

Recall that the forward rate is at a premium when the foreign currency is more expensive in the future and at a discount when the foreign currency is less expensive in the future. So, from the previous example taking the euro as the home currency, one can say that the dollar discount more than offset the interest rate differential. Interest rate parity (IRP) maintains that the return from investing abroad and converting back to the home currency at the forward rate (covered interest arbitrage) is the same as investing domestically. A currency forward premium or discount should exactly offset any difference in interest rates otherwise arbitrage profits will be possible.

The following analysis takes a more formal look at the elements of return from covered interest rate arbitrage and its relation with returns from home investment. A practical example then follows.

Consider a UK investor who attempts covered interest arbitrage. The investor's return from using covered interest arbitrage can be determined given the following:

● The amount of the home currency (UK pounds in our example) that is initially invested (A_h).

● The spot rate (S) in direct form, i.e. pounds to a single unit of foreign currency.

● The interest rate on the foreign deposit (i_f).

● The forward rate (F) in pounds to a single unit of foreign currency.

The amount of the home currency received after investing A_h in a foreign deposit and converting back at the forward rate is denoted as A_n:

$$A_n = (A_h / S) (1 + i_f) F$$

Since F, the forward rate, can be written as the spot rate (S) times one plus the forward premium (called p), i.e. $F = S(1 + p)$, we can rewrite this equation as:

$$A_n = (A_h / S) (1 + i_f) [(S(1 + p)]$$

EXHIBIT 7.8   Comparing arbitrage operations

Locational arbitrage: Capitalizes on discrepancies in exchange rates between two locations.

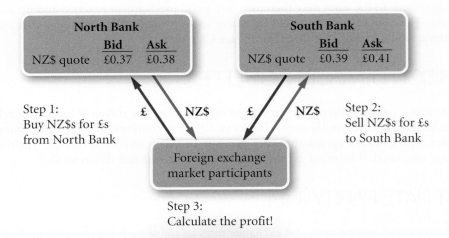

Triangular arbitrage: Capitalizes on discrepancies in cross exchange rates.

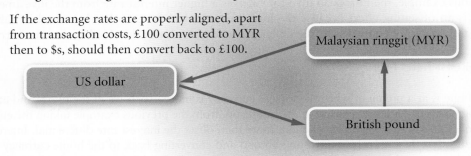

Covered interest arbitrage: Capitalizes on discrepancies between the forward rate and interest rate differentials.

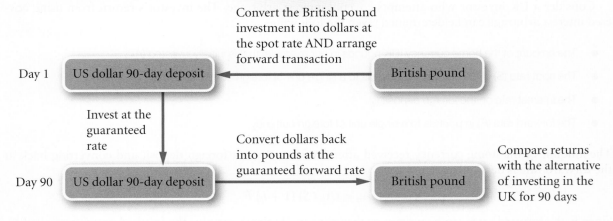

S cancels out so:

$$A_n = A_h\,(1 + i_f)\,(1 + p)$$

The rate of return from investing abroad (called R) is as follows:

$$R = \frac{A_n - A_h}{A_h}$$

Expanding, using the above formula for A_n

$$R = \frac{A_h(1 + i_f)(1 + p) - A_h}{A_h}$$

A_h cancels out, not surprising in that one would not expect a return to depend on the amount invested, so:

$$R = (1 + i_f)\,(1 + p) - 1$$

Returns from covered interest rate arbitrage is made up of the foreign interest rate (i_f) and the movement in the value of the foreign currency (p). Home investment (i_h) should yield a return that is the same as that on foreign investment (R) according to IRP:

$$R = i_h$$

Expanding the return on foreign investment (R) using the above formula we have:

$$(1 + i_f)\,(1 + p) - 1 = i_h$$

By rearranging terms, we can determine what the forward premium (p) of the foreign currency should be under conditions of IRP:

$$(1 + i_f)(1 + p) - 1 = i_h$$
$$(1 + i_f)(1 + p) = 1 + i_h$$
$$(1 + p) = \frac{(1 + i_h)}{(1 + i_f)}$$
$$p = \frac{(1 + i_h)}{(1 + i_f)} - 1$$

In words, where interest rate parity exists, the premium (p) is determined by the ratio of the interest rates. This relationship was used informally in the above example of covered interest rate arbitrage and is illustrated further below.

Determining the forward premium

From the above, the premium or discount can be simply determined.

EXAMPLE

Assume that the South African rand offers an interest rate of 6 per cent, while the British pound offers an interest rate of 5 per cent. From a UK investor's perspective, the British pound is the home currency.

(Continued)

According to IRP, the forward rate premium of the rand with respect to the pound should be:

$$p = \frac{(1 + i_h)}{(1 + i_f)} - 1$$

$$p = \frac{1 + 0.05}{1 + 0.06} - 1 = -0.0094339$$

Thus, the rand should exhibit a forward discount of about 0.943 per cent (rounded). This implies that UK investors would receive 0.943 per cent less when selling rands one year from now (based on a forward sale) than the price they pay for rands today at the spot rate. Such a discount would offset the interest rate advantage of the rand. If the rand's spot rate is £0.10, a forward discount of 0.943 per cent means that the one year forward rate is as follows:

$$F = S(1 + p)$$

$$F = 0.10(1 - 0.00943) = 0.099057$$

At this forward rate, covered interest arbitrage would not be any more profitable than domestic investment. As a brief check: £100 would convert to £100 / £0.10 = 1000 rand which would earn 1000 (1.06) 1060 rand and convert back to pounds at the forward rate calculated above at £0.099057 so 1060 × £0.099057 = £105.00042 a rounding error of £0.00042 means that

the absolute returns of £105.00042 – 0.00042 = £105 are the same as investing domestically at 5 per cent.

Note that the relationship also means that South African investors would get the same return as domestic investment in South Africa, i.e. 6 per cent. Again, a brief check will confirm this relationship. A South African investor with 1000 rand will convert at the spot rate of £0.10 to the rand, so 1000 × £0.10 = £100, which will earn 5 per cent in the UK so the investor will end up with £100 × 1.05 = £105 and convert back at the forward rate of £0.099057 producing absolute returns of £105 / £0.099057 = 1059.99576 rand, a rounding error of 0.00424 rand means that the return will be 1059.99576 + 0.00424 1060 rand, the same amount as would be achieved domestically by investing at 6 per cent.

This is a slightly counter intuitive result in that the forward rate allows UK investors (or rather holders of British pounds) to earn 5 per cent and South African investors to earn 6 per cent. The point is that the 5 per cent is earned in pounds and the 6 per cent is earned in rand. If we assume that the only reason for a difference is a difference in inflation, then the purchasing power of the UK investment would be the same as the purchasing power of the South African investment. In real terms (i.e. what can be bought with the money) they have earned the same rate of return. So the positions of the two investors are not quite as different as at first might seem.

The approximate relationship between forward premium and interest rate differential

The forward premium (p), as a reminder, is derived from:

$$F = S(1 + p)$$

where F is the forward rate and S the spot rate. The premium is simply the amount by which the forward rate is more or less than the spot rate.

The exact relationship between the forward premium (or discount) and the interest rate differential according to IRP is as given above:

$$p = \frac{(1 + i_h)}{(1 + i_f)} - 1$$

Note that the right-hand side is approximately equal to $i_h - i_f$ when the interest rates are low. So, where home interest rates are 6 per cent and foreign interest rates are 4 per cent, the premium on the value of foreign currency should be:

$$p = \frac{(1 + 0.06)}{(1 + 0.04)} - 1 = 0.01923 \text{ or } 1.923\%$$

In approximate form, the premium should be home less foreign interest rates:

$$p = i_h - i_f$$
$$= 6\% - 4\%$$
$$= 2\%$$

Note that the two results are about the same:

$$1.923\% \approx 2\%$$

In many calculations this approximate relationship will suffice, particularly where the interest rate differential is small.

EXAMPLE

Reworking the previous example using the approximate method where: the South African rand has a 6-month interest rate of 6 per cent, the British pound has a 6-month interest rate of 5 per cent and the rand's spot rate is £0.10. Suppose a UK investor has £100:

Step 1: On day 1 the £100 are converted into rand at £0.10 per rand.

£100 / £0.10 per rand = 1000 rand

Step 2. On the first day, the UK investor also sells rand 6 months forward. The number of rand to be sold forward is the anticipated accumulation of rand over the 6-month period, which is estimated as:

1000 rand × (1 + 0.06) = 1060 rand

Step 3. After 6 months, the UK investor withdraws the initial deposit of rand along with the accumulated interest, amounting to a total of 1060 rand. The investor converts the rand into pounds in accordance with the forward contract agreed upon 6 months earlier. The premium for the forward rate using the *approximate process* is:

$$p \approx i_h - i_f = 0.05 - 0.06 = -1\%$$

therefore, the actual forward rate is:

$$F = S(1 + p) = £0.10(1 - 0.01) = 0.099$$

the forward is £0.099 per rand. So the UK investor can expect to receive 1060 rand × £0.099 = £104.94 which is approximately equal to £105, the same return as investing in the UK. The rounding error is only £0.04 and is sufficiently small for most purposes.

Graphic analysis of interest rate parity

The interest rate differential can be compared to the forward premium (or discount) with the use of a graph. All the possible points that represent interest rate parity are plotted on Exhibit 7.9 by using the approximation expressed earlier and plugging in numbers.

Points representing a discount. For all situations in which the foreign interest rate exceeds the home interest rate, the forward rate should exhibit a discount approximately equal to that differential. When the foreign interest rate (i_f) exceeds the home interest rate (i_h) by 1 per cent ($i_h - i_f = -1\%$), then the forward value of the foreign currency should exhibit a discount of 1 per cent. This is represented by point A on the graph. If the foreign interest rate exceeds the home rate by 2 per cent, then the forward value of the foreign currency should exhibit a discount of 2 per cent, as represented by point B on the graph and so on.

Points representing a premium. For all situations in which the foreign interest rate is less than the home interest rate, the forward value of the foreign currency should exhibit a premium approximately equal to

EXHIBIT 7.9   Illustration of interest rate parity

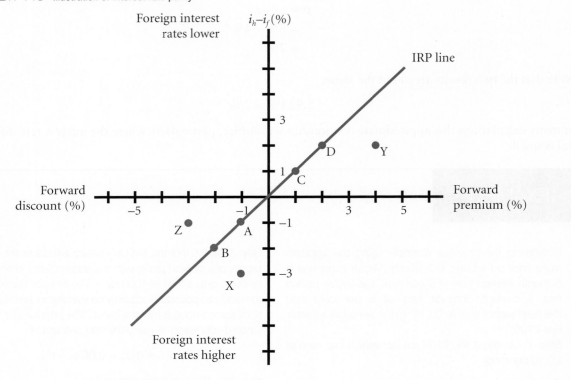

that differential. For example, if the home interest rate exceeds the foreign rate by 1 per cent ($i_h - i_f = 1\%$), then the forward premium should be 1 per cent, as represented by point C. If the home interest rate exceeds the foreign rate by 2 per cent ($i_h - i_f = 2\%$), then the forward premium should be 2 per cent, as represented by point D and so on.

Points representing IRP. Any points lying on the diagonal line cutting the intersection of the axes represent IRP. For this reason, that diagonal line is referred to as the **interest rate parity (IRP) line**. Covered interest arbitrage is not possible for points on the IRP line.

An individual or corporation can at any time examine all currencies to compare forward rate premiums (or discounts) to interest rate differentials. From a UK perspective, interest rates in Japan are usually lower than the home interest rates. Consequently, the forward rate of the Japanese yen usually exhibits a premium and may be represented by points such as C or D or even points above D along the diagonal line in Exhibit 7.9. Conversely, South American and African currencies often have higher interest rates than the UK, so the pound's forward rate often exhibits a discount, represented by point A or B.

Exhibit 7.9 can be used whether or not you annualize the rates, as long as you are consistent. That is, if you annualize the interest rates to determine the interest rate differential, you should also annualize the forward premium or discount.

Points below the IRP line. What if a 3-month deposit represented by a foreign currency offers an annualized interest rate of 10 per cent versus an annualized interest rate of 7 per cent in the home country? Such a scenario is represented on the graph by $i_h - i_f = -3\%$. Also assume that the foreign currency exhibits an annualized forward discount of 1 per cent. The combined interest rate differential and forward discount information can be represented by point X on the graph. Since point X is not on the IRP line, we should expect that covered interest arbitrage will be beneficial for some investors. The investor attains an additional 3 percentage points for the foreign deposit, and this advantage is only partially offset by the 1 per cent forward discount.

Assume that the annualized interest rate in the foreign currency is 5 per cent, as compared to 7 per cent in the home country. The interest rate differential expressed on the graph is $i_h - i_f = 2\%$. However, assume that the forward premium of the foreign currency is 4 per cent (point Y in Exhibit 7.9). Thus, the high forward premium more than makes up what the investor loses on the lower interest rate from the foreign investment.

If the current interest rate and forward rate situation is represented by point X or Y, home country investors can engage in covered interest arbitrage. By investing in a foreign currency, they will earn a higher return (after considering the foreign interest rate and forward premium or discount) than the home interest rate. This type of activity will place upward pressure on the spot rate of the foreign currency, and downward pressure on the forward rate of the foreign currency, until covered interest arbitrage is no longer feasible.

Points above the IRP line. Now shift to the left side of the IRP line. Take point Z, for example. This represents a foreign interest rate that exceeds the home interest rate by 1 per cent, while the forward rate exhibits a 3 per cent discount. This point, like all points to the left of the IRP line, represents a situation in which investors would achieve a lower return on a foreign investment than on a domestic one.

For points such as these, however, covered interest arbitrage is feasible from the perspective of foreign investors. Consider South African investors whose interest rate is 1 per cent higher than the UK interest rate, and the forward rate (with respect to the pound) contains a 3 per cent discount (as represented by point Z). South African investors will sell their home currency in exchange for pounds, invest in pound-denominated securities, and engage in a forward contract to purchase rand forward. Though they earn 1 per cent less on the UK investment, they are able to purchase their home currency for 3 per cent less than what they initially sold it for. This type of activity will place downward pressure on the spot rate of the rand (as it is sold now to invest in the pound) and upward pressure on the pound's forward rate (as investors seek to convert back to rand and consolidate their gain), until covered interest arbitrage is no longer feasible.

How to test whether interest rate parity exists

An investor or firm can plot all realistic points for various currencies on a graph such as that in Exhibit 7.9 to determine whether gains from covered interest arbitrage can be achieved. The location of the points provides an indication of whether covered interest arbitrage is worthwhile. For points to the right of the IRP line, investors in the home country should consider using covered interest arbitrage, since a return higher than the home interest rate (i_h) is achievable. Of course, as investors and firms take advantage of such opportunities, the point will tend to move toward the IRP line. Covered interest arbitrage should continue until the interest rate parity relationship holds.

Interpretation of interest rate parity

As pointed out in the previous example, interest rate parity means that holders of, say, British pounds who invest abroad at a higher interest rate will not get a higher overall return compared to home investment. This is because the forward rate will be at a discount such that any interest rate gain is exactly offset by a fall in the value of the foreign currency in the forward market.

Also, as pointed out in the South African example (above), interest rate parity does *not* mean that all currencies must have the *same* interest rate. One of the major benefits of having an independent currency is that a separate interest rate can be set for that currency and hence the economy where the currency is used. A currency experiencing high inflation and high interest rates, as a result, can neutralize the effect with other currencies by devaluing. Hot money will not flow into the country to exploit the high interest rates because the currency will be quoted at a devalued, lower rate on the forward market.

Does interest rate parity hold?

To determine conclusively whether interest rate parity holds, it is necessary to compare the forward rate (or discount) with interest rate quotations occurring at the same time. If the forward rate and interest rate quotations do not reflect the same time of day, then results could be somewhat distorted. Due to limitations in access to data, it is difficult to obtain quotations that reflect the same point in time.

A comparison of annualized forward rate premiums and annualized interest rate differentials for seven widely traded currencies as of 10 February 2004, is provided in Exhibit 7.10 from a US perspective. At this time, the US interest rate was higher than the Japanese interest rate and lower than the interest rates in other countries. The exhibit shows that the yen exhibited a forward premium, while all other currencies exhibited a discount. The Brazilian real exhibited the most pronounced forward discount, which is attributed to its relatively high interest rate. The forward premium or discount of each currency is in line with the interest rate differential and therefore reflects IRP.

At different points in time, the position of a country may change. For example, if Mexico's interest rate increased while other countries' interest rates stayed the same, Mexico's position would move down along the y-axis. Yet, its forward discount would likely be more pronounced (farther to the left along the x-axis) as well, since covered interest arbitrage would occur otherwise. Therefore, its new point would be farther to the left but would still be along the 45° line.

Numerous academic studies have conducted empirical examination of IRP in several periods. The actual relationship between the forward rate premium and interest rate differentials generally supports IRP. Although there are deviations from IRP, they are often not large enough to make covered interest arbitrage worthwhile, as we will now discuss in more detail.

Considerations when assessing interest rate parity

If interest rate parity does not hold, covered interest arbitrage still may not be worthwhile due to various characteristics of foreign investments, including transaction costs, political risk and differential tax laws.

EXHIBIT 7.10   Forward rate premiums and interest rate differentials for seven currencies

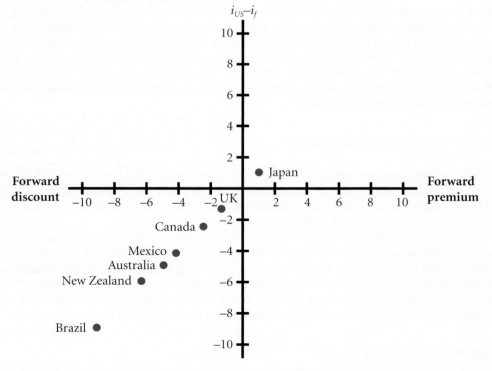

Note: The data are as of 10 February 2004. The forward rate premium is based on the 6-month forward rate and is annualized. The interest rate differential represents the difference between the 6-month annualized US interest rate and the 6-month foreign interest rate. This period has been chosen as it reflects quite large interest rate differentials. The period 2009–10, for instance, experienced much lower differentials. The difference between bid and ask rates and the movements of prices during the day in such periods becomes greater than the premiums and differentials, thus obscuring the relationship.

Transaction costs. If an investor wishes to account for transaction costs, the actual point reflecting the interest rate differential and forward rate premium must be farther from the IRP line to make covered interest arbitrage worthwhile. Exhibit 7.11 identifies the areas that reflect potential for covered interest arbitrage *after* accounting for transaction costs. Notice the band surrounding the IRP line. For points not on the IRP line but within this band, covered interest arbitrage is not worthwhile (because the excess return is offset by costs). For points to the right of (or below) the band, investors residing in the home country could gain through covered interest arbitrage. For points to the left of (or above) the band, foreign investors could gain through covered interest arbitrage.

Political risk. Even if covered interest arbitrage appears feasible after accounting for transaction costs, investing funds overseas is subject to political risk. Though the forward contract locks in the rate at which the foreign funds should be reconverted, there is no guarantee that the foreign government will allow the funds to be reconverted. A crisis in the foreign country could cause its government to restrict any exchange of the local currency for other currencies. In this case, the investor would be unable to use these funds until the foreign government removed the restriction.

Investors may also perceive a slight default risk on foreign investments such as foreign Treasury bills, since they may not be assured that the foreign government will guarantee full repayment of interest and principal upon default. Therefore, because of concern that the foreign Treasury bills may default, they may accept a lower interest rate on their domestic Treasury bills rather than engage in covered interest arbitrage in an effort to obtain a slightly higher expected return.

Differential tax laws. Because tax laws vary among countries, investors and firms that set up deposits in other countries must be aware of the existing tax laws. Covered interest arbitrage might be feasible when considering before-tax returns but not necessarily when considering after-tax returns. Such a scenario would be due to differential tax rates.

EXHIBIT 7.11 Potential for covered interest arbitrage when considering transaction costs

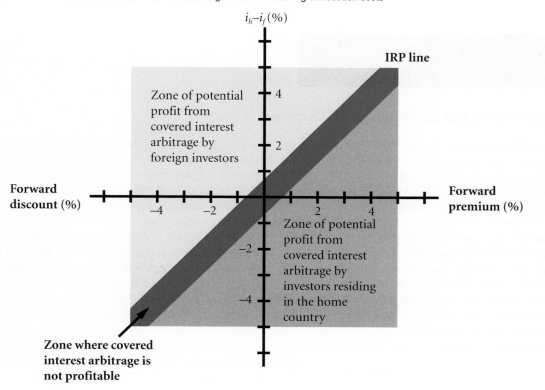

Changes in forward premium. Generally, given low transaction costs and low political and regulatory risk, changes in the forward premium will match changes in the relative interest rates. Where a particular foreign interest rate is higher than the home interest rate, then to make a profit without taking a risk one would have to invest abroad and convert back at the end of the period at the guaranteed forward rate. However, as we have seen, the forward rate will 'close off' any such possibility by being at a discount – a lower value. What you gain on the interest rate you lose on the exchange rate. This relationship must hold otherwise a riskless profit could be made through arbitrage – an efficient market will not allow investors to make profits through buying and selling or borrowing and investing without taking a risk. Equally, a fall in foreign interest rates will not make foreign interest rates less attractive as there will be a lessening of the discount. In this way currency acts as a financial 'lubricant' allowing different currency areas to have their own interest rates and hence their own monetary policy. A corollary of this is to consider countries with a fixed forward rate between each other, as is the case between countries in the Eurozone. A higher interest rate of one of the member countries would be more attractive to investors of another country *within that zone* as there would be no offsetting forward rate. Thus countries within a currency area are forced through arbitrage to have similar interest rates – the only difference being risk. A common interest rate means similar monetary policies – borrowing and spending levels – and it has been excessive borrowing that has been the cause of the 2009 Greek crisis.

It is tempting to think that changes in interest rates cause changes in the forward rate. But governments sometimes seek to protect their currencies by buying them on the forward market. This will in turn affect interest rates in order to avoid riskless profits. The direction of causality is never clear and to avoid the problem, forward rates and interest rates are sometimes referred to as being co-determined.

USING THE WEB

Forward rates

Forward rates of the Canadian dollar, British pound, euro and Japanese yen are provided for various periods at: http://markets.ft.com/ft/markets/currencies.asp.

MANAGING FOR VALUE

How interest rate parity affects IBM's hedge

Many MNCs (and one may think of a multinational company such as Renault or IBM) have subsidiaries based in Brazil. Since the Brazilian real has historically depreciated against the dollar, MNCs naturally consider hedging any funds that its Brazilian subsidiaries plan to remit to the parent. Forward and futures contracts can be used to hedge the future transactions in which the Brazilian real will be converted into dollars. Due to interest rate parity, however, the forward or futures rate of the Brazilian real is unfavourable relative to its spot rate. Since the Brazilian interest rate is higher than the European interest rate, IRP forces the forward rate of the Brazilian real to exhibit a discount. The discount is especially pronounced when the Brazilian interest rate is very high. Thus, if an MNC hedges its future conversions of Brazilian real to dollars, it must accept a heavily discounted exchange rate for conversion in the future. This exchange rate may not be as favourable as the prevailing spot rate at that future time, even if today's spot rate declines over time. This is an important cost of doing business in countries with high interest rates. Since high interest rates are usually caused by a high level of expected inflation, this example illustrates the indirect effect that a foreign country's expected inflation can have on an MNC. IBM, Renault and other MNCs can increase their value by identifying countries that will have a high degree of expected inflation and limiting their exchange rate exposure in those countries.

SUMMARY

- Locational arbitrage may occur if foreign exchange quotations differ among banks. The act of locational arbitrage should force the foreign exchange quotations of banks to become realigned, and locational arbitrage will no longer be possible.

- Triangular arbitrage is related to cross exchange rates. A cross exchange rate between two currencies is determined by the values of these two currencies with respect to a third currency. If the actual cross exchange rate of these two currencies differs from the rate that should exist, triangular arbitrage is possible. The act of triangular arbitrage should force cross exchange rates to become realigned, at which time triangular arbitrage will no longer be possible.

- Covered interest arbitrage is based on the relationship between the forward rate premium and the interest rate differential. The size of the premium or discount exhibited by the forward rate of a currency should be about the same as the differential between the interest rates of the two countries of concern. In general terms, the forward rate of the foreign currency will contain a discount (premium) if its interest rate is higher (lower) than the home interest rate. The forward premium should never deviate substantially from the interest rate differential as that would imply a profit from covered interest rate arbitrage. In effect this would be a riskless profit. Efficient markets do not allow riskless profits to be made.

- Interest rate parity (IRP) is a theory that states that the size of the forward premium (or discount) on the spot rate should be equal to the interest rate differential between the two countries of concern. When IRP exists, the carry trade (borrowing in one currency and lending in another and converting back at the prevailing spot rate at the end of the lending period), would not result in profits as any interest rate advantage in the foreign country will be offset by the discount on the prevailing spot rate in the future. However, profits (and losses) are made from the carry trade as IRP does not in general hold except in extreme circumstances.

CRITICAL DEBATE

Should arbitrage be more regulated?

Proposition. Yes. Large financial institutions have the technology to recognize when one participant in the foreign exchange market is trying to sell a currency for a higher price than another participant. They also recognize when the forward rate does not properly reflect the interest rate differential. They use arbitrage to capitalize on these situations, which results in large foreign exchange transactions. In some cases, their arbitrage involves taking large positions in a currency and then reversing their positions a few minutes later. This jumping in and out of currencies can cause abrupt price adjustments of currencies and may create more volatility in the foreign exchange market. Regulations should be created that would force financial institutions to maintain their currency positions for at least one month. This would result in a more stable foreign exchange market.

Opposing view. No. When financial institutions engage in arbitrage, they create pressure on the price of a currency that will remove any pricing discrepancy. If arbitrage did not occur, pricing discrepancies would become more pronounced. Consequently, firms and individuals who use the foreign exchange market would have to spend more time searching for the best exchange rate when trading a currency. The market would become fragmented, and prices could differ substantially among banks in a region, or among regions. If the discrepancies became large enough, firms and individuals might even attempt to conduct arbitrage themselves. The arbitrage conducted by banks allows for a more integrated foreign exchange market, which ensures that foreign exchange prices quoted by any institution are in line with the market.

With whom do you agree? State your reasons. Use InfoTrac or search engines recommended by your institution to access academic journals subscribed to by your institution. The keyword 'arbitrage' is probably the best means of selecting relevant articles. Such articles often conduct statistical tests of some sophistication. It is the conclusions from these tests and the discussion surrounding their design and the literature review that is the real contribution to the debate. Do not be put off by the rather more obscure aspects of the statistical tests. For this subject, newspapers are *not* a good source as they often confuse speculation with arbitrage. Speculation is considered in the next chapter.

SELF TEST

Answers are provided in Appendix A at the back of the text.

1 Assume that the following spot exchange rates exist today:

$$1 = \$1.50$$
$$C\$1 = \$0.75$$
$$1 = C\$2$$

Assume no transaction costs. Based on these exchange rates, can triangular arbitrage be used to earn a profit? Explain.

2 Assume the following information:

Spot rate of $1 = 0.625
180 day forward rate of $1 = 0.641
180 day British interest rate = 4%
180 day US interest rate = 3%

Explain in words what is happening to the value of the dollar over the 180-day period. Calculate the change in the value of the dollar as a percentage and compare with the difference in interest rates.

Based on this information, is covered interest arbitrage by UK investors feasible (assume a UK investor has £100 to possibly invest in the US)? Explain.

3 Using the information in the previous question, outline how the market might react to the given rates.

4 Explain in general terms how various forms of arbitrage can remove any discrepancies in the pricing of currencies.

5 Assume that the US dollar's 1-year forward rate exhibits a premium. Assume that interest rate parity continually exists. Explain how the premium on the US dollars' 1-year forward rate would change if British 1-year interest rates rose by 3 percentage points while US 1-year interest rates rose by 2 percentage points.

QUESTIONS AND APPLICATIONS

1 **Locational arbitrage.** Explain the concept of locational arbitrage and the scenario necessary for it to be plausible.

2 **Locational arbitrage.** Assume the following information:

	Beal Bank	Yardley Bank
Bid price of New Zealand dollar	£0.020	£0.018
Ask price of New Zealand dollar	£0.022	£0.019

Given this information, is locational arbitrage possible? If so, explain the steps involved in locational arbitrage, and compute the profit from this arbitrage if you had £1 000 000 to invest. What market forces would occur to eliminate any further possibilities of locational arbitrage?

3 **Triangular arbitrage.** Explain the concept of triangular arbitrage and the scenario necessary for it to be plausible.

4 **Triangular arbitrage.** Assume the following information:

	Quoted price
Value of Canadian dollar in British pounds	£0.60
Value of New Zealand dollar in British pounds	£0.20
Value of Canadian dollar in New Zealand dollars	NZ$3.02

Given this information, is triangular arbitrage possible? If so, explain the steps that would reflect triangular arbitrage, and compute the profit from this strategy if you had £1 000 000 to invest.

What market forces would occur to eliminate any further possibilities of triangular arbitrage?

5 **Covered interest arbitrage.** Explain the concept of covered interest arbitrage and the scenario necessary for it to be plausible.

6 **Covered interest arbitrage.** Assume the following information:

Spot rate of Canadian dollar	= £0.4400
90-day forward rate of Canadian dollar	= £0.4345
90-day Canadian interest rate	= 4%
90-day UK interest rate	= 2.5%

Given this information, what would be the yield (percentage return) to a UK investor who used covered interest arbitrage? (Assume the investor invests £1 000 000.)

What market forces would occur to eliminate any further possibilities of covered interest arbitrage?

7 **Covered interest arbitrage.** Assume the following information:

Spot rate of Mexican peso	= 14.00 euros
180-day forward rate of Mexican peso	= 13.72 euros
180-day Mexican interest rate	= 6%
180-day euro interest rate	= 5%

Given this information, is covered interest arbitrage worthwhile for Mexican investors who have pesos to invest? Explain your answer.

8 **Effects of September 11.** The terrorist attack on the USA on September 11, 2001, caused expectations of a weaker US economy. Explain how such expectations could have affected US interest rates and therefore have affected the forward rate premium (or discount) on various foreign currencies.

9 **Interest rate parity.** Explain the concept of interest rate parity. Provide the rationale for its possible existence.

10 **Inflation effects on the forward rate.** Why do you think currencies of countries with high inflation rates tend to have forward discounts?

11 **Covered interest arbitrage in both directions.** Assume that the existing UK 1-year interest rate is 10 per cent and the EU 1-year interest rate is 11 per cent. Also assume that interest rate parity exists. Should the forward rate of the euro exhibit a discount or a premium?

If UK investors attempt covered interest arbitrage, what will be their return?

If Eurozone investors attempt covered interest arbitrage, what will be their return?

12 **Interest rate parity.** Why would UK investors consider covered interest arbitrage in France when the interest rate on euros in France is lower than the UK interest rate?

13 **Interest rate parity.** Consider investors who invest in either US or British 1-year Treasury bills. Assume zero transaction costs and no taxes.

   a 'If interest rate parity exists, then the return for UK investors who use covered interest arbitrage will be the same as the return for US investors who invest in UK Treasury bills.'

   Is this statement true or false? If false, correct the statement.

   b 'If interest rate parity exists, then the return for British investors who use covered interest arbitrage will be the same as the return for British investors who invest in British Treasury bills.'

   Is this statement true or false? If false, correct the statement.

14 **Changes in forward premiums.** Assume that the Japanese yen's forward rate currently exhibits a premium of 6 per cent and that interest rate parity exists. If Eurozone interest rates decrease, how must this premium change to maintain interest rate parity? Why might we expect the premium to change?

15 **Changes in forward premiums.** Assume that the forward rate premium of the euro was higher last month than it is today. What does this imply about interest rate differentials between the USA and Europe today compared to those last month?

16 **Interest rate parity.** If the relationship that is specified by interest rate parity does not exist at any period but does exist on average, then covered interest arbitrage should not be considered by MNCs. Do you agree or disagree with this statement? Explain.

17 Covered interest arbitrage in both directions.
The 1-year interest rate in New Zealand is 6 per cent. The 1-year UK interest rate is 10 per cent. The spot rate of the New Zealand dollar (NZ$) is £0.25. The forward rate of the New Zealand dollar is £0.27. Is covered interest arbitrage feasible for UK investors? Is it feasible for New Zealand investors? In each case, explain why a profit from covered interest arbitrage is or is not feasible.

18 Limitations of covered interest arbitrage.
Assume that the 1-year UK interest rate is 11 per cent, while the 1-year interest rate in Malaysia is 40 per cent. Assume that a UK bank is willing to purchase the currency of that country from you 1 year from now at a discount of 13 per cent. Would covered interest arbitrage be worth considering? Is there any reason why you should not attempt covered interest arbitrage in this situation? (Ignore tax effects.)

19 Covered interest arbitrage in both directions.
Assume that the annual US interest rate is currently 8 per cent and Germany's annual interest rate is currently 9 per cent. The euro's 1-year forward rate currently exhibits a discount of 2 per cent.

  a Does interest rate parity exist?
  b Can a US firm benefit from investing funds in Germany using covered interest arbitrage?
  c Can a German subsidiary of a US firm benefit by investing funds in the USA through covered interest arbitrage?

20 Covered interest arbitrage. The South African rand has a 1-year forward premium of 2 per cent. One-year interest rates in France are 3 percentage points higher than in South Africa. Based on this information, is covered interest arbitrage possible for a French investor if interest rate parity holds?

21 Deriving the forward rate. Assume that annual interest rates in the UK are 4 per cent, while interest rates in France are 6 per cent.

  a According to IRP, what should the forward rate premium or discount of the euro be?
  b If the euro's spot rate is £0.66, what should the 1-year forward rate of the euro be?

22 Covered interest arbitrage in both directions.
The following information is available:

- You have £500 000 to invest.
- The current spot rate of the Moroccan dirham is £0.06.
- The 60-day forward rate of the Moroccan dirham is £0.05.
- The 60-day interest rate in the UK is 1 per cent.
- The 60-day interest rate in Morocco is 2 per cent.

  a What is the yield to a UK investor who conducts covered interest arbitrage? Did covered interest arbitrage work for the investor in this case?
  b Would covered interest arbitrage be possible for a Moroccan investor in this case?

ADVANCED QUESTIONS

23 Economic effects on the forward rate. Assume that Mexico's economy has expanded significantly, causing a high demand for loanable funds there by local firms. How might these conditions affect the forward discount of the Mexican peso?

24 Differences among forward rates. Assume that the 30-day forward premium of the euro with the British pound is − 1 per cent, while the 90-day forward premium of the euro is 2 per cent. Explain the likely interest rate conditions that would cause these premiums. Does this ensure that covered interest arbitrage is worthwhile?

25 Testing interest rate parity. Describe a method for testing whether interest rate parity exists. Why are transaction costs, currency restrictions and differential

tax laws important when evaluating whether covered interest arbitrage can be beneficial?

26 Deriving the forward rate. Before the Asian crisis began, Asian central banks were maintaining a somewhat stable value for their respective currencies. Nevertheless, the forward rate of South East Asian currencies exhibited a discount. Explain.

27 Interpreting changes in the forward premium.
Assume that interest rate parity holds. At the beginning of the month, the spot rate of the Canadian dollar is £0.35, while the 1-year forward rate is £0.34. Assume that UK interest rates increase steadily over the month. At the end of the month, the 1-year forward rate is higher (foreign currency costs more) than it was at the beginning of the month. Yet,

the 1-year forward discount is larger (the 1-year premium is more negative) at the end of the month than it was at the beginning of the month. Explain how the relationship between the UK interest rate and the Canadian interest rate changed from the beginning of the month until the end of the month.

28 **Interpreting a large forward discount.** The interest rate in Indonesia is commonly higher than the interest rate in the UK and the Eurozone, which reflects a high expected rate of inflation there. Why should European MNCs consider hedging their future remittances from Indonesia to their parent even when the forward discount on the currency (rupiah) is so large?

29 **Change in the forward premium.** At the end of this month, you (the owner of a German firm) are meeting with a Japanese firm to which you will try to sell supplies. If you receive an order from that firm, you will obtain a forward contract to hedge the future receivables in yen. As of this morning, the forward rate of the yen and spot rate are the same. You believe that interest rate parity holds.

This afternoon, news occurs that makes you believe that the Eurozone interest rates will increase substantially by the end of this month, and that the Japanese interest rate will not change. However, your expectations of the spot rate of the Japanese yen are not affected at all in the future. How will your expected euro amount of receivables from the Japanese transaction be affected (if at all) by the news that occurred this afternoon? Explain.

30 **Testing IRP.** The 1-year interest rate in Singapore is 11 per cent. The 1-year interest rate in the USA is 6 per cent. The spot rate of the Singapore dollar (S$) is $0.50 and the forward rate of the S$ is $0.46. Assume zero transactions costs.

a Does interest rate parity exist?
b Can a US firm benefit from investing funds in Singapore using covered interest arbitrage?

PROJECT WORKSHOP

31 **Forward rates.** Using interest rates (preferably LIBOR) from the newspaper or other source, and forward rates from the website: http://www.bmo.com/economic/regular/fxrates.html or http://www.ft.com or using your own institutions data sources, calculate whether the 1 year forward premium between the British pound and the US dollar is in the right direction (note that all required data can be found in a financial newspaper such as the *Financial Times*):

a Estimate the accuracy of your calculations and suggest reasons for the inaccuracy.
b Perform the same calculation for other currencies.

DISCUSSION IN THE BOARDROOM

This exercise can be found on our dedicated CourseMate platform for students.

RUNNING YOUR OWN MNC

This exercise can be found on our dedicated CourseMate platform for students.

Essays/discussion and articles can be found at the end of Part II.

BLADES PLC CASE STUDY

Assessment of potential arbitrage opportunities

Recall that Blades, a UK manufacturer of roller blades, has chosen Thailand as its primary export target for 'Speedos', Blades' primary product. Moreover, Blades' primary customer in Thailand, Entertainment Products, has committed itself to purchase 180 000 Speedos annually for the next 3 years at a fixed price denominated in baht, Thailand's currency. Because of quality and cost considerations, Blades also imports some of the rubber and plastic components needed to manufacture Speedos.

Lately, Thailand has experienced weak economic growth and political uncertainty. As investors lost confidence in the Thai baht as a result of the political uncertainty, they withdrew their funds from the country. This resulted in an excess supply of baht for sale over the demand for baht in the foreign exchange market, which put downward pressure on the baht's value. As foreign investors continued to withdraw their funds from Thailand, the baht's value continued to deteriorate. Since Blades has net cash flows in baht resulting from its exports to Thailand, a deterioration in the baht's value will affect the company negatively.

Ben Holt, Blades' finance director, would like to ensure that the spot and forward rates Blades' bank has quoted are reasonable. If the exchange rate quotes are reasonable, then arbitrage will not be possible. If the quotations are not appropriate, however, arbitrage may be possible. Under these conditions, Holt would like Blades to use some form of arbitrage to take advantage of possible mispricing in the foreign exchange market. Although Blades is not an arbitrageur, Holt believes that arbitrage opportunities could offset the negative impact resulting from the baht's depreciation, which would otherwise seriously affect Blades' profit margins.

Ben Holt has identified three arbitrage opportunities as profitable and would like to know which one of them is the most profitable. Thus, he has asked you, Blades' financial analyst, to prepare an analysis of the arbitrage opportunities he has identified. This would allow Holt to assess the profitability of arbitrage opportunities very quickly.

1 The first arbitrage opportunity relates to locational arbitrage. Holt has obtained spot rate quotations from two banks in Thailand: Minzu Bank and Sobat Bank, both located in Bangkok. The bid and ask prices of Thai baht for each bank are displayed in the table below:

	Minzu Bank	Sobat Bank
Bid	£0.0149	£0.0152
Ask	£0.0151	£0.0153

Determine whether the foreign exchange quotations are appropriate. If they are not appropriate, determine the profit you could generate by withdrawing £100 000 from Blades' cheque account and engaging in arbitrage before the rates are adjusted.

2 Besides the bid and ask quotes for the Thai baht provided in the previous question, Minzu Bank has provided the following quotations for the pound and the Japanese yen:

	Quoted bid price	Quoted ask price
Value of a Japanese yen in British pounds	£0.0057	£0.0058
Value of a Thai baht in Japanese yen	¥2.69	¥2.70

Determine whether the cross exchange rate between the Thai baht and Japanese yen is appropriate. If it is not appropriate, determine the profit you could generate for Blades by withdrawing £100 000 from Blades' current account and engaging in triangular arbitrage before the rates are adjusted.

3 Ben Holt has obtained several forward contract quotations for the Thai baht to determine whether covered interest arbitrage may be possible. He was quoted a forward rate of £0.015 per Thai baht for a 90-day forward contract. The current spot rate is £0.0151. Ninety-day interest rates

available to Blades in the UK are 2 per cent, while 90-day interest rates in Thailand are 3.75 per cent (these rates are not annualized). Holt is aware that covered interest arbitrage, unlike locational and triangular arbitrage, requires an investment of funds. Thus, he would like to be able to estimate the British pound profit resulting from arbitrage over and above the amount available on a 90-day UK deposit.

Determine whether the forward rate is priced appropriately. If it is not priced appropriately, determine the profit you could generate for Blades by withdrawing £100 000 from Blades'

current account and engaging in covered interest arbitrage. Measure the profit as the excess amount above what you could generate by investing in the UK money market.

4 Why are arbitrage opportunities likely to disappear soon after they have been discovered? To illustrate your answer, assume that covered interest arbitrage involving the immediate purchase and forward sale of baht is possible. Discuss how the baht's spot and forward rates would adjust until covered interest arbitrage is no longer possible. What is the resulting equilibrium state called?

SMALL BUSINESS DILEMMA

Assessment of prevailing spot and forward rates by the Sports Exports Company

As the Sports Exports Company from Ireland exports basketballs to the UK, it receives British pounds. The cheque (denominated in pounds) for last month's exports just arrived. Jim Logan (owner of the Sports Exports Company) normally deposits the cheque with his local bank and requests that the bank convert the cheque to euros at the prevailing spot rate (assuming that he did not use a forward contract to hedge this payment). Jim's local bank provides foreign exchange services for many of its business customers who need to buy or sell widely traded currencies. Today, however, Jim decided to check the quotations of the spot rate at other banks before converting the payment into euros.

1 Do you think Jim will be able to find a bank that provides him with a more favourable spot rate than his local bank? Explain.

2 Do you think that Jim's bank is likely to provide more reasonable quotations for the spot rate of the British pound if it is the only bank in town that provides foreign exchange services? Explain.

3 Jim is considering using a forward contract to hedge the anticipated receivables in pounds next month. His local bank quoted him a spot rate of 1.45 euros and a 1-month forward rate of 1.4435 euros. Before Jim decides to sell pounds 1 month forward, he wants to be sure that the forward rate is reasonable, given the prevailing spot rate. A 1-month Treasury security in Ireland currently offers a yield (not annualized) of 1 per cent, while a 1-month Treasury security in the UK offers a yield of 1.4 per cent. Do you believe that the 1-month forward rate is reasonable given the spot rate of 1.45 euros?

CHAPTER 8 RELATIONSHIPS AMONG INFLATION, INTEREST RATES AND EXCHANGE RATES

LEARNING OBJECTIVES

The specific objectives of this chapter are to:

● Explain the purchasing power parity (PPP) theory and its implications for exchange rate changes.

● Explain the international Fisher effect (IFE) theory and its implications for exchange rate changes.

● Compare the PPP theory, the IFE theory and the theory of interest rate parity (IRP), which was introduced in the previous chapter.

Inflation rates and interest rates can have a significant impact on exchange rates (as explained in Chapter 4) and therefore can influence the value of multinational corporations (MNCs). Here, the concern is exclusively with how the spot or present rate behaves over time. MNC treasurers who do not take out forward rate protection (see previous chapter) will need to understand the relationship between exchange rates, interest rates and inflation in order to understand how the extensive debates in the financial press over inflation and interest rates are likely to affect exchange rates. Also, where a government seeks to control exchange rates, it is important to understand the effect on inflation and interest rates in that country. We assume in this chapter, unless stated otherwise, that exchange rates are free floating and wholly determined by non-government market forces.

PURCHASING POWER PARITY (PPP)

In Chapter 4 the expected impact of relative inflation rates on exchange rates was discussed. Recall from this discussion that when the inflation rate in country A (for example) rises, the demand for its currency declines as its exports decline (due to its higher prices). In addition, consumers and firms in country A tend to increase their importing (increasing the supply of home currency for foreign currency). The reduced demand for country A's currency and the increased supply of country A's home currency for foreign currency, both place downward pressure on A's currency.

Inflation rates often vary among countries, causing international trade patterns and exchange rates to adjust accordingly. One of the most popular and controversial theories in international finance is the **purchasing power parity (PPP) theory**. The theory bases its predictions of exchange rate movement on changing patterns of trade due to different inflation rates between countries.

Interpretations of purchasing power parity

There are two forms of PPP theory: the absolute form and the broader relative form.

Absolute form of PPP. The **absolute form of PPP** is based on the notion that without international trade barriers and transport costs, consumers shift their demand to wherever prices are lower. It suggests that prices of the same basket of products in two different countries should be equal when measured in a common currency. If there is a discrepancy in prices as measured by a common currency, demand should shift so that these prices converge.

EXAMPLE

If the same basket of products is produced by the USA and the UK, and the price in the UK is lower when measured in a common currency, US consumers should seek to import the cheaper UK products. Consequently, the actual price charged in each country may be affected, and/or the exchange rate may adjust. Remember that for a US resident seeking to import the cheaper goods from the UK, an increase in the value of the British pound represents a price rise just as much as an increase in the price of the goods themselves. There are two purchases by the US importer; the currency has to be purchased in order to buy the goods. Overall, market demand would cause the prices of the baskets to be similar when measured in a common currency. Exchange rates are a part of the price adjustment process.

Realistically, the existence of transportation costs, tariffs and quotas may prevent the absolute form of PPP. If transportation costs were high in the preceding example, the demand for the baskets of products might not shift as suggested. Thus, the discrepancy in prices would continue.

Relative form of PPP. The **relative form of PPP** accounts for the possibility of market imperfections such as transportation costs, tariffs and quotas. This version acknowledges that because of these market imperfections, prices of the same basket of products in different countries will not necessarily be the same when measured in a common currency. It does state, however, that the *rate of change* in the prices of the baskets should be similar when measured in a common currency, as long as the transportation costs and trade barriers are unchanged.

EXAMPLE

Assume that the USA and the UK trade extensively with each other and initially have zero inflation. Now assume that the USA experiences a 9 per cent inflation rate, while the UK experiences a 5 per cent inflation rate. All goods in the USA are going to appear to be 9% − 5% = 4% more expensive to the UK resident. Under these conditions, PPP theory suggests that the US dollar should depreciate by approximately 4 per cent − the difference in inflation rates. The reduced demand for dollars by British pounds and the increased supply of dollars for pounds will, in a free floating exchange rate regime, lower the value of the dollar against the pound. Thus, the exchange rate should adjust to offset the differential in the inflation rates of the two countries. If this occurs, then the difference in prices that existed before the inflation changes will remain after the inflation changes. If a particular washing machine costs 6 per cent more in the USA before the inflation change, it will still cost 6 per cent more after the inflation change.

Therefore the exchange rate adjusts so that *relative* prices are undisturbed by inflation differences. Relative PPP does not require that prices translated into one currency are the same, merely that the differences remain constant.

Rationale behind purchasing power parity theory

PPP is based on international trade in goods and services rather than investment in stocks and shares. In our previous example, the relatively high US inflation should cause US consumers to increase imports from the UK and British consumers to lower their demand for US goods (since prices of British goods have increased by a lower rate). Such forces place downward pressure on the value of the dollar when measured in pounds. As a result, US importers will find that the pound is becoming more expensive.

The shifting in consumption spending from the USA to the UK will continue until the British pound's value has appreciated to the extent that the price of British goods relative to US goods is not altered by the different inflation rates. Absolute PPP states that the relative prices should be such that the same goods cost the same whether purchased in the USA or the UK (after allowing for transport costs) − a relative difference of zero. Relative PPP states merely that whatever differences exist should remain constant − goods costing X per cent more should remain costing X per cent more.

The relationship between exchange rates and inflation, as will be shown more formally, is approximately additive (see Appendix B). To get an intuitive feel for the problem, refer back to the previous example. The conclusion was that the value of the British pound would increase relative to the dollar by about 4 per cent. Assume an exchange rate of $1.80 to the pound. For a US consumer, goods costing £100 in the UK would, before inflation, cost £100 × 1.8 = $180. After UK inflation of 5 per cent, the UK cost would be £105 or in dollars £105 × 1.8 = $189. But as the value of the pound had increased by 4 per cent the exchange rate would have changed. A 4 per cent increase in the value of the pound would mean that the pound would cost 1.8 × 1.04 = $1.872 to the pound. So the full cost to the US importer of the British goods would be £105 × 1.872 = $196.56. The total increase in cost to the US importer would be ($196.56 − $180)/$180 = 9.2%. In approximate terms this is the increase in the value of the British pound of 4 per cent plus the increase in British prices of 5 per cent, a total of 9 per cent.

From the British point of view, the pound will now buy $1.872 or 4 per cent more dollars than before the inflation. Goods costing $1000 will now cost $1090 after the 9 per cent inflation in the USA. But as the dollar is now cheaper for the UK importer, the total cost to the UK importer will be $1090/$1.872 = £582.26. Before inflation, the cost in terms of pounds would have been $1000/1.8 = £555.56. So the net increase taking into account US inflation and the change in the value of the dollar would be (£582.26 − £555.56)/£555.56 = 4.8 per cent. The 9 per cent US inflation less the 4 per cent fall in the value of the dollar results in a net increase in the value of US goods to UK importers of approximately 5 per cent or more exactly 4.8 per cent as calculated above (see Appendix B for an explanation of the difference).

So, reviewing the figures, the exchange rate has performed a neat trick. Both the USA and the UK can have their own inflation rates — an important element in having independent economic policies. Yet the relative price of imports compared to domestic goods remains unchanged. Goods imported into the UK from the USA go up by 5 per cent the same rate as UK goods. UK exports to the USA go up by 9 per cent, the same rate as US goods. The exchange rate adjusts for the difference in inflation rates. The important conditions to this result are that the exchange rate is allowed to float freely and that investment flows guided by interest rates do not disturb the relationship. Conversely one can begin to see that controlling the exchange rate will affect inflation. A fixed exchange rate in the previous example would put downward pressure on the price of US goods to compete with UK goods rising at a lower rate. The interest rate effect is discussed later. For now, a more general derivation of PPP is required.

Derivation of purchasing power parity

Inflation is usually measured as the *change* in the price index of a country, where a price index can be thought of as a scale or number which measures the average price. Assume that before inflation, the price indexes of the home country (h) and a foreign country (f) are both set at 100. Now assume that over time, the home country experiences an inflation rate of I_h, while the foreign country experiences an inflation rate of I_f. Due to inflation, the price index of goods in the consumer's home country (P_h) becomes:

$$P_h(1 + I_h)$$

The price index of the foreign country (P_f) will also change due to inflation in that country:

$$P_f(1 + I_f)$$

If home inflation is greater than foreign inflation, $I_h > I_f$, and the exchange rate between the currencies of the two countries does not change, then the consumer's purchasing power is greater when buying foreign goods than buying home goods. In this case, PPP does not exist. If $I_h < I_f$, and the exchange rate between the currencies of the two countries does not change, then the consumer's purchasing power is greater when buying home goods than buying foreign goods. In this case also, PPP does not exist.

The PPP theory suggests that the exchange rate will not remain constant but will adjust to maintain the parity in purchasing power. If inflation occurs and the exchange rate of the foreign currency changes, the foreign price index from the home consumer's perspective becomes:

$$P_f(1 + I_f)(1 + e_f)$$

where e_f represents the percentage change in the value of the foreign currency. It is worth stressing that it is the change in the value of the currency (e_f) that we are seeking to measure, not the actual exchange rate itself. The actual future rate can be easily worked out using the current spot and the expected change in the value of the currency.

According to PPP theory, the percentage change in the foreign currency (e_f) should change to maintain parity between the new price indexes of the two countries. We can solve for e_f under conditions of PPP by setting the formula for the new price index of the foreign country equal to the formula for the new price index of the home country, as follows:

$$P_f(1 + I_f)(1 + e_f) = P_h(1 + I_h)$$

Solving for e_f, we obtain:

$$(1 + e_f) = \frac{P_h(1 + I_h)}{P_f(1 + I_f)}$$

$$e_f = \frac{P_h(1 + I_h)}{P_f(1 + I_f)} - 1$$

Since P_h equals P_f (because price indexes were initially assumed equal in both countries), they cancel, leaving:

$$e_f = \frac{(1 + I_h)}{(1 + I_f)} - 1$$

This formula reflects the relationship between relative inflation rates and the exchange rate according to PPP. Notice that if $I_h > I_f$, e_f should be positive. This implies that the foreign currency will appreciate when the home country's inflation exceeds the foreign country's inflation. Conversely, if $I_h < I_f$, then e_f should be negative. This implies that the foreign currency will depreciate when the foreign country's inflation exceeds the home country's inflation. Students often wrongly think that this relationship is automatic. In the real world this relationship is *not* automatic and is precisely why the purchasing power of currencies gain and lose over time. This aspect is explored further below in discussing real exchange rates.

Returning to the PPP analysis, in approximate terms for relatively low levels of inflation:

$$e_f = \frac{(1 + I_h)}{(1 + I_f)} - 1 \approx I_h - I_f$$

Thus if $I_h = 4$ per cent and $I_f = 3$ per cent the exact approach gives 0.0097 whereas the approximate approach is 0.01 (i.e. 4% − 3% = 1%), a difference of 0.0003. Whereas if the inflation rates were 54 per cent and 53 per cent the error would be 0.0034, over ten times greater but still possibly not too large (see rounding in Appendix B). From now on we follow the convention that '=' will replace '≈' for the approximate approach.

A useful way of thinking about the relationship is to separate the foreign and home effects:

$$I_h = I_f + e_f$$

The offsetting effect of percentage changes in the value of foreign currency (e_f) and foreign inflation (I_f) becomes clear.

Using PPP to estimate exchange rate effects

The relative form of PPP can be used to estimate how an exchange rate will change in response to differential inflation rates between countries.

EXAMPLE

Assume that the exchange rate is in equilibrium initially. Then the home currency experiences a 5 per cent inflation rate, while the foreign country experiences a 3 per cent inflation rate. According to PPP, the foreign currency will adjust as follows:

$$e_f = \frac{(1 + I_h)}{(1 + I_f)} - 1$$

$$e_f = \frac{(1 + 0.05)}{(1 + 0.03)} - 1$$

$$= 0.0194 \text{ or } 1.94\%$$

Thus, according to this example, the foreign currency should appreciate by 1.94 per cent in response to the higher inflation of the home country relative to the foreign country. If this exchange rate change does occur, the effective price index of the foreign country will be as high as the index in the home country from the perspective of home country consumers. Even though inflation is lower in the foreign country, appreciation of the foreign currency pushes the foreign country's price index up from the perspective of consumers in the home country. When considering the exchange rate effect, price indexes of both countries rise by 5 per cent from the home country perspective. Thus, consumers' purchasing power is the same for foreign goods and home goods.

EXAMPLE

EXAMPLE

This example examines the situation when foreign inflation exceeds home inflation. Assume that the exchange
rate is in equilibrium initially. Then the home country
experiences a 4 per cent inflation rate, while the foreign
country experiences a 7 per cent inflation rate. According to PPP, the foreign currency will adjust as follows:

$$e_f = \frac{(1 + I_h)}{(1 + I_f)} - 1$$

$$e_f = \frac{(1 + 0.04)}{(1 + 0.07)} - 1$$

$$= -0.028 \text{ or } -2.8\%$$

Thus, according to this example, the foreign currency should depreciate by 2.8 per cent in response to the
higher inflation of the foreign country relative to the home country. Even though the inflation is lower in the
home country, the depreciation of the foreign currency places downward pressure on the foreign country's
prices from the perspective of consumers in the home country. When considering the exchange rate impact,
prices of both countries rise by 4 per cent. Thus, PPP still exists due to the adjustment in the exchange rate.

Using a simplified PPP relationship. The simplified relationship derived above is:

$$e_f = I_h - I_f$$

or

$$I_h = I_f + e_f$$

Applied to the first of the two previous examples where home inflation is 5 per cent and foreign inflation
is 3 per cent, in approximate terms, the change in the value of one unit of foreign currency (e_f) is $I_h - I_f =$
$5\% - 3\% = 2\%$ so that $I_h = 5\%$ and $I_f + e_f = 3\% + 2\% = 5\%$. Foreign goods increase in price at the
same rate as home goods.

In the second example, home inflation is 4 per cent and foreign inflation is 7 per cent, in approximate
terms, the change in the value of one unit of foreign currency (e_f) is $I_h - I_f = 4\% - 7\% = -3\%$ so that $I_h =$
4% and $I_f + e_f = 7\% - 3\% = 4\%$. Again foreign goods increase in price at the same rate as home goods.

Graphic analysis of purchasing power parity

Using PPP theory, we should be able to assess the potential impact of inflation on exchange rates.
Exhibit 8.1 is a graphic representation of PPP theory. The points on the exhibit suggest that given an
inflation differential between the home and the foreign country of X per cent, the foreign currency
should adjust by X per cent due to that inflation differential.

PPP line. The diagonal line connecting all these points together is known as the PPP line. Point A represents
our earlier example in which the US and British inflation rates were assumed to be 9 per cent and 5 per
cent, respectively, so that $I_h - I_f = -4$ per cent (taking the home country to be the UK). Recall that this led
to the anticipated depreciation in the US dollar of 4 per cent, as illustrated by point A. Point B reflects a situation in which the UK and foreign inflation rates are 5 per cent and 2 per cent, respectively, so that $I_h - I_f$
$= 3$ per cent. This leads to anticipated appreciation of the foreign currency by 3 per cent, as illustrated by
point B. If the exchange rate does respond to inflation differentials as PPP theory suggests, the actual points
should lie on or close to the PPP line.

Purchasing power disparity. Exhibit 8.2 identifies areas of purchasing power disparity. In such cases the
exchange rate does not offset the difference in inflation rates over the given period. Assume an initial

EXHIBIT 8.1   Illustration of purchasing power parity

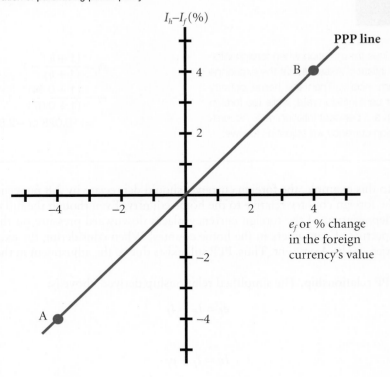

EXHIBIT 8.2   Identifying disparity in purchasing power

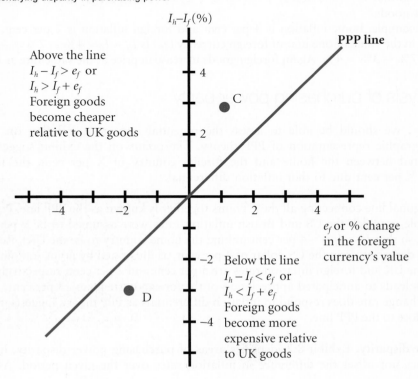

equilibrium situation, then a change in the inflation rates of the two countries. If the exchange rate does not move as PPP theory suggests, there is a disparity in the purchasing power of the two countries.

Point C in Exhibit 8.2 represents a situation where home inflation (I_h) exceeds foreign inflation (I_f) by 3 per cent. Yet, the foreign currency appreciated by only 1 per cent in response to this inflation differential. Consequently, purchasing power disparity exists. Home country consumers' purchasing power for foreign goods has become more favourable relative to their purchasing power for the home country's goods. The PPP theory suggests that such a disparity in purchasing power should exist only in the short run. Over time, as the home country consumers take advantage of the disparity by purchasing more foreign goods, upward pressure on the foreign currency's value will cause point C to move toward the PPP line. All points to the left of (or above) the PPP line represent more favourable purchasing power for foreign goods than for home goods.

Point D in Exhibit 8.2 represents a situation where home inflation is 3 per cent below foreign inflation. Yet, the foreign currency has depreciated by only 2 per cent. Again, purchasing power disparity exists. The purchasing power for foreign goods has become less favourable relative to the purchasing power for the home country's goods. The PPP theory suggests that the foreign currency in this example should have depreciated by 3 per cent to fully offset the 3 per cent inflation differential. Since the foreign currency did not weaken to this extent, the home country consumers may cease purchasing foreign goods, causing the foreign currency to weaken to the extent anticipated by PPP theory. If so, point D would move toward the PPP line. All points to the right of (or below) the PPP line represent more favourable purchasing power for home country goods than for foreign goods.

Testing the purchasing power parity theory

The PPP theory not only provides an explanation as to how relative inflation rates between two countries can influence an exchange rate, but it also provides information that can be used to forecast exchange rates.

Conceptual tests of PPP. One way to test the PPP theory is to choose two countries (say, the UK and another country) and compare the differential in their inflation rates to the percentage change in the foreign currency's value during several time periods. Using a graph similar to Exhibit 8.2, each point representing the inflation differential and exchange rate percentage change for each specific time period could be plotted. The result could then be compared to the PPP line as drawn in Exhibit 8.2. If the points deviate significantly from the PPP line, then the percentage change in the foreign currency is not being influenced by the inflation differential in the manner PPP theory suggests.

As an alternative test (known as cross-sectional analysis), several foreign countries could be compared with the home country over a given time period. Each foreign country will exhibit an inflation differential relative to the home country, which can be compared to the exchange rate change during the period of concern. Thus, a point can be plotted on a graph such as Exhibit 8.2 for each foreign country analyzed. If the points deviate significantly from the PPP line, then the exchange rates are not responding to the inflation differentials in accordance with PPP theory. One would suspect from the theory that the greater the level of trade with the country the more likely PPP will hold.

Statistical test of PPP. A somewhat simplified statistical test of PPP can be developed by applying regression analysis to historical exchange rates and inflation differentials (see Appendix B for more information on regression analysis). To illustrate, let's focus on one particular exchange rate. The quarterly percentage changes in the foreign currency value (e_f) can be regressed against the inflation differential that existed at the beginning of each quarter, as shown here:

$$e_f = a_0 + a_1 \left[\frac{(1 + I_{UK})}{(1 + I_f)} - 1 \right] + \mu$$

where a_0 is a constant, a_1 is the slope coefficient, and μ is an error term. Regression analysis could be applied to quarterly data to determine the regression coefficients. The hypothesized values of a_0 and a_1 are 0 and 1.0, respectively. These coefficients imply that for a given inflation differential, there is an equal offsetting percentage change in the exchange rate, on average. The appropriate t-test for each regression coefficient requires a comparison to the hypothesized value and division by the standard error (s.e.) of the coefficient as follows:

$$\text{Test for } a_0 = 0 \quad \text{Test for } a_1 = 1$$
$$t = \frac{a_0 - 0}{\text{s.e. of } a_0} \qquad t = \frac{a_1 - 0}{\text{s.e. of } a_1}$$

Then the t-table is used to find the critical t-value. If either t-test finds that the coefficients differ significantly from what is expected, the relationship between the inflation differential and the exchange rate differs from that stated by PPP theory. Further problems with testing for PPP are discussed below.

Results of tests of PPP. Much research has been conducted to test whether PPP exists. Studies by Mishkin, Adler and Dumas, and Abuaf and Jorion[1] found evidence of significant deviations from PPP that persisted for lengthy periods. A related study by Adler and Lehman[2] provided evidence against PPP even over the long term.

Hakkio[3], however, found that when an exchange rate deviated far from the value that would be expected according to PPP, it moved toward that value. Although the relationship between inflation differentials and exchange rates is not perfect even in the long run, it supports the use of inflation differentials to forecast long-run movements in exchange rates. A review paper is included at the end of Part II.

Tests of PPP for each currency. To further examine whether PPP is valid, Exhibit 8.3 illustrates the relationship between relative inflation rates and exchange rate movements over time taking the UK as the

EXHIBIT 8.3   Comparison of annual inflation differentials with exchange rate movements 1993 to 2009

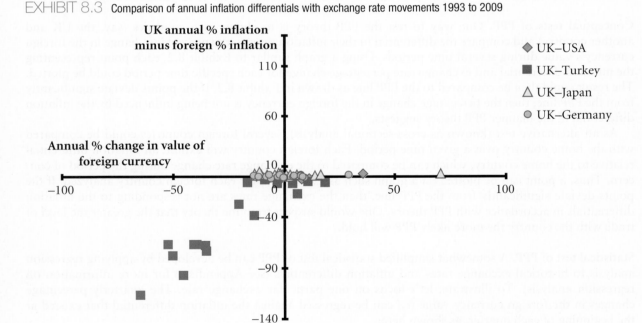

[1]Frederic S. Mishkin (1984) 'Are Real Interest Rates Equal Across Countries? An Empirical Investigation of International Parity Conditions', *Journal of Finance*, December, 1345–57; M. Adler and B. Dumas (1983) 'International Portfolio Choice and Corporate Finance: A Synthesis', *Journal of Finance*, June, 925–84; N. Abuaf and P. Jorion (1990) 'Purchasing Power in the Long Run', *Journal of Finance*, March, 157–74.

[2]M. Adler and B. Lehman (1983) 'Deviations from Purchasing Power Parity in the Long Run', *Journal of Finance*, December, 1471–87.

[3]Craig S. Hakkio (1986) 'Interest Rates and Exchange Rates – What Is the Relationship?', *Economic Review*, Federal Reserve Bank of Kansas City, November, 33–43.

home currency. The implications of PPP would suggest that observations should lie on the PPP line (Exhibit 8.2). For the relationship between most countries, and the example of the UK in Exhibit 8.3 is typical in this respect, the change in the value of the currency is far greater than inflation differentials. Furthermore, there appears to be no top right / bottom left pattern. Only in the case of Turkey where there were very large differences in inflation was there anything like conformity to the PPP line. Thus, when there is very high inflation (as in the case of Turkey) there clearly is evidence that a currency will devalue to offset the higher rate but otherwise there are generally other much stronger influences affecting the value of currencies.

USING THE WEB

Country inflation rates

Information about inflation for each country is provided by the IMF World Economic Outlook Report as an excel spreadsheet and the Trading Economics website.

Why purchasing power parity does not occur

Statistical tests are a joint test of the theory and the model. If results prove to be poor, it may be the model that is at fault rather than the theory. One obvious problem with the model is that there is an unspecified period of change. Although an arbitrage (riskless) trade process according to the theory drives the relationship, it is not clear how long it takes for an exchange rate to adjust to an imbalance of prices. Should an exchange rate in the third quarter of the year change according to inflation differences in the third, second or first quarter of the year, or some other time period? The measurement of inflation is also problematic. Should the index include goods and services not exported? Preferably not, but then the index will not be weighted according to trade levels appropriate to any single exchange rate. So there will always be an element of approximation. The theory also has important *ceteris paribus* assumptions – other factors such as interest rates are assumed to not affect the relationship. In the real world, of course, other factors are changing all the time and will affect the exchange rate. It would not be unreasonable to argue, in view of these problems, that the relationship may well be untestable in many circumstances. However, where the foreign country experiences much higher inflation than the home country it is observably the case that the foreign currency depreciates. In extreme conditions, therefore, where inflation is clearly the most important economic phenomenon, PPP will hold. In less extreme conditions, the importance of inflation differences is less clear. A more detailed consideration follows.

Confounding effects. The PPP theory presumes that exchange rate movements are driven completely by the inflation differential between two countries. Yet, recall from Chapter 4 that a change in a currency's spot rate is influenced by the following factors:

$$e = f(\Delta INF, \Delta INT, \Delta INC, \Delta GC, \Delta EXP)$$

Where:

e = percentage change in the spot rate
ΔINF = change in the differential between home inflation and the foreign country's inflation
ΔINT = change in the differential between the home interest rate and the foreign country's interest rate
ΔINC = change in the differential between the home income level and the foreign country's income level
ΔGC = change in government controls
ΔEXP = change in expectations of future exchange rates

Since the exchange rate movement is not driven solely by ΔINF, the relationship between the inflation differential and the exchange rate movement is not as simple as suggested by PPP.

EXAMPLE

Assume that Venezuela's inflation rate is 5 per cent above the Eurozone inflation rate. From this information, PPP theory would suggest that the Venezuelan bolivar should depreciate by about 5 per cent against the euro. Yet, if the government of Venezuela imposes trade barriers against Europe, Venezuela's consumers and firms will not be able to adjust their spending in reaction to the inflation differential. Therefore, the exchange rate will not adjust as suggested by PPP.

The idea behind PPP theory is that as soon as the prices become relatively higher in one country, consumers in the other country will stop buying imported goods from that country and shift to purchasing domestic goods instead. This shift influences the exchange rate. But, if substitute goods are not available domestically, consumers may not stop buying the more expensive imported goods. In such cases the low inflation country would be 'importing' inflation from the high inflation country. PPP would still hold, but the adjustment process would involve the inflation rates as well as the exchange rates.

The real exchange rate

Discussion of purchasing power parity in newspapers and the press is usually in terms of the **real exchange rate**. The real exchange rate is the exchange rate adjusted for inflationary effects in the two countries of concern. As it is not an actual exchange rate but rather an adjusted rate, it is normally expressed as an index. Rather than consider just one currency the rate is usually measured against a basket of currencies weighted according to the level of trade. Thus for the British pound, the exchange rate with the euro would be given the highest weighting in the basket, followed by the US dollar and so on. The strict term for such a rate is the 'real effective exchange rate'. But this is often abbreviated to the 'real exchange rate' or 'the real value of the currency'. It is this value that is important in foreign trade.

As is normally the case, the significance of the index number is not the actual number itself but how it has changed. Thus, if the real (effective) exchange rate of the British pound increases from 120 to 132, there has been an increase in the purchasing power of the pound compared to foreign currencies by 10 per cent $((132 - 120) / 120 = 0.10)$. That is, holders of pounds will find that they can now buy 10 per cent more foreign goods (on average). But also, foreign earners will find that they can on average buy 10 per cent fewer British goods. So an increase in the real value of a currency is associated with decreased competitiveness of the home currency. Similarly, a decrease in the real exchange rate index of a currency would be associated with an increase in competitiveness, as goods would become relatively cheaper for foreign currency holders.

There are two causes of a change in the real value of a currency, a change in the exchange rate (e) and relative inflation. The similarity with purchasing power parity (PPP) should now be apparent. If a home currency weakens (lowers in value) by 10 per cent but its inflation is 10 per cent more than foreign inflation, the real exchange rate has not changed. From the foreign perspective, the weakness of the currency is offset by the higher inflation. In other words, an unchanged real value of a currency means that PPP has been maintained.

The link between the real exchange rate and PPP can be worked out more formally in the following.

The first cause of a change in the real value of a home currency (the pound) is e_h – the percentage change in the exchange rate value of the pound or home currency. This is an indirect quote rather than the more normal direct quote. The second factor outlined above is the effect of inflation. Remember that inflation is inflation of prices *and* incomes. So higher domestic inflation means *on its own* that the real value of the home currency will increase – residents will be able to buy more goods abroad as their earnings will have increased (as well as domestic prices) but the pound will still be buying the same number of euros, dollars, pesos, etc. so with more pounds due to inflation and no change in the exchange rate the real value of the pound will increase. Relative inflation is therefore $I_h - I_f$, if home inflation is higher, the real value of the home currency will be greater. We can therefore add the two sources of a change in the real value together as follows:

$$\Delta R_h = e_h + (I_h - I_f)$$

Where:

$\Delta R_h =$ percentage change in the real value of the home currency
$e_h =$ percentage change in the exchange rate value of one unit of home currency
$I_h, I_f =$ the home inflation rate and foreign inflation rate respectively

What is the relation between this equation and PPP? We have asserted that PPP implies that there is no change in the real value of the home currency, so we can set:

$$\Delta R_h = 0$$

which implies that

$$e_h = I_f - I_h$$

using approximate processes, e_h is roughly equal to $-e_f$. As an example, a 5 per cent depreciation in the pound (as home currency) against all foreign currencies is approximately the same as a 5 per cent appreciation in foreign currencies against the pound. Therefore:

$$-e_f = I_f - I_h$$

and therefore:

$$e_f = I_h - I_f$$

which is the PPP formulation. Therefore testing for changes in the real exchange rate and testing for PPP are one and the same thing. No change in the real exchange rate implies that PPP holds. The real exchange rate addresses purchasing power and therefore has direct trade implications.

EXAMPLE

Armington Ltd is seeking to export slimming products to the USA. Over the last year the value of the pound increased from $1.50 to $1.65 or 10 per cent. Inflation in the UK for this particular year was 1 per cent and in the USA was 4 per cent. Using the formula: $\Delta R_h = e_h + (I_h - I_f)$ the real value of the pound increased by 10% + (1% − 4%) = 7% making the exports less competitive. The Finance Director explained to the Managing Director: 'The pound cost them 10 per cent more, on top of that, our prices went up by 1 per cent. However, their domestic prices went up by 4 per cent, but that still left a 7 per cent increase in our prices relative to theirs. Of course, if we priced the goods in dollars, then we would lose 7 per cent compared to selling here. The real value of the pound goes up which is fine for holiday makers and importers, but we are less competitive.'

Purchasing power parity in the long run

Purchasing power parity can be tested over the long run by assessing a 'real' exchange rate between two currencies over time. If the real exchange rate reverts to some mean level over time, this suggests that it is constant (or stationary) in the long run, and any deviations from the mean are temporary. Conversely, if the real exchange rate follows a random walk, this implies that it moves randomly without any predictable pattern (non-stationary). That is, it does not tend to revert to some mean level and therefore cannot be viewed as constant in the long run. Under these conditions, the notion of PPP is rejected because the movements in the real exchange rate appear to be more than temporary deviations from some equilibrium value.

A very large statistical literature has grown over the years attempting to measure whether the movements in the real exchange rates are stationary or non-stationary. Early studies showed a half life (the time taken for a disturbance to halve its impact) that implied a 'glacially slow' adjustment. This gave rise to what was termed the PPP puzzle, if adjustment was so slow, why did the exchange rate change so often? More recent studies have suggested that the earlier findings were in part due to a lack of sophistication in the models and that the half-life for many currencies is much shorter. This finding eases the PPP puzzle accepting that in the short run there are many temporary disturbances. It is not uncommon to hear on the news that 'the pound fell (rose) on worries (news of) …'. When the equilibrium value is not a clear figure but is at best a range of values such variation must be expected. In the medium term and longer, however, the evidence is mounting that the exchange rate does not 'wander' in the manner of a random walk but does experience a 'gravitational pull' to a range of rated when it wanders beyond. Evidence that in practice PPP is influential.

Although there is evidence to support PPP it is very far from being so strong that it can be used as a planning tool by MNCs. It should be stressed that the deviations are at times large and persistent over many years. For the purposes of planning in the shorter term, the random walk model can serve as a model of real exchange rate behaviour that may err on the side of overstating the potential variation of a currency, but will provide a simply calculated and slightly pessimistic (conservative) predictions – this is dealt with in Part III.

It seems visually clear that real exchange rates do not wander in the manner of a random walk in the medium to long term – see Exhibit 8.3A. There are nevertheless large short run changes that may have a considerable effect on MNCs.

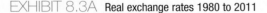

EXHIBIT 8.3A   Real exchange rates 1980 to 2011

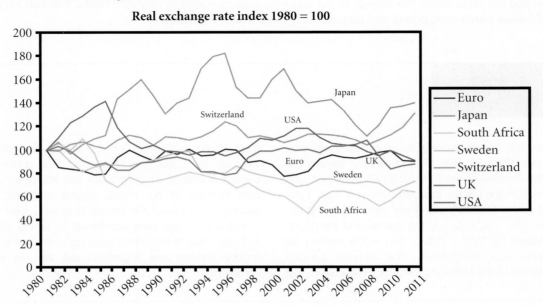

MANAGING FOR VALUE

Indirect impact of purchasing power parity on MNCs

The purchasing power parity relationship, though not exact, can explain how some events can have major effects on MNCs through their impact on exchange rates. One common example is the impact of oil prices on inflation and therefore on exchange rates. During the year 2000, the market price of oil increased substantially, placing upward pressure on inflation rates in countries that import oil. The European countries that participate in the euro import oil, and were subjected to the higher prices of oil. Since the UK produces its own oil, it was not directly affected by the higher market price of oil. Its MNCs, however, were adversely affected as a result of their business with the other European countries. Inflation increased in Europe during 2000, which placed downward pressure on the euro relative to the British pound. MNCs in the UK that export to these Eurozone countries were adversely

affected because the pound became more expensive relative to the euro, reducing the demand for British products.

MNCs based in EuroZone countries were also affected. Those that export to the UK benefited because their products became cheaper to British consumers. However, the inflation in the EuroZone countries caused the European Central Bank to raise interest rates in an attempt to reduce the inflationary pressure. Consequently, the economies of these countries weakened, and the local demand for the products produced by the MNCs was reduced.

MNCs that recognize their susceptibility to foreign inflation rates are motivated to monitor foreign inflation and limit their exposure to countries that may experience an abrupt increase in inflation.

INTERNATIONAL FISHER EFFECT (IFE)

Along with PPP theory, another major theory in international finance is the international Fisher effect (IFE) theory. It uses interest rate rather than inflation rate differentials to explain why exchange rates change over time. The theory is closely related to the PPP theory because interest rates are often highly correlated with inflation rates. High inflation is typically accompanied by high interest rates. According to Fisher the monetary or nominal rate is approximately the sum of the real and inflation rates. If it is assumed that investors in different countries require the same real (non-inflation) return for the same level of risk, then the only reason for interest rates to differ for a given risk is differences in expected inflation (see Exhibit 8.4).

Relationship with purchasing power parity

Recall that PPP theory suggests that exchange rate movements are caused by inflation rate differentials. If differences in expected inflation are the only reason for any difference in nominal interest rates then interest rates and inflation differences should be the same. The IFE theory suggests that foreign currencies with relatively high interest rates will depreciate the same way as currencies with high inflation rates (Exhibit 8.4). The following analysis will concentrate on investments that are risk-free, in the sense of guaranteeing the monetary or nominal return – the actual cash. The rates offered by a central bank would be one such example.

EXAMPLE

The nominal interest rate is 8 per cent in the UK. Investors in the UK expect a 6 per cent rate of inflation, which means that they expect to earn a real return of 2 per cent over 1 year. The nominal interest rate in Canada is 13 per cent. Given that investors in Canada also require a real return of 2 per cent, the expected inflation rate in Canada must be 11 per cent. According to PPP theory, the Canadian dollar is expected to depreciate by approximately 5 per cent against the British pound (i.e. 6% − 11% = −5%, Canadian inflation rate is 5 per cent higher). Therefore, UK investors would not benefit from investing in Canada because they would earn 13 per cent from their investment in Canada but find that when the Canadian dollar is converted back into pounds it is worth 5 per cent less, giving a net return of 13% − 5% = 8%, the same rate as investing in the UK.

The link with PPP is therefore that inflation differences provide a rationale for interest rate differences. In this sense PPP enriches the IFE theory. But it should be stated that the Fisher interpretation of interest rates is not necessary in the use of interest rates to explain exchange rate movements. If interest rates are higher in country H than in country L, and funds are not moving from L to H, there must be the market expectation that the value of country H's currency will fall relative to L for whatever reason. Expressed in this manner the relationship is termed uncovered interest rate parity. Investing abroad with no exchange rate protection (uncovered) yields a net return (interest rate plus exchange rate movement) that has parity with the domestic return.

Implications of the IFE for the foreign investment market

The IFE theory disagrees with the notion introduced in Chapter 4 that a high interest rate may entice investors from various countries to invest there and could place upward pressure on the currency. This would only happen where the high interest rate was *unexpected*. The term unexpected in this context means that the exchange rate has not adjusted to the change. Where the higher interest rate is expected there is no reason to believe that there will be upward pressure placed on the currency as the high interest rate compensates for an expected devaluation of the currency as suggested by PPP. The following example illustrates this effect.

EXAMPLE

Brazil's prevailing nominal interest rate is frequently very high because of the high inflation there. With inflation levels sometimes exceeding 100 per cent annually, people tend to spend now before prices rise. Rather than saving, they are very willing to borrow even at high interest rates to buy products now because the alternative is to defer the purchase and have to pay a much higher price later. Thus, the high nominal interest rate is attributed to the high expected inflation. Given these expectations of high inflation, even interest rates exceeding 50 per cent will not entice foreign investors because they recognize that high inflation could cause Brazil's currency (the Brazilian real) to decline by more than 50 per cent in a year, fully offsetting the high interest rate. Thus, the high interest rate in Brazil does not attract investment from foreign investors and therefore will not cause the Brazilian real to strengthen. Instead, the high interest rate in Brazil may indicate potential depreciation of the Brazilian real, which places downward pressure on the

(Continued)

currency's value. Thus, as with IFE theory, a higher interest rate compensates for an expected fall in the value of the currency.

Now consider a second currency, the Chilean peso, and assume that there is a sudden increase in interest rates to a higher level than in the developed world. Chile normally has relatively low inflation, so foreign investors are not as concerned that the Chilean peso's value will decline due to inflationary pressure. In this context, any increase in Chilean interest rates would be unexpected, investors would have no reason to expect a compensating fall in the value of the Chilean peso. Therefore, they may attempt to capitalize on the higher interest rate in Chile. The increase in investment in Chile would not amount to a deluge as there is always the risk that expectations may be wrong and that the peso does indeed devalue. More cautious money would stay at home!

Exchange rates reflect market expectations; the IFE is a theory of market expectations. It maintains that on average changes in the exchange rate offset interest rate differences. The example of Chile above does not therefore contradict the example of Brazil due to the fact that, in Chile, the changes were not anticipated by the market.

In addition, one should caution against over-simple analysis. Here it has been suggested that an unexpected increase in interest rates in Chile would attract foreign investment. But one could also argue that the market would take this unexpected piece of news as a signal that the Chilean government, in possession of more information than the market, has reason to believe that the value of the peso will fall. Existing investors, particularly the least content, may decide that this is a hint to the market and pull out. The reaction of the market is rarely simple and rarely unified. Some may increase their investment in Chile, others may withdraw their funds. The spot exchange rate will reflect the net effect of these varying reactions. Perhaps the only safe conclusion is that any test of the theory cannot be expected to yield particularly strong evidence in normal times.

The implications are similar for foreign investors who attempt to capitalize on relatively high home interest rates. Foreign investors may wish to invest in the home market to take advantage of the high interest rates, but where there is no flood of inward investment, the market must be expecting that the value of the home currency will fall. On average across different time periods, the currency value will fall if the foreign exchange market is efficient.

These possible investment opportunities are summarized in Exhibit 8.4. Note that whether investors of a given country invest their funds at home or abroad, the expected nominal or market return to the investor is the same (i.e. the extreme left and right columns in Exhibit 8.4).

EXHIBIT 8.4   **Illustration of the international Fisher effect (IFE) from various investor perspectives**

a) The elements of the nominal (newspaper) interest rates. If real rates are the same then the only reason for a difference in the nominal rate is a difference in the inflation rate.

	Country A	Country B	Difference
Time preference	1%	1%	0%
+ Risk	2%	2%	0%
= Real rate	3%	3%	0%
+ Inflation	8%	2%	6%
= Nominal rate	11%	5%	6%

(Continued)

b) IFE states that the exchange rate offsets any difference in (nominal) interest rates, so:

$$e_f = I_h - I_f \, (\text{UK as home country})$$

The returns from foreign investment are therefore the same as home investment, with some simple algebra we have from the above equation:

$$I_h = I_f + e_f$$

	UK as home country	Eurozone	USA
Real return	3%	3%	3%
+ Inflation	2%	4%	1%
= Interest rate (nominal)	5%	7%	4%
+ Implied change in the value of the foreign currency during the investment period abroad according to IFE	N/A	−2%	1%
= Net return from investment home or abroad	**5%**	**5%**	**5%**

c) As with (b) only with the Eurozone defined as the home country

	UK	Eurozone as home currency	USA
Real return	3%	3%	3%
+ Inflation	2%	4%	1%
= Interest rate (nominal)	5%	7%	4%
+ Implied change in the value of the foreign currency during the investment period abroad according to IFE	2%	N/A	3%
= Net return from investment home or abroad	**7%**	**7%**	**7%**

Notes:
1 Using the approximate method.
2 The exchange rate performs a neat 'trick' in allowing UK residents to earn 5 per cent whether they invest abroad or at home (b) and at the same time from the EuroZone perspective residents there earn 7 per cent whether investing at home or abroad (c) and by extension US residents would earn 4 per cent whether they invest at home or abroad.

Derivation of the international Fisher effect

The precise relationship between the interest rate differential of two countries and the expected exchange rate change according to the IFE can be derived more formally as follows. First, the actual return to investors who invest in money market securities (such as short-term bank deposits) in their home country is simply the interest rate offered on those securities. The actual return to investors who invest in a foreign money market security, however, depends on not only the foreign interest rate (i_f) but also the percentage change in the value of the foreign currency (e_f) denominating the security. The formula for the actual or 'effective' (exchange-rate-adjusted) return on a foreign bank deposit (or any money market security) is:

$$r_f = (1 + i_f)(1 + e_f) - 1$$

According to the IFE, the effective return on a foreign investment should, on average, be equal to the effective return on a domestic investment. Therefore, the IFE suggests that the expected return on a foreign money market investment is equal to the interest rate on a local money market investment:

$$E\left(r_f\right) = i_h$$

where r is the effective return on the foreign deposit and i_h is the interest rate on the home deposit. We can determine the degree by which the foreign currency must change in order to make investments in both countries generate similar returns. Take the expansion of r from the previous formula, and set it equal to i_h as follows:

$$r_f = i_h$$
$$(1 + i_f)(1 + e_f) - 1 = i_h$$

Now solve for e_f:

$$(1 + i_f)(1 + e_f) = (1 + i_h)$$
$$(1 + e_f) = \frac{(1 + i_h)}{(1 + i_f)}$$
$$e_f = \frac{(1 + i_h)}{(1 + i_f)} - 1$$

Thus IFE theory contends that when $i_h > i_f$ then e_f will be positive because the lower foreign interest rate reflects lower inflationary expectations in the foreign country. That is, the foreign currency will appreciate when the foreign interest rate is lower than the home interest rate. This appreciation will improve the foreign return to investors from the home country, making returns on foreign securities similar to returns on home securities.

Conversely, when $i_f > i_h$ then e_f will be negative. That is, the foreign currency will depreciate when the foreign interest rate exceeds the home interest rate. This depreciation will reduce the return on foreign securities from the perspective of investors in the home country, making returns on foreign securities no higher than returns on home securities.

Numerical example based on the derivation of IFE. Given two interest rates, the value of e_f can be determined from the formula that was just derived, and used to forecast the exchange rate.

Assume that the interest rate on a 1-year home country bank deposit is 11 per cent, and the interest rate on a 1-year foreign bank deposit is 12 per cent. For the actual returns of these two investments to be similar from the perspective of investors in the home country, the foreign currency would have to change over the investment horizon by the following percentage:

$$e_f = \frac{(1 + i_h)}{(1 + i_f)} - 1$$
$$= \frac{(1 + 0.11)}{(1 + 0.12)} - 1$$
$$= -0.0089 \text{ or } -0.89\%$$

The implications are that the foreign currency denominating the foreign deposit would need to depreciate by 0.89 per cent to make the actual return on the foreign deposit equal to 11 per cent from the perspective of investors in the home country. This would make the return on the foreign investment equal to the return on a domestic investment.

Simplified relationship. A more simplified but less precise relationship specified by the IFE is:

$$e_f \approx i_h - i_f$$

That is, the percentage change in the exchange rate over the investment horizon will equal the interest rate differential between two countries. This approximation provides reasonable estimates only when the interest rate differential is small. The similarity with the PPP approximate formula is apparent, interest rates are substituted for inflation rates.

Graphic analysis of the international Fisher effect

Exhibit 8.5 displays the set of points that conform to the argument behind IFE theory. For example, point E reflects a situation where the foreign interest rate exceeds the home interest rate by three percentage points. Yet, the foreign currency has depreciated by 3 per cent to offset its interest rate advantage. Thus, an investor setting up a deposit in the foreign country achieves a return similar to what is possible domestically. Point F represents a home interest rate 2 per cent above the foreign interest rate. If investors from the home country establish a foreign deposit, they are at a disadvantage regarding the foreign interest rate. However, IFE theory suggests that the currency should appreciate by 2 per cent to offset the interest rate disadvantage.

Point F in Exhibit 8.5 also illustrates the IFE from a foreign investor's perspective. The home interest rate will appear attractive to the foreign investor. However, IFE theory suggests that the foreign currency will appreciate by 2 per cent, which, from the foreign investor's perspective, implies that the home country's currency denominating the investment instruments will depreciate to offset the interest rate advantage.

EXHIBIT 8.5   Illustration of IFE line (when exchange rate changes perfectly offset interest rate differentials)

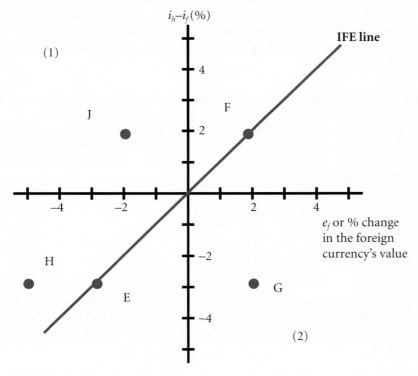

Notes:
- Above the line $(i_h - i_f) > e_f$ or $i_h > (e_f + i_f)$; in words, the returns from investing at home are greater than investing abroad.
- Below the line $(i_h - i_f) < e_f$ or $i_h < (e_f + i_f)$; in words, the returns from at home are less than investing abroad.

Points on the IFE line. All the points along the so-called **IFE line** in Exhibit 8.5 reflect exchange rate adjustments to offset the differential in interest rates. This means investors will end up achieving the same yield (adjusted for exchange rate fluctuations) whether they invest at home or in a foreign country.

To be precise, IFE theory does not suggest that this relationship will exist continuously over each time period. The point of IFE theory is that if an MNC periodically makes foreign investments to take advantage of higher foreign interest rates, it will achieve a yield that is sometimes above and sometimes below the domestic yield. Periodic investments by an MNC corporation in an attempt to capitalize on the higher interest rates will, on average, achieve a yield similar to that by a corporation simply making domestic deposits periodically.

Points below the IFE line. Points below the IFE line generally reflect the higher returns from investing in foreign deposits. For example, point G in Exhibit 8.5 indicates that the foreign interest rate exceeds the home interest rate by 3 per cent. In addition, the foreign currency has appreciated by 2 per cent. The combination of the higher foreign interest rate plus the appreciation of the foreign currency will cause the foreign yield to be higher than what is possible domestically. If actual data were compiled and plotted, and the vast majority of points were below the IFE line, this would suggest that investors of the home country could consistently increase their investment returns by establishing foreign bank deposits. Such results would refute the IFE theory.

Points above the IFE line. Points above the IFE line generally reflect returns from foreign deposits that are lower than the returns possible domestically. For example, point H reflects a foreign interest rate that is 3 per cent above the home interest rate. Yet, point H also indicates that the exchange rate of the foreign currency has depreciated by 5 per cent, more than offsetting its interest rate advantage.

As another example, point J represents a situation in which an investor of the home country is hampered in two ways by investing in a foreign deposit. First, the foreign interest rate is lower than the home interest rate. Second, the foreign currency depreciates during the time the foreign deposit is held. If actual data were compiled and plotted, and the vast majority of points were above the IFE line, this would suggest that investors of the home country would receive consistently lower returns from foreign investments as opposed to investments in the home country. Such results would refute the IFE theory.

Tests of the international Fisher effect

If the actual points (one for each period) of interest rates and exchange rate changes were plotted over time on a graph such as Exhibit 8.5, we could determine whether the points are systematically below the IFE line (suggesting higher returns from foreign investing), above the line (suggesting lower returns from foreign investing), or evenly scattered on both sides (suggesting a balance of higher returns from foreign investing in some periods and lower foreign returns in other periods).

Exhibit 8.6 is an example of a set of points that tend to support the IFE theory. It implies that returns from short-term foreign investments are, on average, about equal to the returns that are possible domestically. Notice that each individual point reflects a change in the exchange rate that does not exactly offset the interest rate differential. In some cases, the exchange rate change does not fully offset the interest rate differential. In other cases, the exchange rate change more than offsets the interest rate differential. Overall, the results balance out such that the interest rate differentials are, on average, offset by changes in the exchange rates. Thus, foreign investments have generated yields that are, on average, equal to those of domestic investments.

Risk premiums. If foreign yields are expected to be about equal to domestic yields, an MNC would probably prefer the domestic investments. The firm would know the yield on domestic short-term securities (such as bank deposits) in advance, whereas the yield to be attained from foreign short-term securities would be uncertain because the firm would not know what spot exchange rate would exist at the securities' maturity. Investors generally prefer an investment whose return is known over an investment whose return is uncertain, assuming that all other features of the investments are similar. The approximate

EXHIBIT 8.6 Illustration of IFE concept (when exchange rate changes offset interest rate differentials on average)

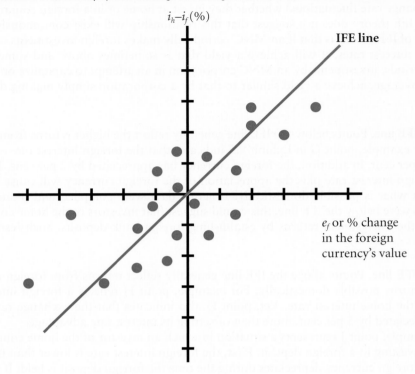

equation can be developed to include a risk premium (by tradition, the term premium is used to include a negative premium or discount):

$$e_f + \rho_f = i_h - i_f$$

where ρ_f is the risk premium for the period of investment being considered. Risk premiums in international finance, and one might add in finance generally, are not well understood. Theoretical models including premiums are not well supported in practice.

EXAMPLE

Mr Trader observes that for most months Australian interest rates are higher than Japanese interest rates by about 3 per cent i.e. $(i_h - i_f) \approx 3$ per cent. IFE implies that the Australian dollar would fall by 3 per cent offsetting any gain; but the value of the Australian dollar sometimes does not fall at all against the yen, sometimes it even increases. So he reasons: 'If I borrow in yen and invest Australian dollars I will make about a 3 per cent profit a year on average. Some months the value of the Australian dollar may fall by

say 2 per cent (annualized) in which case my profit will be reduced to 1 per cent, but I should make a profit most months.' This strategy is all very well except that there is a risk that the Australian dollar like any currency can fall dramatically in value. In May 2011 the Australian dollar fell nearly 20 per cent over the following 4 months. A higher inflation rate and a risk of a fall in the currency explains the difference and a return can easily look like a profit until such very large losses are made.

Results from testing the IFE. Whether the IFE holds in reality depends on the particular time period examined. Although the IFE theory may hold during some time frames, there is evidence that it does not consistently hold. A study by Thomas[4] tested the IFE theory by examining the results of: (1) purchasing currency futures contracts of currencies with high interest rates that contained discounts (relative to the spot rates) and (2) selling futures on currencies with low interest rates that contained premiums. If the high-interest-rate currencies depreciated and the low-interest-rate currencies appreciated to the extent suggested by the IFE theory, this strategy would not generate significant profits. However, 123 (57 per cent) of the 216 transactions created by this strategy were profitable. In addition, the average gain was much higher than the average loss. This study indicates that the IFE relationship in practice is more complex than the simple form would suggest. For example, a risk premium may indicate why high interest rate currencies are apparently a better investment on average. On average, insurance is not worthwhile, but it is still purchased to guard against a sudden fall. The same argument may apply to futures contracts, though the exact relationship has yet to be clearly established.

Statistical test of the IFE. A somewhat simplified statistical test of the IFE can be developed by applying regression analysis to historical exchange rates and the nominal interest rate differential:

$$e_f = a_0 + a_1 \left(\frac{(1 + i_h)}{(1 + i_f)} - 1 \right) + \mu$$

where a_0 is a constant, a_1 is the slope coefficient, and μ is an error term. Regression analysis would determine the regression coefficients. The hypothesized values of a_0 and a_1 are 0 and 1.0, respectively.

The appropriate t-test for each regression coefficient requires a comparison to the hypothesized value and then division by the standard error (s.e.) of the coefficients, as follows:

$$\text{Test for } a_0 = 0 \quad \text{Test for } a_1 = 1$$
$$t = \frac{a_0 - 0}{\text{s.e. of } a_0} \qquad t = \frac{a_1 - 0}{\text{s.e. of } a_1}$$

The t-table is then used to find the critical t-value. If either t-test finds that the coefficients differ significantly from what was hypothesized, the IFE is not supported by the data.

Why the international Fisher effect does not occur

The IFE model cannot be rejected, only not supported by tests. Poor performance may be due to an oversimplistic model or measurement problems.

Exchange rates can be affected by factors other than interest rates. The relation between interest rates and inflation rates suggested by Fisher may not always hold. Assume a nominal interest rate in a foreign country that is 3 per cent above the US rate because expected inflation in that country is 3 per cent above expected US inflation. Even if these nominal rates properly reflect inflationary expectations, the exchange rate of the foreign currency will react to other factors in addition to the inflation differential. If these other factors put upward pressure on the foreign currency's value, they will offset the downward pressure from the inflation differential. Consequently, foreign investments will achieve higher returns for the US investors than domestic investments.

[4]Lee R. Thomas (1985) 'A Winning Strategy for Currency – Futures Speculation', *Journal of Portfolio Management*, Fall, 65–9.

COMPARISON OF THE IRP, PPP AND IFE THEORIES

At this point, it is helpful to compare three related theories of international finance: (1) interest rate parity (IRP) or covered interest rate arbitrage, discussed in Chapter 7, (2) purchasing power parity (PPP) and (3) the international Fisher effect (IFE), sometimes referred to as uncovered interest rate arbitrage, uncovered because the investor takes the risk that the future spot rate (value) of the currency of an investment may fall. Exhibit 8.7 summarizes the main themes of each theory. Note that although all three theories relate to the determination of exchange rates, they have different implications. The IRP theory focuses on why the forward rate differs from the spot rate and on the degree of difference that should exist. It relates to a specific point in time. In contrast, the PPP theory and IFE theory focus on how a currency's spot rate will change over time. Whereas PPP theory suggests that the spot rate will change in accordance with inflation differentials, IFE theory suggests that it will change in accordance with interest rate differentials.

Nevertheless, PPP is related to IFE because expected inflation differentials influence the nominal interest rate differentials between two countries.

Some generalizations about national economies can be made from these theories. High inflation countries tend to have high nominal interest rates (due to the **Fisher effect**). In other words, investors want to be compensated for the high level of inflation. The currencies of high inflation countries tend to weaken over time (because of the PPP and IFE), and the forward rates of their currencies normally exhibit large discounts (due to IRP). There is no doubt that inflation and interest rates play a part in affecting the value of a currency when these values are large.

Where the interest rate and inflation rate differential are smaller the relationships are far less clear. It seems unlikely that the fundamentals of interest rates and inflation rates are no longer relevant, but other factors become relatively more significant. Models that predict future spot rates effectively at lower levels of interest and inflation rates have yet to be developed. The general problems of prediction are examined in the following section. The contribution of the basic theory, as outlined in this chapter, is to provide a strong logical argument for exchange rate behaviour that can serve as the starting point for prediction. In the appendix to this chapter we move on a little more and consider some of the more recent attempts to understand exchange rate behaviour.

EXHIBIT 8.7 Comparison of the IRP, PPP and IFE theories

Theory	Key variables of theory		Summary of theory
Interest rate parity (IRP) or covered interest rate arbitrage	Forward rate premium (or discount)	Interest rate differential	The forward rate of one currency with respect to another will contain a premium (or discount) that is determined by the differential in interest rates between the two countries. As a result, covered interest arbitrage will provide a return that is no higher than a domestic return.
Purchasing power parity (PPP)	Percentage change in spot exchange rate	Inflation rate differential	The spot rate of one currency with respect to another will change in reaction to the differential in inflation rates between the two countries. Consequently, the purchasing power for consumers when purchasing goods in their own country will be similar to their purchasing power when importing goods from the foreign country.
International Fisher effect	Percentage change in spot exchange rate	Interest rate differential	The spot rate of one currency with respect to another will change in accordance with the differential in interest rates between the two countries. Consequently, the return on uncovered foreign money market securities will, on average, be no higher than the return on domestic money market securities from the perspective of investors in the home country.

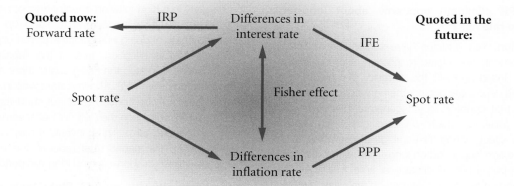

SUMMARY

- Purchasing power parity (PPP) theory specifies a precise relationship between relative inflation rates of two countries and their exchange rate. In inexact terms, PPP theory suggests that the equilibrium exchange rate will adjust by the same magnitude as the differential in inflation rates between two countries. Though PPP continues to be a valuable concept, there is evidence of sizable deviations from the theory in the real world.

- The international Fisher effect (IFE) specifies a precise relationship between relative interest rates of two countries and their exchange rates. It suggests that an investor who periodically invests in foreign interest-bearing securities will, on average, achieve a return similar to what is possible domestically. This implies that the exchange rate of the country with high interest rates will depreciate to offset the interest rate advantage achieved by foreign investments. However, there is evidence that during some periods the IFE does not hold. Thus, investment in foreign short-term securities may achieve a higher return than what is possible domestically. If a firm attempts to achieve this higher return, however, it does incur the risk that

the currency of the foreign security might depreciate against the investor's home currency during the investment period. In this case, the foreign security could generate a lower return than a domestic security, even though it exhibits a higher interest rate.

- The PPP theory focuses on the relationship between the inflation rate differential and future exchange rate movements. The IFE focuses on the interest rate differential and future exchange rate movements. The theory of interest rate parity (IRP) focuses on the relationship between the interest rate differential and the forward rate premium (or discount) at a given point in time.

- If IRP exists, it is not possible to benefit from covered interest arbitrage. Investors can still attempt to benefit from high foreign interest rates if they remain uncovered (do not sell the currency forward). But IFE suggests that this strategy will not generate higher returns than what are possible domestically because the exchange rate is expected to decline, on average, by the amount of the interest rate differential.

CRITICAL DEBATE

Does PPP eliminate concerns about long-term exchange rate risk?

Proposition. Yes. Studies have shown that exchange rate movements are related to inflation differentials in the long run. Based on PPP, the currency of a high-inflation country will depreciate against the home currency. A subsidiary in that country should generate inflated revenue from the inflation, which will help offset the adverse exchange effects when its earnings are remitted to the parent. If a firm is focused on long-term performance, the deviations from PPP will offset over time. In some years, the exchange rate effects may exceed the inflation effects, and in other years the inflation effects will exceed the exchange rate effects.

Opposing view. No. Even if the relationship between inflation and exchange rate effects is consistent, this does not guarantee that the effects on the firm will be offsetting.

A subsidiary in a high-inflation country will not necessarily be able to adjust its price level to keep up with the increased costs of doing business there. The effects vary with each MNC's situation. Even if the subsidiary can raise its prices to match the rising costs, there are short-term deviations from PPP. The investors who invest in an MNC's stock may be concerned about short-term deviations from PPP, because they will not necessarily hold the stock for the long term. Thus, investors may prefer that firms manage in a manner that reduces the volatility in their performance in short-run and long-run periods.

With whom do you agree? State your reasons. Examine the exchange rate policies of the major multinationals by referring to their annual reports. The Forbes listing of major multinationals on the web is a good starting point. In particular, consult the reports of Renault (France) and Philips (Holland).

SELF TEST

Answers are provided in Appendix A at the back of the text.

1 A UK importer of Japanese computer components pays for the components in yen. The importer is not concerned about a possible increase in Japanese prices (charged in yen) because of the likely offsetting effect caused by purchasing power parity (PPP). Explain what this means.

2 Use what you know about tests of PPP to answer this question. Using the information in the first question, explain why the UK importer of Japanese computer components should be concerned about its future payments.

3 Use PPP to explain how the values of the currencies of Eastern European countries might change if those countries experience high inflation, while the UK and the Eurozone experience low inflation.

4 Assume that the Canadian dollar's spot rate is £0.57 and that the Canadian and UK inflation rates are similar. Then assume that Canada experiences 4 per cent inflation, while the UK experiences 3 per cent inflation. According to PPP, what will be the new value of the Canadian dollar after it adjusts to the inflationary changes? (You may use the approximate formula to answer this question.)

5 Assume that the Australian dollar's spot rate is £0.30 and that the Australian and UK 1-year interest rates are initially 6 per cent. Then assume that the Australian 1-year interest rate increases by 5 percentage points, while the UK 1-year interest rate remains unchanged. Using this information and the international Fisher effect (IFE) theory, forecast the spot rate for 1 year ahead.

6 In the previous question, the Australian interest rates increased from 6 per cent to 11 per cent. According to the IFE, what is the underlying factor that would cause such a change? Give an explanation based on the IFE of the forces that would cause a change in the Australian dollar. If UK investors believe in the IFE, will they attempt to capitalize on the higher Australian interest rates? Explain.

QUESTIONS AND APPLICATIONS

1 **PPP.** Explain the theory of purchasing power parity (PPP). Based on this theory, what is a general forecast of the values of currencies in countries with high inflation?

2 Rationale of PPP. Explain the rationale of the PPP theory.

3 Testing PPP. Explain how you could determine whether PPP exists. Describe a limitation in testing whether PPP holds.

4 Testing PPP. Inflation differentials between the USA and other industrialized countries have typically been a few percentage points in any given year. Yet, in many years annual exchange rates between the corresponding currencies have changed by 10 per cent or more. What does this information suggest about PPP?

5 Limitations of PPP. Explain why PPP does not hold.

6 Implications of IFE. Explain the international Fisher effect (IFE). What is the rationale for the existence of the IFE? What are the implications of the IFE for firms with excess cash that consistently invest in foreign Treasury bills? Explain why the IFE may not hold.

7 Implications of IFE. Assume UK interest rates are generally above foreign interest rates. What does this suggest about the future strength or weakness of the British pound based on the IFE? Should UK investors invest in foreign securities if they believe in the IFE? Should foreign investors invest in UK securities if they believe in the IFE?

8 Comparing parity theories. Compare and contrast interest rate parity (discussed in the previous chapter), purchasing power parity (PPP), and the international Fisher effect (IFE).

9 Real interest rate. One assumption made in developing the IFE is that all investors in all countries have the same real interest rate. What does this mean?

10 Interpreting inflationary expectations. If investors in the UK and Canada require the same real interest rate, and the nominal rate of interest is 2 per cent higher in Canada, what does this imply about expectations of UK inflation and Canadian inflation? What do these inflationary expectations suggest about future exchange rates?

11 PPP applied to the euro. Assume that several European countries that use the euro as their currency experience higher inflation than the USA, while two other European countries that use the euro as their currency experience lower inflation than the USA. According to PPP, how will the euro's value against the dollar be affected?

12 Source of weak currencies. Currencies of some Latin American countries, such as Brazil and Venezuela, frequently weaken against most other currencies. What concept in this chapter explains this occurrence? Why don't all US-based MNCs use forward contracts to hedge their future remittances of funds from Latin American countries to the USA if they expect depreciation of the currencies against the dollar?

13 PPP. Japan has typically had lower inflation than the USA. How would one expect this to affect the Japanese yen's value? Why does this expected relationship not always occur?

14 IFE. Assume that the nominal interest rate in Mexico is 48 per cent and the interest rate in the USA is 8 per cent for 1-year securities that are free from default risk. What does the IFE suggest about the differential in expected inflation in these two countries? Using this information and the PPP theory, describe the expected nominal return to US investors who invest in Mexico.

15 IFE. Shouldn't the IFE discourage investors from attempting to capitalize on higher foreign interest rates? Why do some investors continue to invest overseas, even when they have no other transactions overseas?

16 Changes in inflation. Assume that the inflation rate in Brazil is expected to increase substantially. How will this affect Brazil's nominal interest rates and the value of its currency (called the real)? If the IFE holds, how will the nominal return to UK investors who invest in Brazil be affected by the higher inflation in Brazil? Explain.

17 Comparing PPP and IFE. How is it possible for PPP to hold if the IFE does not?

18 Estimating depreciation due to PPP. Assume that the spot exchange rate of the British pound is $1.73. How will this spot rate adjust according to PPP if the UK experiences an inflation rate of 7 per cent while the USA experiences an inflation rate of 2 per cent?

19 Forecasting the future spot rate based on IFE. Assume that the spot exchange rate of the Singapore dollar is £0.35. The 1-year interest rate is 11 per cent in the UK and 7 per cent in Singapore. What will the spot rate be in 1 year according to the IFE? (You may use the approximate formula to answer this question.)

20 Deriving forecasts of the future spot rate. As of today, assume the following information is available:

	UK	Mexico
Real rate of interest required by investors	2%	2%
Nominal interest rate	11%	15%
Spot rate	–	£0.05
1-year forward rate	–	£0.049

   a Use the forward rate to forecast the percentage change in the Mexican peso over the next year.

   b Use the differential in expected inflation to forecast the percentage change in the Mexican peso over the next year.

   c Use the spot rate to forecast the percentage change in the Mexican peso over the next year.

21 Inflation and interest rate effects. The opening of Russia's market has resulted in a highly volatile Russian currency (the rouble). Russia's inflation has commonly exceeded 20 per cent per month. Russian interest rates commonly exceed 150 per cent, but this is sometimes less than the annual inflation rate in Russia.

   a Explain why the high Russian inflation has put severe pressure on the value of the Russian rouble.

b Does the effect of Russian inflation on the decline in the rouble's value support the PPP theory? How might the relationship be distorted by political conditions in Russia?

c Does it appear that the prices of Russian goods will be equal to the prices of UK goods from the perspective of Russian consumers (after considering exchange rates)? Explain.

d Will the effects of the high Russian inflation and the decline in the rouble offset each other for UK importers? That is, how will UK importers of Russian goods be affected by the conditions?

22 IFE application to the Asian crisis. Before the Asian crisis, many investors attempted to capitalize on the high interest rates prevailing in the South East Asian countries although the level of interest rates primarily reflected expectations of inflation. Explain why investors behaved in this manner. Why does the IFE suggest that the South East Asian countries would not have attracted foreign investment before the Asian crisis despite the high interest rates prevailing in those countries?

23 IFE applied to the euro. Given the recent conversion of several European currencies to the euro, explain what would cause the euro's value to change against the dollar according to the IFE.

ADVANCED QUESTIONS

24 IFE. Beth Miller does not believe that the international Fisher effect (IFE) holds. Current 1-year interest rates in Europe are 5 per cent, while 1-year interest rates in the USA are 3 per cent. Beth converts $100 000 to euros and invests them in Germany. One year later, she converts the euros back to dollars. The current spot rate of the euro is $1.10.

   a Acording to the IFE, what should the spot rate of the euro in 1 year be?

   b If the spot rate of the euro in 1 year is $1.00, what is Beth's percentage return from her strategy?

   c If the spot rate of the euro in 1 year is $1.08, what is Beth's percentage return from her strategy?

   d What must the spot rate of the euro be in 1 year for Beth's strategy to be successful?

25 Integrating IRP and IFE. Assume the following information is available for the USA and Europe:

	USA	Europe
Nominal interest rate	4%	6%
Expected inflation	2%	5%
Spot rate	–	$1.13
1-year forward rate	–	$1.10

   a Does IRP hold?

   b According to PPP, what is the expected spot rate of the euro in 1 year?

   c According to the IFE, what is the expected spot rate of the euro in 1 year?

   d Reconcile your answers to parts (a) and (c).

26 IRP. The 1-year risk-free interest rate in Mexico is 10 per cent. The 1-year risk-free rate in the UK is 2 per cent. Assume that interest rate parity exists. The spot rate of the Mexican peso is £0.14.

a What is the forward rate premium?

b What is the 1-year forward rate of the peso?

c Based on the international Fisher effect, what is the expected change in the spot rate over the next year?

d If the spot rate changes as expected according to the IFE, what will be the spot rate in 1 year?

e Compare your answers to (b) and (d) and explain the relationship.

27 Testing the PPP. How could you use regression analysis to determine whether the relationship specified by PPP exists on average? Specify the model, and describe how you would assess the regression results to determine if there is a *significant* difference from the relationship suggested by PPP.

28 Testing the IFE. Describe a statistical test for the IFE.

29 Impact of barriers on PPP and IFE. Would PPP be more likely to hold between the UK and Hungary if trade barriers were completely removed and if Hungary's currency were allowed to float without any government intervention? Would the IFE be more likely to hold between the UK and Hungary if trade barriers were completely removed and if Hungary's currency were allowed to float without any government intervention? Explain.

30 Interactive effects of PPP. Assume that the inflation rates of the countries that use the euro are very low, while other European countries that have their own currencies experience high inflation. Explain how and why the euro's value could be expected to change against these currencies according to the PPP theory.

31 Applying IRP and IFE. Assume that Mexico has a 1-year interest rate that is higher than the UK 1-year interest rate. Assume that you believe in the international Fisher effect (IFE) and interest rate parity. Assume zero transactions costs.

Ed is based in the UK and attempts to speculate by purchasing Mexican pesos today, investing the pesos in a risk-free asset for a year, and then converting the pesos to pounds at the end of 1 year. Ed did not cover his position in the forward market.

Maria is based in Mexico and attempts covered interest arbitrage by purchasing pounds today and

simultaneously selling pounds 1-year forward, investing the pounds in a risk-free asset for a year, and then converting the pounds back to pesos at the end of 1 year.

Do you think the rate of return on Ed's investment will be higher than, lower than, or the same as the rate of return on Maria's investment? Explain.

32 Arbitrage and PPP. Assume that locational arbitrage ensures that spot exchange rates are properly aligned. Also assume that you believe in purchasing power parity. The spot rate of the British pound is $1.80. The spot rate of the Swiss franc is £0.30. You expect that the 1-year inflation rate will be 7 per cent in the UK, 5 per cent in Switzerland and 1 per cent in the USA. The 1-year interest rate is 6 per cent in the UK, 2 per cent in Switzerland and 4 per cent in the USA. What is your expected spot rate of the Swiss franc in 1 year with respect to the US dollar? Show your work.

33 IRP versus IFE. You believe that interest rate parity and the international Fisher effect hold. Assume that the UK interest rate is presently much higher than the New Zealand interest rate. You have receivables of 1 million New Zealand dollars that you will receive in 1 year. You could hedge the receivables with the 1-year forward contract. Or, you could decide to not hedge. Is your expected British pound amount of the receivables in 1 year from hedging higher, lower, or the same as your expected British pound amount of the receivables without hedging? Explain.

34 IRP, PPP, and speculating in currency derivatives. The UK 3-month interest rate (un-annualized) is 1 per cent. The Canadian 3-month interest rate (un-annualized) is 4 per cent. Interest rate parity exists. The expected inflation over this period is 5 per cent in the UK and 2 per cent in Canada. A call option with a 3-month expiration date on Canadian dollars is available for a premium of £0.02 and a strike price of £0.44. The spot rate of the Canadian dollar is £0.45. Assume that you believe in purchasing power parity.

a Determine the pound amount of your profit or loss from buying a call option contract specifying C$100 000.

b Determine the pound amount of your profit or loss from buying a futures contract specifying C$100 000.

PROJECT WORKSHOP

35 Using a graph similar to Exhibit 8.2, represent the inflation differential and exchange rate percentage change for at least ten time periods between two chosen currencies. Plot the results and compare with the PPP line. Where there are deviations, consult e-newspaper sources (available at your institution) to try to determine causes of misalignment. If your institution does not provide these resources, search the Internet for causes.

36 Currency interest rates. The 'Market' section of the Bloomberg website provides interest rate quotations for numerous currencies. Its address is http://www.bloomberg.com.

   a Go to the 'Markets' section and then to 'International Yield Curves'. Determine the prevailing 1-year interest rate of the Australian dollar, the Japanese yen and the British pound. Assuming a 2 per cent real rate of interest for savers in any country, determine the expected rate of inflation over the next year in each of these countries that is implied by the nominal interest rate (according to the Fisher effect).

   b What is the approximate expected percentage change in the value of each of these currencies against the dollar over the next year, when applying PPP to the inflation level of each of these currencies versus the dollar?

37 Using your institution's databases, test one of the following equations:

$$e_f = a_0 + a_1 (i_h - i_f) + \varepsilon$$

or

$$e_f = a_0 + a_1 (I_h - I_f) + \varepsilon$$

where:

e	= percentage change in the value of foreign currency
i	= interest rate
I	= inflation rate
f	= foreign country
h	= home country
a_0, a_1	= parameters
ε	= residual term

choose:

- Two countries (one exchange rate)
- A time period, e.g. 1990 to 2010
- A frequency (annually, quarterly, monthly, daily).

Review your results, then perform a secondary test in response to your findings. The secondary test may, for example:

- Alter the lag structure of the explanatory variables, e.g. quarter 4 exchange rate change regressed against quarter 1 inflation differential
- Alter the time periods
- Alter the frequency.

Compare your secondary test with the first test to see if there has been an improvement.

38 From a reading of Appendix 8, carry out a variance ratio test measuring Z(k) for a particular currency chosen from your institution's database or from Oanda.com. Choose at least 30 observations for the longer time period (e.g. 30 months or 30 quarters).

   a Carry out the test for real exchange rates and nominal exchange rates.

   b Explain the meaning of your results.

   As a practical note if you need to convert daily data into monthly quarterly data or even simply take every fifth or tenth, etc. quotet, this can be done using a basic EXCEL package. The following is a guide suitable only for those familiar with EXCEL. Typically the information is in two columns 'mm/dd/yy' and the 'exchange rate' in columns A and B respectively. To select the first exchange rate in every month use the 'text to columns' feature under the 'data' heading and isolate the month, day and year into separate columns. Then in blank columns copy the date and exchange rate if the exchange rate is the first of the month as follows. The formula: '=IF(A2 = A1,'''',B2' (or whatever you want to copy) will copy the data into the blank cell *if* it is the first quote of the month *otherwise* the cell will be left blank. Create the first line and Block Copy down the column. Then Block Copy all these cells and paste them as a block into their existing location using the paste special formula checking the 'values' radio button, this gets rid of the IF formulas. Block the whole area and sort on the year in ascending order. Exchange rates are now in monthly intervals!

   To get every fifth or tenth quote, etc. replace the months column as follows: put a 1 in the top cell, say A1, below that in A2 enter '= IF(A1 = 5, 1,A1 + 1)' and block copy down the column. Then proceed as above from the amended formula '= IF(A2 = 5,'''', B2' (or whatever you want to copy)!

DISCUSSION IN THE BOARDROOM

This exercise can be found on our dedicated Course-Mate platform for students.

RUNNING YOUR OWN MNC

This exercise can be found on our dedicated Course-Mate platform for students.

Essays/discussion and articles can be found at the end of Part II.

BLADES PLC CASE STUDY

Assessment of purchasing power parity

Blades, the UK-based roller blades manufacturer, is currently both exporting to and importing from Thailand. The company has chosen Thailand as an export target for its primary product, 'Speedos', because of Thailand's growth prospects and the lack of competition from both Thai and UK roller blade manufacturers in Thailand. Under an existing arrangement, Blades sells 180 000 pairs of Speedos annually to Entertainment Products, Inc., a Thai retailer. The arrangement involves a fixed, baht-denominated price and will last for 3 years. Blades generates approximately 10 per cent of its revenue in Thailand.

Blades has also decided to import certain rubber and plastic components needed to manufacture Speedos because of cost and quality considerations. Specifically, the weak economic conditions in Thailand resulting from recent events have allowed Blades to import components from the country at a relatively low cost. However, Blades did not enter into a long-term arrangement to import these components and pays market prices (in baht) prevailing in Thailand at the time of purchase. Currently, Blades incurs about 4 per cent of its cost of goods sold in Thailand.

Although Blades has no immediate plans for expansion in Thailand, it may establish a subsidiary there in the future. Moreover, even if Blades does not establish a subsidiary in Thailand, it will continue exporting to and importing from the country for several years. Due to these considerations, Blades' management is very concerned about recent events in Thailand and neighbouring countries, as they may affect both Blades' current performance and its future plans.

Ben Holt, Blades' finance director, is particularly concerned about the level of inflation in Thailand. Blades' export arrangement with Entertainment Products, while allowing for a minimum level of revenue to be generated in Thailand in a given year, prevents Blades from adjusting prices according to the level of inflation in Thailand. In retrospect, Holt is wondering whether Blades should have entered into the export arrangement at all. Because Thailand's economy was growing very fast when Blades agreed to the arrangement, strong consumer spending there resulted in a high level of inflation and high interest rates. Naturally,

Blades would have preferred an agreement whereby the price per pair of Speedos would be adjusted for the Thai level of inflation. However, to take advantage of the growth opportunities in Thailand, Blades accepted the arrangement when Entertainment Products insisted on a fixed price level. Currently, however, the baht is freely floating, and Holt is wondering how a relatively high level of Thai inflation may affect the baht-pound exchange rate and, consequently, Blades' revenue generated in Thailand.

Ben Holt is also concerned about Blades' cost of goods sold incurred in Thailand. Since no fixed-price arrangement exists and the components are invoiced in Thai baht, Blades has been subject to increases in the prices of rubber and plastic. Holt is wondering how a potentially high level of inflation will impact the baht-pound exchange rate and the cost of goods sold incurred in Thailand now that the baht is freely floating.

When Holt started thinking about future economic conditions in Thailand and the resulting impact on Blades, he found that he needed your help. In particular, Holt is vaguely familiar with the concept of purchasing power parity (PPP) and is wondering about this theory's implications, if any, for Blades. Furthermore, Holt also remembers that relatively high interest rates in Thailand will attract capital flows and put upward pressure on the baht.

Because of these concerns, and to gain some insight into the impact of inflation on Blades, Ben Holt has asked you to provide him with answers to the following questions

1 What is the relationship between the exchange rates and relative inflation levels of the two countries? How will this relationship affect Blades' Thai revenue and costs given that the baht is freely floating? What is the net effect of this relationship on Blades?

2 What are some of the factors that prevent PPP from occurring in the short run? Would you expect PPP to hold better if countries negotiate trade arrangements under which they commit themselves to the purchase or sale of a fixed

number of goods over a specified time period? Why or why not?

3 How do you reconcile the high level of interest rates in Thailand with the expected change of the baht-pound exchange rate according to PPP?

4 Given Blades' future plans in Thailand, should the company be concerned with PPP? Why or why not?

5 PPP may hold better for some countries than for others. Given that the Thai baht has been freely floating for only a short period of time, how do you think Blades can gain insight into whether PPP will hold for Thailand?

SMALL BUSINESS DILEMMA

Assessment of the IFE by the Sports Exports Company

Every month, the Sports Exports Company receives a payment denominated in British pounds for the basketballs it exports to the UK. Jim Logan, owner of the Sports Exports Company, decides each month whether to hedge the payment with a forward contract for the following month. Now, however, he is questioning whether this process is worth the trouble. He suggests that if the international Fisher effect (IFE) holds, the pound's value should change (on average) by an amount that reflects the differential between the interest rates of the two countries of concern.

Since the forward premium reflects that same interest rate differential, the results from hedging should equal the results from not hedging on average.

1 Is Jim's interpretation of the IFE theory correct?

2 If you were in Jim's position, would you spend time trying to decide whether to hedge the receivables each month, or do you believe that the results would be the same (on average) whether you hedged or not?

APPENDIX 8
FURTHER NOTES ON EXCHANGE RATE MODELS

One would have thought that after over 50 years of research during which time space travel and convincing explanations of the origins of the universe have been accomplished, the relatively small matter of explaining the movement of exchange rates would by now be fully understood. Unfortunately human financial behaviour appears to be even more complex than the aforementioned problems. There are as yet no models that convincingly explain the movements of the exchange rate. Results are found that are statistically significant, but the term must not be misinterpreted. Such results are better described as discernable rather than significant, certainly they are not sufficient to predict results in a useful manner. In this section we restate the problem and add in a few more attempts to explain matters.

The dominant theory for explaining changes in the exchange rate is Purchasing Power Parity or PPP. Changes in price levels drive changes in interest rates according to the Fisher explanation and thus influence international trade and investment which are the main reasons for exchanging currencies. As discussed above, if PPP holds then the exchange rate adjusts for changes in the relative price levels. Thus, the purchasing power of a currency or its real value remains constant. In this chapter we looked at the real value of the home currency in terms of foreign currency which is the normal usage of the term in practice. Newspapers report an index of the real value of the pound, the euro, the dollar and so on, meaning their purchasing power in relation to foreign currencies. Academic modelling looks at the relationship the other way, the real value of foreign currency in relation to home currency, an equivalent view with easier notation. Thus the absolute version of PPP is:

$$P^h_t = S_t P^f_t \text{ or } S_t = P^h_t / P^f_t$$

where P is the price level for a basket of goods and S is the spot value of a foreign currency unit.

Using small letters to represent logs, the equation in log form is:

$$s_t = p^h_t - p^f_t$$

Putting this into a regression equation to test the relationship yields:

$$s_t = \alpha + \beta^h p^h_t + \beta^f p^f_t + \varepsilon_t$$

where the expectation would be that β^h would be 1 and β^f would be -1. To test the relative form, the equation would be based on differences thus:

$$\Delta s_t = \alpha + \beta^h \, \Delta p^h{}_t + \beta^f \, \Delta p^f{}_t + \varepsilon_t$$

It is hardly necessary to use the log form and approximating Δp_t as a percentage change in the price level or inflation and Δs_t as the percentage change in the spot rate is satisfactory. Results from this equation in whatever form are spectacularly inaccurate. Except in conditions of extreme inflation, one is generally fortunate in finding any of the parameters significantly different from 0, even when they are, the direction is often wrong. A typical example of the overall picture is given in Exhibit 8.3.

This finding has led researchers to ask a slightly different question of the data. Essentially they ask: 'given that there are random news-related changes to the exchange rate, is there a tendency for the exchange rate to move back to a form of long run equilibrium?' Simple regression is insufficient to answer this question in that a correcting trend over time is being suggested. A regression takes each observation for a particular time period independently as the residuals (ε_t) are assumed to be independent over time. This question is suggesting a form of negative autocorrelation, that is, an error on average would be corrected over time by errors in the other direction. Three concepts express this idea, a random walk, stationarity and the unit root test; they all encapsulate the same idea.

A random walk can be expressed as:

$$s_t = s_{t-i} + \varepsilon_t$$

or in first difference form as:

$$\Delta s_t = s_t - s_{t-1} = \varepsilon_t$$

Here the exchange rate is determined over time by a random step from the previous rate. In this sense the movements in exchange rate have no memory in the sense that February, March etc. do not need to know January's movement and if this is the case there can be no correcting process. Suppose that in January the value of the dollar increases by 1 per cent for reasons unconnected with relative inflation rates, a random walk for February takes the January rates and moves either up or down with equal probability from that point. If there were mean reversion then there would on average be a more likely fall in the value of the dollar than a rise. So for example if it were found that:

$$s_t = \alpha + \beta \, s_{t-1} + \varepsilon_t$$

where β was 0.9 then February's value of the dollar would be a random movement (according to randomly good or bad news) from a 10 per cent step down from the January value. In other words, a fall in value would be more likely. In fact, March would have 0.9^2 or 0.81 of the January valuation and after six-and-a-half months the influence of the January valuation would be 50 per cent of the original ($0.9^{6.5} = 0.5$). The process would have a half-life of six-and-a-half months. Clearly there is a correcting process. The jump in January will fade and in this process there will be a long run value of $\alpha/(1 - \beta)$. These processes are also classified as stationary processes in that the expected value is the same no matter what segment of time we choose. The third concept is the unit root and this measure tests for the influence of past prices. A random walk has a unit root in that it takes the previous value with a parameter of 1, i.e. all of the previous value on average and therefore shows no element of reversion to a mean. The unit root test is more sophisticated than this but is tantamount to determining whether or not there is some systematic reversion of previous movements. When the parameters of previous movements sum to 1 there is a unit root and no reversion, at less than 1 there is some reversion.

A more recent test of the relationship between price differentials and changes in the exchange rate is to see if they are co-integrated. Here the test is to see if a linear combination of the two variables is itself stationary. Disappointingly, tests fail to reject non-stationarity or establish colinearity.

Fundamental to the problem of all such models is the extreme volatility of the exchange rate compared to price differentials. Of the few tests that do find a mean reversion, a half-life of some 3 to 5 years appears to be the general finding. But how can such a slow change exist when there is such large short-term volatility? There also exists some conflict with the efficient markets reasoning. We cannot claim that market prices move randomly as news is randomly good or bad and at that same time claim that the movements are mean reverting as that would make them predictable. There is as yet no answer to this conundrum.

An alternative simple test of the behaviour of exchange rates was proposed by Cochrane (1988). If the exchange rate behaves as a random walk and there is no mean reverting process, then the variance (var) of, say, daily exchange rate changes should be 1/30th of the variance of monthly exchange rate changes (there being about 30 days in the average month). This is a basic property of a random walk — variance of monthly data should be 30 times the variance of daily data, the variance of half yearly data should be six times the variance of monthly data and so on. Put more succinctly:

$$Z(k) = 1/k \frac{\text{var}[(q_t - q_{t-k})/q_{t-k}]}{\text{var}[(q_t - q_{t-1})/q_{t-1}]} = 1/k \frac{\text{var}(q_t/q_{t-k})}{\text{var}(q_t - q_{t-1})}$$

where q is the exchange rate adjusted for relative inflation (i.e. the real exchange rate) and k is the number of smaller time periods in the larger time period and is therefore greater than 1. So if the top is looking at months and the lower half is looking at days as suggested above, k will be 30. By applying the scaling factor $1/k$, a random walk should approximate $Z(k)$ as 1. If it is less than 1, then over time there is a dampening or mean reversion effect because the variance does not increase by as much as a random walk process predicts. If $Z(k)$ is greater than 1 the system is growing by more than even a random walk would suggest and is clearly unstable.

There is also a simple practical point to be made here. MNCs using the random walk to approximate the uncertainty of exchange rate changes into the future are likely to be slightly overestimating the risk. As an error it is likely to lead to rejection of a profitable opportunity which is somewhat less expensive than an MNC accepting an unprofitable opportunity — a likely consequence of underestimating uncertainty. The random walk approach therefore is a good practical model of future uncertainty.

Of course, it is possible to interpret deviations from PPP as a change in the fundamental PPP relationship. Productivity increases could be one such cause. But the daily nature of movements in the exchange rate suggests that this is unlikely. A better source of explanation is based on models concerned with the money supply and portfolio investment. Because investment flows are large and take place on a daily basis, there is a chance that they may be able to explain exchange rate variability. To get a flavour of such approaches it is instructive to consult the UK Government's Debt and Reserve Management Report, 2009–10 currently at http://webarchive. nationalarchives.gov.uk/+/http://www.hm-treasury.gov.uk/d/Budget2009/bud09_drmr_2034.pdf. The report records issues of government debt thus we also learn that the size of the weekly tenders rose from a total of £1.6 billion, split across 1 month, 3 months and 6 months maturity Treasury bills, at the start of 2008–09, to £3.3 billion by the end of the year.

This is just one small snapshot of the workings of the money markets, their size and influence. The over-subscription in Exhibit 8A.1 suggests that many institutions (mainly insurance and pension companies) have funds that will have to be invested elsewhere. The portfolio balance model suggests that investments abroad are very much part of the portfolio of investments made by such companies. A change in the risk return features in the UK or foreign markets will alter the relative attractiveness of investing abroad. Insurance companies may move funds abroad if investment there becomes relatively more attractive or repatriate funds if UK investment returns improve. Clearly there are exchange rate implications. The Dornbusch 'sticky price model' argues that a shock to the money supply (e.g. a sudden greater availability of cash and credit due to government open market operations) will initially lead to portfolio investments such as Treasury bills and shares and will affect interest rates and therefore exchange rates. There are also inflationary effects that take longer to develop (hence the 'sticky price'). Such price effects again have exchange rate implications. Exchange rates may, therefore, have to adjust quite frequently to balance monetary and inflationary effects. Although these are persuasive arguments, attempts to model their predicted effects on the exchange rate have not been particularly successful – but this is not to say that such influences are unimportant.

The predictive ability of a model is a test both of the underlying theory that gives rise to the model and the model's ability to measure the variables. In the last couple of decades theory has remained relatively

EXHIBIT 8A.1 Central Government Net Cash Requirement (CGNCR) and gross gilt sales 1998–99 to 2008–09

Financial year	CGNCR	Gross gilt sales
	(£ billion)	(£ billion)
1998–99	−4.5	8.2
1999–00	−9.1	14.4
2000–01[1]	−35.6	10
2001–02	2.8	13.7
2002–03	21.8	26.3
2003–04	39.4	49.9
2004–05	38.5	50.1
2005–06	40.8	52.3
2006–07	37.1	62.5
2007–08	32.6	58.5
2008–09	162.4	146.5

[1]Reflecting the proceeds from the 3G (mobile phone) Spectrum auction.
Source: HM Treasury/Debt Management Office.

static while most of the effort has gone into modelling. It is not surprising that two of the last four Nobel prizes for economics have gone to econometricians and the third (Edward Prescott) raised a famous problem from measurement rather than theory (the share premium puzzle).

The question remains as to why measurement is so difficult. To understand something of the possible answer, suppose we were given the 'right' model for predicting exchange rates. Looking at the variables, all correctly measured, suppose we noted that over the months of April to June for a particular year there was no change in the variables. Would the exchange rate have changed? The answer is probably 'yes'. The market price reflects not just the actual values but also speculation as to what those values might be in the future. Such speculation may be affected by the quality of the information, a new newspaper, or an article that changes the views of influential investors. The result is that even in periods where economic factors (fundamentals) do not change, the exchange rate can be expected to vary due to changes in beliefs about a future that may or may not occur.

The term 'news models' has been applied to an approach that looks at the broad information set that might inform the market opinion forming process. On the left-hand side of a regression equation is the difference between the spot and the forward prediction of that spot as a percentage of the previous spot rate, or similar measure. On the right-hand side is news. Potentially, this could be an article expressing a different opinion – clearly there are measurement problems. Often economic data are used; to be news, such data must be unexpected and there are ways of measuring differences between actual figures and expectations. Empirical results are mixed; sometimes news is relevant, sometimes not. But even if results were strong, from a more applied MNC point of view, such tests appear to be no more than semi-strong market efficiency tests. What is being tested is whether or not the exchange rate changes as a result of market information - the semi-strong hypothesis. One form of uncertainty, the movement of the exchange rate, is being substituted for another form of uncertainty, unexpected information about employment, inflation rates, growth and so on. Predictive ability is not greatly advanced.

In general it is difficult to see how the opinion forming process itself can be modelled; certainly there is no consistent measurable model of such processes. As a result, predicting exchange rates accurately on a consistent basis may well have to remain a largely unaccomplished goal. Instead, models offer explanations of linkages in the economic system which in extreme circumstances may on occasion be measurable (e.g. a devaluing currency when there is hyperinflation) but ordinarily a model's predictions will be part of a noisy process. More recent modelling attempts simply try to simulate the volatility and jumps found in practice (deGauwe and Grimaldi, 2005) with models that combine technical and fundamental elements. The fundamental model they choose as a random walk without drift and the technical model one of mean reversion. The results establish plausibility but as yet do little to increase predictive power.

At least we can attempt to model uncertainty itself using ideas such as random walks and stationarity and learn to manage the result - hence the emphasis on scenarios in this and succeeding chapters.

REFERENCES

Sarno, L. and Taylor, M.P. (2002) 'Purchasing Power Parity and the Real Exchange Rate', *IMF Staff Papers,* 49 (1), 65–105.

Cochrane, J.H. (1988) 'How Big Is the Random Walk in GNP?', *Journal of Political Economy,* 96, 893–920.

deGrauwe, P. and Grimaldi, M. (2005) 'The Exchange Rate and its Fundamentals in a ComplexWorld', *Review of International Economics,* (13 (3), 549–75.

PART 2 Integrative problem

EXCHANGE RATE BEHAVIOUR

Questions

1 As an employee of the foreign exchange department for a large company, you have been given the following information:

Beginning of Year
Spot rate of £ = **$1.596**
Spot rate of Australian dollar (A$) = **$0.70**
Cross exchange rate: £1 = **A$2.28**
One-year forward rate of A$ = **$0.71**
One-year forward rate of £ = **$1.58004**
One-year US interest rate = **8.00%**
One-year British interest rate = **9.09%**
One-year Australian interest rate = **7.00%**

Suppose you are a foreign currency trader and that you are managing £100 000:

a Determine whether triangular arbitrage is feasible and, if so, how it should be conducted to make a profit.
b Determine whether covered interest arbitrage is feasible and, if so, how it should be conducted to make a profit.
c For the beginning of the year, use the international Fisher effect (IFE) theory to forecast the annual percentage change in the British pound's value over the year.
d Assume that at the beginning of the year, the pound's value is in equilibrium. Assume that over the year the British inflation rate is 6 per cent, while the US inflation rate is 4 per cent. Assume that any change in the pound's value due to the inflation differential has occurred by the end of the year. Using this information and the information provided in question 1, determine how the pound's value changed over the year.
e Assume that the pound's depreciation over the year was attributed directly to central bank intervention. Explain the type of direct intervention that would place downward pressure on the value of the pound.

PART 2 Essays/discussion and academic articles

1   Eichengren, B. (1999) 'Kicking The Habit: Moving From Pegged Exchange Rates To Greater Exchange Rate Flexibility', *The Economic Journal,* 109, C1-C9. A nontechnical discussion reflecting on (relatively) recent economic history.

2   Willet, T.D. (1998) 'Credibility and Discipline Effects of Exchange Rates as Nominal Anchors: The Need to Distinguish Temporary from Permanent Pegs. A Discussion on the Problems and Reasons for Government Management of Exchange Rates', *World Economy,* 21 (6), 803–26.
    Q   *'Developing countries need fixed exchange rates.' Discuss (article 1 or 2).*

3   Amann, E. and Baer, W. (2000) 'The Illusion of Stability: The Brazilian Economy under Cardoso', *World Development,* 28 (10), 1805–18. A look at the relationship between government and the exchange rate.
    Q   *Explain how the exchange rate can act as an economic instrument - does the failure of the Plano Real suggest that exchange rates should not be managed? Discuss.*

4   Eichengren, B. (2000) 'Taming Capital Flows', *World Development,* 28 (6), 1105–16. A look at the disruptive effect of massive flows of portfolio investment.
    Q   *Explain why capital flows are seen by some authors as disruptive – evaluate Eichengren's proposed solution.*

5   Lenain, P. and de Serres, A. (2002) 'Is The Euro Area Converging or Diverging? Implication for Policy Coordination', *The World Economy,* 25 (10), 1501–19. The start of a proper analysis of the actual as opposed to the intended effects of monetary union.

6   Wyplosz, C. (2006) 'European Monetary Union: The Dark Sides of a Major Success', *Economic Policy,* 21 (46), 207–61.

7   Mussa, M. (1997) 'Political and Institutional Commitment to a Common Currency', *The American Economic Review,* 87 (2), 217–20. A commentary on the political implications of the euro.
    Q   *Far from creating unity, is the euro becoming another vehicle for creating further divisions in Europe? Discuss (articles 5, 6, 7 or 11).*

8   Tobin, J. (2000) 'Financial Globalisation', *World Development,* 28 (6), 1101–04. Nobel prize winning economist considers the relative merits of exchange rate regimes and the problem of capital flows using an impossibility theorem.
    Q   *Outline Tobin's impossibility theorem. Consider the possible solutions.*

9   Rogoff, K. (1996) 'The Purchasing Power Parity Puzzle', *Journal of Economic Literature,* 34 (2), 647–68. An excellent review of PPP.
    Q   *Evaluate the attempts to explain why exchange rates can be so volatile and PPP adjustment so slow.*

10 LeBaron, B. and McCulloch, R. (2000) 'Floating, Fixed, or Super-Fixed? Dollarization Joins the Menu of Exchange-Rate Options', *The American Economic Review,* 90 (2), 32–7. The effects of dollarization.

11 Mundell, R.A. (1961) 'A Theory of Optimum Currency Areas', *The American Economic Review,* 51 (4), 657–65. The original article.
    Q   *Describe and evaluate the effects of adopting the currency of another country (article 11 or 12).*

12 Reinhart, C.M. and Rogoff, K.S. (2004), 'The Modern History of Exchange Rate Arrangements: A Reinterpretation', *The Quarterly Journal of Economics,* 119 (1), 1–48. Examines the reality behind general exchange rate classifications.
    Q   *Evaluate the evidence provided to justify the claim the IMF classifications are misleading.*

13 Gulcin Ozkan, F. (2005) 'Currency and Financial Crises in Turkey 2000–2001: Bad Fundamentals or Bad Luck?', *World Economy,* 28 (4), 541–72. An examination of one particular crisis with reflections on other crises.
    Q   *In what sense can the Turkish currency crisis be described as a typical currency crisis? Discuss.*

PART III
EXCHANGE RATE RISK MANAGEMENT

PART 3 (Chapters 9–12) explains the various functions involved in managing exposure to exchange rate risk. Chapter 9 describes various methods used to forecast exchange rates and explains how to assess forecasting performance. Chapter 10 demonstrates how to measure exposure to exchange rate movements. Given a firm's exposure and forecasts of future exchange rates, Chapters 11 and 12 explain how to hedge that exposure.

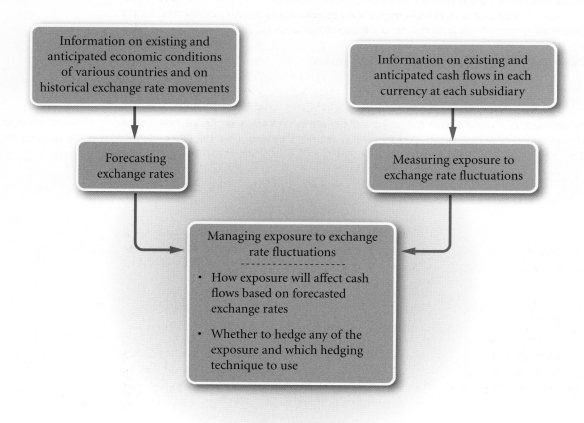

CHAPTER 9
FORECASTING
EXCHANGE RATES

LEARNING OBJECTIVES

The specific objectives of this chapter are to:

● Explain how firms can benefit from forecasting exchange rates.

● Describe the common techniques used for forecasting.

● Explain how forecasting performance can be evaluated.

Many decisions of multinational corporations (MNCs) are influenced by exchange rate projections. Financial managers must understand how to forecast exchange rates so that they can make decisions that maximize the value of their MNCs.

WHY FIRMS FORECAST EXCHANGE RATES

While the academic models of purchasing power parity (PPP) and interest rate parity (IRP) or the international Fisher effect (IFE) provide powerful rationales for explaining changes in exchange rates, in practice, their predictive power is poor. Typically statistical models in practice based on PPP and IRP or IFE will explain 10 per cent or less of the variation in exchange rates. Even if models were to explain actual movements much better there would still be the problem of 'fat tails'. This is the finding that the normal distribution, on which statistical models are based, tends to underestimate extreme movements. Actual distributions tend to have a higher frequency of very high and very low movements hence the high and low values (tails) of the normal distribution are 'fatter' than would be predicted by a normal distribution. This is unfortunate because predicting large movements in exchange rates is much more valuable for a MNC than predicting small movements.

Virtually every operation of an MNC can be influenced by changes in exchange rates. The following are some of the corporate functions for which exchange rate forecasts are necessary:

- *Hedging decision.* MNCs constantly face the decision as to whether to hedge future payments and receipts in foreign currencies. Whether a firm hedges may be determined by its forecasts of foreign currency values.

EXAMPLE

Pierre SA based in France, plans to pay for clothing imported from Mexico in 90 days. If the forecasted value of the peso in 90 days is sufficiently below the 90-day forward rate, the MNC may decide not to hedge. In other words it will not have to pay insurance (hedge) to protect against the possibility of a price rise. Forecasting may therefore enable the firm to make a successful forecast that will reduce expenditure for the firm and increase its cash flows.

- *Short-term financing decision.* When large corporations borrow, they have access to several different currencies. The currency they borrow will ideally: (1) exhibit a low interest rate and (2) decline in value over the financing period and therefore be cheaper to repay.

EXAMPLE

Luigi SpA, an Italian based company, considers borrowing Japanese yen to finance its European operations because the yen has a low interest rate. If the yen depreciates against the euro over the financing period, the firm can pay back the loan with fewer euros (when converting those euro in exchange for the amount owed in yen). The decision as to whether to finance with yen or euro is dependent on a forecast of the future value of the yen.

- *Short-term investment decision.* Corporations sometimes have a substantial amount of excess cash available for a short time period. Large deposits can be established in several currencies. The ideal currency for deposits will: (1) exhibit a high interest rate and (2) strengthen in value over the investment period.

EXAMPLE

Roar ASA, a Norwegian-based company, has excess cash and considers depositing the cash into a British bank account. If the British pound appreciates against the Norwegian krone by the end of the deposit period when pounds will be withdrawn and exchanged for krone, more krone will be received than was invested. Thus, the firm can use forecasts of the pound's exchange rate when determining whether to invest the short-term cash in a British account or a Norwegian account.

- *Capital budgeting decision.* When an MNC's parent assesses whether to invest funds in a foreign project, the firm takes into account that the project may periodically require the exchange of currencies. The capital budgeting analysis can be completed only when all estimated cash flows are measured in the parent's local currency.

EXAMPLE

Decker BV from Belgium wants to determine whether to establish a subsidiary in Thailand. Forecasts of the future cash flows used in the capital budgeting process will be dependent on the future exchange rate of Thailand's currency (the baht) against the euro. This dependency can be due to: (1) future inflows denominated in baht that will require conversion to euros and/or (2) the influence of future exchange rates on demand for the subsidiary's products. Accurate forecasts of currency values will improve the estimates of the cash flows and therefore enhance the MNC's decision-making.

- *Earnings assessment.* The parent's decision about whether a foreign subsidiary should reinvest earnings in a foreign country or remit earnings back to the parent may be influenced by exchange rate forecasts. If a strong foreign currency is expected to weaken substantially against the parent's currency, the parent may prefer to convert the foreign earnings before the foreign currency weakens.

  Exchange rate forecasts are also useful for forecasting an MNC's earnings. When earnings of an MNC are reported, subsidiary earnings are consolidated and translated into the currency representing the parent firm's home country.

EXAMPLE

Monroe Ltd has its home office in the UK and subsidiaries in Canada and the USA. It must decide whether its Canadian and US subsidiaries should remit their earnings. This involves comparing the amount of dollar cash flows that would be received today (if the subsidiaries remit the earnings) to the potential dollar cash flows that would be received in the future (if the subsidiaries reinvest the earnings). The decision is influenced by Monroe's forecast of the value of the Canadian dollar and the US dollar at the time when

(Continued)

the future earnings of the subsidiaries would be remitted.

For accounting purposes, the Canadian subsidiary's earnings in Canadian dollars must be measured by translating them to British pounds. The US subsidiary's earnings in dollars must also be measured by translation to pounds. 'Translation' does not mean that the earnings are physically converted to British pounds. It is simply a periodic recording process so that consolidated earnings can be reported in a single currency. In this case, appreciation of the Canadian dollar will boost the Canadian subsidiary's earnings when they are reported in (translated to) pounds. Forecasts of exchange rates thus play an important role in the overall forecast of an MNC's consolidated earnings.

- *Long-term financing decision.* Corporations that issue bonds to secure long-term funds may consider denominating the bonds in foreign currencies. They prefer the currency borrowed to depreciate over time against the currency they are receiving from sales. To estimate the cost of issuing bonds denominated in a foreign currency, forecasts of exchange rates are required.

EXAMPLE

Harold plc, a UK-based company needs long-term funds to support its UK business. It can issue 10-year bonds denominated in Japanese yen at a 1 per cent coupon rate, which is 5 percentage points less than the prevailing coupon rate on British pound-denominated bonds. However, Harold will need to convert pounds to yen to make the coupon or principal payments on the yen-denominated bond. So if the yen's value rises, the yen-denominated bond could be more costly to Harold than a pound-denominated bond. Harold's decision to issue yen-denominated bonds versus pound-denominated bonds will be dependent on its forecast of the yen's exchange rate over the 10-year period.

Although most forecasting is applied to currencies whose exchange rates fluctuate continuously, forecasts are also derived for currencies whose exchange rates are fixed at the time of investigation.

EXAMPLE

Even though the Argentine peso's value was still pegged to the US dollar in 2001, some MNCs anticipated that it would be devalued. They therefore made forecasts of its unpegged value. The peso was devalued in 2002, and its exchange rate is no longer tied to the US dollar (see Chapter 6). The Hong Kong dollar has been tied to the US dollar since 1983, but some MNCs still prepare long-term forecasts of the Hong Kong dollar in anticipation that it may be revalued.

An MNC's motives for forecasting exchange rates are summarized in Exhibit 9.1. The motives are distinguished according to whether they can enhance the MNC's value by influencing its cash flows or its cost of capital. The need for accurate exchange rate projections should now be clear. The following section describes the forecasting methods available.

EXHIBIT 9.1 Corporate motives for forecasting exchange rates

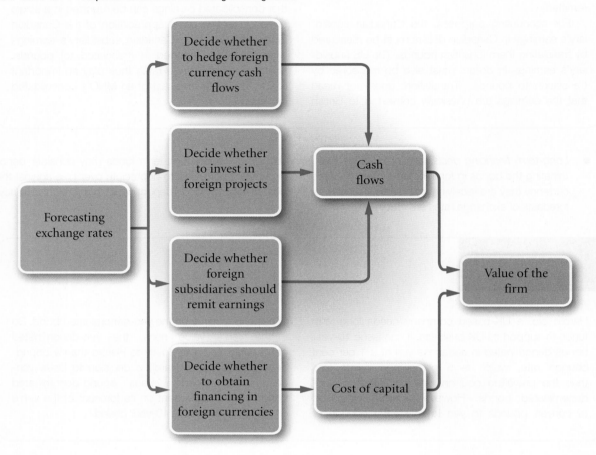

FORECASTING TECHNIQUES

The numerous methods available for forecasting exchange rates can be categorized into four general groups: (1) technical, (2) fundamental, (3) market-based and (4) mixed. The concept of market efficiency puts these methods in context.

Market efficiency

The efficiency of the foreign exchange market has implications for the approach to predicting movements as the efficient markets hypothesis (often referred to as EMH) attempts to answer the question: why do prices change? If the reason for a price change is established then it will be possible to select which models should perform better.

The simple idea behind the efficient markets hypothesis is that prices change as a result of news. If the news is good, the price goes up; if the news is bad, the price goes down. What is meant by news, however, needs to be clearly understood. In the ordinary meaning of the word news means information. In this contest however news is taken to mean the unexpected, literally what is new. We can therefore write:

$$\text{News} = \text{'Actual information'} - \text{'Expected information'}$$

This simple formula has important implications in understanding markets. For example, to say that the publication of a positive balance of payments is good news and the exchange rate should as a result increase is in itself a misunderstanding, as a positive balance of payments could be good or bad news. To illustrate:

Good News = Published current account balance $10bn positive − Market expectation $6bn

Bad News = Published current account balance $10bn positive − Market expectation $12bn

The impact of any single piece of information can therefore be positive or negative. This means that in times of economic hardship the market price is still as likely to go up or down. Although the news in absolute terms may be bad, it may yet be better or worse than expected depending on expectations. The argument is therefore that in a market context it is news that is the driving force behind a change in the market price. The logic of this reasoning is very attractive.

With this understanding of news, the efficient markets hypothesis is traditionally divided into 'weak', 'semi-strong' and 'strong'. These rather odd terms refer to the degree to which news is identified.

If the foreign exchange market is **weak-form efficient**, the price reflects estimates of the *future* value of the currency. All known information about the *future* is discounted into the *current* price. This implies that historical information has no role to play in explaining a change in price. Such information whether it is about past events or future expected events is already included in the current expectation (the current price) and therefore cannot be news. This has three implications.

First, technical analysis has no role to play in estimating changes in the exchange rate. Technical forecasting attempts to find patterns in exchange rates, and a pattern over time by its very definition is determined by movements in the past as the pattern unfolds. A head and shoulder pattern predicts a fall when past movements indicate that the exchange rate has reached the top of the head and so on. So a pattern is inherently backward looking.

The second implication is that the movement of the exchange rate should be random as there can, by definition, be no pattern. Weak form tests are confined to establishing that the movements of market prices such as shares and exchange rates are random and without a pattern. Randomness is therefore the 'footprint' of a price that is reacting to news but the tests do not identify any piece of news as such, hence the term 'weak'.

The third implication is that if the movement is random, the changes should be normally distributed. If there is an equal chance of a rise or fall over successive days the probabilities of the price changes over time should be normally distributed. Demonstrations from repeated lots of two flips of a coin representing 2 days (with heads as a rise and tails as a fall) will show that on average two flips will result in a 25 per cent chance of two rises, 25 per cent of two falls in value and a 50 per cent chance of a rise and a fall. A histogram of this result already has the basic shape of a normal distribution and as the number of flips (days) is extended so the results look closer and closer to that of a normal distribution[1]. Reversing the argument, the assumption that changes in the exchange rate are normally distributed relies on the assumption that the market is efficient.

If the foreign exchange market is **semi-strong-form efficient**, then the exchange rate reacts in an immediate and unbiased way to all publicly available information. This builds on the notion of news being a *possible* explanation in the weak form. With a semi-strong test the piece of news is identified and attempts are made to gauge the effect, if any, on the exchange rate. In the case of currencies a typical piece of news would be the announcement of the balance of payments. If it is unexpected, does the exchange rate react immediately? It would be very unusual if it did not, one does not have to look far to see that the exchange rate is constantly being scrutinized in the press. Markets are regulated to try to ensure that they are semi-strong-form efficient. That is, everyone has equal access to information. Price movements are reactions to new information available to all or are revised interpretations of existing information.

If foreign exchange markets are **strong-form efficient**, then all relevant public and private information is already reflected in today's exchange rates. This form of efficiency is difficult to test with regard to exchange rates as it is difficult to clearly define private information, unlike say shares where private information becomes public on specified announcement dates. This is an undesirable form of efficiency as some

---

[1] The emerging normal distribution is the same as histograms of successive layers of Pascal's triangle, each level represents an extra day starting from the top.

traders (referred to as 'insider traders') in this market know more than others and the price at any given time will not reflect all that is knowable about the currency, interest rate or MNC share price.

Tests of market efficiency generally show that markets are, as desired, semi-strong efficient. Weak-form tests confirm that the movement in market prices over the short to medium term are random – confirming that information *may* be the cause[2]. Direct semi-strong tests show that prices react to information almost immediately. Often however an unusual movement in a price will occur before an announcement. Whether this is because of insider trading or clever anticipation is very difficult to distinguish. Direct strong-form tests are difficult as private information by its nature is difficult to collect. However, prosecutions of insider traders have revealed alarming levels of contacts with major multinationals as in the case of Raj Rajaratnam. He was found guilty in 2011 of insider trading, profiting by over $50m from illegally obtained insider information from major multinationals including Google, Hilton and Goldman Sachs.

As a note of caution, tests of market efficiency in the academic literature are in danger of overstating the case for efficiency. With regard to weak form testing, the set of patterns is infinite so all that is being found is that there is little evidence of the existence of the patterns being tested – the tests say nothing about untested patterns. Semi strong and strong form tests are only tests of particular items of information, the tests do not of themselves imply that prices only react to news, insider trading is not ruled out.

A few further general points are relevant about market efficiency. The hypothesis is probably the most fundamental in all finance. Without market efficiency being *generally* true, the whole price mechanism would fail. The price must represent all that is knowable about the product and this is true for the efficiency of all markets, cars, food as well as financial instruments. The reason why it is so important in finance is that news about the product (a share, currency, etc.) changes every day, every hour. For cars and food, etc. the information set is very much more stable.

A second general implication is that market efficiency implies that how the information is disclosed does not greatly matter. Tests show that the market is good at interpreting information from whatever source and however presented.

Thirdly, market efficiency does not mean that the estimate is necessarily accurate. The market may be wrong in its estimation of the effect of any piece of news but it is not wrong in any consistent way, it does not consistently underestimate the value of any particular currency – that would create a pattern. Statements that the market is undervaluing a share or a currency should therefore be treated as probably incorrect. It may be true in retrospect that a share was underpriced but that is to assume information not known at the time of setting the price.

Finally, the definition of information as news does much to explain why models based on news (i.e. not determined by arbitrage) can be inaccurate. As has been shown above, a piece of information on its own is not necessarily good or bad news, it depends on what was expected. Thus if a model is built such that for any particular time period

$$\text{Change in currency value} = a + b \, (\text{Change in the current account balance}) + \text{Error term}$$

The change in the current account balance is news, calculated by the government statistical services and published. If it is news it should therefore be unexpected. This would be true if the market always assumed that there would be no change but this is obviously not true. However, as expectations are almost impossible to measure, the crude assumption of no expected change is often an implied feature of such models.

Technical forecasting

Technical forecasting involves the use of historical exchange rate data to predict future values based on patterns in past prices. Academics in general do not support this approach to forecasting. Prices move in reaction to information and not past price movements as is found in weak form testing. Yet in the press there are often comments that appear to support the view that prices are following a pattern of sorts. For example, a comment such as: 'the exchange rate has fallen back as a result of 3 days' increases' suggests that it

---

[2]Long-term tests are almost impossible to sample and panel testing (for example, five-year movements in a price across a range of countries) is still a developing area in statistics.

has done so *because* it has risen for 3 days in a row. The movement of the next day's exchange rate is not known and a pattern that suggests that after every 3 days of increases a reduction is more likely can be tested and is almost certainly not present. However, there is no doubt that technical forecasting is popular in practice. More recently many sceptics have reconsidered their position in the face of unexplained apparent patterns over the longer term, particularly in the share price market.

As statistics cannot prove that there are absolutely no patterns, the existence of patterns as sought by technical forecasting cannot wholly be denied.

EXAMPLE

Tomorrow Freeda GmbH (Austria) has to pay 10 million Brazilian real for supplies that it recently received from Brazil. Today, the real has appreciated by 3 per cent against the euro. Freeda could send the payment today so that it would avoid the effects of any additional appreciation tomorrow. Based on an analysis of historical time series, Freeda has determined that whenever the real appreciates against the euro by more than 1 per cent, it experiences a reversal of about 60 per cent of that amount on the following day. That is:

$$e_{t+1} = e_t \times (-60\%) \text{ when } e_t > 1 \%$$

Applying this tendency to the current situation in which the peso appreciated by 3 per cent today, Freeda forecasts that tomorrow's exchange rate will change by:

$$e_{t+1} = e_t \times (-60\%)$$
$$= (3\%) \times (-60\%)$$
$$= -1.8\%$$

Given this forecast that the real will depreciate tomorrow, Freeda decides that it will make its payment tomorrow instead of today.

USING THE WEB

http://www.ny.frb.org/markets/foreignex.html and http://www.oanda.com provide historical exchange rate data that may be used to create technical forecasts of exchange rates.

Corporations tend to make only limited use of technical forecasting because it typically focuses on the near future, which is not very helpful for developing corporate policies. Most technical forecasts apply to very short-term periods such as 1 day or 1 week. A short-term forecast obviously yields quicker returns and more limited losses and is therefore attractive to potential clients.

Both sceptics and proponents would agree that even if technical forecasting cannot provide accurate predictions of the exchange rate itself, it can give some idea of the *range* of possible future rates. Random price movements can move within a predictable range of prices. For example, spinning a coin yields an outcome that one cannot predict with certainty; but one can predict that the outcome will be either heads or tails (barring some freak accident of physics). Because technical analysis typically cannot estimate future exchange rates in precise terms, it is not, by itself, an adequate forecasting tool for financial managers of MNCs.

As noted above, technical factors are often cited in the financial press as the main reason for changing speculative positions that cause an adjustment in a currency's value. For example, headlines often attribute a change in the value of a currency to technical factors, typical examples are:

- Technical factors overwhelmed economic news.

- Technical factors triggered sales of pounds.

- Technical factors indicated that euros had been recently oversold, triggering purchases of euros.

As these examples suggest, technical forecasting appears to be widely used by speculators who attempt to capitalize on day-to-day exchange rate movements.

Technical forecasting models have helped some speculators in the foreign exchange market at various times. However, a model that has worked well in one particular period will not necessarily work well in another. With the abundance of technical models existing today, some are bound to generate speculative profits in any given period. If the pattern of currency values over time appears to be random, then technical forecasting is not appropriate. Unless historical trends in exchange rate movements can be identified, examination of past movements will not be useful for indicating future movements.

Finally, mention should be made of the trading effects of technical forecasting models. Many foreign exchange participants argue that even if a particular technical forecasting model is shown to lead consistently to speculative profits, it will no longer be useful once other participants begin to use it. Trading based on the model's recommendation will push the currency value to a position that negates the profit. For example, if a method identifies that the prices always rise on a Tuesday, the extra demand on a Monday that is seeking to exploit the pattern will, of itself, push up the price and destroy the very pattern it is seeking to exploit. The notion that something as public and valuable as a pattern in prices can remain undetected by all but the few is rather fanciful. Technical forecasting nevertheless remains popular in practice. Perhaps like gambling, its justification is behavioural rather than logical.

MANAGING FOR VALUE

How MNCs' earnings depend on currency values

Like many publicly traded companies, Renault SA, the French vehicle manufacturer, analyze their exposure to currency changes in their accounts. The calculation is not easy. In some countries, or more relevantly, in some currency areas Renault will produce as well as sell cars and lorries. Devaluation in such a currency would reduce the value of the revenues in terms of Renault's home currency, the euro; but also, there would be an offsetting reduction in the value of the costs. So the exposure is the net of the revenue figure less the costs in the foreign currency. In other currency areas there may be an excess of purchases and in yet others, an excess of sales. To help investors appreciate how currency changes affect earnings, Renault in their 2009 Annual Report explain that: 'Automobile's revenue contribution declined to €31 951 million in 2009, from €35 791 million in 2008 on a consistent basis. The 10.7 per cent decline was due to: a contraction in volumes, accounting for −0.6 points. . . . a negative currency effect, accounting for − 2.5 points, due to depreciation against the euro on several Group markets, especially the Korean won, the pound sterling, the Russian ruble and the Romanian leu' (p. 76).

With costs mainly in euros and revenues in other currencies the fall in value of the other currencies will adversely affect sales measured in euros. How much of this is realized as a loss depends on the cash flow transactions. The consolidated cash flow statement refers rather vaguely to an increase in cash flows of some €57m due to 'effect of changes in exchange rate and other changes' so clearly there have been offsetting gains.

Fundamental forecasting

Fundamental forecasting is based on fundamental relationships between economic variables and exchange rates. Recall from Chapter 4 that a change in a currency's spot rate is influenced by the following factors:

$$e = f(\Delta INF, \Delta INT, \Delta INC, \Delta GC, \Delta EXT)$$

Where:

e = percentage change in the spot rate

ΔINF = the difference between home inflation and the foreign country's inflation

ΔINT = the difference between the home interest rate and the foreign country's interest rate

ΔINC = the difference between the home income level and the foreign country's income level

ΔGC = change in government controls

ΔEXT = change in expectations of future exchange rates

Given current values of these variables along with their historical impact on a currency's value, corporations can develop exchange rate projections.

A forecast may arise simply from a subjective assessment of the degree to which general movements in economic variables in one country are expected to affect exchange rates. MNCs typically use in-house economists to make such projections. From a statistical perspective, a forecast would be based on quantitatively measured impacts of factors on exchange rates. Pure statistical models are highly unlikely to be accurate. They are nevertheless useful in informing the subjective estimates of managers. The following example illustrates the nature of statistical modelling but without a high R^2 and high T-scores for the explanatory variables such models have little value on their own.

EXAMPLE

The focus here is on only two of the many factors that affect currency values. Before identifying them, consider that the corporate objective is to forecast the percentage change (rate of appreciation or depreciation) in the US dollar with respect to the British pound during the next quarter. For simplicity, assume the firm's forecast for the dollar is dependent on only two factors that affect the dollar's value:

1 Inflation in the USA relative to inflation in the UK.

2 Income growth in the USA relative to income growth in the UK (measured as a percentage change).

The first step is to determine how these variables have affected the percentage change in the dollar's value based on historical data. This is commonly achieved with regression analysis. First, quarterly data are compiled for the inflation and income growth levels of both the UK and the USA. The dependent variable (the left-hand side of a regression) is the quarterly percentage change in the dollar value. The independent variables (the right-hand side of a regression) may be set up as follows:

1 Previous quarterly percentage inflation differential (British inflation rate minus US inflation rate), referred to as INF_{t-1}.

2 Previous quarterly percentage income growth differential (British income growth minus US income growth), referred to as INC_{t-1}.

The regression equation can be defined as:

$$e_{\$,t} = b_0 + b_1 INF_{t-1} + b_2 INC_{t-1} + \mu_t$$

Where:

INF_{t-1} = British inflation less US inflation for time $t-1$, the previous period to time t

INC_{t-1} = British income growth less US income growth for time $t-1$, the previous period to time t

$e_{\$,t}$ = percentage change in the value of the dollar over time t

b_0 = a constant

b_1 = the sensitivity of $e_{\$,t}$ to changes in INF_{t-1}

b_2 = the sensitivity of $e_{\$,t}$ to changes in INC_{t-1}

μ_t = the error term.

A set of historical data is used to obtain previous values of dollar, INF and INC. Using this data set, regression analysis will generate the values of the regression coefficients (b_0, b_1 and b_2). That is, regression analysis determines the direction and degree to which *changes* in the dollar are affected by each independent variable over the sample. The coefficient b_1 will exhibit a positive sign if, when INF_{t-1} and $e_{\$t}$ change in the same direction over time (other things held constant). A negative sign indicates that $e_{\$t}$ and INF_{t-1} move in opposite directions. In the equation given, b_1 is expected to exhibit a positive sign because when UK inflation increases relative to inflation in the USA, upward pressure is exerted on the

(Continued)

dollar's value (dollar goods appear cheaper leading to a greater demand for dollars).

The regression coefficient b_2 (which measures the impact of INC_{t-1} on $e_{\$t}$) is expected to be positive because when British income growth exceeds US income growth, there is upward pressure on the dollar's value. These relationships have already been thoroughly discussed in Chapter 4.

Once regression analysis is employed to generate values of the coefficients, these coefficients can be used to forecast. To illustrate, assume the following values: $b_0 = 0.002$, $b_1 = 0.8$ and $b_2 = 1.0$. The coefficients can be interpreted as follows. For a one-unit percentage change in the inflation differential, the dollar is expected to change by 0.8 per cent in the same direction, other things held constant. For a one-unit percentage change in the income differential, the dollar is

expected to change by 1.0 per cent in the same direction, other things held constant. To develop forecasts, assume that the most recent quarterly percentage change in INF_{t-1} (the inflation differential) is 4 per cent, and that INC_{t-1} (the income growth differential) is 2 per cent. Using this information along with our estimated regression coefficients, the forecast for $e_{\$t}$ is:

$$e_{\$,t} = b_0 + b_1 INF_{t-1} + b_2 INC_{t-1} + \mu_t$$
$$= 0.002 + 0.8(4\%) + 1(2\%)$$
$$= 0.2\% + 3.2\% + 2\%$$
$$= 5.4\%$$

Thus, given the current figures for inflation rates and income growth, the dollar should appreciate by 5.4 per cent during the next quarter.

This example is simplified to illustrate how fundamental analysis can be implemented for forecasting. A full-blown model might include many more than two factors, but the application would still be similar. Unfortunately, a relationship that held in the past is not necessarily going to hold in the future. Models that have in a sense 'thrown in' all relevant variables into the right-hand side of the equation are likely to produce a reasonably good prediction, given that the model chooses the parameters b_1, b_2, etc. that offer the best fit as measured by the adjusted R^2. But the more variables included in the right-hand side the weaker the rationale and the greater the statistical problem of multicollinearity (correlation among the explanatory variables). One can have little confidence in the longevity of a model that has no clear justification other than that it worked well over a particular time period.

Use of sensitivity analysis for fundamental forecasting. When a regression model is used for forecasting, and the values of the influential factors have a lagged impact on exchange rates, the actual value of those factors can be used as input for the forecast. For example, if the inflation differential has a lagged impact on exchange rates, the inflation differential in the previous period may be used to forecast the percentage change in the exchange rate over the future period. Some factors, however, have an instantaneous influence on exchange rates. Since these factors obviously cannot be known, forecasts must be used. Firms recognize that poor forecasts of these factors can cause poor forecasts of the exchange rate movements, so they may attempt to account for the uncertainty by using **sensitivity analysis**, which considers more than one possible outcome for the factors exhibiting uncertainty.

EXAMPLE

Phoenix GmbH (Germany) develops a regression model to forecast the percentage change in the Mexican peso's value. It believes that the real interest rate differential and the inflation differential are the only

factors that affect exchange rate movements, as shown in this regression model:

$$e_{p,t} = a_0 + a_1 INT_t + a_2 INF_{t-1} + \mu_t$$

(Continued)

Where:

INT_t = euro interest rate less Mexican interest rate for time t

INF_{t-1} = euro inflation rate less Mexican inflation rate for the previous period time $t-1$

$e_{p,t}$ = percentage change in the value of the peso over time t

a_0 = a constant

a_1 = the sensitivity of $e_{p,t}$ to changes in INT_t

a_2 = the sensitivity of $e_{p,t}$ to changes in INF_{t-1}

μ_t = the error term

Regression coefficient	Estimate
a_0	0.001
a_1	−0.7
a_2	0.6

The negative sign of a_1 indicates a negative relationship between INT_t and the peso's movements, while the positive sign of a_2 indicates a positive relationship between INF_{t-1} and the peso's movements.

To forecast the peso's percentage change over the upcoming period, INT_t and INF_{t-1} must be estimated. Assume that INF_{t-1} was 1 per cent. However, INT_t is not known at the beginning of the period and must therefore be forecasted. Assume that Phoenix GmbH has developed the following probability distribution for INT_t:

Historical data are used to determine values for $e_{p,t}$ along with values for INT_t and INF_{t-1} for several periods (preferably, 30 or more periods are used to build the database). The length of each historical period (quarter, month, etc.) should match the length of the period for which the forecast is needed. The historical data needed per period for the Mexican peso model are: (1) the percentage change in the peso's value, (2) the euro real interest rate minus the Mexican real interest rate and (3) the euro inflation rate in the previous period minus the Mexican inflation rate in the previous period. Assume that regression analysis has provided the following estimates for the regression coefficients and that the model has a high R^2 and the coefficients have a high T-score!:

Probability	Possible outcome
20%	−3%
50%	−4%
30%	−5%
100%	

A separate forecast of e_t can be developed from each possible outcome of INT_t as follows:

Forecast of *INT*	Forecast of e_t	Probability
−3%	0.1% + (−0.7)(−3%) + 0.6(1%) = 2.8%	20%
−4%	0.1% + (−0.7)(−4%) + 0.6(1%) = 3.5%	50%
−5%	0.1% + (−0.7)(−5%) + 0.6(1%) = 4.2%	30%

If the firm needs forecasts for other currencies, it can develop the probability distributions of their movements over the upcoming period in a similar manner.

As a note of caution, it should be remembered that most statistical based models have a low R^2 and poor T-scores and therefore make poor forecasts.

Use of PPP for fundamental forecasting. Recall that the theory of PPP specifies the fundamental relationship between the inflation differential and the exchange rate. In simple terms, PPP states that the currency of the relatively inflated country will depreciate by an amount that reflects that country's inflation differential. Recall that according to PPP, the percentage change in the foreign currency's value (e_f) over a period should reflect the differential between the home inflation rate (I_h) and the foreign inflation rate (I_f) over that period.

EXAMPLE

The UK inflation rate is expected to be 1 per cent over the next year, while the Australian inflation rate is expected to be 6 per cent. According to PPP, the Australian dollar's exchange rate should change as follows:

$$e_f = \frac{(1 + I_{UK})}{(1 + I_A)} - 1$$

$$= \frac{(1.01)}{(1.06)} - 1$$

$$\approx -4.7\%$$

This forecast of the percentage change in the Australian dollar can be applied to its existing spot rate to forecast the future spot rate at the end of 1 year. If the existing spot rate (S_t) of the Australian dollar is £0.40, the expected spot rate at the end of 1 year, $e(S_{t+1})$, will be about 0.3812:

$$e(S_{t+1}) = S_t(1 + e_f)$$

$$= £0.40[1 + (-0.047)]$$

$$= £0.3812$$

In reality, the inflation rates of two countries over an upcoming period are uncertain and therefore would have to be forecasted when using PPP to forecast the future exchange rate at the end of the period. This complicates the use of PPP to forecast future exchange rates. Even if the inflation rates in the upcoming period were known with certainty, PPP might not be able to forecast exchange rates accurately.

If the PPP theory were accurate in reality, there would be no need to even consider alternative forecasting techniques. However, using the inflation differential of two countries to forecast their exchange rate is not always accurate. Problems arise for several reasons:

1   The timing of the impact of inflation fluctuations on changing trade patterns, and therefore on exchange rates, is not known with certainty.

2   Data used to measure relative prices of two countries may be somewhat inaccurate.

3   Barriers to trade can disrupt the trade patterns that should emerge in accordance with PPP theory.

4   Other factors, such as the interest rate differential between countries, can also affect exchange rates.

For these reasons, the inflation differential by itself is not sufficient to accurately forecast exchange rate movements. Nevertheless, it should be included in any fundamental forecasting model.

Limitations of fundamental forecasting. Although fundamental forecasting accounts for the expected fundamental relationships between factors and currency values, the following limitations exist:

1   The precise timing of the impact of some factors on a currency's value is not known. It is possible that the full impact of inflation on exchange rates will not occur until two-, three- or four-quarters later. The regression model would need to be adjusted accordingly.

2   As mentioned earlier, some factors exhibit an immediate impact on exchange rates. They can be usefully included in a fundamental forecasting model only if forecasts can be obtained for them. Forecasts of these factors should be developed for a period that corresponds to the period for which a forecast of exchange rates is necessary. In this case, the accuracy of the exchange rate forecasts will be somewhat dependent on the accuracy of these factors. Even if a firm knows exactly how movements in these factors affect exchange rates, its exchange rate projections may be inaccurate if it cannot predict the values of the factors.

3 Some factors that deserve consideration in the fundamental forecasting process cannot be easily quantified. For example, what if large Australian exporting firms experience an unanticipated labour strike, causing shortages? This will reduce the availability of Australian goods for British consumers and therefore reduce British demand for Australian dollars. Such an event, which would put downward pressure on the Australian dollar value, normally is not incorporated into the forecasting model.

4 Coefficients derived from the regression analysis will not necessarily remain constant over time. In the previous example, the coefficient for INF_{t-1} (a_2) was 0.6, suggesting that for a 1 per cent change in INF_{t-1}, the Mexican peso would appreciate by 0.6 per cent. Yet, if the Mexican government or the European Union imposed new trade barriers, or eliminated existing barriers, the impact of the inflation differential on trade (and therefore on the Mexican peso's exchange rate) could be affected.

These limitations of fundamental forecasting have been discussed to emphasize that even the most sophisticated forecasting techniques (fundamental or otherwise) cannot provide consistently accurate forecasts. MNCs that develop forecasts must allow for some margin of error and recognize the possibility of error when implementing corporate policies.

Market-based forecasting

The process of developing forecasts from market indicators, known as **market-based forecasting**, is usually based on either: (1) the spot rate or (2) the forward rate. In this section we examine in greater detail matters first raised in Chapter 7.

Use of the spot rate. Today's spot rate may be used as a forecast of the spot rate that will exist on a future date. Using the spot rate is the same as forecasting that there will be no change in the exchange rate. To see why the spot rate can serve as a market-based forecast, assume the dollar was expected to appreciate against the pound in the very near future. This expectation will have encouraged speculators to buy the dollar with pounds today in anticipation of its appreciation, and these purchases will have forced the dollar's value up immediately. So the current price of the dollar will include the expectation that the value of the dollar will rise.

Conversely, if the dollar was expected to depreciate against the pound, speculators will have sold off dollars hoping to purchase them back at a lower price after their decline in value. Such actions will have forced the dollar to depreciate immediately. Thus, the current value of the dollar should reflect the expectation of the dollar's decline in value. Corporations can use the spot rate to forecast, since it represents the market's expectation of the spot rate in the near future. In an efficient market there is a 50 per cent chance of a rise or a fall making the spot the best estimate.

Use of the forward rate. A forward rate quoted for a specific date in the future is commonly recommended as the forecasted spot rate on that future date. Within the buy and ask rate margin it is possibly the case that the rate does indicate market expectations as no arbitrage profit can be made by investing abroad and converting back at the forward rate. However, apart from this relatively narrow band the forward rate should be no better than the current spot as a prediction except where there is a large difference in inflation.

As stated in Chapter 7, the information set that informs the forward rate is the same as the information set that informs the spot. The only difference between the two rates is time and that is accounted for by the difference between the foreign and home interest rates. Where there is a large difference in inflation (a time related effect), the interest rate difference is likely to be significant. The forward rate will capture this information and quote a discount in the value of the currency with the higher inflation. In such circumstances, the forward estimate should be better than the spot. Nevertheless, in the far more common instances where the interest rate differences are small, inflation will not be a factor and the forward rate will be no better than the spot rate.

Long-term forecasting with forward rates. Long-term exchange rate forecasts can be derived from long-term forward rates.

EXAMPLE

Assume that the spot rate of the dollar is currently 1.20 euros, while the 5-year forward rate of the dollar is 1.02 euros. This forward rate can serve as a forecast of 1.02 euros for the dollar in 5 years, which reflects a 15% depreciation in the dollar over the next 5 years.

Forward rates are normally available for periods of 2 to 5 years or even longer, but the bid/ask spread is wide because of the limited trading volume. Although such rates are rarely quoted in financial newspapers, the quoted interest rates on risk-free instruments of various countries can be used to determine what the forward rates would be under conditions of interest rate parity. The wider bid ask spread ensures that covered interest arbitrage is not possible and that only risk averse investors wanting to insure against a large fall in the value of the currency would be interested in buying forward in this way.

EXAMPLE

Raymond plc a UK company is expecting to have to make a large contract payment in dollars in 5 years' time. The company has been quoted a 5-year forward *ask* rate on dollars of £0.70 and a *bid* rate of £0.52 by a UK bank. Interest rates in the USA are quoted at 30 per cent over the 5 years and in the UK a rate of 40 per cent has been quoted (note that this is not a per year interest rate but the total interest rate charge over the 5 years). The current spot rate is £0.59 to the dollar.

Raymond notes that £100 would convert now to $169 (£100 / 0.59) and be worth $220 at the end of the 5-year investment period in the USA ($169 × 1.30); the investment would then convert back to £114 ($220 × 0.52), a return of only 14 per cent and considerably less than investing in the UK.

Also, $100 would convert to £59 ($100 × 0.59) and be worth £83 (£59 × 1.4) at the end of the 5-year investment period in the UK. The investment would then convert back to $119 at the end of the period (£83 / 0.70), a return of only 19 per cent and considerably less than investing in the USA. So covered interest rate arbitrage is not possible.

Raymond, however, is thinking of taking out a forward contract to sell dollars at the bank bid rate of £0.52 for a dollar as the discount on the current spot rate of 12 per cent ([£0.52 − £0.59]/£0.59) is considered worthwhile to protect against an even further possible fall in the value of the dollar. Raymond's financial manager predicts that such a fall might well be possible and that the company should insure its returns in this way.

As a note, the governments of some emerging markets (such as those in Latin America) do not issue long-term fixed-rate bonds very often. Consequently, long-term interest rates are not available and covered interest rate arbitrage would not be possible.

USING THE WEB

Forward rates as forecasts

Forward rates for the euro, British pound, Canadian dollar and Japanese yen for 1-month, 3-month, 6-month and 1-year maturities are available on the *Financial Times* website at: http://www.ft.com/ by following the market data tab. These rates are determined by the spot and interest rates.

The forward rate is easily accessible and therefore serves as a convenient and free forecast. Like any method of forecasting exchange rates, the forward rate is typically more accurate when forecasting exchange rates for short-term horizons than for long-term horizons. Exchange rates tend to wander farther from expectations over longer periods of time.

Implications of the IFE and IRP for forecasts using the forward rate. Recall that if interest rate parity (IRP) holds, the forward rate premium reflects the interest rate differential between two countries. Also recall that if the international Fisher effect (IFE) holds, a currency that has a higher interest rate than the UK interest rate should depreciate against the pound because the higher interest rate implies a higher level of expected inflation in that country than in the UK. Since the forward rate captures the nominal interest rate (and therefore the expected inflation rate) between two countries, it should provide more accurate forecasts for currencies in high-inflation countries than the spot rate.

EXAMPLE

Alvi SpA is an Italian firm that trades in Brazil, and it needs to forecast the exchange rate of the Brazilian real for 1 year ahead. It considers using either the spot rate or the forward rate to forecast the real. The spot rate of the Brazilian real is 0.30 euros. The 1-year interest rate in Brazil is 20 per cent, versus 5 per cent in Italy. The 1-year forward rate is 0.2625 euros, which reflects a discount to offset the interest rate differential according to IRP (check this yourself using the exact method). Alvi believes that the future exchange rate of the real will be driven by the inflation differential between Brazil and Italy. It also believes that the real rate of interest (i.e. without inflation rate) in both Brazil and Italy is 3 per cent. This implies that the expected inflation rate for next year is 17 per cent in Brazil and 2 per cent in Italy. The forward rate discount is based on the interest rate differential, which in turn is related to the inflation differential. In this example, the forward rate of the Brazilian real reflects a large discount, which means that it implies a forecast of substantial depreciation of the real against the euro. Conversely, using the spot rate of the real as a forecast would imply that the exchange rate at the end of the year will be what it is today. Since the forward rate forecast indirectly captures the differential in expected inflation rates, it is a more appropriate forecast method than the spot rate.

Firms may not always believe that the forward rate provides more accurate forecasts than the spot rate. If a firm is forecasting over a very short-term horizon such as a day or a week, the interest rate (and therefore expected inflation) differential may not be as influential. Second, some firms may believe that the interest rate differential may not even be influential in the long run. Third, if the foreign country's interest rate is usually similar to the US rate, the forward rate premium or discount will be close to zero, meaning that the forward rate and spot rate will provide similar forecasts.

Mixed forecasting

Because no single forecasting technique has been found to be consistently superior to the others, some MNCs prefer to use a combination of forecasting techniques. This method is referred to as mixed forecasting. Various forecasts for a particular currency value are developed using several forecasting techniques. The techniques used are assigned weights in such a way that the weights total 100 per cent, with the techniques considered more reliable being assigned higher weights. The actual forecast of the currency is a weighted average of the various forecasts developed.

EXAMPLE

Pergreen plc needs to assess the value of the Mexican peso because it is considering expanding its business in Mexico. The conclusions drawn from each forecasting technique are shown in Exhibit 9.2. Notice that, in this example, the forecasted direction of the peso's value is dependent on the technique used. The fundamental forecast predicts the peso will appreciate, but the technical forecast and the market-based forecast predict it will depreciate. Also, notice that even though the fundamental and market-based forecasts are both driven by the same factor (interest rates), the results are distinctly different.

EXHIBIT 9.2   Forecasts of the Mexican peso drawn from each forecasting technique

	Factors considered	Situation	Forecast
Technical forecast	Recent movement in peso	The peso's value declined below a specific threshold level in the last few weeks.	The peso's value will continue to fall now that it is beyond the threshold level.
Fundamental forecast	Economic growth, inflation, interest rates	Mexico's interest rates are high and inflation should remain low.	The peso's value will rise as euro investors capitalize on the high interest rates by investing in Mexican securities.
Market-based forecast	Spot rate, forward rate	The peso's forward rate exhibits a significant discount which is attributed to Mexico's relatively high interest rates.	Based on the forward rate, which provides a forecast of the future spot rate, the peso's value will decline.

Sometimes MNCs assign one technique a lower weight when forecasting in one period, but a higher weight when forecasting in a later period. Some firms even weight a given technique more for some currencies than for others at a given point in time. For example, a firm may decide that a market-based forecast provides the best prediction for the pound, but that fundamental forecasting works best for the New Zealand dollar, and technical forecasting for the Mexican peso.

While each forecasting method has its merits, some changes in exchange rates are not anticipated by any method.

EXAMPLE

During the Asian crisis, the Indonesian rupiah depreciated by more than 80 per cent against the dollar within a 9-month period. Before the rupiah's decline, neither technical factors, nor fundamental factors, nor the forward rate indicated any potential weakness. The depreciation of the rupiah was primarily attributed to concerns by institutional investors about the safety of their investments in Indonesia, which encouraged them to liquidate the investments and convert the rupiah into other currencies, putting downward pressure on the rupiah.

Weakness in some currencies may best be anticipated by a subjective assessment of conditions in a particular country and not by the quantitative methods described here. Thus, MNCs may benefit from using the methods described in this chapter along with their own sense of the conditions in a particular country. Nevertheless, it is still difficult to anticipate that a currency will weaken before a speculative outflow occurs. By that time, the currency will have weakened as a result of the outflow.

FORECASTING SERVICES

The corporate need to forecast currency values has prompted the emergence of several forecasting service firms, including Business International, Conti Currency, Predex and Wharton Econometric Forecasting Associates. In addition, large investment banks offer forecasting services. Many consulting services use at least two different types of analysis to generate separate forecasts and then determine the weighted average of the forecasts. Some forecasting services focus on technical forecasting, while others focus on fundamental forecasting.

USING THE WEB

Exchange rate forecasts

A useful source for the type of data used in making forecasts can be found at: www.fxstreet.com but beware of the mixture of technical and fundamental approaches to forecasting.

Forecasts are even provided for currencies that are not widely traded. Forecasting service firms provide forecasts on any currency for time horizons of interest to their clients, ranging from 1 day to 10 years from now. In addition, some firms offer advice on international cash management, assessment of exposure to exchange rate risk, and hedging. Many of the firms provide their clients with forecasts and recommendations monthly, or even weekly, for an annual fee.

Performance of forecasting services

Given the recent volatility in foreign exchange markets, it is quite difficult to forecast currency values. One way for a corporation to determine whether a forecasting service is valuable is to compare the accuracy of its forecasts to that of publicly available and free forecasts. The forward rate serves as a benchmark for comparison here, since it is quoted in many newspapers and magazines.

Some studies have compared several forecasting services' forecasts for different currencies to the forward rate, and found that the forecasts provided by services are no better than using the forward rate. Such results are frustrating for the corporations that have paid substantial amounts for expert opinions.

Perhaps some corporate clients of these forecasting services believe the fee is justified even when the forecasting performance is poor, if other services (such as **cash management**) are included in the package. Alternatively, one may argue that the value of the services is not in necessarily being able to predict exchange rates on a day-to-day basis, but rather being able to anticipate high-risk situations and predict large changes in the exchange rate as with Black Wednesday 1992 in the UK, or the unpegging of the Argentine peso with the dollar in 2002 (see Chapter 6). It is also possible that a corporate treasurer, in recognition of the potential for error in forecasting exchange rates, may prefer to pay a forecasting service firm for its forecasts. Then the treasurer is not directly responsible for corporate problems that result from inaccurate currency forecasts. Not all MNCs hire forecasting service firms to do their forecasting, some may have in-house economists, others may hedge as a matter of policy.

EVALUATION OF FORECAST PERFORMANCE

An MNC that forecasts exchange rates must monitor its performance over time to determine whether the forecasting procedure is satisfactory. For this purpose, a measurement of the forecast error is required.

There are various ways to compute forecast errors. One popular measurement will be discussed here and is defined as follows:

$$\text{Absolute forecast error as a fraction of the realized value} = \frac{|\text{Forecasted value} - \text{Realized value}|}{\text{Realized value}}$$

The error is computed using an absolute value because this avoids a possible offsetting effect when determining the mean forecast error. If the forecast error is 0.05 in the first period and −0.05 in the second period (if the absolute value is not taken), the mean error is zero. Yet, that is misleading because the forecast was not perfectly accurate in either period. The absolute value avoids such a distortion.

When comparing a forecasting technique's performance among different currencies, it is often useful to adjust for their relative sizes.

EXAMPLE

Consider the following forecasted and realized values by Old Hampshire plc during one period:

	Forecasted value	Realized value
US dollar	£0.60	£0.58
Japanese yen	£0.005	£0.006

In this case, the difference between the forecasted value and the realized value is £0.02 for the dollar and £0.001 for the yen. This does not necessarily mean that the forecast for the yen is more accurate. When the *relative* size of what is forecasted is considered (by dividing the difference by the realized value), one can see that the dollar has been predicted with more accuracy on a percentage basis. With the data given, the forecasting error (as defined earlier) of the British pound is:

Absolute forecast error as a percentage of the realized value $= \frac{|£0.60 - £0.58|}{£0.58}$
$= 3.4\%$

In contrast, the forecast error of the Japanese yen is:

Absolute forecast error as a percentage of the realized value $= \frac{|£0.005 - £0.006|}{£0.006}$
$= 16.7\%$

It is the percentage difference between actual and forecast that matters when translating large sums of money, not the absolute amount. Thus, the yen has been predicted with less accuracy as a percentage even though the absolute error in the exchange rate is a smaller number. Translating yen into pounds would differ from expectations by 16.7 per cent as opposed to only 3.4 per cent if translating the US dollar into pounds.

Forecast accuracy over time

The efficient markets hypothesis has the rather hidden assumption that the best forecast of a future exchange rate is the current one, the spot rate. In effect this is a prediction of no change. If an MNC uses the current spot to predict the rate 30 days forward the implication is that there will be no change between the current spot and the actual 30 days. Hence, why should this prediction be accurate? Surely all the discussion in the newspapers about a currency strengthening and another weakening etc. implies that the market is predicting future movements and a 1 month forward rate would include such a prediction. But the efficient markets hypothesis says that *all* information about a product is included in the *current* price. That information is about the *future* not the past. Therefore any expectations about a rise in the value of the dollar should be included in the *current* price. The only difference between the spot rate and our prediction *now* of some future rate is the relative cost of time between the two currencies. Other than that, all the information that is included in the estimate of say a forward rate will also be included in the spot rate.

Exhibit 9.3 examines the euro dollar exchange rate but the results would be the same for any two currencies over any time period. There are two predictions of the spot rate in 1-month's time. First, the 1 month forward prediction of the spot rate and second, the no change prediction from just using the current spot. One can see clearly that the two predictions are very similar. In fact the mean absolute forecast error as a percentage of the realized value is 2.3 per cent using the forward prediction and 2.4 per cent using the no change or spot prediction. Not only are the errors similar, Exhibit 9.4 shows that they are highly correlated. This is what we would expect because the efficient markets hypothesis tells us that all the information in the spot should be in the forward and all the information in the forward should also be in the spot. The only exception is the difference in interest rates. Because the forward rate is at a different point in time, the difference in interest rates (the cost of time) must be accounted for (see Chapter 7).

Statistical test of forecasts – the de-trending problem

A wrong method of testing a forecast is to apply the following regression model to historical data:

$$S_t = a_0 + a_1 F_{t-1,\, t} + \mu_t$$

Where:

S_t = the spot rate in direct form (i.e. per unit of foreign currency) at time t
$F_{t-1,t}$ = the forward rate prediction, again in direct form, for time t made at time $t-1$
μ_t = error term for period t
a_0 = the intercept
a_1 = the regression coefficient

The problem with this model as a prediction is that it is not de-trended. The results appear to produce in most instances a regression model of very high significance and therefore good prediction with a high R^2. Do not be fooled. The model is measuring error from using the model compared to the error made by no

EXHIBIT 9.3 Forward prediction, no change prediction and actual spot

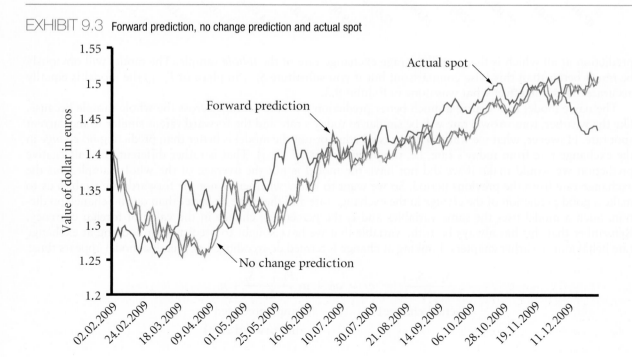

EXHIBIT 9.4 Percentage prediction error

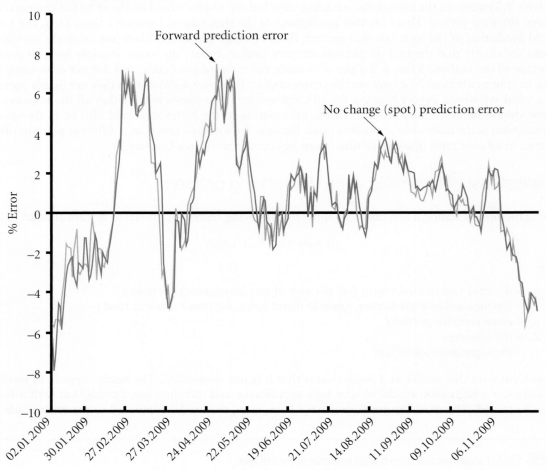

prediction at all which is the overall average exchange rate of the *whole* sample. The model will obviously be much better than this false comparison; but if you substitute S_{t-1} in place of $F_{t-1,t}$ the model is equally accurate! This is in effect what was done in Exhibit 9.3.

The naïve model is of course a much better prediction than the average across the whole sample because, like the weather, tomorrow's rate will be similar to today's rate and the forward rate is similar to the current spot rate. However, what we want to know is whether or not the model is better than predicting *no change* in the exchange rate from today's rate, i.e. the *previous period* (S_{t-1}). That is rather different. The alternative prediction we would make if we did not have the model is not the average of the whole sample, but the exchange rate from the previous period. So we want to know whether or not the forward rate enables us to make a good prediction of the *change* in the exchange rate and therefore be better than our no change prediction. Such a model uses the same variables and e_f the percentage change in the value of foreign currency. Remember that this has always been the variable that we have sought to predict when looking at exchange rate behaviour in earlier chapters. Looking at change is termed de-trending, a de-trended model appears thus:

$$\frac{S_t - S_{t-1}}{S_t} = e_f = a_0 + a_1 \frac{F_{t-1} - S_t}{S_t} + \mu_t$$

(actual change)   (change predicted by

the forward rate)

If the forward rate is unbiased, the intercept should equal zero, and the regression coefficient a_1 should equal 1.0. The t-test for a_1 is:

$$t = \frac{a_1 - 1}{\text{Standard error of } a_1}$$

If $a_0 = 0$ and a_1 is significantly less than 1.0, this implies that the forward rate is systematically overestimating the spot rate. For example, if $a_0 = 0$ and $a_1 = 0.90$, the prediction of the change in the spot rate (as in the de-trended model) is estimated to be 90 per cent of the change forecast generated by the forward rate.

Conversely, if $a_0 = 0$ and a_1 is significantly greater than 1.0, this implies that the forward rate is systematically underestimating the value of 1 unit of foreign currency – the spot rate. For example, if $a_0 = 0$ and $a_1 = 1.1$, the future spot rate is estimated to be 1.1 times the forecast generated by the forward rate.

It is generally the case that statistical models make very poor predictions of future exchange rate changes. Again the efficient markets hypothesis tells us that we should not be too surprised by this result. The semi-strong and strong forms of the hypothesis identify news as the cause of price changes. By definition, news is the unexpected. Now let us suppose that we have a regression model to predict changes in the exchange rate (e_f) that is:

$$e_f = a_0 + a_1\, X_1 + a_2\, X_2 + \ldots$$

The explanatory variables X_1, X_2, ... could be differences in the money supply, changes in current account balances and so on. To return to an earlier argument, what we are measuring is not the effect of news because we do not know what the market expected. It was shown that in terms of news, if the market expected a worsening of the current account balance, the actual worsening would not be news and we would not expect to see a change in the exchange rate even though the current account worsened. The assumption of the model is in effect that all changes are news and this is not the case. The evidence is that news is the predominant influence as suggested by the efficient markets hypothesis. A visual representation of this is in Exhibit 9.3, where the gap between the actual spot and the forward prediction is caused by news. In a no-news world the forward rate would be more or less accurate, determined by interest and inflation. Only when inflation is extreme as in the case of Turkish inflation cited earlier will inflation dominate. The fact that news is randomly good or bad means that the no change prediction, the current spot, has a sound theoretical basis. This is confirmed in weak form tests of the efficient markets hypothesis.

Should MNCs make exchange rate forecasts?

The answer to this question is both yes and no. In what is a reasonably efficient market, expecting an MNC to make regular forecasts of the exchange rate and to act on those predictions would be misleading. On occasions the company would profit and at other times make a loss. On average, however, the MNC will not be able to 'beat the market' and should not be engaging in what are essentially speculative activities.

On the other hand, monitoring exchange rates because of the risk of changes in the exchange rate is sensible. Actual changes do not occur in quite the way that theory predicts. The difference is apparent when comparing Exhibit 9.5a with Exhibit 9.5b, the first shows 7 years of actual changes in the £:$1 exchange rate and the second shows the changes that would be predicted by a random walk – the theoretical basis of the price movements.

Two differences are immediately apparent. The first is that the percentage change in Exhibit 9.5b occurs evenly throughout the range whereas in Exhibit 9.5a the changes are quite irregular. Not only are there periods of heightened movement during the world financial crisis but also there are periods of extremely low movement before the crisis. The variation is uneven, a phenomenon referred to as 'bunching' by Benoit Mandelbrot. The second very apparent difference is that in practice (Exhibit 9.5a) there are extreme changes that are not predicted by theory. Of the 2556 observations there are 19 with a probability of less than three in a million of occurring. This is sometimes referred to as 'sigma events' in this case four-sigma events and above, i.e. 4 standard deviations from the mean. This phenomenon is known as 'fat tails' in that there are more observations in the extreme ends of the distribution than would be predicted from a normal distribution.

EXHIBIT 9.5a   US $ to UK £ percentage daily change in exchange rate of the UK £ value of $1

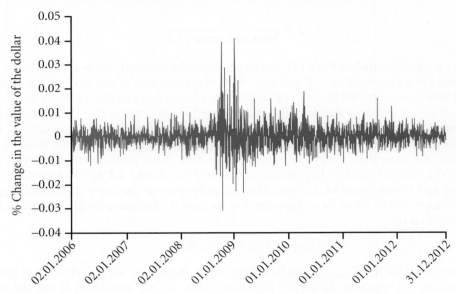

EXHIBIT 9.5b   Percentage change from a random walk with the same mean and standard deviation as Exhibit 9.5a – this is the theoretical model of exchange rate changes

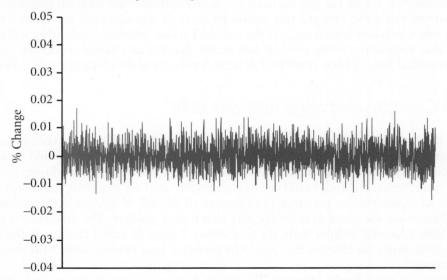

A less obvious difference is the 'peakiness' of the distribution. There are more smaller movements than would be predicted resulting in a pointed rather than a rounded distribution as one would expect from a normal distribution, see Exhibit 9.5c.

This mixture of excessively quiet periods mixed with extreme variation both of which are not predicted by the normal distribution is difficult to manage. For some periods, protection in the form of derivatives may seem unnecessary and risk taking may seem profitable. In the very short term this may well be true;

EXHIBIT 9.5c   Distribution of changes in the exchange rate. The actual distribution

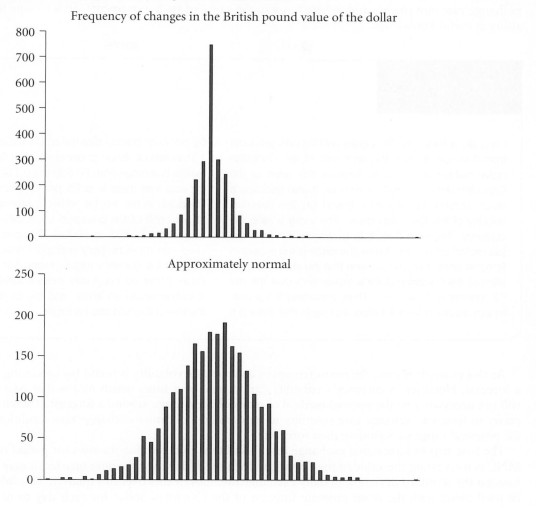

but where it is not true, large losses will be made. Certainly, one cannot rely on statistics (the analysis of past data) and the ergodic assumption (the future will replicate the past). To understand surprises in the market, more must be understood about the driving force of the exchange rate changes. This requires being able to understand the nature of a crisis and its implications through interpreting the newspapers and other news sources. Fortunately for the reader, MNCs need managers who understand international financial management!

EXCHANGE RATE VOLATILITY

Stock market efficiency suggests that an MNC, like an investor, cannot outpredict the market in attempting to forecast the actual future exchange rate. The efficiency concept in a sense does not allow anyone to consistently outpredict the market. But predicting volatility is still 'allowable' in that knowledge of future volatility does not suggest any particular buying or selling strategy that will affect prices. Speculators may take out straddles (see Chapter 8) but this is not, of itself, a hedge on a price rise or fall. For an MNC, the knowledge that an exchange rate is going to become more volatile is nevertheless useful for managing uncertainty; it can take the market forecast and the range around the forecast. Where volatility is predicted to increase, an MNC can take a more cautious strategy to protect itself from the effects of exchange rate movements and, where known, the cause of such movements. So a change in expected volatility is useful knowledge.

EXAMPLE

Harp plc is based in Shropshire and imports products from Canada. It uses the spot rate of the Canadian dollar (valued at £0.70) to forecast the value of the Canadian dollar 1 month from now. It also specifies a range around its forecasts, based on the historical volatility of the Canadian dollar. The more volatile the currency, the more likely it is to wander far from the forecasted value in the future (the larger is the expected forecast error). Harp determines that the standard deviation of the Canadian dollar's movements over the last 12 months is 2 per cent. Thus, assuming the movements are normally distributed, it expects that there is a

68 per cent chance that the actual value will be within 1 standard deviation (2 per cent) of its forecast, which results in a range from £0.686 to £0.714. In addition, it expects that there is a 95 per cent chance that the Canadian dollar will be within 2 standard deviations (4 per cent) of the predicted value, which results in a range from £0.672 to £0.728. By specifying a range, Harp can more properly anticipate how far the actual value of the currency might deviate from its predicted value. If the currency was more volatile, its standard deviation would be larger, and the range surrounding the forecast would also be larger.

As this example shows, the measurement of a currency's volatility is useful for specifying a range around a forecast. However, a currency's volatility can change over time, which means that past volatility levels will not necessarily be the optimal method of establishing a range around a forecast. Therefore, MNCs may prefer to forecast exchange rate volatility using estimates of future exchange rate conditions to determine the potential range surrounding their forecast.

The first step in forecasting exchange rate volatility is to determine the relevant period of concern. If an MNC is forecasting the value of the Canadian dollar each day over the next quarter, it may also attempt to forecast the standard deviation of daily exchange rate movements over this quarter. This information could be used along with the point estimate forecast of the Canadian dollar for each day to derive confidence intervals around each forecast.

Methods of forecasting exchange rate volatility

The volatility of exchange rate movements for a future period can be forecast using: (1) recent exchange rate volatility, (2) historical time series of volatilities and (3) the implied standard deviation derived from currency option prices.

Use of short-term volatility to predict long-term volatility. The volatility of historical exchange rate movements over a recent period can be used to forecast the short-, medium- and long-term future. In our example, the standard deviation of monthly exchange rate movements in the Canadian dollar during the previous 12 months could be used to estimate the future volatility of the Canadian dollar over the next month. If the volatility conditions of the monthly figures in the 12-months' sample is thought to be typical for the next year, the predicted monthly standard deviation can be converted to an annual predicted standard deviation by the simple formula:

$$\text{s.d.}_t = \text{s.d.}_m \times \sqrt{(t \, / \, m)}$$

Where:

    s.d. = standard deviation

    t, m = time periods in the same unit of time where t is the longer time period and m the shorter time period (so a monthly prediction converted to a prediction of the standard deviation for a year can be calculated by setting $t = 12$ months and $m = 1$ month)

The assumptions are that the exchange rate movements are not correlated over time and follow a random walk. In practice, levels of stationarity will mean that this is a slight overestimate of future volatility (see Appendix 8).

EXAMPLE

The standard deviation of monthly changes in the value of currency Y for the last 12 months has been 1 per cent. Winston Ltd estimates that these conditions will last for at least 1 year and wants to know the estimated standard deviation for the exchange rate 1 year hence rather than 1 month hence. Using the above equation, $t = 12$ months and $m = 1$ month.

So the implied annual standard deviation of the 1-year estimate is:

$$\text{s.d.}_t = \text{s.d.}_m \times \sqrt{(t/m)}$$
$$3.46\% = 1\% \times \sqrt{(12/1)}$$

Assuming a random walk and a current spot of £0.50:1 Y, the 95 per cent confidence interval for Y will be:

1.96 standard deviations × 3.46% = 6.78% of the expected value, so:

£0.50 × (1 − 6.78%) < £0.50 < £0.50 × (1 + 6.78%)

£0.4661 < £0.50 < £0.5339

Use of a historical pattern of volatilities. Since historical volatility can change over time, the standard deviation of monthly exchange rate movements in the last 12 months is not necessarily an accurate predictor of the volatility of exchange rate movements in the next month. To the extent that there is a pattern to the changes in exchange rate volatility over time, a series of time periods may be used to forecast volatility in the next period. Being able to predict stock market volatility does not violate weak-form efficiency. The actual value of a currency may not follow a pattern or be predictable but the variance can be predictable. Just as with a lottery, knowing the range of outcomes and their equal probability does not (alas) help to predict the actual number.

EXAMPLE

The standard deviation of monthly exchange rate movements in the dollar can be determined for each of the last several years. Then, a time series trend of these standard deviation levels can be used to form an estimate for the volatility of the dollar over the next month. The forecast may be based on a weighting scheme such as 60 per cent times the standard deviation in the last year, plus 30 per cent times the standard deviation in the year before that, plus 10 per cent times the standard deviation in the year before that. This scheme places more weight on the most recent data to derive the forecast but allows data from the last 3 years to influence the forecast. Normally, the weights that achieved the most accuracy (lowest forecast error) over previous periods and the number of previous periods (lags) would be used when applying this method.

Various economic and political factors can cause exchange rate volatility to change abruptly, however, so even sophisticated time series models do not necessarily generate accurate forecasts of exchange rate volatility. This method differs from the first method in that it uses information from periods beyond the previous 12 months.

Implied standard deviation. A third method for forecasting exchange rate volatility is to derive the exchange rate's implied standard deviation (ISD) from the currency option pricing model. Recall that the premium on a call option for a currency is dependent on factors such as the relationship between the spot exchange rate and the exercise (strike) price of the option, the number of days until the expiration date of the option, and the anticipated volatility of the currency's exchange rate movements. The actual values of each of these factors are known, except for the anticipated volatility. By plugging in the prevailing option premium paid by investors for that specific currency option, however, it is possible to derive the market's anticipated volatility for that currency. The volatility is measured by the standard deviation, which can be used to develop a probability distribution surrounding the forecast of the currency's exchange rate.

Subjective estimation. As a concluding note it should be emphasized that statistical techniques do no more than inform what is essentially a subjective judgement. Implied volatilities are market judgements and will include information from statistical modelling. To that extent the implied volatilities in option prices are a better source of estimation as market efficiency implies that the estimate is well informed.

USING THE WEB

Implied volatilities

Implied volatilities of major currencies are provided at: www.fednewyork.org/markets/ impliedvolatility.html. The implied volatility can be used to measure the market's expectations of a specific currency's volatility in the future. Implied volatilities are shown for different expiration dates, which allows for forecasts of volatility over periods up to those expiration dates.

SUMMARY

- MNCs need exchange rate forecasts to make decisions on hedging payables and receivables, short-term financing and investment, capital budgeting, and long-term financing.

- The most common forecasting techniques can be classified as: (1) technical, (2) fundamental, (3) market-based and (4) mixed. Each technique has limitations, and the quality of the forecasts produced varies. Yet, due to the high variability in exchange rates, it should not be surprising that forecasts are not always accurate.

- Forecasting methods can be evaluated by comparing the actual values of currencies to the values predicted by the forecasting method. To be meaningful, this comparison should be conducted over several periods. Two criteria used to evaluate performance of a forecast method are bias and accuracy. When comparing the accuracy of forecasts for two currencies, the absolute forecast error should be divided by the realized value of the currency to control for differences in the relative values of currencies.

CRITICAL DEBATE

What should an MNC use to forecast when budgeting?

Proposition: use the spot rate to forecast. When an MNC firm conducts financial budgeting, it must estimate the values of its foreign currency cash flows that will be received by the parent. Since it is well documented that firms cannot accurately forecast future values, MNCs should use the spot rate for budgeting. Changes in economic conditions are difficult to predict, and the spot rate reflects the best guess of the future spot rate if there are no changes in economic conditions.

Opposing view: use the forward rate to forecast. The spot rates of some currencies do not represent accurate or even unbiased estimates of the future spot rates. Many currencies of developing countries have generally declined over time. These currencies tend to be in countries that have high inflation rates. If the spot rate

had been used for budgeting, the dollar cash flows resulting from cash inflows in these currencies would have been highly overestimated. The expected inflation in a country can be accounted for by using the nominal interest rate. A high nominal interest rate implies a high level of expected inflation. Based on interest rate parity, these currencies will have pronounced discounts. Thus, the forward rate captures the expected inflation differential between countries because it is influenced by the nominal interest rate differential. Since it captures the inflation differential, it should provide a more accurate forecast of currencies, especially those currencies in high-inflation countries.

With whom do you agree? Use InfoTrac or some other search engine to learn more about this issue. Which argument do you support? Offer your own opinion on this issue.

SELF TEST

Answers are provided in Appendix A at the back of the text.

1 Assume that the annual UK interest rate is expected to be 7 per cent for each of the next 4 years, while the annual interest rate in India is expected to be 20 per cent. Determine the appropriate 4-year forward rate premium or discount on the Indian rupee, which could be used to forecast the percentage change in the rupee over the next 4 years.

2 Consider the following information

Currency	90-day forward rate	Spot rate that occurred 90-days later
Canadian dollar	0.80 euros	0.82 euros
Japanese yen	0.012 euros	0.011 euros

Assuming the forward rate was used to forecast the future spot rate, determine whether the Canadian dollar or the Japanese yen was forecasted with more

accuracy, based on the absolute forecast error as a percentage of the realized value.

3 An analyst has stated that the British pound seems to increase in value over the 2 weeks following announcements by the Bank of England (the British central bank) that it will raise interest rates. If this statement is true, what are the inferences regarding weak-form or semi-strong-form efficiency?

4 Assume that Russian interest rates are much higher than UK interest rates. Also assume that interest rate parity (discussed in Chapter 7) exists. Would you expect the rouble to appreciate or depreciate? Explain.

5 Warden plc is considering a project in Venezuela, which will be very profitable if the local currency (bolivar) appreciates against the British pound. If the bolivar depreciates, the project will result in losses. Warden plc forecasts that the bolivar will appreciate. The bolivar's value historically has been very volatile. As a manager of Warden plc, would you be comfortable with this project? Explain.

QUESTIONS AND APPLICATIONS

1 Motives for forecasting. Explain corporate motives for forecasting exchange rates.

2 Technical forecasting. Explain the technical technique for forecasting exchange rates. What are some limitations of using technical forecasting to predict exchange rates?

3 Fundamental forecasting. Explain the fundamental technique for forecasting exchange rates. What are some limitations of using a fundamental technique to forecast exchange rates?

4 Market-based forecasting. Explain the market-based technique for forecasting exchange rates. What is the rationale for using market-based forecasts? If the euro appreciates substantially against the dollar during a specific period, would market-based forecasts have overestimated or underestimated the realized values over this period? Explain.

5 Mixed forecasting. Explain the mixed technique for forecasting exchange rates.

6 Detecting a forecast bias. Explain how to assess performance in forecasting exchange rates. Explain how to detect a bias in forecasting exchange rates.

7 Measuring forecast accuracy. You are hired as a consultant to assess a firm's ability to forecast. The firm has developed a point forecast for two different currencies presented in the following table. The firm asks you to determine which currency was forecasted with greater accuracy.

Period	Yen forecast	Actual yen value	Dollar forecast	Actual dollar value
1	£0.0050	£0.0051	£0.60	£0.61
2	0.0048	0.0052	0.62	0.61
3	0.0053	0.0052	0.63	0.65
4	0.0055	0.0056	0.58	0.62

8 Limitations of a fundamental forecast. Wellington Ltd believes that future real interest rate movements will affect exchange rates, and it has applied regression analysis to historical data to assess the relationship. It will use regression coefficients derived from this analysis, along with forecasted real interest rate movements, to predict exchange rates in the future. Explain at least three limitations of this method.

9 Consistent forecasts. Brinnington plc is a UK-based MNC with subsidiaries in most major countries. Each subsidiary is responsible for forecasting the future exchange rate of its local currency relative to the British pound. Comment on this policy. How might Brinnington ensure consistent forecasts among the different subsidiaries?

10 Forecasting with a forward rate. Assume that the 4-year annualized interest rate in the UK is 9 per cent and the 4-year annualized interest rate in Singapore is 6 per cent. Assume interest rate parity holds for a 4-year horizon. Assume that the spot rate of the Singapore dollar is £0.40. If the forward rate is used to forecast exchange rates, what will be the forecast for the Singapore dollar's spot rate in 4 years? What percentage appreciation or depreciation does this forecast imply over the 4-year period?

11 Foreign exchange market efficiency. Assume that foreign exchange markets were found to be weak-form efficient. What does this suggest about utilizing technical analysis to speculate in euros? If MNCs believe that foreign exchange markets are strong-form efficient, why would they develop their own forecasts of future exchange rates? That is, why wouldn't they simply use today's quoted rates as indicators about future rates? After all, today's quoted rates should reflect all relevant information.

12 Forecast error. The director of currency forecasting at Champaign-Urbana Ltd says, 'The most critical task of forecasting exchange rates is not to derive a point estimate of a future exchange rate but to assess how wrong our estimate might be.' What does this statement mean?

13 Forecasting exchange rates of currencies that previously were fixed. When some countries in Eastern Europe initially allowed their currencies to fluctuate against the dollar, would the fundamental technique based on historical relationships have been useful for forecasting future exchange rates of these currencies? Explain.

14 Forecast error. Royce Ltd is a UK firm with future receivables 1 year from now in Canadian dollars and Brazilian real. Its Brazilian real receivables are known with certainty, and its estimated Canadian dollar receivables are subject to a 2 per cent error in either direction. The pound values of both types of receivables are similar. There is no chance of default by the customers involved. Royce's treasurer says that the estimate of pound cash flows to be generated from the Brazilian real receivables is subject to greater uncertainty than that of the Canadian dollar receivables. Explain the rationale for the treasurer's statement.

15 Forecasting the euro. Cooper plc periodically obtains euros to purchase German products. It assesses UK and German trade patterns and inflation rates to develop a fundamental forecast for the euro. How could Cooper possibly improve its method of fundamental forecasting as applied to the euro?

16 Forward rate forecast. Assume that you obtain a quote for a 1-year forward rate on the Mexican peso. Assume that Mexico's 1-year interest rate is 40 per cent, while the UK 1-year interest rate is 7 per cent.

Over the next year, the peso depreciates by 12 per cent. Do you think the forward rate overestimated the spot rate 1 year ahead in this case? Explain.

17 Forecasting based on purchasing power parity versus the forward rate. You believe that the Singapore dollar's exchange rate movements are mostly attributed to PPP. Today, the nominal annual interest rate in Singapore is 18 per cent. The nominal annual interest rate in the UK is 3 per cent. You expect that annual inflation will be about 4 per cent in Singapore and 1 per cent in the UK. Assume that interest rate parity holds. Today the spot rate of the Singapore dollar is £0.41. Do you think the 1-year forward rate would underestimate, overestimate or be an unbiased estimate of the future spot rate in 1 year? Explain.

18 Interpreting an unbiased forward rate. Assume that the forward rate is an unbiased but not necessarily accurate forecast of the future exchange rate of the yen over the next several years. Based on this information, do you think Raven Ltd should hedge its remittance of expected Japanese yen profits to the UK parent by selling yen forward contracts? Why would this strategy be advantageous? Under what conditions would this strategy backfire?

ADVANCED QUESTIONS

19 Probability distribution of forecasts. Assume that the following regression model was applied to historical quarterly data:

$$e_t = a_0 + a_1 INT_t + a_2 INF_{t-1} + \mu_t$$

Where:

e_t = percentage change in the exchange rate of the Japanese yen in period t

INT_t = average real interest rate differential (UK interest rate minus Japanese interest rate) over period t

INF_{t-1} = inflation differential (UK inflation rate minus Japanese inflation rate) in the previous period

a_0, a_1, a_2 = regression coefficients

μ_t = error term.

Assume that the regression coefficients had high T-scores and were estimated as follows:

$$a_0 = 0.0$$
$$a_1 = 0.9$$
$$a_2 = 0.8$$

Also assume that the inflation differential in the most recent period was 3 per cent. The real interest rate differential in the upcoming period is forecasted as follows:

Interest rate differential	Probability
0%	30%
1	60
2	10

If Stillwater Ltd uses this information to forecast the Japanese yen's exchange rate, what will be the probability distribution of the yen's percentage change over the upcoming period?

20 **Testing for a forecast bias.** You must determine whether there is a forecast bias in the forward rate. You apply regression analysis to test the relationship between the actual spot rate and the forward rate forecast (F):

$$S = a_0 + a_1(F)$$

The regression results are as follows:

Coefficient	Standard error
$a_0 = 0.006$	0.011
$a_1 = 0.800$	0.05

Based on these results, is there a bias in the forecast? Verify your conclusion. If there is a bias, explain whether it is an overestimate or an underestimate.

21 **Effect of September 11 on forward rate forecasts.** The September 11, 2001 terrorist attack on the USA was quickly followed by lower interest rates in the USA. How would this affect a fundamental forecast of foreign currencies? How would this affect the forward rate forecast of foreign currencies?

22 **Interpreting forecast bias information.** The treasurer of Glencoe Ltd detected a forecast bias when using the 30-day forward rate of the euro to forecast future spot rates of the euro over various periods. He believes he can use this information to determine whether imports ordered every week should be hedged (payment is made 30 days after each order). Glencoe's managing director says that in the long run the forward rate is unbiased and that the treasurer should not waste time trying to 'beat the forward rate' but should just hedge all orders. Who is correct?

23 **Forecasting Latin American currencies.** The value of each Latin American currency relative to the euro is dictated by supply and demand conditions between that currency and the dollar. The values of Latin American currencies have generally declined substantially against the euro over time. Most of these countries have high inflation rates and high interest rates. The data on inflation rates, economic growth, and other economic indicators are subject to error, as limited resources are used to compile the data.

a If the forward rate is used as a market-based forecast, will this rate result in a forecast of appreciation, depreciation, or no change in any particular Latin American currency? Explain.

b If technical forecasting is used, will this result in a forecast of appreciation, depreciation, or no change in the value of a specific Latin American currency? Explain.

c Do you think that UK firms can accurately forecast the future values of Latin American currencies? Explain.

24 **Selecting between forecast methods.** Suppose Bolivia has a nominal 1-year risk-free interest rate of 40 per cent, which is primarily due to the high level of expected inflation. The euro nominal 1-year risk-free interest rate is 8 per cent. The spot rate of Bolivia's currency (called the boliviana) is 0.14 euro. The 1-year forward rate of the boliviana is 0.108 euro. What is the forecasted percentage change in the boliviana if the spot rate is used as a 1-year forecast? What is the forecasted percentage change in the boliviana if the 1-year forward rate is used as a 1-year forecast? Which forecast do you think will be more accurate? Why?

25 **Comparing market-based forecasts.** For all parts of this question, assume that interest rate parity exists, the prevailing 1-year UK nominal interest rate is low, and that you expect UK inflation to be low this year.

a Assume that the country Dinland engages in much trade with the UK and the trade involves many different products. Dinland has had a zero trade balance with the UK (the value of exports and imports is about the same) in the past. Assume that you expect a high level of inflation (about 40 per cent) in Dinland over the next year because of a large increase in the prices of many products that Dinland produces. Dinland presently has a 1-year risk-free interest rate of more than 40 per cent. Do you think that the prevailing spot rate or the 1-year forward rate would result in a more accurate forecast of Dinland's currency (the din) 1 year from now? Explain.

b Assume that the country Freeland engages in much trade with the UK and the trade involves many different products. Freeland has had a zero trade balance with the UK (the value of exports and imports is about the same) in the past. You expect high inflation (about 40 per cent) in Free-land over the next year because of a large increase in the cost of land (and therefore hous-ing) in Freeland. You believe that the prices of products that Freeland produces will not be affected. Freeland presently has a 1-year risk-free interest rate of more than 40 per cent. Do you think that the prevailing 1-year forward rate of

Freeland's currency (the fre) would overestimate, underestimate, or be a reasonably accurate fore-cast of the spot rate 1 year from now? (Presume a direct quotation of the exchange rate, so that if the forward rate underestimates, it means that its value is less than the realized spot rate in one year. If the forward rate overestimates, it means that its value is more than the realized spot rate in one year.)

PROJECT WORKSHOP

26 **CME exchange rates.** The website of the Chicago Mercantile Exchange (CME) provides information about the exchange and the futures contracts offered on the exchange. Its address is http://www.cme.com.

a   Go to the section on 'Prices' and then to the 'Daily and Weekly Charts'. Describe the trend of a peso futures contract over the last few months. What does this trend suggest about changes in fore-casts of the peso over the period assessed (assuming that the futures rate was used as a forecasting method)? What do you think caused the futures prices to change over the last few months?

b   Select a peso futures contract that has at least 1 month until its settlement date. Determine whether that futures contract would have under-estimated or overestimated the spot rate as of the settlement date if it had been used to forecast the future spot rate. Was the forecast accurate?

27 Select an exchange rate and a forward rate for a given period.

a   Calculate:

$$S_t = a_0 + a_1 F_{t-1,t} + \mu_t$$

Where:

S_t = the spot rate at time t

$F_{t-1,t}$ = the forward rate prediction for time t made at time $t-1$

μ_t = error term for period t

a_0 = the intercept

a_1 = the regression coefficient, and note the R^2. Does this prove that the future is a good predictor?

b   Now calculate the equation:

$$S_t = a_0 + a_1 S_{t-1} + \mu_t$$

compare your result with the equation in section (a). How do you explain the good performance of the model in this section, given that it is only using an old rate $(t-1)$ to predict the rate at time t?

c   Finally calculate the equation:

$$\frac{S_t - S_{t-1}}{S_t} = a_0 + a_1 \frac{F_{t-1} - S_t}{S_t} + \mu_t$$

Is this a better model? Explain with reference to de-trending.

DISCUSSION IN THE BOARDROOM

This exercise can be found on our dedicated Course-Mate platform for students.

RUNNING YOUR OWN MNC

This exercise can be found on our dedicated Course-Mate platform for students.

Essays/discussion and articles can be found at the end of Part III.

BLADES PLC CASE STUDY

Forecasting exchange rates

Recall that Blades plc the UK-based manufacturer of roller blades, is currently both exporting to and importing from Thailand. Ben Holt, Blades' chief financial officer (CFO), and you, a financial analyst at Blades plc are reasonably happy with Blades' current performance in Thailand. Entertainment Products, Inc., a Thai retailer for sporting goods, has committed itself to purchase a minimum number of Blades' 'Speedos' annually. The agreement will terminate after 3 years. Blades also imports certain components needed to manufacture its products from Thailand. Both Blades' imports and exports are denominated in Thai baht. Because of these arrangements, Blades generates approximately 10 per cent of its revenue and 4 per cent of its cost of goods sold in Thailand.

Currently, Blades' only business in Thailand consists of this export and import trade. Ben Holt, however, is thinking about using Thailand to augment Blades' UK business in other ways as well in the future. For example, Holt is contemplating establishing a subsidiary in Thailand to increase the percentage of Blades' sales to that country. Furthermore, by establishing a subsidiary in Thailand, Blades will have access to Thailand's money and capital markets. For instance, Blades could instruct its Thai subsidiary to invest excess funds or to satisfy its short-term needs for funds in the Thai money market. Furthermore, part of the subsidiary's financing could be obtained by utilizing investment banks in Thailand.

Due to Blades' current arrangements and future plans, Ben Holt is concerned about recent developments in Thailand and their potential impact on the company's future in that country. Economic conditions in Thailand have been unfavourable recently. Movements in the value of the baht have been highly volatile, and foreign investors in Thailand have lost confidence in the baht, causing massive capital outflows from Thailand. Consequently, the baht has been depreciating.

When Thailand was experiencing a high economic growth rate, few analysts anticipated an economic downturn. Consequently, Holt never found it necessary to forecast economic conditions in Thailand even though Blades was doing business there. Now, however, his attitude has changed. A continuation of the unfavourable economic conditions prevailing in Thailand could affect the demand for Blades' products in that country. Consequently, Entertainment Products may not renew its commitment for another 3 years.

Since Blades generates net cash inflows denominated in baht, a continued depreciation of the baht could adversely affect Blades, as these net inflows would be converted into fewer pounds. Thus, Blades is also considering hedging its baht-denominated inflows.

Because of these concerns, Holt has decided to reassess the importance of forecasting the baht-pound exchange rate. His primary objective is to forecast the baht-pound exchange rate for the next quarter. A secondary objective is to determine which forecasting technique is the most accurate and should be used in future periods. To accomplish this, he has asked you, a financial analyst at Blades, for help in forecasting the baht-pound exchange rate for the next quarter.

Holt is aware of the forecasting techniques available. He has collected some economic data and conducted a preliminary analysis for you to use in your analysis. For example, he has conducted a time series analysis for the exchange rates over numerous quarters. He then used this analysis to forecast the baht's value next quarter. The technical forecast indicates a depreciation of the baht by 6 per cent over the next quarter from the baht's current level of £0.015 to £0.014. He has also conducted a fundamental forecast of the baht-pound exchange rate using historical inflation and interest rate data. The fundamental forecast, however, depends on what happens to Thai interest rates during the next quarter and therefore reflects a probability distribution. There is a 30 per cent chance that Thai interest rates will be such that the baht will depreciate by 2 per cent, a 15 per cent chance that the baht will depreciate by 5 per cent, and a 55 per cent chance that the baht will depreciate by 10 per cent.

Ben Holt has asked you to answer the following questions:

1 Considering both Blades' current practices and future plans, how can it benefit from forecasting the baht-pound exchange rate?

2   Which forecasting technique (i.e. technical, fundamental, or market-based) would be easiest to use in forecasting the future value of the baht? Why?

3   Blades is considering using either current spot rates or available forward rates to forecast the future value of the baht. Available forward rates currently exhibit a large discount. Do you think the spot or the forward rate will yield a better market-based forecast? Why?

4   The current 90-day forward rate for the baht is £0.014. By what percentage is the baht expected to change over the next quarter according to a market-based forecast using the forward rate? What will be the value of the baht in 90 days according to this forecast?

5   Assume that the technical forecast has been more accurate than the market-based forecast in recent weeks. What does this indicate about market efficiency for the baht–pound exchange rate? Do you think this means that technical analysis will always be superior to other forecasting techniques in the future? Why or why not?

6   What is the expected percentage change in the value of the baht during the next quarter based on the fundamental forecast? What is the forecasted value of the baht using this forecast? If the value of the baht 90 days from now turns out to be £0.0147, which forecasting technique is the most accurate? (Use the absolute forecast error as a percentage of the realized value to answer the last part of this question.)

7   Do you think the technique you have identified in question 6 will always be the most accurate? Why or why not?

SMALL BUSINESS DILEMMA

Exchange rate forecasting by the Sports Exports Company

The Sports Exports Company converts euros into British pounds every month. The prevailing spot rate is about 1.45 euros, but there is much uncertainty about the future value of the euro. Jim Logan, owner of the Sports Exports Company, expects that British inflation will rise substantially in the future. In previous years when British inflation was high, the pound depreciated. The prevailing British interest rate is slightly higher than the prevailing euro interest rate. The pound has risen slightly over each of the last several months. Jim wants to forecast the value of the pound for each of the next 20 months.

1   Explain how Jim can use technical forecasting to forecast the future value of the euro. Based on the information provided, do you think that a technical forecast will predict future appreciation or depreciation in the pound?

2   Explain how Jim can use fundamental forecasting to forecast the future value of the euro. Based on the information provided, do you think that a fundamental forecast will predict appreciation or depreciation in the pound?

3   Explain how Jim can use a market-based forecast to forecast the future value of the euro. Do you think the market-based forecast will predict appreciation, depreciation, or no change in the value of the pound?

4   Does it appear that all of the forecasting techniques will lead to the same forecast of the euro's future value? Which technique would you prefer to use in this situation?

CHAPTER 10
MEASURING EXPOSURE TO EXCHANGE RATE FLUCTUATIONS

LEARNING OBJECTIVES

The specific objectives of this chapter are to:

- Discuss the relevance of an multinational corporation's (MNC's) exposure to exchange rate risk.

- Explain how transaction exposure can be measured.

- Explain how economic exposure can be measured.

- Explain how translation exposure can be measured.

Exchange rate risk can be broadly defined as the risk that a company's performance will be affected by exchange rate movements. MNCs closely monitor their operations to determine how they are exposed to various forms of exchange rate risk. Financial managers must understand how to measure the exposure of their MNCs to exchange rate fluctuations so that they can determine whether and how to protect their companies from such exposure.

IS EXCHANGE RATE RISK RELEVANT?

Some have argued that exchange rate risk is irrelevant. These contentions, in turn, have resulted in counter-arguments, as summarized here.

Purchasing power parity argument

One argument for exchange rate irrelevance is that, according to purchasing power parity (PPP) theory, exchange rate movements are just a response to differentials in price changes between countries. Therefore, the exchange rate effect is offset by the change in prices.

EXAMPLE

Hokkaido Ltd of Japan denominates its exports to Europe in euros. If the euro weakens by 3 per cent due to PPP, that implies that European inflation is about 3 per cent higher than Japanese inflation. If European competitors raise their prices in line with European inflation, Hokkaido can increase its euro prices by 3 per cent without losing any customers. Thus, the increase in its price of 3 per cent offsets the 3 per cent reduction in the value of the euro.

PPP does not necessarily hold, however, so the exchange rate will not necessarily change in accordance with the inflation differential between the two countries. Since a perfect offsetting effect is unlikely, the firm's competitive capabilities may indeed be influenced by exchange rate movements. Even if PPP did hold over a very long period of time, this would not comfort managers of MNCs that are focusing on the next quarter or year.

The investor hedge argument

A second argument for exchange rate irrelevance is that investors in MNCs can hedge exchange rate risk on their own. Therefore companies need not concern themselves with currency risk. The investor hedge argument assumes that investors have sufficient information on corporate exposure to exchange rate fluctuations as well as the capabilities to correctly insulate their individual exposure. To the extent that investors prefer that corporations perform the hedging for them, exchange rate exposure is relevant to corporations. An MNC may be able to hedge at a lower cost than individual investors. In addition, it has more information about its exposure and can more effectively hedge its exposure.

Currency diversification argument

Another argument is that if an MNC is well diversified across numerous countries, its value will not be affected by exchange rate movements because of offsetting effects. Correlations between currencies can be high and complete offsetting impossible.

Stakeholder diversification argument

Some critics also argue that if stakeholders (such as creditors or shareholders) are well diversified, they will be somewhat insulated against losses experienced by an MNC due to exchange rate risk. The exact nature of the currency risk of MNCs' is not disclosed so protection can only be approximate.

Response from MNCs

Creditors who provide loans to MNCs can experience large losses if the MNCs experience financial problems. Thus, creditors may prefer that the MNCs maintain low exposure to exchange rate risk.

To the extent that MNCs can stabilize their earnings over time by hedging their exchange rate risk, they may also reduce their general operating expenses over time (by avoiding costs of downsizing and restructuring caused by more variable earnings over time). Many MNCs show concern over the need to avoid excessive swings in earnings caused by exchange rate risk and engage in relatively short-term hedging (12 months or less). The following extracts from the annual accounts of selected MNCs give a flavour of their attitude to currency risk:

Nokia uses the Value-at-Risk (VaR) methodology to assess the Group exposures to foreign exchange (FX), interest rate, and equity risks. The VaR gives estimates of potential fair value losses in market risk sensitive instruments as a result of adverse changes in specified market factors, at a specified confidence level over a defined holding period.

In Nokia, the FX VaR is calculated with the Monte Carlo method which simulates random values for exchange rates in which the Group has exposures and takes the non-linear price function of certain FX derivative instruments into account. The variance-covariance methodology is used to assess and measure the interest rate risk and equity price risk.

(Nokia Annual Financial Reports 2011, p. 66)

During 2011, the Group continued to use derivatives to limit interest and exchange rate risk on otherwise unhedged positions, and to adapt its debt structure to market conditions.

There then follows a very comprehensive list of its hedging position illustrating the complexity of the operation.

(Telefonica S.A. Annual Report 2011)

With respect to currency exposure linked to long term assets in foreign currencies, the Company makes an effort to reduce the associated currency exposure by financing in the same currency ... Short term currency exposure is periodically monitored with limits set by the Company's management. The Group's treasury department manages this currency exposure.

(Total Annual Financial Report 2004, p. 173)

Foreign exchange risk management. Our principal objective is to reduce the risk to short term profits of exchange rate volatility. Transactional currency exposures that could impact the profit and loss account are hedged, typically using forward purchases or sales of foreign currencies and currency options. We hedge the majority of our investment in our international subsidiaries via foreign exchange transactions in matching currencies. Our objective is to maintain a low cost of borrowing and hedge against material movements to our balance sheet value. We translate overseas profits at average exchange rates which we do not currently seek to hedge.

(Tesco Annual Financial Report 2005, p. 7)

These major MNCs attempt to stabilize their earnings with hedging strategies because exchange rate risk is significant. All annual reports of major companies contain sections on exchange risk management.

MANAGING FOR VALUE

The German car maker BMW was in a position such that less than 20 per cent of its sales were in Germany. As a result a very large exchange rate risk had developed that either had to be borne by the company or the customer. In a competitive market BMW could not afford to pass on the costs to the customer. BMW's response was to offset its foreign revenues with foreign costs. This it did by setting up factories abroad increasing its foreign production to nearly 50 per cent. Where possible it also purchased in foreign currency. The effect was that if the value of the foreign currency fell revenues suffered as before; but this was now offset by cheaper costs, company exposure was then only the difference between the revenues and the costs. The factories in Spartanburg (USA) and Shenyang (China) are the result of this strategy. In the short to medium term the company engages in currency swaps with what they assure shareholders are carefully vetted counterparties.

TYPES OF EXPOSURE

As mentioned in the previous chapter, exchange rates cannot be forecasted with perfect accuracy, but the firm can at least measure its exposure to exchange rate fluctuations. If the firm is highly exposed to exchange rate fluctuations, it can consider techniques to reduce its exposure. Such techniques are identified in the following chapter. Before choosing among them, the firm should first measure its degree of exposure.

Exposure to exchange rate fluctuations comes in three forms:

- Transaction exposure

- Economic exposure

- Translation exposure.

Each type of exposure will be discussed in turn.

TRANSACTION EXPOSURE

The value of a firm's cash *inflows* received in various currencies will be affected by the respective exchange rates of these currencies when they are converted typically into the home currency. Similarly, the value of a firm's cash *outflows* in various currencies will be dependent on the respective exchange rates of these currencies. The degree to which the value of future cash transactions can be affected by exchange rate fluctuations is referred to as **transaction exposure.**

Transaction exposure can have a substantial impact on a firm's earnings. It is not unusual for a currency to change by as much as 10 per cent in a given year. If an exporter denominates its exports in a foreign currency, a 10 per cent decline in that currency will reduce the dollar value of its receivables by 10 per cent. This effect could possibly eliminate any profits from exporting.

To assess transaction exposure, an MNC needs to: (1) estimate its net cash flows in each currency and (2) measure the potential impact of the currency exposure.

Estimating 'net' cash flows in each currency

MNCs tend to focus on transaction exposure over an upcoming short-term period (such as the next month or the next quarter) for which they can anticipate foreign currency cash flows with reasonable accuracy. Since MNCs commonly have foreign subsidiaries spread around the world, they need an information system that can track their currency positions.

To measure its transaction exposure, an MNC needs to project the consolidated *net* amount in currency inflows or outflows for all its subsidiaries, categorized by currency. One foreign subsidiary may have inflows of a foreign currency while another has outflows of that same currency. In that case, the MNC's net cash flows of that currency overall may be negligible. If most of the MNC's subsidiaries have future inflows in another currency, however, the net cash flows in that currency could be substantial. Estimating the consolidated net cash flows per currency is a useful first step when assessing an MNC's exposure because it helps to determine the MNC's overall position in each currency.

EXAMPLE

Youth plc, a UK company, conducts its international business in four currencies. Its objective is first to measure its exposure in each currency in the next quarter and then estimate its consolidated cash flows for one-quarter ahead, as shown in Exhibit 10.1. For example, Youth expects Swiss franc inflows of 12 000 000 SFr and outflows of 2 000 000 SFr over the next quarter. Thus, Youth expects net inflows of 10 000 000 SFr. Given an expected exchange rate of £0.44 to the Swiss franc at the end of the quarter, it can convert the expected net inflow of Swiss francs into an expected net inflow of £4 400 000 (estimated as 10 000 000 SFr × £0.44).

The same process is used to determine the net cash flows of each of the other three currencies. Notice from the last column of Exhibit 10.1 that the expected net cash flows in three of the currencies are positive, while the net cash flows in Japanese yen are negative (reflecting cash outflows). Thus, Youth will be favourably affected by the appreciation of the euro, US dollar and Swiss franc. Conversely, it will be adversely affected by the appreciation of the yen.

EXHIBIT 10.1   Consolidated net cash flow assessment of Youth plc

Currency	Total inflow	Total outflow	Net inflow or outflow	Expected exchange rate at end of quarter	Net inflow or outflow as measured in £s
Euros	17 000 000 euros	7 000 000 euros	+10 000 000 euros	£0.68	+£6 800 000
Swiss francs	12 000 000 SFr	2 000 000 SFr	+10 000 000 SFr	£0.44	+£4 400 000
Japanese yen	200 000 000 yen	900 000 000 yen	−700 000 000 yen	£0.005	−£3 500 000
US dollars	$10 000 000	$7 000 000	+$3 000 000	£0.55	+£1 650 000

EXHIBIT 10.2   Estimating the range of net inflows or outflows for Youth plc

Currency	Expected net inflow or outflow	Range of possible exchange rates at end of quarter (company is 95% confident that the exchange rate will lie between these values)	Range of possible net inflows or outflows in British pounds (based on the range of possible exchange rates)
Euros	+10 000 000 euros	£0.65 to £0.71	+£6 500 000 to +£7 100 000
Swiss francs	+10 000 000 SFr	£0.40 to £0.48	+£4 000 000 to +£4 800 000
Japanese yen	−700 000 000 yen	£0.004 to £0.006	−£2 800 000 to −£4 200 000
US dollars	+$3 000 000	£0.52 to £0.58	+£1 560 000 to +£1 740 000

EXAMPLE

The information in Exhibit 10.1 has been converted into British pounds so that Youth plc can assess the exposure of each currency by using a common measure. Notice that Youth has a smaller pound amount of exposure in yen and US dollars than in the other currencies. However, this does not necessarily mean that Youth will be less affected by these exposures, as will be explained shortly.

Recognize that the net inflows or outflows in each foreign currency and the exchange rates at the end of the period are uncertain. Thus, Youth might develop a range of possible exchange rates for each currency, as shown in Exhibit 10.2, instead of a point estimate. In this case, there is a range of net cash flows in pounds rather than a point estimate. Notice that the range of pound cash flows resulting from Youth's transactions is variable. Where uncertainty is high, there is a wide range of exchange rate estimates and as a consequence a wide range of possible pound values over the next quarter.

Youth plc assessed its net cash flow situation for only one-quarter. It could also derive its expected net cash flows for other periods, such as a week or a month. Some MNCs assess their transaction exposure during several periods by applying the methods just described to each period. The further into the future an MNC attempts to measure its transaction exposure, the less accurate will be the measurement due to the greater uncertainty about inflows or outflows in each foreign currency, as well as future exchange rates, over periods further into the future. An MNC's overall exposure can be assessed only after considering each currency's variability and the correlations among currencies. The overall exposure of Youth plc will be assessed after the following discussion of currency variability and correlations.

Measuring the potential impact of the currency exposure

The net cash flows of an MNC can be viewed as streams of cash flows in differing currencies. Their value converted into the home currency will vary due to both business risk and exchange rate risk. The currency values over time are bound to be correlated to some degree. If there is inflation in the UK, for instance, the pound will depreciate against all currencies, not just one currency. Business risk may also be correlated between different countries; recession can affect economic areas made up of many countries. A successful new drug, for instance, will be effective in a range of markets in different countries. Here we look just at currency exposure and assume that the cash flow in the foreign currency is known and it is only the exchange rate that is uncertain. A company needs to be able to assess its overall exposure to exchange rate variation. To do this it needs to be able to combine the individual estimates of variation due to exchange rate changes as outlined in Exhibit 10.2.

One way of combining the risk from different sources to achieve an overall estimate is to see the returns as a portfolio of cash flows and use the model developed in Chapter 3 to assess the overall portfolio risk of the cash flows. Here the absolute form of the model (see Appendix B) is used. Thus the standard deviation in terms of the converted value of the foreign cash flows is used rather than a percentage. So, absolute cash flows are used rather than percentages and weights. Combining the variability of cash flows originating from two different currencies can be achieved as follows:

$$\sigma_P = \sqrt{\sigma_X^2 + \sigma_Y^2 + 2\sigma_X^2 \sigma_Y^2 CORR_{XY}}$$

Where:

σ_p = the standard deviation of the converted value of foreign cash flows
σ_X^2, σ_Y^2 = the variance in terms of converted net cash flows from currencies X and Y respectively
σ_X and σ_Y = standard deviation for X and Y respectively
$CORR_{XY}$ = correlation coefficient of the converted value of cash flows in currencies X and Y

In practice, companies will want to assess the overall variability from more than just two different currency sources. Here again, approaches from earlier chapters are adapted as outlined in the next sections.

Measurement of currency variability. The standard deviation statistic measures the degree of movement for each currency. In any given period, some currencies clearly fluctuate much more than others. The exact causes of fluctuation and hence standard deviation in a currency are not well understood. Where countries trade extensively with each other, the standard deviation tends to be lower, though other factors may intervene. Also where there are stable economies, variation in the value of the currency tends to be lower. Thus, the US dollar-Canadian dollar exchange rate has always been stable; the British pound-US dollar rate has been less stable given recent problems with the dollar (see Chapter 3); the British pound-euro exchange rate has been relatively stable. Currencies in emerging markets can be very unstable. It is also easy to underestimate the variability due to the 'peso effect' or 'the dog that never barked'. Such currencies can have long quiet periods followed by episodes of complete collapse. If measurement is taken during the long quiet period, the collapse will not be recorded in the sample (the 'dog' didn't bark) and the expected variability underestimated.

As well as crises being able to change currency variability, a change of government policy or a change of economic policy or external changes such as an oil price rise, or war, can have an effect on measures of variability. It should be remembered that the object of measuring variability is to try to predict *future* variation. In looking at historic periods, it is important to select a time span that represents conditions likely to prevail in the future. A representative period is not necessarily the last 5 years. In retrospect, history in finance does repeat itself with alarming similarity and regularity. It is just that we never know which period of history is going to repeat itself at any one point in time!

Measurement of currency correlations. The correlation coefficient measures the degree to which two currencies move in relation to each other. As noted in an earlier chapter a correlation is the same as a covariance except that a correlation is mapped on to a scale of −1.0 through to +1.0. The extreme case is perfect positive correlation, which is represented by a correlation coefficient equal to 1.00. In such cases when the change in one currency is a little above its mean, the change in the other currency is also a little above its mean. When one currency change is very much below its mean, the change in the other currency is also very much below its mean. Correlations can also be negative, reflecting an inverse relationship between individual movements, the extreme case being −1.00. When the change in one currency is a little *above* its mean, the change in the other currency is a little *below* its mean. Here they move in opposite directions and offset each other. Negative correlations are obviously useful in reducing risk; but so are poor correlations instead of high correlations. Exhibit 10.5 shows the correlation coefficients (based on daily data) for several currency pairs. It is clear that some currency pairs exhibit a much higher correlation than others. The £:euro and £:SFr are highly correlated whereas the £:dollar and the $:SFr had almost zero correlation over the time in question. As there is no clear understanding as to what causes a correlation, prediction and stability of correlations must be treated with great caution.

Applying currency correlations to net cash flows. The implications of currency correlations for a particular MNC depend on the cash flow characteristics of that MNC.

Positive cash flows in highly correlated currencies result in higher exchange rate risk for the MNC. However, many MNCs have negative net cash flow positions in some currencies; in these situations, the correlations can have different effects on the MNC's exchange rate risk. To measure currency correlations in a relatively practical way we now turn to an extended multicurrency example.

Multicurrency exposure. In practice, MNCs will want to value the cash flows from more than just two currencies as in the above model. The extension to a multicurrency position as in Exhibit 10.3 requires the use of a variance-covariance model as first developed in Chapter 3 (see also Appendix B) as follows: As an example, the variance-covariance matrix can be applied to Youth plc.

EXHIBIT 10.3 Variance-covariance matrix for MNC cash flows

	Currency A	Currency B	Currency C
Currency A	**Var(A)**	Cov(A,B)	Cov(A,C)
Currency B	Cov(A,B)	**Var(B)**	Cov(B,C)
Currency C	Cov(A,C)	Cov(B,C)	**Var(C)**

Notes:
- The overall variance is the total of all the values in the matrix. The overall standard deviation is the square root of the overall variance.
- Values of (A), (B), (C), (A,B), (A,C), etc. are measured as cash flows converted into the home currency.
- Var(A) etc. is the variance of the converted value of currency A, etc.
- Cov(A,B) etc. stands for the covariance between converted cash flows of currency A and B, it can be calculated as
  $Cov(A,B) = \sigma_A \times \sigma_B \times Correlation\ (A,B)$. Also, $cov(A,B) = cov(B,A)$ where σ_A is the standard deviation of A, σ_B the standard deviation of B.
- Extending the analysis to more than three currencies simply requires an extension of the pattern of variances and covariances.

EXAMPLE

The expected cash flows anticipated by Youth plc are given in Exhibit 10.4. The spread of outcomes represent a subjective estimate with 95 per cent confidence that the true value will lie between the limits. If this notion is translated into the statistical 95 per cent confidence interval then the standard deviation can be estimated as there are 3.92 standard deviations in a 95 per cent confidence interval, i.e. $1.96 \times 2 = 3.92$. With this assumption, Exhibit 10.4 gives the expected value and calculates the standard deviation of each of the foreign cash flows. The *expected* cash flows are additive, so Youth can expect to receive £9 350 000 at

EXHIBIT 10.4 Expected cash flows and standard deviations for Youth plc

Source of foreign cash flow	Expected converted value of cash flow	Subjective estimate of standard deviation of cash flows (see notes below)
Euros	+£6 800 000	£153 061
Swiss francs	+£4 400 000	£204 082
Japanese yen	−£3 500 000	£357 143
US dollars	+£1 650 000	£45 918
Total expected return	£9 350 000	

Note:
- Standard deviation estimate assumes a normal distribution about the expected value, hence the 95 per cent confidence interval spread is 1.96 standard deviations above and below the mean, therefore:

$$high = £6\,800\,000 + 1.96 \times £153\,061 = £7\,100\,000$$
$$low = £6\,800\,000 - 1.96 \times £153\,061 = £6\,500\,000$$
$$spread = £7\,100\,000 \text{ to } £6\,500\,000.$$

(Continued)

the end of the next month. The standard deviation of the combined receipts are *not* additive and must be calculated using a variance-covariance matrix. As a covariance (A,B) = correlation (A,B) $\times$ σ_A $\times$ σ_B, and we have estimates of the standard deviations σA and σB, the correlation is all that is required to complete the calculation.

The Exhibit in 10.6 simply applies the variance-covariance matrix as in 10.3 to Youth plc, using the correlations and standard deviations calculated in 10.4 and 10.5. Note that as the Japanese yen is an *outflow* so the correlations are *negative for this example,* this is simply the positive correlation of Exhibit 10.5 multiplied by -1.0.

EXHIBIT 10.5 Correlations of exchange rate movements of rates with the British pound (daily percentage changes October 2004 to October 2005)

	Euros	Swiss francs	Japanese yen	US dollars
Euros	1	0.76	0.29	0.22
Swiss francs		1	0.27	0.04
Japanese yen			1	0.32
US dollars				1

EXHIBIT 10.6 Overall cash flow risk faced by Youth plc-variance covariance matrix

	Euros	Swiss francs	Japanese yen	US dollars
Euros	23 427 669 721	23 740 116 202	−15 852 752 770	1 546 216 100
Swiss francs	23 740 116 202	41 649 462 724	−19 679 343 586	374 841 491
Japanese yen	−15 852 752 770	−19 679 343 586	127 551 122 449	−5 247 773 528
US dollars	1 546 216 100	374 841 491	−5 247 773 528	2 108 462 724
Expected value (from Exhibit 10.4)	£9 350 000			
Variance of combined cash flows (total of matrix)	£ 164 499 325 436			
Standard deviation of combined cash flows (square root of variance)	£405 585			
Standard deviation / expected return =		0.04	or 4%	

Notes:
- The variance of the portfolio is the sum of all the values of the matrix.
- The matrix is normally calculated using a spreadsheet (see Appendix C).
- Japanese covariances are negative as they relate to a cash outflow.
- Calculation: as an example, top left, variance of euros: $153\,061^2 = 23\,427\,66\,721$.
- Second column top row, correlation (SFr, euro) $\times$ $\sigma_{sFr} \times$ $\sigma_{euro} = 0.76 \times 153\,061 \times 204\,082 = 23\,740\,116\,202$.

(Continued)

These calculations involve large numbers and would normally be done using a spreadsheet (see support material for an example). Looking at the calculation overall, Youth plc is expecting a cash inflow of £9 350 000 (Exhibit 10.4) and a standard deviation of £405 585 or 4 per cent of that expected value (Exhibit 10.6). The confidence interval of 1.96 standard deviations implies a spread of outcomes of:

$$£8\,555\,053 \quad \underset{-1.98 \times £405\,585}{\longleftarrow} \quad £9\,350\,000 \quad \underset{+1.98 \times £405\,585}{\longleftarrow} \quad £10\,144\,947$$

for Youth plc. The decision is whether to hedge or not hedge. That decision depends on whether a potential return of only £8 555 053 is acceptable. The value at risk approach, discussed below, elaborates on this decision.

More generally, one can see from the example of Youth plc that:

1   Setting cash outflows against inflows of foreign currency helps to offset the overall currency risk. In simple terms, the negative values in the matrix in Exhibit 10.6 represent the outflows and lower the overall variance and hence the risk. If the cash flows were predominantly negative, then inflows would offset the outflows and lower the risk.

2   In the case of cash flows that are either all negative or all positive, higher positive correlations implies higher risk and lower correlations lower risk. Again looking at the variance-covariance matrix, correlation is part of the covariance calculation and affects all the off diagonal entries. The closer the correlation coefficient is to zero the lower the overall risk.

Exhibit 10.7 summarizes the combined effect.

Currency correlations over time. Exhibit 10.8 shows the trends of exchange rate movements of various currencies against the pound.

Assessing transaction exposure based on value-at-risk

A related method for assessing exposure is termed value-at-risk (VAR). This is a measure that incorporates volatility and correlations to determine the potential maximum 1 day (or any other period) loss on the value of positions held by an MNC. In the case of international finance, the cause of the risk could be exchange rates, economic performance, interest rates and so on. Obviously, the maximum can be exceeded, but only at a chosen low probability. So, for example, if one wanted only a 1 per cent chance of the maximum loss being exceeded, then from the normal distribution, the level chosen should be such that there is a 99 per cent chance that the outcome will be better. So a 1 per cent value at risk of £100 000 means that there is a 1 per cent chance of a loss or cost of *more than* £100 000 for any 1 day or whatever time period is chosen; conversely a 99 per cent chance that it is better.

Note that VAR calculations rely on the outcomes being normally distributed. We have commented that the 'fat tails' phenomenon is evidence that the normal distribution tends to underestimate the spread of returns, so it might be more appropriate to be 99.9 per cent sure that the actual will be better than the value at risk (just over three standard deviations). Conceptually VAR adds no more than what can be understood from the normal distribution; its great advantage is that it does not employ statistical terms and is therefore more user-friendly. The danger is that it can provide false assurance. It is not clear that value at risk of £100 000 means at least £100 000 and the omission of the probability also makes the term somewhat ambiguous.

EXHIBIT 10.7   Impact of cash flow and correlation conditions on an MNC's exposure

If the MNC's expected cash flow situation is:	And the currencies are:	The MNC's exposure is relatively:
Equal amounts of net inflows in two currencies	Highly correlated	High
Equal amounts of net inflows in two currencies	Slightly positively correlated	Moderate
Equal amounts of net inflows in two currencies	Negatively correlated	Low
A net inflow in one currency and a net outflow of about the same amount in another currency	Highly correlated	Low
A net inflow in one currency and a net outflow of about the same amount in another currency	Slightly positively correlated	Moderate
A net inflow in one currency and a net outflow of about the same amount in another currency	Negatively correlated	High

EXHIBIT 10.8   Correlation of movements of major currencies against the British pound

Correlation of changes in the exchange rate – 30-day sliding window

— Correlation £:1€ and £:$1
— Correlation £:1€ and £:1SFr

Notes:
From September 2011 the Swiss National Bank has acted in the exchange market to control the level of the Swiss franc against the euro at 1.2 Swiss francs to the euro in order to halt the fall of the euro against the Swiss franc (in 2010 it was 1.5 Swiss francs). Since that time the euro has floated freely and gained slightly in value.
The top line represents the correlation of the value of euro and Swiss franc in terms of the British pound. The bottom line shows the correlation of the value of dollar and euro again in terms of the British pound.

EXAMPLE

Celia Ltd will receive 10 million Norwegian krone (NKr) tomorrow as a result of providing consulting services to a Norwegian oil firm. It wants to determine the maximum 1-day loss due to a potential decline in the value of the krone, based on a 95 per cent confidence level, i.e. a 5 per cent chance only of the krone being a lower value. It estimates the standard deviation of daily percentage changes of the Norwegian krone to be 1.2 per cent over the last 100 days. If these daily percentage changes are normally distributed, the maximum 1-day loss is determined by the lower boundary (the left tail) of the probability distribution, which is about 1.65 standard deviations away from the expected percentage change in the krone (this is a one tail distribution as we are only interested in a fall in value, so it is not the more familiar 1.96 standard deviations). Assuming an expected percentage change of 0 per cent (implying no expected change in the krone) during the next day, the maximum 1-day loss is:

$$\text{Maximum 1-day loss} = E(e_t) - (1.65 \times \sigma_{\text{krone}})$$
$$= 0\% - (1.65 \times 1.2\%)$$
$$= -0.0198, \text{ or } -1.98\%$$

Assume the spot rate of the krone is £0.09. The maximum 1-day loss of −1.98 per cent implies a krone value of:

$$\text{Krone based on maximum 1-day loss}$$
$$= S \times [1 + E(e_t)]$$
$$= £0.09 \times [1 + (-0.0198)]$$
$$= £0.088218$$

Thus, if the maximum 1-day loss occurs, the krone's value will have declined to £0.088218. If Celia has 10 million NKr, this represents an expected value of £900 000 (at £0.09 per krone), so a decline in the krone's value to £0.088218 would result in a loss of 10 million krone × (£0.088218 − £0.09) = −£17 820.

Factors that affect the maximum 1-day loss. The maximum 1-day loss of a currency is dependent on three factors. First, it is dependent on the expected percentage change in the currency for the next day. If the expected outcome in the previous example is −0.2 per cent instead of 0 per cent, the maximum loss over the 1-day period is

$$\text{Maximum 1-day loss} = E(e_t) - (1.65 \times \sigma_{\text{krone}})$$
$$= -0.2\% - (1.65 \times 1.2\%)$$
$$= -0.0218 \text{ or } -2.18\%$$

Second, the maximum 1-day loss is dependent on the confidence level used. A higher confidence level will cause a more pronounced maximum 1-day loss, holding other factors constant. If the confidence level in the example is 97.5 per cent instead of 95 per cent, the lower boundary is 1.96 standard deviations from the expected percentage change in the krone. Thus, the maximum 1-day loss is:

$$\text{Maximum 1-day loss} = E(e_t) - (1.96 \times \sigma_{\text{krone}})$$
$$= -0\% - (1.96 \times 1.2\%)$$
$$= -0.02352 \text{ or } -2.352\%$$

Third, the maximum 1-day loss is dependent on the standard deviation of the daily percentage changes in the currency over a previous period. If the krone's standard deviation in the example is 1 per cent instead of 1.2 per cent, the maximum 1-day loss is:

$$\text{Maximum 1-day loss} = E(e_t) - (1.65 \times \sigma_{\text{krone}})$$
$$= -0\% - (1.65 \times 1.0\%)$$
$$= -0.0165 \text{ or } -1.65\%$$

Applying VAR to longer time horizons. The VAR method can also be used to assess exposure over longer time horizons. To predict monthly standard deviation it seems sensible to take monthly observations, but to predict the standard deviation 5 years' hence, taking five yearly observations would be impractical, 30 observations would go back 150 years! The following example uses the analysis from the previous chapter to resolve this problem.

EXAMPLE

Laffe SA (France) expects to receive US dollars in 1 month for products that it exported. It wants to determine the maximum 1-month loss due to a potential decline in the value of the dollar, based on a 95 per cent confidence level. It estimates the standard deviation of the percentage changes of the US dollar to be 2 per cent per month over the last 40 months. If these monthly percentage changes are normally distributed, the maximum 1-month loss is determined by the lower boundary (the left tail) of the probability distribution, which is about 1.65 standard deviations away from the expected percentage change in the dollar. Assuming an expected percentage change of -1 per cent during the next month, the maximum 1-month loss is:

$$\text{Maximum 1-month loss} = E(e_t) - (1.65 \times \sigma_\$)$$
$$= -1\% - (1.65 \times 2.0\%)$$
$$= -0.043, \text{ or } -4.3\%$$

If Laffe is uncomfortable with the magnitude of the potential loss, it can hedge its position as explained in the next chapter.

Laffe is also wondering about the change in the value of the dollar in 5 years' time as it is thinking of undertaking a long-term contract in the USA. It considers that the last 40 months are representative of the future conditions over the next 5 years. We could not take 40 observations or even ten observations of 5-year changes as the exchange rates would reach back to different times. However, given that the last 40 months are seen as representing future conditions, we can easily solve this very practical problem by assuming that the future possible returns are normally distributed and that the currency is weak-form efficient and follows a random walk. Note that these assumptions are approximate and err on the side of caution. As a reminder, the formula for calculating long time horizons from shorter periods under these conditions is:

$$\sigma_t = \sigma_m \sqrt{(t/m)}$$

Where:

t = the longer time period
m = shorter time period, both expressed in common time units
σ = standard deviation of the foreign currency

In this case m is 1 month and t is 60 months (i.e. 5 years $\times$ 12 months) so $t/m = 60$. The 5-year standard deviation is therefore:

$$\text{Five-year standard deviation} = 2\% \times \sqrt{(60)} = 15.5\%$$

If our expected value is no change in the exchange rate over the 5 years, the maximum 5-year loss under such conditions is:

$$\text{Maximum 5-year loss} = E(e_t) - (1.65 \times \sigma_\$)$$
$$= 0\% - (1.65 \times 15.5\%)$$
$$= -0.256, \text{ or } -25.6\%$$

Laffe might want to take measures to protect itself from this potential risk. Longer-term hedging is possible, also it may wish to structure its operations to minimize the risk as explained in the next chapter. Note from Chapter 9 that the exchange rate variance increases at slightly less than that predicted by the random walk model.

Applying VAR to transaction exposure of a portfolio. Since MNCs are commonly exposed to more than one currency, they may apply the VAR method to a currency portfolio. Once the standard deviation of the portfolio is calculated (see above) the VAR approach can proceed as for one currency. An example of applying VAR to a two-currency portfolio is provided here.

EXAMPLE

Benny AB, a Swedish exporting firm, expects to receive substantial payments denominated in Indonesian rupiah and Thai baht in 1 month. Based on today's spot rates, the Swedish krone value of the funds to be received is estimated at 600 000SKr for the rupiah and 400 000SKr for the baht. Thus, Benny is exposed to a currency portfolio weighted 60 per cent in rupiah and 40 per cent in baht. Benny wants to determine the maximum 1-month loss due to a potential decline in the value of these currencies, based on a 95 per cent confidence level. Based on data for the last 20 months, it estimates the standard deviation of monthly percentage changes to be 7 per cent for the rupiah and 8 per cent for the baht, and a correlation coefficient of 0.50 between the rupiah and baht. The portfolio's standard deviation is:

$$\sigma_P = \sqrt{(0.36)(0.0049) + (0.16)(0.0064) + 2(0.60)(0.40)(0.07)(0.08)(0.50)}$$
$$= \text{about } 0.0643 \text{ or about } 6.43\%$$

We assume joint normality, that is to say the combined return of the currencies is normally distributed. The maximum 1-month loss of the currency portfolio is determined by the lower boundary (the left tail) of the probability distribution. To be 95 per cent sure that the outcome will be higher (the 5 per cent value at risk) the 1 month VAR should be the mean less 1.65 standard deviations. Assuming an expected percentage change of 0 per cent for each currency during the next month (and therefore an expected change of zero for the portfolio), the maximum 1-month loss is:

$$\text{Maximum 1-month loss of currency portfolio} = E(e_t) - (1.65 \times \sigma_P)$$
$$= 0\% - (1.65 \times 6.43\%)$$
$$= -0.1061 \text{ or } -10.61\%$$

Compare this maximum 1-month loss to that of the rupiah or the baht:

$$\text{Maximum 1-month loss of rupiah} = 0\% - (1.65 \times 7\%)$$
$$= -0.1155 \text{ or } -11.55\%$$
$$\text{Maximum 1-month loss of baht} = 0\% - (1.65 \times 8\%)$$
$$= -0.132 \text{ or } -13.2\%$$

Notice that the maximum 1-month loss for the portfolio is less than the maximum loss for either individual currency, which is attributed to the diversification effects. Even if one currency experiences its maximum loss in a given month, the other currency is not likely to experience its maximum loss in that same month. The lower the correlation between the movements in the two currencies, the greater is the diversification benefit.

Given the maximum losses calculated here, Benny AB may decide to hedge its rupiah position, its baht position, neither position or both positions. The decision of whether to hedge is discussed in the next chapter.

ECONOMIC EXPOSURE

The degree to which a firm's future cash flows can be influenced by exchange rate fluctuations is referred to as **economic exposure** to exchange rates. All types of anticipated future transactions that cause transaction exposure also cause economic exposure because these transactions represent cash flows that can be influenced by exchange rate fluctuations. Thus economic exposure is the general term for the financial effects of exchange rates, it includes transaction exposure and indirect effects on revenues and costs.

MANAGING FOR VALUE

Intel invoices about 65 per cent of its chip exports in US dollars. Although Intel is not subject to transaction exposure for its dollar-denominated exports, it is subject to economic exposure. If the euro weakens against the dollar, European importers of those chips from Intel may decide to purchase chips from European manufacturers instead. Consequently, Intel's cash flows from its exports will be affected by changes in the value of the dollar even though it is invoicing in dollars.

Some of the more common international business transactions that typically subject an MNC's cash flows to economic exposure are listed in the first column of Exhibit 10.9. Transactions listed in the exhibit that require conversion of currencies, and thus reflect transaction exposure, include exports denominated in foreign currency, interest received from foreign investments, imports denominated in foreign currency and interest owed on foreign loans. The other transactions, which do not require conversion of currencies and therefore do not reflect transaction exposure, are also a form of economic exposure because the cash flows resulting from these transactions can be influenced by exchange rate movements. Indirect effects of exchange rates can be greater than the direct effects.

The second and third columns of Exhibit 10.9 indicate how each transaction can be affected by the appreciation and depreciation, respectively, of the firm's home (local) currency. The next sections discuss these effects in turn.

Economic exposure to home currency appreciation

The following discussion is related to the second column of Exhibit 10.9. With regard to the firm's cash inflows, its home sales are expected to decrease if the home currency appreciates because the firm will face increased foreign competition. Home customers will be able to obtain foreign substitute products cheaply with their strengthened currency. The extent of the decline in home sales will depend on the price sensitivity of customers otherwise termed the price elasticity of demand.

A firm's exports in home currency will decline if the value of the home currency increases as the exports will now be more expensive. If however the exports are denominated in the foreign currency then the firm

EXHIBIT 10.9 Economic exposure to exchange rate fluctuations

Transactions that influence a firm's cash inflows in home currency terms	Impact of home currency gain in value	Impact of a fall in value of the home currency
Home sales when affected by foreign competition in home markets	Decrease	Increase
Firm's exports denominated in home currency	Decrease	Increase
Firm's exports denominated in foreign currency	Decrease	Increase
Interest received from foreign investments	Decrease	Increase
Transactions that influence a firms' cash outflows in its home currency		
Firm's imported supplies denominated in home currency	No change	No change
Firm's imported supplies denominated in foreign currency	Decrease	Increase
Interest owed on foreign funds borrowed	Decrease	Increase

will lose out in that the foreign revenue will be worth less. The choice as to whether to invoice in home or foreign currency is therefore in part a choice between a decline in demand due to higher prices (the customer bears the risk) and the alternative of invoicing in the foreign currency and having probably no change in demand but a fall in the value of the revenue (the firm nears the risk). Most firms choose the latter.

EXAMPLE

Molone plc, an Irish firm, arranged to sell software to UK customers. Its sales are invoiced in euros. Recently, the pound depreciated against the euro increasing the price of the software to British cus- tomers. Consequently, some British customers shifted their purchases to British software producers, and Molone's sales to Britain declined.

Interest received from foreign investments will be like sales in foreign currency in that there will be no change in the foreign currency amount, only a change in the value of the earnings.

With regard to the firm's cash outflows, the cost of imported supplies denominated in the *home* currency (e.g. a UK firm paying pounds for its imports) will not be directly affected by changes in exchange rates. If the home currency appreciates, however, the cost of imported supplies denominated in the *foreign* currency against which the pound is increasing in value, will be reduced. If the home currency depreciates, the cost of the imports will increase. Whether or not the firm changes the volume of its purchases because of the change in price depends on its price sensitivity, its elasticity of demand.

Finally, interest owed on foreign funds borrowed will be paid in foreign currency. If the value of the foreign currency rises (home currency falls in value), then the home currency cost of the payments will increase. By the same reasoning if the foreign currency falls in value the home currency cost of the payments will decrease. In that sense, all foreign interest payments are variable.

Appreciation in the firm's own home currency causes a reduction in both cash inflows and outflows. The impact on a firm's net cash flows will depend on whether the inflow transactions are affected more or less than the outflow transactions. If, for example, the firm is in the exporting business but obtains its supplies and borrows funds locally, its inflow transactions will be reduced by a greater degree than its outflow transactions. In this case, net cash flows will be reduced. Conversely, cash inflows of a firm concentrating its sales locally with little foreign competition will not be severely reduced by appreciation of the home currency. If such a firm obtains supplies and borrows funds overseas, its outflows will be reduced. Overall, this firm's net cash flows will be enhanced by the appreciation of its home currency.

MANAGING FOR VALUE

Philips Electronics' exposure to exchange rate risk

Philips Electronics incurs much of its expenses in euros but earns substantial amounts in dollars and dollar-related currencies. When the dollar strengthens, Philips is at an advantage with respect to its US competitors as its euro costs reduce in comparison. When the dollar is relatively weak, the company can potentially lose. To manage this risk the company hedges the dollar value. A decline in the value of the dollar increases the value of its derivatives and therefore offsets the potential exchange rate losses. When the value of the dollar rises, the value of the derivatives falls and hence some of the gain is lost. In this way Philips is able to reduce the impact of its exposure to the dollar.

Economic exposure to home currency depreciation

If the firm's home currency depreciates (see the third column of Exhibit 10.9), its transactions will be affected in a manner opposite to the way they are influenced by appreciation. Home sales should increase due to reduced foreign competition, because prices denominated in strong foreign currencies will seem high to the home customers. The firm's exports denominated in the home currency will appear cheap to importers, thereby increasing foreign demand for those products. Even exports denominated in the foreign currency can increase cash flows because a given amount in foreign currency inflows to the firm will convert to a larger amount of the home currency. In addition, interest or dividends from foreign investments will now convert to more of the home currency.

With regard to cash outflows, imported supplies denominated in the home currency will not be directly affected by any change in exchange rates. The cost of imported supplies denominated in the foreign currency will rise, however, because more of the weakened home currency will be required to obtain the foreign currency needed. Any interest payments paid on financing in foreign currencies will increase.

In general, depreciation of the firm's home currency causes an increase in both cash inflows and outflows. A firm that concentrates on exporting and obtains supplies and borrows funds locally is likely to benefit from a depreciated home currency. This is the case for Philips Electronics and Renault both of whom earn substantial foreign income. Conversely, a firm that concentrates on home sales, has very little foreign competition, and obtains foreign supplies (denominated in foreign currencies), will likely be hurt by a depreciated home currency.

Economic exposure of domestic firms

Although our focus is on the financial management of MNCs, even purely domestic firms are affected by economic exposure.

EXAMPLE

Bridlington Ltd is a UK manufacturer of steel that purchases all of its supplies locally and sells all of its steel locally. Because its transactions are solely in the home currency, Bridlington is not subject to transaction exposure. It is subject to economic exposure, however, because it faces foreign competition in its home markets. If the exchange rate of the foreign competitor's invoice currency depreciates against the pound, customers interested in steel products will shift their purchases toward the foreign steel producer. Consequently, demand for Bridlington's steel is likely to decrease, and so will its net cash inflows. Thus, Bridlington is subject to economic exposure even though it is not subject to transaction exposure.

Measuring economic exposure

Since MNCs are affected by economic exposure, they should assess the potential degree of exposure that exists and then determine whether to insulate themselves against it.

Sensitivity of earnings to exchange rates. One method of measuring an MNC's economic exposure is to forecast a range of exchange rates and for each rate develop a subjective prediction of the costs and revenues that make up the income statement for the firm. By reviewing how the earnings forecast in the income statement changes in response to alternative exchange rate scenarios, the firm can assess the influence of currency movements on its earnings and cash flows.

Unlike transaction exposure, the problem of economic exposure is that the original foreign currency amounts are uncertain due to the economic effects of a change in the exchange rate. A common cause of such uncertainty is a change in the volumes of sales and consequent change in the variable costs of production that both occur directly as a result of a change in the exchange rate. Although very evident in practice, it should be remembered that foreign costs are likely to vary with all sales including sales in the home market. Production for an MNC can be anywhere for any market.

Economic exposure therefore has a volume as well as a currency or price effect. A simple set of rules that ensures that both effects are included, is for each scenario to:

1   Calculate the volume changes *in the currency where they occur* – such change is typically as a result of a change in the level of sales. You may need to convert from pounds back to the original currency before applying the volume adjustment.

2   Convert to the reporting (home) currency at the exchange rate for the chosen scenario.

The following example illustrates the problem in context.

EXAMPLE

Mannerton plc is a UK-based MNC that conducts a portion of its business in Europe. Its UK sales are denominated in British pounds, while its European sales are denominated in euros. Its pro forma income statement for next year is shown in Exhibit 10.10(a). The income statement items are segmented into those

EXHIBIT 10.10(a)   Revenue and cost estimates based on an exchange rate of £0.60:1 euro: Mannerton plc

	UK business £ million	European business millions of euros
Sales	300.00	40
less Cost of goods sold	50.00	200
Gross profit	250.00	−160
less Operating expenses:		
Fixed	30.00	–
Variable	30.72	–
Total	60.72	–
Earnings before interest and taxes (EBIT)	189.28	−160
less Interest expense	3.00	10
Earnings before taxes (EBT)	186.28	−170

Note:
- European goods are translated from pounds to euros at a rate of approximately £0.60:1 euro so European sales represents 40m euros × £0.60 = £24 million or about 24/(300 + 24) = 7.4 per cent of total sales.

(Continued)

EXHIBIT 10.10(b)   Exchange rate scenarios with sales and volume changes

Possible values of the euro	Forecasted UK sales (in millions)	Volume increase over £0.60 rate assume no price changes
£0.60	£300	–
£0.70	304	$1\frac{1}{3}\%$ (304/300 – 1)
£0.80	307	$2\frac{1}{3}\%$ (307/300 – 1)

Note:
UK volume of sales will increase as the pound is cheaper. The volume of sales in Europe will not be affected as the goods are priced in euros, though the assumption is being made that European customers will not switch to cheaper foreign goods.

for the UK and for Europe. Note that Mannerton undertakes much of the manufacturing of UK goods in Europe. Assume that Mannerton plc desires to assess how its income statement items would be affected by three possible exchange rate scenarios for the euro over the period of concern: (1) £0.60, (2) £0.70 and (3) £0.80. The estimated impact is outlined in Exhibit 10.10(b) and the implications for the profit and loss account are analyzed in the second, third and fourth columns of Exhibit 10.10(c).

Mannerton's sales in the UK are higher when the euro is stronger (Exhibit 10.10(b)), because European competitors are priced out of the UK market.

The impact of an exchange rate on home sales for any firm will depend on the foreign competition. Historical data can be used to assess how home sales were affected by exchange rates in the past. It may be possible to construct a probability distribution from historic data or historic data may be used to inform an essentially subjective estimate of the effect of exchange rates.

We assume in Exhibit 10.10(c) that the cost of sales and variable costs vary with volume and that the manufacturing in Europe is for UK as well as European goods. Given this information, Mannerton plc can determine how its *pro forma* statement would be affected by each exchange rate scenario, as shown in Exhibit 10.10(c). The assumed impact of exchange rates on UK sales is shown in line 1. Line 2 shows the amount in pounds to be received as a result of European sales (after converting the forecasted 40 million euros of European sales into pounds). Line 3 shows the estimated pounds to be received from total sales, which is determined by combining lines 1 and 2. Line 4 shows the cost of

goods sold in the UK which is subject to the volume changes. Line 5 converts the estimated 200 million euro cost of goods sold into pounds after adjusting for volume changes. Line 6 measures the estimated pounds needed to cover the total cost of goods sold, which is determined by combining lines 4 and 5. Line 7 estimates the gross profit in pounds, determined by subtracting line 6 from line 3. Lines 8 through to 10 shows estimated operating expenses, and line 11 subtracts total operating expenses from gross profit to determine earnings before interest and taxes (EBIT). Line 12 estimates the interest expenses paid in the UK, while line 13 estimates the pounds needed to make interest payments in Europe. Line 14 combines lines 12 and 13 to estimate total pounds needed to make all interest payments. Line 15 shows earnings before taxes (EBT), estimated by subtracting line 14 from line 11.

The effect of exchange rates on Mannerton's revenues and costs can now be reviewed. Exhibit 10.10(c) illustrates how both UK sales and the pound value of European sales would increase as a result of a stronger euro. Because Mannerton's European cost of goods sold exposure (200 million euro) is much greater than its European sales exposure (40 million euro), a strong euro has a negative overall impact on gross profit. The total amount in pounds needed to make interest payments is also higher when the euro is stronger. In general therefore, Mannerton plc would be adversely affected by a stronger euro. By the same argument, the company would be favourably affected by a weaker euro because the reduced value of total revenue would be more than offset by the reduced cost of goods sold and interest expenses.

(Continued)

EXHIBIT 10.10(c) Impact of possible exchange rate movements in earnings of Mannerton plc – see 'Mannerton ch10.xls' on the CourseMate for a spreadsheet version

Exchange rate scenarios			
	£ million		
	Scenario 1	Scenario 2	Scenario 3
Value of euro	£0.60	£0.70	£0.80
(1) UK sales	300.00	304.00	307.00
2) European sales invoiced in euros (40 million euros in each scenario)	24.00	28.00	32.00
3) Total	324.00	332.00	339.00
less Cost of goods sold:			
4) UK costs	50.00	50.62	51.08
(5) European costs	120.00	141.73	163.46
(6) Total	170.00	192.35	214.54
(7) Gross profit	**154.00**	**139.65**	**124.46**
less Operating expenses:			
(8) UK: Fixed	30.00	30.00	30.00
less (9) UK: Variable costs (by volume of output)	30.72	31.10	31.38
(10) Total	60.72	61.10	61.38
(11) EBIT (earnings before interest and tax)	**93.28**	**78.56**	**63.08**
less Interest expense:			
(12) UK	3.00	3.00	3.00
(13) European 10 million euros	6.00	7.00	8.00
(14) Total	9.00	10.00	11.00
(15) EBT (earnings before tax)	**84.28**	**68.56**	**52.08**

Note:

Total volume changes compared to Scenario 1: European sales are 0.074 or 7.4 per cent of total sales in Scenario 1 (see Exhibit 10.10(a)) and do not change. So using the volume changes from Exhibit 10.10(b) and taking a weighted average, the volume changes are: Scenario 2: 0.074 × 0% + (1–0.074) × 1⅓% = **1.235%;** Scenario 3: 0.074 × 0% + (1–0.074) × 2⅓% = **2.16%** (0% represents no change to the European sales).

Line 4: UK cost of goods sold is variable and presumed to relate to all sales. Applying the volume changes (above) for Scenarios 2 and 3, 50 + 1.235 % × 50 = 50.62 and 50 + 2.16% × 50 = 51.08.

Line 5: European costs are incurred in the production of both UK and European goods. So for scenarios 2 and 3 applying the volume changes above:

Scenario 2: 200 + 200 × 1.235% = 202.47 euros

Scenario 3: 200 + 200 × 2.16 % = 204.32 euros

And the £ valuations are Scenario 1: 200 × 0.6 = 120; Scenario 2: 202.47 × 0.70 = 141.73; Scenario 3: 204.32 × 0.80 = 163.46.

Line 9: UK variable costs are subject to the volume changes above, 30.72 as given for Scenario 1, for Scenario 2 it is 30.72 + 1.235% × 30.72 = 31.10 and 30.72 + 2.16% × 30.72 = 31.38 for Scenario 3.

A general conclusion from this example is that firms with more (less) in foreign costs than in foreign revenue will be unfavourably (favourably) affected by a stronger foreign currency. An estimation of the impact, however, can be determined only by utilizing the kind of scenario analysis outlined here. The example is based on a one-period time horizon. Multi-period analysis becomes more complex very rapidly and is better handled by repeating the one period model in a Monte Carlo simulation as may be carried out on a spreadsheet. Alternatively regression analysis using past inputs may also give some idea as to the likely future outcomes.

Sensitivity of cash flows to exchange rates. A firm's economic exposure to currency movements can also be assessed by applying regression analysis to historical cash flow and exchange rate data as follows:

$$PCF_t = a_0 + a_1 e_t + \mu_t$$

Where:

PCF_t = percentage change in inflation-adjusted cash flows measured in the firm's home currency over period t

e_t = percentage change in the exchange rate of the currency over period t

μ_t = random error term

a_0 = intercept

a_1 = slope coefficient

The regression coefficient a_1, estimated by regression analysis, indicates the sensitivity of PCF_t to e_t. If the firm anticipates no major adjustments in its operating structure, it will expect the sensitivity detected from regression analysis to be somewhat similar in the future.

This regression model can be revised to handle more complex situations. For example, if additional currencies are to be assessed, they can be included in the model as additional independent variables. Each currency's impact is measured by estimating its respective regression coefficient. If an MNC is influenced by numerous currencies, it can measure the sensitivity of PCF_t to an index (or composite) of currencies.

The analysis just described for a single period can also be extended over separate sub-periods, as the sensitivity of a firm's cash flows to a currency's movements may change over time. This would be indicated by a shift in the regression coefficient, which may occur if the firm's exposure to exchange rate movements changes.

Some MNCs may prefer to use their share price as a proxy for the firm's value and then assess how their share price changes in response to currency movements. Regression analysis could also be applied to this situation by replacing PCF_t with the percentage change in share price in the model specified here. It is however unlikely that there will be a regular multi-period discernable (significant) relationship such that it is measurable using regression analysis. Unfortunately, in practice, there appears to be a large range of influences on share prices most of which are unmeasurable and irregular in their effect.

EXAMPLE

Volkswagen AG engages in what it calls 'natural hedging'. By producing in Mexico and Brazil, they lower their exchange rate risk. Because the currency of these cash outflows matches better with the currency of Volkswagen's inflows from abroad, they reduce their exposure to exchange rate risk. If revenues fall due to the value of the currency of foreign sales falling against the euro, costs will also fall due to the fact that they are in similarly behaving currencies such as the Brazilian real and the Mexican peso.

TRANSLATION EXPOSURE

An MNC creates its financial statements by consolidating all of its individual subsidiaries' financial statements. A subsidiary's financial statement is normally measured in its local currency. To be consolidated, each subsidiary's financial statement must be translated into the currency of the MNC's parent. Since exchange rates change over time, the translation of the subsidiary's financial statement into a different currency is affected by exchange rate movements. The exposure of the MNC's consolidated financial statements to exchange rate fluctuations is known as **translation exposure**. In particular, subsidiary earnings translated into the reporting currency on the consolidated income statement are subject to changing exchange rates.

The process of consolidating financial statements is governed by accounting standards. In the UK the standard is Financial Reporting Standard 23, in the USA the standard is set by the Financial Accounting Standards Board (FASB) in FASB 52. The International Accounting Standard (IAS) 21 will represent the common accounting standard to be used by all major reporting countries. To obtain a quote on a stock exchange, companies must produce reports in conformity with the standard of that country. Standards also exist for translating currency derivative contracts, in the UK FRS 39.

Does translation exposure matter?

The relevance of translation exposure can be argued based on a cash flow perspective or a stock price perspective.

Cash flow perspective. Translation of financial statements for consolidated reporting purposes does not by itself affect an MNC's cash flows. The subsidiary earnings do not actually have to be converted into the parent's currency only reported in that currency. If a subsidiary's local currency is currently weak, the earnings could be retained rather than converted and sent to the parent. The earnings could be reinvested in the subsidiary's country if feasible opportunities exist.

An MNC's parent, however, may rely on funding from periodic remittances of earnings by the subsidiary. Even if the subsidiary does not need to remit any earnings today, it will remit earnings at some point in the future. To the extent that today's spot rate serves as a forecast of the spot rate that will exist when earnings are remitted, a weak foreign currency today results in a forecast of a weak exchange rate at the time that the earnings are remitted. In this case, the expected future cash flows are affected by the prevailing weakness of the foreign currency.

Stock price perspective. Many investors tend to use earnings when valuing firms, either by deriving estimates of expected cash flows from previous earnings or by applying a price-earnings (P/E) ratio to expected annual earnings to derive a value per share of stock. Since an MNC's translation exposure affects its consolidated earnings, it can affect the MNC's valuation. If the market is efficient, investors will realize that negative exchange rate adjustments to earnings are not necessarily actual cash flow losses. As long as the information is fully revealed to the market, investors will be able to make an unbiased valuation of the firm. The very open and detailed reports on risk (including currency risk) in the accounts of MNCs, are in recognition of this efficiency argument.

Determinants of translation exposure

Some MNCs are subject to a greater degree of translation exposure than others. An MNC's degree of translation exposure is dependent on the following:

- The proportion of its business conducted by foreign subsidiaries.
- The locations of its foreign subsidiaries, in particular, the volatility of the currency in relation to the home currency.
- The accounting methods that it uses.

Proportion of its business conducted by foreign subsidiaries. The greater the percentage of an MNC's business conducted by its foreign subsidiaries, the larger the percentage of a given financial statement item that is susceptible to translation exposure.

EXAMPLE

Locus Ltd and Zeuss Ltd each generate about 30 per cent of their sales from foreign countries. However, Locus Ltd generates all of its international business by exporting, whereas Zeuss Ltd has a large subsidiary in India that generates all of its international business. Locus Ltd is not subject to translation exposure (although it is subject to economic exposure), while Zeuss has substantial translation exposure.

Locations of foreign subsidiaries. The locations of the subsidiaries can also influence the degree of translation exposure because the financial statement items of each subsidiary are typically measured by the home currency of the subsidiary's country.

EXAMPLE

Zum Ltd (UK) and Canton SA (France) each have one large foreign subsidiary that generates about 30 per cent of their respective sales. However, Zum Ltd is subject to a much higher degree of translation exposure because its subsidiary is based in India, and the rupee's value is volatile. In contrast, Canton's subsidiary is based in Switzerland, and the Swiss franc is very stable against the euro.

Accounting methods. An MNC's degree of translation exposure can be greatly affected by the accounting procedures it uses to translate when consolidating financial statement data. The guidelines for UK statement FRS 23 incorporates IAS 21. The main points of IAS 21 are:

1   The functional currency of an entity is the currency of the economic environment in which the entity operates. This is normally the local currency where the subsidiary operates. But if the subsidiary is in India but sells and buys in France, the euro would be the functional currency. SAB (Miller) has a main quote on the London Stock Exchange but has the dollar as its functional (reporting) currency.

2   The current exchange rate as of the reporting date is used to translate monetary assets and liabilities of a foreign entity from its functional currency into the reporting or presentation currency. Non-monetary assets and liabilities are translated at the rate current when the transaction was recorded, or when there was a revaluation.

3   The weighted average exchange rate over the relevant period is used to translate revenue, expenses and gains and losses of a foreign entity from its functional currency into the reporting currency. The weights reflect the level of sales and expense activity. In some cases, such as depreciation, a simple average may be used.

4   Translated income gains or losses arise mainly due to the different rate applied to when the transaction took place and when the resultant assets and liabilities are reported. Thus, sales recorded at an average rate result in

an increase in monetary assets (cash and debtors) recorded at the reporting date – hence the difference. These differences are due to presentation only and are not taken into the current period income or expense.

5 *Realized* income gains or losses due to foreign currency transactions are recorded in current net income, although there are some exceptions.

Under IAS 21, consolidated earnings are sensitive to the functional currency's weighted average exchange rate.

EXAMPLE

A US subsidiary of Provenance plc (a UK company) earned $10 000 000 in Year 1 and $10 000 000 in Year 2. When these earnings are consolidated along with other subsidiary earnings, they are translated into pounds at the weighted average exchange rate in that year. Assume the weighted average exchange rate of the dollar is £0.60 in Year 1 and reporting period in British pounds are determined as £0.55 in Year 2. The translated earnings for each are as follows:

Reporting period	Local earnings of US subsidiary	Weighted average exchange rate of the dollar over the period	Translated UK pound earnings of the US subsidiary
Year 1	$10 000 000	£0.60	£6 000 000
Year 2	$10 000 000	£0.55	£5 500 000

Notice that even though the subsidiary's earnings in dollars were the same each year, the translated consolidated pound earnings were reduced by £0.5 million in Year 2. The discrepancy here is due to the change in the weighted average of the British pound exchange rate. The drop in earnings is not the fault of the subsidiary, but rather of the weakened dollar that makes its Year 2 earnings look small (when measured in pounds).

Examples of translation exposure

Consolidated earnings of Black & Decker, Philips, Renault, The Coca-Cola Company and other MNCs are very sensitive to exchange rates because more than a third of their assets and sales are overseas. Their earnings in foreign countries are reduced when foreign currencies depreciate against the dollar.

In the 2000–01 period, the weakness of the euro caused several US-based MNCs to report lower earnings than they had expected. In September 2000, when DuPont announced that its consolidated earnings would be affected by its translation exposure to the euro, investors responded quickly by dumping DuPont's shares. The stock price of DuPont declined 10 per cent on that day. Other MNCs including Colgate-Palmolive, Gillette, Goodyear and McDonald's followed with similar announcements.

In 2002 and 2003, however, the euro strengthened, and the consolidated income statements of US-based MNCs improved as a result. IBM stated that in the first quarter of 2003, more than half of its 11 per cent increase in revenue was attributed to favourable translation effects. In that same quarter, translation effects accounted for more than two-thirds of Colgate-Palmolive's 20 per cent increase in revenue.

Conversely, the strong euro and pound affected MNCs in Europe. In 2004 when the pound reached $1.88 and the euro was worth $1.31 difficulties were created for European MNCs, Volkswagen saw its US sales fall by 14 per cent, whereas BMW were less affected as they had a production plant in South Carolina that supplied the US market. Adidas-Salomon were also protected in that the source of the majority of their products was from Asia and they were billed in dollars.

SUMMARY

- MNCs with less risk can obtain funds at lower financing costs. Since they may experience more volatile cash flows because of exchange rate movements, exchange rate risk can affect their financing costs. Thus, MNCs may benefit from hedging exchange rate risk.

- Transaction exposure is the exposure of an MNC's future cash transactions to exchange rate movements. MNCs can measure their transaction exposure by determining their future payables and receivables positions in various currencies, along with the variability levels and correlations of these currencies. From this information, they can assess how their revenue and costs may change in response to various exchange rate scenarios.

- Economic exposure is any exposure of an MNC's cash flows (direct or indirect) to exchange rate movements. MNCs can attempt to measure their economic exposure by determining the extent to which their cash flows will be affected by their exposure to each foreign currency.

- Translation exposure is the exposure of an MNC's consolidated financial statements to exchange rate movements. To measure translation exposure, MNCs can forecast their earnings in each foreign currency and then determine the potential exchange rate movements of each currency relative to their home currency.

CRITICAL DEBATE

Should investors care about an MNC's translation exposure?

Proposition. No. The present value of an MNC's cash flows is based on the cash flows that the parent receives. Any impact of the exchange rates on the financial statements is not important unless cash flows are affected. MNCs should focus their energy on assessing the exposure of their cash flows to exchange rate movements and should not be concerned with the exposure of their financial statements to exchange rate movements. Value is about cash flows, and investors focus on value.

Opposing view. Investors do not have sufficient financial data to derive cash flows. They commonly use earnings as a base, and if earnings are distorted, so will be their estimates of cash flows. If they underestimate cash flows because of how exchange rates affected the reported earnings, they may underestimate the value of the MNC. Even if the value is corrected in the future once the market realizes how the earnings were distorted, some investors may have sold their stock by the time the correction occurs. Investors should be concerned about an MNC's translation exposure. They should recognize that the earnings of MNCs with large translation exposure may be more distorted than the earnings of MNCs with low translation exposure.

With whom do you agree? As well as looking at translation exposure, you might like to review the concept of market efficiency.

SELF TEST

Answers are provided in Appendix A at the back of the text.

1   Given that shareholders can diversify away an individual firm's exchange rate risk by investing in a variety of firms, why are firms concerned about exchange rate risk?

2   Brume SA (France) considers importing its supplies from either Switzerland (denominated in Swiss francs) or South Africa (denominated in rand) on a monthly basis. The quality is the same for both sources. Once the firm completes the agreement with a supplier, it will be obliged to continue using that

supplier for at least 3 years. Based on existing exchange rates, the euro amount to be paid (including transportation costs) will be the same. The firm has no other exposure to exchange rate movements. Given that the firm prefers to have less exchange rate risk, which alternative is preferable? Explain.

3 Assume your firm Paris SA (France) currently exports to the USA on a monthly basis. The goods are priced in dollars. Once material is received from a source, it is quickly used to produce the product in France, and then the product is exported. Currently, you have no other exposure to exchange rate risk. You have a choice of purchasing the material from Canada (denominated in C$), from the USA (denominated in dollars), or from within Europe (denominated in euros). The quality and your expected cost are similar across the three sources. Which source is preferable, given that you prefer minimal exchange rate risk?

4 Using the information in the previous question, consider a proposal to price the exports to the USA in euros and to use the French source for material. Would this proposal eliminate the exchange rate risk?

5 Assume that the euro is expected to strengthen against the dollar over the next several years. Explain how this will affect the consolidated earnings of Europe-based MNCs with subsidiaries in the USA.

QUESTIONS AND APPLICATIONS

1 **Transaction versus economic exposure.** Compare and contrast transaction exposure and economic exposure. Why would an MNC consider examining only its 'net' cash flows in each currency when assessing its transaction exposure?

2 **Assessing transaction exposure.** Your employer, a large MNC, has asked you to assess its transaction exposure. Its projected cash flows are as follows for the next year:

Currency	Total inflow	Total outflow	Value of currency
C$ (Canadian dollar)	C$3.2m	C$ 2.56m	£0.43
$ (US dollar)	$2m	$1m	£0.60

Provide your assessment as to your firm's degree of transaction exposure (as to whether the exposure is high or low). Explain your answer.

3 **Factors that affect a firm's transaction exposure.** What factors affect a firm's degree of transaction exposure in a particular currency? For each factor, explain the desirable characteristics that would reduce transaction exposure.

4 **Currency correlations.** Kopetsky SA (Poland) has net receivables in several currencies that are highly correlated with each other. What does this imply about the firm's overall degree of transaction exposure? Are currency correlations perfectly stable over time? What does your answer imply about Kopetsky or any other firm using past data on correlations as an indicator for the future?

5 **Currency effects on cash flows.** How should appreciation of a firm's home currency generally affect its cash inflows? How should depreciation of a firm's home currency generally affect its cash outflows?

6 **Transaction exposure.** Fischer Ltd exports products from Europe to the USA. It obtains supplies and borrows funds locally. How would the appreciation of the dollar be likely to affect its net cash flows? Why?

7 **Exposure of domestic firms.** Why are the cash flows of a purely domestic firm exposed to exchange rate fluctuations?

8 **Measuring economic exposure.** Boston Ltd (UK) hires you as a consultant to assess its degree of economic exposure to exchange rate fluctuations. How would you handle this task? Be specific.

9 **Factors that affect a firm's translation exposure.** What factors affect a firm's degree of translation exposure? Explain how each factor influences translation exposure.

10 **Translation exposure.** Consider a period in which the US dollar weakens against the euro. How will this affect the reported earnings of a European-based MNC with US subsidiaries? Consider a period in which the US dollar strengthens against most foreign currencies. How will this affect the reported earnings of a European-based MNC with subsidiaries all over the world?

11 **Transaction exposure.** Aggie plc (UK) produces chemicals. It is a major exporter to the USA, where its main competition is from other European exporters. All of these companies invoice the products in US dollars. Is Aggie's transaction exposure likely to

be significantly affected if the euro strengthens or weakens? Explain. If the euro weakens for several years, can you think of any change that might occur in the global chemicals market?

12 **Economic exposure.** Holbein BV (Netherlands) produces hospital equipment. Most of its revenues are in the USA. About half of its expenses are in Philippine pesos (to pay for Philippine materials). Most of Holbein's competition is from US firms that have no international business at all. How will Holbein be affected if the peso strengthens?

13 **Economic exposure.** Enid Ltd (UK) produces furniture and has no international business. Its major competitors import most of their furniture from Brazil and then sell it out of retail stores in the UK. How will Enid be affected if Brazil's currency (the real) strengthens over time?

14 **Economic exposure.** Laurette SA is a French wholesale company that imports expensive high-quality luggage and sells it to retail stores around Europe. Its main competitors also import high-quality luggage and sell it to retail stores. None of these competitors hedge their exposure to exchange rate movements. The treasurer of Laurette told the board of directors that the firm's performance would be more volatile over time if it hedged its exchange rate

exposure. How could a firm's cash flows be more stable as a result of such high exposure to exchange rate fluctuations?

15 **PPP and economic exposure.** Boulder plc exports chairs to the USA (invoiced in euros) and competes against local US companies. If purchasing power parity exists, why would Boulder not benefit from a stronger dollar?

16 **Measuring changes in economic exposure.** Renault SA measures the sensitivity of its profits to the pound and dollar exchange rate (relative to the euro). Explain how regression analysis could be used for such a task. Identify the expected sign of the regression coefficient if Renault primarily exports to the USA. If Renault established new plants in the USA, how might the regression coefficient on the exchange rate variable change?

17 **Impact of exchange rates on earnings.** Cieplak NV is a Dutch-based MNC that has expanded into Asia. Its Dutch parent exports to some Asian countries, with its exports denominated in the Asian currencies. It also has a large subsidiary in Malaysia that serves that market. Offer at least two reasons related to exposure to exchange rates why Cieplak's earnings were reduced during the Asian crisis.

ADVANCED QUESTIONS

18 **Speculating based on exposure.** During the Asian crisis in 1998, there were rumours that China would weaken its currency (the yuan) against the US dollar and many European currencies. This caused investors to sell stocks in Asian countries such as Japan and Singapore. Offer an intuitive explanation for such an effect. What types of Asian firms would have been affected the most?

19 **Dual currency.** In the early 1990s the UK government suggested that what is now called the euro could be used alongside local currencies. How would such a currency arrangement affect MNCs?

20 **Using regression analysis to measure exposure.**

   a How can a UK company use regression analysis to assess its economic exposure to fluctuations in the euro?

   b In using regression analysis to assess the sensitivity of cash flows to exchange rate movements, what is the purpose of breaking the database into sub-periods?

   c Assume the regression coefficient based on assessing economic exposure was much higher in the second sub-period than in the first sub-period. What does this tell you about the firm's degree of economic exposure over time? Why might such results occur?

21 **Transaction exposure.** Crediton plc is a UK firm that exports most of its products to Europe. It historically invoiced its products in euros to accommodate the importers. However, it was adversely affected when the euro weakened against the British pound. Since Crediton did not hedge, its euro receivables were converted into a relatively small amount of pounds. After a few more years of continual concern about possible exchange rate movements, Crediton called its customers and requested that they pay for future orders with pounds instead of euros. At this time, the European pound was valued at £0.81. The customers decided to oblige, since the number of euros to be converted into pounds when importing

the goods from Crediton was still slightly smaller than the number of euros that would be needed to buy the product from a European manufacturer. Based on this situation, has transaction exposure changed for Crediton plc? Has economic exposure changed? Explain.

22 **Measuring economic exposure.** Using the following cost and revenue information shown for DeKalb plc (UK) determine how the costs, revenue, and earnings items would be affected by three possible exchange rate scenarios for the New Zealand dollar (NZ$): (1) NZ$ = £0.40, (2) NZ$ = £0.44 and (3) NZ$ = £0.48. (Assume UK sales will be unaffected by the exchange rate.) Assume that NZ$ earnings will be remitted to the UK parent at the end of the period.

Revenue and cost estimates for DeKalb plc		
	UK business £m	New Zealand business NZ$m
Sales	800	800
Cost of goods sold	500	100
Gross profit	300	700
Operating expenses	300	0
Earnings before and taxes interest	0	700
Interest expense	100	0
Earnings before taxes	**−100**	**700**

23 **Changes in economic exposure.** Walt Disney World built an amusement park in France that opened in 1992. How do you think this project has affected Disney's economic exposure to exchange rate movements? Think carefully before you give your final answer. There is more than one way in which Disney's cash flows may be affected. Explain.

24 **Lagged effects of exchange rate movements.** Uton plc is an exporter of products to Singapore. It wants to know how its share price is affected by changes in the Singapore dollar's exchange rate. It believes that the impact may occur with a lag of one to three quarters. How could regression analysis be used to assess the impact?

25 **Potential effects if the UK adopted the euro.** The British pound's interest rate has historically been higher than the euro's interest rate. The UK has considered adopting the euro as its currency. There have

been many arguments about whether it should do so.

Discuss the likely effects on the UK economy if the UK were to adopt the euro. For each of the ten statements below, insert either *increase* or *decrease* in the first blank and complete the statement by adding a clear, short explanation (perhaps one to three sentences) as to why the UK's adoption of the euro would have that effect.

To help you narrow your focus, follow these guidelines. Do not base your answer on whether the pound would have been stronger than the euro in the future. Also, do not base your answer on an unusual change in economic growth in the UK or in the Eurozone if the euro is adopted.

a The economic exposure of British firms that are heavy exporters to the Eurozone would___ because . . .

b The translation exposure of firms based in the Eurozone that have British subsidiaries would___ because . . .

c The economic exposure of US firms that conduct substantial business in the UK and have no other international business would___ because . . .

d The translation exposure of US firms with British subsidiaries would___because . . .

e The economic exposure of US firms that export to the UK and whose only other international business is importing from firms based in the Eurozone would___because . . .

f The discount on the forward rate paid by US firms that periodically use the forward market to hedge payables of British imports would___ because . . .

g The earnings of a foreign exchange department of a British bank that executes foreign exchange transactions desired by its European clients would___ because . . .

h Assume that the Swiss franc is more highly correlated with the British pound than with the euro (the opposite is in fact the case). A US firm has substantial monthly exports to the UK denominated in the British currency and also has substantial monthly imports of Swiss supplies (denominated in Swiss francs). The economic exposure of this firm would___because . . .

i Assume that the Swiss franc is more highly correlated with the British pound than with the euro. A US firm has substantial monthly exports to the UK denominated in the British currency and also has substantial monthly exports to Switzerland (denominated in Swiss francs). The economic exposure of this firm would___because . . .

j The British government's reliance on monetary policy (as opposed to fiscal policy) as a means of fine-tuning the economy would___because . . .

26 Invoicing policy to reduce exposure. Blackstone is a UK firm that exports its products to Canada. It faces competition from many firms in Canada. Its price to customers in Canada has generally been lower than those of the competitors, primarily because the British pound has been strong. It prices its exports in Canadian dollars, and then converts the Canadian dollar receivables into pounds. All of its expenses are in the UK and are paid for with pounds. It is concerned about its economic exposure. It considers a change in its pricing policy, in which it will price its products in pounds instead of Canadian dollars. Offer your opinion on why this will or will not significantly reduce its economic exposure.

27 Exposure of an MNC's subsidiary. Le Rozier SA is a French firm with a Chinese subsidiary that produces cell phones in China and sells them in Japan. This subsidiary pays its wages and its rent in Chinese yuan, which is presently tied to a basket of major currencies. The cell phones sold to Japan are denominated in Japanese yen. Assume that Le Rozier SA expects that the Chinese yuan will continue to stay fixed against the dollar. The subsidiary's main goal is to generate profits for itself and it reinvests the profits. It does not plan to remit any funds to the French parent.

a Assume that the Japanese yen strengthens against the euro over time. How would this be expected to affect the profits earned by the Chinese subsidiary?

b If Le Rozier SA had established its subsidiary in Tokyo, Japan instead of China, would its subsidiary's profits be more exposed or less exposed to exchange rate risk?

c Why do you think that Le Rozier SA established the subsidiary in China instead of Japan? Assume no major country risk barriers.

d If the Chinese subsidiary needs to borrow money to finance its expansion and wants to reduce its exchange rate risk, should it borrow euros, Chinese yuan or Japanese yen?

PROJECT WORKSHOP

28 Daily exchange rates and annual reports. The following website provides daily exchange rate data for several currencies over the last few months: http://www.oanda.com.

a Use this website to assess the volatility of recent daily exchange rates of the euro and US dollar over the last 2 months. Which currency appears to be more volatile? What are the implications for UK firms with cash flows denominated in US dollars and euros?

b The following website contains lists of the worlds top 2000 companies http://www.forbes.com. Select *lists* and then *Forbes 2000,* then select 'Sort list by' *country*. Select a Continental European country (Germany, France, Netherlands, etc.). By clicking on the firm's name you will be able to access the home page of the company and by following the financial links *investor relations* or *annual accounts* find the latest annual report stored as a pdf file (choose another firm if your first selection does not work, the more well-known firms are usually more informative). By searching on the word 'risk' review the company's policy on transaction exposure, economic exposure and translation exposure. Summarize the MNC's exposure based on the comments in the annual report.

DISCUSSION IN THE BOARDROOM

This exercise can be found on our dedicated Course-Mate platform for students.

RUNNING YOUR OWN MNC

This exercise can be found on our dedicated Course-Mate platform for students.

Essays/discussion and articles can be found at the end of Part III.

BLADES PLC CASE STUDY

Assessment of exchange rate exposure

Blades plc is currently exporting roller blades to Thailand and importing certain components needed to manufacture roller blades from that country. Under a fixed contractual agreement, Blades' primary customer in Thailand has committed itself to purchase 180 000 pairs of roller blades annually at a fixed price of 4594 Thai baht (THB) per pair. Blades is importing rubber and plastic components from various suppliers in Thailand at a cost of approximately THB2871 per pair, although the exact price (in baht) depends on current market prices. Blades imports materials sufficient to manufacture 72 000 pairs of roller blades from Thailand each year. The decision to import materials from Thailand was reached because rubber and plastic components needed to manufacture Blades' products are inexpensive, yet high quality, in Thailand. Blades has also conducted business with a Japanese supplier in the past. Although Blades' analysis indicates that the Japanese components are of a lower quality than the Thai components, Blades has occasionally imported components from Japan when the prices were low enough. Currently, Ben Holt, Blades' finance director, is considering importing components from Japan more frequently. Specifically, he would like to reduce Blades' baht exposure by taking advantage of the recently high correlation between the baht and the yen. Since Blades has net inflows denominated in baht and would have outflows denominated in yen, its net transaction exposure would be reduced if these two currencies were highly correlated. If Blades decides to import components from Japan, it would probably import materials sufficient to manufacture 1700 pairs of roller blades annually at a price of ¥7440 per pair.

Holt is also contemplating further expansion into foreign countries. Although he would eventually like to establish a subsidiary or acquire an existing business overseas, his immediate focus is on increasing Blades' foreign sales. Holt's primary reason for this plan is that the profit margin from Blades' imports and exports exceeds 25 per cent, while the profit margin from Blades' domestic production is below 15 per cent. Consequently, he believes that further foreign expansion will be beneficial to the company's future.

Though Blades' current exporting and importing practices have been profitable, Ben Holt is contemplating extending Blades' trade relationships to countries in different regions of the world. One reason for this decision is that various Thai roller blade manufacturers have recently established subsidiaries in the UK. Furthermore, various Thai roller blade manufacturers have recently targeted the UK market by advertising their products over the Internet. As a result of this increased competition from Thailand, Blades is uncertain whether its primary customer in Thailand will renew the current commitment to purchase a fixed number of roller blades annually. The current agreement will terminate in 2 years. Another reason for engaging in transactions with other, non-Asian, countries is that the Thai baht has depreciated substantially recently, which has somewhat reduced Blades' profit margins. The sale of roller blades to other countries with more stable currencies may increase Blades' profit margins.

While Blades will continue exporting to Thailand under the current agreement for the next 2 years, it may also export roller blades to Jogs Inc a US retailer. Preliminary negotiations indicate that Jogs would be willing to commit itself to purchase 200 000 pairs of 'Speedos', Blades' primary product, for a fixed price of $80 per pair.

Holt is aware that further expansion would increase Blades' exposure to exchange rate fluctuations, but he believes that Blades can supplement its profit margins by expanding. He is vaguely familiar with the different types of exchange rate exposure but has asked you, a financial analyst at Blades plc to help him assess how the contemplated changes would affect Blades' financial position. Among other concerns, Holt is aware that recent economic problems in Thailand have had an effect on Thailand and other Asian countries. Whereas the correlation between Asian currencies such as the Japanese yen and the Thai baht is generally not very high and very unstable, these recent problems have increased the correlation among most Asian currencies. Conversely, the correlation between the British pound and the Asian currencies is quite low. To aid you in your analysis, Holt has provided you with the following data:

Currency	Expected exchange rate	Range of possible exchange rates
US dollar	£0.67	£0.68 to £0.65
Japanese yen	£0.0055	£0.0053 to £0.0058
Thai baht	£0.016	£0.013 to £0.019

Holt has asked you to answer the following questions:

1 What type(s) of exposure (i.e. transaction, economic or translation exposure) is Blades subject to? Why?

2 Using a spreadsheet, conduct a consolidated net cash flow assessment of Blades plc and estimate the range of net inflows and outflows for Blades for the coming year. Assume that Blades enters into the agreement with Jogs Inc.

3 If Blades does not enter into the agreement with the US firm and continues to export to Thailand and import from Thailand and Japan, do you think the increased correlations between the Japanese yen and the Thai baht will increase or reduce Blades' transaction exposure?

4 Do you think Blades should import components from Japan to reduce its net transaction exposure in the long run? Why or why not?

5 Assuming Blades enters into the agreement with Jogs Inc, how will its overall transaction exposure be affected?

6 Given that Thai roller blade manufacturers located in Thailand have begun targeting the UK roller blade market, how do you think Blades' UK sales were affected by the depreciation of the Thai baht? How do you think its exports to Thailand and its imports from Thailand and Japan were affected by the depreciation?

SMALL BUSINESS DILEMMA

Assessment of exchange rate exposure by the Sports Exports Company

At the current time, the Sports Exports Company (Ireland) is willing to receive payments in British pounds for the monthly exports it sends to the UK. While all of its receivables are denominated in pounds, it has no payables in pounds or in any other foreign currency. Jim Logan, owner of the Sports Exports Company, wants to assess his firm's exposure to exchange rate risk.

1 Would you describe the exposure of the Sports Exports Company to exchange rate risk as transaction exposure? Economic exposure? Translation exposure?

2 Jim Logan is considering a change in the pricing policy in which the foreign importer must pay in euros, so that Jim will not have to worry about converting pounds to euros every month. If implemented, would this policy eliminate the transaction exposure of the Sports Exports Company? Would it eliminate Sports Exports' economic exposure? Explain.

3 If Jim decides to implement the policy described in the previous question, how would the Sports Exports Company be affected (if at all) by appreciation of the pound? By depreciation of the pound? Would these effects on Sports Exports differ if Jim retained his original policy of pricing the exports in British pounds?

CHAPTER 11
MANAGING
TRANSACTION
EXPOSURE

LEARNING OBJECTIVES

The specific objectives of the chapter are to:

● Identify the commonly used techniques for hedging transaction exposure.

● Explain how each technique can be used to hedge future payables and receivables.

● Compare the advantages and disadvantages of the different hedging techniques.

● Suggest other methods of reducing exchange rate risk when hedging techniques are not available.

Recall from the previous chapter that a multinational corporation (MNC) is exposed to exchange rate fluctuations in three ways: (1) transaction exposure, (2) economic exposure and (3) translation exposure. This chapter focuses on the management of transaction exposure, while the following chapter focuses on the management of economic and translation exposure. By managing transaction exposure, financial managers can:

● *Reduce the risk of future earnings,*
● *Protect the firm from adverse price movements for a limited period thus:*
    ● *protecting the profits of that period, and*
    ● *giving the firm time to adjust future transactions so that they remain profitable given an adverse price movement.*

TRANSACTION EXPOSURE

Transaction exposure exists when the anticipated future cash transactions of a firm are affected by exchange rate fluctuations. A UK-based MNC that *purchases* French goods may need euros to buy the goods. Though it may know exactly how many euros it will need, it doesn't know how many British pounds will be needed to be exchanged for those euros. This uncertainty occurs because the exchange rate between euros and the pound fluctuates over time. A UK-based MNC that will be *receiving* a foreign currency is exposed because it does not know how many pounds it will obtain when it exchanges the foreign currency for pounds, though here again it may know the foreign currency units it expects to receive.

If transaction exposure exists, the firm faces three major tasks. First, it must identify its degree of transaction exposure. Second, it must decide whether to hedge this exposure. Finally, if it decides to hedge part or all of the exposure, it must choose among the various hedging techniques available. Each of these tasks is discussed in turn.

Identifying net transaction exposure

Before an MNC makes any decisions related to hedging, it should identify the individual **net transaction exposure** on a currency-by-currency basis. The term net here refers to the difference between expected inflows and outflows for a particular time and currency. If a firm at the end of the month is going to receive 1000 Australian dollars and has to pay 800 Australian dollars then it can use its earnings to pay what it owes no matter what happens to the value of the Australian dollar. Only the net amount of 200 Australian dollars will be affected by changes in value, as the firm seeks to convert that amount back to its home currency.

For a multinational company the overall picture is more complex, the management of each subsidiary plays a vital role in reporting its expected inflows and outflows. Then a centralized group consolidates the subsidiary reports to identify, for the MNC as a whole, the expected net positions in each foreign currency during several upcoming periods.

The MNC can identify its exposure by reviewing this consolidation of subsidiary positions. For example, one European subsidiary may have net receivables in dollars 3 months from now, while a different subsidiary has net payables in dollars. If the dollar appreciates, this will be favourable to the first subsidiary and unfavourable to the second subsidiary. For the MNC as a whole, however, the impact is at least partially offset. Each subsidiary may desire to hedge its net currency position in order to avoid the possible adverse impacts on its performance due to fluctuation in the currency's value. The overall performance of the MNC, however, may already be insulated by the offsetting positions between subsidiaries. Therefore, hedging the position of each individual subsidiary may not be necessary.

Adjusting the invoice policy to manage exposure

In some circumstances, the UK firm may be able to modify its pricing policy to hedge against transaction exposure. That is, the firm may be able to invoice (price) its exports in the same currency that will be needed to pay for imports. Alternatively, a firm may choose to purchase some of its supplies from the country where it is selling, thus netting off foreign earnings with foreign payments. A firm may even choose to produce in the countries of its sales. It is interesting that avoiding transaction exposure encourages MNCs to produce abroad. In these simple but very effective ways, the net exposure can be reduced.

EXAMPLE

Clarkson plc (UK) has continual payables in euros because a German exporter sends goods to Clarkson invoiced in euros. Clarkson also exports products (invoiced in UK pounds) to other corporations in Germany. If Clarkson changes its invoicing policy from pounds to euros, it can use the euro receivables from its exports to pay off its future payables in euros. It is unlikely, however, that Clarkson would be able to: (1) invoice the precise amount of euro receivables to match the euro payables and (2) perfectly time the inflows and outflows to match each other.

MANAGING FOR VALUE

Centralized management of exposure

Fiat, the Italian auto manufacturer, implemented a centralized system to monitor 421 subsidiaries dispersed among 55 countries. It uses a comprehensive reporting system that keeps track of its aggregate cash flows in each currency. The net inflow or outflow position for each currency can then be assessed to determine whether and how the position should be balanced out.

Cadbury Schweppes plc (UK) seeks to relate its borrowings to the trading cash flows, matching receipts as far as possible with interest payments in that currency.

Renault SA (France) are monitored through Renault's Central Cash Management and Financing Department. The transactions are executed by its specialist subsidiary Renault Financing. Where cash surpluses are reported in weak currencies deposits are made in strong currencies where possible.

DuPont Co. uses a centralized approach to determine its net inflow or outflow in each currency. Using this approach, it recently anticipated a net inflow position of more than one billion British pounds. It used hedging techniques to hedge almost all of its net exposure in pounds. The hedge generated substantial savings for DuPont because the pound's value had declined by the time the pounds were received.

The important point here is that a hedging decision cannot be made until the firm has determined its exposure to all currencies. The centralized approach enables the MNC to determine its net transaction exposure in each currency so that it can decide whether to hedge these individual positions having considered the complete picture.

Because the matching of inflows and outflows in foreign currencies does have its limitations, an MNC will normally be exposed to some degree of exchange rate risk and, therefore, should consider the various hedging techniques identified next.

TECHNIQUES TO ELIMINATE TRANSACTION EXPOSURE

If an MNC decides to hedge part or all of its transaction exposure, it may select from the following hedging techniques:

- Futures hedge
- Forward hedge
- Money market hedge
- Currency option hedge.

Before selecting a hedging technique, MNCs normally compare the cash flows that would be expected from each technique along with the reduced risk associated with the hedging. Hedging techniques can vary over time, as the relative advantages of the various techniques may change over time. Each technique is discussed in turn, with examples provided. After all techniques have been discussed, a comprehensive example illustrates how all the techniques can be compared to determine the appropriate technique to hedge a particular position.

Futures hedge

Currency futures can be used by firms that desire to hedge transaction exposure.

Purchasing currency futures. A firm that buys a currency futures contract is entitled to receive a specified amount in a specified currency for a stated price on a specified date. To hedge a payment on future payables in a foreign currency, the firm may purchase a currency futures contract for the currency it will need in the near future. By holding this contract, it locks in the amount of its home currency needed to make the payment. If the currency is the currency of the underlying payment and the maturity date of the futures contract is the same as the payment date there is no risk. As compensation in a futures contract is based on movements of the futures contract price and not the currency itself, the two may differ slightly, this is known as basis risk. The currency may also not be the currency that the MNC is purchasing but one that behaves similarly, known as cross hedging. Finally, the company may choose not to hedge the whole payment and thus will be exposed to some variation. See Chapter 5 for further details.

Selling currency futures. A firm that sells a currency futures contract is entitled to sell a specified amount in a specified currency for a stated price on a specified date. To hedge the home currency value of future receivables in a foreign currency, the firm may sell a currency futures contract for the currency it will be receiving. Therefore, the firm knows how much of its home currency it will receive after converting the foreign currency receivables into its home currency. By locking in the exchange rate at which it will be able to exchange the foreign currency for its home currency, the firm insulates the value of its future receivables from the fluctuations in the foreign currency's spot rate over time.

Forward hedge

Like futures contracts, forward contracts can be used to lock in the future exchange rate at which an MNC can buy or sell a currency. A forward contract hedge is very similar to a futures contract hedge, except that forward contracts are commonly used for large transactions, whereas futures contracts tend to be used for smaller amounts. Also, MNCs can request forward contracts that specify the exact number of units that they desire, whereas futures contracts represent a standardized number of units for each currency.

Forward contracts are commonly used by large companies for hedging the risk associated with underlying transactions. There has to be an underlying transaction as MNCs are not allowed to speculate, though the distinction may at times be difficult when the value of the underlying transaction is uncertain. The size of the contracts is often large, for example, DuPont Co. often has the equivalent of $300 million to $500 million in forward contracts at any one time to cover open currency positions (net transaction exposure). To recognize the uses of forward contracts, consider the following quotations from the annual reports of MNCs:

> We use foreign currency forward contracts, currency swaps and currency option contracts for the purpose of managing the risk of fluctuations in foreign exchange rates on forecasted transactions in foreign currencies. Gains or losses arising from changes in the value of the contracts that qualify for hedge accounting are deferred and recognized in the period in which corresponding losses or gains from transactions being hedged by such contracts are recognized.
>
> (Japan Tobacco Inc., Annual Report 2009, p. 68)

The Group has transactional currency exposures arising from sales or purchases by operating subsidiaries in currencies other than the subsidiaries' functional currency. Under the Group's foreign exchange policy, such transactional exposures are hedged once they are known.

(GKN plc, Annual Report 2004, p. 29)

Our most significant foreign currency exposures relate to Japan, Korea and western European countries. We selectively enter into foreign exchange forward and option contracts with durations generally 15 months or less to hedge our exposure to exchange rate risk on foreign source income and purchases. The hedges are scheduled to mature coincident with the timing of the underlying foreign currency commitments and transactions. The objective of these contracts is to neutralize the impact of exchange rate movements on our operating results. We also enter into foreign exchange forward contracts when situations arise where our foreign subsidiaries or Corning enter into lending situations, generally on an intercompany basis, denominated in currencies other than their local currency.

(Owens Corning Co., Annual Report 2004, p. 98)

Forward contracts. Recall that forward contracts are negotiated between the firm and a commercial bank and specify the currency, the exchange rate and the date of the forward transaction. MNCs that need a foreign currency in the future can negotiate a forward contract to purchase the currency forward, thereby locking in the exchange rate at which they will obtain the currency on a future date. MNCs wishing to sell a foreign currency in the future can negotiate a forward contract to sell the currency forward, thereby locking in the exchange rate at which they sell the currency on a future date.

Forward hedge versus no hedge on payables. Although forward contracts are easy to use for hedging, that does not mean that every exposure to exchange rate movements should be hedged. In some cases, an MNC may prefer not to hedge its exposure to exchange rate movements. It may decide that the gains and losses will even themselves out or it may have offsetting transactions such that its net exposure is low.

Forward rates for hedging. Forward rates are available for the euro, US dollar and Japanese yen for 1-month, 3-month and 12-month maturities at http://www.marketprices.ft.com/markets/currencies/ab. These forward rates indicate the exchange rates at which positions in these currencies can be hedged for specific time periods.

The decision as to whether to hedge a position with a forward contract or to keep it unhedged can be made by comparing the known result of hedging to the possible results of remaining unhedged.

EXAMPLE

Durham plc (UK) will need $100 000 in 90 days to pay for US imports. Today's 90-day forward rate of the US dollar is £0.55 to the dollar. To assess the future value of the US dollar, Durham may develop a probability distribution, as shown in Exhibit 11.1. This is graphically illustrated in Exhibit 11.2, which breaks down the probability distribution. Both exhibits can be used to determine the probability that a forward hedge will be more costly than no hedge. This is achieved by estimating the expected cost of hedging payables (ECH_p).

(Continued)

EXHIBIT 11.1   Feasibility analysis for hedging

1	2	3	4	5	6
Possible spot rate of dollar in 90 days (pounds to the dollar)	Cost of *hedging* $100 000 using the forward rate of £0.55:$1 (CH)	Amount in £s needed to buy *$100 000* if firm remains *unhedged* (column 1 × $100 000) (CNH)	Cost of hedging for each possible spot (column 2 − column 3) negative = saving	Probability (%) of spot in column 1 occurring	Expected value calculation (column 4 × column 5)
£0.45:$1	£55 000	**£45 000**	**£10 000**	5%	£500
0.47	55 000	**47 000**	**8 000**	10	800
0.49	55 000	**49 000**	**6 000**	15	900
0.51	55 000	**51 000**	**4 000**	20	800
0.53	55 000	**53 000**	**2 000**	20	400
0.55	55 000	**55 000**	**0**	15	0
0.57	55 000	**57 000**	**2 000**	10	−200
0.60	55 000	**60 000**	**5 000**	5	−250
				100%	
		Overall expected cost of hedged payables *(ECH$_p$)*			£2 950

EXHIBIT 11.2   Comparison of costs of hedging versus no hedge

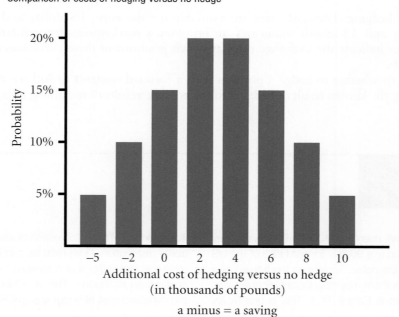

Additional cost of hedging versus no hedge
(in thousands of pounds)

a minus = a saving

(Continued)

The expected cost of hedging measures the overall expected additional expenses beyond those incurred without hedging. The expected cost of payables when hedged is measured as:

$$ECH_p = \Sigma[(CH_p - CNH_p) \times P_i]$$

Where:

ECH_p = expected cost of hedged payables (see total of column 6, Exhibit 11.1)

CH_p = cost of payables when hedged for a given possible exchange rate (column 2, Exhibit 11.1)

CNH_p = cost of payables *without* hedging for a given possible exchange rate (column 3, Exhibit 11.1)

P_i = probability of given exchange rate (column 5, Exhibit 11.1)

$\Sigma[.]$ = overall average being the total of the expression in the squared brackets for all possible exchange rates (see total of column 6, Exhibit 11.1)

When the expected cost of hedging payables is negative, this implies that hedging is more favourable than not hedging. The cost of hedging for each exchange rate scenario $(CH_p - CNH_p)$ is estimated for each exchange rate scenario (column 4, Exhibit 11.1). While CH_p is certain, CNH_p is uncertain, causing ECH_p to be uncertain.

Though Durham plc doesn't know the actual cost of hedging in advance, it can at least use the information in Exhibits 11.1 and 11.2 to decide whether a hedge is feasible. The spread of possible returns is as important as the expected return. An informal review of the range of possible outcomes shows that there is a 15 per cent chance that the cost of hedging will be cheaper than the unhedged position (the last two entries in column 4). But the unhedged position is anticipated to cost less or as much for 85 per cent of the time. So Durham is faced with losing out by an expected £2950 through hedging with only a 15 per cent chance of the actual cost of hedging being cheaper. Providing that the potential cost of buying the $100 000 at £57 000 and £59 000 is bearable (has no special consequences), Durham would do better not to hedge.

The hedge-versus-no-hedge decision is based on the firm's degree of risk aversion. Firms with a greater desire to avoid risk will hedge their open positions in foreign currencies more often than firms that are less concerned about risk. The exact criteria is unclear as currency risk is an individual risk that the shareholder can diversify away. So, in theory, perhaps there should be no hedging. A counter argument is that the losses may be so large as to damage the future of the firm. Alternatively it could distort the risk profile of the company making estimates of systematic risk difficult. Arguably a food firm's profits should vary with the market for food and not with the price of the currency of its main supplies. Finally, if the risk is outside the area of expertise of the firm it could be argued that hedging avoids unnecessary losses.

If the forward rate is an accurate predictor of the future spot rate, the expected cost of hedging will be zero. This means that although in practice the forward rate will sometimes underestimate or overestimate the future spot rate for any particular period, on average, the actual cost of hedging will be zero over time. On that basis hedging would seem worthwhile because on average it will not be costly and in any one particular period it will avoid possible adverse outcomes. For instance, if the actual rate turned out to be £0.59 to the US dollar in the Durham example, the company will be pleased to have hedged and purchased at the forward price of only £0.55 to the dollar. Even if on average the hedged position proves to be more expensive, the firm might still choose to hedge. If there are potentially very adverse outcomes that could happen in a period, for example a 40 per cent depreciation in the value of foreign currency earnings, then avoiding such outcomes by hedging might be seen as worthwhile. Companies are accountable to shareholders on an annual basis and might well feel uncomfortable with arguing that their losses in 1 year will be recouped in future years.

Forward hedge versus no hedge on receivables. For firms with exposure in receivables, the expected cost of hedging receivables (ECH_r) can be estimated as with payables namely:

$$ECH_r = \Sigma[(CNH_r - CH_r) \times P_i]$$

Where:

ECH_r = expected cost of hedging receivables

CH_r = receivables when hedged for a given possible exchange rate

CNH_r = receivables when *not* hedged for a given possible exchange rate

P_i = probability of a given exchange rate

$\Sigma[.]$ = overall average being the total of the expression in the squared brackets for all possible exchange rates

The terms in the '( )' above are reversed so that a positive value means that hedging is more costly than not hedging as with the previous cost equation.

As with payable positions, firms can determine whether to hedge receivable positions by first developing a probability distribution for the future spot rate and then using it to develop a probability distribution of possible outcomes as in Exhibit 11.2. Again the consideration is of the expected value and the range of possible outcomes. An MNC might consider as with payables that a year on year net cost of hedging as opposed to not hedging might be worthwhile if the immediate consequences of exceptionally adverse exchange rate movements can be avoided.

Measuring the cost of hedging with forward contracts. The cost of hedging has been defined here in terms of the currency of the MNC's home country. It can also be expressed as a percentage of the hedged amount. This may be a useful measurement when comparing the cost of hedging for various currencies. A percentage expected cost of hedging applies to all currencies as an easily applicable measure.

The cost of hedging has two uncertainties, first, the exchange rate, and second, the actual amount involved. Adidas (sports equipment) express their policy as follows:

> *Due to the Group's global activity, currency management is a key focus of the Group's Treasury department. Hedging US dollars is a central part of our programme. This is a direct result of our Asian-denominated sourcing, which is largely denominated in US dollars …As outlined in our Group's Treasury Policy, we have established a rolling 12–24 month hedging system, under which the vast majority of the anticipated seasonal hedging volume is secured six months prior to the start of a season…. The use or combination of different hedging instruments, such as forward contracts, currency options and swaps protected us against unfavourable currency movements, while retaining the potential to benefit from future favourable exchange rate developments.*

(Adidas Annual Report 2009, p. 131)

As is often the case, companies use derivatives in combination.

Money market hedge

A money market hedge involves taking a money market position to cover a future payables or receivables position (see Exhibit 11.3). Money market hedges on payables and receivables will be discussed separately.

Money market hedge on payables. If a firm has a payment required in a foreign currency in 6 months time, it can buy the required amount of foreign currency now and deposit it in a bank account denominated in that currency. In 6 months time the money can be used to make the payment. In this way, uncertainty due to exchange rate fluctuation can be avoided. Furthermore, the firm will not have to convert the full amount of the payment. Only the discounted value will need to be converted. When the payment is due, the converted sum plus interest will amount to the payment.

EXHIBIT 11.3 **Money market hedges**

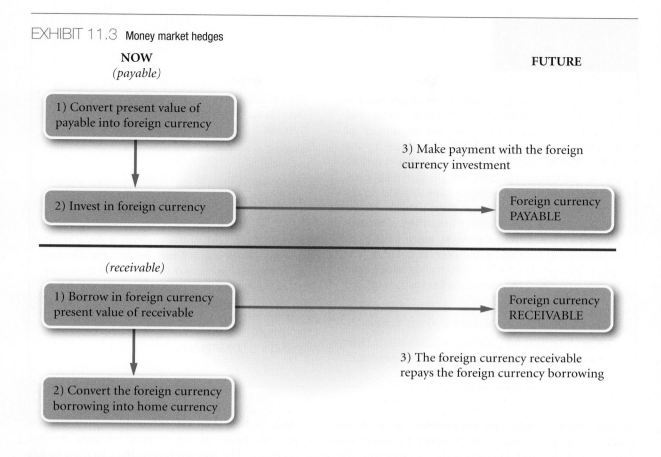

EXAMPLE

Ashland plc needs NZ$1 000 000 (New Zealand dollars) in 30 days, and it can earn 6 per cent annualized (0.5 per cent for 30 days) on a New Zealand security over this period. In this case, the amount needed to purchase a New Zealand 1-month security is:

$$\text{Deposit amount to hedge NZ\$ payables} = \frac{\text{NZ\$1 000 000}}{(1 + 0.005)} = \text{NZ\$995 025}$$

Assuming that the New Zealand dollar's spot rate is £0.40, then £398 010 is needed to purchase the New Zealand security (computed as NZ$995 025 × £0.40). In 30 days, the security will mature and provide NZ$1 000 000 to Ashland plc which can then use this money to cover its payables. Regardless of how the New Zealand dollar exchange rate changes over this period, Ashland's investment in the New Zealand security will be able to cover its payables position.

In many cases, MNCs prefer to hedge payables without using their own cash balances. A money market hedge can still be used in this situation, but it requires two money market positions: (1) borrowed funds in the home currency and (2) a short-term investment in the foreign currency.

EXAMPLE

Reconsider the previous example, in which Ashland plc needs NZ$1 000 000 in 30 days. Recall that £398 010 is needed to obtain the investment of NZ$995 025, which in turn will accumulate to the NZ$1 000 000 needed in 30 days. If Ashland has no excess cash, it can borrow £398 010 from a UK bank and exchange those pounds for New Zealand dollars in order to purchase the New Zealand security.

Because the New Zealand investment will cover Ashland's future payables position, the firm needs to be concerned only about the pounds owed on the loan in 30 days. The firm's money market hedge used to hedge payables can be summarized as follows:

Step 1. Borrow £398 010 from a UK bank; assume a 0.7 per cent interest rate over the 30-day loan period.

Step 2. Convert the £398 010 to NZ$995 025, given the exchange rate of £0.40 per New Zealand dollar.

Step 3. Use the New Zealand dollars to purchase a New Zealand security that offers 0.5 per cent over 1 month.

Step 4. Pay the NZ$1million with the maturing security.

Step 5. Repay the UK loan in 30 days, plus interest; the amount owed is £400 796 (computed as £398 010 × 1.007).

Note that the cost of the exercise is the interest paid to the UK bank at 0.7 per cent less the effective discount for early payment of 0.5 per cent – a net cost of 0.2 per cent (0.002) or more accurately: 400 000 – 398 010 = £1990 saved through early payment at a cost of 398 010 × 0.007 = £2786 a net cost of £796 (1990 – 2786). The approximate version is £400 000 × 0.002 = £800.

Money market hedge on receivables. If, in 6 months' time, a firm expects receivables in a foreign currency, it can hedge this position by borrowing the present value of the receivables now in that foreign currency and converting the amount into the home currency. The foreign receivable can then be left to repay the foreign borrowing and will therefore not be converted.

EXAMPLE

Bakerstown Ltd is a UK firm that transports goods to Singapore and expects to receive 400 000 Singapore dollars (S$) in 90 days. To avoid exchange rate uncertainty, Bakerstown can today borrow Singapore dollars and convert the amount into British pounds. The

Singapore dollar receipt can then be 'left' to repay the Singapore dollar loan in 90 days. Assuming an annualized interest rate of 8 per cent, or 2 per cent over the 90-day period, the amount of Singapore dollars to be borrowed to hedge the future receivables is:

$$\text{Borrowed amount to hedge the S\$ receivables} = \frac{\text{S\$400 000}}{1 + 0.02}$$
$$= \text{S\$392 157}$$

If Bakerstown borrows S$392 157 now and converts those Singapore dollars to British pounds, then it can use the receivables of S$400 000 to pay off the Singapore dollar loan in 90 days. Meanwhile, the converted value of the S$392 157 can now be used by

Bakerstown. The company will not be affected by any change in the S$ value as it will not be converting the receivables in 90 days. The cost is the interest rate on borrowing in Singapore dollars less the benefit of receiving the converted money early (not shown here).

Hedging with a money market hedge versus a forward hedge. Should an MNC implement a forward contract hedge or a money market hedge? The forward hedge and the money market hedge are directly comparable. Both eliminate currency risk. The forward rate guarantees a rate now for the future point in time; whereas the money market hedge converts the present value of the receivable or payable at the current spot rate. As the effect is the same for the MNC, the cost cannot differ greatly. However, the money market hedge is a drain on the working capital of the MNC. Box 1 in Exhibit 11.3 for receivables and payables both represent an increase in the MNC's short-term liabilities (overdraft) either through borrowing now (the receivable) or paying early (the payable). For this reason the money market hedge is less attractive when considering the strategies in isolation. If the MNC was borrowing anyway, then hedging the receivable by switching borrowing to the currency of the receivable would be an attractive money market hedge. If the MNC had surplus cash, hedging the payable by depositing the present value of the payable in the foreign currency might also be an attractive prospect.

Implications of IRP for the money market hedge. If interest rate parity (IRP) exists, and transaction costs do not exist, the money market hedge will yield the same results as the forward hedge. This is so because, as established in Chapter 5, the forward premium on the forward rate reflects the interest rate differential between the two currencies. The money market hedge also reflects the interest rate differential. The position for payables and receivables is illustrated in Exhibit 11.3. For payables, the MNC earns the foreign interest rate but 'pays' the equivalent of the home interest rate by paying early (for example, the overdraft may increase by the amount of the early payment). For receivables, the MNC pays interest on the foreign borrowing but earns the equivalent of home interest on the money borrowed.

Even if the forward premium generally reflects the interest rate differential between countries, the existence of transaction costs may cause the results from a forward hedge to differ from those of the money market hedge.

Currency option hedge

Firms recognize that hedging techniques such as the forward hedge and money market hedge can backfire when payables are made in a currency that depreciates or a receivables earned in a currency that appreciates over the hedged period. In these situations, an unhedged strategy is likely to outperform the forward hedge or money market hedge. The ideal hedge would insulate the firm from adverse exchange rate movements but allow the firm to benefit from favourable exchange rate movements. Currency options exhibit these attributes. However, a firm must assess whether the advantages of a currency option hedge are worth the price (premium) paid for it. Details on currency options are provided in Chapter 5. The following discussion illustrates how they can be used in hedging.

Hedging payables with currency call options. A currency call option provides the right to buy a specified amount of a particular currency at a specified price (the exercise price) within a given period of time. Yet, unlike a futures or forward contract, the currency call option *does not oblige* its owner to buy the currency at that price. If the spot rate of the currency remains lower than the exercise price throughout the life of the option, the firm can let the option expire and simply purchase the currency at the existing spot rate. On the other hand, if the spot rate of the currency appreciates over time, the call option allows the firm to purchase the currency at the exercise price. That is, the firm owning a call option has locked in a maximum price (the exercise price) to pay for the currency. Yet, it also has the flexibility to let the option expire and obtain the currency at the existing spot rate when the currency is to be sent for payment.

EXAMPLE

Clement Ltd (UK) has payables of $100 000 to be made 90 days from now. Assume there is a call option available with an exercise price of £0.62 for 1 dollar. Assume also that the option premium is £0.03 per unit. For options that cover the 100 000 units, the total premium is £3000 (100 000 × £0.03). If the cost of a dollar at the time of maturity is below the option strike price of £0.62 per dollar, Clement will not have to exercise the option.

Clement expects the spot rate of the dollar to be either £0.58, £0.63 or £0.66 when the payables are due. The effect of each of these scenarios on Clement's cost of payables is shown in Exhibit 11.4. Columns 1 and 2 simply identify the scenario to be analyzed. Column 3 applies the rule for exercising: where spot is greater than the exercise price it is cheaper to buy using the option, therefore the option is exercised; if the spot is less than the exercise price then it is cheaper to buy on the spot market and not exercise the option. Column 4 shows the premium per unit paid on the option, which is the same regardless of the spot rate that occurs when payables are due - note that this is a fixed or sunk cost and should not play a part in our decision whether or not to exercise.

Column 5 shows the amount that Clement would pay per dollar for the payables under each scenario, the amount varies depending on whether or not the option is exercised. If Scenario 1 occurs, Clement will let the options expire and purchase dollars on the spot market for £0.58 each. If Scenario 2 occurs Clement will exercise the option because the option price is £0.62 which is less than the spot of £0.63. Similarly for Scenario 3, the spot cost of the dollar is greater than the option cost and therefore it is cheaper to buy dollars using the spot rate. Column 6, which is the sum of Columns 4 and 5, shows the amount paid per unit when the premium paid on the call option is included. Note that the Scenario 2 total cost of £0.65 is higher than the spot rate of £0.63. It is a common error to argue that the option should therefore not have been exercised. The premium, however, is a sunk cost. If the option had not been exercised in Scenario 2, the premium would still have to be paid and therefore the total cost would have been £0.66 (i.e. £0.63 + £0.03), more than if the option had been exercised. Column 7 converts Column 6 into a total dollar cost, based on the $100 000 hedged.

EXHIBIT 11.4 Use of currency call options for hedging the US dollar payables for a UK company
(exercise price = £0.62; premium £0.03)

(1)	(2)	(3)	(4)	(5)	(6) = (5) + (4)	(7) = (6) × $100 000
Scenario	Spot rate when payables are due	Exercise price £0.62 per $ Exercise?	Premium per unit paid on call options	Amount paid per unit when owning call options	Total amount paid per unit (including the premium) when owning call options	£ amount paid for $100 000 when owning a call option on dollars
1	£0.58	NO	£0.03	£0.58	£0.61	£61 000
2	0.63	YES	0.03	0.62	0.65	65 000
3	0.66	YES	0.03	0.62	0.65	65 000

Hedging receivables with currency put options. Like currency call options, currency put options can be a valuable hedging device. A currency put option provides the right to sell a specified amount in a particular currency at a specified price (the exercise price) within a given period of time. Firms can use a currency put option to hedge future receivables in foreign currencies, since it guarantees a certain price (the exercise price) at which the future receivables can be sold. The currency put option *does not oblige* its owner to sell the currency at a specified price. If the existing spot rate of the foreign currency is above the exercise price when the firm receives the foreign currency, the firm can sell the currency received at the spot rate and let the put option expire.

EXAMPLE

Lebenstadt GmbH (Germany), transports goods to Brazil (the real, R$) and expects to receive R$600 000 in about 90 days. Because Lebenstadt is concerned that the Brazilian real may depreciate against the euro, the company is considering purchasing put options to cover its receivables. The Brazilian real put options considered here have an exercise price of 0.32 euros and a premium of 0.02 euros per unit. Lebenstadt anticipates that the spot rate of the real in 90 days will be either 0.30 euros, 0.33 euros or 0.35 euros. The amount to be received as a result of owning currency put options is shown in Exhibit 11.5. Columns 2 through to 6 are on a per-unit basis. Column 7 is determined by multiplying the per-unit amount received in Column 5 by 600 000 units.

EXHIBIT 11.5 Use of currency put options to hedge a Brazilian real receivable to be converted to euros (exercise price 0.32 euros for R$1; premium 0.02 euros)

(1)	(2)	(3)	(4)	(5)	(6) = (5) + (4)	(7) = (6) × R$600 000
Scenario	Spot rate when receivables are received	Exercise price 0.32 euros for R$1 Exercise?	Premium per unit paid on put options	Amount received per unit when owning put options	Net amount received per unit (after paying the premium) when owning put options.	Euro amount received for R$600 000 when owning put options
1	0.30 euros	YES	0.02 euros	0.32 euros	0.30 euros	R$180 000
2	0.33	NO	0.02	0.33	0.31	186 000
3	0.35	NO	0.02	0.35	0.33	198 000

Hedging contingent exposure. Currency call options are also useful for hedging contingent exposure, in which an MNC's exposure is contingent on a specific event happening.

James plc (UK) is negotiating to acquire an Australian company in 3 months, but the deal is contingent on approval by the Australian government. The British pound price that will be paid for the company is dependent on the value of the Australian dollar in 3 months. James wants to lock in the rate at which it will exchange pounds for Australian dollars because it is worried that the Australian dollar may appreciate. Yet, it does not want to be obliged to obtain Australian dollars unless the acquisition is approved. It can purchase call options on Australian dollars to hedge its contingent exposure.

Comparison of hedging techniques

Each of the hedging techniques is briefly summarized in Exhibit 11.6. When using a futures hedge, forward hedge or money market hedge, the firm can estimate the funds (denominated in its home currency) that it will need for future payables, or the funds that it will receive after converting foreign currency receivables. Thus, it can compare the costs or revenue and determine which of these hedging techniques is appropriate.

EXHIBIT 11.6   **Review of techniques for hedging transaction exposure**

Hedging technique	To hedge payables	To hedge receivables
1. Futures hedge	Purchase a currency futures contract (or contracts) representing the currency and amount related to the payables.	Sell a currency futures contract (or contracts) representing the currency and amount related to the receivables.
2. Forward hedge	Negotiate a forward contract to purchase the amount of foreign currency needed to cover the payables.	Negotiate a forward contract to sell the amount of foreign currency that will be received as a result of the receivables.
3. Money market hedge	Borrow local currency and convert to currency denominating payables. Invest these funds until they are needed to cover the payables.	Borrow the currency denominating the receivables, convert it to the local currency and invest it. Then pay off the loan with cash inflows from the receivables.
4. Currency option hedge	Purchase a currency call option (or options) representing the currency and amount related to the payables.	Purchase a currency put option (or options) representing the currency and amount related to the receivables.

In contrast, the cash flow associated with the currency option hedge cannot be determined with certainty because the costs of purchasing payables and the revenue generated from receivables are not known ahead of time. Therefore, firms need to forecast cash flows from the option hedge based on possible exchange rate outcomes.

Comparison of techniques to hedge payables. A comparison of hedging techniques should focus on obtaining a foreign currency at the lowest possible cost. To reinforce an understanding of the hedging techniques, a comprehensive example is provided here.

EXAMPLE

Assume that Bracken Ltd (UK) will need $200 000 in 180 days. It considers using: (1) a forward hedge, (2) a money market hedge, (3) an option hedge or (4) no hedge. Its analysts develop the following information, which can be used to assess the alternative solutions:

- Spot rate of the dollar as of today = £0.60 for $1.
- 180-day forward rate of pound as of today = £0.61 for $1.
  Interest rates are as follows:

	UK	USA
180-day deposit rate	4.5%	4%
180-day borrowing rate	5.5%	5%

- A call option on pounds that expires in 180 days has an exercise price of £0.61 and a premium of $0.021.
- A put option on pounds that expires in 180 days has an exercise price of £0.59 and a premium of £0.004.

Bracken forecasts the future spot rate in 180 days as follows:

Possible outcomes	Probability
0.75	1%
0.70	9
0.66	22
0.63	33
0.59	23
0.56	10
0.53	2
	100%

(Continued)

Bracken then assesses the alternative solutions, as shown in Exhibit 11.7. Each alternative is analyzed to estimate the cost of paying in pounds for the payables denominated in dollars.

The cost is known with certainty for the forward rate hedge and money market hedge. When using the call option or leaving the payment unhedged, the cost is dependent on the spot rate 180 days from now. The costs of the four alternatives are illustrated using probability distributions as shown in Exhibit 11.8. A review of this exhibit shows that the money market hedge is superior to the forward hedge by £269 (£122 000 – £121 731). This is a very small amount and the order could be easily reversed by differing tax treatments or further administration cost differences.

Whereas the forward and the money market hedges are offering a single known exchange rate, both the option and the no hedge positions have uncertain outcomes. There is in Exhibit 11.8, an estimated 35 per cent chance that the call option will be cheaper than a money market or forward hedge. A cheaper outcome could be £110 200 (2 per cent) or 116 200 (10 per cent) or 120 200 (23 per cent), the total percentage probability of these outcomes is 35 per cent. There is also a 65 per cent chance that it will cost about 3.5 per cent more than the forward hedge at £126 200 (i.e. (126 200 – 122 000) / 122 000 = 0.034 or about 3.5 per cent) and similarly so for the money market hedge. For the no hedge position the outcomes and probabilities are: £150 000 (1 per cent), 140 000 (9 per cent), 132 000 (22 per cent), 126 000 (33 per cent), 118 000 (23 per cent), 112 000 (10 per cent) and 106 000 (2 per cent). Here again, there is a 35 per cent chance that the cost of the $200 000 payable could be cheaper than either the forward or money market hedges.

There is no clear decision as to which is the best form of hedge. A company may well be prepared to take a 65 per cent chance of paying about 3.5 per cent more in order to potentially benefit from the 35 per cent chance of paying less than the cost of a fixed hedge.

EXHIBIT 11.7 Comparison of hedging alternatives for Bracken Ltd wishing to purchase $200 000 in 180 days' time (point of comparison is in 180 days' time)

Forward hedge

To purchase dollars 180 days forward

British pounds needed in 180 days = forward rate of dollar × payables in dollars

$$= £0.61 × \$200\,000$$
$$= \pounds122\,000$$

Money market hedge

Borrow in pounds the present value of the payable, convert to dollars and invest, then allow the investment to pay the payable when due.

$$\text{Amount in dollars that has to be invested} = \frac{\$200\,000}{(1 + 0.04)}$$
$$= \$192\,308$$

Amount in £s needed to convert into $s for investment = $192 308 × £0.60 = £115 385
Interest and principal owed on £ loan after 180 days = £115 385 × (1 + 0.055) = **£121 731**

(Continued)

Call option

Exercise price £0.61, premium = £0.021

Possible spot rate in 180 days	Premium per unit paid for option	Exercise option at £0.61 per dollar	Total price (including option premium) paid per unit)	Total Price paid for $200 000	Probability
£0.75	£0.021	YES	£0.631	£126 200	1 per cent
0.70	0.021	YES	0.631	126 200	9
0.66	0.021	YES	0.631	126 200	22
0.63	0.021	YES	0.631	126 200	33
0.58	0.021	NO	0.601	120 200	23
0.56	0.021	NO	0.581	116 200	10
0.53	0.021	NO	0.551	110 200	2
			Expected value	123 500	

Remain unhedged

Possible spot rate in 180 days	British pounds needed to pay for $200 000	Probability
£0.75	£150 000	1%
0.70	140 000	9
0.66	132 000	22
0.63	126 000	33
0.58	116 000	23
0.56	112 000	10
0.53	106 000	2
Expected value	124 720	

EXHIBIT 11.8 British pound cost of dollar denominated payables

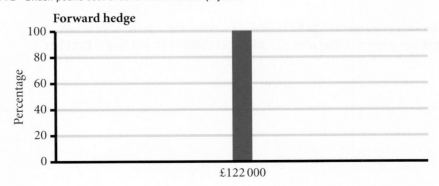

Forward hedge

£122 000

(Continued)

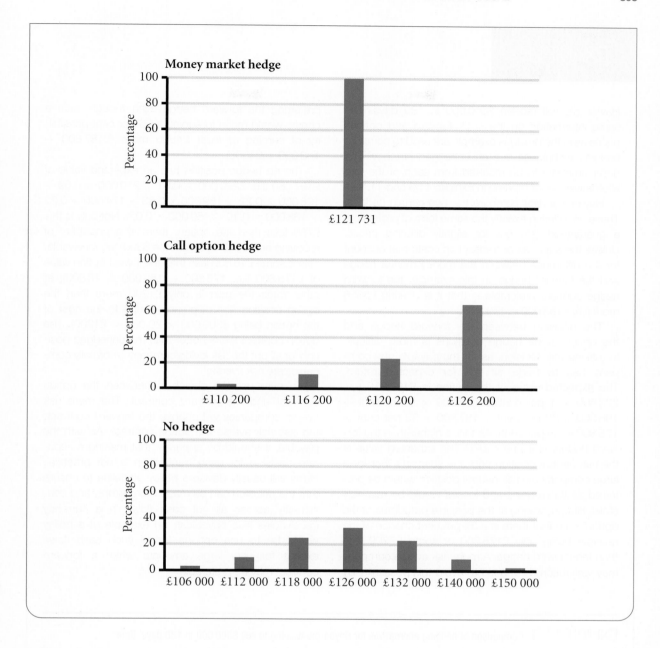

Often there are too many transactions in a company to take the decision on a transaction by transaction basis. Company policy will offer overall guidance. As an example, for transactions up to a certain size, the company may as a matter of policy use options; but above a certain size, decide on a transaction by transaction basis whether or not to use forward rates. As well as looking at transactions, a company may well look at its overall exposure across all transactions for selected currencies. Where a certain overall exposure level for each currency is reached, the company may well decide to take out protection against variation in the currency by means of a futures or forward contract.

Comparison of techniques to hedge receivables. If a firm desires to hedge receivables, it will conduct a similar analysis of transaction exposure. From an MNC's perspective, the comparison should focus on selecting a technique that will maximize the dollars to be received as a result of hedging.

EXAMPLE

Haytor plc will receive $300 000 in 180 days. The same information on the spot, forward and options prices as in the previous example are used to compare hedging techniques and an unhedged strategy. The dollar amounts to be received from each of the four alternatives are compared in Exhibits 11.9 and 11.10.

Haytor can first compare the two certain hedges. These are offering exactly the same form of protection, a guaranteed rate but for slightly differing prices. Unless there are tax or transaction costs that account for the difference between the money market hedge and the forward hedge, in this example, the forward hedge appears preferable in that it is offering £3858 more (i.e. £183 000 − 179 142).

The decision between the forward hedge and the option or no hedge positions is more difficult. In making the decision, as for the payable, the company has to trade off risk for expected return. The expected value of the option is £187 830 (i.e. 223 800 × 1 per cent + 208 800 × 9 per cent + 196 800 × 22 per cent + 187 800 × 33 per cent + 175 800 × 35 per cent). As this is higher than the forward hedge, is it preferable? The expected value is the risk neutral position and one suspects that for a large company the risk neutral position would be preferred as these gains and losses would be relatively small. But, in looking at the possible outcomes of the option, note that there is a 35 per cent chance of the receipts being only £175 800 or some £7200 less than the forward hedge. A more risk averse company may well rationally choose to avoid this possibility by preferring the forward hedge even though such a choice would mean foregoing a 65 per cent possibility of earning *at least* £4800 more (£187 800 − 183 000 = £4800).

The no hedge position has an expected value of £187 080 (i.e. £225 000 × 0.01 + 210 000 × 0.09 + 198 000 × 0.22 + 189 000 × 0.33 + 174 000 × 0.23 + 168 000 × 0.10 + 159 000 × 0.02). Not only is this £750 less than the option, there is a possibility of receiving only £159 000 from the $300 000 receivable. This is some £16 800 less than the lowest option value of £175 800 (i.e. 175 800 − 159 000 = 16 800); at other rates the gain is only £1200 more than the option position (the difference is due to the cost of the option being $300 000 × £0.004 = £1200). The option contract looks better than the unhedged position for all but the risk loving company – normally companies are risk averse.

To sum up, the choice is between the option contract and the forward contract. The more risk averse companies will choose the forward contract; the less risk averse the option contract. As with the payable, it should be apparent that making a separate decision for each transaction is not practical. Firms will usually devise a policy guideline to ensure that the decision can be made more simply and consistently across all net cash flows in a currency (receivables less payables). An example of a policy would be to use options for all such cash flows except for very large amounts when a forward contract may be preferable.

EXHIBIT 11.9 **Comparison of hedging alternatives for Haytor plc wishing to sell $300 000 in 180 days' time**

Forward hedge

To sell dollars 180 days forward

$$\text{British pounds value of dollars in 180 days} = \text{forward rate of dollar} \times \text{receivables in dollars}$$
$$= £0.61 \times \$300\,000$$
$$= \mathbf{£183\,000}$$

(Continued)

Money market hedge

Borrow in dollars the present value of the receivable, convert to pounds then allow the dollar receivable to repay the borrowing when due.

$$\text{Amount in dollars borrowed} = \frac{\$300\,000}{(1 + 0.05)}$$
$$= \$285\,714$$

£s received from converting \$s = \$285\,714 × £0.60 = £171\,428
Interest and principal on £s invested 180 days = £171\,428 × (1 + 0.045) = **£179\,142**
(This is done to compare with other hedges all valued in 180 days' time.)

Put option

Exercise price £0.59, premium = £0.004

Possible spot rate in 180 days	Premium per unit paid for option	Exercise option at £0.61 per dollar	Total price (net of option premium) received per unit)	Total price received for $300 000	Probability
£0.75	£0.004	NO	£0.746	£223 800	1%
0.70	0.004	NO	0.696	208 800	9
0.66	0.004	NO	0.656	196 800	22
0.63	0.004	NO	0.626	187 800	33
0.58	0.004	YES	0.586	175 800	23
0.56	0.004	YES	0.586	175 800	10
0.53	0.004	YES	0.586	175 800	2
			Expected value	187 830	

Remain unhedged

Possible spot rate in 180 days	British pounds received from converting $300 000	Probability
£0.75	£225 000	1%
0.70	210 000	9
0.66	198 000	22
0.63	189 000	33
0.58	174 000	23
0.56	168 000	10
0.53	159 000	2
Expected value	187 080	

(Continued)

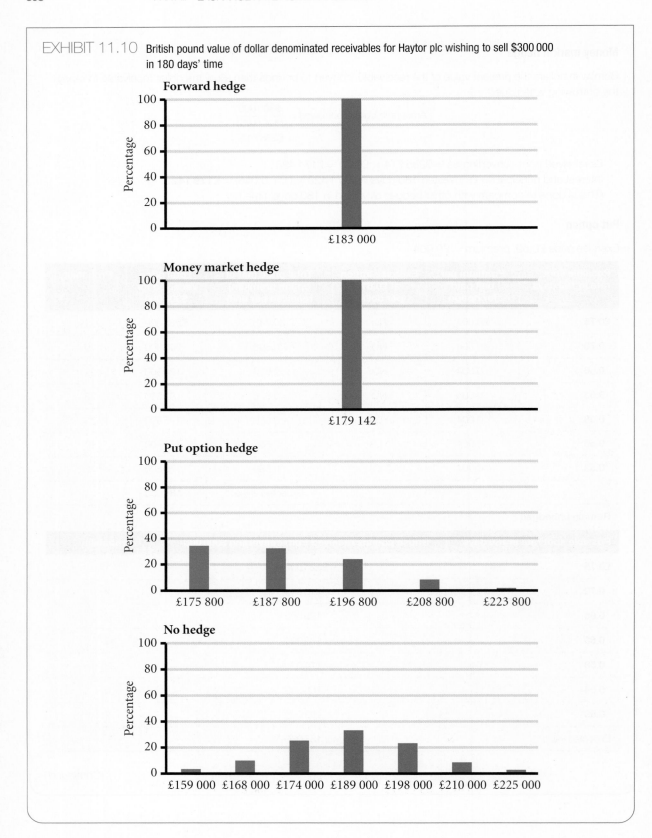

EXHIBIT 11.10 British pound value of dollar denominated receivables for Haytor plc wishing to sell $300 000 in 180 days' time

Comparing alternative currency option contracts. Although the preceding example assessed only one particular currency option, several alternative currency options are normally available with different exercise prices. When hedging payables, a firm can reduce the premium paid by choosing a call option with a higher exercise price. Of course, the tradeoff is that the maximum amount to be paid for the payables will be higher. Similarly, a firm hedging receivables can reduce the premium paid by choosing a put option with a lower exercise price. In this case, the trade-off is that the minimum amount to be received for the receivables will be lower. Firms generally compare the available options first to determine which is most appropriate. Then, this particular option is compared to the other hedging techniques to determine which technique (if any) should be used.

When MNCs purchase call options to hedge payables, they can finance their purchase by selling put options. This was outlined in Appendix 5B, Chapter 5.

EXAMPLE

Haytor in the previous example was considering a put option at £0.59 to the dollar exercise price, the spot being £0.60 to the dollar. Although the premium was only £0.004 per dollar, the total cost was $300 000 × 0.004 = £1200. One way of 'paying' for the option is to offer (probably to the seller of the option) a call contract for that same amount ($300 000) at a similar premium. Using the Black Scholes formula (not shown here) such a strike price would be at about £0.67. In other words, to pay for the put, Haytor can sell a call at a strike price of 0.67 for a premium of £0.004 per dollar. The company is now in a position of having to pay £0.004 for the put and receive £0.004 for selling or writing the call. Therefore no net payment need be made. If the counterparty is a bank, then Haytor would

be fully compensated by the bank if the value of the dollar falls below £0.59 to the dollar. To pay for this service, if the value of the dollar rises above £0.67, Haytor will in effect have paid the bank the difference out of its converted $300 000 revenue at a higher rate. So Haytor will at most convert the receivables at £0.67 (anything above that amount is paid to the bank). In return Haytor will not receive anything less than £0.59 for each dollar of revenue. Anything less is compensated by the bank. The spread of possible returns for Haytor is shown in Exhibit 11.11.

Note that if the amount were to be a payment, then Haytor could purchase a call and finance the purchase by writing a put option. The graph in Exhibit 11.11 would be similar.

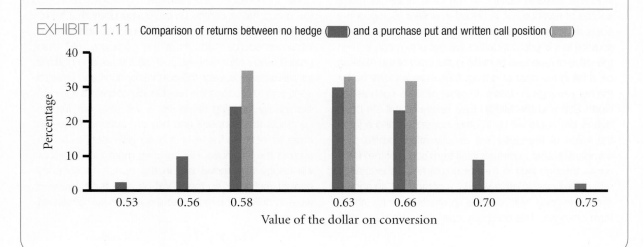

EXHIBIT 11.11 Comparison of returns between no hedge (███) and a purchase put and written call position (███)

Hedging policies of MNCs

In general, hedging policies vary with the MNC management's degree of risk aversion. An MNC may choose to hedge most of its exposure, to hedge none of its exposure or to selectively hedge.

Hedging most of the exposure. Some MNCs hedge most of their exposure so that their value is not highly influenced by exchange rates. MNCs that hedge most of their exposure do not necessarily expect that hedging will always be beneficial. In fact, such MNCs may even use some hedges that are likely to result in slightly worse outcomes than no hedges at all, just to avoid the possibility of a major adverse movement in exchange rates. They prefer to know what their future cash inflows or outflows in terms of their home currency will be in each period because this improves corporate planning. A hedge allows the firm to know the future cash flows (in terms of the home currency) that will result from any foreign transactions that have already been negotiated.

Hedging none of the exposure. MNCs that are well diversified across many countries may consider not hedging their exposure. This strategy may be driven by the view that a diversified set of exposures will limit the actual impact that exchange rates will have on the MNC during any period.

LIMITATIONS OF HEDGING

Although hedging transaction exposure is effective and widely practiced by multinationals, the protection it offers is limited in a number of ways.

MANAGING FOR VALUE

BP hedging strategy

BP, Philips Electrical and Cadbury Schweppes and a number of other European multinationals have considerable sales in dollars. In the case of BP its major source of revenue, oil, is priced in dollars. Some of the costs as in its Alaskan oil fields will be in dollars as well; so a fall in the price of dollars will not only mean a fall in the value of revenues but also in the case of the Alaskan oil, a fall in the cost of drilling. Exposure will only be for the net earnings in dollars. In other oil fields such as the North Sea and the Middle East revenues will still be in dollars but costs will be in other currencies and a fall in the value of the dollar will directly affect profits. The company is able to protect itself from some of the differences through lags in market adjustment to exchange rate differences. In other words, a contract at an agreed exchange rate will provide protection from short-term changes. The company can also switch to other

suppliers in reaction to exchange rate changes. Nevertheless there remains a significant exposure to the dollar in particular. To manage its hedging strategy the group has a central co-ordinating body that takes the net of inflows and outflows of each currency from whatever source throughout the company. BP then uses a range of derivatives such as futures and options as well as swaps, over-the-counter options and forward contracts to manage the residual exposure. As it is predominantly hedging revenues, it will take out futures contracts to sell dollars and buy put options. Finally, in order to increase the level of dollar payments to set off against the revenues, BP borrows mostly in dollars or will hedge any movement in the borrowed currency against the dollar so that it will be as if the borrowing were in dollars. Interest rates are also mainly swapped into dollars.

Limitation of hedging an uncertain amount

Some international transactions involve an uncertain amount of goods ordered and therefore involve an uncertain transaction amount in a foreign currency. Consequently, an MNC may create a hedge for a larger number of units than it will actually need and hedging can then easily turn into speculating.

EXAMPLE

Recall the previous example on hedging receivables, which assumed that Haytor plc will receive $300 000 in 180 days. Now assume that the receivables amount could actually be much lower. If Haytor sells the $300 000 forward and the receivables amount to only $200 000, it will in effect be speculating on the $100 000 balance. If the future spot value of the dollar is above the forward rate, the company will lose out; if below, it will gain by the difference over $300 000, more than the revenue it was trying to hedge.

This example shows how **over-hedging** (hedging a larger amount in a currency than the actual transaction amount) can adversely affect a firm. A solution to avoid over-hedging is to hedge only known amounts. As a result an MNC will tend to be under-hedged and more exposed to currency fluctuations. In our example, if the future receivables were as low as $200 000, Haytor could hedge this amount. Under these conditions, however, the firm may not have completely hedged its position. If the actual transaction amount turns out to be $300 000 as expected, Haytor will be only partially hedged and will need to sell the extra $100 000 in the spot market.

Firms commonly face this type of dilemma because the precise amount to be received in a foreign currency at the end of a period can be uncertain, especially for firms heavily involved in exporting. Based on this example, it should be clear that most MNCs cannot completely hedge all of their transactions. Nevertheless, by hedging a portion of those transactions that affect them, they can reduce the sensitivity of their cash flows to exchange rate movements.

Limitation of repeated short-term hedging

The continual hedging of repeated transactions that are expected to occur in the near future has limited effectiveness over the long run. A hedge gives the MNC time to rearrange its affairs. If the company still has to purchase goods in an appreciating currency, the higher rate will have to be paid after the period of protection afforded by the hedge. Similarly for a depreciating currency, revenues in a depreciating currency can be protected for the period of the hedge, but beyond that period the revenues will translate at the lower value. As stated at the beginning of this chapter, the hedge as well as protecting the profitability of the transactions during the hedge also gives a firm time to adjust to new price regimes.

EXAMPLE

Renghini SpA (Italy) is an importer that specializes in importing particular CD players in one large shipment per year and then selling them to retail stores throughout the year. Assume that today's exchange rate of the Japanese yen is worth 0.005 euro and that the CD players are worth ¥60 000 or 300 euro. The forward rate of the yen generally exhibits a small premium over the currency spot. But such a premium may be absorbed by a strengthening yen. Exhibit 11.12 shows the euro value of the yen to be paid by the importer over time. As the spot rate changes, the forward rate will change by a similar amount given that

(Continued)

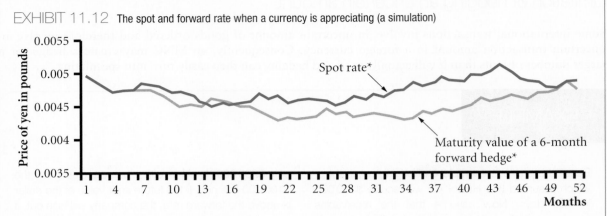

EXHIBIT 11.12 The spot and forward rate when a currency is appreciating (a simulation)

* Where the forward rate line is below the spot line, the forward contract will have been worthwhile for purchasing yen. Otherwise the spot rate will have been cheaper.

the interest rate differential will not change greatly. Thus, if the spot rate increases by 10 per cent over the year, the forward rate will increase by about the same amount and the importer will pay 10 per cent more for next year's shipment (assuming no change in the yen price quoted by the Japanese exporter).

The use of a 1-year forward contract during a strong-yen cycle is preferable to no hedge in this case but will still result in subsequent increases in prices paid by the importer each year under existing conditions. The hedge does however give the importer time to rearrange finances to account for the change in the value of the currency. Renghini may seek to negotiate lower prices. The company may look elsewhere for supplies. Or the company may try to earn revenues in yen. All these actions would help to reduce the financial cost of an appreciating currency.

If the hedging techniques can be applied to longer-term periods, they can more effectively insulate the firm from exchange rate risk over the long run. That is, Renghini could, as of Time 0, create a hedge for shipments to arrive at the end of each of the next several years. During a strong-yen cycle, such a strategy would save a substantial amount of money but there could be large losses if the yen were to weaken. It should be remembered that hedging is a person to person contract and that any gains by Renghini will be paid for by the losses of the counterparty. In an efficient market, those gains and losses should even out. With this in mind, Renghini should find that the longer-term forward contracts will offer increasingly less attractive rates for purchasing the yen compared to converting at spot. No strategy offers the prospect of certain gains in the financial markets.

HEDGING LONG-TERM TRANSACTION EXPOSURE

Some MNCs are almost certain of having cash flows of a certain amount denominated in foreign currencies for several years and attempt to use long-term hedging. For example, Walt Disney Co hedged its Japanese yen cash flows that will be remitted to the USA (from its Japanese theme park) 20 years ahead.

Firms that can accurately estimate foreign currency payables or receivables that will occur several years from now commonly use three techniques to hedge such long-term transaction exposure:

● Long-term forward contract

● Currency swap

● Parallel loan

● Borrowing policy.

Each technique is discussed in turn.

Long-term forward contract

Until recently, **long-term forward contracts**, or long forwards, were seldom used. Today, the long forward is quite popular. Most large international banks routinely quote forward rates for terms of up to 5 years for British pounds, Canadian dollars, Japanese yen and Swiss francs. Long forwards are especially attractive to firms that have set up fixed-price exporting or importing contracts over a long period of time and want to protect their cash flow from exchange rate fluctuations.

Like a short-term forward contract, the long forward can be tailored to accommodate the specific needs of the firm. Maturities of up to 10 years or more can sometimes be set up for the major currencies. Because a bank trusts that the firm will fulfil its long-term obligation specified in the forward contract, it will consider only very creditworthy customers.

Currency swap

A **currency swap** is a second technique for hedging long-term transaction exposure to exchange rate fluctuations. It can take many forms. One type of currency swap accommodates two firms that have different long-term needs.

EXAMPLE

Bellevue Ltd, a UK firm, is hired to build an oil pipeline in Alaska. It expects to receive payment in US dollars in 5 years when the job is completed. At the same time, a US firm is hired by a UK bank for a long-term consulting project. Assume that this US firm will be paid in British pounds and that much of the payment will occur in 5 years. Thus, Bellevue Ltd will be receiving US dollars in 5 years, and the US firm will be receiving pounds in 5 years. These two firms could arrange a currency swap that allows for an exchange of pounds for dollars in 5 years at some negotiated exchange rate. In this way, Bellevue can lock in the number of pounds the US dollar earnings will convert to in 5 years. Likewise, the US firm can lock in the number of US dollars its earnings will convert to in 5 years. This is an example of disintermediation in the forward market. Instead of going to the forward market and taking out long forwards, the same protection is gained by cutting out the market and having a person-to-person swap deal.

In practice the other party to swap may well be a bank and is likely to be a member of the International Swaps and Derivatives Association (http://www.isda.org/). Large banks and investment firms employ brokers who act as intermediaries for swaps. Corporations that want to eliminate transaction exposure to specific currencies at certain future dates contact a broker. The role of the broker is to find one firm that needs a currency and another firm that wants to sell the same currency and then match them up. The broker receives a fee for the service. A swap may be non-deliverable, as in the case where one of the currencies is restricted. In such cases payments are made between the two parties to reflect the net effect of an actual swap.

In the above example the swap was of a single amount. Often a firm will be engaged in earning regular amounts in a foreign currency and want some form of protection against exchange rate fluctuations over time. In such cases interest payments on loans can be exchanged. Suppose that in the above example Bellevue, as is normal for businesses, had a number of loans in British pounds requiring regular interest payments in pounds. The company may want to swap the interest payments it makes on its borrowings for dollar interest payments. The dollar payments would not be of the exact amount of dollar earnings nor would they be at the same time. But if the value of the dollar were to decrease, the less expensive interest payments would help offset the decline in value of the dollar earnings. Such a swap arrangement is likely to be cheaper for the company than an equivalent series of long forwards.

Over time, the currency swap obligation may become undesirable to one of the parties involved. The parties can mutually agree to end the arrangement. Or a contract with opposite offsetting terms can be drawn up either with the original counterparty (as a mirror swap) or with another party. As with closing out of futures contracts, if one is due to receive £x and pay £x at the same time, the net liability is zero. Finally, an arrangement similar to daily settlement may require periodic payments from one party to the other to account for exchange rate movements. Such an arrangement will reduce the possibility that one party will not fulfill its obligation by the time the exchange of currencies is supposed to occur.

Parallel loan

A **parallel loan** (or 'back-to-back loan') involves an exchange of loans in different currencies between two parties, they then agree to pay the interest on each other's loan and repay the amount borrowed on maturity. A parallel loan is interpreted by accountants as a loan and is therefore recorded on financial statements. At first this behaviour may seem rather odd. The critical aspect of the arrangement is that companies will find themselves paying interest in the currency of their choice which due to circumstances may not be the currency of the original loan (similar to the swap arrangement discussed above). If an MNC finds that it has significant yen revenues and wants to protect itself from changes in the value of the yen, it can do so by arranging more of its payments in yen.

Borrowing policy

For many MNCs the exposure of their profits to exchange rate changes will be predictable as the pattern of trade will not change greatly. For such companies such knowledge will over time guide their choice of currency in which to borrow.

> *The currency disposition of the borrowings is used as a partial, long-term hedge of the cash flows arising from investments overseas and as a hedge against any future business disposal proceeds. Consequently, a large part of the Group's borrowings (after taking account of swaps and forward contracts) are denominated in US Dollars.*
>
> (ICI Annual Report 2005, p. 22)

ALTERNATIVE HEDGING TECHNIQUES

A firm may engage in a number of less direct hedging activities which reduce exposure to exchange rate fluctuation. Such methods include the following:

- Leading and lagging
- Cross-hedging
- Currency diversification.

Each method is discussed in turn.

Leading and lagging

Leading and lagging strategies involve adjusting the timing of a payment request or disbursement to reflect expectations about future currency movements.

EXAMPLE

Zlatica AG is based in Austria and has subsidiaries dispersed around the world. The focus here will be on a subsidiary in the USA that has built up a considerable cash surplus. If Zlatica AG expects that the dollar will soon depreciate against the euro, it may attempt to make the payment before the dollar depreciates. This strategy is referred to as **leading**.

As a second scenario, assume that the US subsidiary expects the dollar to appreciate against the euro soon. In this case, the US subsidiary may attempt to stall its payment until after the dollar appreciates. This strategy is referred to as **lagging**.

MNCs commonly use leading and lagging strategies in countries that allow them. In some countries, the government limits the length of time involved in leading and lagging strategies so that the flow of funds into or out of the country is not disrupted. However, the form of payment is varied and not easy to control. It may include tightening or extending credit, early or late settlement of inter-subsidiary accounts, reinvesting funds or repatriating them, adjusting transfer prices and dividend payments. There are, in short, many ways in which an MNC can minimize the time it has funds denominated in weakening currencies and maximize the length of time funds are held in strengthening currencies.

Cross-hedging

Cross-hedging is a common method of reducing transaction exposure when the currency cannot be hedged.

EXAMPLE

Greeley plc, a UK firm, has payables in zloty (Poland's currency) 90 days from now. Because it is worried that the zloty may appreciate against the British pound, it may desire to hedge this position. If forward contracts and other hedging techniques are not possible for the zloty, Greeley may consider cross-hedging. In this case, it needs to first identify a currency that can be hedged and is highly correlated with the zloty. Greeley notices that the euro has recently been moving in tandem with the zloty and decides to set up a 90-day forward contract on the euro. If the movements in the zloty and euro continue to be highly correlated relative to the British pound (that is, they move in a similar direction and degree against the British pound), then the exchange rate between these two currencies should be somewhat stable over time. By buying euros using a 90-days forward contract, Greeley plc will gain if the euro unexpectedly gains in value, because the euro is highly correlated with the zloty, that gain will help offset the more expensive zloty.

How much protection in euros should Greeley take out? The amount will depend on the relative standard deviations of the euro and zloty and the correlation between the two. If there is perfect correlation and the standard deviations are the same then the same amount in euros as the revenue in zloty should be covered in euro forwards. If the standard deviation of the euro is less than the zloty then more euros will need to be sold forward. The more highly correlated the currencies, the more effective the strategy (see Appendix 11A).

Currency diversification

A third method for reducing transaction exposure is currency diversification, which can limit the potential effect of any single currency's movements on the value of an MNC. Some MNCs claim that their exposure to exchange rate movements is significantly reduced because they diversify their business among numerous countries.

The dollar value of future inflows in foreign currencies will be more stable if the foreign currencies received are *not* highly positively correlated. The reason is that lower positive correlations or negative correlations can reduce the variability of the dollar value of all foreign currency inflows. If the foreign currencies were highly correlated with each other, diversifying among them would not be a very effective way to reduce risk. If one of the currencies substantially depreciated, the others would do so as well, given that all these currencies move in tandem.

SUMMARY

- MNCs use the following techniques to hedge transaction exposure: (1) futures hedge, (2) forward hedge, (3) money market hedge and (4) currency options hedge.

- To hedge payables, a futures or forward contract on the foreign currency can be purchased. Alternatively, a money market hedge strategy can be used; in this case, the MNC borrows its home currency and converts the proceeds into the foreign currency that will be needed in the future. Finally, call options on the foreign currency can be purchased.

- To hedge receivables, a futures or forward contract on the foreign currency can be sold. Alternatively, a money market hedge strategy can be used. In this case, the MNC borrows the foreign currency to be received and converts the funds into its home currency; the loan is to be repaid by the receivables. Finally, put options on the foreign currency can be purchased.

- Futures contracts and forward contracts normally yield similar results. Forward contracts are more flexible because they are not standardized. The money market hedge yields results similar to those of the forward hedge if interest rate parity exists. The currency options hedge has an advantage over the other hedging techniques in that the options do not have to be exercised if the MNC would be better off unhedged. A premium must be paid to purchase the currency options, however, so there is a cost for the flexibility they provide.

- When hedging techniques are not available, there are still some methods of reducing transaction exposure, such as leading and lagging, cross-hedging and currency diversification.

CRITICAL DEBATE

Should MNCs hedge?

Proposition. No. when investors buy shares in an MNC they are in part wanting to benefit from the currency risk that they believe that the MNC is exposed to when trading. If the dollar is unexpectedly strong, UK investors may choose a company that has strong sales in the USA. If the MNC hedges all its dollar revenues the hedging losses caused by a strong dollar will offset any benefits. The shareholder will be deceived. The only benefit of hedging is to protect the jobs and bonuses of current management.

The accounts state clearly the effect of exchange rates on profits and the shareholders can use this information to isolate their effect when judging the management. The better quality company reports also tell you the effect on profits of a 1 per cent change in their major trading currencies. Shareholders who want protection from currency changes can invest in bonds or in other shares less sensitive but the market should not be denied this important source of risk.

Opposing view. MNCs should hedge. Foreign exchange variation is not really part of a business. Predicting its value is not in the expertise of companies whose goals are to make profits through providing goods or services or both. It is also the duty of management to maintain steady profits so that shareholders who have to sell their shares because they are faced with unexpected bills, do not have to do so when the companies' price is low due to adverse currency conditions. Dividend payments should also be kept as regular as possible for investors who want steady income. Large exchange rate losses could jeopardize such payments. Shareholders wanting to benefit from a strong dollar could take out futures contracts instead.

With whom do you agree? Examine the arguments on both sides. How well do the points made support the case? Whom do you support and why?

SELF TEST

Answers are provided in Appendix A at the back of the text.

1   Montclair plc, a UK firm, plans to use a money market hedge to hedge its payment of 3 000 000 Australian dollars for Australian goods in 1 year. The UK interest rate is 7 per cent, while the Australian interest rate is 12 per cent. The spot rate of the Australian dollar is £0.45, while the 1-year forward rate is £0.44. Determine the amount of British pounds needed in 1 year if a money market hedge is used.

2   Using the information in the previous question, would Montclair be better off hedging the payables with a money market hedge or with a forward hedge?

3   Using the information about Montclair from the first question, explain the possible advantage of a currency option hedge over a money market hedge for Montclair. What is a possible disadvantage of the currency option hedge?

4   Sanibel Ltd purchases US goods (and pays in dollars) every month. It negotiates a 1-month forward contract at the beginning of every month to hedge its payables. Assume the US dollar appreciates consistently over the next 5 years. Will Sanibel be affected? Explain.

5   Using the information from question 4, suggest how Sanibel Ltd could more effectively insulate itself from the possible long-term appreciation of the US dollar.

6   Hopkins Ltd transported goods to Switzerland and will receive 2 000 000 Swiss francs in 3 months. It believes the 3-month forward rate will be an accurate forecast of the future spot rate. The 3-month forward rate of the Swiss franc is £0.35. A put option is available with an exercise price of £0.36 and a premium of £0.02. Would Hopkins prefer a put option hedge to no hedge? Explain.

QUESTIONS AND APPLICATIONS

1   **Consolidated exposure.** Quincy Corp. estimates the following cash flows in 90 days at its subsidiaries as follows:

Net position in each currency measured in the parent's currency (in 100s of units)

Subsidiary	Currency 1	Currency 2	Currency 3
A	+200	−300	−100
B	+100	−40	−10
C	−180	+200	−40

Determine the consolidated net exposure of the MNC to each currency.

2   **Money market hedge on receivables.** Assume that Hartland Point Ltd (UK) has net receivables of 100 000 Singapore dollars in 90 days. The spot rate of the S$ is £0.32, and the Singapore interest rate is 2 per cent over 90 days. Suggest how the UK firm could implement a money market hedge. Be precise.

3   **Money market hedge on payables.** Assume that Belmont plc has net payables of 200 000 Mexican pesos in 180 days. The Mexican interest rate is 7 per cent over 180 days, and the spot rate of the Mexican peso is £0.05. Suggest how the UK firm could implement a money market hedge. Be precise.

4   **Invoicing strategy.** Assume that Citadel plc purchases some goods in Chile that are denominated in Chilean pesos. It also sells goods denominated in

British pounds to some firms in Chile. At the end of each month, it has a large net payables position in Chilean pesos. How can it use an invoicing strategy to reduce this transaction exposure? List any limitations on the effectiveness of this strategy.

5 **Hedging with futures.** Explain how a UK company could hedge net receivables in US dollars with futures contracts. Explain how a UK company could hedge net payables in Japanese yen with futures contracts.

6 **Hedging with forward contracts.** Explain how a UK company could hedge net receivables in Malaysian ringgit with a forward contract. Explain how a UK company could hedge payables in euros with a forward contract.

7 **The cost of hedging payables.** Assume that Loras (UK) Ltd imported goods from New Zealand and needs 100 000 New Zealand dollars 180 days from now. It is trying to determine whether to hedge this position. Loras has developed the following probability distribution for the New Zealand dollar:

Possible value of the New Zealand dollar in 180 days	Probability
£0.40	5%
0.45	10
0.48	30
0.50	30
0.53	20
0.55	5
	100%

The 180-day forward rate of the New Zealand dollar is £0.52. The spot rate of the New Zealand dollar is £0.49. Develop a table showing a feasibility analysis for hedging. That is, determine the possible differences between the costs of hedging versus no hedging. What is the probability that hedging will be more costly to the firm than not hedging? Determine the expected value of the additional cost of hedging.

8 **Benefits of hedging.** If hedging is expected to be more costly than not hedging, why would a firm even consider hedging?

9 **Cost of hedging payables.** Assume that Suffolk plc negotiated a forward contract to purchase $200 000 in 90 days. The 90-day forward rate was £0.70 to the US dollar. The dollars to be purchased were to be used to purchase US supplies. On the day the dollars were delivered in accordance with the forward contract, the spot rate of the British pound was £0.69. What was the cost of hedging the payables for this UK firm compared with not hedging?

10 **Cost of hedging receivables.** Assume that Bentley Ltd negotiated a forward contract to sell 100 000 Canadian dollars in 1 year. The 1-year forward rate on the Canadian dollar was £0.55. This strategy was designed to hedge receivables in Canadian dollars. On the day the Canadian dollars were to be sold in accordance with the forward contract, the spot rate of the Canadian dollar was £0.53. What was the cost of hedging receivables for this UK firm compared with not hedging?

Repeat the question, except assume that the spot rate of the Canadian dollar was £0.60 on the day the Canadian dollars were to be sold in accordance with the forward contract. What was the cost of hedging receivables in this example compared with not hedging?

11 **Forward versus money market hedge on payables.** Assume the following information:

90-day UK interest rate	4%
90-day Malaysian interest rate	3%
90-day forward rate of Malaysian ringgit	£0.25
Spot rate of Malaysian ringgit	£0.2525

Assume that Saint Barnabus plc in the UK will need 300 000 ringgit in 90 days. It wishes to hedge this payables position. Would it be better off using a forward hedge or a money market hedge? Substantiate your answer with estimated costs for each type of hedge.

12 **Forward versus money market hedge on receivables.** Assume the following information:

90-day UK interest rate	8%
90-day US interest rate	9%
90-day forward rate of US dollar	£0.65
Spot rate of US dollar	£0.64

Assume that Riverside Ltd (UK) will receive $400 000 in 180 days. Would it be better off using a forward hedge or a money market hedge? Substantiate your answer with estimated revenue for each type of hedge.

13 Currency options. Relate the use of currency options to hedging net payables and receivables. That is, when should currency puts be purchased, and when should currency calls be purchased?

Why would Bristol Ltd consider hedging net payables or net receivables with currency options rather than forward contracts? What are the disadvantages of hedging with currency options as opposed to forward contracts?

14 Currency options. Can Birstall plc determine whether currency options will be more or less expensive than a forward hedge when considering both hedging techniques to cover net payables in euros? Why or why not?

15 Long-term hedging. How can a firm hedge long-term currency positions? Elaborate on each method.

16 Leading and lagging. Under what conditions would Zoot Ltd's subsidiary consider using a 'leading' strategy to reduce transaction exposure? Under what conditions would Zoot's subsidiary consider using a 'lagging' strategy to reduce transaction exposure?

17 Cross-hedging. Explain how a firm can use cross-hedging to reduce transaction exposure.

18 Currency diversification. Explain how a firm can use currency diversification to reduce transaction exposure.

19 Hedging with put options. As treasurer of Tupperman (a UK exporter to New Zealand), you must decide how to hedge (if at all) future receivables of 250 000 New Zealand dollars 90 days from now. Put options are available for a premium of £0.02 per unit and an exercise price of £0.24 per New Zealand dollar. The forecasted spot rate of the NZ$ in 90 days follows:

Future spot rate	Probability
£0.25	30%
0.24	50
0.22	20

Given that you hedge your position with options, create a probability distribution for British pounds to be received in 90 days.

20 Forward hedge. Would Devon Ltd's cost of hedging Australian dollar payables every 90 days have been positive, negative, or about zero on average over a period in which the British pound weakened unexpectedly? What does this imply about the forward rate as an unbiased predictor of the future spot rate? Explain.

21 Implications of IRP for hedging. If interest rate parity exists, would a forward hedge be more favourable, equally favourable or less favourable than a money market hedge on euro payables? Explain.

22 The cost of hedging. Would Monkton Ltd's cost of hedging Japanese yen receivables have been positive, negative or about zero on average over a period in which the British pound unexpectedly weakened? Explain.

23 Forward versus options hedge on payables. If you are a US importer of Mexican goods and you believe that today's forward rate of the peso is a very accurate estimate of the future spot rate, do you think Mexican peso call options would be a more appropriate hedge than the forward hedge? Explain.

24 Forward versus options hedge on receivables. You are an exporter of goods to the USA and you believe that today's forward rate of the US dollar substantially underestimates the future spot rate. Company policy requires you to hedge your dollar receivables in some way. Would a forward hedge or a put option hedge be more appropriate? Explain.

25 Forward hedging. Explain how a Malaysian firm can use the forward market to hedge periodic purchases of UK goods denominated in British pounds. Explain how a French firm can use forward contracts to hedge periodic sales of goods sold to the USA that are invoiced in dollars. Explain how a British firm can use the forward market to hedge periodic purchases of Japanese goods denominated in yen.

26 Continuous hedging. Cornwall Ltd (UK) purchases computer chips denominated in euros on a monthly basis from a Dutch supplier. To hedge its exchange rate risk, this UK firm negotiates a 3-month forward contract 3 months before the next order will arrive. In other words, Cornwall is always covered for the next three monthly shipments. Because Cornwall consistently hedges in this manner, it is not concerned with exchange rate movements. Is Cornwall insulated from exchange rate movements? Explain.

27 Hedging payables with currency options. Malibu, Inc. is a US company that imports British goods. It plans to use call options to hedge payables of £100 000 in 90 days. Three call options are available that have an expiration date 90 days from now. Fill in the number of dollars needed to pay for the payables (including the option premium paid) for each option available under each possible scenario.

Scenario	Spot rate of pound 90 days from now	Exercise price = $1.74; premium = $.06	Exercise price = $1.76; premium = $.05	Exercise price = $1.79; Premium = $.03
1	$1.65			
2	1.70			
3	1.75			
4	1.80			
5	1.85			

If each of the five scenarios had an equal probability of occurrence, which option would you choose? Explain.

28 Forward hedging. Wedco Technology (UK) exports plastics products to the USA. Wedco decided to price its exports in British pounds. Telematics International plc (of Scotland) exports computer network systems to the USA (denominated in US dollars) and other countries. Telematics decided to use hedging techniques such as forward contracts to hedge its exposure.

  a Does Wedco's strategy of pricing its materials for US customers in pounds avoid transaction exposure? Explain.

  b Explain why the earnings of Telematics International plc were affected by changes in the value of the pound. Why might Telematics leave its exposure unhedged sometimes?

29 The long-term hedge dilemma. St Weonards Ltd which relies on exporting, denominates its exports in euros and receives euros every month. It expects the euro to weaken over time. St Weonards recognizes the limitation of monthly hedging. It also recognizes that it could remove its transaction exposure by denominating its exports in British pounds but it would still be subject to economic exposure. The long-term hedging techniques are limited, and the firm does not know how many euros it will receive in the future, so it would have difficulty even if a long-term hedging method was available. How can this business realistically reduce its exposure over the long term?

30 Long-term hedging. Since Llancloudy Ltd conducts much business in Japan, it is likely to have cash flows in yen that will periodically be remitted by its Japanese subsidiary to the UK parent. What are the limitations of hedging these remittances one year in advance over each of the next 20 years? What are the limitations of creating a hedge today that will hedge these remittances over each of the next 20 years?

31 Hedging during the Asian crisis. Describe how the Asian crisis could have reduced the cash flows of a UK firm that exported products (denominated in British pounds) to Asian countries. How could a UK firm that exported products (denominated in British pounds) to Asia, and anticipated the Asian crisis before it began, have insulated itself from any currency effects while continuing to export to Asia?

ADVANCED QUESTIONS

32 Comparison of techniques for hedging receivables.

  a Assume that Carbondale Ltd expects to receive S$500 000 in one year. The existing spot rate of the Singapore dollar is £0.40. The one-year forward rate of the Singapore dollar is £0.41. Carbondale created a probability distribution for the future spot rate in one year as follows:

Future spot rate	Probability
£0.41	20%
0.43	50
0.47	30

Assume that 1-year put options on Singapore dollars are available, with an exercise price of £0.40 and a premium of £0.025 per unit. One-year call options on Singapore dollars are available with an exercise price of £0.39 and a premium of £0.02 per unit. Assume the following money market rates:

	UK	Singapore
Deposit rate	8%	5%
Borrowing rate	9	6

Given this information, determine whether a forward hedge, a money market hedge or a currency options hedge would be most appropriate. Then compare the most appropriate hedge to an unhedged strategy, and decide whether Carbondale should hedge its receivables position.

b Assume that Black Rod plc expects to need S$1 million in 1 year. Using any relevant information in part (a) of this question, determine whether a forward hedge, a money market hedge or a currency options hedge would be most appropriate. Then, compare the most appropriate hedge to an unhedged strategy, and decide whether Black Rod should hedge its payables position.

33 Comparison of techniques for hedging payables. SMU Ltd has future receivables of 4 000 000 New Zealand dollars (NZ$) in 1 year. It must decide whether to use options or a money market hedge to hedge this position. Use any of the following information to make the decision. Verify your answer by determining the estimate (or probability distribution) of dollar revenue to be received in 1 year for each type of hedge.

Spot rate of NZ$	£0.36	
1-year call option	Exercise price = £0.33; premium = £0.046	
1-year put option	Exercise price = £0.35; premium = £0.02	
	UK	New Zealand
1-year deposit rate	9%	6%
1-year borrowing rate	11	8

Spot rate of NZ$	£0.36	
1-year call option	Exercise price = £0.33; premium = £0.046	
1-year put option	Exercise price = £0.35; premium = £0.02	
	Rate	Probability
Forecasted spot rate of NZ$	£0.33	20%
	0.34	50
	0.35	30

34 Devon Ltd manufactures plastic moulding machines. Annual company sales are £3 million in the UK and £12 million in the rest of Europe (invoiced in euros, average exchange rate £0.60:1 euro). The cost of goods sold are £11 million, half of which is incurred in the euro area again at £0.60:1 euro (about half the product is actually made in Europe and half in the UK). Devon estimates that for every 1 per cent increase in the value of the euro its UK sales increase by 0.2 per cent and its euro sales decrease by 0.5 per cent. Profits are generally translated into British pounds at the end of the year.

a Calculate the percentage change in the gross profit based on a 10 per cent increase in the value of the euro. Explain your result.

b Suggest how gross profits might be made less sensitive to the value of the euro.

35 Hedging with a bull spread. (See the chapter appendix.) Evar Imports Ltd buys chocolate from Switzerland and resells it in the UK. It just purchased chocolate invoiced at SFr62 500. Payment for the invoice is due in 30 days. Assume that the current exchange rate of the Swiss franc is £0.49. Also assume that three call options for the franc are available. The first option has a strike price of £0.49 and a premium of £0.02; the second option has a strike price of £0.51 and a premium of £0.005; the third option has a strike price of £0.53 and a premium of £0.004. Evar Imports is concerned about a modest appreciation in the Swiss franc.

a Describe how Evar Imports could construct a bull spread using the first two options. What is the cost of this hedge? When is this hedge most effective? When is it least effective?

b Describe how Evar Imports could construct a bull spread using the first option and the third option. What is the cost of this hedge? When is this hedge most effective? When is it least effective?

c Given your answers to parts (a) and (b), what is the trade-off involved in constructing a bull spread using call options with a higher exercise price?

36 Hedging with a bear spread. (See the chapter appendix.) Marsden Ltd has customers in Canada and frequently receives payments denominated in Canadian dollars (C$). The current spot rate for the Canadian dollar is £0.50. Two call options on Canadian dollars are available. The first option has an exercise price of £0.47 and a premium of £0.02. The second option has an exercise price of £0.49 and a premium of £0.01. Marsden Ltd would like to use a bear spread to hedge a receivable position of C$50 000, which is due in 1 month. Marsden is concerned that the Canadian dollar may depreciate to £0.48 in 1 month.

a Describe how Marsden Ltd could use a bear spread to hedge its position.

b Assume the spot rate of the Canadian dollar in 1 month is £0.48. Was the hedge effective?

37 Hedging with forward versus option contracts. As treasurer of Temple plc you are confronted with the following problem. Assume the 1-year forward rate of the US dollar is £0.62. You plan to receive $1 million in 1 year. A 1-year put option is available. It has an exercise price of £0.63. The spot rate as of today is £0.63 and the option premium is £0.03 per unit. Your forecast of the percentage change in the spot rate was determined from the following regression model:

$$e_t = a_0 + a_1 DINF_{t-1} + a_1 DINT_t + \varepsilon$$

Where:

$e_t =$ percentage change in British pound value over period t

$DINF_{t-1} =$ differential in inflation between the USA and the UK in period $t - 1$

$DINT_t =$ average differential between US interest rate and British interest rate over period t

$a_0, a_1,$ and $a_2 =$ regression coefficients

$\varepsilon =$ error term

The regression model was applied to historical annual data, and the regression coefficients were estimated as follows:

$$a_0 = 0.0$$
$$a_1 = 1.1$$
$$a_2 = 0.6.$$

Assume last year's inflation rates were 3 per cent for the USA and 8 per cent for the UK. Also assume that the interest rate differential ($DINT_t$) is forecasted as follows for this year:

Forecast of $DINT_t$	Probability
1%	40%
2	50
3	10

Using any of the available information, should the treasurer choose the forward hedge or the put option hedge? Show your workings.

38 Hedging with straddles. (See the Appendix B.) Bach GmbH (a German company) imports wood from Morocco. The Moroccan exporter invoices in Moroccan dirham. The current exchange rate of the dirham is 0.10 euro. Bach has just purchased wood for 2 million dirham and should pay for the wood in 3 months. It is also possible that Bach will receive 4 million dirham in 3 months from the sale of refinished wood in Morocco. Bach is currently in negotiations with a Moroccan importer about the refinished wood. If the negotiations are successful, Bach will receive the 4 million dirham in 3 months, for a net cash outflow of 2 million dirham. The following option information is available:

- Call option premium on Moroccan dirham = 0.003 euro.
- Put option premium on Moroccan dirham = 0.002 euro.
- Call and put option strike price = 0.098 euro.
- One option contract represents 500 000 dirham.

a Describe how Bach could use a straddle to hedge its possible positions in dirham.

b Consider three scenarios. In the first scenario, the dirham's spot rate at option expiration is equal to the exercise price of 0.98 euro. In the second scenario, the dirham depreciates to 0.08 euro. In the third scenario, the dirham appreciates to 0.11 euro. For each scenario, consider both the case when the negotiations are successful and the case when the negotiations are not successful.

Assess the effectiveness of the long straddle in each of these situations by comparing it to a strategy of using long call options to hedge.

39 **Hedging with straddles versus strangles.** (See Appendix B.) Refer to the previous problem. Assume that Bach believes the cost of a long straddle is too high. However, call options with an exercise price of 0.105 euro and a premium of 0.002 euro and put options with an exercise price of 0.09 euro and a premium of 0.001 euro are also available on Moroccan dirham. Describe how Bach could use a long strangle to hedge its possible dirham positions. What is the trade-off involved in using a long strangle versus a long straddle to hedge the positions?

PROJECT WORKSHOP

41 **Evaluating exchange rate movement** Find the home page of a large multinational by referring to the lists on the website http://www.forbes.com and find the latest annual report – including all the accounting policies.

a Review the annual report of your choice. Look for any comments in the report that describe the MNC's hedging of transaction exposure. Summarize the MNC's hedging of transaction exposure based on the comments in the annual report

40 **Hedging decision.** You believe that IRP presently exists. The nominal annual interest rate in Mexico is 14 per cent. The nominal annual interest rate in the UK is 6 per cent. You expect that annual inflation will be about 4 per cent in Mexico and 5 per cent in the UK. The spot rate of the Mexican peso is £0.65. Put options on pesos are available with a 1-year expiration date, an exercise price of £0.70 and a premium of £0.07 per unit. You will receive 1 million pesos in 1 year.

a Determine the expected amount of British pounds that you will receive if you use a forward hedge.

b Determine the expected amount of pounds that you will receive if you do not hedge and believe in purchasing power parity.

c Determine the amount of pounds that you will expect to receive if you use a currency put option hedge. Account for the premium you would pay on the put option.

(an easy way to find the right section is to use the search function using the word 'risk').

b The following website http://www.oanda.com provides exchange rates, select the FXhistory option. Based on the exposure of the MNC you assessed in part (a), determine whether the exchange rate movements of whatever currency (or currencies) the MNC is exposed to moved in a favourable or unfavourable direction over the last few months.

DISCUSSION IN THE BOARDROOM

This exercise can be found on our dedicated Course-Mate platform for students.

RUNNING YOUR OWN MNC

This exercise can be found on our dedicated Course-Mate platform for students.

Essays/discussion and articles can be found at the end of Part III.

BLADES PLC CASE STUDY

Management of transaction exposure

Blades plc has recently decided to expand its international trade relationship by exporting to the USA. Jogs Inc a US retailer, has committed itself to the annual purchase of 200 000 pairs of 'Speedos', Blades' primary product, for a price of $80 per pair. The agreement is to last for 2 years, at which time it may be renewed by Blades and Jogs.

In addition to this new international trade relationship, Blades continues to export to Thailand. Its primary customer there, a retailer called Entertainment Products, is committed to the purchase of 180 000 pairs of Speedos annually for another 2 years at a fixed price of 4594 Thai baht per pair. When the agreement terminates, it may be renewed by Blades and Entertainment Products.

Blades also incurs costs of goods sold denominated in Thai baht. It imports materials sufficient to manufacture 72 000 pairs of Speedos annually from Thailand. These imports are denominated in baht, and the price depends on current market prices for the rubber and plastic components imported.

Under the two export arrangements, Blades sells quarterly amounts of 50 000 and 45 000 pairs of Speedos to Jogs and Entertainment Products, respectively. Payment for these sales is made on the first of January, April, July and October. The annual amounts are spread over quarters in order to avoid excessive inventories for the British and Thai retailers. Similarly, in order to avoid excessive inventories, Blades usually imports materials sufficient to manufacture 18 000 pairs of Speedos quarterly from Thailand. Although payment terms call for payment within 60 days of delivery, Blades generally pays for its Thai imports upon delivery on the first day of each quarter in order to maintain its trade relationships with the Thai suppliers. Blades feels that early payment is beneficial, as other customers of the Thai supplier pay for their purchases only when it is required.

Since Blades is relatively new to international trade, Ben Holt, Blades' chief financial officer (CFO), is concerned with the potential impact of exchange rate fluctuations on Blades' financial performance. Holt is vaguely familiar with various techniques available to hedge transaction exposure, but he is not certain whether one technique is superior to the others. Holt would like to know more about the forward, money market and option hedges and has asked you, a financial analyst at Blades, to help him identify the hedging technique most appropriate for Blades. Unfortunately, no options are available for Thailand, but dollar call and put options are available for $50 000 per option.

Ben Holt has gathered and provided you with the following information for Thailand and the USA:

	Thailand (baht)	USA (dollar)
Current spot rate	£0.0153	£0.66
90-day forward rate	£0.0143	£0.67
Put option premium	Not available	£0.013 per unit
Put option exercise price	Not available	£0.68
Call option premium	Not available	£0.010 per unit
Call option exercise price	Not available	£0.68
90-day borrowing rate (non-annualized)	4%	2%
90-day lending rate (non-annualized)	3.5%	1.8%

In addition to this information, Ben Holt has informed you that the 90-day borrowing and lending rates in the USA are 2.3 per cent and 2.1 per cent, respectively, on a non-annualized basis. He has also identified the following probability distributions for the exchange rates of the British pound and the Thai baht in 90 days:

Probability	Spot rate for the dollar in 90 days	Spot rate for the Thai baht in 90 days
5%	£0.690	£0.0133
20	0.680	0.0142
30	0.675	0.0145
25	0.671	0.0147
15	0.666	0.0153
5	0.658	0.0157

Blades' next sales to and purchases from Thailand will occur one-quarter from now. If Blades decides to hedge, Holt will want to hedge the entire amount subject to exchange rate fluctuations, even if it requires over-hedging (i.e., hedging more than the needed amount). Currently, Holt expects the imported components from Thailand to cost approximately 3000 baht per pair of Speedos. Holt has asked you to answer the following questions for him:

Questions

1 Using a spreadsheet, compare the hedging alternatives for the Thai baht with a scenario under which Blades remains unhedged. Do you think Blades should hedge or remain unhedged? If Blades should hedge, which hedge is most appropriate?

2 Using a spreadsheet, compare the hedging alternatives for the dollar receivables with a scenario under which Blades remains unhedged. Do you think Blades should hedge or remain unhedged? Which hedge is the most appropriate for Blades?

3 In general, do you think it is easier for Blades to hedge its inflows or its outflows denominated in foreign currencies? Why?

4 Would any of the hedges you compared in question 2 for the dollars to be received in 90 days require Blades to over-hedge? Given Blades' exporting arrangements, do you think it is subject to over-hedging with a money market hedge?

5 Could Blades modify the timing of the Thai imports in order to reduce its transaction exposure? What is the trade-off of such a modification?

6 Could Blades modify its payment practices for the Thai imports in order to reduce its transaction exposure? What is the trade-off of such a modification?

7 Given Blades' exporting agreements, are there any long-term hedging techniques Blades could benefit from? For this question only, assume that Blades incurs all of its costs in the UK.

SMALL BUSINESS DILEMMA

Hedging decisions by the Sports Exports Company

Jim Logan, owner of the Sports Exports Company (Ireland), will be receiving about £10000 about 1 month from now as payment for exports produced and sent by his firm. Jim is concerned about his exposure because he believes that there are two possible scenarios: (1) the pound will depreciate by 3 per cent over the next month or (2) the pound will appreciate by 2 per cent over the next month. There is a 70 per cent chance that Scenario 1 will occur. There is a 30 per cent chance that Scenario 2 will occur.

Jim notices that the prevailing spot rate of the pound is 1.45 euros, and the 1-month forward rate is about 1.445 euros. Jim can purchase a put option over the counter from a securities firm that has an exercise (strike) price of 1.445 euros, a premium of 0.020 euros and an expiration date of 1 month from now.

1 Determine the amount of euros received by the Sports Exports Company if the receivables to be received in 1 month are not hedged under each of the two exchange rate scenarios.

2 Determine the amount of euros received by the Sports Exports Company if a put option is used to hedge receivables in 1 month under each of the two exchange rate scenarios.

3 Determine the amount of euros received by the Sports Exports Company if a forward hedge is used to hedge receivables in 1 month under each of the two exchange rate scenarios.

4 Summarize the results of euros received based on an unhedged strategy, a put option strategy and a forward hedge strategy. Select the strategy that you prefer based on the information provided.

APPENDIX 11A
CALCULATING THE OPTIMAL SIZE OF A CROSS CURRENCY HEDGE

Suppose I expect to receive Polish zloty to the value of £10 000 with a standard deviation of £1000 at current spot rates in 90 days. If there is no market for a forward or futures rate with the zloty (giving a guaranteed exchange rate in 90 days), a cross hedge can be arranged with a closely correlated currency – the euro for example. Instead of taking out a forward contract to sell zloty for a fixed rate, a forward contract is taken out to sell euro at a fixed rate. The idea is that if the value of the zloty unexpectedly falls, the euro value will also fall as the two currencies are well correlated. A forward euro contract in such circumstances will have gained (buy the now unexpectedly cheaper euros and sell at the higher fixed forward rate); but this gain will depend on the correlation between the euro and the zloty. If the correlation between euros and zloty were perfect positive and the standard deviation were the same, then one would take out a contract for £10 000 worth of euros. The gain in the euro forward contract would exactly offset the loss due to the fall in value of the zloty. But where the standard deviations are different and the correlation not perfect, one wants to know the ratio of euro to zloty in taking out a forward contract that would afford the best protection (e.g. the ratio could be euros to the value of 1.2 times the £10 000 or 0.8 times the £10 000 and so on). The formula for the optimum ratio and hence the amount to invest in euros is:

$$(\sigma_{zloty}/\sigma_{euro}) \times \text{correlation (zloty, euro)}.$$

If the correlation coefficient between euros and zloty is 0.75 and the standard deviation of £10 000 worth of euros is £666.66 (and £1000 for zloty), maximum protection (i.e. minimum overall variance of cash flows) is gained through taking out a forward sell on euros. The ratio is: 1000/666.66 × 0.75 = 1.125, therefore the size of the cross hedge is: £10 000 × 1.125 = £11 250. Any less, and one could lower prospective variation by increasing the euros being sold forward, any more and euro variation would actually increase the overall variation in the total returns.

The expected variation of the combined return from the forward contract and the zloty can be calculated by using a variance-covariance matrix with weights of 1 for the zloty receipt and −1 for the euro forward contract. The expected return on the euro would be 0 as it is a forward contract and the standard deviation would be £666.66 × £11 250 / £10 000 = £750. The zloty return and standard deviations are £10 000 and £1000 respectively. Place these values in the portfolio cash flow model spreadsheet (see support material) as follows:

	Weights	SD	Returns
Zloty	1	£1000	£10 000
Euro	−1	£750	£0
Correlation (zloty/euro) = 0.75			

The variance-covariance matrix is:

	Zloty	Euro
Zloty	1 000 000	−562 500
Euro	−562 500	562 500

where wzloty * SDzloty * weuro * SDeuro * correlation (zloty/euro) = 1000 × 750 × 1 ×−1 × 0.75 = −562 500, see notes on the variance-covariance matrix. The total of the matrix is the variance 1 000 000 − 562 500 = £437 500. The standard deviation of the returns to the zloty and euro combination is the square root i.e. £437 500$^{1/2}$ = £661.44. Thus the variation in zloty is countered by the euro forward variation having an opposite effect.

More generally the formula is:

$$R=(\sigma_{hedged}/\sigma_{hedging}) \times \rho_{(hedged,\ hedging)}$$

Where:

R = ratio of hedging amount to hedged currency
σ_{hedged} and $\sigma_{hedging}$ = expected standard deviation of the hedged and hedging currency respectively
$\rho_{(hedged,\ hedging)}$ = correlation of hedged and hedging currency

APPENDIX 11B
NON-TRADITIONAL HEDGING TECHNIQUES

While traditional hedging techniques were covered in the chapter, many other techniques may be appropriate for an MNC's particular situation. Some of these non-traditional techniques are described in this appendix.

HEDGING WITH CURRENCY STRADDLES

In reality, some MNCs do not know whether they will have net cash inflows or outflows as a result of their transactions in a specific currency over a particular period of time. A long straddle (purchase of a call option and put option with the same exercise price) is an effective tool to hedge under these conditions.

EXAMPLE

Hunter Ltd conducts business in Switzerland and expects to need SFr4 000 000 to cover specific expenses. If it is unable to renew a business deal with the Swiss government (its biggest customer), it will receive a total of SFr3 000 000 in revenue in 1 month, which will result in net cash flows of −SFr1 000 000. Conversely, if it is able to renew the business deal with the government, it will receive a total of SFr5 000 000, which will result in net cash flows of +SFr1 000 000. The prevailing spot rate of the Swiss franc is £0.45. If Hunter has excess Swiss francs in 1 month, it will convert them to British pounds. Conversely, if Hunter does not have enough Swiss francs in 1 month, it will use pounds to obtain the amount that it needs. Hunter would like to hedge its exchange rate risk, regardless of which scenario occurs.

Currently, call options for Swiss francs with settlement dates in 1 month are available with an exercise price of £0.45 (the same as the spot rate) and a premium of £0.004 per franc. Put options for Swiss francs with the same exercise price and settlement date of 1 month are available for a premium of £0.005 per franc. Options for Swiss francs are denominated in 250 000 francs per option contract.

(Continued)

Hunter could hedge its possible position of having positive net cash flows of SFr1 000 000 by purchasing put options on Swiss francs. It would pay a premium of £5000 (1 000 000 units × £0.005). It could hedge its possible position of needing SFr1 000 000 by purchasing call options. It would pay a premium of £4000 (1 000 000 units × £0.004). Assume that Hunter constructs a straddle to hedge both possible outcomes and pays £9000 for the call options and put options on francs. Assume that Hunter exercises the options in 1 month, if at all.

Consider the following scenarios that could occur 1 month from now:

1 If Hunter has net cash flows of +SFr1 000 000 and the franc's value is £0.51, it would let its put options expire and would convert its francs to pounds in the spot market, receiving £510 000 (1 000 000 units × £0.51) from this transaction. It would also exercise its call option by purchasing 1 000 000 francs at £0.45 and selling them in the spot market for £0.51. This transaction would generate a gain of (0.51 − 0.45) × 1 000 000 = £600 00. Overall, Hunter would receive £510 000 + £600 00 = £570 000, minus the £9000 in premiums paid for the options.

2 If Hunter has net cash flows of +SFr1 000 000 and the franc depreciates to £0.44, it would exercise its put options and let the call options expire. Overall, Hunter would receive £450 000 (1 000 000 units × £0.45) from exercising the options, minus the £9000 in premiums paid for the options.

3 If Hunter has net cash flows of +SFr1 000 000 and the franc is £0.45, it would let its call and put options expire. It would receive £450 000 (1 000 000 × £0.45) from selling francs in the spot market, minus the £9000 in premiums paid for the options.

4 If Hunter has net cash flows of −SFr1 000 000, and the franc's value is £0.51, it would exercise its call options and let its put options expire. Overall, Hunter would pay a total of £459 000, which consists of the £450 000 (1 000 000 × £0.45) from exercising the call option and the £9000 in premiums paid for the options.

5 If Hunter has net cash flows of −SFr1 000 000 and the franc's value is £0.44, it would let its call options expire and buy francs in the spot market. It would also buy 1 000 000 francs and then sell them by exercising its put options. This transaction would generate a gain of (0.45 − 0.44) × 1 000 000 = £10 000. Overall, Hunter would pay a total of £439 000, which consists of the £440 000 paid to obtain the francs it needs, plus the £9000 in premiums paid for the options, minus the £10 000 gain generated from its put options.

6 If Hunter has net cash flows of −SFR1 000 000 and the franc's value is £0.45, it would let its call and put options expire. It would pay a total of £459 000, which consists of the £450 000 paid to obtain francs and the £9000 in premiums paid for the options. Many other scenarios could also occur, but a summary of the possible scenarios and the actions taken by Hunter appears in Exhibit 11B.1(a) and (b).

EXHIBIT 11B.1(a) Possible scenarios for Hunter Co. when hedging with a straddle

Panel A: Hunter has net cash flows of + SFr1 000 000 in 1 month	
SFr value > £0.45 in 1 month	• Hunter converts excess Swiss francs to pounds in the spot market. • It lets the put options expire. • It exercises its call options and sells the francs obtained from this transaction in the spot market; the proceeds recapture part of the premiums that were paid for the options.
SFr value < £0.45 in 1 month	• Hunter converts excess francs to pounds at £0.45, by exercising its put options. • It lets the call options expire.
SFr value = £0.45 in 1 month	• Hunter converts excess francs to pounds in the spot market. • It lets its call options and put options expire.

(Continued)

Panel B: Hunter has net cash flows of −SFr1 000000 in 1 month	
SFr value > £0.45 in 1 month	• Hunter converts pounds to francs by exercising its call options. • It lets the put options expire.
SFr value < £0.45 in 1 month	• It lets the call options expire. • It buys francs in the spot market and sells the francs obtained by exercising the put options; the proceeds recapture part of the premiums that were paid for the options.
SFr = £0.45 in 1 month	• Hunter converts pounds to francs in the spot market. • It lets its call and put options expire.

EXHIBIT 11B.1(b)   Contingency diagram for hedging with a straddle (Hunter Ltd)

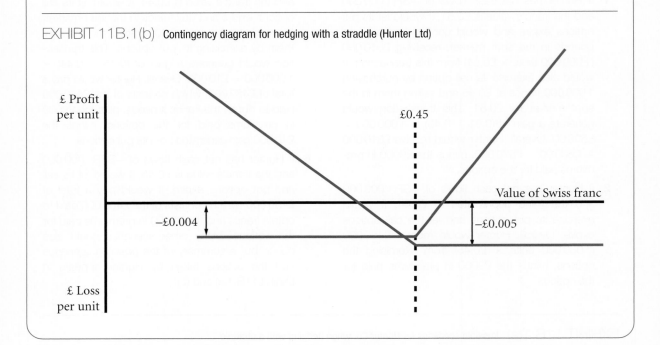

HEDGING WITH CURRENCY STRANGLES

In the hedging example just provided for Hunter Ltd, consider that the expected value of the amount that Hunter would pay or receive based on today's spot rate is £450 000 (SFr1 000 000 × £0.45). The option premiums paid for the options (£9000) represent 2 per cent of that expected value. Thus, the straddle is a relatively expensive means of hedging. The exercise price at which Hunter hedged was equal to the spot rate ('at the money'). If Hunter is willing to accept exposure to small exchange rate movements in the Swiss franc, it could reduce the premiums paid for the options. Specifically, it would use a *long strangle* by purchasing a call option and a put option that have different exercise prices. By purchasing a call option that has an exercise price higher than £0.45, and a put option that has an exercise price lower than £0.45, Hunter can reduce the premiums it will pay on the options (see Exhibit 11B.2).

Reconsider the example in which Hunter Ltd expects that it will have net cash flows of either +SFr1 000 000 or −SFr1 000 000 in 1 month. To reduce the premiums it pays for hedging with options, it can purchase options that are out of the money. Assume that it can obtain call options for Swiss francs

EXHIBIT 11B.2 Contingency diagram for hedging with a strangle (Hunter Ltd)

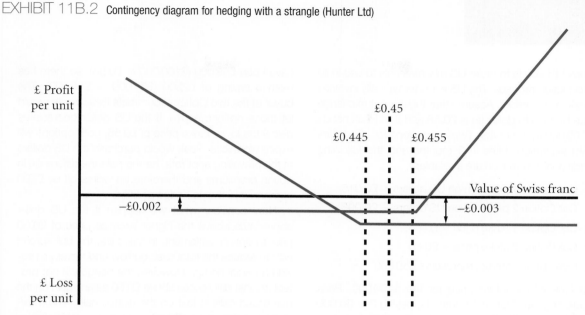

Note:
• Notice the smaller costs compared with the straddle (Exhibit 11B.1) and the reduced protection.

with an expiration date of 1 month, an exercise price of £0.455 and a premium of £0.002 per Swiss franc. It can also obtain put options for Swiss francs with an expiration date of 1 month, an exercise price of £0.445 and a premium of £0.003 per Swiss franc.

Hunter Ltd could hedge its possible position of needing SFr1 000 000 by purchasing call options. It would pay a premium of £2000 (1 000 000 units × £0.002) – note that the term units is used instead of the particular currency involved, in this case Swiss francs. It could also hedge its possible position of having positive net cash flows of SFr1 000 000 by purchasing put options. It would pay a premium of £3000 (1 000 000 units × £0.003). Overall, Hunter would pay £5000 for the call options and put options on francs, which is substantially less than the £9000 it would pay for the straddle in the previous example. However, the options do not offer protection until the spot rate deviates by more than £0.005 from its existing level. If the spot rate remains within the range of the two exercise prices (from £0.445 to £0.455), Hunter will not exercise either option.

This example of hedging with a strangle is a compromise between hedging with the straddle in the previous example and no hedge. For the range of possible spot rates between £0.445 and £0.455, there is no hedge. For scenarios in which the spot rate moves outside the range, Hunter is hedged. It will have to pay no more than £0.455 if it needs to obtain francs and will be able to sell francs for at least £0.445 if it has francs to sell.

HEDGING WITH CURRENCY BULL SPREADS

Where MNCs find call options too expensive a bull spread can be constructed to lower the cost as the following example illustrates.

HEDGING WITH CURRENCY BEAR SPREADS

In certain situations, MNCs can use currency bear spreads to hedge their receivables denominated in a foreign currency.

EXAMPLE

Peak Ltd needs to order US raw materials to use in its production process. The US exporter typically invoices Peak in US dollars. Assume that the current exchange rate for the US dollar ($) is £0.55 and that Peak needs $100 000 in 3 months. Two call options for US dollars with expiration dates in 3 months and the following additional information are available:

- Call Option 1 premium on US dollars = £0.015.
- Call Option 2 premium on US dollars = £0.008.
- Call Option 1 strike price = £0.55.
- Call Option 2 strike price = £0.60.
- One option contract represents $50 000.

To lock into a future price for the $100 000, Peak could buy two Option 1 contracts, paying 2 × 50 000 × £0.015 = £1500. This would effectively lock in a maximum price of £0.55 that Peak would pay in 3 months, for a total maximum outflow of £56 500 (100 000 × £0.55 + £1500). If the spot price for US dollars at option settlement is below £0.55, Peak has the right to let the options expire and buy the $100 000 in the open market for the lower price. Naturally, Peak would still have paid the £1500 total premium in this case.

If Peak believes that the US dollar will appreciate in the next 3 months but is very unlikely to be above £0.60, it should consider constructing a bull spread to hedge its US dollar payables. To do so, Peak would purchase two Option 1 contracts. To help finance this cost Peak should *write* (or sell) two Option 2 contracts (see Exhibit 11B.3). The total cash outflow necessary to construct this bull spread is 2 × $50 000 × (£0.015 − £0.008) = £700, since Peak would receive the premiums from writing the two Option 2 contracts. Constructing the bull spread has reduced the cost of hedging by £800 (£1500 − £700).

If the spot price of the US dollar at option expiration is below the £0.60 strike price, the bull spread will have provided an effective hedge. For example, if the spot price at option expiration is £0.58, Peak will exercise the two Option 1 contracts it purchased, for a total maximum outflow of £55 700 ($100 000 × £0.55 + $700). If Peak had not hedged then the cost would

have been £58 000 ($100 000 × £0.58), so there has been a saving of £2300 (£58 000 − £55 700). The buyer of the two Option 2 contracts Peak wrote would let those options expire. If the US dollar depreciates below the lower strike price of £0.55, both options will expire worthless. Peak would purchase the US dollars at the prevailing spot rate, having paid the difference in option premiums and therefore be worse off by £700 compared to the no hedge position.

Now consider what will happen if the US dollar appreciates above the higher exercise price of £0.60 prior to option settlement. In this case, the bull spread will still reduce the total cash outflow and therefore provide a partial hedge. However, the hedge will not protect against differences above £0.60 as any gain on the purchased calls is lost on the written calls. The maximum benefit will be (£0.60 − £0.55) × $100 000 − £700 = £4300.

To illustrate, assume the US dollar appreciates to a spot price of £0.70 in 3 months. Peak will still exercise the two Option 1 contracts it purchased. However, the two Option 2 contracts it wrote will also be exercised. The gain on the two Option 1 contracts will be (£0.70 − £0.55) × 100 000 = £15 000. But Peak will lose on the two written Option 2 contracts by (£0.60 − £0.70) × 100 000 = £10 000, a net gain of only £5000 (£15 000 − £10 000). The gain of £5000 has been at the cost of purchasing the option contracts at a cost of £700 (see above) so the net gain is £4300. The total cost to Peak will be the purchase at spot of the $100 000, so $100 000 × £0.70 = £70 000 less the net gain from the options of £4300 making a total cost of £65 700 (£70 000 − £4300), still better than the no protection cost of £70 000. To repeat, for every £0.01 or penny increase in the spot rate above £0.60 to the dollar, Option 1 *pays to Peak £0.01* per $1 covered but Option 2 *requires a payment of £0.01* per $1 covered. The two contracts cancel out for movements above the £0.60 to the dollar exchange rate. So Peak is not covered for increases in spot rates above £0.60 to the dollar. Consequently, MNCs should hedge using bull spreads only for relatively stable currencies that are not expected to appreciate drastically prior to option settlement.

(Continued)

EXHIBIT 11B.3 Contingency diagram for hedging with a bull spread (Peak Ltd) per unit (dollars) and total cost (not drawn to scale)

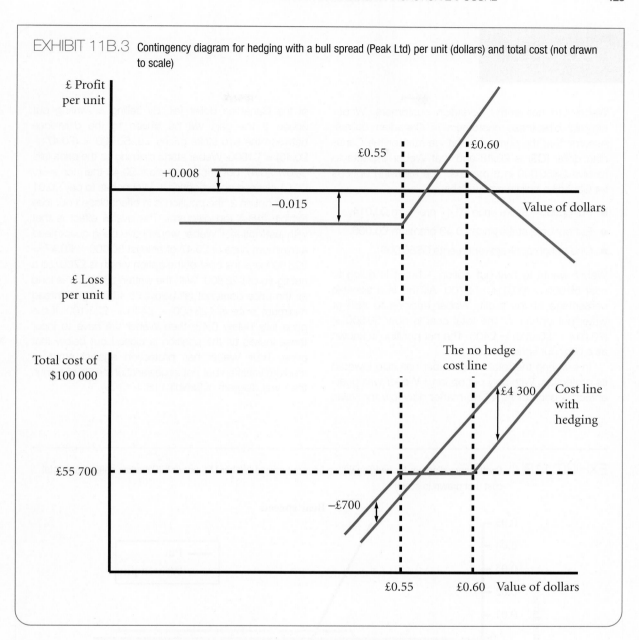

EXAMPLE

Weber Ltd has some Canadian customers, Weber typically bills these customers in Canadian dollars. Assume that the current exchange rate for the Canadian dollar (C$) is £0.48 and that Weber expects to receive C$50 000 in 3 months. The following options for Canadian dollars are available.

- Put option 1 strike price £0.47 premium £0.014.
- Put option 2 strike price £0.43 premium £0.006.
- One option contract represents C$50 000.

Weber wants to buy put option 1 but it is going to cost 50 000 × £0.014 = £700. As this is a sizeable percentage of the profit, Weber decides to sell, or write, put option 2. The total cost is now 50 000 × (£0.014 − £0.006) = £400. The net position is known as a bear put spread.

In lowering the total cost, Weber has also lowered its protection. With only put option 1 Weber was guaranteed a price of £0.47 no matter how low the value of the Canadian dollar fell. By selling or writing put option 2 the gain will be limited to the difference between the two strike prices, i.e. 50 000 × (£0.47 − £0.43) = £1500. Weber starts claiming as the price falls below £0.47 but if it goes below £0.43 then for every £0.01 claimed on put option 1, Weber has to pay £0.01 on put option 2, the position is in effect closed out (see Exhibit 11B.4 top diagram). The overall effect is that with just option 1 Weber would have been guaranteed a minimum price of £0.47 or at least 50 000 × £0.47 = £23 500 less the cost of the option which is £700, so a net figure of £22 800. With the written option 2, as long as the price does not fall below £0.43 the guaranteed minimum price is £23 500 − £400 = £23,100. If the price falls below 0.43, then Weber will have to incur those losses as the position is closed out below that price. Thus Weber has protection against small to medium variation but not large variations as is shown in the lower diagram of Exhibit 11B.4.

EXHIBIT 11B.4   Contingency diagram for hedging with a bear put spread (Weber Ltd) per unit (Canadian dollars) and total cost (not drawn to scale)

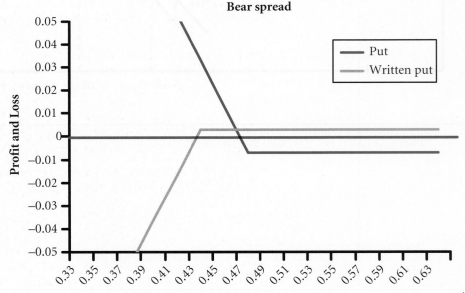

(Continued)

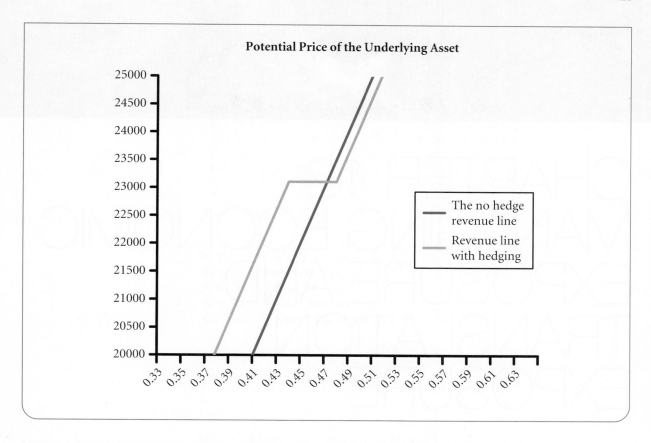

EVALUATION OF NON-TRADITIONAL HEDGING TECHNIQUES

Options used in combination offer a very flexible form of protection from currency variation. Many such combinations are popular with speculators who want to benefit from imagined patterns in currency prices or who want to take out unusual bets. Straddles and strangles, for example, are bets on the standard deviation, if the currency varies sufficiently either up or down a profit is made with the purchased puts and calls. If the puts and calls are written, a profit is made if the currency does not vary greatly. For the multinational the protection is likely to be rather simpler. MNCs seek protection from extreme rates. Such protection avoids unexpected losses and gives the company time to rearrange affairs. For the most part this would involve buying a put or a call option. Helping to reduce the cost of the option is probably best achieved through collars or range forwards. Thus, buying a put option can in part be financed by selling a call at a higher strike price (see Chapter 5). A cheap put at a low strike price protects revenue denominated on foreign currency from being translated at an unexpectedly low price. If the price of the foreign currency is unexpectedly high, some of the gain will be lost as the purchaser of the call option will claim the difference between the high call strike and the even higher spot. How an MNC defines extreme rates and high and low will depend on the financial circumstances. Where margins are small, transactions infrequent and significant, a high level of protection may be desired. For companies with larger margins and frequent transactions there will be greater tolerance of currency changes. For such companies, protection may only be desired for large adverse changes. In any event, the rationale for non-traditional options must be carefully worked out as it is very easy to accidentally start to speculate on currencies when the original intention was simply to protect against adverse movements. See Appendix 5B and the companion website for a spreadsheet that models two option combinations.

CHAPTER 12
MANAGING ECONOMIC EXPOSURE AND TRANSLATION EXPOSURE

LEARNING OBJECTIVES

The specific objectives of this chapter are to:

● Explain how an MNC's economic exposure can be hedged.

● Explain how an MNC's translation exposure can be hedged.

When the British pound value of, for example, the Argentine peso changes, the cost in pounds of all goods and services denominated in pesos will change. Any transaction by an multinational corporation (MNC) that involves converting pounds to pesos or pesos to pounds will be directly affected (transaction exposure). There will also be indirect effects caused by changes in the pattern of demand for goods and services as a result of the new exchange rate. Together these risks are termed economic exposure.

Even if an MNC is protected from all economic exposure, the reported profits of an MNC may still be affected by exchange rate changes. This is because reported profits are in the home currency and therefore a conversion of foreign sales etc. has to be made even if no such conversion has taken place. Accounting conventions help to clarify and minimize the effect of converting currencies for reporting purposes, but there remains a concern that a loss that is solely as a result of reporting practices may yet reflect badly on MNCs. This form of risk is termed translation exposure.

In this chapter we examine how an MNC may organize its affairs and use the financial markets to protect itself from both forms of exposure.

ECONOMIC EXPOSURE

From a multinational's perspective, transaction exposure represents only the exchange rate risk when *converting* net foreign cash inflows to its home currency or when making payments in foreign currency. Economic exposure includes this concept but also represents *any* impact of exchange rate fluctuations on a firm's future cash flows. A firm whose production and sales are in the home market with no sales or purchases from abroad can be affected by foreign currency movements *if* competitors are affected. Therefore, firms cannot focus just on hedging their foreign currency payables or receivables but must also attempt to determine how all their cash flows will be affected by possible exchange rate movements.

EXAMPLE

Adidas' economic exposure comes in various forms. First, it is subject to transaction exposure because of its numerous purchase and sale transactions in foreign currencies, particularly dollars. This transaction exposure is a subset of economic exposure. Second, any remitted earnings from foreign subsidiaries to the German parent also reflect transaction exposure. Third, a change in exchange rates that affects the demand for shoes at other athletic shoe companies (such as Nike) can indirectly affect the demand for Adidas' athletic shoes. All these effects when taken together amount to economic exposure. Adidas gives special mention to options as a means of protecting against an appreciation of the dollar and at the same time allowing the firm to benefit from a depreciation. Adidas also purchase forward contracts and engage in currency swaps as well as trying to increase purchases in the currency of their sales. The company attempts to hedge some of its transaction exposure typically up to 18 months in advance, but it cannot eliminate transaction exposure because it cannot predict all future transactions ahead of time. Moreover, even if it could eliminate its transaction exposure, it cannot perfectly hedge its remaining economic exposure; it is difficult to determine exactly how a specific exchange rate movement will affect the demand for a competitor's athletic shoes and, therefore, how it will indirectly affect the demand for Adidas' shoes.

The following comments by Marshall and McLennan Companies summarize the dilemma faced by many MNCs that assess economic exposure.

> *We are subject to exchange rate risk because some of our subsidiaries receive revenue other than in their functional currencies, and because we must translate the financial results of our foreign subsidiaries into US dollars. Our US operations earn revenue and incur expenses primarily in US dollars. In certain jurisdictions (primarily the UK), however, our Risk and Insurance Services operations generate revenue in a number of different currencies, but expenses are almost entirely incurred in local currency. Due to fluctuations in foreign exchange rates, we are subject to economic exposure as well as currency translation exposure on the profits of our operations. Exchange rate risk could have a material adverse effect on our financial condition, results of operations or cash flow...*

(Marshall and McLennan Companies Annual Report 2008, p. 18)

USING THE WEB

MNCs' Annual Reports can be downloaded from the web (the name of the firm plus the keywords 'Annual Report' and 'pdf' is the most direct route). Part of the reporting requirements is an account of the risk management policy of the firm. The use of financial derivatives, the types of derivative used, natural hedges, an estimate of the degree of exposure and the way in which risk is managed are all part of the report.

Use of the income statement to assess economic exposure

An MNC must determine its economic exposure before it can manage its exposure. It can determine its exposure to each currency in terms of its cash inflows and cash outflows. The income statements for each subsidiary can be used to derive estimates.

EXAMPLE

Recall from Chapter 10 that Mannerton plc is subject to economic exposure. Mannerton can assess its economic exposure to exchange rate movements by determining the sensitivity of its expenses and revenue to various possible exchange rate scenarios.

Exhibit 12.1 reproduces Mannerton's revenue and expense information from Exhibit 10.10(c) of Chapter 10. The UK revenues are assumed to be sensitive to different exchange rate scenarios because of the foreign competition. Regardless of the exchange rate scenario, European sales are expected to be 40 million euros, but the British pound amount received from these sales will depend on the scenario. The cost of goods sold attributable to UK orders is assumed to be £50 million for Scenario 1; Scenarios 2 and 3 are sensitive to the volume effects on UK sales of exchange rate. The cost of goods sold attributable to European and UK orders is 200 million euros for Scenario 1. The British pound amount of this cost varies with the exchange rate scenario *and* the volume changes in UK sales as a result of the differing exchange rates. The gross profit shown in Exhibit 12.1 is determined by subtracting the total pound value of cost of goods sold from the total pound value of sales.

Operating expenses are separated into fixed and variable categories. The fixed expenses are £30 million per year, while the projected variable expenses are dictated by projected sales volumes. The earnings before interest and taxes are determined by the total British pound amount of gross profit minus the total British pound amount of operating expenses. The interest owed to UK banks is insensitive to the exchange rate scenario, but the projected amount of pounds needed to pay interest on existing European loans varies with the exchange rate scenario. Earnings before taxes are estimated by subtracting total interest expense from earnings before interest and taxes.

Exhibit 12.1 enables Mannerton to assess how its income statement items will be affected by different exchange rate movements. A stronger euro increases Mannerton's UK sales and the pound value of the revenue earned from European sales. On the negative side, there is also a large increase in Mannerton's cost of materials purchased from Europe and the pound amount needed to pay interest on loans from European banks.

The higher expenses more than offset the higher revenue in this scenario. Hence, the amount of Mannerton's earnings before taxes is inversely related to the strength of the euro. A 17 per cent rise in the value of the euro (£0.70 / £0.60 − 1 = 0.17) results in an estimated fall in profits of 19 per cent (£68.56m/£84.28m − 1 = 0.19). Equivalent figures for Scenario 3 are a 33 per cent rise in the value of the euro compared to Scenario 1 resulting in a 38 per cent fall in profits. To convey some idea of this risk, Mannerton could report in the annual accounts that a 1 per cent rise in the value of the euro will result in an estimated £0.9m fall in profits ((84.28 − 68.56)/17 ≈ 0.9). Renault SA in their 2009 report present a table showing the effect on earnings of a 10 per cent increase in the value of the euro against the US dollar and the British pound and also a 10 per cent increase in the value of the US dollar against the Japanese yen, bearing in mind its links with Nissan.

If the euro strengthens consistently over the long run, Mannerton's cost of goods sold and interest expense will rise at a higher rate than its UK revenues. Consequently, it may wish to institute some policies to ensure that movements of the euro will have a more balanced impact on its revenue and expenses. At the current time, Mannerton's high exposure to exchange rate movements occurs because its expenses are more susceptible than its revenue to the changing value of the euro.

Now that Mannerton has assessed its exposure, it recognizes that it can reduce this exposure by either increasing European sales or reducing orders of European materials. These actions would allow some offsetting of cash flows and therefore reduce its economic exposure.

(Continued)

EXHIBIT 12.1   Original impact of exchange rate movements on earnings: Mannerton plc

	Exchange rate scenarios		
Item	Scenario 1	Scenario 2	Scenario 3
Value of euro	£0.60	£0.70	£0.80
		£ million	
(1) UK sales	300.00	304.00	307.00
(2) European sales (40 million euros in each scenario)	24.00	28.00	32.00
(3) Total	324.00	332.00	339.00
less Cost of goods sold:			
(4) UK costs	50.00	50.62	51.08
(5) European costs	120.00	141.73	163.46
(6) Total	170.00	192.35	214.54
(7) Gross profit	**154.00**	**139.65**	**124.46**
less Operating expenses:			
(8) UK: Fixed	30.00	30.00	30.00
less (9) UK: Variable costs (by volume of output)	30.72	31.10	31.38
(10) Total	60.72	61.10	61.38
(11) EBIT (earnings before interest and tax)	**93.28**	**78.56**	**63.08**
less Interest expense:			
(12) UK	3.00	3.00	3.00
(13) European 10 million euros	6.00	7.00	8.00
(14) Total	9.00	10.00	11.00
(15) EBT	**84.28**	**68.56**	**52.08**

Notes:

Total volume changes compared to Scenario 1: European sales are 0.074 or 7.4 per cent of total sales in Scenario 1 (see Exhibit 10.10(a)) and do not change. So using the volume changes from Exhibit 10.10(b) and taking a weighted average, the volume changes are: Scenario 2: 0.074×0 per cent $+ (1 - 0.074) \times 1\frac{1}{3}$ per cent = **1.235 per cent;** Scenario 3: 0.074×0 per cent $+ (1 - 0.074) \times 2\frac{1}{3}$ per cent = **2.16 per cent.**

Line 4:   Cost of goods sold is variable and presumed to relate to all sales. Applying the volume changes (above) for Scenarios 2 and 3, $50 + 1.235$ per cent $\times 50 = 50.62$ and $50 + 2.16$ per cent $\times 50 = 51.08$.

Line 5:   European costs are incurred in the production of both UK and European goods. So for Scenarios 2 and 3 applying the volume changes above:

Scenario 2: $200 + 200 \times 1.235$ per cent $= 202.47$ euros

Scenario 3: $200 + 200 \times 2.16$ per cent $= 204.32$ euros
And the £ valuations are Scenario 1: $200 \times 0.6 = 120$; Scenario 2: $202.47 \times 0.70 = 141.73$;
Scenario 3: $204.32 \times 0.80 = 163.46$.

Line 9:   UK variable costs are subject to the volume changes above, 30.72 as given for Scenario 1, for Scenario 2 it is $30.72 + 1.235$ per cent $\times 30.72 = 31.10$ and $30.72 + 2.16$ per cent $\times 30.72 = 31.38$ for Scenarios 2 and 3.

How restructuring can reduce economic exposure

MNCs may restructure their operations to reduce their economic exposure. The restructuring involves shifting the sources of costs or revenue to other locations in order to match cash inflows and outflows in foreign currencies.

EXAMPLE

Reconsider the previous example of Mannerton plc which has more cash outflows than cash inflows in euros as it produces mainly in Europe. Mannerton could create more balance by increasing European sales. It believes that it can achieve European sales of 60 million euro if it spends £2 million more on advertising (which is part of its fixed operating expenses). The increased sales will also require an additional expenditure of £10 million on materials from UK suppliers and a £1m increase in variable operating expenses. In addition, it plans to reduce its reliance on European suppliers and increase its reliance on UK suppliers. Mannerton anticipates that this strategy will reduce the cost of goods sold attributable to European suppliers by 100 million euros and increase the cost of goods sold attributable to UK suppliers by £70 million (not including the £10 million increase resulting from increased sales to the European market). Furthermore, it plans to borrow additional funds in the UK and retire some existing loans from European banks. The result will be an additional interest expense of £3.5 million to UK banks and a reduction of 5 million euros owed to European banks. Exhibit 12.2 shows the anticipated impact of these strategies on Mannerton's income statement. For each of the three exchange rate scenarios, the initial projections are in the left column, and the revised projections (as a result of the proposed strategy) are in the right column.

Note first that there is an increase in projected total sales in response to Mannerton's plan to penetrate the European market. Second, the UK cost of goods sold is now £130 million higher as a result of the £10 million materials increase to accommodate increased European sales and the £70 million increase due to the shift from European suppliers to UK suppliers. The European cost of goods sold decreases from 200 million euros to 100 million euros as a result of this shift to the UK. The revised fixed operating expenses of $32 million include the increase in advertising expenses

necessary to penetrate the European market. The variable operating expenses are revised by £1m because of revised estimates for total sales. The interest expenses are revised because of the increased loans from the UK banks and reduced loans from European banks.

If Mannerton increases its euro inflows and reduces its euro outflows as proposed, its revenue and expenses will be affected by movements of the euro. Exhibit 12.3 illustrates the sensitivity of Mannerton's earnings before taxes to the three exchange rate scenarios (derived from Exhibit 12.2). The reduced sensitivity of Mannerton's proposed restructured operations to exchange rate movements is clear. There is nevertheless a cost to be considered. Taking Scenario 1 to be the most likely, Mannerton is in effect having to consider reducing its earnings in the most likely scenario in order to improve earnings in the less favourable but less likely scenarios.

The way a firm restructures its operations to reduce economic exposure to exchange rate risk depends on the form of exposure. For Mannerton plc future expenses are more sensitive than future revenue to the possible values of a foreign currency. Therefore, it can reduce its economic exposure by increasing the sensitivity of revenue and reducing the sensitivity of expenses to exchange rate movements. Firms that have a greater level of exchange rate-sensitive revenue than expenses, however, would reduce their economic exposure by decreasing the level of exchange rate-sensitive revenue or by increasing the level of exchange rate-sensitive expenses. The net effect is to match as far as possible revenues and costs in each currency.

Some revenue or expenses may be more sensitive to exchange rates than others. An increase in the value of the euro in the previous example could mean a very large increase in domestic demand as big customers switch to Mannerton's products.

(Continued)

EXHIBIT 12.2 Impact of possible exchange rate movements on earnings under two alternative operational structures (in millions)

£ million	Scenario 1 £0.60:1euro		Scenario 2 £0.70:1euro		Scenario 3 £0.80:1euro	
	Original	**Proposed**	**Original**	**Proposed**	**Original**	**Proposed**
(1) UK sales	300.00	300.00	304.00	304.00	307.00	307.00
(2) European sales						
(40 million euros and 60 million − proposed)	24.00	36.00	28.00	42.00	32.00	48.00
(3) Total	324.00	336.00	332.00	346.00	339.00	355.00
Cost of goods sold:						
(4) UK	50.00	130.00	50.62	131.55	51.08	132.71
(5) European costs	120.00	60.00	141.73	70.83	163.46	81.67
(6) Total	170.00	190.00	192.35	202.38	214.54	214.38
(7) Gross profit	**154.00**	**146.00**	**139.65**	**143.62**	**124.46**	**140.63**
Operating expenses:						
(8) UK: Fixed	30.00	32.00	30.00	32.00	30.00	32.00
(9) UK: Variable (by volume of output)	30.72	31.72	31.10	32.10	31.38	32.38
(10) Total	60.72	63.72	61.10	64.10	61.38	64.38
(11) EBIT	**93.28**	**82.28**	**78.55**	**79.52**	**63.08**	**76.24**
Interest expense:						
(12) UK	3.00	6.50	3.00	6.50	3.00	6.50
(13) European 10 million euros	6.00	3.00	7.00	3.50	8.00	4.00
(4) Total	9.00	9.50	10.00	10.00	11.00	10.50
(5) EBT	**84.28**	**72.78**	**68.55**	**69.52**	**52.08**	**65.74**

Summary of strategy
1. European sales increase of 20 million euro from spending £2 million more on advertising (which is part of its fixed operating expenses) £10 million on materials from UK suppliers and £1m on operating expenses.
2. Reduce the European cost of goods sold by 100 million euros and increase the UK cost of goods sold by £50 million (not including the £10 million increase resulting from increased sales to the European market).
3. Increase UK borrowing by £3.5 million to UK banks and reduce borrowing from European banks by 5 million euros.

For Scenarios 2 and 3 the volume effects are applied as outlined in Chapter 10.
Line 2: European sales increased to 60m euros so Scenario 1: 60 × 0.60 = 36.00
Line 4: £10m for European sales plus £50m switch from European costs, Scenario 1 £50m + £10m + £70m = £110m.
Line 5: Decrease in costs of 100m euros so Scenario 1: £120m − 100m euros × 0.6 = £60m,
Line 8: plus the £2m on advertising.
Line 9: plus the £1m on operating expenses for European sales.
See Exhibit 10.10(c) for the orginal plan.

(Continued)

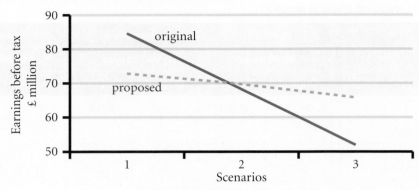

EXHIBIT 12.3   Economic exposure–earnings in different scenarios

Note:

These are earnings in different scenarios: the steeper the slope the greater the risk. Note that the proposed changes lessen the risk faced by the company but offers a lower overall spread of returns – see 'mannerton ch. 12.xls' on the CourseMate.

The volume effects of economic exposure mean that the simple matching of costs and revenues may not be sufficient. The firm can best evaluate a proposed restructuring of operations by forecasting various income statement items for various possible exchange rate scenarios (as shown in Exhibit 12.2) and then assessing the sensitivity of earnings to these different scenarios as in Exhibit 12.3.

Using computer spreadsheets. Determining the sensitivity of earnings before taxes to alternative exchange rate scenarios can be helped by using a computer to create a spreadsheet similar to Exhibit 12.2. The analyst then inputs forecasts for items such as sales, cost of goods sold, and fixed operating expenses. A formula is used to define the remaining items so that the computer can provide estimates after the forecasts are input. For example, the exchange rate forecast influences projections of: (1) pounds received from European sales, (2) cost of goods sold attributable to purchases of European materials and (3) amount in dollars needed to cover the European interest payments. By revising the input to reflect various possible restructurings, the analyst can determine how each operational structure would affect the firm's economic exposure.

Recall that Mannerton plc assessed one alternative operational structure in which it increased European sales by 20 million euros, reduced its purchases of European materials by 100 million euros, and reduced its interest owed to European banks by 5 million euros. By using a computerized spreadsheet, Mannerton can easily assess the impact of alternative strategies, such as increasing European sales by other amounts and/or reducing the European expenses by other amounts. This provides Mannerton with more information about its economic exposure under various operational structures and enables it to devise the operational structure that will reduce its economic exposure to the degree desired.

Issues involved in the restructuring decision

Restructuring operations to reduce economic exposure is a more complex task than hedging any single foreign currency transaction. By managing economic exposure, however, the firm is developing a long-term solution because once the restructuring is complete, it should reduce economic exposure over the long run. In contrast, the hedging of transaction exposure deals with each foreign currency transaction separately. Note, however, that it can be very costly to reverse or eliminate restructuring that was undertaken to reduce economic exposure. Therefore, MNCs must be very confident about the potential benefits before they decide to restructure their operations.

When deciding how to restructure operations to reduce economic exposure, one must address the following questions:

- Should the firm attempt to increase or reduce sales in new or existing foreign markets?

- Should the firm increase or reduce its dependency on foreign suppliers?

- Should the firm establish or eliminate production facilities in foreign markets?

- Should the firm increase or reduce its level of debt denominated in foreign currencies?

Each of these questions reflects a different part of the firm's income statement. The first relates to foreign cash inflows and the remaining ones to foreign cash outflows. Some of the more common solutions to balancing a foreign currency's inflows and outflows are summarized in Exhibit 12.4. Any restructuring of operations that can reduce the periodic difference between a foreign currency's inflows and outflows can reduce the firm's economic exposure to that currency's movements.

MNCs that have production and marketing facilities in various countries may be able to reduce any adverse impact of economic exposure by shifting the allocation of their operations.

EXHIBIT 12.4   How to restructure operations to balance the impact of adverse currency changes

Recommended action when a company has net cash inflows in the foreign currency	Recommended action when a company has net cash outflows in the foreign currency
Reduce foreign currency sales or invoice in home currency	Increase foreign currency sales
Increase foreign supply orders (costs)	Reduce foreign supply orders (costs)
Restructure debt to increase debt payments in foreign currency	Restructure debt to reduce debt payments in foreign currency

EXAMPLE

Hartland plc produces products in the UK, Japan and France and sells these products to several countries. The products are denominated in the currency where they are produced – so Japanese production is sold in yen even when exported. If the Japanese yen strengthens against many currencies, Hartland may boost production in France, expecting a decline in demand for the Japanese subsidiary's exported products. Hartland may even transfer some machinery from Japan to France and allocate more marketing funds to the French subsidiary at the expense of the Japanese subsidiary. By following this strategy, however, Hartland may have to forgo economies of scale that could be achieved if it concentrated production at one subsidiary while other subsidiaries focused on warehousing and distribution.

A CASE STUDY IN HEDGING ECONOMIC EXPOSURE

The complexity of MNC operations presents further difficulties. First, an MNC's economic exposure may not be so obvious. An analysis of the income statement for an entire MNC may not necessarily detect its economic exposure. The MNC may be composed of various business units, each of which attempts to achieve high performance for its shareholders. Each business unit may have a unique cost and revenue structure. One unit of an MNC may focus on computer consulting services in the UK and have no exposure to exchange rates. Another unit may also focus on sales of personal computers in the UK, but this unit may be adversely affected by weak foreign currencies because its UK customers may buy computers from foreign firms.

A multinational can more effectively hedge its economic exposure if it can pinpoint the underlying source of the exposure. Yet, even if the MNC can pinpoint the underlying source of the exposure, there may not be a perfect hedge. No textbook formula can provide the perfect solution, but a combination of actions may reduce the economic exposure to a tolerable level, as illustrated in the following example.

Case Study – Silverton Ltd's dilemma

Silverton Ltd (a UK firm), is primarily concerned with its exposure to the euro. It wants to pinpoint the source of its exposure so that it can determine a hedging strategy. Silverton has three units that conduct some of their business in Europe. Because each unit has established a wide variety of business arrangements, it is not obvious whether all three units have a similar exposure. Each unit tends to be independent of the others, and the managers of each unit are compensated according to that unit's performance. Silverton may want to hedge its economic exposure, but it must first determine whether it is exposed and the source of the exposure.

MANAGING FOR VALUE

How auto manufacturers restructure to reduce exposure

To illustrate how the shifting of production can reduce economic exposure, consider the actual case of Honda, the Japanese automobile producer. By developing plants in the USA to produce automobiles for sale there, Honda not only circumvents possible trade restrictions but also reduces its economic exposure to exchange rate risk. When Honda exported automobiles to the USA, the US demand for Hondas would decline if the yen appreciated because the dollar cost of the autos would increase. Thus, Honda's cash flows were adversely affected when a strong yen reduced demand for its exports. By producing automobiles in the USA and invoicing them in dollars, Honda has reduced the sensitivity of US demand for its automobiles to the value of the Japanese yen. Nevertheless, Honda is not completely insulated from exchange rate risk for two reasons. First, the Honda plants in the USA purchase various components from Japan (invoiced in yen), so the dollar costs of these components rises when the yen appreciates. Second,

earnings remitted from Honda's plants in the USA to its parent in Japan convert to a smaller number of yen when the yen appreciates. Nevertheless, by transferring production to the location where the product is sold, Honda has reduced its economic exposure.

Honda's British subsidiary has also restructured to reduce the adverse effects of its economic exposure. When the euro declined against the British pound, consumers throughout Europe reduced their demand for vehicles produced at Honda's subsidiary in the UK and denominated in pounds. Consequently, Honda shifted some of its supply sources from the UK to European countries that have adopted the euro. This strategy is intended to reduce the impact of the euro on the performance of Honda's British subsidiary. When the euro declines, the decline in revenue (because of a reduced demand for Hondas produced in the UK) is partially offset by a decline in the costs of obtaining supplies denominated in euros. When the euro's value increases, Honda's cost of euro-denominated supplies rises, but the demand for its pound-denominated vehicles (and therefore its revenue) also increases (see Exhibit 12.5). By shifting its operations, Honda has reduced its exposure to exchange rate risk, thereby increasing its value.

As a result of Honda's decision to use suppliers in the Eurozone countries to hedge its exposure, it is buying less from suppliers in the UK. Thus, the UK auto suppliers have lost local business because of Honda's desire to offset its exposure. Ironically, these auto suppliers are subject to increased economic exposure as a result of Honda's decision to reduce its exposure.

EXHIBIT 12.5   **Honda's decision to obtain supplies outside the United Kingdom**

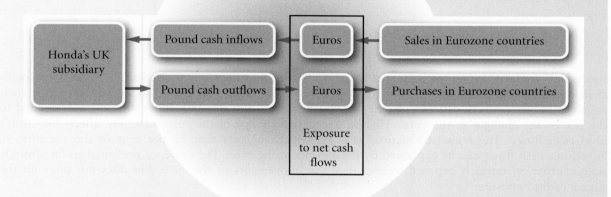

- Weak euro: weak European demand for Honda's pound denominated vehicles offset by reduced cost of euro denominated supplies.
- Strong euro: strong European demand for Honda's pound denominated vehicles offset by high cost of euro denominated supplies.

Assessment of economic exposure

Because the exact nature of its economic exposure to the euro is not obvious, Silverton attempts to assess the relationship between the euro's movements and each unit's cash flows over the last nine-quarters. A firm may want to use more data, but nine-quarters are sufficient to illustrate the point. The cash flows and movements in the euro are shown in Exhibit 12.6. First, Silverton applies regression analysis (as discussed in the previous chapter) to determine whether the percentage change in its total cash flow *(PCF,* shown in Column 5) is related to the percentage change in the euro (%Δ percentage change in the euro, shown in Column 6) over time:

$$PCF_t = a_0 + a_1(\%\Delta)_t + \mu$$

EXHIBIT 12.6   Assessment of Silverton's cash flows and the euro's movements

(1) Quarter	(2) Per cent change in unit A's cash flows	(3) Per cent change in unit B's cash flows	(4) Per cent change in unit C's cash flows	(5) Per cent change in total cash flows	(6) Per cent change in the value of the euro
1	−3	2	1	0	2
2	0	1	3	4	5
3	6	−6	−1	−1	−3
4	−1	1	−1	−1	0
5	−4	0	−1	−5	−2
6	−1	−2	−2	−5	−5
7	1	−3	3	1	4
8	−3	2	1	0	2
9	4	−1	0	3	−4

Regression analysis derives the values of the constant, a_0, and the slope coefficient, a_1. The slope coefficient represents the sensitivity of PCF_t to movements in the euro. Based on this analysis, the slope coefficient is positive and statistically significant, which implies that the cash flows are positively related to the percentage changes in the euro. That is, a negative change in the euro adversely affects Silverton's total cash flows. The r-squared statistic is 0.31, which suggests that 31 per cent of the variation in Silverton's cash flows can be explained by movements in the euro. The evidence presented so far strongly suggests that Silverton is exposed to exchange rate movements of the euro, but does not pinpoint the source of the exposure.

Assessment of each unit's exposure

To determine the source of the exposure, Silverton applies the regression model separately to each individual unit's cash flows. The results are shown here (apply the regression analysis yourself as an exercise):

Unit	Slope coefficient
A	Not significant
B	Not significant
C	Coefficient = 0.45, which is statistically significant (r-squared = 0.80)

The results suggest that the cash flows of Units A and B are not subject to economic exposure. However, Unit C is subject to economic exposure. Approximately 80 per cent of Unit C's cash flows can be explained by movements in the value of the euro over time. The regression coefficient suggests that for a 1 per cent decrease in the value of the euro, the unit's cash flows will decline by about 0.45 per cent. Exhibit 12.6, which shows the euro's exchange rate movements and the cash flows for Silverton's individual units, confirms the strong relationship between the euro's movements and Unit C's cash flows.

Identifying the source of the unit's exposure

Now that Silverton has determined that one unit is the cause of the exposure, it can pinpoint the characteristics of that unit that cause the exposure. Silverton believes that the key components that affect Unit C's cash flows are income statement items such as its UK revenue, its cost of goods sold, and its operating expenses. This unit conducts all of its production in the UK.

Silverton first determines the value of each income statement item that affected the unit's cash flows in each of the last nine-quarters. It then applies regression analysis to determine the relationship between the percentage change in the euro and each income statement item over those quarters. Assume that it finds:

- A significant positive relationship between Unit C's sales and the euro's value.

- No relationship between the unit's cost of goods sold and the euro's value.

- No relationship between the unit's operating expenses and the euro's value.

These results suggest that when the euro weakens, the unit's revenue from UK customers declines substantially. Its UK customers shift their demand to foreign competitors when the euro weakens and they can obtain imports at a low price. Thus, Silverton's economic exposure could be due to foreign competition. A firm's economic exposure is not always obvious, however, and regression analysis may detect exposure that was not suspected by the firm or its individual units. Furthermore, regression analysis can be used to provide a more precise estimate of the degree of economic exposure, which can be useful when deciding how to manage the exposure.

It is important to stress, however, that findings from regression analysis should be supported by other evidence. In this case, customers may not be sensitive to a weakening euro. It could be that the regression happened to be measured during a period of weakening euro when customers were moving away from Silverton's products for entirely different reasons. A correlation, no matter how strong, must be supported by other evidence before being acted upon.

Possible strategies to hedge economic exposure

Now that Silverton has identified the source of its economic exposure, it can develop a strategy to reduce that exposure.

Pricing policy. Silverton recognizes that there will be periods in the future when the euro will depreciate against the pound. Under these conditions, Unit C may attempt to be more competitive by reducing its prices. If the euro's value declines by 10 per cent and this reduces the prices that UK customers pay for the foreign products by 10 per cent, then Unit C can attempt to remain competitive by discounting its prices by 10 per cent. Although this strategy can retain market share, the lower prices will result in less revenue and therefore less cash flows. Therefore, this strategy does not completely eliminate Silverton's economic exposure. Nevertheless, this strategy may still be feasible, especially if the unit can charge relatively high prices in periods when the euro is strong and UK customers have to pay higher prices for European products. In essence, the strategy might allow the unit to generate abnormally high cash flows in a strong-euro period to offset the abnormally low cash flows in a weak-euro period. The adverse effect during a weak-euro period will still occur, however. Given the limitations of this strategy, other strategies should be considered.

Hedging with forward contracts. Silverton's Unit C could sell euros forward for the period in which it wants to hedge against the adverse effects of the weak euro. Assume the spot and 3-month forward rates on the euro are £0.80. If the euro weakens, the cash flows from normal operations will still be adversely affected. However, the unit would generate a gain on the forward contract because it will be able to purchase euros at the spot rate at the end of the period at a lower exchange rate than the rate at which it will have to sell those euros to fulfill the forward contract. The weaker the euro, the more pronounced will be the adverse effects on the unit's cash flows from normal operations, but the gains from the forward contract will also be more pronounced.

Using a forward contract has definite limitations, however. Since the economic exposure is likely to continue indefinitely, the use of a forward contract in the manner described here hedges only for the period of the contract. It does not serve as a continuous long-term hedge against economic exposure.

Purchasing foreign supplies. Another possibility is for the unit to purchase its materials in Europe, a strategy that would reduce its costs (and enhance its cash flows) during a weak-euro period to offset the adverse effects of the weak euro. However, the cost of buying European materials may be higher than the cost of buying local materials, especially when transportation expenses are considered.

Financing with foreign funds. The unit could also reduce its economic exposure by financing a portion of its business with loans in euros. It could convert the loan proceeds to pounds and use the pounds to support its business. It will need to make periodic loan repayments in euros. If the euro weakens, the unit will need fewer pounds to cover the loan repayments. This favourable effect can partially offset the adverse effect of a weak euro on the unit's revenue. If the euro strengthens, the unit will need more pounds to cover the loan repayments, but this adverse effect will be offset by the favourable effect of the strong euro on the unit's revenue. This type of hedge is more effective than the pricing hedge because it can offset the adverse effects of a weak euro in the same period (whereas the pricing policy attempts to make up for lost cash flows once the euro strengthens).

This strategy also has some limitations. First, the strategy only makes sense if Silverton needs some debt financing. It should not borrow funds just for the sake of hedging its economic exposure. Second, Silverton might not desire this strategy when the euro has a very high interest rate. Though borrowing in euros can reduce its economic exposure, it may not be willing to enact the hedge at a cost of higher interest expenses than it would pay in the UK.

Third, this strategy is unlikely to create a perfect hedge against Silverton's economic exposure. Even if the company needs debt financing and the interest rate charged on the foreign loan is low, Silverton must attempt to determine the amount of debt financing that will hedge its economic exposure. The amount of foreign debt financing necessary to fully hedge the exposure may exceed the amount of funding that Silverton needs.

Revising operations of other units. Given the limitations of hedging Unit C's economic exposure by adjusting the unit's operations, Silverton may consider modifying the operations of another unit in a manner that will offset the exposure of Unit C. However, this strategy may require changes in another unit that will not necessarily benefit that unit. For example, assume that Unit C could partially hedge its economic exposure by borrowing euros (as explained above) but that it does not need to borrow as much as would be necessary to fully offset its economic exposure. Silverton's top management may suggest that Units A and B also obtain their financing in euros, so that the MNC's overall economic exposure is hedged. Thus, a weak euro would still adversely affect Unit C because the adverse effect on its revenue would not be fully offset by the favourable effect on its financing (debt repayments). Yet, if the other units have borrowed euros as well, the combined favourable effects on financing for Silverton overall could offset the adverse effects on Unit C.

However, Units A and B will not necessarily desire to finance their operations in euros. Recall that these units are not subject to economic exposure. Also recall that the managers of each unit are compensated according to the performance of that unit. By agreeing to finance in euros, Units A and B could become exposed to movements in the euro. If the euro strengthens, their cost of financing increases. So, by helping to offset the exposure of Unit C, Units A and B could experience weaker performance, and their managers would receive less compensation.

A solution is still possible if Silverton's top managers who are not affiliated with any unit can remove the hedging activity from the compensation formula for the units' managers. That is, top management could instruct Units A and B to borrow funds in euros, but could reward the managers of those units based on an assessment of the units' performance that excludes the effect of the euro on financing costs. In this way, the managers will be more willing to engage in a strategy that increases their economic exposure while reducing Silverton's.

Silverton's hedging solution

In summary, Silverton's initial analysis of its units determined that only Unit C was highly subject to economic exposure. Unit C could attempt to use a pricing policy that would maintain market share when the euro weakens, but this strategy would not eliminate the economic exposure because its cash flows would still be adversely affected. Borrowing euros can be an effective strategy to hedge Unit C's exposure, but it does not need to borrow the amount of funds necessary to offset its exposure. The optimal solution for Silverton is to instruct its other units to do their financing in euros as well. This strategy effectively increases their exposure, but in the opposite manner of Unit C's exposure, so that the MNC's economic exposure overall is reduced. The units' managers should be willing to co-operate if their compensation is not reduced as a result of increasing the exposure of their individual units.

Limitations of Silverton's optimal hedging strategy

Even if Silverton is able to achieve the hedge described above, the hedge will still not be perfect. The impact of the euro's movements on Silverton's cash outflows needed to repay the loans is known with certainty. But the impact of the euro's movements on Silverton's cash inflows (revenue) is uncertain and can change over time. If the amount of foreign competition increases, the sensitivity of Unit C's cash flows to exchange rates would increase. To hedge this increased exposure, it would need to borrow a larger amount of euros. An MNC's economic exposure can change over time in response to shifts in foreign competition or other global conditions, so it must continually assess and manage its economic exposure.

HEDGING EXPOSURE TO FIXED ASSETS

Up to this point, the focus has been on how economic exposure can affect periodic cash flows. The effects may extend beyond periodic cash flows, however. When an MNC has fixed assets (such as buildings or machinery) in a foreign country, the cash flows to be received from the ultimate sale of these assets is subject to exchange rate risk.

EXAMPLE

Wagner SA, a French firm, pursued a 7-year project in Russia. It purchased a manufacturing plant from the Russian government in 2002 for 500 million roubles. Since the rouble was worth €0.03 at the time of the investment, Wagner needed €15 million to purchase the plant. The Russian government guaranteed that it would repurchase the plant for 500 million roubles in 2009 when the project was completed. In 2009, how-

ever, the rouble was worth only €0.023, so Wagner received only €11.5 million (computed as 500 million x €0.023) from selling the plant. Even though the price of the plant in roubles at the time of the sale was the same as the price at the time of the purchase, Wagner lost €3.5 million (€15m – €11.5m) due to the fall in the value of the euro.

Some MNCs may not worry about the exchange rate effect on fixed assets because they normally expect to retain the assets for several years. Given the frequent restructuring of global operations, however, MNCs should consider hedging against the possible sale of these assets in the distant future. A sale of fixed assets can be hedged by creating a liability that matches the expected value of the assets at the point in the future when they may be sold. In essence, the sale of the fixed assets generates a foreign currency cash inflow that can be used to pay off the liability that is denominated in the same currency.

EXAMPLE

In the previous example, Wagner could have financed part of its investment in the Russian manufacturing plant by borrowing roubles from a local bank, with the loan structured to have zero interest payments and a lump-sum repayment value equal to the expected sales price set for the date when Wagner expected to sell the plant. Thus, the loan could have been structured to have a lump-sum repayment value of 500 million roubles in July 2009. Any loss in expected revenue would therefore be matched by the reduced cost of repaying the loan.

The limitations of hedging a sale of fixed assets are that an MNC does not necessarily know the date when it will sell the assets or the price in local currency at which it will sell them. Consequently, it is unable to create a liability that perfectly matches the date and amount of the sale of the fixed assets. Nevertheless, any hedging strategy that reduces the time the exposure is unhedged is valuable – any residual unhedged periods will be much shorter and therefore present far less risk to the firm.

EXAMPLE

Even if the Russian government would not guarantee a purchase price of the plant, Wagner could create a liability that reflects the earliest possible sale date and the lowest expected sale price. If the sale date turns out to be later than the earliest possible sale date, Wagner might be able to extend its loan period to match the sale date. By structuring the lump-sum loan repayment to match the minimum sale price, Wagner will not be perfectly hedged if the fixed assets turn out to be worth more than the minimum expected amount. Nevertheless, Wagner would at least have reduced its exposure by offsetting a portion of the fixed assets with a liability in the same currency.

Long-term forward contracts may also be a possible way to hedge the distant sale of fixed assets in foreign countries, but they may not be available for many emerging market currencies.

MANAGING TRANSLATION EXPOSURE

Translation exposure occurs when an MNC translates each subsidiary's financial data to its home currency for consolidated financial statements. Even if translation exposure does not affect cash flows, it is a concern of many MNCs because it can reduce an MNC's consolidated earnings and risks causing a decline in its share price. Thus, some MNCs may consider hedging their translation exposure. Annual reports of multinationals for the most part make statements along the lines of:

While the Group uses short term hedging for trading activities, the Company does not believe that it is appropriate or practicable to hedge long term translation exposure.

(Cadbury Schweppes)

A statement that does not preclude the following:

In addition the Group hedges balance sheet risk selectively.

(Adidas)

Occasionally more committed statements are made:

The company does not hedge the exposure arising from translation exposure of net income in foreign entities. Translation exposure of equity invested in consolidated foreign entities financed by equity is partially hedged.

(Philips)

The phrase 'the Company does not believe that it is appropriate' in the first quote is interesting. Changes in profits due solely to reporting practices are not relevant to the future prosperity of the firm because they do not represent actual transactions. Hedging a translation exposure should not further the wealth of the shareholders and therefore is not appropriate as expenditure. But this argument critically relies on the semi-strong form of efficient market, namely, that all public information is interpreted in a timely and unbiased manner (i.e. without consistent errors). The company has every chance in the annual report to distinguish translation exposure from other types of exposure. If the market interprets the information correctly and sees that shareholder wealth is not affected, there should indeed be no need to hedge such exposure. Nevertheless, multinationals are perfectly entitled to hedge translation risk. Some companies are very exposed to such risk and may well argue that a failure to protect against such risk may be interpreted as a signal of weakness on the part of management. The consequent fall in share price would affect the wealth of shareholders and therefore justify hedging.

A paper by Bonini *et al.* (2007)[1] found that in a survey of 622 firms 47 per cent actively managed translation risk. Those firms reporting to international rather than national standards showed a greater tendency to manage translation risk as a matter of policy. This is a rather disappointing finding, suggesting that there is a lack of confidence by firms in the market's ability to differentiate between measurement effects and the economic reality.

Use of forward contracts to hedge translation exposure

MNCs can use forward contracts or futures contracts to hedge translation exposure. Specifically, they can sell the currency forward that their foreign subsidiaries receive as earnings. In this way, they create a cash outflow in the currency to offset the earnings received in that currency.

EXAMPLE

Callia SA is a Greek-based MNC with just one subsidiary. As of the beginning of its fiscal year, the subsidiary, which is located in the UK, forecasts that its annual earnings will be £20 million. The subsidiary plans to reinvest the entire amount of earnings within the UK and does not plan to remit any earnings back to the parent in Greece. While there is no foreseeable

transaction exposure in the near future from the future earnings (since the pounds will remain in the UK), Callia is exposed to translation exposure.

In the consolidated profit and loss account, the British earnings will be translated at the weighted average value of the pound over the course of the year. If the British pound is currently worth 1.30 euros and its

(Continued)

---

[1]Bonini, Stefano, Dallocchio, Maurizio, Raimbourg, Philippe and Salvi, Antonio, (2007) Do Firms Hedge Translation Risk? Available at SSRN: http://ssrn.com/abstract=1063781 or http://dx.doi.org/10.2139/ssrn.1063781

value remains constant during the year, the forecasted translation of British earnings into euros would be 26 million euros (computed as £20 million × 1.30 euros per pound).

Callia SA may be concerned that the translated value of the British earnings will be reduced if the pound's value declines during the year. To hedge this translation exposure, Callia can implement a forward hedge using futures contracts on the expected earnings by selling £20 million 1-year forward. Assume the futures rate at that time is 1.30 euros, the same as the spot rate. At the end of the year, if the spot rate has fallen to, say, 1.20 euros to the pound, Callia *will have received* the difference of 0.10 euros × £20m or £200 000 through daily settlement. This amount matches the arbitrage profit on maturity that the Greek company could have made

by buying £20m at the spot rate of 1.20 euros and selling at the higher futures rate of 1.30 euros. If the pound appreciates during the fiscal year, then Callia will have to pay the difference between 1.30 euros and the higher rate. This payment or loss reflects the operation of buying £20m at the above 1.30 euro rate and fulfilling the contract by selling at the lower 1.20 euro rate. In such a case Callia will have incurred a real loss in a failed attempt to save a potential paper loss.

The precise level of income generated by the forward contract will depend on the spot rate of the pound at the end of the fiscal year. Under conditions in which the pound depreciates, the translation loss will be somewhat offset by the gain generated from the forward contract position.

Limitations of hedging translation exposure

There are five limitations in hedging translation exposure.

Inaccurate earnings forecasts. A subsidiary's forecasted earnings for the end of the year are not guaranteed. In the previous example involving Callia SA, British earnings were projected to be £20 million. If the actual earnings turned out to be much higher, and if the pound weakens during the year, the translation loss would likely exceed the gain generated from the forward contract strategy.

Inadequate forward contracts for some currencies. A second limitation is that forward contracts are not available for all currencies. Thus, an MNC with subsidiaries in some smaller countries may not be able to obtain forward contracts for the currencies of concern.

Accounting distortions. A third limitation is that the forward rate gain or loss reflects the difference between the forward rate and the future spot rate, whereas the translation gain or loss reflects the difference between the average exchange rate over the period of concern and the future spot rate. In addition, the translation losses are not tax deductible, whereas gains on forward contracts used to hedge translation exposure are taxed.

Increased transaction exposure. The fourth and most critical limitation with a hedging strategy (forward or money market hedge) on translation exposure is that the MNC may be increasing its transaction exposure. For example, consider a situation in which the subsidiary's currency appreciates during the fiscal year, resulting in a translation gain. If the MNC enacts a hedge strategy that results in losses if the foreign currency appreciates, this strategy will generate a transaction (real) loss that will partly offset the translation gain.

A translation loss is not a real loss. It has already been noted that reporting a loss that is due purely to accounting conventions rather than actual losses should not affect the value of a multinational in an efficient stock market. A translation gain is simply a paper gain arising out of the need to report in one currency. In the Callia example, none of the British pound earnings were translated into the home currency of euros; but an appreciation of the pound would have increased the accounting profits of Callia overall. The appreciation of the pound does affect expectations of future profits, but whether or not one reporting convention is used as opposed to another should not affect the valuation of the company. As actual cash flows are not affected, the value of the company should not be affected in an efficient stock market. Conversely, the loss resulting from a hedge strategy is a *real* loss; that is, the net cash flow to the parent will be reduced due to this loss. Incurring a real loss to avoid a paper loss is not a policy that is actively pursued by multinationals as the extract from accounts given above illustrate.

SUMMARY

- Economic exposure can be managed by balancing the sensitivity of revenue and expenses to exchange rate fluctuations. To accomplish this, however, the firm must first recognize how its revenue and expenses are affected by exchange rate fluctuations. For some firms, revenue is more susceptible. These firms are most concerned that their home currency will appreciate against foreign currencies, since the unfavourable effects on revenue will more than offset the favourable effects on expenses. Conversely, firms whose expenses are more sensitive to exchange rates than their revenue are most concerned that their home currency will depreciate against foreign currencies. When firms reduce their economic exposure, they reduce not only these unfavourable effects but

  also the favourable effects if the home currency value moves in the opposite direction.

- Translation exposure can be reduced by selling forward the foreign currency used to measure a subsidiary's income. If the foreign currency depreciates against the home currency, the adverse impact on the consolidated income statement can be offset by the gain on the forward sale in that currency. If the foreign currency appreciates over the time period of concern, there will be a loss on the forward sale that is offset by a favourable effect on the reported consolidated earnings. However, many MNCs would not be satisfied with a 'paper gain' that offsets a 'cash loss'.

CRITICAL DEBATE

Should an MNC reduce expected profits by hedging as in the Mannerton example in order to limit losses in less likely scenarios?

Proposition. Yes. Extreme losses will disrupt the running of the company and put future earnings in jeopardy. By protecting against such losses the company is protecting shareholders' long-term interests.

Opposing view. No. Investors know the risk. Part of the reason for investing in a multinational is to benefit from the exchange rate risk. If a company hedges against such risk, they are only protecting themselves at the expense of the shareholders.

With whom do you agree? Which argument do you support? Offer your own opinion on this issue.

SELF TEST

Answers are provided in Appendix A at the back of the text.

1 Salem Exporting Ltd (UK) purchases chemicals from UK sources and uses them to make pharmaceutical products that are exported to US hospitals. Salem

prices its products in dollars and is concerned about the possibility of the long-term depreciation of the dollar against the pound. It periodically hedges its exposure with short-term forward contracts, but this does not insulate against the possible trend of continuing dollar depreciation. How could Salem offset some of its exposure resulting from its export business?

2 Using the information in question 1, give a possible disadvantage of offsetting exchange rate exposure from the export business.

3 Neve NV is a Dutch firm with a subsidiary in the USA. It expects that the dollar will depreciate this year. Explain Neve's translation exposure. How could Neve hedge its translation exposure?

4 Cheriton plc has substantial translation exposure in US subsidiaries. The treasurer of Cheriton plc suggests that the translation effects are not relevant because the earnings generated by the US subsidia-ries are not being remitted to the UK parent, but are simply being reinvested in the USA. Nevertheless, the director of finance of Cheriton plc is concerned about translation exposure because the stock price is highly dependent on the consolidated earnings, which are dependent on the exchange rates at which the earnings are translated. Who is correct?

5 Lincolnshire Ltd manufactures wholly in the UK and exports 80 per cent of its total production to Latin America. Kalafa Ltd sells all the goods it produces to Latin America, but it has a subsidiary in Spain that usually generates about 20 per cent of its total earn-ings. Compare the translation exposure of these two UK firms.

QUESTIONS AND APPLICATIONS

1 **Reducing economic exposure.** Banter plc is an Irish based MNC that obtains 10 per cent of its sup-plies from US manufacturers. Of its revenues, 60 per cent are due to exports to the USA, where its prod-uct is invoiced in dollars. Explain how Banter can attempt to reduce its economic exposure to exchange rate fluctuations in the dollar.

2 **Reducing economic exposure.** UVA Ltd is a UK-based MNC that obtains 40 per cent of its foreign supplies from Thailand. It also borrows Thailand's currency (the baht) from Thai banks and converts the baht to pounds to support UK operations. It currently receives about 10 per cent of its revenue from Thai customers. Its sales to Thai customers are denomi-nated in baht. Explain how UVA Ltd can reduce its economic exposure to exchange rate fluctuations.

3 **Reducing economic exposure.** Alright Ltd is a UK-based MNC that has a large government con-tract with Australia. The contract will continue for sev-eral years and generate more than half of Albany's total sales volume. The Australian government pays Albany in Australian dollars. About 10 per cent of Albany's operating expenses are in Australian dollars; all other expenses are in pounds. Explain how Alright can reduce its economic exposure to exchange rate fluctuations.

4 **Trade-offs when reducing economic exposure.** When an MNC restructures its operations to reduce its economic exposure, it may sometimes forgo economies of scale. Explain.

5 **Exchange rate effects on earnings.** Explain how an MNC's consolidated earnings are affected when foreign currencies depreciate.

6 **Hedging translation exposure.** Explain how a firm can hedge its translation exposure.

7 **Limitations of hedging translation exposure.** Bartunek Co. is a US-based MNC that has European subsidiaries and wants to hedge its translation expo-sure to fluctuations in the euro's value. Explain some limitations when it hedges translation exposure.

8 **Effective hedging of translation exposure.** Would a more established MNC or a less established MNC be better able to effectively hedge its given level of translation exposure? Why?

9 **Comparing degrees of economic exposure.** Carlton Ltd and Palmer Ltd are UK-based MNCs with subsidiaries in Brazil that distribute medical sup-plies (produced in the UK) to customers throughout Latin America. Both subsidiaries purchase the prod-ucts at cost and sell the products at 90 per cent mark-up. The other operating costs of the subsidia-ries are very low.

Carlton has a research and development centre in the UK that focuses on improving its medical technol-ogy. Palmer has a similar centre based in Brazil. The parent of each firm subsidizes its respective research and development centre on an annual basis. Which firm is subject to a higher degree of economic expo-sure? Explain.

10 **Comparing degrees of translation exposure.**
Nelson Ltd is a UK firm with annual export sales to
Singapore of about £20 million. Its main competitor is
Hamilton Ltd, also based in the UK, with a subsidiary
in Singapore that also generates about £20 million in
annual sales. Any earnings generated by the subsidiary are reinvested to support its operations.

Based on the information provided, which firm is
subject to a higher degree of translation exposure?
Explain.

ADVANCED QUESTIONS

11 **Managing economic exposure.** St Paul Ltd (a UK
company) does business in the UK and New Zealand. In attempting to assess its economic exposure,
it compiled the following information.

a St Paul's UK sales are somewhat affected by the
value of the New Zealand dollar (NZ$), because it
faces competition from New Zealand exporters. It
forecasts the UK sales based on the following
three exchange rate scenarios:

Exchange rate of NZ$	Revenue from UK business (in millions)
NZ$ = £0.32	£100
NZ$ = 0.33	£105
NZ$ = 0.36	£110

b Its New Zealand dollar revenues on sales to New
Zealand invoiced in New Zealand dollars are
expected to be NZ$600 million.

c Its anticipated cost of goods sold is estimated at
£200 million from the purchase of UK materials
and NZ$100 million from the purchase of New
Zealand materials.

d Fixed operating expenses are estimated at £30
million.

e Variable operating expenses are approximated
as 20 per cent of total sales (after including New
Zealand sales, translated to a pound amount).

f Interest expense is estimated at £20 million
on existing UK loans, and the company has no
existing New Zealand loans.

Create a forecasted income statement for St Paul
under each of the three exchange rate scenarios.
Explain how St Paul's projected earnings before
taxes are affected by possible exchange rate movements. Explain how it can restructure its operations
to reduce the sensitivity of its earnings to exchange
rate movements without reducing its volume of business in New Zealand.

12 **Assessing economic exposure.** Alhambra plc
plans to create and finance a subsidiary in Argentina
that produces computer components at a low cost
and exports them to other countries. It has no other
international business. The subsidiary will produce
computers and export them to Africa and will invoice
the products in pounds. The values of the currencies
in Africa are expected to remain very stable against
the pound. The subsidiary will pay wages, rent and
other operating costs in Argentine pesos. The subsidiary will remit earnings monthly to the parent.

a Would Alhambra's cash flows be favourably or
unfavourably affected if the Argentine peso
depreciates over time?

b Assume that Alhambra considers partial financing
of this subsidiary with peso loans from Argentine
banks instead of providing all the financing with
its own funds. Would this alternative form of
financing increase, decrease or have no effect on
the degree to which Alhambra is exposed to
exchange rate movements of the peso?

13 **Hedging continual exposure.** Consider this
common real-world dilemma faced by many firms
that rely on exporting. Clearlake Ltd produces its
products in its factory in the UK and exports most of
the products to Europe each month. The exports are
denominated in euros. Clearlake recognizes that
hedging on a monthly basis does not really protect
against long-term movements in exchange rates. It
also recognizes that it could eliminate its transaction
exposure by denominating the exports in British
pounds, but that it still would have economic exposure because European consumers would reduce
demand if the euro weakened. Clearlake does not
know how many euros it will receive in the future, so
it would have difficulty even if a long-term hedging
method were available. How can Clearlake realistically deal with this dilemma and reduce its exposure
over the long term? (There is no perfect solution, but
in the real world, there rarely are perfect solutions.)

PROJECT WORKSHOP

14 Researching MNCs and exposure. The following website provides annual reports of numerous MNCs: http://reportgallery.com. You may also access annual reports via the FT website http://www.ft.com and international reports via http://www.forbes.com choosing lists.

a   Review an annual report of an MNC of your choice. Look for any comments that relate to the MNC's economic or translation exposure. Does it appear that the MNC hedges its economic exposure or translation exposure? If so, what methods does it use to hedge its exposure?

b   The following website provides exchange rate movements between currencies over time http://www.oanda.com.

Based on the translation exposure of the MNC you assessed in exercise (a), determine whether the exchange rate movements of whatever currency (or currencies) it is exposed to moved in a favourable or unfavourable direction over the reporting period.

Further notes: search the annual reports using the keyword 'risk'. You will find the MNC's policy on currency risk. Fuller details are given by the major multinationals. These can include: estimates of the sensitivity of profits to a 1 per cent currency change; derivative returns from currency change; the main types of hedging used and principal type of exposure. Do not just report their calculations; make your own estimates from the data provided.

DISCUSSION IN THE BOARDROOM

This exercise can be found on our dedicated Course-Mate platform for students.

RUNNING YOUR OWN MNC

This exercise can be found on our dedicated Course-Mate platform for students.

Essays/discussion and articles can be found at the end of Part III.

BLADES PLC CASE STUDY

Assessment of economic exposure

Blades plc has been exporting to Thailand since its decision to supplement its declining UK sales by exporting there. Furthermore, Blades has recently begun exporting to a retailer in the USA. The suppliers of the components needed by Blades for roller blade production (such as rubber and plastic) are located in the UK and Thailand. Blades decided to use Thai suppliers for rubber and plastic components needed to manufacture roller blades because of cost and quality considerations. All of Blades' exports and imports are denominated in the respective foreign currency; for example, Blades pays for the Thai imports in baht.

The decision to export to Thailand was supported by the fact that Thailand had been one of the world's fastest growing economies in recent years. Furthermore, Blades found an importer in Thailand that was willing to commit itself to the annual purchase of 180 000 pairs of Blades' 'Speedos', which are among the highest quality roller blades in the world. The commitment began last year and will last another 2 years, at which time it may be renewed by the two parties. Due to this commitment, Blades is selling its roller blades for 4594 baht per pair (approximately £60 at current exchange rates) instead of the usual £72 per pair. Although this price represents a substantial discount from the regular price for a pair of Speedo blades, it still constitutes a considerable mark-up above cost. Because importers in other Asian countries were not willing to make this type of commitment, this was a decisive factor in the choice of Thailand for exporting purposes. Although Ben Holt, Blades' financial director, believes the sports product market in Asia has very high future growth potential, Blades has recently begun exporting to Jogs Ltd, a US retailer. Jogs has committed itself to purchase 200 000 pair of Speedos annually for a fixed price of $80 per pair.

For the coming year, Blades expects to import rubber and plastic components from Thailand sufficient to manufacture 80 000 pairs of Speedos, at a cost of approximately 3000 baht per pair of Speedos.

You, as Blades' financial analyst, have pointed out to Ben Holt that events in Asia have fundamentally affected the economic condition of Asian countries, including Thailand. For example, you have pointed out that the high level of consumer spending on leisure products such as roller blades has declined considerably. Thus, the Thai retailer may not renew its commitment with Blades in 2 years. Furthermore, you are worried that the current economic conditions in Thailand may lead to a substantial depreciation of the Thai baht, which would affect Blades negatively.

Despite recent developments, however, Ben Holt remains optimistic; he is convinced that South East Asia will exhibit high potential for growth when the impact of recent events in Asia subsides. Consequently, Holt has no doubt that the Thai customer will renew its commitment for another 3 years when the current agreement terminates. In your opinion, Holt is not considering all of the factors that might directly or indirectly affect Blades. Moreover, you are worried that he is ignoring Blades' future in Thailand even if the Thai importer renews its commitment for another 3 years. In fact, you believe that a renewal of the existing agreement with the Thai customer may affect Blades negatively due to the high level of inflation in Thailand.

Since Holt is interested in your opinion and wants to assess Blades' economic exposure in Thailand, he has asked you to conduct an analysis of the impact of the value of the baht on next year's earnings to assess Blades' economic exposure. You have gathered the following information:

- Blades has forecasted sales in the UK of 520 000 pairs of Speedos at regular prices; exports to Thailand of 180 000 pairs of Speedos for 4594 baht a pair; and exports to the USA of 200 000 pairs of Speedos for $80 per pair.

- Cost of goods sold for 80 000 pairs of Speedos are incurred in Thailand; the remainder is incurred in the USA, where the cost of goods sold per pair of Speedos runs to approximately £70.

- Fixed costs are £2 million, and variable operating expenses other than costs of goods sold represent approximately 11 per cent of UK sales. All fixed and variable operating expenses other than cost of goods sold are incurred in the USA.

- Events in Asia have increased the uncertainty regarding certain Asian currencies considerably, making it extremely difficult to forecast the value of the baht at which the Thai revenues will be converted. The current spot rate of the baht is £0.0147, and the current spot rate of the dollar is £0.67. You have created three scenarios and derived an expected value on average for the upcoming year based on each scenario:

Scenario	Effect on the average value of the baht	Average value of the baht	Average value of the dollar
1	No change	£0.015	£0.654
2	Depreciate by 5 per cent	£0.01425	0.6213
3	Depreciate by 10 per cent	£0.0135	£0.5886

● Blades currently has no debt in its capital structure. However, it may borrow funds in Thailand if it establishes a subsidiary in the country.

Ben Holt has asked you to answer the following questions:

1 How will Blades be negatively affected by the high level of inflation in Thailand if the Thai customer renews its commitment for another 3 years?

2 Holt believes that the Thai importer will renew its commitment in 2 years. Do you think his assessment is correct? Why or why not? Also, assume that the Thai economy returns to the high growth level that existed prior to the recent unfavourable economic events. Under this assumption, how likely is it that the Thai importer will renew its commitment in 2 years?

3 For each of the three possible values of the Thai baht and the dollar, use a spreadsheet to construct a *pro forma* income statement for the next year. Briefly comment on the level of Blades' economic exposure.

4 Now repeat your analysis in question 3 but assume that the US dollar and the Thai baht are perfectly correlated. For example, if the baht depreciates by 5 per cent, the dollar will also depreciate by 5 per cent. Under this assumption, is Blades subject to a greater degree of economic exposure? Why or why not?

5 Based on your answers to the previous three questions, what actions could Blades take to reduce its level of economic exposure to Thailand?

SMALL BUSINESS DILEMMA

Hedging the Sports Exports Company's economic exposure to exchange rate risk

Jim Logan, owner of the Sports Exports Company (Ireland), remains concerned about his exposure to exchange rate risk. Even if Jim hedges his transactions from one month to another, he recognizes that a long-term trend of depreciation in the British pound could have a severe impact on his firm. He believes that he must continue to focus on the British market for selling his basketballs. However, he plans to consider various ways in which he can reduce his economic exposure. At the current time, he obtains material from a local manufacturer and uses a machine to produce the basketballs, which are then exported. He still uses his garage as a place of production and would like to continue using his garage to maintain low operating expenses.

1 How could Jim adjust his operations to reduce his economic exposure? What is a possible disadvantage of such an adjustment?

2 Offer another solution to hedging the economic exposure in the long run as Jim's business grows. What are the disadvantages of this solution?

PART 3 Integrative problem

EXCHANGE RATE RISK MANAGEMENT

Vogel Ltd is a UK firm conducting a financial plan for the next year. It has no foreign subsidiaries, but more than half of its sales are from exports. Its foreign cash inflows to be received from exporting and cash outflows to be paid for imported supplies over the next year are shown in the following table:

Currency	Total inflow	Total outflow
Canadian dollar (C$)	C$32 000 000	C$2 000 000
New Zealand dollar (NZ$)	NZ$5 000 000	NZ$1 000 000
Mexican peso (MXP)	MXP11 000 000	MXP10 000 000
Singapore dollar (S$)	S$4 000 000	S$8 000 000

The spot rates and 1-year forward rates as of today are shown below:

Currency	Spot rate	1-Year forward rate
C$	£0.60	£0.63
NZ$	0.40	0.39
MXP	0.14	0.12
S$	0.42	0.41

Questions

1 Based on the information provided, determine Vogel's net exposure to each foreign currency in dollars.

2 Assume that today's spot rate is used as a forecast of the future spot rate 1 year from now. The New Zealand dollar, Mexican peso and Singapore dollar are expected to move in tandem against the British pound over the next year. The Canadian dollar's movements are expected to be unrelated to movements of the other currencies. Since exchange rates are difficult to predict, the forecasted net pound cash flows per currency may be inaccurate. Do you anticipate any offsetting exchange rate effects from whatever exchange movements do occur? Explain.

3 Given the forecast of the Canadian dollar along with the forward rate of the Canadian dollar, what is the expected increase or decrease in pound cash flows that would result from hedging the net cash flows in Canadian dollars? Would you hedge the Canadian dollar position?

4 Assume that the Canadian dollar net inflows may range from C$20 000 000 to C$40 000 000 over the next year. Explain the risk of hedging C$30 000 000 in net inflows. How can Vogel Ltd avoid such a risk? Is there any trade-off resulting from your strategy to avoid that risk?

5 Vogel recognizes that its year-to-year hedging strategy hedges the risk only over a given year and does not insulate it from long-term trends in the Canadian dollar's value. It has considered establishing a subsidiary in Canada. The goods would be sent from the UK to the Canadian subsidiary and distributed by the subsidiary. The proceeds received would be reinvested by the Canadian subsidiary in Canada. In this way, Vogel would not have to convert Canadian dollars to pounds each year. Has Vogel eliminated its exposure to exchange rate risk by using this strategy? Explain.

PART 3 Essays/discussion and academic articles

1 Bodnar, G.M. (1999) 'Derivative Usage in Risk Management by US and German Non Financial Firms', *Journal of International Financial Management and Accounting*, 10, (3), 153–87.

Q *Describe the usage of derivatives by US and German firms. Discuss possible trends in Europe; will usage inevitably become more like the US model?*

2 Dominguez, K.M.E. and Tesar, L.L. (2006) 'Exchange Rate Exposure', *Journal of International Economics,* 68, 188–218. Some relatively simple regression analysis looking at MNC valuation and exchange rates.

Q *What can be learned from the Dominguez and Tesar article that can be of practical use to a Finance Director of an MNC? Discuss.*

3 Dhanani, A. (2003) 'Foreign Exchange Risk Management: A Case in the Mining Industry', *British Accounting Review,* 35, 35–63. An excellent review and case study.

Q *Evaluate the way in which the exchange rate risk management of ABC plc in the mining industry (as described by Dhanani) differs from the exchange rate risk management of other multinationals. More generally, how important are the activities of multinationals in determining exchange rate risk policy?*

4 Solomon, J.F. (1999) 'Do Institutional Investors in the UK Adopt a Dual Strategy for Managing Foreign Exchange Risk', *British Accounting Review,* 31, 205–24. This is, in fact, an excellent survey of the factors influencing foreign investment.

Q *Combine the survey results in Solomon's article to produce an overall description of the factors influencing portfolio investment. Assess the extent to which practice differs from theory.*

5 Dhanani, A. and Groves, R. (2001) 'The Management of Strategic Exchange Risk: Evidence from Corporate Practices', *Accounting and Business Research*, 31 (4), 275–90.

Q *From a reading of the Dhanani and Groves article, discuss the organizational issues involved in managing exchange rate risk.*

6 Makar, S.D, J. de Bruin and Huffman, S.P. (1999) 'The Management of Foreign Currency Risk: Derivatives Use and the Natural Hedge of Geographic Diversification', *Accounting & Business Research,* 29 (3), 229–37.

Q *Explain the hypothesis advanced by Makar et al. concerning the use of derivatives. Assess the strength of their findings.*

7 Bonini, Stefano, Dallocchio, Maurizio, Raimbourg, Philippe and Salvi, Antonio, Do Firms Hedge Translation Risk? (latest revision March 30, 2012). Available at SSRN: http://ssrn.com/abstract=1063781 or http://dx.doi.org/10.2139/ssrn.1063781

Q *Evaluate the arguments for and against hedging translation exposure, is it a waste of shareholders' funds?*

PART IV
LONG-TERM ASSET AND LIABILITY MANAGEMENT

PART 4 (Chapters 13–16) focuses on how multinational corporations (MNCs) manage long-term assets and liabilities. International investments face a much higher degree of political, economic and regulatory risk than domestic investments. Chapter 13 examines the problem of valuing such investments. Chapter 14 describes how the political and regulatory risk can be measured and managed. Chapter 15 addresses the problem of long term international finance. Finally, Chapter 16 discusses the ethical dimension of investment and its financial implications.

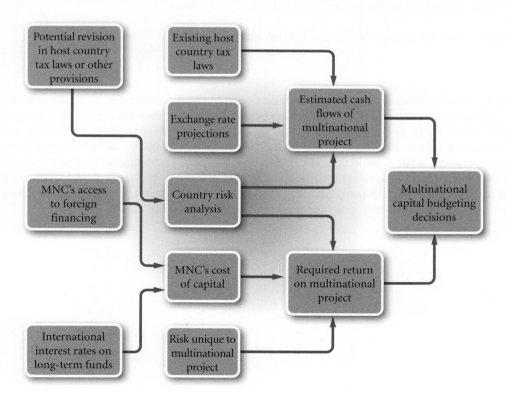

CHAPTER 13
FOREIGN DIRECT
INVESTMENT

LEARNING OBJECTIVES

The specific objectives of this chapter are to:

● Describe models of investment appraisal in an international context.

● Describe common motives for initiating foreign direct investment.

● Examine relations between host governments and multinational companies.

● Illustrate the theoretical and empirical effects of international diversification.

Multinational corporations (MNCs) commonly capitalize on foreign business opportunities by engaging in foreign direct investment (FDI), which is investment in real assets (such as land, buildings or even existing plants) in foreign countries. They engage in joint ventures with foreign firms, acquire foreign firms and form new foreign subsidiaries. Any of these types of FDI (usually defined as involving at least a 10 per cent ownership interest in a legally recognized foreign entity) can generate high returns when managed properly. However, FDI requires a substantial investment and can therefore put much capital at risk. Given these return and risk characteristics of FDI, MNCs need to carefully analyze the potential benefits and costs before implementing any type of FDI. Financial managers must understand the potential return and risk associated with FDI so that they can make investment decisions that maximize the MNC's value.

INVESTMENT APPRAISAL – THE MODERN APPROACH

The modern approach to investment appraisal is of particular importance to international financial management. The broader scope that this approach offers explains better the very rich and complex environment of international investment.

For many years the net present value model was regarded as the only method of investment appraisal. Assessing projects by estimating the expected cash flows and discounting them to the present produced a valuation that represented the value of the investment to the company.

Then in the 1970s following the growth of the financial options market (see Chapter 5) it was realized that investments could include options in the form of decisions that are only made if the investment outcome gets to a certain level. For example, if the investment were successful the firm could consider a takeover of a company in the same area. It was realized that these and other options, including the option to delay, were not part of the net present value (NPV) calculation and needed to be added. Although options can be valued very precisely in the financial markets, the same is not true of the real investment 'market'. Input values in particular are very much more difficult to establish. A looser approach of 'options thinking' has been advocated in an attempt to maintain in the overall valuation process the important possibilities offered by options.

In the 1990s following the huge increase in the game theory literature a number of academics pointed out that existing investment valuation models, based on NPV and options, did not account for the reaction of competitors to an investment (the essence of a 'game'). More generally, game theory analysis includes the reaction of any party to an investment, not just a competitor and in an international context the reaction of the local host government. The inclusion of game theory has been more difficult, in part, because it is a very different form of analysis compared to options and NPV. However, even if game theory does not provide direct valuations, it is nevertheless an important critique of any investment valuation, particularly in an international context.

Taken together options and game theory change investment valuation from a relatively clear well defined process to a far more subjective and uncertain exercise. This is probably a good development as many surveys over the years confirm that in practice companies use many measures of investment and refuse to confine themselves to just using NPV. The practicing businessman, one suspects, is likely to be far more comfortable with a valuation model that includes possibilities (options) that are dependent on outcomes and the reaction of competitors and governments.

Net present value

The NPV model uses the equations of borrowing and lending and applies them to investment projects. Thus a project is seen as an initial investment (outflow) followed by a series of cash inflows in the same way as investing in a bond or an interest bearing deposit account. Valuation uses the actuarial equation as follows:

$$NPV = -IO + \left(\sum_{t=1}^{n} \frac{CF_t}{(1+k)^t} \right) + \frac{SV_n}{(1+k)^n}$$

Where:

NPV = net present value
IO = initial outlay (investment)
CF_t = cash flow in period t
k = required rate of return on the project
n = lifetime of the project (number of periods)
SV = Salvage Value = terminal value

EXAMPLE

Stumble Ltd estimate the following cash flows for project X in £s '000:

Now	Year 1	Year 2	Year 3	Year 4	Year 5
−800	400	500	600	200	100

Using the NPV model and a discount rate or required rate of return of 14 per cent the financial manager for Stumble estimates the NPV to be:

$$\text{NPV } 511 = -800 + \frac{400}{(1.14)} + \frac{500}{(1.14)^2} + \frac{600}{(1.14)^3} + \frac{200}{(1.14)^4} + \frac{100}{(1.14)^5}$$

Not only will the company get a 14 per cent return on its investment but it will be better off by £511 000 if it undertakes this project. If Stumble were to sell the investment, it should be paid £511 000.

Of course, it is recognized that the cash flows are only estimates and that they could be higher or lower than originally planned. How much higher or lower defines the risk of the project and affects the required rate of return – the higher the risk, the higher the required rate of return. In the more refined Capital Asset Pricing Model risk is defined relative to the market return but the risk return relationship is the same. The higher the relative market risk the higher the required return.

Once established, risk is often treated as constant over the years of the investment, why is this so? Consider the price or value of the investment as finding a pathway through the lattice structure in Exhibit 13.1. At each node there is a 50:50 chance of the value of the investment either going up by x per cent of going down by x per cent. The size of x per cent depends as indicated earlier on the risk of the investment. Suppose that nodes 2 and 3 represent increases and decreases respectively of 10 per cent on the original valuation at node 1. From node 2 or node 3 the prospect can be the same, a 10 per cent increase or decrease. All other nodes can have a risk that is the same, a 10 per cent increase or decrease. Therefore, the discount rate for those other periods can be the same. Rates can of course change over time, so the prospect from nodes 2 and 3 may be of a larger change and hence risk than from nodes 4, 5 and 6. The important point is that the rate may change over time but does not depend in this model on the actual level at a point in time, i.e. whether it is 4, 5 or 6.

Although this lattice diagram is implied but not strictly needed for the NPV model, it turns out to be useful for the two developments of real options and game theory.

Real options

The real options approach considers what can be done to improve the value of the investment *if* it reaches any particular node – a contingent plan. For example if the investment value reaches node 4 the investor could consider carrying out the same project in another country; if the investment value falls to node 6, the project could be abandoned. These decisions are distinct from the operational decisions required for returns to move from, say, 5 to 8 on good news or 3 to 6 on bad news.

A decision that occurs at node 1 is not to undertake the project. If the conditions that would give rise to node 2 arise then invest but if conditions are such that after the first period the value of the investment has fallen to 3 and the prospects are of either 5 or 6 then do not even start the project.

These post investment potential decisions destroy the neat symmetry of the lattice structure. Abandoning at 6 will mean that 10 will not be reached. This will be an important consideration at node 3 but will not be of any value should the investment reach node 2.

EXHIBIT 13.1   The lattice diagram of price movement over time

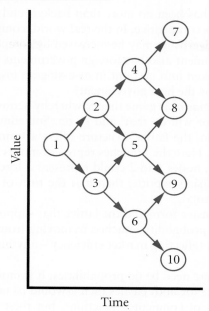

The option pricing model offers a means of valuing these possibilities. Unfortunately, the input requirements to the model are difficult to estimate even subjectively and the real world situations it seeks to model are often a complex multiple of options. Nevertheless, this does not mean that the value of such options should be ignored and for this reason options thinking is seen as a way of including post investment decisions that are contingent on outcomes.

EXAMPLE

Really Ltd is considering an investment of £5m with an expected return of £8m per year for the foreseeable future but with a standard deviation of £6m. This is deemed to be highly risky and the directors think that a return of 40 per cent is required. The valuation of such a project is (£8m / 0.40) – £5m = £15m using the perpetuity formula.[1]

The financial manager points out that the project is not that risky with the inclusion of an option. He explains that one option would be to wait and if after 6 months conditions seemed to be more in favour of the investment the chances of an adverse outcome would

be greatly reduced. The director argues that in 6-months time much of the competitive advantage would be lost and the returns greatly reduced.

As an alternative, the financial manager argues that the project could go ahead now at a slightly greater cost due to contracts that would enable Really to exercise the option to terminate the project should the conditions deteriorate.

The director agrees with this suggestion. The NPV shows enough potential profit to allow for the purchase of what is in effect a real option to abandon the project in its early stages.

[1] The formula for the present value of a constant cash flow in perpetuity is CF_t / i (where CF is cash flow and i is interest) so in this case it is £8m / 0.40 = £20m.

Game theory and strategy

For NPV and options, competition has been no more than background noise. It is the reason why returns are not higher, because the market is competitive. In the real world, competition may be reactive to the outcome of a particular investment. Advertising may be increased by competitors, prices cut, similar products launched. The international environment also has foreign governments reacting to the actions of multinational companies. This has to be taken into account in assessing an investment, how will the competition react, what actions might be taken by the host government?

The model for analyzing such scenarios is game theory whereby action is mapped against reaction, 'if we do this, the government / competitor will do that' and so on. Sometimes the term strategy is used which implies a game type scenario. Again, the lattice structure offers a framework for analyzing such 'moves' known as a game in extensive form. Here the branches represent moves by the 'players'. Referring again to the lattice structure of Exhibit 13.1, nodes 1 to 2 could represent a foreign investment by a multinational, and 1 to 3 the alternative of increasing exports; then it is the turn of the government which may be to encourage (2 to 4) or discourage (2 to 5).

The link between a game in extensive form and the lattice that supports NPV and real options differs in two important respects. Firstly, the probability attached to moving from one node to the other in the NPV and real option model is 50 per cent reflecting market efficiency – anything different would create a pattern, a greater tendency to rise or fall.

In the game theory approach, there need be no probabilities. It is more in the nature of an investigation. If there is a mutually beneficial route for both parties then it would be taken barring mistakes. Probabilities may be used to reflect the chances of competitor reactions; but these probabilities are really degrees of belief and have no particular distribution. Often there are no probabilities attached and it is simply a case of 'if I do this, he will do that' as in a game of chess. This game or competitive element considerably obscures the original rather neat and tidy analysis using NPV.

EXAMPLE

Really2 Ltd is considering investing in a gold mining concession in Nigeria. The financial manager uses the NPV model to work out that the present value of the concession is about £50m though with different assumptions about the price of gold, the value could rise to as much as £70m.

The director responds that the real uncertainty is not the price of gold, but whether or not a rival mining company puts in a bid for the concession. It knows that we can only bid for one concession whereas the rival can bid for all three that are coming up in the next 6 months. If it outbids us on every concession, it may end up paying far more than if it lets us win the first of the next three in the knowledge that we will then not compete for the other two.

NPV is useful in letting Really2 know the sensible range in which to bid but the profitability of the concession depends more on the bidding strategy of its main rival than the price of gold.

EXAMPLE

Foodico plc has an international chain of supermarkets. A rival company, Eatmore plc has recently started to develop a chain of stores in country X where Foodico is dominant. The directors of Foodico are

(Continued)

considering whether or not to resist the move by having a local price war or to do nothing and acquiesce in the move. NPV calculations show that resisting would be much more expensive than acquiescing.

The directors decide to resist the move and start a local price war. They explain their actions as follows: It may be much cheaper for us to acquiesce but if we send out the message that we will not resist then the same is likely to happen at our other stores across the world. If we acquiesce in every case it will be very expensive, far better to resist and lose money in one country and deter competition in the other countries than to lose less on a store by store basis but lose more overall as the competition spreads.

This is an adaptation of what is known as the supermarket game and highlights the importance of understanding the full consequences of any one investment project, in particular, the need for a project to be consistent with a strategic policy.

A combined view

The three models of investment appraisal each represent important aspects of an investment. The NPV model values the basic proposal without any elaboration against a largely unresponsive market environment. The real options approach adds possibilities and contingent plans to exploit or avert outcomes creating something of a strategy – that is a course of action for each outcome. The game theory approach considers direct responses to the outcomes of a particular investment, how will governments react, how will competitors react?

For certain valuation problems, the NPV model may well be sufficient. In valuing a company, *overall* competitor reaction to its value may be very limited and contingent actions again not of great significance. By contrast, projects that make up the company may experience fierce competition and have to implement important market based strategies – the use of options. In the case of foreign direct investment, the relations with the host government may be the dominant influence – the game theory model. Here, the precise valuation of the project may be the lesser factor. It may seem odd that at the company level competition may not be a significant factor, whereas at project level it is significant in certain cases. All one can point to is a certain offsetting effect and differences in the nature of various projects.

In sum, there is no fixed relationship between the models and hence no overall valuation model. How to combine any two is not at all clear and even valuation for options and game based models on their own is unclear. Given such uncertainty, NPV has the undoubted merit of offering a starting point to the valuation process. Including options and game theory can be seen as a development in that critical opportunities (options) and reactions (games) are identified and serve to modify the original valuation. The end result is nevertheless largely a matter of subjective judgement. More theoretical development is required. Exhibit 13.2 shows the relationship between the models.

EXHIBIT 13.2 **A classification of decision models**

	Only consider the investment decision: invest or do not invest *now*	Decisions after initial investment decision (including delay)
Assuming no reaction from competitors and governments	NPV	NPV + Real options
Including reaction from competitors and governments	NPV + Strategy / Game Theory	NPV + Real options + Game Theory / Strategy

MOTIVES FOR FOREIGN DIRECT INVESTMENT

MNCs commonly consider foreign direct investment because it can improve their profitability and enhance shareholder wealth. In most cases, MNCs engage in FDI because they are interested in boosting revenues, reducing costs or both. The following list is adapted from Dunning's eclectic model of internationalisation.

Firm specific advantages

These are motives to invest abroad to protect and develop specific advantages of a company.

- Proprietary technology – the company has a particular set of patents that it seeks to exploit by taking its business abroad.

- Managerial/ marketing skills – the company makes a profit by taking over other companies and running them using their management and marketing skills. Eventually those companies will be from abroad.

- Trademarks – the company seeks to promote its brand in competition with other brands that are international and inevitably an international image is required.

- Economies of scale – only by selling on the world market can a profit be made due to large capital requirements.

Internalization advantages

These are advantages to having a presence abroad rather than merely exporting or franchising an operation.

- High enforcement costs – a weak legal structure may mean that a physical presence abroad is required to ensure that the company's wishes are carried out.

- Buyer uncertainty over value – if buyers are uncertain over the value of a product then the company may have to carry out at least the sales and marketing operation in that country by investing directly abroad.

- Need to control production. Some items such as food and drink are not easily exported and need to be produced in a manner that cannot be easily replicated.

Country specific advantages

- Natural resources – exploitation of natural resources necessarily requires a foreign presence.

- Technology – countries may develop expertise in certain production or service industries that can only be exploited by being physically close to such sources.

- Labour force – cheap labour may represent a significant cost saving.

- Tax – some countries have particularly low tax regimes and can be part of an overall strategy to minimize tax payments.

- Trade barriers – to avoid restrictions on exports it may be better to produce in the country concerned. Investment by multinationals in the European Union (EU) is sometimes cited as evidence of the effect of restrictions on international trade.

MANAGING FOR VALUE

Japanese automobile manufacturers (notably Toyota and Honda) established plants in the UK in anticipation that their exports to the EU would be subject to more stringent trade restrictions. Japanese companies recognized that trade barriers could be established that would limit or prohibit their exports. By producing automobiles in the UK, Japanese manufacturers could avoid such trade barriers.

MANAGING FOR VALUE

The removal of trade barriers within the EU by the Single European Act allowed MNCs to achieve greater economies of scale. Some US-based MNCs consolidated their European plants because the removal of tariffs between countries in the EU enabled firms to achieve economies of scale at a single European plant without incurring excessive exporting costs. The act also enhanced economies of scale by making regulations on television ads, automobile standards and other products and services uniform across the EU. As a result, Colgate-Palmolive Co. and other MNCs are manufacturing more homogeneous products that can be sold in all EU countries. The adoption of the euro also encouraged consolidation by eliminating exchange rate risk within these countries.

Use foreign factors of production. Labour and land costs can vary dramatically among countries. MNCs often attempt to set up production in locations where land and labour are cheap. Due to market imperfections (as discussed in Chapter 1) such as imperfect information, relocation transaction costs, and barriers to industry entry, specific labour costs do not necessarily become equal among markets. Thus, it is worthwhile for MNCs to survey markets to determine whether they can benefit from cheaper costs by producing in those markets.

MANAGING FOR VALUE

Many MNCs have established subsidiaries in Mexico to achieve lower labour costs. Mexico has attracted almost $5 billion in FDI from firms in the automobile industry, primarily because of the low-cost labour. Mexican workers at General Motors' subsidiaries who manufacture estates and trucks earn daily wages that are less than the average hourly rate for similar workers in the UK. Ford is also producing trucks at subsidiaries based in Mexico.

Volkswagen produces its Beetle in Mexico. DaimlerChrysler manufactures its 12-wheeler trucks in Mexico and Nissan Motor Co. of Japan produces some of its wagons in Mexico.

Other Japanese companies are also increasingly using Mexico and other low-wage countries for production. For example, Sony Corp. recently established a plant in Tijuana. Matsushita Electrical Industrial Co. has a large plant in Tijuana.

MANAGING FOR VALUE

General Motors (Vauxhall and Opel) expanded its production in Poland, Peugeot increased its production in the Czech Republic, Toyota expanded its production in Slovakia, Audi expanded in Hungary and Renault expanded in Romania. Volkswagen expanded its capacity in Slovenia, and cut jobs in Spain. While it originally established operations in Spain because the wages were about half of those in Germany, wages in Slovenia are less than half of those in Spain. Peugeot has also moved production from the UK to Eastern Europe. The expansion of the EU allows new member countries to transport products throughout Europe at reduced tariffs.

USING THE WEB

Foreign direct investment indicators

Visit Morgan Stanley's Global Economic Forum for analyses, discussions, statistics and forecasts related to non-US economies at: http://www.morganstanley.com/ by searching for 'FDI' on the internal search engine.

USING THE WEB

Also, visit http://www.imf.org and click on 'country info', and http://www.worldbank.org and click on 'countries'.

EXAMPLE

Plymouth Ltd, a large clothing manufacturer, is thinking of producing clothes in Country X. The company determines that the direct costs of production would be lower in Country X. However, there are some other indirect costs of FDI that should also be considered. Plymouth Ltd determines that economic conditions in Country X are uncertain, that government restrictions might be imposed on a subsidiary there, and that inflation and exchange rate movements might be unfavourable. Most importantly, the safety of employees who would be sent there to manage the subsidiary might be threatened by terrorist groups. After considering all the costs, Plymouth Ltd decides not to pursue FDI in Country X.

USING THE WEB

Foreign direct investment

Valuable updated country data that can be considered when making FDI decisions is provided at: http://www.worldbank.org.

EXAMPLE

Rodez SA (a French firm) is contemplating FDI in Thailand where it would produce and sell mobile phones. It had decided that costs were too high. Now it is reconsidering because costs in Thailand have declined. Rodez could rent office space at a low cost. It could also purchase a manufacturing plant at a lower cost because factories that recently failed are standing empty. In addition, the Thai baht has depreciated substantially against the euro, so Rodez could invest in Thailand at a time when the British pound can be exchanged at a favourable exchange rate.

Rodez also discovers, however, that while the cost-related characteristics have improved, the revenue-related characteristics are now less desirable. A new subsidiary in Thailand might not attract new sources of demand due to the country's weak economy. In addition, Rodez might be unable to earn excessive profits there because the weak economy might force existing firms to keep their prices very low in order to survive.

MANAGING FOR VALUE

Yahoo's decision to expand internationally

Laminar Medica, a UK-based manufacturer of transport systems for healthcare facilities, has so far invested 1.7m euro in constructing a plant in the Czech Republic. The 204 square metre operation is located at Vodnany, south of Prague, in Bohemia. 'We started the search for a suitable site in eastern Europe 2 years ago', said Stuart Allcock, managing director of Laminar. 'We were looking for ways to enhance our service to an expanding customer base on the eastern side of Western Europe. We considered other options – namely Poland and, to a lesser extent, Hungary and Austria.'

A key player in the establishment of the Vodnany operation was CzechInvest, the inward investment organization. 'It saved us a lot of leg work,' Mr Allcock said. 'The agency gave us phenomenal help with our research, and also set up meetings with local officials and helped us pinpoint suitable sites.' Identifying local staff presented no problems. With about 9 per cent unemployment in the area, there were a lot of enthusiastic potential employees to choose from, said Mr Allcock. The Vodnany plant is expected to become as large as Laminar's UK operation within 5 years.

Crucial in the early stages of production is the initial qualifying process, which is undertaken directly with customers, according to regulations set down by the regulatory bodies. This can take months, but it is vital that products made at the plant are of a consistent quality to those produced at the company's Tring HQ in the UK.

Mr Allcock conceded that lower costs in the Czech Republic would help to take cost out of the delivered products. 'Costs are significantly lower than they are in the UK. I'd be naive to say that wasn't of interest, but the main reason for setting up in Vodnany was strategic. It will be a huge benefit for our customers on the eastern side of Europe to have greater access to our service to enhance their cold chain,' he said.

Laminar Medica was established in 1975 and, with the backing of the CliniMed Group since 1996, is now the leading manufacturer and supplier of insulated shipping systems in Europe.

(Financial Times, FDI, Internet magazine, 1 August 2005)

BENEFITS OF INTERNATIONAL DIVERSIFICATION

An international project can reduce a firm's overall risk as a result of international diversification benefits. The key to international diversification is selecting foreign projects whose performance levels are not highly correlated over time. In this way, the various international projects should not experience poor performance simultaneously.

Diversification analysis of international projects

Like any investor, a MNC with projects positioned around the world is concerned with the risk and return characteristics of the projects when considered altogether. The same model of portfolio risk as developed in Chapter 3 applies to the risk of the investment returns. The model for combining exchange rates that vary is the same as the model we use for combining foreign profits that vary which is the general model for combining standard deviations from differing risky sources of return.

EXAMPLE

Merriweather Ltd (a UK firm) plans to invest in a new project in either the UK or the USA. Once the project is completed, it will constitute 30 per cent of the firm's total funds invested. The remaining 70 per cent of its investment is exclusively in the UK. Characteristics of the proposed project are forecasted for a 5-year period for both a US and a British location, as shown in Exhibit 13.3.

Merriweather Ltd plans to assess the feasibility of each proposed project based on expected risk and return, using a 5-year time horizon. Its expected annual after-tax return on investment on its prevailing business is 20 per cent, and its variability of returns (as measured by the standard deviation) is expected to be 0.10. The firm can assess its expected overall performance based on developing the project in the USA and in the UK. In doing so, it is essentially comparing two portfolios. In the first portfolio, 70 per cent of its total funds are invested in its prevailing UK business, with the remaining 30 per cent invested in a new project located in the UK. In the second portfolio, again 70 per cent of the firm's total funds are invested in its prevailing business, but the remaining 30 per cent are invested in a new project located in the USA. Therefore, 70 per cent of the portfolios' investments are identical. The difference is in the remaining 30 per cent of funds invested.

If the new project is located in the UK, the firm's overall expected after-tax return (r_p) is:

$r_p =$	(70%	$\times$	20%)	$+$	(30%	$\times$	25%)	$= 21.5\%$
	% of funds invested in prevailing business		Expected return on prevailing business		% of funds invested in new UK project		Expected return on new UK project	Firm's overall expected return

This computation is based on weighting the returns according to the percentage of total funds invested in each investment.

If the firm calculates its overall expected return with the new project located in the USA instead of the UK, the results are unchanged. This is because the new project's expected return happens in this case to be the same regardless of the country of location. Therefore, in terms of return, neither new project has an advantage.

With regard to risk, the new project is expected to exhibit slightly less variability in returns during the 5-year period if it is located in the UK (see Exhibit 13.3). Since firms typically prefer more stable returns

(Continued)

EXHIBIT 13.3   Evaluation of proposed projects in alternative locations

	Characteristics of proposed project	
	If located in the UK	**If located in the USA**
Mean expected annual return on investment (after taxes)	25% (0.25)	25% (0.25)
Standard deviation of expected annual after-tax returns on investment	0.09	0.11
Correlation of expected annual after-tax returns on investment with after-tax returns of prevailing UK business	0.80	0.02

on their investments, this is an advantage. However, estimating the risk of the individual project without considering the overall firm would be a mistake. The expected correlation of the new project's returns with those of the prevailing business must also be consid-

ered. Recall that portfolio variance is determined by the individual variability of each component as well as their pair-wise correlations. The variance of a portfolio ($Var\ (P)$) composed of only two investments (A and B) is computed as:

$$Var(P) = w_A^2 var(A) + w_B^2 var(B) + 2w_A w_B\ stdev(A) stdev(B) corr(A, B)$$

where w_A and w_B represent the percentage of total funds allocated to Investments A and B, respectively, *stdev(A) stdev(B)* are the standard deviations of returns on Investments A and B, respectively, and *corr (A, B)* is the correlation coefficient of returns between Investments A and B. This equation for portfolio

variance can be applied to the problem at hand. The portfolio reflects the overall firm. First, compute the overall firm's variance in returns assuming it locates the new project in the UK (based on the information provided in Exhibit 13.3). This variance *(Var (P))* is:

$$
\begin{aligned}
Var(P_{UK}) &= (0.70)^2(0.10)^2 + (0.30)^2(0.09)^2 + 2(0.70)(0.30)(0.10)(0.09)(0.80) \\
&= (0.49)(0.01) + (0.09)(0.0081) + 0.003024 \\
&= 0.0049 + 0.000729 + 0.0003024 \\
&= 0.008653
\end{aligned}
$$

If Merriweather Ltd decides to locate the new project in the USA instead of the UK, its overall variability in returns will be different, because that project differs from the new UK project in terms of individual variability in returns and

correlation with the prevailing business. The overall variability of the firm's returns based on locating the new project in the USA is estimated by variance in the portfolio returns *(Var(P))*:

$$
\begin{aligned}
Var(P_{US}) &= (0.70)^2(0.10)^2 + (0.30)^2(0.11)^2 + 2(0.70)(0.30)(0.10)(0.11)(0.02) \\
&= (0.49)(0.01) + (0.09)(0.0121) + 0.0000924 \\
&= 0.0049 + 0.001089 + 0.0000924 \\
&= 0.0060814
\end{aligned}
$$

Thus, Merriweather will generate more stable returns if the new project is located in the USA. The firm's overall variability in returns is almost 29.7 per cent less if the new project is located in the USA rather than in the UK.

The variability is reduced when locating in the foreign country because of the correlation of the new

project's expected returns with the expected returns of the prevailing business. If the new project is located in Merriweather's home country (the UK), its returns are expected to be more highly correlated with those of the prevailing business than they would be if the project was located in the USA.

Comparing portfolios. When considering a major new investment, it is not just the individual risk that is important, but how that risk contributes to the overall risk of the portfolio of projects that a MNC is undertaking. A MNC has therefore to consider its portfolio of investments before and after the foreign direct investment to assess whether or not the project is a valuable addition.

Foreign direct investments tend to be large undertakings, care should be taken in assessing the costs and benefits of a project as they may well be wider than the physical project itself (see the Really2 example above). References to a strategy and policies are terms often used to incorporate these wider issues.

Exhibit 13.4 compares the existing risk return profile with the potential post investment profiles. Return here is defined as the *expected* increase in the market value of shares in the company plus dividends. The term 'expected' is dropped here as is the convention but it should be remembered that the *actual return* could be very different. Because this is a market definition, an investment that is offering options and strategic gains would benefit the share value though not necessarily the immediate earnings. Risk is measured here as the standard deviation of returns. Systematic or non-diversifiable risk would in theory be a better measure but measurement problems in practice and theory make it an impractical measure. Where investors are international, the relevant stock market return will differ. Not surprisingly, surveys of practice show beta measures to be the least popular and the most variable of the measures of risk.

The analysis of the risk return relationship is similar to Exhibit 3.8 of Chapter 3. If the new foreign direct investment moves the MNC's risk profile (in the centre) to point A then the project should be accepted in that the overall return has increased from 13 per cent to 15 per cent and the risk has reduced. This would be the case where the returns of the foreign direct investment were negatively related to the existing returns of the company. For opposite reasons, if the movement is to point D, the proposed project would normally be rejected as risk has increased and return decreased. The holder of £100 worth of shares would be worse off. If the foreign direct investment moves the overall risk profile of the MNC from the centre to either points B or C, then the MNC needs to assess whether the increased risk for point B is justified by the increased return and for C the loss of return is justified by the lower risk.

Diversification among countries

Risk reduction is achieved through diversification, investing in projects whose returns are not well correlated with the existing returns. How might this be achieved for a MNC? The intuitive answer is to invest in differing

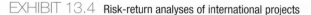

EXHIBIT 13.4   Risk-return analyses of international projects

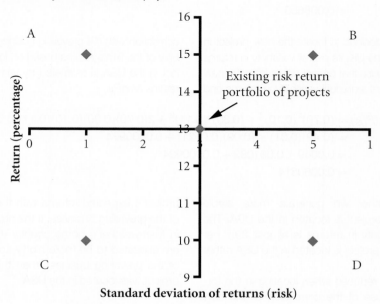

economies. The less than perfect synchronization of economic activity would seem to offer a natural diversification, economy X may be doing well when the 'home' economy is performing less well. On its own, this effect would indeed lower risk. However, where the foreign economy is less well developed and the project naturally more risky than a home project, the variation of returns can be expected to be higher. So there are potentially two conflicting influences. Greater risk as the foreign economies are likely to be more volatile and the project naturally riskier compared to lower risk as the returns are more likely to be unsynchronized or 'out of step' with the home economy. They vary independently. Not surprisingly, surveys of firms with varying degrees of international involvement offer no strong effect on risk of international diversification.

EXAMPLE

Eurosteel plc forges steel in Europe and sells exclusively to European nations. The company is considering building steel plants in Egypt and South Africa. Both projects are thought to offer potentially very high returns though both would have a much higher risk of failure than a similar project in Europe – a higher expected return but a higher risk. On the other hand, the South African economy and the Egyptian economy may perform well when the European economies are performing poorly thus offering Eurosteel a measure of risk reduction. Overall, the directors of Eurosteel see a higher expected return than an equivalent investment in Europe but a higher risk that has been nevertheless reduced by the fact that the Egyptian and South African economies vary independently from the European economies.

USING THE WEB

Foreign direct investment information for a particular country

FDI in specific countries can be assessed by reviewing websites focused on those countries. For example, conditions in China are described at: http://www.business-china.com.

HOST GOVERNMENT VIEWS OF FOREIGN DIRECT INVESTMENT

The relationship between host governments and MNCs over direct investment has varied greatly over the years. There have been instances of outright opposition as evidenced by Indian government opposition to Pepsi and other MNCs as in the dictum of the times: 'computer chips yes ... potato chips no'. This mistrust has given way to a bargaining type relationship and now a desire to attract foreign investment. This aspect of investment illustrates the importance of strategy and real options in the overall consideration of investment appraisal as outlined at the start of this chapter.

MANAGING FOR VALUE

India throws open doors to foreign supermarkets, again
Reuters Fri Sep 14, 2012 6:32 pm BST
India opened its retail sector to foreign supermarkets on Friday, a major economic reform that has been stalled for months by political gridlock and came as part of a package of measures aimed at reviving growth.

Following are key aspects of the policy ... Foreign retailers will have to source almost a third of their

(Continued)

manufactured and processed goods from industries with a total plant and machinery investment of less than $1 million... Foreign retailers will have to invest a minimum of $100 million, and put at least half of their total investment into so-called 'back-end' infrastructure, such as warehousing and cold storage facilities. The aim is to meet one of the key justifications for opening the supermarket sector to foreign players – revamping the country's crumbling infrastructure and unclogging bottlenecks.

The bargaining model

The bargaining approach serves as a model whereby the country gets long-term benefits in return for allowing MNCs to operate in their country. Bargaining is at two levels, the fist level is between governments including international institutions and the second level is between governments and individual MNCs.

Negotiations at intergovernmental level may be bilateral as between two countries or unilateral. In the example above as part of India's opening up to world trade, an issue discussed at intergovernmental level, the change in their laws allows MNCs from whatever country to invest.

Bilateral investment treaties (BITs) are aimed at allowing often developed countries' industries to invest in a host country. The USA and other developed countries have signed a great many such agreements prompting the observation that developed countries are promoting their interests 'BIT by BIT'. A typical agreement might guarantee investors the right to move funds in and out of a country without penalties, prevent countries from imposing local content requirements or export requirements or a local manager quota or local legal jurisdiction on international matters. Countries may also protect investments by their MNCs by imposing penalties for hostile actions by the other country. This may involve the withdrawal of aid, the withdrawal of lower tariffs or the withdrawal of support for loans from international lending bodies. In brief, all governments see a close link between the interests of their MNCs and national interests.

The second level of the MNC host country relationship is between the MNC and the government. The governments want technology, employment, taxes and managerial knowledge. They have control over natural and human resources, regulations and law enforcement. Their ability to use these measures to promote their interests is tempered by BITs and other international agreements. The MNC want to maximize profits for their shareholders and other sponsors. Their interests in a particular country therefore are purely financial but this does not preclude giving way on lesser restrictions such as local content and local employment as a cost of obtaining agreement from the host country.

EXAMPLE

Vietnam maps out strategy to attract FDI in supporting industries:

To make Vietnam more attractive to foreign small and medium-sized enterprises, the Ministry of Industry and Trade proposed the government adjust regulations on import and export taxes that would give supporting industry investors more incentives; but only if they built supporting industry facilities and used local market input materials ... the strategy demands reform ... detailing import and export duty regulations, with supporting industry firms to be eligible for 5-year import duty exemption.

It added that big foreign companies' investment in the past had failed to help Vietnam develop supporting industries, because capital was focused on assembling facilities to take advantage of cheap labour.

Source: Adapted from US Chamber of Commerce report, June 2012

Bargaining is of course in place of conflict. There are a number of areas where MNCs can come into conflict with the host government:

- *FINANCE* . . . does the MNC raise money locally or borrow from abroad?

- *TRADE BALANCE* . . . how much does a MNC import or export?

- *ECONOMIC DEVELOPMENT* . . . to what extent should an MNC pass on its knowledge to the country by for example investment in local R&D facilities?

- *COMPETITION* . . . what effect will the MNC have on local companies?

- *ENVIRONMENT* . . . is the MNC there principally to exploit low standards? Financial institutions are encouraged not to exploit countries in this way by subscribing to the Equator Principles (http://www.equator-principles.com)

- *CULTURE* . . . does the MNC blend in with local culture or compete?

- *EMPLOYMENT* . . . how much local employment?

- *TECHNOLOGY* . . . how much sharing? College courses etc?

- *POLITICS* . . . can a MNC always be neutral?

- *LAW* . . . is the law implemented? Host countries may feel under pressure as implementing the law may mean the loss of the investment.

- *TAXES* . . . the MNC may seek to reduce its tax bill through transfer prices with other parts of the company in a way that conceals the true profit being made in that country in order to avoid taxation.

MANAGING FOR VALUE

Tax paid by some global firms in UK 'an insult'

Global firms in the UK that pay little or no tax are an 'insult' to British businesses, a committee of MPs says . . . Multinationals such as Starbucks and Amazon have come under fire for paying little or no corporation tax . . . Starbucks, for example, sold nearly £400m worth of goods in the UK last year, but paid no corporation tax at all, because it transferred some of the money to a sister company in the Netherlands in the form of royalty payments, bought its coffee beans from Switzerland and paid high interest rates to borrow money from other parts of the business.

BBC 3 December 2012

MANAGING FOR VALUE

The decision by Allied Research Associates, Inc. (a US-based MNC), to build a production facility and office in Belgium was highly motivated by Belgian government subsidies. The Belgian government subsidized a large portion of the expenses incurred by Allied Research Associates and offered tax concessions and favourable interest rates on loans to Allied.

MANAGING FOR VALUE

In France, the Treasury can reject any deal if the acquirer is based outside the EU. The French government may also reject a deal if the target is in some closely monitored industry, such as defence or health care. The Monopolies Commission of France also reviews acquisitions to prevent any combined firms from controlling more than 25 per cent of an industry or from severely reducing competition.

The European Union Commission assesses mergers that may affect competition in Europe. The EU Commission rejected the merger between General Electric and Honeywell because it believed that the merger would have resulted in a monopoly.

Acquisitions in Japan are reviewed by the Fair Trade Commission. Japan has historically imposed barriers to discourage international acquisitions. Recently, however, these barriers have been reduced (as long as the Japanese target is agreeable), enabling US-based MNCs such as Corning Glass Works, Data General, Eastman Kodak and Motorola to acquire Japanese firms.

Acquisitions in the USA are also reviewed by several agencies, including the Securities and Exchange Commission, which regulates the conduct of acquisitions, and the Justice Department and Federal Trade Commission, which analyzes the potential impact on competition.

MANAGING FOR VALUE

Many governments in Asia and Latin America have traditionally restricted foreign majority ownership. In recent years, however, these restrictions have been reduced. Governments of Asian countries removed restrictions on international acquisitions during the

Asian crisis to encourage MNCs to develop new business there. Mexico also recently announced that it would allow foreign companies to own 100 per cent of their subsidiaries established in Mexico.

MANAGING FOR VALUE

Spain's government allowed Ford Motor Co. to set up production facilities in Spain only if it would abide by certain provisions. These included limiting Ford's local sales volume to 10 per cent of the previous year's local automobile sales. In addition, two-thirds of the total

volume of automobiles produced by Ford in Spain must be exported. The idea behind these provisions was to create jobs for workers in Spain without seriously affecting local competitors. Allowing a subsidiary that primarily exports its product achieved this objective.

SUBSIDIARY VERSUS PARENT PERSPECTIVE

Should capital budgeting for a multinational project be conducted from the viewpoint of the subsidiary that will administer the project or the parent that will most likely finance much of the project? Some would say the subsidiary's perspective should be used because it will be responsible for administering the project and there will be shareholders with interests only in the subsidiary. However, if the parent is financing the project, then it should be evaluating the results from its point of view. The feasibility of the capital budgeting analysis can vary with the perspective because the net after-tax cash inflows to the subsidiary can differ substantially from those to the parent. Such differences can be due to several factors, some of which are discussed here.

Tax differentials

If the earnings due to the project will someday be remitted to the parent, the MNC needs to consider how the parent's government taxes these earnings. If the parent's government imposes a high tax rate on the remitted funds, the project may be feasible from the subsidiary's point of view, but not from the parent's point of view. Under such a scenario, the parent should not consider implementing the project, even though it appears feasible from the subsidiary's perspective.

Restricted remittances

Consider a potential project to be implemented in a country where government restrictions require that a percentage of the subsidiary earnings remain in the country. Since the parent may never have access to these funds, the project is not attractive to the parent, although it may be attractive to the subsidiary. One possible solution is to let the subsidiary obtain partial financing for the project within the host country. In this case, the portion of funds not allowed to be sent to the parent can be used to cover the financing costs over time.

Excessive remittances

Consider a parent that charges its subsidiary very high administrative fees because management is centralized at the headquarters. To the subsidiary, the fees represent an expense. To the parent, the fees represent revenue that may substantially exceed the actual cost of managing the subsidiary. In this case, the project's earnings may appear low from the subsidiary's perspective and high from the parent's perspective. The feasibility of the project again depends on perspective. In most cases, neglecting the parent's perspective will distort the true value of a foreign project.

Exchange rate movements

When earnings are remitted to the parent, they are normally converted from the subsidiary's local currency to the parent's currency. The amount received by the parent is therefore influenced by the existing exchange rate. If the subsidiary project is assessed from the subsidiary's perspective, the cash flows forecasted for the subsidiary do not have to be converted to the parent's currency.

Summary of factors

Exhibit 13.5 illustrates the process from the time earnings are generated by the subsidiary until the parent receives the remitted funds. The exhibit shows that the earnings are reduced initially by corporate taxes paid to the host government. Then, some of the earnings are retained by the subsidiary (either by the subsidiary's choice or according to the host government's rules), with the residual targeted as funds to be remitted. Those funds that are remitted may be subject to a withholding tax by the host government. The remaining funds are converted to the parent's currency (at the prevailing exchange rate) and remitted to the parent.

Given the various factors shown here that can drain subsidiary earnings, the cash flows actually remitted by the subsidiary may represent only a small portion of the earnings it generates. The feasibility of the project from the parent's perspective is dependent not on the subsidiary's cash flows but on the cash flows that the parent ultimately receives.

The parent's perspective is appropriate in attempting to determine whether a project will enhance the firm's value. Given that the parent's shareholders are its owners, it should make decisions that satisfy its shareholders. Each project, whether foreign or domestic, should ultimately generate sufficient cash flows to

EXHIBIT 13.5   Process of remitting subsidiary earnings to the parent

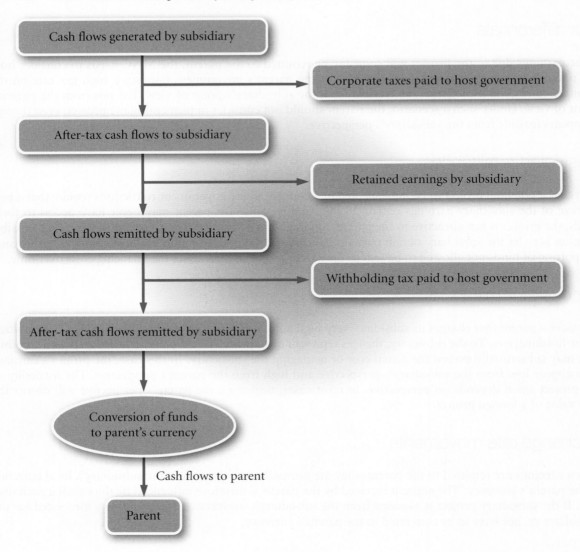

the parent to enhance shareholder wealth. Any changes in the parent's expenses should also be included in the analysis. The parent may incur additional expenses for monitoring the new foreign subsidiary's management or consolidating the subsidiary's financial statements. Any project that can create a positive NPV for the parent should enhance shareholder wealth.

One exception to the rule of using a parent's perspective occurs when the foreign subsidiary is not wholly owned by the parent and the foreign project is partially financed with retained earnings of the parent and of the subsidiary. In this case, the foreign subsidiary has a group of shareholders that it must satisfy. Any arrangement made between the parent and the subsidiary should be acceptable to the two entities only if the arrangement enhances the values of both. The goal is to make decisions in the interests of both groups of shareholders and not to transfer wealth from one entity to another.

Although this exception occasionally occurs, most foreign subsidiaries of MNCs are wholly owned by the parents. Examples in this text implicitly assume that the subsidiary is wholly owned by the parent (unless noted otherwise) and therefore focus on the parent's perspective.

SUMMARY

- Foreign Direct Investment requires the consideration of the original investment (as valued in the NPV model), post investment decisions (real options) and the effect of competition and host governments (game theory).

- MNCs have a variety of motives for wanting to have a foreign presence. Broadly they are: (a) motives specific to the firm, (b) the need to have control over the process (internalization) and (c) country specific motives (the resources).

- International diversification is a common motive for FDI. It allows an MNC to reduce its exposure to domestic economic conditions. This is counterbalanced by the greater risk of a foreign investment. The overall effect has to be considered in relation to the portfolio of investments undertaken by the MNC.

- The MNC relations with the host government is one of potential conflict that is avoided through bargaining. Intergovernmental relations are also an important influence on the MNC's ability to invest in a particular country.

CRITICAL DEBATE

Should MNCs avoid FDI in countries with liberal child labour laws?

Proposition. Yes. An MNC should maintain its hiring standards, regardless of what country it is in. Even if a foreign country allows children to work, an MNC should not lower its standards. Although the MNC forgoes the use of low-cost labour, it maintains its global credibility.

Opposing view. No. An MNC will not only benefit its shareholders, but will create employment for some children who need support. The MNC can provide reasonable working conditions and perhaps may even offer educational programmes for its employees.

With whom do you agree? Review sites such as http://www.corporatewatch.org and contrast http:www.cleanclothes.org/companies/adidas00-05-05.htm with http://www.adidas-group.com/en/overview/corporate_governance/sea/default.asp. Also see http://cbae.nmsuedu/~dboje/AA/academics_reebok.html; for a more sympathetic view of MNCs see http://www.fdimagazine.com/ (keywords being 'Corporatewatch', 'Adidas', 'Cleanclothes', 'Standards of Engagement', 'academics studying' and 'FDI'). But remember that these sites and others are not impartial and often present a distorted picture. *You must take care to think of both sides of the argument.*

SELF TEST

Answers are provided in Appendix A at the back of the text.

1 Offer some reasons why UK firms might prefer to direct their FDI to Europe rather than Latin America.

2 Offer some reasons why UK firms might prefer to direct their FDI to Latin America rather than Europe.

3 One UK executive said that Europe was not considered as a location for FDI because of the euro's value. Interpret this statement.

4 Why do you think UK firms commonly use joint ventures as a strategy to enter China?

5 Why would the UK offer a foreign automobile manufacturer large incentives for establishing a production subsidiary in the UK? Isn't this strategy indirectly subsidizing the foreign competitors of UK firms?

6 The following projected net cash flows are for a proposed bridge building project in country H

costing £30m for which the company will be allowed 4-years worth of toll revenue.

Years	1	2	3	4
£m	5	10	15	20

a) The company applies a 10 per cent discount rate to such projects. Calculate the NPV of the project.

b) The company is worried about potential conflict with the government authorities in country H. What steps might be taken to cope with this risk?

QUESTIONS AND APPLICATIONS

1 **Motives for FDI.** Describe some potential benefits to an MNC as a result of FDI. Elaborate on each type of benefit. Which motives for FDI do you think encouraged Nike (a US company) to expand its footwear production in Latin America?

2 **Impact of a weak currency on feasibility of FDI.** Tilda AB, a Swedish producer of computer disks, plans to establish a subsidiary in the Ukraine in order to penetrate the Middle Eastern market. Tilda's executives believe that the Ukrainian hryvnia's value is relatively strong and will weaken against the Swedish krone over time. If their expectations about the hryvnia's value are correct, how will this affect the feasibility of the project? Explain.

3 **FDI to achieve economies of scale.** Max AG and Marie AG are German automobile manufacturers that desire to benefit from economies of scale. Max has decided to establish distributorship subsidiaries in various countries, while Marie has decided to establish manufacturing subsidiaries in various countries. Which firm is more likely to benefit from economies of scale?

4 **FDI to reduce cash flow volatility.** Rideau Chemical SA and Robert Sarl (both French companies) have similar intentions to reduce the volatility of their cash flows. Rideau implemented a long-range plan to establish 40 per cent of its business in Canada. Robert implemented a long-range plan to establish 30 per cent of its business in Europe and Asia, scattered among 12 different countries. Which company will more effectively reduce cash flow volatility once the plans are achieved?

5 **Impact of import restrictions.** If the UK imposed long-term restrictions on imports, would the amount of FDI by non-UK MNCs in the UK increase, decrease or be unchanged? Explain.

6 **Capitalizing on low-cost labour.** Some MNCs establish a manufacturing facility where there is a relatively low cost of labour. Yet, they sometimes close the facility later because the cost advantage dissipates. Why do you think the relative cost advantage of these countries is reduced over time? (Ignore possible exchange rate effects.)

7 **Opportunities in less developed countries.** Offer your opinion on why economies of some less developed countries with strict restrictions on international trade and FDI are somewhat independent from economies of other countries. Why would MNCs desire to enter such countries? If these countries relaxed their restrictions, would their economies continue to be independent of other economies? Explain.

8 Consider the effects on FDI of a major **political incident** involving the host country of the MNC making the investment.

9 **FDI strategy.** Luigi SpA (an Italian company) has decided to establish a subsidiary in China that will produce stereos and sell them there. It expects that the cost of producing these stereos will be one-third the cost of producing them in Italy. Assuming that its production cost estimates are accurate, is Luigi's strategy sensible? Explain.

10 **Risk resulting from international business.** This chapter concentrates on possible benefits to a firm that increases its international business.

   a What are some risks of international business that may not exist for local business?

   b What does this chapter reveal about the relationship between an MNC's degree of international business and its risk?

11 **Motives for FDI.** Starter Ltd (UK) produces sportswear that is licensed by professional sports teams. It recently decided to expand in Europe. What are the potential benefits for this firm from using FDI?

12 Disney's FDI motives. What potential benefits do you think were most important in the decision of the Walt Disney Co. to build a theme park in France?

13 FDI strategy. Once an MNC establishes a subsidiary, FDI remains an ongoing decision. What does this statement mean?

14 Host government incentives for FDI. Why would foreign governments provide MNCs with incentives to undertake FDI there?

15 FDI valuation XH plc is considering the following cash flows for project Y (mining rare earth) in country K that requires an initial investment of £2.5m

£000			
Year 1	Year 2	Year 3	Year 4
800	1200	1000	1000

a) Calculate the NPV using the companies weighted average cost of capital of 12 per cent – is the project worth undertaking?

b) A director points out that as the investment is in a country that is relatively unstable, a more appropriate discount rate would be 25 per cent. Recalculate the NPV at 25 per cent and reconsider your answer to part (a).

c) A second director argues that the risk is in fact about whether or not a licence will be granted to mine rare earth. If it is not granted then XH plc can withdraw immediately with a loss of about £300 000. Reconsider your answer to the first two parts of this question.

d) A third director points out that should XH not go ahead, a local mining company CC will almost certainly put in for a licence and is likely to collaborate with a rival US company. Other deposits are thought to be present. Reconsider your previous answers.

e) Identify the real option and game theoretic (competitive) elements of this question.

ADVANCED QUESTIONS

16 FDI strategy. JC Penney (a real US company) has recognized numerous opportunities to expand in foreign countries and has assessed many foreign markets, including Brazil, Greece, Mexico, Portugal, Singapore and Thailand. It has opened new stores in Europe, Asia and Latin America. In each case, the firm was aware that it did not have sufficient understanding of the culture of each country that it had targeted. Consequently, it engaged in joint ventures with local partners who knew the preferences of the local customers.

a What comparative advantage does JC Penney have when establishing a store in a foreign country, relative to an independent variety store?

b Why might the overall risk of JC Penney decrease or increase as a result of its recent global expansion?

c JC Penney has been more cautious about entering China. Explain the potential obstacles associated with entering China.

17 FDI location decision. Pimlico Ltd is a UK firm with a Chinese subsidiary that produces mobile phones in China and sells them in Japan. This subsidiary pays its wages and its rent in Chinese yuan, which is presently tied to a basket of currencies. The mobile phones sold to Japan are denominated in Japanese yen. Assume that Pimlico Ltd expects that the Chinese yuan will continue to keep its value against the dollar. The subsidiary's main goal is to generate profits for itself and reinvest the profits. It does not plan to remit any funds to the UK parent.

a Assume that the Japanese yen strengthens against the US dollar over time. How would this be expected to affect the profits earned by the Chinese subsidiary?

b If Pimlico Ltd had established its subsidiary in Tokyo, Japan instead of China, would its subsidiary's profits be more exposed or less exposed to exchange rate risk?

c Why do you think that Pimlico Ltd established the subsidiary in China instead of Japan? Assume no major country risk barriers.

d If the Chinese subsidiary needs to borrow money to finance its expansion and wants to reduce its exchange rate risk, should it borrow US dollars, Chinese yuan or Japanese yen?

18 **FDI valuation** AQ plc is considering expanding its operations into country X for a cost of £40m. The following possibilities exist.

i) A rival firm JQ plc also decides to expand its operations into country X. Estimated annual earnings would be about £8.

ii) If JQ does not follow AQ then the earnings would be about £13m.

iii) If AQ does not go ahead but JQ does then there could be some reputational damage to AQ which could affect current operations – a director estimates that the potential cost would be about the equivalent of a loss of £2m sales per year.

The finance director wants to apply NPV calculations but the managing director says that he is happy using the annual earnings as an estimate of the benefits.

a) Consider the managing director's viewpoint.

b) Consider the problems of combining NPV calculations with competitive scenarios as described in this question.

PROJECT WORKSHOP

19 Select three articles from the online *FDI* magazine (registration for the search function is free) at http://www.fdimagazine.com/. For search-words choose well-known MNCs or countries. For each article assess what good and bad aspects of FDI are supported by the article.

DISCUSSION IN THE BOARDROOM

This exercise can be found on our dedicated Course-Mate platform for students.

RUNNING YOUR OWN MNC

This exercise can be found on our dedicated Course-Mate platform for students.

Essays/discussion and articles can be found at the end of Part IV.

BLADES PLC CASE STUDY

Consideration of foreign direct investment

For the last year, Blades plc has been exporting to Thailand in order to supplement its declining UK sales. Under the existing arrangement, Blades sells 180 000 pairs of roller blades annually to Entertainment Products, a Thai retailer, for a fixed price denominated in Thai baht. The agreement will last for another 2 years. Furthermore, to diversify internationally and to take advantage of an attractive offer by Jogs Inc., a US retailer, Blades has recently begun exporting to the USA. Under the resulting agreement, Jogs will purchase 200 000 pairs of 'Speedos', Blades' primary product, annually at a fixed price of $80 per pair.

Blades' suppliers of the needed components for its roller blade production are located primarily in the UK, where Blades incurs the majority of its cost of goods sold. Although prices for inputs needed to manufacture roller blades vary, recent costs have run approximately £70 per pair. Blades also imports components from Thailand because of the relatively low price of rubber and plastic components and because of their high quality. These imports are denominated in Thai baht, and the exact price (in baht) depends on prevailing market prices for these components in Thailand. Currently, inputs sufficient to manufacture a pair of roller blades cost approximately 3000 Thai baht per pair of roller blades.

Although Thailand had been among the world's fastest growing economies, recent events in Thailand have increased the level of economic uncertainty. Specifically, the Thai baht, which had been pegged to the dollar, is now a freely floating currency and has depreciated substantially in recent months. Furthermore, recent levels of inflation in Thailand have been very high. Hence, future economic conditions in Thailand are highly uncertain.

Ben Holt, Blades' financial director, is seriously considering FDI in Thailand. He believes that this is a perfect time to either establish a subsidiary or acquire an existing business in Thailand because the uncertain economic conditions and the depreciation of the baht have substantially lowered the initial costs required for FDI. Holt believes the growth potential in Asia will be extremely high once the Thai economy stabilizes.

Although Holt has also considered FDI in the USA, he would prefer that Blades invest in Thailand as opposed to the USA. Forecasts indicate that the demand for roller blades in the USA is similar to that in the UK; since Blades' UK sales have recently declined because of the high prices it charges, Holt expects that FDI in the USA will yield similar results. Furthermore, both domestic and foreign roller blade manufacturers are relatively well established in the USA, so the growth potential there is limited. Holt believes the Thai roller blade market offers more growth potential.

Blades can sell its products at a lower price but generate higher profit margins in Thailand than it can in the UK. This is because the Thai customer has committed itself to purchase a fixed number of Blades' products annually only if it can purchase Speedos at a substantial discount from the UK price. Nevertheless, since the cost of goods sold incurred in Thailand is substantially below that incurred in the USA, Blades has managed to generate higher profit margins from its Thai exports and imports than in the UK.

As a financial analyst for Blades plc you generally agree with Ben Holt's assessment of the situation. However, you are concerned that Thai consumers have not been affected yet by the unfavourable economic conditions. You believe that they may reduce their spending on leisure products within the next year. Therefore, you think it would be beneficial to wait until next year, when the unfavourable economic conditions in Thailand may subside, to make a decision regarding FDI in Thailand. However, if economic conditions in Thailand improve over the next year, FDI may become more expensive both because target firms will be more expensive and because the baht may appreciate. You are also aware that several of Blades' UK competitors are considering expanding into Thailand in the next year.

If Blades acquires an existing business in Thailand or establishes a subsidiary there by the end of next year, it would fulfil its agreement with Entertainment Products for the subsequent year. The Thai retailer has expressed an interest in renewing the contractual agreement with Blades at that time if Blades establishes operations in Thailand. However, Holt believes that Blades could charge a higher price for its products if it establishes its own distribution channels.

Holt has asked you to answer the following questions:

1 Identify and discuss some of the benefits that Blades plc could obtain from FDI.

2 Do you think Blades should wait until next year to undertake FDI in Thailand? What is the trade-off if Blades undertakes the FDI now?

3 Do you think Blades should renew its agreement with the Thai retailer for another 3 years? What is the trade-off if Blades renews the agreement?

4 Assume a high level of unemployment in Thailand and a unique production process employed by Blades plc. How do you think the Thai government would view the establishment of a subsidiary in Thailand by firms such as Blades? Do you think the Thai government would be more or less supportive if firms such as Blades acquired existing businesses in Thailand? Why?

SMALL BUSINESS DILEMMA

Foreign direct investment decision by the Sports Exports Company

Jim Logan's business, the Sports Exports Company (Ireland) continues to grow. His primary product is the basketballs he produces and exports to a distributor in the UK. However, his recent joint venture with a British firm has also been successful. Under this arrangement, a British firm produces other sporting goods for Jim's firm; these goods are then delivered to that distributor. Jim intentionally started his international business by exporting because it was easier and cheaper to export than to establish a place of business in the UK. However, he is considering establishing a firm in the UK to produce the basketballs there instead of in

Ireland. This firm would also produce the other sporting goods that he now sells, so he would no longer have to rely on another British firm (through the joint venture) to produce those goods.

1 Given the information provided here, what are the advantages to Jim of establishing the firm in the UK?

2 Given the information provided here, what are the disadvantages to Jim of establishing the firm in the UK?

APPENDIX 13
INCORPORATING INTERNATIONAL TAX LAWS IN THE INVESTMENT DECISION

Tax laws can vary among countries in many ways, but any type of tax causes an MNC's after-tax cash flows to differ from its before-tax cash flows. To estimate the future cash flows that are to be generated by a proposed foreign project (such as the establishment of a new subsidiary or the acquisition of a foreign firm), MNCs must first estimate the taxes that they will incur due to the foreign project. This appendix provides a general background on some of the more important international tax characteristics that an MNC must consider when assessing foreign projects. Financial managers do not necessarily have to be international tax experts because they may be able to rely on the MNC's international tax department or on independent tax consultants for guidance. Nevertheless, they should at least be aware of international tax characteristics that can affect the cash flows of a foreign project and recognize how those characteristics can vary among the countries where foreign projects are considered.

VARIATION IN TAX LAWS AMONG COUNTRIES

Each country generates tax revenue in different ways. The UK relies on corporate and individual income taxes for federal revenue. Other countries may depend more on a *value-added tax (VAT)* or excise taxes. Since each country has its own philosophy on whom to tax and how much, it is not surprising that the tax treatment of corporations differs among countries. Because each country has a unique tax system and tax rates, MNCs need to recognize the various tax provisions of each country where they consider investing in a foreign project. The more important tax characteristics of a country to be considered in an MNC's international tax assessment are: (1) corporate income taxes, (2) withholding taxes, (3) personal and excise tax rates, (4) provision for carry backs and carry forwards, (5) tax treaties, (6) tax credits and (7) taxes on income from intercompany transactions. A discussion of each characteristic follows.

USING THE WEB

The PriceWaterhouseCoopers site at: http://www.pwcglobal.com provides access to country-specific information such as general business rules and regulations and tax environments.

Corporate income taxes

In general, countries impose taxes on corporate income generated within their borders, even if the parents of those corporations are based in other countries. Each country has its unique corporate income tax laws. The USA, for example, taxes the worldwide income of US *persons,* a term that includes corporations. As a general rule, however, foreign income of a foreign subsidiary of a US company is not taxed until it is transferred to the US parent by payment of dividends or a liquidation distribution. This is the concept of deferral.

An MNC planning direct foreign investment in foreign countries must determine how the anticipated earnings from a foreign project will be affected. Tax rates imposed on income earned by businesses (including foreign subsidiaries of MNCs) or income remitted to a parent are shown in Exhibit 13A.1 for several countries. The tax rates may be lower than what is shown for corporations that have relatively low levels of earnings. This exhibit shows the extent to which corporate income tax rates can vary among host countries and illustrates why MNCs closely assess the tax guidelines in any foreign country where they consider conducting direct foreign investment. Given differences in tax deductions, depreciation, business subsidies and other factors, corporate tax differentials cannot be measured simply by comparing quoted tax rates across countries.

EXHIBIT 13A.1 Comparison of tax characteristics among countries

	Corporate tax	Withholding tax on dividends*
Brazil	34	15/25
China	25	10
Egypt	25	0
Norway	28	0/25
France	33.33	0/30
Germany	15	0/25
Nigeria	30	10
South Africa	28	15
Switzerland	8.5	0/35
UK	23	0
USA	35	30

* Varies depending on matters such as tax treaties, residency and economic area
Source: http://www.dits.deloitte.com

Corporate tax rates can also differ within a country, depending on whether the entity is a domestic corporation. Also, if an unregistered foreign corporation is considered to have a permanent establishment in a country, it may be subject to that country's tax laws on income earned within its borders. Generally, a permanent establishment includes an office or fixed place of business or a specified kind of agency *(independent agents are normally excluded)* through which active and continuous business is conducted. In some cases, the tax depends on the industry or on the form of business used (e.g. corporation, branch, partnership).

Withholding taxes

The following types of payments by an MNC's subsidiary are commonly subject to a withholding tax by the host government: (1) a subsidiary may remit a portion of its earnings, referred to as *dividends,* to its parent since the parent is the shareholder of the subsidiary, (2) the subsidiary may pay interest to the parent or to other non-resident debtholders from which it received loans and (3) the subsidiary may make payments to the parent or to other non-resident firms in return for the use of patents (such as technology) or other rights. The payment of dividends reduces the amount of reinvestment by the subsidiary in the host country. The payments by the subsidiary to non-resident firms to cover interest or patents reflect expenses by the subsidiary, which will normally reduce its taxable income and therefore will reduce the corporate income taxes paid to the host government. Thus, withholding taxes may be a way for host governments to tax MNCs that make interest or patent payments to non-resident firms.

Since withholding taxes imposed on the subsidiary can reduce the funds remitted by the subsidiary to the parent, the withholding taxes must be accounted for in a capital budgeting analysis conducted by the parent. As with corporate tax rates, the withholding tax rate can vary substantially among countries.

Reducing exposure to withholding taxes. Withholding taxes can be reduced by income tax treaties (discussed shortly). Because of tax treaties between some countries, the withholding taxes may be lower when the MNC's parent is based in a county participating in the treaties.

If the host country government of a particular subsidiary imposes a high withholding tax on subsidiary earnings remitted to the parent, the parent of the MNC may instruct the subsidiary to temporarily refrain from remitting earnings and to reinvest them in the host country instead. As an alternative approach, the MNC may instruct the subsidiary to set up a research and development division that will enhance subsidiaries elsewhere. The main purpose behind this strategy is to efficiently use the funds abroad when the funds cannot be sent to the parent without excessive taxation. Since international tax laws can influence the timing of the transfer of funds to the parent, they affect the timing of cash flows on proposed foreign projects. Therefore, the international tax implications must be understood before the cash flows of a foreign project can be estimated.

Personal and excise tax rates

An MNC is more likely to be concerned with corporate tax rates and withholding tax rates than individual tax rates because its cash flows are directly affected by the taxes incurred. However, a country's individual tax rates can indirectly affect an MNC's cash flows because the MNC may have to pay higher wages to employees in countries (such as in Europe) where personal income is taxed at a relatively high rate. In addition, a country's VAT or excise tax may affect cash flows to be generated from a foreign project because it may make the products less competitive on a global basis (reducing the expected quantity of products to be sold).

Provision for carrybacks and carryforwards

Negative earnings from operations can often be carried back or forward to offset earnings in other years. The laws pertaining to these so-called net operating loss carrybacks and carryforwards can vary among countries. An MNC generally does not plan to generate negative earnings in foreign countries. If negative earnings do occur, however, it is desirable to be able to use them to offset other years of positive earnings. Most foreign countries do not allow negative earnings to be carried back but allow some flexibility in carrying losses forward. Since many foreign projects are expected to result in negative earnings in the early years, the tax laws for the country of concern will affect the future tax deductions resulting from these losses and will therefore affect the future cash flows of the foreign project.

Tax treaties

Countries often establish income tax treaties, whereby one partner will reduce its taxes by granting a credit for taxes imposed on corporations operating within the other treaty partner's tax jurisdiction. Income tax treaties help corporations avoid exposure to double taxation. Some treaties apply to taxes paid on income earned by MNCs in foreign countries. Other treaties apply to withholding taxes imposed by the host country on foreign earnings that are remitted to the parent.

Without such treaties, subsidiary earnings could be taxed by the host country and then again by the parent's country when received by the parent. To the extent that the parent uses some of these earnings to provide cash dividends for shareholders, triple taxation could result (since the dividend income is also taxed at the shareholder level). Because income tax treaties reduce taxes on earnings generated by MNCs, they help stimulate direct foreign investment. Many foreign projects that are perceived as feasible would not be feasible without income tax treaties because the expected cash flows would be reduced by excessive taxation.

Tax credits

Even without income tax treaties, an MNC may be allowed a credit for income and withholding taxes paid in one country against taxes owed by the parent if it meets certain requirements. Like income tax treaties, tax credits help to avoid double taxation and stimulate direct foreign investment.

Tax credit policies vary somewhat among countries, but they generally work like this. Consider a UK-based MNC subject to a UK tax rate of 30 per cent. Assume that a foreign subsidiary of this corporation has generated earnings taxed at less than 30 per cent by the host country's government. The earnings remitted to the parent from the subsidiary will be subject to an additional amount of UK tax to bring the total tax up to 30 per cent. From the parent's point of view, the tax on its subsidiary's remitted earnings are 30 per cent overall, so it does not matter whether the host country of the subsidiary or the UK receives most of the taxes. From the perspective of the governments of these two countries, however, the allocation of taxes is very important. If subsidiaries of UK corporations are established in foreign countries, and if these countries tax income at a rate close to 30 per cent, they can generate large tax revenues from income earned by the subsidiaries. The host countries receive the tax revenues at the expense of the parent's country (the UK, in this case). The UK has double taxation agreements with over 100 countries.

If the corporate income tax rate in a foreign country is greater than 30 per cent, the UK generally does not impose any additional taxes on earnings remitted to a UK parent by foreign subsidiaries in that country. In fact, some countries allow the excess foreign tax to be credited against other taxes owed by the parent, due on the same type of income generated by subsidiaries in other lower-tax countries. In a sense, this suggests that some host countries could charge abnormally high corporate income tax rates to foreign subsidiaries and still attract direct foreign investment. If the MNC in our example has subsidiaries located in some countries with low corporate income taxes, the UK tax on earnings remitted to the UK parent will normally bring the total tax up to 30 per cent. Yet, credits against excessive income taxes by high-tax countries on foreign subsidiaries could offset these taxes that would otherwise be paid to the UK government. Due to tax credits, therefore, an MNC might be more willing to invest in a project in a country with excessive tax rates.

Basic information on a country's current taxes may not be sufficient for determining the tax effects of a particular foreign project because tax incentives may be offered in particular circumstances, and tax rates can change over time. Consider an MNC that plans to establish a manufacturing plant in country Y rather than country X. Assume that while many economic characteristics favour country X, the current tax rates in country Y are lower. However, whereas tax rates in country X have been historically stable and are expected to continue that way, they have been changing every few years in country Y. In this case, the MNC must assess the future uncertainty of the tax rates. It cannot treat the current tax rate of country Y as a constant when conducting a capital budgeting analysis. Instead, it must consider possible changes in the tax rates over time and, based on these possibilities, determine whether country Y's projected tax advantages *over time* sufficiently outweigh the advantages of country X. One approach to account for possible changes in the tax rates is to use sensitivity analysis, which measures the sensitivity of the *NPV* of after-tax cash flows to various possible tax changes over time. For each tax scenario, a different *NPV* is projected. By accounting for each possible tax scenario, the MNC can develop a distribution of possible *NPV*s that may occur and can then compare these for each country.

Two critical, broadly defined functions are necessary to determine how international tax laws affect the cash flows of a foreign project. The first is to be aware of all the current (and possible future) tax laws that exist for each country where the MNC does (or plans to do) business. The second is to take the information generated from the first function and apply it to forecasted earnings and remittances to determine the taxes, so that the proposed project's cash flows can be estimated.

Taxes on income from intercompany transactions

Many of an MNC's proposed foreign projects will involve intercompany transactions. For example, a US-based MNC may consider acquiring a foreign firm that will produce and deliver supplies to its UK subsidiaries. Under these conditions, the MNC must use **transfer pricing**, which involves pricing the transactions between two entities (such as subsidiaries) of the same corporation. When MNCs consider new foreign projects, they must incorporate their transfer pricing to properly estimate cash flows that will be generated from these projects. Therefore, before the feasibility of a foreign project can be determined, transfer pricing decisions must be made on any anticipated intercompany transactions that would result from the new project. MNCs are subject to some guidelines on transfer pricing, but they usually have some flexibility and tend to use a transfer pricing policy that will minimize taxes while satisfying the guidelines.

EXAMPLE

Oakland Ltd has established two subsidiaries to capitalize on low production costs. One of these subsidiaries (called Hitax Sub) is located in a country whose government imposes a 50 per cent tax rate on before-tax earnings. Hitax Sub produces partially finished products and sends them to the other subsidiary (called Lotax Sub) where the final assembly takes place. The host government of Lotax Sub imposes a 20 per cent tax on before-tax earnings. To simplify the example, assume that no dividends are to be remitted to the parent in the near future. Given this information, *pro forma* income statements would be as shown in the top part of Exhibit 13A.2 for Hitax Sub (second column), Lotax Sub (third column), and the combined subsidiaries (last column). The income statement

items are reported in UK pounds to illustrate how a revised transfer pricing policy can affect earnings and cash flows.

The sales level shown for Hitax Sub matches the cost of goods sold for Lotax Sub, indicating that all Hitax Sub sales are to Lotax Sub. The additional expenses incurred by Lotax Sub to complete the product are classified as operating expenses.

Notice from Exhibit 13A.2 that both subsidiaries have the same earnings before taxes. Yet, because of the different tax rates, Hitax Sub's after-tax income is £7.5 million less than Lotax Sub's. If Oakland Ltd can revise its transfer pricing, its combined earnings after taxes will be increased. To illustrate, suppose that the price of products sent from Hitax Sub to Lotax Sub is

(Continued)

reduced, causing Hitax Sub's sales to decline from £100 million to £80 million. This also reduces Lotax Sub's cost of goods sold by £20 million. The revised *pro forma* income statement resulting from the change in the transfer pricing policy is shown in the bottom part of Exhibit 13A.2. The two subsidiaries' forecasted earnings before taxes now differ by £40 million, although the combined amount has not changed. Because earnings have been shifted from Hitax Sub to Lotax Sub, the total tax payments are reduced to £11.5 million from the original estimate of £17.5 million. Thus, the corporate taxes imposed on earnings are now forecasted to be £6 million lower than originally expected.

EXHIBIT 13A.2   Impact of transfer pricing adjustment on *pro forma* earnings and taxes: Oakland Ltd (in thousands)

	Original estimates		
	Hitax Sub	**Lotax Sub**	**Combined**
Sales	£100 000	£150 000	£150 000
less Cost of goods sold	50 000	100 000	50 000
Gross profit	50 000	50 000	100 000
less Operating expenses	20 000	20 000	40 000
Earnings before interest and taxes	30 000	30 000	60 000
Interest expense	5 000	5 000	10 000
Earnings before taxes	25 000	25 000	50 000
Taxes (50% for Hitax and 20% for Lotax)	12 500	5000	17 500
Earnings after taxes	£12 500	£20 000	£32 500
	Revised estimates based on adjusting transfer pricing policy		
	Hitax Sub	Lotax Sub	Combined
Sales	£80 000	£150 000	£150 000
less Cost of goods sold	50 000	80 000	50 000
Gross profit	30 000	70 000	100 000
less Operating expenses	20 000	20 000	40 000
Earnings before interest and taxes	10 000	50 000	60 000
Interest expense	5000	5000	10 000
Earnings before taxes	5000	45 000	50 000
Taxes (50% for Hitax and 20% for Lotax)	2500	9000	11 500
Earnings after taxes	£2500	£36 000	£38 500

Note:

The combined numbers are shown here for illustrative purposes only and do not reflect the firm's official consolidated financial statements. When consolidating sales and cost of goods sold, intercompany transactions have been eliminated. This example is intended simply to illustrate how total taxes paid by subsidiaries are lower when transfer pricing is structured to shift some gross profit from a high-tax subsidiary to a low-tax subsidiary.

It should be mentioned that possible adjustments in the transfer pricing policies may be limited because host governments may restrict such practices when the intent is to avoid taxes. Transactions between subsidiaries of a firm are supposed to be priced using the principle of 'arm's-length' transactions. That is, the price should be set as if the buyer is unrelated to the seller and should not be adjusted simply to shift tax burdens.

Nevertheless, there is some flexibility on transfer pricing policies, enabling MNCs from all countries to attempt to establish policies that are within legal limits, but also reduce tax burdens. Even if the transfer price reflects the 'fair' price that would normally be charged in the market, one subsidiary can still charge another for technology transfers, research and development expenses or other forms of overhead expenses incurred.

The actual mechanics of international transfer pricing go far beyond the example provided here. The UK laws in this area are particularly strict. Nevertheless, there are various ways that MNCs can justify increasing prices at one subsidiary and reducing them at another.

There is substantial evidence that MNCs based in numerous countries use transfer pricing strategies to reduce their taxes. Moreover, transfer pricing restrictions can be circumvented in several ways. Various fees can be implemented for services, research and development, royalties and administrative duties. Although the fees may be imposed to shift earnings and minimize taxes, they have the effect of distorting the actual performance of each subsidiary. To correct for any distortion, the MNC can use a centralized approach to account for the transfer pricing strategy when assessing the performance of each subsidiary.

USING THE WEB

Country corporate tax rates

An MNC must determine a country's corporate tax rates before it can properly estimate its cash flows from establishing direct foreign investment there. Information about taxes imposed by each country is provided at: http://www.pwcglobal.com. Enter 'tax' into the search section and review information about corporate income taxes, dividend withholding tax, interest withholding tax, and royalties and fees withholding tax.

CHAPTER 14
COUNTRY RISK
ANALYSIS

LEARNING OBJECTIVES

The specific objectives of this chapter are to:

- Identify the common factors used by MNCs to measure a country's political risk.

- Identify the common factors used by MNCs to measure a country's financial risk.

- Explain the techniques used to measure country risk.

- Explain how MNCs use the assessment of country risk when making financial decisions.

An multinational corporation (MNC) conducts country risk analysis when assessing whether to continue conducting business in a particular country. The analysis can also be used when determining whether to implement new projects in foreign countries. Country risk can be partitioned into the country's political risk and its financial risk. Financial managers must understand how to measure country risk so that they can make investment decisions that maximize their MNC's value.

WHY COUNTRY RISK ANALYSIS IS IMPORTANT

Country risk is the potentially adverse impact of a country's environment on an MNC's cash flows. Investments with all the normal business guarantees attached against non-payment, including government guarantees, can become worthless overnight. Loan repayments can be delayed or reduced without warning. Such financial crises are a regular phenomenon in international finance. If the credit risk level of a particular country begins to increase, the MNC may consider divesting its subsidiaries located there. MNCs can also use country risk analysis as a screening device to avoid conducting business in countries with excessive risk. Events that heighten country risk tend to discourage direct foreign investment in that particular country.

Country risk analysis is not restricted to predicting major crises. An MNC may also use this analysis to revise its investment or financing decisions in light of recent events. In any given week, the following unrelated international events might occur around the world:

- A terrorist attack.

- A major labour strike in an industry.

- A political crisis due to a scandal within a country.

- Concern about a country's banking system that may cause a major outflow of funds.

- The imposition of trade restrictions on imports.

- A declaration of non-payment of debts by a government.

Any of these events could affect the potential cash flows to be generated by an MNC or the cost of financing projects and therefore affect the value of the MNC.

Even if an MNC reduces its exposure to all such events in a given week, a new set of events will occur in the following week. For each of these events, an MNC must consider whether its cash flows will be affected and whether there has been a change in policy to which it should respond. Country risk analysis is an ongoing process. Most MNCs will not be affected by every event, but they will pay close attention to any events that may have an impact on the industries or countries in which they do business. They also recognize that they cannot eliminate their exposure to all events but may at least attempt to limit their exposure to any single country-specific event.

POLITICAL RISK FACTORS

An MNC must assess country risk not only in countries where it currently does business but also in those where it expects to export or establish subsidiaries. Several risk characteristics of a country may significantly affect performance, and the MNC should be concerned about the likely degree of impact for each.

As one might expect, many country characteristics related to the political environment can influence an MNC. An extreme form of political risk is the possibility that the host country will take over a subsidiary. In some cases of expropriation, some compensation (the amount decided by the host country government) is awarded. In other cases, the assets are confiscated and no compensation is provided. Expropriation can take place peacefully or by force. The following are some of the more common forms of country-related risk:

- Attitude of consumers in the host country

- Actions of host government

- Blockage of fund transfers

- Currency inconvertibility

- War
- Bureaucracy
- Corruption.

Each of these characteristics will be examined in turn.

Attitude of consumers in the host country

A mild form of political risk (to an exporter) is a tendency of residents to purchase only locally produced goods. Even if the exporter decides to set up a subsidiary in the foreign country, this philosophy could prevent its success. All countries tend to exert some pressure on consumers to purchase from locally owned manufacturers. (In the UK, consumers have in the past been encouraged to purchase locally made goods under the 'buy British' slogan.) MNCs that consider entering a foreign market (or have already entered that market) must monitor the general loyalty of consumers toward locally produced products. If consumers are very loyal to local products, a joint venture with a local company may be more feasible than an exporting strategy.

Actions of host government

Various actions of a host government can affect the cash flow of an MNC. For example, a host government might impose pollution control standards (which affect costs) and additional corporate taxes (which affect after-tax earnings) as well as withholding taxes and fund transfer restrictions (which affect after-tax cash flows sent to the parent).

Some MNCs use turnover in government members or political beliefs as a proxy for a country's political risk. While this can significantly influence the MNC's future cash flows, it alone does not serve as a suitable representation of political risk. A subsidiary will not necessarily be affected by changing governments. Furthermore, a subsidiary can be affected by new policies of the host government or by a changed attitude toward the subsidiary's home country (and therefore the subsidiary), even when the host government has no risk of being overthrown.

A host government can use various means to make an MNC's operations coincide with its own goals. It may, for example, require the use of local employees for managerial positions at a subsidiary. In addition, it may require social facilities (such as an exercise room or non-smoking areas) or special environmental controls (such as air pollution controls). Furthermore, it is not uncommon for a host government to require special permits, impose extra taxes or subsidize competitors. All of these actions represent political risk, in that they reflect a country's political characteristics and could influence an MNC's cash flows.

EXAMPLE

In March 2004, antitrust regulators representing the European Union (EU) countries decided to fine Microsoft about 500 million euros (equivalent to about $610 million at the time) for abusing its monopolistic position in computer software. They also imposed restrictions on how Microsoft can bundle its Windows Media Player (needed to access music or videos) in its portable computers sold in Europe. Microsoft argued that the fine was unfair because it was not subject to such restrictions in its home country, the USA. Some critics argue, however, that the European regulators are not being too strict, but rather that the US regulators are being too lenient.

Lack of restrictions. In some cases, MNCs are adversely affected by a lack of restrictions in a host country, which allows illegitimate business behaviour to take market share. One of the most troubling issues for MNCs is the failure by host governments to enforce copyright laws against local firms that illegally copy the MNC's product. For example, local firms in Asia commonly copy software produced by MNCs and sell it to customers at lower prices. Software producers lose an estimated £2 billion in sales annually in Asia for this reason. Furthermore, the legal systems in some countries do not adequately protect a firm against copyright violations or other illegal means of obtaining market share.

Blockage of fund transfers

Subsidiaries of MNCs often send funds back to the headquarters for loan repayments, purchases of supplies, administrative fees, remitted earnings or other purposes. In some cases, a host government may block fund transfers, which could force subsidiaries to undertake projects that are not optimal (just to make use of the funds). Alternatively, the MNC may invest the funds in local securities that provide some return while the funds are blocked. But this return may be inferior to what could have been earned on funds remitted to the parent.

Currency inconvertibility

Some governments do not allow the home currency to be exchanged into other currencies. Thus, the earnings generated by a subsidiary in these countries cannot be remitted to the parent through currency conversion. When the currency is inconvertible, an MNC's parent may need to exchange it for goods to extract benefits from projects in that country.

War

Some countries tend to engage in constant conflicts with neighbouring countries or experience internal turmoil. This can affect the safety of employees hired by an MNC's subsidiary or by salespeople who attempt to establish export markets for the MNC. In addition, countries plagued by the threat of war typically have volatile business cycles, which make the MNC's cash flows generated from such countries more uncertain. The terrorist attack on the USA on September 11, 2001, aroused the expectation that the USA would be involved in a war. MNCs were adversely affected by their potential exposure to terrorist attacks, especially if their subsidiaries were located in countries where there might be anti-US sentiment. Even if an MNC is not directly damaged due to a war, it may incur costs from ensuring the safety of its employees.

The 2003 war in Iraq. As a result of the 2003 war in Iraq, MNCs' cash flows were affected in various ways. The war caused friction between the USA and some countries in the Middle East. Consequently, MNCs faced the possibility that their buildings or offices overseas might be destroyed and that their employees might be attacked. Furthermore, demand for US products and services by consumers in the Middle East declined. In addition, because of friction between the USA and France over how the situation in Iraq should be handled, French demand for some products produced by US-based MNCs also declined. To a lesser extent, there were protests by citizens in other countries, which could have reduced the demand for products produced by US firms. This form of country risk is not limited to US-based MNCs. Friction periodically arises between many countries. Just as French consumers reduced their demand for US products during the war, US consumers reduced their demand for French wine and reduced their travel to France. The French Government Tourist Office estimated that revenue received in France due to US tourism in 2003 was about $500 million less than in the previous year.

   Even if MNCs were not directly affected by the various protests, there was substantial uncertainty about how the war might adversely affect MNCs by weakening economic conditions. There was concern that oil prices would rise because of the possible destruction of oil wells, and higher oil prices have a direct impact on transportation and energy costs. Higher interest rates were feared because of the substantial funding needed to finance the military spending. Some of the more pessimistic predictions suggested there would be a major world recession combined with high inflation. Thus, MNCs were concerned about the potential higher costs of supplies and the potential impact of high US inflation or interest rates on exchange rates. Given all this uncertainty, MNCs restricted their expansion until the impact of the war on oil prices, the US budget deficit and the political relationships between the USA and other countries was clear.

Bureaucracy

Another country risk factor is government bureaucracy, which can complicate an MNC's business. Although this factor may seem irrelevant, it was a major deterrent for MNCs that considered projects in Eastern Europe in the early 1990s. Many of the Eastern European governments were not experienced at facilitating the entrance of MNCs into their markets.

Corruption

Corruption can adversely affect an MNC's international business because it can increase the cost of conducting business or it can reduce revenue. Various forms of corruption can occur between firms or between a firm and the government. For example, an MNC may lose revenue because a government contract is awarded to a local firm that paid off a government official. Laws and their enforcement vary among countries, however. For example, in the USA, it is illegal to make a payment to a high-ranking government official in return for political favours, but it is legal in most countries for companies to make contributions to political parties.

USING THE WEB

The index for the top 30 (least corrupt) countries is shown in Exhibit 14.1.

EXHIBIT 14.1   Corruption Perception Index (CPI) ratings for selected countries (High ratings indicate low corruption.)

Country rank, 2012	Country	CPI 2012 score
1	New Zealand	90
1	Denmark	90
1	Finland	90
4	Sweden	88
5	Singapore	87
6	Switzerland	86
7	Norway	85
7	Australia	85
9	Netherlands	84
9	Canada	84

(Continued)

Country rank, 2012	Country	CPI 2012 score
11	Iceland	82
12	Luxembourg	80
13	Germany	79
14	Hong Kong	77
15	Barbados	76
16	Belgium	75
17	Japan	74
17	UK	74
19	USA	73
20	Chile	72
20	Uruguay	72
22	Bahamas	71
22	France	71
22	Saint Lucia	71
25	Austria	69
25	Ireland	69
27	Qatar	68
27	United Arab Emirates	68
29	Cyprus	66
30	Spain	65
30	Botswana	65

Source: Transparency International Index
Note: The maximum CPI score is 100.

FINANCIAL RISK FACTORS

Along with political factors, financial factors should be considered when assessing country risk. One of the most obvious financial factors is the current and potential state of the country's economy. An MNC that exports to a country or develops a subsidiary in a country is highly concerned about that country's demand for its products. This demand is, of course, strongly influenced by the country's economy. A recession in the country could severely reduce demand for the MNC's exports or products sold by the MNC's local subsidiary. Renault carmakers who operate in 118 countries state in their 2009 Annual Report that:

> *The automotive market is expected to grow by 3 per cent in 2010 compared with 2009, but with significant disparities between regions. In two of the main regions in which Renault is present, Europe and Euromed, markets are expected to shrink by around 10 per cent on 2009.*

(p. 2)

Later on citing developing markets such as Russia, Romania, Brazil and India as a 'key source of growth' (p. 20).

Indicators of economic growth

A country's economic growth is dependent on several financial factors:

- *Interest rates.* Higher interest rates tend to slow the growth of an economy and reduce demand for the MNC's products. Lower interest rates often stimulate the economy and increase demand for the MNC's products.

- *Exchange rates.* Exchange rates can influence the demand for the country's exports, which in turn affects the country's production and income level. A strong currency may reduce demand for the country's exports, increase the volume of products imported by the country, and therefore reduce the country's production and national income. A very weak currency can cause speculative outflows and reduce the amount of funds available to finance growth by businesses.

- *Inflation.* Inflation can affect consumers' purchasing power and therefore their demand for an MNC's goods. It also indirectly affects a country's financial condition by influencing the country's interest rates and currency value. A high level of inflation may also lead to a decline in economic growth.

Most financial factors that affect a country's economic condition are difficult to forecast. Thus, even if an MNC considers them in its country risk assessment, it may still make poor decisions because of an improper forecast of the country's financial factors.

Some financial conditions may be caused by political risk. For example, the September 11, 2001 terrorist attack on the USA affected US-based MNCs because of political risk and financial risk. Political uncertainty caused uncertainty about economic conditions, which resulted in a reduction in spending by consumers and, therefore, a reduction in cash flows of MNCs. Analysts have cited concerns over the political will of the Greek government as a cause of the higher yield (return) required for Greek bonds in 2010.

Types of country risk assessment

Although there is no consensus as to how country risk can best be assessed, some guidelines have been developed. The first step is to recognize the difference between: (1) an overall risk assessment of a country without consideration of the MNC's business and (2) the risk assessment of a country as it relates to the MNC's type of business. The first type can be referred to as **macroassessment** of country risk and the latter type as a **microassessment**. Each type is discussed in turn.

Macroassessment of country risk

A macroassessment involves consideration of all variables that affect country risk except those unique to a particular firm or industry. This type of risk is convenient in that it remains the same for a given country, regardless of the firm or industry of concern; however, it excludes relevant information that could improve the accuracy of the assessment. Although a macroassessment of country risk is not ideal for any individual MNC, it serves as a foundation that can then be modified to reflect the particular business of the MNC.

Any macroassessment model should consider both political and financial characteristics of the country being assessed:

- *Political factors.* Political factors include the relationship of the host government with the MNC's home country government, the attitude of people in the host country toward the MNC's government, the historical stability of the host government, the vulnerability of the host government to political takeovers, and the probability of war between the host country and neighbouring countries. Consideration of such political factors will indicate the probability of political events that may affect an MNC and the magnitude of the impact.

● *Financial factors.* The financial factors of a macroassessment model should include GDP growth, inflation trends, government budget levels (and the government deficit), interest rates, unemployment, the country's reliance on export income, the balance of trade and foreign exchange controls. The list of financial factors could easily be extended several pages. The factors listed here represent just a subset of the financial factors considered when evaluating the financial strength of a country.

Uncertainty surrounding a macroassessment. There is clearly a degree of subjectivity in identifying the relevant political and financial factors for a macroassessment of country risk. There is also some subjectivity in determining the importance of each factor for the overall macroassessment for a particular country. For instance, one assessor may assign a much higher weight (degree of importance) to real GDP growth than another assessor. Finally, there is some subjectivity in predicting these financial factors. Because of these various types of subjectivity, it is not surprising that risk assessors often arrive at different opinions after completing a macroassessment of country risk.

Microassessment of country risk

While a macroassessment of country risk provides an indication of the country's overall status, it does not assess country risk from the perspective of the particular business of concern. A microassessment of country risk is needed to determine how the country risk relates to the specific MNC.

The specific impact of a particular form of country risk can affect MNCs in different ways.

EXAMPLE

Country Z has been assigned a relatively low macro-assessment by most experts due to its poor financial condition. Two MNCs are deciding whether to set up subsidiaries in Country Z. Carco Ltd is considering developing a subsidiary that would produce automobiles and sell them locally, while Milco Ltd plans to build a subsidiary that would produce military supplies. Carco's plan to build an automobile subsidiary does not appear to be feasible, unless there is a shortage of automobile producers in Country Z.

Country Z's government may be committed to purchasing a given amount of military supplies, regardless of how weak the economy is. Thus, Milco's plan to build a military supply subsidiary may still be feasible, even though Country Z's financial condition is poor.

It is possible, however, that Country Z's government will order its military supplies from a locally owned firm because it wants its supply needs to remain confidential. This possibility is an element of country risk because it is a country characteristic (or attitude) that can affect the feasibility of a project. Yet, this specific characteristic is relevant only to Milco Ltd and not to Carco.

This example illustrates how an appropriate country risk assessment varies with the firm, industry, and project of concern and therefore why a macroassessment of country risk has its limitations. A microassessment is also necessary when evaluating the country risk related to a particular project proposed by a particular firm.

In addition to political variables, financial variables must also be included in a micro assessment of country risk. Microfactors include the sensitivity of the firm's business to real GDP growth, inflation trends, interest rates and other factors. Due to differences in business characteristics, some firms are more susceptible to the host country's economy than others. Exhibit 14.2 reports a survey of risk factors as perceived by large MNCs.

EXHIBIT 14.2 Survey of top 1000 multinationals (2004) – percentage of total respondents listing item as a critical risk

Most critical risk to firm operations	%
Government regulations/legal decision	64
Country financial risk	60
Currency interest rate volatility	51
Political and social disturbances	46
Corporate governance	30
Absence of rule of law	29
Theft of intellectual property	28
Terrorist attack	26
Security threats to employees and assets	26
Disruption of key supplier/customer/partner	23
Product quality and safety problems	20
IT disruption	19
Employee fraud or sabotage	10
Natural disasters	6
Activist attacks on global or corporate brands	5

Source: FDI Confidence Index®, copyright A.T. Kearney, 2004. All rights reserved. Reprinted with permission. http://www.atkearney.com/gbpc/foreign-direct-investment-confidence-index

In summary, the overall assessment of country risk consists of four parts:

1   Macropolitical risk

2   Macrofinancial risk

3   Micropolitical risk

4   Microfinancial risk.

Although these parts can be consolidated to generate a single country risk rating, it may be useful to keep them separate so that an MNC can identify the various ways its direct foreign investment or exporting operations are exposed to country risk.

TECHNIQUES TO ASSESS COUNTRY RISK

Once a firm identifies all the macro- and microfactors that deserve consideration in the country risk assessment, it may wish to implement a system for evaluating these factors and determining a country risk rating.

Various techniques are available to achieve this objective. The following are some of the more popular techniques:

● Check list approach

● Delphi technique

- Quantitative analysis
- Inspection visits
- Combination of techniques.

Each technique is briefly discussed in turn.

Check list approach

A check list approach involves making a judgement on all the political and financial factors (both macro and micro) that contribute to a firm's assessment of country risk. Ratings are assigned to a list of various financial and political factors, and these ratings are then consolidated to derive an overall assessment of country risk. Some factors (such as real GDP growth) can be measured from available data, while others (such as probability of entering a war) must be subjectively measured.

A substantial amount of information about countries is available on the Internet. This information can be used to develop ratings of various factors used to assess country risk. The factors are then converted to some numerical rating in order to assess a particular country. Those factors thought to have a greater influence on country risk should be assigned greater weights. Both the measurement of some factors and the weighting scheme implemented are subjective.

Delphi technique

The **Delphi technique** involves the collection of independent opinions on country risk without group discussion by the assessors (such as employees or outside consultants) who provide these opinions. Though the Delphi technique can be useful, it is based on subjective opinions, which may vary among assessors. The MNC can average these opinions in some manner and even assess the degree of disagreement by measuring the dispersion of opinions.

Quantitative analysis

Once the financial and political variables have been measured for a period of time, models for quantitative analysis can attempt to identify the characteristics that influence the level of country risk. For example, regression analysis may be used to assess risk, since it can measure the sensitivity of one variable to other variables. A firm could regress a measure of its business activity (such as its percentage increase in sales) against country characteristics (such as real growth in GDP) over a series of previous months or quarters. Results from such an analysis will indicate the susceptibility of a particular business to a country's economy. This is valuable information to incorporate into the overall evaluation of country risk.

Although quantitative models can quantify the impact of variables on each other, they do not necessarily indicate a country's problems before they actually occur (preferably before the firm's decision to pursue a project in that country). Nor can they evaluate subjective data that cannot be quantified. In addition, historical trends of various country characteristics are not always useful for anticipating an upcoming crisis.

Inspection visits

Inspection visits involve travelling to a country and meeting with government officials, business executives and/or consumers. Such meetings can help clarify any uncertain opinions the firm has about a country. Indeed, some variables, such as intercountry relationships, may be difficult to assess without a trip to the host country.

Combination of techniques

A survey of 193 corporations heavily involved in foreign business found that about half of them have no formal method of assessing country risk. This does not mean that they neglect to assess country risk, but rather that there is no proven method to use. Consequently, many MNCs use a variety of techniques, possibly using a check list approach to develop an overall country risk rating and then using the Delphi technique, quantitative analysis and inspection visits to assign ratings to the various factors.

EXAMPLE

Mission Ltd recognizes that it must consider several financial and political factors in its country risk analysis of the Ukraine, where it plans to establish a subsidiary. Mission creates a check list of several factors and assigns a rating to each factor. It uses the Delphi tech- nique to rate various political factors. It uses quantita- tive analysis to predict future economic conditions in the Ukraine so that it can rate various financial factors. It conducts an inspection visit to complement its assessment of the financial and political factors.

MEASURING COUNTRY RISK

Deriving an overall country risk rating using a check list approach requires separate ratings for political and financial risk. First, the political factors are assigned values within some arbitrarily chosen range (such as values from 1 to 5, where 5 is the best value/lowest risk). Next, these political factors are assigned weights (representing degree of importance), which should add up to 100 per cent. The assigned values of the factors times their respective weights can then be summed to derive a political risk rating.

The process is then repeated to derive the financial risk rating. All financial factors are assigned values (from 1 to 5, where 5 is the best value/lowest risk). Then the assigned values of the factors times their respective weights can be summed to derive a financial risk rating.

Once the political and financial ratings have been derived, a country's overall country risk rating as it relates to a specific project can be determined by assigning weights to the political and financial ratings according to their perceived importance. The importance of political risk versus financial risk varies with the intent of the MNC. An MNC considering direct foreign investment to attract demand in that country must be highly concerned about financial risk. An MNC establishing a foreign manufacturing plant and planning to export the goods from there should be more concerned with political risk.

If the political risk is thought to be much more influential on a particular project than the financial risk, it will receive a higher weight than the financial risk rating (together both weights must total 100 per cent). The political and financial ratings multiplied by their respective weights will determine the overall country risk rating for a country as it relates to a particular project.

EXAMPLE

Assume that Cougar plc plans to build a steel plant in Country X. It has used the Delphi technique and quan- titative analysis to derive ratings for various political and financial factors. The discussion here focuses on how to consolidate the ratings to derive an overall country risk rating.

(Continued)

Exhibit 14.3 illustrates Cougar's country risk assessment of Country X. Notice in Exhibit 14.3 that two political factors and five financial factors contribute to the overall country risk rating in this example.

Cougar plc will consider projects only in countries that have a country risk rating of 3.5 or higher, based on its country risk rating.

EXHIBIT 14.3   Determining the overall country risk rating

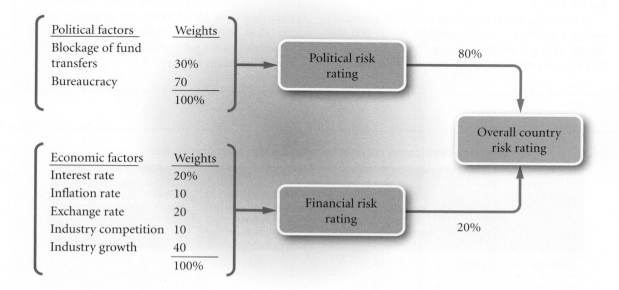

Variation in methods of measuring country risk

Country risk assessors have their own individual procedures for quantifying country risk. The procedure described here is just one of many. Most procedures are similar, though, in that they somehow assign ratings and weights to all individual characteristics relevant to country risk assessment.

The number of relevant factors comprising both the political risk and the financial risk categories will vary with the country being assessed and the type of corporate operations planned for that country. The assignment of values to the factors, along with the degree of importance (weights) assigned to the factors, will also vary with the country being assessed and the type of corporate operations planned for that country.

EXAMPLE

Cougar plc has assigned the values and weights to the factors as shown in Exhibit 14.4. In this example, the company generally assigns the financial factors higher ratings than the political factors. The financial

(Continued)

condition of Country X has therefore been assessed more favourably than the political condition. Industry growth is the most important financial factor in Country X, based on its 40 per cent weighting. The bureaucracy is thought to be the most important political factor, based on a weighting of 70 per cent; regulation of international fund transfers receives the remaining 30 per cent weighting. The political risk rating is estimated at 3.3 by adding the products of the assigned ratings (Column 2) and weights (Column 3) of the political risk factors.

The financial risk is computed to be 3.9, based on adding the products of the assigned ratings and the weights of the financial risk factors. Once the political and financial ratings are determined, the overall country

risk rating can be derived (as shown at the bottom of Exhibit 14.4), given the weights assigned to political and financial risk. Column 3 at the bottom of Exhibit 14.4 indicates that Cougar perceives political risk (receiving an 80 per cent weight) to be much more important than financial risk (receiving a 20 per cent weight) in Country X for the proposed project. The overall country risk rating of 3.42 may appear low given the individual category ratings. This is due to the heavy weighting given to political risk, which in this example is critical from the firm's perspective. In particular, Cougar views Country X's bureaucracy as a critical factor and assigns it a low rating. Given that Cougar considers projects only in countries that have a rating of at least 3.5; it decides not to pursue the project in Country X.

EXHIBIT 14.4 Derivation of the overall country risk rating for country based on assumed information

(1)	(2)	(3)	(4) = (2) × (3)
	Rating assigned by company to factor within a range of 1–5	Weight assigned by company to factor according to importance	Weighted value of factor
Blockage of fund transfers	4	30%	1.2
Bureaucracy	3	70	2.1
Political risk factors		100%	3.3 = **Political risk rating**
Interest rate	5	20%	1.0
Inflation rate	4	10	0.4
Exchange rate	4	20	0.8
Industry competition	5	10	0.5
Industry growth	3	40	1.2
Financial risk factors		100%	3.9 = **Financial risk rating**
(1)	(2)	(3)	(4) = **(2)** × **(3)**
Weight assigned	Rating as determined above	Weight assigned by company to each risk factor	Weighted rating
Political risk	3.3	80%	2.64
Financial risk	3.9	20	0.78
		100%	3.42 = **Overall country risk rating 1**

Using the country risk rating for decision-making

If the country risk is too high, then the firm does not need to analyze the feasibility of the proposed project any further. Some firms may contend that no risk is too high when considering a project. Their reasoning is that if the potential return is high enough, the project is worth undertaking. When employee safety is a concern, however, the project may be rejected regardless of its potential return.

Even after a project is accepted and implemented, the MNC must continue to monitor country risk. With a labour-intensive MNC, the host country may feel it is benefiting from a subsidiary's existence (due to the subsidiary's employment of local people), and the chance of expropriation may be low. Nevertheless, several other forms of country risk could suddenly make the MNC consider divesting the project. Furthermore, decisions regarding subsidiary expansion, fund transfers to the parent, and sources of financing can all be affected by any changes in country risk. Since country risk can change dramatically over time, periodic reassessment is required, especially for less stable countries.

Regardless of how country risk analysis is conducted, MNCs are often unable to predict crises in various countries. MNCs should recognize their limitations when assessing country risk and consider ways they might limit their exposure to a possible increase in that risk.

COMPARING RISK RATINGS AMONG COUNTRIES

An MNC may evaluate country risk for several countries, perhaps to determine where to establish a subsidiary. One approach to comparing political and financial ratings among countries, advocated by some foreign risk managers, is a foreign investment risk matrix (FIRM), which displays the financial (or economic) and political risk by intervals ranging across the matrix from 'poor' to 'good'. Each country can be positioned in its appropriate location on the matrix based on its political rating and financial rating.

USING THE WEB

Country risk ratings

If an MNC wants to consider a country risk assessment by outside evaluators, it can obtain a country risk rating for any country at: http://www.oecd.org and search for 'Country Risk Classification' within the site.

MARKET APPROACH TO COUNTRY RISK RATING

Government bond interest rates are, like any other interest rate, made up of three main factors: time preference (the reward purely for delayed spending), inflation and risk. Assuming that time preference is the same across countries, differences in the real interest rates (that is the total market rate less the inflation rate) must be due to a risk premium. Exhibit 14.5 lists an estimate of risk premiums by a selection of countries.

INCORPORATING COUNTRY RISK IN CAPITAL BUDGETING

If the risk rating of a country is in the tolerable range, any project related to that country deserves further consideration. Country risk can be incorporated in the capital budgeting analysis of a proposed project by adjusting the discount rate or by adjusting the estimated cash flows. Each method is discussed here.

EXHIBIT 14.5 An estimate of market risk premiums March 2013

	Interest	Inflation	Risk premium	Credit rating (Standard and Poor's)
Greece	10.8	0.2	10.6	B−
Portugal	6.19	0.2	5.99	BB
New Zealand	3.78	0.9	2.88	AA
Ireland	3.8	1.2	2.6	BBB+
Spain	5.25	2.68	2.57	BBB−
Italy	4.56	2.2	2.36	BBB+
Sweden	2.04	0	2.04	AAA
Canada	1.88	0.5	1.38	AAA
Australia	3.39	2.2	1.19	AAA
Switzerland	0.79	−0.3	1.09	AA
France	2.2	1.2	1	AA+
Belgium	2.44	1.46	0.98	AA
Japan	0.68	−0.1	0.78	AA−
Denmark	1.73	1.3	0.43	AAA
USA	1.86	1.6	0.26	AA+
Finland	1.74	1.6	0.14	AAA
Germany	1.54	1.7	−0.16	AAA
UK	2.08	2.7	−0.62	AAA
Austria	1.91	2.8	−0.89	AA+
Netherlands	1.81	2.97	−1.16	AAA

Note: Time preference is assumed to be constant across all countries and has been set at 0 per cent. The risk premium is therefore the same as the real rate of interest being the interest rate less inflation. Interest rates are of 10-year government bonds.

Adjustment of the discount rate

The discount rate of a proposed project is supposed to reflect the required rate of return on that project. Thus, the discount rate can be adjusted to account for the country risk. The lower the country risk rating, the higher the perceived risk and the higher the discount rate applied to the project's cash flows. This approach is convenient in that one adjustment to the capital budgeting analysis can capture country risk. However, there is no precise formula for adjusting the discount rate to incorporate country risk. The adjustment is somewhat arbitrary and may therefore cause feasible projects to be rejected or infeasible projects to be accepted.

Adjustment of the estimated cash flows

Perhaps the most appropriate method for incorporating forms of country risk in a capital budgeting analysis is to estimate how the cash flows would be affected by each form of risk. For example, if there is a 20 per cent probability that the host government will temporarily block funds from the subsidiary to the parent, the MNC should estimate the project's *NPV* under these circumstances, realizing that there is a 20 per cent chance that this *NPV* will occur.

MANAGING FOR VALUE

Ireland invests in Spain

In 1995 Ireland's Electricity Supply Board (ESB) a government owned firm started looking to build electricity power plants abroad and supply electricity abroad. The legal framework for such development was not in place in either Germany or France. They eventually chose Spain as offering a suitable legal framework. The area they chose was the Basque Country because of its good infrastructure, education and local supply of natural gas needed to produce the electricity. They set up a wholly owned subsidiary called Bizkaia Energia and waited for reports by the central government and the Basque parliament concerning the environmental impact of their plans. They also had to take into account the possibility of terrorist group ETA demanding Basque independence. ESB estimated that ETA would not be a threat. Reasons were not given, indeed MNCs rarely report their precise country risk calculations as such judgements are obviously politically sensitive. In this case, one would have good reason to believe that ETA would not see an Irish company as hostile or as a symbol of suppression. Ireland historically had been part of the British Empire and had to fight for its freedom, a path that ETA aspired to. It is also a part of the Celtic fringe of Europe along with Brittany, Wales and Scotland with whom the Basque maintained cultural links. In fact over the subsequent 9 years there were no incidents with employees. In 2005, the company sold 50 per cent of its electricity producing plant to a Japanese multinational Osaka Gas. Shell will sell gas to and buy electricity from the ESB plant in Spain. By judging the political risk correctly at a national and local level and by having certain cultural advantages, ESB was able to develop electricity supply before other major MNCs.

If there is a chance that a host government takeover will occur, the foreign project's *NPV* under these conditions should be estimated. Then the company should engage in 'what if' analysis by assessing the options available at possible levels of outcomes. Real options analysis may help in valuing these opportunities. Finally, the relationship with the host government needs to be assessed. In this case, game theory may help on analyzing scenarios.

How country risk affects financial decisions

Country risk analysis is a separate source of risk particular to international investment. Unlike other sources of risk, country risk tends to be concerned with the possibility of sudden big events described as crises. This can be in the form of a sudden collapse in the value of the currency, such as the Russian rouble (see below). Or it can be in the form of a sudden collapse in the economy, or both. In contrast, other sources of risk in international investment, such as business risk and currency risk, lead to outcomes that can be represented by the normal probability curve. They offer a range of outcomes from being a little better or worse than expected to being much better or worse than expected. The normal probability curve captures the greater likelihood of smaller deviations from expectations compared to larger deviations. However, where a crisis is anything more than a very remote possibility, combining such a one off risk with currency and business risk becomes difficult. Scenario analysis can be useful, particularly worst case scenarios. As a result, two investments offering the same return may be chosen on the basis of their ability to cope with crises rather than the normal measure of risk, i.e. the standard deviation of returns. The history of international finance (see Chapter 6), is littered with such crises as the following further examples illustrate.

Gulf War. As a result of the crisis that culminated in the Gulf War in 1991, many MNCs attempted to reassess country risk. Terrorism became a major concern. MNCs used various methods to protect against terrorism. Cross-country travel by executives was reduced, as MNCs used teleconference calls instead. Some MNCs with subsidiaries in Saudi Arabia temporarily closed some of their operations, allowing employees from other countries to return home. Some projects that were being considered for countries that could be subject to terrorist attacks were postponed. Even projects that appeared to be feasible from a financial perspective were postponed because of the potential danger to employees.

In addition to the threat of terrorism, the crisis influenced cash flows of MNCs in many other ways. The effects varied with the characteristics of each MNC. The more obvious effects of the crisis were reduced travel and higher oil prices. The reduction in travel adversely affected airlines, hotels, restaurants, luggage manufacturers, tourist attractions, rental car agencies and cruise lines.

Asian crisis. As a result of the 1997–98 Asian crisis, MNCs realized that they had underestimated the potential financial problems that could occur in the high-growth Asian countries. Country risk analysts had concentrated on the high degree of economic growth, even though the Asian countries had high debt levels and their commercial banks had massive loan problems. The loan problems were not obvious because commercial banks were typically not required to disclose much information about their loans. Some MNCs recognized the potential problems in Asia, though, and discontinued their exports to those Asian businesses that were not willing to pay in advance.

Russian crisis. Large government budget deficits in 1996 and 1997 led to a build-up of government debts. To reduce the debt the government introduced austerity packages which resulted in political unrest and discontent with the Prime Minister. In July of 1998 the IMF made a loan to the Russian government of $15bn which was accompanied by $22.6bn from international lenders. In addition the Asian crisis led to withdrawal by investors in emerging markets, such as Russia, causing adverse balances on the financial (capital) account. On 17 August 1998 the government set a partial moratorium (non-payment) on foreign debt; the currency fell by 10 per cent. The following day the parliament called for the President Boris Yeltsin to resign. On the 23rd the President sacked the Prime Minister. The Russian stock market fell. On the 25th, the government announced rouble debt restructuring that foreign investors said amounts to default. On 26 August rouble-dollar trading was suspended by the central bank and there was a run on Russian banks (customers withdrew their deposits in cash). Many banks were unable to meet their commitments. September 4, inflation was reported as having jumped to 15 per cent per month; the value of the rouble had fallen by 64 per cent compared to 25 August. September 11, the government failed to pay $685 million in interest payments. October 21, the State backed railway company defaulted on its bond payments. The gross domestic product (value of all output) was reported as having fallen by 10 per cent year on year. Inflation was over 50 per cent higher than the previous year and shares hit all-time lows. The following year Putin became Prime Minister and subsequently President. The effect of these events on the value of the rouble is illustrated in Exhibit 14.6.

The Russian crisis combined with the earlier Asian crisis is also thought to have prompted the Brazilian crisis in January 1999 when the Brazilian real abandoned its crawling peg arrangement and became freely floating. During that month the real declined by 40 per cent against the British pound.

REDUCING EXPOSURE TO HOST GOVERNMENT TAKEOVERS

Although direct foreign investment offers several possible benefits, country risk can offset such benefits. The most severe country risk is a host government takeover. This type of takeover may result in major losses, especially when the MNC does not have any power to negotiate with the host government.

EXHIBIT 14.6 Russian currency crisis

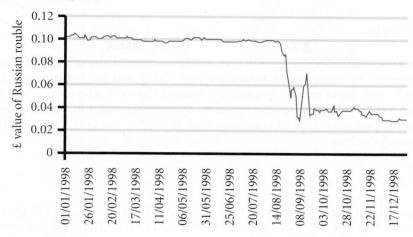

The following are the most common strategies used to reduce exposure to a host government takeover:

● Use a short-term horizon.

● Rely on unique supplies or technology. Hire local labour.

● Borrow local funds.

● Purchase insurance.

● Use project finance.

Use a short-term horizon

An MNC may concentrate on recovering cash flow quickly so that in the event of expropriation, losses are minimized. An MNC would also exert only a minimum effort to replace worn-out equipment and machinery at the subsidiary. It may even phase out its overseas investment by selling off its assets to local investors or the government in stages over time.

Rely on unique supplies or technology

If the subsidiary can bring in supplies from its headquarters (or a sister subsidiary) that cannot be duplicated locally, the host government will not be able to take over and operate the subsidiary without those supplies. Also the MNC can cut off the supplies if the subsidiary is treated unfairly.

If the subsidiary can hide the technology in its production process, a government takeover will be less likely. A takeover would be successful in this case only if the MNC would provide the necessary technology, and the MNC would do so only under conditions of a friendly takeover that would ensure that it received adequate compensation.

Hire local labour

If local employees of the subsidiary would be affected by the host government's takeover, they can pressure their government to avoid such action. However, the government could still keep those employees after taking over the subsidiary. Thus, this strategy has only limited effectiveness in avoiding or limiting a government takeover.

Borrow local funds

If the subsidiary borrows funds locally, local banks will be concerned about its future performance. If for any reason a government takeover would reduce the probability that the banks would receive their loan repayments promptly, they might attempt to prevent a takeover by the host government. However, the host government may guarantee repayment to the banks, so this strategy has only limited effectiveness. Nevertheless, it could still be preferable to a situation in which the MNC not only loses the subsidiary but also still owes home country creditors.

Purchase insurance

Insurance can be purchased to cover the risk of expropriation. For example, the UK government provides insurance through the Export Credit Guarantee Department (ECGD). The insurance premiums paid by a firm depend on the degree of insurance coverage and the risk associated with the firm. Typically, however, any insurance policy will cover only a portion of the company's total exposure to country risk.

Many home countries of MNCs have investment guarantee programmes that insure to some extent the risks of expropriation, wars or currency blockage. Some guarantee programmes have a 1-year waiting period, or longer before compensation is paid on losses due to expropriation. Also, some insurance policies do not cover all forms of expropriation. Furthermore, to be eligible for such insurance, the subsidiary might be required by the country to concentrate on exporting rather than on local sales. Even if a subsidiary qualifies for insurance, there is a cost. Any insurance will typically cover only a portion of the assets and may specify a maximum duration of coverage, such as 15 or 20 years. A subsidiary must weigh the benefits of this insurance against the cost of the policy's premiums and potential losses in excess of coverage. The insurance can be helpful, but it does not by itself prevent losses due to expropriation.

In 1993, Russia established an insurance fund to protect MNCs against various forms of country risk. The Russian government took this action to encourage more direct foreign investment in Russia.

The World Bank has established an affiliate called the Multilateral Investment Guarantee Agency (MIGA) to provide political insurance for MNCs with direct foreign investment in less developed countries. MIGA offers insurance against expropriation, breach of contract, currency inconvertibility, war and civil disturbances.

SUMMARY

- The factors used by MNCs to measure a country's political risk include the attitude of consumers toward purchasing locally produced goods, the host government's actions toward the MNC, the blockage of fund transfers, currency inconvertibility, war, bureaucracy and corruption. These factors can increase the costs of international business.

- The factors used by MNCs to measure a country's financial risk are the country's interest rates, exchange rates and inflation rates.

- The techniques typically used by MNCs to measure the country risk are the check list approach, the Delphi technique, quantitative analysis and inspection visits. Since no one technique covers all aspects of country risk, a combination of these techniques is commonly used. The measurement of country risk is essentially a weighted average of the political or financial factors that are perceived to comprise country risk. Each MNC has its own view as to the weights that should be assigned to each factor. Thus, the overall rating for a country may vary among MNCs.

- Once country risk is measured, it can be incorporated into a capital budgeting analysis by adjustment of the discount rate. The adjustment is somewhat arbitrary, however, and may lead to improper decision-making. An alternative method of incorporating country risk analysis into investment valuation is to account for each factor that affects country risk and value options that may exist if the risk occurs. In addition the investment may be viewed in terms of possible reactions of the host country in which case a game theory setting may offer insights.

CRITICAL DEBATE

Does country risk analysis make other forms of risk meaningless?

Proposition. Where there is a risk of a 40 per cent fall or more in the value of a currency, worrying about a 3 per cent standard deviation makes no sense. Firms should analyze their ability to cope with such disaster scenarios and use this analysis to decide whether the expected returns are worthwhile.

Opposing view. No. These kinds of risks can affect all firms and in a sense is an unavoidable risk of international finance. The lessons of diversification and currency protection from looking at lower levels of risk are all the more relevant given country risk.

With whom do you agree? Which argument do you support? Offer your own opinion on this issue.

SELF TEST

Answers are provided in Appendix A at the back of the text.

1 Key West Co. (a US company) exports highly advanced phone system components to its subsidiary shops on islands in the Caribbean. The components are purchased by consumers to improve their phone systems. These components are not produced in other countries. Explain how political risk factors could adversely affect the profitability of Key West Co.

2 Using the information in question 1, explain how financial risk factors could adversely affect the profitability of Key West Co.

3 Given the information in question 1, do you expect that Key West Co. is more concerned about the adverse effects of political risk or of financial risk?

4 Explain how a terrorist attack might affect an MNC.

5 Rockford Ltd plans to expand its successful business by establishing a subsidiary in France. However, it is concerned that after 2 years the French government will either impose a special tax on any income sent back to the US parent or order the subsidiary to be sold at that time. The executives have estimated that either of these scenarios has a 15 per cent chance of occurring. They have decided to add four percentage points to the project's required rate of return to incorporate the country risk that they are concerned about in the capital budgeting analysis. Is there a better way to more precisely incorporate the country risk of concern here?

QUESTIONS AND APPLICATIONS

1 **Forms of country risk.** List some forms of country risk other than a takeover of a subsidiary by the host government, and briefly elaborate on how each factor can affect the risk to the MNC. Identify common financial factors for an MNC to consider when assessing country risk. Briefly elaborate on how each factor can affect the risk to the MNC.

2 **Country risk assessment.** Describe the steps involved in assessing country risk once all relevant information has been gathered.

3 **Uncertainty surrounding the country risk assessment.** Describe the possible errors involved in assessing country risk. In other words, explain why country risk analysis is not always accurate.

4 Diversifying away country risk. Why do you think that an MNC's strategy of diversifying projects internationally could achieve low exposure to country risk?

5 Monitoring country risk. Once a project is accepted, country risk analysis for the foreign country involved is no longer necessary, assuming that no other proposed projects are being evaluated for that country. Do you agree with this statement? Why or why not?

6 Country risk analysis. If the potential return is high enough, any degree of country risk can be tolerated. Do you agree with this statement? Why or why not? Do you think that a proper country risk analysis can replace a capital budgeting analysis of a project considered for a foreign country? Explain.

7 Country risk analysis. Niagra Ltd has decided to call a well-known country risk consultant to conduct a country risk analysis in a small country where it plans to develop a large subsidiary. Niagra prefers to hire the consultant since it plans to use its employees for other important corporate functions. The consultant uses a computer program that has assigned weights of importance linked to the various factors. The consultant will evaluate the factors for this small country and insert a rating for each factor into the computer. The weights assigned to the factors are not adjusted by the computer, but the factor ratings are adjusted for each country that the consultant assesses. Do you think Niagra Ltd should use this consultant? Why or why not?

8 Microassessment. Explain the microassessment of country risk.

9 Incorporating country risk in capital budgeting. How could a country risk assessment be used to adjust a project's required rate of return? How could such an assessment be used instead to adjust a project's estimated cash flows?

10 Reducing country risk. Explain some methods of reducing exposure to existing country risk, while maintaining the same amount of business within a particular country.

11 Managing country risk. Why do some subsidiaries maintain a low profile as to where their parents are located?

12 Country risk analysis. When Jerrik ApS (Danish) considered establishing a subsidiary in Zenland, it performed a country risk analysis to help make the decision. It first retrieved a country risk analysis performed about 1 year earlier, when it had planned to begin a major exporting business to Zenland firms. Then it updated the analysis by incorporating all current information on the key variables that were used in that analysis, such as Zenland's willingness to accept exports, its existing quotas and existing tariff laws. Is this country risk analysis adequate? Explain.

13 Reducing country risk. MNCs such as Alcoa, DuPont, Heinz and IBM donated products and technology to foreign countries where they had subsidiaries. How could these actions have reduced some forms of country risk?

14 Country risk ratings. Assauer Ltd would like to assess the country risk of Glovanskia. Assauer has identified various political and financial risk factors, as shown below.

Political risk factor	Assigned rating	Assigned weight
Blockage of fund transfers	5	40%
Bureaucracy	3	60%

Financial risk factor	Assigned rating	Assigned weight
Interest rate	1	10%
Inflation	4	20%
Exchange rate	5	30%
Competition	4	20%
Growth	5	20%

Assauer has assigned an overall rating of 80 per cent to political risk factors and of 20 per cent to financial risk factors. Assauer is not willing to consider Glovanskia for investment if the country risk rating is below 4.0. Should Assauer consider Glovanskia for investment?

15 Buxton plc is thinking of investing in Country Y. The expected return is 20 per cent with a standard deviation due to currency movements of 5 per cent. However, 10 years ago Country Y's currency fell by 40 per cent. How should Buxton assess this risk?

ADVANCED QUESTIONS

16 **How country risk affects *NPV*.** Hoosier Ltd is planning a project in the USA. It would lease space for 1 year in a shopping mall to sell expensive clothes manufactured in the UK. The project would end in 1 year, when all earnings would be remitted to Hoosier Ltd. Assume that no additional corporate taxes are incurred beyond those imposed by the UK government. Since Hoosier Ltd would rent space, it would not have any long-term assets in the USA and expects the salvage (terminal) value of the project to be about zero.

Assume that the project's required rate of return is 18 per cent. Also assume that the initial outlay required by the parent to fill the store with clothes is £200 000. The pretax foreign earnings are expected to be $300 000 at the end of 1 year. The British pound is expected to be worth $1.60 at the end of 1 year, when the after-tax earnings are converted to pounds and remitted to the UK. The following forms of country risk must be considered:

● The US economy may weaken (probability = 30 per cent), which would cause the expected pretax earnings to be $200 000.

● The US corporate tax rate on income earned by British firms may increase by 25 per cent (probability = 20 per cent).

These two forms of country risk are independent.

Calculate the expected value of the project's *NPV* and determine the probability that the project will have a negative *NPV*.

17 **How country risk affects *NPV*.** Explain how the capital budgeting analysis in the previous question would need to be adjusted if there were three possible outcomes for the dollar along with the possible outcomes for the British economy and corporate tax rate.

18 **JC Penney's country risk analysis.** Recently, JC Penney (an actual US company) decided to consider expanding into various foreign countries; it applied a comprehensive country risk analysis before making its expansion decisions. Initial screenings of 30 foreign countries were based on political and economic factors that contribute to country risk. For the remaining 20 countries where country risk was considered to be tolerable, specific country risk characteristics of each country were considered. One of JC Penney's biggest targets is Mexico, where it planned to build and operate seven large stores.

a Identify the political factors that you think may possibly affect the performance of the JC Penney stores in Mexico.

b Explain why the JC Penney stores in Mexico and in other foreign markets are subject to financial risk (a subset of country risk).

c Assume that JC Penney anticipated that there was a 10 per cent chance that the Mexican government would temporarily prevent conversion of peso profits into dollars because of political conditions. This event would prevent JC Penney from remitting earnings generated in Mexico and could adversely affect the performance of these stores (from the US perspective). Offer a way in which this type of political risk could be explicitly incorporated into a capital budgeting analysis when assessing the feasibility of these projects.

d Assume that JC Penney decides to use dollars to finance the expansion of stores in Mexico. Second, assume that JC Penney decides to use one set of dollar cash flow estimates for any project that it assesses. Third, assume that the stores in Mexico are not subject to political risk. Do you think that the required rate of return on these projects would differ from the required rate of return on stores built in the USA at that same time? Explain.

e Based on your answer to the previous question, does this mean that proposals for any new stores in the USA have a higher probability of being accepted than proposals for any new stores in Mexico?

19 **How country risk affects *NPV*.** Monk Ltd is considering a capital budgeting project in Tunisia. The project requires an initial outlay of 1 million Tunisian dinar; the dinar is currently valued at £0.48. In the first and second years of operation, the project will generate 700 000 dinar in each year. After 2 years, Monk will terminate the project, and the expected salvage value is 300 000 dinar. Monk has assigned a discount rate of 12 per cent to this project. The following additional information is available:

● There is currently no withholding tax on remittances to the UK, but there is a 20 per cent chance that the Tunisian government will impose a withholding tax of 10 per cent beginning next year.

● There is a 50 per cent chance that the Tunisian government will pay Monk 100 000 dinar after 2 years instead of the 300 000 dinar it expects.

● The value of the dinar is expected to remain unchanged over the next 2 years.

a Determine the *NPV* of the project in each of the four possible scenarios.

b Determine the joint probability of each scenario.

c Compute the expected *NPV* of the project and make a recommendation to Monk regarding its feasibility.

20 **How country risk affects *NPV*.** In the previous question, assume that instead of adjusting the estimated cash flows of the project, Monk had decided to adjust the discount rate from 12 per cent to 17 per cent. Re-evaluate the *NPV* of the project's expected scenario using this adjusted discount rate.

21 **The risk and cost of potential kidnapping.** In 2004 following the war in Iraq, some MNCs capitalized on opportunities to rebuild Iraq. However, in April 2004, some employees were kidnapped by local militant groups. How should an MNC account for this potential risk when it considers foreign direct investment (FDI) in any particular country? Should it avoid in any country in which such an event could occur? If so, how would it screen the countries to determine which are acceptable? For whatever countries that it is willing to consider, should it adjust its feasibility analysis to account for the possibility of kidnapping? Should it attach a cost to reflect this possibility or increase the discount rate when estimating the *NPV*? Explain.

22 **Integrating country risk and capital budgeting.** Tovar Cie is a French firm that has been asked to provide consulting services to help Gredia Company (in Country Y) improve its performance. Tovar would need to spend 300 000 euros today on expenses related to this project. In 1 year, Tovar will receive payment from Gredia, which will be tied to Gredia's performance during the year. There is uncertainty about Gredia's performance and about Gredia's tendency for corruption.

Tovar expects that it will receive 400 000 euros if Gredia achieves strong performance following the consulting job. However, there are two forms of country risk that are a concern to Tovar. There is an 80 per cent chance that Gredia will achieve strong performance. There is a 20 per cent chance that Gredia will perform poorly, and in this case, Tovar will receive a payment of only 200 000 euros.

While there is a 90 per cent chance that Gredia will make its payment to Tovar, there is a 10 per cent chance that Gredia will become corrupt, and in this case, Gredia will not submit any payment to Tovar.

Assume that the outcome of Gredia's performance is independent of whether Gredia becomes corrupt. The prevailing spot rate of Country Y's currency is 0.6 euros to the Y, but Tovar expects that currency Y will depreciate by 10 per cent in 1 year, regardless of Gredia's performance or whether it is corrupt.

Tovar's cost of capital is 26 per cent. Determine the expected value of the project's *NPV*. Determine the probability that the project's *NPV* will be negative.

PROJECT WORKSHOP

23 **Political considerations** Enter the terms: 'Financial crisis', 'chronology', 'date' and 'country'. Select a reasonably long article in a search engine of newspaper articles. Your institution should have access to such resources.

a Select events from the financial crisis that would be of concern to a multinational operating in the country.

b From each of the events of the financial crisis, consider how an MNC with investments in that country would be affected and how the MNC might best react.

DISCUSSION IN THE BOARDROOM

This exercise can be found on our dedicated Course-Mate platform for students.

RUNNING YOUR OWN MNC

This exercise can be found on our dedicated Course-Mate platform for students.

Essays/discussion and articles can be found at the end of Part IV.

BLADES PLC CASE STUDY

Country risk assessment

Recently, Ben Holt, Blades' chief financial officer (CFO), has assessed whether it would be more beneficial for Blades to establish a subsidiary in Thailand to manufacture roller blades or to acquire an existing manufacturer, Skates'n'Stuff, which has offered to sell the business to Blades for 1 billion Thai baht. In Holt's view, establishing a subsidiary in Thailand yields a higher *NPV* than acquiring the existing business. Furthermore, the Thai manufacturer has rejected an offer by Blades plc for 900 million baht. A purchase price of 900 million baht for Skates'n'Stuff would make the acquisition as attractive as the establishment of a subsidiary in Thailand in terms of *NPV*. Skates'n'Stuff has indicated that it is not willing to accept less than 950 million baht.

Although Holt is confident that the *NPV* analysis was conducted correctly, he is troubled by the fact that the same discount rate, 25 per cent, was used in each analysis. In his view, establishing a subsidiary in Thailand may be associated with a higher level of country risk than acquiring Skates'n'Stuff. Although either approach would result in approximately the same level of financial risk, the political risk associated with establishing a subsidiary in Thailand may be higher than the political risk of operating Skates'n'Stuff. If the establishment of a subsidiary in Thailand is associated with a higher level of country risk overall, then a higher discount rate should have been used in the analysis. Based on these considerations, Holt wants to measure the country risk associated with Thailand on both a macro and a micro level and then to re-examine the feasibility of both approaches.

First, Holt has gathered some more detailed political information for Thailand. For example, he believes that consumers in Asian countries prefer to purchase goods produced by Asians, which might prevent a subsidiary in Thailand from being successful. This cultural characteristic might not prevent an acquisition of Skates'n'Stuff from succeeding, however, especially if Blades retains the company's management and employees. Furthermore, the subsidiary would have to apply for various licences and permits to be allowed to operate in Thailand, while Skates'n'Stuff obtained these licences and permits long ago. However, the number of licences required for Blades' industry is relatively low compared to other industries. Moreover, there is a high possibility that the Thai government will implement capital controls in the near future, which would prevent funds from leaving Thailand. Since Blades Ltd has planned to remit all earnings generated by its subsidiary or by Skates'n'Stuff back to the UK, regardless of which approach to direct foreign investment it takes, capital controls may force Blades to reinvest funds in Thailand.

Ben Holt has also gathered some information regarding the financial risk of operating in Thailand. Thailand's economy has been weak lately, and recent forecasts indicate that a recovery may be slow. A weak economy may affect the demand for Blades' products, roller blades. The state of the economy is of particular concern to Blades since it produces a leisure product. In the case of an economic turndown, consumers will first eliminate these types of purchases. Holt is also worried about the high interest rates in Thailand, which may further slow economic growth if Thai citizens begin saving more. Furthermore, Holt is also aware that inflation levels in Thailand are expected to remain high. These high inflation levels can affect the purchasing power of Thai consumers, who may adjust their spending habits to purchase more essential products than roller blades. However, high levels of inflation also indicate that consumers in Thailand are still spending a relatively high proportion of their earnings.

Another financial factor that may affect Blades' operations in Thailand is the baht-pound exchange rate. Current forecasts indicate that the Thai baht may depreciate in the future. However, recall that Blades will sell all roller blades produced in Thailand to Thai consumers. Therefore, Blades is not subject to a lower level of UK demand resulting from a weak baht. Blades will remit the earnings generated in Thailand back to the UK, however, and a weak baht would reduce the pound amount of these translated earnings.

Based on these initial considerations, Holt feels that the level of political risk of operating may be higher if Blades decides to establish a subsidiary to manufacture roller blades (as opposed to acquiring Skates'n'Stuff). Conversely, the financial risk of operating in Thailand will be roughly the same whether Blades establishes a subsidiary or acquires Skates'n'Stuff. Holt is not satisfied with this initial assessment, however, and would like to have numbers at hand when he meets with the board of directors next week. Thus, he would like to conduct a quantitative analysis of the country risk associated with operating in Thailand. He has asked you, a financial analyst at Blades, to develop a country risk analysis for Thailand and to adjust the discount rate for the riskier venture (i.e. establishing a subsidiary or acquiring Skates'n'Stuff). Holt has provided the following information for your analysis:

- Since Blades produces leisure products, it is more susceptible to financial risk factors than political risk factors. You should use weights of 60 per cent for financial risk factors and 40 per cent for political risk factors in your analysis.

- You should use the attitude of Thai consumers, capital controls and bureaucracy as political risk factors in your analysis. Holt perceives capital controls as the most important political risk factor. In his view, the consumer attitude and bureaucracy factors are of equal importance.

- You should use interest rates, inflation levels and exchange rates as the financial risk factors in your analysis. In Holt's view, exchange rates and interest rates in Thailand are of equal importance, while inflation levels are slightly less important.

- Each factor used in your analysis should be assigned a rating in a range of 1 to 5, where 5 indicates the most unfavourable rating.

Ben Holt has asked you to provide answers to the following questions for him, which he will use in his meeting with the board of directors:

1 Based on the information provided in the case, do you think the political risk associated with Thailand is higher or lower for a manufacturer of leisure products such as Blades as opposed to, say, a food producer? That is, conduct a micro-assessment of political risk for Blades plc.

2 Do you think the financial risk associated with Thailand is higher or lower for a manufacturer of leisure products such as Blades as opposed to, say, a food producer? That is, conduct a micro-assessment of financial risk for Blades plc. Do you think a leisure product manufacturer such as Blades will be more affected by political or financial risk factors?

3 Without using a numerical analysis, do you think establishing a subsidiary in Thailand or acquiring Skates'n'Stuff will result in a higher assessment of political risk? Of financial risk? Substantiate your answer.

4 Using a spreadsheet, conduct a quantitative country risk analysis for Blades plc using the information Ben Holt has provided for you. Use your judgement to assign weights and ratings to each political and financial risk factor and determine an overall country risk rating for Thailand. Conduct two separate analyses for: (a) the establishment of a subsidiary in Thailand and (b) the acquisition of Skates'n'Stuff.

5 Which method of direct foreign investment should utilize a higher discount rate in the capital budgeting analysis? Would this strengthen or weaken the tentative decision of establishing a subsidiary in Thailand?

SMALL BUSINESS DILEMMA

Country risk analysis at the Sports Exports Company

The Sports Exports Company (Ireland) produces basketballs and exports them to the UK. It also has an ongoing joint venture with a British firm that produces some sporting goods for a fee. The Sports Exports Company is considering the establishment of a small subsidiary in the UK.

1 Under the current conditions, is the Sports Exports Company subject to country risk?

2 If the firm does decide to develop a small subsidiary in the UK, will its exposure to country risk change? If so, how?

CHAPTER 15
LONG-TERM
FINANCING

LEARNING OBJECTIVES

The specific objectives of this chapter are to:

● Explain why MNCs consider long-term financing in foreign currencies.

● Explain how to assess the feasibility of long-term financing in foreign currencies.

● Explain how the assessment of long-term financing in foreign currencies is adjusted for bonds with floating interest rates.

Multinational corporations (MNCs) typically seek to match the duration of their finance with the duration of the investment so that long-term sources of funds are used to finance long-term projects. They have access to both domestic and foreign sources of funds. It is worthwhile for MNCs to consider all possible forms of financing before making their final decisions. Financial managers must be aware of their sources of long-term funds so that they can finance international projects in a manner that maximizes the wealth of the MNC. Financial managers also need to consider the structure of the investment, whether it is a partnership, wholly owned subsidiary or project finance.

LONG-TERM FINANCING DECISION

Since MNCs commonly invest in long-term projects, they rely heavily on long-term financing. Generally, long-term projects take longer to generate funds and are more appropriately financed by investors who are prepared to deposit their funds for the longer term. Shorter-term funding for such investments would mean a constant need for refinancing that is to say repaying one short-term fund by taking out another. The risk is that further funds might not be forthcoming, particularly if the project is at a difficult stage of its development. Those seeking short-term security might be worried that on maturity of their short-term loans the funds might not be available. Equity is one of the major sources of long-term funding able to raise large sums of money. Long-term debt, in the form of debentures is the other major source. The decision to use equity funding versus debt funding was covered in the previous chapter. Once that decision is made, the MNC must consider the possible sources of equity or debt and the cost and risk associated with each source.

Sources of equity

MNCs may consider a domestic equity offering in their home country, in which the funds are denominated in their local currency. Second, they may consider a global equity offering, in which they issue stock in their home country and in one or more foreign countries. They may consider this approach to obtain partial funding in a currency that they need to finance a foreign subsidiary's operations. In addition, the global offering may provide them with some name recognition. Investors in a foreign country will be more interested in a global offering if the MNC places a sufficient number of shares in that country to provide liquidity. The stock will be listed on an exchange in the foreign country so that investors there can sell their holdings of the stock.

Third, MNCs may offer a private placement of equity to financial institutions in their home country. Fourth, they may offer a private placement of equity to financial institutions in the foreign country where they are expanding. Private placements are beneficial because they may reduce transaction costs. However, MNCs may not be able to obtain all the funds that they need with a private placement. The funding must come from a limited number of large investors who are willing to maintain the investment for a long period of time, because the equity has very limited liquidity.

Sources of debt

When MNCs consider debt financing, they have a similar set of options. They can engage in a public placement of debt in their own country or a global debt offering. In addition, they can engage in a private placement of debt in their own country or in the foreign country where they are expanding.

Most MNCs obtain equity funding in their home country. In contrast, debt financing is frequently done in foreign countries. Thus, the focus of this chapter is on how debt financing decisions can affect the MNC's cost of capital and risk.

COST OF DEBT FINANCING

An MNC's long-term financing decision is commonly influenced by the different interest rates that exist among currencies. The actual cost of long-term financing is based on both the quoted interest rate and the percentage change in the exchange rate of the currency borrowed over the loan life. Just as interest rates on short-term bank loans vary among currencies, so do bond yields.

Because bonds denominated in foreign currencies sometimes have lower yields, MNCs often consider issuing bonds denominated in those currencies. Since the total financing cost to an MNC issuing a foreign currency-denominated bond is affected by that currency's value relative to the MNC's main (functional) currency there is no guarantee that the bond will be less costly than a home currency-denominated bond. The borrowing firm must make coupon payments in the currency denominating the bond. If this currency appreciates against the firm's home currency, more funds will be needed to make the coupon payments. For this reason, a firm will not always denominate debt in a currency that exhibits a low interest rate (Exhibit 15.1).

To make the long-term financing decision, the MNC must: (1) determine the amount of funds needed, (2) forecast the price at which it can issue the bond and (3) forecast periodic exchange rate values for the currency denominating the bond. This information can be used to determine the bond's financing costs, which can be compared with the financing costs the firm would incur using its home currency. The uncertainty of the actual financing costs to be incurred from foreign financing must be accounted for as well.

EXHIBIT 15.1   International interest rates 2013

Country	Interest (10-year bond or similar)
Greece	10.8
Nigeria	10.51
Egypt	9.25
South Africa	6.36
Portugal	6.19
Spain	5.25
Italy	4.56
Ireland	3.8
New Zealand	3.78
Australia	3.39
Belgium	2.44
France	2.2
UK	2.08
Sweden	2.04
Austria	1.91
Canada	1.88
USA	1.86
Netherlands	1.81
Finland	1.74
Denmark	1.73
Germany	1.54
Switzerland	0.79
Japan	0.68

Measuring the cost of financing

The cost of financing in a foreign currency is influenced by the value of that currency when the MNC makes coupon payments to its bondholders and when it pays off the principal at the time the bond reaches maturity.

EXAMPLE

Piedmont plc needs to borrow £1 million over a 3-year period. This reflects a relatively small amount of funds and a short time period for bond financing but will allow for a more simplified example. Piedmont believes it can sell pound-denominated bonds at par value if it provides a coupon rate of 14 per cent. It also has the alternative of denominating the bonds in Singapore dollars (S$), in which case it would convert its borrowed Singapore dollars to pounds to use as needed. Then, it would need to obtain Singapore dollars annually to make the coupon payments. Assume that the current exchange rate of the Singapore dollar is £0.3333.

Piedmont needs S$3 million in loans (computed as £1 million / £0.3333 per Singapore dollar) to obtain the £1 million it initially needs. It believes it can sell the Singapore dollar-denominated bonds at par value if it provides a coupon rate of 10 per cent.

The costs of both financing alternatives are illustrated in Exhibit 15.2, which provides the outflow payment schedule of each financing method. The outflow payments if Piedmont finances with UK pound denominated debt fixed interest capital are known. In addition, if Piedmont finances with Singapore dollar-denominated bonds, the number of Singapore dollars

needed at the end of each period is known. Yet, because the future exchange rate of the Singapore dollar is uncertain, the number of pounds needed to obtain the Singapore dollars each year is uncertain. If exchange rates do not change, the annual cost of financing with Singapore dollars is 10 per cent, which is less than the 14 per cent annual cost of financing with pounds.

A comparison between the costs of financing with the two different currencies can be conducted by determining the annual cost of financing with each bond, from Piedmont's perspective. The comparison is shown in the last column of Exhibit 15.2. The annual cost of financing represents the discount rate at which the future outflow payments must be discounted so that their present value equals the amount borrowed. This is similar to the so-called yield to maturity but is assessed here from the borrower's perspective rather than from the investor's perspective. When the price at which the bonds are initially issued equals the par value and there is no exchange rate adjustment, the annual cost of financing is simply equal to the coupon rate. Thus, the annual cost of financing for the British pound-denominated bonds would be 14 per cent.

For Piedmont, the Singapore dollar-denominated debt appears to be less costly. However, it is unrealistic to assume that the Singapore dollar will remain stable over time. Consequently, some MNCs may choose to issue UK pound-denominated debt, even though it appears more costly. The potential savings from issuing bonds denominated in a foreign currency must be weighed against the potential risk of such a method. In this example, risk reflects the possibility that the Singapore dollar will appreciate to a degree that causes Singapore dollar-denominated bonds to be more costly than UK fixed interest debt. There would in fact have to be a considerable change in the exchange rate (40 per cent) for the Singapore loan to be more expensive, as explained in the notes to Exhibit 15.2.

Normally, exchange rates are more difficult to predict over longer time horizons. Thus, the time when the principal is to be repaid may be so far away that it is virtually impossible to have a reliable estimate of the exchange rate at that time. For this reason, some firms may be uncomfortable issuing bonds denominated in foreign currencies.

Impact of a strong currency on financing costs. If the currency that was borrowed appreciates over time, an MNC will need more funds to cover the coupon or principal payments. This type of exchange rate movement increases the MNC's financing costs.

EXHIBIT 15.2   Financing with bonds denominated in British pounds versus Singapore dollars

	End of year			Annual cost of financing
	1	2	3	
Financing alternative				
(1) British pound-denominated debt (coupon rate = 14%) borrow £1 million	**£140 000**	**£140 000**	**£1 140 000**	14%
Or				
(2) Singapore dollar-denominated bonds (coupon rate = 10%) borrow S$3 000 000	S$300 000	S$300 000	S$3 300 000	**10%**
(2) Forecasted exchange rate of S$	£0.3333	£0.3333	£0.3333	–
(2) Payments in pounds	**£100 000**	**£100 000**	**£1 100 000**	10%

Notes:
- At an exchange rate of £0.33 financing with Singapore dollars (2) is cheaper.
- The exchange rate would have to increase to 14% / 10% × £0.3333 = £0.46662 for the loan to be as expensive, this is unlikely unless inflation is higher by about 4% in the UK.

EXAMPLE

After Piedmont decides to issue Singapore dollar-denominated bonds, assume that the Singapore dollar appreciates from £0.3333 to £0.40 at the end of Year 1, to £0.45 at the end of Year 2 and to £0.50 by the end of Year 3. In this case, the payments made by Piedmont are displayed in Exhibit 15.3. By comparing the pound outflows in this scenario with the outflows that would have occurred from a British pound-denominated bond, the risk to a firm from denominating a bond in a foreign currency is evident. The period of the last payment is particularly crucial for bond financing in foreign currencies because it includes not only the final coupon payment but the principal as well. Based on the exchange rate movements assumed here, financing with Singapore dollars was more expensive than financing with pounds would have been.

EXHIBIT 15.3   Financing with Singapore dollars during a strong S$ period

	End of year			Annual cost of financing
	1	2	3	
Payments in Singapore dollars	S$300 000	S$300 000	S$3 300 000	–
Forecasted exchange rate of Singapore dollar	£0.40	£0.45	£0.50	–
Payments in pounds	£120 000	£135 000	£1 650 000	26.20%

Note:
The annual cost (discount rate) is calculated by trial and error on a spreadsheet such that:

$$£1\,000\,000 = \frac{120\,000}{(1 + 0.262)} + \frac{135\,000}{(1 + 0.262)^2} + \frac{1\,650\,000}{(1 + 0.262)^3}$$

an appreciating foreign currency increases the cost of borrowing in that currency.

EXHIBIT 15.4 Financing with Singapore dollars during a weak S$ period

	End of year			Annual cost of financing
	1	2	3	
Payments in Singapore dollars	S$300 000	S$300 000	S$3 300 000	–
Forecasted exchange rate of Singapore dollar	£0.32	£0.30	£0.28	–
Payments in pounds	£96 000	£90 000	£924 000	3.90%

Note:
The annual cost (discount rate) is calculated by trial and error on a spreadsheet such that:

$$£1\,000\,000 = \frac{96\,000}{(1+0.039)} + \frac{96\,000}{(1+0.039)^2} + \frac{924\,000}{(1+0.039)^3}$$

a depreciating foreign currency lowers the cost of borrowing in that currency.

Impact of a weak currency on financing costs. Whereas an appreciating currency increases the periodic outflow payments of the bond issuer, a depreciating currency will reduce the issuer's outflow payments and therefore reduce its financing costs.

EXAMPLE

Reconsider the case of Piedmont plc, except assume that the Singapore dollar depreciates from £0.3333 to £0.32 at the end of Year 1, to £0.30 at the end of Year 2, and to £0.28 by the end of Year 3. In this case, the payments made by Piedmont are shown in Exhibit 15.4.

When one compares the pound outflows in this scenario with the outflows that would have occurred from a K fixed interest debt, the potential savings from foreign financing are evident.

Exhibit 15.5 compares the effects of a weak currency on financing costs to the effects of a stable or a strong currency. An MNC that denominates bonds in a foreign currency may achieve a major reduction in costs, but could incur high costs if the currency denominating the bonds appreciates over time.

Actual effects of exchange rate movements on financing costs

The international Fisher effect suggests that home interest rates (i_h) should be the same as foreign interest rates (i_f) when changes in the exchange rate (e_f) are taken into account. Thus: $i_h = i_f + e_f$. Thus for a UK company borrowing in pounds should be the same as borrowing in another currency and repaying in that currency. If the foreign interest rate is higher, then the foreign currency value should fall to offset the higher interest rate (see Chapter 8). In practice, this is often not the case. Exhibit 15.6 compares UK interest rates as the home rate with other countries' interest rates plus the change in the value of their currency.

EXHIBIT 15.5   Exchange rate effects on outflow payments for Singapore dollar-denominated bonds

	Payment in UK pounds at end of year			
	End of year			
Exchange rate scenario	1	2	3	Annual cost of financing
Scenario 1: No change in S$ value	£100 000	£100 000	£1 100 000	10.00%
Scenario 2: Strong	£120 000	£135 000	£1 650 000	26.20%
Scenario 3: Weak	£96 000	£90 000	£924 000	3.90%

EXHIBIT 15.6   UK interest rates compared with the effective foreign interest rate defined as the foreign interest rate plus changes in the value of the foreign currency

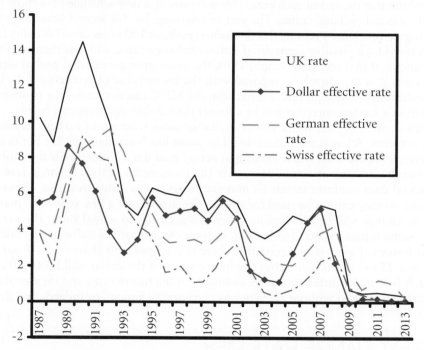

Note: The UK rate appears to be more expensive than borrowing from abroad. However, foreign borrowing is more risky, the foreign rates do not include higher transaction costs and foreign borrowing is likely to include a higher risk premium.

ASSESSING THE EXCHANGE RATE RISK OF DEBT FINANCING

Use of exchange rate probabilities

Apart from looking at the past, another approach to using point estimates of future exchange rates is to develop a probability distribution for an exchange rate for each period in which payments will be made to bondholders. The *expected value* of the exchange rate can be computed for each period by multiplying each possible exchange rate by its associated probability and totalling the products. Then, the exchange rate's expected value can be used to forecast the cash outflows necessary to pay bondholders over each period. The exchange rate's expected value may vary from one period to another. After developing probability distributions and computing the expected values, the MNC can estimate the expected cost of financing and compare that with the cost of financing with a bond denominated in the home currency.

Using this approach, a single outflow estimate is derived for each payment period, and a single estimate is derived for the annual cost of financing over the life of the bond. This approach does not indicate the range of possible results that may occur, however, so it does not measure the probability that a bond denominated in a foreign currency will be more costly than a bond denominated in the home currency.

Use of simulation

After an MNC has developed its probability distributions of the foreign currency's exchange rate at the end of each period, as just described, it can feed those probability distributions into a computer simulation program. The program will randomly draw one possible value from the exchange rate distribution for the end of each year and determine the outflow payments based on those exchange rates. Consequently, the cost of financing is determined. The procedure described up to this point represents one iteration.

Next, the program will repeat the procedure by again randomly drawing one possible value from the exchange rate distribution at the end of each year. This will provide a new schedule of outflow payments reflecting those randomly selected exchange rates. The cost of financing for this second iteration is also determined. The simulation program continually repeats this procedure, perhaps 100 times or so (as many times as desired).

Every iteration provides a possible scenario of future exchange rates, which is then used to determine the annual cost of financing if that scenario occurs. Thus, the simulation generates a probability distribution of annual financing costs that can then be compared with the known cost of financing if the bond is denominated in the home currency. Through this comparison, the MNC can determine the probability that issuing bonds denominated in a foreign currency will be cheaper than dollar-denominated bonds.

Note that in this context we are using actual exchange rates whereas in earlier chapters we have used exchange rate movements. What is the difference? The point has been made earlier but is worth repeating. Exchange rate movements are used when looking at actual past data. Therefore if the probability distributions were drawn up by looking at actual data, only the movements of the exchange rate should be used. This is because actual data contains trends (is non-stationary) or is liable to do so. These trends are only clear after the event, so they cannot be used for profit. The actual rate a few years ago may be out of date, but the tendency to change will be relevant to today. To get back to actual rates, the percentage changes can be applied to some future expected value. So, if one expects that the value of the dollar 1 year hence will be £0.60 and historical analysis suggests that there is a 25 per cent chance of a 5 per cent increase in value, then there is a 25 per cent chance that the future value of the dollar will be £0.60 × 1.05 = £0.63. The other approach is to make direct subjective estimates of the future rates and their probabilities. In such cases the actual rate can be used without reference to percentage changes, or indeed, past data.

REDUCING EXCHANGE RATE RISK

The exchange rate risk from financing with bonds in foreign currencies can be reduced by using one of the alternative strategies described next.

Offsetting cash inflows

Some firms may have inflow payments in particular currencies, which could offset their outflow payments related to bond financing. Thus, a firm may be able to finance with bonds denominated in a foreign currency that exhibits a lower coupon rate without becoming exposed to exchange rate risk. Nevertheless, it is unlikely that the firm would be able to perfectly match the timing and amount of the outflows in the foreign currency denominating the bond to the inflows in that currency. Therefore, some exposure to exchange rate fluctuations will exist. The exposure can be substantially reduced, though, if the firm receives inflows in the particular currency denominating the bond. This can help to stabilize the firm's cash flow.

EXAMPLE

GlaxoSmithKlein policy is to minimize the exposure of overseas operating subsidiaries to transaction risk by matching local currency income with local currency costs ... A significant proportion of Group borrowing including the commercial paper programme, is in US dollars, to benefit from the liquidity of US denominated capital markets. Certain of these and other borrowings are swapped into other currencies as required for group purposes. The Group seeks to denominate borrowings in the currencies of its principal assets.

(GSK Annual Report 2004)

MANAGING FOR VALUE

General Electric's decision to rely on global financial markets

General Electric is a well-diversified MNC that produces lighting products, automation devices, electrical equipment, and many other products. It has subsidiaries scattered throughout the world, which produce products that are sold locally. General Electric obtains funds from many different markets to finance a portion of its investment in foreign countries. It has issued bonds denominated in Australian dollars, British pounds, Japanese yen, New Zealand dollars and Polish zloty to finance its foreign operations. Its subsidiaries in Australia use Australian dollar inflows to pay off their Australian debt. Its subsidiaries in Japan use Japanese yen inflows to pay off their yen-denominated debt. By using various debt markets, General Electric can match its cash inflows and outflows in a particular currency. The decision to obtain debt in currencies where it receives cash inflows reduces the company's exposure to exchange rate risk. If it used dollars to finance all of its foreign investment, the subsidiaries would have to convert much of the local currency they receive to dollars to repay their debt. During periods when the foreign currencies depreciate against the dollar, General Electric would need more foreign currency to pay off the dollar-denominated debt. Thus, by considering its source of cash inflows, General Electric is able to make financing decisions that reduce its exposure to exchange rate risk and maximize its value.

MNCs may be able to offset their exposure to exchange rate risk by issuing bonds denominated in the local currency. Issuing debt denominated in the currencies of some developing countries such as Brazil, Indonesia, Malaysia and Thailand is an example. If an MNC issues bonds denominated in the local currency in one of those countries, there may be a natural offsetting effect that will reduce the MNC's exposure to exchange rate risk because it can use its cash inflows in that currency to repay the debt.

Alternatively, the MNC might obtain debt financing in its home currency at a lower interest rate, but it will not be able to offset its earnings in the foreign currency. Recall that countries where bond yields are high tend to have a high risk-free interest rate and that a high risk-free interest rate usually occurs where inflation is high (the Fisher effect). Also consider that the currencies of countries with relatively high inflation tend to weaken over time (as suggested by purchasing power parity). Thus, a UK-based MNC could be highly exposed to exchange rate risk when using pound-denominated debt to finance business in a country with high costs of local debt because it would have to convert cash inflows generated in a potentially depreciated currency to cover the debt repayments. Thus MNCs face a dilemma when they consider obtaining long-term financing: issue debt in the local currency and reduce exposure to exchange rate risk, or issue debt denominated in its home currency at a lower interest rate but with considerable exposure to exchange rate risk. Neither solution is without problems.

Implications of the euro for financing to offset cash inflows. Since the adoption of the euro by Austria, Belgium, Finland, France, Germany, Greece, Ireland, Italy, Luxembourg, Netherlands, Portugal and Spain (but not Sweden, Denmark or the UK) MNCs from member countries have not had to worry about exchange risk for trade within their area. Exchange rate risk is also lower for MNCs from outside the area as they no longer are exposed to exchange rate risk of sometimes quite small economies. Nevertheless, there is a lessening of the possibilities for diversification. The management of the euro is still a relatively new process that has not had the test of a major financial crisis. There are therefore still considerable currency risks to be hedged.

FORWARD CONTRACTS

When a bond denominated in a foreign currency has a lower coupon rate than the firm's home currency, the firm may consider issuing bonds denominated in that currency and simultaneously hedging its exchange rate risk through the forward market. Because the forward market can sometimes accommodate requests of 5 years or longer, such an approach may be possible. The firm could arrange to purchase the foreign currency forward for each time at which payments are required. However, the forward rate for each horizon will most likely be above the spot rate. Consequently, hedging these future outflow payments may not be less costly than the outflow payments needed if a dollar-denominated bond were issued. The relationship implied here reflects the concept of interest rate parity, which was discussed in earlier chapters, except that the point of view in this chapter is long term rather than short term.

CURRENCY SWAPS

A currency swap enables firms to exchange currencies at periodic intervals. The motive for such swaps is to make payments in a currency where revenues are being earned and thereby reduce exposure to exchange rate movements.

EXAMPLE

Milltop plc, a UK firm, desires to issue a bond denominated in euros because it could make payments with euro revenues to be generated from existing operations. However, Milltop is not well known to investors who would consider purchasing euro-denominated bonds. Meanwhile Beck GmbH of Germany desires to issue pound-denominated bonds because it has large revenues in pounds. However, it is not well known to the investors who would purchase these bonds.

If Milltop is known in the pound-denominated market while Beck is known in the euro-denominated market,

the following transactions are appropriate. Milltop issues pound-denominated bonds, while Beck issues euro-denominated bonds. Milltop will provide euro payments to Beck in exchange for pound payments from Beck. The two companies will in effect swap their interest rate bills. They will also typically swap the principal. This swap of currencies allows the companies to lower their exchange rate exposure by making interest payments in a revenue earning currency.

This type of currency swap is illustrated in Exhibit 15.7.

EXHIBIT 15.7   Illustration of an interest rate swap

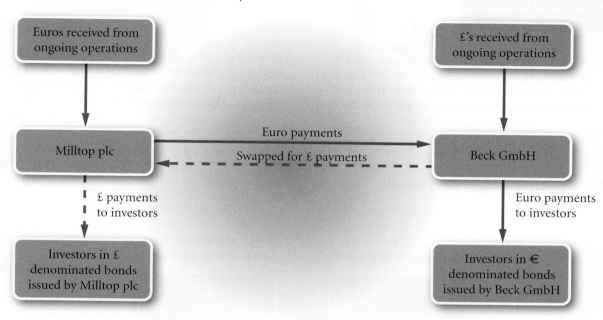

The swap just described was successful in reducing exchange rate risk for both Milltop and Beck. Milltop essentially passes the euros it receives from ongoing operations through to Beck and passes the pounds it receives from Beck through to the investors in the pound-denominated bonds. Thus, even though Milltop receives euros from its ongoing foreign operations, the effect of a change in value of the euro is reduced in that it now makes offsetting interest payments in euros. The same logic applies to Beck GmbH on the other side of the transaction.

Many MNCs simultaneously swap interest payments and currencies at agreed rates. Rates can also be fixed with forwards and futures. The Gillette Co. engaged in swap agreements that converted $500 million in fixed rate dollar-denominated debt into multiple currency variable rate debt. PepsiCo enters into **interest rate swaps** and currency swaps to reduce borrowing costs.

The differing conditions for each of the loans mean that a mutually agreed arrangement can be difficult. The large commercial banks that serve as financial intermediaries for currency swaps sometimes take positions. That is, they may agree to swap currencies with firms, rather than simply search for suitable swap candidates.

Swaps have also been used for window dressing balance sheets - an attempt to deceive the investment markets. Both the Greek and Italian governments have been accused of this practice that originated in Japan and was given the name 'tobashi' or 'make go away'. In essence the MNC arranges a swap with the counterparty at very unfavourable rates. In return the counterparty makes a payment which the MNC then uses to pay off debt. As the swap deal is not reported as a debt the MNC borrowings appear to simply reduce when in fact they have been rolled over but into a format that does not appear as borrowing.

Parallel loans

Firms can also obtain financing in a foreign currency through a parallel (or back-to-back) loan, which occurs when two parties provide simultaneous loans with an agreement to repay at a specified point in the future.

EXAMPLE

A UK company, Siddington Ltd operates a subsidiary in France and a French company, LePierre SA operates a subsidiary in the UK. Both wish to invest in their respective subsidiaries but wish to avoid exchange rate risks.

LePierre therefore lends euros to the French subsidiary of Siddington and in return Siddington lends to the UK subsidiary of LePierre. The loans are repaid in the same currencies as shown in Exhibit 15.8.

EXHIBIT 15.8   Illustration of a parallel loan

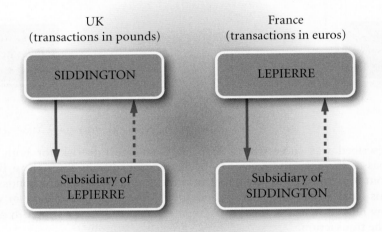

Note:
The continuous line arrow represents the loan and the dashed line arrow the repayment.

Using parallel loans to hedge exchange rate risk for foreign projects. The ability to reduce or eliminate exchange rate risk can also affect the attractiveness of projects in foreign countries. Sometimes, parallel loans can function as a useful alternative to forward or futures contracts as a way to finance foreign projects. The use of parallel loans is particularly attractive if the MNC is conducting a project in a foreign country, will receive the cash flows in the foreign currency and is worried that the foreign currency will depreciate substantially. If the foreign currency is not heavily traded, other hedging alternatives, such as forward or futures contracts, may not be available, and the project may have a negative net present value (NPV) if the cash flows remain unhedged.

Diversifying among currencies

A UK firm may denominate bonds in several foreign currencies, rather than a single foreign currency, so that substantial appreciation of any one currency will not drastically increase the number of pounds needed to cover the financing payments.

EXAMPLE

Never plc, a UK-based MNC, is considering four alternatives for issuing bonds to support its US operations:

1 Issue bonds denominated in British pounds (14 per cent).

2 Issue bonds denominated in Japanese yen (8 per cent).

3 Issue bonds denominated in US dollars (8 per cent).

4 Issue some bonds denominated in Japanese yen and some bonds denominated in US dollars.

Never plc has no net exposure in either Japanese yen or US dollars. The coupon rate for a UK pound-denominated bond is 14 per cent, while the coupon rate is 8 per cent for a yen- or US dollar-denominated bond. It is expected that any of these bonds could be sold at par value. The foreign currency would then be converted to British pounds for use and then at the end of the term of the bond Never will have to purchase the foreign currency to repay the loan. The exchange rate movement over the life of the loan will affect the cost of the loan.

If the US dollar appreciates against the British pound by more than 14 per cent − 8 per cent = 6 per cent, Never's actual financing cost from issuing US dollar-denominated bonds may be higher than that of the British pound-denominated bonds. If the Japanese yen appreciates substantially against the British pound, Never's actual financing cost from issuing yen-denominated bonds may be higher than that of the British pound-denominated bonds. If the exchange rates of the US dollar and Japanese yen move in opposite directions against the British pound, then both types of bonds could not simultaneously be more costly than British pound-denominated bonds, so financing with both types of bonds would almost ensure that the Never's overall financing cost would be less than the cost from issuing British pound-denominated bonds.

There is no guarantee that the exchange rates of the US dollar and Japanese yen will move in opposite directions. The movements of these two currencies are not highly correlated, however, so it is unlikely that both currencies will simultaneously appreciate to an extent that will offset their lower coupon rate advantages. Therefore, financing in bonds denominated in more than one foreign currency can increase the probability that the overall cost of foreign financing will be less than that of financing with the dollars. Never decides to issue bonds denominated in US dollars and in yen.

The preceding example involved only two foreign currencies. In reality, a firm may consider several currencies that they feel are going to cost less after taking into account the interest rate of the bond and the expected exchange rate movement and issue a portion of its bonds in each of these currencies. Such a strategy can increase the other costs (advertising, printing, etc.) of issuing bonds, but those costs may be offset by a reduction in cash outflows to bondholders.

Currency cocktail bonds. A firm can finance in several currencies without issuing various types of bonds (thus avoiding higher transaction costs) by developing a **currency cocktail bond**, denominated in not one, but a mixture (or 'cocktail' or 'basket') of currencies. A currency cocktail simply reflects a multicurrency unit of account. Several currency cocktails have been developed to denominate international bonds, and some have already been used in this manner. One of the more popular currency cocktails is the special drawing right (SDR), which was originally devised as a unit of account for the International Monetary Fund and is made up of a cocktail of currencies but is now also used to denominate bonds and bank deposits and to price various services. With the creation of the euro, the use of currency cocktail bonds in Europe is limited because numerous European countries now use a single currency.

Such multicurrency instruments will protect companies from the depreciation of one particular currency and protection may be enhanced by selecting currencies with relatively low correlations. However, unless earnings are similarly diverse there will be a net exposure to particular currencies. The preference is for matching outflows with inflows of a particular currency and only being exposed to the difference. Currency cocktails in that context would be far less attractive. It should be remembered that the cost of a bond will also be a function of the credit rating of the company whatever the currency.

Shares too can be raised in differing currencies. Portfolio theory suggests that the capital asset pricing model should determine the risk premium and for multinational companies an international capital asset pricing model should prevail. That is there should be a world market risk premium and a world beta for international projects. The predominant finding is, however, that companies react only to their own home markets no matter how multinational their activities. In other words, for a MNC, a domestic capital asset pricing model is a better predictor of market behaviour than an international version of the model.

INTEREST RATE RISK FROM DEBT FINANCING

Regardless of the currency that an MNC uses to finance its international operations, it must also decide on the maturity that it should use for its debt. Its goal is to use a maturity that will minimize the total payments on the debt needed for each business unit. Normally, an MNC will not use a maturity that exceeds the expected life of the business in that country.

When it uses a relatively short maturity, the MNC is exposed to interest rate risk, or the risk that interest rates will rise, forcing it to refinance at a higher interest rate. It can avoid this exposure by issuing a long-term bond (with a fixed interest rate) that matches the expected life of the operations in the foreign country. The disadvantage of this strategy is that long-term interest rates may decline in the near future, but the MNC will be obliged to continue making its debt payments at the higher rate. There is no perfect solution, but the MNC should consider the expected life of the business and the yield curve of the country in question when weighing the trade-off.

The yield curve is the difference in the per annum rate for bonds of differing maturities (e.g. a 10-year bond may charge 7 per cent per annum but a 3-year bond may charge 5 per cent per annum). The difference is shaped by the demand and supply of funds for varying maturities (2, 5, 10 years and so on) in a country's debt market.

The debt maturity decision

Before making the debt maturity decision, MNCs assess the yield curves of the countries in which they need funds. If a MNC wants to borrow for 15 years, should it issue 15-year bonds or should it issue 5-year bonds and seek to refinance every 5 years? The yield curve gives some idea of the different rates for differing periods of borrowing (maturities) at a point in time. Examples of yield curves for the UK and the USA are shown in Exhibit 15.9. First, notice that at any given debt maturity, the interest rate varies among countries. Second, notice that the shape of the yield curve varies between countries and over time within one country. The typical slope is as for 2009 in both the USA and the UK for mid-March and has an upward-sloping yield curve, which means that the per annum interest rates are lower for short-term debt than for long-term debt. Over time however, short-term debt can easily be more expensive than long-term debt. In the USA a 20-year bond in 2006 proved less expensive than a 5-year bond a mere 2 years before and 3 years after.

There are a number of rationales to try to explain the shape of the yield curve but there is no single accepted analysis. One argument for the upward slope is that investors may require a higher rate of return on long-term debt as compensation for lower liquidity. This is known as the liquidity hypothesis. Alternatively, the market value of long-term debt is more sensitive to market interest rate movements than short-term debt, so investors face a greater risk of a loss if they need to sell the debt before its maturity hence they will require a higher return. This is known as the market segmentation hypothesis. The yield curve is not always upward sloping because other forces such as interest rate expectations may affect the demand and supply conditions for debt at various maturity levels. Sometimes the yield curve is flat as in mid-March 2006 in the USA and the UK and can be even downward sloping. There is no necessary similarity between the USA and the UK as the yield curves for 2004 demonstrate.

Some MNCs may use a country's yield curve to compare annualized rates among debt maturities, so that they can choose a maturity that has a relatively low rate. Other MNCs use a yield curve to assess the prevailing market demand for and supply of funds for particular debt maturities, which may indicate the future movement in interest rates. This type of information may help an MNC decide whether to lock in a long-term rate or borrow for a short-term period and re-finance in the near future.

EXAMPLE

Withington Ltd expects to generate earnings in Indonesia, Malaysia and Thailand for the next 10 years. It expects that the Indonesian rupiah and Malaysian ringgit will weaken substantially against the pound over that period, and therefore plans to finance the respective operations with local debt from those countries. Its earnings from Thailand may be discontinued in 5 years when a contract with the Thai government expires.

Withington's best guess is that the Thai baht's future value will be similar to today's spot rate, but it is concerned about the exchange rate risk of its baht-denominated revenue. The 10-year bond yield is about 12 per cent for each country, but the yield curve is upward sloping (implying lower annualized yields for shorter debt maturities) in Malaysia and Thailand and downward sloping (higher annualized yields for shorter debt maturities) in Indonesia. It expects that future interest rates in these countries should be somewhat stable over time.

Withington Ltd decides to issue Thai notes with a maturity of 5 years to finance the Thai operations because it does not want to have debt in the business beyond the period when its operations may be discontinued. In addition, the upward-sloping yield curve allows it to issue 5-year notes at a lower annualized yield than a 10-year bond in Thai baht. Withington decides to issue 10-year bonds to finance its operations in Indonesia; because the yield curve is downward sloping, if it issued shorter-term debt, it would have to pay a higher annualized yield and would then be exposed to the possibility of higher interest rates when it re-finances the debt. Finally, it decides to issue short-term debt to finance its operations in Malaysia because it will pay a lower annualized yield on short-term debt. In this case, Withington will be exposed to the possibility that interest rates will increase by the time it re-finances the debt.

The fixed versus floating rate decision

MNCs that wish to use a long-term maturity but wish to avoid the prevailing fixed rate on long-term bonds may consider floating rate bonds. In this case, the coupon rate will fluctuate over time in accordance with interest rates. For example, the coupon rate is frequently tied to the London Interbank Offer Rate (LIBOR), which is a rate at which banks lend funds to each other. As LIBOR increases, so does the coupon rate of a

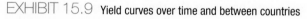

EXHIBIT 15.9 **Yield curves over time and between countries**

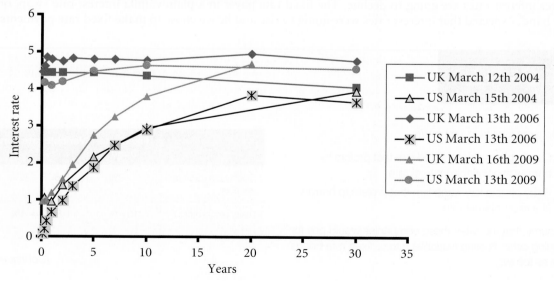

floating rate bond. A floating coupon rate can be an advantage to the bond issuer during periods of decreasing interest rates, when otherwise the firm would be locked in at a higher coupon rate over the life of the bond. It can be a disadvantage during periods of rising interest rates. In some countries, such as those in South America, most long-term debt has a floating interest rate.

If the coupon rate is floating, then forecasts are required for interest rates as well as for exchange rates. Simulation can be used to incorporate possible outcomes for the exchange rate and for the coupon rate over the life of the loan and can develop a probability distribution of annual costs of financing.

Hedging with interest rate swaps

When MNCs issue bonds that expose them to interest rate risk, they may use interest rate *swaps* to hedge the risk. Interest rate swaps enable a firm to exchange fixed rate payments for variable rate payments. Bonds issuers use interest rate swaps because they may reconfigure the future cash flows in a manner that offsets (better matches) their outflow payments to bondholders. In this way, MNCs can reduce their exposure to interest rate movements.

Financial institutions such as commercial and investment banks and insurance companies often act as dealers in interest rate swaps. Financial institutions can also act as brokers in the interest rate swap market. As a broker, the financial institution simply arranges an interest rate swap between two parties, charging a fee for the service, but does not actually take a position in the swap. MNCs frequently engage in interest rate swaps to hedge or to reduce financing costs.

Note that as with much in finance there are alternative ways of achieving the same result. In this case, a firm may take out a futures contract on bonds. A bond price varies inversely with any change in the interest rate. If interest rates go up, bond prices fall to offer a similarly attractive return and *vice versa*. Selling bond futures will mean that an MNC will receive money (through daily settlement) when interest rates go up implying a fall in bond prices and the MNC will pay out when interest rates fall and bond prices go up. Closing out will ensure that no bonds are actually sold on the forward market. So the price of a swap must not be greater than this alternative approach.

Plain vanilla swap

A plain vanilla swap is a standard contract without any unusual contract additions. In a plain vanilla swap, the floating rate payer is typically highly sensitive to interest rate changes and seeks to reduce interest rate risk. A firm with a large amount of highly interest rate-sensitive assets may seek to exchange floating rate payments for fixed rate payments. In general, the floating rate payer, at the time of arranging the loan, believes interest rates are going to decline. The fixed rate payer in a plain vanilla interest rate swap, on the other hand, expected that interest rates were going to rise and hence chose to make fixed rate payments.

EXAMPLE

Two firms plan to issue bonds:

- Quality plc is a highly rated firm that prefers to borrow at a variable interest rate.
- Risky plc is a low-rated firm that prefers to borrow at a fixed interest rate.

Assume that the rates these companies would pay for issuing either floating (variable) rate or fixed rate bonds are as follows:

	Fixed rate bond	Variable rate bond
Quality plc (prefers variable)	9%	LIBOR +½%
Risky plc (prefers fixed)	10½%	LIBOR + **1%**

(Continued)

LIBOR changes over time. Based on the information given, Quality plc has an advantage when issuing either fixed rate or variable rate bonds, but more of an advantage with fixed rate bonds. Quality plc could issue fixed rate bonds while Risky plc issues variable rate bonds; then, Quality could provide variable rate payments to Risky in exchange for fixed rate payments.

Assume that Quality plc negotiates with Risky plc to provide variable rate payments at LIBOR + one-half per cent in exchange for fixed rate payments of nine-and-a-half per cent. The interest rate swap arrangement is shown in Exhibit 15.10. Quality plc benefits because the fixed rate payments it receives on the swap exceed the payments it owes to bondholders by one-half per cent. Its variable rate payments to Risky plc are the same as what it would have paid if it had issued variable rate bonds. Risky plc is receiving LIBOR + one-half per cent on the swap, which is one-half per cent less than what it must pay on its variable rate bonds. Yet, it is making fixed rate payments of nine-and-a-half per cent, which is 1 per cent less than what it would have paid if it had issued fixed rate bonds. Overall, Risky plc saves 1-to-2 per cent per year of financing costs.

EXHIBIT 15.10 Illustration of an interest rate swap

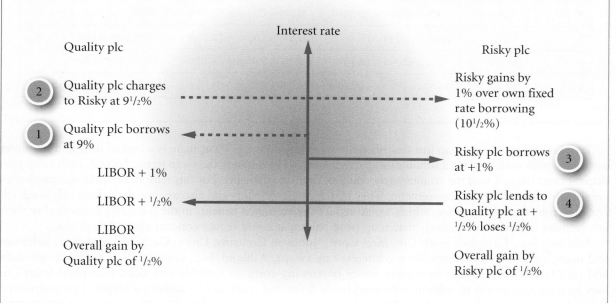

Notes:

- Risky wants a fixed rate loan; Quality a variable rate loan.
- Risky's position: Paying a fixed rate at nine-and-a-half per cent is 1 per cent cheaper than issuing at ten-and-a-half per cent at a cost of losing one-half per cent on the variable (LIBOR) rate deal. A net gain of half a per cent.
- Quality's position: Variable loan is the same as if it had issued directly. But by issuing at fixed rate instead and charging nine-and-a-half per cent to Risky, it gains one-half per cent.

Determining swap payments. The payments in an interest rate swap are typically determined using some **notional value** agreed upon by the parties to the swap and established contractually. Importantly, the notional amount itself is never exchanged between the parties, but is used only to determine the swap payments. Once the swap payments have been determined using the notional amount, the parties periodically exchange only the net amount owed instead of all payments. Payments are typically exchanged either annually or semi-annually.

EXAMPLE

Continuing with the previous example involving Quality plc and Risky plc, assume that the notional value agreed upon by the parties is £50 million and that the two firms exchange net payments annually.

From Quality plc's viewpoint, the complete swap arrangement now involves payment of LIBOR + one-half per cent annually, based on a notional value of £50 m. From Risky plc's viewpoint, the swap arrangement involves a fixed payment of nine-and-a-half per cent annually based on a notional value of £50 m. The following table below illustrates the payments based on LIBOR over time.

Year	LIBOR	Quality plc payment	Risky plc payment	Net payment
1	8.0%	8.5% × £50 m = £4.25 m	9.5% × £50 m = £4.75 m	Risky pays quality £0.5 m
2	7.0%	7.5% × £50 m = £3.75 m	9.5% × £50 m = £4.75 m	Risky pays quality £1 m
3	5.5%	6.0% × £50 m = £3 m	9.5% × £50 m = £4.75 m	Risky pays quality £1.75 m
4	9.0%	9.5% × £50 m = £4.75 m	9.5% × £50 m = £4.75 m	No payment is made
5	10.0%	10.5% × £50 m = £5.25 m	9.5% × £50 m = £4.75 m	Quality pays Risky £0.5 m

Two limitations of the swap just described are worth mentioning. First, there is a cost of time and resources associated with searching for a suitable swap candidate and negotiating the swap terms. Second, each swap participant faces the risk that the counterparty could default on payments. For this reason, financial intermediaries are usually involved in swap agreements. They match up participants and also assume the default risk involved. For their role, they charge a fee, which would reduce the estimated benefits in the preceding example, but their involvement is critical to effectively match up swap participants and reduce concern about default risk.

Ashland, Inc., Campbell Soup Co., Intel Corp., Johnson Controls, Union Carbide and Adidas Salomon and many other MNCs commonly use interest rate swaps. Ashland, Inc., commonly issues fixed rate debt and uses interest rate swaps to achieve lower borrowing costs on variable rate debt. Campbell Soup Co. uses interest rate swaps to minimize its worldwide financing costs and to achieve a targeted proportion of fixed rate versus variable rate debt. Adidas use interest rate swaps and cross currency interest rate swaps, thereby reducing foreign currency exposure as well.

Other types of interest rate swaps. Continuing financial innovation has resulted in various additional types of interest rate swaps in recent years. Listed below are some examples:

- *Accretion swap.* An accretion swap is a swap in which the notional value is increased over time.

- *Amortizing swap.* An amortizing swap is essentially the opposite of an accretion swap. In an amortizing swap, the notional value is reduced over time.

- *Basis (floating-for-floating) swap.* A basis swap involves the exchange of two floating rate payments. For example, a swap between 1-year LIBOR and 6-month LIBOR is a basis swap.

- *Callable swap.* As the name suggests, a callable swap gives the fixed rate payer the right to terminate the swap. The fixed rate payer would exercise this right if interest rates fall substantially.

- *Forward swap.* A forward swap is an interest rate swap that is entered into today. However, the swap payments start at a specific future point in time.

- *Putable swap.* A putable swap gives the floating rate payer the right to terminate the swap. The floating rate payer would exercise this right if interest rates rise substantially.

- *Zero-coupon swap.* In a zero-coupon swap, all fixed interest payments are postponed until maturity and are paid in one lump sum when the swap matures. However, the floating rate payments are due periodically.

- *Swaption.* A swaption gives its owner the right to enter into a swap. The exercise price of a swaption is a specified fixed interest rate at which the swaption owner can enter the swap at a specified future date. A payer swaption gives its owner the right to switch from paying floating to paying fixed interest rates at the exercise price. A receiver swaption gives its owner the right to switch from receiving floating rate to receiving fixed rate payments at the exercise price.

Standardization of the swap market. As the swap market has grown in recent years, one association in particular is frequently credited with its standardization. The International Swaps and Derivatives Association (ISDA) is a global trade association representing leading participants in the privately negotiated derivatives industry. This encompasses interest rate, currency, commodity, credit and equity swaps, as well as related products such as caps, collars, floors and swaptions. The ISDA was chartered in 1985, after a group of 18 swap dealers began work in 1984 to develop standard terms for interest rate swaps. Today, the ISDA has over 600 member institutions from 46 countries. These members include most of the world's major institutions that deal in derivative instruments, as well as leading end-users of privately negotiated derivatives and associated service providers and consultants.

Since its inception, the ISDA has pioneered efforts to identify and reduce the sources of risk in the derivatives and risk management business. The ISDA's two primary objectives are: (1) the development and maintenance of derivatives documentation to promote efficient business conduct practices and (2) the promotion of the development of sound risk management practices.

One of the ISDA's most notable accomplishments is the development of the ISDA Master Agreement. This agreement provides participants in the private derivatives markets with the opportunity to establish the legal and credit terms between them for an ongoing business relationship. The key advantage of such an agreement is that the general legal and credit terms do not have to be renegotiated each time the parties enter into a transaction. Consequently, the ISDA Master Agreement has contributed greatly to the standardization of the derivatives market (see http://www.isda.org).

USING THE WEB

Long-term foreign interest rates

Long-term interest rates for major currencies such as the Canadian dollar, Japanese yen and British pound for various maturities are provided at: http://www.bloomberg.com. You can develop a yield curve from this information.

Project finance

An important method of reducing risk in medium-to-long-term projects is to engage in project finance. Rather than reduce risk by managing prices, this approach reduces risk by creating a legal structure that protects the investor in the event of a strong negative outcome. The distinguishing aspect of project finance is the creation of a special purpose vehicle (SPV) sometimes referred to as a special purpose enterprise. The MNC in this context becomes an investor in a project and is rewarded through dividends. If the project fails the creditors cannot seek redress from the investing company's assets of its main business but only from the assets of the SPV. The details of the investment may also be less visible on the balance sheet. If the

SPV is not a subsidiary (the ownership is less than 50 per cent) then the assets are not consolidated and the SPV appears as an investment only without revealing the individual assets. To this extent the investment is 'off the balance sheet'.

Surrounding the SPV are a web of contracts designed to reduce risk and increase performance.

On the cost side, an offtake agreement is a contract to purchase all or most of the output of the project at an agreed price formula. A put or pay or a throughput agreement is a contract to supply or pay the difference between the supply price and the price of an alternative supplier. A multicurrency agreement is between the SPV and lenders allowing the SPV to choose the currency of the loan.

On the revenue side where there is a public private partnership (confusingly referred to as PPP) revenues due to the SPV depend on the contractual agreement. A contract may be BOT (build operate transfer) the private builders are allowed to operate the project (collect tolls, charge fees, etc.) and at the end of a designated period, the facility is transferred to public ownership without payment of any fees. BOOT contracts (Build Operate Own Transfer) are the same as the BOT contracts except that a fee is paid on transfer. Finally BOO contracts have no element of transfer to the public sector.

MANAGING FOR VALUE

In the UK some 10 per cent of prisons are run by the private sector most of whose jails have also been privately built. Newspapers report excessive windfall profits by private companies and ministers commissioning the projects and, when out of office, being 'hired' for 'consultancy' by the private parties to the contract.

Project finance represents a contractual approach rather than a market or managerial approach to managing risk and guaranteeing performance. In theory it would be possible to lay off or protect against all the risk of a project, but in an efficient market the cost of doing so should be as much if not more than the profit from the project.

The investors must decide the risks the SPV should take on and the risks that it must protect against. Examples of project finance include the construction of bridges, toll roads, schools, the supply of water and sewage plants and cross border renewable energy projects. Many projects involve government and large construction companies with joint interest in a SPV or simply acting as the customer of a SPV – this has been termed the 'Private Finance Initiative' or PFI. From the government's point of view such projects require less or no government borrowing compared to an investment wholly financed by the government. This benefit, however, comes at a cost as the contracts and clauses usually amount to a more expensive construction in the longer term, the extra cost being paid by future generations. The guarantees provided by government in the form of various offtake agreements has been viewed as a nationalization of risk giving private investors an excess return for the risk at the expense of the taxpayer. There is however something of a political return for the government in that the alternative would be to raise taxes or increase government borrowing both of which would be unpopular.

SUMMARY

- Some MNCs may consider long-term financing in foreign currencies to offset future cash inflows in those currencies and therefore reduce exposure to exchange rate risk. Other MNCs may consider long-term financing in foreign currencies to reduce financing costs. If a foreign interest rate is relatively low or the foreign currency borrowed depreciates over the financing period, long-term financing in that currency can result in low financing costs.

- An MNC can assess the feasibility of financing in foreign currencies by applying exchange rate forecasts to the periodic coupon payments and the principal payment. In this way, it determines the amount of its home currency that is necessary per period to cover the payments. The annual cost of financing can be estimated by determining the discount rate that equates the periodic payments on the foreign financing to the initial amount borrowed (as measured in the domestic currency). The discount rate derived from this exercise represents the annual cost of financing in the foreign currency, which can be compared to the cost of domestic financing. The cost of long-term financing in a foreign currency is dependent on the currency's exchange rate over the financing period and therefore is uncertain. Thus, the MNC will not automatically finance with a foreign currency that has a lower interest rate, since its exchange rate forecasts are subject to error. For this reason, the

MNC may estimate the costs of foreign financing under various exchange rate scenarios over time.

● For bonds that have floating interest rates, the coupon payment to be paid to investors is uncertain. This creates another uncertain variable (along with exchange rates) in estimating the amount in the firm's domestic currency that is required per period to make the payments. This uncertainty can be accounted for by estimating the coupon payment amount necessary under various interest rate scenarios over time. Then, with the use of these estimates, the amount of the firm's domestic currency required to make the payments can be estimated, based on various exchange rate scenarios over time.

CRITICAL DEBATE

Are swaps deceiving the market?

Proposition. Yes. Interest rates are charged to firms because the market estimates that the risk is appropriate for the borrower. For MNCs to then swap the loans is to ignore this judgement and puts lenders at risk and hence the interests of the shareholders.

Opposing view. No. The difference in rates is often small and hardly related to non-payment. There are other rea-

sons for swaps to do with currencies and changing the nature of the loan, so there is no second guessing the market.

With whom do you agree? Provide a reasoned argument as to why you agree or disagree with one of the above views.

SELF TEST

Answers are provided in Appendix A at the back of the text.

1 Explain why a firm may issue a bond denominated in a currency different from its home currency to finance local operations. Explain the risk involved.

2 Trulane plc is considering issuing a 20-year Swiss franc-denominated bond. The proceeds are to be converted to pounds to support the firm's UK operations. Trulane has no Swiss operations but prefers to issue the bond in francs rather than pounds because the coupon rate is two percentage points lower. Explain the risk involved in this strategy. Do you think the risk here is greater or less than it would be if the bond proceeds were used to finance Swiss operations? Why?

3 Some large companies based in Latin American countries could borrow funds (through issuing bonds

or borrowing from UK banks) at an interest rate that would be substantially less than the interest rates in their own countries. Assuming that they are perceived to be creditworthy in the UK why might they still prefer to borrow in their local countries when financing local projects (even if they incur interest rates of 80 per cent or more)?

4 A respected economist recently predicted that even though Japanese inflation would not rise, Japanese interest rates would rise consistently over the next 5 years. Abend GmbH, a German firm with no foreign operations, has recently issued a Japanese yen-denominated bond to finance German operations. It chose the yen denomination because the coupon rate was low. Its vice president stated, 'I'm not concerned about the prediction because we issued fixed rate bonds and are therefore insulated from risk.' Do you agree? Explain.

5 Long-term interest rates in some Latin American countries commonly exceed 100 per cent annually. Offer your opinion as to why these interest rates are so much higher than those of industrialized countries and why some projects in these countries are feasible for local firms, even though the cost of funding the projects is so high.

QUESTIONS AND APPLICATIONS

1 **Floating rate bonds**

   a What factors should be considered by a UK firm that plans to issue a floating rate bond denominated in a foreign currency?

   b Is the risk of issuing a floating rate bond higher or lower than the risk of issuing a fixed rate bond? Explain.

   c How would an investing firm differ from a borrowing firm in the features (i.e. interest rate and currency's future exchange rates) it would prefer a floating rate foreign currency-denominated bond to exhibit?

2 **Risk from issuing foreign currency-denominated bonds.** What is the advantage of using simulation to assess the bond financing position?

3 **Exchange rate effects**

   a Explain the difference in the cost of financing with foreign currencies during a strong-pound period versus a weak-pound period for a UK firm.

   b Explain how a UK-based MNC issuing bonds denominated in euros may be able to offset a portion of its exchange rate risk.

4 **Bond offering decision.** Columbia plc is a UK company with no foreign currency cash flows. It plans to issue either a bond denominated in euros with a fixed interest rate or a bond denominated in UK pounds with a floating interest rate. It estimates its periodic pound cash flows for each bond. Which bond do you think would have greater uncertainty surrounding these future pound cash flows? Explain.

5 **Currency diversification.** Why would a UK firm consider issuing bonds denominated in multiple currencies?

6 **Financing that reduces exchange rate risk.** Kerr plc, a major UK exporter of products to Japan, denominates its exports in pounds and has no other international business. It can borrow pounds at 9 per cent to finance its operations or borrow yen at 3 per cent. If it borrows yen, it will be exposed to exchange rate risk. How can Kerr borrow yen and possibly reduce its economic exposure to exchange rate risk?

7 **Exchange rate effects.** Katina plc is a UK firm that plans to finance with bonds denominated in euros to obtain a lower interest rate than is available on pound-denominated bonds. What is the most critical point in time when the exchange rate will have the greatest impact?

8 **Financing decision.** Ivax plc (based in Germany) is a drug company that has attempted to capitalize on new opportunities to expand in Eastern Europe. The production costs in most Eastern European countries are very low, often less than one-quarter of the cost in Germany or Switzerland. Furthermore, there is a strong demand for drugs in Eastern Europe. Ivax penetrated Eastern Europe by purchasing a 60 per cent stake in Galena AS, a Czech firm that produces drugs.

   a Should Ivax finance its investment in the Czech firm by borrowing euros that would then be converted into koruna (the Czech currency) or by borrowing koruna from a local Czech bank? What information do you need to know to answer this question?

   b How can borrowing koruna locally from a Czech bank reduce the exposure of Ivax to exchange rate risk?

   c How can borrowing koruna locally from a Czech bank reduce the exposure of Ivax to political risk caused by government regulations?

ADVANCED QUESTIONS

9 **Bond financing analysis.** Sambuka plc can issue bonds in either UK pounds or in Swiss francs. Pound-denominated bonds would have a coupon rate of 15 per cent; Swiss franc-denominated bonds would have a coupon rate of 12 per cent. Assuming that Sambuka can issue bonds worth £10 000 000 in

either currency, that the current exchange rate of the Swiss franc is £0.47, and that the forecasted exchange rate of the franc in each of the next 3 years is £0.50, what is the annual cost of financing for the franc-denominated bonds? Which type of bond should Sambuka issue?

10 Bond financing analysis. Hatton Ltd just agreed to a long-term deal in which it will export products to Japan. It needs funds to finance the production of the products that it will export. The products will be denominated in pounds. The prevailing UK long-term interest rate is 9 per cent versus 3 per cent in Japan. Assume that interest rate parity exists, and that Hatton believes that the international Fisher effect holds.

a   Should Hatton finance its production with yen and leave itself open to exchange rate risk? Explain.

b   Should Hatton finance its production with yen and simultaneously engage in forward contracts to hedge its exposure to exchange rate risk?

c   How could Hatton plc achieve low-cost financing while eliminating its exposure to exchange rate risk?

11 Cost of financing. Assume that Seminole plc considers issuing a Singapore dollar-denominated bond at its present coupon rate of 7 per cent, even though it has no incoming cash flows to cover the bond payments. It is attracted to the low financing rate, since UK pound-denominated bonds issued in the UK would have a coupon rate of 12 per cent. Assume that either type of bond would have a 4-year maturity and could be issued at par value. Seminole needs to borrow £10 million. Therefore, it will issue either UK pound-denominated bonds with a par value of £10 million or bonds denominated in Singapore dollars with a par value of S$20 million. The spot rate of the Singapore dollar is £0.33. Seminole has forecasted the Singapore dollar's value at the end of each of the next 4 years, when coupon payments are to be paid:

End of year	Pound exchange rate of Singapore dollar
1	£0.34
2	0.35
3	0.38
4	0.33

Determine the expected annual cost of financing with Singapore dollars. Should Seminole plc issue bonds denominated in UK pounds or Singapore dollars? Explain.

12 Interaction between financing and invoicing policies. Assume that Hurricane plc is a UK company that exports products to the USA, invoiced in pounds. It also exports products to Denmark, invoiced in pounds. It currently has no cash outflows in foreign currencies, and it plans to issue bonds in the near future. Hurricane could issue bonds at par value in: (1) pounds with a coupon rate of 12 per cent, (2) Danish kroner with a coupon rate of 9 per cent or (3) dollars with a coupon rate of 15 per cent. It expects the kroner and dollar to strengthen over time. How could Hurricane revise its invoicing policy and make its bond denomination decision to achieve low financing costs without excessive exposure to exchange rate fluctuations?

13 Swap agreement. Grant plc is a well-known UK firm that needs to borrow 10 million dollars to support a new business in the USA. However, it cannot obtain financing from US banks because it is not yet established within the USA. It decides to issue pound-denominated debt (at par value) in the UK, for which it will pay an annual coupon rate of 10 per cent. It then will convert the pound proceeds from the debt issue into dollars at the prevailing spot rate (the prevailing spot rate is 1 pound = $1.70). Over each of the next 3 years, it plans to use the revenue in dollars from the new business in the USA to make its annual debt payment. Grant plc engages in a currency swap in which it will convert dollars to pounds at an exchange rate of $1.70 per pound at the end of each of the next 3 years. How many pounds must be borrowed initially to support the new business in the USA? How many dollars should Grant plc specify in the swap agreement that it will swap over each of the next 3 years in exchange for pounds so that it can make its annual coupon payments to the UK creditors?

14 Interest rate swap. Janutis plc has just issued fixed rate debt at 10 per cent. Yet, it prefers to convert its financing to incur a floating rate on its debt. It engages in an interest rate swap in which it swaps variable rate payments of LIBOR plus 1 per cent in exchange for payments of 10 per cent. The interest rates are applied to an amount that represents the principal from its recent debt issue in order to determine the interest payments due at the end of each year for the next 3 years. Janutis plc expects that the LIBOR will be 9 per cent at the end of the first year, eight-and-a-half per cent at the end of the second year, and 7 per cent at the end of the third year. Determine the financing rate that Janutis plc expects to pay on its debt after considering the effect of the interest rate swap.

PROJECT WORKSHOP

15 **Long-term cost of debt.** The Bloomberg website provides interest rate data for many countries and various maturities. Its address is http://www. bloomberg.com.

Go to the 'Market Data' section of the website and then to 'Rates and Bonds'. Consider a subsidiary of a US-based MNC that is located in Australia. Assume that when it borrows in Australian dollars, it would pay 1 per cent more than the risk-free (government) rates shown on the website. What rate would the subsidiary pay for 1-year debt? For 5-year debt? For 10-year debt? Assuming that it needs funds for 10 years, do you think it should use 1-year debt, 5-year debt, or 10-year debt? Explain your answer.

DISCUSSION IN THE BOARDROOM

This exercise can be found on our dedicated Course-Mate platform for students.

RUNNING YOUR OWN MNC

This exercise can be found on our dedicated Course-Mate platform for students.

Essays/discussion and articles can be found at the end of Part IV.

BLADES PLC CASE STUDY

Use of long-term foreign financing

Recall that Blades plc is considering the establishment of a subsidiary in Thailand to manufacture 'Speedos', Blades' primary roller blade product. Alternatively, Blades could acquire an existing manufacturer of roller blades in Thailand, Skates'n'Stuff. At the most recent meeting of the board of directors of Blades plc, the directors voted to establish a subsidiary in Thailand because of the relatively high level of control it would afford Blades.

The Thai subsidiary is expected to begin production by early next year, and the construction of the plant in Thailand and the purchase of necessary equipment to manufacture Speedos are to commence immediately. Initial estimates of the plant and equipment required to establish the subsidiary in Bangkok indicate costs of approximately 550 million Thai baht. Since the current exchange rate of the baht is £0.0153, this translates to a pound cost of £8.43 million. Blades currently has £1.76 million available in cash to cover a portion of the costs. The remaining £6.67 million (436 million baht), however, will have to be obtained from other sources.

The board of directors has asked Ben Holt, Blades' financial director, to line up the necessary financing to cover the remaining construction costs and purchase of equipment. Holt realizes that Blades is a relatively small company whose stock is not widely held. Furthermore, he believes that Blades' stock is currently undervalued because the company's expansion into Thailand has not been widely publicized at this point. Because of these considerations, Holt would prefer debt to equity financing to raise the funds necessary to complete construction of the Thai plant.

Ben Holt has identified two alternatives for debt financing: issue the equivalent of £8.43 million yen denominated notes or issue the equivalent of approximately £8.43 million baht-denominated notes. Both types of notes would have a maturity of 5 years. In the fifth year, the face value of the notes will be repaid together with the last annual interest payment.

Due to recent unfavourable economic events in Thailand, expansion into Thailand is viewed as relatively risky; Holt's research indicates that Blades would have to offer a coupon rate of approximately 10 per cent on the yen-denominated notes to induce investors to purchase these notes. Conversely, Blades could issue baht-denominated notes at a coupon rate of 15 per cent. Whether Blades decides to issue baht- or yen-denominated notes, it would use the cash flows generated by the Thai subsidiary to pay the interest on the notes and to repay the principal in 5 years. For example, if Blades decides to issue yen-denominated notes, it would convert baht into yen to pay the interest on these notes and to repay the principal in 5 years.

Although Blades can finance with a lower coupon rate by issuing yen-denominated notes, Ben Holt suspects that the effective financing rate for the yen-denominated notes may actually be higher than for the baht-denominated notes. This is because forecasts for the future value of the yen indicate an appreciation of the yen (versus the baht) in the future. Although the precise future value of the yen is uncertain, Holt has compiled the following probability distribution for the annual percentage change of the yen versus the baht:

Annual % change in yen (versus the baht)	Probability
0%	20%
2	50
3	30

Holt suspects that the effective financing cost of the yen-denominated notes may actually be higher than for the baht-denominated notes once the expected appreciation of the yen (versus the baht) is taken into consideration.

Holt has asked you, a financial analyst at Blades plc, to answer the following questions for him:

1 Given that Blades expects to use the cash flows generated by the Thai subsidiary to pay the interest and principal of the notes, would the effective financing cost of the baht-denominated notes

be affected by exchange rate movements? Would the effective financing cost of the yen-denominated notes be affected by exchange rate movements? How?

2 Construct a spreadsheet to determine the annual effective financing percentage cost of the yen-denominated notes issued in each of the three scenarios for the future value of the yen. What is the probability that the financing cost of issuing yen-denominated notes is higher than the cost of issuing baht-denominated notes?

3 Using a spreadsheet, determine the expected annual effective financing percentage cost of issuing yen-denominated notes. How does this expected financing cost compare with the expected financing cost of the baht-denominated notes?

4 Based on your answers to the previous questions, do you think Blades should issue yen- or baht-denominated notes?

5 What is the trade-off involved?

SMALL BUSINESS DILEMMA

Long-term financing decision by the Sports Exports Company

The Sports Exports Company continues to focus on producing basketballs in Ireland and exporting them to the UK. The exports are denominated in pounds, which has continually exposed the firm to exchange rate risk. It is now considering a new form of expansion where it would sell specialty sporting goods in the USA. If it pursues this US project, it will need to borrow long-term funds. The dollar-denominated debt has an interest rate that is slightly lower than the pound-denominated debt.

1 Jim Logan, owner of the Sports Exports Company, needs to determine whether dollar-denominated debt or pound-denominated debt would be most appropriate for financing this expansion, if he does expand. He is leaning toward financing the US project with dollar-denominated debt, since his goal is to avoid exchange rate risk. Is there any reason why he should consider using pound-denominated debt to reduce exchange rate risk?

2 Assume that Jim decides to finance his proposed US business with dollar-denominated debt, if he does implement the US business idea. How could he use a currency swap along with the debt to reduce the firm's exposure to exchange rate risk?

CHAPTER 16
ETHICS

LEARNING OBJECTIVES

The specific objectives of this chapter are to:

- Evaluate the importance of ethical issues.

- Describe the principles and practice of ethical investment.

- Describe the principles and practice of Islamic finance.

- Assess the arguments of globalization and its discontents.

Whether or not a multinational corporation (MNC) decides to invest in a particular country has important implications for particular locations, organizations and for the country in general. As an unelected and hence undemocratic organization, a MNC is in the difficult position of having considerable power without responsibility other than to its owners, for the most part shareholders.

Understanding the issues and attitudes of sections in society that criticize the actions of MNCs is important for understanding the financial environment within which MNCs operate. There have been sufficient scandals, court cases and fines for financial management to be seen as more than just profit maximization. The concerns of other stakeholders need to be considered. Accordingly, this chapter examines alternative perspectives to the simple profit maximization motive that underlies analysis in other chapters.

WHAT ARE ETHICS?

Ethics are a set of directions or a code that acts as a guide to individual and social behaviour. Normally the code is acknowledged by a significant group in society, and will hence often form the basis of the legal and regulatory framework. The code is sometimes partially written but never wholly described in this way; what is ethical within a particular group is always subject to discussion and development in the face of new challenges.

THE IMPORTANCE OF ETHICAL ISSUES

The implied ethical code of finance is simply described as profit maximization for the owners, usually shareholders. The structure of a MNC is with few exceptions, hierarchical with the feature that the ultimate owners, the shareholder, often have little influence on the actions of the company. In a typical organization the shareholders appoint the managing director (also known as the chief executive officer or CEO) and members to the board of directors to act as their agents to fulfil the objectives as laid out in the articles of association. In large publically held organizations in the UK, the USA and most other common law countries, directors are rarely judged on anything other than financial performance. Indeed attempts by shareholders to influence the decisions of the company on ethical grounds is regarded as exceptional and referred to as shareholder activism. In non-common law countries, companies are more likely to be controlled by a few major shareholders narrowing the gap between ownership and control. Shareholders in such companies have a greater say in their actions, but this does not mean that it is necessarily more responsible.

Despite the focus on maximizing returns for owners, MNCs increasingly recognise that other sections of society, in particular pressure groups, feel significantly affected by their actions and that such groups can adversely affect the MNC's own profit maximizing goals by influencing government rules and legislation.

MANAGING FOR VALUE

On Friday 13th June Friends of the Earth, Grassroots Action on Food and Farming, Banana Link, the Small and Family Farms Alliance, farm and National Sheep Association attended the Tesco AGM to expose the company's record of putting profit before people and the environment, despite the claims in its Annual Report and Corporate Social Responsibility report.

... Friends of the Earth and GAFF are therefore calling on the Government to:

- Legislate to ensure that retailers trade fairly with their suppliers by imposing a new stricter Code of Practice on the biggest supermarkets, and appoint a watchdog with teeth to ensure it is being complied with.

- Stop any further consolidation of power by blocking all the Safeway merger bids.

Friends of the Earth is also seeking changes in Company Law so that communities can hold companies like Tesco to account for their impacts ...

Tesco says: 'We have a long-standing commitment to source as much UK produce as possible.' Tesco refers to its 'commitment to UK farming' and claims that it has 'consistently supported British farmers over recent years. As our business has grown, so has that of our suppliers.' 'We have developed long-term working relationships with our suppliers and by working together to meet customer needs we have both grown our market share.'

Extract from (Grassroots Action of Food and Farming) http://www.gaff.org.uk/ tesco-exposed/#more-26 27/12/12

MANAGING FOR VALUE

The New Friends of the Earth?

January 23, 2007

The superstores are suddenly competing to be green. Can we trust them?

The superstores' green conversion is astonishing, wonderful, disorienting. If Tesco and Walmart have become friends of the earth, are any enemies left?

These were the most arrogant of the behemoths. They have trampled their suppliers, their competitors and even their regulators. . . .

We environmentalists developed a picture of the world which seemed to be repeatedly confirmed by experience. Big corporations destroy the environment. They are the enemies of society. The bigger they become, the less they can be constrained by either democracy or consumer power. The politics of scale permit them to bully governments, tear up standards, reshape the world to suit themselves.

Then, as a result of powerful campaigns against sweatshops in the USA and Europe, some of the big clothing and sports retailers broke ranks. Soon after that, the energy companies started announcing big investments in renewable technologies (though not, unfortunately, any corresponding disinvestments in fossil fuel). But the supermarkets have shifted faster than anyone else. Environmental campaigners are partly responsible (listen to how the superstore bosses keep name-checking the green pressure groups); even so, their sudden conversion leaves us reeling.

Embarrassingly, for those of us who have scorned the idea of corporate social responsibility, some of these companies now claim to be setting higher standards than any government would dare to impose on them. Marks and Spencer, for example, has promised to become carbon neutral and to cease sending waste to landfill by 2012, and to stop stocking any fish, wood or paper which has not been sustainably sourced. Tesco promises to attach a carbon label to all its goods. Walmart now says it will run its US stores entirely on renewable energy.

These standards, moreover, are rather higher than those the British government sets for itself. M&S has pledged to use carbon offsets (paying other people to make cuts on its behalf) only as 'a last resort'. The government uses them as a first resort. Could it be true, as the neoliberals insist, that markets can do more to change the world than governments?

. . .

The big retailers are competing to convince us that they are greener than their rivals, and this should make us glad. But we still need governments, and we still need campaigners.

An extract of the full article By George Monbiot. Published in the Guardian 23rd January 2007, also available at http://www.monbiot.com

Just as companies have gained power through expanding and becoming multinational so have the pressure groups.

USING THE WEB

There are numerous instances of accusations of unethical activity by companies. One of the best sources is http://www.corporatewatch.org.uk which is part of a whole network of 'watchers' that can be accessed by visiting the Corporatewatch website for the links:

Other watchers

Multinational Monitor, Corporate Europe Observatory, CorpWatch (USA), CounterCorp (USA), BankWatch Network, BiofuelWatch, GeneWatch, GM Watch, IFIwatch, Media Lens, Press Action, Oil Watch, PR Watch, Spin Watch, State Watch, Nor Watch (Norway).

(Continued)

Anti-corporate campaigns: Baby Milk Action, Compassion in World Farming, Boycott Nike, Boycott Israeli Goods Camapign, Campaign Against Arms Trade, Coalition against Bayer Dangers, Communities Against Toxics, Do or Die, Hands Off Iraqi Oil, Labour Behind the Label, McSpotlight, Mines and Communities, No New Coal No Sweat, Shell Boycott, SmashEDO, Sprawl Busters, Stop Huntingdon Animal Cruelty (SHAC), Bretton Woods Project, Corporate Ethics Center for Corporate Policy, Corporate Accountability, International Endgame, Research Services (US), Essential Information, New Economics Foundation (nef), Ultimate Holding Company.

Other grassroots campaigns and groups: Action for Solidarity, Equality, Environment & Development (ASEED Europe), Banana Link, Down to Earth, Earth First! in Britain, ETC Group, Genetic Engineering Network, GenetiX Snowball, Norfolk Genetic Information Network, Grassroots Action on Food and Farming, (GAFF) INQUEST, International Rivers Network, LetsLink UK, Pesticide Action Network, Primal Seeds, Practical Action, Public Concern at Wor,k Reclaim The Streets, Radical Routes, Rainforest Action Network, Stop Deportation, Survival International, Sustain, The Land is Ours, Uncaged Campaigns, WaterWatch, Women's Environmental Network, Free Range Activism, Freedom to Care, Action on Smoking & Health (ASH), Corner House, Friends of the Earth, Greenpeace UK, Iraq Occupation Focus, The Stop the War Coalition, People & Planet, Peoples Global Action PLATFORM, World Development Movement, Women Working Worldwide.

Alternative media: Adbusters, Clearer Channel, Envirolink, Network Ethical Consumer, Earth First!, Action Reports, Action Update (newsletter), Greenpepper, Indymedia, Indymedia UK, Information for Action, New Internationalist, News Alternative, Peace News, Radical Activist Network, Red Pepper, SchNEWS, The Ecologist, UKWatch, Undercurrents, VisionOnTV, ZNet.

Other: Banksy, George Monbiot, Naomi Klein.

A number of campaigns involve MNCs. There has been a long-standing campaign against genetically modified crops. Campaigners see the development of seeds that do not reproduce as creating a dependence of farming on large MNCs. Others object on the grounds of unforeseen consequences. Animal rights organisations are against testing products and carrying out research on animals for ethical reasons – causing pain and suffering. Multinationals have been accused of running sweatshops in developing countries and of putting downward pressure on wages and standards in their own countries. Specific examples are easily found on the Internet. The green agenda often comes into conflict with MNCs, not surprisingly as green non-polluting technology is often more expensive.

As an example, the efficient farming industry in the developed world is accused of destroying local food production:

> *Cheap imports and food dumping create a vicious circle: they drive developing country farmers out of their local markets because they can no longer compete, local production falls, farmers abandon their land, the whole of the rural economy shrinks, people are forced to move to the cities for work and more food must be imported.*

http://www.corporatewatch.org.uk/?lid=2627 (27/12/12)

At the same time food is being imported from the developing world by the large food retailers. The overall picture in this and many other instances is never that clear. MNCs and pressure groups typically cite different evidence to support their cases with little by way of an overall assessment.

Even if MNCs wish to behave in an ethical manner there are difficulties. What is 'right' in one country, for example child labour, is seen as unacceptable in another. Are MNCs to respect the customs and practices of the country in which they operate or are they to adopt a rather vaguely defined concept of global ethical standards? The latter approach is finding more favour amongst some MNCs but it is not a general picture; for every MNC that adopts higher standards than strictly required by law, a cheaper rival with no such standards will compete.

It may be argued that it is the law that is deficient and not the MNCs – if it is legal it is 'right'. The dilemma is highlighted by the revelations in the UK in 2013 that large MNCs such as Amazon, Google and

Starbucks were paying little or no corporation tax. Their defence was 'we pay every penny we owe' which is indeed true. However, many hold the view that what is legal is not always ethical; hence there is a proliferation of pressure groups most of whom want to change the law in some aspect.

Poor regulation of markets

The permissiveness of legal frameworks across the world has a number of explanations. Generally, the politicians in developed countries are reluctant to regulate in any of the economic markets. The current capitalist based economic view is that regulations obstruct wealth creation in markets and that however distasteful some of the consequences may be, it is to be preferred to over-regulated markets that stifle the efficient use of capital. This is the rationale that, for instance, leads the UK government to seek 'growth built on cuts in workers' terms and conditions' (*Guardian* 13/05/12).

A second rationale for the relatively poor regulation of markets is the technological change in markets through the Internet and greater financial sophistication. Markets are created at times with a view to avoiding regulation. The rapid increase in the Eurodollar market in the 1960s was due in the main to regulation Q restricting the lending of dollars in the USA, so the markets simply traded dollars outside the USA. The newly created bitcoin market is an Internet currency where payment is person to person (peer to peer) over the Internet and is beyond government control. These markets thrive because individual governments cannot effectively legislate to regulate international markets – they do not have the authority on an international scale. Furthermore, international regulatory bodies such as the International Monetary Fund (IMF) require international agreement, this is difficult to obtain.

A third reason for poor regulation is the rapid increase in communication that has led to disintermediation – there is no market to regulate. In the recent world financial crisis, credit derivatives were sold largely over the counter and were not subject to market scrutiny – mispricing was almost an inevitable consequence. Imposing some form of central clearing of such instruments is seen by many (including the IMF) as an essential requirement.

Fourthly international non-governmental organizations are either committed to the economic argument of reduced regulation as is the case with the IMF, or are ineffective as is often said of UNCTAD (the United Nations Conference on Trade and Development) incorporating UNCTC (The United Nations Centre of Transnational Corporations). This unfortunately is a reflection of the lack of common responsibility amongst nations.

Given the reluctance to regulate, MNCs are almost inevitably caught in a moral vacuum between investors who want to maximize returns, governments that impose minimum regulations, international organizations that appear ineffective and pressure groups that seek to further their own moral standards.

A sensible reaction is for a MNC to adopt its own set of moral standards – failure to do so is in danger of leading to questionable behaviour that can have severe consequences as societies belatedly impose their ethical standards. Mis-selling of sub-prime loans, mis-selling of payment protection insurance (in the UK), fixing the LIBOR rate, money laundering (in the UK) and the horsemeat scandal are some of the more recent ethical scandals all of which had financial consequences.

MANAGING FOR VALUE

British banks face US suit over 'mis-selling' £1.6bn of sub-prime loans

HSBC, Barclays and RBS are among 15 Wall Street banks accused by a US investment firm of mis-selling a total of $2.4bn (£1.6bn) in mortgage-backed securities.

Cambridge Place Investment Partners, a fund based in Boston, Massachusetts, is suing US branches of the three British banks in a suit filed on Friday. It is also targeting JP Morgan, Citigroup, Credit Suisse, Deutsche

(Continued)

Bank, Merrill Lynch, UBS, Goldman Sachs and Morgan Stanley in what could turn out to be a test case for funds seeking restitution for their losses during the financial crisis.

The lawsuit filed in Boston states that Barclays, HSBC and RBS all sold mortgage-backed securities based on 'untrue statements'. Cambridge Place also blames the 'mortgage originators' – the sub-prime lenders responsible for assessing borrowers – for bending the truth about the worth of the loans. It says banks failed to conduct proper due diligence before packaging the loans into financial instruments and repeated untrue statements about the sub-prime mortgages in their prospectuses and sales pitches.

It also pointed out that the banks often had representatives on site at the mortgage lenders and gave them billions of dollars in credit. As a result, the suit alleges that they were 'complicit in creating an environment of improper lending practices.'

'The Wall Street bank defendants fostered the environment for, permitted and profited from the mortgage originators' rampant violations of sound lending practices,' the suit says.

'Driven to profit from the lucrative securitization business, the defendants demanded enormous volumes of loans, leading to erosion in lending standards' . . .
The suit claims that Barclays and the other British banks assured the investor that employees were on-site with the largest lenders 'quality controlling' the underwriting process . . .

Extract from The Telegraph 28/12/12
http://www.telegraph.co.uk/finance/newsbysector/banksandfinance/7884322/British-banks-face-US-suit-over-misselling-1.6bn-of-sub-prime-loans.html

ETHICAL BEHAVIOUR

As an example of moral standard setting the Marubeni Corporation claimed the following corporate principles formulated in 1998 quoted in their 2012 report:

1   Conduct fair and open business activities.

2   Develop a globally connected company.

3   Create new value through business vision.

4   Respect and encourage individuality and originality.

5   Promote good corporate governance.

6   Safeguard ecological and cultural diversity.

It is not clear whether any of the issues of especial interest to pressure groups such as child labour or animal experimentation would be specifically excluded by these corporate principles. Furthermore, pressure groups quoted above detail many instances of companies that do not always conform to their own code of behaviour. If not easily actionable, the standards in the Marubeni example nevertheless illustrate the difficult social and ethical position that MNCs now find themselves.

History provides encouraging examples of ethical behaviour with many examples of companies who owe their success to a strong personal moral code. Religious groups, particularly dissenting religions, have founded major businesses. The Quakers founded Lloyds TSB and Barclays two major UK banks, one reason it is said is that their 'aye meant aye and their nay meant nay,' they kept their word. Mennonites were tolerated in certain parts of Europe despite their pacifist doctrine because of their business skills.

In the following sections we look at three examples of concern over ethical standards. The first is the Green Movement founded on sustainability and respect for the environment. The second is a continuation of the long history of religious objections to finance in the form of Islamic finance which embraces a code of ethics that gives some assurance of ethical standards. The third example is entitled globalization and its discontents which is a concern for the ethical and social consequences of the existing form of the global economy.

THE GREEN MOVEMENT

The green movement is a pressure group in some countries and a political party in others. It is certainly less economically orientated than traditional political parties and is less focussed on furthering the interests of any particular faction in society. The most recent expression of those values (the Global Greens Charter) is the following six principles:

- Ecological wisdom
- Social justice
- Participatory democracy
- Nonviolence
- Sustainability
- Respect for diversity.

Unfortunately, this seems to be about as operational as the six principles of the Marubeni Corporation. Nevertheless, a green policy is generally understood to include the following elements:

- Waste reduction – encourage reuse and recycling. Use resources such as water as sparingly as possible.
- Purchasing – consider the resources used in production, is it an item shipped across the world when it could have been made locally? Could the resource be shared? Is there a commitment to the community that has produced the item? Does the purchase price allow a fair wage for workers including adequate social and pension provisions?
- Energy – as far as possible use renewable energy, create as little pollution as possible by reducing consumption
- Travel – are journeys necessary? Are there alternatives to arranging meetings? Can the journey be arranged such that the pollution is minimized.
- Can carbon credits be purchased to offset consumption?
- Is the worker provided with an acceptable working environment?

Most of these policies imply higher costs. In some cases, such as importing cheap clothes from impoverished countries with poor conditions for workers and no social security or health system, the whole business model would fail if it had to conform to an ethical code.

MANAGING FOR VALUE

Ethical procurement

Our ethical objective is to ensure that people in the supply-chain are treated with respect and have rights with regard to employment including the rights to freely choose employment, freedom of association, payment of a living wage, working hours that comply with national laws, equal opportunities, recognized employment relationship, freedom from intimidation and to a safe and healthy working environment.

Morrisons plc http://www.morrisonplc.com/files/ story_download/downloads/119/original/Procurement_- _Ethical_Procurement_Policy.pdf? 1323090041 28/12/12

MANAGING FOR VALUE

Historically, the lack of visibility of homeworkers in supply chains, combined with their complicated employment status in many countries, has made them a vulnerable group of workers. Many homeworkers have been underpaid and unsafe. We believe that one of the first steps towards reducing the vulnerability of these workers is to take an open and positive position towards homeworking. By reacting negatively to instances of homeworkers in our supply chain, there is a danger of:

1 Sending homeworkers underground and thus preventing any progress on improving their labour conditions.

2 Triggering unintended consequences whereby workers could have their sole means of income removed.

Primark plc http://www.ethicaltrade.org/sites/ default/files/resources/Primark %20homeworker%20policy.pdf

It may seem environmentally absurd to be importing goods such as shirts and woolly hats from the other side of the world when they could have been made within a short distance of the consumer; but there is an ethical rationale. Buying a country's goods is arguably more generous than giving aid. Giving aid provides little incentive to improve and if the aid is in the form of goods, food, clothing, etc. it can harm local businesses. In the form of cash, it can end up in the wrong hands. Buying a country's produce helps the society to organize itself, develop and administer an adequate legal framework to enforce contracts and honour agreements and pay ordinary people. The evidence is that national wealth increases faster through trade than through aid. Also it tends to be the case that wealth eventually becomes more evenly distributed in society.

The Green movement is also vulnerable to the argument that it is a form of cultural imperialism. The West has developed economies that were as environmentally polluting as the developing economies of today, to ask developing economies of today to reduce their carbon footprint is to an extent hypocritical.

MANAGING FOR VALUE

The Kyoto protocol is an international agreement to reduce greenhouse emissions. It came into force in 2005 with the significant omission of the USA that signed but did not ratify the agreement and Canada that withdrew in 2011. The Doha agreement of 2012 created a second round of reductions covering 2012 to 2020. It seems likely that Russia, Ukraine, Belarus and Kazakhstan will not ratify the new treaty.

The flaws in the Green agenda however do not justify ignoring the issues they raise. Multinational companies are keen to comply with an ethical agenda close to the requirements of the Green movement. Minimizing costs as the only ethical criteria is clearly an overly simplistic approach as illustrated in the Ikea example.

MANAGING FOR VALUE

IKEA apologises for benefitting from forced prison labour in communist East Germany 30 years ago

– East German prisoners, including many political dissidents, were involved in the

(Continued)

manufacture of goods supplied to IKEA 25 to 30 years ago.
- Swedish furniture giant has said it 'deeply regrets' its use of suppliers involved in forced prison labour.

The Swedish furniture giant released a report showing that East German prisoners, among them many political dissidents, were involved in the manufacture of goods that were supplied to IKEA 25 to 30 years ago. The report concluded that IKEA managers were aware of the possibility that prisoners would be used in the manufacture of its products and took some measures to prevent this, but they were insufficient.

Daily Mail http://www.dailymail.co.uk/news/article-2234050/IKEA-apologises-benefitting-forced-prison-labour-communist-East-Germany-30-years-ago.html (28/12/12)

MNCs are part of a world economy that operates without a world government. Instead there are pressure groups such as the Green movement, international organizations that operate by agreement and world public opinion as evidenced on the Internet. In this smaller world of the 'global village' MNCs are having to realize that profit maximization to be anything other than purely short term, has to have self-regulation guided by an ethical code.

ISLAMIC FINANCE

The second ethical construct that has international prominence is Islamic finance. The best known feature of which is the prohibition on interest or riba which in past times has also been banned in the Jewish faith (amongst themselves) and Christianity where it was seen as usury.

EXAMPLE

Former president Obasanjo speaking to international creditors:

'All that we had borrowed up to 1985 or 1986 was around $5 billion and we have paid about $16 billion. Yet we are still being told that we owe about $28 billion. That $28 billion came about because of the injustice in the foreign creditors' (lenders) interest rates. If you ask me what is the worst thing in the world, I will say it is compound interest.'

Jubilee 2000 News Update, August 2000

The reason for the dislike of interest in the Muslim faith is that money is regarded not an asset but only a measure. The ancient Greek philosopher Aristotle expressed similar views as follows:

Usury is most reasonably hated because its gain comes from money itself and not from that for the sake of which money was invented. For money was brought into existence for the purpose of exchange, but interest increases the amount of the money itself (poiei pleon); (and this is the actual origin of the Greek word: offspring resembles parent, and interest is money born of money); consequently this form of the business of getting wealth is of all forms the most contrary to nature (para phusin).

Aristotle, (350 BC) Politics 1, iii, 23 350BC quoted in Usury and the Church of England by Rev. Henry Swabey p.3 Cesc publications

The somewhat cynical view expressed by non-users of Islamic finance (which is open to non-Muslims) is that the Islamic alternatives are really the same as paying interest. This is not true in that interest is only part of the finance structure and taken together amounts to a different approach to lending. It may be true for those organizations who wish only to appear to conform to Islamic principles; but Islamic finance should be entered into willingly by both parties and therefore provide little incentive to those who may only want to borrow in the capitalist manner – that option is open to Muslims and of course all others.

The ethical arguments of capitalist interest rates

The ethical foundation of capitalist interest rates should perhaps be stated to understand the contrast with Islamic finance. The Fisher analysis is that interest consists of three elements:

1 Time preference: the reward for non-consumption.

2 Inflation: the maintenance of the purchasing power of the loan.

3 Risk: the possibility of non-repayment.

Thus, for example, if time preference is 1 per cent and estimate of inflation 3 per cent and risk at 5 per cent then the overall interest rate will be approximately the sum of these elements, i.e. 9 per cent. Many banking operations, have through the ages regarded money lending, in particular, as a form of exploitation. Borrowing at one rate and lending at a higher rate is seen as 'making money'. The margin is justified on four principal grounds. Firstly the process is one of maturity transformation, short-term lenders (those holding current accounts for the most part) are lending to long-term borrowers. The banking operation is taking on a risk that it will not be able to meet the demands of the depositors when they wish to withdraw their money. Secondly, risk transformation, in a banking operation a lot of small deposits are being lent out to relatively fewer large borrowers. Thirdly, liquidity, borrowers are able to go to one lender who has amassed the savings of many lenders to provide the large loan. Fourthly, allocative efficiency, the lending operation is deciding what are the worthy or profitable operations and what are not worth pursuing. These it can be argued are significant services to society justifying the use of an interest rate.

MANAGING FOR VALUE

OFT gives the green light to 2000 per cent interest rates*

Are payday loans a terrible money-making scheme that preys on the vulnerable, or do they provide a useful service? Mike Thomas reports.

Now the Office of Fair Trading (OFT) has backed away from recommending price controls on expensive forms of short-term borrowing, I bet the sub-prime market can't believe its luck. It means letting firms such as QuickQuid can continue to charge up to 2278 per cent interest on a payday loan.

So why has the OFT allowed this market to continue to operate with such high interest rates and is it the right decision?

As far back as July 2009 the OFT decided to have an in-depth look at the way payday loans, pawnbrokers and home-credit worked for consumers. Many debt advisers had also called for a review

because they felt, as I do, that these firms prey on the desperate and the vulnerable – people who can't get money from a mainstream lender, so are forced to turn to more desperate measures . . .

This means people in a fix, who have no credit rating and need to raise some cash end up going to the secondary (or sub-prime) market, which is worth around £7.5 billion, according to the OFT. That's enormous and so are the profits.

The OFT has said that although this form of borrowing is expensive, it actually serves a purpose for those on low incomes, who need short-term borrowing, so they are wary of barring it. It also felt that intervention would not necessarily address the problems in the sector because controls may reduce competition in the area.

(Continued)

The review conducted by the OFT also found many consumers were unaware of the options available to them. ...

It just does not seem fair or justifiable for those on low incomes to have to pay extortionate rates of interest if they fall behind with their payments, for the profits of the lenders.

Payday loans are banned in 15 states in the USA because of the way lenders rack up the interest rates once a borrower falls behind with the payments. Should we think of banning them here as well?

The bottom line is that a Payday loan is really only suitable for anyone looking to pay back after just a few days.

Mike Thomas Moneywise Jun 17th, 2010 downloaded 29/12/12 http://www.moneywise.co.uk/ cards-loans/cut-your-debts/oft-gives-the-green- light-to-2000-interest-rates

*Credit Unions are limited by law to charging no more than 2 per cent per month or 26.8 per cent per year. Many charge less.

If the interest rate is helping to fund all these operations then why is it seen as unworthy? Aristotle's view that using money to make a profit with no substantive service being provided is not really the case – the services of maturity and risk transformation and liquidity and allocative efficiency are vital to wealth creation. Nevertheless MNCs have to accept that finance is held in low esteem in many parts of the world. Although MNC operations do not usually involve banking operations any form of financial decision-making that involves negative social consequences is likely to incur social opprobrium from quarters of society. A clear ethical defence is important.

Islamic finance principles[1]

For Islamic finance the apparent unethical nature of free market finance is a matter of religious conviction. There are five guiding principles based on the Koran:

1. Belief in divine guidance. The Muslim faith is not restricted to worship but provides guidance for almost every aspect of life including financial transactions. This is part of the debate as to whether government should be secular (independent of religion) or non-secular, abiding, in this case, by the Islamic faith in its actions, including tolerance of other religions.

2. The charging of interest (riba) is prohibited. This does not mean that money is lent money free of charge. Typically, the loan will be linked with the underlying transaction and payment will be made from a combination of fees and profit sharing. Interest is trading money for money, generally there is a ban on profiting from buying and selling the same asset, which is also the essence of speculation. In this sense a loan can be thought of as selling money in return for even more money at a later date. Any form of delay in a contract that is artificial in the sense of not physically necessary is also banned as this could easily form the basis of an interest based contract.

3. No banned (haram) investments. In similar fashion to the Green movement, investment in products deemed to be physically or socially harmful are banned. Thus tobacco, alcohol, arms, pornography are banned.

4. Risk sharing is to be encouraged. This is an important element of the general distancing from the Western concept of an 'arms length transaction'. In a finance context in the UK, for instance, a bank charges interest based on the risk that it perceives to its loan. If the borrower can offer security in the form of assets, land and buildings for example, then the bank will not be especially concerned with the purpose of the loan. If it is successful, the borrower stands to gain significant profits, the bank's involvement will be limited to the interest charged. If the project is unsuccessful then the bank can claim the assets to help repay the loan. In this way, the bank need have little involvement in the activities of the borrower. This has been a much criticised aspect of finance as it also implies that there is little knowledge transfer between the parties. The banks' financial skills are not transferred.

In making risk sharing part of the contract the lender now has to take an interest in the purpose of the loan as well as the security of the borrower. The intention is to promote sharing and to avoid excessive profiting by either party at the expense of the other. Risk sharing on its own does not achieve this and indeed it would be easy to

---

[1]See Abdullah, D.V. and Chee, K. (2010) *Islamic Finance: Understanding its Principles and Practices*, Marshall Cavendish

construct a risk sharing contract that favours banks even more than an arms length transaction. Risk sharing does no more than create a structure within which mutual co-operation and trust can be enhanced more easily.

5   Financing should be based on real assets. A loan should be for the purposes of buying real assets rather than say purchasing shares. Borrowing to buy shares is a form of speculation that leads to share values rising at a faster rate than the economic growth – a situation that in the long run is unsustainable.

These five principles form the basis of what is termed Shariah compliant investment. Whether or not a transaction is Shariah compliant is a matter of scholarly debate and standards vary across countries. Regulatory bodies have evolved being the Accounting and Auditing Organization for Islamic Financial Institutions (AAOIFI), the Islamic Financial Services Board (IFSB) and the organization of International Islamic Financial Market (IIFM).

The lack of clear definition is in many ways a strength of the system. Hard targets introduce game playing and it seems right that, apart from the most basic of arrangements, no one scheme should be assured of being Shariah compliant.

Prohibitions and encouraged practices

The first prohibition is riba or interest, which is discussed above as one of the five principles.

The second is gharar or uncertainty. Whereas risk is to be shared, it should not be excessive. Excessive risk is not clearly defined but it should not be due to extreme complexity of an agreement, which amounts to deceit or fraud. Nor, as in moral hazard, should uncertainty be caused by the withholding of information; for example, an employee withholding information from his or her superior. Outcomes must as far as possible be ascertainable. Thus, for instance, the sale of fish not yet caught would be deemed to be gharar or excessively risky; but paying someone to fish for 5 hours in return for the catch would not be anything other than taking on unavoidable risk and therefore permitted.

Thirdly, maysir or gambling is prohibited. Closing out derivatives in particular futures and option contracts are seen as a form of gambling as there is no actual delivery (see Chapter 5). However, derivatives where there is a clear underlying asset with a risk that the company wishes to insure would ordinarily be permissible.

In addition practices that are forbidden or discouraged include:

Price manipulation, prices should be determined by fair and open trading in the market, i.e. an efficient market.

There should be equal access to information on both sides of the contract. The sale of land and buildings where the seller fails to reveal significant defects would not be Shariah compliant.

Mutual co operation should be encouraged. This is evidenced in the profit sharing schemes and the sharing of information. Also Muslims are obligated to give a portion of their wealth to the less well off in the what is known as zakat.

Islamic financial transactions

Bai bithaman ajil (BBA) This is a loan to meet long-term financing. Note the role of the real asset. In the case of for example a house purchase.

1   The house is identified by the buyer.

2   Bank agrees to finance the purchase.

3   The bank purchases the asset and sells it to the buyer for the cost plus a mark-up. The bank may previously have appointed the buyer as an agent thus ensuring an obligation to buy.

4   You pay the price to the bank over an agreed time period.

Note that the asset and the mark-up are evident in this transaction. In the case of a variable rate mortgage the interest element would not be as clear. There are variable rate products but with limitations to differentiate between risk and gharar.

Murabaha(h)

This is very similar to a BBA except that it is normally for shorter periods and used for example for financing working capital.

1   The buyer wishes to purchase raw material for a business.

2   The bank purchases the goods.

3   The bank sells the goods to the buyer for an agreed mark-up price.

4   Payment made in 30 days time by the buyer to the bank.

As with BBA the customer may be appointed as an agent.

Ijara(h)

An operating lease (a lessor lends an asset – a car for example – to a lessee who leases the asset for an extended period) a typical configuration might be:

1   The bank appoints the lessee as an agent giving ownership responsibilities to the lessee.

2   The lessee identifies the asset and buys it on behalf of the bank.

3   Ownership is transferred to the bank.

4   The lessee then uses the asset.

5   At the end of the lease period the asset is returned to the bank.

6   The bank may lease the asset to another customer or sell the asset.

Note that contracts are not allowed to run in parallel thus the agency contract terminates when the lease contract begins.

A financial lease ends with the lessee having the right to purchase the asset. This is termed Al-Ijarah-Themmal Al-Bai (AITAB) or Ijarah Muntahia Bittamleek (IMB). This is the same as the operating lease with the addition of a sales contract at the end of the lease period.

Mudharaba(h)

This is a joint venture between the borrower and the bank, the bank provides the funding and the borrower the expertise. The borrower runs the business. Payment to the bank is by an agreed profit sharing ratio. If there is a loss, the bank is solely responsible unless there is negligence or other form of wrongdoing by the borrower. The bank's liability is limited to the capital it has provided. Any further liability is due to the borrower who has incurred the extra debt as a result of managing the enterprise.

Note that this is almost the exact opposite of the Western approach to a financing arrangement where the borrower takes on most of the unsecured risk in the event of failure.

Musharaka(h)

Similar to the Mudharabah except that losses are shared in proportion to the amount of capital contributed by each party. The business is run jointly by the borrower and the bank. Each party has unlimited liability.

A variant is diminishing Musharakah whereby the borrower can use some of the profits to repay the capital that the bank has contributed. Thus, the bank's share of the profits gradually diminishes in line with the diminished share of the capital. This process can for example be used for a house purchase where the borrower's deposit and the bank's contribution form the initial capital sharing and the borrower gradually over time buys out the bank's contribution.

Sukuk

The Islamic bonds is known as a sukuk. The bond holders appoint a manager to oversee the underlying assets which are assigned to the bondholders as the owners. The sukuk holder participates in the profit generated by the bond and also the potential losses. This arrangement adheres to the principles of no interest being paid and the need to have underlying assets to support financial transactions.

Scholars who are seen as the judges of shariah compliance actively debate these Islamic financial transactions and contracts and their many and growing variations. From the ethical perspective their interest is in the way in which they attempt to express the principles of Islamic finance. The process is not easy as there is often a small but important distinction between a profit that exploits a business opportunity and one that exploits other people or encourages unproductive behaviour.

The two ethical codes of Green economics and Islamic finance offer widely differing views on ethical behaviour. The essentially scientific orientation of the Green movement is focussed on the object of expenditure; the Islamic code more on social behaviour. A MNC needs to be aware that the perspective of these stakeholders and others in society have an important voice in the regulation of business in different countries. It cannot be assumed in any society that financial management can be guided solely by profit maximization.

GLOBALIZATION AND ITS DISCONTENTS

The final area of ethical concern is from those who accept the profit maximization philosophy, but are concerned that it is leading to a catastrophic end, chiefly as a result of globalization. Such advocates seek modification in the form of greater regulation to international trade and the investment process.

Globalization

Globalization was described by the economist and diplomat Peter Jay as:
'Any entrepreneur anywhere can draw on savings accumulated anywhere and on technologies and managerial skills located anywhere to create a productive unit anywhere, employing local labour, and selling its products anywhere to everyone.'[2] Although this definition is not yet literally true, it is this scenario that is implied by the free market philosophy of the IMF and major nations of the developed world. For many, this apparent ideal brings with it national and international problems in the form of significant social and economic change that is so disruptive as to imply a general lowering rather than increase in wealth. A recent study of US imports from China concluded: 'Our analysis finds that exposure to Chinese import competition affects local labour markets not just through manufacturing employment, which unsurprisingly is adversely affected, but also along numerous other margins. Import shocks trigger a decline in wages that is primarily observed outside of the manufacturing sector. Reductions in both employment and wage levels lead to a steep drop in the average earnings of households. These changes contribute to rising transfer payments through multiple federal and state programs, revealing an important margin of adjustment to trade that the literature has largely overlooked.'[3]

---

[2]Kennedy, P. and Jay, P. (1996) Globalization and its Discontents, BBC Analysis Lecture tape No. SLN621/96VT1022. This section is based on the arguments of this prescient programme

[3]Autor, D.H. Dorn, D. and Hanson, G.H. (2012) The China Syndrome: Local Labor Market Effects of Import Competition in the United States, *American Economic Review*, Forthcoming

Ricardo's law of comparative advantage (see Chapter 1) underwrites the rationale for free trade. This is, in essence, showing that where countries have differing productivities, the world economic output can be increased by allowing a degree of specialization and then trading the surpluses. In this way, all countries can be better off even those who are less productive in all aspects but relatively less unproductive in some. The price mechanism should support this process, the lower cost resources being those of the more productive processes. However, there is a growing problem with this rationale. The benefits reduce as the productivity differences reduce between countries. In the extreme example of equal productivity everywhere, there would be no benefit through international trade.

The free market and technology are achieving an equalization of technology for many products and services. Production can indeed be anywhere and increasingly so for services with the use of the Internet. In such cases, the lower cost is due to government grants, less rigorous regulations and less expensive employment. Countries with no pension provision, poor hospital services and no social security attract investment to take advantage of the lower employment costs. These goods are then exported to the developed world where, in the early part of this century, governments have maintained artificially high standards by excessive borrowing. MNCs are actively involved in bringing about these changes through foreign direct investment (FDI) and international trade.

Discontent

The discontent of analysts is due to the view that this is not a stable scenario. The large movement of production out of the developed world reduces the national income in those countries that are then unable to fund pensions and social services. To compete, firms in the developed world must lower their standards – a process known as the 'race to the bottom'. MNCs find themselves in the difficult position of implementing these developments, more part-time work, fewer apprenticeships, closing factories and moving to the Far East.

As a note, the socialist model of the European Union was at one time to create a critical mass of free trade economies that would keep out production from countries that did not observe minimum workers rights. This model appears to have failed; in its place is what is termed the Anglo Saxon model of free trade.

This lowering of standards is not a new phenomenon. The industrial revolution replaced the old guild and mercantilist economies leading to a worsening of conditions. Many see the current changes as dismantling social structures that have taken over 100 years to achieve.

A second source of discontent is the liberalization of exchange controls and investment. Restrictions on foreign owned shares and foreign investment have largely been lifted. This has led to huge increases in portfolio and real investment. The volume of trade on the foreign exchanges in one day is larger than the UK gross national income. This increase has enabled countries to borrow on the international exchanges, issuing bonds to foreign investors to fund domestic spending promises. For many years the US national debt (government bonds) has had significant ownership from Japan and more recently China as well. About 30 per cent of US equity and 38 per cent US government bonds are foreign owned. This phenomenon is not confined to the USA; in Australia, for instance, about half the equities and bonds are foreign owned.

If foreign investors were to sell their bonds, interest rates would rise in the country concerned resulting in a reduction in the growth of economic activity. Generally, this does not happen as the lender will lose from a fall in the value of the bonds caused through selling (they cannot be sold all in one go). Thus there is a dependency between the lender and the borrower. There is also a dependency created between the borrowing country and the financial markets. Government actions and policy are actively constrained by concern over the views of the market; 'what the market will think' is now an active political concern for most countries. One of the more easily observed sources of market views are the credit agencies such as Standard and Poor, Fitch or Moodys. Politicians feel that they are being judged, as indeed they are, by an unelected unaccountable organization that is making essentially political judgements. The market however is free to ignore the judgements of the credit agencies as indeed was the case when the USA was downgraded, there was no effect on interest rates.

As a result of government borrowing, there has been a loss of national sovereignty to the financial markets. The lack of democratic accountability and indeed any clear governing structure of the markets represents a worrying loss of control from the point of view of the discontents.

MANAGING FOR VALUE

S&P downgrades France and Austria

The EuroZone debt crisis returned with a vengeance on Friday as Standard & Poor's, the credit rating agency, downgraded France and Austria . . .

'It is not good news . . . but it is not a catastrophe,' said François Baroin, France's finance minister. 'It is not the rating agencies that dictate the policies of France' . . .

S&P said last month's EU summit, which saw Euro-Zone leaders agree steps towards fiscal union, had 'not produced a breakthrough of sufficient size.'

By Gerrit Wiesmann, Peter Spiegel and Robin Wigglesworth
FT.com January 14, 2012 9:34 am
Here we see rating agencies making economic judgements with political consequences that are clearly seen as influencing government policies.

A third source of discontent is the communications revolution through the development of the Internet. Ideas, copyright and patents are easily stolen and transmitted worldwide. Weak international legislation can do little to prevent these developments. Business models as a result are increasingly uncertain, the publishing industry, the music industry and services either are, or could be, radically changed by the Internet.

The fourth concern is the huge labour force in South America, Indonesia, India, China and the rest of South East Asia with approximately 1.2 thousand million (billion) workers willing to work for a fraction of the wages in the developed world. This factor combined with the reduction in the technological advantage of the developed world due to the ease with which technology can be exported, combined with the Internet and international financial markets is enabling MNCs to produce efficiently anywhere. The problem that this creates is that in taking production away from the developed world, demand is also being removed. A wage cost for one company is a source of demand for another. Eventually, of course, the developing world itself will become a source of demand but there are two major problems. The first is that the demand on which the exporting nations depend may be disrupted by the failure of the economies in the developed world to adapt. The current debt crisis of the developed countries is evidence of this possibility. The second is that the political and social changes that are likely to accompany the increasing wealth of the developing (producing) countries may also disrupt the changes.

A fifth and final concern is the argument of what might be called the New Malthusians. In 1798 Thomas Malthus published his treatise: 'An Essay on the Principle of Population'. His concern was that the growth in population would outstrip their means of support leading to widespread poverty. For many years this argument was discounted. Huge advances in technology in the nineteenth and twentieth centuries meant that the means of support grew at a faster rate than Malthus thought possible. Also, populations showed a natural tendency to restrict growth as they became wealthier.

The rejection of Malthus' gloomy doctrine relied on these two factors, technology or scientific advances and a diminishing growth rate in the population. The new Malthusians attack both these points.

The once almost free energy of oil and gas is rapidly becoming more expensive as sources are harder to exploit. Scientific breakthroughs are not reliable and if present trends continue, resources will become increasingly expensive. Developing countries in such an event would find it difficult to support their populations. Sub-Saharan Africa is already suffering increased poverty due to rising food prices.

With regard to population, there have indeed been dramatic reductions in the rate of growth of populations. China's growth rate is only one-half per cent and Japan, Russia, Germany and many other countries have negative growth rates. Countering these trends however is the growth in the consumer population. The move away from agrarian subsistence to urban consumerism lifestyles in China is producing rapidly increasing demands for wheat, oil, coal and other resources similar to the effect of population growth. A future scenario of a decline in living standards along with social unrest based on a shortage of resources is, according to the New Malthusians, the inevitable result.

This is a pessimistic view of the future and is deepened by the fact that there appears to be little control over this process. There is no effective international government. Furthermore, the international nature of financial markets has made them remarkably difficult to regulate being beyond the control or influence of any one government. MNCs are also poorly regulated, the recent revelation that Amazon, Google and Starbucks paid almost no UK tax illustrates how control is difficult even for a developed nation. It is ironic that free trade and movement of capital that have been the source of wealth, are the very features that appear to be the cause of much of the 'discontent'.

MNCs in responding to governments, pressure groups and the press need to be aware of these international concerns as the MNCs are often blamed unfairly for being the cause of the problem. Their first duty, however, is to maximize returns for their shareholders and in doing so appear as helpless to influence many of these trends as any other party.

INTERNATIONAL CORPORATE GOVERNANCE[4]

Increasing concern over the way in which companies are managed has been motivated by financial scandals such as Enron, Arthur Andersen and WorldCom and earlier corporate scandals in the 1990s. Of particular concern has been the unethical behaviour of company directors who have benefitted themselves at the expense of the shareholder. The result has been legislation and codes of conduct around the world designed to increase the power of the shareholder and limit the influence of individual directors – the relationship, however, is not uniform. International corporate governance is concerned with the differing governance regimes within companies around the world and why there are differences. From a financial management perspective, joint ventures and partnerships require an appreciation of the differing control structures of foreign companies to be effective.

Corporate governance and outside parties

Corporate governance is questioned particularly by the Green movement over issues such as the environment and child labour. Also, MNCs are accused of regulation arbitrage, moving to countries where the tax or environmental or employment or other legislation is particularly favourable. Examples quoted earlier in this chapter provide ample evidence of the dilemma these MNCs face.

Differing control structures[5]

The basic common format for ownership is of shareholding in a legal entity that engages in commercial activities. One of the main international differences is in the nature of the relation between the owner and the managers or directors. In this regard the UK along with the USA are markedly different from other major industrialized countries. The influence of shareholders on managers depends in large measure on the size of the shareholding. A small shareholding has little influence in voting and hence cannot influence decision. This is generally the case in both the UK and the USA. Less than 5 per cent of listed firms have majority shareholders in these countries. This is in sharp contrast to the rest of the world where the percentages are much higher. In Austria, Belgium and Germany there is a majority shareholder in over 60 per cent of the listed companies. Control can be exercised by shareholders with blocking power set usually at 25 per cent. This is true of over 80 per cent of companies in these three countries plus the Netherlands with Spain Italy and Sweden at over 60 per cent. By contrast in the UK 15% of companies have blocking shareholders and in the USA below 10 per cent. The situation is even more extreme in East Asia with the exception of Japan and similarly so in Eastern Europe. In other words apart from the UK and the USA there is a much closer relationship between ownership and control.

---

[4]See M. Goergen (2012) *International Corporate Governance*, Pearson
[5]See Barca, F. and Becht, M. (2001) *The Control of Corporate Europe*, Oxford University Press.

The advantage of having large shareholders is that information asymmetry is far less. The investors will have access to the detailed accounts of the company in that they will be able to nominate directors to the board. Where the major shareholder is a bank or financial institution the company may benefit from its financial expertise. The disadvantages are that major shareholders reduce the flexibility of the company. A major shareholder will be reluctant to increase the shareholding and dilute its influence or in any way damage its interests elsewhere.

In addition the benefit of a major shareholder depends in part on their identity. Here again research reveals large differences. In Italy, for example, a survey found that 69 per cent of shareholders holding over 5 per cent were individuals or families, in the UK the figure was 2 per cent. Banks in France and Germany (through proxy votes) are particularly influential. In East Asia families are also the predominant influence. There are also links between firms through cross holding of shares and bank investments. In Japan such structures are termed keiretsus and in Korea chaebols. China similarly displays a narrow shareholder ownership, a study found that the largest shareholder held on average 43 per cent of the shares with the government being the identity of the shareholder in 67 per cent of the cases. A MNC seeking to go into partnership with a company or even to purchase the company is therefore likely to be dealing with a family or other large shareholder rather than the directors as the ultimate influence.

Why do governance structures differ?

Researchers have sought to explain the cause of the large differences in corporate governance. Of particular interest is the large difference between the 'Anglo Saxon' model of the USA and the UK where there is a strong division between shareholders and directors and the continental model where the division is far less. The question of interest is whether or not this difference is a symptom of other features of the societies to which they belong.

A number of distinguishing features have been suggested as causal factors of the differences. An early study sought to distinguish between bank based and market based economies. The UK and the USA have the most highly developed stock markets and are therefore attractive to a range of investors thus widening the ownership base. The bank offers an alternative source performing much the same functions as the market providing risk and maturity transformation, diversification and liquidity. This would suggest that the growth of stock markets would be accompanied by the dilution of ownership. Yet the European countries show a markedly narrow ownership despite large stock markets.

Other researchers have pointed to the very large difference in the legal structures. The UK and the USA are governed by common law which is case based. Judges decisions set a legal precedent, that is to say that they add to the law passed by parliament. The alternative is civil law based on Roman law which is rule or principal based. The argument is that common law is more flexible and hence more attractive to investors as it adapts more quickly to changing circumstances. The civil law system with its lesser concern with the concept of fairness and greater adherence to the letter of the law is deemed less reassuring. Judges rulings under common law are lengthy as the judge wrestles with the concepts of fairness and conformity with precedents, whereas the civil law judgements are briefer, concerned solely with the application of the law.

Evidence that common law is more flexible is also in the larger number of measures restricting the power of directors in a company. The concern of corporate governance is over the misuse of company resources by directors. So evidence that common law countries protect ordinary shareholders to a much greater extent would support the more widely held shareholding.

In sum, ownership and control varies greatly between countries and between companies. Possible causes point to fundamental differences in the economies. The ethical concern of directors defrauding shareholders is possibly less in countries where the shareholder is influential on the board of directors. Here the concern is that minority shareholders lose out. Where the shareholding is more diluted there is markedly more protection for the shareholder, matching their lesser influence on directors' decisions.

SUMMARY

- MNCs have to be aware of the potential regulatory threat posed indirectly by pressure groups and directly by governments who feel threatened by the actions of MNCs.

- There are a number of alternative views of business that can potentially conflict with the profit maximization process including concern for the environment, animal rights and employment.

- MNCs need to develop a response to the alternative views of business and develop codes or statements of ethical behaviour.

- The Green movement offers a detailed agenda as to what is ethical expenditure. The actions of MNCs are scrutinised by a large number of international pressure groups.

- Islamic finance presents an alternative model of financial transactions according to a set of

principles based on the Koran. Business conducted according to these principles is becoming increasingly popular.

- Advocates of the free market and capitalism are also concerned that free trade is going to create huge disruptions due to the international transferability of technology, production and finance. MNCs are sometimes accused as being the cause of the disruption.

- Ethics is also an important element of corporate governance. Differences in governance between countries have a number of possible causes that may help to explain the differences such as the use of the bank or the stock market as a source of finance.

CRITICAL DEBATE

Importing

Proposition. MNCs should seek to obey the laws of each country within which they operate. To do more would mean that they are not maximizing profits and potentially lead them into appearing as a political force in a particular country.

Opposing view. MNCs should have a single set of values to guide their investments. Otherwise they will appear to be hypocritical and exploitative.

With whom do you agree? Remembering that a MNC is bound to maximize returns for its shareholders, should their actions be guided by the law or an independent set of ethical standards?

SELF TEST

1 Define globalization for a MNC.

2 Give three examples of the application of Green movement principles that have financial consequences.

3 Outline the principles of Islamic finance.

QUESTIONS AND APPLICATIONS

1 Explain why recent technological developments are causing some commentators to question the effect of a free market.

2 Why is the charging of interest prohibited in Islamic finance?

3 Describe a Murabaha contract and explain why it is ethically superior according to Islamic finance.

4 What are the justifications for charging 2000 per cent?

5 How does a sukuk differ from an ordinary bond?

6 What is the role of profit sharing in Islamic finance contracts?

7 Should MNCs adopt more expensive green technology?

8 Why is the law of comparative advantage less effective in the current business environment?

9 Explain why interest rates differ?

10 'It is not the rating agencies that dictate the policies of France' . . . is this true?

ADVANCED QUESTIONS

11 Devise a set of five principles that conform to the ethics of the Green movement?

12 Is Islamic finance just a matter of engaging in Islamic contracts or is it relevant to MNCs who engage in ordinary financial contracts?

13 ABC plc seeks to move production to the Far East. What ethical considerations if any should it take into account in assessing the profitability of the exercise?

14 ABC plc seeks to buy shares in a gold mining company. Discuss the ethical considerations of this investment.

15 Prepare a report for the directors of a MNC outlining the principle differences between Islamic finance and the mainstream finance that the company currently employs.

16 Is trade better than aid? Discuss.

17 To what extent is the law of comparative advantage undermined by recent developments.

18 Are MNCs to blame for trade imbalances? Discuss.

19 Is 'We pay every penny we owe in taxes' an ethical defense? Discuss.

PROJECT WORKSHOP

20 Devise a set of five principles that you feel would be adequate in guiding the financial activities of a MNC.

21 Investigate and summarize the use of tax havens by companies in the developed world. Is this behaviour justified?

BLADES PLC CASE STUDY

Ethical debate

In a conference call by investors after publishing the year-end figures Ben Holt is accused of exploiting the workforce in Thailand. He explains that they do not produce goods in Thailand. The caller who he later learns is from a British trade union says that this is not the case. Although Blades technically does not own the suppliers, Blades is by far and away the biggest customer of the suppliers. The caller quotes an email from Blades complaining about the cost of the components imported and threatening to transfer the order to Cambodia. The caller quotes the conditions in one of the major suppliers of rubber and plastic components in Cambodia and says that they are considerably worse than in Thailand. This the caller explains was by British standards already low. Thai workers did not enjoy anything like the real value of pay compared with British workers, pension schemes in the Thai factory were also very poor and in some cases non-existent. The caller further states that the poor conditions are poor by Thai standards as well, that the company is regarded as a poor employer in Thailand.

Ben Holt is surprised by the call and is worried that other investors who are sensitive to pressure groups and some of whom have an ethical investment policy might be concerned about these accusations. He therefore decides to make a reasonably robust defence. Firstly he says that he had no idea that Blades was the main customer of the company and stressed that it had no shares or other interests other than being a customer. Secondly, being the main customer did not mean that they were the problem, it may be that the other customers were getting even lower prices. Thirdly, that he had a duty to shareholders to maximize returns and obtaining the best value for money from suppliers was part of that process. One of the larger investors then responds asking Ben if he has an ethical purchasing policy. Ben is caught off guard by this but decides that he had better sound a bit more sympathetic. He responds that they do not have an ethical policy *per se*; but were they to have matters brought to their attention regarding the conditions in the factories of their suppliers, they would certainly look into the matter. The investor replies that they have recently come under pressure to ensure that their investments were ethical and conformed with Islamic principles. He asks Ben whether he engaged in any form of Islamic finance. Ben has to be direct with this question and admits that he does not; though he argues that he would be sympathetic to any concerns that their company engaged in practices that might be considered unacceptable under Islamic principles. The unionist responds saying that Mr Holt seems to be sympathetic to a lot of things but only when they are brought to his attention in a conference call. His sympathy seems to fade rapidly when the call is over. He then asked whether he had any sympathy for the workers and the families of the workers who had had their employment terminated at their former UK suppliers. Also whether he had any sympathy for the Thai workers and their conditions which were poor even by Thai standards. Ben Holt replies that the company is not in a position to rectify these issues, that it is a matter for governments. He adds that he is in competition and if he did not seek the lowest price then a competitor would do so and take market share away from Blades. He then presses the point by saying that perhaps the caller should educate the customers and encourage them not to purchase goods on the basis of value for money. If the customer took into account the conditions of the workers who produced the goods then it would be a lot easier for us to take these issues into account as well.

After the call Ben Holt asks you as the company financial analyst to report on the following concerns:

1 Draft out an ethical purchasing policy for Blades and identify the key cost areas.

2 Ben Holt remembers that on a trip to Thailand the factory which is in the south has mainly Muslim employees. He asks you whether there is anything that can be done to make the relationship more sympathetic to the Muslim faith.

3 Ben Holt is also wondering whether or not it would be a good idea to have a clear ethical policy that might combine all of the concerns of the callers. He is nevertheless concerned about the cost implications and asks you to investigate the matter.

SMALL BUSINESS DILEMMA

Obtaining finance

Jim Logan is aware that he might have problems in refinancing his working capital from his existing bank as they are now very reluctant to take on any risky investment and he knows from a friend that they have recently been refusing requests to renew arrangements with firms that Jim thought were perfectly sound. He notes that an Islamic bank has recently opened near the Sports Exports Company and he is wondering whether or not they might be a future source of funds. The literature they give him is very similar to his existing bank; but he wonders whether or not they might be more sympathetic to an Islamic type loan or financial arrangement. To get a better idea as to whether Islamic based finance would be a possibility or not he asks you to identify how Islamic finance could help him and his business.

PART 4 Integrative problem

LONG-TERM ASSET AND LIABILITY MANAGEMENT

Gandor plc is a UK firm that is considering a joint venture with a Chinese firm to produce and sell video-cassettes. Gandor will invest £12 million in this project, which will help to finance the Chinese firm's production. For each of the first 3 years, 50 per cent of the total profits will be distributed to the Chinese firm, while the remaining 50 per cent will be converted to dollars to be sent to the UK. The Chinese government intends to impose a 20 per cent income tax on the profits distributed to Gandor. The Chinese government has guaranteed that the after-tax profits (denominated in yuan, the Chinese currency) can be converted to British pounds at an exchange rate of £0.13 per yuan and sent to Gandor plc each year. At the current time, no withholding tax is imposed on profits sent to the UK as a result of joint ventures in China. Assume that after considering the taxes paid in China, an additional 10 per cent tax is imposed by the UK government on profits received by Gandor plc. After the first 3 years, all profits earned are allocated to the Chinese firm.

The expected total profits resulting from the joint venture per year are as follows:

Year	Total profits from joint venture (in yuan)
1	60 million
2	80 million
3	100 million

Gandor's average cost of debt is 13.8 per cent before taxes. Its average cost of equity is 18 per cent. Assume that the corporate income tax rate imposed on Gandor is normally 30 per cent. Gandor uses a capital structure composed of 60 per cent debt and 40 per cent equity. Gandor automatically adds four percentage points to its cost of capital when deriving its required rate of return on international joint ventures. Though this project has particular forms of country risk that are unique, Gandor plans to account for these forms of risk within its estimation of cash flows.

Gandor is concerned about two forms of country risk. First, there is the risk that the Chinese government will increase the corporate income tax rate from 20 per cent to 40 per cent (20 per cent probability). If this occurs, additional tax credits will be allowed, resulting in no UK taxes on the profits from this joint venture. Second, there is the risk that the Chinese government will impose a withholding tax of 10 per cent on the profits that are sent to the UK (20 per cent probability). In this case, additional tax credits will not be allowed, and Gandor will still be subject to a 10 per cent UK tax on profits received from China. Assume that the two types of country risk are mutually exclusive. That is, the Chinese government will adjust only one of its taxes (the income tax or the withholding tax), if any.

Questions

1 Determine Gandor's cost of capital. Also, determine Gandor's required rate of return for the joint venture in China.

2 Determine the probability distribution of Gandor's net present values for the joint venture. Capital budgeting analyses should be conducted for these three scenarios:

- *Scenario 1.* Based on original assumptions.
- *Scenario 2.* Based on an increase in the corporate income tax by the Chinese government.
- *Scenario 3.* Based on the imposition of a withholding tax by the Chinese government.

3 Would you recommend that Gandor participate in the joint venture? Explain.

4 What do you think would be the key underlying factor that would have the most influence on the profits earned in China as a result of the joint venture?

5 Is there any reason for Gandor to revise the composition of its capital (debt and equity) obtained from the UK when financing joint ventures like this?

6 When Gandor was assessing this proposed joint venture, some of its managers recommended that Gandor borrow the Chinese currency rather than dollars to obtain some of the necessary capital for its initial investment. They suggested that such a strategy could reduce Gandor's exchange rate risk. Do you agree? Explain.

PART 4 Essays/discussion and academic articles

1 Buch, C.M., Kleinert, J., Lipponer, A. and Toubal, F. (2005) 'Determinants and Effects of Foreign Direct Investment: Evidence from German firms level data', *Economic Policy*, Jan., 51–110.

    Q *Evaluate the principal determinants of FDI as reported by Buch et al. in their survey of German firms. Is there any clear lesson for the future?*

2 Doukas, J.A. and Lang, L.H.P. (2003) 'Foreign Direct Investment, Diversification and Firm Performance', *Journal of International Business Studies,* 34 (2), 153–72.

    Q *Writing as a Finance Director, prepare a report outlining the main findings in this paper and assessing their significance for a non-diversified multinational. Take care to assess the size as well as significance of any relationships.*

3 Blonigen, B.A. (2005) 'A Review of the Empirical Literature on FDI Determinants', *Atlantic Economic Journal, 3*, 383–403. A review of the issues, a bit heavy going especially as the studies are not particularly conclusive. Nevertheless it does give a good idea of the issues and problems.

    Q *From a reading of Blonigen's review, select the three most convincing (partial) models of FDI. Evaluate these models and explain why you think these models have the potential for greater development.*

4 Brink, N. and Viviers, W. (2003) 'Obstacles on Attracting Increased Portfolio Investment into Southern Africa,' *Development Southern* Africa, 20 (2), 213–36. This is an excellent study of portfolio investment in the widely differing economies of Southern Africa.

    Q *With reference to the Brink and Viviers article, is there a mismatch? Discuss (you are being asked to discuss the ways in which the economies of southern Africa fail to meet the needs of foreign investors and evaluate the extent to which foreign investment fails to meet the development needs of southern Africa).*

5 Xing, Y. and Wan, G. (2006) 'Exchange Rates and Competition for FDI in Asia', *The World Economy,* 29 (4), 419–34.

    Q *How important are exchange rates in determining the significance of FDI? Discuss.*

6 Demirag, I.S. (1986) 'The Treatment of Exchange Rates in Internal Performance Evaluation', *Accounting & Business Research,* 16(2), 157–64.

    Q *Describe the differing methods of treating exchange rates in the budget process. Discuss how a survey today might differ from Demirag's findings.*

PART V
SHORT-TERM
ASSET AND
LIABILITY
MANAGEMENT

PART V (Chapters 17–19) focuses on the MNC's management of short-term assets and liabilities. Chapter 17 describes methods by which MNCs can finance their international trade. Chapter 18 identifies sources of short-term funds and explains the criteria used by MNCs to make their short-term financing decisions. Chapter 19 describes how MNCs optimize their cash flows and explains the criteria used to make their short-term investment decisions.

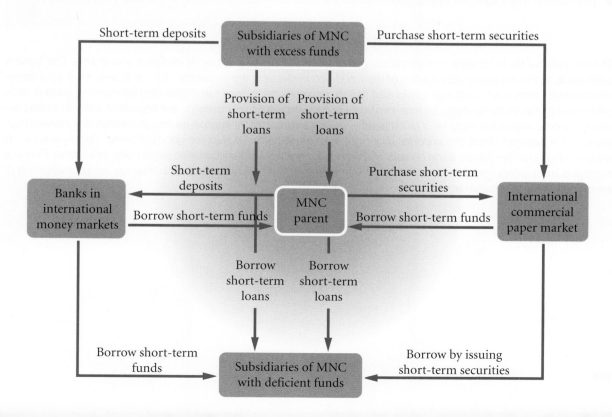

CHAPTER 17
FINANCING INTERNATIONAL TRADE

LEARNING OBJECTIVES

The specific objectives of this chapter are to:

- Describe methods of payment for international trade.

- Explain common trade finance methods.

- Describe the major agencies that facilitate international trade with export insurance and/or loan programmes.

The international trade activities of multinational corporations (MNCs) have grown in importance over time. This trend is attributable to the increased globalization of the world economies and the availability of trade finance from the international banking community. Although banks also finance domestic trade, their role in financing international trade is more critical due to the additional complications involved. First, the exporter might question the importer's ability to make payment. Second, even if the importer is credit worthy, the government might impose exchange controls that prevent payment to the exporter. Third, the importer might not trust the exporter to ship the goods ordered. Fourth, even if the exporter does ship the goods, trade barriers or time lags in international transportation might delay arrival time. Financial managers must recognize methods that they can use to finance international trade so that they can conduct exporting or importing in a manner that maximizes the value of an MNC.

PAYMENT METHODS FOR INTERNATIONAL TRADE

In any international trade transaction, credit is provided by the supplier (exporter), the buyer (importer), one or more financial institutions, or any combination of these. The supplier may have sufficient cash flow to finance the entire trade cycle, beginning with the production of the product by the exporter until payment is eventually made by the importer. This form of credit is known as **supplier credit**. In some cases, the exporter may require bank financing to augment its cash flow. On the other hand, the exporter may not desire to provide financing, in which case the buyer will have to finance the transaction itself, either internally or externally, through its bank. Banks on both sides of the transaction can thus play an integral role in trade financing.

In general, five basic methods of payment are used to settle international transactions, each with a different degree of risk to the exporter and importer (Exhibit 17.1):

- Prepayment
- Letters of credit
- Drafts (sight/time)
- Consignment
- Open account.

Prepayment

Under the **prepayment** method, the exporter will not ship the goods until the buyer has remitted payment to the exporter. This method affords the supplier the greatest degree of protection, and it is normally

EXHIBIT 17.1   **Comparison of payment methods**

Method	Usual time of payment	Goods available to buyers	Risk to exporter	Risk to importer
Prepayment	Before shipment	After payment	None	Relies completely on exporter to ship goods as ordered
Letter of credit	When shipment is made	After payment	Very little or none, depending on credit terms	Assured shipment made, but relies on exporter to ship goods described in documents
Sight draft; documents against payments	On presentation of draft to buyer	After payment	If draft unpaid must dispose of goods	Same as above unless importer can inspect goods before payment
Time draft; documents against acceptance	On maturity of drafts	Before payment	Relies on buyer to pay drafts	Same as above
Consignment	At time of sale by buyer	Before payment	Allows importer to sell inventory before paying exporter	None; improves cash flow of buyer
Open account	As agreed	Before payment	Relies completely on buyer to pay account as agreed	None

requested of first-time buyers whose creditworthiness is unknown or whose countries are in financial difficulty. Most buyers, however, are not willing to bear all the risk by prepaying an order.

Letters of credit (L/C)

A **letter of credit (L/C)** is an instrument issued by a bank on behalf of the importer (buyer) promising to pay the exporter (beneficiary) upon presentation of shipping documents in compliance with the terms stipulated therein. In effect, the bank is substituting its credit for that of the buyer. The exporter is assured of receiving payment from the issuing bank as long as it presents documents in accordance with the L/C. The importer must still rely upon the exporter to ship the goods as described in the documents, since the L/C does not guarantee that the goods purchased will be those invoiced and shipped. Letters of credit will be described in greater detail later in this chapter.

Drafts

A **draft (or bill of exchange)** is an unconditional promise drawn by one party, usually the exporter, instructing the buyer to pay the face amount of the draft upon presentation. It can be thought of as a you-owe-me note. The person owed the money usually draws up the bill simply to ensure that it is in a legally enforceable format. The draft represents the exporter's formal demand for payment from the buyer. A draft affords the exporter less protection than an L/C, because the banks are not obliged to honour payments on the buyer's behalf.

Most trade transactions handled on a draft basis are processed through banking channels. In banking terminology, these transactions are known as **documentary collections**. If shipment is made under a sight draft, the exporter is paid once shipment has been made and the draft is presented to the buyer for payment. The buyer's bank will not release the shipping documents to the buyer until the buyer has paid the draft. This is known as **documents against payment**.

If a shipment is made under a time draft, the exporter instructs the buyer's bank to release the shipping documents against acceptance (signing) of the draft. This method of payment is sometimes referred to as **documents against acceptance**. By accepting the draft, the buyer is promising to pay the exporter at the specified future date. This accepted draft is also known as a **trade acceptance**. This method affords some credit to the buyer. The added risk is that if the buyer fails to pay the draft at maturity, the bank is not obliged to honour payment. The exporter is assuming all the risk.

Consignment

Under a **consignment** arrangement, the exporter ships the goods to the importer while still retaining actual title to the merchandise. The importer has access to the items but does not have to pay for the goods until they have been sold to a third party. The exporter is trusting the importer to remit payment for the goods sold at that time. If the importer fails to pay, the exporter has limited recourse because no draft is involved and the goods have already been sold. As a result of the high risk, consignments are seldom used except by affiliated and subsidiary companies trading with the parent company.

Open account

The opposite of prepayment is the **open account transaction** in which the exporter ships the merchandise and expects the buyer to remit payment according to the agreed upon terms. The exporter is relying fully upon the financial creditworthiness, integrity and reputation of the buyer. Open account transactions are widely utilized, particularly among the industrialized countries in North America and Europe. Although there is no legal recourse for non-payment, where transactions are relatively small and frequent there is an implied security in the sense that failure to pay will result in no more business and possible difficulty in obtaining supplies from elsewhere.

TRADE FINANCE METHODS

As mentioned in the previous section, banks on both sides of the transaction play a critical role in financing international trade. The following are some of the more popular methods of financing international trade:

- Accounts receivable financing

- Factoring

- Letters of credit (L/C)

- Banker's acceptance

- Working capital financing

- Medium-term capital goods financing (forfaiting)

- Countertrade.

Each of these methods is described in turn.

Accounts receivable financing

In some cases, the exporter of goods may be willing to ship goods to the importer without an assurance of payment from a bank. This could take the form of an open account shipment or a time draft. If the exporter is willing to wait for payment, it will extend credit to the buyer.

If the exporter needs funds immediately, it may require financing from a bank. In what is referred to as **accounts receivable financing**, the bank will provide a loan to the exporter secured by an assignment of the account receivable (to be paid by the importer) as security. The length of a financing term is usually 1 to 6 months. To mitigate the additional risk of a foreign receivable, exporters and banks often require export credit insurance before financing foreign receivables.

Factoring

When an exporter ships goods before receiving payment, the accounts receivable (or debtors) balance increases. Unless the exporter has received a loan from a bank, it is initially financing the transaction and must monitor the collections of receivables. Since there is a danger that the buyer will never pay at all, the exporting firm may consider selling the accounts receivable to a third party, known as a **factor**. The factor then assumes all administrative responsibilities involved in collecting from the buyer and the associated credit exposure. The factor usually purchases the receivable at a discount and also receives a flat processing fee.

Since it is the importer who must be creditworthy from a factor's point of view, **cross-border factoring** is often used. This involves a network of factors in various countries who assess credit risk. The exporter's factor contacts a correspondent factor in the buyer's country to assess the importer's creditworthiness and handle the collection of the receivable.

Letters of credit (L/C)

Introduced earlier, the letter of credit (L/C) is one of the oldest forms of trade finance still in existence. Because of the protection and benefits it accords to both exporter and importer, it is a critical component of many international trade transactions. The L/C is an undertaking by a bank to make payments on behalf of a specified party to a beneficiary under specified conditions. The beneficiary (exporter) is paid upon presentation of the required documents in compliance with the terms of the L/C. The L/C process normally involves two banks, the exporter's bank and the importer's bank. The issuing bank is substituting its credit for that of the importer. It has essentially guaranteed payment to the exporter, provided the exporter complies with the terms and conditions of the L/C.

EXAMPLE

Nike can attribute part of its international business growth in the 1970s to the use of L/Cs. In 1971, Nike (which was then called BSR) was not well known to businesses in Japan or anywhere else. Nevertheless, by using L/Cs, it was still able to subcontract the production of athletic shoes in Japan. The L/Cs assured the Japanese shoe producer that it would receive payment for the shoes it would send to the USA and thus facilitated the flow of trade without concern about credit risk. Banks served as the guarantors in the event that the Japanese shoe company was not paid in full after transporting shoes to the USA. Without such agreements, Nike (and many other firms) would not be able to order shipments of goods.

Types of letters of credit. Trade-related letters of credit are known as commercial letters of credit or import/export letters of credit. (For an example of an irrevocable letter of credit, see Exhibit 17.2.) The documentary credit procedure is depicted in the flow chart in Exhibit 17.3. In what is commonly referred to as a *re-financing of a sight* L/C, the bank arranges to fund a loan to pay out the L/C instead of charging the importer's account immediately. The importer is responsible for repaying the bank both the principal and interest at maturity. This is just another method of providing extended payment terms to a buyer when the exporter insists upon payment at sight.

The typical documentation required under an L/C before payment can be made includes a draft (sight or time), a commercial invoice and a bill of lading. Depending upon the agreement, product or country, other documents (such as a certificate of origin, inspection certificate, packing list or insurance certificate) might be required. The three most common documents to accompany L/Cs are drafts, bills of lading and commercial invoices.

EXHIBIT 17.2   **Example of an irrevocable letter of credit**

Name of issuing bank

Address of issuing bank

Name of exporter

Address of exporter

We establish our irrevocable letter of credit: for the account of *(importer name)*, in the amount of *(value of exports)*, expiring *(date)*, available by your draft at *(time period)* days sight and accompanied by: (any invoices, packing lists, bills of lading, etc., that need to be presented with the letter of credit) Insurance provided by *(exporter or importer)* covering shipment of *(merchandise description)*

From: *(port of shipment)*

To: *(port of arrival)*

(Authorized Signature)

Draft. Also known as a bill of exchange, a draft (introduced earlier). A **banker's acceptance** is a time draft drawn on and accepted by a bank. When presented under an L/C, the draft represents the exporter's formal demand for payment. The time period, or **tenor**, of most time drafts is usually anywhere from 30 to 180 days.

Bill of lading. The key document in an international shipment under an L/C is the **bill of lading (B/L)**. It serves as *a receipt for shipment* and a summary of freight charges; most importantly, it conveys title to the merchandise. If the merchandise is to be shipped by boat, the carrier will issue what is known as an **ocean bill of lading**. When the merchandise is shipped by air, the carrier will issue an **airway bill**. The carrier presents the bill to the exporter (shipper), who in turn presents it to the bank along with the other required documents for payment.

A significant feature of a B/L is its negotiability. When a B/L is made out to order, it is said to be in negotiable form. The exporter normally endorses the B/L to the bank once payment is received from the bank, the bank may now sell the bill and recoup most of the payment.

The bank holding the bill when due will not endorse the B/L over to the importer until payment has been made. The importer needs the original B/L to pick up the merchandise. With a **negotiable B/L**, title passes to the holder of the endorsed B/L. Because a negotiable B/L grants title to the holder, banks can take the merchandise as collateral. A B/L usually includes the following provisions:

- A description of the merchandise
- Identification marks on the merchandise
- Evidence of loading (receiving) ports
- Name of the exporter (shipper)
- Name of the importer
- Status of freight charges (prepaid or collect)
- Date of shipment.

EXHIBIT 17.3 **Documentary credit procedure**

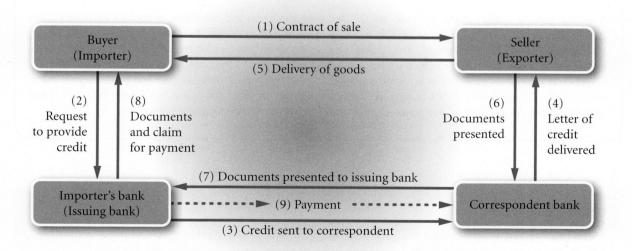

Commercial invoice. The exporter's (seller's) description of the merchandise being sold to the buyer is the commercial invoice, which normally contains the following information:

- Name and address of seller

- Name and address of buyer

- Date

- Terms of payment

- Price, including freight, handling and insurance if applicable

- Quantity, weight, packaging, etc.

- Shipping information.

Under an L/C shipment, the description of the merchandise outlined in the invoice must correspond exactly to that contained in the L/C.

Variations of the L/C. There are several variations of the L/C that are useful in financing trade. A **standby letter of credit** can be used to guarantee invoice payments to a supplier. It promises to pay the beneficiary if the buyer fails to pay as agreed. In an international or domestic trade transaction, the seller will agree to ship to the buyer on standard open account terms as long as the buyer provides a standby L/C for a specified amount and term. As long as the buyer pays the seller as agreed, the standby L/C is never funded. The buyer's bank is essentially guaranteeing that the buyer will make payment to the seller.

A **transferable letter of credit** is a variation of the standard commercial L/C that allows the first beneficiary to transfer all or a part of the original L/C to a third party. The new beneficiary has the same rights and protection as the original beneficiary. This type of L/C is used extensively by brokers, who are not the actual suppliers.

EXAMPLE

A broker asks a foreign buyer to issue an L/C for £100 000 in his favour. The L/C must contain a clause stating that the L/C is transferable. The broker has located a supplier who will provide the product for £80 000, but requests payment in advance from the broker. With a transferable L/C, the broker can transfer £80 000 of the original L/C to the supplier under the same terms and conditions, except for the amount, the latest shipment date, the invoice and the period of validity. When the supplier ships the product, it presents its documents to the bank. When the bank pays the L/C, £80 000 is paid to the supplier and £20 000 goes to the broker. In effect, the broker has utilized the credit of the buyer to finance the entire transaction.

USING THE WEB

Many banks have a website that explains the variety of trade financing that they can provide for firms. Try, for example, searching for 'NatWest bank letter of credit' in an Internet search engine.

Banker's acceptance

Introduced earlier, a banker's acceptance (shown in Exhibit 17.4) is a bill of exchange, or time draft, drawn on and accepted by a bank. It is the accepting bank's obligation to pay the holder of the draft at maturity.

For the first step in creating a banker's acceptance, the importer orders goods from the exporter. The importer then requests its local bank to issue an L/C on its behalf. The L/C will allow the exporter to draw a time draft on the bank in payment for the exported goods. The exporter presents the time draft along with shipping documents to its local bank, and the exporter's bank sends the time draft along with shipping documents to the importer's bank. The importer's bank accepts the draft, thereby creating the banker's acceptance. If the exporter does not want to wait until the specified date to receive payment, it can request that the banker's acceptance be sold in the money market. By doing so, the exporter will receive less funds from the sale of the banker's acceptance than if it had waited to receive payment. This discount reflects the time value of money.

If the exporter holds the acceptance until maturity, it provides the financing for the importer as it does with accounts receivable financing. In this case, the key difference between a banker's acceptance and accounts receivable financing is that a banker's acceptance guarantees payment to the exporter by a bank.

A banker's acceptance can be beneficial to the exporter, importer and issuing bank. The exporter does not need to worry about the credit risk of the importer and can therefore penetrate new foreign markets without concern about the credit risk of potential customers. In addition, the exporter faces little exposure to political risk or to exchange controls imposed by a government because banks normally are allowed to meet their payment commitments even if controls are imposed. In contrast, controls could prevent an importer from paying, so without a banker's acceptance, an exporter might not receive payment even though the importer is willing to pay. Finally, the exporter can sell the banker's acceptance at a discount before payment is due and thus obtain funds up front from the issuing bank.

The importer benefits from a banker's acceptance by obtaining greater access to foreign markets when purchasing supplies and other products. Without banker's acceptances, exporters may be unwilling to accept the credit risk of importers. In addition, due to the documents presented along with the acceptance, the importer is assured that goods have been shipped. Even though the importer has not paid in advance, this assurance is valuable because it lets the importer know if and when supplies and other products will arrive. Finally, because the banker's acceptance allows the importer to pay at a later date, the importer's payment is financed until the maturity date of the banker's acceptance. Without an acceptance, the importer is likely to be forced to pay in advance, thereby tying up funds.

The bank accepting the drafts benefits in that it earns a commission for creating an acceptance. The commission that the bank charges the customer reflects the customer's perceived creditworthiness. The interest rate charged to the customer, commonly referred to as the **all-in-rate**, consists of the discount rate plus the

EXHIBIT 17.4   Banker's acceptance

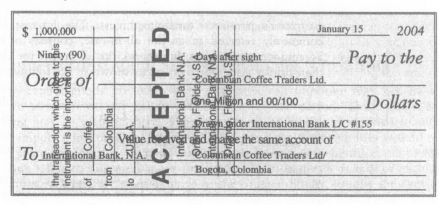

acceptance commission. In general, the all-in-rate for acceptance financing is lower than prime-based borrowings, as shown in the following comparison:

	Loan	Acceptance
Amount	£1 000 000	£1 000 000
Term	180 days	180 days
Rate	Prime + 1.5 %	Banker's acceptance rate + 1.5 %
	10.0 % + 1.5 % = 11.5 %	7.60 % + 1.5 % = 9.10 %
Interest cost	£57 500	£45 500

In this case, the savings in interest for a 6-month period is £12 000 (i.e. £57 500 – £45 500). Since the banker's acceptance is a marketable instrument with an active secondary market, the rates on acceptances usually fall between the rates on short-term Treasury bills and the rates on commercial paper. Investors are usually willing to purchase acceptances as an investment because of their yield, safety and liquidity. When a bank creates, accepts and sells the acceptance, it is actually using the investor's money to finance the bank's customer. As a result, the bank has created an asset at one price, sold it at another and retained a commission (spread) as its fee.

EXAMPLE

Slow Bank has accepted a time draft from WellKnown plc for £1 500 000 to be paid to WellKnown in 6-months' time. WellKnown wants the money now and has asked its own bank, MyBank, to sell the bill. MyBank charges a 10 per cent discount to WellKnown. So WellKnown receives £1 500 000 × (1–10 per cent) = £1 350 000. MyBank then sells the bill to BigInsurance plc for £1 400 000. In effect, MyBank has operated as a go-between and has created an asset, the bill to be paid by Slow Bank, for a cost of £1 350 000 (buying it from WellKnown) and sold it for £1 400 000. BigInsurance plc has purchased this asset and in effect has used its spare cash ultimately to help provide finance to WellKnown. BigInsurance will collect £1 500 000 from Slow bank in 6-months' time a return of (£1 500 000 − £1 400 000) / £1 500 000 = 0.0666 or 6.66 per cent. This is a return of $1.066^2 - 1 = 0.136$ or 13.6 per cent per year and presumably it is a good return given the low risk of non-payment by Slow Bank.

Banker's acceptance financing can also be arranged through the refinancing of a sight letter of credit. In this case, the beneficiary of the L/C (the exporter) may insist on payment at sight. The bank arranges to finance the payment of the sight L/C under a separate acceptance-financing agreement. The importer (borrower) simply draws drafts upon the bank (a 'you, the bank, owe me' note). The bank in turn accepts and discounts the drafts (i.e. sells the bills on the money markets) on condition that the importer will pay with say a promissory note. The proceeds are used to pay the exporter. At maturity of the discounted acceptance, the money market investor presents the bill to the bank, who pay, and the importer then pays the money to the bank honouring the promissory note. Why is it done in this way? Well, it is important that to the money markets the bank is the debtor – the discount will be less. So the bank creates this debt to the importer with the backing that the importer will pay.

Acceptance financing can also be arranged without the use of an L/C under a separate acceptance agreement. Similar to a regular loan agreement, it stipulates the terms and conditions under which the bank is prepared to finance the borrower using acceptances instead of promissory notes. As long as the acceptances meet one of the underlying transaction requirements, the bank and borrower can utilize banker's acceptances as an alternative financing mechanism. The life cycle of a banker's acceptance is illustrated in Exhibit 17.5.

Working capital financing

As just explained, a banker's acceptance can allow an exporter to receive funds immediately, yet allow an importer to delay its payment until a future date. The bank may even provide short-term loans beyond the banker's acceptance period. In the case of an importer, the purchase from overseas usually represents the acquisition of inventory. The loan finances the working capital cycle that begins with the purchase of inventory and continues with the sale of the goods, creation of an account receivable, and finally conversion to cash. With an exporter, the short-term loan might finance the manufacture of the merchandise destined for export (pre-export financing) or the time period from when the sale is made until payment is received from

EXHIBIT 17.5 Life cycle of a typical banker's acceptance (B/A)

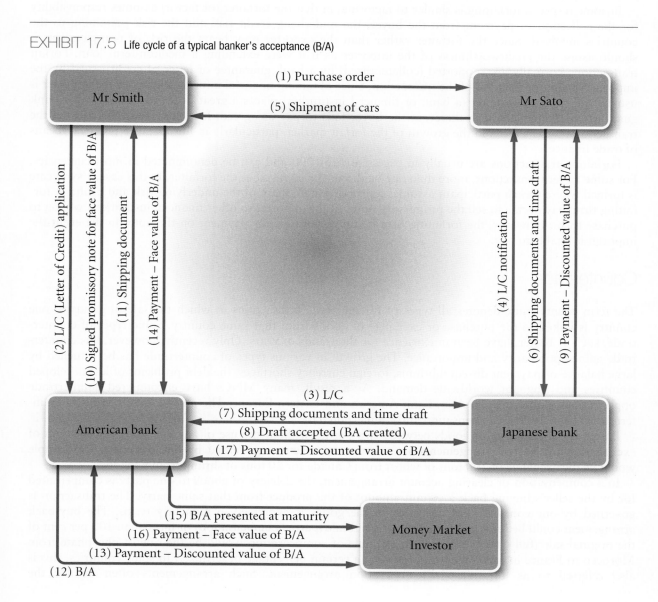

the buyer. For example, the firm may have imported foreign beer, which it plans to distribute to grocery and liquor stores. The bank can provide a letter of credit for trade finance, and also finance the importer's cost from the time of distribution and collection of payment.

Medium-term capital goods financing (forfaiting)

Because capital goods are often quite expensive, an importer may not be able to make payment on the goods within a short time period. Thus, longer-term financing may be required here. The exporter might be able to provide financing for the importer but may not desire to do so, since the financing may extend over several years. In this case, a type of trade finance known as forfaiting could be used. The forfaiter buys the bills or promissory notes from the exporter. These financial obligations are usually guaranteed by the importer (payer's) bank. The importer thus finds that payment has to be made to a financial institution rather than the exporter. Thus, for a fee, the forfaiter enables the exporter to receive the money immediately and the importer at the same time has a period of credit before payment has to be made.

In some respects, forfaiting is similar to factoring, in that the forfaiter (or factor) assumes responsibility for the collection of payment from the buyer, the underlying credit risk and the risk pertaining to the countries involved. Since the forfaiter rather than the exporter now bears the risk of non-payment, it should assess the creditworthiness of the importer as if it were extending a medium-term loan. Forfait transactions normally are supported (collateralized) by a bank guarantee or letter of credit issued by the importer's bank for the term of the transaction. Since obtaining financial information about the importer is usually difficult, the forfaiter (a bank or financial institution) places a great deal of reliance on the bank guarantee as the collateral in the event the buyer fails to pay as agreed. It is this guarantee backing the transaction that has fostered the growth of the forfait market, particularly in Europe, as a practical means of trade finance.

Forfaiting transactions are usually in excess of £250 000 and can be denominated in most currencies. For some larger transactions, more than one bank may be involved as the forfaiter. In this case, a syndicate is formed wherein each participant assumes a proportionate share of the underlying risk and profit. A forfaiting firm may decide to sell the promissory notes of the importer to other financial institutions willing to purchase them. However, the forfaiting firm is still responsible for payment on the notes in the event the importer is unable to pay.

Countertrade

The term countertrade denotes all types of foreign trade transactions in which the sale of goods to one country is linked to the purchase or exchange of goods from that same country. Some types of countertrade, such as barter, have been in existence for thousands of years. Only recently, however, has countertrade gained popularity and importance. The growth in various types of countertrade has been fuelled by large balance-of-payment dis-equilibriums, foreign currency shortages, the debt problems of less developed countries and stagnant worldwide demand. As a result, many MNCs have encountered countertrade opportunities, particularly in Asia, Latin America and Eastern Europe. The most common types of countertrade include barter, compensation and counterpurchase.

Barter is the exchange of goods between two parties without the use of any currency as a medium of exchange. Most barter arrangements are one-time transactions governed by one contract. An example would be the exchange of 100 tons of wheat from Canada for 20 tons of shrimp from Ecuador.

In a compensation or clearing-account arrangement, the delivery of goods to one party is compensated for by the seller's buying back a certain amount of the product from that same party. The transaction is governed by one contract, and the value of the goods is expressed in monetary terms. The buy-back arrangement could be for a fraction of the original sale (partial compensation) or more than 100 per cent of the original sale (full compensation). An example of compensation would be the sale of phosphate from Morocco to France in exchange for purchasing a certain percentage of fertilizer. In some countries, this is also referred to as an industrial co-operation arrangement. Such arrangements often involve the construction of large projects, such as power plants, in exchange for the purchase of the project's output over an extended period of time. For example, Brazil sold a hydroelectric plant to Argentina and in exchange purchased a percentage of the plant's output under a long-term contract.

The term counterpurchase denotes the exchange of goods between two parties under two distinct contracts expressed in monetary terms. Delivery and payment of both goods are technically separate transactions.

Despite the economic inefficiencies of countertrade, it has become much more important in recent years. The primary participants are governments and MNCs, with assistance provided by specialists in the field, such as attorneys, financial institutions and trading companies. The transactions are usually large and very complex. Many variations of countertrade exist, and the terminology used by the various market participants is still forming as the countertrade market continues to develop.

GOVERNMENT AGENCIES FOR INTERNATIONAL TRADE

Due to the inherent risks of international trade, government institutions and the private sector offer various forms of export credit, export finance and guarantee programmes to reduce risk and stimulate foreign trade. The private sector is generally reluctant to provide financial support for investments with high risk. Usually such investments are in countries with poorly developed or unreliable financial systems. To provide cover for such transactions most developed countries have a government backed agency whose principal goal is to provide credit and finance for exports.

In the UK export services are provided by the Export Credit Guarantee Department (ECGD). For a fee, it provides a guarantee of payment to UK exporters on transactions ranging from £25 000 to over £100 million. As with a forfaiter, it will also offer loans to importers thus enabling exporters to receive payment immediately and at the same time give time for foreign importers to pay in accordance with the conditions of the loan. Government backing of the ECGD and like organizations elsewhere ensures that the guarantees are well respected in the marketplace and may of themselves be sufficient for a company to then get private finance to support an export transaction. The ECGD also offers insurance against political risk for UK investors of up to 15 years.

As with all government agencies a moral as well as a practical rationale is required to justify their role. On the virtuous side, Third World countries termed Heavily Indebted Poor Countries (HIPC – this is an official International Monetary Fund (IMF) term) often have poor credit records. Credit guarantees and loans to importers in those countries encourage trade with HIPCs helping their economies to grow. Thus the ECGD, by offering generous credit terms to HIPCs is providing a form of foreign aid. It is arguable that such help is much better than straight gift-based aid in that trade is encouraged, and trade is generally seen as the principal means of becoming a developed economy.

Some trade is, of course, with governments. The ECGD holds most of the sovereign (government) debt owed to the UK. The agency therefore has a crucial role in any debt relief programme. HIPCs are supported by IMF and World Bank programmes. Satisfactory compliance is measured as achieving a 'completion point' that triggers a debt relief programme. Developed countries in the form of the Paris Club will reduce payments to a sustainable level for countries that achieve their completion point, and in the case of the UK, will write off old debts completely. Thus the ECGD is heavily involved in aid packages.

There is also, surprisingly, a less virtuous argument. First, IMF debt relief programmes are seen by some as intrusive, unaccountable and ineffective. Visit the IMF website – http://www.imf.org – and search under the term 'ineffective IMF' – a good example of openness. The progress towards developed nation status is generally recognized as having been slow to non-existent for most HIPCs over the last 50 years. This leads to the second counter argument that the true purpose of the ECGD is to finance and thereby subsidize domestic industry with little real concern for the recipient country. The aid given to Third World countries to purchase exports from developed countries is in fact a way of helping MNCs sell goods to customers of doubtful credit. Although such aid purports to be to help the customer, the suspicion is that the real purpose is to help the MNC. Arms sales, in particular, are difficult to justify as necessary for a developing country. In tacit acknowledgement of this critique the ECGD sets out a broad mission statement that includes a commitment that:

> *ECGD will when considering support look not only at the payment risks but also at the underlying quality of the project including its environmental, social and human rights impact.*
>
> (Statement of ECGD Business Principles, 2000)

There is also a special procedure over financial help for arms exports (some 24 per cent of ECGD business). In addition to the special licences, for less developed countries it also applies a 'productive expenditure test'. The relevant form asks:

> *Please explain how it (the project) will contribute to economic and social development:*
>   *You may care to give details of how the project will:*

- Meet priority human development needs
- Promote the inclusion of the poor in economic activity
- Build or rehabilitate essential infrastructure
- Promote economic growth, or
- Promote development of the indigenous private sector.

For some, these stated intentions are not borne out by practice and there is a campaign for Export Credit Agencies (ECAs) to improve their practices (see http://www.fern.org/ and use their internal search engine). Undoubtedly, financing international trade has a political dimension. Similar issues can be found in examining 'soft loans' policies, for more information see http://www.bankwatch.org and search for 'EIB'. MNCs need to be aware that requesting government help requires an ethical as well as a financial justification.

SUMMARY

- The common methods of payment for international trade are: (1) prepayment (before goods are sent), (2) letters of credit, (3) drafts, (4) consignment and (5) open account.

- The most popular methods of financing international trade are: (1) accounts receivable financing, (2) factoring, (3) letters of credit, (4) banker's acceptances, (5) working capital

- financing, (6) medium-term capital goods financing (forfaiting) and (7) countertrade.

- The major agencies that facilitate international trade with export insurance and/or loan programmes are: (1) Export-Import Bank, (2) Private Export Funding Corporation and (3) Overseas Private Investment Corporation.

CRITICAL DEBATE

Do government agencies promoting exports benefit the recipient country?

Proposition. Yes. They enable countries to import vital supplies needed to develop their economies. The commercial world would not necessarily export to these countries because of the risks that they face. They are in a catch 22 position, they cannot get credit unless they are developed and they cannot develop unless they have

credit to purchase goods. Government agencies are the ideal bodies to break this vicious circle. In addition, the agencies can and do promote a social and economic agenda working with the World Bank and the IMF.

Opposing view. No. The commercial world will lend to these countries and has done so to a greater extent in colonial days before World War I. Developing countries must realize that a stable currency and a stable economy is a top priority and that instability is more than just a technical problem. Corruption, over-ambitious economic policies and social unrest caused by oppression all result in unstable economies. Giving credit and guarantees to these countries has unfortunately served to support poor government practice rather than cure it. Developed countries are concerned with helping their own firms in competition with other developed countries and any desire to promote standards is lost in the need to protect home industry against competition.

With whom do you agree? Reread the section on the ECGD and follow the website links.

SELF TEST

Answers are provided in Appendix A at the back of the text.

1 Explain why so many international transactions require international trade credit facilitated by commercial banks.

2 Explain the difference in the risk to the exporter between accounts receivable financing and factoring.

3 Explain how the Export-Import Bank can encourage UK firms to export to less developed countries where there is political risk.

QUESTIONS AND APPLICATIONS

1 **Banker's acceptances**

a Describe how foreign trade would be affected if banks did not provide trade-related services.

b How can a banker's acceptance be beneficial to an exporter, an importer and a bank?

2 **Export financing**

a Why would an exporter provide financing for an importer?

b Is there much risk in this activity? Explain.

3 **Role of factors.** What is the role of a factor in international trade transactions?

4 **ECGD**

a What is the role today of the ECGD?

b Describe the basis of the political opposition to the ECGD.

5 **Bills of lading.** What are bills of lading, and how do they facilitate international trade transactions?

6 **Forfaiting.** What is forfaiting? Specify the type of traded goods for which forfaiting is applied.

7 Should the **World Bank** be in charge of providing finance for exports?

8 **Government programmes.** What motivates a government to establish/intervene in the credit markets?

9 **Countertrade.** What is countertrade?

10 **Impact of a financial crisis.** What steps should Brunch take if a crisis occurs in country X which is a major exporting destination for Brunch Ltd?

ADVANCED QUESTIONS

11 **Letters of credit.** Channel Traders (UK) is a firm based in Grimsby, that specializes in seafood exports and commonly uses letters of credit (L/C) to ensure payment. It recently experienced a problem, however. Channel Traders had an irrevocable L/C issued by a Russian bank to ensure that it would receive payment upon shipment of 16 000 tons of fish to a Russian firm. This bank backed out of its obligation, however, stating that it was not authorized to guarantee commercial transactions.

a Explain how an irrevocable L/C would normally facilitate the business transaction between the Russian importer and Channel Traders (the UK exporter).

b Explain how the cancellation of the L/C could create a trade crisis between the UK and Russian firms.

c Why do you think situations like this (the cancellation of the L/C) are rare in industrialized countries?

d Can you think of any alternative strategy that the UK exporter could have used to protect itself better when dealing with a Russian importer?

PROJECT WORKSHOP

12 Compare and contrast the web provision for exporters from the UK and the USA. For the US provision visit http://www.exim.gov and for the UK provision visit http://www.ecgd.gov.

DISCUSSION IN THE BOARDROOM

This exercise can be found on our dedicated CourseMate platform for students.

RUNNING YOUR OWN MNC

This exercise can be found on our dedicated CourseMate platform for students.

Essays/discussion and articles can be found at the end of Part V.

BLADES PLC CASE STUDY

Assessment of international trade financing in Thailand

Blades plc has recently decided to establish a subsidiary in Thailand to produce 'Speedos', Blades' primary roller blade product. In establishing the subsidiary in Thailand, Blades was motivated by the high growth potential of the Thai roller blade market. Furthermore, Blades has decided to establish a subsidiary, as opposed to acquiring an existing Thai roller blade manufacturer for sale, in order to maintain its flexibility and control over the operations in Thailand. Moreover, Blades has decided to issue yen-denominated notes to partially finance the cost of establishing the subsidiary. Blades has decided to issue notes denominated in yen instead of baht to avoid the high effective interest rates associated with the baht-denominated notes.

Currently, Blades plans to sell all roller blades manufactured in Thailand to retailers in Thailand. Furthermore, Blades plans to purchase all components for roller blades manufactured in Thailand from Thai suppliers. Similarly, all of Blades' roller blades manufactured in the UK will be sold to retailers in the UK and all components needed for Blades' UK production will be purchased from suppliers in the UK. Consequently, Blades will have no exports and imports once the plant in Thailand is operational, which is expected to occur early next year.

Construction of the plant in Thailand has already begun, and Blades is currently in the process of purchasing the machinery necessary to produce Speedos. Besides these activities, Ben Holt, Blades' financial director, has been actively lining up suppliers of the needed rubber and plastic components in Thailand and identifying Thai customers, which will consist of various sports product retailers in Thailand.

Although Holt has been successful in locating both interested suppliers and interested customers, he is discovering that he has neglected certain precautions for operating a subsidiary in Thailand. First, although Blades is relatively well known in the USA, it is not recognized internationally. Consequently, the suppliers Blades would like to use in Thailand are not familiar with the firm and have no information about its reputation. Moreover, Blades' previous activities in Thailand were restricted to the export of a fixed number of

Speedos annually to one customer, a Thai retailer called Entertainment Products. Holt has little information about the potential Thai customers that would buy the roller blades produced by the new plant. He is aware, however, that although letters of credit (L/C) and drafts are usually employed for exporting purposes, these instruments are also used for trade within a country between relatively unknown parties.

Of the various potential customers Blades has identified in Thailand, four retailers of sports products appear particularly interested. Because Blades is not familiar with these firms and their reputations, it would like to receive payment from them as soon as possible. Ideally, Blades would like its customers to prepay for their purchases, as this would involve the least risk for Blades. Unfortunately, none of the four potential customers have agreed to a prepayment arrangement. In fact, one potential customer, Cool Runnings Inc., insists on an open account transaction. Payment terms in Thailand for purchases of this type are typically 'net 60', indicating that payment for the roller blades would be due approximately 2 months after a purchase was made. Two of the remaining three retailers, Sports Equipment Inc., and Major Leagues Inc., have indicated that they would also prefer an open account transaction; however, both of these retailers have indicated that their banks would act as intermediaries for a time draft. The fourth retailer, Sports Gear Inc., is indifferent as to the specific payment method but has indicated to Blades that it finds a pre-payment arrangement unacceptable.

Blades also needs a suitable arrangement with its various potential suppliers of rubber and plastic components in Thailand. Because Blades' financing of the Thai subsidiary involved a UK bank, it has virtually no contacts in the Thai banking system. Because Blades is relatively unknown in Thailand, Thai suppliers have indicated that they would prefer pre-payment or at least a guarantee from a Thai bank that Blades will be able to make payment within 30 days of purchase. Blades does not currently have accounts receivable in Thailand. It does, however, have accounts receivable in the UK resulting from its UK sales.

Ben Holt would like to please Blades' Thai customers and suppliers in order to establish strong business relationships in Thailand. However, he is worried that Blades may be at a disadvantage if it accepts all of the Thai firms' demands. Consequently, he has asked you, a financial analyst for Blades plc to provide him with some guidance regarding international trade financing. Specifically, Holt has asked you to answer the following questions for him:

1 Assuming that banks in Thailand issue a time draft on behalf of Sports Equipment Inc., and Major Leagues Inc., would Blades receive payment for its roller blades before it delivers them? Do the banks issuing the time drafts guarantee payment on behalf of the Thai retailers if they default on the payment?

2 What payment method should Blades suggest to Sports Gear Inc.? Substantiate your answer.

3 What organization could Blades contact in order to insure its sales to the Thai retailers? What type of insurance does this organization provide?

4 How could Blades use accounts receivable financing or factoring, considering that it does not currently have accounts receivable in Thailand? If Blades uses a Thai bank to obtain this financing, how do you think the fact that Blades does not have receivables in Thailand would affect the terms of the financing?

5 Assuming that Blades is unable to locate a Thai bank that is willing to issue an L/C on Blades' behalf, can you think of a way Blades could utilize its bank in the UK to effectively obtain an L/C from a Thai bank?

6 What organizations could Blades contact to obtain working capital financing? If Blades is unable to obtain working capital financing from these organizations, what are its other options to finance its working capital needs in Thailand?

SMALL BUSINESS DILEMMA

Ensuring payment for products exported by the Sports Exports Company

The Sports Exports Company (Ireland) produces basketballs and exports them to a distributor in the UK. It typically sends basketballs in bulk and then receives payment after the distributor receives the shipment. The business relationship with the distributor is based on trust. Although the relationship has worked thus far, Jim Logan (owner of the Sports Exports Company) is concerned about the possibility that the distributor will not make its payment.

1 How could Jim use a letter of credit to ensure that he will be paid for the products he exports?

2 Jim has discussed the possibility of expanding his export business through a second sporting goods distributor in the USA; this second distributor would cover a different territory than the first distributor. The second distributor is only willing to engage in a consignment arrangement when selling basketballs to retail stores. Explain the risk to Jim beyond the typical types of risk he incurs when dealing with the first distributor. Should Jim pursue this type of business?

CHAPTER 18
SHORT-TERM
FINANCING

LEARNING OBJECTIVES

The specific objectives of this chapter are to:

● Explain why MNCs consider foreign financing.

● Explain how MNCs determine whether to use foreign financing.

● Illustrate the possible benefits of financing with a portfolio of currencies.

All firms make short-term financing decisions periodically. Beyond the trade financing discussed in the previous chapter, MNCs obtain short-term financing to support other operations as well. Because MNCs have access to additional sources of funds, their short-term financing decisions are more complex than those of other companies. Financial managers must understand the possible advantages and disadvantages of short-term financing with foreign currencies so that they can make short-term financing decisions that maximize the value of the MNC.

SOURCES OF SHORT-TERM FINANCING

MNC parents and their subsidiaries typically use various methods of obtaining short-term funds to satisfy their liquidity needs. When financing in a foreign currency, it is increasingly the case that the bank or financial market providing the finance will not be in the country of the currency. When this is the case the term 'euro' is used. Thus a eurodollar bank account is an account that will probably be situated in London and will be denominated in dollars. A eurobank is a bank that makes loans and accepts deposits in foreign currencies.

Euronotes

One method increasingly used in recent years is the issuing of euronotes, or unsecured debt securities. These are bonds issued by MNCs with an interest payment and a fixed term after which the MNC will repay the nominal (agreed) amount. The interest rates on these notes are based on LIBOR (the interest rate eurobanks charge on interbank loans). Euronotes typically have maturities of 1, 3, or 6 months. Some MNCs continually roll them over as a form of intermediate-term financing. That is to say, they issue new euronotes to repay ones that are maturing and need to be repaid by the MNC. The MNCs in this way extend the term of the loan to themselves. Commercial banks underwrite (guarantee) the notes for MNCs, and some commercial banks purchase them for their own investment portfolios.

Euro-commercial paper

In addition to euronotes, MNCs also issue euro-commercial paper to obtain short-term financing. This is a promissory note (an iou note) issued by a large reputable MNC needing to borrow for a very short term or any stated length usually about 180 days but can be for 1 year. It is a bearer note, that is the holder is the owner rather like a currency note such as £5 only these notes are for a minimum of $500 000! Dealers issue this paper for MNCs without the backing of an underwriting syndicate, so a selling price is not guaranteed to the issuers. Maturities can be tailored to the issuer's preferences. Dealers make a secondary market by offering to repurchase euro-commercial paper before maturity.

Eurobank loans

Direct loans from eurobanks, which are typically utilized to maintain a relationship with eurobanks, are another popular source of short-term funds for MNCs. If other sources of short-term funds become unavailable, MNCs rely more heavily on direct loans from eurobanks. Most MNCs maintain credit arrangements with various banks around the world. Some MNCs have credit arrangements with more than 100 foreign and domestic banks.

INTERNAL FINANCING BY MNCS

Before an MNC's parent or subsidiary in need of funds searches for outside funding, it should check other subsidiaries' cash flow positions to determine whether any internal funds are available.

EXAMPLE

The French subsidiary of Shrimport Ltd (UK) has experienced strong earnings and invested a portion of the earnings locally in money market securities. Meanwhile, Shrimport's Mexican subsidiary has generated lower earnings recently but needs funding to support expansion. Shrimport can instruct the French subsidiary to loan some of its excess funds to the Mexican subsidiary.

This process is especially useful during periods when the cost of obtaining funds in the parent's home country is relatively high.

Parents of MNCs can also attempt to obtain financing from their subsidiaries by increasing the mark-ups on supplies they send to the subsidiaries. In this case, the funds the subsidiary gives to the parent will never be returned. This method of supporting the parent can sometimes be more feasible than obtaining loans from the subsidiary because it may circumvent restrictions or taxes imposed by national governments. In some cases, though, this method itself may be restricted or limited by host governments where subsidiaries are located. The practice may also transgress double taxation agreements where intra (within) company trade should be conducted 'at arm's-length', i.e. as if they were independent companies.

WHY MNCS CONSIDER FOREIGN FINANCING

Regardless of whether an MNC parent or subsidiary decides to obtain financing from subsidiaries or from some other source, it must also decide which currency to borrow. Even if it needs its home currency, it may prefer to borrow a foreign currency. Reasons for this preference follow.

Foreign financing to offset foreign currency inflows

A large firm may finance in a foreign currency to offset a net receivables position in that foreign currency.

EXAMPLE

Plenty Ltd (UK) has net receivables denominated in dollars and needs pounds now for liquidity purposes. It can borrow dollars and convert them to British pounds to obtain the needed funds. Then, the net receivables in dollars will be used to pay off the loan. In this example, financing in a foreign currency reduces the firm's exposure to fluctuating exchange rates (see Chapter 12). This strategy is especially appealing if the interest rate of the foreign currency is low and the currency is not appreciating.

How Avon used foreign financing during the Asian crisis. During the Asian crisis in 1997 and 1998, many MNCs with Asian subsidiaries were adversely affected by the weakening of Asian currencies against the dollar. Avon Products Inc. used various methods to reduce its economic exposure to the weak Asian currencies. Given that Avon had more cash inflows than cash outflows in Asian currencies, it used strategies that reduced the excess of cash inflows denominated in those currencies. First, it purchased more materials locally. Second, it borrowed funds locally to finance its operations so that it could use some of its cash inflows in Asian currencies to repay the debt. Third, it hired more local salespeople (rather than relying on marketing from the USA) to help sell its products locally. Fourth, it began to remit its earnings more frequently so that excess cash flows denominated in Asian currencies would not accumulate.

Foreign financing to reduce costs

Even when an MNC parent or subsidiary is not attempting to cover foreign net receivables, it may still consider borrowing foreign currencies if the interest rates on those currencies are relatively low and the currency stable. Since interest rates vary among currencies, the cost of borrowing can vary substantially among countries. MNCs that conduct business in countries with high interest rates and a currency that is not depreciating to compensate, incur a high cost of short-term financing if they finance in the local currency. Thus, they may consider financing with another currency that has a lower interest rate. By shaving one percentage point off its financing rate, an MNC can save £1 million annually on debt of £100 million. Thus, MNCs are motivated to consider in detail various currencies when financing their operations.

Exhibit 18.1 compares interest rates among countries for a given point in time. In most periods, the interest rate in Japan is relatively low, while the interest rates in many developing countries are relatively high. Countries with a high rate of inflation tend to have high interest rates.

EXHIBIT 18.1   Central Bank interest rates February 2013

Country	Current rate
Australia	3%
Brazil	7.25%
Canada	1%
Chile	5%
China	6%
Czech Republic	0.75%
Denmark	1.25%
Egypt	9.25%
Hong Kong SAR	0.50%
Hungary	5.25%
Iceland	6%
India	7.75%
Indonesia	5.75%
Japan	0.10%
New Zealand	2.50%
Norway	1.50%
Philippines	5.50%
Poland	3.75%
Romania	5.25%
South Africa	5%
Sweden	1%
Switzerland	0%
Turkey	5.50%
UK	0.50%
USA	0.25%

Source: http://www.fxstreet.com/fundamental/interest-rates-table/

EXAMPLE

Salon SA is a French firm that needs euros to expand its European Union operations. Assume the euro financing rate is 9 per cent, while the Japanese yen financing rate is 4 per cent. Salon can borrow Japanese yen and immediately convert those yen to euros for use. When the loan repayment is due, Salon will need to obtain Japanese yen to pay off the loan. If the value of the Japanese yen in terms of euros has not changed since the time Salon obtained the loan, it will pay 4 per cent on that loan. If, however, the Japanese yen has increased in value by 2 per cent over the period then the total cost of the loan will be the 4 per cent plus the extra 2 per cent of the cost of buying the yen to repay the loan (using the approximate method). The total cost will therefore be 4 per cent + 2 per cent = 6 per cent, still much cheaper than the 9 per cent cost of borrowing in euros. So when choosing a currency for the loan, Salon has to decide whether the lower interest rate in a foreign currency is going to be taken up by the increasing value of that currency. The international Fisher effect (IFE) suggests that the currency will increase in value such that any saving in interest rates will be taken up entirely by the increase in value of the currency and hence the cost of repayment. Salon is hoping that the IFE will not hold if it decides to borrow in yen.

USING THE WEB

Forecasts of interest rates

When an MNC borrows funds in a specific currency, its choice of a maturity is partially based on expectations of future interest rates in that country. Forecasts of interest rates in the near future for each country are provided by a number of websites that can be accessed by search engines; try http://www.investica.co.uk/rateforecasts.htm.

DETERMINING THE EFFECTIVE FINANCING RATE

As has been pointed out, the actual cost of financing by the debtor firm will depend on: (1) the interest rate charged by the bank that provided the loan and (2) the movement in the borrowed currency's value over the life of the loan. Thus, the actual or 'effective' financing rate may differ from the quoted interest rate. This point is further illustrated in the following example.

EXAMPLE

Deckborn Ltd (UK) obtains a 2-year loan in New Zealand dollars (NZ$) worth £1 000 000 at the quoted interest rate of 8 per cent – a full 2 per cent less than an equivalent loan offered to Deckborn in the UK. When Deckborn receives the New Zealand loan, it converts the New Zealand dollars to British pounds to pay a supplier for materials. The exchange rate at that time is £0.40 per New Zealand dollar, so the NZ$2 500 000 is converted to £1 000 000 (computed as NZ$2 500 000 × £0.40 per NZ$ = £1 000 000). One year later, Deckborn pays interest of NZ$200 000 (computed as 8 per cent × NZ$2 500 000). Two years

(Continued)

later, Deckborn pays back the loan of NZ\$2 500 000 plus a second interest payment instalment of NZ\$200 000 a total of NZ\$2 700 000. Assume that the New Zealand dollar unexpectedly appreciates from £0.40 to £0.50 shortly after receiving the loan and before any repayments are made. The interest pay-ment at the end of the first year will therefore cost Deckborn NZ\$200 000 × 0.50 or £100 000. At the end of the second year Deckborn will have a bill for NZ\$2 700 000, this will cost £1 350 000 (computed as NZ\$2 700 000 × £0.50 per NZ\$). The cash flows are as follows:

	Start of period 1 or t_0	End of period 1 or t_1	End of period 2 or t_2
Cash flows in NZ\$s	NZ\$2 500 000	NZ\$200 000	NZ\$2 700 000
Exchange rate £s per NZ\$	£0.40	£0.40	£0.40
Cash flows in £s	+£1 000 000	−£80 000	−£1 080 000
	Start of period 1 or t_0	End of period 1 or t_1	End of period 2 or t_2
Cash flows in NZ\$s	NZ\$2 500 000	NZ\$200 000	NZ\$2 700 000
Exchange rate £s per NZ\$	£0.40	£0.50	£0.50
Cash flows in £s	+£1 000 000	−£100 000	−£1 350 000

The effective cost is the interest rate that 'equates' the repayments with the initial loan. The interest rate is a cost so the basic formula is repayment less cost equals the original loan. The formula is:

$$\text{Initial loan} + £1\,000\,000 = \text{Repayment}\frac{-£100\,000}{(1+r)^1} + \text{Repayment}\frac{-£1\,350\,000}{(1+r)^2}$$

$$\text{Cost of borrowing}$$

A two-period model can be solved by formula but the simplest approach is to solve such problems by trial and error using a spreadsheet (where the cost of borrowing is r (10 per cent = 0.10 etc.) the formula for the present value in another cell is =1 000 000 − 100 000 / (1+r) − 1 350 000 / (1+r)^2). A sufficiently close result is achieved with an interest rate of 21.3 per cent thus:

$$+£1\,000\,000 = \frac{-£100\,000}{(1+0.213)^1} + \frac{-1\,350\,000}{(1+0.213)^2}$$

Originally, Deckborn was seeking to obtain a loan for 8 per cent some 2 per cent cheaper than the UK equiva-lent. But because of the increase in the value of the NZ dollar, Deckborn is now having to pay 21.3 per cent.

MANAGING FOR VALUE

Outsourcing short-term asset and liability management

SkyePharma is a UK-based drug delivery company, focused on the development of prescription pharma-ceuticals utilizing proprietary controlled release tech-nologies. In May 1996 the company listed on the main board of the London Stock Exchange and in 1998 achieved a US NASDAQ listing.

In June 2000, SkyePharma issued a 5-year 6 per cent convertible bond raising £60 million to fund key

(Continued)

research and development projects. The company's strategy is to earn a greater share of product revenues and profits through: 1) providing customers with a wider range of services and 2) taking selected key products to later stages in the development process independently.

Given this background, SkyePharma's finance function was focused on value added support activities such as strategic risk management rather than day-to-day operational treasury activities.

SkyePharma has specific requirements with regard to the management of the convertible bond proceeds:

- Credit risk has to be diversified across a number of institutions to a minimum credit rating of A+.

- Cash has to be managed in line with stated cash burn obtaining a consistently competitive rate of return.

In addition it was recognized that, to help support the stated business strategy, SkyePharma would require access to an active foreign exchange and interest rate deal execution and hedging resource going forward.

Driven by the costs and management time involved in providing these services in house, a strategic decision was taken to outsource this function. The Royal Bank of Scotland's Agency Treasury Services team was chosen as the preferred outsourcing supplier. The bank was mandated to act as SkyePharma's agent and deal with all aspects of treasury risk.

The services provided fall into three categories:

- Liquidity management
- Foreign exchange and interest rate risk management
- Treasury administration and support.

Liquidity management

As a first step, an investment model was created for management of the convertible bond proceeds, which reflected SkyePharma's cash flow requirements and risk/reward parameters. This model covered:

- Credit limits – maximum maturity to be authorized
- Counterparty list – list of authorized banks/financial institutions and credit ratings
- Instruments permitted – range of authorized financial instruments and approved amount per instrument
- Time limits – tenor per counterparty and financial instrument

- Authorized signatories – list of designated personnel who could approve changes to the agreed investment policy.

This model provides the basis for SkyePharma's investment portfolio. Liquidity is managed out to a pre-agreed panel of counterparties using a competitive tender approach. Working to an ongoing cashflow forecast, cash is repatriated in line with requirements and the portfolio is constantly updated to reflect both ongoing investment needs and alterations in the shape of the sterling yield curve.

Foreign exchange and interest rate risk management

With overseas operations in Europe and the USA, SkyePharma has forex exposures in the Swiss franc, euro and US dollar. To ensure effective control over management of foreign exchange risk, a hedging policy has been pre-agreed. Similar in nature to the liquidity management policy, it covers products, tenors, credit limits and authorized signatories.

In practice, as soon as a foreign exchange exposure has been identified, it is notified to the bank. Under the terms of the outsourcing mandate, it is analyzed and a range of solutions to hedge the risk arising are created for approval. SkyePharma select the solution most appropriate to business needs, and this is then executed on the company's behalf in the marketplace.

In terms of interest rate risk management, early on an opportunity was identified to lower the servicing costs on the convertible bond through interest rate risk management. The structuring, execution and settlement aspects of this issue were also outsourced.

Treasury administration and support

To reduce costs within the finance function, SkyePharma has outsourced all confirmations, settlements, payments and transfers activity. A performance benchmarking service forms part of the outsourcing mandate, with performance reported on a monthly basis against a pre-agreed benchmark. This benchmark is appropriate to the service being utilized, i.e. a LIBID-related benchmark for liquidity management and appropriate foreign exchange budget rates (LIBID is the London Interbank bid rate, the rate banks offer to buy eurocurrency deposits hence determining the interest rate).

(Continued)

Interest rates can be broken down into differing elements. The relationship is multiplicative. Thus if the overall rate is called the effective financing rate (denoted as r_{eff}) then breaking the rate down into two elements can be represented as:

$$r_{eff} = (1 + r_1)(1 + r_2) - 1$$

or three elements as:

$$r_{eff} = (1 + r_1)(1 + r_2)(1 + r_3) - 1$$

When managing international loans a natural division to examine is how much of the effective interest rate is due to foreign interest rates (i_f) and how much due to the percentage change in the exchange rate (e_f). Thus:

$$r_{eff} = (1 + i_f)(1 + e_f)$$

Taking the case of Deckborn, $i_f = 0.08$ or 8 per cent and the effective rate is 21.3 per cent. So the portion of the effective rate due to changes in the exchange rate (e_f) is:

$$0.213 = (1 + 0.08)(1 + e_f) - 1$$

thus:

$$e_f = 1.213/1.08 - 1$$
$$= 0.123 \text{ or } 12.3\%$$

Deckborn was charged 8 per cent interest but incurred a further 12.3 per cent due to the fact that the value of the NZ\$ went up from £0.40 to £0.50. As a result interest payments in NZ\$s were more expensive and the loan was also more expensive to repay. But the value of the NZ\$ could have fallen in which case the loan could have been even cheaper.

Assume the same details as in the previous example, only the value of the NZ\$ fell from £0.40 per NZ\$ to £0.35 per NZ\$.

	Start of period 1 or t_0	End of period 1 or t_1	End of period 2 or t_2
Cash flows in NZ\$s	NZ\$2 500 000	NZ\$200 000	NZ\$2 700 000
Exchange rate £s per NZ\$	£0.40	£0.35	£0.35
Cash flows in £s	+£1 000 000	−£70 000	−£945 000

We are now seeking a rate of return that will solve the following equation:

$$+£1\,000\,000 = \frac{-£70\,000}{(1+r)^1} + \frac{-945\,000}{(1+r)^2}$$

Again using trial and error and a spreadsheet the solution is 0.77 per cent so:

$$+£1\,000\,000 = \frac{-£70\,000}{(1 + 0.0077)^1} + \frac{-945\,000}{(1 + 0.0077)^2}$$

If the NZ dollar were to fall in value in this way, the loan would virtually be free. Thus Deckborn is taking a risk by borrowing in a foreign currency: the cost could be much cheaper than a domestic loan, but if the value of the foreign currency increases, the cost of the loan could be greater. An MNC should therefore consider the expected rate of appreciation or depreciation as well as the quoted interest rates of foreign currencies.

USING THE WEB

Short-term foreign interest rates

Short-term interest rates for major currencies such as the Canadian dollar, Japanese yen and British pound for various maturities are provided at: http://www.bloomberg.com. The short-term interest rates provided at this site reflect the government cost of borrowing; an MNC would have to pay a slightly higher interest rate than the rate shown. A review of the data illustrates how short-term interest rates can vary among currencies at a given point in time.

CRITERIA CONSIDERED FOR FOREIGN FINANCING

A more formal consideration of the factors relevant to short-term financing should include:

- Interest rate parity

- Exchange rate forecasts.

These criteria can influence the MNC's decision regarding which currency or currencies to borrow. Each is discussed in turn.

Interest rate parity

Recall that covered interest arbitrage was described as a short-term foreign investment with a simultaneous forward sale of the foreign currency denominating the foreign investment. From a financing perspective, covered interest arbitrage can be conducted as follows. First, borrow a foreign currency and convert that currency to the home currency for use. Also, simultaneously purchase the foreign currency forward to lock in the exchange rate of the currency needed to pay off the loan. If the foreign currency's interest rate is low, this may appear to be a feasible strategy. However, such a currency will, in an efficient market, exhibit a forward premium that offsets the differential between its interest rate and the home interest rate. Therefore borrowing in the foreign currency will incur the same cost as borrowing domestically. So if a foreign interest rate is 2 per cent cheaper, the currency on the forward market will exhibit a 2 per cent premium (i.e. be more expensive by 2 per cent) and this premium will offset the lower interest rate. Thus there is no benefit through borrowing from abroad.

More formally interest rate parity can be expressed as:

$$r_{eff} = (1 + i_f)(1 + p) - 1$$

Where:

r_{eff} = the overall cost of financing in a foreign currency
i_f = foreign currency interest rate
p = the forward rate premium − currency more expensive (or discount − currency cheaper)

If interest rate parity exists then:

$$r_{eff} = i_h$$

Where:

i_h = home interest rate
and therefore:

$$i_h = (1 + i_f)(1 + p) - 1$$

and:

$$p = \frac{(1 + i_h)}{(1 + i_f)} - 1 \text{ and approximately for small differences } p = i_h - i_f$$

which is a more formal way of saying that the premium will reflect the difference in interest rates.

Covered interest rate arbitrage is one of the relationships that hold well in the marketplace. If there are differences with domestic returns than administration costs or restrictions will ensure that no riskless (arbitrage) profit can be made.

An MNC has a choice when borrowing internationally, in can cover its position by taking out a forward or futures contract thus ensuring a return similar to domestic returns. Alternatively it can leave its position uncovered. In such a case:

$$r_{eff} = (1 + i_f)(1 + e_f) - 1$$

Where:

e_f = the change in value of the foreign currency

The forward rate premium (p) had to reflect the difference in interest rates to avoid arbitrage profits; but in this case interest rate parity may or may not exist as there is no implied forward or futures contract in e_f. So a firm may have experiences as in the Deckborn example.

Finally, an MNC may choose to half cover its position by taking out a derivative such as a forward or futures or option contract that protects against some of the risk. In the case of forwards and futures, taking out contracts that do not fully cover the position would mean that some risk remains. In the Deck born example the New Zealand loan was 2 per cent cheaper therefore the forward rate for the first year can be expected to be 2 per cent more expensive to offset the difference. The current spot was £0.40 per NZ$ so the forward rate should be £0.408 per NZ$ for the first year (i.e. (0.408 − 0.40)/0.40 = 0.02 or 2 per cent). If Deckborn only covers (by taking out a forward or futures contract) for NZ$100 000 of the NZ$200 000 due after the first year, then there is no cover for the cost of repaying the remaining NZ$100 000, there may be gains or losses compared to domestic lending. Alternatively, an option may be taken out. In this case, Deckborn may take out a call option to buy NZ$200 000 at £0.42. So that if the NZ$ increased by more than 5 per cent (i.e. (0.42 − 0.40) / 0.40 = 0.05 or 5 per cent) Deckborn could exercise the option and lock in a maximum effective interest rate of 3 per cent more than the domestic (UK) equivalent (5 per cent extra at the £0.42 rate less the 2 per cent lower NZ charge compared to the domestic charge). Similar calculations can be made for the year 2 payments.

Exhibit 18.2 summarizes the implications of a variety of scenarios relating to interest rate parity.

Finally, an issue dealt with in Chapter 15 and earlier, is the effect of the borrowing on the overall exchange rate exposure of the MNC. Short-term financing in a foreign currency implies cash outflows in

EXHIBIT 18.2 Financing alternatives and immediate implications

Scenario	Implications
All repayments fully covered by forward or futures contracts.	The effective interest rate will be about the same as the domestic rate (there may be differences due to transaction costs and market imperfections).
All repayments made at the prevailing exchange rate.	If interest parity holds, the effective rate will be similar to the domestic rate. If interest rate parity does not hold, the effective cost could be higher or lower than the domestic rate depending on the change in value of the foreign currency.
Some repayments covered by a futures or forwards contract.	As in scenario 1 for the elements covered by the contract and as in scenario 2 for the uncovered element.
Repayments covered by options.	Assuming that the option is out of the money (the exercise price is above the currency spot), if the value of the foreign currency goes above the level determined by the strike or exercise price, the option will be exercised and the increased cost of payment restricted to that of the exercise price.

that currency. Where there are earnings in that currency as well, the borrowing will give a degree of protection from exchange rate exposure. So, if the value of the currency falls, the adverse effect on translation of earnings into the home currency will be offset partially (or even fully) by the saving made by the cheaper cost home currency of payments of interest and capital in the foreign currency. The matching is not an exact science but setting any cash outflow in a currency against an inflow will help protect against the effects of changes in the value of that currency.

Exchange rate forecasts

While the forecasting capabilities of firms are somewhat limited, some firms may make decisions based on their estimation of the future value of the currency. The estimate may be based on market forecasts through a stockbroker subscription service or the quoted futures rate may be taken as a prediction of the future rate (effectively assuming that interest rate parity holds). Or a firm may use its own in-house economists to make an estimate. Methods of prediction used by staff may range from sophisticated econometric techniques to purely subjective judgements.

A point estimate or prediction of a single rate is rarely sufficient. Most MNCs will want to have an idea of the potential variation in the rate that could occur in the future. Only by knowing these possibilities can some impression of risk be gained. In looking at future possibilities two approaches are common. The first is to develop a probability distribution, looking at the varying rates and their probabilities. This is the dominant approach in financial theory leading to measures of spread such as the standard deviation and also to measures of association as in covariance or correlation. A second approach is to assess scenarios. Probabilities may or may not be used, for instance, if a firm wants to adopt a policy of protecting against the three worst scenarios, no probability calculations would be required. Scenarios are not confined to predicting the value of the exchange rate. There may, for instance, be a series of scenarios whereby the value of the foreign currency falls by 5 per cent, but the differences in the scenarios is what is happening to other exchange rates or to international regulations or government policies. So this approach is more than merely approximating a distribution of exchange rates.

Starting with a prediction of a single future rate, once the firm develops a forecast or series of forecasts for the exchange rate's percentage change over the financing period (e_f), it can use this forecast along with the foreign interest rate to forecast the effective financing rate of a foreign currency. The forecasted rate can then be compared to the domestic financing rate.

EXAMPLE

Danya Ltd (Ireland) needs funds for 1 year and is aware that the 1-year interest rate in euros is 12 per cent while the interest rate from borrowing Swiss francs is 8 per cent. Danya forecasts that the Swiss franc will appreciate from its current rate of 0.64 euros to 0.6528 euros or by 2 per cent over the next year. The expected value for e_f [written as $E(e_f)$] will therefore be 2 per cent. Thus, the expected effective financing rate [$E(r_f)$] will be:

In this example, financing in Swiss francs is expected to be less expensive than financing in euros. However, the value for e_f is forecasted and therefore is not known with certainty. Thus, there is no guarantee that foreign financing will truly be less costly.

$$E(r_{eff}) = (1 + i_f)(1 + E(e_f)) - 1$$
$$= (1 + 0.08)(1 + 0.02) - 1$$
$$= 0.1016 \text{ or } 10.16\%$$

Deriving a value for e_f that equates domestic and foreign rates. Continuing from the previous example, Danya Ltd may attempt at least to determine what value of e_f would make the effective rate from foreign financing the same as domestic financing. To determine this value, note that e_f plays the same role as 'p' above so:

$$e_f = \frac{(1 + i_h)}{(1 + i_f)} - 1 \text{ and approximately for small differences } e_f = i_h - i_f$$

$i_h = 12$ per cent and $i_f = 8$ per cent so the change in value of foreign currency (e_f) that equates domestic and foreign rates is 12 per cent − 8 per cent = 4 per cent. The more accurate calculation is:

$$ef = \frac{(1 + 0.12)}{(1 + 0.08)} = 0.037037 \text{ or } 3.704\%$$

This suggests that the Swiss franc would have to appreciate by about 3.7 per cent over the loan period to make the Swiss franc loan as costly as a loan in euros. Any smaller degree of appreciation would make the Swiss franc loan less costly. Danya can use this information when determining whether to borrow euros or Swiss francs. If it expects the Swiss franc to appreciate by more than 3.7 per cent over the loan life, it should prefer borrowing in euros. If it expects the Swiss franc to appreciate by less than 3.7 per cent or to depreciate, its decision is more complex. If the potential savings from financing with the foreign currency outweigh the risk involved, then the firm should choose that route. The final decision here will be influenced by Danya's degree of risk aversion.

Use of probability distributions. To gain more insight about the financing decision, a firm may wish to develop a probability distribution for the percentage change in value for a particular foreign currency over the financing horizon. Since forecasts are not always accurate, it is sometimes useful to develop a probability distribution instead of relying on a single point estimate. Using the probability distribution of possible percentage changes in the currency's value, along with the currency's interest rate, the firm can determine the probability distribution of the possible effective financing rates for the currency. Then, it can compare this distribution to the known financing rate of the home currency in order to make its financing decision.

EXAMPLE

Caroline Ltd (UK) is deciding whether to borrow Swiss francs for 1 year. It finds that the bank quote for Caroline to borrow in Swiss francs is 8 per cent and the quoted rate for the pound is 15 per cent. It then develops a probability distribution for the Swiss franc's possible percentage change in value over the life of the loan.

The probability distribution is displayed in Exhibit 18.3. The first row in Exhibit 18.3 shows that there is a 5 per cent probability of a 6 per cent depreciation in the Swiss franc over the loan life. If the Swiss franc does depreciate by 6 per cent, the effective financing rate would be 1.52 per cent. Thus, there is a 5 per cent probability that Caroline will incur a 1.52 per cent effective financing rate on its loan. The second row shows that there is a 10 per cent probability of a 4 per

cent depreciation in the Swiss franc over the loan life. If the Swiss franc does depreciate by 4 per cent, the effective financing rate would be 3.68 per cent. Thus, there is a 10 per cent probability that Caroline will incur a 3.68 per cent effective financing rate on its loan.

For each possible percentage change in the Swiss franc's value, there is a corresponding effective financing rate. We can associate each possible effective financing rate (third column) with its probability of occurring (second column). By multiplying each possible effective financing rate by its associated probability, we can compute an expected value for the effective financing rate of the Swiss franc. Based on the information in Exhibit 18.3, the expected value of the effective financing rate, referred to as $E(r_f)$, is computed as:

$$
\begin{aligned}
E(r_f) &= 5\%\,(1.52\%) + 10\%\,(3.68\%) + 15\%\,(6.92\%) + 20\%\,(9.08\%) + 20\%\,(12.32\%) + 15\%\,(14.48\%) \\
&\quad + 10\%\,(16.64\%) + 5\%\,(18.80\%) \\
&= 0.076\% + 0.368\% + 1.038\% + 1.816\% + 2.464\% + 2.172\% + 1.664\% + 0.94\% \\
&= 10.538\%
\end{aligned}
$$

Thus, the decision for Caroline is whether to borrow pounds (at 15 per cent interest) or Swiss francs (with an expected value of 10.538 per cent for the effective financing rate). Using Exhibit 18.3, the risk reflects the 5 per cent chance (probability) that the effective financing

rate on Swiss francs will be 18.8 per cent and the 10 per cent chance that the effective financing rate on Swiss francs will be 16.64 per cent. Either of these possibilities represents a greater expense to Caroline than it would incur if it borrowed British pounds.

To further assess the decision regarding which currency to borrow, the information in the second and third columns of Exhibit 18.3 is used to develop the probability distribution in Exhibit 18.4. This exhibit illustrates the probability of each possible effective financing rate that may occur if Caroline borrows Swiss francs. Notice that the UK interest rate (15 per cent) is included in Exhibit 18.4 for comparison purposes. There is no distribution of possible outcomes for the UK rate since the rate of 15 per cent is known with certainty (no exchange rate risk exists). There is a 15 per cent probability that the UK rate will be lower than the effective rate on Swiss francs and an 85 per cent chance that the UK rate will be higher than the effective rate on Swiss francs. This information can assist the firm in its financing decision. Given the potential savings relative to the small degree of risk, Caroline decides to borrow Swiss francs.

ACTUAL RESULTS FROM FOREIGN FINANCING

The fact that some firms utilize foreign financing suggests that they believe reduced financing costs can be achieved. To assess this issue, the effective financing rates of a Swiss franc loan to a UK company compared to a UK loan are compared in Exhibit 18.5. The somewhat artificial assumption is that for both loans the variable monthly deposit rate is charged for the month and then the loan is repaid at the end of the month – the rates have been annualized. We look at the cost as a percentage of the original loan for each month

EXHIBIT 18.3   Analysis of financing with a foreign currency

Possible rate of change in the Swiss franc over the life of the loan	Probability of occurrence	Effective financing rate if this rate of change in the (e_f) Swiss franc does occur (r_{eff})
−6%	5%	(1.08)[1 + (−6%)] − 1 = 1.52%
−4	10	(1.08)[1 + (−4%)] − 1 = 3.68
−1	15	(1.08)[1 + (−1%)] − 1 = 6.92
+1	20	(1.08)[1 + (1%)] − 1 = 9.08
+4	20	(1.08)[1 + (4%)] − 1 = 12.32
+6	15	(1.08)[1 + (6%)] − 1 = 14.48
+8	10	(1.08)[1 + (8%)] − 1 = 16.64
+10	<u>5</u>	(1.08)[1 + (10%)] − 1 = 18.80
	100%	

EXHIBIT 18.4   Probability distribution of effective financing rates

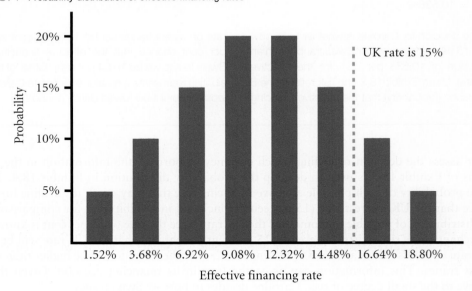

from 2000 to 2013. For the Swiss loan, the payment is in Swiss francs; so if the Swiss franc has fallen by more than the interest rate, the repayment could be less than the original loan! This indeed happened for nearly 30 per cent of the months. The average interest rate of the Swiss loan was 1.5 per cent compared to 3.25 per cent for a domestic loan. However, the standard deviation of the Swiss loan was 3.2 per cent compared to 2.1 per cent for the UK loan. As with longer term foreign borrowing, the cheaper Swiss interest rates do not take into account the higher transactions costs not the greater risk premium that a Swiss bank is likely to charge. The greater variation caused by the exchange rate fluctuations also makes the Swiss borrowing less attractive as would be the case with all foreign borrowing.

EXHIBIT 18.5 Comparison of the monthly British pound cost of financing a Swiss franc loan compared with a UK loan

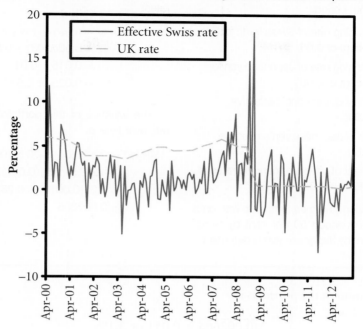

FINANCING WITH A PORTFOLIO OF CURRENCIES

Where more than one currency is part of the financing package, the overall cost of financing can be measured using the portfolio model of Chapter 3. The difference is that the effective financing rate rather than the interest rate alone is relevant. The effective rate is approximately for, say, 1 month: the interest rate for that month *plus* the change in the value of the currency over that month. Thus the variance of a two-currency portfolio's effective financing rate [VAR(r_p)] over time is computed as:

$$VAR(r_p) = w_A^2 \sigma_A^2 + w_B^2 \sigma_B^2 + 2w_A w_B \sigma_A \sigma_B CORR_{AB}$$

where w_A^2 and w_B^2 represent the percentage of total funds financed from Currencies A and B, respectively; σ_A^2 and σ_B^2 represent the individual variances of each currency's effective financing rate over time; and $CORR_{AB}$ reflects the correlation coefficient of the two currencies' effective financing rates. Since the percentage change in the exchange rate plays an important role in influencing the effective financing rate, it should not be surprising that $CORR_{AB}$ is strongly affected by the correlation between the exchange rate fluctuations of the two currencies. A low correlation between movements of the two currencies may force $CORR_{AB}$ to be low.

EXAMPLE

Valparaiso SA (Spain) considers borrowing a portfolio of Japanese yen and Swiss francs to finance its euro operations. Half of the needed funding would come from each currency. To determine how the variance in this portfolio's effective financing rate is related to characteristics of the component currencies, assume

(Continued)

the following information based on historical information for several 3-month periods:

- Mean effective financing rate of Swiss franc for 3 months = 3 per cent or 0.03.
- Mean effective financing rate of Japanese yen for 3 months = 2 per cent or 0.02.
- Standard deviation of Swiss franc's effective financing rate = 0.04.
- Standard deviation of Japanese yen's effective financing rate = 0.09.
- Correlation coefficient of effective financing rates of these two currencies = 0.10.

Given this information, the mean effective rate on a portfolio (r_p) of funds financed 50 per cent by Swiss francs and 50 per cent by Japanese yen is determined by totalling the weighted individual effective financing rates:

$$
\begin{aligned}
r_P &= w_{SFr}r_{SFr} + w_{Yen}r_{Yen} \\
&= 0.50(0.03) + 0.50(0.02) \\
&= 0.015 + 0.01 \\
&= 0.025 \text{ or } 2.5\%
\end{aligned}
$$

The variance of this portfolio's effective financing rate over time is:

$$
\begin{aligned}
VAR(r_P) &= 0.5^2(0.04)^2 + 0.5^2(0.09)^2 \\
&\quad + 2(0.5)(0.5)(0.04)(0.09)(0.10) \\
&= 0.25(0.0016) + 0.25(0.0081) + 0.00018 \\
&= 0.002605
\end{aligned}
$$

The standard deviation of the portfolio is:

$$
\sqrt{0.002605} = 0.051 \text{ or } 5.1\%
$$

Valparaiso can use this same process to compare various financing packages to see which package would be most appropriate. It may be more interested in estimating the mean return and variability for repeated financing in a particular portfolio in the future. There is no guarantee that past data will be indicative of the future. Yet, if the individual variability and paired correlations are somewhat stable over time, the historical variability of the portfolio's effective financing rate should provide a reasonable forecast.

To recognize the benefits from financing with two currencies that are not highly correlated, reconsider how the variance of the portfolio's effective financing rate would have been affected if the correlation between the two currencies was 0.90 (very high correlation) instead of 0.10. The variance would be 0.004045, which is more than 50 per cent higher than the variance when the correlation was assumed to be 0.10.

The assessment of a currency portfolio's effective financing rate and variance is not restricted to just two currencies. The mean effective financing rate for a currency portfolio of any size will be determined by totalling the respective individual effective financing rates weighted by the percentage of funds financed with each currency. Solving the variance of a portfolio's effective financing rate becomes more complex as more currencies are added to the portfolio; the underlying model, however, is the variance/covariance matrix first encountered in Chapter 3.

SUMMARY

- MNCs may use foreign financing to offset anticipated cash inflows in foreign currencies so that exposure to exchange rate risk will be minimized. Alternatively, some MNCs may use foreign financing in an attempt to reduce their financing costs. Foreign financing costs may be lower if the foreign interest rate is relatively low or if the foreign currency borrowed depreciates over the financing period.

- MNCs can determine whether to use foreign financing by estimating the effective financing rate for any foreign currency over the period in which financing will be needed. The expected effective financing rate is dependent on the quoted interest rate of the foreign currency and the forecasted percentage change in the currency's value over the financing period.

- When MNCs borrow a portfolio of currencies that have low interest rates, they can increase the probability of achieving relatively low financing costs if the currencies' values are not highly correlated.

CRITICAL DEBATE

Do MNCs increase their risk when borrowing foreign currencies?

Proposition. Yes. MNCs should borrow the currency that matches their cash inflows. If they borrow a foreign currency to finance business in a different currency, they are essentially speculating on the future exchange rate movements. The results of the strategy are uncertain, which represents risk to the MNC and its shareholders.

Opposing view. No. If MNCs expect that they can reduce the effective financing rate by borrowing a foreign

currency, they should consider borrowing that currency. This enables them to achieve lower costs and improves their ability to compete. If they take the most conservative approach by borrowing whatever currency matches their inflows, they may incur higher costs and have a greater chance of failure.

With whom do you agree? Which argument do you support? Offer your own opinion on this issue.

SELF TEST

Answers are provided in Appendix A at the back of the text.

1 Assume that the interest rate in New Zealand is 9 per cent. A UK firm plans to borrow New Zealand dollars, convert them to UK pounds, and repay the loan in 1 year. What will be the effective financing rate if the New Zealand dollar depreciates by 6 per cent? If the New Zealand dollar appreciates by 3 per cent?

2 Using the information in question 1 and assuming a 50 per cent chance of either scenario occurring, determine the expected value of the effective financing rate.

3 Assume that the Japanese 1-year interest rate is 5 per cent, while the UK 1-year interest rate is 8 per cent. What percentage change in the Japanese yen would cause a UK firm borrowing yen to incur the same effective financing rate as it would if it borrowed pounds?

4 The spot rate of the Australian dollar is £0.40. The 1-year forward rate of the Australian dollar is £0.38. The Australian 1-year interest rate is 9 per cent. Assume that the forward rate is used to forecast the future spot rate. Determine the expected effective financing rate for a UK firm that borrows Australian dollars to finance its UK business.

5 Omaha SA (France) plans to finance its UK operations by repeatedly borrowing two currencies with low interest rates whose exchange rate movements are highly correlated. Will the variance of the two-currency portfolio's effective financing rate be much lower than the variance of either individual currency's effective financing rate? Explain.

QUESTIONS AND APPLICATIONS

1 **Financing from subsidiaries.** Explain why an MNC parent would consider financing from its subsidiaries.

2 **Foreign financing.**
   a Explain how a firm's degree of risk aversion enters into its decision of whether to finance in a foreign currency or a local currency.

   b Discuss the use of specifying a break-even point when financing in a foreign currency.

3 **Probability distribution.**
   a Discuss the development of a probability distribution of effective financing rates when financing in a foreign currency. How is this distribution developed?

b Once the probability distribution of effective financing rates from financing in a foreign currency is developed, how can this distribution be used in deciding whether to finance in the foreign currency or the home currency?

4 Financing and exchange rate risk. How can a UK firm finance in euros and not necessarily be exposed to exchange rate risk?

5 Short-term financing analysis. Assume that Tilly Ltd needs £3 million for a 1-year period. Within 1 year, it will generate enough British pounds to pay off the loan. It is considering three options: (1) borrowing pounds at an interest rate of 6 per cent, (2) borrowing Japanese yen at an interest rate of 3 per cent or (3) borrowing Canadian dollars at an interest rate of 4 per cent. Tilly expects that the Japanese yen will appreciate by 1 per cent over the next year and that the Canadian dollar will appreciate by 3 per cent. What is the expected 'effective' financing rate for each of the three options? Which option appears to be most feasible? Why might Tilly not necessarily choose the option reflecting the lowest effective financing rate?

6 Effective financing rate. How is it possible for a firm to incur a negative effective financing rate?

7 IRP application to short-term financing.

a If interest rate parity does not hold, what strategy should Connect Ltd consider when it needs short-term financing?

b Assume that Connect Ltd needs pounds. It borrows euros at a lower interest rate than that for pounds. If interest rate parity exists and if the forward rate of the euro is a reliable predictor of the future spot rate, what does this suggest about the feasibility of such a strategy?

c If Connect Ltd expects the current spot rate to be a more reliable predictor of the future spot rate, what does this suggest about the feasibility of such a strategy?

8 Break-even financing. Akron Ltd needs dollars. Assume that the local 1-year loan rate is 15 per cent, while a 1-year loan rate on euros is 7 per cent. By how much must the euro appreciate to cause the loan in euros to be more costly than a UK loan?

9 IRP application to short-term financing. Assume that interest rate parity exists. If a firm believes that

the forward rate is an unbiased predictor of the future spot rate, will it expect to achieve lower financing costs by consistently borrowing a foreign currency with a low interest rate?

10 Effective financing rate. Boca, SA (Spain) needs 4 million euros for 1 year. It currently has no business in Japan but plans to borrow Japanese yen from a Japanese bank because the Japanese interest rate is three percentage points lower than the euro rate. Assume that interest rate parity exists; also assume that Boca believes that the 1-year forward rate of the Japanese yen will exceed the future spot rate 1 year from now. Will the expected effective financing rate be higher, lower, or the same as financing with euros? Explain.

11 IRP application to short-term financing. Assume that the UK interest rate is 7 per cent and the euro's interest rate is 4 per cent. Assume that the euro's forward rate has a premium of 4 per cent (is 4 per cent more expensive in terms of £s?). Determine whether the following statement is true: 'Interest rate parity does not hold; therefore, UK firms could lock in a lower financing cost by borrowing euros and purchasing euros forward for 1 year.' Explain your answer.

12 Break-even financing. Orlando plc is a UK-based MNC with a subsidiary in Mexico. Its Mexican subsidiary needs a 1-year loan of 10 million pesos for operating expenses. Since the Mexican interest rate is 70 per cent, Orlando is considering borrowing pounds, which it would convert to pesos to cover the operating expenses. By how much would the pound have to appreciate against the peso to cause such a strategy to backfire? (The 1-year UK interest rate is 9 per cent.)

13 Financing in a crisis. What actions can a firm take with regard to its short-term financing when there are concerns that there might be a currency crisis in the country of one of its subsidiaries.

14 Effects of currency change. Homewood Ltd commonly finances some of its expansion in Europe by borrowing in euros. The interest rate for the euro then increases with no prospect of a fall in value of the euro against the pound. Should Homewood refinance in pounds? Explain.

ADVANCED QUESTIONS

15 **Probability distribution of financing costs.** Missoula Ltd decides to borrow Japanese yen for 1 year. The interest rate on the borrowed yen is 8 per cent. Missoula has developed the following probability distribution for the yen's degree of fluctuation against the pound:

Possible degree of fluctuation of yen against the pound	Percentage probability
-4%	**20%**
Probability 1	**30**
0	10
3	40

Given this information, what is the expected value of the effective financing rate of the Japanese yen from Missoula's perspective?

16 **Analysis of short-term financing.** Jackson Ltd is a UK-based firm that needs £600 000. It has no business in Japan but is considering 1-year financing with Japanese yen because the annual interest rate would be 5 per cent versus 9 per cent in the UK. Assume that interest rate parity exists.

a Can Jackson benefit from borrowing Japanese yen and simultaneously purchasing yen 1 year forward to avoid exchange rate risk? Explain.

b Assume that Jackson does not cover its exposure and uses the forward rate to forecast the future spot rate. Determine the expected effective financing rate. Should Jackson finance with Japanese yen? Explain.

c Assume that Jackson does not cover its exposure and expects that the Japanese yen will appreciate by either 5 per cent, 3 per cent or 2 per cent, and with equal probability of each occurrence. Use this information to determine the probability distribution of the effective financing rate. Should Jackson finance with Japanese yen? Explain.

17 **Financing with a portfolio.** Pfeffer GmbH (Germany) considers obtaining 40 per cent of its 1-year financing in Canadian dollars and 60 per cent in Japanese yen. The forecasts of appreciation in the Canadian dollar and Japanese yen for the next year are as follows:

Currency	Possible percentage change in the spot rate over the loan life	Probability of that percentage change in the spot rate occurring
Canadian dollar	4%	70%
Canadian dollar	7	30
Japanese yen	6	50
Japanese yen	9	50

The interest rate on the Canadian dollar is 9 per cent, and the interest rate on the Japanese yen is 7 per cent. Develop the possible effective financing rates of the overall portfolio and the probability of each possibility based on the use of joint probabilities (assume independence).

18 **Financing with a portfolio.**

a Does borrowing a portfolio of currencies offer any possible advantages over the borrowing of a single foreign currency?

b If a firm borrows a portfolio of currencies, what characteristics of the currencies will affect the potential variability of the portfolio's effective financing rate? What characteristics would be desirable from a borrowing firm's perspective?

19 **Financing with a portfolio.** Raleigh Ltd needs to borrow funds for 1 year to finance an expenditure in the USA. The following interest rates are available:

	Borrowing rate
USA	10%
Canada	6
Japan	5

The percentage changes in the spot rates of the Canadian dollar and Japanese yen over the next year are as follows:

Canadian dollar		Japanese yen	
Probability	Percentage change in spot rate	Probability	Percentage change in spot rate
10%	5%	20%	6%
90	2	80	1

If Raleigh Ltd borrows a portfolio, 50 per cent of funds from Canadian dollars and 50 per cent of funds from yen, determine the probability distribution of the effective financing rate of the portfolio. What is the probability that Raleigh will incur a higher effective financing rate from borrowing this portfolio than from borrowing US dollars?

PROJECT WORKSHOP

20 **Yields for foreign currencies.** The Bloomberg website provides interest rate data for many different foreign currencies over various maturities. Its address is: http://www.bloomberg.com.

a   Go to the section that shows yields for different foreign currencies. Review the 3-month yields of currencies. Assume that you could borrow at a rate one percentage point above the quoted yield for each currency. Which currency would offer you the lowest quoted yield?

b   As a cash manager of a UK-based MNC that needs dollars to support UK operations, where would you borrow funds for the next 3 months? Explain.

DISCUSSION IN THE BOARDROOM

This exercise can be found on our dedicated Course-Mate platform for students.

RUNNING YOUR OWN MNC

This exercise can be found on our dedicated Course-Mate platform for students.

Essays/discussion and articles can be found at the end of Part V.

BLADES PLC CASE STUDY

Use of foreign short-term financing

Blades plc just received a special order for 120 000 pairs of 'Speedos', its primary roller blade product. Ben Holt, Blades' financial director, needs short-term financing to finance this large order from the time Blades orders its supplies until the time it will receive payment. Blades will charge a price of 5000 baht per pair of Speedos. The materials needed to manufacture these 120 000 pairs will be purchased from Thai suppliers. Blades expects the cost of the components for one pair of Speedos to be approximately 3500 baht in its first year of operating the Thai subsidiary.

Because Blades is relatively unknown in Thailand, its suppliers have indicated that they would like to receive payment as early as possible. The customer that placed this order insists on open account transactions, which means that Blades will receive payment for the roller blades approximately 3 months subsequent to the sale. Furthermore, the production cycle necessary to produce Speedos, from purchase of the materials to the eventual sale of the product, is approximately 3 months. Because of these considerations, Blades expects to collect its revenues approximately 6 months after it has paid for the materials, such as rubber and plastic components, needed to manufacture Speedos.

Ben Holt has identified at least two alternatives for satisfying Blades' financing needs. First, Blades could borrow Japanese yen for 6 months, convert the yen to Thai baht, and use the baht to pay the Thai suppliers. When the accounts receivable in Thailand are collected, Blades would convert the baht received to yen and repay the Japanese yen loan. Second, Blades could borrow Thai baht for 6 months in order to pay its Thai suppliers. When Blades collects its accounts receivable, it would use these receipts to repay the baht loan. Thus, Blades will use revenue generated in Thailand to repay the loan, whether it borrows the money in yen or in baht.

Holt's initial research indicates that the 180-day interest rates available to Blades in Japan and in Thailand are 4 per cent and 6 per cent, respectively. Consequently, Holt favours borrowing the Japanese yen, as he believes this loan will be cheaper than the baht-denominated loan. He is aware that he should somehow incorporate the future movements of the yen-baht exchange rate in his analysis, but he is unsure how to

accomplish this. However, he has identified the following probability distribution of the change in the value of the Japanese yen with respect to the Thai baht and of the change in the value of the Thai baht with respect to the dollar over the 6-month period of the loan:

Possible rate of change in the Japanese yen relative to the Thai baht over the life of the loan	Possible rate of change in the Thai baht relative to the pound over the life of the loan	Probability of occurrence
2%	−3%	30%
1	−2	30
0	−1	20
1	0	15
2	1	5

Holt has also informed you that the current spot rate of the yen (in baht) is THB0.347826, while the current spot rate of the baht (in pounds) is £0.0015.

As a financial analyst for Blades, you have been asked to answer the following questions for Ben Holt:

1 What is the amount, in baht, that Blades needs to borrow to cover the payments due to the Thai suppliers? What is the amount, in yen, that Blades needs to borrow to cover the payments due to the Thai suppliers?

2 Given that Blades will use the receipts from the receivables in Thailand to repay the loan and that Blades plans to remit all baht-denominated cash flows to the UK parent whether it borrows in baht or yen, does the future value of the yen with respect to the baht affect the cost of the loan if Blades borrows in yen?

3 Using a spreadsheet, compute the expected amount (in pounds) that will be remitted to the UK in 6 months if Blades finances its working capital requirements by borrowing baht versus borrowing yen. Based on your analysis, should Blades obtain a yen- or baht-denominated loan?

SMALL BUSINESS DILEMMA

Short-term financing by the Sports Exports Company

At the current time, the Sports Exports Company (Ireland) focuses on producing basketballs and exporting them to a distributor in the UK. The exports are denominated in British pounds. Jim Logan, the owner, plans to develop other sporting goods products besides the basketballs that he produces. His entire expansion will be focused on the UK, where he is trying to make a name for his firm. He remains concerned about his firm's exposure to exchange rate risk but does not plan to let that get in the way of his expansion plans because he believes that his firm can continue to penetrate the British sporting goods market. He has just negotiated a joint venture with a British firm that will produce other sporting goods products that are popular in the USA but will be sold in the UK. Jim will pay the British manufacturer in British pounds. These products will be delivered directly to the British distributor rather than to Jim, and the distributor will pay Jim with British pounds.

Jim's expansion plans will result in the need for additional funding. Jim would prefer to borrow on a short-term basis now. Jim has an excellent credit rating and collateral and therefore should be able to obtain short-term financing. The British interest rate is one-quarter of a percentage point above the US interest rate.

1 Should Jim borrow dollars or pounds to finance his joint venture business? Why?

2 Jim could also borrow euros at an interest rate that is lower than the US or British rate. The values of the euro and pound tend to move in the same direction against the dollar but not always by the same degree. Would borrowing euros to support the British joint venture result in more exposure to exchange rate risk than borrowing pounds? Would it result in more exposure to exchange rate risk than borrowing dollars?

CHAPTER 19
INTERNATIONAL CASH MANAGEMENT

LEARNING OBJECTIVES

The specific objectives of this chapter are to:

- Explain the difference in analyzing cash flows from a subsidiary perspective and from a parent perspective.

- Explain the various techniques used to optimize cash flows.

- Explain common complications in optimizing cash flows.

- Explain the potential benefits and risks from foreign investing.

The term cash management can be broadly defined to mean optimization of cash flows and investment of excess cash. From an international perspective, cash management is very complex because laws pertaining to cross-border cash transfers differ among countries. In addition, exchange rate fluctuations can affect the value of cross-border cash transfers. Financial managers need to understand the advantages and disadvantages of investing cash in foreign markets so that they can make international cash management decisions that maximize the value of the multinational corporation (MNC).

CASH FLOW ANALYSIS: SUBSIDIARY PERSPECTIVE

The management of working capital (such as inventory, accounts receivable and payable – debtors and creditors – and cash) has a direct influence on the amount and timing of cash flows. Working capital management and the management of cash flow are integrated. First, we discuss these elements before focusing on cash management.

Subsidiary expenses

Begin with outflow payments by the subsidiary to purchase raw materials or supplies. The subsidiary will normally have a more difficult time forecasting future outflow payments if its purchases are international rather than domestic because of exchange rate fluctuations. In addition, there is a possibility that payments will be substantially higher due to appreciation of the invoice currency. Consequently, the firm may wish to maintain a large inventory of supplies and raw materials so that it can draw from its inventory and cut down on purchases if the invoice currency appreciates. Still another possibility is that imported goods from another country could be restricted by the host government (through quotas etc.). In this event, a larger inventory would give a firm more time to search for alternative sources of supplies or raw materials. A subsidiary with domestic supply sources would not experience such a problem and therefore would not need such a large inventory.

Outflow payments for supplies will be influenced by future sales. If the sales volume is substantially influenced by exchange rate fluctuations, its future level becomes more uncertain, which makes its need for supplies more uncertain. Such uncertainty may force the subsidiary to maintain larger cash balances to cover any unexpected increase in supply requirements.

Subsidiary revenue

If subsidiaries export their products, their sales volume may be more volatile than if the goods were only sold domestically. This volatility could be due to the fluctuating exchange rate of the invoice currency. Importers' demand for these finished goods will most likely decrease if the invoice currency appreciates. The sales volume of exports is also susceptible to business cycles of the importing countries. If the goods were sold domestically, the exchange rate fluctuations would not have a direct impact on sales, although they would still have an indirect impact since the fluctuations would influence prices paid by local customers for imports from foreign competitors.

Sales can often be increased when credit standards are relaxed. However, it is important to focus on cash inflows due to sales rather than on sales themselves. Looser credit standards may cause a slowdown in cash inflows from sales, which could offset the benefits of increased sales. Accounts receivable management is an important part of the subsidiary's working capital management because of its potential impact on cash inflows.

Subsidiary dividend payments

The subsidiary may be expected to periodically send dividend payments and other fees to the parent. These fees could represent royalties or charges for overhead costs incurred by the parent that benefit the subsidiary. An example is research and development costs incurred by the parent, which improve the quality of goods produced by the subsidiary. Whatever the reason, payments by the subsidiary to the parent are often necessary. When dividend payments and fees are known in advance and denominated in the subsidiary's currency, forecasting cash flows is easier for the subsidiary. The level of dividends paid by subsidiaries to the parent is dependent on the liquidity needs of each subsidiary, potential uses of funds at various subsidiary locations, expected movements in the currencies of the subsidiaries, and regulations of the host country government.

Subsidiary liquidity management

After accounting for all outflow and inflow payments, the subsidiary will find itself with either excess or deficient cash. It uses liquidity management to either invest its excess cash or borrow to cover its cash deficiencies. If it anticipates a cash deficiency, short-term financing is necessary, as described in the previous chapter. If it anticipates excess cash, it must determine how the excess cash should be used. Investing in foreign currencies can sometimes be attractive, but exchange rate risk makes the effective yield uncertain. This issue is discussed later in this chapter.

Liquidity management is a crucial component of a subsidiary's working capital management. Subsidiaries commonly have access to numerous lines of credit and overdraft facilities in various currencies. Therefore, they may maintain adequate liquidity without substantial cash balances. While liquidity is important for the overall MNC, it cannot be properly measured by liquidity ratios. Potential access to funds is more relevant than cash on hand.

CENTRALIZED CASH MANAGEMENT

Each subsidiary should manage its working capital by simultaneously considering all of the points discussed thus far. Often, though, each subsidiary is more concerned with its own operations than with the overall operations of the MNC. Thus, a **centralized cash management** group may need to monitor, and possibly manage, the parent-subsidiary and intersubsidiary cash flows. This role is critical since it can often benefit individual subsidiaries in need of funds or overly exposed to exchange rate risk.

EXAMPLE

The treasury department of Kraft Foods is centralized to manage liquidity, funding and foreign exchange requirements of its global operations. And Monsanto has a centralized system for pooling different currency balances from various subsidiaries in Asia that saves hundreds of thousands of dollars per year.

Exhibit 19.1 is a complement to the following discussion of cash flow management. It is a simplified cash flow diagram for an MNC with two subsidiaries in different countries. Although each MNC may handle its payments in a different manner, Exhibit 19.1 is based on simplified assumptions that will help illustrate some key concepts of international cash management. The exhibit reflects the assumption that the two subsidiaries periodically send loan repayments and dividends to the parent or send excess cash to the parent (where the centralized cash management process is assumed to take place). These cash flows represent the incoming cash to the parent from the subsidiaries. The parent's cash outflows to the subsidiaries can include loans and the return of cash previously invested by the subsidiaries. The subsidiaries also have cash flows between themselves because they purchase supplies from each other.

While each subsidiary is managing its working capital, there is a need to monitor and manage the cash flows between the parent and the subsidiaries, as well as between the individual subsidiaries. This task of international cash management should be delegated to a centralized cash management group. International cash management can be segmented into two functions: (1) optimizing cash flow movements, and (2) investing excess cash. These two functions are discussed in turn.

The centralized cash management division of an MNC cannot always accurately forecast events that affect parent – subsidiary or intersubsidiary cash flows. It should, however, be ready to react to any event by considering: (1) any potential adverse impact on cash flows and (2) how to avoid such an adverse impact. If the cash flow situation between the parent and subsidiaries results in a cash squeeze on the

EXHIBIT 19.1   Cash flow of the overall MNC

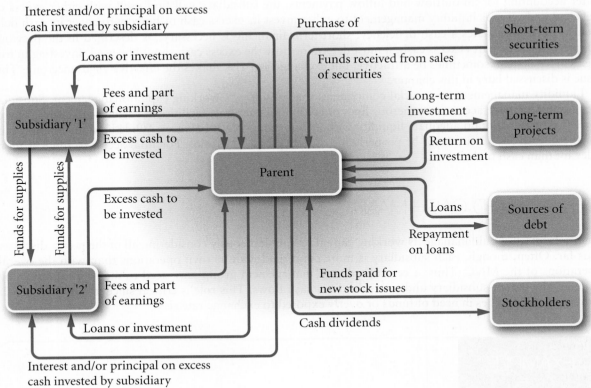

parent, it should have sources of funds (credit lines) available. On the other hand, if it has excess cash after considering all outflow payments, it must consider where to invest funds. This decision is thoroughly examined shortly.

MANAGING FOR VALUE

Flexsys' decision to use a multibank payments system

Flexsys is a large chemical company with more than 20 subsidiaries in Europe, the USA and Asia. To improve its liquidity, it wanted to create a system that would enable its treasury department to continuously monitor all payments at each subsidiary. Since the inception of the euro, Flexsys has had euro balances at several subsidiaries and consolidates these balances so that it can maximize the interest earned on the balances. It uses technology that allows all payments due to be recorded and transmitted to the treasury

department. The treasury nets all payments due between subsidiaries so that only net payments need to be made to cover the payments due between subsidiaries. Flexsys' system is especially effective because it is 'transparent', meaning that the payments due at each subsidiary can be easily monitored by the subsidiaries.

Flexsys uses multiple banks rather than branches of a single bank so that each subsidiary can use the bank it prefers. Having a multibank system

(Continued)

complicates the reporting of payments, but allows each subsidiary to choose the bank that provides it with the best service. Thus, Flexsys' decision to use a multibank system can ensure optimal service at its subsidiaries. At the same time, however, its centralized payments network ensures that cash is utilized properly so that it can maximize its value.

TECHNIQUES TO OPTIMIZE CASH FLOWS

Cash inflows can be optimized by the following techniques:

- Accelerating cash inflows
- Minimizing currency conversion costs
- Managing blocked funds
- Managing intersubsidiary cash transfers.

Each of these techniques is discussed in turn.

Accelerating cash inflows

The first goal in international cash management is to accelerate cash inflows, since the more quickly the inflows are received, the more quickly they can be invested or used for other purposes. Several managerial practices are advocated for this endeavour, some of which may be implemented by the individual subsidiaries. First, a corporation may establish **lockboxes** around the world, which are post office boxes to which customers are instructed to send payment. When set up in appropriate locations, lockboxes can help reduce mailing time (**mail float**). A bank usually processes incoming checks at a lockbox on a daily basis. Second, cash inflows can be accelerated by using **preauthorized payments**, which allow a corporation to charge a customer's bank account up to some limit. Both preauthorized payments and lockboxes are also used in a domestic setting. Because international transactions may have a relatively long mailing time, these methods of accelerating cash inflows can be quite valuable for an MNC.

Minimizing currency conversion costs

Another technique for optimizing cash flow movements, **netting**, can be implemented with the joint effort of subsidiaries or by the centralized cash management group. This technique optimizes cash flows by reducing the administrative and transaction costs that result from currency conversion.

EXAMPLE

Mount plc has subsidiaries located in France and in Hungary. Whenever the French subsidiary needs to purchase supplies from the Hungarian subsidiary, it needs to convert euros into Hungary's currency (the forint) to make payment. Hungary's subsidiary must convert its forint into euros when purchasing supplies

(Continued)

from the French subsidiary. Mount plc has instructed both subsidiaries to net their transactions on a monthly basis so that only one net payment is made at the end of each month. By using this approach, both subsidiaries avoid (or at least reduce) the transaction costs of currency conversion.

Over time, netting has become increasingly popular because it offers several key benefits. First, it reduces the number of cross-border transactions between subsidiaries, thereby reducing the overall administrative cost of such cash transfers. Second, it reduces the need for foreign exchange conversion since transactions occur less frequently, thereby reducing the transaction costs associated with foreign exchange conversion. Third, the netting process imposes tight control over information on transactions between subsidiaries. Thus, all subsidiaries engage in a more co-ordinated effort to accurately report and settle their various accounts. Finally, cash flow forecasting is easier since only net cash transfers are made at the end of each period, rather than individual cash transfers throughout the period. Improved cash flow forecasting can enhance financing and investment decisions.

A **bilateral netting system** involves transactions between two units: between the parent and a subsidiary, or between two subsidiaries. A **multilateral netting system** usually involves a more complex interchange among the parent and several subsidiaries. For most large MNCs, a multilateral netting system would be necessary to effectively reduce administrative and currency conversion costs. Such a system is normally centralized so that all necessary information is consolidated. From the consolidated cash flow information, net cash flow positions for each pair of units (subsidiaries, or whatever) are determined, and the actual reconciliation at the end of each period can be dictated. The centralized group may even maintain inventories of various currencies so that currency conversions for the end-of-period net payments can be completed without significant transaction costs.

MNCs commonly monitor the cash flows between their subsidiaries with the use of an intersubsidiary payments matrix.

EXAMPLE

Exhibit 19.2(a) is an example of an intersubsidiary payments matrix that totals each subsidiary's individual payments to each of the other subsidiaries. The first row indicates that the Canadian subsidiary owes the equivalent of £40 000 to the French subsidiary, the equivalent of £90 000 to the Japanese subsidiary, and so on. During this same period, these subsidiaries have also received goods from the Canadian subsidiary, for which payment is due. The second column (under Canada) shows that the Canadian subsidiary is owed the equivalent of £60 000 by the French subsidiary, the equivalent of £100 000 by the Japanese subsidiary, and so on.

Since subsidiaries owe each other, the first step is to charge only the net amounts between each other as illustrated in 19.2 (b) and (c). Since the Canadian subsidiary owes the French subsidiary the equivalent of £40 000 but is owed the equivalent of £60 000 by the French subsidiary, the net payment required is the equivalent of £20 000 from the French subsidiary to the Canadian subsidiary. This is known as bilateral netting.

Further economies can be made through multilateral netting (Exhibit 19.3). Canada owes £40 000 in total and is owed £30 000 in total and therefore can clear net indebtedness by paying £10 000. The Canadian subsidiary would not be especially concerned as to which other subsidiary it paid the net indebtedness. Similarly, France owes a net amount of £20 000.

The only country owed money is the UK, so if Canada pays £10 000, France £20 000 and Switzerland £30 000 all to the UK, all debts will have been

(*Continued*)

EXHIBIT 19.2(a)   Intersubsidiary payments matrix

Payments OWED BY subsidiary located in:	British pound value (in thousands) OWED TO subsidiary located in:				
	Canada	*France*	*Japan*	*Switzerland*	*UK*
Canada	—	40	90	20	40
France	60	—	30	60	50
Japan	100	30	—	20	30
Switzerland	10	50	10	—	50
UK	10	60	20	20	—

EXHIBIT 19.2(b)   Bilateral netting (arrows show the example of Canada)

Payments OWED BY subsidiary located in:	British pound value (in thousands) OWED TO subsidiary located in:				
	Canada	*France*	*Japan*	*Switzerland*	*UK*
Canada	—	40	90	20	40
France	60	—	30	60	50
Japan	100	30	—	20	30
Switzerland	10	50	10	—	50
UK	10	60	20	20	—

EXHIBIT 19.2(c)   Bilateral netting – the net position (arrows show the example of Canada)

Payments OWED BY subsidiary located in:	British pound value (in thousands) OWED TO subsidiary located in:				
	Canada	*France*	*Japan*	*Switzerland*	*UK*
Canada	—	0	0	10	30
France	20	—	0	10	0
Japan	10	0	—	10	10
Switzerland	0	0	0	—	30
UK	0	10	0	0	—

EXHIBIT 19.3 Multilateral netting schedule

Payments OWED BY subsidiary located in:	British pound value (in Thousands) OWED TO subsidiary located in:						
	Canada	France	Japan	Switzerland	UK	Total owed by:	Net payments by:
Canada	—	0	0	10	30	40	10
France	20	—	0	10	0	30	20
Japan	10	0	—	10	10	30	30
Switzerland	0	0	0	—	30	30	0
UK	0	10	0	0	—	10	0
Total owed to:	30	10	0	30	70		
Net owed to:	0	0	0	0	60		60

paid. Thus three payments will have accounted for a payments schedule that at the outset amounted to 20 payments! Note that the bilateral stage could be skipped by simply totalling the columns and rows in the original matrix and making the net payers pay the net receivers.

Managing blocked funds

Cash flows can also be affected by a host government's blockage of funds, which might occur if the government requires all funds to remain within the country in order to create jobs and reduce unemployment. To deal with funds blockage, the MNC may implement the same strategies used when a host country government imposes high taxes. To make efficient use of these funds, the MNC may instruct the subsidiary to set up a research and development division, which incurs costs and possibly generates revenues for other subsidiaries.

Another strategy is to use transfer pricing in a manner that will increase the expenses incurred by the subsidiary. A host country government is likely to be more lenient on funds sent to cover expenses than on earnings remitted to the parent. Most tax treaties require that transfer pricing be conducted at market rates. Therefore a policy of artificially inflated transfer prices resulting in subsidiaries in developing countries paying very high prices for 'services' or 'goods' from Head Office is of dubious legality and ethics.

When subsidiaries are restricted from transferring funds to the parent, the parent may instruct the subsidiary to obtain financing from a local bank rather than from the parent. By borrowing through a local intermediary, the subsidiary is assured that its earnings can be distributed to pay off previous financing. Overall, most methods of managing blocked funds are intended to make efficient use of the funds by using them to cover expenses that are transferred to that country.

> ### EXAMPLE
>
> Wittenberg GmbH, a German-based MNC, has a subsidiary in the Philippines. During a turbulent period, the subsidiary was prevented from exchanging its Philippine pesos into euros to be sent home. Wittenberg held its corporate meeting in Manila so that it could use the pesos to pay the expenses of the meeting (hotel, food, etc.) in pesos. In this way, it was able to use local funds to cover an expense that it would have incurred anyway. Ordinarily, the corporate meeting would have been held in the parent's country, and the parent would have paid the expenses.

Managing intersubsidiary cash transfers

Proper management of cash flows can also be beneficial to a subsidiary in need of funds.

> ### EXAMPLE
>
> Essex Ltd has two foreign subsidiaries called Short Sub and Long Sub. Short Sub needs funds, while Long Sub has excess funds. If Long Sub purchases supplies from Short Sub, it can provide financing by paying for its supplies earlier than necessary. This technique is often called leading. Alternatively, if Long Sub sells supplies to Short Sub, it can provide financing by allowing Short Sub to lag its payments. This technique is called lagging.

The leading or lagging strategy can make efficient use of cash and thereby reduce debt. Some host governments prohibit the practice by requiring that a payment between subsidiaries occur at the time the goods are transferred. Thus, an MNC needs to be aware of any laws that restrict the use of this strategy.

COMPLICATIONS IN OPTIMIZING CASH FLOW

Most complications encountered in optimizing cash flow can be classified into three categories:

- Company-related characteristics
- Government restrictions
- Characteristics of banking systems.

Each complication is discussed in turn.

Company-related characteristics

In some cases, optimizing cash flow can become complicated due to characteristics of the MNC. If one of the subsidiaries delays payments to other subsidiaries for supplies received, the other subsidiaries may be forced to borrow until the payments arrive. A centralized approach that monitors all intersubsidiary payments should be able to minimize such problems.

Government restrictions

The existence of government restrictions can disrupt a cash flow optimization policy. Some governments prohibit the use of a netting system, as noted earlier. In addition, some countries periodically prevent cash from leaving the country, thereby preventing net payments from being made. These problems can arise even for MNCs that do not experience any company-related problems. Countries in Latin America commonly impose restrictions that affect an MNC's cash flows.

Characteristics of banking systems

The abilities of banks to facilitate cash transfers for MNCs vary among countries. Banks in the developed world are advanced in this field, but banks in some other countries do not offer services. MNCs prefer some form of zero-balance account, where excess funds can be used to make payments but earn interest until they are used. In addition, some MNCs benefit from the use of lockboxes. Such services are not available in some countries.

In addition, a bank may not update the MNC's bank account information sufficiently or provide a detailed breakdown of fees for banking services. Without full use of banking resources and information, the effectiveness of international cash management is limited. In addition, an MNC with subsidiaries in, say, eight different countries will typically be dealing with eight different banking systems. Much progress has been made in foreign banking systems in recent years. As time passes and a more uniform global banking system emerges, such problems may be alleviated.

INVESTING EXCESS CASH

Many MNCs have at least £100 million in cash balances across banks in various countries. If they can find a way to earn an extra 1 per cent on those funds, they will generate an extra £1 million each year on cash balances of £100 million. Thus, their short-term investment decision affects the amount of their cash inflows. Their excess funds can be invested in domestic or foreign short-term securities. In some periods, foreign short-term securities will have higher interest rates than domestic interest rates. The differential can be substantial, as illustrated in Exhibit 19.4. However, firms must account for the possible exchange rate movements when assessing the potential yield on foreign investments.

How to invest excess cash

International money markets have grown to accommodate corporate investments of excess cash. MNCs may use international money markets in an attempt to earn higher returns than they can achieve domestically.

Eurocurrency deposits are one of the most commonly used international money market instruments. Many MNCs establish large deposits in various currencies in the eurocurrency market, with eurodollar deposits being the most popular. The dollar volume of eurodollar deposits has more than doubled since 1980. Eurodollar deposits commonly offer MNCs a slightly higher yield than bank deposits in the USA. Though eurodollar deposits still dominate the market, the relative importance of nondollar currencies has increased over time.

In addition to using the eurocurrency market, MNCs can also purchase foreign treasury bills and commercial paper. Improved telecommunications systems have increased access to these securities in foreign markets and allow for a greater degree of integration among money markets in various countries.

EXHIBIT 19.4   Short-term annualized interest rates

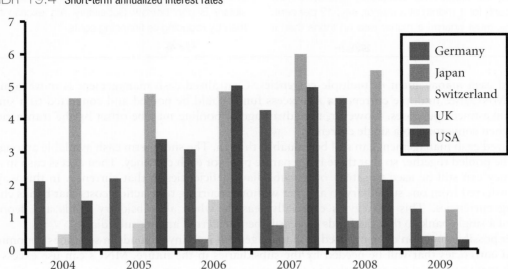

Centralized cash management

An MNC's short-term investing policy can either maintain separate investments for all subsidiaries or employ a centralized approach. Recall that the function of optimizing cash flows can be improved by a centralized approach, since all subsidiary cash positions can be monitored simultaneously. With regard to the investing function, centralization allows for more efficient usage of funds and possibly higher returns. Here the term *centralized* means that excess cash from each subsidiary is pooled until it is needed by a particular subsidiary.

Centralization when subsidiaries use the same currency. To understand the advantages of a centralized system, consider that the rates paid on short-term investments such as bank deposits are often higher for larger amounts. Thus, if two subsidiaries have excess cash of £50 000 each for 1 month, the rates on their individual bank deposits may be lower than the rate they could obtain if they pooled their funds into a single £100 000 bank deposit. In this manner, the centralized (pooling) approach generates a higher rate of return on excess cash.

The centralized approach can also facilitate the transfer of funds from subsidiaries with excess funds to those that need funds.

EXAMPLE

Subsidiary A of Moorhead Ltd has excess cash of £50 000 during the next month, while Subsidiary B of Moorhead Ltd needs to borrow £50 000 for 1 month.

If cash management is not centralized, Subsidiary A may use the £50 000 to purchase a 1-month bank certificate earning, say, 10 per cent (on an annualized

(Continued)

basis). At the same time, Subsidiary B may borrow from a bank for 1 month at a rate of, say, 12 per cent. The bank must charge a higher rate on loans than it offers on deposits. With a centralized approach, Subsidiary B can borrow Subsidiary A's excess funds, thereby reducing its financing costs.

Centralized cash management of multiple currencies. Centralized cash management is more complicated when the MNC uses multiple currencies. All excess funds could be pooled and converted to a single currency for investment purposes. However, the advantage of pooling may be offset by the transaction costs incurred when converting to a single currency.

Centralized cash management can still be valuable, though. The short-term cash available among subsidiaries can be pooled together so that there is a separate pool for each currency. Then excess cash in a particular currency can still be used to satisfy other subsidiary deficiencies in that currency. In this way, funds can be transferred from one subsidiary to another without incurring transaction costs that banks charge for exchanging currencies. This strategy is especially feasible when all subsidiary funds are deposited in branches of a single bank so that the funds can easily be transferred among subsidiaries.

Another possible function of centralized cash management is to invest funds in securities denominated in the foreign currencies that will be needed by the subsidiaries in the future. MNCs can use excess cash to invest cash in international money market instruments so that they can cover any payables positions in specific foreign currencies. If they have payables in foreign currencies that are expected to appreciate, they can cover such positions by creating short-term deposits in those currencies. The maturity of a deposit would ideally coincide with the date at which the funds are needed.

Impact of technology on centralized cash management. International cash management requires timely information across subsidiaries regarding each subsidiary's cash positions in each currency, along with interest rate information about each currency. A centralized cash management system needs a continual flow of information about currency positions so that it can determine whether one subsidiary's shortage of cash can be covered by another subsidiary's excess cash in that currency. Given the major improvements in online technology in recent years, all MNCs can easily and efficiently create a multinational communications network among their subsidiaries to ensure that information about cash positions is continually updated.

EXAMPLE

To understand how such a communications network works, consider Jax plc which creates a cash balances website that specifies the cash balance of every currency for each subsidiary. Near the end of each day, each subsidiary revises the website to provide the latest update of its cash balance for each currency. Each subsidiary also specifies the period of time in which the excess or deficiency will persist. The parent's treasury department monitors the updated data and determines whether any cash needs identified by a subsidiary in a particular currency can be accommodated by another subsidiary that has excess cash in that same currency. The treasury department then emails instructions to the subsidiaries about fund transfers. If it notices that the Canadian subsidiary has an excess of Canadian dollars for the next 26 days, and the Belgian subsidiary needs Canadian dollars tomorrow (but will have inflows of Canadian dollars in 17 days), it provides the following instructions: 'The Canadian subsidiary should transfer C$60 000 to the Belgian subsidiary and will be repaid by the Belgian subsidiary in 17 days.' The fund transfers are essentially short-term loans, so a subsidiary that borrows funds will repay them with interest. The interest charged on a loan creates an incentive for subsidiaries to make their excess cash available and an incentive for subsidiaries with cash deficiencies to return the funds as soon as possible.

The electronic communications network may be more sophisticated than the one described here, but this description illustrates how easy it is for an MNC's parent to continuously monitor the cash balances of each subsidiary and communicate instructions among subsidiaries. The process of transferring funds among subsidiaries may be especially easy when all the MNC's subsidiaries use branches of the same bank. A communications network allows the MNC to make the best use of each subsidiary's cash, which can reduce the amount of external financing needed and reduce the MNC's exchange rate risk.

Determining the effective yield

Firms commonly consider investing in a deposit denominated in a currency with a high interest rate and then converting the funds back to dollars when the deposit matures. This strategy will not necessarily be feasible, since the currency denominating the deposit may depreciate over the life of the deposit. If it does, the advantage of a higher interest rate may be more than offset by the depreciation in the currency representing the deposit.

Consequently, it is the deposit's *effective yield*, not its interest rate, that is most important to the cash manager. The effective yield of a bank deposit considers both the interest rate and the rate of appreciation (or depreciation) of the currency denominating the deposit and can therefore be very different from the quoted interest rate on a deposit denominated in a foreign currency. An example follows to illustrate this point.

EXAMPLE

Quant plc a large UK corporation with £1 000 000 in excess cash, could invest in a 1-year deposit at 6 per cent but is attracted to higher interest rates in Australia. It creates a 1-year deposit denominated in Australian dollars (A$) at 9 per cent. The exchange rate of the Australian dollar at the time of the deposit is £0.45. The British pounds are first converted to A$2 222 222 (since £1 000000 / £0.45 = $2 222 222) and then deposited in a bank.

One year later, Quant receives A$2 422 222, which is equal to the initial deposit plus 9 per cent interest on the deposit (A$2 222 222*1.09). At this time, Quant plc has no use for Australian dollars and converts them into pounds. Assume that the exchange rate at this time is £0.48. The funds will convert to £1 162 667 (computed as A$2 422 222 × £0.48 per A$). Thus, the yield on this investment is:

$$\frac{£1\,162\,667 - £1\,000\,000}{£1\,000\,000} = 0.1627 \text{ or } 16.27\%$$

The high yield is attributed to the relatively high interest rate earned on the deposit, plus the appreciation in the currency denominating the deposit over the investment period.

If the currency had depreciated over the investment period, however, the effective yield to Quant plc would have been less than the interest rate on the deposit and could even have been lower than the interest rate available on UK investments. For example, if the Australian dollar had *depreciated* from £0.45 at the beginning of the investment period to £0.43 by the end of the investment period, Quant plc would have received £1 041 555 (computed as A$2 422 222 × £0.43 per A$). In this case, the yield on the investment to the UK company would have been:

$$\frac{£1\,041\,555 - £1\,000\,000}{£1\,000\,000} = 0.0416 \text{ or } 4.16\%$$

The preceding example illustrates how appreciation of the currency denominating a foreign deposit over the deposit period will force the effective yield to be above the quoted interest rate. Conversely, depreciation will create the opposite effect.

The previous computation of the effective yield on foreign deposits was conducted in a real world setting. A quicker method is shown here:

$$r = (1 + i_f)(1 + e_f) - 1$$

The effective yield on the foreign deposit is represented by r (for simpler notation the r_{eff} from the previous chapter has been dropped here), i_f is the quoted foreign interest rate, and e_f is the percentage change (from the day of deposit to the day of withdrawal) in the value of the currency representing the foreign deposit. In this chapter, the interest rate of concern is the deposit rate on the foreign currency.

EXAMPLE

Given the information for Quant plc, the effective yield on the Australian deposit can be estimated. The term e_f represents the percentage change in the Australian dollar (against the pound) from the date Australian dollars are purchased (and deposited) until the day they are withdrawn (and converted back to pounds). The Australian dollar appreciated from £0.45 to £0.48, or by 6.66 per cent over the life of the deposit [(0.48-0.46)/0.46]. Using this information as well as the quoted deposit rate of 9 per cent, the effective yield to

the UK firm on this deposit denominated in Australian dollars is:

$$\begin{aligned} r &= (1 + i_f)(1 + e_f) - 1 \\ &= (1 + 0.09)(1 + 0.0666) - 1 \\ &= 0.1627 \text{ or } 16.27\% \end{aligned}$$

This estimate of the effective yield corresponds with the return on investment determined earlier for Quant plc.

If the currency had depreciated, Quant plc would have earned an effective yield that was less than the interest rate.

EXAMPLE

In the revised example for Quant plc the Australian dollar depreciated from £0.45 to £0.43, or by 4.44 per cent. Based on the quoted interest rate of 9 per cent and the depreciation of 4.44 per cent, the effective yield is:

$$\begin{aligned} r &= (1 + i_f)(1 + e_f) - 1 \\ &= (1 + 0.09)(1 + -0.0444) - 1 \\ &= 0.0416 \text{ or } 4.16\% \end{aligned}$$

which is the same rate computed earlier for this revised example.

The effective yield can be negative if the currency denominating the deposit depreciates to an extent that more than offsets the interest accrued from the deposit.

> ## EXAMPLE
>
> Northampton Ltd invests in a bank deposit denominated in euros that provides a yield of 9 per cent. The euro depreciates against the dollar by 12 per cent over the 1-year period. The effective yield is:
>
> $$r = (1 + i_f)(1 + e_f) - 1$$
> $$= (1 + 0.09)(1 + -0.12) - 1$$
> $$= -0.0408 \text{ or } -4.08\%$$
>
> This result indicates that Northampton will end up with 4.08 per cent less in funds than it initially deposited.

As with bank deposits, the effective yield on all other securities denominated in a foreign currency is influenced by the fluctuation of that currency's exchange rate. Our discussion will continue to focus on bank deposits for short-term foreign investment, but the implications of the discussion can be applied to other short-term securities as well.

Implications of interest rate parity

Recall that covered interest arbitrage is described as a short-term foreign investment – with a simultaneous forward sale of the foreign currency denominating the foreign investment. One might think that a foreign currency with a high interest rate would be an ideal candidate for covered interest arbitrage. However, such a currency will normally exhibit a forward discount that reflects the differential between its interest rate and the investor's home interest rate. This relationship is based on the theory of interest rate parity. Investors cannot lock in a higher return when attempting covered interest arbitrage if interest rate parity exists.

Even if interest rate parity does exist, short-term foreign investing may still be feasible but would have to be conducted on an uncovered basis (without use of the forward market). That is, short-term foreign investing may result in a higher effective yield than domestic investing, but it cannot be guaranteed.

Use of the forward rate as a forecast

If interest rate parity exists, the forward rate serves as a break-even point to assess the short-term investment decision. When investing in the foreign currency (and not covering the foreign currency position), the effective yield will be more than the domestic yield if the spot rate of the foreign currency after 1 year is more than the forward rate at the time the investment is undertaken. Conversely, the yield of a foreign investment will be lower than the domestic yield if the spot rate of the foreign currency after 1 year turns out to be less than the forward rate at the time the investment is undertaken.

Relationship with the international Fisher effect. When interest rate parity exists, MNCs in the UK that use the forward rate as a predictor of the future spot rate expect the yield on foreign deposits to equal that on UK deposits. Though the forward rate is not necessarily an accurate predictor, it may provide unbiased forecasts of the future spot rate. If the forward rate is unbiased, it does not consistently underestimate or overestimate the future spot rate with equal frequency. Thus, the effective yield on foreign deposits is equal to the domestic yield, on average. MNCs that consistently invest in foreign short-term securities would earn a yield similar on average to what they could earn on domestic securities.

Our discussion here is closely related to the international Fisher effect (IFE). Recall that the IFE suggests that the exchange rate of a foreign currency is expected to change by an amount reflecting the differential between its interest rate and the UK interest rate. The rationale behind this theory is that a high nominal interest rate reflects an expectation of high inflation, which could weaken the currency (according to purchasing power parity).

If interest rate parity exists, the forward premium or discount reflects that interest rate differential and represents the expected percentage change in the currency's value when the forward rate is used as a predictor of the future spot rate. The IFE suggests that firms cannot consistently earn short-term yields on foreign securities that are higher than those on domestic securities because the exchange rate is expected to adjust to the interest rate differential on average. If interest rate parity holds and the forward rate is an unbiased predictor of the future spot rate, we can expect the IFE to hold.

A look back in time reveals that the IFE is supported for some currencies in some periods. Moreover, it may be difficult for an MNC to anticipate when the IFE will hold and when it will not. For virtually any currency, it is possible to identify previous periods when the forward rate substantially underestimated the future spot rate, and an MNC would have earned very high returns from investing short-term funds in a foreign money market security. However, it is also possible to identify other periods when the forward rate substantially overestimated the future spot rate, and the MNC would have earned low or even negative returns from investing in that same foreign money market security.

Conclusions about the forward rate. The key implications of interest rate parity and the forward rate as a predictor of future spot rates for foreign investing are summarized in Exhibit 19.5. This exhibit explains the conditions in which investment in foreign short-term securities is feasible.

EXHIBIT 19.5   Considerations when investing excess cash

Scenario	Implications for investing in foreign money markets
1. Interest rate parity exists.	Covered interest arbitrage is not worthwhile.
2. Interest rate parity exists, and the forward rate is an accurate forecast of the future spot rate.	An uncovered investment in a foreign security is not worthwhile.
3. Interest rate parity exists, and the forward rate is an unbiased forecast of the future spot rate.	An uncovered investment in a foreign security will on average earn an effective yield similar to an investment in a domestic security.
4. Interest rate parity exists, and the forward rate is expected to overestimate the future spot rate.	An uncovered investment in a foreign security is expected to earn a lower effective yield than an investment in a domestic security.
5. Interest rate parity exists, and the forward rate is expected to underestimate the future spot rate.	An uncovered investment in a foreign security is expected to earn a higher effective yield than an investment in a domestic security.
6. Interest rate parity does not exist; the forward premium (discount) exceeds (is less than) the interest rate differential.	Covered interest arbitrage is feasible for investors residing in the home country.
7. Interest rate parity does not exist; the forward premium (discount) is less than (exceeds) the interest rate differential.	Covered interest arbitrage is feasible for foreign investors but not for investors residing in the home country.

Use of exchange rate forecasts

Although MNCs do not know how a currency's value will change over the investment horizon, they can use the formula for the effective yield provided earlier in this chapter and plug in their forecast for the percentage change in the foreign currency's exchange rate (e_f). Since the interest rate of the foreign currency deposit (i_f) is known, the effective yield can be forecasted given a forecast of e_f. This projected effective yield on a foreign deposit can then be compared with the yield when investing in the firm's local currency.

EXAMPLE

Latrobe SA is a French firm with funds available to invest for 1 year. It is aware that the 1-year interest rate on a euro deposit is 11 per cent and the interest rate on an Australian deposit is 14 per cent. Assume that the French firm forecasts that the Australian deposit will depreciate from its current rate of 0.60 euros to 0.594 euros, or a 1 per cent decrease. The expected value for e_f [$E(e_f)$] will therefore be −1 per cent. Thus, the expected effective yield [$E(r)$] on an Australian dollar-denominated deposit is:

$$E(r) = (1 + i_f)(1 + E(e_f)) - 1$$
$$= (1 + 0.14)(1 + -0.01) - 1$$
$$= 0.1286 \text{ or } 12.86\%$$

Thus, this example, investing in an Australian dollar deposit is expected to be more rewarding than investing in a euro-denominated deposit.

Keep in mind that the value for e_f is forecasted and therefore is not known with certainty. Thus, there is no guarantee that foreign investing will truly be more lucrative.

Deriving the value of e_f that equates foreign and domestic yields. From the preceding example, Latrobe may attempt to at least determine what value of e_f would make the effective yield from foreign investing the same as that from investing in a euro deposit. To determine this value, begin with the effective yield formula and solve for e_f as follows:

$$r = (1 + i_f)(1 + e_f) - 1$$
$$(1 + r) = (1 + i_f)(1 + e_f)$$
$$(1 + e_f) = \frac{(1 - r)}{(1 + i_f)}$$
$$e_f = \frac{(1 + r)}{(1 + i_f)} - 1$$

Since the euro deposit rate was 11 per cent in our previous example, that is the rate to be plugged in for r. We can also plug in 14 per cent for i_f, so the break-even value of e_f would be:

$$e_f = \frac{(1 + r)}{(1 + i_f)} - 1$$
$$= \frac{(1 + 0.11)}{(1 + 0.14)} - 1$$
$$= -2.63\%$$

This suggests that the Australian dollar must depreciate by about 2.63 per cent to make the Australian dollar deposit generate the same effective yield as a deposit in euros. With any smaller degree of depreciation, the Australian dollar deposit would be more rewarding. Latrobe SA can use this information when determining whether to invest in a euro or Australian dollar deposit. If it expects the Australian dollar to depreciate by more than 2.63 per cent over the deposit period, it will prefer investing in euros. If it expects the Australian dollar to depreciate by less than 2.63 per cent, or to appreciate, its decision is more complex. If the potential reward from investing in the foreign currency outweighs the risk involved, then the firm should choose that route. The final decision here will be influenced by the firm's degree of risk aversion.

Use of probability distributions. Since even expert forecasts are not always accurate, it is sometimes useful to develop a probability distribution instead of relying on a single prediction. An example of how a probability distribution is applied follows.

EXAMPLE

Opera Ltd (UK) is deciding whether to invest in Australian dollars for 1 year. It finds that the quoted interest rate for the Australian dollar is 14 per cent, and the quoted interest rate for a pound deposit is 11 per cent. It then develops a probability distribution for the Australian dollar's possible percentage change in value over the life of the deposit.

The probability distribution is displayed in Exhibit 19.6. From the first row in the exhibit, we see that there is a 5 per cent probability of a 10 per cent depreciation in the Australian dollar over the deposit's life. If the Australian dollar does depreciate by 10 per cent,

the effective yield will be 2.60 per cent. This indicates that there is a 5 per cent probability that Opera Ltd will earn a 2.60 per cent effective yield on its funds. From the second row in the exhibit, there is a 10 per cent probability of an 8 per cent depreciation in the Australian dollar over the deposit period. If the Australian dollar does depreciate by 8 per cent, the effective yield will be 4.88 per cent, which means there is a 10 per cent probability that Opera will generate a 4.88 per cent effective yield on this deposit.

For each possible percentage change in the Australian dollar's value, there is a corresponding effective

EXHIBIT 19.6   Analysis of investing in a foreign currency

Possible rate of change in the Australian dollar over the life of the investment (e_f)	Probability of occurrence	Effective yield if this rate of change in the Australian dollar does occur (combining the 14% interest rate with the change in the value of the currency)
−10%	5%	$(1.14)[1 + (−0.10)] − 1 = 0.0260$, or 2.60%
−8	10	$(1.14)[1 + (−0.08)] − 1 = 0.0488$, or 4.88%
−4	15	$(1.14)[1 + (−0.04)] − 1 = 0.0944$, or 9.44%
−2	20	$(1.14)[1 + (−0.02)] − 1 = 0.1172$, or 11.72%
+1	20	$(1.14)[1 + (0.01)] − 1 = 0.1514$, or 15.14%
+2	15	$(1.14)[1 + (0.02)] − 1 = 0.1628$, or 16.28%
+3	10	$(1.14)[1 + (0.03)] − 1 = 0.1742$, or 17.42%
+4	5	$(1.14)[1 + (0.04)] − 1 = 0.1856$, or 18.56%
	100%	

yield. Each possible effective yield (third column) is associated with a probability of that yield occurring (second column). An *expected value* of the effective yield of the Australian dollar is derived by multiplying each possible effective yield by its corresponding probability. Based on the information in Exhibit 19.6, the expected value of the effective yield, referred to as $E(r)$, is computed this way:

$$E(r) = 5\%(2.60\%) + 10\%(4.88\%) + 15\%(9.44\%) + 20\%(11.72\%) + 20\%(15.14\%)$$
$$+ 15\%(16.28\%) + 10\%(17.42\%) + 5\%(18.56\%)$$
$$= 0.13\% + 0.488\% + 1.416\% + 2.344\% + 3.028\% + 2.442\% + 1.742\% + 0.928\%$$
$$= 12.518\%$$

Thus, the expected value of the effective yield when investing in Australian dollars is approximately 12.6 per cent.

To further assess the question of which currency to invest in, the information in the second and third columns from Exhibit 19.6 is used to develop a probability distribution in Exhibit 19.7, which illustrates the probability of each possible effective yield that may occur if Opera Ltd invests in Australian dollars. Notice that the UK interest rate (11 per cent) is known with certainty and is included in Exhibit 19.7 for comparison purposes. A comparison of the Australian dollar's probability distribution against the UK interest rate suggests that there is a 30 per cent probability that the UK rate will be more than the effective yield from investing in Australian dollars and a 70 per cent chance that it will be less.

If Opera Ltd invests in a British pound deposit, it knows with certainty the yield it will earn from its investment. If it invests in Australian dollars, its risk is the 5 per cent chance (probability) that the effective yield on the Australian dollar deposit will be 2.60 per cent, or the 10 per cent chance that the effective yield on the Australian dollar deposit will be 4.88 per cent or the 15 per cent chance that the effective yield on Australian dollars will be 9.44 per cent. Each of these possibilities represents a lower return to Opera Ltd than what it would have earned had it invested in a UK deposit. Opera Ltd concludes that the potential return on the Australian deposit is not high enough to compensate for the risk and decides to invest in the UK deposit.

EXHIBIT 19.7 Probability distribution of effective yields

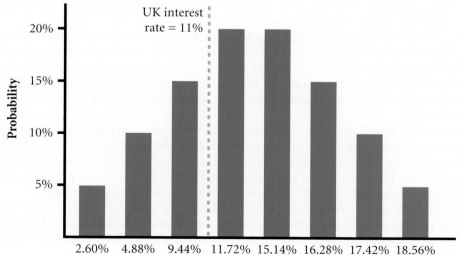

Diversifying cash across currencies

Because an MNC is not sure how exchange rates will change over time, it may prefer to diversify cash among securities denominated in different currencies. Limiting the percentage of excess cash invested in each currency will reduce the MNC's exposure to exchange rate risk.

The degree to which a portfolio of investments denominated in various currencies will reduce risk depends on the currency correlations. Ideally, the currencies represented within the portfolio will exhibit low or negative correlations with each other. When currencies are likely to be affected by the same underlying event, their movements tend to be more highly correlated, and diversification among these types of currencies does not substantially reduce exposure to exchange rate risk.

EXAMPLE

In 1997, the interest rates in most Asian countries were higher than the interest rate in the UK. However, Asian currencies, such as the Indonesian rupiah, the Malaysian ringgit, the South Korean won and the Thailand baht, depreciated by more than 50 per cent against the pound in less than 1 year. Consequently, subsidiaries based outside Asia that attempted to benefit from the high Asian interest rates earned negative effective yields on their investments, so they received less than what they initially invested. Diversification of cash among these currencies was not beneficial in this case because all of the currencies weakened in response to the Asian crisis.

Dynamic hedging

Some MNCs continually adjust their short-term positions in currencies in response to revised expectations of each currency's future movement. They may engage in dynamic hedging, which is a strategy of applying a hedge when the currencies held are expected to depreciate and removing the hedge when the currencies held are expected to appreciate. In essence, the objective is to protect against downside risk while benefiting from the favourable movement of exchange rates.

For example, consider a treasurer of a UK firm who plans to invest in US money market securities. If the British pound begins to decline and is expected to depreciate further, the treasurer may sell dollars forward in the foreign exchange market for a future date at which the dollar's value is expected to turn upward. The treasurer is likely to take out a futures contract as these contracts are easier to buy and sell than forward contracts. If the treasurer is very confident that the dollar will depreciate in the short run, most or all of the position will be hedged.

Now assume that the pound begins to appreciate before the futures contract date. Since the contract will preclude the potential benefits from the pound's appreciation, the treasurer may buy pounds forward to offset the existing futures sale contracts. In this way, the treasurer has removed the existing hedge (or closed out the position). Of course, if the forward rate at the time of the futures purchase exceeds the forward rate that existed at the time of the futures sale, a cost is incurred to offset the hedge.

The treasurer may decide to remove only part of the hedge, offsetting only some of the existing futures sales with futures purchases. With this approach, the position is still partially protected if the pound depreciates further. Overall, the performance from using dynamic hedging is dependent on the treasurer's ability to forecast the direction of exchange rate movements.

SUMMARY

- Each subsidiary of an MNC can assess its cash flows by estimating expected cash inflows and outflows to forecast its balance in each currency. This will indicate whether it will have excess cash to invest or a cash deficiency. The MNC's parent may prefer to use a centralized perspective, which consolidates the cash flow positions of all subsidiaries. In this way, funds can be transferred among subsidiaries to accommodate cash deficiencies at particular subsidiaries.

- The common techniques to optimize cash flows are: (1) accelerating cash inflows, (2) minimizing currency conversion costs, (3) managing blocked funds and (4) implementing intersubsidiary cash transfers.

- The efforts by MNCs to optimize cash flows are complicated by: (1) company-related characteristics, (2) government restrictions and (3) characteristics of banking systems.

- MNCs can possibly achieve higher returns when investing excess cash in foreign currencies that either have relatively high interest rates or may appreciate over the investment period. If the foreign currency depreciates over the investment period, however, this may offset any interest rate advantage of that currency.

CRITICAL DEBATE

Should an MNC's subsidiaries operate their own cash management policies?

Proposition. Yes. Ultimately cash management means that everything is controlled from the centre. Different countries and indeed different products have very different working capital requirements. Centralization could easily lead to poor working capital management and cash flow difficulties.

Opposing view. No. Trade between subsidiaries accounts for a large percentage of world exports, so there has to be co-ordination between subsidiaries. Also customers can be MNC's so co-ordination is also required in debt collection. Also, there are considerable exchange rate savings to be made.

With whom do you agree? Think carefully about the arguments for and against allowing subsidiaries to manage their own cash. What are the problems with each of the arguments? Is there a solution that avoids the main drawbacks?

SELF TEST

Answers are provided in Appendix A at the back of the text.

1 Country X typically has a high interest rate, and its currency is expected to strengthen against the pound over time. Country Y typically has a low interest rate, and its currency is expected to weaken against the pound over time. Both countries have imposed a 'blocked funds' restriction over the next 4 years on the two subsidiaries owned by a UK firm. Which subsidiary will be more adversely affected by the blocked funds, assuming that there are limited opportunities for corporate expansion in both countries?

2 Assume that the Australian 1-year interest rate is 14 per cent. Also assume that the Australian dollar is expected to appreciate by 8 per cent over the next year against the British pound. What is the expected effective yield on a 1-year deposit in Australia by a UK firm?

3 Assume that the 1-year forward rate is used as the forecast of the future spot rate. The Malaysian ringgit's spot rate is £0.12, while its 1-year forward rate is £0.11. The Malaysian 1-year interest rate is 11 per cent. What is the expected effective yield on a 1-year deposit in Malaysia by a UK firm?

4   Assume that the Venezuelan 1-year interest rate is 90 per cent, while the UK 1-year interest rate is 6 per cent. Determine the break-even value for the percentage change in Venezuela's currency (the bolivar) that would cause the effective yield to be the same for a 1-year deposit in Venezuela as for a 1-year deposit in the UK.

5   Assume interest rate parity exists. Would European firms possibly consider placing deposits in countries with high interest rates? Explain.

QUESTIONS AND APPLICATIONS

1   **International cash management.** Discuss the general functions involved in international cash management. Explain how the MNC's optimization of cash flow can distort the profits of each subsidiary.

2   **Netting.** Explain the benefits of netting. How can a centralized cash management system be beneficial to the MNC?

3   **Leading and lagging.** How can an MNC implement leading and lagging techniques to help subsidiaries in need of funds?

4   **International Fisher effect.** If a US firm believes that the international Fisher effect holds, what are the implications regarding a strategy of continually attempting to generate high returns from investing in currencies with high interest rates?

5   **Investing strategy.** Trumpington Ltd has £2 million in excess cash that it has invested in Mexico at an annual interest rate of 60 per cent. The UK interest rate is 9 per cent. By how much would the Mexican peso have to depreciate to cause such a strategy to backfire?

6   **Investing strategy.** Why would a UK firm consider investing short-term funds in euros even when it does not have any future cash outflows in euros?

7   **Covered interest arbitrage.** Granville SA has 2 million euros in cash available for 90 days. It is considering the use of covered interest arbitrage, since the euro's 90-day interest rate is higher than the euro interest rate. What will determine whether this strategy is feasible?

8   **Effective yield.** Corlins plc has £1 million in cash available for 30 days. It can earn 1 per cent on a 30-day investment in the UK. Alternatively, if it converts the pounds to South African rand, it can earn one-and-a-half per cent on a rand deposit. The spot rate of the rand is £0.09. The spot rate 30 days from now is expected to be £0.08. Should Corlins invest its cash in the UK or in South Africa? Explain your answer.

9   **Effective yield.** Rollins plc has £3 million in cash available for 180 days. It can earn 7 per cent on a UK Treasury bill or 9 per cent on a US Treasury bill. The US investment does require conversion of pounds to dollars. Assume that interest rate parity holds and that Rollins believes the 180-day forward rate is a reliable predictor of the spot rate to be realized 180 days from now. Would the British investment provide an effective yield that is below, above, or equal to the yield on the US investment? Explain your answer.

10 **Effective yield.** Repeat question 9, but this time assume that Rollins plc expects the 180-day forward rate of the dollar to substantially overestimate the spot rate to be realized in 180 days.

11 **Effective yield.** Repeat question 9, but this time assume that the Rollins plc expects the 180-day forward rate of the dollar to substantially underestimate the spot rate to be realized in 180 days.

12 **Effective yield.** Assume that the 1-year UK interest rate is 10 per cent and the 1-year US interest rate is 13 per cent. If a UK firm invests its funds in the USA, by what percentage will the dollar have to depreciate to make its effective yield the same as the UK interest rate from the UK firm's perspective?

13 **Investing in a currency portfolio.** Why would a firm consider investing in a portfolio of foreign currencies instead of just a single foreign currency?

14 **Interest rate parity.** Trellis Ltd has determined that the interest rate on euros is 16 per cent while the UK interest rate is 11 per cent for 1-year Treasury bills. The 1-year forward rate of the euro has a discount of 7 per cent. Does interest rate parity exist? Can Trellis achieve a higher effective yield by using covered interest arbitrage than by investing in UK Treasury bills? Explain.

15 **Diversified investments.** Hofstra Ltd has no business outside the UK but has cash invested in six European countries, each of which uses the euro as its local currency. Are Hofstra's short-term investments

well diversified and subject to a low degree of exchange rate risk? Explain.

16 **Investing strategy.** Should McNeese Ltd consider investing funds in Latin American countries where it may expand facilities? The interest rates are high, and the proceeds from the investments could be used to help support the expansion. When would this strategy backfire?

ADVANCED QUESTIONS

18 **Investing in a portfolio.** Poppleton Ltd plans to invest its excess cash in South African rand for 1 year. The 1-year South African interest rate is 19 per cent. The probability of the rand's percentage change in value during the next year is shown below:

Possible rate of change in the South African rand over the life of the investment	Probability of occurrence
−15%	20%
−4	50%
0	30%

What is the expected value of the effective yield based on this information? Given that the UK interest rate for 1 year is 7 per cent, what is the probability that a 1-year investment in pesos will generate a lower effective yield than could be generated if Poppleton Ltd simply invested domestically?

19 **Effective yield of portfolio.** Ithaca (Greece) considers placing 30 per cent of its excess funds in a 1-year Singapore dollar deposit and the remaining 70 per cent of its funds in a 1-year US dollar deposit. The Singapore 1-year interest rate is 15 per cent, while the US 1-year interest rate is 10 per cent.

17 **Impact of a crisis.** Palos SA (Spain) commonly invests some of its excess euros in foreign government short-term securities in order to earn a higher short-term interest rate on its cash. Describe how the potential return and risk of this strategy may be affected by financial crisis.

The possible percentage changes in the two currencies for the next year are forecasted as follows:

Currency	Possible percentage change in the spot rate over the investment horizon	Probability of that change in the spot rate occurring
Singapore dollar	−2%	20%
Singapore dollar	1	60
Singapore dollar	3	20
US dollar	1	50
US dollar	4	40
US dollar	6	10

Given this information, determine the possible effective yields of the portfolio and the probability associated with each possible portfolio yield. Given a 1-year euro interest rate of 8 per cent, what is the probability that the portfolio's effective yield will be lower than the yield achieved from investing in the USA? (Assume that the movements on the two currencies are not correlated.)

PROJECT WORKSHOP

20 **Foreign currency yields.** The Bloomberg website provides interest rate data for many different foreign currencies over various maturities. Its address is http://www.bloomberg.com.

● Go to the section that shows yields for different foreign currencies. Review the 1-year yields of currencies. Assume that you could borrow at a

rate one percentage point above the quoted yield for each currency. Which currency would offer you the highest quoted yield?

● As a cash manager of an MNC based in the UK that has extra pounds that can be invested for 1 year, where would you invest funds for the next year? Explain.

- If you were working for a foreign subsidiary based in Japan and could invest Japanese yen for 1 year until the yen are needed to support local operations, where would you invest the yen? Explain.

DISCUSSION IN THE BOARDROOM

This exercise can be found on our dedicated Course-Mate platform for students.

RUNNING YOUR OWN MNC

This exercise can be found on our dedicated Course-Mate platform for students.

Essays/discussion and articles can be found at the end of Part V.

BLADES PLC CASE STUDY

International cash management

Recall from Chapter 18 that the new Thailand subsidiary of Blades plc received a one-time order from a customer for 120 000 pairs of 'Speedos', Blades' primary product. There is a 6-month lag between the time when Blades needs funds to purchase material for the production of the Speedos and the time when it will be paid by the customer. Ben Holt, Blades' chief financial officer (CFO), has decided to finance the cost by borrowing Thai baht at an interest rate of 6 per cent over a 6-month period. Since the average cost per pair of Speedos is approximately 3500 baht, Blades will borrow 420 million baht. The payment for the order will be used to repay the loan's principal and interest.

Ben Holt is currently planning to instruct the Thai subsidiary to remit any remaining baht-denominated cash flows back to the UK. Just before Blades receives payment for the large order, however, Holt notices that interest rates in Thailand have increased substantially. Blades would be able to invest funds in Thailand at a relatively high interest rate compared to the UK rate. Specifically, Blades could invest the remaining baht-denominated funds for 1 year in Thailand at an interest rate of 15 per cent.

If the funds are remitted back to the UK parent, the excess pound volume resulting from the conversion of baht will either be used to support the UK production of Speedos, if needed, or be invested in the UK. Specifically, the funds will be used to cover the cost of goods sold in the UK manufacturing plant. Since Blades used a significant amount of cash to finance the initial investment to build the plant in Thailand and purchase the necessary equipment, its UK operations are strapped for cash. Consequently, if the subsidiary's earnings are not remitted back to the UK, Blades will have to borrow funds at an interest rate of 10 per cent to support its UK operations. Any funds remitted by the subsidiary that are not used to support UK operations will be invested in the USA at an interest rate of 8 per cent. Holt estimates that approximately 60 per cent of the remitted funds will be needed to

support UK operations and that the remaining 40 per cent will be invested in the UK. Consequently, Holt must choose between two alternative plans. First, he could instruct the Thai subsidiary to repay the baht loan (with interest) and invest any remaining funds in Thailand at an interest rate of 15 per cent. Second, he could instruct the Thai subsidiary to repay the baht loan and remit any remaining funds back to the UK, where 60 per cent of the funds would be used to support UK operations and 40 per cent would be invested at an interest rate of 8 per cent. Assume no income or withholding taxes on the earnings generated in Thailand.

Ben Holt has contacted you, a financial analyst at Blades plc to help him analyze these two options. Holt has informed you that the current spot rate of the Thai baht is £0.015 and that the baht is expected to depreciate by 5 per cent over the coming year. He has provided you with the following list of questions he would like you to answer.

1 There is a trade-off between the higher interest rates in Thailand and the delayed conversion of baht into pounds. Explain what this means.

2 If the net baht received from the Thailand subsidiary are invested in Thailand, how will UK operations be affected?

3 Construct a spreadsheet that compares the cash flows resulting from the two plans. Under the first plan, net baht-denominated cash flows (received today) will be invested in Thailand at 15 per cent for a 1-year period, after which the baht will be converted to pounds. Under the second plan, net baht-denominated cash flows are converted to pounds immediately and 60 per cent of the funds will be used to support UK operations, while 40 per cent are invested in the UK for 1 year at 8 per cent. Which plan is superior given the expectation of the baht's value in 1 year?

SMALL BUSINESS DILEMMA

Cash management at the Sports Exports Company

Ever since Jim Logan began his Sports Exports Company (Ireland), he has been concerned about his exposure to exchange rate risk. The firm produces basketballs and exports them to a distributor in the UK, with the exports being denominated in British pounds. Jim has just entered into a joint venture in the UK in which a British firm produces sporting goods for Jim's firm and sells the goods to the British distributor. The distributor pays pounds to Jim's firm for these products. Jim recently borrowed pounds to finance this venture, which created some cash outflows (interest payments) that partially offset his cash inflows in pounds. The interest paid on this loan is equal to the British Treasury bill rate plus three percentage points. His original business of exporting has been very successful recently, which has caused him to have reve-

nue (in pounds) that will be retained as excess cash. Jim must decide whether to pay off part of the existing British loan, invest the cash in the euro-denominated Treasury bills, or invest the cash in British Treasury bills.

1   If Jim invests the excess cash in UK Treasury bills, would this reduce the firm's exposure to exchange rate risk?

2   Jim decided to use the excess cash to pay off the British loan. However, a friend advised him to invest the cash in British Treasury bills, stating that 'the loan provides an offset to the pound receivables, so you would be better off investing in British Treasury bills than paying off the loan.' Is Jim's friend correct? What should Jim do?

PART 5 Integrative problem

SHORT-TERM ASSET AND LIABILITY MANAGEMENT

Kent plc is a large UK firm with no international business. It has two branches within the UK, a southern branch and a northern branch. Each branch currently makes investing or financing decisions independently, as if it were a separate entity. The northern branch has excess cash of £15 million to invest for the next year. It can invest its funds in Treasury bills denominated in pounds or in any of four foreign currencies. The only restriction enforced by the parent is that a maximum of £5 million can be invested or financed in any foreign currency.

The southern branch needs to borrow £15 million over 1 year to support its UK operations. It can borrow funds in any of these same currencies (although any foreign funds borrowed would need to be converted to pounds to finance the UK operations). The only restriction enforced by the parent is that a maximum equivalent of £5 million can be borrowed in any single currency. A large bank serving the international money market has offered Kent plc the following terms:

Currency	Annual interest rate on deposits	Annual interest rate charged on loans
British pound	6%	9%
Australian dollar	11	14
Canadian dollar	7	10
New Zealand dollar	9	12
Japanese yen	8	11

The parent of Kent plc has created 1-year forecasts of each currency for the branches to use in making their investing or financing decisions:

Currency	Today's spot exchange rate	Forecasted annual percentage change in exchange rate
Australian dollar	11	14
Canadian dollar	7	10
New Zealand dollar	9	12
Japanese yen	8	11

Questions

1   Determine the investment portfolio composition for Kent's northern branch that would maximize the expected effective yield while satisfying the restriction imposed by the parent.

2   What is the expected effective yield of the investment portfolio?

3   Based on the expected effective yield for the portfolio and the initial investment amount of £15 million, determine the annual interest to be earned on the portfolio.

4   Determine the financing portfolio composition for Kent's southern branch that would minimize the expected effective financing rate while satisfying the restriction imposed by the parent.

5   What is the expected effective financing rate of the total amount borrowed?

6   Based on the expected effective financing rate for the portfolio and the total amount of £15 million borrowed, determine the expected loan repayment amount beyond the principal borrowed.

7   When the expected interest received by the northern branch and paid by the southern branch of Kent plc are consolidated, what is the net amount of interest received?

8   If the northern branch and the southern branch worked together, the northern branch could loan its £15 million to the southern branch. Nevertheless, one could argue that the branches could not take advantage of interest rate differentials or expected exchange rate effects among currencies. Given the data provided in this example, would you recommend that the two branches make their short-term investment or financing decisions independently, or should the northern branch lend its excess cash to the southern branch? Explain.

PART 5 Essays/discussion and academic articles

1   Shenk, C.R. (1997) 'The Origins of the Eurodollar Market in London 1955–1963', *Explorations in Economic History*, 35, 221–38. A readable account of financial innovation being a mixture of market competition, margins and governments.

   Q *To what extent is the control of national financial economics out of the hands of any one government? Discuss in relation to international financial arrangements (the euro-dollar market being one such example).*

2   Easterly, W. (2002) 'How Did Heavily Indebted Poor Countries Become Heavily Indebted? Reviewing two decades of debt relief', *World Development*, 30 (10), 1677–96. Required reading for any discussion of debt relief.

   Q *Is it sensible for governments of rich countries to offer better trade terms for poorer countries? Discuss.*

3   Menzler-Hokkanen, I. (1989) 'Countertrade Arrangements in International Trade: A Tool for Creating Competitive Advantage', *Scandinavian Journal of Management*, 5 (2), 105–22. Never mind the date; this paper looks at the relationship between business and finance – a subject that deserves more attention.

   Q *Use Menzler-Hokkanen's article to assess the advantages and disadvantages of using financial schemes to promote trade. In particular, what factors need to be considered?*

4   Durbin, E. and Ng, D. (2005) 'The Sovereign Ceiling and Emerging Market Corporate Bond Spreads', *Journal of International Money and Finance*, 24, 631–49. A look at bond spreads.

   Q *Based on the study by Durbin and Ng, assess the extent to which companies' credit is limited by their home countries' credit worthiness.*

5   De Boyrie, M.E., Pak, S.J. and Zdaniwicz, J.S. (2005) 'Estimating the Magnitude of Capital Flight Due to Abnormal Pricing in International Trade, the Russia-USA Case', *Accounting Forum*, 29, 249–70. Over and under invoicing.

   Q *Describe how the authors establish mispricing of exports and imports. Discuss the effects of such mispricing – is it all bad?*

CHAPTER 20
CONCLUDING
COMMENTS

Textbooks can easily appear to be manuals explaining how things work. This is not their intended role. A textbook is no more than an explanation of the current state of knowledge. As a reminder of this function, it is a valuable exercise to outline the areas where there have been gains and also where further development is required.

THE SIGNIFICANCE OF INTERNATIONAL FINANCIAL MANAGEMENT

One of the most significant facts in the world of finance is to be found in the rather dryly named 'Triennial Central Bank Survey of Foreign Exchange and Derivatives Market Activity in April 2010' published by the Monetary and Economic Department of the Bank for International Settlements. Daily turnover of foreign exchange (spot, swaps and forward transactions) total $4.0 trillion (12 zeros). This is more than the gross national product of the UK. The sheer size of the international markets means that governments cannot pursue their own economic policies without the market's tacit approval. Currency crises that can follow a loss of confidence by the international markets as in Argentina, Asia, Russia, Mexico and elsewhere show how countries can be brought to the point of social and economic chaos. Perhaps the loss of sovereignty by being a member of the Eurozone is not so great. In addition, the World Trade Organization pursues a policy of free-er trade, reducing a government's ability to protect and subsidize its own industries. Multinational companies close factories in one country and open elsewhere with fewer restrictions than ever before. Multinational corporations (MNCs) can borrow in any currency and increasingly invest freely. In sum, MNCs and international financial markets are experiencing greater influence and the nation state less influence over our economic lives.

Understanding the motives for international investment, the reasons for exchange rate changes and the problems of international financial management is becoming a study of the new 'engine' of economic wealth. International financial management is, rather surprisingly, a topic of increasing importance beyond finance.

SUMMARY OF THE BOOK

This book has taken as its reference point, in what is a very broadly defined area, the MNC. The first two parts of the book examined the general international environment and financial environment with particular reference to the exchange rate. It is hoped that the reader now appreciates that currencies and its exchange rate in many ways defines an economy. Within a currency area there has to be a degree of uniformity in economic policy. This is an issue that clearly is at the heart of current European economic difficulties. Different countries within the euro area cannot pursue widely differing policies any more than local governments can within a country. An exchange rate is similar to a border, it defines the 'edge' of the currency area. The exchange rate adjusts so that the currency area is not automatically affected by outside economic events. Turkey can have high inflation when just over the border, Greece has low inflation – they have different currencies.

Understanding the driving forces of the exchange rate is important to MNC management. Dramatic devaluations as in Argentina and Russia directly affect profits; even movements between major currencies can be significant. The international financial markets allow MNCs to manage these risks to much finer levels of detail than in the past. Part III of the book explained the many market and non-market methods that MNCs can now use. Evidence of the increasing management of such risks is to be found in the expanding risk management sections of the Annual Reports of MNCs. MNCs even publish estimated sensitivities of their profits to exchange rate changes.

The final two parts of the book explored the financial management of long-term and short-term assets and liabilities in the international environment. The management and valuation of long-term projects and shorter-term cash flows need to account for international risks. Many of the issues represent an extension of single economy analysis focusing, in particular, on the currency risk analysis that is a feature of most international transactions.

ADVANCES

There have been two major advances in the last 50 years. The first has been the management of risk. Derivatives markets enable MNCs to choose what risk they want to take and how much of that risk the company should bear. Some risk has to be taken, otherwise there will be no return, at least not in an efficient market. Financial markets themselves are now better understood. The risk return trade-off, the concept of market efficiency and the significance of random walks all help MNCs to understand and manage their investments. Markets are now more open and more heavily scrutinized than ever before. The result is arguably greater stability in the marketplace and an improved ability to avoid panics and to adjust to change. Crashes still occur as does hyperinflation, but without the devastating consequences of the earlier part of the twentieth century.

The demand for more tools to manage risk has been occasioned in no small part by the second major advance, the worldwide freeing up of investment, both real and portfolio. Not only has the alternative economic organization of communism been dismantled, but also, restrictions in the capitalist world have largely been lifted. Globalization, investing anywhere and producing anywhere, is now an economic reality.

Together these advances *should* lead to greater economic wealth for all nations in the manner of the law of comparative advantage. For some, the economic depression of 2007 onwards is part of that change, for others it is evidence that this process is not working. Certainly international trade has brought wealth to large areas of the world in a manner that charity could not possibly match. In 1981 according to the World Bank 84 per cent of China's population were in poverty, in 2008 the rate had dropped to 13 per cent. MNCs and the international trade that they promote has in large measure been the vehicle of this remarkable change.

REMAINING ISSUES

International financial management faces a great number of unresolved issues. The international element opens up the often limited economic models to a very diversified environment that is in many ways beyond current analysis. The following does little more than itemize the future challenges.

The early years of certainty over investment analysis have given way to increasing doubt. The Capital Asset Pricing Model in the international environment gives rise to difficult questions. How is the risk of investing in developing countries to be measured? It does not seem right to just apply systematic risk; such investments might even appear safer under such approaches. In a world where portfolios are imperfectly diversified, exactly what index to use and other relevant non-diversifiable risks are not clear. The size of the discount rate to apply is also problematic. The equity premium puzzle highlights the size of the market premium – it appears too large given the historic risk of such investment compared to safer fixed interest instruments.

There has also been a development in the academic modelling of real investment appraisal (projects). Models developed over the last 20 years address issues that seem unavoidable in an international environment. The certainties of net present value (NPV) have given way to an appreciation of the need to include options in the valuation process – opportunities that may or may not be undertaken depending on the outcome. Also, the reaction of competitors, again contingent on the outcome of a project, is significant. For MNCs investing abroad, it is hard to imagine these issues being anything other than very significant. Both options and competitive reactions are not included in the NPV formula. Unfortunately, including such extra considerations has proved to be difficult in the sense that the precision of the actuarial formula of NPV is lost. In its place are either option pricing formulae that are excessively demanding in terms of judgement and calculation; or strategic models, that only seem to require very basic valuation. NPV still has a part to play, but it is no longer seen as providing a reliable invest / do not invest signal. How these three differing perspectives are to be combined is an unresolved issue. A future text on financial management may well include far more on strategy and real options than is currently the case.

There is also the purchasing power parity (PPP) puzzle. Why do exchange rates change so often when the underlying causes appear relatively static? Perhaps the information process itself or the opinion forming process should be included, or indeed, can they be included? Are there aspects of the process that are inherently not measurable?

There are also international economic unresolved issues that are relevant to financial management. International Monetary Fund (IMF) recovery packages (conditionality) are challenged by many as ineffective. The almost permanent status of many countries as less developed countries is depressing. Are free market policies, advocated by the IMF and others, the answer? Or should there be greater management and responsibility? Then there are trade issues. The persistence of price differential between countries is not well understood. The adjustment to the tremendous price differentials between Europe and developing countries such as China and India raises issues about the progress of globalization. To what extent should resources such as labour be transferable?

The global financial crisis shows the illusory nature of much diversification in times of crisis. Crisis management or prevention is still largely an unresolved issue. The contagion effect in a crisis is as virulent as it was in 1982 the start of the Third World Debt crisis. When graphs of changing financial prices are looked at again, more attention is being given to the outliers (the so called 'fat tails'), why are they bunched over time (calm and 'stormy' periods) and why are they more frequent than predicted by random variation? The 'flash crash' in the Dow Jones on May 6 2010 (an echo of October 1987) presents us with the alarming picture of crashes with no real explanation. There are no simple solutions, Robert Engle wryly observed that 'circuit breakers' in the market (a temporary suspension of trade) would be programmed into the trading computer programmes but that they would not necessarily offer greater stability. We do not appear to have models for predicting crises or effective means of preventing them and that is a considerable shortcoming. Even if we did, their reliability would always be suspect, models work until they do not work.

Finally, regulation of the financial markets as evidenced in the repeated financial crises and bubbles is poor. Trade and investment is multinational but regulation is weak at an international level. Competition does not distinguish between a low price due to greater efficiency and a low price due to lower standards. Competing by having lower standards is seen by some as part of a 'race to the bottom'. The implementation of worldwide regulation to match the freedom given to trade and investment is a pressing issue.

It should be said, of course, that with all the above questions, something is known of the answer, it is simply that the answers are evidently incomplete. The list of unresolved issues should, I hope, encourage the reader; there remains much to be done. The need for more development merely supports and explains why international financial management remains a well-rewarded profession.

APPENDIX A
ANSWERS TO
SELF-TEST QUESTIONS

ANSWERS TO SELF-TEST QUESTIONS FOR CHAPTER 1

1   MNCs can capitalize on comparative advantages. *Firm specific advantages:* i) proprietary technology – licensing; ii) managerial/marketing skills – franchising; iii) trademarks; iv) economies of scale; v) large capital requirements. *Internalization advantages:* i) high enforcement costs (e.g. weak legal systems mean that an MNC is better doing it itself rather than contracting with local companies); ii) buyer uncertainty over value; iii) need to control production; iv) tax. *Country specific advantages:* i) natural resources; ii) labour force (cheap); iii) trade barriers (e.g. a US multinational may seek to avoid barriers by producing in the EU). Many MNCs initially penetrate markets by exporting but ultimately establish a subsidiary in foreign markets and attempt to differentiate their products as other firms enter those markets (product cycle theory).

2   The EU seeks to create a unified market across all member states. Common rules and regulations particularly on takeovers will make expansion for MNCs easier, though this area as the text explains remains restrictive. The euro as a common currency across most of the EU except for UK, Denmark and Sweden reduces exchange rates risk for MNCs. The large increase in portfolio investment by MNCs will be helped by this reduction in uncertainty. Eastern European countries also offer opportunities for MNCs to use relatively cheaper resources in countries such as the Czech Republic.

3   First, there is the risk of poor economic conditions in the foreign country. High inflation, a slump in demand, high interest rates, labour and material shortages can all severely affect MNC performance. Second, there is country risk, which reflects the risk of changing government or public attitudes towards the MNC. Funds can be blocked, taxes increased and regulations made more restrictive. Third, there is exchange rate risk, which can affect the financial performance of the MNC in the foreign country.

ANSWERS TO SELF-TEST QUESTIONS FOR CHAPTER 2

1   Each of the economic factors is described, holding other factors constant.

   a   *Inflation.* A relatively high UK inflation rate relative to other countries can make UK goods less attractive to UK and non-UK consumers, which results in fewer UK exports, more UK imports, and a lower (or more negative) current account balance. A relatively low UK inflation rate would have the opposite effect.

b *National income.* A relatively high increase in the UK national income (compared to other countries) tends to cause a large increase in demand for imports and can cause a lower (or more negative) current account balance. A relatively low increase in the UK national income would have the opposite effect.

c *Exchange rates.* A weaker pound tends to make UK products cheaper to non-UK firms and makes non-UK products expensive to UK firms. Thus, UK exports are expected to increase, while UK imports are expected to decrease. However, some conditions can prevent these effects from occurring, as explained in the chapter. Normally, a stronger pound causes UK exports to decrease and UK imports to increase because it makes UK goods more expensive to non-UK firms and makes non-UK goods less expensive to UK firms.

d *Government restrictions.* When the UK government imposes new barriers on imports, UK imports decline, causing the UK balance of trade to increase (or be less negative). When non-UK governments impose new barriers on imports from the UK, the UK balance of trade may decrease (or be more negative). When governments remove trade barriers, the opposite effects are expected.

2 When the UK imposes tariffs on imported goods, foreign countries may retaliate by imposing tariffs on goods exported by the UK. Thus, there is a decline in UK exports that may offset any decline in UK imports.

3 The Asian crisis caused a decline in Asian income levels and therefore resulted in a reduced demand for UK exports. In addition, Asian exporters experienced problems, and some UK importers discontinued their relationships with the Asian exporters. The large devaluations in Asian currencies also attracted speculators looking for investments that appeared to be undervalued.

ANSWERS TO SELF-TEST QUESTIONS FOR CHAPTER 3

1 Sunny Bank is buying US dollars at £0.58 and selling dollars at £0.60. The spread is:

$$\text{Bid/Ask spread} = \frac{\text{Ask rate} - \text{bid rate}}{\text{Ask rate}}$$

$$\text{Bid/Ask spread} = \frac{£0.60 - £0.58}{£0.60}$$

$$= 0.0333$$

$$= 3^{1}/_{3}\%$$

2 Cloudy Bank is buying the new sol at £0.09 and selling the new sol at £0.12. The spread is:

$$\text{Bid/Ask spread} = \frac{\text{Ask rate} - \text{bid rate}}{\text{Ask rate}}$$

$$\text{Bid/Ask spread} = \frac{£0.12 - £0.09}{£0.12}$$

$$= 0.25$$

$$= 25\%$$

Greater currency variability, order costs, inventory costs and competition costs account for the difference in spreads (see chapter).

3 MNCs use the spot foreign exchange market to exchange currencies for immediate delivery. They use the forward foreign exchange market and the currency futures market to lock in the exchange rate at which currencies will be exchanged at a future point in time. They use the currency options market when they wish to lock in the maximum (minimum) amount to be paid (received) in a future currency transaction but maintain flexibility in the event of favourable exchange rate movements.

MNCs use the eurocurrency market to engage in short-term investing or financing or the eurocredit market to engage in medium-term financing. They can obtain long- term financing by issuing bonds in the eurobond market or by issuing stock in the international markets.

ANSWERS TO SELF-TEST QUESTIONS FOR CHAPTER 4

1   Economic factors affect the yen's value as follows:

   a   If UK inflation is higher than Japanese inflation, the UK demand for Japanese goods may increase (to avoid the higher UK prices), and the Japanese demand for UK goods may decrease (to avoid the higher UK prices). Consequently, there is upward pressure on the value of the yen.

   b   If UK interest rates increase and exceed Japanese interest rates, the UK demand for Japanese interest-bearing securities may decline (since UK interest-bearing securities are more attractive), while the Japanese demand for UK interest-bearing securities may rise. Both forces place downward pressure on the yen's value in terms of British pounds.

   c   If UK national income increases more than Japanese national income, the UK demand for Japanese goods may increase more than the Japanese demand for UK goods. Assuming that the change in national income levels does not affect exchange rates indirectly through effects on relative interest rates, the forces should place upward pressure on the yen's value.

   d   If government controls reduce the UK demand for Japanese goods, they place downward pressure on the yen's value. If the controls reduce the Japanese demand for UK goods, they place upward pressure on the yen's value.

   The opposite scenarios of those described here would cause the expected pressure to be in the opposite direction.

2   UK capital flows with Country A may be larger than UK capital flows with Country B. Therefore, the change in the interest rate differential has a larger effect on the capital flows with Country A, causing the exchange rate to change. If the capital flows with Country B are non-existent, interest rate changes do not change the capital flows and therefore do not change the demand and supply conditions in the foreign exchange market.

3   Smart Banking plc should not pursue the strategy because a loss would result, as shown here.

   a   Borrow £5 million.
   b   Convert £5 million to $8 333 333 (based on the spot exchange rate of £0.60 per $).
   c   Invest the dollars at 9 per cent annualized, which represents a return of 0.15 per cent over 6 days, so the dollars received after 6 days = $8 345 833 (computed as $8 333 333 × [1 + 0.0015]).
   d   Convert the dollars received back to UK pounds after 6 days: $8 345 833 = £4 924 041 (based on anticipated exchange rate of £0.59 per dollar after 6 days).
   e   The interest rate owed on the UK pound loan is 0.10 per cent over the 6-day period (0.06 * 6 / 360). Thus, the amount owed as a result of the loan is £5 005 000 (computed as $5 000 000 × [1 + 0.001]).
   f   The strategy is expected to cause a loss of ($4 924 041 − $5 005 000) = −£80 959.

   In approximate terms the value of the dollar is expected to decline *in 6 days* from £0.60 to £0.59 or 1.66 per cent. The difference in the lending and borrowing rate produces a small surplus of 3 per cent (i.e. 9% − 6%) *over 1 year* – this is a 6-day gain of approximately 3% / (360/6) = 0.0005 or 0.05% as in the calculations above. The benefit through borrowing at a low rate and investing at a higher rate is therefore considerably outweighed by expected decline in the value of the dollar.

ANSWERS TO SELF-TEST QUESTIONS FOR CHAPTER 5

1   The net profit to the speculator is £0.65 − £0.60 − £0.06 = −£0.01 per unit.
   The net profit to the speculator for one contract is −£500 (computed as −£.01 × 50 000 units).
   The spot rate would need to be £0.66 for the speculator to break even.
   The net profit to the seller of the call option is +£0.01 per unit calculated as £0.60 − 0.65 + 0.06 = +£0.1.

2   The speculator should exercise the option.
   The net profit to the speculator is (£0.53 − £0.50) − £0.02 = £0.01 per unit.
   The net profit to the seller or writer of the put option is equal and opposite to −£0.01.

3   The premium paid is higher for options with longer expiration dates (other things being equal). Firms may prefer not to pay such high premiums.

ANSWERS TO SELF-TEST QUESTIONS FOR CHAPTER 6

1   Market forces cause the demand and supply of dollars and euros in the foreign exchange market to change, which causes a change in the equilibrium exchange rate. The central banks could intervene to affect the demand or supply conditions in the foreign exchange market, but they would not always be able to off set the changing market forces. For example, if there were a large increase in the US demand for euros and no increase in the supply of euros for sale, the central banks would have to increase the supply of euros in the foreign exchange market to offset the increased demand.

2   The ECB could use direct intervention by selling some of its euro reserves in exchange for dollars in the foreign exchange market. It could also use indirect intervention by attempting to reduce euro interest rates through monetary policy. Specifically, it could increase the euro money supply, which places downward pressure on the euro's interest rates (assuming that inflationary expectations do not change). The lower euro interest rates should discourage foreign investment in the euros area and encourage increased investment by euros investors in foreign securities. Both forces tend to weaken the euro's value.

3   A weaker home currency tends to increase the demand for home goods because the price paid for a specified amount in home currency by foreign firms is reduced. In addition, the home demand for foreign goods is reduced because it takes more home currency to obtain a specified amount in foreign currency once the home currency weakens. Both forces tend to stimulate the home economy and therefore improve productivity and reduce unemployment in the home country.

ANSWERS TO SELF-TEST QUESTIONS FOR CHAPTER 7

1   No. The pound buys \$1.50 or C\$2.00, the indirect or implied rate is \$1.50 = C\$2.00 as they are both worth £1. Taking \$1.50 = C\$2.00 and dividing both sides by 2.00 we have C\$1 = \$0.75 which is the direct rate, so there is no gain to be made through triangular arbitrage.

2   Covered interest arbitrage involves the exchange of pounds for dollars. Assuming that the investors begin with £1 million (the starting amount will not affect the final conclusion), the pounds would be converted to dollars as shown here:

$$£1 \text{ million} \times \$1.50 = \$1\ 500\ 000$$

The US investment would accumulate interest over the 180-day period, resulting in

$$\$1\ 500\ 000 \times 1.03 = \$1\ 545\ 000$$

After 180 days, the dollars would be converted to pounds:

$$\$1\ 545\ 000 \times £0.673 \text{ per dollar} = \$1\ 039\ 785$$

This amount reflects a return of 3.9875 per cent a small amount below the domestic return from an investment of 4 per cent. Thus, UK investors would earn less using the covered interest arbitrage strategy than investing in the UK.

3   No strong reaction. The forward rate premium on the dollar almost matches the interest rate difference between the two countries. It is likely that the margin required by banks, their bid and ask spreads and other transaction costs, would make any attempt to capitalize on those differences unprofitable.

4   If there is a discrepancy in the pricing of a currency, one may capitalize on it by using the various forms of arbitrage described in the chapter. As arbitrage occurs, the exchange rates will be pushed toward their appropriate levels because arbitrageurs will buy an underpriced currency in the foreign exchange market (increase in demand for currency places upward pressure on its value) and will sell an overpriced currency in the foreign exchange market (increase in the supply of currency for sale places downward pressure on its value).

5   The 1-year forward premium on dollars in terms of £s would increase as a UK investor would lose a further 1 per cent relative to UK investment by investing in the USA. So what the UK investor loses in terms of interest rates must be made up for in terms of change in the value of the currency for interest rate parity to hold – the value of the dollar would therefore have to increase by 1 per cent to offset the difference. Arbitrage would, in any case, ensure that the premium would rise.

ANSWERS TO SELF-TEST QUESTIONS FOR CHAPTER 8

1   If the Japanese prices rise because of Japanese inflation, the value of the yen should decline. Thus, even though the importer might need to pay more yen, it would benefit from a weaker yen value (it would pay fewer pounds for a given amount in yen). Thus, there could be an offsetting effect if PPP holds. The real value of the yen would therefore possibly remain the same, the higher inflation on its own increases the real value (purchasing power) of the yen and this is offset by the fall in the value of the yen on the exchange markets. If there were an exact offset there would be no change in the purchasing power of the yen (its real value) and hence no change in the cost of Japanese goods.

2   PPP does not necessarily hold. In our example, Japanese inflation could rise (causing the importer to pay more yen), and yet the Japanese yen would not necessarily depreciate by an offsetting amount, or at all. Therefore, the pound amount to be paid for Japanese supplies could increase over time.

3   High inflation is likely to result in a decline in the value of the Eastern European currencies relative to the euro and the British pound. The higher prices in Eastern Europe will result in a decline in demand for their goods and an increase in demand by resident people and companies in Eastern Europe for euros and UK goods. On the foreign exchange there will be a decline in demand for Eastern European currency and an increase in the supply of Eastern European currency for euros and pounds. Both forces will result in a decline in the value of the Eastern European currencies. These forces will only cease when the decline in the value of Eastern European currencies offsets the change in relative inflation rates. So, using the approximate approach, if inflation in an Eastern European currency had increased by 5 per cent more than in the UK, it is only after a 5 per cent fall in the value of the Eastern European currency that the old levels of demand and supply will be restored. Demand for Eastern European goods will then pick up as they will now cost the same relative to UK and euro goods as before and Eastern European demand for UK and euro goods from Eastern Europe will decline as they become more expensive due to the fall in value of Eastern European currencies and the implied increase in value of the euro and the pound for holders of Eastern European currency.

4   The approximate formula is:

$$e_f = I_h - I_f$$

Taking the UK as the home currency:

$$= 3\% - 4\%$$
$$= 0.01 \text{ or } -1\%$$
$$S_{t+1} = S_t(1 + e_f)$$
$$= £0.57(1 + (-0.01))$$
$$= £0.5643$$

5

$$e_f = (1 + i_h)/(1 + i_f) - 1$$
$$= 1.06/1.11 - 1$$
$$= -0.045 \text{ or } -4.5\% \text{ approximately}$$
$$S_{t+1} = S_t(1 + e_f)$$
$$= £0.30(1 + (-0.045))$$
$$= £0.2865$$

6   According to the IFE, the increase in interest rates by five percentage points reflects an increase in expected inflation by five percentage points.

   If the inflation adjustment occurs, the balance of trade should be affected, as Australian demand for UK goods rises while the UK demand for Australian goods declines. Thus, the Australian dollar should weaken.

If UK investors believed in the IFE, they would not attempt to capitalize on higher Australian interest rates because they would expect the Australian dollar to depreciate over time.

ANSWERS TO SELF-TEST QUESTIONS FOR CHAPTER 9

1 UK 4-year interest rate = $(1 + 0.07)^4 - 1 = 0.3108$ or 31.08%. Indian 4-year interest rate = $(1 + 0.20)^4 - 1 = 1.0736$ or 107.36%.

Percentage change = $(1 + i_h) / (1 + i_f) - 1 = 1.3108/2.0736 - 1 = -0.3679$ or -36.79% decline in the value of the Indian rupee offsetting any gain through higher interest rates.

2 Canadian dollar absolute of $[(0.80 - 0.82) / 0.82] = 2.44\%$

Japanese yen absolute of $[(0.012 - 0.011) / 0.011] = 9.09\%$

The forecast error was larger for the Japanese yen; remember that error is measured as a percentage so the yen error is greater even though the actual number is smaller.

3 Semi-strong-form efficiency would be refuted since the currency values do not adjust immediately to useful public information.

4 The rouble should decline in value relative to the pound, the higher interest rates should compensate for higher inflation and PPP suggests that the rouble should decline in value to maintain the same real value or purchasing power.

5 As the chapter suggests, forecasts of currencies are subject to a high degree of error. Thus, if a project's success is very sensitive to the future value of the bolivar, there is much uncertainty. This project could easily result in losses because the future value of the bolivar is very uncertain.

ANSWERS TO SELF-TEST QUESTIONS FOR CHAPTER 10

1 Managers have more information about the firm's exposure to exchange rate risk than do shareholders and may be able to hedge it more easily than shareholders could. Shareholders may prefer that the managers hedge for them. Also, cash flows may be stabilized as a result of hedging, which can reduce the firm's cost of financing.

2 The Swiss supplies would have less exposure to exchange rate risk because historically the Swiss franc is less volatile with respect to the euro than the South African rand.

3 The US source would be preferable because the firm could use dollar inflows to make payments for material that is imported thus reducing your exposure to changes in the value of the dollar.

4 No. If exports are priced in euros, the euro cash flows received from exporting will depend on US demand, which will be influenced by the dollar's value. If the dollar depreciates, US demand for the French exports is likely to decrease. Exposure would be economic rather than translation exposure as there would now be no need to convert dollars to euros.

5 The earnings generated by the European subsidiaries will be translated to a smaller amount in euro earnings if the euro strengthens. Thus, the consolidated earnings of the Europe-based MNCs will be reduced.

ANSWERS TO SELF-TEST QUESTIONS FOR CHAPTER 11

1 Invest the present value of the payment in A$s by using borrowed money in £s and converting at the current spot rate (thus avoiding exchange rate risk).

The A$s to be invested today is A$3 000 000 / (1 + 0.12) = A$2 678 571

£s needed to be borrowed in order to buy these A$s: A$2 678 571 × £0.45 = £1 205 357. At a cost of 7 per cent, the amount owing after 1 year will be 1 205 357 × 1.07 = £1 289 732.

2 The money market hedge would be more appropriate. Given a forward rate of £0.44, Montclair would need £1 320 000 in 1 year (computed as A$3 000 000 × £0.44) when using a forward hedge. Thus more is needed in 1-year's time using the forward hedge than the money market hedge where the amount needed is only £1 289 732.

3 Montclair could purchase currency call options in Australian dollars. The option could hedge against the possible appreciation of the Australian dollar. Yet, if the Australian dollar depreciates, Montclair could let the option expire and purchase the Australian dollars at the spot rate at the time it needs to send payment. A disadvantage of the currency call option is that a premium must be paid for it. Thus, if Montclair expects the Australian dollar to appreciate over the year, the money market hedge would probably be a better choice, since the flexibility provided by the option would not be useful in this case.

4 Even though Sanibel Ltd is insulated from the beginning of a month to the end of the month, the forward rate will become higher each month because the forward rate moves with the spot rate. Thus, the firm will pay more dollars each month, even though it is hedged during the month. Sanibel will therefore be adversely affected by the consistent appreciation of the dollar. The effect will be lagged (delayed) by 1 month. If the appreciation is very high, it may use the delay gained from hedging to find an alternative supplier.

5 Sanibel Ltd could engage in a series of forward contracts today to cover the payments in each successive month. In this way, it locks in the future payments today and does not have to agree to the higher forward rates that may exist in future months.

6 A put option allows Hopkins Ltd to sell SFs at £0.36, higher than the expected future spot of £0.35 (forward rate). Unfortunately to sell at the rate of £0.36 will cost £0.02 per SF, so the net revenue will be £0.36 − £0.02 = £0.34 less than the expected future spot of £0.35. Hopkins has a difficult choice. Based on expected values, no hedge would be preferable. Such a decision would make sense if Hopkins were risk neutral and would be willing to risk a loss (i.e. below £0.35) for the possible gain (i.e. above £0.35). If Hopkins is satisfied with the forward rate of £0.35 but is worried that it might be less, then a forward contract at the £0.35 rate would be best. If Hopkins is willing to risk the possibility of getting only £0.34 but wants to take the chance that it might rise to above £0.35 then the option would be preferable. The amount of revenue involved (about £700 000 = 2 000 000*0.35)) will affect Hopkins' attitude to risk. If this is a small amount for Hopkins, it is more likely that the company will be risk neutral.

ANSWERS TO SELF-TEST QUESTIONS FOR CHAPTER 12

1 Salem could attempt to purchase its chemicals from US sources. Then, if the $ depreciates, the reduction in dollar inflows resulting from its exports to the USA will be partially offset by a reduction in dollar outflows needed to pay for the imports.

An alternative possibility for Salem is to finance its business with US dollars, but this would probably be a less efficient solution.

2 A possible disadvantage is that Salem would forgo some of the benefits if the $ appreciated over time.

3 We do not know if the subsidiary is a net cost (say a production unit) or a net earner for Neve. If there are net earnings, the consolidated earnings of Neve will be adversely affected if the dollar depreciates because the dollar earnings will be translated into euros for the consolidated income statement at a lower exchange rate. Neve could attempt to hedge its translation exposure by selling dollars forward. If the dollar depreciates, it will benefit from its forward position, which could help offset the translation effect. If the subsidiary is a net cost then the prospect of a depreciating dollar will be attractive as the translated cost will be lower.

4 This argument has no perfect solution. It appears that shareholders penalize the firm for poor earnings even when the reason for poor earnings is a weak euro that has adverse translation effects. It is possible that translation effects could be hedged to stabilize earnings, but Cheriton may consider informing the shareholders that the major earnings changes have been due to translation effects and not to changes in consumer demand or other factors. Perhaps shareholders would not respond so strongly to earnings changes if they were well aware that the changes were primarily caused by translation effects. In an efficient market, one would expect that the investors would appreciate that translation effects do not have direct wealth implications. It is up to Cheriton to point this out to their shareholders in the annual and interim reports.

5   Lincolnshire has no translation exposure since it has no foreign subsidiaries. Kalafa has translation exposure resulting from its subsidiary in Spain.

ANSWERS TO SELF-TEST QUESTIONS FOR CHAPTER 13

1   Possible reasons may include:
   - More demand for the product (depending on the product)
   - Better technology in Europe
   - Fewer restrictions (less political interference)
   - No exchange rate risk
   - Low political risk.

2   Possible reasons may include:
   - More demand for the product (depending on the product)
   - Greater probability of earning superior profits (since many goods have not been marketed in Latin America in the past)
   - Cheaper factors of production (such as land and labour)
   - Possible exploitation of monopolistic advantages.

3   UK firms normally would prefer that the foreign currency appreciate after they invest their pounds to develop the subsidiary. The executive's comment suggests that the euro is too strong and is likely to depreciate in the future, so any UK investment of pounds into Europe will lose value in the future.

4   It may be easier to engage in a joint venture with a Chinese firm, which is already well established in China, to circumvent barriers.

5   The government may attempt to stimulate the economy in this way.

6   The NPV is £7.74m $= -30 + 5/(1.10)^1 + 10/(1.10)^2 + 15/(1.10)^3 + 20/(1.10)^4$
   - Possible steps:
     - Go into partnership with a local company
     - Employ more local managers and employees
     - Set up a research centre
     - Contribute to the local infrastructure (schools etc.)
     - Purchase supplies locally.

ANSWERS TO SELF-TEST QUESTIONS FOR CHAPTER 14

1   First, consumers on the islands could develop a philosophy of purchasing home-made goods. Second, they could discontinue their purchases of exports by Key West Co as a form of protest against specific US government actions. Third, the host governments could impose severe restrictions on the subsidiary shops owned by Key West Co. (including the blockage of funds to be remitted to the US parent).

2   First, the islands could experience poor economic conditions, which would cause lower income for some residents. Second, residents could be subject to inflation that is greater than the increase in their salaries or higher interest rates, which would reduce the income that they could allocate towards exports. Depreciation of the local currencies could also raise the local prices to be paid for goods imported from the USA. All factors described here could reduce the demand for goods exported by Key West Co.

3   Financial risk is probably a bigger concern. The political risk factors are unlikely, based on the product produced by Key West Co. and the absence of substitute products available in other countries. The financial risk factors deserve serious consideration.

4   A terrorist attack usually heightens concern about the particular target (office, underground, a checkpoint). Firms can seek to insure employees or seek safer ways of communicating. There may be cultural elements, and some people will be more affected by such events than others. Projects may be delayed or redesigned or abandoned as a result of revised risk assessments.

5   Rockford Ltd could estimate the *NPV* of the project under three scenarios: (1) include a special tax when estimating cash flows back to the parent (probability of scenario = 15 per cent), (2) assume the project ends in 2 years and include a salvage value when estimating the *NPV* (probability of scenario = 15 per cent), and (3) assume no French government intervention (probability = 70 per cent). This results in three estimates of *NPV*, one for each scenario. This method is less arbitrary than the one considered by Rockford's executives.

ANSWERS TO SELF-TEST QUESTIONS FOR CHAPTER 15

1   A firm may be able to obtain a lower coupon rate by issuing bonds denominated in a different currency. The firm converts the proceeds from issuing the bond to its local currency to finance local operations. Yet, there is exchange rate risk because the firm will need to make coupon payments and the principal payment in the currency denominating the bond. If that currency appreciates against the firm's local currency, the financing costs could become larger than expected. If there are revenues earned in that country then the bond payments will serve to reduce the company's net exposure to the currency and thereby reduce risk.

2   The risk is that the Swiss franc would appreciate against the pound over time since the European subsidiary will periodically convert some of its pound cash flows to francs to make the coupon payments.

The risk here is less than it would be if the proceeds were used to finance UK operations. The Swiss franc's movement against the pound is much more volatile than the Swiss franc's movement against the euro. The Swiss franc and the euro have historically moved in tandem to some degree against the pound, which means that there is a somewhat stable exchange rate between the two currencies.

3   If these firms borrow pounds and convert them to finance local projects, they will need to use their own currencies to obtain pounds and make coupon payments. These firms would be highly exposed to exchange rate risk.

4   Abend GmbH is exposed to exchange rate risk. If the yen appreciates, the number of euros needed for conversion into yen will increase. To the extent that the yen strengthens, Abend's cost of financing when financing with yen could be higher than when financing with euros.

5   The nominal interest rate incorporates expected inflation (according to the Fisher effect). Therefore, the high interest rates reflect high expected inflation. Cash flows can be enhanced by inflation because a given profit margin converts into larger profits as a result of inflation, even if costs increase at the same rate as revenues.

ANSWERS TO SELF-TEST QUESTIONS FOR CHAPTER 16

1   Globalization is the ability of firms to invest anywhere, borrow in any currency, purchase supplies from any country and sell in any country.

2   The potential financial effects of the Green movement are mostly of greater expenditure on:
   ● A waste reduction programme
   ● Obtaining supplies locally from ethical production
   ● Using renewable energy wherever possible
   ● Reducing travel by holding virtual meetings, video conferences, etc
   ● The purchase of carbon credits to offset pollution
   ● Providing acceptable working conditions.

3   Islamic finance principles are:
   ● Belief in divine guidance
   ● Prohibition of interest (riba)

- No banned (haram) investments
- Risk sharing is to be encouraged
- Financing should be based on real assets.

ANSWERS TO SELF-TEST QUESTIONS FOR CHAPTER 17

1   The exporter may not trust the importer or may be concerned that the government will impose exchange controls that prevent payment to the exporter. Meanwhile, the importer may not trust that the exporter will ship the goods ordered and therefore may not pay until the goods are received. Commercial banks can help by providing guarantees to the exporter in case the importer does not pay.

2   In accounts receivable financing, the bank provides a loan to the exporter secured by the accounts receivable. If the importer fails to pay the exporter, the exporter is still responsible to repay the bank. Factoring involves the sales of accounts receivable by the exporter to a so-called factor, so that the exporter is no longer responsible for the importer's payment.

3   The Export Credit Guarantee Department provides medium-term protection against the risk of non-payment by the foreign buyer due to political risk.

ANSWERS TO SELF-TEST QUESTIONS FOR CHAPTER 18

1   If the New Zealand dollar depreciates by 6 per cent, in approximate terms the return will be:

Cost of borrowing in NZ$s	9%
Less gain from reduction in value of the NZ$:	6%
Net cost of borrowing	3%

Using the exact approach: $(1 + 9\%)(1 + -6\%) - 1 = 1.09 \times 0.94 - 1 = 0.0246$ or 2.46%. If the New Zealand dollar appreciates by 3 per cent, in approximate terms the return will be:

Cost of borrowing in NZ$s	9%
Plus loss due to increase in value of the NZ$:	3%
Net cost of borrowing	12%

Using the exact approach: $(1 + 9\%)(1 + 3\%) - 1 = 1.09 \times 1.03 - 1 = 0.01227$ or 12.27%.

2   Using the exact measures: $50\% \times 2.46\% + 50\% \times 12.27\% = 0.5 \times 2.46 + 0.5 \times 12.27 = 7.365\%$.

3   IFE is based on the notion that the cost of borrowing should be the same at home as abroad (there should be one price). Using the approximate method the IFE formula is $e_f = i_h - i_f$ or $i_h = i_f + e_f$. Plugging in the variables from the question we have $8\% = 5\% + e_f$. By inspection we can see that e_f should take the value 3 per cent for the same effective borrowing rate in the UK as in Japan. Using the exact approach IFE states that:

$$e_f = \frac{(1 + i_h)}{(1 + i_f)} - 1 = \frac{1.08}{1.05} - 1 = 0.286 \text{ or } 2.86\% \text{ or about } 3\%$$

4   The expected gain or loss from conversion will be due to the expected difference in the exchange rates

$$Ee_{ff} = (\text{Forward rate} - \text{sport rate})/\text{spot rate}$$
$$= (£0.38 - 0.40)/£0.40 = -0.05 \text{ or } -5$$

The expected effective financing rate $E(r_{eff}) = -5\% + 9\%$ or 4% the exact rate would be $(1 + -5\%)(1 + 9\%) - 1 = 0.0355 = 3.55\%$.

5   The two-currency portfolio will not exhibit much lower variance than either individual currency because the currencies tend to move together. Thus, the diversification effect is limited.

ANSWERS TO SELF-TEST QUESTIONS FOR CHAPTER 19

1   The subsidiary in Country Y should be more adversely affected because the blocked funds will not earn as much interest over time. In addition, the funds will likely be converted to pounds at an unfavourable exchange rate because the currency is expected to weaken over time.

2   Well, when a firm invests abroad the returns are affected by the profitability of the operation in the country and changes in the exchange rate. Using the approximate method, returns from investment in Australia is:

Return on Australian investment in A$s	= 14%
Change in the value of the A$	= 8%
Total return	= 22%

Using the exact method, the return is $(1 + 14\%)(1 + 8\%) - 1 = 0.2312$ or 23.12%.

3   The percentage change in the value of the ringgit is $(£0.11 - £0.12)/£0.12 = -0.0833$ or −8.33%. A 1-year investment earns 11 per cent. Using the approximate method, returns from investment in Malaysia is:

Return on Malaysian investment in ringgit	= 11.00%
Change in the value of the ringgit	= −8.33%
Total return	= 2.67%

Using the exact method, the return is $(1 + 11\%)(1 - 8.33\%) - 1 = 0.017537$ or 1.75%.

4   If the cost of borrowing should be the same at home as abroad according to the IFE (there should be one price). Using the approximate method, the IFE formula is $e_f = i_h - i_f$ or $i_h = i_f + e_f$. Plugging in the variables from the question we have $6\% = 90\% + e_f$, implying that $e_f = -84\%$. But caution should be advised because the approximate method is only suitable for relatively small interest rates. The exact method produces a very different rate:

$$e_f = \frac{(1 + i_h)}{(1 + i_f)} - 1 = \frac{1.06}{1.90} - 1 = -0.4421 \text{ or } -44.21\%$$

As a check, $1.90 \times (1 - 0.4421) - 1 = 0.06001$, a small rounding error of 0.00001. Therefore, the point at which the returns would be the same is if the bolivar depreciates by less than 44.21 per cent against the pound over the 1-year period, a 1-year deposit in Venezuela will generate a higher effective yield than a 1-year UK deposit.

5   Well, only on the basis that interest rate parity will not actually hold. As long as the firms believe that the currency will not depreciate to offset the interest rate advantage, they may consider investing in countries with high interest rates.

APPENDIX B
MATHS AND
STATISTICS SUPPORT

This section is aimed specifically at students who are experiencing difficulties with the more numerate aspects of the text. It therefore offers a more descriptive version of measures used in the text as opposed to the mathematical definitions that are widely available. It may also serve as a quick reminder of basic issues to those who are experiencing less difficulty. Some attention is also paid to linguistic issues which is occasionally a problem where English is a second language. The subjects addressed are:

- Return
- Siegel's paradox
- Rounding
- Indexes
- Variance and standard deviation
- Covariance and correlation
- Regression analysis.

RETURN

A return is the most fundamental measure in finance; it is therefore worth spending a little time considering its various forms. A return is a measure of an increase or decrease over an initial investment. If I invest £100 today and receive £110 tomorrow, I have made a return of £10 in absolute terms. Often the return is expressed as a percentage, this is a price paid by the borrower and received by the investor per £1 invested. So the return on the £100 above is:

$$\text{Return} = \frac{\text{End value} - \text{Start value}}{\text{Start value}}$$

$$\frac{£110 - £100}{£100} = 0.10 \text{ or } 10\%$$

an alternative formulation that is arithmetically the same is:

$$\text{Return} = \frac{\text{End value}}{\text{Start value}} - 1$$

$$\frac{110}{100} - 1 = 0.10 \text{ or } 10\%$$

The end value can be defined as the value at the end of the period of any amount invested (the principal) plus any payments received or paid such as interest rates, dividends and so on. The start period is the start of that particular month if the period is defined as months. So monthly returns for a particular year would start with 1 January to 31 January, followed by 1 February to 28 February, then 1 March to 31 March and so on.

The problem with expressing the return as a percentage is that the investor (or the borrower) does not know how much will be received (or paid). This may sound trivial; surely the investor knows how much he or she is investing? To be told that the investment offers a return of 10 per cent only requires a small calculation to work out that £100 invested will yield a return of £10. But in the text, we deal with investment in several different sources and look at the combined effect. To be told that the £100 will be invested in a combination of one venture that will yield a return of 10 per cent and another that will yield a return of 5 per cent, does not allow calculation of the overall return because we do not know how much is invested in each source. To measure that we need to know the weights, these are the proportions of the total investment in each source. So for two investments A and B the symbols w_A and w_B are used and they should add up to 1.00 so that the whole of the investment is explained. If A yields 10 per cent and B yields 5 per cent and 60 per cent is invested in A implying that 40 per cent is invested in B ($w_A = 0.60$ and $w_B = 0.40$) then the overall return is $0.60 \times 0.10 + 0.40 \times 0.05 = 0.08$ or 8 per cent. For this reason, when looking at portfolio returns and standard deviation when a percentage is being used (e.g. the standard deviation is 3 per cent), we need a weight (w_A etc.) to tell us how much of our total investment will be affected in this way. Note that this is not a problem if returns are expressed in absolute terms, thus one would be told that investment A has a return of £6 and investment B a return of £2 so it is immediately apparent that the overall return is £8 and as a percentage 8 per cent. The problem with absolute returns is that they are unwieldy and difficult to generalize; percentage returns are much more 'portable' between problems.

When measuring return over time, there are three types of measure: simple, compound and continuous. In this text we use the most popular type namely compound. In words this means that interest is earned on interest and is credited per period. So investment of £100 for 1 year at 10 per cent results in a return of £110 (£100 × 1.1); for 2 years it is this amount multiplied by 1.1 or (£100 × 1.1) × 1.1 = £100 × 1.1^2 = £121. Interest rates are expressed as being per year unless otherwise stated. In databases, all interest rates are expressed on an annual basis. So a 30-day rate is not the rate over 30 days but the 30-day rate over 1 year. So, without explanation, converting a 30-day rate quoted as an *annualized* rate to the rate for 30 days is calculated as follows:

30-day rate as quoted in the database: 8 per cent implies a rate over 30 days of:

$$(1 + 8\%)^{30/360} - 1 = (1.08)^{0.833} - 1 = 0.006434 \text{ or } 0.6434\%$$

Note that 360 days rather than 365 days are used in finance, simply because it is easier to halve, quarter and so on. It also results in a slightly higher charge by the lender (the bank) and is a hidden source of profit.

Sometimes a simple approach is used to approximate the amount, thus in the above example, the rate would be given as 8% × (30 / 360) = 0.6667% which is about the same as 0.6434 per cent. Often in financial contracts, such as mortgages, the simple method is used to calculate payments. The reason for its use is because, as you can see from this example, the approximate or simple approach errs on the side of charging a higher amount – once again!

Generally, databases give very short-term, short-term, medium- and long-term rates. When comparing interest rates of different countries, it may not be possible to get an exact match of rates. Instead an approximate time match should be used. So, short-term rates should not be mixed with long-term rates, the risk profile is not comparable. As a rule, very short-term rates (often described as overnight rates) should be avoided altogether – their annualized rates are often very high.

There is frequent reference in the text to using the approximate method when combining returns. Thus, investment abroad results in a return from movement of the currency and a return from investing in the foreign share, bond or whatever. Suppose that these are 3 per cent and 2 per cent respectively. The combined return is $(1.03) \times (1.02) - 1 = 0.0506$ or 5.06% for the exact approach. This is approximately the same as $3\% + 2\% = 5\%$ a method referred to as the approximate approach. This is always true for low rates. But if the rates were 30 per cent and 20 per cent then the exact approach gives $(1.30) \times (1.20) - 1 = 0.56$ or 56% whereas the approximate approach yields $30\% + 20\% = 50\%$. Whether or not these differences matter depends on the context of the question (see rounding below). The benefit of using the approximate method is that the analysis of return is much clearer – it is therefore almost always used in this text.

The language used for return differs according to the context. Where it is an investment in a bank or other financial institution it is an interest rate or borrowing rate. Where the return is from a change in the value of a currency the term premium (a positive return) or discount (a negative return) tends to be used. For convenience, often the term premium is used even where the return is negative, so one can have a negative premium. But the term 'positive discount' is never used! In investment analysis the terms 'discount rate' or 'internal rate of return' are used to describe the interest rate in NPV calculations. When looking to calculate current values in the future, 'interest rate' is used; when valuing future cash flows in the present, the term 'discount rate' is used. Finally, where the investment is in shares, return might be expressed as being a dividend.

SIEGEL'S PARADOX

In all examples the home country has been carefully specified. The reason for this is that in many problems, different answers are obtained depending on which country is designated as being the home country. Also, in triangular arbitrage going around the 'triangle' in one direction does not yield an equal and opposite return from going around in the other direction. The effect is known as Siegel's paradox and is included here as a warning to the student who notices this phenomenon – do not spend hours checking your calculations! Occasionally the paradox is mentioned in the research literature but it is not currently thought to have any consequences. As a practical guide, one has to be aware that taking a different perspective may yield slightly differing results. The example in Exhibit B1 illustrates the effect.

EXHIBIT B1   Siegel's paradox

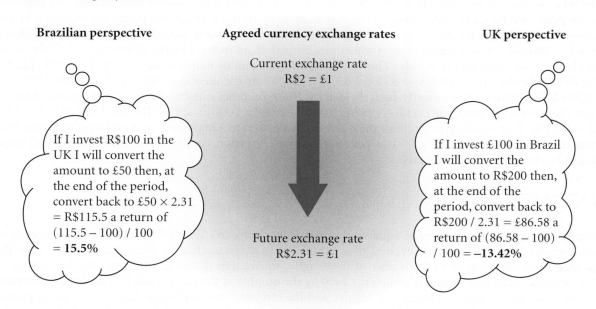

Brazilian perspective

If I invest R$100 in the UK I will convert the amount to £50 then, at the end of the period, convert back to £50 × 2.31 = R$115.5 a return of $(115.5 - 100) / 100$ = **15.5%**

Agreed currency exchange rates

Current exchange rate
R$2 = £1

Future exchange rate
R$2.31 = £1

UK perspective

If I invest £100 in Brazil I will convert the amount to R$200 then, at the end of the period, convert back to R$200 / 2.31 = £86.58 a return of $(86.58 - 100) / 100 = $ **−13.42%**

Notes:
- The paradox is that the returns are not equal and opposite: 15.5% × −1.0 is not equal to −13.42%.
- Note that the percentage change in the exchange rate is the e_f of the equations in the text, therefore the Brazilian perspective will be expecting different inflation and interest rate differences compared to the UK perspective.

ROUNDING

The most common issue raised by students is the problem of rounding. How accurate does one need to be? A practical response is to ask the lecturer. Some lecturers prefer to issue an overall guideline for the course such as all currencies are to be rounded to four decimal places; others prefer to leave the decision to the student.

Rounding is a problem in practice as well as in study. If you are translating $100 into British pounds in 3-months' time and the bureau de change rounds the figure from the actual quote of $1.7277 to the pound to $1.73 saying that 'it is our practice to round the rates for convenience', this will mean that you will receive $100/1.73 = £57.80 instead of £57.88 – not a great difference. However, if the amount is $1 million, then the translated amount should be £578 804 and you receive £578 035 – a difference of £769. Why should their convenience cost you nearly £800? You will note that in illustrating this case, the figures themselves have been rounded, the translated amounts are to the nearest pound! So what is the basis for rounding? The simple answer is that it depends on the context. If rounding does not make much of a difference to the answer, then round. If there is a big difference, then do not round or at least round to a level that will only make a small difference to the answer. If the answer is simply a rate such as the exchange rate, then you again need to look at the context. If the problem concerns exchange rates that vary between, say, 1.7277 and 1.7315 then clearly the answer should be to four decimal places or even five places. If the problem is looking at exchange rates that vary between 1.7 and 1.9 then one decimal place possibly or two just to be safe! Managing the rounding problem forces one to look at the context of the problem and not just to see it as a game of numbers – so it is useful to have to consider the issue.

INDEXES

In international finance, indexes are almost always concerned with prices and exchange rates. Databases contain numerous consumer price indexes and manufacturing price indexes and so on. Price indexes can be thought of as 'average prices'; a change in the index is a measure of the change in the average price and hence a measure of the rate of inflation. So if the index is 3245 at the end of month 1 and 3251 at the end of month 2 and 3576 at the end of month 3, the inflation over the second month is (3251 − 3245) / 3245 = 0.001849 (rounded) or 0.1849 per cent and over the third month is (3576 − 3251) / 3251 = 0.10 or 10%. The type of index to use depends on the problem. If one is dealing with exports then an index of exported goods prices would seem appropriate. Note that in making up the average, the prices are weighted by the importance of the goods. So the price of high revenue earning exports would receive a higher weighting than low revenue items. Finally, there is sometimes a break in an index. Usually this occurs when the index number gets too high and unwieldy. Thus one might have a run of numbers such as: 8329, 9995, 12, 13. The first inflation rate is (9995 − 8329) / 8329 = 20% but the second is NOT (12 − 9995) / 9995 = −100%! The numbers have clearly been divided by 1000, no other number would give a sensible answer. Thus the second inflation rate is (12 − [9995 / 1000]) / [9995 / 1000] = 20%. The third rate is (13 − 12) / 12 = 8.33%. You should always check the numbers being used in a regression or correlation to ensure that there are no odd values such as −100 per cent . Most regression packages will give outliers and these should be checked for just such errors.

VARIANCE AND STANDARD DEVIATION

In words, a variance is the average 'squared distance from the mean'. Where the input data are a history of actual exchange rate changes converted to a column of percentage changes from the past, you take the distance from the mean of each member of the sample, square that distance, and then find the average of these squared difference figures (dividing the total by the number in the sample less 1). Exhibit B2 illustrates this method. Where there is no relevant history and the estimates are of possible future rates accompanied by their probability, the squared differences are multiplied by their probabilities and totalled to get the variance – consult a statistics textbook for further details.

EXHIBIT B2   Prediction of a change in the exchange rate

1 Year	2 Exchange rate: $s to the £1	2a Year on year change, e.g. (1.1 − 1.3) / 1.3 = −0.1538 or −15.38%	3 The difference from the mean: column 2a less 0.119	4 The square of the difference from the mean: square of column 3	
1	1.30				
2	1.10	−0.1538	−0.2728	0.0744	
3	1.80	0.6364	0.5174	0.2677	
4	1.50	−0.1667	−0.2857	0.0816	
5	1.60	0.0667	−0.0523	0.0027	
6	1.94	0.2125	0.0935	0.0087	
Total			0.00000	0.4352	
Average or mean change (e_f) =		0.1190 or 11.9%	Variance =	0.1088	
			Standard deviation =	0.3298	i.e. 32.98%

Notes:
- The variance is the total of column 4 divided by the number of observations less 1 i.e. 5 − 1 = 4. The 1 is concerned with degrees of freedom. So, variance = 0.4352 / (5 − 1) = 0.1088; standard deviation = $\sqrt{(0.1088)}$ = 0.3298.
- Note that this is the expected *change in the exchange rate* (11.9%) and the standard deviation of the *change* (32.98%). So, for example, 1 standard deviation above the change would be as 11.9% + 32.98% = 44.88%.
- The expected change is the same as e_f in the text, it is therefore the object of prediction for IFE and PPP theories.

The variance figure often looks rather odd. To make it more intuitive, the standard deviation or the square root of the figure is often reported. As both measures order the level of spread in the same way (a larger variance implies a larger standard deviation), the term variance is often used in analysis even where the actual figure might be the standard deviation.

There are two types of variance in international finance, the variance in the prediction of an actual exchange rate and the variance in the prediction of *changes* in the exchange rate. Scenario analysis, as used extensively in this text, uses predictions of actual rates and their probability estimated subjectively (i.e. gut feeling).

When looking at databases, the better approach is to estimate *changes* in the exchange rate and look at the average change and measure standard deviation of the changes in the exchange rate - this is illustrated in Exhibit B2. Why are changes in the rate a more interesting measure than the actual rate? The answer is that, as in the Exhibit, the exchange rate from 5-years ago may not now be relevant because of trends and general changes in the economic environment. One does not expect the rate today to suddenly change to the rate 5-years ago! But we can expect the history of *change* to continue. Thus if the exchange rate habitually in the past changed 5 per cent to 10 per cent a year up or down, i.e. was extremely volatile, one can expect such behaviour to continue. So how the figures *changed* 5-years ago is relevant but not the actual figures. Variance of course does itself change over time and statistical methods do attempt to predict such change (the ARCH and GARCH models); but in using just the variance of past changes in exchange rate as a prediction of the future variance we assume no change. The statistical models do no more than try to identify patterns in past variances in the exchange rate, they do not provide explanatory variables such as interest rates to attempt to explain why variance changes – the actual reasons for changes in variance is not well understood. With regard to predicting the actual rate, using the current rate is better than using past actual rates because market efficiency states that the current rate includes all information about the future value discounted into the current price. So the rate 5-years ago is definitely inferior. Also, although we cannot predict the actual future rate any better than the present price, the variance remains predictable. Unfortunately, one cannot make a profit from such knowledge because we do not know the direction of the change! Note also that IFE and PPP talk about the change in the value of a currency, not the actual rate. Again they take the current rate and current information as the starting point as advocated by market efficiency.

There are many other measures of spread. One could take the absolute distance from the mean, that is, simply treat the negatives as positives and take the average absolute distance from the mean. Alternatively, one could take just the downside variance, that is, the variance that is unattractive. With regard to a cost, unattractive variance would be the variation above the mean; with revenue, the variation below the mean would be unattractive. In practice, such measures do not produce radically different conclusions about the spread of a distribution. The advantage of the variance over the other methods is that the variance is more tractable - easier to manipulate in measurement generally - hence variance has remained the most popular measure of spread.

COVARIANCE AND CORRELATION

A covariance is, as the name suggests, a measure as to what extent two variables co-vary or move together. Exhibit B3 illustrates the relation between the measure and one's intuitive idea of varying together. Notice that the measure is taken in relation to the mean, i.e. being above or below the mean. The calculation of the measure of covariance is in practice much like the measure of variance and is illustrated in Exhibit B4. The correlation, also illustrated in Exhibit B4, is based on the same differences from the mean of the dollar and the euro (columns 3 and 5). The effect of dividing the total differences (column 6) by the standard deviations of the two exchange rates is to map the covariance on to a scale of −1 for perfect negative correlation, to 0 for absolutely no correlation and no relationship, to the highest value of 1 representing perfect positive correlation. A correlation is therefore a covariance mapped on to a −1 to 1 scale. Thus one may talk about a correlation when in fact the measure used is a covariance. As with standard deviations and variances the terms relate to the same phenomenon measures in a slightly different way. The spreadsheet for Exhibit B4 is available on the CourseMate.

EXHIBIT B3 Intuitive measures of covariance

High covariance / correlation	Change in exchange rate 2 is *above* the average change	Change in exchange rate 2 is *below* the average change
When change in exchange rate 1 is *above* the average change	Often	Rarely
When change in exchange rate 1 is *below* the average change	Rarely	Often
Low covariance / correlation	**Change in exchange rate 2 is *above* the average change**	**Change in exchange rate 2 is *below* the average change**
When change in exchange rate 1 is *above* the average change	Sometimes	Occasionally
When change in exchange rate 1 is *below* the average change	Occasionally	Sometimes

EXHIBIT B4   Correlation and covariance

1	2	2a	3	4	4a	5	6
Year	Exchange rate: $s to the £1 (dollar)	Year on year % change (dollar)	Column 2a less average (0.119) (dollar)	Exchange rate: euros to the £1 (euro)	Year on year % change (euro)	Column 2a less −0.0302 (euro)	Squared differences columns 3 × 5 (both)
1	1.30			1.40			
2	1.10	−0.1538	−0.2728	1.10	−0.2143	−0.1841	0.0502
3	1.80	0.6364	0.5174	1.20	0.0909	0.1211	0.0627
4	1.50	−0.1667	−0.2857	1.20	0.0000	0.0302	−0.0086
5	1.60	0.0667	−0.0523	0.90	−0.2500	−0.2198	0.0115
6	1.94	0.2125	0.0935	1.10	0.2222	0.2525	0.0236
Total			0.00000			0.00000	0.1394
Average		0.119			−0.0302		
Standard deviation		0.3298			0.2009		
Number of observations = 5							
Covariance = 0.1394 / 5 = 0.02788							
Correlation = 0.0279 / (0.3298 * 0.2009) × 5/4 = 0.526							

Notes:
- The ratio 5/4 reverses the degrees of freedom in the standard deviation. This adjustment becomes less important the larger the sample (normally the sample would be much larger in project work, 30 at least). For, say, 50 observations the adjustment would be 50/49. Note that the degree of freedom is only an issue for actual observations. If the variables are estimated using probabilities, the degree of freedom is not relevant.
- To understand covariance, examine columns 3 and 5. For the dollar exchange rate (column 3) (−0.1538 − 0.119) = −0.2728, is quite a bit below the mean, whereas for the euro the same calculation is (−0.2143 − −0.0302) = −0.1841, again below the mean by the second highest amount. So the two currencies moved in similar directions in year 2. In year 3 they were both above their means, the dollar rate at 0.5174 and the euro at 0.1211, so the pound rose in value that year against both currencies. In year 4, however, there was a sharp fall in the dollars to the pound, the change was −0.2857 below the mean. Whereas for the euro there was no change, the no change was 0.0302 above the average negative change of that amount. So with respect to the mean the two currencies moved in opposite directions against the pound − note the resultant negative value in column 6 with the effect of lowering the covariance and correlation. In year 5 the change in the currencies are both less than the average change but the euro is more negative and in year 6 the changes are both more than the average changes and the euro is again moving rather more in that it is more positive than the dollar. It may be rather surprising that the changes in the euro value against the pound are on average less than the dollar (the standard deviation is less). The cause is the early years where the dollar is changing rather more, in particular the year 3 change is very large for the dollar. If the covariance is being used to apply to future changes then there may be concerns that the change in year 3 is exceptional and not relevant to predicting the future. The point here is that these exchange rate movements are more than mere numbers but rather are the result of economic events.

REGRESSION ANALYSIS

Businesses often use **regression analysis** to measure relationships between variables when establishing policies. For example, a firm may measure the historical relationship between its sales and its accounts receivable. Using the relationship detected, it can then forecast the future level of accounts receivable based on a forecast of sales. Alternatively, it may measure the sensitivity of its sales to economic growth and interest rates so that it can assess how susceptible its sales are to future changes in these economic variables. In international financial management, regression analysis can be used to measure the sensitivity of a firm's performance (using sales or earnings or stock price as a proxy) to currency movements or economic growth of various countries.

Regression analysis can be applied to measure the sensitivity of exports to various economic variables. This example will be used to explain the fundamentals of regression analysis. The main steps involved in regression analysis are:

1   Specifying the regression model

2   Compiling the data

3   Estimating the regression coefficients

4   Interpreting the regression results.

Specifying the regression model

Assume that your main goal is to determine the relationship between percentage changes in UK exports to Australia (called $CEXP$) and percentage changes in the value of the Australian dollar (called $CAUS$). The percentage change in the exports to Australia is the **dependent variable** since it is hypothesized to be influenced by another variable. Although you are most concerned with how $CAUS$ affects $CEXP$, the regression model should include any other factors (or so-called **independent variables**) that could also affect $CEXP$. Assume that the percentage change in the Australian GDP (called $CGDP$) is also hypothesized to influence $CEXP$. This factor should also be included in the regression model. To simplify the example, assume that $CAUS$ and $CGDP$ are the only factors expected to influence $CEXP$. Also assume that there is a lagged impact of one-quarter. In this case, the regression model can be specified as:

$$CEXP_t = b_0 + b_1(CAUS_{t-1}) + b_2(CGDP_{t-1}) + \mu_t$$

Where:

b_0 = a constant
b_1 = regression coefficient that measures the sensitivity of $CEXP_t$ to $CAUS_{t-1}$
b_2 = regression coefficient that measures the sensitivity of $CEXP_t$ to $CGDP_{t-1}$
μ_t = an error term.

The t subscript represents the time period. Some models, such as this one, specify a *lagged impact* of an independent variable on the dependent variable and therefore use a $t-1$ subscript. In this case we assume that the lag is 1 year, the size of the lag is usually an educated guess. The lag could be 2 or even 3 years. Often researchers simply try differing lag patterns to see which is best by including independent variables with lags of 1, 2 and 3 years in the same equation, in this case $CAUS_{t-1}$ $CAUS_{t-2}$ and $CAUS_{t-3}$ and $CGDP_{t-1}$ $CGDP_{t-2}$ and $CGDP_{t-3}$.

Compiling the data

Now that the model has been specified, data on the variables must be compiled. The data are normally input on to a spreadsheet or into a statistics package such as *MINITAB* or *SPSS* as follows:

Period (t)	CEXP	CAUS	CGDP
1	0.03	−0.01	0.04
2	−0.01	0.02	−0.01
3	−0.04	0.03	−0.02
4	0.00	0.02	−0.01
5	0.01	−0.02	0.02
.	...	...	...
.	...	...	...
.	...	...	...

The column specifying the period is not necessary to run the regression model but is normally included in the data set for convenience.

The difference between the number of observations (periods) and the regression coefficients (including the constant) represents the degrees of freedom. For our example, assume that the data covered 40 quarterly periods. The degrees of freedom for this example are $40 - 3 = 37$. As a general rule, analysts usually try to have at least 30 degrees of freedom when using regression analysis.

Some regression models involve only a single period. For example, if you desired to determine whether there was a relationship between a firm's degree of international sales (as a percentage of total sales) and earnings per share of MNCs, last year's data on these two variables could be gathered for many MNCs, and regression analysis could be applied. This example is referred to as cross-sectional analysis, whereas our original example is referred to as a time series analysis.

Estimating the regression coefficients

Once the data have been input into a data file, a regression program can be applied to the data to estimate the regression coefficients. There are various packages such as *Excel* and *Lotus, MINITAB* and *SPSS* that contain a regression analysis application.

The actual steps conducted to estimate regression coefficients are somewhat complex. For more details on how regression coefficients are estimated, see any econometrics textbook.

Interpreting the regression results

Most regression programs provide estimates of the regression coefficients along with additional statistics. For our example, assume that the following information was provided by the regression programme:

	Estimated regression coefficient	Standard error of regression coefficient	t-Statistic
Constant	0.002		
$CAUS_{t-1}$	80	0.32	2.50
$CGDP_{t-1}$	0.36	0.50	0.72
Coefficient of determination (R^2)	$= 0.33$		

The independent variable $CAUS_{t-1}$ has an estimated regression coefficient of 0.80, which suggests that a 1 per cent increase in $CAUS$ is associated with an 0.8 per cent increase in the dependent variable $CEXP$ in the following period. This implies a positive relationship between $CAUS_{t-1}$ and $CEXP_t$. The independent variable $CGDP_{t-1}$ has an estimated coefficient of 0.36, which suggests that a 1 per cent increase in the Australian GDP is associated with a 0.36 per cent increase in $CEXP$ one period later.

Many analysts attempt to determine whether a coefficient is statistically different from zero. Regression coefficients may be different from zero simply because of a coincidental relationship between the independent variable of concern and the dependent variable. One can have more confidence that a negative or positive relationship exists by testing the coefficient for significance. A *t*-test is commonly used for this purpose as follows:

Test to determine whether $CAUS_{t-1}$ affects $CEXP_t$

$$\text{Calcuated } t\text{-statistic} = \frac{\text{Estimated regression coefficient for } CAUS_{t-1}}{\text{Standard error of the regression coefficient}} = \frac{0.80}{0.42} = 2.50$$

Test to determine whether $CGDP_{t-1}$ affects $CEXP_t$

$$\text{Calcuated } t\text{-statistic} = \frac{\text{Estimated regression coefficient for } CGDP_{t-1}}{\text{Standard error of the regression coefficient}} = \frac{0.36}{0.50} = 0.72$$

The calculated t-statistic is sometimes provided within the regression results. It can be compared to the critical t-statistic to determine whether the coefficient is significant. The critical t-statistic is dependent on the degrees of freedom and confidence level chosen. For our example, assume that there are 37 degrees of freedom and that a 95 confidence level is desired. The critical t-statistic would be 2.02, which can be verified by using a t-table from any statistics book. Based on the regression results, the coefficient of $CAUS_{t-1}$ is significantly different from zero, while $CGDP_{t-1}$ is not. This implies that one can be confident of a positive relationship between $CAUS_{t-1}$ and $CEXPt$, but the positive relationship between $CGDP_{t-1}$ and $CEXP_t$ may have occurred simply by chance.

In some particular cases, one may be interested in determining whether the regression coefficient differs significantly from some value other than zero. In these cases, the t-statistic reported in the regression results would not be appropriate. See an econometrics text for more information on this subject.

The regression results indicate the **coefficient of determination** (called R^2) of a regression model, which measures the percentage of variation in the dependent variable that can be explained by the regression model. R^2 can range from 0 to 100 per cent. It is unusual for regression models to generate an R^2 of close to 100 per cent, since the movement in a given dependent variable is partially random and not associated with movements in independent variables. In our example, R^2 is 33 per cent, suggesting that one-third of the variation in $CEXP$ can be explained by movements in $CAUS_{t-1}$ and $CGDP_{t-1}$.

Some analysts use regression analysis to forecast. For our example, the regression results could be used along with data for $CAUS$ and $CGDP$ to forecast $CEXP$. Assume that $CAUS$ was 5 per cent in the most recent period, while $CGDP$ was −1 per cent in the most recent period. The forecast of $CEXP$ in the following period is derived from inserting this information into the regression model as follows:

$$\begin{aligned}
CEXP_t &= b_0 + b_1(CAUS_{t-1}) + b_2(CGDP_{t-1}) \\
&= 0.0002 + (0.80)(0.05) + (0.36)(-0.01) \\
&= 0.002 + 0.0400 - 0.0036 \\
&= 0.0420 - 0.0036 \\
&= 0.0384
\end{aligned}$$

Thus, the $CEXP$ is forecasted to be 3.84 per cent in the following period. Some analysts might eliminate $CGDP_{t-1}$ from the model because its regression coefficient was not significantly different from zero. This would alter the forecasted value of $CEXP$.

When there is not a lagged relationship between independent variables and the dependent variable, the independent variables must be forecasted in order to derive a forecast of the dependent variable. In this case, an analyst might derive a poor forecast of the dependent variable even when the regression model is properly specified, if the forecasts of the independent variables are inaccurate.

As with most statistical techniques, there are some limitations that should be recognized when using regression analysis. These limitations are described in most statistics and econometrics textbooks.

Using Excel to conduct regression analysis

Various software packages are available to run regression analysis. The following example is run on Excel to illustrate the ease with which regression analysis can be run. Assume that a firm wants to assess the influence of changes in the value of the Australian dollar on changes in its exports to Australia based on the following data:

Period	Value (in thousands of dollars) of exports to Australia	Average exchange rate of Australian dollar over that period
1	110	$0.50
2	125	0.54
3	130	0.57
4	142	0.60
5	129	0.55
6	113	0.49
7	108	0.46
8	103	0.42
9	109	0.43
10	118	0.48
11	125	0.49
12	130	0.50
13	134	0.52
14	138	0.50
15	144	0.53
16	149	0.55
17	156	0.58
18	160	0.62
19	165	0.66
20	170	0.67
21	160	0.62
22	158	0.62
23	155	0.61
24	167	0.66

Assume that the firm applies the following regression model to the data:

$$CEXP = b_0 + b_1 \, CAUS + \mu$$

Where:

$CEXP$ = percentage change in the firm's export value from one period to the next
$CAUS$ = percentage change in the average exchange rate from one period to the next
μ = error term.

The first step is to input the data for the two variables in two columns on a file using Excel. Then, the data can be converted into percentage changes. This can be easily performed with a COMPUTE statement in the third column (Column C) to derive *CEXP* and another COMPUTE statement in the fourth column (Column D) to derive *CAUS*. These two columns will have a blank first row, since the percentage change cannot be computed without the previous period's data. Many students already know how to use Excel to create a COMPUTE statement and to apply the COMPUTE statement to all of the data within a column. If you do not, ask a friend for a few minutes of help.

Once you have derived *CEXP* and *CAUS* from the raw data, you can perform regression analysis as follows. On the main menu, select 'Tools'. This leads to a new menu, in which you should click on 'Data Analysis'. Next to the 'Input Y Range', identify the range C2 to C24 for the dependent variable as C2:C24. Next to the 'Input X Range', identify the range D2 to D24 for the independent variable as D2:D24. The 'Output Range' specifies the location on the screen where the output of the regression analysis should be displayed. In our example, F1 would be an appropriate location, representing the upper-left section of the output. Then, click on OK, and within a few seconds, the regression analysis will be complete. For our example, the output is listed below:

SUMMARY OUTPUT

Regression statistics	
Multiple R	0.8852
R Square	0.7836
Adjusted R Square	0.7733
Standard error	2.9115
Observations	23.0000

ANOVA

	Df	SS	MS	F	Significance F
Regression	1.0000	644.6262	644.6262	76.0461	0.0000
Residual	21.0000	178.0125	8.4768		
Total	22.0000	822.6387			

	Coefficients	Standard error	t-Statistic	P-value
Intercept	0.7951	0.6229	1.2763	0.2158
X Variable 1	0.8678	0.0995	8.7204	0.0000

	Lower 95%	Upper 95%	Lower 95.0%	Upper 95.0%
Intercept	−0.5004	2.0905	−0.5004	2.0905
X Variable 1	0.6608	1.0747	0.6608	1.0747

The estimate of the so-called slope coefficient is about 0.8678, which suggests that every 1 per cent change in the Australian dollar's exchange rate is associated with a 0.8678 per cent change (in the same direction) in the firm's exports to Australia. The *t*-statistic is also estimated to determine whether the slope coefficient is significantly different from zero. Since the standard error of the slope coefficient is about 0.0995, the *t*-statistic is $(0.8678 / 0.0995) = 8.72$. This would imply that there is a significant relationship between *CAUS* and *CEXP*. The R-Square statistic suggests that about 78 per cent of the variation in *CEXP* is explained by *CAUS*. The correlation between *CEXP* and *CAUS* can also be measured by the correlation coefficient, which is the square root of the R-Square statistic.

If you have more than one independent variable (multiple regression), you should place the independent variables next to each other in the file. Then, for the X-RANGE, identify this block of data. The output for the regression model will display the coefficient, standard error and *t*-statistic for each of the independent variables. For multiple regression, the R-Square statistic is interpreted as the percentage of variation in the dependent variable explained by the model as a whole.

Using the 'COPY' command

If you need to repeat a particular type of computation for several different cells, you can use the COPY command. You must highlight the particular cells in which the computation is performed and instruct Excel (by clicking on 'Edit') to copy that computation to whatever range of cells you desire.

GLOSSARY

absolute advantage When one country is more efficient at producing a product or service than its trading partner.

absolute form of purchasing power parity This theory explains how inflation differentials affect exchange rates. It suggests that prices of two products of different countries should be equal when measured by a common currency.

accounts receivable financing Indirect financing provided by an exporter for an importer by exporting goods and allowing for payment to be made at a later date.

agency problem Conflict of goals between a firm's shareholders and its managers.

airway bill Receipt for a shipment by air, which includes freight charges and title to the merchandise.

all-in-rate Rate used in charging customers for accepting banker's acceptances, consisting of the discount interest rate plus the commission.

American depository receipts (ADRs) Certificates representing ownership of foreign stocks, which are traded on stock exchanges in the USA.

appreciation Increase in the value of a currency.

arbitrage Action to capitalize on a discrepancy in quoted prices; in many cases, there is no investment of funds tied up for any length of time.

Asian dollar market Market in Asia in which banks collect deposits and make loans denominated in US dollars.

ask price Price at which a trader of foreign exchange (typically a bank) is willing to sell a particular currency.

balance of payments Statement of inflow and outflow payments for a particular country.

balance of trade Difference between the value of merchandise exports and merchandise imports.

balance on goods and services Balance of trade, plus the net amount of payments of interest and dividends to foreign investors and from investment, as well as receipts and payments resulting from international tourism and other transactions.

Bank for International Settlements (BIS) Institution that facilitates co-operation among countries involved in international transactions and provides assistance to countries experiencing international payment problems.

Bank Letter of Credit Policy Policy that enables banks to confirm letters of credit by foreign banks supporting the purchase of US exports.

banker's acceptance Bill of exchange drawn on and accepted by a banking institution; it is commonly used to guarantee exporters that they will receive payment on goods delivered to importers.

barter Exchange of goods between two parties without the use of any currency as a medium of exchange.

Basel Accord Agreement among country representatives in 1988 to establish standardized risk-based capital requirements for banks across countries.

bid price Price that a trader of foreign exchange (typically a bank) is willing to pay for a particular currency.

bid/ask spread Difference between the price at which a bank is willing to buy a currency and the price at which it will sell that currency.

bilateral netting system Netting method used for transactions between two units.

bill of exchange (draft) Promise drawn by one party (usually an exporter) to pay a specified amount to another party at a specified future date, or upon presentation of the draft.

bill of lading Document serving as a receipt for shipment and a summary of freight charges and conveying title to the merchandise.

call See *currency call option.*

call option on real assets Project that contains an option of pursuing an additional venture.

capital account Account reflecting changes in country ownership of long-term and short-term financial assets.

carry cost The net cost incurred by owning an asset from the time of the spot quote to the time of the forward rate. This normally includes the cost of borrowing, storage costs (where relevant) and any revenue earned by possession of the underlying asset over the time period.

carryforwards Tax losses that are applied in a future year to offset income in the future year.

cash management Optimization of cash flows and investment of excess cash.

central exchange rate Exchange rate established between two European currencies through the European Monetary System arrangement; the exchange rate between the two currencies is allowed to move within bands around that central exchange rate.

centralized cash management Policy that consolidates cash management decisions for all MNC units, usually at the parent's location.

clearing house An organization that matches buyers and sellers and ensures creditworthiness.

coefficient of determination Measure of the percentage variation in the dependent variable that can be explained by the independent variables when using regression analysis.

co-financing agreements Arrangement in which the World Bank participates along with other agencies or lenders in providing funds to developing countries.

commercial invoice Exporter's description of merchandise being sold to the buyer.

commercial letters of credit Trade-related letters of credit.

comparative advantage Theory suggesting that a degree of specialization by countries in products and services where they are more efficient than other products and services they produce will increase worldwide production.

compensation Arrangement in which the delivery of goods to a party is compensated for by buying back a certain amount of the product from that same party.

compensatory financing facility (CFF) Facility that attempts to reduce the impact of export instability on country economies.

consignment Arrangement in which the exporter ships goods to the importer while still retaining title to the merchandise.

contingency graph Graph showing the net profit to a speculator in currency options under various exchange rate scenarios.

counterpurchase Exchange of goods between two parties under two distinct contracts expressed in monetary terms.

countertrade Sale of goods to one country that is linked to the purchase or exchange of goods from that same country.

country risk Characteristics of the host country, including political and financial conditions, that can affect an MNC's cash flows.

covered interest arbitrage Investment in a money market security with a simultaneous ... sale of the currency denominating that security.

cross-border factoring Factoring by a network of factors across borders. The exporter's factor can contact correspondent factors in other countries to handle the collections of accounts receivable.

cross exchange rate Exchange rate between currency A and currency B, given the values of currencies A and B with respect to a third currency.

cross-hedging Hedging an open position in one currency with a hedge on another currency that is highly correlated with the first currency. This occurs when for some reason the common hedging techniques cannot be applied to the first currency. A cross-hedge is not a perfect hedge, but can substantially reduce the exposure.

cross-sectional analysis Analysis of relationships among a cross section of firms, countries or some other variable at a given point in time.

currency board System for maintaining the value of the local currency with respect to some other specified currency.

currency call option Contract that grants the right to purchase a specific currency at a specific price (exchange rate) within a specific period of time.

currency cocktail bond Bond denominated in a mixture (or cocktail) of currencies.

currency diversification Process of using more than one currency as an investing or financing strategy. Exposure to a diversified currency portfolio typically results in less exchange rate risk than if all of the exposure was in a single foreign currency.

currency futures contract Contract specifying a standard volume of a particular currency to be exchanged on a specific settlement date.

currency put option Contract granting the right to sell a particular currency at a specified price (exchange rate) within a specified period of time.

currency swap Agreement to exchange one currency for another at a specified exchange rate and date. Banks commonly serve as intermediaries between two parties who wish to engage in a currency swap.

current account Broad measure of a country's international trade in goods and services.

daily settlement Payment between holders and sellers of a derivative based on movements of the underlying asset price before the maturity date.

Delphi technique Collection of independent opinions without group discussion by the assessors who provide the opinions; used for various types of assessments (such as country risk assessment).

dependent variable Term used in regression analysis to represent the variable that is dependent on one or more other variables.

depreciation Decrease in the value of a currency.

derivative A financial instrument (or tradable promise) whose value depends on the price of another asset. An option is a derivative, its value depends on the price of the underlying asset, e.g. a foreign currency. A futures contract is the other main example.

devaluation A reduction in the value of a currency.

developing country The IMF considers per capita income levels, the extent of integration into the world financial community and the range of exports i.e., not a single export country.

direct foreign investment (DFI) Investment in real assets (such as land, buildings or even existing plants) in foreign countries.

Direct Loan Program Programme in which the Ex-Im Bank offers fixed-rate loans directly to the foreign buyer to purchase US capital equipment and services.

direct quotations Exchange rate quotations representing the value measured by the number of dollars per unit.

discount As related to forward rates, represents the percentage amount by which the forward rate is less than the spot rate.

disintermediation Direct exchange between buyer and seller without the marketplace as an intermediary.

documentary collections Trade transactions handled on a draft basis.

documents against acceptance Situation in which the buyer's bank does not release shipping documents to the buyer until the buyer has accepted (signed) the draft.

documents against payment Shipping documents that are released to the buyer once the buyer has paid for the draft.

dollarization The use of a foreign currency (normally the dollar) as the national currency.

double-entry book-keeping Accounting method in which each transaction is recorded as both a credit and a debit.

draft (bill of exchange) Unconditional promise drawn by one party (usually the exporter) instructing the buyer to pay the face amount of the draft upon presentation.

dumping Selling products overseas at unfairly low prices (a practice perceived to result from subsidies provided to the firm by its government).

dynamic hedging Strategy of hedging in those periods when existing currency positions are expected to be adversely affected, and remaining unhedged in other periods when currency positions are expected to be favourably affected.

economic exposure Degree to which a firm's present value of future cash flows can be influenced by exchange rate fluctuations.

economies of scale Achievement of lower average cost per unit by means of increased production.

effective yield Yield or return to an MNC on a short-term investment after adjustment for the change in exchange rates over the period of concern.

efficient frontier Set of points reflecting risk-return combinations achieved by particular portfolios (so-called efficient portfolios) of assets.

equilibrium exchange rate Exchange rate at which demand for a currency is equal to the supply of the currency for sale.

eurobanks Commercial banks that participate as financial intermediaries in the Eurocurrency market.

eurobonds Bonds sold in countries other than the country represented by the currency denominating them.

euro-clear Telecommunications network that informs all traders about outstanding issues of eurobonds for sale.

euro-commercial paper Debt securities issued by MNCs for short-term financing.

eurocredit loans Loans of 1 year or longer extended by eurobanks.

eurocredit market Collection of banks that accept deposits and provide loans in large denominations and in a variety of currencies. The banks that comprise this market are the same banks that comprise the eurocurrency market; the difference is that the eurocredit loans are longer term than so-called eurocurrency loans.

eurocurrency market Collection of banks that accept deposits and provide loans in large denominations and in a variety of currencies.

eurodollar Term used to describe US dollar deposits placed in banks located in Europe.

euronotes Unsecured debt securities issued by MNCs for short-term financing.

European Central Bank (ECB) Central bank created to conduct the monetary policy for the countries participating in the single European currency, the euro.

European Currency Unit (ECU) Unit of account representing a weighted average of exchange rates of member countries within the European Monetary System.

exchange rate mechanism Method of linking European currency values with the European Currency Unit (ECU).

exercise price (strike price) Price (exchange rate) at which the owner of a currency call option is allowed to buy a specified currency; or the price (exchange rate) at which the owner of a currency put option is allowed to sell a specified currency.

Export-Import Bank (Ex-Im Bank) Bank that attempts to strengthen the competitiveness of US industries involved in foreign trade.

factor Firm specializing in collection on accounts receivable; exporters sometimes sell their accounts receivable to a factor at a discount.

factoring Purchase of receivables of an exporter by a factor without recourse to the exporter.

financial account A term used by the International Monetary Fund to replace all but minor entries in the capital account.

Financial Institution Buyer Credit Policy Policy that provides insurance coverage for loans by banks to foreign buyers of exports.

Fisher effect Theory that nominal interest rates are composed of a real interest rate and anticipated inflation.

fixed exchange rate system Monetary system in which exchange rates are either held constant or allowed to fluctuate only within very narrow boundaries.

floating rate notes (FRNs) Provision of some eurobonds, in which the coupon rate is adjusted over time according to prevailing market rates.

foreign bond Bond issued by a borrower foreign to the country where the bond is placed.

foreign direct investment Long-term participation by one country into another country, usually involving participation in management, joint-venture, transfer of technology and expertise.

foreign exchange market Market composed primarily of banks, serving firms and consumers who wish to buy or sell various currencies.

foreign investment risk matrix (FIRM) Graph that displays financial and political risk by intervals, so that each country can be positioned according to its risk ratings.

forfaiting Method of financing international trade of capital goods.

forward contract Agreement between a commercial bank and a client about an exchange of two currencies to be made at a future point in time at a specified exchange rate.

forward discount Percentage by which the forward rate is less than the spot rate; typically quoted on an annualized basis.

forward premium Percentage by which the forward rate exceeds the spot rate; typically quoted on an annualized basis.

forward rate Rate at which a bank is willing to exchange one currency for another at some specified date in the future.

franchising Agreement by which a firm provides a specialized sales or service strategy, support assistance and possibly an initial investment in the franchise in exchange for periodic fees.

freely floating exchange rate system Monetary system in which exchange rates are allowed to move due to market forces without intervention by country governments.

full compensation An arrangement in which the delivery of goods to one party is fully compensated for by buying back more than 100% of the value that was originally sold.

fundamental forecasting Forecasting based on fundamental relationships between economic variables and exchange rates.

General Agreement on Tariffs and Trade (GATT) Agreement allowing for trade restrictions only in retaliation against illegal trade actions of other countries.

hedge To insulate a firm from exposure to exchange rate fluctuations.

hostile takeovers Acquisitions not desired by the target firms.

imperfect market The condition where, due to the costs to transfer labour and other resources used for production, firms may attempt to use foreign factors of production when they are less costly than local factors.

import/export letters of credit Trade-related letters of credit.

independent variable Term used in regression analysis to represent the variable that is expected to influence another (the 'dependent') variable.

indirect quotations Exchange rate quotations representing the value measured by the number of units per dollar.

interbank market Market that facilitates the exchange of currencies between banks.

Interest Equalization Tax (IET) Tax imposed by the US government in 1963 to discourage US investors from investing in foreign securities.

interest rate parity (IRP) Theory specifying that the forward premium (or discount) is equal to the interest rate differential between the two currencies of concern.

interest rate parity (IRP) line Diagonal line depicting all points on a four-quadrant graph that represent a state of interest rate parity.

interest rate parity theory Theory suggesting that the forward rate differs from the spot rate by an amount that reflects the interest differential between two currencies.

interest rate swap Agreement to swap interest payments, whereby interest payments based on a fixed interest rate are exchanged for interest payments based on a floating interest rate.

International Bank for Reconstruction and Development (IBRD) Bank established in 1944 to enhance economic development by providing loans to countries. Also referred to as the World Bank.

International Development Association (IDA) Association established to stimulate country development; it was especially suited for less prosperous nations, since it provided loans at low interest rates.

International Financial Corporation (IFC) Firm established to promote private enterprise within countries; it can provide loans to and purchase stock from corporations.

international Fisher effect Theory specifying that a currency's exchange rate will depreciate against another currency when its interest rate (and therefore expected inflation rate) is higher than that of the other currency.

international Fisher effect (IFE) line Diagonal line on a graph that reflects points at which the interest rate differential between two countries is equal to the percentage change in the exchange rate between their two respective currencies.

International Monetary Fund (IMF) Agency established in 1944 to promote and facilitate international trade and financing.

international mutual funds (IMFs) Mutual funds containing securities of foreign firms.

intracompany trade International trade between subsidiaries that are under the same ownership.

irrevocable letter of credit Letter of credit issued by a bank that cannot be cancelled or amended without the beneficiary's approval.

J-curve effect Effect of a weaker dollar on the US trade balance, in which the trade balance initially deteriorates; it only improves once US and non-US importers respond to the change in purchasing power that is caused by the weaker dollar.

joint venture Venture between two or more firms in which responsibilities and earnings are shared.

lagging Strategy used by a firm to stall payments, normally in response to exchange rate projections.

law of one price Generally in markets, one product should have one price. If there are two prices then arbitrage is possible to profit from the difference (buying at the lower price and selling at the higher price). In international finance the application is to internationally traded products. When converted to a common currency, the prices should be the same. The difference in price is usually ascribed to market imperfections and differences in tastes.

leading Strategy used by a firm to accelerate payments, normally in response to exchange rate expectations.

letter of credit (L/C) Agreement by a bank to make payments on behalf of a specified party under specified conditions.

licensing Arrangement in which a local firm in the host country produces goods in accordance with another firm's (the licensing firm's) specifications; as the goods are sold, the local firm can retain part of the earnings.

locational arbitrage Action to capitalize on a discrepancy in quoted exchange rates between banks.

lockbox Post office box number to which customers are instructed to send payment.

London Interbank Offer Rate (LIBOR) Interest rate commonly charged for loans between Eurobanks.

long-term forward contracts Contracts that state any exchange rate at which a specified amount of a specified currency can be exchanged at a future date (more than 1 year from today). Also called long forwards.

Louvre Accord 1987 agreement between countries to attempt to stabilize the value of the US dollar.

macroassessment Overall risk assessment of a country without considering the MNC's business.

mail float Mailing time involved in sending payments by mail.

maintenance margin The minimum balance required by a clearing house or similar organization to cover for potential contract losses.

managed float Exchange rate system in which currencies have no explicit boundaries, but central banks may intervene to influence exchange rate movements.

margin requirement Deposit placed on a contract (such as a currency futures contract) to cover the fluctuations in the value of that contract; this minimizes the risk of the contract to the counterparty.

market-based forecasting Use of a market-determined exchange rate (such as the spot rate or forward rate) to forecast the spot rate in the future.

marking to market Daily settlement as if the current day's price of a derivative is the price at maturity.

Medium-term Guarantee Program Programme conducted by the Ex-Im Bank in which commercial lenders are encouraged to finance the sale of US capital equipment and services to approved foreign buyers; the Ex-Im Bank guarantees the loan's principal and interest on these loans.

microassessment The risk assessment of a country as related to the MNC's type of business.

mixed forecasting Development of forecasts based on a mixture of forecasting techniques.

money market hedge Use of international money markets to match future cash inflows and outflows in a given currency.

multibuyer policy Policy administered by the Ex-Im Bank that provides credit risk insurance on export sales to many different buyers.

Multilateral Investment Guarantee Agency (MIGA) Agency established by the World Bank that offers various forms of political risk insurance to corporations.

multilateral netting system Complex interchange for netting between a parent and several subsidiaries.

multinational restructuring Restructuring of the composition of an MNC's assets or liabilities.

negotiable bill of lading (B/L) Contract that grants title of merchandise to the holder, which allows banks to use the merchandise as collateral.

net operating loss carrybacks Practice of applying losses to offset earnings in previous years.

net operating loss carryforwards Practice of applying losses to offset earnings in future years.

netting Combining of future cash receipts and payments to determine the net amount to be owed by one subsidiary to another.

net transaction exposure Consideration of inflows and outflows in a given currency to determine the exposure after offsetting inflows against outflows.

nominal exchange rate The exchange rate as announced in the newspapers.

non-deliverable forward contracts (NDFs) Like a forward contract, represents an agreement regarding a position in a specified currency, a specified exchange rate and a specified future settlement date, but does not result in delivery of currencies. Instead, a payment is made by one party in the agreement to the other party based on the exchange rate at the future date.

non-sterilized intervention Intervention in the foreign exchange market without adjusting for the change in money supply.

notional value An agreed amount that is not traded directly between two parties but is used as the basis for other calculations.

ocean bill of lading Receipt for a shipment by boat, which includes freight charges and title to the merchandise.

open account transaction Sale in which the exporter ships the merchandise and expects the buyer to remit payment according to agreed-upon terms.

over-hedging Hedging an amount in a currency larger than the actual transaction amount.

parallel bonds Bonds placed in different countries and denominated in the respective currencies of the countries where they are placed.

parallel loan Loan involving an exchange of currencies between two parties, with a promise to re-exchange the currencies at a specified exchange rate and future date.

partial compensation An arrangement in which the delivery of goods to one party is partially compensated for by buying back a certain amount of product from the same party.

pegged exchange rate Exchange rate whose value is pegged to another currency's value or to a unit of account.

perfect forecast line A 45° line on a graph that matches the forecast of an exchange rate with the actual exchange rate.

petrodollars Deposits of dollars by countries that receive dollar revenues due to the sale of petroleum to other countries; the term commonly refers to OPEC deposits of dollars in the Eurocurrency market.

Plaza Accord Agreement among country representatives in 1985 to implement a co-ordinated programme to weaken the dollar.

political risk Political actions taken by the host government or the public that affect the MNC's cash flows.

portfolio The holding of a variety of assets (invest-ments) usually of varying risk and return.

preauthorized payment Method of accelerating cash inflows by receiving authorization to charge a customer's bank account.

premium As related to forward rates, represents the percentage amount by which the forward rate exceeds the spot rate. As related to currency options, represents the price of a currency option.

prepayment Method that exporter uses to receive payment before shipping goods.

price-elastic Sensitive to price changes.

privatization Conversion of government-owned businesses to ownership by shareholders or individuals.

product cycle theory Theory suggesting that a firm initially establishes itself locally and expands into foreign markets in response to foreign demand for its product; over time, the MNC will grow in foreign markets; after some point, its foreign business may decline unless it can differentiate its product from competitors.

Project Finance Loan Program Programme that allows banks, the Ex-Im Bank, or a combination of both to extend long-term financing for capital equipment and related services for major projects.

purchasing power parity (PPP) line Diagonal line on a graph that reflects points at which the inflation differential between two countries is equal to the percentage change in the exchange rate between the two respective currencies.

purchasing power parity (PPP) theory Theory suggesting that exchange rates will adjust over time to reflect the differential in inflation rates in the two countries; in this way, the purchasing power of consumers when purchasing domestic goods will be the same as that when they purchase foreign goods.

put See *currency put option*.

put option on real assets Project that contains an option of divesting part or all of the project.

quota Maximum limit imposed by the government on goods allowed to be imported into a country.

random walk A process whereby prices move up or down from the previous price in an unpredictable way. There is no memory further back than the previous price (i.e. no trend). Sometimes referred to as a process with a 'unit root'.

real cost of hedging The additional cost of hedging when compared to not hedging (a negative real cost would imply that hedging was more favourable than not hedging).

real exchange rate The purchasing power of a currency against another currency, usually measured as an index against a basket of currencies (the real effective exchange rate index). An increase in the real exchange rate of a home currency implies that the currency is able to buy more goods than the foreign currency due to an increase in the value of the home currency and/or higher inflation in the home currency, this also implies that home currency goods are more expensive.

real interest rate Nominal (or quoted) interest rate minus the inflation rate.

real options Implicit options on real assets.

regression analysis Statistical technique used to measure the relationship between variables and the sensitivity of a variable to one or more other variables.

regression coefficient Term measured by regression analysis to estimate the sensitivity of the dependent variable to a particular independent variable.

re-invoicing centre Facility that centralizes payments and charges subsidiaries fees for its function; this can effectively shift profits to subsidiaries where tax rates are low.

relative form of purchasing power parity Theory stating that the rate of change in the prices of products should be somewhat similar when measured in a common currency, as long as transportation costs and trade barriers are unchanged.

Semi-strong-form efficient Description of foreign exchange markets, implying that all relevant public information is already reflected in prevailing spot exchange rates.

sensitivity analysis Technique for assessing uncertainty whereby various possibilities are input to determine possible outcomes.

separation theorem Investors' risk preferences are separated from that of their investments by virtue of the marketplace.

settlement date The date at which a financial contract ends.

simulation Technique for assessing the degree of uncertainty. Probability distributions are developed for the input variables; simulation uses this information to generate possible outcomes.

Single-Buyer Policy Policy administered by the Ex-Im Bank that allows the exporter to selectively insure certain transactions.

Single European Act Act intended to remove numerous barriers imposed on trade and capital flows between European countries.

Small Business Policy Policy providing enhanced coverage to new exporters and small businesses.

snake Arrangement established in 1972, whereby European currencies were tied to each other within specified limits.

special drawing rights (SDRs) Reserves established by the International Monetary Fund; they are used only for intergovernment transactions; the SDR also serves as a unit of account (determined by the values of five major currencies) that is used to denominate some internationally traded goods and services, as well as some foreign bank deposits and loans.

spot market Market in which exchange transactions occur for immediate exchange.

spot rate Current exchange rate of currency.

standby letter of credit Document used to guarantee invoice payments to a supplier; it promises to pay the beneficiary if the buyer fails to pay.

sterilized intervention Intervention by the Federal Reserve in the foreign exchange market, with simultaneous intervention in the Treasury securities markets to offset any effects on the dollar money supply; thus, the intervention in the foreign exchange market is achieved without affecting the existing dollar money supply.

straddle Combination of a put option and a call option.

strike price *See exercise price.*

strong-form efficient Description of foreign exchange markets, implying that all relevant public information and private information is already reflected in prevailing spot exchange rates.

Structural Adjustment Loan (SAL) Facility Facility established in 1980 by the World Bank to enhance a country's long-term economic growth through financing projects.

supplier credit Credit provided by the supplier to itself to fund its operations.

syndicate Group of banks that participate in loans.

syndicated eurocredit loans Loans provided by a group (or syndicate) of banks in the Eurocredit market.

target zones Implicit boundaries established by central banks on exchange rates.

tariff Tax imposed by a government on imported goods.

technical forecasting Development of forecasts using historical prices or trends.

tenor Time period of drafts.

time series analysis Analysis of relationships between two or more variables over periods of time.

time series models Models that examine series of historical data; sometimes used as a means of technical forecasting by examining moving averages.

trade acceptance Draft that allows the buyer to obtain merchandise prior to paying for it.

trade sanctions Government imposed restrictions on international trade.

transaction exposure Degree to which the value of future cash transactions can be affected by exchange rate fluctuations.

transfer pricing Policy for pricing goods sent by either the parent or a subsidiary to a subsidiary of an MNC.

transferable letter of credit Document that allows the first beneficiary on a standby letter of credit to transfer all or part of the original letter of credit to a third party.

translation exposure Degree to which a firm's consolidated financial statements are exposed to fluctuations in exchange rates.

triangular arbitrage Action to capitalize on a discrepancy where the quoted cross exchange rate is not equal to the rate that should exist at equilibrium.

umbrella policy Policy issued to a bank or trading company to insure exports of an exporter and handle all administrative requirements.

unilateral transfers Accounting for government and private gifts and grants.

volatility The standard deviation.

weak-form efficient Description of foreign exchange markets, implying that all historical and current exchange rate information is already reflected in prevailing spot exchange rates.

Working Capital Guarantee Program Programme conducted by the Ex-Im Bank that encourages commercial banks to extend short-term export financing to eligible exporters; the Ex-Im Bank provides a guarantee of the loan's principal and interest.

World Bank Bank established in 1944 to enhance economic development by providing loans to countries.

World Trade Organization (WTO) Organization established to provide a forum for multilateral trade negotiations and to settle trade disputes related to the GATT accord.

writer Seller of an option.

Yankee stock offerings Offerings of stock by non-US firms in the US markets.

INDEX

History of Costume

written and designed by
Rosemary Lowndes and Claude Kaïler
for Macdonald and Jane's . London .

How to use this book

This book will make up into your own gallery of fashion. By simply cutting out the pages you will have :
9 three dimensional costume models 20cm (8") high ready to cut out, fold and glue, together with easy to follow visual instructions.
9 fashion plates to cut out and frame or pin up on a wall.
A complete illustrated booklet of costume through the ages to cut out and bind, which can be used as a descriptive guide for each model.

GENERAL INSTRUCTIONS FOR MAKING THE MODELS

You will need :
Good sharp scissors
A tube of transparent glue
Some cardboard for mounting the backgrounds
Time and patience

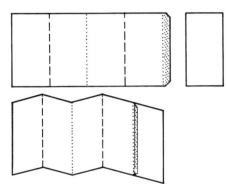

Remember always to :
Cut along black lines
Fold these lines outwards
Fold these lines inwards
Glue these areas

IMPORTANT

When you have cut out the pieces place them the right side up on a table on a sheet of paper so as not to lose them.
Fold and bend the pieces carefully following the assembly order as shown by the photographs and make sure that you have got the shapes and folds correct before finally glueing them in place.
If you have difficulty glueing tubular pieces such as necks, it is a good idea to roll them around a pencil whilst glueing them in shape. Then use the pencil or scissors to push the glue covered flanges up inside the neck afterwards.
Make the model first, then cut out the background carefully leaving the fashion plates and booklet till the end.

HOW TO MOUNT THE BACKGROUNDS so they stand up behind each model.
Paste each background onto a piece of stiff cardboard cut to the same size, cut another piece of cardboard into a wedge shape. Fold it in half, glue one half to the back as shown on the photograph.
When you have made up the models and their backgrounds, turn to the last page of the book for instructions and ideas on how to make the booklet and display the fashion plates.

©Rosemary Lowndes and Claude Kailer 1977

First published in Great Britain in 1977 by
Macdonald and Jane's Publishers, Ltd.
Paulton House
8, Shepherdess Walk
London N1 7LW
Printed and bound in Great Britain by
Hazell Watson & Viney Ltd, Aylesbury, Bucks
ISBN 356 084 183

EGYPTIAN   GREEK   ROMAN   BYZANTINE

1230   1350   1410   1460

BURGUNDIAN

1 Nature had failed to protect early man with abundant fur which meant that he was forced to kill wild animals for their coats to keep himself warm. Because he was a hunter the hides he used had to be shaped to give him freedom of movement.

With the passage of time he found that fleece could be clipped, spun and woven on a loom. This was the beginning of cloth as we know it today. As the Assyrian, Babylonian, Egyptian and Greek civilizations progressed, they draped and folded the cloth, and gave certain styles to each individual ; be it man or woman, slave or master, high priest or king. Wars between nations forced the vanquished to wear the fashions of the victors, so that when the Romans created an empire throughout Europe and North Africa they introduced their own style of clothing but also adopted the garments of the people whom they had conquered. Influenced by the Gauls and Celts they shortened their togas and began to wear a version of knee length trousers.

In the twelfth century Christian Knights from all over Europe banded together to repel the hordes of Moslems who had overrun the Christian countries of the Near East. These crusaders not only returned home with wealth and power, but in their travels extended their knowledge of other peoples and cultures, including a new style of Gothic architecture. The soaring pointed Gothic arch replaced the simple rounded Roman arch ; buildings were high and narrow ; the clothes copied the architecture, and it became fashionable for ladies to look tall and slender.

The men of the thirteenth century wore long belted robes called 'surcotes' over their under tunics, short breeches and long hose (or stockings). Their cloaks were fastened at the front, or on the shoulder, by brooches, and the women wore similar gowns and cloaks.   In the fourteenth century a parti-coloured tunic called the cotehardie, with a

hooded shoulder cape became fashionable for men ; a decorated belt was slung on the hips, and the women wore tight fitting cotehardies under loose, sideless surcotes.

By the early fifteenth century clothes were decorated by fluttering leaf shapes called 'daggings' cut out from the edges of the sleeves and tunics.

The fourteenth and fifteenth centuries, in spite of long and almost continuous wars, were years of adventure and riches for the nobles. During the fifteenth century the Princes of the proud state of Burgundy lived in magnificent wealth and extravagance. No expense was spared on clothing and fabrics. Rich velvets, soft silks, heavy damasks and shimmering satins, combined with precious jewels, added beauty and splendour to the age of chivalry. A courtier's head was easily turned by the elegance and loveliness of ladies dresses. Vanity and admiration caused exaggeration and gowns trailed, sleeves flowed from the arms, and headdresses became huge towering structures.

The most flattering woman's dress of this period was the 'houppelande' gown. This was high waisted, worn with a broad belt below the breast. Usually decorated with circles, stars or flower designs, the belt was thought to have magical powers. The low-cut neckline of the gown was filled in with a 'modesty' vest and it was considered improper for a woman to display her bare arms. So the sleeve was made long and tight, with fur-trimmed cuffs either worn folded down to cover half the hand, or else folded back over the wrist. The sleeve was so narrow that it had to be fastened with small buttons.

The skirt of the gown was full, and edged with fur, forming a long train which swept the ground at the back, and fell only a little shorter at the front and sides.In order to walk, a lady had to hold up the voluminous folds of her skirts, clasping them under her breast, with her head drooping forward, her shoulders back, bottom tucked in and her stomach pushed out which gave the medieval woman the peculiar pregnant look fashionable at the time. Her shoes were flat, so to make her look taller she wore a high cone-shaped headdress called the 'hennin' which could reach heights of 90 centimetres (three feet) or more. The hennin, worn far back on the head, was stiffened and covered in silver or gold brocade, or silk, sometimes bordered in velvet and topped by a delicate, floating transparent veil, which was shaped and wired into two or three wings. Fashion demanded that no hair should show beneath the headdress so women removed their eyebrows and the hair from the nape of their necks and foreheads.

A version of the houppelande was worn by men, but unlike those of the ladies did not reach the ground. By the middle of the fifteenth century however, the very short tunic became popular for younger men. The body of the tunic was padded, with flat pleats which came together at the waist and then flared out in the short skirt, sometimes edged with fur. The shoulders were padded and puffed out to add to the overall impression of slim waist and broad masculine chest and shoulders. The round, or slightly square neckline showed the collar of the 'undertunic'. Sleeves were often cut with an opening at elbow level to push the arms through, (showing off the decorative patterns of the undertunic) and allowing the rest of the sleeve to hang free. With the short tunic were worn hose, tailored of wool or cotton in various colours. These were close fitting, cut to the shape of the leg and tied at the waist.

Shoes were normally made of soft leather, but velvet, brocade and other materials were also used. Styles of men's shoes varied from decorated short boots, laced or buckled at the side, to snug-fitting shoes with very long pointed toes turned up at the end. So lengthy and impractical were the points of the shoes—sometimes reaching a length of 45 centimetres (eighteen inches)—that it became necessary to tie the end back onto the shoe. This rather absurd fashion went to such extremes that a law was eventually passed fining any man wearing shoes with points longer than 5 centimetres (two inches).

Most men throughout this period were clean-shaven with their hair cut at collar length and brushed down, with the ends turned in and curled under.

Jewelled neck chains were worn over the tunics ; purses and daggers with decorated hilts were slung from the belts adding to the romantic splendours of the costumes.

With the lavish elegance of the court of Burgundy the excitement of wearing something new and different launched costume amongst the ruling classes into the beginning of a continuous chain of changing fashion.

1460

1

2

3

4

5

6

7

8

9

10

11

12

13

14

15

16

On the next two pages you will find a costume model of 1460
Cut out the pages carefully along the cutting lines.
When making the model it is important to follow the assembly
order by numbers as shown above.

For general instructions on cutting, folding and glueing see
page 4.

On the back of the cutout pages there are patchwork patterns.
These form the patterned linings to the dresses, hats and ribbons etc.

1500 ITALY

1515 GERMANY   1545 SPAIN   1540 GERMANY

1570 SPAIN   1570 FRANCE   1590 FRANCE

2   The end of the Medieval period heralded the start of Italian Renaissance fashions. Instead of the towering hennins of previous years, headdresses became lower and flatter. Sleeves grew larger and wider, and were detachable. The gowns were made of separate skirts and bodices sewn together at the waist opening on to under-skirts of great beauty. Women's necklines became square and the men's neckline lower, shoes were broad and as short as the foot instead of long and pointed. Men began to wear breeches and a curious German fashion called 'slashing' became popular. This consisted of pulling a vividly coloured contrasting lining through slits in the outer material of sleeves, doublet, and breeches. The male shirt became visible, eventually developing into a finely pleated affair worn under the doublet ending in a standing collar gathered in a small frill at the neck.

The flamboyant German influence of men's clothes with huge padded shoulders and lavish doublets in brilliant colours, hanging to the knee, gave way to the tight-laced, proud bearing and sombre colours of the Spanish court.

With the discovery of America, gold and precious stones poured into Spain, the wealthy, anxious to show off their new riches, encrusted their clothes with jewels—as safe a place as any to parade them as no banks existed. The ladies of fashion throughout Europe wore these richly embroidered fabrics tightly stretched over their bodices and hanging to the ground over cone-shaped Spanish farthingales which were made of canvas stiffened by hoops of wood or whalebone.

Later the French farthingale was introduced. This was either an enormous stuffed bolster called a 'bum-roll' tied below the waist, or a wheel of radiating spokes made of whalebone. These were worn under the skirt making the fabric spring out at the hip by as much as 60 centimetres (two feet) all the way round before dropping sharply to the ground.

To hide the hard line of the wheel or bum-roll a circular frill, called a flounce, was added. The hole for the waist was nearer the front of the skirt so that the wider portion at the back sloped upwards. To overcome the problem of sitting down comfortably a special farthingale chair was made.

Down the front of the bodice ending in a long point below the waist a piece of material called the 'stomacher' was pinned or laced. Heavily padded sleeves with tight wrist bands were tied on with ribbons or laces at the shoulders and armpits, with false hanging sleeves attached under the small 'wings' on the shoulders of the dress. The sleeves and stomachers were interchangeable so that they provided the wearer with different colour schemes in contrast to the overgown.

Cruel corsets enforced the rigid pose shown in paintings and portraits of the time. At first they were made of wooden laths held together by tapes and then metal corsets hinged at one side, padded and covered in velvet. These machines of torture rubbed the skin raw as they squeezed the flesh into the required stiff shape of tiny waist and flat bosom. Even children wore the same formal dresses and corsets as their parents; hardly surprising, as at the age of thirteen a girl from a wealthy family was considered ready to marry and take on the responsibilities of a husband and household, having mastered the difficulties of Latin, tapestry and embroidery together with an appreciation of art and music which she had learnt from tutors at home. Her prowess at sewing would have been helpful, for men and women spent large sums of money on clothes.

Ruffs, which had begun as a small frill round the neck of the shirt developed into huge status symbols, proving by their size that the wearer was not involved in manual work. Some were so wide that eating was difficult and spoons with extra long handles had to be made so that food could be conveyed safely from plate to mouth. The ruffs were made of cambric decorated by lace edgings shaped by heated metal setting sticks and stiffened by wires and starch paste. Unmarried ladies wore heart-shaped ruffs and the married ones wore circular cartwheel ruffs.

Because of the elaborate ruffs it was now necessary for ladies to pile the hair on top of their heads, either turned back from the face over a pad or brushed over a high wired support, the back hair coiled or plaited was generally hidden by a jewelled hair net. Hair was dyed, often with disastrous results; and wigs and false hair pieces were worn to cover the baldness caused by the use of dangerous concoctions of herbs and chemicals. Ladies painted their faces and bosoms with white powdered lead, and tinted their cheeks with vermilion to give a fashionable pink and white complexion and also to disguise blemishes and pock marks caused by smallpox and other diseases. The poisonous lead caused the early death of many vain women.

Men also wore large ruffs and make-up for them was not unusual, they also put oil and pomade on their faces and hands at night as well as plucking their eyebrows and moustaches to form a finer line. But the most important features of masculine charm were the beards; these were trimmed and cut into various forms long or short, pointed or spade shaped.

Gentlemen wore splendid doublets embroidered with an abundance of gold braid, lace, ribbons and jewels over padded 'bombasts' which curved outwards from the chest into a pot-bellied ridge down the front ending in a point below the tightly-laced waists. These bombasts were stuffed with horsehair, wool, flock or even bran; an accidental tear in the cloth could result in a sudden deflation of the silhouette!

A short circular cloak, sometimes with sleeves, flared out from the shoulders. Breeches ballooned like giant pumpkins, slashed and puffed with padding. Both men and women wore knitted stockings of fine silk or wool, and shoes of similar styles made in leather, silk or velvet.

Scented gloves were worn by both sexes and pomanders hanging on chains from the ladies waists probably helped to keep away the less pleasant odours rising from the open sewers in the streets.

The inequality between rich and poor was marked by the difference in clothing. Instead of the silks and velvets worn by the merchant's wife, the poorer woman possessed one gown of rough wool, just as the squalor of rat infested hovels contrasted with the sumptuous furnishings, fine rugs and silver goblets of the wealthy.

1595

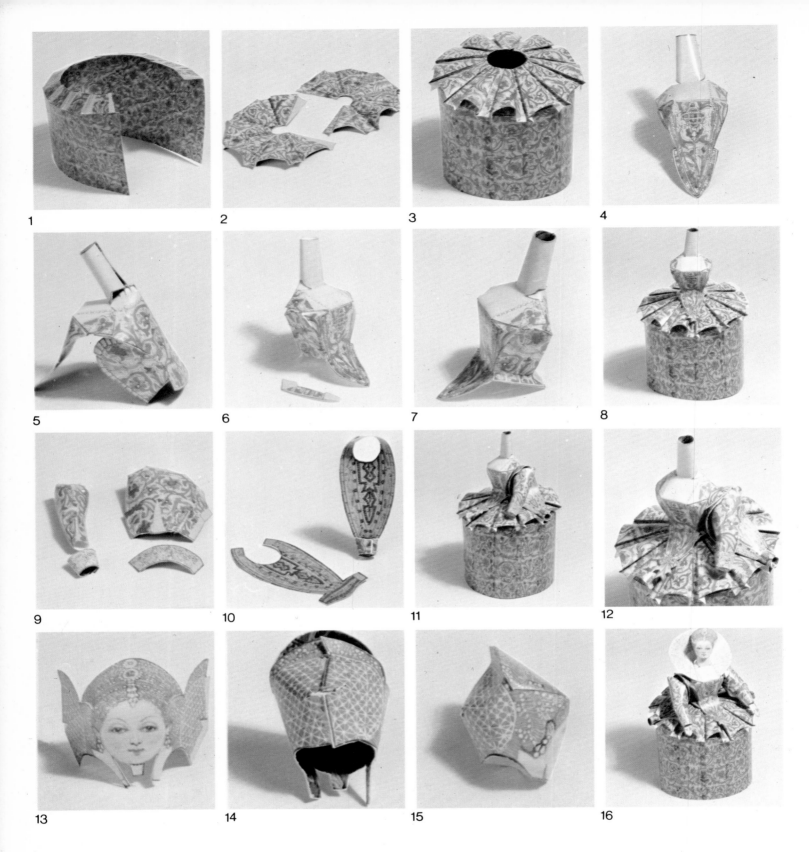

1

2

3

4

5

6

7

8

9

10

11

12

13

14

15

16

On the next two pages you will find a costume model of 1595
Cut out the pages carefully along the cutting lines.
When making the model it is important to follow the assembly
order by numbers as shown above.

For general instructions on cutting, folding and glueing see
page 4.

On the back of the cutout pages there are patchwork patterns.
These form the patterned linings to the dresses, hats and ribbons etc.

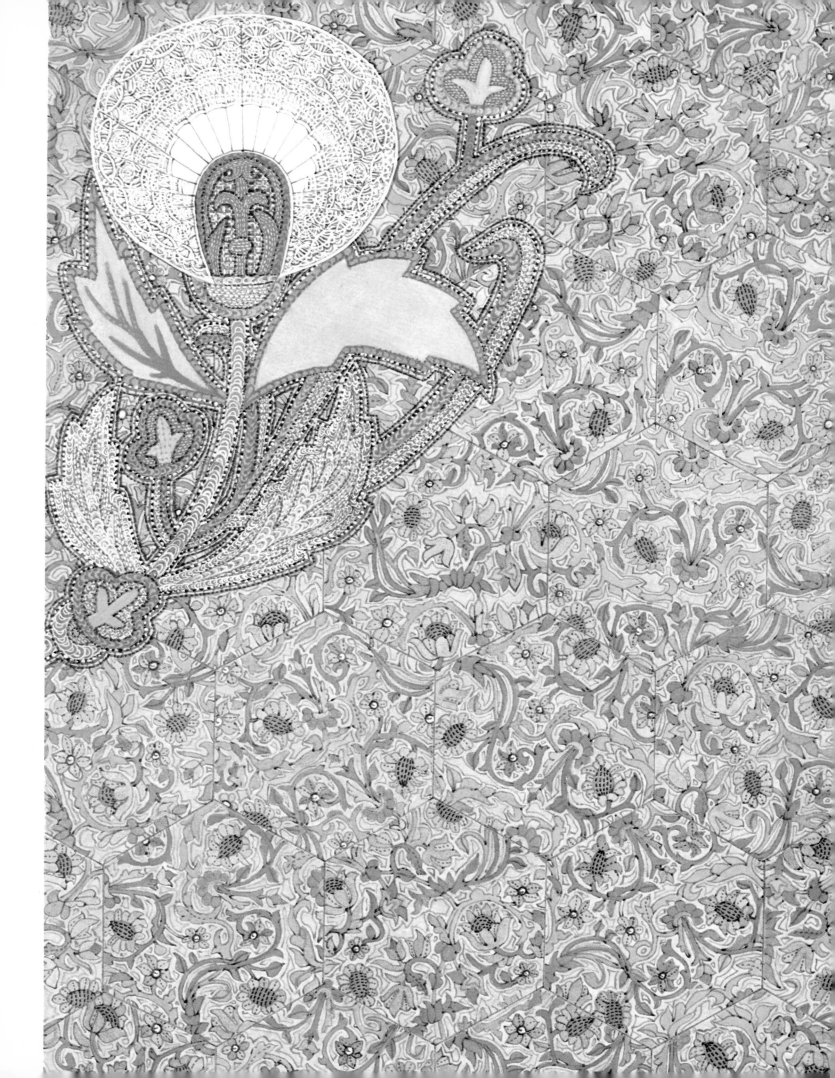

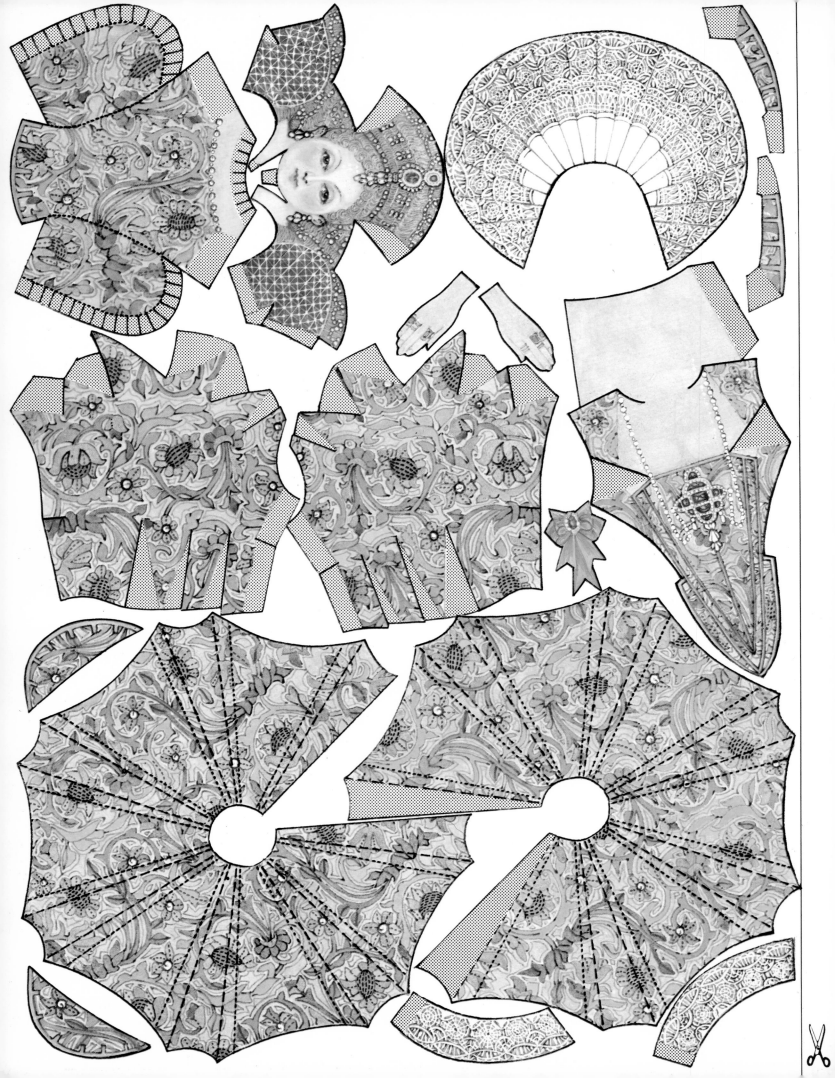

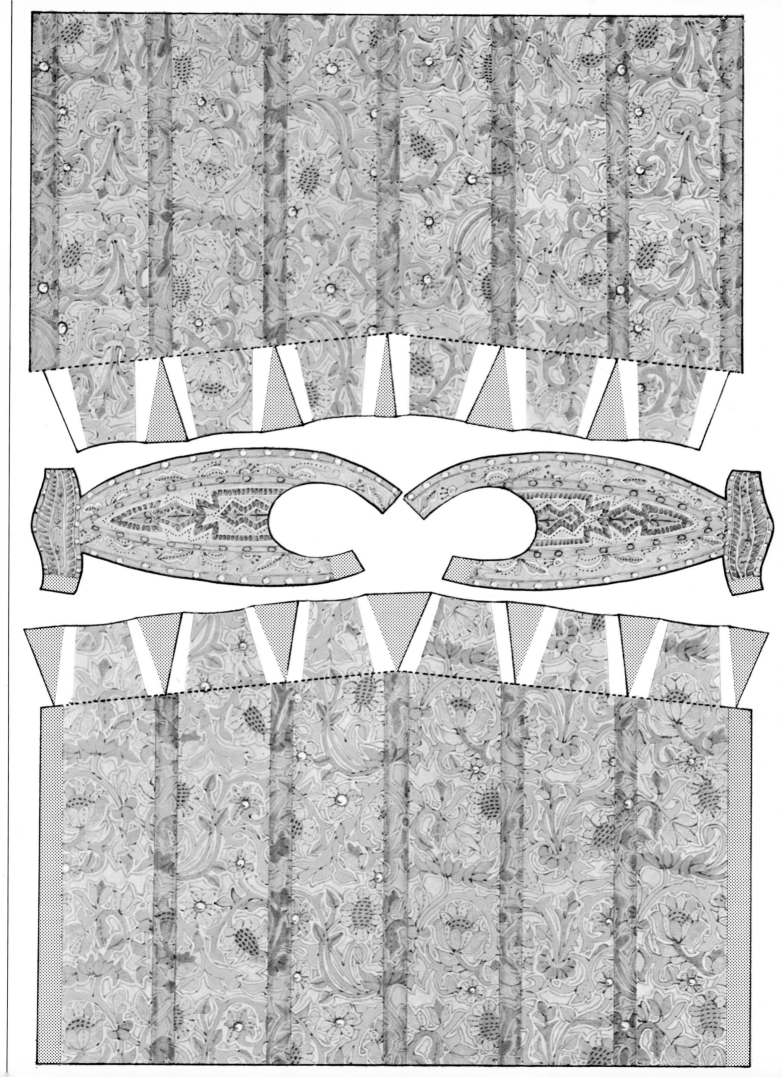

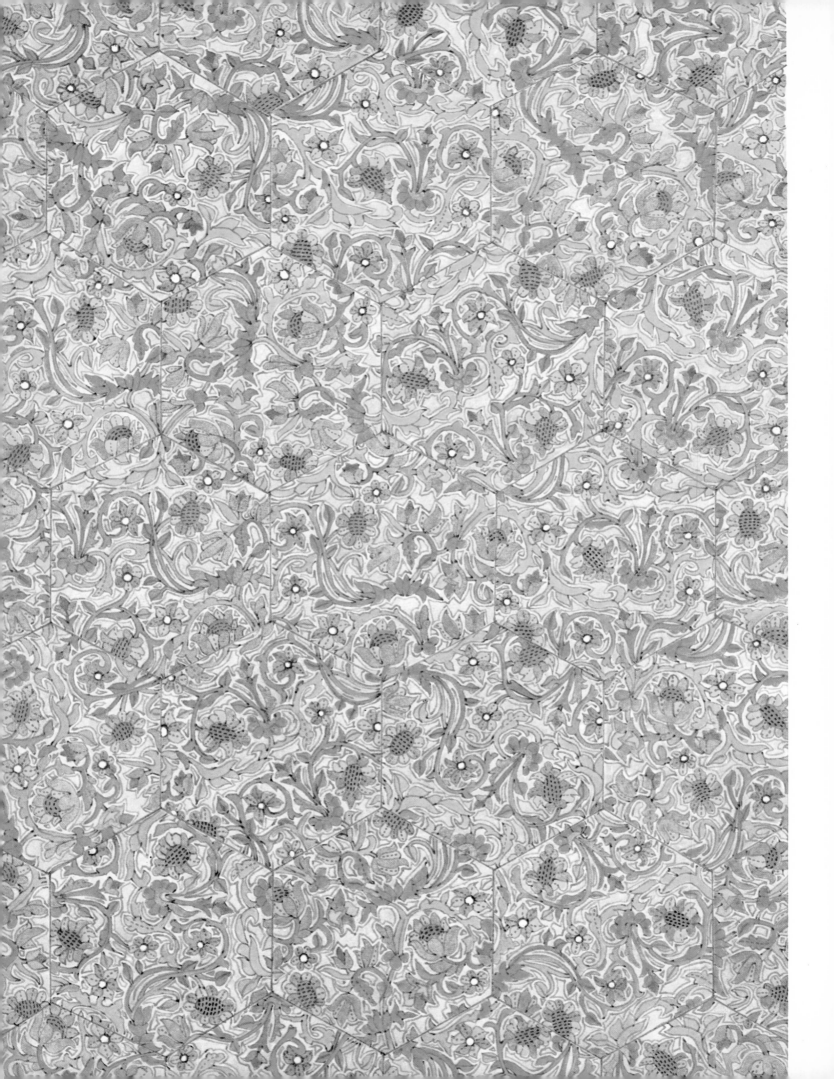

1615

1625

1630

1640

1640 PURITANS

3   In spite of the frequent periods of war and destruction throughout Europe, costume continued to develop in elegance and refinement, moving from formality towards a more relaxed look. During these times, styles of clothing were most strongly influenced by the French, and to a lesser extent, the Dutch.

Gradually ladies, no longer restricted by the severity of stiff corsets and excessive padding, gained not only comfort but a naturalness and simplicity of style. Instead of the farthingale, the long full-skirted gown hung free from the waist over slight padding, often pinned up in front or at the sides, to display a bright decorative petticoat or underskirt.

By 1640 waisted jackets were worn over the skirts, the jackets were laced down the chest over a small stomacher, and sashed under the breast with a silk ribbon belt tied with bows. Similar ribbons, bows and rosettes decorated the large puffed slashed 'virago' sleeves which ballooned out from the shoulder and were then caught in again at one or two places with jewelled clasps or ribbons. The hanging sleeve at the back had become smaller and shorter and now stopped at the elbow, the sleeves ended in turned-up lace cuffs, a little way above the wrists leaving the lower arm bare.

The starched ruff after having become gradually smaller disappeared to be replaced by a large collar made of layers of lace which fell gracefully over the shoulders and around the deep neckline of the low-cut dress.

Stiff brocades were no longer admired; instead soft draperies of satin, velvet and silks were skilfully and subtly blended in contrasting colours and materials, trimmed with a variety of ribbons and lace. The rich luxury of gleaming coloured silks caught the light in the gathered folds of materials expressing the flamboyant and romantic spirit of the time.

Ladies wore their hair shoulder-length brushed flat on top, with a small fringe and frizzed out at the sides often gathered into a cluster of ringlets and prettily tied together with charming bows or strings of pearls. It was now fashionable to have dark hair, so fair young ladies coloured their hair with brown powder. It was the custom to do away with a head-covering indoors, but out of doors ladies would protect their fair complexions with broad brimmed felt or beaver-skin hats topped with flowing ostrich plumes, like those of the men, and worn at a jaunty angle. Ladies venturing out of the house often wore masks to protect their faces from the weather, or to conceal their identity. Make-up was heavy, and consisted of powdered white lead, flour, rice, quicksilver or bismuth, patches were stuck to the face and seductively placed on the bosom.

Women's shoes were beautifully embroidered and expensive, so specially constructed wooden soles fastened over the shoes with leather straps called 'pattens' or 'chopines', were worn to protect the elegant footwear from the mud in the streets. At times the soles were so high that they lifted the wearer many inches off the ground.

To keep their hands warm in the winter, both men and women carried large muffs made of velvet, satin or fur. Men, too, adopted the custom of sticking on small face patches cut out of black silk or taffetta in the forms of stars or crescents or various other shapes. The dashing worldliness of the men of these times has seldom been equalled. With their rich lace and bright sashes, their short cloaks nonchalantly tossed over a shoulder to show off the contrasting coloured lining, young men of good birth were less restricted than women in the display of lace and linen on the cuffs and wide falling collars, over their velvet or satin suits.

Men now wore a form of unpadded doublet which was not buttoned right up to the neck and fell open below the waist to show off the shirt, usually made of fine white linen or silk. Doublet sleeves were slashed to show the full shirt beneath and the tightly fastened wrists were trimmed with deep turned back cuffs of lace.

In time longer breeches replaced the short trunk hose and lost their padding, gradually developing away from the previous baggy and loose shape, and narrowing from the waist to be fastened just below the knee by rosettes or bows of ribbon.

The materials used for doublets and breeches although rich, were plain and unadorned and colours were paler with contrasting trimmings.

With the breeches, bucket top boots of soft wrinkled leather were worn, either pushed down so that they hung loose and flopping below the knee, or else pulled up to the thigh for riding. Stockings or boot-hose were trimmed with a deep lace flounce which frothed over the tops of the boots. As well as boots, shoes of leather with thick high heels, squared toes and elaborate buckles, often decorated with huge rosettes, were worn ; scarlet heels being popular with full dress or Court wear. With the shoes, silk stockings were gartered at the top with fancy ribbons and rosettes and to enhance the shape of the leg, men's stockings were sometimes padded to make up for nature's deficiency.

Although tradesmen and workers wore their hair 'bobbed' or of medium length the man of fashion, having discarded the stiff starched ruff, now wore his hair in shoulder length flowing locks and sometimes when courting a lady he attached a ribbon bow to a curl. Beards were trimmed to a fashionable point and the upturned moustache was curled with hot curling tongs.

In addition to the profusion of lace and ribbons, jewelled brooches and buttons adorned both men and women. Although men favoured a single ear ring, pearl drop ear rings were fashionable for women throughout this period. Sword hilts were also elaborately made of precious metals and decorated with jewels.

The distinction in dress which separated the nobility from the mass of the people was as great as ever. However, the merchant, with his new found wealth, began to copy the aristocracy, which forced the nobles to change styles constantly in order to maintain a difference of social class that was immediately obvious in their clothing.

Whilst the dashing cavalier and his lady dressed in a dazzling array of colours, lace and ribbons, some of the British puritans and the Dutch Protestants went to equal extremes of severe simplicity, wearing dark colours such as black, greys and browns, and proving their religious beliefs by the quiet modesty and humility of their dress.

1640

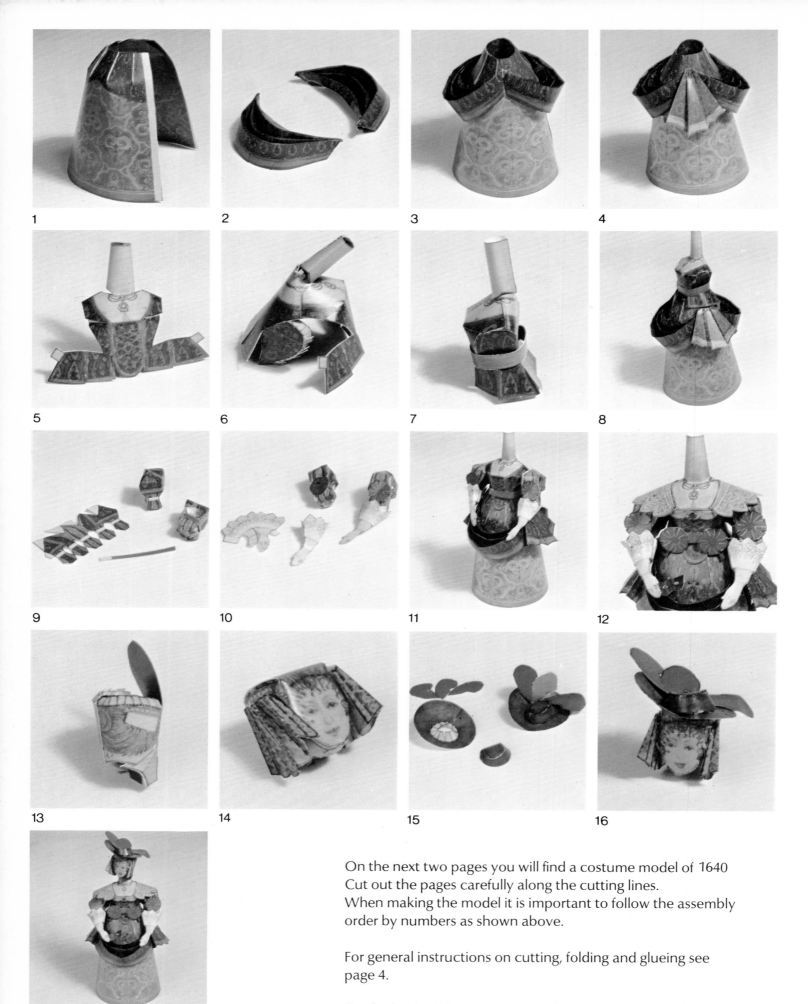

1

2

3

4

5

6

7

8

9

10

11

12

13

14

15

16

17

On the next two pages you will find a costume model of 1640
Cut out the pages carefully along the cutting lines.
When making the model it is important to follow the assembly
order by numbers as shown above.

For general instructions on cutting, folding and glueing see
page 4.

On the back of the cutout pages there are patchwork patterns.
These form the patterned linings to the dresses, hats and ribbons etc.

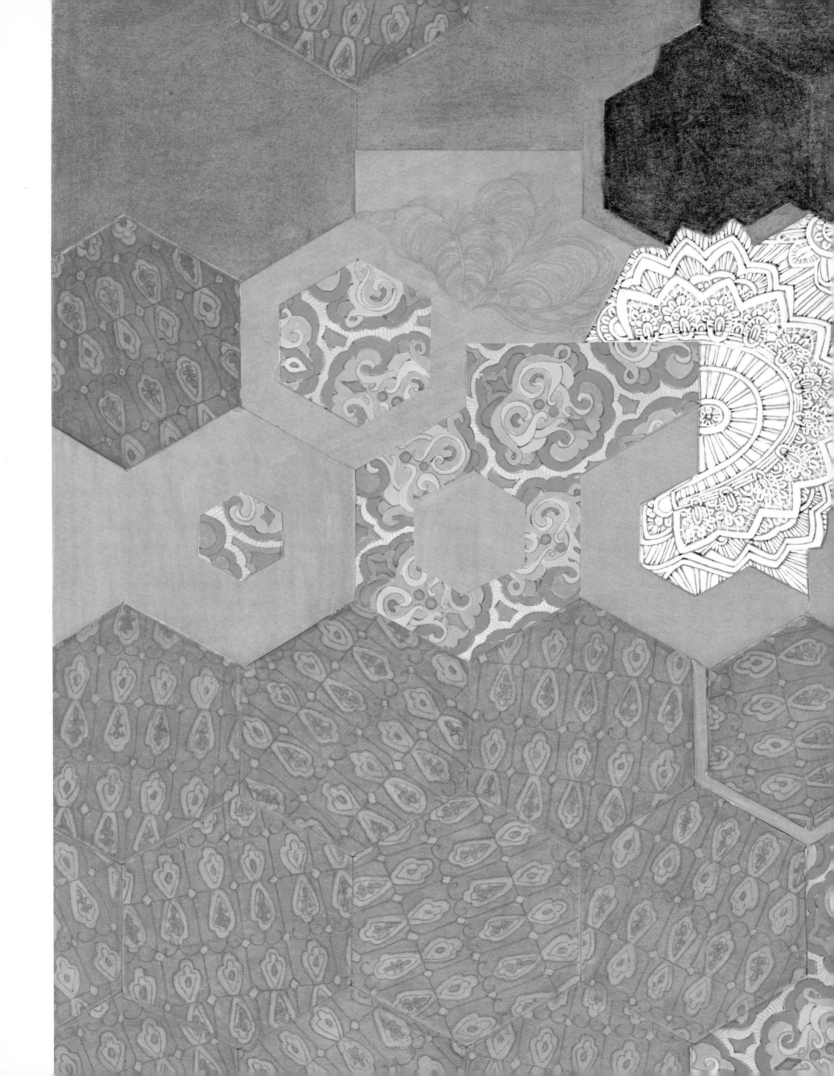

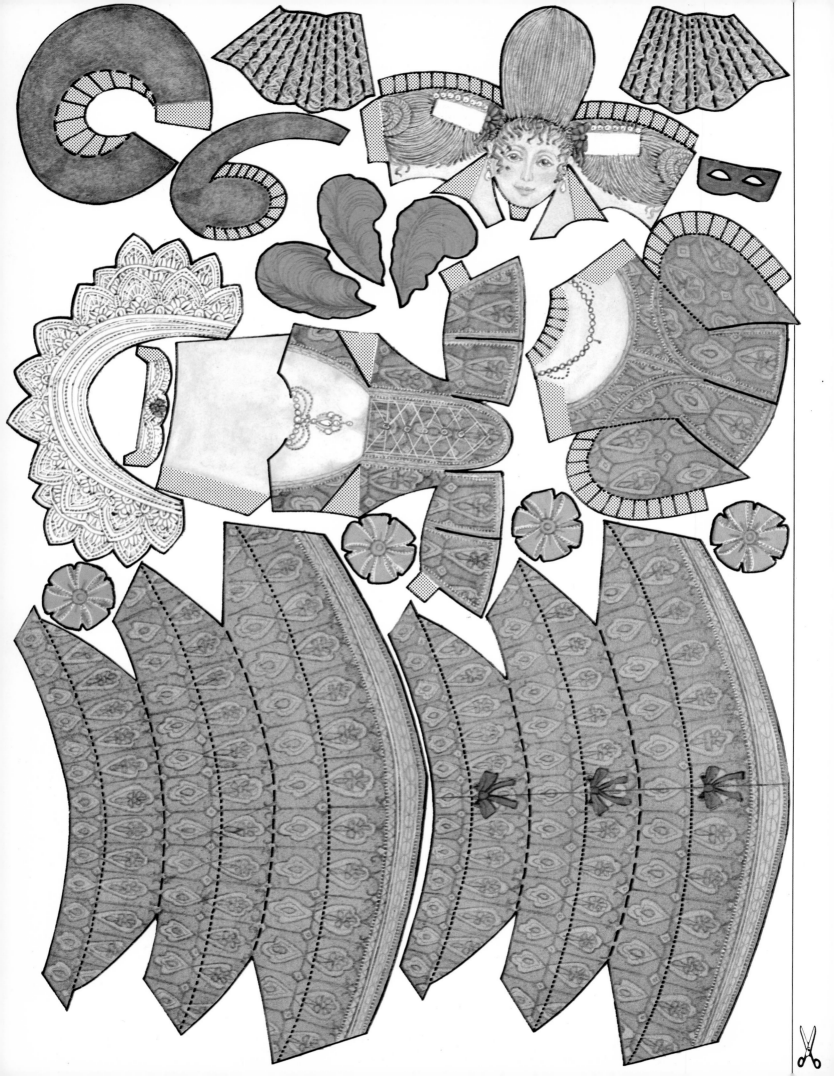

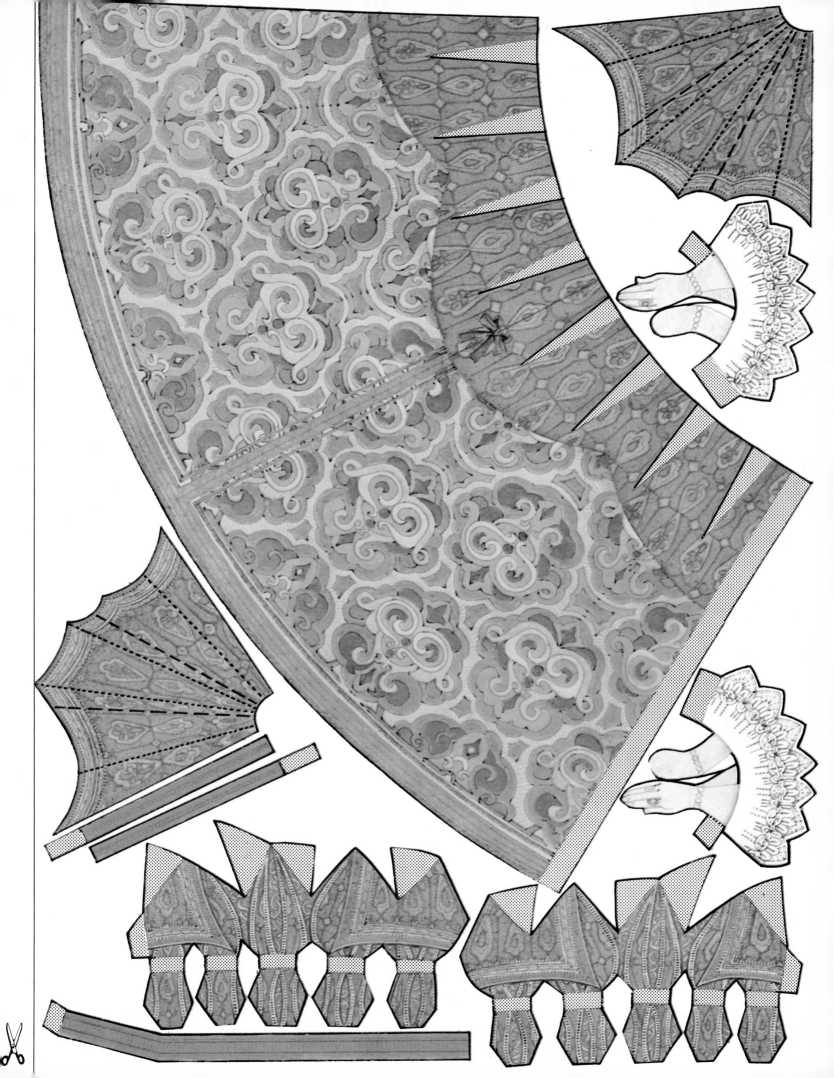

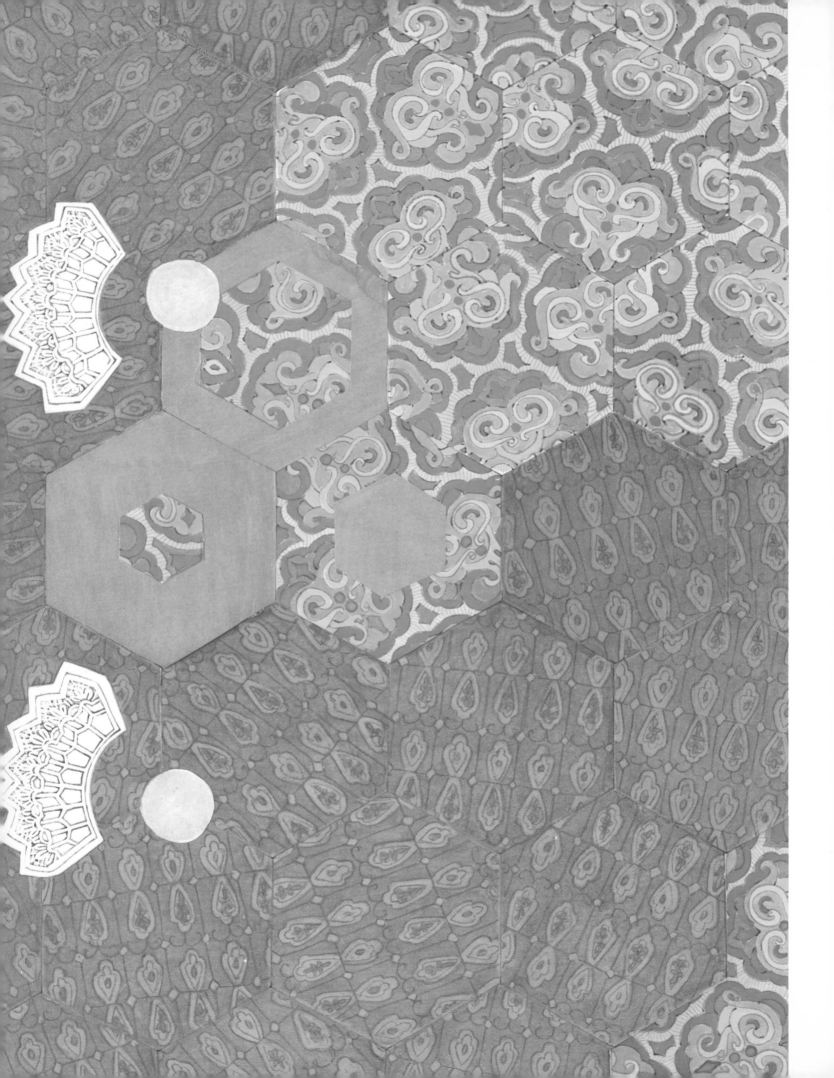

1646

1660

1670

1695

1730

1740

1756

4 Fashions continued for a while in the lavish styles of the 1640s. Then jackets and virago sleeves disappeared and dresses with low collars were opened in the front to show beautiful elaborate underskirts. Gentlemen wore wide baggy trousers, with shorter jackets allowing the shirts to be pulled out at the waist.

In the 1690s the grandiose splendour of Louis XIV's Court at Versailles, developed a new, stiff elegance of costume to match the architecture. For the ladies the open skirt was now pulled back and piled up at the rear on a support, exposing petticoats made of heavily embroidered brocades, opulently tasselled and fringed in gold cords and braids. The bodice was cut low and square and the stomacher accentuated the tiny corseted waist, as the sleeves grew tighter, ending in ruffles below the elbow. The hair was decorated by a high wired 'Fontange' cap of pleated lace.

Gentlemen wore knee-breeches under tight-waisted coats which were stiffened below the waist to flare out into wide long pleated skirts. Gold braids outlined the shape of the coat with the huge turned back cuffs and low pockets. Wigs gradually became larger, with a centre parting ending in trailing masses of curls and ringlets.

The stuffy formality of these clothes gave way eventually to a new delicacy and lightness. By the early 1700s a new gaiety and easy grace was displayed in the interior decoration; as mirrors, furniture and panellings were carved and moulded into twisted fanciful shell-like shapes. A new softness and prettiness was introduced into women's clothes in France as they ceased to be made by tailors and instead were cut and styled by ladies dressmakers.

After 1730 the shape of ladies' skirts changed from a circle to an oval as the front and back of the skirt was flattened and the sides spread out extending to as wide as 180 centimetres (two yards) either side of the hips. This was supported by wide hoops at the sides called 'Panniers' (from the French word for baskets). To pass through doorways the wide

hipped women had to sidle sideways, until this was eventually overcome by the invention of hinged panniers which could be folded up and held under the arms.

Necklines became square and low, with a series of graduated pretty ribbon bows forming ladders (échelles) which ran down the front of the stomacher, to the waist. the skirt generally opened in the front and was bordered with ruffles or flowers and lace over a decorative flounced underskirt. Long vertical box pleats were stitched at the top of the back of the shoulders, hanging loose behind and falling in elegant folds to the ground, with a short train. The dresses cut tightly to fit the corsetted waist, were made of light, fine Indian silks and muslins, in fresh clean colours and pale tones of white, rose-pinks, cream, or soft apple greens, edged in ruffled bands of silk with flower motifs—materials which were ideal for this enchantingly delicate fashion. The short, tight, elbow-length sleeves ending in more ruffles and the diminutive waist, combined with the little light running steps, as though they were gliding across the floor on wheels, all stressed the effect of the fragile, frivolous woman.

Hair was drawn back, swept up into a small bun or plait and powdered white with wheatmeal or rice meal. Special closets or cabinets were reserved for this procedure, the woman hiding her face in a bag as the scented powder was sprayed up into the air to fall evenly over her head.

In the early 18th century hats were hardly ever worn, later the swept up hair-style was enhanced by flattering small hats, with upturned brims often three-cornered (tricorne), in shape. The simple country style, adopted from England, led to the wearing of wide brimmed, rustic straw hats trimmed and tied with ribbons, over a small close-fitting milkmaid mob-cap of white muslin.

Ladies' shoes had pointed toes and were made in silk, satin, brocade or kid decorated with valuable jewelled metal buckles, with very tall heels, often red.

At this time there was a certain restraint in the wearing of jewellery; however with beautiful buttons, elbow length gloves, small handsome muffs and fans and maybe, a little black boy to carry the long handled painted silk parasol over the lady of fashion, there seemed little need for other accessories.

This was an age of interest in the arts, and ladies of high society presided over salons (drawing rooms), entertaining the famous writers, painters, politicians, and philosophers. Fashion now followed high society rather than imitating noble courtiers.

This was also reflected in the dress of the men in their clean-cut, fitted costumes. Their tight-waisted narrow-shouldered coats ended just above the knee, the coat skirts were re-inforced with canvas and horsehair so that they stood out from the hips. Coats were made of rich satins, silks, plush, velvets and brocades, with elaborate embroidery on the large pocket flaps and buttoned cuffs. The waistcoat was a veritable work of art in rich embroidery, stiffened with buckram or coarse linen to spring out from the hips in front of the coat. The neck cravat made of linen or muslin, was loosely knotted and tucked into the frilled shirt, whose ruffled shirt sleeves protruded from under the coat cuffs.

The knee-breeches were made with a full seat which was tightened by buckles at the back; the legs of these breeches were buttoned just below the knees.

Men's shoes became more rounded at the toe, with bold buckles; the tonges and the heels now smaller than before, and red heels were still fashionable for dress wear. Stockings were ribbed or chequered, and were made of different colours.

Men wore wigs in a variety of styles. They were usually powdered, and the lock of hair behind was caught back and tied in a ribbon low on the neck. Because of the powdered wigs, the three-cornered hat, its brim bound with braid, was more often than not carried under the arm rather than worn.

The man about town took as much trouble as the ladies over his make-up; he reddened his lips, decorated his cheeks with patches, scented his linen, carefully dressed his wig and plucked his eyebrows. He carried a lace handkerchief as an accessory, which he casually held between his fingers. It was said at the time that "a slovenly fellow might hustle into his clothes in an hour but a gentleman could scarcely dress in less than two!"

1750

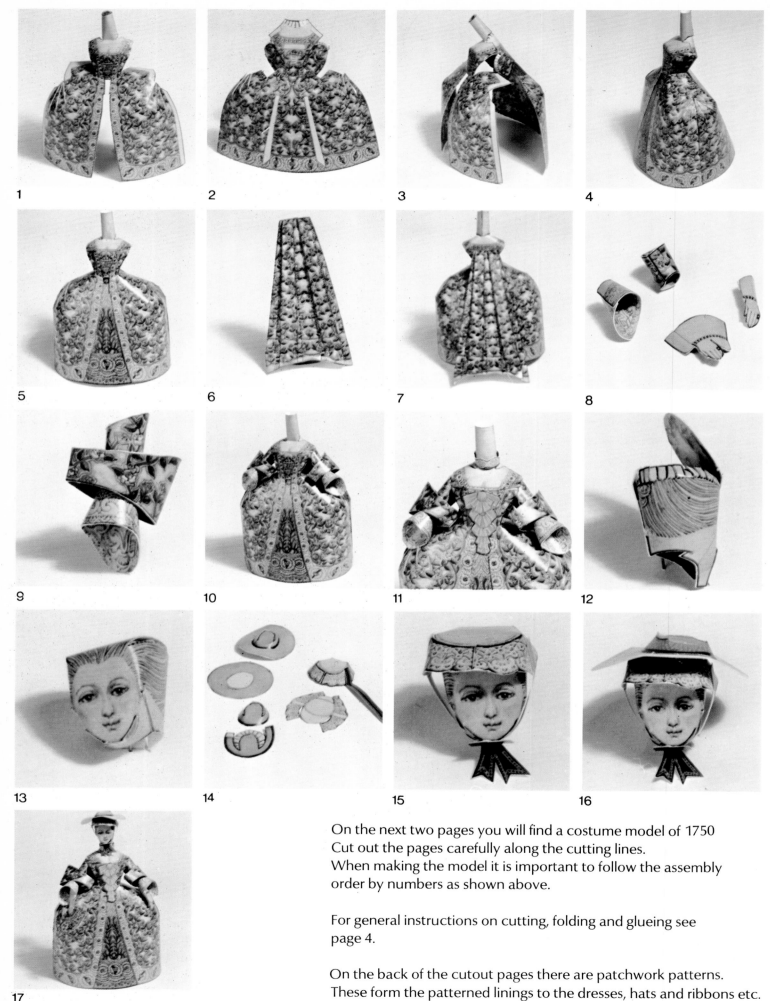

1

2

3

4

5

6

7

8

9

10

11

12

13

14

15

16

17

On the next two pages you will find a costume model of 1750
Cut out the pages carefully along the cutting lines.
When making the model it is important to follow the assembly order by numbers as shown above.

For general instructions on cutting, folding and glueing see page 4.

On the back of the cutout pages there are patchwork patterns.
These form the patterned linings to the dresses, hats and ribbons etc.

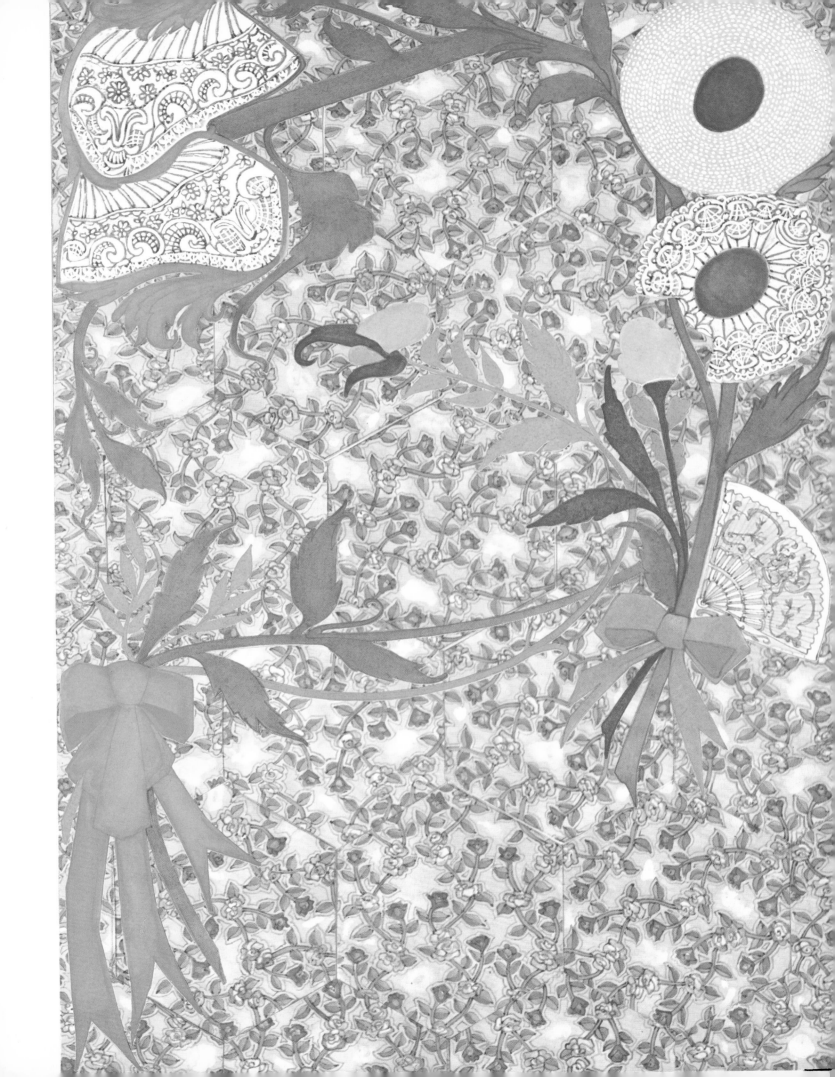

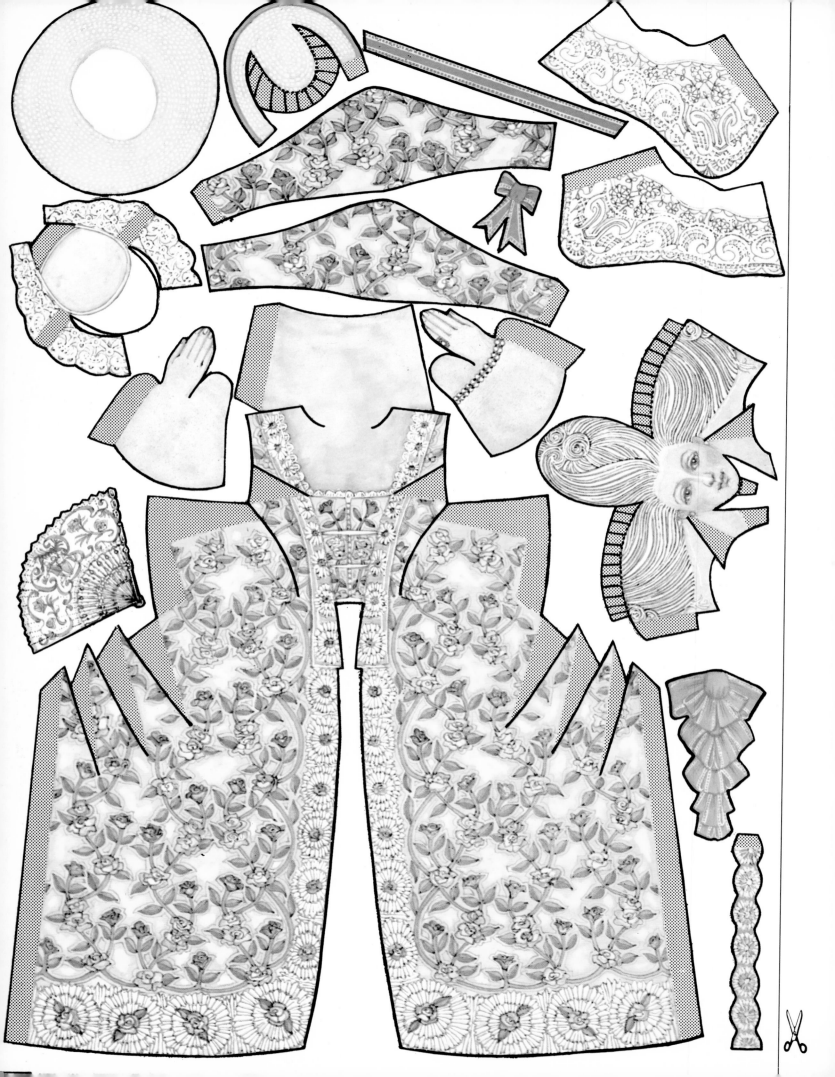

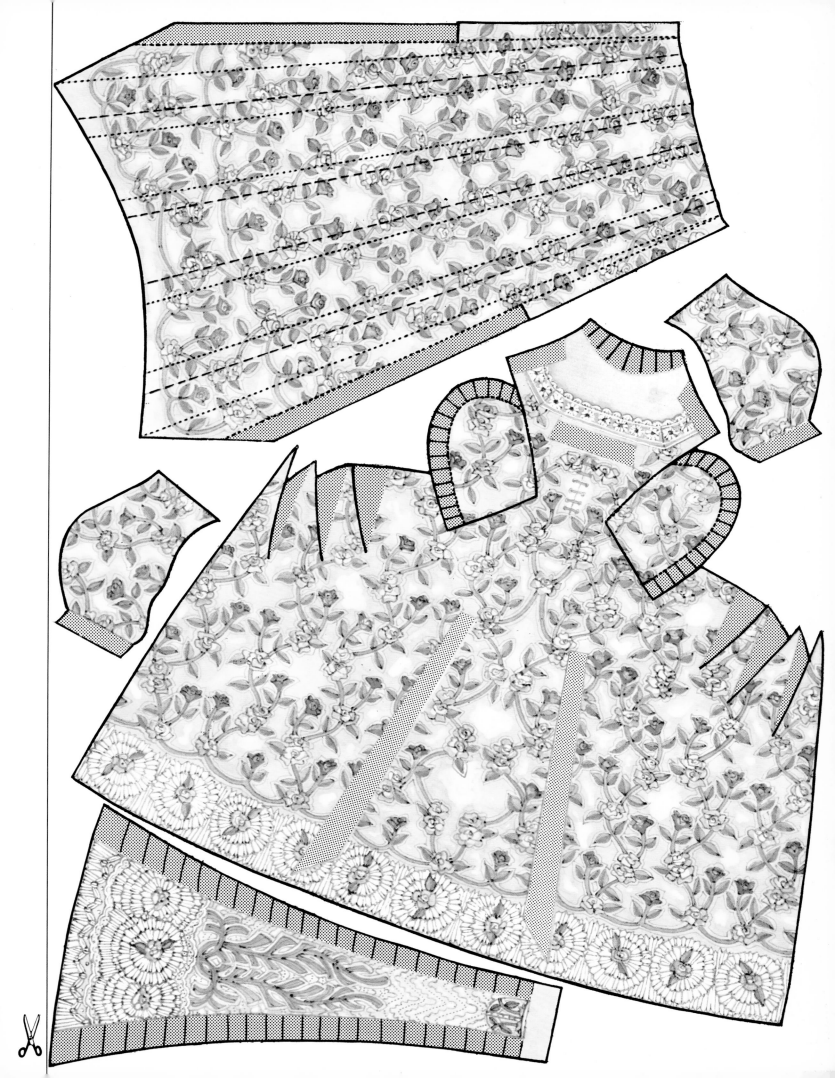

1765

1770

1772

1775

1780

5   The rise of industry in the eighteenth century brought new wealth created by the invention of many new machines. The grand life of the rich and powerful contrasted strongly to the hardship, poverty, and squalor suffered by the labouring classes. However, amongst many far-thinking people, it was a time of growing awareness of social injustices. The revolutionary war in America which won Americans complete independence from England was later to encourage the poor people of France to rise up against the indifference of their rulers. France not only sent naval and military aid to America but French fashions, too, were readily accepted by wealthy colonists, for France was still the leader in matters of style. Fashionable women eagerly awaited the arrival of the carefully constructed boxes containing detailed fashion dolls, beautifully formed in paper, showing the latest Paris styles. Towards the end of the eighteenth century, hand painted, engraved fashion plates replaced the dolls, and dressmakers could use these engravings to discuss dresses with their customers.

The Queen of France, Marie Antoinette, was indeed the Queen of fashion. Completely out of touch with reality, the Queen and ladies of her Court enjoyed their extravagant tastes, adapting and romantising their own frivolous version of the dresses of milkmaids and shepherdesses, as they amused themselves with a farm built specially for them in the grounds of the Palace of Versailles. There is little doubt that the costly whims of the Queen and her Court helped to build up the smouldering resentment that led to the raging fire of the French Revolution and her eventual execution at the guillotine.

Panniers and hoops were only worn at court, otherwise they vanished and were replaced by an existing fashion, which was altered and adapted for everyday wear, called the Polonaise.

Most dresses were made with an opening in the side seams, so that women could reach into the special side pockets which were tied by tapes around the waist beneath the petticoat. As the petticoat was slightly shorter than the dress, the more active ladies gathered up the two bottom corners of the over-gown and pushed them through the opening in the side seams, looping up the skirts as they did so to give the effect of festoons of material. This fashion continued, until by 1780 the skirts were draped by cords or tapes pulled through rings sewn inside the dress, to hold the folds more firmly and permanently in place. The low neckline of the Polonaise was tied at the bosom with a large bow. A small scarf or kerchief lay around the shoulders, folded over with the ends tucked into the neckline. Dresses were made of satin, silk, printed cotton, or muslin in plain or striped materials. The waistline was natural and a small bustle or false rump was worn to give padding to the skirt.

The extravagance of the French fashion was nowhere better to be seen than in the women's hairdressing, where the grotesque elaborate fantasies of false plaits and tresses were supported on pads and piled up and raised to absurd and exaggerated heights of over 90 centimetres (three feet). These creations were smeared with scented ointment and then heavily powdered. Into the hair were fastened pins, ribbons, feathers and various ornaments, such as artificial birds, cardboard cupids, bunches of vegetables, models of coaches, windmills, and even ships in full sail. These monstrous structures became so cumbersome that women had to sit on the floor when riding in coaches. Once built, the heavily powdered construction remained in place for days or even weeks, providing a warm comfortable hiding place for fleas so that a long-handled scratching-stick was a practical accessory!

To protect these large wigs out of doors, a large collapsible 'calash' hood, made like a pram hood, of hoops and whalebone, padded and covered in silk, could be opened up or closed down over the hair by means of cords. Less ostentatious ladies wore simpler, smaller wigs or dusted over their own hair with grey powder, this was then dressed with ringlets framing the face, hanging at times to touch the shoulders. Often perched on top of the head and held there with pins was a straw tricorne or turban hat trimmed with gauze or feathers. Ladies' shoes were made of silk or brocades decorated with jewels and buckles, with high curved heels.

Men's clothes in France still consisted of close-fitting, embroidered dress coats in satin or velvet, cut away in front to narrow coat-tails ending at the back of the knees. The double-breasted coats were generally buttoned up so that only the bottom of the waistcoat was seen. The collar was high, turned down and faced with velvet. The embroidered waistcoat was shorter than before and cut-away ending in two v-shaped points. Tight breeches in black velvet or satin extended just below the knee and were buckled or fastened by ribbons.

Men's wigs became smaller and more discreet and were worn in many styles, but towards the end of the century two or three horizontal rolls of hair were placed at the sides, and the whole crown of the hair was swept back without a parting. Beneath the wig the natural hair was cut short, and at night the wig would rest beside the bed on a wig stand. The most popular hat was the tricorne which was almost always black, edged with fringing or gold braid. Shoes were flat-soled and made of black leather, with shining silver buckles. A silver knobbed cane and a quizzing glass suspended from a black ribbon helped to complete the wardrobe of the French gentleman.

A fresh wind of change was blowing over from England, as the English simplicity of style now began to influence some of the French ideas of dress. The English noblemen, unlike their French equivalents, generally disliked Court life and preferred the freedom of their large estates. When they came to town on business or pleasure, they wore the same casual clothing made of woollen cloth in practical colours, that were designed for riding and shooting. The English lady borrowed and adapted the sporting masculine styles of the English men wearing long riding coats with shoulder capes, large lapels, bold buttons triple collars, and pocket flaps, over her dresses, as well as sensible skirts and jackets.

These English fashions rapidly gained in popularity in France, where the over-dressed French nobleman promenading with his lady was about to witness the French Revolution, and the disintegration of the world as they knew it.

1780

Kailu . Lowndes

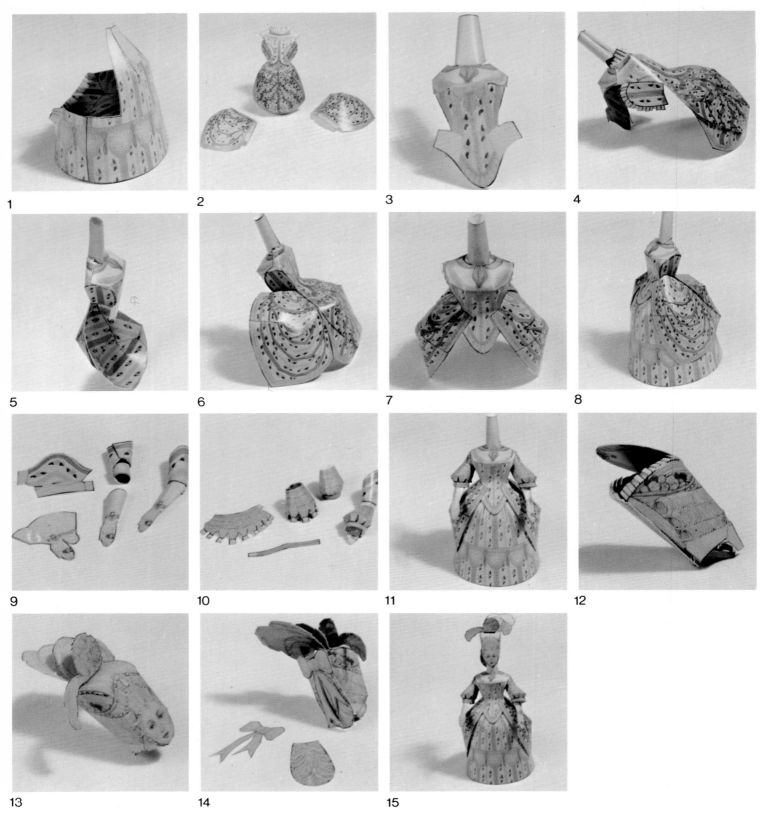

1

2

3

4

5

6

7

8

9

10

11

12

13

14

15

On the next two pages you will find a costume model of 1780
Cut out the pages carefully along the cutting lines.
When making the model it is important to follow the assembly
order by numbers as shown above.

For general instructions on cutting, folding and glueing see
page 4.

On the back of the cutout pages there are patchwork patterns.
These form the patterned linings to the dresses, hats and ribbons etc.

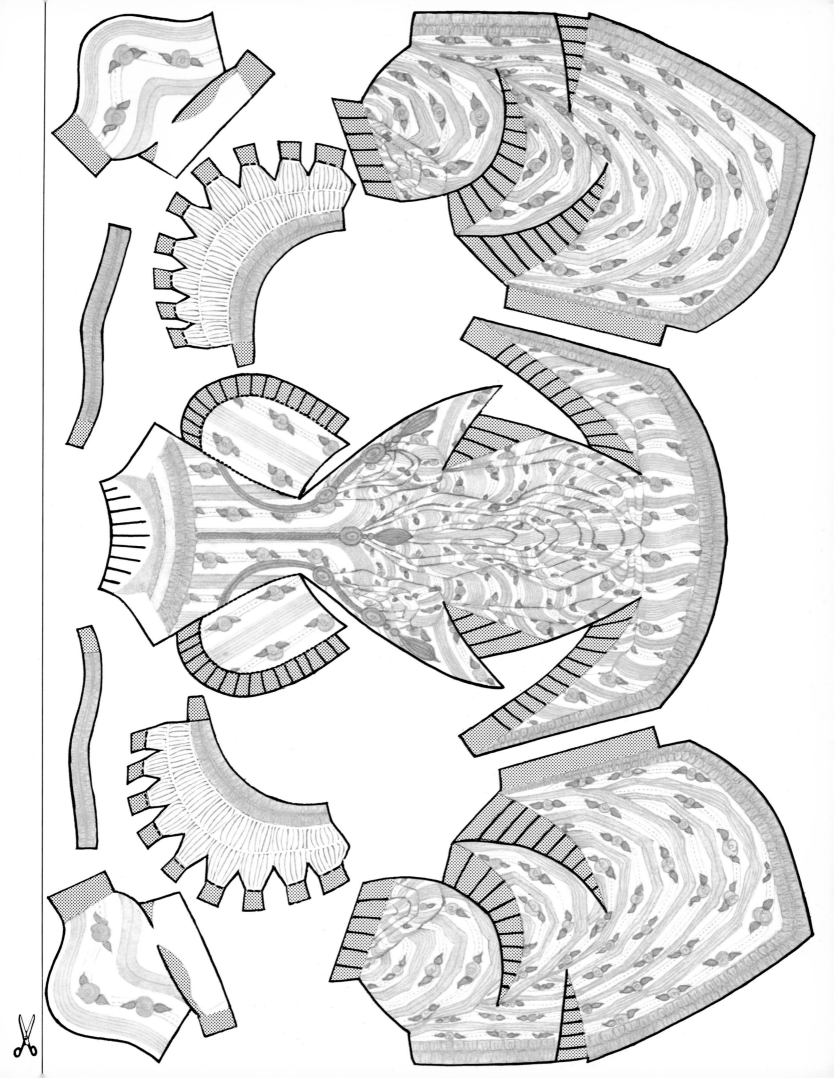

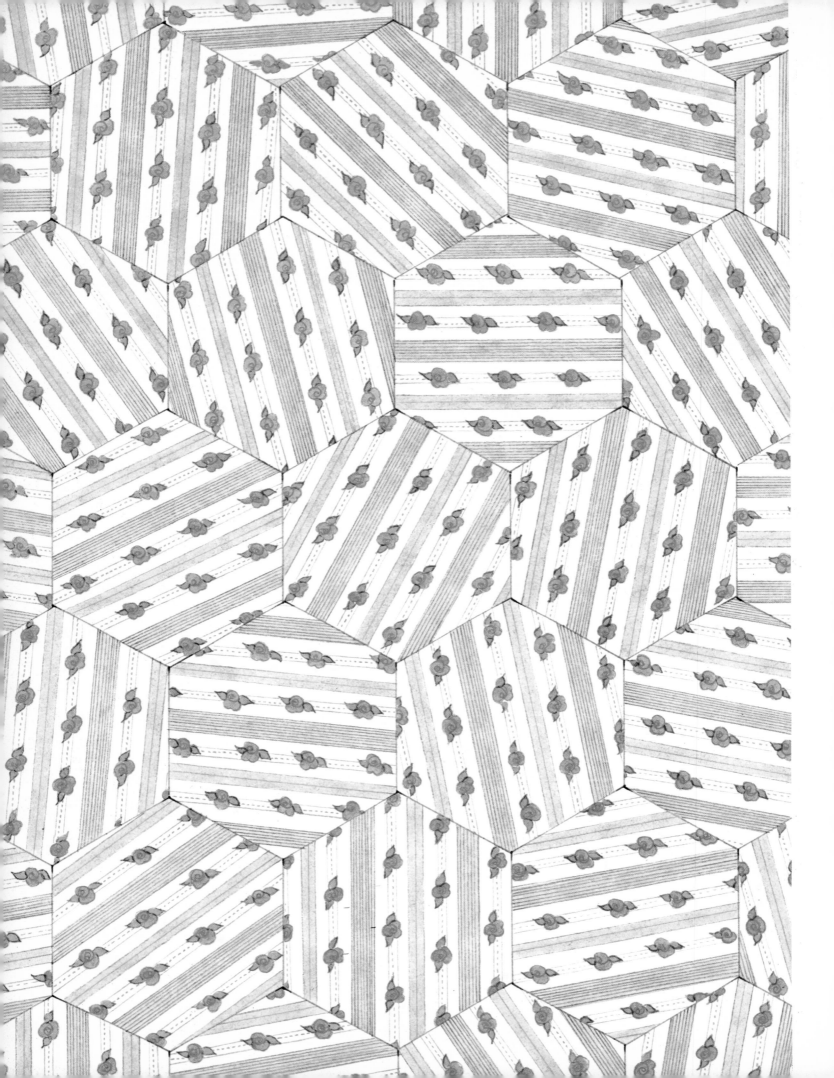

1780

1790

1795

1796

1802

1815

6   The English country styles continued in popularity throughout Europe and gentlemen's clothes were more sober and well cut. As ladies hairdressing became simpler, their hats grew larger and more flamboyant. Gentle muslin dresses were worn with a natural waistline and a soft fichu (scarf) puffed out and draped around the neck to look pigeon-chested, Then came the French Revolution and a dramatic change in fashion.

   No one could survive the reign of Terror during the French Revolution if they continued the customs and flaunted the clothes of the Royalists. To escape attention and avoid denunciation and the danger of death at the guillotine it was necessary to dress as one of the people. Therefore fashion meant a display of simplicity, liberty and equality in costume. When the threat of the guillotine had passed, there was an upsurge of freedom of expression that was immediately reflected in the fashions worn by the carefree and spirited youth. They dressed in outrageous clothes ; the young men called 'incroyables' (incredibles), wore high collars with enormous cravats that covered not only the neck, but the chin as well, and generally carried their clothing to extremes of ridiculous exaggeration. The young women 'merveilleuses' (the marvellous ones), admired the classic Greek and Roman dress, which they adapted into high waisted and transparent dresses, daringly slit from waist to hem, worn with open Roman sandals on their feet and rings on their toes. Hair of both sexes was wild, short, straggly and totally dishevelled.

   Revolutionary France was caught up in wars with neighbouring nations. In the beginning, victories in Italy, Spain and Portugal brought General Bonaparte power and fame. In 1804 Napoleon, at the age of thirty, became Emperor of the French.

   The dream of Napoleon was a romantic vision of the Roman empire, so the flowing classical lines of ancient Roman

clothes were transformed into fragile white muslin and the delicate textures of net, gauze and lace. The dresses were semi-transparent sheaths with the necklines low-cut and square exposing most of the bosom, and the arms were bare. Immediately below the breasts, the high waists were encircled with a narrow belt, allowing the skirt to fall in graceful, soft folds to the feet. Underneath the dress was worn a flesh coloured body stocking which gave a daring impression of nudity. It was not long before Napoleon decided that the dignity of the state was in question, which brought in a new sense of modesty to Frenchwomen, and through them to the rest of Europe and America. The bare arms were covered in long coloured gloves to be replaced gradually by long narrow sleeves with small puffs on the shoulders. The bare bosom was filled in with gauze and ended in a ruffled collarette around the neck. The smartest fashion accessory was the brightly coloured shawl, the more expensive ones came from Kashmir in India, but cheaper imitations were made and found an instant market. There was an art to wearing the shawl, it could be draped behind the back and over the arms, or else trailed along the floor.

The simple sheath dress was now no longer semi-transparent. Made of heavier silks it was embroidered with floral decorative motifs; the hem of the skirt was padded and swags of ruched ribbons or fabrics were added to give greater richness and weight.

Since the light weight gowns gave no protection from the cold winter, even though stiffened petticoats and knee drawers were worn underneath, an outer garment was introduced in the form of a fur-lined coat with a hood. This was the origin of the coat as we know it today.

The Napoleonic wars influenced women's dress in Europe; froggings, epaulettes and braid—the trimmings of military uniforms—became part of the fashion-conscious ladies' wardrobe. At first women's hair was cut short—a fashionable reminder of preparations for the guillotine. Later it was arranged in the soft flattering forms of the ancient Greek style. This led to the wearing of all types of bonnets and turbans fitting closely to the head, the most popular hat was the tall-crowned French bonnet decorated with sprays of artificial flowers, tied under the chin with bright ribbons with the wide brim sweetly framing the face. To achieve a pale, fragile, interesting look, white face powder was used, without rouge.

For walking front-laced boots of soft kid were comfortable and for evening wear and dancing white satin slippers were fashionable and pretty. Both had small, very low heels or no heels at all, and white silk stockings showed off a delightful trim ankle.

It was necessary to carry small fabric bags, for dresses allowed no place for pockets. Fans were small and discreet and jewellery was worn sparingly.

From the French Revolution onwards the centre of fashion for the man passed from Paris to London. The informality and independence of the English gentleman with his dislike of fussy detail in his casual country wear, was carried to the ultimate elegance in the carefully fitted and perfectly tailored suits encouraged by the Prince Regent, and his dandy friends such as Beau Brummel.

Ornate silk embroidery disappeared from men's clothes to be replaced by a new crisp concept of scrupulous cleanliness.

The double breasted tail coat was cut square and then sloped away from the waist leaving the thighs free. The coats were of plain colours usually in dark blue, black, olive green or plum. Beneath the waistcoat was worn a linen shirt with a muslin frill at the neck or else high starched white collars with the points reaching the cheeks, tied by a broad tightly-wrapped cravat, the meticulous knotting of which was the most important part of a man's dress.

The tight, light-coloured breeches were fastened by small buttons on the outside of the legs below the knees and were tucked into highly polished black leather riding boots with tan-coloured tops.

During the daytime out of doors, single breasted greatcoats trimmed with fur collars and cuffs were worn, for evening wear the greatcoats were exchanged for cloaks. Hairstyles for men were classical, cut fairly short and brushed forward onto the face without a parting, in soft curls or strands. All gentlemen wore hats of silk or beaver, with curled up brims; the crowns were large but of moderate height, in colours of black, fawn or grey. Men's jewellery was inconspicuous, consisting merely of a gold watch, fob and chain.

For the first time in the history of fashion it was now stylish to be discreet.

1815

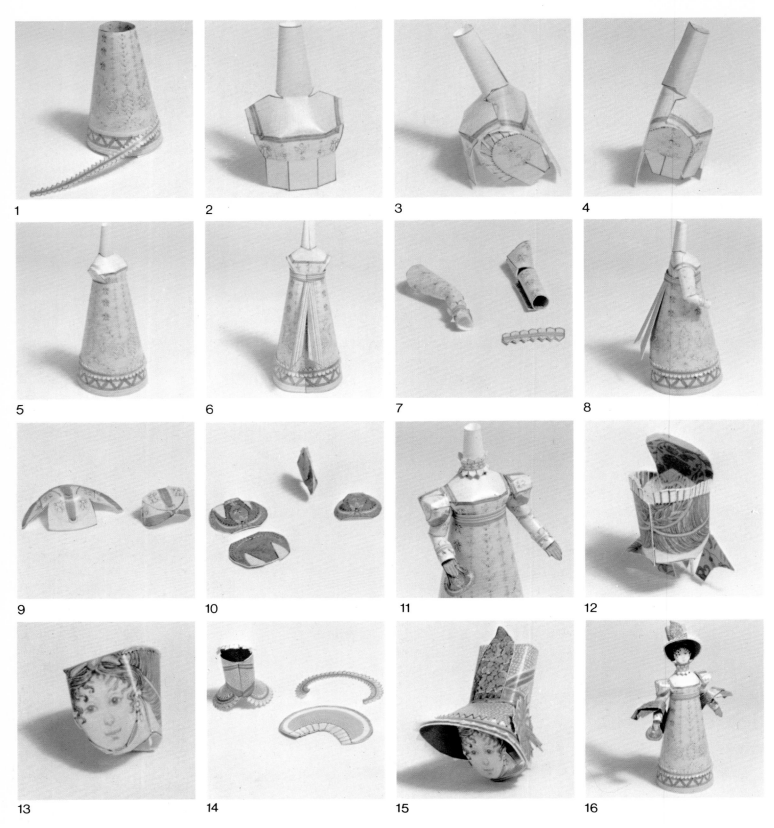

1 2 3 4

5 6 7 8

9 10 11 12

13 14 15 16

On the next two pages you will find a costume model of 1815
Cut out the pages carefully along the cutting lines.
When making the model it is important to follow the assembly
order by numbers as shown above.

For general instructions on cutting, folding and glueing see
page 4.

On the back of the cutout pages there are patchwork patterns.
These form the patterned linings to the dresses, hats and ribbons etc.

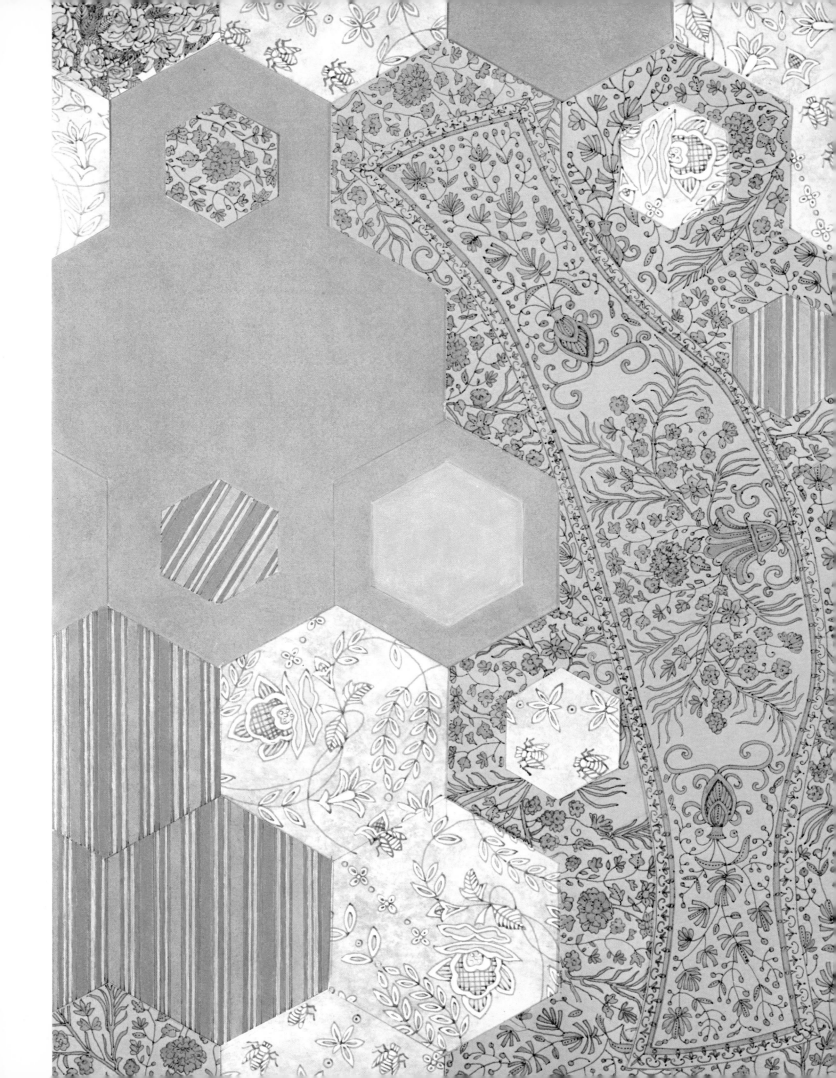

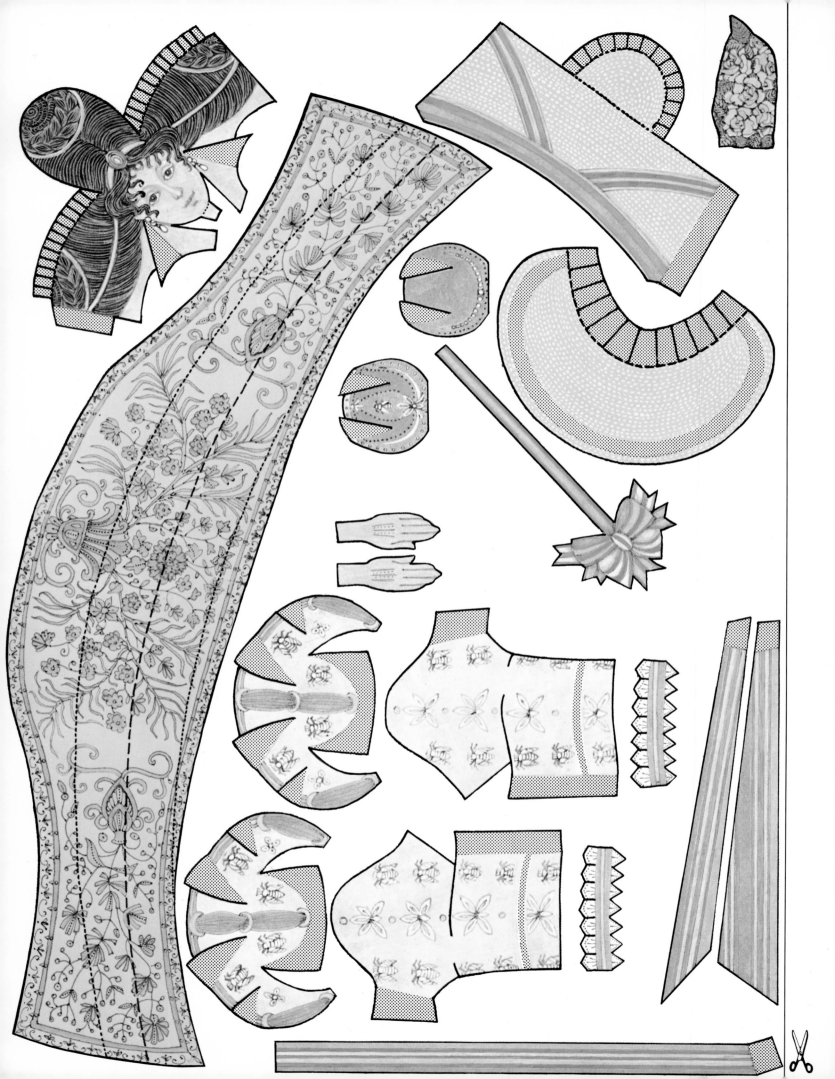

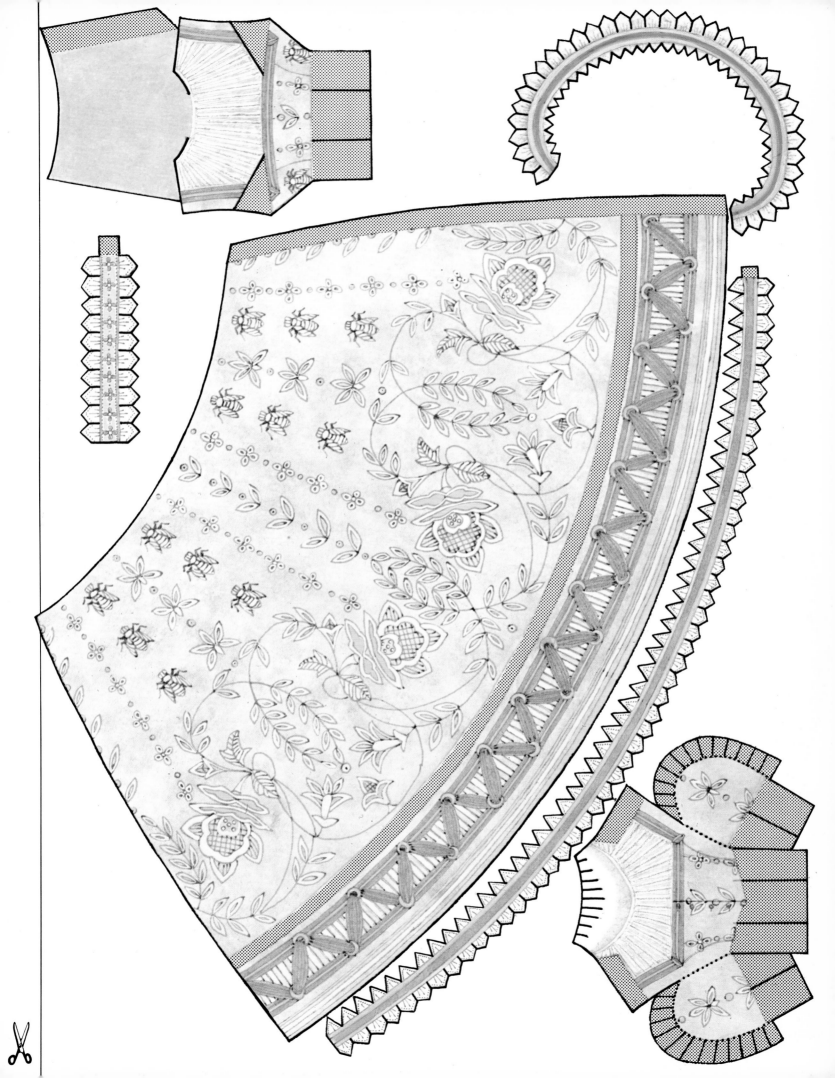

1825

1835

1850

1860

7   In Paris in the 1820s the Empire waistline dropped to its natural position immediately above the hips. Tightly laced corsets squeezed and compressed the waist into the now fashionable hour-glass figure. Sleeves were puffed out, giving a top heavy downward sloping appearance at the shoulder line whilst the skirt was widened at the hem with padded bands and decorations. This was topped by wide hats and bonnets decorated with streaming ribbons and fluttering feathers.

Following similar lines as the women, the fashionable men of this period wore an ample loose frock coat thrown open to display deep rolling padded collars and wide lapels, emphasising the narrow waist and retaining a military swagger and self-confidence showed in the variety of colours used for waistcoats, gloves, and cravats. This was virtually the last splash of colour to be seen in men's dress.

After 1830 trousers were well and truly established. First introduced in the early 1800s, they were at first skin-tight and ended above the ankle, then fell loosely to the feet fastened under the shoes by means of straps. In contrast to the dark coats in sombre hues of blue or brown, trousers were light grey or fawn. For town wear a symbol of respectability was the tall shiny cylindrical top hat with a large brim later reducing in width.

Every year the spread of the ladies' skirt made a wider circle, supported by up to seven petticoats made of starched muslin, flannel, padded cotton or quilted down, these became so heavy that walking was difficult.

Fashion was undergoing one of those strange changes for which it is famous. From the simple comfortable sheath-like dress of the Empire period, the almost incredible crinoline arrived on the scene. To support the volume of these large gowns which covered the women's long lace trimmed pantaloons, at first pads of horse hair (crin in French) were

introduced to make their skirts stand out. Later a stiff dome-shaped crinoline cage was introduced, consisting of an ever increasing circumference towards the hem, of bamboo, whalebone or steel hoops suspended on tapes; its lightness gave a much greater freedom of movement.

The crinoline stayed in fashion for over twenty years during which time even the charming habit of a gentleman giving his arm to a lady had to be abandoned, and to sit beside a woman on a sofa was impossible, as women were made unapproachable by their skirts. You could hold their hands but not embrace them.

This was a time when a desire to dwell on the tragedies of life was reflected in the cultivated delicate appearance, to look pale and faint into a trance was considered to be delightfully feminine. But with the increase in width of the dress women seemed to develop a self-confidence in society and the fragile angel of the 1800s was transformed into the heavily draped matronly woman of the 1860s.

From 1860 crinoline cages were flattened in front, and the fullness was concentrated at the back, extending in length almost into a train. The day dress was usually high-necked and the tiny waist was squeezed into a boned and laced corset. Large decorated 'pagoda' sleeves were worn over under-sleeves of white tulle or puffed muslin which were gathered in at the wrist and enriched with rows of lace. Large heavily fringed and braided shawls or capes were draped over the huge sleeves and voluminous skirts during the winter months. Pastel shades and white were popular for evening wear. Evening gowns were in silks and other light materials, with deeply cut necklines to expose the shoulders.

Deep purple, magenta, dark green and brown materials were fashionable during the daytime; the dresses heavily decorated with stripes and bands in contrasting colours, of silk, velvet or plush edged with rows of tassels and fringes.

The impracticability of the crinolines led to the short-lived introduction of loose baggy trousers gathered in at the ankles, by the courageous American Mrs. Amelia Bloomer, who at least if not able to establish a new fashion gave her name to womens knickers until more recent times.

The hair was brushed down smoothly from a centre parting, kept simple in style, with a low bun circular plaits over the ears, or side curls falling onto the cheeks.

At first the brim of the poke bonnets rose high from the forehead but after 1840 it shrank in size, no longer hiding the face but worn well back on the head, with ruchings and long tabs tied under the chin. Bonnets were made in velvet and silk or light straw and were often trimmed inside or out with feathers or bows of fine ribbons.

Outdoor shoes were long and narrow with square toes and high shaped heels. Boots of white satin, kid or coloured silks were also worn to just above the ankle, either laced or buttoned up or with elastic at the inner side, usually with white stockings.

Hands were covered in gloves or lace mittens and handbags were made of velvet and silks, decorated with needlework or beads.

Very young boys and girls dressed so alike that it was difficult to tell them apart. Both wore dresses over ankle-length pantaloons. Older boys wore sailor suits which remained the fashion for many years. The older girls copied their mothers, but with shorter dresses.

Unlike women's clothes men's fashions did not change dramatically. Gradually by 1860, men lost the romantic dash and individuality of colour of the early 1800s, becoming heavier with the arrival of the dark unimaginative woollen frock coat, which, accompanied by a plain waistcoat, was only slightly relieved by the coloured, checked or striped trousers without creases or turnups.

A simple form of bow tie replaced the elegant cravat worn over a starched, pleated shirt.

Hair was fairly long, parted in the centre or side and brushed forward to curl over the ears with side whiskers, sometimes accompanied by a moustache. Country hats for men were low crowned and broad brimmed. The essential tall, cylindrical top hat, of silk or felt, in fawn, grey or black, completed the town gentleman's wardrobe.

Leather shoes and boots, tended to be narrow in the foot and square at the toe, often with gaiters.

The clothes for men and women of this period, although lacking in originality and imagination, gave an impression of reassuring dependability similar to the rich drapes and stuffy hangings which were crammed into the parlours and sitting rooms; this heavy claustrophobic extravagance was reflected in the formal clothes of the time.

1860

Kailer Lowndes

1   2   3   4

5   6   7   8

9   10   11   12

13   14   15   16

On the next two pages you will find a costume model of 1860
Cut out the pages carefully along the cutting lines.
When making the model it is important to follow the assembly
order by numbers as shown above.

For general instructions on cutting, folding and glueing see
page 4.

On the back of the cutout pages there are patchwork patterns.
These form the patterned linings to the dresses, hats and ribbons etc.

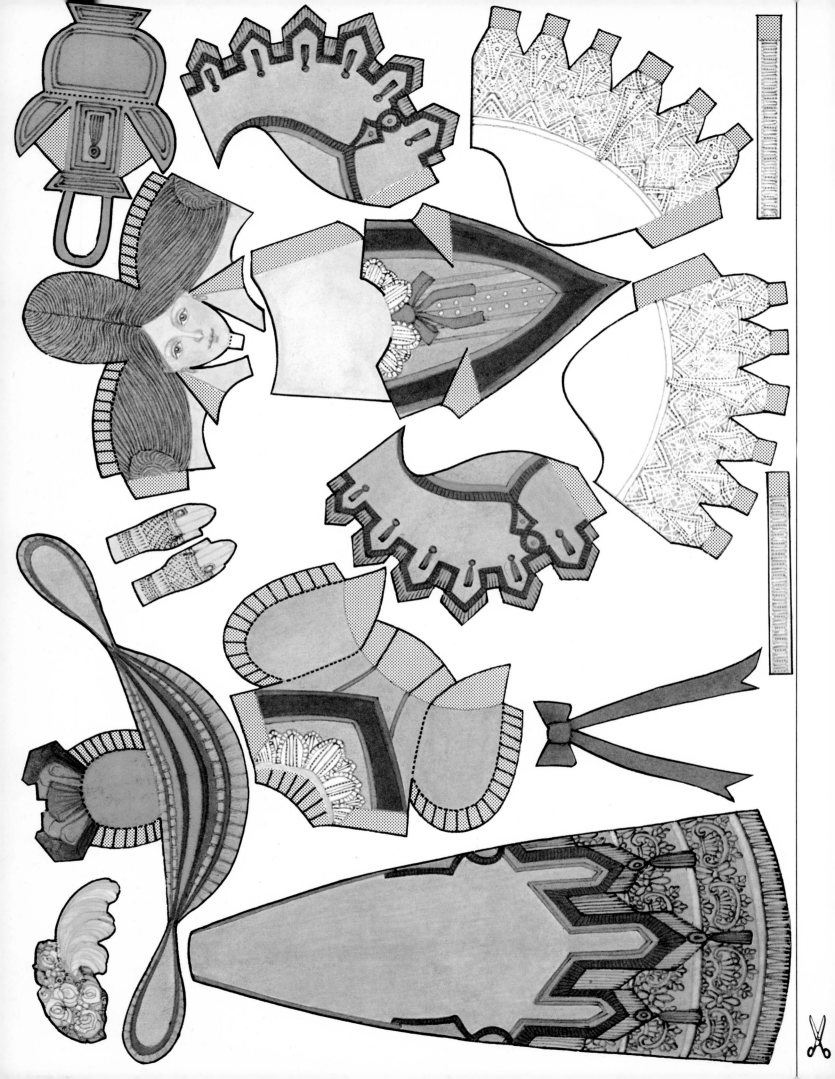

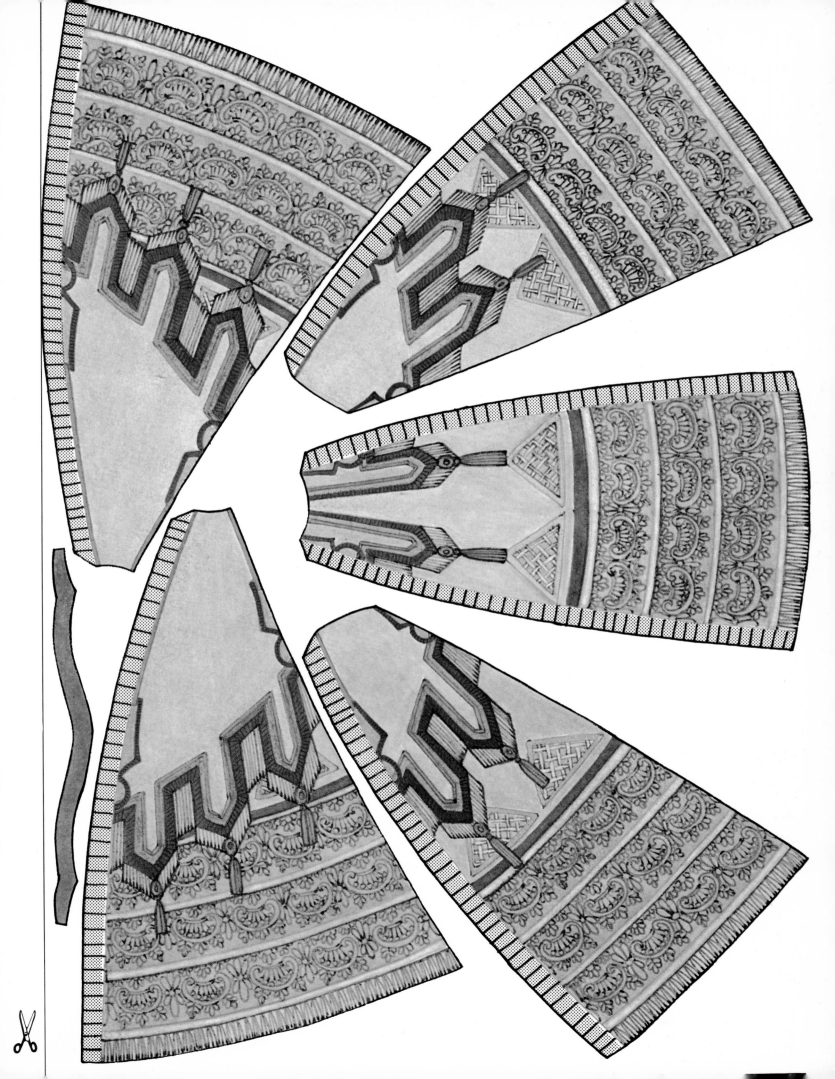

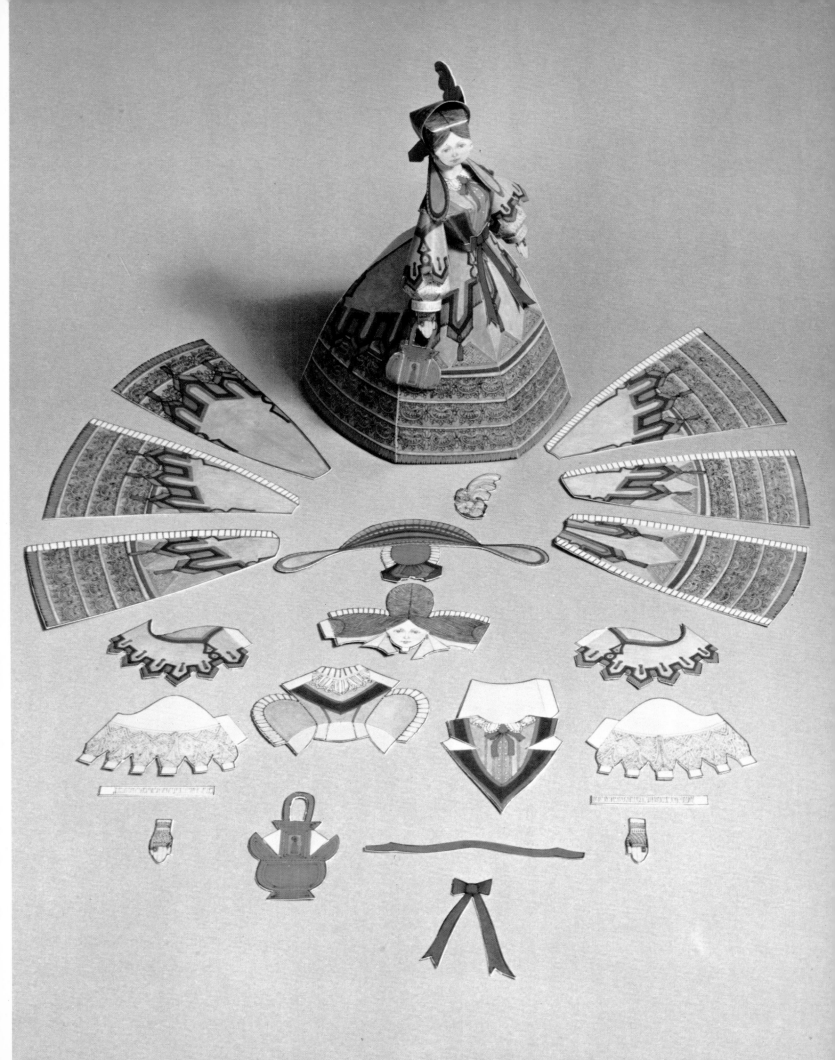

1865

1868

1870

1875

8   Fashion magazines with illustrations of the latest modes made it not only possible for all women to follow the latest styles, but also to choose patterns for themselves, thus expressing their individual personalities.

By 1867 it was recorded that America was manufacturing two hundred thousand sewing machines each year for the world market and with the introduction of these time-and-labour-saving devices, the ready-to-wear clothing industry grew rapidly, although ladies of society still ordered their dresses from the dressmakers. However, a young Englishman, Charles Worth, who worked in Paris, had the new idea of preparing a collection of dresses to offer his customers and the first Haute Couture fashion house of Paris was born. Paris collections showing complete ensembles, assured French supremacy over women's clothes throughout the world; Paris dictated the fashion and everyone followed.

The crinoline had grown larger and larger until, like most extremes of fashion, it became ridiculous—and with lighted candles and gas lamps—highly dangerous as it was so easy for the huge skirts to catch fire. After a few modifications, such as a half crinoline called a crinolette, it finally disappeared from favour by 1870 and it then became as important to reveal the shape of the female figure as it had been to conceal it under the mushrooming crinoline. Women's hips, previously hidden from view, came back into sight as the skirts were draped closely around the body and then bunched up behind over a 'dress improver'—a boned half-cage which supported the back of the skirt, so that the material fell from it into a long train which swept the floor. The skirt, looped up and back, was adorned with frills, ribbons and flounces. The half-cage was soon replaced by the small jaunty 'bustle' which jutted out from the lower back and was made of rolls of braided wire in a stuffed cushion shape tied around the waist by tapes. The

feminine shape under the sweeping gown was further enhanced and shown off to advantage by a stylish tight-fitting tailor-made jacket with long tight sleeves, the tiny waist emphasised by a line of buttons down the front. The back of the jacket sat on top of the bustle, with the skirt flowing down to the ground in a great many flounces.

For wealthy society women it was important to dress according to the occasion. Clothes for the morning and afternoon, clothes for formal dinners, and clothes for the theatre. Rich shot-silks, taffetas, satins, delightful striped or checked patterned cottons and linen were all used to subtle effect. Glossy and dull materials were mixed together and draped into pleats and swags in the same dress. Day dresses, with the introduction of the newly-discovered aniline dyes, were garish in bright hues such as royal blue, emerald green, cerise and plum.

For evening wear white was still predominant, with gowns cut daringly low and square at the bosom, with short sleeves.

Hair, like the dresses, was drawn back and piled high in a chignon, or bun, on top of the head with falling loops and twists of hair hanging down to the shoulders. Small perky hats were worn well forward over the forehead in a great variety of styles, decorated with feathers, lace, flowers or ribbons. For the evening the hair was entwined with sprays of flowers, ribbon streamers or jewelled clasps.

Precious stones in heavy, ornate settings were fashionable jewellery, and at night close-fitting necklaces encircled the delicate throat, with large matching earrings almost reaching the shoulders. During the day short silk or kid gloves protected the pale hands, and the fashionably fair skin was shielded from the sun's rays by a long-handled parasol.

Brocaded slippers, often with small heels, were worn indoors. High heeled boots, laced up in front or buttoned at the side were worn out of doors.

Women could now take up simple sports. Free at last from the cumbersome clumsiness of the swaying crinoline their clothes took on a lively, pretty and pert appearance helped by the bewitching twitch of the bustle and the figure-flattering jackets.

Essentially men's fashions became simplified, for evening wear the cut-away coat was necessary and for morning wear a coat with the front sloping away at the sides was to remain in fashion for many years. However, the single or double-breasted frock coat, shaped at the waist and fully buttoned, in fawn, greys or black was considered correct for town.

Trousers were light in colour, in plain greys or striped, fitting the legs loosely, but narrowing slightly below the knees. A new informality was creeping into men's dress by the introduction of the short jacket, the ancestor of the modern jacket and for daytime a starched round collar was worn with a cravat, or the less formal turned down collar with a knotted or bow tie.

With the growing interest in various sporting activities it was necessary to wear more comfortable clothes. A craze for bicycling initiated a strange outfit consisting of a jacket in checked rough material with matching 'knickerbockers' stopping just below the knee. Thick woollen stockings filled in the gap between the knickerbockers and the black or brown ankle boots, which were sometimes topped with leather gaiters. Men of this era felt undressed without a hat, during daytime and for evening wear. For visits to town the top hat was essential with the frock coat, although the low crowned black or fawn bowler hat (or 'Derby' as it is called in America), with the brim slightly curved up at the sides was becoming fashionable. The sporting version of the bowler was covered in tweed material, soft caps of similar fabrics were popular, and the deerstalker with peaks at front and back was worn for fishing and shooting.

For evening a black tail-coat was worn with a front pleated white shirt, short white waistcoat and white bow tie.

Hair was cut quite short and parted in the middle or side. Side whiskers and moustaches helped the young men to look older and more responsible, whilst the older men strived to look like wise sages, under large beards. Inconspicuous jewellery was acceptable, being confined to a gold ring and perhaps a gold watch and chain, as well as a tie pin set with jewels, gold cuff links and shirt studs set with pearls or diamonds.

The tremendous progress in the manufacture of superb cloths, both plain and woven, enabled men and women to take pride in the cut and quality of their clothes, and to possess a selection for different occasions, ranging from theatre going to roller skating.

1875

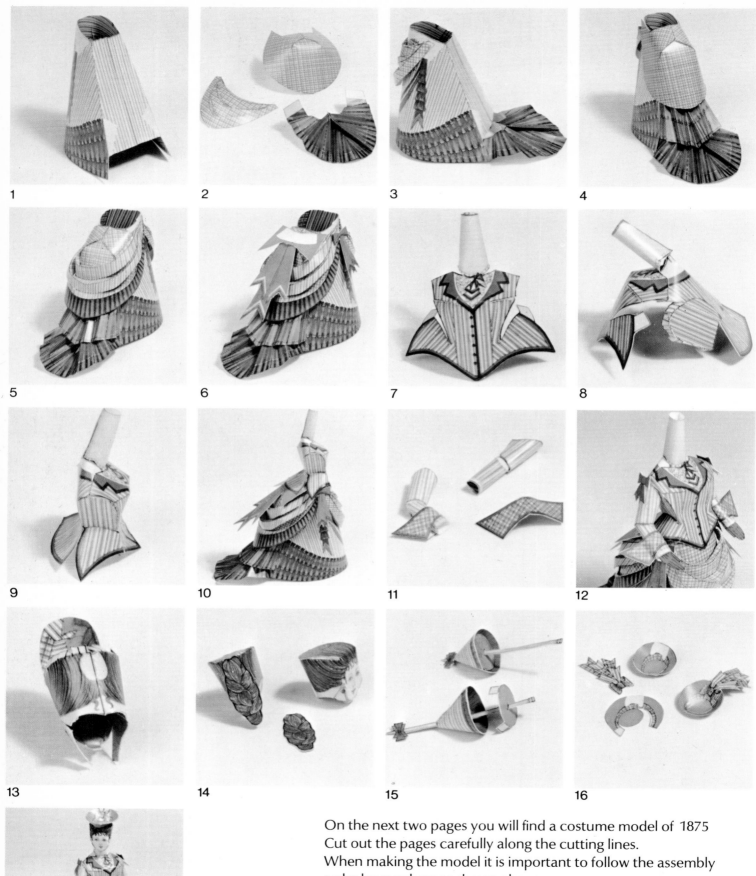

1

2

3

4

5

6

7

8

9

10

11

12

13

14

15

16

17

On the next two pages you will find a costume model of 1875
Cut out the pages carefully along the cutting lines.
When making the model it is important to follow the assembly
order by numbers as shown above.

For general instructions on cutting, folding and glueing see
page 4.

On the back of the cutout pages there are patchwork patterns.
These form the patterned linings to the dresses, hats and ribbons etc.

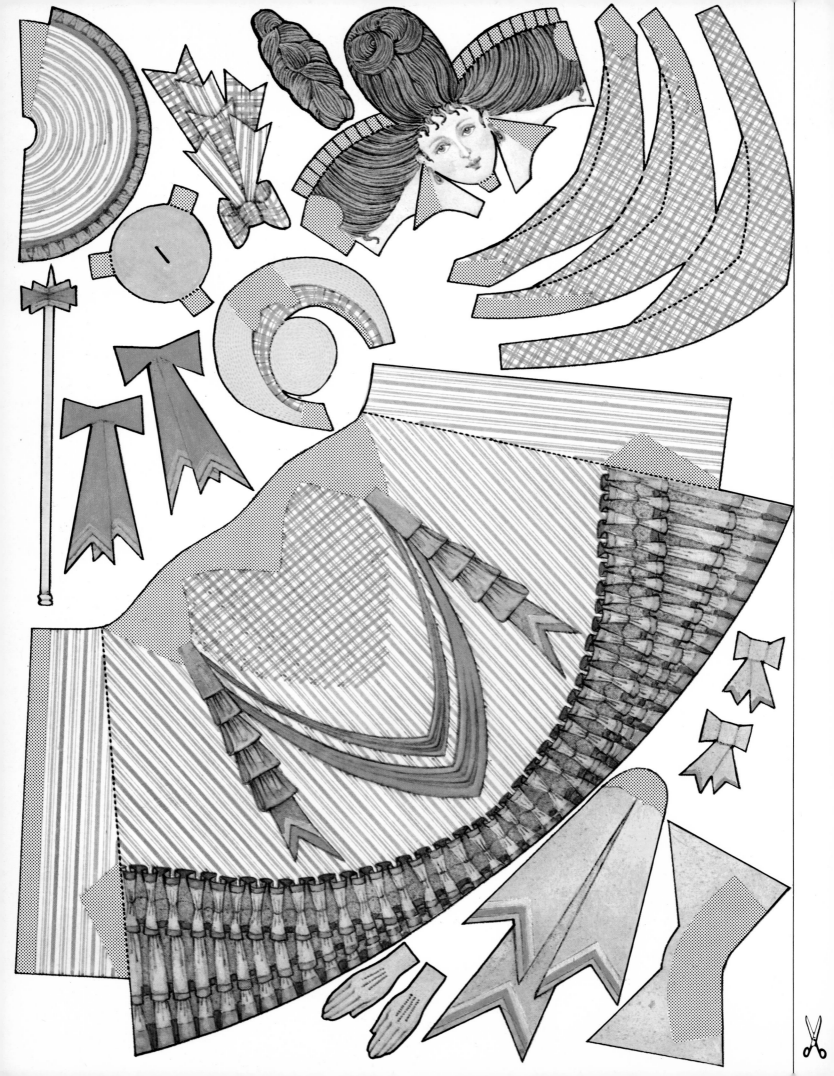

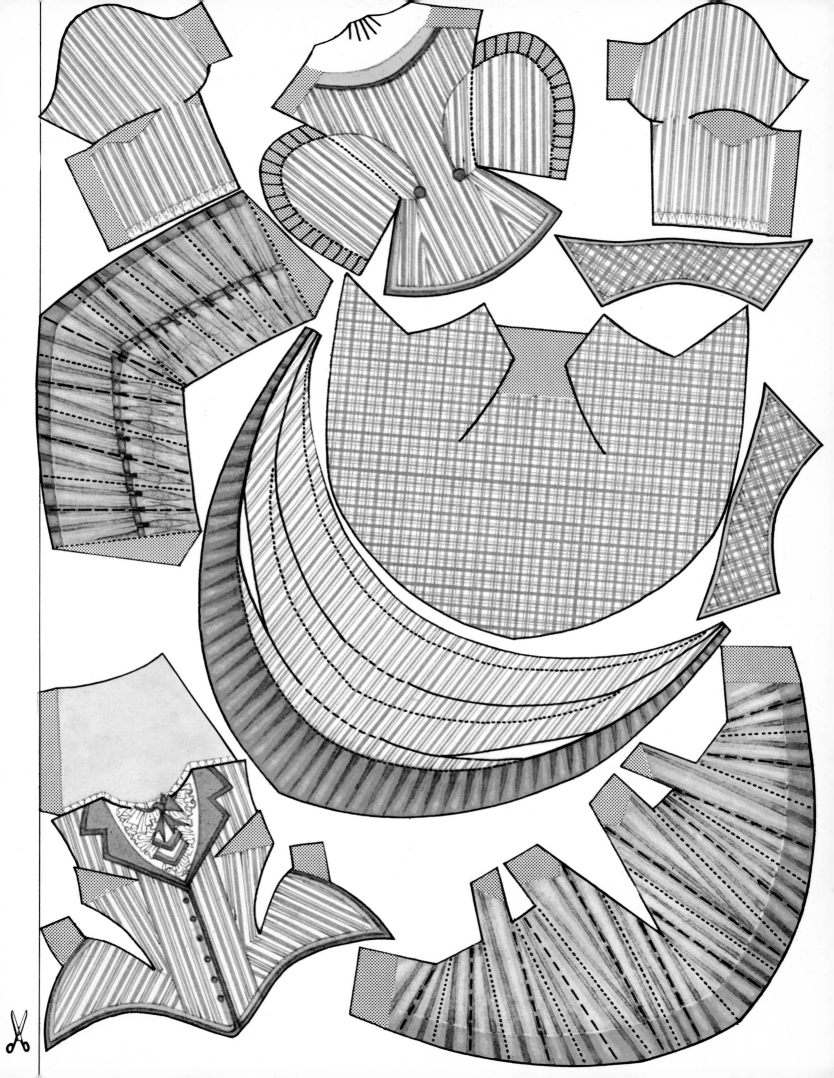

1878

1885

1895

1900

1905

9   The bustle grew higher and larger until by 1887 it gained truly exaggerated dimensions. Then it disappeared, although the waist was still kept small by the well tailored and boned seams of the bodice. During the daytime the collar remained high with abundant trimmings of lace. 'Gigot', or leg-of-mutton, sleeves were puffed out at the shoulder narrowing to a tight fit from the elbow to the wrist.

Towards the end of the 1800s a new practical dress was now worn by the young women earning their livings as typists and shop assistants. Close fitting, tailored, hip length jackets, were worn over elaborate blouses with either a high lace collar, or a stiff masculine collar and tie, with a long flared, simply cut, ground length skirt, tightly belted at the narrow waist allowing the blouse to pouch out over it. The whole effect gave a crisp clean line suitable for the informality of games and sports such as archery, tennis, croquet, skating or bicycling.

The Wright Brothers flew their first aeroplane in 1903, and the cinema was opening up a new world to everybody. Materials became soft and clinging, the flowing lines of the gowns harmonizing with the twisting curving flowing lines of the Art Nouveau style in decorative art. Chiffon, tulle, linen, muslin, and voile were made into attractive dresses and the more expensive natural subtle coloured silks, satins, brocades and velvets, lavishly outlined with lace, minute tucks, tiny beads, miniature buttons and narrow ribbons, were in great demand by elegant society women.

Delicate hues and gentle pastel shades were all the rage for blouses, coats and skirts in light pink, blue, green and yellow, light brown or grey. Although at the same time, French couturiers influenced by the costume designs for the Russian ballet, preferred the bold contrasts of brilliant exotic oriental colours.

These highly sophisticated gowns demanded exaggerated curves, achieved by the new foundation garment which

moulded the figure into a curious S shape, by pushing the bust forward over a tiny waist; the back arched inwards at the waistline and the stomach was flattened. The women of fashion had to look heavy in the bust and rear, so padded corsets helped enormously.

The tightly belted trumpet shaped skirt was composed of sections flaring outwards at the hem, making it necessary to lift the skirt daringly when out walking, showing the flounces of the petticoat.

The blouse was high-necked with a deep lace yoke and high collar boned at the sides to stand up round the neck with a satin or silk neckband.

With the aids of pads, combs, slides and hair pins the hair was piled on top of the head in a bun with a loose upward sweep. The front arranged softly in puffs and waves made a foundation for the vast hats, perched high on the head, laden with ostrich feathers and flowers and anchored in place by means of a long elaborate hat pin. It was still not considered proper for a lady to wear more than the slightest suspicion of make-up.

Daytime accessories consisted of vanity bags, long handled parasols, and large muffs in winter. Long feathered boas fluttered round the lace collared necks and long kid or silk gloves were worn outdoors during daytime or with evening dress.

The cool sophisticated, wealthy woman with her wardrobe of outfits for every occasion, was equally matched by the men. Men's formal dress had altered little, although the black morning suit was now more fashionable with the jacket bound at the edges with silk, worn with dark striped or checked trousers. The man's short dinner jacket was first worn at this time for comfort during the long evenings. The new fashion for ironing a crease down each trouser leg did away with the baggy unkempt look. The short jacket of the lounge suit with a slit in the back became universal and was worn with matching trousers.

For motoring through the countryside gentlemen wore tweed Norfolk jackets with broad pleats at the back and a wide belt above large pockets, with knee breeches. Stiff cuffs and starched upright, or turned-down, collars with bow or knotted tie were obligatory, but when boating or bicycling during the heat of the summer, the light summer suit kept the wearer cool.

Although silk top hats remained in favour, bowler hats were common. The new straw boater or straw panama with a silk band brightened the summer days, while sporting tweed hats kept the head warm in the winter countryside. Hair was quite short at the back and sides and brushed backwards usually with a centre parting. Beards were worn by elderly men, but the young man was clean shaven, apart from a moustache trimmed in a variety of styles.

Laced, polished black or brown, leather boots were changed in summer for white buckskin or canvas boots or shoes. Elegance demanded few masculine accessories, a silver topped cane, a simple tie pin, and a pair of gloves completed the gentleman's wardrobe.

From 1905 onwards faster transport and speedy means of communication appeared to reduce the size of the world, and women's fashion was to become more uniformly international. The American influence of the hobble skirt followed in 1910—with the new craze for dancing tangos. Later in the 1920s the Charleston brought in the age of the Flapper. Never before had girls worn waistless, knee length skirts nor dared to cut their hair quite so short, and tight corsets were abandoned altogether.

There were gradual adjustments in the styles for men who began to wear the lounge suits more and more. These have only changed in cut to become more casual and relaxed during recent years.

During and after the Second World War women learnt to wear utilitarian, masculine styles with padded high shoulders and trousers became gradually acceptable wear.

Fashion has always changed whenever a style had been pushed to an extreme. Just as panniers and hoops gave way to sheath dresses, so the masculine clothes became more feminine with the more romantic 'new look' after the Second World War. Skirts, pullovers, suits and dresses continued to be modified and changed in cut, without any really startling variation, until in the 1960s skirt hems shot up, and nearly vanished with the mini skirt. Having gone so far, down it came again! Perhaps the greatest fashion change of all in present times is the lack of any real definite style to follow. Most people now wear exactly what they please to suit the contemporary scene.

1905

Kailer Lowndes

1

2

3

4

5

6

7

8

9

10

11

12

13

14

15

16

17

On the next two pages you will find a costume model of 1905
Cut out the pages carefully along the cutting lines.
When making the model it is important to follow the assembly
order by numbers as shown above.

For general instructions on cutting, folding and glueing see
page 4.

On the back of the cutout pages there are patchwork patterns.
These form the patterned linings to the dresses, hats and ribbons etc.

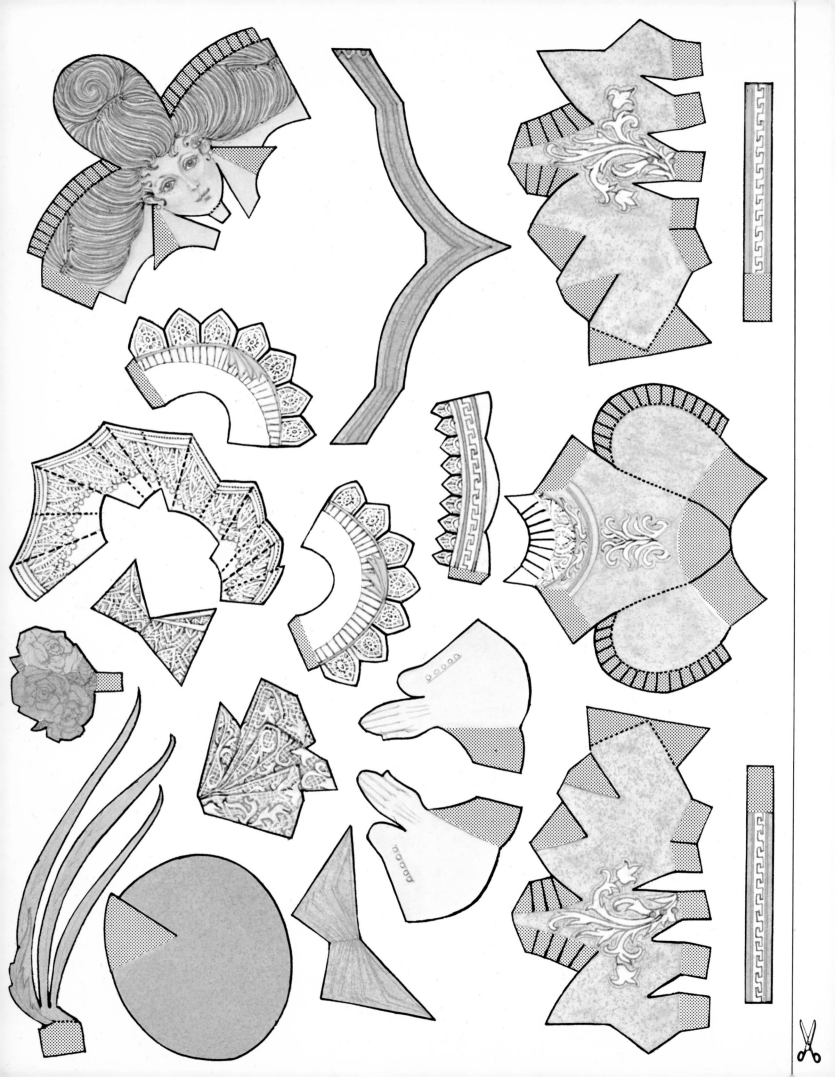

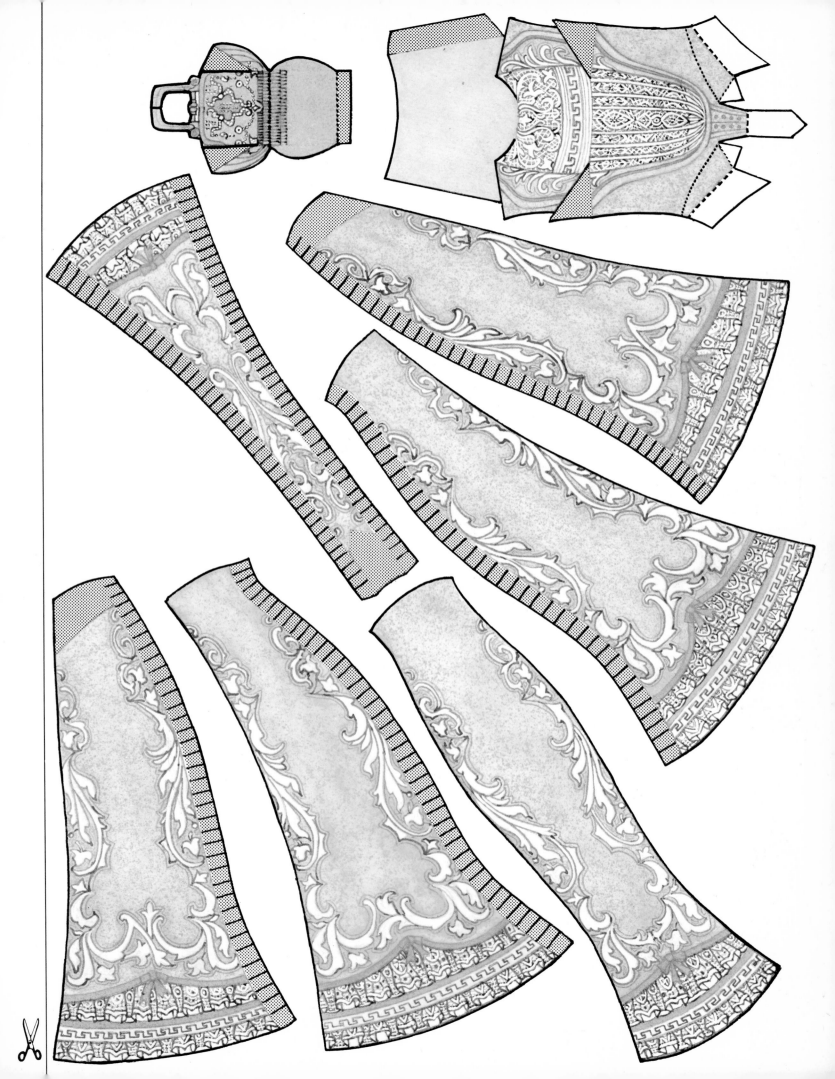

When you have made the models and their backgrounds.

Cut out the booklet pages carefully along the black line. Punch holes at intervals along the margin, bind with metal rings, or thread ribbon, loosely tied, through the holes.

Cut out each fashion plate carefully along the black line. Pin them on the wall or else paste them first onto a coloured background as shown.

You will now have a complete costume collection of your own.

Special thanks are due to
Trevor Jones and Diana Hall
for all their help, and to
Donald Southern for all
the photographs.
R. L. and C. K.